OXFORD
TWENTY-FIRST CENTURY
APPROACHES TO LITERATURE

Frontispiece: Andrea Mantegna, *A Sibyl and a Prophet, c.*1495. Reproduced by permission of the Cincinnati Art Museum

OXFORD
TWENTY-FIRST CENTURY
APPROACHES TO LITERATURE

Cultural Reformations: Medieval and Renaissance in Literary History

Edited by

BRIAN CUMMINGS

and

JAMES SIMPSON

OXFORD
UNIVERSITY PRESS

OXFORD
UNIVERSITY PRESS

Great Clarendon Street, Oxford OX2 6DP

Oxford University Press is a department of the University of Oxford.
It furthers the University's objective of excellence in research, scholarship,
and education by publishing worldwide in

Oxford New York

Auckland Cape Town Dar es Salaam Hong Kong Karachi
Kuala Lumpur Madrid Melbourne Mexico City Nairobi
New Delhi Shanghai Taipei Toronto

With offices in

Argentina Austria Brazil Chile Czech Republic France Greece
Guatemala Hungary Italy Japan Poland Portugal Singapore
South Korea Switzerland Thailand Turkey Ukraine Vietnam

Oxford is a registered trade mark of Oxford University Press
in the UK and in certain other countries

Published in the United States
by Oxford University Press Inc., New York

First published 2010

British Library Cataloguing in Publication Data
Data available

Library of Congress Cataloging-in-Publication Data
Data available

Typeset by SPI Publisher Services, Pondicherry, India
Printed and bound in Great Britain by
CPI Antony Rowe, Chippenham, Wiltshire
ISBN 978–0–19–921248–4

1 3 5 7 9 10 8 6 4 2

ACKNOWLEDGEMENTS

The editors warmly thank Andrew McNeillie, *olim* Commissioning Editor at Oxford University Press, for inspiring this volume. We also thank James Simpson's research assistant Nicole Miller, for her indefatigable work on the minutiae of each essay. Finally, we thank our contributors for producing their essays with exemplary promptness (no minor virtue in academic life).

CONTENTS

Part IV LEGALITIES

Part V OUTSIDE THE LAW

Part VI LITERATURE

Part VII COMMUNITIES

Part VIII LABOUR

Part IX SELFHOOD

LIST OF ILLUSTRATIONS

LIST OF ABBREVIATIONS

BL	British Library (manuscripts)
CCSL	*Corpus Christianorum Series Latina* (Turnholt: Brepols)
CSEL	*Corpus Scriptorum Ecclesiasticorum Latinorum*
EEBO	Early English Books Online <http://eebo.chadwyck.com/home>
EETS	Early English Text Society
L&P	*Henry VIII: Letters and Papers, Foreign and Domestic, of the Reign of Henry VIII*... calendared by J. S. Brewer et al., 21 vols. (Longman, Green, Longman and Roberts, 1862–1910)
MED	*Middle English Dictionary*, ed. H. Kurath, S. M. Kuhn, and R. E. Lewis (Ann Arbor: University of Michigan Press, 1954–2001)
ODNB	*Oxford Dictionary of National Biography* <http://www.oxforddnb.com>
o.s.	Original series
PG	*Patrologia Cursus Completus... Series Graeca*, ed. J.-P. Migne, 161 vols. (Paris: J.-P. Migne, 1857–1866)
SR	*Statutes of the Realm*, ed. T. E. Tomlins, et al., 11 vols. (Dawsons, 1810–28; repr. 1963)
STC	*A Short-Title Catalogue of Books Printed in England, Scotland and Ireland and of English Books Printed Abroad 1475–1640*, ed. A. W. Pollard and G. R. Redgrave, 2nd edn rev. W. A. Jackson et al., 3 vols. (Bibliographical Society, 1976–91)

LIST OF CONTRIBUTORS

David Aers Duke University

Alexander Barratt University of Waikato

Sarah Beckwith Duke University

Thomas Betteridge Oxford Brookes University

Julia Boffey Queen Mary, University of London

Colin Burrow All Souls' College, University of Oxford

Ardis Butterfield University College London

Helen Cooper Magdalene College, University of Cambridge

Brian Cummings University of Sussex

Margreta De Grazia University of Pennsylvania

Vincent Gillespie Lady Margaret Hall, University of Oxford

Stephen Greenblatt Harvard University

Andrew Hadfield University of Sussex

Lorna Hutson University of St Andrews

David Scott Kastan Yale University

James Kearney University of California at Santa Barbara

Jesse Lander Notre Dame University

Seth Lerer University of California at San Diego

David Loewenstein University of Wisconsin-Madison

Tim William Machan Marquette University

Janel Mueller University of Chicago

Maura Nolan University of California at Berkeley

John Parker University of Virginia

Cathy Shrank University of Sheffield

James Simpson Harvard University

Lynn Staley Colgate University

Paul Strohm Columbia University

Jennifer Summit Stanford University

Ramie Targoff Brandeis University

Gordon Teskey Harvard University

Greg Walker University of Edinburgh

David Wallace University of Pennsylvania

Nicholas Watson Harvard University

CHAPTER 1

INTRODUCTION

BRIAN CUMMINGS AND JAMES SIMPSON

'A Sibyl and a Prophet' is the title that has been given to a beautiful painting in grisaille by Andrea Mantegna, perhaps from the last decade of the fifteenth century (reproduced as the frontispiece to this volume).[1] The image is a sumptuous imitation of a bronze relief, almost a *trompe-l'oeil*, with highlights of gold against a base colour of pink-brown. This is the surface burnish of a scene of underlying dramatic intensity. A conversation is taking place, or better a debate, marked out starkly against the backdrop of a jet black open doorway. The empty space behind the figures only serves to accentuate the relationship between the two talking heads, which are in any case in iconographic opposition. The figures represent female versus male, young versus old, perhaps secular versus priestly. The argument between the two has been best described by Edgar Wind: 'While the Prophet holds the sacred script, the sibyl explains it to him with persuasive clairvoyance, *numine afflata*, touching the crucial passage like a divine enchantress, while he listens with awe to her inspired utterances.'[2]

Wind's authorship of that classic work of Renaissance historiography and iconography, *Pagan Mysteries in the Renaissance*, may suggest to us an inevitable dichotomy between the sibyl and the prophet in Mantegna's image.[3] Is there a subliminal message of cultural transformation here, between old and new worlds, or old and new ways of learning? Is the prophet a medieval scholar, and the sibyl a humanist critic? They argue over a text, which appears as if it may be written in Hebrew. The tight grip of the scroll between the thumb and forefinger of the older,

[1] The date is uncertain but it has been suggested that it was painted in 1495. Although the original purpose is unknown, it is possible that it was hung at a height above eye level, perhaps over one of the doors of the Studiolo of Isabella d'Este in the Corte Vecchia in the Ducal Palace at Mantua. By 1603 it was in the collection of Cardinal Pietro Aldobrandini in Rome. It is now owned by the Cincinnati Art Museum. See *Andrea Mantegna*, ed. Jane Martineau (Milan: Electa, 1992), 401–3.

[2] 'Michelangelo's Prophets and Sibyls', *Proceedings of the British Academy*, 51 (1965), 47–84, at 60–1.

[3] *Pagan Mysteries in the Renaissance* (London: Faber & Faber, 1958). Wind was of course himself a formidable medievalist and a brilliant opponent of cultural stereotypes.

male, master suggests a method which is exegetical, critical, and learned; while the younger, female interpreter, depicted by Mantegna with a virtuoso *di sotto in sù* view of her hand, is visionary, inspired, and improvisatory.

This book fights hard against the stereotypes that might encourage any such iconographic division between medieval and Renaissance modes of thinking. Before we rush to associate the sibyl with an incipient classical and scientific methodology poised against the prophet's scholastic appeal to authority, it is worth pausing to consider that the modern title given to the work is only conjectural. The painting may in fact be a fragment of a larger whole that might yield an entirely different meaning to the figures in front of us. This problem is a good emblem for the philosophical pitfalls of the historiography of culture, and especially for the idea of periodization and the division of cultural history into separated eras. Scholars conceive of these eras as discrete, and as inviting a description of their distinguishing features, yet the motivation for identifying their autonomy lies in the needs of historical analysis: the features scholarship discovers are more often than not predetermined by expectations of the material. After all, the sibyl is a major symbolic figure in medieval narrative from Macrobius to Dante, while there is no reason at all for us not to find in the prophet an icon of Renaissance method: pedantic, immersed in ancient texts, and overwhelmingly male.

Cultural Reformations is an exercise in redrawing historical categories, or in the period unbound. It is a study of the idea of change or else of resistance to change; perhaps better, of process, or of historical temporality itself. Yet it is pre-eminently also an exercise in collective scholarship, which represents heterogeneous approaches to heterogeneous materials. Half of us are professionally tied to what for want of a better term we call the Middle Ages, and half to what we now tend to name, with no better intrinsic reason, the 'early modern'. In investigating the invisible boundary line between us, and the grounds for conceiving of any gap between us in the first place, we have all undertaken to examine material either side of the jubilee year of 1500, each in relation to a topic that has, in modern academic study, been taken to be a site of cultural change.

Yet we do not consider ourselves immune to the historical boundaries which define our subject. Nor do we write outside their consequences. Revolutions not only attract revolutionaries; they also attract historians, partly because historians need to generate explanatory narratives from apparently seminal, liberating starting points; revolutionary moments claim to provide those liberating points of origin. Such moments, to a much greater degree even than decisive wars, characteristically claim to restart the very measures of time and sequence. Historians may also be drawn to revolutionary zero points because they sympathize with the new cultural order ushered in by the revolution.

Historiography is, then, deeply connected with revolutions in and of time. Since the end of the eighteenth century, at least, most Europeans and Americans are, whether they like it or not (and whether they know it or not), profoundly revolutionary creatures, necessarily shaped as they have been, one way or another, by the formative revolutions of our epoch. Our very conception of historical periods, divisible into detachable segments of time punctuated by liberating convulsions, is itself the product of revolutionary aspiration to neutralize the pathologies of time and start afresh. The philological tools of our historiographical enquiry, designed as they are to erase the accretions of tradition and to give us access to worlds freshly perceived 'in their own terms', are also themselves revolutionary tools.

Many periodic terms across English literary history embed ideological claims within apparently neutral periodic divisions. But the deepest periodic division in that history has been between the medieval and the early modern, not least because the cultural investments in maintaining that division are exceptionally powerful. Narratives of national and religious identity and freedom; of individual liberties; of the history of education and scholarship; of reading or the history of the book; of the very possibility of sophisticated individual self-consciousness, and of persuasive historical consciousness: each of these narratives (and more) has been motivated by positing a powerful break around 1500. None of these claims for a profound historical and cultural break at the turn of the fifteenth into the sixteenth centuries is negligible. But the very habit of working within those periodic bounds (either medieval or early modern) tends, however, simultaneously to affirm and to ignore the rupture. It affirms the rupture by staying within standard periodic bounds, but it ignores it by never examining the rupture itself. The moment of profound change is either, for medievalists, just over an unexplored horizon; or, for early modernists, a zero point behind which more penetrating examination is unnecessary.

Institutionally, too, our intellectual life is organized, before we have begun to consider the matter, within these periodic bounds. Publishing houses tend to insist on commissioning and marketing journals and books within tightly periodic frames. Many academic departments or alliances also organize intellectual practice within the terms given us by revolutionary consciousness. This is especially true of 'Medieval Studies' and its pair 'Renaissance', since these terms imply the notion of civilizations entire unto themselves.

Such institutional formations tend to privilege synchronic relations of analogy between different discursive fields, within the same 'period'. The merging of literary history and cultural history, to produce what might be called 'cultural poetics', has for some decades been extraordinarily fertile, not to say exhilarating. That said, that scholarly practice has remained, until recently, resolutely held within synchronic boundaries, underwritten as it has been by a Foucauldian archaeology of knowledge (itself built on an archaeological substratum of the French Revolution). That archaeology posits unbridgeable epistemic crevasses between periods. Committed as they are to synchrony for profound reasons, both medievalists and early modernists have tended to rest steadily within set chronological frames, rehearsing well-worn clichés about what came afterwards or went before.

Cultural Reformations takes a dynamically diachronic approach to cultural history. Many of the essays range in the full span between the fourteenth and the seventeenth centuries, we could say from Lollardy to the Commonwealth, or from the Lancastrian *coup d'état* to the British Civil Wars. This is not only to bring the perspective of a *longue durée* to literary history. It is because the chronological divisions that we are arguing about first come to be framed within this time period. To continue to exist politely on either side of the divide is to ignore the way that the works we study, and the way in which we study them, are implicated in the complex history of that terminology and its making. The term *media tempestas* seems to have been first used in 1469 by Giovanni Andrea de' Bussi, Pope Paul II's librarian.[4] For a literary historian, there is a wonderful power in the fact that he coins the word to describe a history of books. A century before this, Petrarch had begun to identify an age of barbarism intervening to obscure the richness of the classical past. Following in his wake, and with increasing confidence, Italian humanists such as Flavio Biondo, Marsilio Ficino, and Lorenzo Valla proposed the modern era as a bridge to the culture of the past, an age of renewal of the glories of the antique. The intervening middle age, lending the new its spectacular identity, was an age of intellectual oblivion. In England *medium aevum* first appears, in more neutral terms as a period in history, in John Selden, the jurist and historian of Judaism, in 1610.[5]

One prevalent version of cultural history is that the Renaissance invented the 'modern'. A more interesting analysis, or irony, would be that the humanists of the late fifteenth and early sixteenth centuries conceptualized their own place in history not so much by inventing the modern as by inventing the 'medieval'. They created the third term as a conscious polemic. And increasingly in the sixteenth century, most eloquently in the work of Erasmus, they postulated as the distinguishing features of the new age, in relation to the middle age, methods and concepts that are central to the practice of modern literary history: philology, textual criticism, and the idea of 'literature' (or *bonae literae*) itself. This fact alone means that literary history has a need to investigate this claim.

In April 1517, Erasmus predicted in a letter to Pope Leo X that *saeculo huic nostro* ('in our time') a new golden age might be upon us, and that the revival of learning would bring with it the restoration of Christian unity.[6] Even in a history of

[4] Apuleius, *Opera*, ed. Johannes Andreas (Rome: [Conradus Sweynheym and Arnoldus Pannartz], 1469).

[5] *Iani Anglorum facies altera Memoria* (London: Thomas Snodham, 1610). For the development of periodic terms for both medieval and Renaissance, see the evergreen study by Wallace K. Ferguson, *The Renaissance in Historical Thought: Five Centuries of Interpretation* (Boston: Houghton Mifflin, 1948).

[6] *Epistola* No. 566, *Opus epistolarum Erasmi*, ed. P. S. Allen, 12 vols. (Oxford: Clarendon Press, 1906–58), 2: 527.

spectacularly bad predictions this would have a proud place. The Lutheran Reformation, and the peculiar English one that followed it, only served to exacerbate and reinforce the distinctions embodied in the *medium aevum*. Indeed the Reformation gave ideological exactitude and political compulsion to emerging prejudices.

Nonetheless, even a decade ago the Reformation barely had a place in English literary history. The Reformation in literary terms was seen as the rebarbative and recondite home of a few special interests. Now, at the beginning of the twenty-first century, it seems that, after all, the huge ritual, social, political, and economic rifts of the sixteenth century could hardly be more relevant to the way that we write a history of literature. That this is the case is due in part to the past work of the contributors here assembled. But it has also happened because of an interesting, we might say glacial, shift in the subject and its period boundaries. Medievalists have come forward into the Reformation just as early modernists have moved backwards from Shakespeare to mid-century. There has been an interesting renegotiation in the middle.

We are therefore at a peculiarly appropriate moment to reassess the energies of literature between the fourteenth and seventeenth centuries. It is timely for us to examine once again, in a more general way than is possible by any single scholar, what the creative and destructive anxieties of the Reformation were, and what their legacy is. This gives a special stringency to the historiography of cultural history and cultural change. For the idea of change propels the Reformation moment into creating the modern version of the Middle Ages, by rejecting its values in the first place. The concepts by which we frame our subjects as either 'Medieval Studies' or 'Renaissance Studies' or 'Reformation Studies' or 'Early Modern Studies' occlude the historiographical certainties of the revolutionary moment, whether of 'reformed' religion or humanist philology.

A more complex understanding of English cultural history is the impossible project of this volume. Fredric Jameson might be correct in saying that 'we cannot not periodize', but in this volume we nevertheless want to try.[7] Or, rather, we want to initiate new periodic conversations in reaction to *Cultural Reformations*, in particular across the standard boundaries of the 'medieval' and the early modern, or Renaissance, or Reformation. In our view, both 'periods' look different when set into dialogue with each other. We propose that there is a good deal of unfinished business to be transacted within English literary history.

*

We invited contributors to focus on a theme, of their own choosing, that connects pre- and post-Reformation cultures. The volume is not designed to summarize what is known in a given field, not least because the 'field' we hope to outline does not yet exist. Neither does it provide 'coverage', since we wanted our

[7] *A Singular Modernity: Essay on the Ontology of the Present* (New York: Verso, 2002), 29.

authors to write to their passions, and that meant giving them freedom to pursue those passions. In many cases the themes chosen are of apparently less pressure for either medievalists or early modernists, until set into periodic dialogue, when their importance is suddenly perceived afresh. We had, we underline, no party line, no implicitly expected or desired view of continuity, rupture, or permutations of the two. In the following essays, on the contrary, many models of the relation between pre- and post-Reformation cultures emerge. In some cases the relation is one of stark contrast of the new and old, of new post-Reformation worlds that were impossible or undreamed of before 1500. In other cases the relation is one of continuity, even if that continuity might be visible only after the event, when pre-Reformation materials begin to look prophetic of the convulsions to come. In other cases still, the relation is one of visible continuity. In yet others, pre- and post-Reformation cultures stand in a relation of what might be called a hydraulics of culture: if one powerful aspect of a culture is depressed, it will resurface later, one way or another, in disguised form, as the return of the repressed. Such a notion is applicable, for example, to the notion of place, on which many of our essayists chose to focus: repress monastic and conventual sites of contemplation, and they resurface, one way or another, in noble households. Or, to take another example, repress the forensics of conscience in the sacrament of penance, and it will resurface, one way or another, in dramatic and legal forensics. Cultural forces migrate, under pressure, from one discourse to another. Repression of the religious life of contemplation can even produce the enclosed 'experimentum' of the empirical science.

Even where the emphasis is on continuity, that continuity might not be obvious: materials forged for a pre-Reformation historical moment are suddenly rediscovered, and redeployed, for a largely different historical need, in which those materials gain a sudden new urgency and relevance that their original shapers could not have foreseen. The pre-Reformation clerics who posed anti-fraternal attacks on idleness could not have predicted how their ideological materials would be wielded by Reformation polemicists against the Catholic Church at large. Or, in other cases, the continuity remains for the most part unobserved simply because we as scholars tend to read books produced by authors in our given periods; we tend not to read books by long-dead vernacular authors, even if those books continued to be printed in large numbers and avidly read, as the works of Chaucer were in the sixteenth century, for example. Other essays disabuse us of continuity, by pointing out that the continuity is only apparent: historical players might continue to deploy the same key words as they put themselves on the line ('sacrament' is an example; 'despair' and 'saint' are others), but the words' deeper meaning is utterly transformed, or their referent changed, by circumstance.

The emphases of the last paragraph might suggest that the Reformation is the centre of this volume, and that what might emerge from these essays is a new 'period', running from the late fourteenth to the mid-seventeenth century, a period characterized by the origin and final triumph of reformed religion. There might be considerable mileage in such a proposition. It makes a certain historical sense. It might suit the strategic needs of both medievalists and early modernists in a contemporary academic culture in which 'the past' (always conceived as something definitively ended) is considered to stop at 1800. Despite, however, the centrality of the Reformation in any discussion of periodic sense, we did not wish to make the Reformation the single, non-negotiable pivot of this volume.

True, contemporary world history is investing the cultural poetics of religion with a commanding attention. True, too, that late medieval and early modern religion stand in very significant asymmetry with 'secular' culture in societies where relatively few could read but all were deeply involved, one way or another, with the practice of their religion through visual art, liturgy, and, not least, the fate of their souls. This is an especially fertile moment for the cultural study of pre- and post-Reformation English religion. Historical scholarship has revised deep-set persuasions about the Reformation in Britain; that scholarship increasingly envisions the Reformation moment as less of a break with, and more of a deep expression of, powerful currents within late medieval religious experience.

What is more, phenomena that had been taken to be purely 'secular', characteristic of the 'increasingly secular' Renaissance, turn out instead to be deep reflexes of a post-Reformation religion that, so far from waning, is instead becoming too hot to handle. By this account, even when post-Reformation texts are silent about religion, that silence might be very loud. 'Secular' love lyric, for example, apparently most resistant to and insouciant about religion, turns out to be deeply informed by it. Autobiography finds newly experimental forms and media even as it reabsorbs older forms of penitential and confessional practice. The very notion of 'secularity' itself, after all, turns out to be the product of long *religious* histories. Certainly, European secularity is a reflex of the Reformation centuries, repudiating as it does the visceral, non-negotiable hatreds of intra- and extra-Christian violence. But secularity also has a more specifically Christian history, as the upshot, *mutatis mutandis*, of the late medieval Church's turn to the *saeculum* out of the enclosure of the monastery, a turn initiated in the early thirteenth century.

Those essays that do address religious cultures avoid the error of treating confessional identities as reified and constant essences; instead, they define the unstably variant nature of such confessional identities. Confessionalization is rather the product than the motor of change.

*

The situation in which we find ourselves at the present moment within the field is an odd one. The term 'Renaissance' occupies a strange intellectual no-man's-land. It continues to have a currency with the general reading public, and in common culture, that is happily borrowed for course design or for the entitling of books. Yet academically its power is etiolated beyond recognition: the rejection of Jakob Burckhardt's paradigm of *The Civilization of the Renaissance in Italy* is so widespread as to be a minor industry. The term 'Renaissance' no longer encourages much faith, and has become a bastard term. This has partly been due to what has been called 'the revolt of the medievalists'—a powerful rebuttal of the claims in Burckhardt, especially around the idea of the birth of individualism and subjectivity. Yet this phrase was first coined by Wallace Ferguson in 1948, and there has been no corresponding revolt against the idea of the medieval.[8] If anything, medievalists are surprisingly happy with a term that was first invented to exclude and disenfranchise them.

Here we should note the curious asymmetry between the different terms in use. We use the combinations 'Medieval and Renaissance' or 'Medieval and Early Modern' routinely and interchangeably, whereas the words themselves are incapable of signifying commensurate states. The 'medieval' is a concept of long-term continuity. If we find it difficult to say when it begins and when it ends, this is because the word means something non-terminal in the first place and is an intrinsically medial signifier. The 'Renaissance', on the other hand, is not a temporal term at all. It describes an event, or better a state of mind or feeling or body. In historical significance it tends towards the idealization of the momentary, the ruptural and the sudden. It has now largely been replaced in technical parlance by 'Early Modern', sometimes on the basis that this new term is less prejudicial and ideological. That is a very odd view. 'Early Modern' in relation to 'Medieval' does quite different work, but the juxtaposition is just as divisive. It is a strange phrase: at once proleptic and parasitic, implying a state that is both with it, and not quite there yet.

Yet it is modernity we are always half arguing about anyway. Does modernity have a beginning? If not now, when? The debates are endless, timeless, sometimes tiresome. Yet they are hardly irrelevant to our volume. One common view of the transition between medieval and Renaissance is that it encompasses the very birth of the modern. In questioning the models of both medieval and Renaissance that inform this, we may also be understood as questioning that view, too. Yet this should make us think all the harder about what we mean by 'modernity'. Modernity is not the subject of these essays, but it is the unseen spectre, or the uninvited guest at the feast. We both welcome this guest and propose some education of its rather boorish manners. For while modernity, as an experience, could be said to be as old as time itself, it is not such a very old *idea*. Indeed, it is a medieval idea. The Latin word *modernus*, appropriately enough, is post-classical. It first came into use in the fifth and sixth centuries among grammarians attempting to construct a history of literature and of linguistic usage. Priscian (*fl.* 500) routinely distinguishes between a Latin grammar or style used *apud antiquissimos* from one used *apud modernos*.[9]

[8] *The Renaissance in Historical Thought*, 100.

[9] *Institutiones grammaticarum libri XVIII*, ed. Martin Hertz, *Grammatici Latini*, ed. Heinrich Keil, 8 vols., repr. ed. (Hildesheim: G. Olms, 1961), e.g. 2: 11.

Whereas now we tend automatically to valorize the newness of the new, it is salutary to recall that Priscian routinely prefers the most ancient sources to those of the present day. Cassiodorus (d.585), betraying a more modernist sensibility, refers to a contemporary as not only copying the ancients (*antiquorum imitator*) but also inspiring writers of his own times (*modernorum institutor*).[10] Later medieval usage is equally ambiguous or perhaps sometimes neutral: it is never quite clear whether (on the grounds of timeliness alone, as opposed to scholarly method) in fourteenth-century universities the scholastic *via antiqua* was more valued for its authority or the *via moderna* for its logical novelty. It is difficult to believe, however, that the *moderni* did not have some smugness about trumping their predecessors, much like post-structuralists in a latter-day Paris in relation to their merely structuralist professors.

The burden of the modern is not one equally shared among scholars of the medieval and the Renaissance. Perhaps the latter group are too much in thrall to modernity, in the forlorn hope that their own object of study thereby becomes more exciting. Probably it is more rewarding to think of the modern as always a relative term, and therefore always in flux. These essays are written in the hope that we can continue to be alive to the paradoxes and reversals of time as well as to its inexorable teleology. Our title is Medieval *and* (not *to*) Renaissance, since our default position is that historiography moves both backward and forward. As cultural historians who receive our historical categories from history, that is, we move from Renaissance to medieval as much, if not more than, the other way around. Yet *Cultural Reformations* is not primarily conceived in the spirit of setting out a new chronology. Rather it is an ongoing conversation, or debate, between different kinds of modernity in the past, and others still in the future.

[10] Cassiodorus, *Variae*, 4.51 ('Symmacho Patricio Theodoricus Rex').

PART I

HISTORIES

CHAPTER 2

ANACHRONISM

MARGRETA DE GRAZIA

In the field of literary studies, as presently historicized, nothing could be worse than to be accused of anachronism. The Annaliste historian Lucien Febvre judged anachronism 'the worst of all sins, the sin that cannot be forgiven'.[1] He did not mean, of course, those venial little slips whereby something from a later period is attributed to an earlier (an article of dress, for example, or a custom or an invention); these errors are easily forgiven and amended. The unpardonable sin occurs when a present way of thinking is imposed upon the past. Sometimes this happens when a conceptual category is used that did not exist during the period in question, like 'autobiography' or 'democracy' or 'masochist'. And sometimes it happens when such a term is used that *did* exist then, but signified quite differently: like 'individual' or 'fact' or 'race'. These are more serious offenses, if not against the Holy Ghost, at least against History. Indeed the failure to differentiate the world of the present-subject from that of the past-object is a violation of the basic principle of epistemology: the viewing subject must remain distinct from the viewed object. When one collapses into the other, knowledge cannot take place.

But to be guilty of anachronism implies another kind of wrongdoing. Our stance toward other periods has implications for our stance toward other persons. Indeed the way we talk about historical periods encourages us to think of them as persons. We anthropomorphize them, individuating one period from another by an animating spirit (*Zeitgeist*) and an informing consciousness (*mentalité*, mindset, *episteme*, *Weltanschauung*, world view). With periods as with persons, we have an

[1] Lucien Febvre, *The Problem of Unbelief in the Sixteenth Century: The Religion of Rabelais*, trans. Beatrice Gottlieb (Cambridge, MA: Harvard University Press, 1982), 5. On 'psychological anachronism' in 'History and Psychology', see Lucien Febvre, *A New Kind of History from the Writings of Febvre*, ed. Peter Burke and trans. K. Folca (New York, Evanston, San Francisco: Routledge & Kegan Paul, 1973), 1–11; Quentin Skinner on the 'sin' of anachronistic translations of the past into the present in 'Encountering the Past: An Interview', *Finnish Year Book of Political Thought*, 6 (2002), 32–63, at 59; and Quentin Skinner, 'Meaning and Understanding', in *Meaning and Context: Quentin Skinner and his Critics*, ed. James Tully (Princeton: Princeton University Press, 1988), 29–67, especially 32–5.

obligation to respect difference. The reduction of the other to the same constitutes an effacement of the other, and for Lévinas, of the self as well.[2] Not to recognize the distinguishing features of another period is thus more than an error of methodology or epistemology: it is an ethical failure.

Or so it would seem...

*

That anachronism is such a charged critical term at present attests to the close attachment of literary studies to the discipline of history. If *Always Historicize* has been the mandate of the past generation, *Never Anachronize* may be its tacit corollary. Of course, the imperative to historicize is not so easy to follow. What does it mean to do *history*? Like *race* and *author*, *history* is one of those semantic false friends that looks and sounds now as it did then but no longer signifies in the same way. From antiquity through the Renaissance, *history* had a close semantic link to *story*, a word that is now its near opposite. While Aristotle in his *Poetics* had attempted to draw a firm line between history and poetry, Cicero in *De inventione* included both *historia* and *fabula* as branches of *narratio*. The historian D. R. Woolf has nicely captured the interchangeability of the two terms. After reviewing the various forms of narrative that were called *histories*—plays, poems, reports of current events, romances, and didactic pieces—he concludes: '[Histories] tell stories, true or false, about real or imaginary men and women who lived in the remote or the recent past'.[3] The ambiguity continues to linger at the edges of our present disciplinary boundaries. In recent decades, at the same time that literary studies came under the purview of the new historicism, history took a decidedly rhetorical (or linguistic) turn. And both movements were then countered with a re-entrenchment of disciplinary lines, with literature reasserting its formalist center and history reclaiming its basis in research.

Unlike *history*, *anachronism* has no ancient lineage. Coined from the Middle Greek *anacronismos*, anachronism does not emerge in the vernacular until the seventeenth century.[4] Its appearance has been credited to Joseph Scaliger, 'the father of chronology', who in the second edition of *De Emendatio Temporum* (1629) used it several times in its Greek form.[5] Scaliger spent most of his life

[2] Emmanuel Lévinas, *Otherwise than Being, or Beyond Essence*, trans. Alphonso Lingis (The Hague: M. Nijhoff; Hingham, MA: Kluwer Bowson, 1981).

[3] D. R. Woolf, *The Idea of History in Early Stuart England* (Toronto, London, and Buffalo, NY: University of Toronto Press, 1990), 16–17. See also Patrick Collinson, 'History', in *A Companion to English Renaissance Literature and Culture*, ed. Michael Hattaway (Oxford: Blackwell, 2000), 58–70, at 59.

[4] Herman L. Ebeling, 'The Word Anachronism', *Modern Language Notes*, 52 (1937), 120–1; Peter Burke, 'The Sense of Anachronism from Petrarch to Poussin', in *Time in the Medieval World*, ed. Chris Humphrey and W. M. Ormrod (Rochester, NY: York Medieval Press, 2001), 157–73, at 173.

[5] For a compendious account of Scaliger's chronological interests, see Anthony Grafton, *Joseph Scaliger: A Study in the History of Classical Scholarship*, vol. 2: *Historical Chronology* (Oxford: Clarendon Press; New York: Oxford University Press, 1993). For a briefer account, see Anthony

working on various aspects of chronology; reevaluating Greek and Roman annals in light of astronomical calculations and philological evidence, coordinating events from Greek, Roman, Persian, Babylonian, Egyptian, and Jewish history with biblical genealogies, and devising a system, the Julian Period, for computing universal time extending from Creation. When *anachronism* appears in English, it retains its association with this highly specialized study, as its earliest lexical entries make clear. The first, Thomas Blount's *Glossographia or a Dictionary* (1656), defines it as 'an errour in Chronology'; the second, Edward Phillips's *The New World of English Words* (1658), after defining it as 'a word used in Chronology', distinguishes two types: *metachronism*, the placing of an event after it has occurred, and *prochronism*, the placing of it before.[6] Thomas Hearne in *Ductor Historicus* (1698), a guide to universal history, defines *chronology* as 'the Doctrine of Times' and *anachronism* as 'an Error or Mistake in the Computation of Time'.[7]

While *anachronism* enters the language in the mid-seventeenth century under the auspices of chronology, *chronology* itself had recently undergone semantic change. *Chronologia* (or *chronographia*) was associated not with abstruse calculations but, like *historia*, with narration. In his *Art of English Poesy* (1589), George Puttenham anglicizes the term as 'Counterfeit Time', reports that '[e]xamples are every where to be found' and groups it among other mimetic figures like 'Counterfeit Persons' (*Prosopopeia*) and 'Counterfeit places' (*Topographia*).[8] In his entry on *Chronographia*, Henry Peacham in *The Garden of Eloquence* (1593) lists the various temporal units it describes, diurnal and seasonal times, but also 'the time of war, the time of peace, the old time'.[9] The early dictionaries pick up this rhetorical definition. Edmund Coote in *The English School-master* (1596) defines *chronologie* as 'story of times'; Robert Cawdrey in *A Table Alphabetical* (1604) as 'storie of times past'; John Bullokar in *An English Expositor* (1616) and Henry Cockeram in *English Dictionary* (1623) as 'the knowledge of old Stories'. The flashbacks and flash-forwards which the chronologies call *metachronism* and *prochronism* have precedents in the rhetorical figures of *analepsis* and *prolepsis*. Also to be found in the rhetorics is the figure most closely approximating anachronism, *hysteron proteron*, anglicized by Puttenham as the 'Preposterous'.[10] Among the many kinds of order it

Grafton, 'Scaliger's Chronology: Philology, Astronomy, World History', in his *Defenders of the Text: The Traditions of Scholarship in an Age of Science, 1450–1800* (Cambridge, MA, and London: Harvard University Press, 1991), 104–44.

[6] All definitions from sixteenth- and seventeenth-century dictionaries have been quoted from *Lexicons of Early Modern English*, University of Toronto <www.chass.utoronto.ca/epc/chwp/CHC2003/Lancashire2.htm>.

[7] Thomas Hearne, *Ductor Historicus: or, A Short System of Universal History* (London, 1698), 7.

[8] George Puttenham, *The Art of English Poesy*, ed. Frank Whigham and Wayne A. Rebhorn (Ithaca and London: Cornell University Press, 2007), 324.

[9] Henry Peacham, *The Garden of Eloquence*, ed. William G. Crane (Gainesville, FL: Scholars' Facsimiles and Reprints, 1954), 142–3.

[10] Puttenham, *The Art of English Poesy*, ed. Whigham and Rebhorn, 253. For the relation of *hysteron proteron* to anachronicity, see K. K. Ruthven, 'Preposterous Chatterton', *English Literary History*, 71

inverts is that of time, as in Francis Bacon's famous apothegm, *Antiquitas seculi Iuuentus Mundi* ('The age of antiquity is the youth of the world'). By Bacon's preposterous gloss, time's forward movement is retrograde: 'These [present] times are the ancient times when the world is ancient, and not those which we account antient *Ordine retrogrado*, by a computation backward from our selves'.[11]

After the mid-seventeenth century, *chronologia* shifts from its rhetorical provenance to become a field of study in its own right. Thomas Blount's 1656 *Glossographia* begins with the familiar rhetorical definition ('a speaking of times') but also introduces a new one: 'the Art of numbring the yeers from the beginning of the world'. He turns to the cosmographer Peter Heylyn for his definition and illustrations: 'Heylin saith, Chronologies are onely bare supputations of the times without any regard of the acts then happening, such are the Chronologies of Funccius, Scaliger, and Helvicus'.[12] In Edward Phillips's *The New World of English Words*, published two years later, no trace remains of the word's original rhetorical classification: 'a computation of years, whereby is shown the coherence of Histories'. Once a story about time, chronology now has no narrative content at all ('without any regard of acts then happening'), its 'coherence' the result of numerical sequencing ('bare supputation'), starting from Creation and stretching forward to the time of writing.

It is precisely because chronology referred and related to nothing outside its own calibration that it became the dominant mode of measuring time past. Any event from any place could be located on its continuum and put in relation to any other event there. It was absolute, like Newtonian space. (Indeed Newton worked on chronology throughout his life; his *Abstract of Chronology* was published a year before his death in 1727, his *Chronology of Ancient Kingdoms Amended* in 1728.)[13] Yet that chronology had migrated out of the realm of the narrational into that of the quantifiable suggests that it might be nothing more than a particularly ingenious and useful 'storie of time past', or in Puttenham's taxonomy, a brilliant example of 'Counterfeit Time', the result of human invention and construction with extremely wide (indeed universal) applicability. In the eighteenth century, a vast literature propagated this numerate formatting of time, including Samuel Johnson's curricular recommendations in the preface to *The Preceptor* (1748):

(2004), 345–75, especially 345–9; on the figure more generally, see Patricia Parker, *Shakespeare from the Margins: Language, Culture, Context* (Chicago: Chicago University Press, 1996), 20–55.

[11] Francis Bacon, *The Advancement of Learning*, ed. Michael Kiernan (Oxford: Clarendon Press, 2000), 29. For an analysis of several anachronic schemas for narrating the past (chronicles, chorographies, antiquarianism, analogy, euhemerism, and prophecy) in Spenser, the 'Poet-historical', see Bart van Es, *Spenser's Forms of History* (Oxford: Oxford University Press, 2002).

[12] Blount's reference is to Peter Heylyn, *Cosmographie in Foure Books* (London, 1652), 20.

[13] On the supersession of relative time by absolute time, see Donald J. Wilcox, 'The Rise and Fall of Absolute Time', in his *The Measure of Times Past: Pre-Newtonian Chronologies and the Rhetoric of Relative Time* (Chicago and London: University of Chicago Press, 1987), 16–50.

> [The student may begin with] *Le Clerc's Compendium of History*; and afterwards may, for the Historical Part of *Chronology*, procure *Helvicus's* and *Isaacson's* Tables; and, if he is desirous of attaining the technical Part, may first peruse *Holder's Account of Time*, *Hearne's Ductor Historicus*, *Strauchius*, the first Part of *Petavius's Rationarium Temporum*; and, at length, *Scaliger de Emendatione Temporum*. And, for instruction in the Method of his Historical Studies, he may consult *Hearne's Ductor Historicus*, *Wheare's Lectures*, *Rawlinson's Directions for the Study of History*; and, for Ecclesiastical History, *Cave* and *Dupin*, *Baronius* and *Fleury*.[14]

Edward Gibbon appears to have taken naturally to such a course of study. In his *Memoirs of My Life*, he describes his early obsession with the chronology: he devised his own timelines drawn from the various chronologies at his disposal (of Strauchius, Helvicus, Anderson, Ussher, Prideaux, Scaliger, Petavus, Marsham, and Newton): 'I engraved the multitude of names and dates in a clear and indelible series'; and lost sleep over discrepancies: 'my sleep has been disturbed by the difficulty of reconciling the Septuagint with the Hebrew Computation'.[15] Such a 'clear and indelible series' subtended not only his memoirs but also his six-volume magnum opus, *The Decline and Fall of the Roman Empire*; the table of contents to the first edition (1776–88) features a marginal timeline slotted along the side of the seventy-one chapter headings, enabling the reader to follow the longest downward slope on record—thirteen centuries—from the Antonines in 98 CE to the fall of Constantinople in 1453, and on three continents. In his *Memoirs*, he provides the precise dates for both the inception and completion of his six-volume opus, as if out of consideration for the posterity which would one day chronologize his life and works: 'It was at Rome on the fifteenth of October 1764 ... that the idea of writing the decline and fall of the City first started to my mind'; 'It was on the day or rather the night of the 27th of June 1787, between the hours of eleven and twelve that I wrote the last lines of the last page'.[16]

Another account of Rome—of its foundation rather than demise—provided the *locus classicus* for anachronism. Seventeenth- and eighteenth-century critics pointed out that the most celebrated episode in the most celebrated work of antiquity depended on a gross anachronism: Dido and Aeneas had lived two or three hundred years apart. In *Ductor Historicus* (1698), Hearne illustrated his definition of *anachronism* by announcing that Virgil's two lovers 'lived 300 Years distance one from another': using Scaliger's Julian Period, he dates Aeneas at 'Years of the World 2829' and Dido at 'Years 3112'.[17] Both Johnson in his 1755 *Dictionary*

[14] Samuel Johnson, 'Preface', *The Preceptor: containing a general course of education* (London, 1758; first published 1748), xxi–xxii.

[15] Edward Gibbon, *Memoirs of My Life*, ed. Georges A. Bonnard (New York: Funk and Wagnalls, 1962), 43.

[16] Gibbon, *Memoirs*, ed. Bonnard, 136 n. 7 and 180.

[17] Hearne, *Ductor Historicus*, 8.

and Diderot in his 1751 *Encyclopédie* feature the discrepancy as the sole illustration of anachronism.[18]

In the dedication to his translation of the *Aeneid*, John Dryden instructs that *anachronism* is a euphemism for 'falsehood', 'the polite term' or 'civil expression' for an 'errour in chronology', before he charges Virgil with having 'committed an anachronism'. He proposes to defend Virgil's 'famous anachronism, in making Æneas and Dido contemporaries' even though 'it is certain that the hero lived almost two hundred years before the building of Carthage'.[19] As Dryden allows, Virgil could not have known of this disparity, because 'Neither he nor the Romans had ever read the bible, by which only his false computation of times can be made out against him'.[20]

Subsequent commentators on Virgil, of course, *had* read the Bible. Commentators on the *Aeneid* from Servius to Petrarch noted the discrepancy between the building of Carthage and the fall of Troy in discussions over the fictional versus the historical status of Virgil's epic. From the time of Augustine, commentators had also grappled with the problem of how to justify Aeneas' seduction and abandonment of Dido. Numerous writers attempted to supplant Virgil's account (it was also Ovid's in his epistolary *Heroides*) with an older legend, found in Servius and Macrobius, in which Dido had indeed fled to Carthage after her husband's murder but Aeneas en route to Rome had never lighted there.[21] Petrarch relies heavily on the account in several of his works, maintaining that Virgil's two lovers had never in fact encountered one another.[22]

Clearly more than the Bible was needed to detect Virgil's 'false computation of times' for the fall of Troy or the building of Carthage.[23] Dryden lifts his account

[18] See also the anonymous, *Verdicts of the learned concerning Virgil and Homer's heroic poem* (London, 1697), 8, which charges Virgil with both *Achronism* [sic] and *Slander*: the first, by making 'that Princess Elder by 300 Years than in reality she was': the second by ruining her reputation.

[19] Virgil, *The Works of Virgil: Translated into English Verse by Mr. Dryden*, 4 vols., trans. John Dryden (London: J. Rivington and Sons, etc., 1792), 2: 143.

[20] Virgil, *The Works of Virgil*, trans. Dryden, 2: 144.

[21] Diane Purkiss, 'The Queen on Stage: Marlowe's *Dido, Queen of Carthage* and the Representation of Elizabeth I', in *A Woman Scorn'd: Responses to the Dido Myth*, ed. Michael Burden (Faber and Faber, 2000; first published 1998), 151–67, at 165 n. 7. For the historical chaste Dido versus the fictitious wanton Dido, see Marilynn Desmond, *Reading Dido: Gender, Textuality and the Medieval Aeneid* (Minneapolis and London: University of Minnesota Press, 1994), 24–33.

[22] For Petrarch's refutation of Virgil's history in *Trionfi*, *Africa*, and *Epistolae Seniles*, see James Simpson, 'Subjects of Triumph and Literary History: Dido and Petrarch in Petrarch's *Africa* and *Trionfi*', *Journal of Medieval and Early Modern Studies*, 35 (2005), 489–508.

[23] For a list of ancient and medieval attempts to relate the fall of Troy to the founding of Carthage, see Arthur Stanley Pease, *Publii Vergilii Maronis Aeneidos: Liber Quartus* (Cambridge, MA: Harvard University Press, 1935), 58–9. Smalley credits the Oxford friar John Ridevall in his manuscript commentary on *De civitate dei* (*c.*1332) for proving on chronological grounds that Virgil's account of Dido and Aeneas was not historically true, in Beryl Smalley, *English Friars and Antiquity in the Fourteenth Century* (Oxford: Basil Blackwell, 1960), 130–1, and Appendix I, 320–1; thanks to David Wallace for this reference. Marilynn Desmond also discusses Ridevall; see Desmond, *Reading Dido*, 26.

from the preface to the French translation of the *Aeneid* by Jean Regnault de Segrais (1668) who, in a section entitled 'De l'Anacronisme', in turn had drawn it from a recently deceased renowned classical and biblical scholar.[24] According to this source, the date of the fall of Troy had already been calculated from Greek documents (Plato, Herodotus, Erasthones) and dated in relation to Chronicles and Kings: sixty years before the reign of Saul first king of Israel.[25] The date Carthage was built, however, could not be ascertained until the discovery of the Tyrian royal chronicles, set down by the first-century Judaean historian Flavius Josephus.[26] The Tyrian chronicle recorded an event also described in the Bible: the Tyrian King Hiram felled cedars in Lebanon which the Hebrew Solomon used for building his temple in Jerusalem.[27] With this convergence, the Tyrian line of kings could be slotted into the Biblical chronology. The reign of Dido's brother Pygmalion (as dated in the Tyrian chronicle) was contemporary with that of Jehu in Israel and Athaliah in Judah (as dated in Kings). The fall of Troy (as had been previously calculated) occurred sixty years before the reign of Saul. The duration between the reigns of Jehu and Judah (and therefore of Dido's brother) and that of Saul (sixty years after the fall of Troy), was between two and three centuries.

Dryden defends Virgil's anachronism by appealing to poetic license ('a man may be an admirable poet, without being an exact chronologer') while advising poets that if they cannot avoid such anachronisms, they should 'choose an obscure and a remote Æra, where they may invent at pleasure, and not be easily contradicted'.[28] Exposing and defending anachronism in literature becomes one of the routine tasks of eighteenth-century critics, applying chronology to poetry about the past in order to expose anachronisms and then excusing them by appealing to 'poetic license'. It becomes one of the many ways in which the Whiggish Augustan age asserts its literary superiority over its less refined predecessors.[29] Not only Lydgate, Gower, and Chaucer but also Spenser, Sidney, and above all Shakespeare are arraigned for anachronisms.[30] At the same time, literary criticism is itself being

[24] Jean Regnault de Segrais, 'De l'Ancronisme, & de la question, si Eneé a ésté en Italie', *Traduction de l'Eneïde de Virgile, par Mr. De Segrais*, two volumes in one, trans. Jean Regnault de Segrais (Paris, 1668), 27–8. Segrais derives his dates from Samuel Bochart, and prints his letter on the topic at the start of his commentary to Virgil, *Traduction de l'Eneïde de Virgile*, trans. de Segrais, Book 4, 88–91.

[25] For Scaliger's attempt to date the fall of Troy, see A. T. Grafton and N. M. Swerdlow, 'Greek Chronography in Roman Epic: The Calendrical Date of the Fall of Troy in the Aeneid', *The Classical Quarterly*, New Series, 36 (1986), 212–18.

[26] First translated into English by William Whiston in 1737, the fragmentary Tyrian Annals are included in Isaac Preston Cory, *Ancient Fragments of the Phoenician, ChaldÆan, Egyptian, Tyrian, Carthaginian, Indian, Persian, And Other Writers* (London: W. Pickering, 1832; first published 1828), 193–200; on the contemporaneity of Solomon and Hiram, see 196, 198.

[27] II Samuel 5:11 and I Chronicles 14:1.

[28] Virgil, *The Works of Virgil*, trans. Dryden, 2: 144, 145.

[29] John T. Lynch, *The Age of Elizabeth in The Age of Johnson* (Cambridge University Press, 2003).

[30] Ruthven, 'Preposterous Chatterton', 356.

organized along chronological timelines. In the case of Shakespeare, separate chronologies were devised for the life, work, and times of the author so that the three could be brought in sync and interrelated: history, biography, and the canon.[31]

Perhaps the last holdout against computational chronology is Giambattista Vico's *New Science* (1744). As Anthony Grafton has noted, Vico wrote his great mythopoetic history of civilization in part to show that the calculations of Scaliger and Petavius, for all their erudition, were off by a thousand years because they had discounted the stories of the gods and heroes.[32] Chronologists had assumed that the beginning of time coincided with the earliest astronomical calculations, but Vico maintained that the events recorded in the myths of the gods and heroes antedated them by a millennium. For Vico, the chronologists' miscalculation exemplifies the first of his four types of anachronism: 'the attribution of no events to a period full of events'.[33] So defined, an anachronism would be less a chronological error than a rhetorical solecism: an incommensurate relation between *copia verborum* and *copia rerum*. The second type of anachronism is an inversion of the first: 'when many events are attributed to a period that is eventless'. The third and fourth types are errors of *coniunctio* and *disiunctio*: 'when times are connected that should be separated', and 'when times are separated that should be connected'. The rhetorical bent of these definitions accords with the tropological terms of Vico's tripartite division of universal history into eras or *corsi*, each correspondent with a trope or figure of speech: the first or 'age of giants' with metaphor, the second or 'age of heroes' with metonymy and synecdoche, and the third or 'age of men' with irony. Vico places his own times in the third age in which men by submitting to the tyranny of reason have committed *barbarie della riflessione*: among those dim barbarisms was chronology uninformed by myth. Recalling chronology's earlier affiliation with the arts of language, Vico entitles his own fabulous and innumerate arrangement of events in time 'Poetic Chronology'.[34]

*

Though the word *anachronism* does not surface until the beginning of the seventeenth century, and then only in its Greek form and in an esoteric treatise, a grasp

[31] Margreta de Grazia, *Shakespeare Verbatim: The Reproduction of Authenticity and the 1790 Apparatus* (Oxford: Clarendon Press, 1991), 141–52.

[32] Anthony T. Grafton, 'Joseph Scaliger and Historical Chronology: The Rise and Fall of a Discipline', *History and Theory*, 14 (1975), 156–7.

[33] Giambattista Vico, *The New Science of Giambattista Vico, translated from the Third edition (1744)*, trans. Thomas Goddard Bergin and Max Harold Fisch (Ithaca and London: Cornell University Press, 1976, first published 1948), 279–84.

[34] On Vico's *New Science* as an alternative to 'linear, evolutionary, plot-driven, and informative histories', see Rita Copeland, 'History of Rhetoric and the *Longue Durée*: Ciceronian Myth and Its Medieval Afterlives', *Journal of English and Germanic Philology*, 106 (2007), 176–202, at 182.

of the concept has been identified much earlier. Scholars credit the quattrocento Italian humanists with mastering the principle, particularly Lorenzo Valla: 'The Italians, notably Lorenzo Valla, worked out in detail the concept of anachronism'; 'Valla had an acute sense of anachronism'.[35] In his treatise *De falso credita et ementita Constantini donatione declamatio* (1440), Valla exposes as forgery the Donation of Constantine, the document by which the papacy derived its temporal powers. Written in the person of the newly converted emperor Constantine, the Donation confers upon Pope Sylvester and his apostolic successors dominion over the whole of the Eastern Empire ('Judaea, Greece, Asia, Thrace, Africa, and Italy as well as various islands') in addition to the imperial capital of Rome and unspecified 'western territories', all in gratitude for the Pope's having baptized him and cured him (the next day) of leprosy.[36] As modern accounts routinely maintain, Valla's treatise proved the document was spurious by exposing its ubiquitous anachronisms. 'His familiarity with the customs, legal forms, and language of the fourth century is extensive enough to declare the *Donation* at once anachronistic.'[37] Valla's ability to distinguish the usages and references of one period from another is seen to lay the foundations for modern textual criticism. 'The use of anachronisms as an instrument of historical analysis was a real turning point, which had an enormous long-term impact leading to the textual criticism of Richard Bentley and A. E. Housman.'[38]

Yet Valla hardly seems interested in questions of antedating and postdating. Modern scholarship credits him with having 'proved that the so-called Donation of Constantine could not be a genuinely fourth-century document because it contained eighth-century usages'.[39] But whatever Valla proved, it could not have been that: he never identifies Constantine with the fourth century and the forger with the eighth. He never mentions centuries at all, a unit for organizing time that appears not to have been widespread until, at the earliest, the seventeenth century.[40] Modern scholars regularly cite as one of the forger's anachronisms the date of the Donation's subscription, 'Given at Rome[. . .]when the distinguished

[35] Burke, 'The Sense of Anachronism', 160.

[36] Appendix, 'The Donation of Constantine', in Lorenzo Valla, *On the Donation of Constantine*, trans. G. W. Bowersock (Cambridge, MA, and London: The I Tatti Renaissance Library, Harvard University Press, 2007), paragraphs 13, 17. All references to Valla's treatise will be included parenthetically in text, by paragraph numbers.

[37] Joseph M. Levine, *Humanism And History: Origins of Modern Historiography* (Ithaca: Cornell University Press, 1987), 71.

[38] Carlo Ginzburg, *History, Rhetoric, and Proof* (Hanover, NH and London: University Presses of New England, 1999), 64.

[39] Ruthven, 'Preposterous Chatterton', 352. Compare Donald J. Wilcox on Valla's demonstration 'that the language [of the Donation] was commonly used not in the imperial chancery of the fourth century but in the papal chancery of the ninth': Wilcox, *The Measure of Times Past*, 243.

[40] Wilcox, *The Measure of Time Past*, 9; and Daniel S. Milo, *Trahir Le Temps (Histoire)* (Paris: Les Belles Lettres, 1991), 68–70.

consuls were our lord Flavius Constantine Augustus for the fourth time and Gallicanus':[41] on the basis of the modern reconstruction of the consular list, they point out that Constantine and Gallicanus never served as consul in the same year.[42] Valla, however, comments not on the misdating but on the unlikely coincidence of both men having been consuls for four years running (70). He also emphasizes the implausibility of Constantine's having made the public appearances required by this office when disfigured by leprosy, 'a disease [which] stands out among others like an elephant among beasts' (70).

As G. W. Bowersock, Valla's most recent translator, observes, the treatise refers to itself as an 'oratio' and Valla in a letter describes it as a speech more rhetorical than anything he had written (viii); it is a 'bravura exercise in rhetoric and philology' (x). Without question, Valla's favorite rhetorical device is *prosopopeia*, or 'the personation of characters', praised by both Cicero and Quintilian for its force, variety, and animation. It enables the orator 'to invent persuasions, or reproaches, or complaints, or eulogies, or lamentations, and put them into the mouths of characters likely to utter them'.[43] The characters can then converse with one another as well as with the orator. Clearly the device encourages anachronism, for the characters can be dead or alive, as well as animate or inanimate, mortal or immortal. In the opening of his treatise, Valla imagines himself in an assembly of kings and princes, and feigns 'to address them as if they were present in front of me' (6). He addresses the deceased Constantine (6–18), Pope Sylvester (21–6), some of his successors (33), and above all the mendacious imposter who pretended to be Constantine: 'I prefer to attack him as if he were present before me' (40). Addressed as if present in the present, these persons respond in kind. The deceased Constantine, his sons, representatives of the Roman senate and people, and Sylvester all give speeches demonstrating the implausibility of the gift. With splendid irony, Valla berates his opponent for the same histrionics he himself so outrageously exploits: 'This is what it really means to be a *hypocrite*, if we take the Greek word literally—to hide your own identity under someone else's' (italics added), 'mouthing words the way actors do' (65).[44]

Nor are the treatise's philological analyses concerned with temporal discrepancies. It is not the forger's anachronisms that incense Valla, but his barbarisms. He denies Constantine's authorship of the document not because it refers to

[41] Valla, *On the Donation of Constantine*, trans. Bowersock, 20.

[42] Valla, *On the Donation of Constantine*, trans. Bowersock, xv, n. 19; 198 n. 2.

[43] Quintilian, *Institutiones Oratoriae*, ed. and trans. Donald A. Russell (Cambridge, MA, and London: Harvard University Press, 2001), 9: 2, 30–8, at 30; see also, Cicero, *Rhetorica ad Herennium*, trans. Harry Caplan (Cambridge, MA: Harvard University Press, 1954), IV.LII.66. On impersonation and histrionics, see John Parker, 'Persona', in this volume.

[44] Valla's charge nicely illustrates John Parker's apt definition of hypocrisy as 'a technical designation for the brand of feigning that pretends to repudiate the mimetic practice it most depends on', in Parker, *The Aesthetics of Antichrist: From Christian Drama to Christopher Marlowe* (Ithaca and London: Cornell University Press, 2007), 16–17.

phenomena that postdate Constantine but because he never would have written such bad Latin. Valla calls the 'hypocrite' *barbara*, identifying him with the invading Nordic hordes which destroyed Rome and corrupted Latin culture. The forger is betrayed by his 'linguistic barbarisms' (*barbariem sermonis*) and 'foolishness of words' (*verborum stoliditatem*), as Valla repeatedly stresses: 'Uncultivated people [*barbari homines*] commonly talk and write this way' (44, 55, 58). Valla provides numerous examples of Barbara's linguistic incompetence, especially of his lack of discrimination, as when he refers to the cloth of the papal crown as gold; the free subjects who are the SPQR as 'people subject'; a grant as a 'privilege' ('how great barbarousness is there in these words?'); Byzantium as a province when it is a city. He berates and mocks the forger not for historical errors, but for grammatical solecisms and stylistic infelicities: for his abundant 'contraria, impossibilia, stulta, barbara, ridicula' (5), the kind of errors inventoried under *Errors of Latinitas* in Heinrich Lausberg's compendia of rhetorical figures.[45] His critique may at times look as if it were targeting anachronism, most notably when he asks (rhetorically), 'doth not the very barbarousness of the manner of speaking witness openly: that this carol hath been feigned not in the time of Constantine but in a time more late?' But it is not asynchronicity that is the problem, the collapsing of the reign of Constantine (306–337) with that of the Gothic or Germanic rulers (after the sack of Rome in 410 or the deposition of last Roman emperor in 476). It is rather the disparity between the proper Latin he imagines Constantine to have used and the corrupt Latin deployed by the post-imperial barbarian.

That Valla's analysis of the Donation differs from that attributed to him by modern scholars can be ascertained by looking at its most famous anachronism, singled out by Bowersock as 'grotesque' and 'damning'.[46] The forger uses the word *satrapa* three times to refer to an official in the Roman Senate.[47] On the authority of two scholarly monographs (1956 and 2007), his translator concludes, 'The word satrap was not applied to high officials in Rome before the mid-eighth century' (190–1 n. 47). Carlo Ginzburg has also seen in *satraps* 'proof that the alleged date of the *Constitutum Constantini* was untenable'.[48] But it is not the untimeliness of the term that exercises Valla:

> Why do you want to bring in *satraps*? You blockhead, you dolt! Do emperors talk that way? Are Roman decrees normally drafted like that? Who ever heard of satraps being named in the deliberations of the Romans? I cannot recall reading that anyone, either in Rome or even in the provinces of the Romans, was ever named a satrap. (42)

[45] Heinrich Lausberg, *Handbook of Literary Rhetoric: A Foundation for Literary Study* ed. David E. Orton and R. Dean Anderson (Leiden: Brill, 1998) §§475–527, 1066.

[46] Valla, *On the Donation of Constantine*, trans. Bowersock, xii, 190, n.47.

[47] Wolfram Brandes, 'The Satraps of Constantine', in Johannes Fried, *Donation of Constantine and Constitutum Constantini: The Misinterpretation of a Fiction and its Original Meaning* (Berlin and New York: Walter de Gruyter, 2007), 115–27, at 115–16.

[48] Ginzburg, *History, Rhetoric, and Proof*, 64.

In this denunciation, Valla scrolls down a hierarchy of speakers, from emperor to citizen to provincial, until there is no one left—inside the walls of Rome, that is. By contrast to the Donation, Valla's refutation is written in impeccable Latin, polished and supple. His purpose conforms to that declared in his treatise *On the Elegancies of the Latin Language* (1444): 'to restore the language of Rome to the Romans, to return it to the purity that was its glory before the barbarian corruption'.[49] Erasmus in the next century honored him for the same accomplishment: 'a man who with so much energy, zeal, and labour, refuted the stupidities of the Barbarians, saved half-buried letters from extinction, restored Italy to her ancient splendour of eloquence, and forced even the learned to express themselves henceforth with more circumspection'.[50]

Valla's declamation appears to have had little consequence: not for Valla, not for the papacy.[51] In 1444, Valla was arraigned before the Inquisition at Naples not for challenging papal authority but for the Epicureanism of his *De vero bono* and the determinism of *De libero arbitro*; in 1448 he was appointed apostolic *scriptor* by Pope Nicholas V and in 1455 apostolic secretary by Pope Calixtus III. Not until 1559, over a century after its composition, is Valla's oration put on the Index of Prohibited Books. Nor were the Pope's worldly claims in any way curtailed. Indeed the unspecified 'western territories' conferred by the Donation were later taken to refer to lands undiscovered in Valla's time. In 1493, Pope Alexander VI asserted his dominion over the New World by drawing a meridian through the Atlantic Ocean to divide the New World between Spain and Portugal. In 1533, a fresco depicting Constantine handing the Donation to the Pope was completed by Raphael's workshop for the 'Sala di Costantino' of the Vatican palace. Here, too, the presence of elements long postdating Constantine's fourth-century world in no way invalidates the documentation: Sylvester I is portrayed as Pope Clement VII, the pope when the frescos were executed; the event occurs not in the fourth century but in the recently renovated St. Peter's Basilica; with twisted Solomonic columns in the background believed to have been transported by Constantine from the Temple of Solomon in Jerusalem, though later identified as elements from a second-century eastern church.[52]

[49] Paul Oskar Kristeller, *Eight Philosophers of the Italian Renaissance* (Stanford, CA: Stanford University Press, 1964), 25.

[50] Desiderius Erasmus, *Epistles of Erasmus*, ed. Francis Morgan Nichols, 3 vols. (New York: Russell and Russell, 1962; first published 1901), 3: 71.

[51] On the enduring importance of the Donation after its refutation by Nicholas of Cusa, Valla, and Reginald Pecock, see Robert Black, 'The Donation of Constantine: A New Source for the Concept of the Renaissance?', in *Language and Images of Renaissance Italy*, ed. Alison Brown (Oxford: Clarendon Press, 1995), 51–85.

[52] J. B. Ward-Perkins, 'The Shrine of St. Peter's and its Twelve Spiral Columns', *The Journal of Roman Studies*, 42 (1952), 21–33; Pauline Moffitt Watts, 'The Donation of Constantine, Cartography, and Papal *Plenitudo Potestatis* in the Sixteenth Century', A Paper for Salvatore Camporeale, *Modern Language Notes*, 119 (2004), 688–707.

Valla's refutation might well have faded into obscurity, had it not been for the Reformation. It is not published until 1506 and then only in the proto-Protestant North: in Strasbourg (1506 and 1520), Basle (1518 and 1519, 1540), Cologne (1535), and Leyden (1620). It is also translated: into Czech (c.1519), French (1520), German (1524, 1526), English (1534), and Italian (1546).[53] Once translated into the vernaculars, the treatise perforce ceases to showcase Latin eloquence by stigmatizing bad Latin.[54] It is pure polemic: an attack on the instrument establishing the papacy's claim to temporal power. In 1520, Luther marveled that so many were taken in by the Donation's falsehoods, 'so crude and clumsy that I should imagine any drunken peasant could lie more adroitly and skillfully'.[55] In 1537 he published an annotated translation of the Donation to prove that the Pope was Antichrist who had used the Donation to usurp 'for himself half the Roman empire' and foisted it upon believers as an article of faith.[56] Valla's English translator, William Marshall, reports to Thomas Cromwell, 'Surely I thinke there was never better boke made and sett forthe for the defasing of the Pope of Rome than this.'[57] In his *Acts and Monuments*, Foxe summarizes twelve arguments proving the Donation 'falsely fayned and forged'.[58] Only one involves a chronological incongruity, though it could just as easily be an example of *hysteron proteron*: the Donation refers to the see of Constantinople before the building of Constantinople.

The discrediting of the Donation is critical to the Reformation, not only in dissolving the Pope's claim to power, but in preparing the way for Elizabeth's. *Constantine* is the first word of the dedication to Elizabeth in the 1563 *Acts and Monuments*; enthroned in the capacious first initial of the emperor's name, sits Elizabeth. She has replaced Pope Sylvester as Constantine's immediate successor. Like the Donation, the *Book of Martyrs* passes the imperial mantle to its favored head of Church. As Elizabeth succeeds Constantine, so too the Reformed Church picks up where the Primitive Church left off, and Foxe continues the narrative of Christian persecution begun by Eusebius, Constantine's great chronicler. The leap

[53] See 'Nota Bibliografica', in Giovanni Antonazzi, *Lorenzo Valla e la polemica sulla donazione di Costantino* (Rome: Edizioni di Storia e Letteratura, 1985), 189–92.

[54] On the difficulty of preserving Valla's masterful Latin in translation as well as the acumen of his critique, see Valla, *On the Donation of Constantine*, trans. Bowersock, x–xii.

[55] Martin Luther, *To the Christian Nobility of the German Nation*, trans. Charles M. Jacobs, in *Luther's Works*, 55 vols., ed. Jaroslav Pelikan (Saint Louis: Concordia Publishing House, 1955–1986), 44: 166. For the influence of Valla on Luther, see David M. Whitford, 'The Papal Antichrist: Martin Luther and the Underappreciated Influence of Lorenzo Valla', *Renaissance Quarterly*, 61 (2008), 26–52.

[56] Quoted by Black, 'The Donation of Constantine', 76.

[57] Antonazzi, 'Nota Bibliografica', 191.

[58] John Foxe, *Acts and Monuments* [...] (1576 edition), [online]. (hriOnline, Sheffield). Available from: <http://www.hrionline.shef.ac.uk/foxe>. (Accessed: 12 October 2008.)

in genealogy from the fourth to the sixteenth century might be called anachronism. But isn't it typology?

*

Through most of the last century, a grasp of anachronism has been attributed not only to Valla but to the Renaissance period in general. It might well seem a rather minor feature to play an epoch-making role, especially when the capacity to diagnose it is figured as a 'nose', 'ear', or 'eye' for anachronism. (Periods have physiognomies as well as psychologies.) But the ability to detect and avoid anachronism has been taken as nothing less than evidence of historical consciousness. It requires an awareness that the past differs from the present and that the various periods of the past differ from one another. The Renaissance, it is often said, was not only conscious of diachrony but also conscious that it was conscious of it: in recognizing itself as a distinct period, both from remote antiquity (to which it would draw closer) and from the proximate dark ages (from which it would distance itself).

Petrarch is the epochal figure here, particularly as he represents himself in his address to *Africa* (1338): poised on the outermost verge of his own dark epoch, looking back longingly at luminous antiquity while at the same time glimpsing a new shining epoch ahead.[59] Petrarch is also among the many humanists who, like Valla, is lauded for his exposure of forgery, particularly letters from Caesar and Nero. At the same time, he himself feigns a correspondence with the ancients, not only writing but also receiving letters from Homer. As Anthony Grafton has recently demonstrated, both forgery and textual criticism require a grasp of the principle of anachronism: a text from a given period cannot contain usages from or references to anything in a later. And the Renaissance is the best point at which to observe the convergence of these two practices: 'In the Renaissance, even more than in previous periods, forger and critic marched in lockstep'.[60]

The *Dictionary of Historical Concepts* finds a consensus among numerous early modern historians on the periodizing function of anachronism: 'it seems that the sense of anachronism was virtually non-existent in the Middle Ages and appears to have begun to develop seriously only from about the fourteenth century onwards'.[61] No historian has maintained this more adamantly or persistently than Peter Burke, in four separate works spanning from 1968 to 2001.[62] In his

[59] Theodore E. Mommsen, 'Petrarch's Conception of the "Dark Ages"', *Speculum*, 17 (1942), 226–42.

[60] Anthony Grafton, *Forgers and Critics: Creativity and Duplicity in Western Scholarship* (Princeton, NJ: Princeton University Press, 1990), 31.

[61] Harry Ritter, *Dictionary of Historical Concepts* (New York, Westport, CT, and London: Greenwood Press, 1986), 9–13, at 10.

[62] Peter Burke, 'The Sense of Historical Perspective in Renaissance Italy', *Journal of World History*, 11 (1968), 615–32; *The Renaissance Sense of the Past* (London: Edward Arnold, 1969); 'The Renaissance

1969 *The Renaissance Sense of the Past*, he made the sweeping claim that '[d]uring the whole millennium 400–1400, there was no "sense of history" even among the educated'.[63] Thirty years later, he defends this assertion against two objections that had been repeatedly raised against it: (1) that there is sensitivity to anachronism before 1400, and (2) that there is no such sensitivity until after 1600. His solution is easy: extend the termini at either end, and assume in between a more gradual and more finely calibrated chronological development of historical consciousness: a 'more or less acute awareness of anachronism'.[64] By this revision, his moment of emergent anachronism has a *longue durée* indeed, from the *duecento* sculptor Nicola Pisano to the neoclassical painter Nicolas Poussin.

Daniel R. Woolf has also revisited his own earlier work on the subject by giving a more nuanced and exacting analysis of what is meant by the Renaissance 'sense of the past'. In his recent analysis of changes in historical consciousness from 1500 to 1700, the first shift he notes is 'the articulation of a sense of period, and the acquisition... of a historical map', that is, a serial or diachronic disposition of time on which any event can be situated, the temporal counterpart to the world map on which any place can be located.[65] Several Tudor historians have claimed that Reformation England produced a heightened sense of anachronism when Protestantism's split with the old faith Catholicism deepened humanism's break with past scholasticism. In 1967, Fritz Levy concluded that the concept of anachronism was 'one of the most important ideas underlying the Reformation' and that by the early seventeenth century, 'the application of the concept of anachronism had become well nigh second nature'.[66] While those assessments now seem extreme, several recent studies have emphasized how the dissolution of the monasteries sharpened England's sense of its own antiquity; like Rome, it had its own ruins bearing witness to a bygone time.[67] Patrick Collinson has turned attention to Elizabethan antiquarianism for an emergent understanding of anachronism: a sense 'of the past as another country where they did things differently, and as an ever shifting target, the essence of historical thought'.[68]

Sense of the Past Revisited', *Culture and History*, 12 (1994), 42–56; 'The Sense of Anachronism from Petrarch to Poussin', in *Time in the Medieval World*, ed. Humphrey and Ormrod, 157–73.

63 Burke, *The Renaissance Sense of the Past*, 1.

64 Burke, 'The Sense of Anachronism from Petrarch to Poussin', 173.

65 Daniel R. Woolf, 'From Hystories to the Historical: Five Transitions in Thinking About the Past, 1500–1700', *Huntington Library Quarterly*, 68 (2005), 33–70, at 38.

66 Fred Jacob Levy, *Tudor Historical Thought* (San Marino, CA: Huntington Library, 1967), ix.

67 Levy, *Tudor Historical Thought*, 22. For other works, including his own, arguing for the presence of a humanist 'modern historical consciousness' in Reformation England, see Daniel R. Woolf, *The Social Circulation of the Past: English Historical Culture 1500–1730* (Oxford and New York: Oxford University Press, 2003), 3, 5.

68 Patrick Collinson, 'One of Us? William Camden and the Making of History', *Transactions of the Royal Historical Society*, 6th series, 8 (1998), 139–63.

As these historians readily acknowledge, it is from an art historian that they derive their conviction that the Renaissance's claim to period status depended on its awareness of itself as a period distinct from both the Middle Ages and Antiquity. 'From the fourteenth through the sixteenth century, then, and from one end of Europe to the other, the men of the Renaissance were convinced that the period in which they lived was a "new age" as sharply different from the mediaeval past as the mediaeval past had been from classical antiquity.'[69] Prior to 1400, there had been periodic returns to ancient arts and letters: the Carolingian renaissance in the ninth century, the Ottonian and Anglo-Saxon *renovatii* of around 1000, and the proto-Renaissance of the twelfth century. All these movements, however, were no more than generic lower-case *renascences* for one simple reason: they never clearly differentiated Antiquity from their own time. That distinction was proper only to the Renaissance: 'The classical past was looked upon, for the first time, as a totality cut off from the present'.[70] As a result, period styles emerged, specifically in Vasari's tripartite identification (not always consistent): *la buona maniera greca antica*, *la maniera greca* (or *tedesca*), and *la buona maniera moderna*, which roughly align with Ancient, Byzantine or Gothic, and Modern. With periods in place, representations of the past could be true to their own particulars: for the first time, artists painted classical subjects with classicizing motifs—classical dress, architecture, and customs. Even the period features of the contemned Middle Ages were respected, as Panofsky exemplified with Vasari's encasement of a sketch by Cimabue with an architectural enframement of 'a pronouncedly Gothicizing style'.[71] The acquisition of historical distance had a striking counterpart in the representation of spatial distance, 'the distance between the eye and the object'.[72] The interposition of an ideal projection plane separated the viewer from the object viewed, prohibiting direct contact, but offering 'a total and rationalized view'.[73] Thus 'cognitive distance' enabled the Renaissance to comprehend both anachronism and perspective, historical change and spatial depth. (Sometimes the two discoveries were at odds, as when classically garbed figures stand on an anachronistically perspectival checkerboard floor.)

The Middle Ages, however, understood neither spatial nor historical distance. 'Just as it was impossible for the Middle Ages to elaborate the modern system of perspective[. . .]so was it impossible to evolve the modern idea of history,

[69] Erwin Panofsky, *Renaissance and Renascences in Western Art* (New York and Evanston, IL: Harper & Row, 1969; first published *c.*1960), 36.

[70] Panofsky, *Renaissance and Renascences*, 106, 113.

[71] Panofsky, 'The First Page of Vasari's *Libro*', in *Meaning in the Visual Arts: Papers in and on Art History* (Garden City, NY: Doubleday & Company, 1955; first published 1939), 169–225, at 175.

[72] Panofsky, 'The First Page', 51.

[73] Panofsky, 'Introduction', *Studies in Iconology: Humanistic Themes in the Art of the Renaissance* (Oxford: Oxford University Press, 1939), 28; and *Renaissance and Renascences*, 108.

based on the realization of an intellectual distance between the present and the past.'[74] For the Middle Ages, the past flowed into the present in a continuous tradition of *Latinitas*. Antiquity still lingered, however worn or fragmentary its condition, to be admired or ignored and above all *used*: pagan *spolia* were integrated into Christian churches, Venus was recast as Eve, Laocöon depicted as a tonsured monk. Because history was uniform, anachronism was the rule: 'I know no exception to the rule that the classical themes transmitted to medieval artists by texts were anachronistically modernized'.[75] Anachronisms abounded but were not detected, not in the visual arts and not in textual criticism; and this could be explained by a simple truism: 'The Middle Ages never knew that they were medieval' and consequently never knew they were not ancient.[76] As a result, they unknowingly depicted Apollo in a medieval tunic; Raphael, however, consciously placed a modern *lira da braccio* in Apollo's hands in his otherwise classicized painting of Parnassus.[77] In the High Renaissance, an anachronistic element might show off an artist's historical consciousness, rather than betraying its lack. Ancient and modern elements could be strategically combined, once the artist knew the difference between them. And, for Panofsky, that difference was as clear as black and white, life and death. And here comes Panofsky's most startling literalization of *Re-naissance*: before it could be born again, Antiquity had first to be dead and buried: 'The Middle Ages had left antiquity unburied', while '[t]he Renaissance stood weeping at its grave'.[78]

Weeping at the grave is precisely where Thomas Greene locates the Renaissance in his magisterial study of Renaissance poetic production: *The Light in Troy: Imitation and Discovery in Renaissance Poetry*. Longing for the past stimulates the desire to imitate it—but always in heartrending view of the millennial abyss that separates the poet from his (*sic*) ancient models. This is the new dilemma of the Renaissance poet: that he must recreate the past in the present knowing full well 'the risk of anachronism'.[79] '*Imitatio* produced a vast effort to deal with the newly perceived problem of anachronism.' Poetic imitation offered to 'heal estrangement', but it could be attempted only by admitting that estrangement. Greene identifies four 'imitative strategies' for acknowledging distance, 'each of which involves a distinct response to anachronism and each an implicit perspective on history' (44). The weakest strategy he calls *reproductive* or *sacramental*: a 'reverent rewriting' that

[74] Panofsky, *Meaning in the Visual Arts*, 51.
[75] Panofsky, *Renaissance and Renascences*, 87.
[76] Panofsky, *Renaissance and Renascences*, 108.
[77] Panofsky, *Renaissance and Renascences*, 202–5. For an overdue critique of Panofsky's association of the Renaissance with a grasp of historical distance that introduces the anachronistic category of temporal 'instantiation', see Alexander Nagel and Christopher S. Wood, 'Interventions: Toward a New Model of Renaissance Anachronism', *Art Bulletin*, 87 (2005), 401–15.
[78] Panofsky, *Renaissance and Renascences*, 113.
[79] Thomas M. Greene, *The Light in Troy: Imitation and Discovery in Renaissance Poetry* (New Haven: Yale University Press, 1982), 30, 37. Subsequent page references appear parenthetically in text.

leaves its faraway classical model virtually untouched, 'beyond alteration and beyond criticism', like a sacred original. Minimally anachronistic, it is also poetically slack. Alternatively, the strongest of his strategies is the most aggressively confrontational: called *dialectical*, it precipitates a 'miniature anachronistic crisis', an agonistic encounter with the past, a dialectical struggle between two rhetorical and semiotic systems (42). Thus the more acutely conscious the poet is of historical distance, the more successful the poem.[80] In such instances, '[a]nachronism becomes a dynamic source of artistic power' (46).

It is also the source of the critic's power. For the critic of the Renaissance also experiences historical estrangement, indeed estrangement twice over, as he looks back both to the Renaissance and to the Renaissance looking back to antiquity. Like the Renaissance humanist, the critic knows the limitations of his encounter with the past: 'The pathos of this incomplete embrace'. Because he too would bring remote texts to life, he too runs the risk of 'damaging anachronism' (33). But wherein lies the risk or damage? Is it the loss of the object's historical specificity that is feared? Would the past vanish if, like Eurydice, it were viewed head on? For Greene, it is curiously not the loss of the distant object that is dreaded, but the loss of the distance that keeps him from that object. To lose it would be to lose historical consciousness, to fall back into the kind of historical oblivion or 'diachronic innocence' (30) with which he has stigmatized the medieval period. It would be a reversion or relapse into the 'naiveté' that is the period feature of his Middle Ages: 'lacking a strong historical sense', making 'no pretense of historical control', and thereby shirking 'its transitive responsibilities' (41). He retains historical distance from the object he would embrace lest he be counted among those medievals who were content to see Aeneas as knight or the maenads as Bacchic nuns: 'No one, so far as I can judge, neither Abelard nor Bernard of Chartres nor John of Salisbury, was fully sensitive to the fact of radical cultural change that would be glimpsed by Dante and then faced in all its overwhelming force by Renaissance humanism' (17). It is the loss of consciousness that is feared, then, the collapse of the barrier that stands between subject and object and holds them apart, with the subject in control. Devoutly wished for, the consummation is really never attempted, for the cost would be too high, as it was for the most beautiful of Milton's fallen angels: 'For who would lose, / Though full of pain, this intellectual being?'[81]

*

It may not be the desire to respect historical otherness that underlies the aversion to anachronism, as this essay began by proposing, but rather the need to retain the

[80] See also Thomas M. Greene, 'History and Anachronism', in *The Vulnerable Text: Essays on Renaissance Literature* (New York: Columbia University Press, 1986), 218–35.

[81] John Milton, *Paradise Lost* in *John Milton*, ed. Stephen Orgel and Jonathan Goldberg (Oxford and New York: Oxford University Press, 1991), 2: 146–7.

'cognitive distance' that is the very basis of our disciplinary knowledge. The disciplines of history, history of art, and literature have all located the Renaissance as the age when the foundations of modern scholarly and critical practices were set down through the interposition of historical distance. There is a subjective corollary to that disciplinary stance: the feeling of solitude and estrangement that, for Greene, saturates not only Renaissance poetry but also his writing about Renaissance poetry. In the Renaissance, that feeling has been diagnosed as *melancholia* and termed its 'period illness'. (Historical periods have chronic diseases and pathologies to go along with their minds and bodies.)

Walter Benjamin recognized these twinned symptoms of abstracted thought and numbing *acedia* in Luther, in Hamlet, and in Dürer's engraving of *Melancholia.*[82] In his 'Theses on the Philosophy of History', his biting critique of 'the continuum of history', he also includes Flaubert among its sufferers.[83] In Thesis VII, he quotes from a letter Flaubert wrote while working on his heavily researched historical novel *Salammbô*, set in Carthage during the first Punic war: 'Peu de gens devineront combien il a fallu être triste pour [entreprendre de] resusciter Carthage'.[84] For Benjamin, Flaubert's empathetic attachment to ancient Carthage betrays an inherited rapport with the victor: the Romans who dominated Carthage in imperial times, the French who were dominating North African Tunisia in Flaubert's colonial times as well as in Benjamin's. His melancholic longing to retrieve the past of victorious Rome marks him as a beneficiary of the colonial legacy, for in narrating that past, he carries it forward, in a process of transmission Benjamin likens to a triumphal procession that mindlessly bears its spoils from one generation to the next.[85] The historical materialist of Benjamin's 'Theses' would bring that progressive and monotonous temporality to a dead halt. While the 'Theses' do not name them, anachronisms—violations of absolute diachronic time—surely belong among the insurrectionary tactics by which historical materialism 'brush[es] history against the grain' of the dominant and oppressive historical continuum.

*

A revision of this essay's opening premise may now be in order. It is not at all clear that sensitivity to anachronism means that we are being properly and ethically

[82] Walter Benjamin, *The Origin of German Tragic Drama*, trans. John Osborne (London and New York: Verso 1985), 138, 140.

[83] Benjamin, 'Theses on the Philosophy of History', in *Illuminations: Essays and Reflections*, trans. Harry Zohn and ed. Hannah Arendt (New York: Schocken Books, 1969), 253–64, at 262.

[84] Benjamin, 'Theses on the Philosophy of History', 256. The quote is from Flaubert's letter to Ernest Feydeau, 29–30 November 1859, in *Correspondance: Gustave Flaubert*, 5 vols., ed. Giovanni Bonaccorso (Saint-Genouph (France): Nizet, 2001), 3: 59. In the quotation, Benjamin stops short of the end of Flaubert's passage: 'C'est là une thébaïde ou le degôut de la vie moderne m'a poussé.'

[85] Compare Scaliger, 'the vanquished have no other system of dating than that of the victor', *De emendatione*, quoted by Grafton, 'Joseph Scaliger and Historical Chronology', 168.

historical or that we are acknowledging that inviolable difference between then and now, the other and the same. Our diachronic sophistication enables us to see the past as our disciplines have configured it: that is, at a distance maintained and gauged by an absolute timeline. It has been easy, all too easy, to unsettle the old (but hardly outdated) critical tradition that—to the detriment of the Middle Ages—credits the Renaissance with having first grasped the fundamental concept of cognitive distance. This essay has argued that sensitivity to anachronism is a later phenomenon more closely coinciding with the formation of the disciplinary divisions under whose aegis we still mainly work. To speak of anachronism *avant la lettre*, then, would itself be an anachronism. But that should not be taken to mean that we have not been sufficiently historical: when our propositions go so self-reflexively circular, it is a sure sign that we are banging our heads against our disciplinary walls.

Suppose instead, as a way of loosening chronology's hold on historical thought, we were to remove the stigma from anachronism or turn that stigma to advantage? For chronology is only one way by which the past can be related to the present. That this essay has itself taken chronological steps in critiquing chronology indicates the extent of chronology's critical sway. In the process, however, it has at least touched upon other possibilities: in an earlier association of chronology with figuration and narrative, in Vico's 'Poetic Chronology', in Valla's prosopopeic impersonations, in Foxe's typological history, in medieval modernizations of antiquity, in Benjaminian dialectical montages; and (were this essay to continue) in the post-colonial critiques of chronology as a system for ordering time exclusive to the West. Even in the history of the West, chronology has not always ruled the day.

FURTHER READING

Didi-Huberman, Georges. 'Before the Image, Before Time: The Sovereignty of Anachronism', in *Compelling Visuality: The Work of Art In and Out of History*, ed. Claire Farago and Robert Zwijnenberg (Minneapolis: University of Minnesota Press, 2003), 31–44

Grafton, Anthony T. 'Joseph Scaliger and Historical Chronology: The Rise and Fall of a Discipline', *History and Theory*, 14.2 (1975), 156–85

Greene, Thomas M. 'Imitation and Anachronism', in *The Light in Troy: Imitation and Discovery in Renaissance Poetry* (New Haven, CT: Yale University Press, 1982), 28–53

Nagel, Alexander and Christopher Wood. *Anachronic Renaissance* (New York: ZONE Books, forthcoming)

CHAPTER 3

NATIONAL HISTORIES

ARDIS BUTTERFIELD

Nation and vernacularity are natural collaborators.[1] Adrian Hastings speaks for many in saying that 'the literary development of a spoken vernacular' is 'the most influential and widespread single internal factor' in the development of nationhood.[2] Spenser's exclamation 'Why a God's name, may not we, as else the Greeks, have the kingdom of our own language?' is used by Richard Helgerson as the starting point for his investigation of nationhood in the Elizabethan era.[3] And Benedict Anderson points to the fragmentation and pluralization of the sacred languages as a crucial marker in the development of national imaginings.[4] Yet it is puzzling how this widespread assumption can be articulated in relation to such disparate historical contexts. For Anderson, as with most modernist students of nation, the context is the late eighteenth century; Helgerson takes it back to the sixteenth, and Hastings further still to the fourteenth. Each argues that the rise of nation occurs at a moment when there is a decisively new burgeoning of the vernacular; yet for each this moment is in a different century. Any attempt to reconcile such discrete perspectives is bound to be perilous, but it seems worth pointing out their self-containment, not least because of the special discipline imposed by this volume's engagement with period division. This essay identifies three issues concerning nation that have particular relevance to cross-period 'cultural reformations'. The first is the relation of nation to modernity; the second,

[1] Note the classic article by V. H. Galbraith, 'Nationality and Language in Medieval England', *Transactions of the Royal Historical Society*, 23 (1941), 113–28.

[2] Adrian Hastings, *The Construction of Nationhood: Ethnicity, Religion and Nationalism* (Cambridge: Cambridge University Press, 1997), 31.

[3] Richard Helgerson, *Forms of Nationhood: the Elizabethan Writing of England* (Chicago: University of Chicago Press, 1992), Introduction, 1.

[4] Benedict Anderson, *Imagined Communities* (London and New York: Verso, 1991; first published 1983), 18–19.

of nation to language; and the third, of nation to England and Englishness. All three, I argue, are radically affected by England's long relationship with France.

Modernity, language, and Englishness

The topic of modernity has a special tension for both medieval and early modern scholars. It is perhaps above all a medievalists' problem, as Margreta de Grazia has amusingly commented, for the division between 'medieval' and 'modern' works with crushing effectiveness to divide the relevant from the irrelevant. It is a 'secular divide' that acts 'less as a historical marker than as a massive value judgement, determining what matters and what does not'.[5] Modernity is like an eagerly claimed prize, grasped at by the title 'early modern', half-claimed, half-repudiated in 'premodern'. Yet both medieval and early modern together are dismissed as irrelevant to nation by modernist historians.[6] Nation is not only claimed for the modern period, it is held to be the definition of modernity: 'the idea of the "nation"... I believe forms *the constitutive element of modernity*', writes Liah Greenfeld (her italics).[7] Commentators on the medieval and early modern periods are offered two choices by the modernists: to disavow any interest in nation, or else to disavow any interest in modernity.

Taking advantage of their self-description as 'early modern', scholars of the sixteenth and seventeenth centuries deny both choices and boldly lay claim to nation. Helgerson's influential study implicitly associates nationhood with the discourse of rebirth that clings to many aspects of change and discovery in the period from 1400 to 1600: Elizabethan travels to the New World, large-scale finds in antique sculpture, the studies of Erasmus, Luther and Tyndale in Greek and Hebrew, the spread of Protestantism, the developing culture of print. The presence of Shakespeare in the period, subsequent icon of Englishness, is powerfully

[5] Margreta de Grazia, 'The Modern Divide: From Either Side', in *Re-Thinking Periodization*, ed. Jennifer Summit and David Wallace, Special Issue of *Journal of Medieval and Early Modern Studies*, 37 (2007), 453–67, at 453. See also her essay in this volume.

[6] The standard expositions include Eric Hobsbawm, 'Introduction: Inventing Traditions', in *The Invention of Tradition*, ed. Eric Hobsbawm and Terence Ranger (Cambridge: Cambridge University Press, 1983), 1–14; and Eric Hobsbawm, *Nations and Nationalism since 1780* (Cambridge: Cambridge University Press, 1990); Ernest Gellner, *Nations and Nationalism* (Oxford: Blackwell, 1983) and his *Encounters with Nationalism* (Oxford: Blackwell, 1994); and John Breuilly, *Nationalism and the State* (Manchester: Manchester University Press, 1982). For some recent considerations of nation across the premodern and modern divide see Krishnan Kumar, *The Making of English National Identity* (Cambridge: Cambridge University Press, 2003); and John Breuilly's essay, 'Changes in the political uses of the nation: continuity or discontinuity?', in *Power and the Nation in European History*, ed. Len Scales and Oliver Zimmer (Cambridge: Cambridge University Press, 2005), 67–101.

[7] Liah Greenfeld, *Nationalism: Five Roads to Modernity* (Cambridge, MA and London: Harvard University Press, 1992), 18.

reinforcing. It is important to remember, however, that none of this cuts much ice with post-eighteenth-century historians, for whom, as Greenfeld's title *Five Roads to Modernity* concisely indicates, such movements are but preludes to the later modernist moment of the nation-state defined, exclusively, as a post-revolutionary phenomenon.

Scholars of earlier periods, caught in a harder place, tend either to insist that nation belongs just as much to a premodern period as it does to the modern, or else seek to redefine the relationship of the premodern to the modern. The term 'premodern', by collapsing 'medieval' and 'early modern', works hard to enable the 'medieval' to join its sister period to form a continuum of premodernity. Its prefiguration of 'postmodern' ingeniously frames the modern as a new middle age.[8] But it does not avoid begging the question of where, in that case, the modern begins. Chaucer works, like Shakespeare for the early modernists, as the literary focus for the modernity of premodernity. Yet, by virtue of his greater antiquity, he is partly eclipsed by Shakespeare in this role. There is a tension between premodern and early modern that is far from being resolved. The 'early modern' claim that nation begins in the sixteenth century does not see continuity with the medieval period but a break.

I will return to this but it is worth remarking more generally that a modernist narrative about nation cannot deal with discontinuity in its own story, since it always begins by positing a prior rupture. Nation is a good example of a term used precisely to create a distinction between past and present. To locate nation historically is to *create* the moment of modernism. But this is why nation is of peculiar interest to our larger topic, because it requires us to reflect on the modernity of the premodern. The danger of claiming a premodern narrative of nation, by contrast, is that the claim tends to be obsessed with denying discontinuity. It becomes a matter simply of moving the goalposts further and further back. Adrian Hastings puts it bluntly: 'the key issue at the heart of our schism [with modernists] lies in the date of commencement.'[9] This actually unites medieval and early modern arguments about nation which are otherwise contradictory: if you want to say that nation begins in the sixteenth century as Helgerson does, then your reasoning is no different from someone who says it begins in the fourteenth, like Hastings, or the twelfth, like John Gillingham, or 'by the seventh century at the very latest', like Alfred P. Smyth.[10] To put it another way, the desire to locate nation in a particular historical moment is a modernist activity, in any period.

[8] See Bruce Holsinger, *The Premodern Condition: Medievalism and the Making of Theory* (Chicago: University of Chicago Press, 2005).

[9] See Hastings, *The Construction of Nationhood*, 9; Anthony D. Smith, *Nationalism and Modernism: A Critical Survey of Recent Theories of Nations and Nationalism* (London and New York: Routledge, 1998), 176.

[10] John Gillingham, *The English in the Twelfth Century: Imperialism, National Identity and Political Values* (Woodbridge: Boydell, 2000); Alfred P. Smyth, 'The Emergence of English Identity, 700–1000',

The second relationship—between nation and language—is often used to provide help in this awkward corner. It seems to be the best argument available for a premodern narrative of nation.[11] Careful to avoid the nuclear term 'print', Hastings sets the scene for the central importance of the vernacular Bible in English nationhood. Language is indeed a key approach to nation—it takes discussion out of narrow political definitions and into the area of how people define themselves through language. But it is a far from easy route towards thinking about nation, especially when we take account of multilingual societies. The most important complication in relation to pre-eighteenth-century England is that its vernacular world, too, was bilingual, in the broad sense that its cultural, intellectual, ecclesiastical, and commercial life was conducted through the medium of French as well as English. Indeed, before 1400, the vast majority of books consumed in England were in Latin and French rather than English, a situation which did not change markedly with printing.[12] Extensive new research on the early continental printed book trade shows that Latin books continued to form its core business throughout the sixteenth century. England was a peripheral market compared to the great centres in Paris, Venice, Cologne, Basle, and Antwerp. Its small-scale production of manuscripts and then printed books throughout the medieval and early modern centuries meant that there was a great reliance on imports. Andrew Pettegree points out that the focus on vernacular production in England was forced by English printers' failure to compete in the Latin market, a conclusion scholars have also reached of earlier periods.[13] We must be careful not to mistake this for a straightforward indication of the growing status of books in English. Continental production of books in French in manuscript and print for the English market was substantial and dominant.[14] We cannot, then, postulate a rise of the vernacular as a symptom or cause of nation if we pay attention exclusively to English. Hastings's terms 'extensive' and 'living' beg many questions, but are particularly problematic when we contemplate the far stronger written presence of French as a vernacular compared to English, in a culture where English was the dominant spoken language.

in *Medieval Europeans: Studies in Ethnic Identity and National Perspectives in Medieval Europe*, ed. Alfred P. Smyth (Basingstoke and London: Macmillan; New York: St Martin's, 1998), 24–52, at 25.

[11] Cathy Shrank, *Writing the Nation in Reformation England, 1530–1580* (Oxford: Oxford University Press, 2004).

[12] Andrew Pettegree, 'Centre and Periphery in the European Book World', *Transactions of the Royal Historical Society*, 18 (2008), 101–28.

[13] Pettegree, 'Centre and Periphery', 14. On the earlier period, see Lotte Hellinga and J. B. Trapp, 'Introduction', in *The Cambridge History of the Book in Britain*, vol. 3: *1400–1557*, ed. Hellinga and Trapp (Cambridge: Cambridge University Press, 1999), 9: 'No other country with a lively book culture... confined its production so much to its own vernacular and was almost reliant for its Latin books on what was produced elsewhere.'

[14] Hellinga and Trapp (eds.), *The Cambridge History of the Book*, Introduction, 8, 20–1; and in two further essays in the same volume: C. Paul Christianson, 'The rise of London's book-trade', 128–47 at 134–35, 140; and Julia Boffey and A. S. G. Edwards, 'Literary texts', 555–75 at 573.

My third area involves the association of nation with England. I must confess, but perhaps this is because I am only half-English, to surprise at how many influential arguments about nation claim that the English nation is the first and founding nation. Greenfeld:

> The significance of the English case is obvious. The birth of the English nation was not the birth of a nation; it was the birth of the nations, the birth of nationalism. England is where the process originated. (23)

Ironically, one of the most eloquent accounts of the assumptions behind such a view was uttered by the French literary historian, Hippolyte Taine. His *Histoire de la littérature anglaise,* first published in 1863, sees the Conquest as a mere ripple on the surface of English, an unfortunate 300-year blip in the otherwise powerfully continuous Saxon spirit of the English poetic genius. What the Normans did was in vain:

> At the end of three hundred years the conquerors themselves were conquered; their speech became English; and owing to frequent intermarriage, the English blood ended by gaining the predominance over the Norman blood in their veins. The race finally remains Saxon. If the old poetic genius disappears after the Conquest, it is as a river disappears, and flows for a while underground. In five centuries it will emerge once more.[15]

Unsurprisingly, this assumption of the primacy of England as a nation is not usually shared by non-English historians, particularly French ones. Pierre Nora describes not England but France as 'the nation-state par excellence and by seniority'.[16] And interestingly, it is Jeanne d'Arc whom Hastings has placed on the cover of his book rather than St George. Nationalist jokes aside, as Anthony D. Smith rightly observes, it is both England *and* France who, in the longevity of their history, have provided 'the litmus test of the antiquity of the concept of the nation and the nature of national sentiment, as well as of the historical continuity of particular nations'.[17] Neither has priority: nation belongs to neither alone, but is framed by the relationship between them. To put it simply, to argue for the singleness and primacy of England the nation is to waive three hundred years of Anglo-French entanglement.

[15] I cite from the popular English edition of his lifetime: Hippolyte A. Taine, *History of English Literature*, trans. H. Van Laun, 2 vols. (Edinburgh: Edmonston and Douglas, 1871), 1: 57. See Hastings, *The Construction of Nationhood*, 44.

[16] Pierre Nora (ed.), *The State*, trans. Mary Trouille, Volume 1 of *Rethinking France: Les Lieux de mémoire*, 2 vols., translation directed by David P. Jordan (Chicago and London: University of Chicago Press, 2001); first published as Nora, ed., *Les Lieux de mémoire*, 7 vols. ((Paris: Gallimard, 1984–92)), 1: xxi.

[17] Smith, *Nationalism and Modernism*, 172.

Asserting nation

This essay is engaged in several kinds of argument. First, it proposes that we need to return to this entanglement between English and French in investigating pre-eighteenth-century nationhood. That we have a binary not a single model of vernacularity in these long centuries deeply affects the sense of modernity, linguistic identity, and historical autonomy in English literary history. I argue that a bifurcated Anglo-French model for vernacularity is not only central to any understanding of nation but also crucially resistant to it. A double rather than a singular perception of linguistic identity prevents us from thinking of nation in isolationist, individualist ways. The Anglo-French culture that existed in England for several centuries prevented either English or French from being a single condition. To communicate in French was no less an English act than to use English. Conversely, to speak English was to speak only one of the English vernaculars. It was a divided and unequal but shared linguistic culture.[18]

My second main thread is that this complex linguistic environment questions the assertiveness that is so characteristic of the critical as well as political language of nation. Bringing back into view England's post-Conquest bi-vernacular condition has repercussions for nation in both medieval and early modern periods. As some of my citations have already indicated, the dominant discourse of nation amongst current commentators is positivist and assertive. So many of us are looking for *the* moment when nation can be claimed, usually *avant la lettre*: we champion isolated instances of nationalist invective or self-description that then act for us as signs of a larger national impulse. But it is often a deeply retrospective exercise. V. H. Galbraith's classic essay, intended to be delivered on 14 December 1939 to the Royal Historical Society at a meeting that was abandoned, is a model of rational calm in those circumstances of impending war, and yet is punctured throughout by the kinds of large-scale generalization that cannot be regarded as anything other than personal assertion. He begins by remarking that 'broadly speaking, the sentiment of nationality is much the same in quality at all times and in all places' (113) and goes on to say 'the sentiment of nationality is thus a continuous thread in the stuff of English history, present in some primitive form from the beginning, but in the Middle Ages still relatively inconspicuous' (117–18).[19]

Benedict Anderson famously turns this kind of generalization (once more) into a condition of modernity. For him, nation can only emerge where horizontal communal imagining is possible, a situation uniquely enabled by journalism.

[18] These arguments are developed in Ardis Butterfield, *The Familiar Enemy: Chaucer, Language and Nation in the Hundred Years War* (Oxford: Oxford University Press, 2009).

[19] Galbraith, 'Nationality and Language'.

Rapid circulation of ephemeral printed material, which Anderson locates in the nineteenth century with the modern newspaper, grants people a sense of public opinion (even if to some extent this is a fictional sense) and the opportunity to imagine themselves part of it.[20] He seems right that in a period or circumstance where this kind of circulation is unavailable, it is much harder—at times, with restricted evidence, impossible—to see that any continuity should necessarily exist between a locally expressed view and one that claims to speak for the whole nation. We might even say, then, that to find a particular author or work in which to locate nation is oddly irrelevant to a case for nation. What is more centrally at issue is the much knottier crux of how we generalize outward from any such author or work.

Thorlac Turville-Petre's *England the Nation,* a pioneering study of the earlier fourteenth century, like Hastings, wants to find nation and assumes this impulse in the writings it studies. The book ends by arguing that the trilingual manuscript BLMS Harley 2253 demonstrates 'the triumphant emergence of English as the language of the national culture' (vii). The difficulty is that such remarks, based in this case on a single, unique manuscript, are hard to take beyond assertion. I want to turn this approach around and rather than reclaim nation, ask what it means to construct nation through difference as opposed to unity. Before the rapid movements of print the intellectual journey from 'single community' to 'one nation' is not at all clear. In certain influential communities in London and Westminster the cultural link between England and the continent was much stronger than that between southern and northern regions of England, a situation which is not wholly unrecognizable even today. An important reason for this was the widespread use of French in court circles, in law, in business, and especially in diplomacy, which meant not merely that French was available as a second language but that French was the language of choice for such circles. In these circles northern English is a foreign language (one recalls John Trevisa's comments on the language of Northumbrians and especially at York, which is 'so scharp, slitting, and frotyng and vnschape, that we southerne men may that longage unnethe understonde'); French, by contrast, is familiar, domestic, and insular.[21] This casts doubt on the capacity of English to command communal, let alone national loyalty: how can it speak for England when French is doing the public work of England's vernacular? The assumption that it is through English that England finds itself to be an English nation is utterly ingrained in discussions of nation. It forms part of the modern scholar's assertive discourse of nation at every turn. But this should not blind us to the possibility that different

[20] Anderson, *Imagined Communities*, 34–6.

[21] Ranulf Higden, *Polychronicon Ranulphi Higden monachi Cestrensis*, Vol. 2 of 9, ed. Churchill Babington, Rerum Britannicarum medii aevi scriptores, 41 (London: Longman, Green, et al., 1865–86), 2: 163.

assumptions constituted the social and cultural practices of England's social and intellectual elite until well after the 'early modern'.

My more local question of nation is therefore not about 'the date of commencement' but about what it means to call something or someone else foreign. This could be said of any national sentiment, but the case of England is especially complex because it involves turning against the self. In English's double-vernacular culture it is about what it means to call French foreign, a development that is convoluted and gradual, and perhaps even now incomplete because it involves only half-articulated forms of allegiance to a vernacular that became over four centuries in some sense more 'English' than English. The act of assertion is so much part of nation that it becomes suspect: we always need to ask who is making the assertion and why, and—often—who in the process is being denied or ignored. More modern (late nineteenth- and early and late twentieth-century) efforts to found nations, to assert independence are of course genuine performative acts with serious repercussions—but they are also acts of imaginative assertion. This makes them vulnerable and fragile. In looking back even further, I suggest we keep in mind that fragility is always part of any claim to unity. Part of this fragility is that any assertion about English has English's other vernacular in the shadows.

Henry IV's speech at the deposition of Richard II is a classic example. As reported by the chronicler, as soon as Richard's speech of abdication had been read out (in his absence), Henry rose to his feet and claimed the realm of England in his mother tongue (*vendicavit in lingua materna*): 'In the name of Fadir, Sone, and Holy Gost, I, Henry of Lancastr' chalenge this rewme of Yngland.'[22] His challenge and claim is given in English, along with a further short speech that he makes in the same public forum after the Archbishop Arundel has placed him on the throne. This is often described as a key moment in the progress of English nationhood, and linked to Henry V's later adoption of English rather than French in his correspondence after 1415.[23] The Lancastrian chronicler evidently wishes to claim the use of English as symbolic; my point is not to detract from that, but to emphasize that its force comes precisely from the sense that this is a surprising, daring act, a moment where English can be risked in public. The public languages are still French and Latin, and official documents do not begin to be written regularly in English until the mid-fifteenth century.[24] Henry's claim, as

[22] P. Brand et al. (eds.), *The Parliament Rolls of Medieval England*, electronic edition, general editor C. Given-Wilson (London: National Archives, 2005) 3: 423, Membrane 18, § 53, accessed 11 March 2009.

[23] Henry used English only in his signet correspondence (the first securely dated letter is from 1417) rather than under the privy seal or in chancery. See John H. Fisher, Malcolm Richardson, and Jane L. Fisher (eds.), *An Anthology of Chancery English*, (Knoxville: University of Tennessee Press, 1984), 84–5. On the broader issues of Lancastrian discourse, see Paul Strohm, *England's Empty Throne* (New Haven, CT and London: Yale University Press, 1998).

[24] Hoccleve's privy seal formulary contains exclusively French documents; chancery continued to function in French and (perhaps surprisingly) increasingly in Latin throughout the fifteenth century;

the official 'Record and Process' represented it, is in that sense anachronistic: he wants it to have proleptic meaning.

Diversity and foreignness

To trace through some of these thoughts, I have therefore chosen, with perhaps contrary logic, a skew of passages that discuss *diversite*. The widespread use of this term, I suggest, is disruptive of the rhetoric of unity that is so important to nation. It is revealing in several directions. It gives us access to people's sense of the English language as a vernacular. The term also acts as a litmus test for multilingual sensitivities: its use registers the wider cultural signification of English in communities where linguistic plurality was common. Moreover, it gives us the opportunity to track such responses right through the 'medieval' and 'early modern', and therefore ponder at close quarters what kind of support they give, if any, to arguments that associate English vernacularity and nation. My selection of examples, encouraged by the brief of this volume, is partly driven by a desire to allow the two literary icons of the medieval and early modern, Chaucer and Shakespeare, into the same discursive space. Chaucer and Shakespeare frame a discussion of nation in their rival claims to English vernacular pre-eminence: since each is the archetype of his period's assertive self-identification, their incompatible claims on the discourse of nation demand attention. As I will show, their remarks on language resonate strongly with the preoccupations of the writers of language treatises.

Chaucer in fact provides one of the most absorbingly entangled references to *diversite* in the English language, and certainly at that date (*c.*1385). It comes near the end of *Troilus and Criseyde*, after his famously grandiloquent claim to poetic fame:

> Go, litel bok, go, litel myn tragedye,
> Ther God thi makere yet, er that he dye,
> So sende myght to make in som comedye!
> But litel book, no makyng thow n'envie,
> But subgit be to alle poesye;
> And kis the steppes where as thow seest pace
> Virgile, Ovide, Omer, Lucan, and Stace. (5.1786–92)

This stanza's overt mission is to set Chaucer in fame's row as the sixth of six among the greatest classical poets he or any age has known. But it hardly does so unambiguously. The puzzlingly self-deprecating reflex 'litel' is a frequent one

see Fisher, Richardson and Fisher (eds.), *Anthology of Chancery English*, 20. The other versions of Henry's accession do not have him speak in English.

in Chaucer; it occurs for instance in Book 4 where he disclaims his 'litel tonge's' ability to transcribe Criseyde's 'heigh compleynte' (4. 799–805). Repeated thrice with careful, rhetorical deliberation, here it echoes his frequent disclaimers about English.[25] Individually, it is easy to take them as part of a rhetorical strategy of inverted self-promotion. Yet there are good reasons to take such insecurity at face value. This *Troilus* stanza is an instance where an assertion of vernacular supremacy is immediately undercut. His 'litel book' must be 'subgit . . . to alle poesye', otherwise it cannot reach for the temple steps.

He follows this through in the next stanza:

> And for ther is so gret diversite
> In Englissh and in writyng of oure tonge,
> So prey I God that non myswrite the,
> Ne the mysmetre for defaute of tonge;
> And red wherso thow be, or elles songe,
> That thow be understonde, God I biseche! (5.1793–98)

This is not ironic, at least not straightforwardly. The two stanzas are written as a tightly connected sequence. The 'defaute of tonge' is real, and so is the 'diversite' and lack of understanding. Chaucer's literary fame in subsequent centuries has weighted our attention to the first stanza rather than the second, which is often read as if it were in brackets. Yet this embarrassing insistence on the inadequacy of English echoes a memorable passage in the *Boece* where Boethius comments on the limitations of fame, which 'may nat strecchen' to many nations, 'what for difficulte of weyes, and what for diversite of langages, and what for defaute of unusage' (*Boece*, Book 2 pr.7.50–9).[26] 'Defaute' and 'diversite' are genuine problems that afflict fourteenth-century English and, as we shall see, are recurrently expressed as such for many decades to come. If there is irony in these two stanzas it comes from the brilliant eloquence of Chaucer's admission of linguistic insufficiency. This vernacular triumph, he says, is constrained to admit that its fame is unlikely to reach beyond the limited circle of those who can read English.

Chaucer qualifies his high-pitching claim to fame by correspondingly extreme, self-lacerating linguistic references, backed up by the neologizing insults 'myswriten' and 'mysmetren', each uniquely attested here. A passage from his *Compleynte of Venus* indicates what is shadowing his vitiating remarks. This three-ballade sequence, translated partially from a five-ballade sequence by Oton de Graunson, has an added oddly self-abasing envoy.[27] The puzzles are many.

[25] For other examples, see *Knight's Tale*, lines 1459–60; *Man of Law's Tale*, lines 778–9; *Squire's Tale*, lines 37–41; *Prologue* to the *Legend of Good Women*, F, lines 66–7; *Complaint of Venus*, line 80.

[26] Geoffrey Chaucer, *Boece*, in *The Riverside Chaucer*, third edition, general editor Larry D. Benson (Oxford: Oxford University Press, 1987), 418.

[27] On envoys, see Ardis Butterfield, 'Chaucerian Vernaculars', *Studies in the Age of Chaucer*, 31 (2009), forthcoming.

Once again, he draws attention to his 'litel suffisaunce' but with strange gestures of defiant virtuosity. This envoy has a larger number of lines than any French envoy. The complaint that English rhymes are scarce is whimsical: in fact Chaucer, by using only two rhyme sounds in the whole stanza performs a much more difficult (and characteristically French) feat than either he or Graunson attempts in the ballades themselves. Many readers read this as Chaucer's way of trumping Graunson (and hence French poetry in general) through an assertive display of English poetic power.[28] If we take this image at its word, however, it suggests a poet in awe of French 'curiosite' throughout his poetic career and more aware than ever with increasing age of English's inadequacies as a vernacular in waiting. I suggest that we are being invited to read both plainly and elaborately. Chaucer seems to be showing that English cannot win over French in a contest of poetic virtuosity except by making a virtue of its 'litel suffisaunce'. But this does not mean that English is 'winning': on the contrary, it is a contest in which the terms and means are constantly under construction.

The word 'diversite' has much behind and around it. Its usage acts as a register of linguistic difference in many different contexts. One of the first datable citations in English occurs in Richard Rolle's *English Psalter* (*c.*1345), but the references cluster in the late fourteenth century and continue well after.[29] What do they tell us? Do we find a period difference between any of them? Do they tell us anything, positively or negatively, about nation?

Several comments can briefly be made. There is an exponential increase in the use of the word in English as language becomes a more overt topic of discussion. This is stimulated in English partly by Boethius's description of other lands and their customs, and also in the English version of *Mandeville's Travels*, where *diversite* is a leitmotif of the narrative.[30] The word also has important associations in and with French. It appears in Walter Bibbesworth's thirteenth-century language treatise *Tretiz de langage* which was repackaged in the fifteenth century in a version known as *Femina nova*.[31] Bibbesworth's treatise is an exuberant exploration of lexis, full of diverting excursions into homonyms and puns. Where he writes in a throwaway line of 'Diversez nouns & merveilous' (68) he reveals the same pleasure

[28] For further discussion see Ardis Butterfield, 'France', in *Chaucer: Contemporary Approaches*, ed. Susanna Fein and David Raybin (Philadelphia, PA: Penn State University Press, 2010), 25–46.

[29] See *OED*: 'diversity' *n.* From the additional evidence of the *MED*, there is a marked clustering of references that occur in texts circulating in the 1420s (*The Wycliffite Bible* (I); *The Cyrurgie of Guy de Chauliac*; *Troilus*; *Boece*; *Rotuli Parliamentorum*) and 1440–50 (Lydgate, *Siege of Thebes*; Pecock, *The Reuele of Crysten Religioun*; *The Life of St Mary of Oignies*; Bokenham, *Mappula Angliae*).

[30] *Mandeville's Travels*, ed. M. C. Seymour (Oxford: Clarendon Press, 1967), 3, 11, 19. The work was first written in French (*c.*1357), seemingly under a pseudonym.

[31] See Andres M. Kristol, 'L'enseignement du français en Angleterre (XIIIe–XVe siècles): Les sources manuscrites', *Romania*, 111 (1990), 289–330; Ruth Dean and M. B. M. Boulton, *Anglo-Norman Literature: A Guide to Texts and Manuscripts* (London: Anglo-Norman Text Society, 1999), numbers 285 and 286.

in linguistic variety that the *Travels* author shows in his marvellous descriptions of foreignness.[32] By the fifteenth century, however, an anxiety about *diversite* is also evident in such writers as Lydgate, Pecock, and Bokenham. As we see in the *General Prologue* to the *Wycliffite Bible*, *diversite* moves from registering the intellectual fascination of observing and accounting for linguistic difference, to the freighted contexts of Biblical translation and its aftermath.[33]

We have some sophisticated accounts of the varied pressures on the choice and usage of English between 1380 and 1520.[34] Among these, as scholars have widely discussed, occur claims for English as a 'common' language, partly in the sense of being a political language of ordinary revolt in the 1381 Rising, and also as a vehicle for 'lewed' men seeking knowledge of the Bible and devotional instruction.[35] But in most of these modern accounts, these claims are considered precisely and exclusively as 'English' claims. My emphasis here is the role of French in defining and shaping such choices and usages. It is too easy to tell this story as if England had only one vernacular, or only one that mattered.[36]

[32] 'Littere e littere sunt divers / Discordaunt dient lez clers', page 18, at lines 398–9; page 67, at line 313, Walter of Bibbesworth, *Le Tretiz*, ed. William Rothwell, (Aberystwyth: Anglo-Norman online hub, 2009).

[33] Note the heavy, even hysterical nuances gained by the Latin term in *De Haeretico Comburendo* (1401) (not picked up in the modern English translation):

> nichilominus diversi perfidi et perversi cujusdam nove secte, de dicta fide, sacramentis ecclesie, et auctoritate ejusdem dampnabiliter sencientes, et contra legem divinam et ecclesiasticam predicacionis officium temere usurpantes, diversas novas doctrinas et opiniones iniquas, hereticas, et erroneas, eidem fidei ac sanctis determinationibus ecclesie sacrosancte contrarias, perverse et maliciose, infra dictum regnum in diversis locis, sub simulate sanctitatis colore, predicant et docent, hiis diebus, publice et occulte.
>
> nevertheless, various perfidious and perverse people of a certain new sect, believing damnable things of the said faith, the sacrament of the church, and its authority, rashly usurping the office of preacher, contrary to divine and ecclesiastical law, perversely and maliciously preach and teach these days, publicly and secretly, under simulation of the colour of sanctity, various new doctrines and wicked, heretical and erroneous opinions, contrary to this same faith and the holy decrees of the sacrosanct church. (*The Parliament Rolls of Medieval England 1275–1504*, general editor, Chris Given-Wilson, 16 vols. (London: Boydell; The National Archives, 2005), 8: 122.)

[34] Nicholas Watson, 'The Politics of Middle English Writing', in *The Idea of the Vernacular: An Anthology of Middle English Literary Theory 1280–1520*, ed. Jocelyn Wogan-Browne, Nicholas Watson, Andrew Taylor, and Ruth Evans (Exeter: University of Exeter Press, 1999), 331–52; Andrew Cole, 'Chaucer's English Lesson', *Speculum*, 77 (2002), 1128–67.

[35] Steven Justice, *Writing and Rebellion: England in 1381* (Berkeley: University of California Press, 1994); Fiona Somerset, *Clerical Discourse and Lay Audience in Late Medieval England* (Cambridge: Cambridge University Press, 1998); Fiona Somerset, Jill C. Havens, and Derrick G. Pitard (eds.), *Lollards and their Influence in Late Medieval England* (Woodbridge: Boydell, 2003); Kathy Lavezzo (ed.), *Imagining a Medieval English Nation* (Minneapolis: University of Minnesota Press, 2004).

[36] It is worth noting both that French was also claimed as a 'commun' language (see, famously, Richard Morris, ed., *Cursor Mundi*: *A Northumbrian Poem of the XIVth century*, EETS, original series, 57, 59, 62, 66, 68, 99, 101 (London: Oxford University Press, 1961–6), lines 73–82: 'French

The famous description in Chapter 59 of Trevisa's glossed translation of Higden's *Polychronicon* is a case in point. This chapter is usually cited, in extract, as 'evidence' that French lost what significance it had as a language in England from 1385 when, so Trevisa says,

> Iohn Cornwaile, a maister of grammar, changed the lore in gramer scole and construccioun of frennsche in to Englische; . . . so that now . . . in alle the gramere scoles of Engelond, children leveth Frensche and construeth and lerneth an Englische.[37] (161)

However, in the context of the whole chapter, Trevisa's point is rather different. This situation, he writes, has 'avauntage in oon side and disavauntage in another side'. The advantage is that children learn grammar more quickly, but the disadvantage is

> that now children of gramer scole conneth na more Frensche than can hir lift heele, and that is harme for hem and they schulle passe the see and travaille in straunge landes and in many other places. Also gentil men haveth now moche i-left for to teche here children Frensche.

We find here a cue for the *Femina nova.* Trevisa is not reading funeral rites over French but bemoaning the difficulties of promoting it in a climate where demand is actually growing. Far from deserting French, the aspiring gentles created an exceptional moment in the history of vernacular language, since for the first time a vernacular medieval language was taught systematically. Uniquely for a vernacular language, French was given school status, and thus treated not so differently from Latin.[38] Serge Lusignan has demonstrated that a consciousness developed in the later Middle Ages of French as a language capable of philosophical enquiry in its own right: ironically, despite some contemporary claims to the contrary, far from working nationalistically in aggressive independence from French, the English in a remarkable move played a crucial role in support of French in the fifteenth century through giving it renewed cultural value and power.[39]

The dialogue (created by Trevisa) between Higden and Trevisa in his gloss develops in even more interesting directions to reflect on *diversite.* Higden, as it were, responds thoughtfully:

> Hit semeth a greet wonder how englische, [that is the burthe tonge of Englisshe] men and her owne langage and tonge, is so dyverse of sown in this oon ilond, and the langage of Normandie is comlynge of another londe, and hath oon manere soun among alle men that speketh hit aright in Engelond.

rimes here I rede / Communely in iche a stede'), and that comments on the worth of the 'commun' were articulated in French: see, for instance: Robert of Gretham, *Anglo-Norman Miroir*, in *The Middle English Miroir . . . with a Parallel Text of the Anglo-Norman Miroir*, ed. Thomas Duncan and Margaret Connolly, Middle English Texts, 34 (Heidelberg: Universitätsverlag Winter, 2003), lines 635–44.

37 Higden, *Polychronicon*, ed. Babington, 2: 161.

38 See Kristol, 'L'enseignement du français'.

39 Serge Lusignan, *Parler vulgairement: Les Intellectuels et la langue française aux XIIIe et XIVe siècles* (Paris: Vrin; Montréal: Les Presses de l'Université de Montréal, 1986), 101.

But this stimulates Trevisa to the sharply perceptive cross-Channel observation that:

> Nevertheles there is as many dyvers manere Frensche in the reem of Fraunce as is dyvers manere Englische in the reem of Engelond.

There is a great deal to say about this—all I have space for here is that it betrays an acute awareness of the power of *diversite* to disrupt notions of unity 'in this oon ilond', a disruptive power that Trevisa seems also to realize was just as operative in France. Trevisa has long been recognized as being an extraordinarily subtle commentator on language. What is less often acknowledged is the extent to which his remarks on the status of English are conditioned by his sense of the significance of French.[40]

In brief, then, *Femina nova* and a range of other teaching materials, such as the *Manières de langage* probably written by the Oxford teacher William Kingsmill, are evidence that the bicultural Anglo-French condition did not slide into antique oblivion in the fifteenth century in the way that arguments tracking English and nation often assert. How could it in the decades when England was most fully confident of its political and military power on the French mainland?[41] I illustrate this, in the last part of this essay, by turning to some sixteenth-century passages taken from three significant writers on language, Thomas Wyatt, Thomas Wilson, and William Turner. It is salutary to follow through these linguistic topoi of self-deprecation into a period well after Chaucer's supposedly transforming effect on the English tongue. Indeed, as Richard Jones in his classic study and more recently Paula Blank have demonstrated, the anxieties increase rather than diminish; it is the recognition of *diversite* that triumphs rather than English itself.[42]

Wyatt, for instance, in his 1529 Prologue to his translation of Petrarch's *Boke of the Quyete of Mynde* makes a familiar complaint about the 'defaute of tonge' as characterized by Chaucer: as he worked,

> the labour began to seme tedious / by superfluous often rehersyng of one thing. which tho paraventure in the latyn shalbe laudable / by plenteous diversite of the spekyng of it . . . yet for lacke of suche diversite in our tong / it shulde want a great dele of the grace.[43]

[40] For further discussion see Butterfield, *The Familiar Enemy*, Chapter 9.

[41] On the adverse implications of this for the influential notion, proposed by John Fisher, that a 'standard English' developed in the fifteenth century, usually attributed to the influence of Chancery practices, see Butterfield, *The Familiar Enemy*, Chapter 9.

[42] Richard Jones, *The Triumph of the English Language* (London: Oxford University Press, 1953); Paula Blank, *Broken English: Dialects and the Politics of Language in Renaissance Writings* (London and New York: Routledge, 1996). See also on Wilson: Andrew Hadfield, *Literature, Politics and National Identity* (Cambridge: Cambridge University Press, 1994), Chapter 4; and Shrank, *Writing the Nation*, Chapter 5.

[43] Thomas Wyatt, *The Quyet of Mynde*, in *Collected Poems of Sir Thomas Wyatt*, ed. Kenneth Muir and Patricia Thomson (Liverpool: Liverpool University Press, 1969), 440–63, at 440. I have emended 'landable' to 'laudable'.

But here Wyatt's use of *diversite* has more in common with Bibbesworth: *diversite* is 'faire' and is a sign of the copiousness of Latin as opposed to the narrowness of English.

Two further passages, one by the evangelical Turner (1548) and the other by Wilson, Cambridge humanist and later lawyer, whose *Art of Rhetorique* was published in 1553, show that a direct and continuing engagement with French are central to English language treatise writing. Both are contributors to a wide debate about the use of neologisms. Ostensibly, they seek to purify the English language from 'straunge ynkehorne termes':

> Among all other lessons this should first be learned, that wee never affect any straunge ynkehorne termes, but to speake as is commonly received... Some seeke so far for outlandish English, that they forget altogether their mothers language...
>
> (*The Art of Rhetorique*)

But their protestations belie their practice, and reveal that the border between *straunge* and familiar is far from agreed or fixed. Wilson wants to argue that there is a right sort of neologism as well as a wrong sort:

> Now whereas wordes be received, aswell Greeke as Latine, to set forth our meaning in the English tongue... it is well doen to use them, and no man therein can be charged for any affectation, when all other are agreed to followe the same waie... The Communion is a fellowship, or a comming together, rather Latin then English... and yet I know no man greeved for these termes, being used in their place, nor yet any one suspected of affectation when such generall wordes are spoken.
>
> (*The Art of Rhetorique*)

If a word has a Greek or Latin root then suddenly it becomes 'generall' and understood by 'all men'. French 'affectations' are quite another thing:

> Some farre iourneyed gentleman at their returne home, like as they love to goe in forraine apparell, so thei wil pouder their talke with oversea language. He that commeth lately out of Fraunce, will talke French English and never blush at the matter. (*The Art of Rhetorique*)[44]

This wonderful oxymoron 'French English' which Turner mimetically embellishes in the phrase 'newe french englishe blossomes' keeps cropping up with a regularity that suggests that it expresses a more intrinsic condition of English than either writer cares to admit.[45] As with Chaucer's use of *diversite* the context and argument is burdened with half-acknowledged denials mixed in with over-emphatic assertions. It would be disingenuous to fail to note the different rich context in Turner and Wilson of a word like 'fellowship', so caught up in matters of ecclesiastical

[44] All passages from *The Art of Rhetorique* (1909), ed. G. H. Mair, 162–5, cited in Jones, *Triumph of the English Language*, 101.

[45] There are many citations in Jones, *Triumph of the English Language*; see especially Chapters 3 and 4, at 99, 114 n. 29, 133, 260–1.

allegiance, or else of the references to Greek and Latin, where their consciousness of the cultural capital of classical writing is so much more overtly linguistic than it is even in *Troilus*, a poem in which classical authors are a constant, if controversial presence. Part of what is going on here, however, seems remarkably continuous: a battle between the status of current, contemporary, spoken vernacular and the written language of the ancients. Most notably, these sixteenth-century comments reveal, like the fourteenth-century ones, that this battle is articulated, not as a contest between English and Latin (or Greek), but between English and French. If English needs bolstering, and everyone agrees that it does, then it is proper to import words from Latin or Greek but disconcerting that so many come in fact from French. In expressing this pique, writers often resort to the discourse of the 'mother tongue'.[46] Native, natural English is to be preferred over the 'outlandissh'. But here confusion arises, almost wilfully. In the twin effort both to support the influence of the classical languages and overcome the cultural power of French, Latin, as in the Wycliffite *General Prologue*, is even claimed as a 'mother tongue'.[47] There are many complicated turns in these passages, but it is particularly interesting to note the effort both men make to describe French as foreign. French is suddenly moved conceptually far away, an 'oversea language' that a 'farre iourneyed' gentleman will parade on his return home. But the obvious strain in this far-fetched characterization is revealed in the way that this language is easily acquired and articulated: it is, after all, 'English'.

That French continues to be more authoritative than English lies at the bottom of these contorted sixteenth-century linguistic posturings.[48] The *diversite* of which Trevisa wrote in his translation of the *Polychronicon* and expanded upon in his preface to his patron, Lord Berkeley, has not vanished into a smooth upward path towards 'clene and pure' English, but become a reinvigorated Babel of tongues in an English more broken than ever.[49] Moreover, French is not yet foreign, as we can see from the exaggerated attempts to make it seem so.

What, then, of *Henry V*? Reading this after Trevisa and Chaucer, I am struck by how little jingoism is the issue and how much the balance of linguistic power between French and English. From Act 2, Scene 4 onwards the play is set entirely in France and it culminates not in Agincourt but in that famous sparring courtship, an Anglo-French enactment of war's cultural legacy. Language is constantly held up

[46] See Margaret W. Ferguson, *Dido's Daughters: Literacy, Gender and Empire in Early Modern England and France* (Chicago and London: University of Chicago Press, 2003); Butterfield, *The Familiar Enemy*, Chapter 9.

[47] *General Prologue*, Chapter 15, in *Selections from English Wycliffite Writings*, ed. Anne Hudson (Cambridge: Cambridge University Press, 1978), 71, at lines 165–8.

[48] It is worth recalling that Du Bellay in his *Deffence et Illustration de la Langue Françoyse* of 1549 has just as great an anxiety to prove French's worth against Greek and Latin.

[49] *Dialogue Between the Lord and the Clerk on Translation* and *Epistle to Thomas, Lord Berkeley on the translation of Higden's Polychronicon*, edited in extract in *The Idea of the Vernacular*, ed. Wogan-Browne, Watson, Taylor, Evans, 130–8.

for inspection, through dialect, comic pronunciation, class, and gender. A whole scene (Act 2, Scene 3) takes place in French, though the French lords are all presented as speaking English, showing that the point is to appose French English with the English French of the final scene.[50]

Shakespeare gives great depth to this language by layering it with Anglo-French references throughout the play. The central scenes work as a sequence of carefully juxtaposed linguistic encounters, starting with the English lesson in Act 3, Scene 4. The central joke of this scene is that it is a *manière de langage* in reverse. The learning of vocabulary in Bibbesworth, the *Femina nova*, Kingsmill, and in language tools more recent to Shakespeare such as *Ortho-Epia Gallica* is translated back both verbally and culturally, so that we are presented with the spectacle of a French queen trying to learn English, because she must ('il faut que j'apprenne à parler', 3.4.4–5). As she learns to speak these English words through the standard pedagogic technique of repetition, she gradually learns to speak a false English that turns out to be vulgar French in disguise. Her new English turns and betrays her through its resemblance to French.

It is easy to forget that the scene works linguistically through a French matrix: the English audience, in other words, is expected to take French as the base language and English only as a translated tongue. The next scene, and the one after a Welsh interlude, provides another reversal by presenting French lords speaking 'natif' English, albeit with French tags for colour. Shakespeare keeps the sense of English as foreign-sounding by the different ploy in the intervening scene of introducing the Welshman, Fluellen. Often played as an instance of snobbish English caricature, along with the portrayals of the Irishman (Captain MacMorris) and the Scot (Captain Jamy), heard against the different kinds of French in the play these characters can be interpreted rather differently. Shakespeare recognizes, within a long history of such recognition, that English and French are equally engaged in issues of diversity. Gower the Englishman's reproof of Pistol after the incident of the leek is a rebuke to such English snobbery, not an expression of it:

> You thought, because he could not speak English in the native garb, he could not therefore handle an English cudgel. You find it otherwise. And henceforth let a Welsh correction teach you a good English condition. (5.1.68–72)

The distance between Catherine's 'natif' pronunciation of English and Fluellen's is not far: both speak true in their false English, and both teach English foreign manners. More than that, the strong presence of French in the play inverts any expectation that French is necessarily more foreign than Welsh, Irish, or Scots. That Henry succeeds in winning Agincourt but immediately has to deal with fighting in his own ranks implies that the strangers at home may be harder to control than the family over the channel, and their speech harder to understand.

[50] Gary Taylor, ed., *Henry V*, The Oxford Shakespeare (Oxford: Clarendon Press, 1982).

Pistol's scene with the French soldier is perhaps the funniest and cleverest of all these cross-linguistic encounters. More is going on than crude linguistic chauvinism. Shakespeare sets up (at least) four linguistic levels: the 'natif' French of the soldier, Pistol's mongrel Anglo-French jargon (wonderfully mixing with an Irish refrain), the boy's unremarked good French, and finally the English exchanged between Pistol and boy (itself wildly fluctuating and of mixed register). Pistol's attempt to sound like a schoolteacher continues the general theme of cultural education: 'Perpend' he says, like Touchstone, Feste, and Polonius. He has the attitude of a long-suffering culturally superior native who patiently tries to make sense of a dim-witted foreigner, and all this in a barbarously hybrid response to the lucid French of the soldier:

French Soldier
O prenez miséricorde! Ayez pitié de moi!
Pistol
'Moy' shall not serve. I will have forty 'moys',
Or I will fetch thy rim out at thy throat
In drops of crimson blood.
French Soldier
Est-il impossible d'échapper la force de ton bras?
Pistol
Brass, cur? Thou damnèd and luxurious mountain goat,
Offer'st me brass? (4.4.12–18)

When we come finally to the Henry–Catherine scene, French is in a complex condition for the audience: a familiar language, spoken fluently by French and English characters alike; a language of flamboyant and learned reference spoken by the enemy (Act 3, Scene 7); and a common vernacular like any other, liable to be misunderstood by those from another region. English, likewise, has been defamiliarized: it has been presented as Irish, Scots, and Welsh as well as English and taught by one Frenchwoman to another as a foreign language. Catherine, having learnt her English so well in 3.4 is now asked by Henry to teach him. But the question of linguistic competence has become tense and full of bluffs and double bluffs. The audience has learnt, through the display of multiple kinds of French and English, not to assume that linguistic knowledge is either easily defined or articulated.[51]

[51] On the legal implications of the use of French in this scene, see Bradin Cormack, '"If We Be Conquered": Legal Nationalism and the France of Shakespeare's English Histories', in his *A Power to Do Justice: Jurisdiction, English Literature, and the Rise of Common Law, 1509–1625* (Chicago and London: University of Chicago Press, 2007), 177–223, at 219. See further David Womersley's argument that *Henry V* is deeply engaged with Henri IV's claim to the English throne, one taken very seriously in the England of 1599: Womersley, 'France in Shakespeare's Henry V', *Renaissance Studies*, 9 (1995), 442–59; Rowland Cotterill, 'The Structural Role of France in Shakespeare's First and Second

Again, at first sight, all is reversed: English brute force has rendered French eloquence mute and stumbling. Henry goads Catherine into English, pretending throughout (though with the occasional deliberate slip into competence) that his French is halting; she in a matching battle of wits plays on her alleged ignorance of this barbarous tongue to prove her cultural superiority if she cannot prove her political supremacy:

> I cannot speak your England. (5.2.102–3)

But Henry, half cruelly, half tenderly teases her into linguistic submission:

> If you will love me soundly with your French heart, I will be glad to hear you confess it brokenly with your English tongue. (5.2.104–6)

He finally absorbs her utterly into English through the ancient Latin-vernacular pun we find in Bede of angle and angel:

> An angel is like you, Kate, and you are like an angel. (5.2.109–10)

She *must* speak English, she must become an English pun: English eloquence is shown to exist in its oldest foreign characterization.[52]

But this is not the end of the scene. Catherine turns the situation round. By asserting her ignorance ('I cannot tell vat is "like me"') she succeeds in mocking Henry's language, even in her broken English: it is the fact that she does not need to know English that trumps his knowledge of French:

> Sauf votre honneur, le français que vous parlez, il est meilleur que l'anglais lequel je parle. (5.2.183–84)

This is a subtle insult rather than a compliment, a boast rather than an admission of weakness.

As the dialogue proceeds, Henry becomes more eloquent in French *and* English. He does not merely parade his plain English as a 'plain king' victorious over 'fausse' French but gives up on the notion that she cannot understand him and bursts into long wooing speeches. Using Alice not as an interpreter but as a mere device to delay and draw attention to his own word games, Henry bears down on Catherine in both languages. For the idea is not for English to triumph but for English to become French and French English:

> That English may as French, French Englishmen,
> Receive each other. (5.2.352–3)

Historical Tetralogies', *Renaissance Studies*, 9 (1995), 460–76; and Leah Marcus's connection of *1 Henry VI* to the English Protestants' participation in the French wars of the 1590s, *Puzzling Shakespeare: Local Reading and its Discontents* (Berkeley: University of California Press, 1988), 51–105.

[52] *Bede's Ecclesiastical History of the English People*, ed. Bertram Colgrave and R. A. B. Mynors (Oxford: Clarendon Press, 1979; first published 1969), 132–5.

This is a view of nation that is remarkably free from brute conquest: reflecting the spirit of Troyes, Shakespeare's Henry has a whole vision of two nations coming together, not of one nation overmastering the other. The mutuality, the linguistic enmeshing, the sheer, as yet uncontrollable diversity of English means that Henry's desires in that final scene are always self-deprecating even at their most assertive.

Retrospectives

So have we after all found the date of commencement of English as a national language? Can we answer Fernand Braudel's question 'Comment l'Angleterre devint une île?' We could say, with Braudel, that it becomes an island when Calais is lost in 1558:

> Entre 1453 et 1558, entre la fin de la guerre de Cent Ans et l'année de la reprise de Calais par François de Guise, l'Angleterre, sans en avoir eu conscience sur le moment, est devenue une île.[53]

This may be one of the few claims for the birth of early modernism that denies it self-consciousness. Calais, for Shakespeare, has indeed been lost, as it had not yet been for Wilson and Turner. Yet despite his poetic description of England prior to this having been long embroiled or dissolved (*dissoute*) 'dans l'immensité du champ opérationnel qu'était la France', Braudel's answer seems too neat, too inconscient of the linguistic entanglements that still held English and French in a tight, if awkward embrace. My answer would be no, not yet, for this is still a local affair.

Reading *Henry V* from the perspective of the fourteenth and fifteenth centuries, it is difficult to discern the jingoistic nationalist fervour so often ascribed to it. Instead we are caught up in different issues. An exercise such as this in dismantling periodization is full of temporal disturbance. We find ourselves trying to read forward *and* backward, forwards and *not* backwards, while also trying to see contemporary moments as contemporary rather than as stretched out towards our present or left dwindling behind in their past. This is axiomatic of any attempt to find nation. In order to allow Henry IV's 'challenge and claim' in 1399 its full force, we must not flatten its temporal warp into a smoothly linear causality, but allow the shock and rupture of a public English used before its time to resonate historically. I have tried to show that both Chaucer and Shakespeare are treacherous if we seek to use them as points of anchorage. Each has been constantly rewritten either as a point of origin or as a moment of modernity, or else both at once, in ways that are confusing and inconsistent yet ingrained.

[53] Fernand Braudel, *Le Temps du monde*, 3 vols. (Paris: Armand Colin, 1979), 3: 302–4, at 302.

If in this essay Chaucer emerges as ahead of his time and Shakespeare as behind it, then this is only partially a consequence of reading forward. I have also argued that it is because for each author the debate about the status of the vernacular is dominated by English's relationship with French. Neither Chaucer nor Shakespeare gives us the time of nation because in neither is English confident of standing alone. In the contemporary moment for each author, English is full of *diversite* and *defaut*. The fact that each author has been judged retrospectively to transcend that temporal condition through his superlative eloquence belongs to a separate chronology and not, I suggest, one that can or should be tied back to nation.

To what extent was Shakespeare really engaged with French? The biographical facts, as ever, are scant, but we know that he stayed for some time in the house of a Huguenot family.[54] The threat of war with France was by no means a romantic memory lodged in the mythological victory of Agincourt but a present concern. Perhaps most convincingly, his play writes and speaks French with ease and with an expectation of public comprehension of its cross-lingual humour. We might grant all this and still feel that English had won: how could it not with Shakespeare? Moreover, Helgerson's impressive demonstration of the sheer vast bulk of Elizabethan ambition in the writing of law, travel, cartography, and chronicle history, let alone drama, as an adventure in English and Englishness seems a compelling account of a new national consciousness given a new energy of articulation.

My response is prompted by looking still further ahead into the mid-seventeenth century. Thomas Blount's remarkable *Glossographia* of 1656 was the first etymological dictionary and the first to include citations for its definitions.[55] Looking backwards, it was the last 'hard words' dictionary, that is, one that did not seek to be comprehensive but instead to compile unusual or difficult words. It could be called an anachronism; it might be truer to say that it compiles anachronisms. In his Preface to the Reader he thus explains that he largely 'shun'd the old Saxon words; as finding them growing every day more obsolete then other'. But some still count for inclusion: 'yet even such of those, as I found still in use, are not here omitted'. Sensitive to the presence of these living anachronisms, he finds himself citing Chaucer's comments on the changing character of language over the centuries from Book 2 of *Troilus and Criseyde*. It is a nice moment of temporal layering: 'old Chaucer', as he calls him, is brought back into the present to authorize his perception that 'unlearned' or 'common' tongues fall and vanish (A4). But perhaps the most revealing phrase occurs in his rhymed address 'To His Honoured Friend Mr T.B.' He gives a quick witty history of English:

[54] S. Schoenbaum, *William Shakespeare: A Documentary Life* (Oxford: Clarendon Press, 1975), 208–13.

[55] Thomas Blount, *Glossographia 1656: A Scolar Press Facsimile*, ed. R. C. Alston, English Linguistics 1500–1800 (A Collection of Facsimile Reprints), 153 (Menston: The Scolar Press, 1969).

But most, in these our Modern times, this Ile
And Language oft became a double spoil
To Foreiners; *Pictish* with *Danish* clung
Into our *Saxo-Belgick-Norman Tongue.* (A7v)

and then comments ruefully that in the mass of jargon, uncouth words, and cant, he can do no more than reacquaint 'our self-stranger Nation / With its disguised self' (A8v). One hundred years on from Wilson, the dominant discourse of a 'National Interpreter', as he styles himself, is still cleverly but cautiously deprecating, presenting English as disguised and foreign even to itself.

The hard facts, in conclusion, are that English is still unknown abroad in the 'early modern' period. Its book trade during the sixteenth and seventeenth centuries was from an international perspective small and undistinguished. One cause was the poor quality of books printed in Britain compared to the continent; another, as P. G. Hoftijzer remarks, 'whereas other modern languages—French, Italian, German, Dutch—were spoken well beyond their respective language barriers, English was hardly known on mainland Europe, with the exception of mercantile ports with direct trade relations with Britain'.[56] Shakespeare was little known abroad, except in German and Dutch, until Voltaire, whose famous remark, repeated by Antonio Conti in his 1726 translation of Julius Caesar: 'Sesper è il Cornelio degl'Inglesi' ('Shakespeare is the Corneille of the English') makes the direction of cultural transfer plainly not that of the island out to the continent. A 'provincial clown' as Voltaire, less kindly, also named him, Shakespeare was received with considerable reservation in Europe until the nineteenth century, and it might be said, even now has a somewhat mixed reception there.[57]

Even in Shakespeare's time, then, we cannot equate public assertion with public confidence in English. It takes more than assertion to create an international language, and there seems little meaning in having a national language unless it is international too. Perhaps the language lesson here is to avoid the desire to equate the time of nation with the chronological imperatives of assertion. The absorbing character of the Anglo-French bilingual condition of post-Conquest England is that it forces a constant exploration of the time of writing and the condition of language, of whether there is a difference between self and stranger, island and continent, and if so, on what terms.

[56] P. G. Hoftijzer, 'British Books Abroad: the Continent', *The Cambridge History of the Book in Britain*, vol. 4: *1557–1695*, ed. John Barnard and D. F. McKenzie (Cambridge: Cambridge University Press, 2002), 735–43, at 735.

[57] A. Luis Pujante and Ton Hoenselaars (eds.), *Four Hundred Years of Shakespeare in Europe* (Newark: University of Delaware Press, 2003); Roger Paulin, *The Critical Reception of Shakespeare in Germany 1682–1914: Native Literature and Foreign Genius*, Anglistische und Amerikanistische Texte Und Studien, 11 (Hildesheim: Olms, 2003).

FURTHER READING

Breuilly, John. 'Changes in the Political Uses of the Nation: Continuity or Discontinuity?', in *Power and the Nation in European History*, ed. Len Scales and Oliver Zimmer (Cambridge: Cambridge University Press, 2005), 67–101

Ferguson, Margaret W. *Dido's Daughters: Literacy, Gender and Empire in Early Modern England and France* (Chicago and London: University of Chicago Press, 2003)

Lavezzo, Kathy (ed.). *Imagining a Medieval English Nation* (Minneapolis: University of Minnesota Press, 2004)

Lusignan, Serge. *La langue des rois au Moyen âge: le français en France et en Angleterre* (Paris: PUF, 2004)

CHAPTER 4

HISTORIOGRAPHY

JESSE LANDER

The True Tragedie of Richard III, an anonymous history play of the 1590s, treats the murder of the two princes in the tower according to the received history of the late Tudor period. Richard III was, of course, a villain and the murder of his two innocent nephews was perhaps his principal act of villainy. However, the play also reveals an arch knowingness, an almost playful response to the serious matter of historiography. This attitude is on display when Myles Forest, one of the hired killers, responds to a question about what has been done with the bodies of the princes:

> I have conveyd them to the staires foote among a heape of stones, and anon I'le carry them where they shall no more be found againe, nor all the cronicles shall ne'er make mention what shall become of them.[1]

This is something more than historical consciousness; it might well be termed historiographical consciousness.[2]

In Shakespeare's more familiar version of this episode, the murderer Forrest does not appear. Instead, Tyrrel narrates: 'The tyrannous and bloody act is done— / The most arch deed of piteous massacre / That ever yet this land was guilty of' (4.3.1–3). This is itself a straightforward expression of a basic form of historical consciousness. Since Thucydides declared his subject matter, the Peloponnesian War, 'the greatest disturbance in the history of the Hellenes', historians have announced the unprecedented nature of

[1] *The True Tragedie of Richard the Third* (London, 1594), F1v.

[2] Historical consciousness is a notoriously slippery concept. See, for example, Anthony Kemp, *The Estrangement of the Past: A Study in the Origins of Modern Historical Consciousness* (Oxford: Oxford University Press, 1991). For an unsparing critique of the concept, see Ashis Nandy, 'History's Forgotten Doubles', *History and Theory*, 34 (1995), 44–66. Jörn Rüsen pluralizes historical consciousness into four types: traditional, exemplary, critical, and genetic in 'Historical Consciousness: Narrative Structure, Moral Function, and Ontogenetic Development', *History and Memory*, 1 (1989), 35–60.

the events they describe.[3] The event emerges as a subject of historical inquiry precisely because it is a departure or a rupture—literally remarkable—a shift in the ordinary course of affairs that merits registration. The superlative—'the most arch deed of piteous massacre'—announces history in the making; Shakespeare's Tyrrel is immediately aware of the magnitude of the crime and the extent of his own complicity. The murder he recounts is indeed 'piteous'—the hardened villains Dighton and Forrest are reduced to tears when they describe the scene. Tyrrel quotes Dighton's confessional report: '"We smothered / The most replenished sweet work of nature / That from the prime creation e'er she framed"' (4.3. 17–19). Again, superlatives are at work—marking the two princes as the embodiment of innocent, prelapsarian nature and seeking an affective response from audience or reader. The declaration of an unprecedented crime or an outstanding victory reveals a form of historical consciousness that is both ubiquitous and relatively straightforward. After all, the memorialization of great deeds is one of the constant features in western historiography from classical antiquity to the present.

The great-deed model of history is uncomplicated: heroes perform feats of courage (*res gestae*) and scribes chronicle their accomplishments (*historia rerum gestarum*). However, even this relatively straightforward procedure of recording has its complexities. As soon as agents imagine themselves either celebrated or vilified in subsequent history writing, a consideration of temporality and writing has entered the picture. Thus, in Malory's *Le Morte Darthur*, the exiled Lancelot anticipates, 'For ever I feare aftir my dayes that men shall cronycle uppon me that I was fleamed oute of thys londe.'[4] Lancelot here refers to his banishment with an old word, *fleamed*, that has Anglo-Saxon roots and would soon be obsolete, but the word used for the subsequent historical description, *chronicle*, is a Middle English term borrowed from the French that was increasingly common in the fifteenth century, suggesting that Lancelot is not alone in his sensitivity to the role played by chronicle writers in establishing and maintaining honour and reputation. So it is that Hotspur, in *1 Henry IV*, incites the reluctant rebels by asserting that their shameful deeds will 'fill up chronicles in time to come' if they fail to resist the perfidious Henry IV (1.3.171). Unlike Lancelot's lament, which takes his historiographical fate as fixed, Hotspur suggests that the shape of a future chronicle remains open, that swift action against Bolingbroke will restore lost honour and lead to fame.

The example from *The True Tragedy* offers something even more complex. It teasingly points to the incompleteness of the historical record; indeed, Forrest declares an intention to confound subsequent historiography. The idea of a

[3] Thucydides, *The History of the War Fought between Athens and Sparta*, ed. Rex Warner (London: Penguin, 1956), 13.

[4] Thomas Malory, *Le Morte Darthur*, ed. Stephen H. A. Shepherd (New York: W.W. Norton & Company, 2004), 670. I would like to thank Vincent Gillespie for drawing my attention to this passage.

historical mystery only makes sense alongside the assumption that the past is recoverable. Under these circumstances, the historical is not limited to the sum of what is recorded and remembered about the past, it has become a duration projected backwards, a continuous succession of moments that will be more or less adequately described by history writers who are compelled to fill the gaps in received knowledge. The emergence of the historical mystery is, then, a symptom of a particular historical sensibility. It is simultaneously an expression of the ambition to know the past completely and an admission that such an ambition is impossible; the historical mystery marks a deep curiosity toward the past and an equally deep alienation from it. At the same time the historical mystery advertises the gap between *res gestae* and *historia rerum gestarum* and promulgates an awareness of history as written.

In what follows I argue that the historiographical consciousness visible in *The True Tragedy* is principally produced by a post-Reformation understanding of history writing as partial in both senses. Reformation era arguments over the near and distant past are crucial not so much for the popularization of history but for making people increasingly aware of the plurality of competing, even contradictory, accounts of the past. The sort of pluralization of historical narratives fostered by post-Reformation polemic is radically distinct from an earlier form of pluralization that involved a willingness to accommodate a range of disparate accounts of the past.

History plays contribute to this development not only by offering sophisticated reflections on the representation of the past, but also by offering competing accounts of various episodes and particular reigns. The dramatist who transforms chronicle material into two hours' traffic on the stage is acutely aware that the sources are at once excessive and deficient; invariably questions about the modes of historical representation find expression in the plays themselves. In Shakespeare's *Richard III*, for instance, the young Prince Edward asks Buckingham whether Julius Caesar built the Tower. In response to Buckingham's affirmation, Edgar wonders, 'Is it upon record, or else reported / Successively from age to age' (3.1.72–3)? The insistence that it is upon record would have perhaps provoked a smile from audience members familiar with Polydore Vergil's attack on this unsubstantiated tradition, but more importantly it provides an occasion for Edward to defend oral history: 'But say, my lord, it were not registered, / Methinks the truth should live from age to age, / As 'twere retailed to all posterity / Even to the general all-ending day' (3.1.75–7). What gives this assertion its particular poignancy is the audience's awareness that the moment when such a confidence in consensual oral report was possible has itself irrevocably passed—the past is now a site of constant struggle and registers play a central role in the contest. While history plays reflect upon the conditions of their own production, they also exist in a crowded and competitive field, positioning themselves in relationship to other genres (most notably tragedy) but also in relationship to other history plays.

However, my argument is not that the plays in a predictably satisfying way problematize the pieties of conventional humanist historiography—an argument made by Phyllis Rackin and Ivo Kamps.[5] Nor do I want to revert to an earlier argument in which the history plays are mere popularizations of serious historiography, guilty of playing fast and loose with the facts in order to create pleasing drama. My argument is instead that the plays are at once a manifestation of and a contributor to the burgeoning historiographical consciousness that emerged in the wake of the Reformation. But plays provide only part of the evidence for a larger argument that examines a range of historical descriptions of the death of the two princes from the late fifteenth century to the early seventeenth century in order to trace the emergence of the category of the historical mystery and to explore its relationship to rewriting, or, to use contemporary idiom, revisionism.

The prominence of rewriting is a consequence of the polemical aspect of post-Reformation English historiography.[6] However, the emergence of critical historiography is usually credited to the humanists, who used the tools of philology to reveal the powerful interests that are sustained by received narratives. Valla's exposure of the fraudulent Donation of Constantine is an emblematic instance of humanist unmasking that deploys philology and historical argument to expose corruption.[7] But Reformation historians transformed humanist historiography by deploying it in pursuit of what Amos Funkenstein has termed counterhistory, 'a specific genre of history written since antiquity'.[8] 'Their function', he writes, 'is polemical. Their method consists of the systematic exploitation of the adversary's most trusted sources against their grain.' Funkenstein also argues that this 'well-defined, literary-polemical genre in antiquity and the Middle Ages' was transformed in the sixteenth century when it began to focus on an 'explicit reinterpretation, rather than an inverted exploitation, of sources'. Funkenstein acknowledges that developments in philology, biblical studies, and legal interpretation all contributed, but he gives special attention to the Reformation: 'Protestant historiography was driven, from its beginning, toward the construction of a counterhistory of the

5 Phyllis Rackin, *Stages of History: Shakespeare's English Chronicles* (Ithaca, NY: Cornell University Press, 1991); Ivo Kamps, *Historiography and Ideology in Stuart Drama* (Cambridge: Cambridge University Press, 1996).

6 As Reinhart Koselleck points, out recording, continuing, and rewriting form the inescapable methodological basis for history writing. See Reinhart Koselleck, 'Transformations of Experience and Methodological Change: A Historical-Anthropological Essay' in his *The Practice of Conceptual History: Timing History, Spacing Concepts*, trans. Todd Samuel Presner (Stanford, CA: Stanford University Press, 2002), 45–83.

7 For an account that stresses the rhetorical aspects of Valla's *Oration*, see Carlo Ginzburg, *History, Rhetoric, and Proof: The Menahem Stern Jerusalem Lectures* (London: University Press of New England, 1999), 54–70; for a thorough critique of the received wisdom concerning Valla and anachronism, see Margreta de Grazia's contribution to this volume.

8 Amos Funkenstein, 'History, Counterhistory, and Narrative', in Saul Friedlander, *Probing the Limits of Representation: Nazism and the Final Solution* (Cambridge, MA: Harvard University Press, 1992), 66–81, at 69.

Church.' The attempt to promote and popularize this counterhistory not only affirmed historiography's role in the legitimation of institutions, it also advertized the degree to which history had become a contested terrain. Of course, history and historiography were both very much contested terrain in the fifteenth century, and the possibility that history was written with an eye toward the validation of dynastic or institutional claims of priority and privilege was readily recognized, and it was possible to encounter partisan accounts of particular episodes.[9] What distinguishes counterhistory is the scope of its reinterpretation and the fact that received history and counterhistory are mutually exclusive. Humanist history takes up from Roman classical historiography a preoccupation with conspiracy, but post-Reformation counterhistory sees the totality of Christian history in conspiratorial terms.

Analysis of the historiographical treatment of the two princes in the Tower from the second continuation of the Crowland chronicle down to George Buck's skeptical account in his *History of Richard III* reveals neither the triumph of humanism, nor the emergence of modern methodical historiography; instead, what we see is a widespread sense that written history is not only susceptible to error but that consensual narratives about the past are subject to wholesale revision. Historians of historiography, it has been noted, have a tendency to treat their subject in teleological terms, focusing on the elements in past historical writing that seem recognizably modern.[10] Antonia Gransden's enormously learned and impressively comprehensive account of medieval historical writing in England falls prey to this temptation by consistently highlighting the 'rational analysis of cause and effect' and indications of 'objective intellectual curiosity'.[11] Gransden's account ends with the humanist historians Polydore Vergil and Thomas More, and, while acknowledging the distinctiveness of their work, she is eager to point not only to the various anticipations that occur in earlier history writing but also to the longevity of habits of thought that have been labeled 'medieval'. Gransden thus scumbles the divide between medieval and renaissance historiography in England, persuasively arguing that there was no radical break in either 1485 or 1500 and that a native tradition of medieval historiography proved remarkably durable throughout the sixteenth century.

Daniel Woolf, a historian of the early modern period, has also downplayed the notion of a revolution in historiography, a claim made most forthrightly by F. Smith Fussner.[12] Most recently Woolf has taken exception to the emphasis

[9] Antonia Gransden, 'Propaganda in English Medieval Historiography', *Journal of Medieval History*, 1 (1975), 363–82; Paul Strohm, *England's Empty Throne: Usurpation and the Language of Legitimation, 1399–1422*, 2nd edn (South Bend, IN: University of Notre Dame Press, 2006; first published 1998).

[10] David Womersley, 'Against the Teleology of Technique', in *The Uses of History in Early Modern England*, ed. Paulina Kewes (Berkeley: University of California Press, 2006), 91–104.

[11] Antonia Gransden, *Historical Writing in England*, 2 vols. (London: Routledge and Kegan Paul, 1974–1982), 2: 300, xiii.

[12] F. Smith Fussner, *The Historical Revolution: English Historical Writing and Thought, 1580–1640* (London: Routledge and Kegan Paul, 1962). For an early engagement with Fussner, see D. R. Woolf, 'Erudition and the Idea of History in Renaissance England', *Renaissance Quarterly*, 40 (1987), 11–48.

placed on humanism as the driving force behind changes in early modern historiography.[13] Indeed, his *The Social Circulation of the Past: English Historical Culture 1500–1730* argues that change is not to be found at the level of historiography at all but is instead to be sought at the level of 'historical culture'. Woolf claims that in the period he covers a distinctive historical culture emerges and the evidence for this historical culture is to be found not simply or even primarily in history books but in an enormous wealth and range of other documents and artifacts.

Though Woolf acknowledges the importance of 'the various polemical ends to which the past was put' in the formation of England's historical culture, it is not a theme that he pursues.[14] The way that the Reformation encouraged polemical history writing is acknowledged, but not deeply considered. Indeed, this has often been the case. F. J. Levy's magisterial account of Tudor history writing, for example, admits that the Reformation increased the prominence of history writing: 'Forced by the pressure of controversy', theologians, 'adopted the latest methods of source controversy and made them serve theology. Foxe and Jewel did more to spread the knowledge of that product of humanism than the schoolmasters.'[15] The Reformers popularize history but do not contribute anything in terms of historiographical methodology. On one level, this is certainly true. Foxe and Bale are not responsible for the sorts of technical innovations that usually feature in the history of historiography. However, they and their followers are responsible for making a broad audience aware of the degree to which received historical narratives were susceptible to wholesale revision.[16]

Though Bale's *A Brief Chronicle Concerning the Examination and Death of Sir John Oldcastle* (1544), *The Examination of William Thorpe*, and *The Examinations of Anne Askew* (1547) served as important precursors to John Foxe's *Acts and Monuments* (1563), his *The Image of both Churches* (1545) was even more influential. What gives *The Image* its extraordinary power is the way in which it combines an Apocalyptic interpretive scheme with the writing of history.[17] The result is a stark, indeed, Manichean vision of the totality of Christian

[13] Daniel Woolf, *The Social Circulation of the Past: English Historical Culture, 1500–1730* (Oxford: Oxford University Press, 2003), 5–6.

[14] Woolf, *The Social Circulation of the Past*, 7.

[15] F. J. Levy, *Tudor Historical Thought* (Toronto: University of Toronto Press, 2004; orig. printed San Marino, CA: Huntington Library, 1967), 123.

[16] Womersley, 'Against the Teleology', 99. See also Rainer Pineas, 'William Tyndale's Use of History as a Weapon of Religious Controversy', *The Harvard Theological Review*, 55 (1962), 121–41; 'William Tyndale's Influence on John Bale's Polemical Use of History', *Archiv für Reformationsgeschichte*, 52 (1962), 79–96.

[17] Richard Bauckham, *Tudor Apocalypse* (Oxford: Sutton Courtenay Press, 1978); Katherine Firth, *The Apocalyptic Tradition in Reformation Britain, 1530–1645* (Oxford: Oxford University Press, 1979); Paul Christianson, *Reformers and Babylon: English Apocalyptic Visions from the Reformation to the Eve of the Civil War* (Toronto: University of Toronto Press, 1978).

history. Using a sevenfold division of history taken from the seven seals of Revelation, Bale mapped the past as a constant struggle between the true church and the church of Antichrist. As a consequence, the long history of the church's struggle with heterodoxy could be reread as a corrupt institution's attempt to suppress the simple truth; in terms of historiographical method, Bale's position licensed an extreme form of skepticism toward received records and narratives. For Bale it is axiomatic that 'monkish chroniclers' are not to be trusted, that their accounts must be read against the grain. In fact, Bale's project for Reformation extends to include English history writing; in the preface to *A Brief Chronicle Concerning the Examination and Death of Sir John Oldcastle*, Bale announces:

> I wolde wyshe some lerned Englyshe manne (as there are now most excellent fresh wyttes) to set forth the Englyshe chronicles in their right shappe, as certen other landes hath done afore them, all affeccyons set a part. I can not thynke a more necessarye thynge to be laboured to the honour of God, beauty of the realme, erudicyon of the people, and commodite of other landes, next the sacred scripture of the Byble, than that worke wolde be. (A5v)

On the face of it, this plea seems innocuous. Bale's desire for history in the 'right shappe', however, is more than a rejection of the formlessness of the chronicles: to put history in shape requires that it be structured according to the enduring conflict between the true and false churches. Moreover, the echo of '*sine ira et studio*', which seems to promise impartiality, is undercut by Bale's preceding excoriation of Polydore Vergil, who is guilty of 'polutynge oure Englyshe chronycles most shamefullye with his Romyshe lyes and other Italyshe beggerye' (A5r). Elsewhere, Bale, discussing the early inhabitants of Britain and their conversion to Christianity, observes that this matter 'hath bene hytherto in all Englysh Chronycles, doubtfullye, unagreablye, yea, and untrulye treated, upon conjecturs, fantasyes, and lyes onlye, by reason of ignoraunce in the scripturs and most auctorysed hystoryes'.[18]

Bale's framework provides the structuring principle for Foxe's enormous *Acts and Monuments*. Foxe also continues Bale's attack on 'monkish chronicles' and provides an elaborate explanation of his own procedures. Foxe's methodological claims emerge most sharply in his response to the hostile criticism of Nicholas Harpsfield, whose *Dialogi sex* (1566) was the first sustained critique of *Acts and Monuments*.[19] In the 1570 and subsequent editions, Foxe responds directly to Harpsfield:

[18] John Bale, *The Actes of the Englysh Votaryes* (Antwerp, 1546), A4^{v}.

[19] For a survey that looks at both sides of the confessional divide, see Felicity Heal, 'Appropriating History: Catholic and Protestant Polemics and the National Past', *Huntington Library Quarterly*, 68 (2005), 109–32.

> As touching the order and ground of writing among these chroniclers, ye must consider, and can not be ignoraunt, that as none of all these by you forenamed, was present at the deede, not wytnes of the fact, so have they nothing of them selves herein certainly to affirme, but eyther must follow publike rumour and hearesaye for theyr autor, or else one of them must borrow of an other.[20]

Harpsfield's citation of Robert Fabyan, Polydore Vergil, and Edward Hall does not satisfy Foxe, who goes on to observe that 'writers of stories for most parte followyng either blind report, or els one taking of an other, use commonly all to sounde together after one tune'; they are not to be credited 'unles the grounde be founde substauntiall whereupon they stande them selves'. Such a substantial ground is, for Foxe, provided by acts, registers, records, in other words archival documents, and his rejection of Fabyan, Vergil, and Hall as scissors-and-paste historians has traction. Foxe, however, makes a second point: in citing chronicles one must also consider 'what place and effect they serve':

> If ye would shewe out of them the order and course of times, what yeares were of dearth and of plentie, where kings kept there Christenmas, what condites were made, what Mayors and Sherifes were in London, what battailes were fought, what triumphes and great feastes were holden, when kynges began their reigne, and when they ended etc. In such vulgare and populare affaires, the narration of the Chronicler serveth to good purpose, and may have his credite, wherein the matter forceth not much, whether it be true or false, or whether any listeth to beleve them. (686–7)

This rejection of public history echoes the accusation in *The Mirror for Magistrates* that 'Unfruitful Fabyan followed the face / Of time and deeds, but let the causes slip.'[21] But Foxe is not principally concerned with causation here; his rejection of the 'face of time and deeds' has more to do with their inessential nature: such events are inconsequential, the superficial froth of history, and because nothing is at stake in such accounts, they make no claim on the reader's belief. However, in situations 'where as a thyng is denyed, and in cases of judgement, and in controversies doubtfull, which are to be decided and boulted out by evidence of just demonstration: I take them neyther for Judges of the bench, nor for arbiters of the cause, nor as witnesses of them selves sufficient necessarely to be sticked unto.' Foxe here sets up a series of important oppositions: the uncontroversial against the controversial, the manifest against the latent, popular and vulgar opinion against informed judgment. This is a brief for revisionism. The accusation that historians all sing the same tune, that consensus history is based not on robust primary sources and eyewitness accounts but on 'public rumor and hearsay', that the hidden truth of events can only be demonstrated by the careful sifting of evidence, is

[20] John Foxe, *Actes and Monuments* (London, 1570), 686.

[21] William Baldwin, *The Mirror for Magistrates*, ed. Lily B. Campbell (Cambridge: Cambridge University Press, 1938), 198.

evidence of a sharply critical sensibility. Moreover, Foxe makes it clear that history writing has become in some essential sense controversial.[22]

The degree to which religious controversy becomes bound up with historical inquiry in Foxe's work is demonstrated by his invocation of Cicero's famous description of history: 'Albeit I deny not but hystories are taken many tymes, and so termed for witnesses of tymes, and glasses of antiquity etc. yet not such witnesses, as whose testimonie beareth always a necessary truth, and bindeth beleefe.' The marginal note warns: 'Historyes not rashely to be beleved.' This echoes the earlier claim that 'vulgar and popular affairs' are things indifferent: it does not matter 'whether it be true or false, or whether any listeth to beleve them'. By dwelling on belief and historiography, Foxe comes close here to acknowledging the fundamental tension between a Protestant theology of *sola scriptura* and historical knowledge. Under what circumstances would it be possible to offer the contingent and transitory material of history as 'necessary truth' that binds belief? The history that matters to Foxe is the history that concerns 'controversies doubtful', and in these cases history serves to vindicate the Protestant cause.

While the extent of Foxe's influence on English history writing is understudied and probably underestimated, the crucial point for the purposes of my argument is that Foxe made revisionist history mainstream. Moreover, the responses that Foxe provoked served to make the contested and contestable nature of history writing visible to a broad audience. For those who lacked the intellectual or financial resources required to gain direct access to post-Reformation history writing, the professional stage provided ample evidence of the ways in which history was being revised and rewritten. Particular reigns attracted competing accounts, so that perhaps the earliest of the chronicle history plays, *The Famous Victories of Henry the Fifth* (*c.*1587), served as both source and provocation for Shakespeare's *Henry V* (1599), just as *The True Tragedie of Richard the Third* existed in rivalry with Shakespeare's *Richard III*. But even more interesting are the history plays that appear in explicit dialogue: the emphatic Protestantism of *The Troublesome Reign of King John* is answered by Shakespeare's more nuanced *The Life and Death of King John*, and Shakespeare's own *1 Henry IV*, with its apparent satire upon Sir John Oldcastle, one of Foxe's martyrs, was answered by the Admiral's Men, who staged *Sir John Oldcastle* as, at least in part, a rebuttal.[23]

22 Patrick Collinson, 'Truth, Lies, and Fiction in Sixteenth-century Protestant Historiography', in *The Historical Imagination in Early Modern Britain: History, Rhetoric, and Fiction, 1500–1800*, ed. Donald R. Kelley and David Harris Sacks (Cambridge: Cambridge University Press, 1997), 37–68; see also Glyn Parry, 'John Foxe, "Father of Lyes", and the Papists', in *John Foxe and the English Reformation*, ed. David Loades (Aldershot, Hants: Scolar Press, 1997), 295–305.

23 David Scott Kastan, '"Killed with Hard Opinions": Oldcastle, Falstaff, and the Reformed Text of *1 Henry IV*', in *Textual Topography: Formations and Reformations*, ed. Thomas L. Berger and Laurie Maguire (Newark: Delaware University Press, 1998), 211–30.

The story of the two princes is a particularly useful example of this trend toward rewriting and revision because it is not directly tied to the ecclesiastical history that preoccupied Foxe. As a consequence it serves as a secular example of a historiographical impulse that first became prominent in the polemical histories written in the wake of England's break with Rome. The first historical text to describe the fate of the two princes, the Crowland Continuation, is described by its editor as 'the only continuous political narrative that offers an alternative to Polydore Vergil and the inter-related Tudor Histories for the Yorkist period as a whole'.[24] But as Gransden emphasizes, the general congruity between Crowland and the Tudor myth, 'provides important evidence showing that the legend which dominated the Tudors' view of fifteenth century history had a very early origin'.[25] According to Gransden, the Continuation is a quasi-humanist text that reveals a 'rational approach to politics',[26] a tendency on display in the passage treating the death of the princes:

> When at last the people round about the city of London and in Kent, Essex, Sussex, Hampshire, Dorset, Devon, Somerset, Wiltshire and Berkshire and also in some other southern counties of the kingdom, just referred to, began considering vengeance, public proclamation having been made that Henry, duke of Buckingham, then living at Brecknock in Wales, being repentant of what had been done would be captain-in-chief in this affair, a rumour arose that King Edward's sons, by some unknown manner of violent destruction, had met their fate. For this reason, all those who had begun this agitation, realizing that if they could not find someone new at their head for their conquest it would soon be all over with them, remembered Henry, earl of Richmond, who had already spent many years in exile in Brittany.[27]

The writer goes on to describe how John Morton, Bishop of Ely, advised Buckingham to send for Richmond 'inviting him to hasten into the kingdom of England as fast as he could reach the shore to take Elizabeth, the dead king's elder daughter, to wife and with her, at the same time, possession of the whole kingdom'. The importance of this context is clear: the rumour that the princes have met a violent death presents a political problem for the conspiracy against Richard, a problem that is quickly resolved by the expedient of recruiting Henry of Richmond. The writer does not dwell on the truth or falsity of the rumour; indeed, the fate of the princes is only returned to at the conclusion in which the writer asserts that the sons of King Edward were 'avenged' at Bosworth.[28]

Polydore Vergil's subsequent handling of the matter does not appear to have been influenced by the Crowland Chronicle. The first full-scale, humanist history of England, *Anglica Historica*, is also the first to go into circumstantial detail concerning the death of the princes. Polydore tells of the order sent to Robert

[24] Nicholas Pronay and John Cox, *The Crowland Chronicle Continuations: 1459–1486* (London: Richard III and Yorkist Trust, 1986), 33.

[25] Gransden, *Historical Writing in England*, 2: 272.

[26] Ibid., 467.

[27] Pronay and Cox, *The Crowland Chronicle Continuations*, 163.

[28] Ibid., 163, 185.

Brackenbury, the Lieutenant of the Tower, Brackenbury's refusal of the 'kinges horryble commyssion', and the employment of James Tyrell, 'who, being forcyd to do the king's commandment, rode sorrowfully to London, and, to the woorst example that hath been almost ever hard of, murderyd those babes of th'yssue royall'.[29] Vergil's preoccupation with psychology—a prominent feature in his work—is evident in his description of a reluctant Tyrell compelled and acting in sorrow; in addition, Vergil here employs the language of exemplarity that features so prominently in subsequent treatments of this episode.[30]

The fact of death is beyond dispute: 'Thys end had Prince Edward and Richarde his brother; but with what kinde of death these sely chyldren wer executyd yt is not certanely known.' Vergil here offers something close to the Crowland Chronicle's 'some unknown manner of violent destruction', but whereas Crowland identifies this as a rumour, Vergil treats it as established fact. Moreover, he immediately continues:

> But King Richard, delyveryd by this fact from his care and feare, kept the slaughter not long secret, who, within few days after, permyttyd the rumor of ther death to go abrode, to th'intent (as we may well beleve) that after the people understoode no yssue male of king Edward to be now left alyve, they might with better mynde and good will beare and sustayne his governement. (188–9)

As in the Crowland Continuation, the rumor of death is bound up with political calculation, but whereas Crowland describes the rumor as a contingency that threatens to derail the conspiracy against Richard III, Vergil describes it as Richard's intentional strategy, an attempt to deprive the opposition of any alternative claimant to the throne.

However, in an example of the irony of unintended consequences, a common theme among humanist historians, Richard's political calculation backfires grievously:

> Whan the fame of this notable fowle fact was dispersyd throwgh the realme, so great griefe stroke generally to the hartes of all men, that the same, subdewing all feare, they wept every wher, and whan they could wepe no more, they cryed owt, 'Ys ther trewly any man lyving so farre at enemytie with God, with all that holy ys and relygyouse, so utter enemy to man, who wold not have abhorryd the myschief of so fowle a murder?' (189)

29 Polydore Vergil, *Three Books of Polydore Vergil's English History*, ed. Sir Henry Ellis (London: Camden Society, 1844), 188.

30 Exemplarity is, of course, a common feature in history writing. For an illuminating account of Renaissance exemplarity, see Timothy Hampton, *Writing from History: The Rhetoric of Exemplarity in Renaissance Literature* (Ithaca, NY: Cornell University Press, 1990). See also Reinhart Koselleck, 'Historia Magistra Vitae: The Dissolution of the Topos into the Perspective of a Modernized Historical Process', in his *Futures Past: On the Semantics of Historical Time* (Cambridge, MA: MIT Press, 1985), 21–38.

It is, of course, a rhetorical question—there is such a monster and he wears the crown. When the 'news' reaches the Queen in sanctuary she gives vent to 'suche passion' that she is herself in danger of death. After a detailed description of a distraught mother's extravagant grief, Vergil reflects on the death of the 'two innocent imps' (190) and points out that it stands as a warning that the offences of ancestors 'do redound to the posterity'. Edward IV, guilty of perjury and the death of his brother, the Duke of Clarence, is identified as culpable for the shameful murder of his own children.

The Italian humanists, according to Anthony Grafton's brusque assessment, 'wove histories out of older chronicles and contemporary diplomatic dispatches in order to make plain the views and policies of their republican or despotic bosses', and Polydore Vergil is often understood in a similar fashion as a commissioned author of official history.[31] Certainly his dire portrait of Richard III contributed to what has come to be called the Tudor myth. And yet his treatment of the murder of the princes is guarded. He concedes that details are not available, but insists on the indisputable fact of the murders and the gravity of the crime, which reveals Richard to be an enemy to God and the human community. It is, however, the work of another humanist that establishes the full picture of Richard III's crime against nature. Thomas More begins his treatment of Richard's reign with the assertion that as he ended it with the best and most righteous death, 'that is to wyt his own: so began he with the most piteous and wicked, I meane the lamentable murder of innoocent nephewes, the young king and his tender brother'.[32] The rhetorical parallelism imputes a pleasing symmetry to events and more importantly points to the humanist preoccupation with narrative structure and the obligation to tell a story with a beginning, middle, and end.[33] And yet More acknowledges that the death of the princes has 'natheles so far comen in question, that some remain yet in doubt, whither they wer in his dayes destroyde or no' (82).

The career of Perkin Warbeck, who for a time successfully impersonated the Duke of York and aspired to the throne of Henry VII, is cited as evidence of the malice and folly of the people. Yet gullibility and mischief are not entirely to blame: 'all thynges wer in late daies so covertly demeaned, one thing pretended and an other ment, that there was nothyng so plain and openly proved, but that yet for the comen custome of close and covert dealing, men had it ever inwardely suspect, as many well counterfaited jewels make the true mistrusted' (82). More here

[31] Anthony Grafton, *What was History? The Art of History in Early Modern Europe* (Cambridge: Cambridge University Press, 2007), 21.

[32] Thomas More, *The History of King Richard III*, ed. Richard S. Sylvester, in *The Complete Works of St. Thomas More*, 15 vols. (New Haven: Yale University Press, 1963), 2: 82.

[33] Thomas Blundeville, *The True Order and Method of Writing and Reading Histories* (London, 1574): 'an History ought to declare the things in such order, as they were done. And because everything hath his beginning, augmentation, state, declination, and end: The writer ought therefore to tell the things, so as thereby a man may perceive and discern, that which appertaineth to every degree' (A3r).

elaborates on one of his principal themes in the *History*; Richard himself is 'close and secrete, a deepe dissimuler'(8) and his treacherous hypocrisy infects the age, becoming a general condition. Suspicion becomes so automatic that even things 'plain and openly proved' are subject to doubt and uncertainty.

In a familiar Tacitean mode, dissimulation is closely tied to conspiracy, another prominent feature in More's *History*, and it is important to notice the way in which the connection works. In the first place, suspicion underwrites a reading of actions that promises to penetrate beneath the apparent or public face of events in order to reveal the secret machinations of power. The murder in custody is a peculiarly potent image of abusive state power, and history writing promises to illuminate these dark matters of state. Unfortunately, as More observes, conspiracy thinking can also undermine belief even in a conspiracy that is 'plain and openly proved'. Certainly, he goes on to give a very elaborate account of the death of the princes, 'not after every way that I have heard, but after that way that I have so hard by suche men and by such meanes, as me thinketh it wer hard but it should be true' (83).

Elsewhere More is happy to tolerate a number of possibilities, but here his narrative considers only one possibility:

> King Richarde after his coronacion, takyng his way to Gloucester to visit in his newe honor, the towne of which he bare the name of his old, devised as he roode, to fulfil that thing which he before had intended. And forasmuch as his minde gave him, that his nephewes living, men woulde not recken that hee could have right to the realm, he thought therfore without delay to rid them, as though the killing of his kinsmen, could amend his cause, and make him a kindly king.[34]

Along with the ironic assessment of this political calculation— emphasized by the punning play on the kindly killing of kinsmen— the most prominent feature in this passage is the number of words describing thinking: 'devised', 'intended', 'mind', 'reckon', 'thought'. The consideration of psychology is, of course, a hallmark of humanist history, and in this regard, More is typical, but it is worth pointing out the way in which this moment of difficulty provokes an intensification of the language of interiority and motive that amounts to mind-reading.

The history that More tells is furnished with a wealth of concrete details: he writes, for example, of the role played by a nameless, 'secrete' page who alerts Richard to the presence among the companions of his bedchamber of Sir James Tyrell, a man willing to perform murder. This exchange occurs while Richard is on the privy stool, 'a convenient carpet for such a counsaile' (83, 84). The page is himself an astute political observer who has marked the way in which Tyrell has been kept 'under' by Ratcliff and Catesby, and he seizes the 'occasion offered'. Not only does More provide details concerning the recruitment of Tyrell, he carefully

[34] More, *The History of Richard III*, ed. Sylvester, 2: 83. For moments where alternative possibilities are entertained, see 2: 9, 32, 33–4, 50.

describes Tyrell's plan to use the villains Miles Forrest—a fellow already 'fleshed in murther'—and John Dighton, a horsekeeper and 'a big brode square strong knave.' These two smother the princes using a featherbed and pillows at 'about midnight'; they then bring Tyrell to see 'their bodies naked out uppon the bed'. Tyrell immediately orders that the bodies be buried at the foot of the stairs 'under a great heape of stones' (85).

At this point the singleness and certainty of More's narrative begins to break down. After gratefully receiving the news that his nephews have been dispatched, Richard expresses a desire to 'have them buried in a better place, because thei wer a kinge's sonnes' (86). 'Whereupon', continues More,

> thei say that a prieste of syr Robert Brakenbury toke up the bodyes again, and secretely entered them in such place, as by the occasion of his deathe, whiche onely knew it could never synce come to light. Very trouthe is it and well knowen, that at such time as syr James Tirell was in the Tower, for treason committed agaynste the moste famous prince king Henry the seventh, both Dighton and he were examined, and confessed the murther in maner above writen, but whither the bodies were removed thei could nothing tel. (86)

'Thei say' gives the description of priestly burial the status either of common knowledge or informed opinion; in either case, it registers a degree of uncertainty. This expression of uncertainty is followed by an emphatic insistence: 'Very trouthe it is and well knowen'. The quasi-judicial examination of Tyrell and Dighton which produces confessions that would presumably have been documented serves as the source for 'the murther in maner above writen' (86). According to More, then, the precise manner of the murder is verified by the eyewitness testimony of the participants, but the final fate of the bodies produces a lingering mystery. Indeed, More's confidence in the story of priestly reburial does not appear especially strong because in his summation he writes: 'theyr bodies cast God wote where by the cruel ambicion of their unnaturall uncle and his dispiteous tormentors'. His account as he acknowledges was 'learned of them that much knew and litle cause had to lye' (86), but this assertion sits uncomfortably alongside the earlier claim about the 'comen custome of close and covert dealing'. Nonetheless, the murder of the princes serves as a rhetorical example: 'God never gave this world a more notable example, neither in what unsuretie standeth this worldly wel, or what mischief worketh the prowde enterprise of an hyghe heart, or finally what wretched end ensueth such dispiteous crueltie' (86).

More presents here a version of humanist history that is attentive to moral exemplarity, that considers psychological causes and exhibits a strong impulsion toward a singular account. This last tendency is in clear contrast with an earlier attitude exemplified by Higden's comments on methodology at the beginning of *Polychronicon*:

> Wherefore we shal not blame makers and wryters of historyes that dyversly speken and wryten. For longe passyng of tyme and elde of dedes make hem unknowen and

> writers to erre. Therfor Jherome sayth it is semely to byleve theyr sawes that gaynsaye not our bileve ne sothnes that is known, wherefor in the wrytyng of this historye I take not upon me to afferme for trouthe alle that I wryte, but suche as I have seen and redde in dyverse bookes.[35]

This equanimity in the face of a variety of competing accounts is replaced by the humanist attempt to arrive at the single true version of events. And in cases where this was in dispute, they were willing to make an argument for the most plausible sequence of events based on their knowledge of both historical circumstance and human psychology.

The subsequent success of More's *History* suggests that English historiography in the sixteenth century absorbed many elements of the humanist program. Roger Ascham praised it as a model for historians, and Sir John Harington claimed at the end of the sixteenth century that 'in all men's opinions' More's account of Richard III was the 'best written part of all our Chronicles'.[36] More's unfinished narrative was taken up in bits and pieces and used by all the major chronicle writers of the sixteenth century; while this might be understood as the broad promulgation of humanist history, it is worth pointing out that the insertion of More's narrative into larger chronicles undoubtedly changed the way the text was read and understood. The compiling of these texts frequently lead to the inclusion of multiple possibilities when an author confronted variations in the narrative sources. In other words, the key elements of humanist history—the development of a critical method for the evaluation of sources and the imposition of narrative structure—are only sporadically found in the great mass of history writing produced during the sixteenth century.[37] For example, Edward Hall, who generally follows More, includes an addition concerning the bodies of the princes gleaned from John Rastell's *The Pastyme of People* (1529).[38] Where More insists that the death of the priest meant that the location of the bodies 'could never synce come to light', Hall writes, 'the very trueth coulde never yet be very wel and perfightly knowen'. *Yet* here seems to hold out a hope that the truth may still be discovered. Unlike More, who insists that this line of inquiry is literally a dead end, Hall is apparently prepared to entertain alternatives:

[35] Ranulf Higden, *Polychronicon*, ed. William Caxton and trans. John Trevisa (London, 1482), VIv–VIIr. For more on Caxton and the medieval tolerance for differing accounts of the past, see Joseph M. Levine, 'Caxton's Histories: Fact and Fiction at the Close of the Middle Ages', in his *Humanism and History: Origins of Modern English Historiography* (Ithaca, NY: Cornell University Press, 1987), 19–53.

[36] For Ascham's remarks, see Walter F. Staton, 'Roger Ascham's Theory of History Writing', *Studies in Philology*, 56 (1959), 125–37, at 130; Sir John Harington, *A New Discourse of a Stale Subject, called the Metamorphosis of Ajax* (London, 1596), D8^{v}.

[37] For an argument concerning Raphael Holinshed that transforms these attributes into political virtue, see Annabel Patterson, 'Rethinking Tudor Historiography', *The South Atlantic Quarterly*, 92 (1993), 185–208.

[38] Edward Hall, *The Union of the Two Noble and Illustre Families of Lancaster and York* (London, 1548), EE3^{v}.

> For some saye that kinge Richard caused the priest to take them up and close them in lead and to put them in a coffyne full of holes hoked at the ends with two hokes of yron, and so to cast them into a place called the Blacke depes at the Themes mouth, so that they should never rise up nor be sene again. (EE3^{v}–EE4^{r})

Rather than illumination, there is a deepening of the mystery. Indeed, the Black Deep, a channel through the treacherous sandbars of the Thames estuary, figures historical oblivion, the deep, backward and abysm of time. Unlike bodies secretly buried within the Tower precincts, bodies cast into the Black Deep are absolutely beyond recovery. Indeed, Rastell explains that story of submersion in the Black Deep was by 'dyvers men conjectured to be trewe because that the bones of the sayd chylderne coude never be founde buryed nother in the Towre nor in no nother place.'[39]

And yet the princes did 'rise up' and were 'sene again'—notably in the person of Perkin Warbeck—but also in the Tudor history plays with which I began. The murder of the princes is a central feature in the dramatic renderings of Richard's reign. The title page of the first quarto of Shakespeare's play advertises it as 'Containing, His Treacherous Plots against his brother Clarence: the pittieful murther of his iunocent nephewes: his tyrannical usurpation: with the whole course of his detested life, and most deserved death' (1597). Similarly, the anonymous *True Tragedy of Richard the Third* (1594) describes a play 'Wherein is showne the death of Edward the fourth, with the smothering of the two yoong Princes in the Tower'. In both instances, the young princes appear on the stage but their deaths are narrated and their bodies never seen. Thomas Heywood predictably shows no such restraint: his *2 Edward IV* includes a scene in which the two princes comfort one another and pray (accompanied by 'solemn music') in the moment before they are assaulted. The murder itself is not staged, but immediately afterward Forrest and Dighton enter from opposite ends of the stage each carrying a body and join James Tyrell. After a brief exchange of guilty accusations, the bodies are placed on the stage, and Tyrell concludes the scene: 'The priest here in the Tower will bury them; / Let us away.'[40] This is clearly an endorsement of More's account and a rejoinder to *The True Tragedy*—there is pathos in abundance here but no great mystery.

That history plays offered emotionally affecting but factually impoverished versions of the past was widely recognized at the time. In Jonson's *The Devil is an Ass*, after Fitzdottrell explains that the Dukedom of Gloucester is fatal, Merecraft offers an unctuous compliment: 'By m'faith you are cunning i'the chronicle, Sir.' Fitzdottrell responds: 'No, I confess I ha't from the playbooks, / And think they are more authentic.'[41] Jonson is here having a fling at Shakespeare, who includes a bit

[39] John Rastell, *The Pastyme of People* (London, 1529), F6^{v}.

[40] Thomas Heywood, *The First and Second Parts of King Edward IV*, ed. Richard Rowland (Manchester: Manchester University Press, 2005), 17.49–50.

[41] Ben Jonson, *The Devil is an Ass: And Other Plays*, ed. Margaret Jane Kidney (Oxford: Oxford University Press, 2001), 2.4.12–14.

of dialogue on this point in *3 Henry VI*: in response to Edward's assertion that he will make Richard Duke of Gloucester, Richard complains 'Gloucester's dukedom is too ominous' (2.6.107). However, the suggestion that the title of Gloucester has been unfortunate can also be found in Polydore Vergil and his followers.[42] One particularly important critic of the sort of history offered on the stage was Sir George Buck, Master of the Revels from 1610 to 1622. Though its textual history is complicated, Buck's *The History of King Richard III* (1619) appears to contain at least one disparaging comment about the stage:

> The ignorant, and never-understandeing vulgare; whose faith (in history) is drawne from Pamphlet and Ballad, and their Reverend and learned Autors, the stage, or those that play the bauds to it, for a liveing, Let them fly their owne pitch, for they are but kytes, and Crowes, and can digest nought (soe well) as stench and filth, to which I leave them.

Another remark, found in the text published in 1646 and probably an editorial interpolation by Buck's great-nephew, attacks dramatic representations of Richard's bad dreams: 'they will dissect his very sleepes, to find prodigious dreames and bug-beares... which they dress in all the fright and horrour fiction and the stage can adde'. [43] Whether authorial or not, these sentiments are in keeping with the general tenor of *The History.*

Buck's *History* is a remarkable example of revisionism that deploys historical learning against received opinion. In attacking the consensus account of Richard III, exemplified not only in popular stage histories but also in the mainstream of historical writing descending from Vergil, More, and Hall, Buck was reading history against the grain in the manner of Bale and Foxe. Foxe is only cited as an authority when Buck offers his scathing assessment of Thomas More, but a discernibly Foxeian mode of history writing is everywhere evident in Buck's text.[44] Like Foxe, he writes in an exculpatory vein, and, like Foxe, he uses original documents and subjects narrative sources to careful scrutiny, always alert for any indication of bias. Buck has the distinction of having been the first to make use of the Croyland Chronicle which was only available in manuscript; in it he discovered a copy of the suppressed *Titulus Regius*, the Act of Parliament that declared Richard King of England in 1483, a document that undermines the standard Tudor charge of usurpation.

Like Foxe, Buck counsels caution in the reading of histories, urging readers to 'consider and examine what they read, and make trial of such doubtful things are as written before they give credit unto them' (125). Buck singles out John Morton, Bishop of Ely, and Thomas More as 'Antirichards' whose work has infected all

[42] Vergil, *Three Books*, ed. Ellis, 73.

[43] Sir George Buck, *The History of King Richard the Third (1619)*, ed. Arthur Noel Kincaid (Gloucester: Alan Sutton, 1979), xxii.

[44] Buck, *The History of King Richard the Third*, ed. Kincaid, 124.

subsequent writing on the subject. Sounding much like E. H. Carr, Buck offers an historical explanation for the problem: 'Therefore, the Read[er] must read their writings warily, and consider what men *they be. For it* is a hard thing to find that prince's story truly and faithfully written, who was so hateful to the writers *then; for when they* wrote they might write no better' (126). Though Buck's invocation of Antirichards suggests a structural similarity to Foxe's work, unlike his predecessor, who consistently assumes that the forces of Antichrist are constitutively opposed to true religion and will work tirelessly to deprave it, Buck posits a secular dynamic. During his lifetime Richard was subject to scandalous reports and false accusations made by 'malicious clerks' (120) who sought to ingratiate themselves with his enemies. After his death, this process continued in the form of official history written in support of the Tudor line. Under the Tudor regime it was impossible to write the true history of Richard III: 'But for these wrongs the times were most at fault, for then it w[as not] only tolerable and allowable to make and to publish such scandalous and infamous writings of him, but also it was meritorious and guerdonable. And on the contrary side to write well and honourably of him was an offense' (120).

In making the case against Richard's many detractors, Buck pays particular attention to the murder of the princes and has little difficulty poking holes in the various accounts. After considering the logical difficulties of the accusations, Buck affirms: 'And [questionless the] princes were not buried in the Tower nor drowned in the seas. Wherefore there must some [better] enquiry and some better search be made for the discovery of this dark mystery' (140). Though Buck does offer some alternatives, it is clear that the fate of the princes remains a 'dark mystery' and, perhaps needless to say, Buck's quixotic attempt to rehabilitate Richard III had little direct impact on the mainstream of English historiography. In his *Church History of Britain* (1655), Thomas Fuller complains that Buck has given Richard III a makeover: he 'eveneth his shoulders, smootheth his back, planeth his teeth, maketh him in all points a comly, and beautiful person'. Fuller allows that it is 'no heresie to maintain a paradox in History', but he objects strongly to the serious attempt 'to pervert peoples judgments, and therein go against all received Records'. For Fuller such 'singularity' is self-evidently perverse.[45] And yet Buck has had his modern followers, though any mention of the Richard III Society probably provokes a knowing smile of condescension, the sort of slightly amused bafflement that is reserved, in Shakespearean circles, for the Anti-Stratfordians. These conspiracy-minded projects share a deep suspicion toward received history and an ingenious use of evidence. But before being entirely dismissive of such marginal enterprises, it is perhaps worth thinking more carefully about the long and inescapable legacy of revisionism within modern historiography.

[45] Thomas Fuller, *The Church-History of Britain* (London, 1655), 197.

FURTHER READING

Gransden, Antonia. *Historical Writing in England*, 2 vols. (London: Routledge and Kegan Paul, 1974–82)

Levy, F. J. *Tudor Historical Thought* (Toronto: University of Toronto Press, 2004)

Woolf, Daniel. *The Social Circulation of the Past: English Historical Culture 1500–1730* (Oxford: Oxford University Press, 2003)

CHAPTER 5

LITERARY HISTORIES

SETH LERER

Will the reader of this chapter be enticed or dissuaded by its title? For the eighteenth-century ecclesiast and critic William Warburton, literary history was 'the most agreeable subject in the world'. But for the early nineteenth-century German poet, Heinrich Heine, literary history was a 'morgue where each seeks out the friend he most loved'.[1] A pleasure or a pain, a subject of delight or mourning, literary history has itself had a mixed history among the readers and the writers of the European traditions. Part of its complex connotation lies in the modern European understanding of the place of literature in national identity formation. For the nineteenth-century pedagogues who set up what we think of today as the disciplines of literary study, verbal artifacts had something of a deeper, almost transcendent value. Friedrich Diez, one of the founders of historical philology, announced in 1821 that 'the serious study of literature reveals utterly characteristic directions and tendencies in the mind of man', while half a century later, Charles Aubertin could announce that 'the history of the origins of language is the history of the very same origins of the nation'. In seminars and lecture halls today, we still bear something of this legacy of such philologists' attempts to locate national identity in the curricula of language study.[2]

[1] I draw these quotations from an advanced search for the phrase 'literary history' in the online *Oxford English Dictionary* (<http://dictionary.oed.com>), with the following references: the first from Thomas Warburton, as quoted in *Boswell's Johnson* I. Introduction, 50 (*OED*, s.v., *agreement*, def.9); the second from G. W. Haven, translator, Heinrich Heine, *Letters, History, and Modern Political Literature in Germany*, 27 (*OED*, s.v., *morgue*, def. 1.a).

[2] These quotations (the first originally in German, the second originally in French), are drawn from material presented in Hans-Ulrich Gumbrecht, '"Un Souffle d'Allemagne ayant passé": Friedrich Diez, Gaston Paris, and the Genesis of National Philologies', *Romance Philology*, 40 (1986), 1–37, at 18 and 26–7, respectively. For the larger question of literary history's place in the history of institutions and in the modern classroom, the following works may be representative of recent approaches: Douglas Bush, 'Literary History and Literary Criticism', in *Literary History and Literary Criticism*, ed. Leon Edel et al. (New York: New York University Press, 1965); Sacvan Bercovich (ed.), *Reconstructing American Literary History*, Harvard English Studies, 13 (Cambridge, MA: Harvard University Press, 1986); David Perkins, *Is Literary History Possible?* (Baltimore, MD: Johns

For any modern teacher or student, whether literary history is a blessing or a curse, it is often a narrative of periods. We like our literary history in easily digestible quanta of dates ('the Eighteenth Century') or christened ages ('the Augustan') or political time-frames ('the Restoration') or lifetimes shaped by a presiding aegis ('the Pound era'). This fracturing of the literary past has led, in turn, to a fractalization of the histories that write it. The age of the *grand récit*, the overarching narrative of progress, has largely passed. Our literary histories of late revel in details of the everyday, analyses of local life, and individuated texts. Works such as *A New History of French Literature* and the companion volume, *A New History of German Literature*, break up their stories into discrete, at times year-by-year entries, some focusing on texts, some on events, some on authors.[3] Such an approach fits with the temperament of recent historical writing generally: to find value in works not just of high culture, but also of popular expression, technical instruction, or personal account. 'It is impossible to say', writes Denis Hollier, the editor of *A New History of French Literature*, where literature 'starts and where it ends... Literature wants to be everything—but beside itself. As a result, the question today is no longer... "What is literature?" but rather "What is not?"'[4]

For English literary history, what was *not* literature was what did not fit into the accepted periods of canonical reading and writing. Some times and writers languish outside our narratives; some decades linger in the terra incognita of the in-between. Perhaps the most enigmatic, and hence most inviting, of such spots of literary time remains the English 1550s. Within the decade, England saw three monarchs, two queens, and at least two different Churches. Yet there remains, at least for canonical literary history, little in the decade that survives. A seeming hiatus between the efflorescence of Wyatt and Surrey in the Henrician period and Sidney and Spenser in the Elizabethan, the middle of the sixteenth century has been virtually ignored.[5] Historians of the book, too, while attentively detailing the productive lives and works of Caxton, de Worde, and Pynson, and while paying great homage to the printers of Shakespeare's plays, have little patience, it would seem, for the great unknown printers of the middle of the sixteenth century (only Richard Tottel seems to spark much interest).[6]

Hopkins University Press, 1992); Seth Lerer (ed.), *Literary History and the Challenge of Philology: The Legacy of Erich Auerbach* (Stanford, CA: Stanford University Press, 1996).

[3] Denis Hollier (ed.), *A New History of French Literature* (Cambridge, MA: Harvard University Press, 1989); David E. Wellbery (ed.), *A New History of German Literature* (Cambridge, MA: Harvard University Press, 2004).

[4] Hollier, 'On Writing Literary History,' in *A New History*, ed. Hollier, xxv.

[5] A notable exception is Brian Cummings, 'Reformed Literature and Literature Reformed', in *The Cambridge History of Medieval English Literature*, ed. David Wallace (Cambridge: Cambridge University Press, 1999), 821–51.

[6] An exception to this trend is the work of Peter Blayney, who has researched in great detail the development of the Stationers' Company and the productions of mid-sixteenth-century printers. See Peter Blayney, *The Stationers' Company Before the Charter, 1403–1557* (London: Worshipful Company

Recent scholarship has only begun to remedy the situation.[7] There is a growing recognition, for example, of the ways in which the older forms of medieval drama were pressed into the service of new polemics.[8] There is a revival of interest in Bale, Leland, and Stowe, as new readers of the medieval past.[9] And there is an awareness that the printers of mid-century saw in that past the possibilities for a recirculation of old texts to new audiences. Robert Crowley printed *Piers Plowman* three times in 1550—it is now known as what James Simpson has called, 'an exemplary document of the evangelical tradition'—while during Mary's reign (1553–58), certain medieval texts that had been deemed too 'Catholic' or 'papist', or too overwrought with quests and allegories out of fashion, came to be reprinted (notice, for example, Hawes's *Pastime of Pleasure*, which Tottel printed in 1554).[10] Even that most famous document of English Renaissance lyricism, Tottel's *Songs and Sonnets*, first appeared in Mary's reign, and recent scholarship by Stephen Hamrick has revealed just how much of its poetry's commitment to the Petrarchan conceits of love dovetails with a Catholic ideology.[11]

What this body of literary productions shares, it seems to me, is an attempt to come to terms with the literary past for a polemical present. *Tottel's Miscellany* looks back to an earlier generation of courtly lyric, and, too, to a Chaucerian inheritance. English literary history finds itself rewritten into newer teleologies.

of Stationers and Newspaper Makers, 2003), and his earlier study, *The Bookshops in Paul's Cross Churchyard* (London: Bibliographical Society, 1999).

[7] While there is no full-length study of the literary culture of the 1550s, and of the Marian period in particular, much work has been stimulated by the assessment of Eamon Duffy, *The Stripping of the Altars* (London: Yale University Press, 1992), especially 524–64. For a general review of the contexts of literary reception in Mary's reign, see Alison Shell, *Catholicism, Controversy and the English Literary Imagination, 1558–1660* (Cambridge: Cambridge University Press, 1999). The collected essays of J. W. Martin, *Religious Radicals in Tudor England* (London: Hambledon Press, 1989), have much to offer. More recent views include those of Susannah Brietz Monta, *Martyrdom and Literature in Early Modern England* (Cambridge: Cambridge University Press, 2005); and of the contributors to Gordon McMullan and David Matthews (eds.), *Reading the Medieval in Early Modern England* (Cambridge: Cambridge University Press, 2007).

[8] See Greg Walker, *Plays of Persuasion* (Cambridge: Cambridge University Press, 1991).

[9] See James Simpson, *Reform and Cultural Revolution*, The Oxford English Literary History, Vol. 2: *1350–1547* (Oxford: Oxford University Press, 2002), 7–33; and Jennifer Summit, *Memory's Library: Medieval Books in Early Modern England* (Chicago: University of Chicago Press, 2008).

[10] Simpson, *Reform and Cultural Revolution*, 332. See also pages 322–82 for Simpson's account of *Piers Plowman*'s place in the literary traditions of ecclesiastical reform and theological debate. For specific studies of *Piers* and its *Nachleben*, see John N. King, 'Robert Crowley's Editions of *Piers Plowman*: A Tudor Apocalypse', *Modern Philology*, 74 (1976), 342–52; John M. Bowers, '*Piers Plowman* and the Police: Notes Toward a History of the Wycliffite Langland', *Yearbook of Langland Studies*, 6 (1992), 1–50; Larry Scanlon, 'Langland, Apocalypse and the Early Modern Editor', in *Reading the Medieval*, ed. McMullan and Matthews, 51–73. For the Marian revival of the interest in Hawes, see the discussion in John N. King, 'The Account Book of a Marian Bookseller, 1553–4,' *British Library Journal*, 13 (1987), 33–57.

[11] Stephen Hamrick, '*Tottel's Miscellany* and the English Reformation', *Criticism*, 44 (2002), 329–61.

Chaucer, for example, could become the author of the *Plowman's Tale* for Protestant argument, while, by contrast, Caxtonian romances could be revived for Catholic claims. What is, in short, the impact of the 1550s on the transmission of medieval English literature and, in turn, on the ideas and ideologies of poetry and print, authority and authorship, in what would become the Elizabethan Renaissance? Perhaps another way of putting it would be to ask how post-Reformation readers read pre-Reformation literature—and in the process of asking this question, we may realize, too, that in the 1550s in particular, the lines between the pre- and post-Reformation are blurry at best.[12]

To understand the Renaissance reception of the medieval literary past, we need to look, first, at the regulations of late Henrician reading. The 1543 Act for the Advancement of True Religion condemned 'printed bokes, printed balades, playes rymes songes and other fantasies' that did not contribute to the maintenance of Henry VIII's rule or his religious reform. This is the Act that famously permitted, in addition to specifically sanctioned prayers and biblical translations, the printing of 'Cronycles Canterbury tales Chaucers bokes Gowers bokes and stories of mennes lieves'—a proviso that kept the works of Chaucer and Gower in circulation but that stanched the reprinting of their later medieval heirs.[13]

And yet, those heirs would have seen print again in Mary's reign. The middle 1550s saw a renewed interest in the old texts, both for their antiquity and for their dogma. Hawes's *Pastime of Pleasure* was reprinted three times soon after Mary's ascendancy in an attempt to find a new audience for old texts condemned by the previous generation, and his *Example of Virtue* may also have appeared again at this time.[14] Paul Bush, a Catholic propagandist of the 1520s who sought the then Princess Mary's patronage, found new favor under her queenship. His *Extripation of Ignorancy*, published in 1526 but clearly read three decades later, blends aureate diction and rigorous theological argument into a set of rhyme royal stanzas which, while not memorable as poetry, are nonetheless remarkable for their ability to press the older literary idioms into the service of contemporary religious polemic. His investment in those post-Chaucerian devices of chivalric allegory and dream fantasy, together with his relentless polemic, would have classed the *Extripation* as one of the condemnable printed volumes for a readership after the 1543

[12] Some of these questions have been asked and answered in ways different from mine by Brian Cummings, *The Literary Culture of the Reformation: Grammar and Grace* (Oxford: Oxford University Press, 2002); Thomas Betteridge, *Literature and Politics in the English Reformation* (Manchester: Manchester University Press, 2004); and Cathy Shrank, *Writing the Nation in Reformation England, 1530–1580* (Oxford: Oxford University Press, 2004).

[13] For The Act for the Advancement of True Religion, see *Statutes of the Realm* (London: Dawson's, 1810–28), 34 and 35 Henry VIII.c.1. For the literary implications of this Act, see the discussion in Cummings, 'Reformed Literature and Literature Reformed', 842–7.

[14] The Marian reprints of the *Pastime of Pleasure* are STC 12950 (John Wayland, 1554), STC 12951 (Richard Tottell, 1555), and STC 12952 (John Waley, 1555).

Act (and would certainly have made it even more subversive in Elizabethan times).[15]

Evidence for other writers survives, too. John N. King has recovered the records of a Marian bookseller from 1553–4 that help explain the literary environment of the period.[16] Works by Hawes and Heywood figure prominently in the bookseller's accounts. For sale, too, were copies of such educational volumes as Cato's *Distichs*, Hugh Rhodes's *Boke of Nurture*, a version of William Caxton's *Book of Good Manners*, and many Latin and English primers, grammars, psalters, and chronicles. There is a selection from *a Boke of hawkynge, huntynge, and fysshynge* for sale. There is, too, a *Boke of secretes*. In keeping with the religious tenor of the moment, there were also books of Catholic observance and polemic: a treatise against the marriage of priests, a Roman rite book of hours, works by John Fisher, a book called *A defence of the blessed masse*, and anti-Lutheran tracts. King's Marian bookseller represents a kind of social filter for the earlier productions of the age of Lydgate and Hawes and their association with mid-sixteenth-century Catholic polemic and linguistic, social, and moral instruction. There are, as I have illustrated elsewhere, many points of contact between the inventory of this bookseller and the contents of a *Sammelband* of quartos, now preserved in the Cambridge University Library, that I have been able to show was in the possession of a recusant family in the later sixteenth and early seventeenth century.[17]

One of the most prominent authors of the Marian reaction, and one represented in this early *Sammelband*, was Miles Hogarde.[18] From what little evidence we have, it seems clear that Hogarde was a hosier in London who had both literary and political aspirations. From the late 1540s to the middle 1550s, he wrote several tracts and poems, many of which appeared in print, and all of which argued, in various ways, for the maintenance of traditional Catholic observance in the face of

15 For a discussion of Bush's publications and his relationship to Chaucerian writing, Tudor politics, and literary culture, see Seth Lerer, 'Paul Bush and the Chaucer Tradition', *Medium Aevum*, 73 (2004), 103–9.

16 John N. King, 'Account Book'. For a development of King's views, see his 'The Book Trade under Edward VI and Mary I', in *The Cambridge History of the Book in Britain*, vol. 3: *1400–1557*, ed. Lotte Hellinga and J. B. Trapp (Cambridge: Cambridge University Press, 1999), 164–78.

17 Seth Lerer, 'Medieval Literature and Early Modern Readers: Cambridge University Library Sel. 5. 51–63', *Papers of the Bibliographical Society of America*, 97 (2003), 311–32. My brief account here does gloss over the surprising continuity in printers' activity from 1553 to 1558, a matter of some debate among historians of the book at present. The position that printing activities were largely commercial, rather than ideological, has motivated the many studies of A. S. G. Edwards.

18 Sometimes spelled Huggard or Huggarde. See J. W. Martin, 'Miles Hogarde: Artisan and Aspiring Author in Sixteenth-Century England', in *Religious Radicals*, 83–106; Betteridge, *Literature and Politics*, 150–73 (the section 'Penance and Poetry in the Work of Miles Hogarde', a remarkable account, but different in focus and argument from my own); Eamon Duffy, 'The Conservative Voice in the English Reformation,' in *Christianity and Community in the West: Essays for John Bossy*, ed. Simon Ditchfield (Aldershot: Ashgate, 2002), 87–105; and the brief remarks in Monta, *Martyrdom and Literature*, 58–9.

Protestant reform. He had early on affiliated himself with Princess Mary, and when she became queen Hogarde was made a royal hosier. We know that Robert Crowley was an arch-antagonist in the pamphlet wars of mid-century, and that later on Anthony Wood noted that, for a writer, he lacked 'academic breeding'. J. W. Martin, in the only sustained modern study of Hogarde, considered him 'one of the new phenomena of print culture, for without Caxton as a predecessor it is hard to imagine a London hosier, no matter how talented and energetic, having Hogarde's literary background and ambitions'.[19]

I focus on Hogarde, not just within the context of his Catholic polemic, but within a more specific set of literary concerns keyed to the establishment of his authorial identity. Hogarde presents himself as something of a poet laureate for the English Counter-Reformation. His dedications to Queen Mary, combined with his unbridled desire to write and publish his work, transform him from an 'artificer' to an author. 'My calling', he wrote in his *Mirror of Love*, 'is not bokes to write . . . / But to folow my busynesse'. And yet, were God's precepts truly followed, 'No bookes I would have pende',

> But God forbyds al men to preache
> The which he hath not sent:
> So hath he not all men to write;
> This is most evident.[20]

Throughout his writings, Hogarde wrestles with his need to write, and his authorial identity emerges through accounts, in particular, of martyrdom. Hogarde makes himself an author through his doctrinal attentions to these problems. His goal is not simply to present an argument, but to present himself. The authorial body stands before us as the narrator of martyrdom—and its most severe critic.

But Hogarde also locates his productions in the history of literature, and throughout he emerges as a polemical reader and adapter of the literary past. Take for example his poem titled, 'The assault of the sacrament of the Altar' (STC 13556, printed by Robert Caly in 1554, but written in 1549).[21] Dedicated to Queen Mary, the poem transforms the devices of Chaucerian dream vision into scriptural narrative and partisan polemic. The poem begins with the conventional astrological dating: Sagittarius is in ascendance, the sign associated in the later Middle Ages with difficult dreams. Hogarde dreams that Morpheus led him into a great palace, on whose tapestried walls he saw biblical stories depicted. Each of these narratives concerns food (e.g. Manna from heaven, the bread and wine brought to Abraham, and so on), and each is subject to figural interpretation which finds in their

[19] Martin, 'Miles Hogarde', 85. [20] Martin, 'Miles Hogarde', 85.
[21] I quote from the copy in the Huntington Library; references to signatures in my text.

meaning an anticipation of the Christian sacrament. In turn, the poem argues, the sacrament itself 'is a figure':

> But not only of Christes body naturall,
> For [that] it containeth, but this we read in scripture
> That the fourme of bred, which we se material,
> Is a figure of Christes body mysticall. (Bii r)

The poem goes on in this vein for quite some time, occasionally breaking into powerful descriptions of the suffering Christ (again, portrayed upon the vision-palace tapestries; Cii r), before launching into a narrative of romance-style battle. The doctrine of transubstantiation finds itself figured as a medieval castle, under successive assault by a range of heretical reformers (from the twelfth-century Berengar of Tours, through Wyclif, Luther, and Hogarde's Protestant contemporaries).[22] The scene is full of inscribed standards, iconic shields, 'armour blacke as any inke', and symbolic accoutrements (for example, the assailants wear a 'woman's foresleeve' on their helmets, a detail which has been interpreted as a sign of their advocacy of a married clergy).[23]

'The assault of the sacrament of the Altar' is extremely weak, derivative, dogmatic poetry (little wonder, perhaps, that it has never been reprinted since its first appearance). But the point is not its literary quality but its literary claims. Hogarde's use of earlier medieval material involves more than just an antiquarian sensibility or an old-fashioned taste. It is keyed to the politics of literary repression in the early Tudor period. The romances, dream visions, and adventure allegories that distinguished a century of post-Chaucerian poetizing were roundly condemned by the Henrician thought machine as papist, retrograde, unworthy of dissemination (only Chaucer and Gower, as I have already noted, escaped this condemnation). By recycling the old visionary idioms and by appealing to a narrative structure grounded in the medieval romance mode, Hogarde makes a profoundly ideological decision. He returns to a Catholic literature for a Catholic Queen. His is, to some extent, a great nostalgia project: an attempt to evoke, once again, a traditional social and religious order by evoking that tradition's literary order.

Now, if Hogarde is, even by contemporary standards, a weak poet, he is a brilliant prose stylist. Indeed, his passagework can compare favorably with anything in Thomas More. In particular, it is in his treatment of contemporary attitudes toward martyrdom and preaching that he claims his literary voice. As in his poetry, his prose looks back (for all its stylistic innovations) to earlier models;

[22] Space does not permit a full review of the theological debates surrounding transubstantiation during this period. For background, see Francis Clark, *Eucharistic Sacrifice and the Reformation*, 2nd edn (Oxford: Blackwell, 1967; first published 1960).

[23] See Martin, 'Miles Hogarde', 87.

but here, it is to authors rather than to idioms. The editions of Hogarde's major prose work, *The Displaying of Protestants*, are full of marginal notes recording sources drawn from almost everyone: Plato, Cicero, Seneca, Virgil; the Greek and Roman Historians; Augustine, Jerome, Bede, Eusebius, and other fathers of the church; enemies such as Luther and John Ponet. *The Displaying* is, among other things, a displaying of Hogarde's own wide reading—a plea for his erudition. But it is, as well (and this is my real point), an attempt to press a literary history into the service of doctrinal debate. It is a record of polemical reading and a claim for his own authorial identity in print.[24]

From the start of *The Displaying*, Hogarde frames his story in a context of old masters, *auctores* who justify his claims. Plato's famous story of the ring of Gyges opens the book, an appeal to what had become by the middle of the sixteenth century one of the great humanist touchstones of allusion (I note in passing that in one copy of the first edition of this work in the Cambridge University Library, an early seventeenth-century reader has written in the margin, 'A ridiculous comparison'; Sig iii r, in the hand of the signer of the title page, '30 March 1627, Eduardi Goldsmyth liber'). This is the learned prose equivalent of Hogarde's vernacular poetic strategy: to rephrase religious polemic in the forms and idioms of the literary past.

Hogarde's world is littered with bodies broken, burned, and bruised. His poetry is rife with images of Christ's marked body (the passion at its most passionate), while his prose is full of human bricolage—bones, limbs, and liquids splayed across the page. Take, for example, his bitter response to the burning of the Protestant 'heretics', and the attendant Protestant claims for elevating these dead to the status of martyrs. Hogarde argues that these people were mere criminals, and that their punishments do not elevate them to the status of martyrs but, rather, confirm their condition as outlaws (39v–41v). As argument, this is nothing remarkable.[25] But as prose, it is quite striking. Look at how Hogarde opens his discussion:

> This faith onely hath wrought so hotlye, the rather then they would forsake their drossie divinitie, whiche they have gathered by their curiositie, they thoughte with fagotes to end their lyves miserably. And in this kynde of death they so arroga[n]tly reioyce, that they be to bolde to compare themselfes with the Martyrs of christes church. (39^{v}–40^{r})

There is a kind of rough poetics to this passage, with its assonating clausal endings (*hotlye, divinitie, curiosite, miserably*), its evocative alliteration (*drossie divinitie*), and its metonymic vision of self-sacrifice ('they thoughte with fagotes to end their

[24] Miles Hogarde, *The Displaying of Protestants*, STC 1,358. I quote from the copy in the Cambridge University Library (Syn. 8.56.11^{2}). In this and subsequent quotations, I have modernized u/v spellings.

[25] See Brad S. Gregory, *Salvation at Stake: Christian Martyrdom in Early Modern Europe* (Cambridge, MA: Harvard University Press, 1999).

lyves'). No argument is made, here, without reference to the literary past, no claim comes unattended without *auctores*. And, so, in his reasoning that these false martyrs should be held as criminals, he strives for a comparison with classical antiquity. The ancient Greeks 'coulde not abide the despisers of their religion', so why should we?

> The Heathen being noseled in their superstitions, a vaine veneration of their fained goddes, yet bare such reverence to their religion, that in no wyse thei could abide the despisers therof. (40ᵛ–41ʳ)

Alcibiades felt their wrath, he goes on, for neglecting the sacrifices to Ceres; and so did Socrates, for his teachings. Then comes the link:

> If the Heathen had suche a regarde to their fayned religions, what wouide they have done, if they had knowen the true and living god, our creator: And what oughte we christians to doe touching the contemners of our true religion? (41ʳ)

If the Protestant pretences to martyrdom raise Hogarde's hackles, then even more does the veneration of the bodies of the martyrs after death. Here, Hogarde aspires to inflect his polemical account with the texture of both classical literature and homespun invective. It is a brilliant performance.

> And because our heretikes wil nedes have their men to be taken for martyrs, some of them counterfayting the trade of the auncient state of the true churche, gather together the burnt bones of these stynking martyrs, entendyng thereby (by lyke) to shryne the same, or to preserve them for relykes, that at suche a tyme as whe[n] an heretike is burnt, ye shal see a route enclosing the fyer, for that purpose. And when the fyer is done, they lye wallowyng like pygges in a stie to scrape in that hereticall dongehill for the sayde bones. Yea and as it is reported, some gossyps and fellowe disciples of these wicked apostles, use the same next to their hartes in the mornyng, beyng grated in a cuppe of ale, to preserve them from the chyncoughe, and suche other maladies incident to suche hoote burning stomakes. (62ᵛ–63ʳ)

It is, he goes on, 'A pretty medicine & apte for such brainesicke pacientes'. And they may be compared, Hogarde notes, to Artemisia in Aulus Gellius, 'who when her husbande was dead she was of such an affectio[n] . . . that after the funeralles was done, she gathered together all the bones and ashes of her husbande, and minglinge the same with perfumes and other swete odours, she dranke them up' (63r). If the extreme behavior of the Protestants compares them with the lovesick madness of a classical heroine, so the extreme feelings of the Catholic polemicist compel him to rise to classical oratorical heights. 'Who cannot play Democritus part continually to laughe at their folly . . . ?' (64r). The fantasies of Protestant martyrologists may be compared, too, with those of the Greeks. 'The heathen poetes never devysed more toyes upon Iupiter, Iuno, Diana, Actaeon, Io, or suche other counterfaites, then the madbraynes of the protestantes have invented tales upon these Ethnikes' (64v–65r). And, if the classical inheritance provides a template for this Catholic critique, so too does the vernacular legacy of post-Chaucerian writing. In an appropriation of the aureate vocabulary of Lydgate and Hawes, Hogarde frames Protestant martyrology as something out of an old allegory.

> Whole lying lippes are so sugred with false reportes, that ye brethe therof is marveylous delectable to a great many of the same generation. (65^{r})

The phrase 'false report' resounds with post-Chaucerian personification allegory, while the image of the sugared lips and the delectable breath takes the old Lydgatean tropes of inspired eloquence and transforms them into pejorative claim. As if this is not enough, Hogarde goes on to compare the oratory of the Protestants with Sinon from Book 2 of Virgil's *Aeneid*, 'who with his disguised habite, and proporcion of body, together with his unhappy oration, begyled the poore Troianes' (65r). And again, now turning to a homespun idiom: 'But al wyse men whiche can beware of other mennes harmes, no doubte wyll take heede of the lytering adders, which hide the[m]selves in the grasse.'

Hogarde emerges on these pages as a great concatenator of the literary and the lay. His quotations and allusions (all signaled in the margins of the printed page by commentary and citation) pile up, as he seeks not just to strengthen his arguments but to make the very printed artifact look like canonical discourse. In the process, he reveals not just the literacy but the theatricality of everyday life.

Towards the close of *The Displaying of Protestants*, Hogarde rises to this level. In his description of an impromptu separatist meeting in a stable, in his portrait of the deceptive Father Browne, in his insertion of himself into the narrative, he offers up an almost novelistic rendering of social upheaval. Here is the preacher and his bevy of other men's wives (121v). And here he is, 'newly crept out of Bedlem', and 'lying at Islington, to rest his sory bones'. Hogarde writes that he had heard of 'many prodigious wonders' that he preached (122^{r}), and so he tried to find him. Together with a friend, Hogarde finds Browne in a 'typplyng house', but his precise location is a 'secrete'.

> At our entrie into the house, there was never a worde but gossep, all was whist. For prively in a corner certen gosseps were in a marveilous secret talke with father Browne: I trowe he was tellyng their fortunes or such lyke. (122^{r})

The women soon depart, giving him 'spices to comforte his weake stomake', and 'salves to grease his bones'. Browne then goes into another parlor, where there is another 'route' assembled. But Hogarde and his friend can only listen at the doorway, 'for no man except he was of speciall acquaintaunce, could be admitted to go in'. Here, Browne was 'secretly' asked questions. A young woman enters, whom he calls mother. A certain 'Jacke prentise' comes in, called 'for his testament, who reaching the same from his girdle, delivered it to his maistres and turning the boke, she turned to a place of S. Mathewes ghospel...' (123r–v). His mother reads a passage, and announces to father Browne, 'what persecution have you suffered fro[m] time to tyme?' Browne and his 'mother' converse back and forth, before they remove themselves to another room. Soon, they reemerge (Browne, mother, Jack Prentise, and a 'sister'), and go into the stable:

> Anone he called in the co[n]gregacion, & amo[n]ges them thrust we. where Browne leanynge upon hys horsebacke, whiche was a iade scarse worth syxe pence, sitting upo[n] the maunger, he beganne to alledge certen places of Ecclesiastes withoute booke, one upon another in heapes. (123^{v})

Hogarde and his friend soon leave after this stable sermon, and on the way they meet many men and women 'of purpose going to Islyngton, to hear the sermon of this pelti[n]g prophet'. This vignette closes:

> But within a whyle after I heard saye, thys father Browne & his brood with the congregacion were removed from that place and were dispersed into corners. Truly pitie it is he is suffred in this sort to range the countreis without restrainte, not only for corrupting the people with ill opinions, but also for disseminating his vaine Prophecies to excite rumors. But this opinion I have of Browne, that he had rather live a proude confessor than burne a stinking martyr. (125^{r}–^{v})

The Father Browne episode becomes the vehicle for Hogarde's reflections on the nature of authorship, the social function of textuality, and the place of the body in the discourses of observant life. Browne is, throughout, a false reader of scripture. He recalls texts from memory, heaps up allusions and quotations, much as the Protestants themselves would heap up the bodies and bones of their 'stinking martyrs'. Jack Prentise's testament, too, is a mockery of textuality: a bogus version of those testaments familiar from the English literary inheritance from Lydgate on. Taken in tandem (and together with those strangely seduced women in Browne's orbit), they stand as the antitypes to what Hogarde aspires. They remain figures of misreading, whisper, secrecy, and false report, bad eloquence in the ale house and the stable. There is a wild theatricality to these scenes in *The Displaying*: a creation of actors and audiences, impromptu stages, and dramatic entrances and exits. It is a world of crowds and costumes—a world in sharp contrast to the ideal literary world of Hogarde's textual citations.

And if, in the end, Browne would prefer to live a proud confessor rather than burn a stinking martyr, his choice may be that of all our everyday performers. His is a life of salves and spices, of ease for weary bones, a narrative of keeping whole rather than burning at the stake and having bones crushed for elixirs. His is a body well preserved and yet, as Hogarde avers, a body that remains a threat to the health of the Christian body politic for whom he writes.

That body politic was close to flames by the end of Mary's reign, and, as Hyder E. Rollins noted long ago, the martyr's fires and their shrieks formed the backdrop to the printing of *Tottel's Miscellany* in June of 1557.[26] If Miles Hogarde's work is

[26] *Tottel's Miscellany*, ed. Hyder E. Rollins, 2 vols. (Cambridge, MA: Harvard University Press, 1928–9), 2: 3.

the least known to modern students of the sixteenth century, then Tottel's must be the best. Long valued as the beautiful repository for the English Petrarchans, the *Miscellany* has of late been reassessed as a profoundly political book: one that gives voice to a distinctive Catholic poetics in the framework of Petrarchan love. As Stephen Hamrick has shown in great detail, '*Tottel's Miscellany* provides a key site at which to read the cultural impact of the Reformation.'[27]

Following Hamrick's lead, I dovetail Tottel with Hogarde as readers of the English literary past and, in particular, as figures who in reading that past come to terms with ideals of authorship in print. Many texts from Tottel may be chosen for this inquiry, but I wish to attend to a pair of the least known of them. Tottel prints a poem titled, 'To leade a vertuous and honest life', but as soon as we read the poem we realize that it is Chaucer's ballade we know as 'Truth'. The other thing we realize about this poem is that the title is printed in the volume not with a period but with a comma. In other words, the title is the opening clause of a larger statement which is finished by the poem's opening lines, 'Flee from the prese & dwell with sothfastnes', and so on. Chaucer's poem has been pressed into the service of advice, as if it completed a recipe for virtue and honesty. Certainly, the place of the poem in the *Miscellany* chimes with Wyatt's verse epistle to John Pointz, which had begun,

> Myne own John Poyntz, since ye delight to know
> The cause why that homeward I me draw
> (And flee the press of courts whereso they go
> Rather than to live thrall under the awe
> Of lordly looks) . . .[28]

But the place of the poem, too, is as a response to the one that precedes it immediately in the volume: 'A comparison of his love with the faithfull and painful love of Troylus to Creside'. The narrator of this poem begins by noting that, 'I read how Troylus served in Troy', and he then reviews not so much the plot as the emotive content, concluding with the plea to his beloved, 'And set me in as happy case, / As Troylus with his lady was.' Then we get the injunction, 'To leade a virtuous and honest life', *comma*, and the first three stanzas of 'Truth'. Taken together, these are stories about reading Chaucer. They are accounts of how the force of Chaucer's poem can provoke the writing of a verse epistle to a lover, and an epistolary response of a friend. The two poems thus form, in Tottel,

[27] Hamrick, '*Tottel's Miscellany* and the English Reformation', 329. Hamrick provides a full bibliography on the *Miscellany* (n. 4), to which I would add Paul A. Marquis, 'Editing and Unediting Richard Tottel's *Songes and Sonnettes*', *The Book Collector*, 56 (2007), 353–75. My own contribution to this study appears in Seth Lerer, *Courtly Letters in the Age of Henry VIII* (Cambridge: Cambridge University Press, 1997), 201–7.

[28] Quoted from the edition of R. A. Rebholz, *Sir Thomas Wyatt: The Complete Poems* (Harmondsworth: Penguin, 1975), 186. I have discussed the relationship between this poem and Chaucer's 'Truth' in Lerer, *Courtly Letters*, 171–7.

a kind of dramatic pair or dialogue. But what they also form is something of a mid-sixteenth-century distillation of the essentially Chaucerian: *Troilus* and 'Truth'. The first text is a personalized reading of a great love poem, the second is an exemplary ballade now presented as a piece of practical advice. The first is private, the second public. The first lives in the study and the chamber, the second in the press of court.

Troilus and 'Truth' emerge as the poles, too, of literary culture in the Marian 1550s. Like many of the poems in the *Miscellany*, Tottel's *Troilus* poem brings together the Petrarchan images of service, grace, and martyrdom in ways that make explicit the relationship between amorous devotion and Catholic ritual. As Hamrick puts it, characterizing the discourses of much sixteenth-century English verse:

> The discourse of Petrarchan adoration shaped by Catholic poetics combined the secular and the devotional. In so doing, it translated Catholic ritual practices to the poetic construction of the deified and adored Petrarchan beloved.[29]

But, he goes on, 'The discourse of Petrarchan adoration shaped by Protestant poetics rejected the Catholic worship of the beloved without rejecting Petrarchan poetics' (331). The *Troilus* poem exemplifies these lyric strategies. For what the poet clearly sees in Chaucer's story is the deep Petrarchan idiom of adoration. There is, of course, the famous 'Canticus Troili' in Book 1 of *Troilus and Criseyde*: Chaucer's translation of Petrarch's 'S'amor non e' placed in the mouth of the Trojan lover.[30] The oxymorons of love are all Chaucer, and throughout his poem as a whole the images of sight and blindness, grace and gratitude, recall the tortured love of Petrarch for his Laura.

So, too, is Troilus martyr to his love. In Book 4, Pandarus tries to counsel the bereft lover, rhetorically throwing up his hands at the end: 'And if thow deye a martyr, go to hevene!' (4.623). Such a phrase recalls the martyrdom of Petrarch's lover/poet, who laments his 'brief solace for so long a martyrdom' ('breve conforto a sì lungo martiro'), and 'the years I have lived tasting this golden martyrdom' ('e gli anni / onde io son vivo e gusto aureo martire').[31]

[29] Hamrick, '*Tottel's Miscellany* and the English Reformation', 331. On the broader traditions of Petrarchan poetics, see in particular Leonard Forster, *The Icy Fire: Five Studies in European Petrarchism* (London: Cambridge University Press, 1969); Roland Greene, *Post-Petrarchism: Origins and Innovations of the Western Lyric Sequence* (Princeton, NJ: Princeton University Press, 1991).

[30] All quotations from and references to Chaucer's *Troilus and Criseyde* are from Geoffrey Chaucer, *The Riverside Chaucer*, 3rd edn, general editor Larry D. Benson (Boston: Houghton Mifflin, 1987). For the text of Petrarch's Sonnet 132, see Robert Durling (ed. and trans.), *Petrarch's Lyric Poems* (Cambridge, MA: Harvard University Press, 1976), 270–1. For critical discussions of Chaucer's use of Petrarch here, and for the place of this lyric moment in the Troilus as a whole, see Thomas Stillinger, *The Song of Troilus* (Philadelphia: University of Pennsylvania Press, 1992); and the sensitive account in Bruce Holsinger, 'Lyrics and Short Poems', in *The Yale Companion to Chaucer*, ed. Seth Lerer (New Haven: Yale University Press, 2006), 185–9.

[31] These quotations are from Durling, *Petrarch's Lyric Poems*, 48–9 and 592–3, respectively.

Tottel's *Troilus* poem brings out the inherent Petrarchism of Chaucer's story: the pains and poisons, aches and oxymorons of desire.

His youth, his sport, his pleasant chere,
His courtly state and company,
In him so straungly altred were,
With such a face of contrary.
That every ioye became a wo,
This poison new had turned him so.[32]

And if the bed is both the place of Petrarchan ache and Chaucerian imagination, so too is it for this Troilus:

His chamber was his common walke,
Wherin he kept him secretely,
He made his bedde the place of talke,
To heare his great extremitie.
In nothing els had he delight,
But even to be a martyr right.[33]

Such lines recall Troilus's bed-ridden lethargy in Chaucer's poem; but they recall, too, their transformation in the hands of Thomas Wyatt. In the poem Tottel titles, 'The lover to his bed, with describing of his unquiet state', Wyatt calls the bed, 'The restfull place, renewer of my smart'. But, he concludes, this rest is 'all for nought: I find no better ease / In bed, or out.' And in his famous ballade with the rich blend of hunting allegory and erotic wiles, Wyatt begins:

They flee from me, that somtime did me seke
With naked fote stalking within my chamber.[34]

Unlike Chaucer, who would wake from his book-inspired sleeps (in such works as the *Book of the Duchess* and the *Parliament of Fowls*), Wyatt concludes this poem: 'It was no dream: for I lay broade awaking.' Chaucer's Troilus has his dreams of violent hunts.[35] But in the *Troilus* poem in the *Miscellany*, we never quite leave the sad imaginations of the lover. No one wakes up here, and indeed, the only recourse for his pain is death itself. Troilus, the poem avers, finds no pleasure save in pining on his love, and in death he might well be love's martyr.

What does it mean to be love's martyr in the summer of the martyr's fires? What does it mean to take this old, Petrarchan imagery of suffering and read it in an age of Hogarde's 'stinking martyrs'? I would not go so far as to say, as Hamrick has of other poems in the *Miscellany*, that the poem on Troilus is an explicitly or narrowly

[32] *Tottel's Miscellany*, ed. Rollins, 1: 183. [33] *Tottel's Miscellany*, ed. Rollins, 1: 184.

[34] I quote here from the versions of the poems in the *Miscellany*, as presented by Rollins: Thomas Wyatt, 'The restfull place, renewer of my smart', in *Tottel's Miscellany*, ed. Rollins, 1: 44; Thomas Wyatt, 'They flee from me, that sometime did me seke', in *Tottel's Miscellany*, ed. Rollins, 1: 39.

[35] Chaucer, *Troilus and Criseyde*, 5.1233–47.

Catholic one. What I would say, however, is that this poem and the following version of Chaucer's 'Truth' offer a sense of what a literary culture on the edge of Reformation thought of its literary past. *Tottel's Miscellany* remains a collection of old books—early texts, epitaphs, elegies, sonnets, love laments, and inscriptions that, whatever their religious or doctrinal content, function as monuments to literary life. Is the *Miscellany* a book of worship, a kind of vernacular psalter to the courtly dead, whose authors stand as intercessors to the reader seeking (in the words of Tottel's preface) profit and delight?

Perhaps what John N. King says about Foxe's *Book of Martyrs* may hold for the *Miscellany.* First published only six years after the first edition of *Miscellany* and reprinted many times, in many versions, throughout the remainder of the sixteenth century, Foxe's *Book* may stand as something of a spiritual counterweight to Tottel's. In King's words, Foxe's *Book*:

> functions in the manner of a symbolic reliquary that preserves for posterity the deeds and words that constitute the essence of saintly sacrifice. The idea of text as relic or book as reliquary presupposes a transformation in the concept of saintliness, because Foxe and his Protestant contemporaries eliminated intercession of the saints of the kind celebrated in traditional hagiographies.[36]

Tottel's Miscellany is also a book of the dead: a book of martyrs, not so much to religious faith as to courtly love. And if the doctrinal status of the volume seems more complex and more varied than the writings of Miles Hogarde, it does share with that polemicist a literary project. Both take bits and pieces of a literary past and relocate them for a political present. Both show figures of verbal authority reading the world for signs and symbols of requited love or grace. Both establish the book maker (whether he be author or editor/printer) as arbiters of authorship, textuality, and the body in culture. These actions imply an idea of literary history, much as Foxe does, too. For what they all share is a concern with documenting and memorializing: with transforming the lives of lovers, martyrs, saints, or sinners into verbal forms that we may read. Recall, now, Heinrich Heine's view of literary history which I had quoted at my opening: a 'morgue where each seeks out the friend he most loved'.

Such a conception of the history of literature might well fit the specific histories of idiom and ideology I have traced here. For in the poetry of love and loss that follows Tottel we may see the fires of martyrdom still burning. George Turberville, writing in the first decades of Elizabeth's reign, yet explicitly looking back to the *Miscellany,* offered a Tottel-like text that strikingly recalls the *Troilus* poem in that volume.[37] In 'The

[36] John N. King, *Foxe's Book of Martyrs and Early Modern Print Culture* (Cambridge: Cambridge University Press, 2006), 8.

[37] Quotations from Turberville are from *Epitaphes, Epigrams, Songs and Sonnets* (London, 1567); reprinted in facsimile by Richard J. Panofsky (Delmar, NY: Scholars' Facsimiles and Reprints, 1977). For critical discussion of Turberville and the location of his poetry in the arc of post-Tottel literary history, I am indebted to Arthur F. Marotti, *Manuscript, Print, and the English Renaissance Lyric* (Ithaca, NY: Cornell University Press, 1995), 299–302.

Lover driven to absent him from his Ladie, bawayles his estate', he similarly locates the speaker's torment in the reading of the Troy story. But he goes back, directly, to the Homeric origins of Criseyde in the figure of the slave-girl Bryseis, and Turberville recalls Achilles' longing for that girl in terms that evoke Tottel's *Troilus* poem:

> The thousande part of pensive care
> The Noble Greeke endured than
> In Bryseis absence, to declare
> It farre surmounts the Wit of man:
> But sure a Martyr right he livde
> Of Bryseis beautie once berivde.

As in so much of his verse, Turberville here re-classicizes the medieval inheritance. Petrarchan love, filtered through Chaucer and the Chaucerian imitators, inspires him to sustain the old, coterie traditions of the *Miscellany*, except with a new and university-trained learning.[38] Turberville's lines, I think, show us the literary history of a trope as something that can be invoked for purposes of archaism (by the 1590s he was, as his contemporaries noted, hopelessly out of date). Surely, his self-deprecating preface to his 1567 volume, *Epitaphes, Epigrams, Songs and Sonnets*, makes possible his later dismissal. These are 'the unripe seedes of my baraine braine', the products of, he states, a 'slender toyle'.[39]

But songs and sonnets of this sort lived on in other slender toils. Recall Abraham Slender in Shakespeare's *The Merry Wives of Windsor*, who would rather have his 'book of Songs and Sonnets' (what everyone takes to be a reference to Tottel's volume) than forty shillings.[40] Shakespeare's responses to the Tottelized legacy of Petrarch and Chaucer are, of course, more socially and politically complex than Turberville's, and I would conclude this chapter with some provocations for locating Shakespeare in the line of literary history triangulated by the poets and the printer. The image of 'love's martyr' that we saw in the Troilan tradition morphs into an ideal of political service in *2 Henry IV* when Mowbray posits 'our royal faiths' as 'martyrs in love' (4.1.193). *Pericles* virtually begins with the image, as Antiochus points to the heads of famous princes: 'Here they stand martyrs slain in Cupid's wars' (1.1.39). Indeed, the legacies of the Petrarchan and the Protestant meld throughout the plays: 'Oldcastle died a martyr', as we learn in *2 Henry IV* (in the Epilogue's lines at the play's close), and in *Henry VIII*, Wolsey addresses Cromwell: 'if thou fall'st... Thou fall'st a blessed martyr. / Serve the king' (3.2.448–50). Wolsey's whole speech here seems to mine the old tropes of desire (part Petrarch, part *Troilus and Criseyde*) in ways that recall the very lines of Henrician poetry itself:

[38] See Marotti, *Manuscript, Print*, 302.

[39] Quoted in Marotti, *Manuscript, Print*, 300.

[40] All quotations of Shakespeare are from William Shakespeare, *The Complete Pelican Shakespeare*, ed. A. R. Braunmuller and Stephen Orgel (New York: Penguin Books, 2002).

Cromwell, I did not think to shed a tear
In all my miseries, but thou hast forced me
(Out of thy honest truth) to play the woman.
Let's dry our eyes, and thus far hear me, Cromwell,
And when I am forgotten, as I shall be,
And sleep in dull cold marble, where no mention
Of me more must be heard of, say I taught thee. (3.2.428–34)

Wolsey surveys the morgues of friendship here, as we might, too, in looking at the afterlife of English literature of the 1550s. What can one generation teach another? Wolsey's address becomes a kind of epitaph, not just for his own life, but also for the teachings of the Tudor past. What would a Jacobean audience have heard in these lines ('Serve the king')? Perhaps they would have heard not just the explicit charges to royal service, but the language of old love: the shards of Petrarch, Chaucer, and the sonneteers (the pervasive imagery, for example, of the ship of love devotion in the lines, 'Say Wolsey... sounded all the depths and shoals of honor', and 'Found thee a way (out of his wrack) to rise in', lines 435–6). They would have heard a Henrician politician speaking like a Henrician lover.

And, in the end, that seems to me precisely the point. The literary tensions of the 1550s lie along the fault lines of political and amorous service, and the inheritance of fourteenth-century literature (whether it be English or Italian) motivates the polemics of the sixteenth century. If literary history is a morgue, it is an eerie one, where every reader turns into a necromancer of the poets, where the dead rise to speak again in printed books and performed plays. Hogarde, as I have suggested, may look forward to novelistic prose to pursue theological polemic; but Shakespeare may look back, long after Henry and Elizabeth were dead, to the love lyrics of the Tudor court. Along their axes, we may see a changing sense not simply of the authors canonized in literary history but of the idea of literary history itself: an idea that embraces books and bodies, born of reading relics—valued, cherished, capable of healing those who may feel martyred in the flames of love.

FURTHER READING

Duffy, Eamon. *The Stripping of the Altars* (New Haven, CT, and London: Yale University Press, 1992)

Hamrick, Stephen. 'Tottel's Miscellany and the English Reformation', *Criticism* 44 (2002): 329–61

Martin, J. W. *Religious Radicals in Tudor England* (London: Hambledon Press, 1989)

Simpson, James. *Reform and Cultural Revolution*, The Oxford English Literary History, Vol. 2: *1350–1547* (Oxford: Oxford University Press, 2002)

PART II

SPATIALITIES

CHAPTER 6

PLACE

JAMES SIMPSON

Thomas Wyatt's *Mine own John Poyntz* was written, most probably, in 1536. The final sequence of this Horatian satire praises retirement in 'Kent and Christendom', and it does so by contrasting Kent with some Continental countries. Wyatt is not, thankfully, in France, Spain, or Flanders. Above all, he is not 'where Christ is given in prey / For money, poison, and treason at Rome – / A common practice used both night and day.'[1] In Kent, Wyatt is 'at lusty leas in liberty' to walk. He may be reminded of the king's jurisdiction by the noisome clog that 'doth hang yet at my heel', but he can still leap hedges and dikes, and there's nothing unwholesome about Kent in Christendom, as there is about betrayal of Christ through money, poison, and treason in Rome. So a lusty Kent might be firmly in Christendom, but the location of Christendom is itself insecure.

The opening lines of Chaucer's *Canterbury Tales* also place a Kentish site within the larger context of Christendom. Chaucer's Kent and Christendom are, however, very different places from Wyatt's. Wyatt wrote two years after the Act of Supremacy of 1534. In that context, Wyatt's Kent stands in a wholly adversarial relationship with Christendom.[2] Chaucer's Kent, by contrast, is part of a larger Christendom across which pilgrims are moving in the same way for the same reasons, 'to ferne halwes, kouthe in sondry londes / And specially from every shires ende of Englelond to Canterbury they wende.'[3] Further, Wyatt could make no mention of the saint whose shrine is the focus of Chaucer's pilgrimage. Chaucer's pilgrims move through Kent 'The holy blisful martyr for to seke / That hem hath holpen whan that they were seeke' (lines 17–18). For if Wyatt's poem was indeed

[1] Thomas Wyatt, *Sir Thomas Wyatt, The Complete Poems*, ed. R. A. Rebholz (London: Penguin, 1978), 188, lines 97–9.

[2] For an excellent discussion of this satire's representation of competing jurisdictions, see Bradin Cormack, *A Power to Do Justice: Jurisdiction, English Literature, and the Rise of Common Law, 1509–1625* (Chicago: University of Chicago Press, 2007), 12–21.

[3] Geoffrey Chaucer, *The Canterbury Tales*, ed. Jill Mann (London: Penguin, 2005), 'General Prologue', lines 14–16. Further line references will be made in the body of the text.

written in 1536, only two years later the very mention of Becket had become a treasonous act. Subject to a *damnatio memoriae*, Becket was to be deleted from the national memory. His festival days were not be observed, and his name was to be 'erased and put out of all the [liturgical] books', so 'that his grace's loving subjects shall be no longer blindly led and abused to commit idolatry as they have done in times past'.[4] Becket's shrine was demolished, and all references to him in windows and books (including the very lines of Chaucer just cited, in some manuscripts) were to be destroyed. So far from being a saintly martyr, Becket had become, in the words of the proclamation damning him, 'a rebel and traitor to his prince'.[5]

In Chaucer's text the location of Canterbury in Christendom is taken for granted, whereas in Wyatt's text it has become problematic. In Chaucer's text the Church is curative of disease, while in Wyatt it produces disease. In this essay I consider these two issues: the place of the Church, and perceived disease in the Church. Why should these two issues be connected?

The unsettling question of the Church's place provoked radically divided answers across the period 1380 to the 1640s and well beyond. It is part of the wider jurisdictional drama of European modernity, a drama of simplified, unified jurisdictions shouldering aside divided jurisdictions. Settling the profoundly disruptive ecclesiological question of where the Church was had unavoidable implications for the following: spiritual geographies, and in particular for the practice of pilgrimage; the material disposition of churches, both exterior and interior; and the management of what is regarded as spiritually disgusting.

The question of where the Church is arose for the first time in England in Lollard polemic precisely because the entire visible, material Church Militant had become suspect. Some Lollard, and then all evangelical revolutionaries, instituted the Donatist concept of an invisible, ideal, transcendent Church of the Elect at the heart of their ecclesiology. A cardinal sign of this True Church was privative: the Church was *placeless*. Once instituted, the True Church must always be in suspicious flight from any material instantiations the Church might take. In the first instance, it must take flight from the material geographies of the saints. Those pilgrimage sites, and their attendant material relics, offer jurisdictions that compete with the true, placeless Church. Those sites imply that spiritual energy is more intensely compacted in one place than another. In the True Church, by contrast, spiritual jurisdiction must be evenly dispersed across a single, unbroken jurisdiction.

Placelessness also has immediate implications for the perception and management of disgust in the face of evident ecclesiastical corruption. A located Church is, as we shall see, a capacious Church. Such a Church is, in its account of itself at any rate, visible, inclusivist, old, and subject to change. Such a Church is unable to

[4] P. L. Hughes and J. F. Larkin (eds.), *The Early Tudors (1485–1553)*, *Tudor Royal Proclamations*, 3 vols. (New Haven, CT: Yale University Press, 1964), 1: 276.

[5] Hughes and Larkin, *Tudor Royal Proclamations*, 1: 276.

make absolute discriminations. The ultimate discrimination between the saved and the damned will only take place at the end of time; in the uncertain meanwhile, the Church is made up of all Christians. This Church knows that disgust is inevitably part of the experience in *and of* the Church, since this is a Church in which there be 'some sick, some hole, and all sickly'. That inclusivist conception puts a brake on hermeneutic overconfidence: an inclusivist Church rejects only heretics, whom it casts out, as Thomas More says, 'for fear of infection'.[6]

A placeless Church, by contrast, produces a more explicitly institutional identity, and it fuels interpretive confidence in the matter of dealing with disgust. The transcendent True Church, invisible and somewhere else, contains only the Elect. Spiritual activity becomes redefined as an attempt to answer the question as to whether or not one belongs to the True Church. Institutional membership becomes *the* commanding question of the evangelical spiritual life. The question 'how may I save my soule?' is translated as 'do I belong to the True Church?'

By virtue of one's membership of the True Church, one's experience of ecclesiastical failing cuts an entirely different profile. Disgust is no longer a trigger for institutional, sacramental instruments to manage one individual's curable disease. Disgust is, instead, the sign of an entirely corrupted and hypocritical institution, whose corruption is, by definition, everywhere. Disgust is no longer the occasion of reformist ecclesiastical satire directed to specific persons in specific places; it is, instead, the occasion for radical ecclesiology directed to a ubiquitous enemy. Disgust is, in short, the sign of ineradicable, systemic hypocrisy. No longer does disgust provoke pity; it has instead become the occasion for non-negotiable distrust and repudiation of an institution.

In this essay I consider two occasions of visceral spiritual disgust in the face of perceived ecclesiastical disease. Both take place on the road to, or from, Canterbury. The representation of that disgust depends wholly, as we shall see, on an understanding of the Church's location. If the True Church is the one we can see, then the disgusting object or person before our eyes is an instance of a single ecclesiastical officer, a sickly person potentially curable within the sacramental systems of the Church. If, on the other hand, we acknowledge only the True Church of the Elect, we are empowered by a new institutional hermeneutics: the object of our spiritual disgust is not so much a person but a sick and disgusting *system*. We interpret disgust by our confidence in our institutional identity, as a member of the True Church, capable of diagnosing irredeemable institutional failing. The Last Judgement is brought forward into the *saeculum*.

My two Kentish moments of powerful disgust are found in pilgrimage narratives: Chaucer's *Pardoner's Tale*, written in the last decade of the fourteenth century,

[6] Thomas More, *A Dialogue Concerning Heresies*, ed. T. M. C. Lawler, Germain Marc'hadour, and Richard Marius, 2 Parts, in *The Complete Works of St Thomas More*, vol. 6 (New Haven: Yale University Press, 1981), 2.4, 1: 205.

and Erasmus's *Pilgrimage of Pure Devotion*, first published in Latin in 1526.[7] Its translation into English, between 1536 and 1540, repackaged the text as stridently evangelical.[8] In both pilgrimage texts I consider how communities might interpret and reincorporate the 'sick', and the disgusting, within these different understandings of where the Church is. A spiritual geography cleared of the saints, whose relics are now themselves described as disgusting, poses the question of how a community incorporates or rejects the repellent.

I might seem to be setting the stage for one version of the pre- and post-Reformation contrast, a contrast as much sociological as theological: pre-Reformation incorporation of the sickly versus evangelical purist exclusivism.[9] In fact, however, the story is more complex, since the Chaucerian, pre-Reformation example, more intensely than the sixteenth-century text, expresses desire for outright exclusion and repudiation of the disgusting hypocrite. It's true that the *Pardoner's Tale* finally contains that desire for exclusion, but only just, and the containment is managed wholly by lay figures.

Let us begin, though, with theoretical discussions of what might seem a peculiar question: where is the Church?

I

The Westminster Assembly, convened 'with a charge to advise parliament on religious matters',[10] produced its influential Confession in 1646. That Confession expresses a deep and abiding commitment to ecclesiological placelessness:

> Neither prayer, nor any other part of religious worship is, now under the gospel, either tied unto, or made more acceptable by, any place in which it is performed, or towards which it is directed: but God is to be worshipped every where in spirit and truth.[11]

[7] For a translation and excellent notes to the Latin text, see Desiderius Erasmus, *Colloquies*, trans. Craig R. Thompson, in *Collected Works of Erasmus*, 86 vols. (Toronto: University of Toronto Press, 1974–2006), 40: 619–74. For bibliographical details about publication of this colloquy, see 619–21.

[8] Desiderius Erasmus, *A dialoge or communication of two persons deuysyd and set forthe in the late[n] tonge, by the noble and famose clarke. Desiderius Erasmus intituled [the] pylgremage of pure deuotyon*, STC (2nd edn) 10454. STC gives the date as 1540. For the 1536 date of the translation, see Erasmus, *Colloquies*, trans. Thompson, 40: 620.

[9] For a classic statement of the post-Reformation aspect of this contrast, see Michael Walzer, *The Revolution of the Saints: A Study in the Origins of Radical Politics* (Cambridge, MA: Harvard University Press, 1965).

[10] Barbara Kiefer Lewalski, *The Life of John Milton: A Critical Biography*, rev. edn (Oxford: Blackwell, 2000), 161.

[11] John H. Leith (ed.), 'The Westminster Confession of Faith (1646)', in *The Creeds of the Churches, A Reader in Christian Doctrine from the Bible to the Present*, rev. edn (Richmond, VA: John Knox

This evangelical refusal to locate the Church in one place more than another had an immediate context, of legislated iconoclasm, in the 1640s. That iconoclasm included violent and systematic attacks on, for example, Canterbury Cathedral, designed to cure the 'malignant disease, called the Cathedrall evill', in the words of Richard Culmer, who was responsible for image breaking at Canterbury (including the post-Reformation embellishments introduced by Archbishop Laud).[12] When they entered the cathedral sometime in 1642, Culmer and his fellows 'knew not where to begin', since the images were so numerous, 'as if the superstitious cathedrall had beene built for no other end, but to be a stable for Idolls' (image 13). Among the many images and statues broken, the prize was a glass window of Becket that had somehow survived the 1538 proclamation a century earlier. One iconoclast climbed a ladder sixty steps high, 'with a whole pike in his hand ratling down proud Becket's glassy bones' (image 14). By Milton's account, God will himself act as iconoclast in Eden to teach mankind an ecological lesson about place: the Archangel Michael explains to Adam that the very mount of paradise will be pushed into the sea, 'with all his verdure spoiled and trees adrift'. The despoliation of Eden is designed 'To teach thee that God attributes to place / No sanctity if none be thither brought'.[13]

Evangelical refusal to locate the Church would also have a powerful future before it, setting as it did the True Church in flight from any material instantiation it might take. That flight included a flight to New England, where, only three years after the Westminster Confession, Thomas Shepard wrote in 1649 that 'Under the New Testament, all places . . . are equally holy.'[14] That New England commitment to spiritual homogeneity across space involved a refusal to use the very word 'Church', since this word implied that one place was more spiritual than another.[15] Homogeneity of spiritual place also determined the interior space of the meeting house. In the sixteenth and seventeenth centuries in England the altar table had moved

Press, 1973), Chapter 21.6, at 217. For discussion of how this conception of placelessness informed Puritan architecture, see Peter W. Williams, 'Metamorphoses of the Meetinghouse: Three Case Studies', in *Seeing Beyond the Word: Visual Arts and the Calvinist Tradition*, ed. Paul Corby Finney (Grand Rapids, MI: Eerdmans, 1999), 479–505.

[12] Richard Culmer, *Cathedrall newes from Canterbury* (London, 1644), image 2. (The term 'image' in these notes refers to digital facsimile editions available on *Early English Books Online.*) For further discussion of this event, see John Phillips, *The Reformation of Images: Destruction of Art in England, 1535–1660* (University of California Press, 1973), 189–90. See also Margaret Aston, 'Puritans and Iconoclasm, 1560–1640', in *The Culture of English Puritanism, 1560–1700*, ed. Christopher Durston and Jacqueline Eales (Basingstoke, Hants.: Macmillan, 1996), 92–121.

[13] John Milton, *Paradise Lost*, ed. Gordon Teskey (New York: Norton, 2005), 11: 836–7. For the intimate relation between placelessness and iconoclasm, see James Simpson, *Under the Hammer: Iconoclasm in the Anglo-American Tradition* (Oxford: Oxford University Press, forthcoming).

[14] Thomas Shepard, *Theses Sabbaticae* (London, 1649). Cited in J. P. Walsh, 'Holy Time and Sacred Space in Puritan New England', *American Quarterly*, 32 (1980), 79–95, at 84, though Shepard's statement is from Thesis 70, not Thesis 69 as stated by Walsh.

[15] Walsh, 'Holy Time and Sacred Space', 85.

back and forth between the chancel arch and the far east end of the traditional parish church, depending on the current regime's belief, or lack of belief, in special places. The New England meeting house resolved that spatial argument by deleting the chancel arch and its recession altogether. The geometrical symmetry and colourlessness of meeting houses effaced any possibility of places set aside, except the pulpit.

However much New England puritans might have tried to establish what one historian has called 'a time and space of homogenous sanctity',[16] the very impulse to do that initiates a permanent revolution of space, a permanent relocation of the True Church to another, ideal place, somewhere else. Thus Joshua Scottow, writing in New England as soon as 1628, already deplored the collapse of the transplanted Church: the 'Churches of old, and late' he wrote, 'have degenerated into anarchy, or confusion, or else given themselves up, unto the dominion of some prelatical teachers to rule at pleasure, which was the poison and bane of other primitive churches.' The upshot of this deep logic of permanent, *locational* supersession is a paradoxically utopian, no-place location of the Church. By this logic, here is not here: 'Corn-fields, orchards, Streets inhabited, and a place of merchandise', wrote Scottow, 'cannot denominate New England . . . NEW ENGLAND is not to be found in NEW ENGLAND, nor BOSTON in BOSTON'.[17] Place takes flight from place, ideal Church from material Church. Disgust at perceived spiritual corruption generates renewed commitment to the true Church, and so, in this case, drives a wedge between two Bostons, one material, one ideal.

By the time of the Westminster Confession of 1646, however, the notion of the Church's unstable dislocation was already an old and powerful one in England. It exists in two forms, as a theoretical ecclesiological issue, and as a more restricted attack on the place of pilgrimage sites. The attack on place surfaced in Wyclif's Latin writings in ecclesiological form. That view finds occasional voice in vernacular Lollard work across the fifteenth century.[18] For the most part, however, Lollard attack on placelessness finds most frequent expression in Lollard attack on pilgrimage.

[16] Walsh, 'Holy Time and Sacred Space', 79. See also James F. White, 'From Protestant to Catholic Plain Style', in *Seeing Beyond the Word*, ed. Finney, 457–77.

[17] Joshua Scottow, *A Narrative of the Planting of the Massachusetts Colony Anno 1628* (Boston: Harris, 1694), image 39. The text is discussed by Anthony Kemp, *The Estrangement of the Past: A Study in the Origins of Modern Historical Consciousness* (New York and Oxford: Oxford University Press, 1991), 140. Kemp's brilliant book elucidates the logic of historical supersession in Christian, especially evangelical thought; everything he says about historical supersession has implications for the supersession of place.

[18] For which see Anne Hudson, *The Premature Reformation: Wycliffite Texts and Lollard History* (Oxford: Clarendon Press, 1988), 314–23. For Lollard institutional identity, see Katherine C. Little, *Confession and Resistance: Defining the Self in Late Medieval England* (Notre Dame, IN: University of Notre Dame Press, 2006), Chapter 1.

Lollard hostility to place is frequently found in discussion of pilgrimage. One early fifteenth-century polemical text attacks the naïve who think that images at pilgrimage sites are themselves responsible for miracles. These simple people, with their disgusting, idolatrous touch, refer to

> 'the sweet rode of Bromholme', 'the swete rode of Grace', 'the sweet rode at the northe dore', 'our dere lavedy of Walsingham', but noght 'our Lavedy of hevene', ny 'oure lord Iesu Crist of hevene', but cleven sadly strokande and kyssand these olde stones and stokkis.[19]

Certainly those who took it upon themselves to engage with Lollard doctrine saw the implications of Lollard placelessness for particular pilgrimage sites. Thus Reginald Pecock, writing in *c.*1449,[20] defended pilgrimage sites on the ground that one place *was* more holy than another. Because, he says, 'God chooseth one place before another forto . . . work holy deeds of miracles and of graces more than in another place, therefore the one place is holier than the other place is.'[21]

Occasionally, in pre-Reformation England, hostility to the idea of particular places being holy rises to an incipient ecclesiology. *The Lanterne of Light* (written before 1415) has all the elements for a fully fledged account of the True Church as placeless, and as positively hostile to place, at its disposal.[22] It stops just short of activating the full ecclesiological implications of those elements. There are, by this writer's account, three Churches. The first is the truest, because it is without place. It consists of the 'congregation, or gathering together of faithful souls that lastingly keepen faith and trouthe . . . and overcoveren, or hillen [cover], this building in perfect charity'.[23] That connection of a newly defined true Church and its ideal architecture underlines the placelessness of this ideal Church. The second Church, the material Church in which the good and the evil come together, is not altogether damned. It *is* a special place, where God hears our prayers 'in special manner'. Yes, but no sooner has the *Lanterne* author preserved the material Church, a Church 'made by man's craft, of lime, of timber and of stone', than he undermines its material foundations. Man, by virtue of God's Word, might 'hallow this place, but

[19] 'Images and Pilgrimages', in *Selections from English Wycliffite Writings*, ed. Anne Hudson (Cambridge: Cambridge University Press, 1978), 83–8, at 87. For Lollard hostility to pilgrimage, see Hudson, *The Premature Reformation*, 307–9.

[20] For Pecock's career, see Wendy Scase, *Reginald Pecock* (Aldershot, Hants.: Variorum, 1996), and James Simpson, 'Pecock and Fortescue', in *A Companion to Middle English Prose*, ed. A. S. G. Edwards (Woodbridge: Boydell and Brewer, 2004), 271–88.

[21] Reginald Pecock, *Repressor of Over Much Blaming of the Clergy*, ed. Churchill Babington, Rolls Series, 2 vols. (London: Her Majesty's Stationery Office, 1860), 1: 222.

[22] For discussion of the ecclesiology of the *Lanterne* and other Lollard vernacular texts, see Hudson, *The Premature Reformation*, 318–20.

[23] Cited in 'The Nature of the Church', in *Selections from English Wycliffite Writings*, ed. Hudson, 116. For the whole text, see *The Lanterne of Light*, ed. Lilian M. Swinburn, EETS, original series, 151 (London: Kegan Paul, Trench and Trübner, 1917).

this place may not hallow man'.[24] The bulk of the text consists in lessons on how to distinguish the good from the evil in the second Church, a hermeneutic task rendered difficult by the outward near-identity of good and bad.[25]

The *Lanterne*'s third Church, the Church of Antichrist, is described in a separate section, but it is already clear that the devil's Church has infiltrated, and looks very much like, the second Church. In short, textual materials for real hostility to place are all available in this text. Those materials are as follows: an exclusivist, spiritual, and purist definition of the true Church; an account of the near identity of the devil's Church with the material Church made of 'lime, of timber and of stone'; and a hermeneutic kit designed to distinguish True Church from its Duessa look-alike, the false hypocritical church of Antichrist.

Only in the sixteenth century, however, do all these available materials lock systematically to produce a coherent account of the True Church as placeless, and as irredeemably hostile to particular places. Thomas More's arguments against placelessness are the richest source of anti-evangelical reflection on the matter. Already in the *Responsio ad Lutherum* of 1523 More cites Luther as saying that

> Christ does away with all place when He says: 'The Kingdom of God comes unawares, and they will not say it is here or there'... What, then, is the madness of the utterly impious papists that they bind to particular and necessary persons and places the church of God, which of all things is most free as to its place and person.[26]

More's response to this argument in the *Responsio* is relatively rapid. He seizes instantly on the Platonism of placelessness: he says that Luther wants to prove that 'the church militant on earth has not been recognized in this palpable and perceptible church'; instead, he wants to place the church 'in some other multitude of Christians, somehow imperceptible and mathematical—like Platonic ideas [*insensilem et mathematicam, Platonicis ideis cognatam*]—which is both in some place and in no place'.[27]

The treatment of place is much more sustained in More's *Dialogue Concerning Heresies* of 1529. Here we can see the different layers of the argument about place in the first two books of that work. In Book 1, More defends the holy places of pilgrimage sites. In Book 2 he answers the larger and more powerful evangelical charge against place, not with regard to pilgrimage sites, but with regard to the entire material Church.

In More's *Dialogue*, discussion of heresy is inseparable from discussion of geography and evangelical disgust. More's interlocutor in that dialogue is a young, potentially evangelical Cambridge scholar. In Book 1, the young man

24 'The Nature of the Church', in *Selections from English Wycliffite Writings*, ed. Hudson, 116.

25 *The Lanterne of Light*, ed. Swinburn, 48.

26 Thomas More, *Responsio ad Lutherum*, ed. John M. Headley, 2 parts, in *The Complete Works of St Thomas More*, vol. 5 (New Haven: Yale University Press, 1969), 1: 10, 163–5.

27 More, *Responsio ad Lutherum*, ed. Headley, 1: 10, 167.

attacks the notion of place. He refers to the possibility of fake relics being put on show in these places of pilgrimage. When, the young scholar says, we go on pilgrimage 'to this place and that place', it smacks of idolatry, as if we were to say that 'God were not lyke strong or not lyke present in every place'. By honouring the images at pilgrimage sites we 'make it seem that God and his saints stood in this place and that place bound to this post and that post cut out and carved in images'. When we consider ourselves better heard by God 'in Kent than at Cambridge, at the north door of Paul's than at the south door', this is proof that we repose our trust in the images rather than in God.[28] The young man also refers to the possibility of fake relics being put on show in these places of pilgrimage, explicitly citing the 'pig's bone' being presented as a relic, 'that was happely some time, as Chaucer sayth, a bone of some holy Jewes shepe'.[29]

More persuades the young man that belief in one place over another has its own credible coherence. One of his arguments foresees that the likely effect of spiritually homogenized space will be spiritually disenchanted space. Even if we can indeed pray anywhere, he says, most of us need a material church. If visible churches 'were once abolished and put away, we were like to have few good temples of God in men's souls, but all would, within a while, wear away clean and fall to nought'.[30] More understands the proximity of a spiritually homogenized space and a space that is entirely disenchanted.[31]

In Book 2 the argument about place returns, with considerably higher stakes. The young man poses a *geographical* riposte to More's argument that God would not allow the Church to err in so central a matter as cultic worship of the saints. What, he asks, if More is right about the unerring Church, but wrong about *where that unerring Church is*. What if the *true* Church were without specific place? 'Paradventure', he says, 'there myght be sayd that it nedeth not to assyngne any place where the very chyrche and true crysten congregacyon is'. All places are, as he suggests, 'indifferent' to the true Church; that Church is made up of 'all the good men and chosen people of god that be predestynate to be saved in what part so ever they be, and how so ever they be scateryd here one and there one'.[32]

[28] More, *A Dialogue Concerning Heresies*, 1.3, 1: 52.

[29] More, *A Dialogue Concerning Heresies*, 1.17, 1: 98. The young man also refers to the Pardoner's bones at 2.9, 1: 217. The reference to Chaucer is drawn from two separate sources, evidence of More's close reading of Chaucer. At Chaucer, *Canterbury Tales*, 'General Prologue', lines 699–700, the Pardoner is said to have 'a crois of latoun ful of stones, / And in a glas he hadde pigges bones'. In the *Pardoner's Prologue*, lines 350–1, he says about himself that he has 'in latoun a shulder-bon, / Which that was of an holy Jewes sheep'.

[30] More, *A Dialogue Concerning Heresies*, 1.3, 1: 58.

[31] For the larger picture of the ways in which Protestant dispersal of sacrality produces secularity, see Charles Taylor, *A Secular Age* (Cambridge, MA: Harvard University Press, 2007).

[32] More, *A Dialogue Concerning Heresies*, 2.1, 1: 189. For a survey of More's ecclesiology, see Richard C. Marius, 'Thomas More's View of the Church', in Thomas More, *The Confutation of*

The evangelical true Church is a thoroughly ideational institution. It is, perforce, nowhere and potentially everywhere, 'both in some place and in no place'. In reply, More articulates the logic that drives evangelical theology to so theoretical a notion of the Church's whereabouts. The heretic, he argues, grants that the Church cannot err in the right faith; the visible Church, however, damns the heretic. Either the heretic is *entirely mistaken*, or else the Church is *entirely elsewhere*. Heretics are, says More, 'drevyn to deny for the chyrche the peple that be knowyn for the chyrche'.[33] As a result, by a logical necessity, they 'go seek another [Church] they neyther know what nor where'. The ghost of More's own *Utopia* (1516) returns to haunt him here, since now it's his enemies who are inventing powerful but wholly ideational institutions: they 'build up in the air a church all so spiritual'.[34] In these arguments More recapitulates, and extends, arguments first made in English in Henry VIII's *Assertio septem sacramentorum* of 1521, which More himself might have ghost written. There, we read, Luther's rejection of all the national Churches must lead Luther to one of two consequences: 'he must either confess Christ's Church to be in no place at all, or else, like the Donatists, he must reduce the Catholic Church to two or three heretics whispering in a corner.'[35]

More delineates the terrible logic of this all or nothing confrontation. Either the evangelical position is entirely mistaken, or else the entire fabric of the visible Church is diabolical error. And if it is error, then the entire visible Church is hypocritical, making pretence to a status it doesn't have, and occluding the true Church in the process. In this super-charged, no-compromise situation, every aspect of the visible Church becomes readable as an ecclesiological theme. If, that is, one aspect of the Church is felt to be corrupt, that is not a containable matter, restricted to one place; on the contrary, it is directly revealing of the entire institution of the Church as Error writ large. Such a persuasion sets up a direct path to ecclesiology, leap-frogging individual morality and ecclesiastical satire: every visible aspect of the Church leads directly to questions of the Church as institution. Ecclesiastical hypocrisy is no longer containable as an individual failing to be dealt with either by the sacraments or by ecclesiastical satire; hypocrisy is instead the motor of the entire institution, to be dealt with by repudiation. Ecclesiastical satire leads irresistibly to radical ecclesiology.

Tyndale's Answer, ed. Louis A. Schuster, Richard Marius, James P. Lusardi, and Richard J. Schoeck, 3 Parts, in *The Complete Works of St Thomas More*, vol. 8 (New Haven: Yale University Press, 1973), 3: 1271–363. See also James Simpson, *Burning to Read: English Fundamentalism and its Reformation Opponents* (Cambridge, MA: Harvard University Press, 2007), Chapter 7.

33 More, *A Dialogue Concerning Heresies*, 2.3, 1: 196.

34 More, *A Dialogue Concerning Heresies*, 1: 196. For the issue of rhetorical place in More's oeuvre as a whole, see James Simpson, 'Thomas More', in *The Oxford Handbook to Tudor Literature, 1485–1603*, ed. Mike Pincombe and Cathy Shrank (Oxford: Oxford University Press, 209) 121–36.

35 Henry VIII, *Assertio septem sacramentorum* (London, 1687; first published 1522), Wing 565: 11, image 66.

The evangelical views More attacked were heterodox in the 1520s and early 1530s.[36] They did nevertheless converge with aspects of official religious policy in the later 1530s. In particular, they converge with official reshaping of geography. Just as Henry VIII's newly claimed jurisdiction over the English Church divided time, so too did it reshape space. If, for evangelical thinkers, no one place could be more spiritually charged than another, so too, under Henrician policy, all space had to be evenly subject to his jurisdiction.

Hagiographic narratives often turn out to be mini-essays in geography: they map webs of spiritual influence across Christendom, and they draw the contours of saintly influence within England.[37] As Henry VIII destroyed the monasteries from 1536, one of the principal symbolic targets had, therefore, to be destruction of the shrines of saints.[38] Above all, all traces of the jurisdictional victory of Thomas Becket had to be obliterated. I have already mentioned the 1538 proclamation, which branded Becket as a 'rebel and a traitor'. A royal circular to Justices of the Peace in 1538 charged them to suppress the talk of those people who complain that Henry was taking away the liberties of the realm originally fought for by Becket. Instead, 'bishop Becket of Canterbury, which they have tofore called Saint Thomas', demanded these liberties 'traitorously against the law of the realm'.[39]

The highly spiritualized ecclesiology of evangelical writers in the 1520s and 1530s coincided, then, with some aspects of royal jurisdictional redefinition. Both involved a newly conceived spiritual geography, in which either divine and/or royal authority was evenly distributed, undivided and uninterrupted by saintly jurisdictions. I now turn to the effects of that anti-place saint-clearance on the formation of communities of pilgrims as they travel to Canterbury. I look in particular to the way in which these contrasting notions of the Church's whereabouts determine a given community's response to the repellent and disgusting, and in particular to the repellent kiss.

[36] For both the smaller scale argument about pilgrimages and the larger scale argument about the placelessness of the True Church, see nuanced arguments by William Tyndale in *An Answer unto Sir Thomas Mores Dialogue*, ed. Anne M. O'Donnell and Jared Wicks (Washington: The Catholic University of America Press, 2000), 62–3 and 110–12, respectively. Concerning pilgrimages, Tyndale allows the virtuous practice, but says that it is idolatrous to believe that 'God will hear thee more in one place than in another' (62); about the definition of the Church, he allows various material definitions, though carefully adds this in conclusion: 'And some times it [i.e. the word 'Church'] is taken specially for the elect only in whose hearts God hath written his lawe with his holy spirit' (112).

[37] For an initial argument regarding late medieval England, see James Simpson, *Reform and Cultural Revolution*, The Oxford English Literary History, vol. 2: *1350–1547* (Oxford: Oxford University Press, 2002), 396–406.

[38] For the treatment of the saints in Henrician and Edwardian legislation, see Eamon Duffy, *The Stripping of the Altars: Traditional Religion in England, c.1400–c.1580* (New Haven, CT: Yale University Press, 1992), 379–477.

[39] *Letters and Papers, Foreign and Domestic, of the Reign of Henry VIII*... calendared by J. S. Brewer et al., 21 vols. in 33 books (Longman, Green, Longman and Roberts, 1862–1910), 13.2: 1171.

II

Thomas More's notion of the Church Militant as the visible, geographically localizable Church is equally, perforce, a notion of the Church as capacious. 'The chyrche', he says in the *Dialogue*, 'must nedys be the comen knowen multytude of crysten men, good and bad togyther, whyle the chyrche is here in erth. For this nette of Cryste hath for the whyle good fysshes and bad. And this felde of Cryste bereth for the whyle good corne and cocle, tyll it shall at the day of dome be puryfyed.'[40] This capaciousness is predicated on institutional ignorance as to how one's life might turn out. The moral possibilities remain open and unknowable: 'For who can know', he says, 'of the multitude who be good in dede and who be noght, sith the bad maye sodaynly be mended unware to the worlde and the good as sodaynly waxen worse.'[41]

With that conception of a materially visible, localizable Church Militant in mind, let us now turn to two pilgrimage narratives, Chaucer's written in the 1390s and Erasmus's in the 1520s. Both are set in Kent, respectively on the way to and from Becket's shrine at Canterbury. Both make the connection between repulsive relics and potentially repulsive people who may be damned by their use of such relics. Both confront the challenge of disgust and kissing in community formation. And both raise the question of the whereabouts of the True Church.

Erasmus made three visits to English pilgrimage sites, two to Walsingham, the second of which was made in 1512, and one to Canterbury, which Erasmus made with John Colet between 1512 and 1514. His *Pilgrimage of Pure Devotion* (the title of the English translation of the colloquy), first published in Latin in 1526, gathers the separate impressions of these visits into a quiet though decisive satire on pilgrimage sites. Erasmus presents a dialogue between a Flemish pilgrim, Ogygius ('primeval'), who's been both to Walsingham and to Canterbury, and his friend Menedemus ('Stay at Home'). The friend is entirely sceptical about relics, miracles, and the efficacy of praying to the saints. Interestingly, however, this 'enlightened' friend does not dominate the conversation or try to persuade his gullible interlocutor. On the whole, he allows credulous gullibility to expose itself.

As the pilgrim describes the gorgeousness of Thomas's shrine, however, the sceptic comes out into the open. He questions the cost of the saints' shrine when the living temples of God, the suffering poor, cry out. The naïve Ogygius seems to bury himself at this point, by describing the relic of St Thomas's handkerchief, on which Thomas wiped the 'filth of his nose'. The attendant at the shrine offers

[40] More, *A Dialogue Concerning Heresies*, 1: 205. The source of this thought can be found in Augustine, Sermon 47, in *Sermons*, ed. John E. Rotelle, Part 3 of *The Works of Saint Augustine*, 11 vols. (Brooklyn, NY: New City Press, 1990), 2: 298–307, at 301.

[41] More, *A Dialogue Concerning Heresies*, 1: 203.

> Certayne torne ragges of lynnen clothe, many havynge yet remaynynge in them the token of the fylthe of the holy mannes nose. With thes (as they say) saynt Thomas dyd wype a way the swett of hys face or hys neke, the fylthe of hys nose, or other lyke fylthynes with whiche mannes body dothe abownde.

Ogygius's companion (the refined Colet) recoils in disgust:

> But Gratian, therewith lyttle pleasede and content, not without an evydent sygne of dyspleasure, toke one of them betwene hys fyngers, and dysdaynyngly layd it down agayne, made a mocke and a mow [grimace] at it, after the maner of puppettes, for thys was hys maner, if any thyng lykede hym not, that he thought worthy to be despysede.[42]

Without anyone in the text actually saying so, Erasmus suggests here that relics are not so much risible, as physically and morally filthy: the dirty handkerchief is part of the system that deprives the poor of their fair share.

That is not, however, the whole story. Just as the filthy handkerchief is about to become a synecdoche for a filthy and disgusting Church, the pilgrim tells of his journey back from Canterbury to London. Ogygius and Colet pass an almshouse outside which fake relics of St Thomas are on sale, when an old almsman asks them to kiss St Thomas's shoe, at a price. The sceptical Colet is disgusted, and refuses to kiss the shoe. The naïve pilgrim Ogygius, on the other hand, pities the old man, kisses the shoe, and gives him some money. Even the normally credulous Ogygius recognizes the fallen state of all this, but, he argues, if something cannot be amended, then it is his habit to draw the best from it. St Thomas was good while he lived, and his legacy is good: it sustains, for example, a company of poor people by means of his shoe. The narration reveals that legacy in action: the poor, God's living temples, are in fact better served by the man who can absorb disgust and kiss the shoe than by the sceptic who is repelled by such a prospect and refuses to give. In the end, then, Erasmus reveals a world on the verge of change. Even the naïve pilgrim recognizes the cheapness of St Thomas's fake shoe. It won't take much for the numinous world of saintly relics to become a disenchanted world of disgusting bric-a-brac. On the other hand, for the moment it's the naïve pilgrim who helps the poor more effectively. Above all, Erasmus's naïve pilgrim and sceptic are having a gentle conversation, and are still in conversation at the end of the dialogue. This is very understated Erasmian polemics.

Erasmus's text was translated into English across the years 1536–40. Across those same years, in 1538, St Thomas's shrine had, as we have seen, been destroyed and his cult forbidden as treasonous. In this context, Erasmus's discreet but forceful satire means something very different and less gentle when translated. The Prologue to the translation is stridently evangelical. It assumes that the text will be read unequivocally as an attack on pilgrimages and belief in relics. The translator clearly

[42] Erasmus, *A dialoge or communication of two persons*, image 44.

wants to enlist Erasmus's influential voice for the evangelical camp. So many, says the translator, have given themselves to death through idolatrous worship of relics; brotherhoods and sisterhoods who 'play the fools sadly on Palm Sunday', invent themselves in order to go on pilgrimage, and, when challenged, make insurrections against God and the King. Most trenchantly, he attacks continued adoration of relics as a refusal to give up 'sodomitical acts', but promises that God's Word shall destroy the sodomitical idolaters. The evangelical translator reduces Erasmus's subtly equivocal text into a wholly straightforward and disgusted condemnation of idolatry, of what he calls

> the supersticyouse worshype and false honor gyvyn to bones, heddes, iawes, armes, stockes, stones, shyrtes, smokes, cotes, cappes, hattes, shoes, mytres, slyppers, sadles, rynges, bedes, gyrdles, bolles, belles, bokes, gloves, ropes, raperes, candelles, bootes, sporres (my breath was almost past me) with many other soche dampnable allusyones of the devylle to use theme as goddes contrary to the immaculate scripture of gode.[43]

He wants, clearly enough, to sweep away all this junk, and to reassert the king's jurisdiction by 'abolishing of the develishe and destestable usurped authorities' of the Church and its traitorous saints.[44]

The two versions of Erasmus's text, the Latin of 1526 and the English translation of 1536–40, present, then, two different versions of the whereabouts of the Church: the 1526 version is divided, recognizing as it does the emptiness of saintly relics, but carrying on for the moment. The late 1530s translation, by contrast, would stop the pilgrimage, destroy the relics, and eject the idolatrous from the True Church.

With the evangelical translator's identification of idolatry and sodomy, and with his disgusted dismissal of both, let us turn to our second Kentish pilgrimage, Chaucer's *Pardoner's Tale.* For there, too, subliminal and not so subliminal connections between idolatry and sodomy provoke the Host's rejection of the Pardoner's offer of absolution. The Host violently refuses to 'kisse thyn olde breech, / And swere it were a relyk of a seint, / Though it were with thy fundement depeint!' That refusal is, however, the prelude to a kiss between Pardoner and Host, and continuation of the pilgrimage towards Canterbury.

I might seem to be about to set up a simple contrast between the evangelical translator of Erasmus's *Pilgrimage of Pure Devotion* and Chaucer's narrative. On the one hand, the evangelical Prologue to the *Pilgrimage of Pure Devotion* would do away with all jurisdictions that interfere with the principal lines of obedience between the Christian and higher powers of God and king. By that account the true Church is, as we have seen, the invisible, placeless Church of the predestinate, a Church that has no place for the wicked, who deserve only rejection. On the other,

[43] Erasmus, *A dialoge or communication of two persons*, images 3–4.
[44] Erasmus, *A dialoge or communication of two persons*, image 6.

we seem to have in Chaucer's text a representation of the visible Church Militant in action, incorporating both good and bad in the knowledge that repentance is always possible.

If that contrast between a post- and pre-Reformation account of the Church were to hold, then we would be interpreting the Pardoner as a one-off representation of sin, rather than as a sign of a hypocritical Church. This is the working assumption of most twentieth-century criticism of the Pardoner, which sets itself the task of diagnosing the Pardoner's individual state of soul.[45] It is also, it should be said, Thomas More's interpretation in the *Dialogue Concerning Heresies.* The Pardoner's fake relic bones are clearly troubling to More: he twice has the young man refer to them in the *Dialogue* as evidence of the Church's hypocritical abuse of lay credulity.[46] More replies to the second of these references. He says that if someone should pay reverence to such fake relics, it does them no harm, and, in any case, a few bad practitioners do not destroy the whole system. For More, the Church remains intact in the face of the Pardoner. More steers interpretation of the tale away from ecclesiological criticism altogether. He even steers it away from ecclesiastical satire. Indeed, later in his career More attempted to repudiate ecclesiastical satire altogether, as in his expressed wish that Erasmus's *Praise of Folly* now, in 1532, be burnt along with his own earlier works.[47]

I might seem, as I say, to have set up a comparison between a revolutionary and a reformist conception of the Church, with the 1540 translator of Erasmus as the revolutionary, and Chaucer as the reformist, with Erasmus's sceptical but irenic text somewhere in the middle. In fact, however, I think More under-reads the tale, and that Chaucer's position is much more equivocal, in the way of Erasmus. For Erasmus, we remember, the system is only just continuing; it is barely viable, and it won't be long before even the credulous see through it. I think Chaucer sows the same doubts, though in even more forceful ways. It is true that a kiss permits his

[45] Twentieth-century writing on the Pardoner is of course considerable. For an overview of the tradition of character analysis in Chaucer criticism, see Lee Patterson, 'Historical Criticism and the Development of Chaucer Studies', in his *Negotiating the Past: The Historical Understanding of Medieval Literature* (Madison: University of Wisconsin Press, 1987), 3–39, at 18-26. For a summary and an example of character readings, see Derek Pearsall, *The Canterbury Tales* (London: Allen and Unwin, 1985), 91–104. For a critique of psychologized readings of the Pardoner, see Lee Patterson, 'Chaucer's Pardoner on the Couch: Psyche and Clio in Medieval Literary Studies', *Speculum*, 76 (2001), 638–80. Patterson argues forcefully for reinterpretation within traditions of Lollard ecclesiology.

[46] Hugh Latimer might have been thinking of the *Pardoner's Tale* reference that clearly troubled More in the following veiled and glancing reference, made in a larger attack on images: 'And yet, as in those [images] there may be much ungodliness committed, so there may here [in saints' relics] some superstition be hid, if that sometime we chance to visit pig's bones instead of saints' relicks, as in time past it hath chanced, I had almost said, in England.' 'Sermon Preached Before the Convocation of the Clergy', in *Sermons by Hugh Latimer*, ed. George Elwes Corrie (Cambridge: Cambridge University Press, 1844), 41–58, at 53-4. The sermon was delivered in 1537.

[47] More, *The Confutation of Tyndale's Answer*, ed. Schuster, Marius, Lusardi, and Schoeck in *The Complete Works*, vol. 8, 1: 179. See Simpson, *Burning to Read*, Chapter 8.

pilgrimage to continue, but that kiss replicates the problem that Chaucer raises throughout the tale about the relation of the Pardoner and the Church. It was the embrace of one rioter with another, after all, that caused his death.

Some pre-Reformation works, like *Piers Plowman*, have the power to see whence the danger to the Church is coming; indeed, one of the issues about which *Piers Plowman* is truly prophetic is precisely the issue of the Church's place. I end this essay by arguing that Chaucer's *Pardoner's Tale* has the same prophetic power. The Pardoner is not containable as one rotten apple; he belongs to and exposes a system. His tale repeatedly unsettles the question of the Church's whereabouts. In the process, the Pardoner raises the real possibility that the whole Church Militant is very well represented in the here and now of the Pardoner. Chaucer raises the possibility at least of the *Pardoner's Tale* being read as powerfully ecclesiological. Reading the Tale through the lens of the sixteenth-century texts brings to the surface the pressing question of place, of where the True Church is.

The Pardoner's basic strategy in duping, or at least embarrassing, his audience of Canterbury pilgrims, is to fool them as to location. One of the effects of drunkenness, by the Pardoner's account, is geographical confusion: a man who drinks too much Spanish wine thinks he's 'at hoom in Chepe' (line 569), when in fact he's in Spain. This geographical confusion very well describes the effect of listening to the Pardoner himself, since he consistently confuses his audience as to where they are. 'In chirches whan I preche' is how he starts his Prologue (line 329): what we think we hear is a *performance* of what really happens and what is really said *elsewhere*, when the Pardoner addresses 'lewed peple'. It is not, so we must repeatedly remind ourselves, really happening in the here and now of the Canterbury pilgrimage. During both Prologue and tale, that confidence in location is, however, repeatedly challenged, principally by the insistent use of apostrophe and deictics. '*Heere* is a miteyn eek' (line 372); '*Now* wol I deffenden hasadrye' (line 590); 'Goode men and women' (line 377); 'But, sires, *now* wol I telle forth my tale' (line 660): such verbal localizations are presented as reminders of what the Pardoner does *elsewhere*, but the very insistence on presence cannot help but suggest that he's also doing it *here*. By the end of the tale, that uncertainty as to the locality of address becomes unavoidable. The Pardoner makes what is unquestionably an address to the Canterbury pilgrims; he suddenly transforms his performance of what happens elsewhere into what is unavoidably happening here: 'But, sires, o word forgat I in my tale: / I have relikes and pardon in my male...' (lines 919–20).

The Pardoner, then, deliberately creates a locational slipperiness. That uncertainty as to the place of discourse makes it difficult to contain the Pardoner in the way More would have us do. In the tale itself, these sudden, almost phantasmagoric transformations have poisonous effects: attractive gold is suddenly turned into hideous death no less rapidly than a peck of rat's poison will kill any creature. The rioters seek what is unfindable (Death), only to find it when they stop looking.

What implications does this rhetoric of dangerous locational slipperiness have for the whereabouts of the Church? I suggest that Chaucer is intensely sensitive to the transformative powers of pathological systems of circulation. The tavern is transformed into an anti-Church, in which, through excess, the gamblers 'doon the devel sacrifise / Within that develes temple in cursed wise' (lines 469–70). Chaucer so unsettles the stability and boundedness of place that, finally, the Pardoner's limitations on space dissolve altogether, thus generating a potential reference to the whole Church. The following passage, for example, is posed by the Pardoner as a citation of what he said *there*, when in fact it gains a terrible resonance once we realise that it might pertain *here*, in the Church of which the Pardoner is no longer accident but substance, or, rather, in which the entire Church has become accident, with its life ground out of it. The Pardoner, who is, after all, not in a church, warns his listeners

> If any wight be in this chirche now
> That hath doon synne horrible, that he
> Dar nat, for shame, of it yshryven be,
> Or any womman, be she yong or old,
> That hath ymaked hir housbonde cokewold,
> Such folk shal have no power ne no grace
> To offren to my relikes in this place. (lines 378–84)

'In *this* chirche *now*'; 'in *this* place': what is the referent of these deictics? As long as we contain the Pardoner, they are in a single, containable place, somewhere else. Once we allow the possibility of the Pardoner as participating in a pathological system of exchange, their reference extends to an entire Church whose penitential systems have been eaten out and exhausted, leaving nothing but the despair of 'no grace', and leaving nothing but fake, material relics, objects left behind not from any sacred event that occurred somewhere else, but just plain, material leftovers in an empty here and now. If More foresees the evangelical disenchantment of space, Chaucer imagines the disenchantment of Catholic space.

Chaucer's position is far from that of the 1540 evangelical translator of Erasmus's *Pilgrimage of Pure Devotion*. The terrible spectre of existential loneliness as expressed by the old man seeking Death (lines 720–38) is not replicated by having the Pardoner rejected from the pilgrimage. The Host's vicious anti-martyrdom of the Pardoner is neutralized. Instead, the Pardoner, on the way to the relics of St Thomas, is provoked to undergo a salutary martyrdom of sorts himself. The pilgrimage group finds the resources within itself to maintain him and itself whole. Host and Pardoner do kiss. The pilgrimage does continue.

For all that, Chaucer's text expresses a position not entirely different from that of Erasmus. Both recognize that relics are part of a corrupt system; the moment a viewer recognises the corruption, numinous relics will appear no less disgusting than the people who peddle them. Both recognize that the Church's fundamental *raison d'être* is being eroded by the abuse of penance. The profile of ecclesiology is more carefully disguised in Chaucer's tale than in Erasmus's text, but the force of that ecclesiology is much darker. The anti-Church of the 'develes temple' in the tavern is potentially an image of the whole Church: both run on pathological systems of circulation. The Church seems incapable of criticizing and of reforming itself: it is the Host who objects to the Pardoner, and it is the Knight who restores a peace of sorts between Host and Pardoner. No ecclesiastical figure is involved in either criticism or governance of the Pardoner. Chaucer leaves entirely open the possibility that the pathological, murderous circulations of the tavern are happening 'in this chirche now', 'in this place'.

That this darker reading was available in the sixteenth century seems certain from the evidence of John Heywood's play, *The Pardoner and the Friar*, printed in 1533. Heywood exploits drama, the literary art *par excellence* of the deictic, to suggest the expandable locational potential of Chaucer's lines. Heywood has his Pardoner cite Chaucer's Pardoner verbatim, although in new, more treacherous circumstances. His Pardoner, who has earlier announced that he has the bone of 'a holy Jewes shepe', encourages the audience 'in this place now' to come up and receive absolution:

> Yf any wyght be in this place now
> That hath done syn so horryble that she
> Dare nat, for shame, therof shryven be;
> Or any woman, be she yonge or olde,
> That hath made her husbande cockolde,
> Such folke shall have no power nor no grace
> To offer to my relikes in this place.[48]

One year before the Act of Supremacy, that is, the 'place' of the Pardoner is, after 140 years, identical. That duration suggests all the more powerfully that 'this place' is everywhere.

FURTHER READING

Cormack, Bradin. *A Power to Do Justice: Jurisdiction, English Literature, and the Rise of Common Law, 1509–1625* (Chicago: University of Chicago Press, 2008)
Kemp, Anthony. *The Estrangement of the Past: A Study in the Origins of Modern Historical Consciousness* (New York and Oxford: Oxford University Press, 1991)
Taylor, Charles. *A Secular Age* (Cambridge, MA: Harvard University Press, 2007)
Walzer, Michael. *The Revolution of the Saints: A Study in the Origins of Radical Politics* (Cambridge, MA: Harvard University Press, 1965)

[48] John Heywood, *The Pardoner and the Friar*, in *The Plays of John Heywood*, ed. Richard Axton and Peter Happé (Cambridge: Brewer, 1991), lines 174–82.

CHAPTER 7

ENCLOSED SPACES

LYNN STALEY

When in 'Upon Appleton House' Andrew Marvell describes the estate of Thomas Fairfax as a place sanctified by nature, history, and design, as at once accessible and discreet, as ambiguously poised between the ways of action and contemplation, and as both a sign of civilization and a reminder of inherent barbarism, he is at once stating the plain facts about the estate (once the site of a Cistercian nunnery) bound within the exigencies of English law and aligning his long and deliberately irresolute meditation with an earlier but still living concern with the outlines and identity of Britain itself. With its concern for boundaries, lineage, and the processes by which sanctity is asserted, 'Upon Appleton House' links what has been described as the last of the country-house poems with a tradition beginning with Gildas and Bede and continuing through monastic myths of origin, the medieval chronicle tradition, and their refractions in a vernacular literature that comes, finally, to celebrate the secular as sacred. Those pre-Conquest texts and traditions that underlie later identifying texts such as Cistercian founding stories and the Wilton Diptych link the nation to the church, suggesting the boundaries afforded by both geography and *ecclesia*. However, it is the permeability of those boundaries that frequently preoccupies efforts to describe or celebrate Britain, the garden whose inviolability is constantly at risk and with it the very identity of Britain itself. The efforts at self-understanding that are adumbrated in such texts to some extent authorize Marvell's poem, which sets Appleton House within a history and a set of concerns that take geographic distinction as their trope.

In describing Britain as an insular *locus amoenus*, Bede at once nods to Gildas's earlier description of it as a fallen garden or bride, provides a new perspective upon British history, and sets the terms later chroniclers and monastic historians would use to describe Britain and its institutions.[1] Like Gildas, Bede describes Britain as

[1] For Bede, see *Bede's Ecclesiastical History of the English People*, ed. and trans. Bertram Colgrave and R. A. B. Mynors (Oxford: Clarendon Press, 1969). See Catherine A. M. Clarke, *Literary Landscapes and the Idea of England, 700–1400* (Cambridge: D.S. Brewer, 2006), 7–35, for the pleasurable island as

beautiful and fertile; however, where Gildas warns the errant bride, Israel, of her disobedience, infidelity, and consequent barbarism, Bede begins with a picture of the fertile island, whose seas and land provide it with bounty. He moves immediately to list its five languages which are unified by the last, Latin, the language of Christian belief and culture. He goes on to tell the story of the Roman conquest of Britain, placing the story of Britain's first martyr, St Alban, immediately thereafter, a founding story for the British church, whose identity is inseparable from that of Britain, the nation. Where Gildas, writing *c.*540 CE, can see Britain only as Israel in disarray, Bede, who finished the *Ecclesiastical History* in 731, writes the story of a nation whose history is the history of its church, whose heroes and foundations define the synthesis of its culture and its future. Where Gildas outlines an exile from grace, Bede traces the gradual story of Britain's reconversion to a Christianity, now enriched by Irish monasticism, as well as by the Germanic peoples who call Britain home.

Bede's appraisal of a nation whose boundaries are at once distinct and porous encapsulates a prolonged meditation upon the limits or, possibly, the duties or dangers of enclosure that is as characteristic of cenobitic self-definition as it is of British. The final chapter of the *Ecclesiastical History* underlines Britain's separation from and involvement in the greater world by recalling the salient points of the history the book constructs. Though once a part of Rome, it remained geographically alien from and yet dependent upon the Continent for defense. Later, other tribes infiltrated Britain, and missionaries arrived from Rome, Ireland, and Scotland. The penultimate chapter outlines the decision of the Scottish church to align with Britain by accepting the Roman date for Easter, as well as the Roman tonsure for its priests. Only the Britons remain outside the bounds and experience subjection to Britain, rather than peace with it, as do the Picts, for now. Just as the Latin language provides Bede with a common tongue for the languages spoken in the island in the book's opening chapter, so, at its close, Roman observance serves as a common experience within the bounds of a Britain whose distinction from and relationship to the world are carefully achieved identifying features of a history that lies beyond the scope of Bede himself.

Bede ends his final chapter by inserting himself into this history, a native Northumbrian, whose life has been lived between the monasteries of Wearmouth and Jarrow, but whose intellectual and religious life has been focused upon the labors of teaching and of commenting upon the works of the Fathers. He signs himself as heir of two traditions, one belonging to one region of Britain, the other to a greater Christian culture whose boundaries now include Britain without erasing Britain's own insular and privileged identity. Bede might have used the

defining trope, which carries over to the founding stories of the fenland monasteries of Ely and Ramsey (pp. 79–84). For a study of England as possessing a special status because of its isolation, see Kathy Lavezzo, *Angels on the Edge of the World: Geography, Literature, and English Community, 1000–1534* (Ithaca, NY: Cornell University Press, 2006).

same method to explore the finely drawn ideals of Benedictine monasticism, whose foundations are in and not of the world.

Bede's account of Britain as a bountiful and beautiful island that is also characterized by an ethnic diversity unified and dignified by its inclusion in mainstream Christian practice and culture is not simply a conventional beginning point for later English historians, but an identifying *topos* for the nation. For English historians like Gervase of Canterbury, Ralph of Diceto, William of Malmesbury, and William of Newburgh, the history of Britain is a history instituted by Gildas and Bede, who established the foundations of a nation whose boundaries enclosed people or peoples, thus an island of marvels and beauties, a place that is the site of the struggles between individuals and of individuals.[2] In other words, the stories to a great degree depend upon the ideation of the island as a place whose restoration or reformation is its history, whether those reformers be Roman, Saxon, Norman, or the Cistercian 'invaders', who restored a Yorkshire turned into a barren wasteland, and whose language of identity has remarkable affinities with Britain's own terms of self-description.[3] Thus Walter Daniel's *Life of Aelred of Rievaulx* describes Aelred's original view of the abbey: 'High hills surround the valley, encircling it like a crown. These are clothed by trees of various sorts and maintain in pleasant retreats the privacy of the vale, providing for the monks a kind of second paradise of wooded delight.' To visual delight is added aural, for the water tumbling down from the rocks made a melody, that, along with the rustling branches of the trees, formed a 'jubilee of harmonious sound, music whose every diverse note is equal to the rest.'[4] Cistercian accounts of their abbeys do more than evoke the natural beauty of Cistercian sitings. In most cases written decades after the foundations themselves and by authors certainly aware of the language of Britain's own founding narratives, they capture the tension between the secluded, the protected, the feminine, and the active world outside the cloister, whose members are drawn to a seclusion, at once insular and permeable and capable of ongoing acts of reformation.[5]

[2] For the latter, see William of Malmesbury's account of King Alfred's attention to learning in R. A. B. Mynors (ed., completed by R. M. Thomson and M. Winterbottom), *William of Malmesbury: Gesta Regum Anglorum. The History of the English Kings* (Oxford: Clarendon Press, 1998), 181ff. See Hugh M. Thomas, *The English and the Normans: Ethnic Hostility, Assimilation, and Identity 1066–1220* (Oxford: Oxford University Press, 2003), 265; W. Stubbs (ed.), *The Historical Works of Master Ralph de Diceto, Dean of London*, 2 vols. (London: Rolls Series, 1876), 10–1. As Stubbs notes, this section on the marvels of Britain is not Diceto's work but appears in slightly different form in many manuscripts.

[3] See Richard Howlett (ed.), *Historia Rerum Anglicarum of William of Newburgh*, in *Chronicles of the Reigns of Stephen, Henry II, and Richard I*, 4 vols. (London: Rolls Series, 1884–89), 1: 50–1.

[4] *The Life of Aelred of Rievaulx by Walter Daniel*, trans. and annotated by F. M. Powicke, introd. Marsha Dutton (Kalamazoo: Cistercian Publications, 1994), 98. See also Elizabeth Freeman, *Narratives of a New Order: Cistercian Historical Writing in England 1150–1220* (Turnholt: Brepols, 2002), 2, 123, 142–4.

[5] On Cistercian founding narratives, see L. G. D. Baker, 'The Genesis of English Cistercian Chronicles: the Foundation History of Fountains Abbey', part 1, *Analecta Cisterciensia*, 25 (1969),

The impulses of Gildas and Bede to write geography as narrative can be seen in the two most important histories of the later Middle Ages, the fabulous *Brut*, which, like Geoffrey of Monmouth's *Historia* might better be called a romance, and Ranulf Higden's *Polychronicon*, which sets the history of Britain within a universal history.[6] The author of the *Brut*, who begins with the story of the monstrous Albina and her sisters, whose engendering of giants is remedied by Brutus, follows Gildas in inscribing the fallen garden onto the map of Britain. Higden anchors the *Polychronicon* in classical and ecclesiastical histories, maintaining its perspective upon history as a struggle against disorder in which the church, frequently in conflict with kings, serves as a stabilizing force. Higden's Britain, like Bede's, is enclosed, beautiful, bountiful, and wholesome, but it is not closed. It is vulnerable to human passions and barbarity, but nonetheless potential—a landscape whose permeability opens it to restorers, seeking to bring order out of chaos.

The image of the garden of Britain and all that it implies (temptation, fall, carnality, experience, vigilance, restoration) cannot be separated from the central image of the biblical pastoral, the *hortus conclusus*, glossed as the Church, the soul, or the Blessed Virgin, beloved of God and bound to the divine by sacred love. The relationship between the two—the island/garden and the *hortus*—implied by monastic chroniclers linked Britain's secular to its ecclesiastical identity, intimating the distinctive and sacralized quality of the nation's own enclosed space.

Perhaps the most well done, and certainly the most beautiful and mysterious, depiction of Britain's sacrality is the Wilton Diptych, created probably in the 1390s, which shows a young Richard II presented by John the Baptist and the English saints, Edward and Edmund, to the Virgin and Child. The angels flanking the Virgin on the right-hand panel wear Richard's badge of the White Hart; one of the angels carries a banner with a red cross, the banner of St George.[7] In 1993, it was

14–41; part 2, *Analecta Cisterciensia*, 31 (1975), 179–212; Constance Hoffman Berman, *The Cistercian Evolution: The Invention of a Religious Order in Twelfth-Century Europe* (Philadelphia, PA: University of Pennsylvania Press, 2000); Christopher Norton, 'Richard of Fountains and the Letter of Thurstan: History and Historiography of a Monastic Controversy, St. Mary's Abbey, York, 1132', in *Perspectives for an Architecture of Solitude: Essays on Cistercians, Art and Architecture in Honour of Peter Fergusson*, ed. Terryl N. Kinder (Turnholt: Brepols, 2004), 9–31.

[6] Friedrich W. D. Brie, *The Brut*, pt. 1, EETS 131 (London, 1906); pt. 2, EETS 136 (London, 1908); *Polychronicon Ranulphi Higden Monachi Cestrensis*, ed. Joseph Rawson Lumby, 9 vols. (London, 1865; Kraus Reprint, 1975). See also Lister M. Matheson, 'Historical Prose', in *Middle English Prose: A Critical Guide to Major Authors and Genres*, ed. A. S. G. Edwards (New Brunswick, NJ: Rutgers University Press, 1984), 209–48; John Taylor, 'The French Prose *Brut*: Popular History in Fourteenth-Century England', in *England in the Fourteenth Century*, ed. W. M. Ormrod (Woodbridge, Suffolk: Boydell Press, 1986), 247–54; Matheson, *The Prose Brut: The Development of a Middle English Chronicle*, Medieval and Renaissance Texts and Studies, 180 (Tempe, AZ: 1998); Emily Steiner, 'Radical Historiography: Langland, Trevisa, and the Polychronicon', *Studies in the Age of Chaucer*, 27 (2005), 171–212; Francis Ingledew, *'Sir Gawain and the Green Knight' and the Order of the Garter* (Notre Dame, IN: University of Notre Dame Press, 2006), Chapter 1.

[7] For the most recent work on the Wilton Diptych, see Dillian Gordon, *Making and Meaning: The Wilton Diptych* (London: National Gallery Publications, 1993); Dillian Gordon, Lisa Monas, and

discovered that the orb (which is one centimeter in diameter) of the banner contains a miniature of an island upon which are a white castle and trees, surrounded by a sea with a boat in sail, and, above, a blue sky. Dillian Gordon has argued that the orb represents England as the *dos Mariae*, the dowry of the Virgin.[8] That the idea of England as Mary's dowry was current is clear from Thomas Arundel's remarks to that effect in 1400, suggesting that at least by the reign of Richard II, England claimed a special relationship with Mary.[9] Certainly his grandfather, Edward III, seemed to have had an easy relationship with the Virgin. In 1352, returning to England after a truce in the war, he met rough weather and lost men to the sea. His remarks are among the last bits of history Higden records, 'My goode lady seynt Marye, what is it, and what bodeth it, that in my wendynge into Fraunce I wynde have and weder and al thing at my wille, and in my comynge agen toward Engelond I have tempest and many hard happes'.[10] The king complains as suitor to lady, as knight to patron, and certainly Mary served as patroness to the Order of the Garter, which was bound to her and to the king in chivalry. Depicting Britain as enclosed and protected by the sea, as Mary by her chastity, donated to the Virgin, and ruled by the young king, the Wilton Diptych offers itself as an icon of sacred kingship and sacred geography.

As I have suggested elsewhere, when placed in conversation with other fourteenth-century texts, the Wilton Diptych loses none of its beauty, but nonetheless seems an ideogram of sanctity and insularity for another age and set of circumstances.[11] A decade or so after Edward's familiar complaint to the Virgin about the difficulties of returning to his island and several years more than that after his creation of the Order of the Garter, William Langland placed into circulation another image, a semi-enclosed space that functions as a radically different sort of sign of national identity: Piers's half acre, close by his croft. In so

Caroline Elam (eds.), *The Regal Image of Richard II and the Wilton Diptych* (London: Harvey Miller Publishers, 1997); especially Nigel Morgan's 'The Signification of the Banner in the Wilton Diptych', 179–88; and Gordon's Introduction, 22–3, which describes and discusses the orb. I would like to thank Matthew Storey, documentation assistant (of the National Gallery), for making it possible for me to use the files on the painting in the Archives of the National Gallery.

[8] Dillian Gordon, 'A New Discovery in the Wilton Diptych', *Burlington Magazine*, 134 (1992), 662–7. As Gordon points out, there were earlier suggestions linking the painting to the *dos Mariae*. The letter of 17 March 1905 from Everard Green to Captain Neville Wilkinson in the National Gallery Archives argues that the Diptych commemorates Richard's dedication of England to the Blessed Virgin. See also Edmund Waterton, *Pietas Mariana Britannica* (London, 1879), 13–14; C. Coupe, 'An Old Picture', *The Month*, 84 (1895), 229–42.

[9] David Wilkins, *Concilia Magnae Britannicae* (London, 1737), vol. 3: 246. See also Edmund Waterton, *Pietas Mariana Britannica*, 13–14; Gordon, 'The Wilton Diptych', in *The Regal Image of Richard II and the Wilton Diptych*, 329–30, n. 40.

[10] *Polychronicon Ranulphi Higden*, vol. 8: 344–5. This is Trevisa's translation; Caxton's later translation includes the passage.

[11] Lynn Staley, *Languages of Power in the Age of Richard II* (University Park: Pennsylvania State University Press, 2005), 355.

doing, Langland draws upon its biblical and parabolic associations, as well as upon its legal and agricultural, creating an image whereby allegory, agriculture, and nation combine in ways that were to become inextricable in English literature.[12] Both the half acre and the croft are grounded in English rural life. The half acre was the average area of the strip, separated by narrow unplowed strips, into which open fields were plowed, and those half acres then allotted to individuals; the croft designated an enclosed small parcel of land, frequently adjoining a house.[13]

Langland uses both terms as concepts in which the language of tropology coexists with that of topography. He employs the term *croft* twice in the *Visio*: first, as part of an image that David Aers has called a type of the preacher's 'picturing model' in Piers's directions to the dwelling of Truth, which are unchanged in all three writings of the poem:[14]

> Thanne shalt thou come be a croft, ac come thou nought thereinne;
> The croft hattith coveite-nought-menis-catel-ne-here-wyves,
> Ne-none-of-here-servantis-that noie-hem-mighte;
> Loke thou breke no bowis there but it be thin owene. (A: 6, 59–62)

Since Piers has just told the pilgrims that they must first wade in a brook and not swear, the croft, which they are not to enter nor to pillage, serves as a spiritual way-station offered by the Law, codified in the Ten Commandments, a stage preceding their arrival at the court of Mercy. However, his next use of *croft* places it in relation to the half-acre, which he invites the pilgrims to help him work (A: 7, 4). He assigns the croft to the Knight's protection as part of an idealized social covenant:

> I shal swynken & sweten & sowe for us bothe,
> A[nd] ek laboure for thi love al my lif tyme,
> In covenaunt that thou kepe holy [k]ir[k]e and myself
> Fro wastours [and wikkide men] that wolde me destroye,
> And go hunte hardily [to] har[is] & to fox[is],

12 For the rhetoric of agriculture, see Nevill Coghill, 'The Character of Piers Plowman', *Medium Ævum*, 2 (1933), 108–35; Stephen A. Barney, 'The Plowshare of the Tongue', *Mediaeval Studies*, 35 (1973), 261–93; Michael Camille, 'Labouring for the Lord: the Ploughman and the Social Order in the Luttrell Psalter', *Art History*, 10 (1987), 423–55; Ralph Hanna III, *William Langland* (Brookfield, VT: Ashgate, 1993), 11.

13 *Piers Plowman by William Langland: an Edition of the C-Text*, ed. Derek Pearsall (Berkeley: University of California Press, 1979), 146; Christopher Dyer, *Lords and Peasants in a Changing Society: the Estates of the Bishopric of Worcester, 680–1540* (Cambridge: Cambridge University Press, 1980), 331; Joan Thirsk, *The Rural Economy of England: Collected Essays* (London: Hambledon Press, 1984), 59–64; Dyer, *An Age of Transition? Economy and Society in England in the Later Middle Ages* (Oxford: Clarendon Press, 2005), 58, 75–7. See the *Middle English Dictionary* for the use of the words in legal documents.

14 David Aers, *Piers Plowman and Christian Allegory* (London: Edward Arnold, 1975), 114. I shall be quoting from the A-text unless otherwise indicated: *Piers Plowman: the A Version*, ed. George Kane (London: Athlone Press, 1988).

And [to] boris & [to] bukkes that breken myn heggis,
And fecche the hom fauconis the foulis to kille,
For thise comith to my croft & croppith my whete. (A: 7, 27–34)

Piers's image comes from the countryside, from the parcels enclosed by hedges held by individual tenants and worked for private profit but usually subject to communal control or censure when the subject was common grazing. Piers's citing of 'wastours' who threaten him does not so much place the croft, the peasant household, within the concerns of the household of the realm, as substitute the croft for the noble household as a counter-symbol for Britain, the nation.[15] Moreover, the foxes that enter into the croft and threaten his livelihood—which evoke the foxes, the temptations or heretics, of Canticle 2.15 that spoil the grapes within the vineyard of the Church or wreck the work within the field of the spirit—along with hares, boars, and bucks are those animals whose very existence was guaranteed by the Law of the Forest, which prevented the peasant from ridding himself of huntable beasts.[16] Langland has not only substituted a rural scene for a tropological pictogram, he here, and briefly, provides another sort of picture, idealized, but nonetheless intended as an image of a realm wherein peasant and knight are bound through the land and where the scene of rural labor is not one pageant within a program depicting the laborer as an appendage to the noble household. Thus, the laborers within the Luttrell Psalter take their reality from the family and its myths manifested in the Psalter, and the peasants in the *Tres Riches Heures* exist in relation to the castles in the backgrounds.[17] Langland's foregrounding of the peasant holding and its needs offers an image of potentially subversive power that he quickly reinserts into another pictogram by naming Piers's wife and children—'Dame werche-whanne-tyme-is', 'do-right-[so]-or thi damme-shal-the bete', 'suffre-thi-sovereynes-to-haven-here-wille / And-deme-hem-noght-for-yif-thou-dost-thou-shalt-it-dere-abiggen, / Let-god-worthe-withal-for-so-his-woord-techith' (A: 7, 70–4). Here, we return to a tropology designed to reify adages fitting the laborer into the necessary strictures of time and power.

This is not to read *Piers Plowman* as simply a social document, but to pull one image from an early scene, an image in subtle contrast to those courts, monasteries, and castles that proliferate in earlier accounts of Britain's insular and sacred

[15] For the magnatial implications of wasting as it applies to household economies, see D. Vance Smith, *Arts of Possession: the Middle English Household Imaginary* (Minneapolis: University of Minnesota Press, 2003), 72–107.

[16] See St Bernard, *Sermones in Cantica*, *PL* 183: cols. 1081, 1084, 1086; D. W. Robertson, Jr., *A Preface to Chaucer* (Princeton, NJ: Princeton University Press, 1962), 251–2. On hunting and the Law of the Forest, see William Perry Marvin, *Hunting Law and Ritual in Medieval England* (Cambridge: D.S. Brewer, 2006).

[17] Jonathan J. G. Alexander, 'Labeur and Paresse: Ideological Representations of Medieval Peasant Labor', *Art Bulletin* 72–3 (1990), 436–52; Michael Camille, *Mirror in Parchment: The Luttrell Psalter and the Making of Medieval England* (Chicago: The University of Chicago Press, 1998).

geography, that suggests a potential critique of those images used to articulate social order. However, lest he be accused of populism, Langland is careful to place the peasant in relation to the knight through the covenant each has sworn—the one to 'swynk and swete', to labor 'for thi love al my lif tyme', the other to protect Church and layman from destructive forces. The social order is not questioned; rather, Piers underlines the bonds holding society in place. But his picture of that society in this section of the poem is a rural one that at once draws upon the agricultural metaphors of the prophets and of Jesus's parables *and* is grounded in Britain's literal agricultural topography. Langland's image of the peasant croft was appropriated in suggestive and subtle ways by Chaucer and the author of *Mum and the Sothseggar* and passed on in the sixteenth- and seventeenth-century literature of the agricultural landscape that, enclosed but permeable, was used to signify or to question a national identity.

In the *Canterbury Tales*, Chaucer depicts a number of peasant households. Some are in varying states of internal disorder, such as those in the Miller's and the Reeve's tales; some, however, are not so much disordered as threatened by figures who misuse their own power, such as the Summoner in the Friar's tale and Walter in the Clerk's. In both the description of the widow's household and of Griselda's, Chaucer emphasizes their poverty and simple thriftiness. The widow's appears to be enclosed, since the Summoner 'clappeth at the wydwes gate'.[18] The account of Griselda's circumstances is fuller (*CT* 4: 197–203, 223–31): her father's house is in a village, within which poor folk keep their animals and their lodgings; Griselda spins, keeps a few sheep, and has one field that is apart from the house, since, when she returns home each night, she brings cabbages or herbs for supper. When Walter rides out hunting, he sees her at her labors. As in the French translation, but not Petrarch's account, Walter watches Griselda when he rides out hunting. Chaucer thus composes a scene that is faithful to his sources while also recalling the scene in *Piers Plowman* and Piers's advice to the knight standing beside him—to hunt in order to protect Piers's croft. Walter hunts for pleasure. Griselda seems to act out the advice encoded in Piers's son's name.[19] If we read the account of Griselda and of the widow in terms of their *literal* circumstances, the questions asked through both scenes concern civil and ecclesiastical power as it touches the lives of the rural poor. Though such questions are compelling for Langland and Chaucer, it is in the Nun's Priest's tale that Chaucer fully and daringly exploits the potential latent within Langland's reference to Piers's croft.

[18] *Friar's Tale* in *The Canterbury Tales* 3: 1581, in *The Riverside Chaucer*, third edn, ed. Larry D. Benson (Boston: Houghton Mifflin Company, 1987). All quotations from the works of Chaucer are taken from this edition and will be cited in the text by fragment and line.

[19] See Thomas J. Farrell and Amy W. Goodwin, 'The Clerk's Tale', in *Sources and Analogues of The Canterbury Tales*, ed. Robert M. Correale and Mary Hamel (Cambridge: D.S. Brewer, 2002), 114–15, 144–5.

Two of Chaucer's sources for the Nun's Priest's tale contain fairly detailed accounts of enclosed yards that would have been recognizable as crofts in Britain.[20] *Le Roman de Renart* describes the household of a very wealthy peasant, whose well-stocked house is close by the farmyard, the whole property 'enclosed with stout, pointed oak stakes reinforced with hawthorn bushes'. Renart enters through a broken stake though Chantecler proclaims the enclosure safe. Similarly, in *Le Roman de Renart le Contrefait*, a wealthy peasant has enclosed his property with walls and hedges 'because he feared for himself a great deal, lest someone should take his possessions or do him grief'; his rooster, Chantecler, feels himself safe because his lord is a rich man. Both D. W. Robertson and Larry Scanlon have pointed out the anti-fraternal satire of the Renart fables, where the smooth-talking fox/friar baffles and captures the foolish rooster/priest, who, lulled by his apparent safety, is easily flattered and almost brought to ruin.[21]

Chaucer alters the design in order to suggest a potential relationship between croft and nation. The tale begins, not with a wealthy, greedy peasant, but with a poor widow, a dairywoman, whose hall is sooty and whose diet is as simple as Griselda's. She has a cottage near a wood, in a valley and 'a yeerd... enclosed al aboute/ With stikkes, and a drye dych withoute' (7: 2847–8), in which she has her rooster, Chauntecleer. Chaucer's description of the rooster (7: 2850–64) has no counterpart in his sources. After praising his crowing, the Nun's Priest goes on:

> His coomb was redder than the fyn coral,
> And batailled as it were a castel wal;
> His byle was blak, and as the jeet it shoon;
> Lyk asure were his legges and his toon;
> His nayles whitter than the lylye flour,
> And lyk the burned gold was his colour. (7: 2859–64)

With red comb, black shiny beak, azure legs and toes, white nails, and burned gold color, Chauntecleer is the very image of a royal rooster ('Real he was'; 'Thus roial, as a prince is in his halle' [7: 3176, 3184]), as splendid as any figure in the Wilton Diptych, as splendid as Richard himself sitting enthroned in his hall.[22] What we see

[20] Edward Wheatley, 'The Nun's Priest's Tale', in *Sources and Analogues of The Canterbury Tales*, 456–7, 474–5. Marie de France's version (454–5) only places the rooster on a dungheap.

[21] Robertson, *A Preface to Chaucer*, 251–2; Larry Scanlon, *Narrative, Authority, and Power: the Medieval Exemplum and the Chaucerian Tradition* (Cambridge: Cambridge University Press, 1994), 230. See especially *Le Roman de Renart Contrefait*, in *Sources and Analogues of The Canterbury Tales*, ll. 31511–33180. See also the picture of preaching fox/friar in G. R. Owst, *Preaching in Medieval England: An Introduction to Sermon Manuscripts of the Period* (Cambridge: Cambridge University Press, 1926), 86.

[22] Elizabeth Salter, 'Medieval Poetry and the Visual Arts', *Essays and Studies*, 22 (1969), 19; Derek Pearsall (ed.), *The Variorum Edition of the Works of Geoffrey Chaucer*, vol. 2, pt. 9: *The Nun's Priest's Tale* (Norman: University of Oklahoma Press, 1984), 150–1; Lynn Staley Johnson, '"To Make in Som Comedy": Chauntecleer, Son of Troy', *Chaucer Review*, 19 (1985): 226–44; Staley, *Languages of Power in the Age of Richard II*, 142–4.

is not a rooster, but the icon of a rooster inserted into a barnyard fable and at a time when Richard began to adapt some of the Valois mannerisms of regality to his public appearances in his own hall.[23]

This poor widow's yard, hedged and ditched, containing a regal rooster, is not invulnerable to the likes of foxes; nor is the rooster impervious to flattery. The fox 'brast / Into the yerd ther Chauntecleer the faire / Was wont, and eek his wyves, to repaire' (7: 3218–20). The courtly epithet and the verb *repaire* describe not chickens but courtiers and, like the apostrophe comparing the fox to Ganelon, Judas, and Sinon and the simile likening the upset of the hens when Chauntecleer is captured to women's cries when Troy, Carthage, or Rome burned (7: 3355–73), assimilate the barnyard disaster to national. The reference a few lines later, comparing the chaos—bees out of the hive, geese honking, dogs barking, people shouting—to the noise during the Rising of 1381 serves to locate the analogies, not in the realm of mythic history, but in Britain's history, its own instance of discord and failure of authority. Langland follows up the account of the half-acre with its gradual dissolution because of greed, wasting, laziness, or chicanery. In B: 19, C: 21, the half-acre and its Plowman return, but this time as an allegory wherein the Plowman sows the seed of charity with the help of the four Evangelists, who are the oxen hauling his plow. Chaucer maintains the careful connection between the widow's croft and the commonwealth, depicting a rooster who now recognizes the dangers of the courtly speech practised by foxes and a henyard now safer, not because of its hedge, but because of its chastened prince.

The image here stands in subtle contrast to the tiny icon on the orb of the banner in the Wilton Diptych, the noble island with its castle surrounded by the sea, given to Mary and returned to the vested young king as his cure. The Nun's Priest provides something more complicated, a poor widow's holding (and if the widow is a figure for the Church, her *dos* is poor, indeed), hedged and ditched, ruled by a rooster, permeable to foxes who speak with oiled phrases, restored through wit, possibly guaranteed through experience. Langland's choice of the half-acre, the croft, as a sign allowing him to think about nation or national order, is startling when juxtaposed to Edward's decision to found the Order of the Garter several years before. In exchange for the noble order with its sumptuous chivalric ideals and furnishings, devoted to the Blessed Virgin, and focused on the king, Langland proffers the peasant's holding, whose need for knightly protection is explicit but which is not identified with or seen as an appendage to noble privilege. Langland then quickly assimilates that image (which stands as a corrective to tournament fields, battle fields, and aristocratic excess) to the spiritual demands of Will's quest for understanding and meaning. There the A text ends, apparently

[23] See Nigel Saul, *Richard II* (New Haven, CT: Yale University Press, 1997), 340–58, for an analysis of the mannerisms of Richard's court.

unfinished, with the assertion that none are further from right belief than clerks who know many books, and

> Ne none sonnere ysavid, ne saddere of conscience,
> Thanne pore peple, as ploughmen, and pastours of bestis,
> Souteris & seweris; suche lewide iottis
> Percen with a paternoster the paleis of hevene
> Withoute penaunce at here partyng, into [the] heighe blisse. (A: 11, 309–13)

Passus 12, added on to the A text, as well as the rewritings of this scene in the B and C texts of the poem, point up the dangers in Will's assumption that it is easier to get to heaven without learning and thus blur the picture A provides of plowmen, shepherds, shoemakers, and sewers piercing the palace of heaven with the Our Father.[24] In the B and C texts of *Piers Plowman*, Langland allows the agricultural references to plowmen and shepherds to assume their full spiritual significance only after Will's apprehension of the Passion and its meaning for earthly systems of order.[25] The half-acre, the croft, becomes a way of seeing the Christian society, whose order acquires meaning from the seed that Piers, the Plowman/Preacher sows with the four Evangelists.

In taking a fable linked to ecclesiastical satire and focusing it upon regal authority, employing the homely image, the barnyard, as the landscape for royal chastening, Chaucer seems to offer both a shrewd reading of Langland's text(s) and a careful critique of the thinking that inspired the Wilton Diptych, if not of the Diptych itself. Chauntecleer may look like a king, but he lives in a croft, and he stays there. At no point does Chaucer suggest we should see the croft as belonging to the rooster or as a gift of his office, though his folly jeopardizes its order. Chauntecleer's office takes meaning from the croft and its residents, not the other way around; he serves his hens and the poor widow, as the coronation service for English kings suggests. As a rooster, he must abide by the laws of nature; as a king, by the laws of the land.

In *Mum and the Sothseggar*, the substitution of the croft for the noble island as a suitable image for Britain is even more apparent.[26] The poem belongs to the reign of Henry IV and describes the narrator's efforts to understand the conditions of a good society. Like *Piers Plowman*, which it imitates, it describes a search, but a search not for theological understanding but for moral and civil. After much confusion about the merits of staying mum about wrong (and thus profiting from his silence) or speaking the truth (and possibly jeopardizing himself in the

[24] See B:10, 465–9; C:11, 292–7, which gives the passage to Recchelessnesse. See also Pearsall, *Piers Plowman... an edition of the C-text*, 208, n. 290a.

[25] See Aers, *Piers Plowman and Christian Allegory*, 113; *Piers Plowman* B:19; C:21.

[26] *Richard the Redeless and Mum and the Sothsegger*, ed. James M. Dean (Kalamazoo, MI: Medieval Institute Publications, 2000); in *Languages of Power in the Age of Richard II*, 323–4, I relate *Mum* to the concerns of the georgic.

name of common profit), the narrator falls asleep. In his dream the narrator moves first through an abundant landscape of laden fields, trees, and bushes, where hares play and hounds chase, where there are sheep and cows and their young, stallions, and an abundance of all sorts of deer—'Foure hunthrid on a herde yheedid ful faire, / Layen lowe in a launde along by the pale, / A swete sight for souvrayns, so me God helpe' (929–31). After the sight of such plenty, including the promise of good hunting, the narrator moves down into a valley, among hedges filled with nesting birds, then sights a 'faire hous with halles and chambres, / A frankeleynis freholde' (945–6). Though the humble croft, the half-acre, has disappeared, the franklin's freehold has an enclosed garden ('the gladdest gardyn that gome ever had', 948), into which the narrator goes.

The poet uses this garden and its ancient, wise gardener, whose exposition upon apiculture links the order of the bees to that of the state, as a figure for nation. The upper landscape, woods and fields filled with delights for ladies (905) and sovereigns, is anchored by the freehold, which contains the secret of the good society, wherein drones who waste the honey that nourishes the hive are identified and destroyed and the order and thrift of the wise king of the bees is maintained in a strictly hierarchical society 'ygouverned / Yn lowlynes and labour and in lawe eeke' (997). The gardener himself seems the personification of that law, for it is he who destroys the drones, he who maintains the king's order, and he who urges the narrator to seek out Truth, to write something that may 'amende many men of thaire misdeedes' (1279). The old man thus links the picture of the common good, figured in an enclosed georgic space, to the art of making a book, copied and clasped, that lays out Truth for knights to copy and read (1286–7). The narrator then wakes and begins again his search in a world where many are mum and few are true. The freehold, which serves as an image for an idealized Britain, suggests how securely the enclosed and working garden has been embedded in the political imagination—not the ecclesiastical garden, but the peasant or the franklin or the gentry garden, maintained by discernment, by truth, by law.[27]

Britain the island/garden became a sort of national trope. In 1436 the author of the *Libelle of Englyshe Polycye*, in which Henry V is praised as a 'master Mariner', describes the sea as a wall around Britain, guaranteeing its peace and prosperity.[28] The connection between insularity and safety, which seems to be alluded to in the tiny image on the orb of the Wilton Diptych, passed into common parlance in John of Gaunt's speech in *Richard II* in which he offers an encomium whose key elements are drawn from this medieval tradition:

[27] For remarks on the gentry garden see Lynn Staley, 'Susanna and English Communities', *Traditio*, 62 (2007), 25–58.

[28] George Warner (ed.), *The Libelle of Englyshe Polycye: A Poem on the Use of Sea-Power 1436* (Oxford: Clarendon Press, 1926), ll. 1092–5.

This royal throne of kings, this sceptred isle,
This earth of majesty, this seat of Mars,
This other Eden, demi-paradise,
This fortress built by Nature for herself
Against infection and the hand of war,
This happy breed of men, this little world,
This precious stone set in the silver sea,
Which serves it in the office of a wall
Or as a moat defensive to a house
Against the envy of less happier lands,
This blessed plot, this earth, this realm, this England...[29]

Gaunt's praise ends in the bitter irony of 'This land... Is now leased out... Like to a tenement or pelting farm' (2.1.57, 59–60). In the next act the gardeners describe the nation in Langlandian terms, as Richard's unlucky and unweeded garden in which 'law and form and due proportion' have been ignored (3.4.41), suggesting that England is less the safe and sacred island than an untended *croft*.

Shakespeare's trope has added resonance when set within the concatenation of images of Britain to be found in the fourteenth and fifteenth centuries. First, Gaunt's encomium defines Britain's majestic earth in relation to noble identifying traits—fortresses, moated homes, and scepters. These are 'farmed out' by Richard's profligacy and greed, the blessed plot become a tenement, rented to the highest bidder. On the other hand, like the old man in *Mum and the Sothseggar*, the gardeners speak for law as restraining majesty, as maintaining a 'firm estate' in '*our* sea-walled garden' (3.4.42–3). The gardeners' easy analogy between *their* garden and the realm, between unruly plants and ambitious men, as well as their casual assumption that the state of the garden concerns them, substitute another image for the 'precious stone set in the silver sea', just as Chaucer's croft and *Mum*'s freehold offer a way of conceptualizing Britain vastly different from the castellated island in the silver sea of the Diptych's orb.[30] The one image rests upon stasis undergirded by privilege, the other upon a law that must be internalized and executed for the good of all in a realm set within necessity or change.

As numerous studies have demonstrated, the language of horticulture translated easily into that of statecraft, particularly in the sixteenth century when those monastic gardens and enclosures that had earlier helped to define the geography of Britain were opened and sold to a rising nobility. Carried over from medieval horticultural tropes, that early modern political rhetoric reflects a similar (and sometimes conflicting) set of interests in insularity and in law as they help to provide focus for a conception of the identity of the realm. This rhetoric falls

[29] *King Richard II*, ed. Charles R. Forker (London: The Arden Shakespeare, 2002), 2.1.40–50. See Forker's notes to the passage, which cite Peele, DuBartas, Greene, Daniel, Sylvester, and Lodge.

[30] See Gordon, *Making and Meaning: the Wilton Diptych*, 82, for the provenance of the Diptych, the earliest record of which is in the collection of Charles I.

roughly into two categories, of husbandry and of aristocratic landscape architecture.[31] Both are employed by Shakespeare in *Richard II*, and both are predicated upon a recognition of loss that is inextricable from the geography of Britain from the Reformation onwards.[32] For example, John Bale's epistle to the reader that prefaces John Leland's *Laboryouse Journey* cites Gildas and goes on to lament Britain's own fall from learning and hence civilization, saying 'neyther the Brytaynes under the Romanes & Saxons, nor yet the Englyshe people under the Danes and Normanes, had ever suche damage of their lerned monuments, as we have seane in our time'.[33] Bale speaks of lost books, the histories that are monuments to the past. Less than a century later, Gervase Markham notes,

> Although... the nature of this worst part of this last age hath converted all things to such wildnesse that whatsoever is truely good is now esteemed most vitious, learning being derided, fortitude drawne into so many definitions that it consisteth in meere words onely, and although nothing is happy or prosperous, but meere fashion & ostentation, a tedious fustian tale at a great man's table...

He then defines a husbandman as 'a good man', 'turning sterrilitie and barrainenesse into fruitfulness and increase, whereby all common wealths are maintained', giving liberty to all vocations, 'Arts, misteries and trades'.[34] If this were the twelfth century, Markham might be introducing the Cistercians, those good husbandmen who turned waste and wildness into order and plenty, as Langland's plowman would attempt to create an image of national order from a half acre and

[31] For medieval horticultural language, see Staley, *Languages of Power in the Age of Richard II*, 291–303. On the subject of early modern husbandry and agrarian reform, see Andrew McRae, *God Speed the Plough: the Representation of Agrarian England, 1500–1660* (Cambridge: Cambridge University Press, 1996); Joan Thirsk, 'Plough and Pen: Agricultural Writers in the Seventeenth Century', in *Social Relations and Ideas: Essays in Honour of R. H. Hilton*, ed. T. H. Aston, P. R. Cross, Christopher Dyer, and Joan Thirsk (Cambridge: Cambridge University Press, 1983), 295–318; Wendy Wall, 'Renaissance National Husbandry: Gervase Markham and the Publication of England', *Sixteenth-Century Journal*, 27 (1996), 767–85. On the subject of the private garden, estate, or great house, see Kari Boyd McBride, *Country House Discourse in Early Modern England: A Cultural Study of Landscape and Legitimacy* (Burlington: Ashgate, 2001); William A. McClung, *The Country House in English Renaissance Poetry* (Berkeley: University of California Press, 1977); Roy Strong, *The Renaissance Garden in England* (London: Thames and Hudson, 1979); Don E. Wayne, *Penshurst: The Semiotics of Place and the Poetics of History* (Madison: Wisconsin University Press, 1984). For essays relevant to the entire field, see Michael Leslie and Timothy Raylor (eds.), *Culture and Cultivation in Early Modern England: Writing and the Land* (Leicester: Leicester University Press, 1992).

[32] See James Simpson, *Reform and Cultural Revolution*, The Oxford English Literary History, Vol. 2: *1350–1547* (Oxford: Oxford University Press, 2002), Chapter 1; Jennifer Summit, 'Leland's *Itinerary* and the Remains of the Medieval Past', in *Reading the Medieval in Early Modern England*, ed. Gordon McMullan and David Matthews (Cambridge: Cambridge University Press, 2007), 159–76.

[33] 'To the Reader', in John Leland, *Laboryouse Journey* (Norwood, NJ: Theatrum Orbis Terrarum/Walter J. Johnson, Inc., 1975), Bii-r.

[34] Gervase Markham, 'Epistle to the Reader', in *The English Husbandman* (1613) (New York: Garland Publishing, 1982).

Hugh Latimer's plowmen/preachers were urged to till the waiting soil of barren hearts.[35]

That same sense of loss and need for reparation invigorated the group around the reformer Samuel Hartlib in the mid-seventeenth century, which included Ralph Austen, Cressy Dimock, and John Beale, all of whom studied agriculture as an 'experimental science to be disseminated for the public good'.[36] Ralph Austen in *A treatise of fruit trees* (1653) drew upon the trope of *anglia hortus*, what Andrew McRae has described as the new agricultural rhetoric of improvement and profit, in his efforts to promote the planting of fruit trees:

> An eminent person once said of this Nation, that it is a very Garden of delights, and a Well that cannot be exhausted: What then would it be, did it abound with goodly Fruit-trees, & other Profits, where now are barren Wastes: Might it not then be called another Canaan, flowing with Milke and hony, of which it is recorded that there were Fruit-trees in abundance. Nehem.9.25

Austen does not link the dearth of fruit trees to the Dissolution, through which the monks' horticultural knowledge was lost, but rather emphasizes the benefits to the 'commonwealth' and to the poor that enclosed orchards would provide.[37]

Where agricultural writers seem interested in improvements to the croft, Ben Jonson and those who wrote encomia to the great houses of the aristocracy provide pictures of estates whose hierarchical order reflects an idealized picture of Britain, the island paradise, at once enclosed and permeable. Thus Jonson asserts of Penshurst that fruit that 'every child may reach' hangs upon its walls, walls that are 'reared with no man's ruin, no man's groan' and provide not a barrier but a point of entry for all, 'the farmer, and the clown'.[38] Set apart and within its land, maintained by its owner, who is its steward, who is, in turn, placed in relation to his king and his God, Penshurst reminds its readers of the ideals undergirding the island/garden of Britain in an age of excess where houses are built for show and walls are signs of exclusion, envy, and hatred. The abundance that Jonson describes

[35] Hugh Latimer, 'Sermon of the Plough', in *Sermons* (London: J.M. Dent, 1906), 54–71.

[36] Rebecca Bushnell, *Green Desire: Imagining Early Modern English Gardens* (Ithaca, NY: Cornell University Press, 2003), 30. On Hartlib, see Timothy Raylor, 'Samuel Hartlib and the Commonwealth of Bees', in *Culture and Cultivation in Early Modern England*, ed. Leslie and Raylor, 91–129.

[37] Ralph Austen, *A Treatise of Fruit Trees* (Oxford, 1653), 'Epistle'. Austen is pro-enclosure, going so far as to recommend setting aside spots for the poor, 'their share', thus enclosing waste and common ground. 'Anglia Hortus' is the title of a poem by Mildmay Fane, second Earl of Westmoreland, in which he draws upon the idea of England as a garden. See Alexander B. Grosart (ed.), *The Poems of Mildmay, Second Earl of Westmoreland (1648)* (privately printed, 1879), 133. For associations between Mildmay and Marvell, see Rosalie L. Colie, *My Ecchoing Song: Andrew Marvell's Poetry of Criticism* (Princeton, NJ: Princeton University Press, 1970), 225; McClung, *The Country House in English Renaissance Poetry*, 154. On the loss of horticultural knowledge with the Dissolution, see Charles Quest-Ritson, *The English Garden: A Social History* (Boston: David Godine, 2003), 34, 37.

[38] 'To Penshurst', in *Ben Jonson: the Complete Poems*, ed. George Parfitt (New Haven, CT: Yale University Press, 1982), 95–8, lines 44, 46, 48.

Penshurst as boasting evokes earlier public tributes to Richard II and Elizabeth I, whose accessions to the throne were heralded with sprouting trees and gushing fountains and, indeed, were described as producing green leaves and wine where there had been only waste.[39] The garden thus stood as a sign of privilege or special favor, a space at once private and bound within a network of communal concerns. Thomas More's wife, Dame Alice, warned him when he was in the Tower that he would lose his garden, one of the eight magnificent gardens along the Thames that bespoke the social position of their owners, a garden in which he had walked and talked intimately with Henry in happier times.[40] Such spaces do not demand agrarian improvement in the name of profit but stand as tokens of the bonds of hierarchical ordering.

In 'Upon Appleton House' Marvell did not simply inherit these images of national identity, he employed them in ways that suggest he understood them as lenses through which to view and perhaps compose a history of Britain.[41] To say Marvell employed images drawn from medieval accounts of Britain is to suggest that he knew them as belonging to a historiographic language. He was certainly in the right time and place for such a venture. By the time Marvell became tutor to Maria Fairfax (late 1650 to late 1652) at Appleton House in Yorkshire where he wrote the poem in 1651, he would have had ample opportunity to investigate the monuments of Britain's history.

Born in Hull, in the East Riding of Yorkshire, Marvell had been educated at Cambridge, and studied law in London. Yorkshire was dense with the ruins of medieval ecclesiastical foundations, both near Hull and further west, near Fairfax's properties. Many of these ruins were Cistercian, as was Nun Appleton, become Appleton House by Marvell's time. Sir Robert Cotton's library in London drew upon the wealth of despoiled books and manuscripts to be found in Yorkshire.[42] Cotton was a friend of William Camden's, both of the generation previous to Marvell's, and both catalysts for the antiquarian energy represented by Sir William

[39] See Gordon Kipling, *Enter the King: Theatre, Liturgy, and Ritual in the Medieval Civic Triumph* (Oxford: Clarendon Press, 1998), 163–7, 234–6; George Kernodle, *From Art to Theatre: Form and Convention in the Renaissance* (Chicago: University of Chicago Press, 1944), 73; Roy Strong, *The Cult of Elizabeth: Elizabethan Portraiture and Pageantry* (London: Thames and Hudson, 1977), 114–63.

[40] C. Paul Christianson, *The Riverside Gardens of Thomas More's London* (New Haven, CT: Yale University Press, 2005), 6–7, 83, 200; A. L. Rowse (ed.), *A Man of Singular Virtue: being a Life of Sir Thomas More... and a selection of More's letters* (London: Folio Society, 1980), 44; Sir Francis Bacon, 'Of Gardens', in *The Essayes or Counsels, Civill and Morall*, ed. Michael Kiernan (Cambridge, MA: Harvard University Press, 1985), 139–45.

[41] All quotations from 'Upon Appleton House' refer to *The Poems of Andrew Marvell*, ed. Nigel Smith, rev. edn (London: Pearson Longman, 2007), 216–41. For evidence of Marvell's historic and political consciousness as it is manifested here, see Annabel Patterson, *Marvell and the Civic Crown* (Princeton, NJ: Princeton University Press, 1978), 95–110; Patsy Griffin, '"Twas no Religious House till now": Marvell's "Upon Appleton House"', *SEL*, 28 (1988), 61–76; Smith's copious notes and Introduction, 210–16.

[42] Colin G. C. Tite, *The Early Records of Sir Robert Cotton's Library* (London: British Library, 2003).

Dugdale, who sought to preserve the knowledge of the past in the face of rising anti-episcopal pressures and, along with Roger Dodsworth, the author of the *Monasticon Anglicanum,* the first volume of which appeared in 1655. The *Monasticon* marks the beginning of monastic history after the Dissolution. Dugdale was also close to Elias Ashmole, who from the 1650s devoted his antiquarian interests to the history of the Order of the Garter.[43]

Martin Dzelzainis and Annabel Patterson have convincingly argued that Marvell had access to and used the library belonging to the earl of Anglesey in London; it is unlikely he ignored either the books in Thomas Fairfax's library or those to be found in that of Henry Fairfax, Thomas's uncle and rector of Bolton Priory, which had once been an Augustinian foundation.[44] Moreover, by this time, there are contemporary references to the Wilton Diptych, which was in the collection of Charles I, as well as antiquarian interest in Edward III and his foundation of the Order of the Garter.[45] While 'Upon Appleton House' certainly can be read within the traditions of the pastoral and/or the georgic address, it can also be described as a secret history of Britain, poised somewhere between hope and regret, a continuation of those medieval attempts to use the tropes of the past to sacralize the present.

There was precedent for Marvell's deployment of pastoral address in the service of history. Both Ben Jonson, to whose 'Penshurst' he alludes in the opening stanzas of 'Upon Appleton House', and John Denham, whose *Cooper's Hill* was published in 1642, construct their historically rooted critiques of the present through pastoral description. Both Jonson and Denham draw upon tropes of insularity to explore the nature of the geographies they describe. Jonson uses Penshurst, its bounty, its proportion, its inclusive insularity as a type of little Britain, focused by its devotion to sovereign and God, bound within a chain of private and public virtues whose very simplicity is a reproach to present excess and a reminder of a lost age. Denham surveys London from Cooper's Hill and, finding it sooty from business and vain labor (ll. 29–31), turns to Windsor where he recalls the history of Edward III and the founding of the Order of the Garter. The encircling blue garter imaginatively expands to become the encircling sea, joined to Britain by the Thames, which reaches around the world, at once protecting Britain and bringing to her tributes

[43] See *Dictionary of National Biography* for both Dugdale and Ashmole. For Dodsworth, see N. Denholm-Young and H. H. E. Craster, 'Roger Dodsworth and His Circle', *Yorkshire Archaelogical Journal,* 32 (1934), 5–32.

[44] Annabel Patterson and Martin Dzelzainis, 'Marvel and the Earl of Anglesey: A Chapter in the History of Reading', *The Historical Journal,* 44 (2001), 703–27. For Thomas Fairfax's books, see F. Madden, H. H. E. Craster, and N. Nenholm-Young (eds.), *A Summary Catalogue of Western Manuscripts in the Bodleian Library at Oxford,* vol. 2, part 2 (Oxford: Clarendon Press, 1937), 770–87. For Henry Fairfax, see the book list in BL MS Sloane 1872, fol. 60–81b. Thanks to Nigel Smith for answers to my questions about these libraries.

[45] See Stephanie Trigg, 'The Vulgar History of the Order of the Garter', in *Reading the Medieval in Early Modern England,* ed. Gordon McMullan and David Matthews (Cambridge: Cambridge University Press, 2007), 91–105.

from other countries (101–86).[46] Denham's account of place is inevitably an account of the history of the place, but he also uses landscape, the river constrained by the greedy husbandman, the greedy water impatient with its narrow channel, to comment upon the necessity for royal measure and popular obedience.

Marvell is less resolute, certainly less forthright, than either Jonson or Denham, channeling history through landscape, suggesting the delights and temptations of insularity, the renewals of the present that are built upon the 'demolishings' of the past, the need for those in the present to invent a sacred myth to give meaning to their own rebuilt ruins. He builds into his account of the Fairfax estate two key tropes that link it to ancient histories of a sacralized Britain of the island garden and of the *dos Mariae.*

That the two are joined as identifying features of Appleton House is apparent from stanza 10, which moves the poem away from its careful nod to Jonson in the first nine stanzas emphasizing the relatively modest and proportioned character of the house and anchors it in myths of Britain. Stanza 10 points up the natural beauty of Appleton House, what Nature has 'laid so sweetly waste; / In fragrant gardens, shady woods, / Deep meadows, and transparent floods'. This beautiful land, like the *Brut*'s legend of Britain's origins, can trace its history to Amazonian unnaturalness, which Marvell recounts in the mini-history of Isabel Thwaites and William Fairfax, whose kidnapping of her in 1518 rescued her from the nuns' grasp, that is embedded in the poem at stanzas 11–35: 'A nunnery first gave it birth'; those nuns serve as crude reminders of Britain's Catholic past, which is conceived of as isolating, rather than as expansively insular. Marvell's nuns are self-described 'virgin Amazons' (106), who desire Thwaites for her fortune and her beauty, which they promise will be cherished each night, when she will lie chastely with another nun, 'All night embracing arm in arm, / Like crystal pure with cotton warm' (191–2). The suggestion links the nuns to the Amazonian Albina and her sisters, whose unnatural dominance and sexuality produced the grotesque giants that Brutus must kill before claiming Britain. In Isabel Thwaites, the nuns claim to see the Virgin's face, which would allow them to embroider the likeness of Mary using their prospective nun as a model:

> But much it to our work would add
> If here your hand, your face we had:
> By it we would Our Lady touch;
> Yet thus She you resembles much.
> Some of your features, as we sewed,

[46] All references to *Cooper's Hill* (1642 edition) are drawn from *The Poetical Works of Sir John Denham*, ed. Theodore Howard Banks, Jr. (New Haven, CT: Yale University Press, 1928), 63–89. See William Rockett, '"Courts Make Not Kings, but Kings the Court": *Cooper's Hill* and the Constitutional Crisis of 1642', *Restoration: Studies in English Literary Culture, 1660–1700*, 17 (1993), 1–14; Rufus Putney, 'The View from Cooper's Hill', *University of Colorado Studies: Series in Language and Literature*, 6 (1957), 13–22.

Through every shrine should be bestowed.
And in one beauty we would take
Enough a thousand saints to make. (17: 129–36)

Line 132, which suggests that the Virgin resembles the girl, rather than vice versa, underlines the nuns' inordinate desire; moreover, they offer her the temptations of Narcissus, whereby she should see her face multiplied throughout the convent, as though it were a pool reflecting her beauty.

However, the convent, the consecrated site of beauty and falsely directed desire, becomes reconsecrated when Fairfax carries Isabel away to marriage. Marvell thus reworks the traditions of Bedan history whereby invasion becomes reconstitution:

At the demolishing, this seat
To Fairfax fell as by escheat.
And what both nuns and founders willed
'Tis likely better thus fulfilled.
For if the virgin proved not their's,
The cloister yet remainèd her's.
Though many a nun there made her vow,
'Twas no religious house till now. (35: 273–80)

Marvell's irony here cuts both ways. He refers not to the Dissolution, a term commonly used to describe the dissolving of the monasteries, but to the 'demolishing', thus underlining the violence visited upon these virgin buildings. He then proclaims that the nuns' wish to give her the convent was ironically fulfilled and ends with ''Twas no religious house till now', asserting the sacrality of chaste marriage over their monstrous chastity. Since Isabel resembles the Virgin, Appleton House remains in the Virgin's gift.

Marvell's treatment of Maria Fairfax, Thomas's daughter and only heir, links her both to Isabel and to the Virgin, patron of Britain's island garden. He describes her as a virgin nymph, 'with the flowers a flower to be' (301–2), and as the ordering principle for the estate's natural beauty (stanzas 82–94), which nourishes her as she grows to her own destiny. In these stanzas, Marvell presents Maria, or Mary, as the source of beauty, ''Tis she that to these gardens gave / That wondrous beauty which they have' (689–90). Maria is also, like the Virgin, the source of evening peace and stillness, 'Maria such, and so doth hush / The world' (681–2), the figure to whom the estate returns its own gifts:

Therefore what first she on them spent,
They gratefully again present:
The meadow carpets where to tread;
The garden flowers to crown her head;
And for a glass the limpid brook
Where she may all her beauties look;
But, since she would not have them seen,
The wood about her draws a screen. (88: 697–704)

Maria refuses the solipsistic delights the brook offers her, but the chain of giving Marvell describes, like that belonging to the Graces, is one in which she is gladly bound, for she gives beauty only to receive it back, and return it once more. Marvell's description of Appleton House and its beauty as being in the gift of Maria backs a poet's fancy with a father's care, for Thomas Fairfax had broken the terms of the entail to settle the estate upon his only child.[47] It was literally the *dos Mariae.* This old name for Britain was current in the seventeenth century, and, if Marvell had ever seen the Wilton Diptych, his account of Maria as the source for vernal beauty might be even more pointed; for, where Richard kneels in a wasteland, Mary and her vanguard stand in flowers, offering a picture of garden loveliness that resonates with Bede's account of this beautiful, bountiful land called Britain.[48]

Marvell describes Appleton House as though it were Britain, surrounded by a 'sea' when the sluicegates of Denton, Fairfax's higher estate, are opened, abounding with loveliness tempting the narrator (and possibly Fairfax) to solipsistic monastic repose, patronized by the young Maria, whose virgin beauty protects and vivifies it. Like Britain, the landscape contains evidence of violence, the mowers who bloody the rails in leveling the meadows (stanzas 50–53), the royal oak weakened by the traitor worm (554) and then hacked down, the power of time itself that may make of it a pilgrimage site in the future and that signals the end of day, the end of the poem. In fact, the final stanza, with its salmon fishermen coming to shore, their shapes now unclear in the dark, ends the poem, not with Ben Jonson's acclamation, 'thy lord dwells', but with the irresolution of darkness, with the impression that the panorama the poet has offered derives whatever meaning it has from its relation to a past that is shadowed in the poem's present. Maria's future is only potential and set within a landscape that is a testimony to 'demolishing'. As to Appleton House, it epitomizes those attempts to construe identity from circumstance and need, to name as sacred a space whose security can only be contingent, locating Marvell within the company of those who wrote Britain's history through its geography.

FURTHER READING

Clarke, Catherine A. M. *Literary Landscapes and the Idea of England, 700–1400* (Cambridge: D.S. Brewer, 2006)

[47] Colie, *My Ecchoing Song*, 222–4; George W. Johnson, *The Fairfax Correspondence: Memoirs of the Reign of Charles the First*, 2 vols. (London: Richard Bentley, 1848), 2: 109.

[48] See T. E. Bridgett, *Our Lady's Dower or How England gained and lost that title* (London: Burns and Oates, 1875); London, BL MS Harley 360, fol. 98v, where a marginal note to this anti-Catholic tract reads, 'England of long time hath bin said to be our Ladyes Dowrie'.

Gordon, Dillian, Lisa Monas, and Caroline Elam (eds.). *The Regal Image of Richard II and the Wilton Diptych* (London: Harvey Miller Publishers, 1997)

MacRae, Andrew. *God Speed the Plough: The Representation of Agrarian England, 1500–1660* (Cambridge: Cambridge University Press, 1996)

Leslie, Michael and Timothy Raylor (eds.). *Culture and Cultivation in Early Modern England: Writing and the Land* (Leicester: Leicester University Press, 1992)

CHAPTER 8

TRAVEL

ANDREW HADFIELD

An Englishman or woman studying maps in 1650 would have seen a very different world from that viewed by his or her ancestor in 1400. Technology had advanced so that trans-ocean travel was now possible and the globe had been circumnavigated by both Portuguese and English ships. The Americas had been discovered and inhabited by southern and northern Europeans.[1] They had established colonies on the new continent, at first rather tentatively and by the middle of the seventeenth century with a certain amount of confidence as native resistance proved unable to repel the invaders. Mapping, as well as navigational possibilities, had progressed a great deal so that it was now possible to represent more accurately much of the known world, an ever expanding series of territories.[2] Travel within Europe had become, if not much more straightforward, then rather easier, more comfortable, and more feasible. The same can be said of internal travel as a form of tourism, and by the end of that century men and a few women of more humble status had started to explore their own nation.[3] Nevertheless, although British travellers required a license and had restricted freedom of movement, some did explore the continent and beyond. The early seventeenth century saw the rise of the travel writer in the form of Fynes Moryson (1566–1630), Thomas Coryat (*c.*1577–1617) and William Lithgow (1582–*c.*1645), all of whom wrote and published substantial accounts of their extensive travels.

Yet we should be extremely cautious about assuming that the world had really changed beyond recognition or that it was perceived in a fundamentally different way, whatever the development of more sophisticated means of travelling and of understanding it. As is well known, Christopher Columbus went to his grave

[1] Samuel Eliot Morison, *The European Discovery of America: The Northern Voyages, A.D. 500–1600* (New York: Oxford University Press, 1971); and *The European Discovery of America: The Southern Voyages, A.D. 1492–1616* (New York: Oxford University Press, 1974).

[2] Paul Binding, *Imagined Corners: Exploring the World's First Atlas* (London: Review, 2003).

[3] Ian Ousby, *The Englishman's England: Taste, Travel and the Rise of Tourism* (Cambridge: Cambridge University Press, 1990).

convinced that he had reached the east coast of the empire of the Great Khan. Although others realised that he had travelled to a new continent, Columbus was too rooted in a reading of Marco Polo and Herodotus to understand the significance of his voyages and that he had discovered a new continent.[4] Columbus imagined that the fierce Caribs that he encountered—or, rather, thought that he encountered—were the man-eating savages he had learned about in Herodotus's *History* as well as soldiers of the Great Khan, a subtle piece of self-deluding mental gymnastics.[5] There was indeed an increasing scepticism about the miraculous and marvellous discoveries of many medieval travellers who found strange and weird creatures hidden away in the furthermost corners of the world, as in the Hereford *Mappa Mundi*, which showed the half-human, half-plant figure of the mandrake, and the sciapod, whose large foot was able to shelter its owner during times of excessive heat.[6] Yet, we should also note that the first serious compiler of English travel narratives, Richard Hakluyt (1552–1616), included the famous medieval work, *The Travels of Sir John Mandeville*, with its descriptions of the Garden of Eden and the land of Prester John, in the first edition of his major work, *The Principall Navigations, Voiages, and Discoveries of the English Nation* (1589), excluding it only in the second, expanded edition of 1598–1600. Columbus, Sir Martin Frobisher, and others consulted Mandeville before setting out on major voyages, citing his work as an inspiration to travellers and explorers.[7]

Moreover, as Mary Floyd-Wilson has noted, the ethnological models that Europeans used in the sixteenth century were hardly modern: 'Despite Europe's contact with the New World, the classification of people and nations during this period still conformed to the ancient tripartite divisions of climatic regions—northern, southern, and temperate zones.'[8] In fact, if we are looking for a progressive narrative that shows a clear path to modernity we may find ourselves surprised at the uneven development of Renaissance knowledge and some obvious problems. While an encounter with the New World genuinely inspired wonder at the scope and diversity of the known universe, it also fed a series of fears which encouraged a heightened xenophobia.[9] Kim Hall has persuasively argued that what we understand by racism is largely a product of the discovery of the Americas:

[4] Peter Hulme, *Colonial Encounters: Europe and the Native Caribbean, 1492–1797* (London: Methuen, 1986), Chapter 1.

[5] Hulme, *Colonial Encounters*, 21–2.

[6] Gabriel Alington, *The Hereford Mappa Mundi* (Leominster: Gracewing, 1996).

[7] Sir John Mandeville, *The Travels of Sir John Mandeville*. ed. C. W. R. D. Moseley (Harmondsworth: Penguin, 1983); Giles Milton, *The Riddle and the Knight: In Search of Sir John Mandeville* (London: Allison and Busby, 1996).

[8] Mary Floyd-Wilson, *English Ethnicity and Race in Early Modern Drama* (Cambridge: Cambridge University Press, 2003), 2. More generally, see Margaret Hodgen, *Early Anthropology in the Sixteenth and Seventeenth Centuries* (Philadelphia: University of Pennsylvania Press, 1971).

[9] Stephen Greenblatt, *Marvelous Possessions: The Wonder of the New World* (Oxford: Clarendon Press, 1991).

> [I]t is England's sense of losing its traditional insularity that provokes the development of 'racialism'. This moment of transition—England's movement from geographic isolation into military and mercantile contest with other countries—sets the stage for the longer process by which pre-existing literary tropes of blackness profoundly interacted with the fast-changing economic relations of white Europeans and their darker 'others' during the Renaissance.[10]

Larger geographical horizons did not necessarily make for a more expansive and generous understanding of humanity, suggesting that travel could narrow as well as broaden the mind.

And there are other more practical considerations that suggest that change was less rapid than we might expect. Mapping had not advanced enough to help the Spanish Armada after their defeat in the English Channel. Circumnavigating the British Isles in an attempt to get home, they did not sail far enough out into the Atlantic for fear of storms because their maps did not represent the rocky outreaches of the Irish coast. More perished than survived.[11] The amount of travel that took place in the early modern period can also be exaggerated, as the economy was still very clearly rooted in the soil in 1650, restricting the possibilities for most people who were tied to the agricultural year. It was only really after this date that the population in Britain began to expand before the advent of industrialization, creating enforced movement and a more obviously migrant people.[12] We should also not forget that travellers had been extremely active throughout the Middle Ages, in a variety of modes that continued into the early modern period.[13] Diplomatic, royal, and aristocratic travel continued much as before. Crossing the channel, for example, was a fraught and sometimes dangerous enterprise well into the eighteenth century, despite the obvious improvements in ship building.[14]

The easiest way to travel, as Thomas Nashe points out in *The Unfortunate Traveller* (1594), was to join the army, a fact that points to an obvious continuity between the Middle Ages and the Renaissance. If anything, the advent of more controlled warfare in the sixteenth century restricted the amount that ordinary

[10] Kim F. Hall, *Things of Darkness: Economies of Race and Gender in Early Modern England* (Ithaca, NY: Cornell University Press, 1995), 3–4; Walter D. Mignolo, *The Darker Side of the Renaissance: Literacy, Territoriality, and Colonization* (Michigan: University of Michigan Press, 1997); Floyd-Wilson, *English Ethnicity*, 14.

[11] T. P. Kilfeather, *Ireland, Graveyard of the Spanish Armada* (Dublin: Anvil, 1967).

[12] D. C. Coleman, *The Economy of England, 1450–1750* (Oxford: Oxford University Press, 1977), 91–115; Keith Wrightson, *English Social History, 1580–1680* (London: Hutchinson, 1982), Chapter 6; Alison Games, 'Migration', in *The British Atlantic World, 1500–1800*, ed. David Armitage and Michael J. Braddick (Basingstoke: Palgrave, 2000), 31–50.

[13] Margaret Wade Labage, *Medieval Travellers: The Rich and the Restless* (London: Hamish Hamilton, 1989); Norbert Ohler, *The Medieval Traveller*, trans. Caroline Hillier (Woodbridge: Boydell, 1989).

[14] Jeremy Black, *The British Abroad: The Grand Tour in the Eighteenth Century* (Stroud: Alan Sutton, 1992).

men could travel, especially after the end of the Crusades, which provide us with a wealth of cultural encounters and travel narratives well into the fifteenth century.[15] Although the European discovery of the Americas is now perceived as the turning point in world history because of what we know about subsequent historical developments, the main focus of Europe's attention was still turned towards the east in the sixteenth and seventeenth centuries and, in particular, to the Ottoman Empire.[16] Although William Shakespeare's *The Tempest* (*c.*1611) has been regularly taught in universities in the past two decades and has inspired numerous arguments about its relationship to American colonial history and colonial writings, it is an unusual play and therefore has been made to bear an excessive interpretative burden.[17] Far more typical are plays about Turks and Moors, suggesting that *Othello, the Moor of Venice* (*c.*1604), albeit unusual in casting a Black African as a tragic hero, is a more representative work.[18]

Perhaps the key impediment to travel was the Reformation, which split Europe in two and so made a large number of areas dangerous or off limits to European travellers. Whereas medieval pilgrims could and would travel easily enough to such central sites as the shrine of Saint James in Santiago de Compostela, their post-Reformation counterparts could not. After the fall of the crusader states in 1291, travel to European shrines increased, as pilgrims were no longer able to reach Jerusalem as easily. Rome and Santiago, in particular, were popular with pilgrims from all over Europe, eager for the experience of the greater pilgrimage (*peregrinatione maiore*). Other lesser sites, such as Aachen, Canterbury (as Chaucer's *Canterbury Tales* illustrates), Padua, Rocamadour, and Trier, also increased in importance and witnessed more traffic. Pilgrims purchased official guides which provided a wealth of useful information, much like modern tourist guides: 'The author gives advice on roads and rivers, bridges and hospices; food and drink; saints who must be honoured on the way... legends and anecdotes... are woven into the text.'[19] After the Reformation such works largely disappeared in England as they no longer served an obvious purpose for Protestants. Instead, it was possible to get hold of a series of guides to major cities, especially Venice, a key tourist location for travellers, because of its liberty, sexual promise (Venetian courtesans were reputed to be the best looking in Europe), as well as more general guides to European travel, most notably, Samuel

[15] Elizabeth Hallam, *Chronicles of the Crusades: Eye-Witness Accounts of the Wars Between Christianity and Islam* (London: Guild, 1989).

[16] Fernand Braudel, *The Mediterranean and the Mediterranean World in the Age of Philip II*, trans. Sian Reynolds, 2 vols. (London: Collins, 1972).

[17] Peter Hulme and William Sherman (eds.), *'The Tempest' and Its Travels* (London: Reaktion, 2000).

[18] Daniel Vitkus (ed.), *Three Turk Plays from early Modern England* (New York: Columbia University Press, 2000).

[19] Ohler, *Medieval Traveller*, 184.

Palmer's *An Essay of the Meanes How to Make Our Travailes More Profitable* (1606).[20]

There were always travellers who were prepared to go beyond what was generally expected or even acceptable. Despite the obvious dangers and discomforts, both Margery Kempe (*c.*1373–1438?) and William Lithgow (1582–1645) travelled to Rome, Jerusalem, and Spain almost exactly two centuries apart, the former in 1414–15 and 1417, the latter during his first major peregrination between 1609 and 1613, and his second in 1620. A comparison of their experiences tells us a great deal about the difference between the expectations of late medieval and Renaissance travellers, as well as the similarities between them. It also shows us that we should never think about travel writing as a subject on its own. Travellers are always embedded in the society in which they live and so interact with other societies according to the norms and expectations that they have learned as normal and natural. What a comparison of the travels of Kempe and Lithgow shows us is that we will have little chance of understanding how people perceived the world in earlier societies if we fail to consider their religious beliefs, a point that numerous historical works have made in recent years.[21]

Although Margery Kempe was an unusually determined and forceful personality, which is why the story of an illiterate businesswoman from King's Lynn has survived, her horizons and expectations were probably not far removed from those of many of her contemporaries. The difference between her and most other provincial men and women of the merchant class was that she accomplished what many of them would have hoped to achieve but would never have had the dedication or single-minded application to carry out. For Kempe, as her spiritual autobiography makes clear, the highpoints of her life were her pilgrimages to the three most significant sites for Medieval Christians: Santiago de Compostela, Rome, and Jerusalem. It was in these places, and during the journeys to them, that her most important religious experiences took place where she felt that she met and communed with God directly. Kempe had absorbed the notion of *peregrinatio*, life as a spiritual journey for those pure enough to make it, leading towards heavenly revelation. This monastic ideal is manifested not simply in religious texts for the spiritual clergy, but for laymen and women who had the necessary dedication, as expounded in works such as the anonymous romance, *The Quest of the Holy Grail (Queste del Saint Graal*), part of the thirteenth-century

[20] Andrew Hadfield, *Literature, Travel and Colonialism in the English Renaissance, 1540–1625* (Oxford: Clarendon Press, 1998), 1.

[21] See, for example, Peter Lake, with Michael Questier, *The Anti-Christ's Lewd Hat: Protestants, Papists and Players in Post-Reformation England* (New Haven, CT: Yale University Press, 2002), 1–54; Eamon Duffy, *The Stripping of the Altars: Traditional Religion in England, c.1400–c.1580* (New Haven: Yale University Press, 1992).

Vulgate cycle, which shows the knights setting out on journeys, representing 'different types of humanity at varying degrees of spiritual development'.[22]

Kempe's life is made meaningful by her ability to transfer the experiences of her earthly life to a spiritual one, so that she is able to replace the trappings of her marriage to her husband, John, with a spiritual marriage to Christ. Her first major religious revelation occurs when she travels to Jerusalem, which she enters riding on an ass, in conscious imitation of Christ:

> And whan this creatur saw Jerusalem, ryding on an asse, sche thankyd God wyth al hir hert, preying hym for hys mercy that, lych as he had browt hir to se this eardly cyte Jerusalem, he wold grawntyn hir grace to se the blysful cite Jerusalem abovyn, the cyte of hevyn. Owyr Lord Jhesu Chryst, answeryng hyr thowt, grawntyd hir to have hir desyr. Than, for joy that sche had and the swetnes that sche felt in the dalyawnce of owyr Lord, sche was in poynt to a fallyn of hir asse, for sche myth not beryn the swetnesse and grace that God wrowte in hir soul.[23]

Kempe understands her life in terms of travel and the encounter with monuments of religious significance. In seeing Jerusalem as the earthly city that imitates the heavenly city, she is making use of the writings of Saint Bridget of Sweden, who was inspired by Saint Augustine's *City of God*, which casts earthly life as a pale shadow of the glories that await the chosen in heaven.[24] Kempe believes that she has been granted the gift of the true pilgrim so that her earthly travels serve as an index of her spiritual state and she can look forward to seeing the real forms of worldly delights—marriage, peace, freedom, the city of Jerusalem—when she enters heaven after her death. The journey will go on beyond her travel to the Holy City until she reaches the destination for those who are good enough to be admitted into the family of Christ. Her faint shows that she is overcome by the joys that have been granted her, a poor, unworthy 'creature'.

On Mount Calvary Kempe experiences the first of her periods of prolonged crying, something that is to mark her out as a devout Christian chosen by God and set her apart from her fellows:

> And this maner of crying enduryd the terme of x yer... And every Good Friday in alle the forseyd yerys sche was wepyng and sobbyng v or vi owrys togedyr, and therwyth cryed ful lowde many tymes, so that sche myth not restreyn hir therfro, whech madyn hir ful febyl and weyke in hir bodily mytys. Sumtyme sche wept on Good Friday an owr for the synne of the pepil, havyng mor sorowe for ther stnnys

[22] Anonymous, *The Quest of the Holy Grail*, trans. P. M. Matarasso (Harmondsworth: Penguin, 1969), 17.

[23] Margery Kempe, *The Book of Margery Kempe*, ed. Barry Windeatt (Woodbridge: Boydell and Brewer, 2000), 160–1. All further references will be made in the body of the text by page number of this edition.

[24] Johannes Jorgensen, *Saint Bridget of Sweden*, 2 vols. (London: Longman, 1954); Saint Augustine, *The City of God*, ed. and trans. Henry Bettenson (Harmondsworth: Penguin, 1984).

> than for hir owyn, in-as-meche as owr Lorde foryaf hir hir owyn synne er sche went to Jerusalem. (*Book*, 276)

The long sentence ends with a reminder that the change in her life took place when she travelled to the most holy of places and that it is impossible to separate her physical and spiritual journeys.

When she visits Rome on her journey back to King's Lynn, Kempe has a similar experience which serves as an index of her spiritual attainment, again making the link between the physical travel and her religious progress. She confesses her sins to a priest

> fro hir childhode unto that owre, and receyved hir penawns ful joyfully. And sithyn sche schewyd hym the secret thyngys of revelacyonys and of hey contemplacyons, and how sche had swech mend in hys Passyon, and so gret compassyon whan God wolde yeve it, that sche fel downe therwyth and myth not beryn it. Than sche wept bittyrly, sche sobbyd boistowsly, and cryed ful lowde and horybly, that the pepil was oftyntymes aferd and gretly astoyned, demyng sche had ben vexyd wyth sum evyl spirit, er a sodeyn sekenes, not levyng it was the werk of God, but rathar sum evyl spiryt, er a sodeyn seknes, er ellys symulacyon and ypocrisy, falsly feyned of hir owyn self. (*Book*, 185–6)

The uncontrollable weeping that she experiences mirrors that in Jerusalem, an appropriate response to a holy place. The hostility and incomprehension demonstrated by those who see her public display of spasms serves to justify her behaviour. Like Christ, who all pilgrims should imitate, she is misunderstood by an unenlightened world. Their reaction demonstrates their lack of spiritual progress as a static crowd who are unable to move forward, unlike the true pilgrim who understands what is really at stake and so is able to commune with God. Kempe's spirituality develops into a purer state the longer she stays in Rome, leading eventually to a spectacular transformation of her life on earth:

> Sche was so meche affectyd to the manhode of Crist that whan sche sey women in Rome beryn children in her armys, yyf sche myth wetyn that thei wer ony men children, sche schuld cryin, roryn and wepyn as thei sche had seyn Crist in hys childhode... whan sche sey a semly man, sche wept and sobbyd ful sor in the manhod of Crist as sche went in the stretys at Rome...
>
> And therefor it was no wondyr yyf sche wer stille and answeryd not the Fadyr of Hevyn, whan he teld hir that sche schuld be weddyd to hys Godhed. Than seyd the Secunde Persone, Crist Jhesu, whoys manhode sche lovyd so meche, to her:
>
> 'What seyst thu, Margery, dowtyr, to my Fadyr of thes wordys that he spekyth to the? Art thu wel plesyd that it be so?'
>
> And than sche wold not answeryn the Secunde Persone, but wept wonder sor, desiryng to have stille hymselfe and in no wyse to be departyd fro hym...
>
> And than the Fadyr toke hir be the hand [spiritually] in hir sowle befor the Sone and the Holy Gost, and the Modyr of Jhesu, and alle the xii apostelys, and Seynt Kateryn and Seynt Margarete and many other seyntys and holy virgynes, wyth gret multitude of awngelys, seying to hir sowle:

> 'I take the, Margery, for my weddyd wyfe, for fayrer, for fowelar, for richar, for powerar, so that thu be buxom and bonyr to do what I byd the do. For, dowtyr, ther was nevyr childe so buxom to the modyr as I schal be to the, bothe in wel and in wo, to help the and comfort the. And therto I make the suyrte.' (*Book*, 190–2)

In pointed contrast to the animated movement that characterizes the text before this point, the moment when Kempe actually becomes a bride of Christ is characterized by stillness (before the outbreak of another bout of weeping). The grace that Kempe thinks has been offered to her is remarkable as brides of Christ were generally small, innocent children, like the dead young girl in the poem, *Pearl* (late fourteenth century) and not mature women in their forties with several children of their own.[25] Both Christ and God speak to her, further emphasizing her state of grace realized in one of Christianity's most holy places. Kempe has reached a key point in her spiritual journey and is now confirmed as a living saint who has access to the presence of God. Later, during her visit to the Basilica of Santa Maria Maggiore, Saint Jerome appears to her from his tomb and validates her behaviour: 'Blissed art thow, dowtyr, in the wepyng that thu wepyst for the peplys synnes, for many schal be saved therby. And, dowtyr, drede the nowt, for it is a synguler and a specyal yyft that God hath yovyn the—a welle of teerys, the whech schal nevyr man take fro the' (*Book*, 210). Kempe is now assured that she has the power to save, that of a living saint; the weeping that sets her apart from others is sign of her value to God and is something that should be celebrated not restricted, whatever the reaction of those around her.

The subsequent pilgrimage to Santiago (1417) is less spectacular in nature but still remarkable in confirming Kempe's ability to perform miracles.[26] Marooned in Bristol for six weeks because Henry V has requisitioned all the ships to service his expedition to France, the pilgrims become restless.[27] Kempe prays regularly and is visited by Jesus who provides her with 'many holy meditacyons and many hy contemplacyonys and many swet comfortys.' Yet again, Kempe's isolation is a sign of her state of grace. When she receives communion she reacts with 'plentyvows terys and boystows sobbyngys, wyth lowde cryingys and schrill shrykyngys', so that many men and women 'skornyd hir and despised hir, banned hir and cursyd hir, seyde meche evyl of hir, slawndryd hir' (*Book*, 222). Despite the attempts of some of her detractors, Kempe is eventually allowed to board the ship although she is warned that if there are any storms at sea they will throw her overboard as she will

[25] Margery is comparing herself to the female mystics, Saint Catherine of Sienna and Saint Bridget of Sweden: see Katherine J. Lewis, 'Margery Kempe and Saint Making in Later Medieval England', in *A Companion to The Book of Margery Kempe*, ed. John H. Arnold and Katherine J. Lewis (Woodbridge: Boydell and Brewer, 2004), 195–215, at 212–15.

[26] Pilgrimages to Santiago were so well-organized and so frequent that a guide was issued for pilgrims; see Ohler, *Medieval Traveller*, 184–98.

[27] Diane Watt, 'Political Prophecy in *The Book of Margery Kempe*', in *Companion to The Book of Margery Kempe*, ed. Arnold and Lewis, 145–60, at 152.

be to blame. But when she prays for good weather, God obliges and they reach Santiago after seven days (*Book*, 227–8).

Kempe says nothing about the actual experience she has of Santiago, because her story is organized around her spiritual progress not her observations of other places and the mode of travel itself. This is not because medieval travellers were incapable of making such observations: witness, to take two very obvious examples, the interest in physical description in *Sir Gawain and the Green Knight* or the numerous chronicles of the crusades which chart the difficulties of life in the Middle East and the encounters that the crusaders had with an alien landscape and people.[28] Rather, it is because of the allegorical cast of Kempe's mind and her desire to see her life as a pilgrimage organized around her journeys to the most important holy places in Christendom.

The observations of William Lithgow on his visits to the same places could hardly be more at odds with those of Kempe. Lithgow, unlike Kempe, describes places that he encounters—in particular, monuments. But, as with Kempe, the religious significance determines his observations. Lithgow shows that he is not indifferent to the beauties of particular buildings. Having enjoyed the 'Library of the auncient *Romans*', which he visits with two fellow travellers, Lithgow sets off on his own to 'view the gorgeous Mosaicall worke of *S. Peters* Church'.[29] He describes his anticipation as he waits to enter the church, unsure of how to behave in the midst of Catholics, before, 'abandoning all scrupulosities', he 'came in boldly' and immediately confronts the great image of Saint Peter 'erected of pure Brasse, and sitting on a brazen Chaire' (17–18). This great statue inspires Lithgow to produce a sustained attack on the idolatrous nature of Catholicism and to assert the superiority of British Protestant culture:

> The fashion of this people is this, entring the Church, they go straight to this Idoll, and, and saluting with many crosses his fleshlesse [?] body, kisse his feete, and euery one of his severall toes: insomuch that those his comfortlesse feete are growne firy red, while his body, save his breasts, remaineth brazen blew: and yet forsooth some of their learned *Rabines* will not have this superstition, but an humble commemoration of their adored Saints...
>
> O wonderful and strange spectacle! That these onely titular Christians, should become worse of knowledge than Ethnicke Pagans, to worship and reverence the workmanship of mens hands. Woe and shame be unto you all blind Hereticall Papists; Why should you make to your selves Idols and Images of gold silver, brasse, yron, stone, earth and tree; And notwithstanding would excuse the matter with a superstitious reason[.] (18)

28 Hallam, *Chronicles of the Crusades*; Malcolm Andrew and Ronald Waldron (eds.), *The Poems of the Pearl Manuscript* (London: Arnold, 1978).

29 William Lithgow, *The Totall Discourse, of The Rare Aduentures, and Painefull Peregrinations of Long Nineteene Yeares Trauayles* (London, 1632), 16–17. Subsequent references to this edition in parentheses in the text.

While Kempe concentrated on her experiences and used places as means of perceiving her spiritual life, Lithgow sets himself at odds with external signs, locating his spirituality within himself and in terms of his own certain knowledge of salvation. What looked as though it would be a description of the mosaics in Saint Peter's turns instead into a dramatic encounter between an austere Protestantism and the idolatry of Catholicism. The description is clearly staged and given an illusory drama, perhaps even suggesting that Lithgow is feigning an interest in the mosaics in order to emphasize his and the reader's shock at the monstrous statue of Saint Peter. Protestants can enjoy beauty but do not let it distort and obscure their spirituality. The statue stands as an index of all that is wrong with the Church of Rome: 'What virtue can be in a lumpe of brasse? Or, what comfort in the devices of handy craft-men? Alas, nothing but eternall sorrow & condemnation. This was one of the lamentable errors I saw in the *Roman* Sea, amongst many other thousands' (18–19).

In some ways a huge gulf separates the world that Lithgow is exploring from that observed by Kempe. Lithgow shows far more interest in objects than Kempe does, precisely because they do not have the spiritual significance that they do for her. For Kempe, external signs reveal the inner truth of the world as revealed by God to man. The world, as has often been pointed out, can be read as God's book of nature, one in which the images are in harmony with the words, reinforcing and supplementing the message that Christendom contains a series of messages for the faithful.[30] Kempe sees no real need to describe the shrines and holy places that she visits because they are there to tell a much great story, one that everyone knows and can understand.

For Lithgow, the world is full of division and only a confrontational and critical attitude can reveal the truth. Images are no longer to be trusted and are often misleading or even inspired by Satan, hence the suspicion exhibited by many 'hotter' Protestants manifested in its most extreme form in iconophobia and the demand for widespread iconoclasm.[31] Holy places are therefore no longer needed or even desirable, which explains why Lithgow devotes so much energy to describing and attacking the great statue of Saint Peter. Or, rather, what Lithgow attacks is not the image as such, but the attitudes of those worshippers who transform a statue into a graven image, as forbidden in the fourth commandment. Lithgow is

[30] Gabriel Josipovici, *The World and The Book: A Study of Modern Fiction* (Basingstoke: Macmillan, 1971), 25–51; Jacques Derrida, *Of Grammatology*, trans. Gayatri Chakravorty Spivak (Baltimore, MD: The Johns Hopkins University Press, 1974), Chapter 1.

[31] Ernest B. Gilman, *Iconoclasm and Poetry in the English Reformation: Down Went Dagon* (Chicago: Chicago University Press, 1986), Chapters 1 and 2; Margaret Aston, *England's Iconoclasts Laws Against Images*, vol. 1 (Oxford: Clarendon Press, 1988). Lithgow's own religious affiliation is hard to pin down. He was brought up as a member of the Scottish kirk, more austere than its English counterpart, and he often sounds like an iconoclast. But the fact that he travelled so widely might suggest that his faith was more complex than has often been assumed.

clearly conscious that the world and the book do not neatly coincide and that a critical attitude to reading is necessary to reveal God's word. The statue may, like the mosaics that are not actually described, be beautiful, but the aesthetic sense of the observer should not influence his or her apprehension of the truth.

The delusive and complex nature of the world as understood after the Reformation inspired the need to describe it more carefully. The world had to be treated with greater suspicion, but it could now be experienced and appreciated more easily outside religious terms. We never do really discover what motivates Lithgow's desire to travel, but he forms one third of a trio of early modern travellers, along with Moryson and Coryat, who published lengthy and eccentric works in the early 1600s, having travelled extensively throughout Europe and the Near East.[32] There was now a greater appetite for accounts and descriptions of far away places—although this point can be overplayed, as it was clear that works such as Mandeville's *Travels* had been immensely popular throughout Europe in the late Middle Ages. Lithgow's account of his extensive travels, although it is clearly influenced by his vociferous religious views, does not automatically appeal to the reader in terms of a shared and assumed religious understanding, which is why Lithgow constantly and aggressively reminds readers of his Protestant perspective on the world, a trait he shares with Moryson (but not Coryat). Lithgow makes use of his status as an eyewitness to argue that if others could see what he has seen then they would think just like he does:

> I dare not persevere longer herein [i.e., in the church]: Although I can; yea, and so truly bewray their all-corrupted estate, that I need no information of any *Romans* Novice Traveller. Of whose sight and experience, would God all the Papists in *Britaine* had the like eie-witnessing approbation as I have had, I am certainly perswaded, with tears & sighes, they would heavily bemone the terrible fal of that *Babylonian* whore, which (in a prophane estimation) is their holy mother Church. (*Totall Discourse*, 19–20)

Like Kempe, Lithgow establishes himself as a reliable truth-teller, although what each tells the reader is different in important ways, Kempe claiming that her separation from her fellow men and women shows that she understands the world better than they do, Lithgow arguing that if they could only see the world through his eyes they would agree with his judgement. Paradoxically, the observer who trusts the world relies on her revelations to secure her story; the observer who claims to be suspicious of images has complete faith in what he sees.

One other detail separates Lithgow from Kempe. Lithgow's judgement that the Romans are 'onely titular Christians', who have become 'worse of knowledge than

[32] Thomas Coryat, *Coryats crudities hastily gobled vp in five moneths trauells in France, Sauoy, Italy, Rhetia co[m]monly called the Grisons country, Heluetia aliàs Switzerland, some parts of high Germany, and the Netherlands* (London, 1611); Fynes Moryson, *An itinerary... containing his ten yeeres trauell through the tvvelue dominions of Germany, Bohmerland, Sweitzerland, Netherland, Denmarke, Poland, Jtaly, Turky, France, England, Scotland, and Ireland* (London, 1617).

Ethnicke Pagans', further reveals how divided and fractured the world appeared to English Protestants in the early seventeenth century. For Kempe, Christians are in opposition to pagans; for Lithgow, again using his personal authority as a traveller who has the status of an eyewitness, Catholics are often far worse than pagans, suggesting that Protestants might well be better off aligning themselves with infidels than treacherous Catholics. It is a point that was made in aggressive, confrontational form in Christopher Marlowe's stage blockbuster, *Tamburlaine the Great, parts one and two* (*c*.1587), which shows Catholics behaving more treacherously than their pagan counterparts and Tamburlaine dying only when he curses and burns the Koran.[33] After the Reformation it was not obvious which side the different oppositional groups were on and who was actually worse. Pagans may well have been pagans simply because they were ignorant of the true faith, whereas Christians who had failed to heed the truth were more obviously corrupt and damned. Alliances between different faiths and different versions of the same faith became increasingly complicated.[34]

Lithgow's account of his visit to the holy sites in Jerusalem shows that pilgrimage is possible for a Protestant and is written in pointed contrast to his description of Rome, in a sober and understated style. Lithgow's point seems to be that one can be reverent without ostentation and unnecessary display, and that there are probably more connections between Protestants and the Ottomans who occupy Jerusalem than there are between Protestants and Catholics, at least in their own countries, because there is an allegiance between strangers who travel together. Lithgow notes that his companions are a mixed group of Europeans—French, German, Venetian, Syrian, and Cypriot—but that they were 'all glad of me, shewing themselves so kind, so careful, so loving, and so honourable in all respects, that they were as kind Gentlemen, as ever I met withal... Such is the love of Strangers, when they meet in Forreign and remote places' (*Totall Discourse*, 229). Lithgow's description of the 'Holy Grave' shows how a religious site should be maintained by its owners and treated by pilgrims:

> The Holy Grave is covered with a little Chapel, standing within a round Quire in the West-end of the Church. It hath two low and narrow Entries: As we entered the first door, three after three, and our shooes cast off, for these two Rooms are wondrous little, the *Guardiano* fell down, *Ingenochiaro* [i.e. genuflecting], and kissed a stone whereupon (he said) the Angel stood, when *Mary Magdelene.* came to the *Sepulchre*, to know if Christ was risen on the third day as he promised: And within the entry of the second door, we saw the place where Christ our *Messias* was buried, and prostrating our selves in great Humility, every Man, according to his Religion offered up his Prayers to God.

[33] Matthew Dimmock, *New Turkes: Dramatizing Islam and the Ottomans in Early Modern England* (Aldershot: Ashgate, 2005), 135–62.

[34] Matthew Dimmock and Andrew Hadfield (eds.), *Religions of the Book: Co-existence and Conflict, 1400–1660* (Basingstoke: Palgrave, 2008).

> The Sepulchre it self, is eight foot and a half in length, and advanced about three foot in height from the ground, and three foot five inches broad, being covered with a fair Marble Stone of white colour.
>
> In this Chapel, and about it, I mean without the inward incirclings of the compassing Quire, there are always burning above fifty Lampes of Oil, maintained by Christian Princes... I demanded of the *Guardiano* if any part of the Tomb was here yet extant, who replied, there was; but because (said he) Christians resorting thither, being devoutly moved with affection to the place, carried away a good part thereof, which caused *St Helen* inclose it under this Stone; whereby some Relicks of it, should always remain. (*Totall Discourse*, 255–6)

Lithgow appears to accept a wider range of forms of devotion outside Europe than he would inside it. The pilgrims are united in their reverence for the site of Christ's death and by their status as fellow Christians abroad. Lithgow's description of the site of the tomb functions on a variety of levels. In an obvious way it is a form of tourist guide, indicating a continuity with the manuals issued to pilgrims to holy sites throughout the Middle Ages. In another way it is a description of how Protestant devotion at holy sites could and should work. There is a sober reflection on the significance of the site for Christians and a sense of awe and wonder that traces of Christ might remain behind for his followers to observe, if not worship. Lithgow is very concerned to separate his devotions from those of Catholics, especially those observed at their sites, most notably, Rome. But, on the other hand, he is keen to suggest that, if certain rules are obeyed, toleration of different forms of worship can be permitted and a variety of religious faiths accommodated in the same place. Religious divisions are not quite as clear cut as they might seem closer to home.

Lithgow, like Kempe, travelled to Spain in 1620 although he did not visit the shrine at Compostela. Why he chose to visit Spain during the prolonged war with England is a mystery, especially as other English travellers who visited the country had warned fellow Protestants in particular of the dangers of visiting the land of the Inquisition.[35] Lewkenor was arrested in Malaga, accused of being a spy, then imprisoned and tortured, before a lucky series of accidents led to his release.

Lithgow provides the reader with graphic accounts of the terrible tortures to which he was subjected leaving him with wounds that did not heal. He provides one of the few accounts by a survivor of the most extreme instrument of torture then available, the rack. Immediately before this particular ordeal, Lithgow directly addresses God:

> O Great and Gracious GOD, it is truly known to thy All-seeing Eye, that I am Innocent of these false and fearful Accusations, and since therefore it is thy Good Will and Pleasure, that I must suffer now by the scelerate [wicked] hands of merciless Men: Lord furnish me with Courage, Strength and Patience, lest by an impatient Mind, and feeling Spirit, I become my own Murtherer, in confessing my self guilty of

[35] Lewis Lewkenor, *A Discourse of the Usage of the English Fugitives by the Spaniard* (London, 1615); Hadfield, *Literature, Travel, and Colonialism*, 48–9.

> Death, to shun present Punishment. And according to the multitude of thy Mercies, O Lord, be merciful to my sinful Soul, and thus for Jesus thy Son and my Redeemer his sake. (*Totall Discourse*, 432)

Lithgow is eager to represent his suffering, looking back to models of Protestant saints, and he undoubtedly has the martyrs who suffered at the hands of the Marian authorities in mind, collected in John Foxe's compendium, *Actes and Monuments of the Christian Church* (1563, 1570), as well as John Bale's *The Vocacyon of Johan Bale to the byshoprycke of Ossorye* (1553). Bale's work, often described as one of the first autobiographies in English, narrates his own sufferings at the hands of the Catholics who drive him out of Ireland when Mary becomes queen, and of the pirates who kidnap him on his way to exile in Europe.[36] Like Bale, Lithgow survives and so stands as a living testimony to the cruelties of Catholicism and the patient suffering of the godly. The reader learns of his torment through vivid description:

> Whereat the Alcade [The Spanish equivalent of a mayor] inraging, set my teeth asunder with a pair of Iron Cadges, detayning them there, at every several turn, both mainly and manually; whereupon my hunger-clung'd Belly waxing great, grew Drum-like imbolstered; for it being a suffocating Pain, in regard of my Head hanging downward, and the Water re-ingorging it self in my Throat with a struggling force, it strangled and swallowed up my Breath from Youling [crying mournfully] and Groaning...
>
> Thus lay I six hours upon the Rack between four a Clock in the Afternoon, and ten a Clock at Night, having had inflicted upon me threescore and seven Torments: Nevertheless they continued me a large half hour (after my Tortures) at the full bending; where my Body being all begorged with Blood, and cut through in every part to the crushed and bruised Bones, I pitifully remained, still Roaring, Howling, Foaming, Bellowing, and gnashing my Teeth, with insupportable Cries, before the Pins were undone, and my Body loosed. (*Totall Discourse*, 435–6)

We have travelled a long way from the tolerant world of the pilgrimage to Jerusalem, where different versions of the same faith can live side by side. Here in Spain, there is violent conflict between Catholics and Protestants. Lithgow is tortured so that he will confess to the authorities but he preserves his silence, providing his tormentors with cries and various noises but not the information they seek. The words are accompanied by a picture of Lithgow on the rack, a further means of emphasizing the resistance he provides to the Catholic powers. His body can be broken but not his spirit, and he recovered sufficiently to attack the Spanish ambassador, the unpopular Count of Gondomar, at court in April

[36] John Bale, *The Vocacyon of Johan Bale*, ed. Peter Happé and John N. King (Binghampton: Medieval and Renaissance Texts and Studies, 1990); Leslie P. Fairfield, '*The Vocacyon of Johan Bale* and Early English Autobiography', *Renaissance Quarterly*, 24 (1971), 227–40.

1622.[37] Lithgow preserves his silence in front of his adversaries, but tells his readers the truth.

The world that Margery Kempe inhabited had, unsurprisingly enough, changed in the two centuries after her death. What is also clear, however, is the continuity between how she experienced the places she travelled to and William Lithgow's understanding of his world, despite their different senses of geography and the boundaries between areas. Lithgow's travels take place in a more dangerous and divided world than Kempe's. Nevertheless, both perceive the places they visit in fundamentally religious terms—which is not to argue that religion is the key to all mythologies, rather, that experience in the Middle Ages and Renaissance always has a religious dimension.[38] While the Ottoman Empire was perceived as the main obstacle to Christian expansion in the Middle Ages, especially after the fall of Jerusalem, once the Reformation had split Christendom the two main Christian factions found themselves spectacularly at odds and often more in sympathy with pagans they could regard as at least partially virtuous.

The discovery of the New World in 1492 made little real difference to these continuities. Fierce debates raged in Spain about the human status of the men and women they had discovered in the Americas, carried out in terms of Aristotelian theology. The fundamental problem was that the native Americans had no knowledge of Christianity. Did this mean that they were 'natural slaves', incapable of proper humanity and could be used as the Spanish saw fit, as the Dominican Juan Ginés de Sepúlveda (1494–1573) argued? Or were they humans who had to be converted in order to enlarge Christ's empire, as his more celebrated opponent, Bartolomé de las Casas (1484–1566) claimed?[39] Protestant debates were less involved but often more urgent, given the primitive state of plans for imperial expansion. Enthusiasts for empire, such as Richard Hakluyt (1552?–1616) were painfully aware of the need for immediate action and made the case that unless an empire was established quickly the religious wars that were being fought in Europe could come to a swift and undesirable conclusion as the Spanish brought back ever larger hoards of gold bullion from the Americas and converted more and more souls to their diabolical cause.[40]

On the one hand, the way forward looked simple enough. There was a need to establish and police a great empire that could preserve the embattled status of

[37] Martin Garrett, 'Lithgow, William,' *ODNB.*

[38] Brian Cummings, *The Literary Culture of the Reformation: Grammar and Grace* (Oxford: Oxford University Press, 2002); Christopher Haigh, *The Plain Man's Pathways to Heaven: Kinds of Christianity in Post-Reformation England* (Oxford: Oxford University Press, 2007).

[39] Anthony Pagden, *The Fall of Natural Man: The American Indian and the Origins of Comparative Ethnology* (Cambridge: Cambridge University Press, 1986).

[40] Richard Hakluyt, 'Discourse of Western Planting', in *The Original Writings and Correspondence of the Two Richard Hakluyts,* ed. E. G. R. Taylor (London: Hakluyt Society, 1935), 211–326; Richard Helgerson, *Forms of Nationhood: The Elizabethan Writing of England* (Chicago: Chicago University Press, 1992), Chapter 4; Hadfield, *Literature, Travel, and Colonialism*, 69–133.

Protestant Europe. But there were a number of detractors who doubted the wisdom of this; the crown was never keen to spend large sums of money on what could be a hazardous enterprise with a limited prospect of success; and many were more interested in establishing privateering bases to harass Spanish shipping than actually building up colonies.[41] And, on the other, there were questions about who exactly the people of the New World really were. Observers were clear that the relatively peaceful and settled peoples they encountered in Virginia bore little resemblance to the fierce man-eaters that the Spanish—deservedly—encountered in South America.[42] Appended to the grand, illustrated edition of Thomas Hariot's *Brief and True Report of the New Found Land of Virginia* (1590, first published 1588) are a series of carefully commissioned illustrations of the native Americans based on the sketches made by John White.[43] The first shows a picture of Adam and Eve, with Adam poised to pick the apple from the tree of knowledge, an illustration that is obviously designed to have symbolic resonance, as it bears no other relationship to the factually based pictures that follow.[44] The picture must surely be intended to remind readers that they were experiencing a seismic change in the state of world knowledge. The discovery of new peoples would force Europeans to ask a series of questions about who they were as well as who the native Americans were, leading to a reevaluation of the status of mankind. Had the encounter happened two centuries earlier, one suspects that Margery Kempe would have seen it in similar terms.

FURTHER READING

Jeremy Black. *The British Abroad: The Grand Tour in the Eighteenth Century* (Stroud: Alan Sutton, 1992)

Margaret Hodgen. *Early Anthropology in the Sixteenth and Seventeenth Centuries* (Philadelphia: University of Pennsylvania Press, 1971)

Peter Hulme. *Colonial Encounters: Europe and the Native Caribbean, 1492–1797* (London: Methuen, 1986)

Norbert Ohler. *The Medieval Traveller*, trans. Caroline Hilier (Woodbridge: Boydell, 1989)

[41] K. R. Andrews, *Trade, Plunder and Settlement: Maritime Enterprise and the Genesis of the British Empire, 1480–1630* (Cambridge: Cambridge University Press, 1986); Jeffrey Knapp, *An Empire Nowhere: England, America, And Literature From Utopia To The Tempest* (Berkeley: University of California Press, 1992).

[42] Karen Ordhal Kupperman, *Settling With The Indians: The Meeting of English and Indian Cultures in America, 1580–1640* (Totowa, NJ: Rowman and Allanheld, 1980).

[43] Thomas Hariot, *A Briefe and True Report of the New Found Land of Virginia*, ed. Paul Hulton (New York: Dover, 1972); Kim Sloan, *A New World: England's First View of America* (London: The British Museum Press, 2007). Hariot's *Report* was published as the first of a series of works representing the knowledge of the New World, *America* (1594), by the Protestant printer, Theodor De Bry (1528–98).

[44] Hadfield, *Literature, Travel, and Colonialism*, 115–17.

PART III

DOCTRINES

CHAPTER 9

THE EUCHARIST

DAVID AERS AND SARAH BECKWITH

> A picture held us captive. And we could not get outside it, for it lay in our language and language seemed to repeat it to us inexorably.
>
> (Ludwig Wittgenstein)

> But let a man examine himself. And so let him eat of that bread, and drink of that cup.
> For he that eateth and drinketh unworthily, eateth and drinketh damnation to himself, not discerning the Lord's body.
>
> (I Corinthians 11:28–9)

> You must sit down, says Love, and taste my meat, So I did sit and eat.
>
> (George Herbert, Love 3)

In the histories, including the literary histories, of Eucharistic discourse, transubstantiation is a picture that has held us captive. This is true for detractors and defenders of the doctrine. The effects of such captivity have been far-reaching. Perhaps most importantly the liturgical, communitarian practices of the Eucharist became subordinated to the dogmatic construal of the mysterious banquet. Discerning the body became a matter of elaborate scholastic articulations, elaborations that were applied as tests of orthodoxy. This led to a terrible paradox: the sacrament of unity, the bond of charity, became a sign of fragmentation, hatred, and the will to burn.

Augustine had seen the Church as a Eucharistic community. Commenting on the sixth chapter of St John's gospel (6:15–44), he argues that eating the meat given by God is believing in Christ: 'To what purpose dost thou make ready teeth and stomach? Believe, and thou hast eaten already.'[1] In Augustine's own contexts this teaching cannot be assimilated either to Wycliffite or Zwinglian ideas of the

[1] St Augustine, *Homilies on the Gospel of John: Homilies on the First Epistle of John;* and *Soliloquies in Nicene and Post-Nicene Fathers*, ed. Philip Schaff, 7 (Grand Rapids, MI: Eerdmans, 1986), Tractate 25.12. For a helpful study of Augustine's Eucharistic theology see Gerald Bonner, 'Augustine's Understanding of the Church as a Eucharistic Community', in *Saint Augustine the Bishop: A Book of Essays*, ed. Fannie Le Moine and Christopher Kleinhenz (New York: Garland, 1994), 38–63.

Eucharist.[2] This is clear enough as one follows his commentary on John 6:41–9. Once again he emphasizes the act of faith and eating: 'For to believe in Him is to eat the living bread. He that believes eats' (26.1). Thinking of the spiritual rock that was Christ (I Corinthians 10:1–4), he observes that 'the virtue of the sacrament' is received by one who eats in heart, 'not who presses with his teeth' (26:12). But this is neither individualistic nor simply inward activity: 'Believers know the body of Christ, if they neglect not to be the body of Christ. Let them become the body of Christ, if they wish to live by the Spirit of Christ. None live by the spirit of Christ but the body of Christ' (26:13).

Wycliffite or Reformation appeals to Augustine, preoccupied with opposing the late medieval doctrine of transubstantiation, impose on the earlier theologian dichotomies quite alien to his thought and the practices of his Church. Characteristically Augustine recalls St Paul's teaching that 'we being many, are one bread, one body, all that partake of one bread' (I Corinthians 10:17). And having done so, having foregrounded the ecclesial and communitarian assumptions of his version of saving faith, he responds ecstatically: 'O mystery of piety! O sign of unity! O bond of charity!' (26:13). The sacrament *is* the collective act of the community of believers responding to the divine-human mediator, past, present, and future. Christ, says Augustine, 'would have this meat and drink to be understood as meaning fellowship of His own body and members, which is the Holy Church' (26:15). In this meal, 'Christ has pointed our minds to His body and blood in those things which from being many are reduced to some one thing. For a unity is formed by many grains forming together; and another unity is effected by the clustering together of many berries' (26:17). Participation in the Church, participation in the sacrament and participation in Christ are inextricably bound together in acts at once single and collective, outer and inner. The consecration could not be extracted from reception so in an Augustinian theology it made no sense to ask such characteristic medieval questions as to whether a priest could 'consecrate all the bread in the marketplace or all the wine in the cellar', questions addressed by such medieval luminaries as Bonaventura and Aquinas.[3] Nor could an Augustinian theology of Eucharist invent, legitimize, and normalize discussions about what exactly happens when a mouse eats a consecrated (therefore transubstantiated) host—we recall Aquinas's argument that the consecrated host could be 'extracted from the mouse's stomach and appropriately used'.[4]

[2] For Wyclif's *De Eucharistia*, see David Aers, *Sanctifying Signs: Making Tradition in Late Medieval England* (Notre Dame, IN: Notre Dame University Press, 2004), Chapter 3. For Zwingli, see for example the work on the Lord's Supper translated in *Zwingli and Bullinger*, ed. G. W. Bromiley (Philadelphia: Westminster Press, 1953).

[3] P. J. Fitzpatrick, *In Breaking of Bread: The Eucharist and Ritual* (Cambridge: Cambridge University Press, 1993), 163; the whole book is an exceptionally powerful work on many of the issues that concern us.

[4] Fitzpatrick, *In Breaking of Bread*, 164, quoting from Aquinas's commentary on the fourth book of Peter Lombard's *Sentences* (4.d, 9, art 2, qu.1a3); Gary Macy, 'Of Mice and Manna: *Quid mus sumit* as

In Sermon 272, preached around year 408, he explains sacraments as events in which 'one thing is seen, another is to be understood'. How does this apply to bread and wine? Characteristically Augustine turns to a major Pauline model of the church as the body of Christ (I Corinthians 12:27). Having quoted this familiar text, very familiar to those who regularly heard the bishop preaching, he tells those participating in the service that it is they themselves who are 'the body of Christ and its members'. This is the sacrament of the altar, 'the mystery meaning you that has been placed on the Lord's table; what you receive is the mystery that means you . . . What you hear, you see, is the body of Christ, and you answer, Amen. So be a member of the body of Christ, in order to make that Amen true.'[5] In this characteristic locution, Augustine leads us to an action, an event in which Christ, the sacrament, and the particular congregation forming the body of Christ in Hippo Regius are inextricably bound together. Here we should recall another pervasive theme in Augustine's Eucharistic theology, one exquisitely represented in the *Confessions*. Here Augustine recounts the limitations of platonic contemplation and metaphysics in approaching the God who is revealed in the one mediator whose flesh had been a serious obstacle to Augustine: 'I found myself far from you "in the region of dissimilarity" [*et inveni longe me esse a te in regione dissimilitudinis*] and heard your voice from on high: "I am the food of the fully grown; grow and you will feed on me. And you will not change me into you like the food your flesh eats, but you will be changed into me." '[6] The participants of the sacrament of the altar are transformed into the source of life, assimilated to become the body of Christ.

In such a theology of the Eucharistic events it is impossible to fixate on the consecrated host, to focus, for example on the physics, or on the optics of Christ's vision, or on the passage of the body of Christ through a mouse's stomach.[7] But by 1059 Berengarius was being compelled by the Roman church to confess that the true body and blood of Christ are present not only sacramentally but sensually (*sensualiter*) and are truly (*in veritate*) crushed (*atteri*) by the teeth of the faithful. Twenty years later he was again compelled, in Rome, to confess that the bread and wine are substantially converted (*substantialiter converti*) into the Galilean body of Christ. These confessions and the debates to which they belong constituted what

a Pastoral Question', *Recherches de Théologie Ancienne et Médiévale*, 58 (1991), 157–66; Anne Hudson, 'The Mouse in the Pyx', *Trivium*, 26 (1991), 40–53.

[5] Sermon 272 in St Augustine, *Sermons* in *The Works of St Augustine: A Translation for the Twenty-First Century*, ed. John Rotelle and trans. Edmund Hill (New York: New City Press, 1993), 3: 7, 300.

[6] St Augustine, *Confessions*, trans. Henry Chadwick (Oxford: Oxford University Press, 1991), 7: 10, 16; the Latin text is St Augustine, *Confessions*, ed. James J. O'Donnell, 3 vols. (Oxford: Oxford University Press, 1992), vol. 1; for 'in regione dissimilitudinis', a major figure in the *Confessions*, see O'Donnell's note, 2: 2, 443–4. It is fascinating, thinking about continuities across the Reformation, to find Christopher Sutton following Augustine's Eucharistic theology in his 'avant-garde conformism': see Kenneth Fincham and Nicholas Tyacke, *Altars Restored: The Changing Face of English Religious Worship 1547–1700* (Oxford : Oxford University Press, 2007), 67–8.

[7] See this essay, n. 5, together with Aers, *Sanctifying Signs*, Chapter 1 and Bibliography.

Henri de Lubac has shown to be a watershed in medieval theology and its understanding of the body of Christ.[8] Explanations of the sacramental body of Christ, the Galilean body under the accidents of bread and wine, generate 'an entire problematic' that is completely different from any that could have assailed a fifth-century mind, or even the general run of those of the ninth or tenth century.[9] The transformations in the theology of the Eucharist and the ecclesial body of Christ described by de Lubac are, in his words, 'revolutionary'.[10] It is a revolution in which 'St Augustine himself becomes incomprehensible'.[11] It is also a revolution that seems to have been forgotten by some of those telling stories about relations between the 'traditional' Christianity of the Middle Ages and the 'revolution' in sixteenth-century Christianity.

We can reflect on some consequences of this revolution by turning to a work written after the death of St Augustine. The author was Guillaume de Deguileville and the unequivocally orthodox work we have in mind is *Le Pèlerinage de Vie Humaine* (*The Pilgrimage of Human Life*). The French poet dates a commission from Grace in his poem as 1331. He wrote a second version *c.*1355 as well as two other pilgrimage poems, one on the soul's life after death, the other on Jesus Christ's life and redemptive work. His poetry is accompanied by immensely rich iconographic programs studied in most detail by Michael Camille.[12] Here we restrict our attention to his treatment of the Eucharist in the first version of the poem which survives in fifty-three manuscripts and was translated into medieval English, German, Spanish, and Latin.[13] This work is an account of the poet's dream of his pilgrimage from birth to death, a pilgrimage which is a lifelong battle with the vices by a Christian endowed by the Grace of God with all the gifts he needs to reach the New Jerusalem. So his Eucharistic sequences open with Bishop Moses showing discontent at a meal consisting merely of bread and wine: the Christian priest demands 'flesh to eat and blood along with it, in order to break the old law saying that blood must not be eaten' (21/1431ff.). Untroubled by this motivation or by its understanding of relations between the old and the new covenant (contrast Matthew 5:17–19), Grace immediately helps him achieve this desire:

> Then I saw a great wonder to which nothing can compare. He changed the bread into living flesh, as Grace had ordained, and he changed the wine into red blood—it seemed very much like the blood of a lamb [*Le pain en char vive mua / Ainsi com*

[8] Henri de Lubac, *Corpus Mysticum: The Eucharist and the Church in the Middle Ages* (London: SCM, 2006), Chapters 4, 7, and 10, at 80.

[9] Lubac, *Corpus Mysticum*, 94.

[10] Lubac, *Corpus Mysticum*, 98–9; displaying this, see Chapters 4, 7–10.

[11] Lubac, *Corpus Mysticum*, 252–3; see especially Chapter 10 and Conclusion.

[12] Michael Camille, *The Illustrated Manuscripts of Guillaume de Deguileville's 'Pèlerinages' 1350-1426*, 2 vols. (Unpublished PhD dissertation, Cambridge University, 1985).

[13] Guillaume de Deguileville, *Le Pèlerinage de Vie Humaine*, ed. J. Stürzinger (London: Printed for the Roxburghe Club by Nichols & Sons, 1893); and *The Pilgrimage of Human Life*, trans. Eugene Clasby (New York: Garland, 1992). References in text to lines in *Le Pèlerinage* and pages in *The Pilgrimage*, respectively.

> *Grace l'ordena, / Le vin mua en sanc vermeil / Qui bien sembloit ester d'aignel*]. Then he wanted to call the ministers to the meal, in courteous fashion, teaching them his knowledge [*son savoir*] and giving them his power [*son pouvoir*] to make this wondrous change [*conversion*]. Then he gave all of them some of this new and perfect food to eat and he ate it with them and drank the blood. I saw it with my own eyes [*Et il menga avec eus / Et du sanc but veant mes iex*]. Never was there a meal like this, that I ever heard of, and never was there a change [*mutation*] like this, so renowned as a miracle [*Qui ait si merveillux renon*]. (21/1445ff.)

Characteristic of late medieval teaching, the Eucharist now centers on the doctrine of transubstantiation. It focuses on the 'mutation' of the elements in the moment of consecration: its teleology seems the presence of *corpus verum*, the earthly body of Christ. It is also significant, especially in relation to Reformation objections, that Deguileville only writes about communion, the reception of Christ's body, as communion by priests. These are the Christians who are granted the power to make the 'conversion' of bread and wine into the flesh and blood of the lamb, the action which for orthodox teachers (as opposed to Wycliffites) constituted the decisive identity of a Catholic priest.[14] We hear nothing about communion of the laity. We see nothing of the men and women who constituted one body in Christ and according to Augustine are 'the sacrifice which the Church continually celebrates in the sacrament of the altar, by which she demonstrates that she herself is offered in the offering she makes to God'.[15] Nor is this surprising given that the laity in the late medieval Church habitually communicated just once a year, at Easter.

Like so much attention to the event of consecration in medieval teaching, Deguileville's is marked by prolixity. In elaborating his commentary on the 'mutation' of bread and wine to body and blood he emphasizes that the pilgrim actually *sees* 'living flesh' (*char vive*) and 'red blood' (*sanc vermeil*). Reiterating that Bishop Moses ate the flesh and blood he stresses his own perception of this event: 'I saw it with my own eyes' (*veant mes iex*) (21/1445ff., quoted above). Although the poet does not suggest his pilgrim has been the recipient of a special miracle to overcome doubts about the Church's doctrine of transubstantiation, his perception is the very stuff of innumerable late medieval exempla designed to explain and justify this teaching. Because a number of recent works have illustrated and discussed these stories at length, we do not need to rehearse them here.[16] All we need to do is recall that in such exempla people are converted to the Church's account of the Eucharist by seeing the converted elements as the dripping blood and bloody flesh.

[14] See for example, Thomas Aquinas, *Summa Theologiae*, ed. Thomas Gilby, 60 vols. (London: Blackfriars, 1964–81), 3.67.2.

[15] See St Augustine, *City of God*, trans. R. W. Dyson (Cambridge: Cambridge University Press, 1998), 10.6.

[16] See Aers, *Sanctifying Signs*, Chapter 1, at 10–12, 23–6; see too the fifteenth-century compilation on the faith written for laypeople, *Memoriale Credencium*, ed. J. H. L. Kengen (Nijmegen: Kengen, 1979), 174–6.

This hegemonic model of transubstantiation tends to occlude the narratives of the Gospels together with the narratives in the New Testament concerning the formation of communities of disciples. Power (divine and priestly) becomes exorbitant and all consuming. In Deguileville's conventional treatment of the Eucharist we hear virtually nothing of reconciliation, forgiveness, sanctification, or the making of the Church's unity through the loving communion of people with Christ and each other.[17] We cannot detect even traces of St Augustine's words, remembered in St Thomas's discussion of the sacrament:

> I knew myself to be far away from you in a region of unlikeness, and I seemed to hear your voice from on high: 'I am food of the mature; grow then, and you will eat me. You will not change me into yourself like bodily food: you will be changed into me.'[18]

Nor do we glimpse the kind of joy celebrated in Aquinas's invocation of the Song of Songs to celebrate communion in the sacrament.[19] Obsession with transubstantiation, reification of the *corpus verum* and its warranting by the application of an abstract and indeterminate model of divine power, sets the framework for teaching Christians about the Eucharist.

These are the theological contexts shaping the late medieval Church's response to Wyclif's rejection of its teachings on the sacrament of the altar. He affirmed, often citing St Augustine, that in this sacrament Christ's body and blood are certainly given to Christians, as witnessed in evangelical texts.[20] But not given in the manner determined by the late medieval Church. He came to reject its teachings about the substance of the bread and wine as well as its teachings about the presence of Christ's Galilean body in the mode of substance. In doing so he was rejecting not only a particular way of understanding the sacramental gift, but what the Church considered the only truly Christian interpretation of the sacrament. As we have seen, the latter had become elevated, in effect, to the status of a necessary article of faith. The consequences of this move would have been predictable. For the Church's teaching, lucidly articulated in St Thomas Aquinas's *Summa Theologiae*, was that the rejection of one article of faith involves a rejection of the faith disclosed in the Church's infallible and divinely given teaching.[21] When baptized Christians chose to oppose the Church in this way they could be licitly compelled to keep the obligations they had promised to fulfill in baptism.[22] If they insisted on adhering to their own willful choice against the Church's teaching they were to be judged to be heretics, excommunicated, and killed.[23] The sacrament that, as St Thomas explained, following St Augustine and the liturgy, is the sacrament of

[17] Contrast *Summa Theologiae*, 3.73.3–4; 3.79.1. Hereafter cited as '*ST*'.

[18] St Augustine, *Confessions*, trans. Maria Boulding (New York: New City Press, 1997) 7:10, 16; see also *ST*, 3.73.3 and 3.73.4.

[19] *Confessions*, Canticles 5.5, and *ST*, 3.79.1.

[20] Aers, *Sanctifying Signs*, Chapter 3, at 63–5; and references to other commentators there.

[21] *ST*, 2-2.5.3. [22] *ST*, 2-2.10.8. [23] *ST*, 2-2.11.1–4.

love, the bond of charity, the source of grace, the perfection of its recipients' spiritual life, the cause of union with God, making the soul drunk with God's perfect goodness, this sacrament also became the key witness in sentencing to death Christians who rejected the doctrine of transubstantiation.[24] The contemporary Roman Catholic church still adheres to the doctrine formulated at Trent, affirmed in the church's catechism, and tenaciously defended by at least some of its theologians.[25] Once the Church made a particular version of the Eucharist a litmus test for Christian orthodoxy, it was inevitable that Christians seeking different accounts of the presence of Christ in the gift of the sacrament would be cast as the 'disciples of antichrist'.[26]

This model begins to obscure the body of Christ as the locus of mutual participation of God in humanity and humanity in God. One of the consequences of such language is an exclusive concentration and focus on one moment of the canon of the mass—the words of consecration—to the virtual exclusion of the dense ritual, liturgical, and social embedding of those words. Eucharistic discourse and practice became assimilated to Eucharistic dogma. The reduction of the former to the latter underestimates the capaciousness of Eucharistic discourse and the forms in which it is articulated. These are not carriers of a meaning located elsewhere but a constitutive part of the processes of knowledge, recognition, participation, and awareness by means of which the body of Christ is itself discerned. Not everybody forgot this. In *Piers Plowman*, for example, it is impossible to abstract any understanding of the sacraments from the dialectical processes which implicate and seek to educate the reader. In the medieval cycle plays too, we see the Eucharist not so much as the confected wafer but as a claim: 'This is my body'; or better, a question, 'Is this my body?' put by Christ to the entire city.[27] So any elaboration of our subject would have to pay sustained attention to different contexts and discourses in which the Eucharist was performed or discoursed.[28]

Despite this caveat, Nicholas Love's treatment of the Last Supper in *The Mirror of the Blessed Life of Jesus Christ*, another immensely popular late medieval text, shows just how the careful distinction between priest and Christ in the canon of the Mass could be collapsed. For Love actually inverts the relationship of Christ and priest in the canon of the mass. There the priest cites the words of Jesus, maintaining the distinction between the words of Christ and the person of the priest. But in Love's

[24] For a beautiful articulation of the virtues of the sacrament see *ST*, 3.79.1 with *ST*, 3.73.3.

[25] See *Catechism of the Catholic Church*, 2nd edn (New York: Doubleday, 1997), 383–5, at paragraphs 1373–7; paragraphs 1374 and 1376 explicitly invoke the Council of Trent's authority and doctrine.

[26] See discussion of Nicholas Love in Aers, *Sanctifying Signs*, 12–21, 23–8.

[27] A perspective explored in the case of the York Cycle; see Sarah Beckwith, *Signifying God: Social Relation and Symbolic Act in the York Corpus Christi Plays* (Chicago: University of Chicago Press, 2001).

[28] The ritual embedding of the Eucharist is central to Fitzpatrick's account in *In Breaking of Bread*; see especially 'The Way of Ritual', at 195ff. and 203: 'It is only by doing justice to the successive ritual settings of what Christ said that we shall do justice to his Eucharistic presence.' See also Beckwith, *Signifying God*, 122.

Mirror, Christ becomes the consecrating priest and the institution of the Eucharist is turned into a confection of the body of Christ. Love begins with a kind of miming of the 'sursum corda' of the mass ('lift we here up oure hertes sovereynly & bethenke we inwardly wonduryng of that moste wothi dignacion & unspeakable charite'[29]) and then proceeds to abandon the careful distinction between speakers in the canon. The effect is to make Christ imitate the priest, rather than to have the priest speak in the words of Christ:

> He toke brede in his holi handes & lift up hees eyene to his fadere almighty god, & blessed the brede & seide the wordes of consecration there overe, by virtue of the wheche wordes brede was turnede in to his body, & then he yaf it to disciples & seide, '*Taketh and eteth for sothely this is my body...*'[30]

Love adds crucial words to the scriptural narrative in a characteristic move which would be challenged in the Reformation as it had been by Wyclif: 'And aftur he yaf hem powere of that consecracion & alle prestes in hem & seyde, (th)is doth ye also oft as ye take it in commemoracion & mynde of me.'[31] So Christ's words here are turned into a consecration which transfers power to the priesthood in such a way that the Eucharistic community is normally narrowed to a receiving priesthood. In the Rheims translation of the New Testament 'Do this' is interpreted even more explicitly as a sacrament of order.[32] But the evangelical narratives are very clear that Jesus kept an open table: it was the feasters who had to discern the body. So all the gospel accounts agree that Judas participates in the Eucharist. Indeed that seems to be the point of Jesus's enigmatic comment in Matthew. None of the disciples imagines himself capable of betraying Christ and they all utter words of startled shock and denial. They began to say 'one after another, "Surely not I?"' Jesus's response is to say: 'The one who has dipped his hand into the bowl with me will betray me' (Matthew 26:23). Stanley Hauerwas comments on this passage: 'The very gesture of cleanliness becomes an act of betrayal.'[33] Hauerwas's larger point here is on the models of ecclesiology enacted in the institution story: '"Surely not I, lord?" They will all betray him; sin is seldom recognized through self-reflection.'[34] All the disciples will of course deny Jesus and so betray him, so this story is not the story of one identifiable outcast but a story in which those memories of betrayal

[29] Nicholas Love, *The Mirror of the Blessed Life of Christ: A Reading Text*, ed. Michael G. Sargent (Exeter: University of Exeter Press, 2004), 149.

[30] Love, *The Mirror of the Blessed Life*, ed. Sargent, 149.

[31] Love, *The Mirror of the Blessed Life*, ed. Sargent, 149.

[32] *The Original and True Rheims New Testament of Anno domini 1582*, ed. Dr William von Peters (1998), 148. The gloss on Luke 22:19 reads: '"Do this": In these words the holy Sacrament is instituted, because power and commission to do the principal act and work of priesthood.'

[33] Stanley Hauerwas, *Matthew*, Brazos Theological Commentary on the Bible (Grand Rapids, MI: Brazos Press, 2006), 217.

[34] Hauerwas, *Matthew*, 217.

will have to be taken up and redeemed in the recognition stories of the post-resurrection Christ.[35]

In the Sarum Rite, Maundy Thursday was the day in which public penitents were reconciled and permitted to share in the Eucharist at the very feast in which it was instituted. But in the Elizabethan Book of Common Prayer the high theater of the medieval Eucharistic liturgy is radically simplified and pruned: there are no palms on Palm Sunday, no ashes on Ash Wednesday, no creeping to the cross, and the penitential rites of exclusion and inclusion are preserved only in the 'Commination Against Sinners' with its lament for the 'godly discipline of the primitive church'.[36] The Book of Common Prayer must make do with a 'general cursing' drawn out of Deuteronomy 27 'until the said discipline will be restored again'.[37] Yet the minister could also at his discretion 'call and advertise' any 'open and notorious evil livers' from communion,[38] while the service for Holy Communion contains a number of exhortations which could be read to encourage and educate parishioners about worthy reception of the sacrament. These use the imagery of St Luke's banquet and St Matthew's wedding feast (Luke 14:15–24; Matthew 22:1–14) and they also use the Pauline injunction which serves as our epigraph.[39]

What is it then for a member of the Church of England to discern the Lord's body? One of the chief reasons why Cranmer and other reformers thought the rejection of transubstantiation was so essential was that it negated the act of repentance and reception. If the body of Christ was *ex opere operato* produced by a confecting priesthood then all could receive worthily at his hands. In the official book of homilies the two-part 'Homily of the Worthy Receiving and Reverent Esteeming of the Sacrament of the Body and Blood of Christ' also has as one of its central texts I Corinthians 11:29. Here Paul was addressing the divisions among the Corinthians. When you come together, he says, it is not to eat the Lord's Supper. 'For when the time comes to eat, each of you goes ahead with your own supper, and one goes hungry and another one becomes drunk.' But according to Paul, it is impossible to worthily receive the body, to participate in the feast if some go hungry, if some are humiliated. This is 'not discerning the body'. So the homilist begins with an understanding of Eucharist as memory and participation against private eating and sacrifice.[40]

[35] A central theme in Rowan Williams, *Resurrection: Interpreting the Easter Gospel* (Harrisburg, PA: Morehouse Publishing, 1982). There is, of course, a difference between panic, fear, loss of nerve in the face of overwhelming violence and Judas's cold-blooded planning (under no duress) and selling to the killing agents.

[36] John E. Booty (ed.), *The Book of Common Prayer, 1559: The Elizabethan Prayer Book* (Charlottesville and London: The University of Virginia Press, 1976), 316. Hereafter cited as '*BCP 1559*'.

[37] *BCP 1559*, 316. The same hope is expressed in the prayer book of 1549 and 1552.

[38] *BCP 1559*, 247. [39] *BCP 1559*, 258.

[40] 'An Homily of the Worthy Reception and Reverent Esteeming of the Sacrament of the Body and Blood of Christ', in *The Homilies Appointed to be Read in Churches* (Brynmill: Preservation Press, 2006), 321. Hereafter cited as *Homilies*.

Yet as the homily goes on to address proper discernment of the body, there are emergent signs that the participation so enjoined is undercut by the very techniques encouraged to reach it. They are subtle, unwitting, yet retrospectively, in the contexts of later developments, invidious. The first is that there is a tendency to render too cognitive the mode of participation. One of the claims made in the homily is that 'the ignorant cannot without fruit and profit, exercise himself in the Lord's sacraments'. This seems unproblematic. But the author then claims that the Corinthian problem was ignorance: 'St Paul, blaming the Corinthians for the profaning of the Lord's Supper, concludeth that ignorance, both of the thing itself, and the signification thereof, was the cause of their abuse; for they came irreverently, not discerning the Lord's body.'[41] But Paul actually writes in reprimand of the greed and individualism that made a mockery of the body of Christ. The implication in the Reformation homily is epistemological: here, an epistemological problem can have an epistemological cure. Those Corinthians did not know what the Lord's body was just as Catholics think that the bread actually is the literal body of Christ. 'For what hath been the cause of the ruin of God's religion but the ignorance therof?'[42] This constitutes a bewilderingly optimistic assessment of the situation; as if knowledge and right doctrine might dispel malice, hatred, vainglory, and contempt, as if Augustine and Calvin had never contested stoic accounts of virtue for their superficial sense of the resources of the human will. This kind of epistemological confidence was not shared by allegorists such as Langland and Spenser or by Shakespeare, who understood that knowledge was bound up with recognition and plumbed the bewildering complexity of this process, including as it did the sheer opacity of things in the world as well as in our own minds.

Secondly, in trying to insist that there will be no surrogation in worship, no sacrificing of the priesthood on behalf of others ('no dumb massing') the homilist comes to insist that 'every one of us ought to celebrate the same, at his table, in our own persons'.[43] So the notion of 'in our own persons' becomes stressed to such an extent that the Pauline interdependencies of the body of Christ are underdeveloped, even unwittingly undermined, at least in the first part of the homily. The effect is to atomize the body even against the explicit desire and aim, as well as the theology of the supper: 'make Christ thine own, apply his merits to thyself. Herein thou needest no other man's help, no other sacrifice or oblation, or sacrificing priest, no mass, no means established by man's invention.'[44]

Finally, the homilist stresses how important it is 'to prove, and try ourselves unfeignedly, without flattering ourselves, whether we be plants of that fruitful olive, living branches of the true vine'.[45] Thus our feeding, our sustenance becomes dependent not so much on the participation in the supper and our enaction of the body of Christ together but on a process of introspection whereby we could check

[41] *Homilies*, 322. [42] *Homilies*, 322. [43] *Homilies*, 325, the Second Part.
[44] *Homilies*, 323. [45] *Homilies*, 324.

our own worthiness. It is just this eradication of a receiving community in the very act of self-knowledge and self-recognition that becomes so exceedingly problematical in this homily and where its confident tones of dispelling the darkness of ignorance only intensify and undermine its most heartfelt aims. Self-scrutiny that has lost its pastoral context in the spectre of popish abuse is subject to relentlessly circular intensifications, restless anxieties of uncertainty, cravings for an impossible assurance. The religious subject begins to be gripped by an interminable problem of knowledge. It leads several of the subjects of Stachniewski's fascinating book into suicides that guarantee certainty at the cost of damnation itself.[46] But we are now coming to see powerful currents of resistance to these trajectories within the Church of England from the 1590s.[47]

One of the central images in the exhortations to Holy Communion in the Book of Common Prayer and also in the 'Homily of the Worthy Reception' is the image of the heavenly banquet where all must be guests 'and not gazers, eaters and not lookers'.[48] The great suggestiveness and longevity of this idea can be seen from the use Shakespeare makes of it in *The Tempest.* In Act 3, Scene 3 of *The Tempest,* several 'strange shapes' bring in a banquet, on which Alonso proposes to feed. But Ariel, by means of a 'quaint device', causes it to vanish and confronts them with their own sin: 'But remember/(For that's my business to you) that you three/From Milan did supplant good Prospero' (3.3.68–70).[49] The prospective feast becomes an act of remembrance, restoring a memory of themselves that disbars participation until that memory has restored them to repentance. The feast depends on being in 'charity'—and this will mean avowals, heart's sorrow, a relinquishment of the usurped fruits of past ill deeds and a restoration of the relations such acts have damaged through forgiveness. Here the work of theatre supports the work of the mass in a substitution of haunting power and equivocation—for the feast can only be realized in those relations of charity. Without them it is insubstantial. Here we have finally moved away from the Aristotelian language of substance that had controlled Eucharistic discussion for so long, to a language of participation. Shakespeare is taking up a dense source of controversy and allusion.

[46] John Stachniewski, *The Persecutory Imagination: English Puritanism and the Literature of Religious Despair* (Oxford: Oxford University Press, 1991); see also David Como, *Blown by the Spirit: Puritanism and the Emergence of an Antinomian Underground in pre-Civil-War England* (Stanford, CA: Stanford University Press, 2004).

[47] See Fincham and Tyacke, *Altars Restored*; Peter Lake, 'Lancelot Andrewes, John Buckeridge, and Avant-Garde Conformity at the Court of James I', in *The Mental World of the Jacobean Court,* ed. Linda Peck (Cambridge: Cambridge University Press, 1991), 113–53; H. C. Porter, *Reformation and Reaction in Tudor Cambridge* (Cambridge: Cambridge University Press, 1958).

[48] *Homilies,* 320; *BCP 1559,* 256.

[49] This and all subsequent quotations are taken from William Shakespeare, *The Norton Shakespeare Based on the Oxford Edition,* general editor Stephen Greenblatt, ed. Walter Cohen, Jean E. Howard, and Katherine Eisaman Maus (New York and London: 1997).

In the Eucharistic debates of the early 1560s, John Jewel and Thomas Harding rehearse exactly this theme and they show what are the stakes of making the presence real in languages that echo in the airy nothings of the play, but also in the way the island substantiates the desires and memories of each of the protagonists. Taking up the central idea that the Eucharist is a 'supper', they both wonder: who can eat at the feast? For John Jewel the Catholic mass is a meal for one, because the congregation does not partake of the bread. What kind of a meal is it when the cup is withdrawn from the guests, when the guests are invited to watch him eat his solitary feast? Can it be a feast at all when only one person eats and the others watch?

> To such a banquet Pasetes the juggler used sometimes to call his friends. There was a great shew of vanity...but, when any of the guests would have touched anything, it vanished suddenly away and was turned to nothing.... Even thus Mr Harding feedeth and feasteth the people of God with shews and ceremonies, and suffereth in the mean to starve for hunger.[50]

The spectators of the feast are not participants at all: they 'heareth nothing, understandeth nothing, eateth nothing, drinketh nothing, tasteth nothing'.[51] This is feast theatricalized and the spectators long for substance as they gaze on at the priest's greedy and selfish plenitude.

But for Harding it is precisely Jewel's denial of transubstantiation that renders the feast a nullity. At Jewel's feast, says Harding, there are only signs and figures; for no matter how strong is the imagination of the participant, the body of Christ is merely bread and wine. So he asks:

> whether of those two is the colder ceremony, and more simple supper, to have bread and wine, with a sign only of flesh and blood, or to have real flesh and blood, with such form of bread and wine as by the power of God do no less bodily nourish us than the substance would have done, we doubt not of men's wise judgment...ye will have your spiritual banquets so lean and carrion as a man may well discern whether ye have more fantasy to your flesh or to your spirit.[52]

It will be apparent how each man wishes to hold onto a version of real presence but understands that we arrive at it in different ways. And each man abhors the other's view, seeing in that view the horror of nullification of the very source and means of salvation. We will understand little about Eucharistic controversy unless we understand how this pattern repeats itself over and over again.

[50] John Jewel, *The Defence of the Apology of the Church of England* in *The Works of John Jewel, Bishop of Salisbury*, ed. John Ayre (Cambridge: The University Press for the Parker Society, 1845–50), 474.

[51] Jewel, *The Defence*, ed. Ayre, 474.

[52] Jewel, *The Defence*, ed. Ayre, 523. Harding makes this good point: 'If I can receive Christ in my house at home by faith and spirit, how is that work proper to his supper which may be brought without his supper?' (524).

In the mass, as in the communion, the Eucharist is judge as well as redeemer. It is diagnostic. What it shows is the shape of sin. That is why Ariel's business is as a reminder to the sinners of what they are. In *The Tempest* the possibilities of sitting down and eating together are going to depend on the art of memory in the activity of forgiveness. Indeed the fundamental premise of this play is that memory is communal: that it cannot be the possession of any one person alone. On Shakespeare's stage all discussion of religious subjects, and any explicit mention of God, or Christ, or the ministry of the national church, is legally out of bounds. Paradoxically, this frees the Shakespearean stage (as here in *The Tempest*) to take up and allude to the participatory forms of his culture, forms so often compromised or vitiated by coercion, torture, and violence that to call them participatory is to make a mockery of the language. For in the context of the newly national Church of England, attendance at communion and then subsequently participation in communion (James I and VI, 1606) was a mandatory, legal requirement, one meant to flush out disloyalty to the head of the English Church. In the 1671 Test Act, taking the Eucharist was to become a criterion for holding office. Eucharistic longings and their dreams of reconciliation thus migrate to the stage, allusively, yet tangibly, and to other places of contemplation, scrutiny, and relative safety—especially in the poetry of Donne, Herbert, and Vaughan.[53] Is this an aestheticization of theology? Is it an embracing of forms that are by nature voluntary, associative, and non-coercive? Is it in the case of the stage, a marketplace of ideas, as well as scripts and bodies?

FURTHER READING

Aers, David. *Sanctifying Signs: Making Christian Tradition in Late Medieval England* (Notre Dame, IN: University of Notre Dame Press, 2004)

Beckwith, Sarah. *Signifying God: Social Relation and Symbolic Act in the York Corpus Christi Play* (Chicago: University of Chicago Press, 2001)

Lubac, Henri de. *Corpus mysticum: The Eucharist and the Church in the Middle Ages* (London: SCM, 2006)

Macy, Gary. *Treasures from the Storeroom: Medieval Religion and the Eucharist* (Collegeville, MN: Liturgical Press, 1999)

Rubin, Miri. *Corpus Christi: The Eucharist in Late Medieval Culture* (Cambridge: Cambridge University Press, 1991)

[53] Regina Schwartz, *Sacramental Poetics at the Dawn of Secularism: When God Left the World* (Stanford, CA: Stanford University Press, 2008).

CHAPTER 10

THE SAINTS

JANEL MUELLER[1]

Who are the saints of Christianity, and how are they to be known? In the authoritative New Testament formulations of St Paul, most accessible perhaps in his epistle to the Romans, the 'saints' are the 'beloved of God' and 'the called of Jesus Christ' for their 'obedience to the faith' in him as 'the Son of God, with power, according to the spirit of holiness, by the resurrection from the dead' (Romans 1:4–7). Paul traces the interworkings of God's love and God's will with respect to 'the saints':

> We know that all things work together for good to them that love God, to them who are the called, according to his purpose.
>
> For whom he did foreknow, he also did predestinate to be conformed to the image of his Son, that he might be the firstborn among many brethren.
>
> Moreover whom he did predestinate, them he also called: and whom he called, them he also justified: and whom he justified, them he also glorified
>
> (Romans 8:27–30).[2]

According to Paul, the saints are to be located on a trajectory running from an eternal divine purpose to the constitution of a select subset of humankind as a timeless community, whose members live and die at various eras throughout history.[3] Creating humans in the foreknowledge that Adam and Eve and all their descendants would fall from obedience and faith into sin—'they are all under sin . . . there is none righteous, no, not one' (Romans 3:9–10)—God nevertheless determined that those whom he foreknew would love him would be justified by his Son, Christ. They would be redeemed from sin and made sharers in his righteousness as 'the body of Christ, and members in particular' (1 Corinthians 12:27);

[1] I am grateful to Bradin Cormack, Brian Cummings, James Simpson, and Christina von Nolcken for their diverse and incisive comments on earlier drafts of this essay.

[2] See Paul's similar serial predications on the saints in Ephesians 1:3–13 and Colossians 1:3–5, 12–20.

[3] Further resonances of communality as concept and practice are developed in Cathy Shrank's essay 'Community', James Simpson's essay 'Place', and Lynn Staley's 'Enclosed Spaces', all in this volume.

they would be glorified with Christ as 'heirs of God, and joint-heirs with Christ' (Romans 8:17). While never to be securely identified with any given assembly or institution on earth, the saints—past, present, and future—are God's true and only church.

Despite his apostolic urgency, despite his keen sense of strengths and backslidings in the saints of the particular churches to whom he wrote his epistles, Paul's condensed, complex theology is difficult to apprehend. It bypasses familiar patterns of association and reasoning, acquired through living in a family and a community, that one must seek protection from someone stronger in order to feel safe, and in order to receive benefits one must cultivate favour with someone who can bestow these. Paul instead routes the exclusive possibility for reestablishing connection between sinful, condemned humankind and an all-powerful God through an abstruse process of foreknowledge, election, predestination, limited atonement, and ultimate reconciliation conferred by the person and office of Christ.

In Peter Brown's account of the Christian communities of the post-apostolic church and later antiquity, 'the cult of the saints'—his title—emerges from beliefs and practices that operate at a remove from Paul's normative definitions.[4] Unfamiliarity and lack of understanding with regard to Christ's roles as mediator and redeemer open a precipitous gap between sinful humans and a judging God. Great fear combines with equally great desire to find some means of accommodation with divine power and holiness. The sharply felt dilemma triggers cultural innovation, as early Christians begin to invert Jewish and pagan burial customs aimed at shunning pollution and distancing dead bodies underground, beyond town and city walls.[5] The inversion is qualitative: the body that receives radically different treatment is that of a 'saint' (holy one), recognized through an exemplary life and witness to the faith. In the earliest era a saint was often a martyr who had been tortured to death by pagan adversaries. A saint's dead body becomes a precious, cherished entity—first, in a tomb honourably prepared for it outside the settlement of the living; later, in a splendid shrine fashioned around the tomb; and still later, in a reliquary that became a focal site in a grand basilica typically erected by a bishop in the city that was the seat of his office. What began among earlier Christians as commemoration and honouring of a saint who had embodied the triumph of good over evil gradates into an impetus to associate and closely identify with the saint by receiving, through proximity, the saint's blessing and beatitude.[6] The faithful

[4] Peter Brown, *The Cult of the Saints: Its Rise and Function in Latin Christianity* (Chicago: University of Chicago Press, 1981), Chapters 1, 4.

[5] Jocelyn M. C. Toynbee situates the graves and grave goods of third- and fourth-century Christian 'catacombs' within the larger context of non-Christian practices in *Death and Burial in the Roman World* (Ithaca, NY: Cornell University Press, 1971), 239–44.

[6] Brian Cummings has reminded me of the cultic incentive afforded by the Latin noun *praesentia* in its range of connotations from 'immediate presence, availability' to 'helpful, powerful, or opportune presence'.

offered prayers to the saint; they experienced healings and other miraculous demonstrations of beneficent power. The ostensible limitation of the saint's efficacy to the physical location of the holy remains was met in two ways: relics could be and were multiplied in ever tinier fragments without diminishing their effectiveness; pilgrimages to the saint's shrine could be undertaken, and the faithful did so in sizeable numbers.

Brown's multifaceted analysis of the cult of the saints in western Christendom focuses not only on the beliefs, expectations, and practices that assumed such major importance in worship but also on the conspicuous facts of the cult's proliferation and tenacity. What explanation can be given for the emergence of a non-biblical route to divine mercy and favour that, alongside the Mass, became the centrepiece of the church's worship for over a millennium? On the one hand, a potent ideology underlay the cult of the saints, whose figures were conceived in the richly ideal and mutually reinforcing roles of the 'friend' (*amicus*) and the 'patron' (*patronus*) in late Roman political and social life. The 'friend' was not merely well disposed, but also devoted, loyal, and active as an adherent or defender. The 'patron' was an influential person who undertook to protect another person or, more broadly, to advance and defend the interests of a community or institution; a 'patron' might also be the former master of a freed slave, a legal guardian, or a pleader for a client in a law court. What was created at a saint's tomb or shrine was a localized outlet for the most valued and vital aspirations conceivable—now raised from a this-worldly to an otherworldly level—by resorting to a fellow human who, as protector and best friend, could avert God's judgement and secure God's mercy.[7]

But the ideology in itself could not assure its survival. The agency of living Christians was required to transform such hope and aspiration into the institution that the cult of the saints became. This agency traces in turn to the care and control of saints' bodies assumed by members of affluent families of respected standing who, after the adoption of Christianity by the emperor Constantine, might be either bishops or laity. Themselves exercising the ideal roles of patronizing and befriending, these eminent persons vied with each other in acquiring and circulating remains and relics, building shrines, and bolstering the cult with their means and their devotion. The benefits, moreover, of this competition in saint worship were not restricted to the prestige and power that accrued to its promoters. The cult of the saints was characterized by a comprehensiveness of outreach and community: the poor, the sick, and the lowly were encouraged to partake and seek their human solace. They embraced the opportunity by following the lead of their social superiors, and an institution of unparalleled durability and inclusiveness took shape.[8]

[7] Brown, *Cult of the Saints*, 124.

[8] Brown, *Cult of the Saints*, 48–9.

Among Brown's proponents of the cult of the saints, Jerome, Ambrose, Augustine, Paulinus of Nola, Victricius of Rouen, and Gregory of Tours figure prominently. Augustine requires special notice because his perspective on 'the saints' encompasses what in other Christian expositors proves a mutually exclusive divide between a Pauline and a cultic conception. Augustine's contributions range, on the one hand, from his energetic promotion of the cult of St Stephen and the urgent recourse to saints that he aroused with his preaching on the torments of purgatory to, on the other hand, his influential projection of the course of world history in *The City of God* (*De civitate Dei*).[9] This takes the form of a gigantic cosmic antithesis—the respective destinies of the 'city of God' (*civitas Dei*) and the 'earthly city' or 'city of the devil' (*civitas terrena, civitas diaboli*).

Augustine's transhistorical composition of his two cities recognizably retraces Paul's serial tracking of the saints who are the true members of Christ's Church. God knew, says Augustine, from all eternity that the humans he created 'would sin and that, being thereby made subject to death . . . would propagate men doomed to die'. In his mercy, however, God resolved to rescue some number of humankind by predestining them to salvation in spite of their sins. These elect are the members of the city of God. Those whom God has not chosen as recipients of his grace are the lost souls who are the members of the earthly city. Augustine goes beyond Paul in deriving the identities of the two cities from the attachments disclosed in their love. 'If we are to discover the character of any people', he remarks, 'we have only to examine what it loves'. 'This is the great difference that distinguishes the two cities . . . The one is a fellowship of godly men, and the other of the ungodly . . . In the one city, love of God has been given pride of place, and, in the other, love of self.'

What Paul leaves enigmatic in equating the predestined and elect with the saints and true members of Christ's Church, Augustine makes more explicit and emphatic without fully dispelling ambiguity. He warns against facile identification of those who are outwardly Christians and Church members in the present age with timeless citizenship in the heavenly city. 'In this wicked world, and in these evil days . . . many reprobate are mingled in the Church with the good. Both are as it were collected in the net of the Gospel; and in this world, as in a sea, both swim together without separation, enclosed in the net until brought ashore.'[10] While we can know the overall moral characters and destinies of the city of God and the city of the devil, we cannot know with certainty who is a member of which city. This will become known only at the Last Judgement when Christ comes to judge the

[9] Brown, *Cult of the Saints*, 91, 60–1. On purgatorial torments, see Augustine, *Enarrationes in Psalmos* 6, secs. 3–7, in *Patrologia Latina Cursus Completus*, 36 (Paris: J.-P. Migne, 1865), 91–4.

[10] Augustine, *The City of God against the Pagans*, ed. and trans. R. W. Dyson (Cambridge: Cambridge University Press, 1998), xviii–xxi; quotations from 12.23, 19.24, 18.40.

living and the dead and dispatch them to their appointed end in one or the other of the two cities.

Despite Augustine's dubiety regarding earthly institutions, he insists that the Church is the sole means of access to the divine grace on which humankind is utterly dependent. He also associates political power with greed, vanity, and lust for domination, possession, and glory. He expects that persecution will frequently be the lot of the members of the heavenly city in this world. Thus a momentous turn is registered when Augustine bestows approval on the emperor Theodosius for submitting to the authority of bishop Ambrose of Milan in 390, hailing the emperor for his readiness 'to assist the church in her labours against the ungodly by means of the most just and merciful laws'.[11] It is true that Augustine denies ultimate ethical significance to any human institution. It is nonetheless also true that his two opposed cities provide the framework for later contestations over state–church relations and for the this-worldly rather than otherworldly agency that identifies 'the saints' subsequently in Lollardy and Puritanism.

While the cult of the saints proliferated in the centuries after Augustine, the legendary exploits of one category of saints—early Christian virgins martyred by pagan oppressors—became a literary sensation across western Europe. England will be the focus of the discussion to follow. In prose or verse, in Latin or the vernacular, narratives of the 'lives' of such saints as Agatha, Barbara, Cecilia, Katherine of Alexandria, Margaret, and others supplemented—and to some degree supplanted—the affective appeal of their cultic status. In their 'lives' these larger-than-life female figures combine sexual attractiveness with sexual inaccessibility as they scale generic heights of steadfast faith, fearless witness, miraculous endurance of gruesome, often sexualized tortures, and ultimate vindication as heavenly 'brides of Christ'. Karen Winstead analyses the medieval English genre of lives of virgin martyrs as a significant, if sometimes enigmatic register of what is exemplary—in the Christian life of faith, in female self-possession, in the conduct of one's relations with others, whether family or friends, suitors or persecutors.[12] Of particular significance is Winstead's finding that the example of the virgin martyr-saint may not always or only be positive. At certain times, in certain contexts, the example may be revisionary, even contestatory, regarding female agency and gender relations.

Winstead distinguishes three phases in the representation of virgin martyrs in English lives written between 1100 and 1450. In the first phase, 1100–1250, persons with religious vocations are the envisaged readership. Portrayed as ethereal brides of Christ, virgin martyrs confirm the defining values of monastic life—chastity, withdrawal from the world, love of God—as lengthy passages of prayer and

[11] Augustine, *City of God*, ed. and trans. Dyson, xxviii–xxix, quotation from 5.26.

[12] Karen A. Winstead, *Virgin Martyrs: Legends of Sainthood in Late Medieval England* (Ithaca, NY, and London: Cornell University Press, 1997).

meditation sublimate the extremity of their physical sufferings. The chief texts, the legends of the so-called Katherine group, 'provide inspiring models of heroism for women' in 'the saints' brash defiance of male authority' while simultaneously appropriating the virgin martyrs' exemplarity to reinforce 'the barrier between the laity and a celibate elite of saints and clerics'. In the final phase, 1400–50, lengthy passages of prayer and meditation again figure prominently in lives of virgin martyrs, but significant differences emerge in the envisaged readership and the characterizations of saintly heroines. Designed for lay readers whose spiritual proficiency and cultivated sensibilities often compared favourably with their clerical counterparts, the saints' lives of Osbern Bokenham, John Capgrave, and John Lydgate transform their subjects into models of 'courtesy, refinement, eloquence, and piety' who 'could be "safely" emulated': 'decorous gentlewomen who best their adversaries through heroic good manners'. In this phase, as Winstead notes, the genre reaches a cultural equilibrium: 'The exemplary virgin martyr suited to the conservative purposes of hagiographers increasingly suited the conservative tastes of middle-class readers.'[13]

However, the intervening phase of English lives of virgin martyrs, 1250–1400, demonstrates anything but cultural equilibrium as speech-and-action-packed narratives turn the spotlight on defiant, domineering, disorderly women saints. Jacobus de Voragine's *Legenda Aurea* sets the precedent in lives of Agatha, Christine, Juliana, and Margaret, whose adversaries—mighty rulers or even the devil incarnate—are no match at all for the invective, derision, or sheer muscle that the virgin martyrs deploy. In the narratives of the *South English Legendary* and the *North English Legendary*, the virgin martyrs' expressions of 'contempt for traditional figures of authority, such as fathers, well-placed suitors, and magistrates, assume a prominent place' and 'the authority, strength, and desires of men are invariably the objects of contempt'. 'By consistently emphasizing that the voices of authority against which the virgin struggles are male voices' and by dramatizing their female subjects' ingenious pursuit of 'economic, sexual, and religious freedom', 'the Middle English hagiographers present their stories as gender conflicts . . . Ongoing gender wars . . . dominate the saints' legends of the thirteenth and fourteenth centuries', profoundly troubling the exemplarity of the virgin-martyr figure.[14]

The conundrum presented by these saints' lives resists simple or single resolution. On the one hand, where the virgin martyrs figure as outspoken critics of secular power, they can be seen as serving the interests of a clerical elite concerned with maintaining ecclesiastical prerogative and authority over an increasingly informed lay public. On the other hand, by associating defiant, insubordinate behaviour with unquestionably virtuous women, these saints' lives call received views of gender into question. The virgin martyrs dissolve the association between

[13] Winstead, *Virgin Martyrs,* 11, 14, 15.

[14] Winstead, *Virgin Martyrs,* 76, 77, 82.

female speech and sexual and moral laxity. They also subvert fantasies of women as sexual objects by dramatizing their utter unattainability by males whose love (or lust) invariably ends in frustration and humiliation. In general these virgin martyrs seem to authorize rejection of patriarchal norms for female conduct.[15]

Natalie Zemon Davis has made an influential case for recognizing multiple representational effects by insisting on the range of ideological functions performed by the 'woman on top': 'Play with the unruly woman is partly a chance for temporary release from the traditional and stable hierarchy; but it is also a part of the conflict over efforts to change the basic distribution of power within society' and 'to prompt new ways of thinking about the system and reacting to it.'[16] For present purposes, what matters about these virgins as saints-in-the making is less their martyrdoms than their this-worldly agency (of which suffering is a part) and their this-worldly impact (revision of received norms).[17] In the later developments of Lollardy and Puritanism, this-worldly agency and impact come to define and identify 'the saints'.

In tandem with the legendary dimensions attained by the virgin-saints, the cultic appeal of the saints more generally was raising devotion to new heights in the churches and cathedrals of western Europe. Eamon Duffy offers a richly circumstantial evocation of 'the men and women of late medieval England... busy surrounding themselves with new or refurbished images of the holy dead, laying out large sums of money to provide lights, jewels, and precious coverings to honour these images'. The church partly imposed such devotion as an obligation: over fifty days in the year, excluding Sundays, were '*festa ferianda*, days solemnly dedicated to the saints on which all except the most essential agricultural work was forbidden'. Above all, however, such devotion became deeply internalized, as English laymen and laywomen

> looked to the saints... as powerful helpers and healers in time of need, whether bodily need or the last spiritual extremity of death and the pains of purgatory...
>
> The saint desired pilgrimage to his shrine, and a promise to visit the saint's relics and there offer a coin or a candle was held to be the most likely way to attract his interest and help...
>
> Accounts of the saints often contained dire warnings of the dangers of failing to fulfil vows undertaken during moments of crisis, and the non-performance of such vows could clearly lie heavy on the conscience, at least as the moment of final reckoning drew near...
>
> There was ample scope for fraud and abuse here.[18]

[15] Winstead, *Virgin Martyrs*, 98–111.

[16] Natalie Zemon Davis, 'Women on Top', in *Society and Culture in Early Modern France* (Stanford, CA: Stanford University Press, 1975), 131, 143.

[17] See further James Simpson, *Reform and Cultural Revolution*, The Oxford English Literary History, Vol. 2: *1350–1547* (Oxford: Oxford University Press, 2002), 406–29.

[18] Eamon Duffy, *The Stripping of the Altars: Traditional Religion in England, c.1400–c.1580* (New Haven, CT, and London: Yale University Press, 1992), Chapter 5; quotations at 156, 178, 183, 194, 196.

Among perceptive observers of the later medieval period, the vulnerability of anxious rank-and-file Christians to various sorts of manipulation and deception by unscrupulous priests and friars aroused considerable negative feeling, whether expressed in a generalized anticlericalism or in critiques that targeted the remoteness of such practices from Jesus's simplicity of life and ministry in the gospels. Such was the climate that, in England, gave rise to John Wyclif. Heterodoxy—and more transformative revampings of the idea and vocabulary of 'sainthood'—lay around the next corner.

During his tenure as an Oxford scholar and cleric and in later retirement as a parish priest in Lutterworth, Wyclif amassed a foundation in theology and metaphysics on which he built out his conception of 'the word of God': the Bible as the unique source and guarantor of the truth accessible to human minds. What drove Wyclif from radicalism to eventual heterodoxy was his relentless reasoning about the character and validity of the Church and its members, the saints false and true. As several scholars have shown, the driving force in Wyclif's thought was his extreme philosophical 'realism'.[19] Humans share in God's eternality, necessity, and indestructibility as his creation, brought into being through his knowledge and intention. Two conjoint principles of ontology and epistemology come to govern Wyclif's thinking: 'the identity of truth and being, so that whatever the mind conceived as an entity corresponded to a reality outside it'; and 'the eternity of all truth and thus of being'.[20] From these principles he deduces the literal truth and the eternal verity of scripture as 'the word of God', as well as the congruence between temporal appearances and their underlying realities and the predestined certainty of all future events.

These conjoint principles of ontology and epistemology served as a filter through which Wyclif read Augustine's *City of God* and extended the dichotomy of the two cities, with its origin in Paul, to its limits and beyond into heterodoxy regarding the institutional Church of his time. While Augustine distinguishes between the earthly and the heavenly cities—respectively, the damned or reprobate and the saved or elect—he also insists that the two are mingled in the membership of the Church, and that they would be separated only at the Last Judgement. For Wyclif, however, the damned and the saved are two eternally distinct conceptual groups corresponding to two eternally distinct modes of being; they could not mix with each other. There must always have been and there must always be a total separation of the saved and the damned.

[19] On Wyclif's philosophical context, see Anthony Kenny, 'The Realism of the *De Universalibus*', in *Wyclif in His Times*, ed. Kenny (Oxford: Clarendon Press, 1986), 17–29; and Stephen E. Lahey, *Philosophy and Politics in the Thought of John Wyclif* (Cambridge and New York: Cambridge University Press, 2003), Chapter 3.

[20] Gordon Leff, *Heresy in the Later Middle Ages: The Relation of Heterodoxy to Dissent, c. 1250–c. 1450* (Manchester: Manchester University Press; and New York: Barnes and Noble, 1967), 2: 498–510; quotations at 508, 510.

Wyclif's ontological and epistemological principles find their most sweeping application in his zeal for wholesale reform.[21] While ascribing to God not only all power but also all knowledge of who was a true member of the Church and who was not, he none the less confidently judges the conduct of the clergy by the single, simple standard of whether their living conforms to Christ's example and teaching in the gospels. Since every pope and many priests and monks of his day manifestly fail to meet this standard, they and the exercise of their offices are not only unavailing but illegitimate.[22] There was ample contextual provocation for such either-or reasoning: the fourteenth century witnessed a series of popes preoccupied with wealth, luxury, and the pursuit of political and military power culminating in the scandal of two pretenders to the Holy See setting up rival courts and jurisdictions in Rome and Avignon, the so-called 'Great Schism' (1309–77). Among unfinished works from the last years of Wyclif's life are two books entitled *De Antichristo* (On the Antichrist) in which he demands the elimination of the pope and the religious orders. Leff reflects on Wyclif's trajectory:

> The progression was complete: from denying the pope's sanctity and the need to believe in him, he came to deny him, as Antichrist, his very existence. If not inevitable it was predictable, granted Wyclif's attitude to the church and the bible.

For Wyclif there was only one implication to be drawn regarding

> the infallibility of the bible and the decretals of the church: the one was from Christ, the other could and did err; they were subject to constant change, one decretal superseding another, often from the same pope. The bible was divine and had to be believed; the church's laws when wrong had to be repudiated.

The utter antinomy that Wyclif perceives makes the claims of the Church and the Bible irreconcilable. The farthest institutional reach of his argument entails nothing less than the repudiation of ecclesiastical power and its replacement by lay power. 'The bible was the agent of the first, the king—so far... as England was concerned—of the second. Taken together, and acted upon, they meant revolution.'[23]

The cult of the saints (*sancti*) comes in for a share of Wyclif's revisionary attentions. Many post-biblical saints have been dubiously canonized, while equally dubious, even morally offensive legends about them have been condoned.

[21] On 'reform' and 'revolution' as fundamental interpretive terms, differently defined, see Simpson, *Reform and Cultural Revolution*, 1–6, 31–3.

[22] Michael Wilks, '*Reformatio regni:* Wyclif and Hus as Leaders of Religious Protest Movements', in *Schism, Heresy and Religious Protest*, ed. Derek Baker (Cambridge: Cambridge University Press, 1972), 109–27; reprinted in *Wyclif—Political Ideas and Practice: Papers by Michael Wilks*, intro. Anne Hudson (Oxford: Oxbow Books, 2000), 63–84.

[23] Leff, *Heresy*, 2:537–9, citing Wyclif, *Opus evangelicum* (Work of the Gospel), bk. 3; *De veritate* (On Truth), bk. 1; *De potestate papae* (On the Power of the Pope); *De ecclesia* (On the Church); *De civili dominio* (On Civil Dominion), bk. 1.

But Wyclif has little to say about pilgrimage, and he acknowledges the potential helpfulness of images to illiterate laypersons in their worship, if they use the images rightly.[24] As Ian Christopher Levy notes,

> even when it is right to venerate a given saint, Wyclif insists that the saint be considered in due proportion to Christ.... When one prays to a saint one's words should be directed principally towards Christ, not the saint... The honoring of saints is pointless unless it leads one to love Christ and prepares one to pray all the more for his assistance.

In the furthest reach of his critical engagement with the subject, Wyclif asserts that 'true sainthood remains a mystery; for there are many as-yet unrecognized saints doing the faithful more good with their prayers than those-so called saints whose feast days receive so much devotion.'[25]

Among Wyclif's non-academic continuators and followers, the term 'the saints' regains its special charge of Pauline meaning and assumes new intensity within the Augustinian dichotomy of the earthly and heavenly cities. The Lollards personalize this meaning, conceiving themselves as a collectivity of true, faithful Christians headed by Christ and opposed by the false, vain, merely nominal Christians headed by Antichrist. Their activism draws its inspiration from Wyclif's call for a return to the true Church of Christ through a refashioning of the present institution by lay intervention. In Leff's words,

> Lollardy can... best be described as militant spirituality. On the one hand, it looked to naked force for the physical overthrow of the existing church; on the other it opposed to it not another church but purity of heart and personal example. This attitude—or perhaps more accurately—ambivalence underlies the majority of Lollard writings.[26]

Thus, characteristically, the Twenty-Five Points, written in 1388 within four years of Wyclif's death, engage frontally with the cult of the saints, attacking the saints' days of the ecclesiastical calendar—in particular that of Thomas Becket, the upholder of papal authority at the expense of royal authority—and denouncing the use of images in worship.

To the hierarchy and sacraments of the church the Lollards opposed Christ's example of poverty and preaching, sustained in present time in the daily lives of ordinary men and women, saints attesting themselves as such. Right living, the only criterion of genuine righteousness, is the individual's own responsibility before God. So much, therefore, for the office of the priest—in place of whom

[24] Anne Hudson, *The Premature Reformation: Wycliffite Texts and Lollard History* (Oxford: Clarendon Press, 1988), 302, 307.

[25] Ian Christopher Levy, 'Wyclif and the Christian Life,' in *A Companion to John Wyclif*, ed. Levy (Leiden: Brill, 2006), 330–2; this section on 'the cult of the saints' cites Wyclif, *Trialogus* 3.30; *De ecclesia* 2.

[26] Leff, *Heresy*, 2: 575.

Wyclif's continuators and followers set Wyclif himself as 'another kind of saint'.[27] Christina von Nolcken surveys a range of Lollard opinions to the effect that Wyclif was a saint because he 'lived and taught so truly' and because he preached 'not of envy but of love... had to the law of Christ and to increase of the people in keeping it'. William Emayn was brought to abjure his view that 'Master John Wyclif was holier and now is more in bliss and higher in heaven glorified than St. Thomas of Canterbury', but in 1431 Thomas Bagley was burned at the stake, in part for holding the same view. John Stilman, condemned to burn in 1518 for relapsing into Lollardy, declared that 'Wyclif is a saint in heaven, and the book called his *Wicket* is good, for therein he showeth the truth.'

The thread of consistency in the Lollard perception of the saints traces to Wyclif's Augustinian conception of the true Church of Christ and the false Church of Antichrist, each with their eternally predetermined membership. In such a framework, von Nolcken observes, 'There is no room for saints as these were popularly conceived, for it is impossible that saints should be able in any way to affect the eternally defined state of the individual.'[28] The redefinition given to the saints by Wyclif's followers and what von Nolcken characterizes as 'their frequent positive use of the term *sancti*, or *saints*' provide a fresh impetus toward cultural innovation. Undoubtedly a by-product of their intense advocacy and study of vernacular scripture, the ideology that undergirds the Lollards' impetus consists in their recovery of Paul's serial equivalences among the 'saints', the 'predestined', the 'chosen', the 'just', and the 'saved'—terms also found frequently in their writings.[29] To the Lollards the eternal identities of the saints are crucial, not their cultic functions or legendary attributes. The saints—the members of the true Church, in and beyond time—are to carry out God's purposes in and for the world during their lives. 'The fullest exemplification of the Lollard concept of the church is to be found in chapters 6–10 of *The Lantern of Light* (c. 1409–15).'[30]

Yet again, ideology in itself could not assure its survival. The agency of living Christians—specifically identified with laymen who would undertake the reconstitution of the church—was required to carry out God's purposes in and for the world. This agency initially takes the form of agitation within existing institutional channels. The Twelve Conclusions displayed on the doors of Westminster Hall and St Paul's Cathedral during the parliamentary session of 1395 compounded scathing

[27] Christina von Nolcken, 'Another Kind of Saint: A Lollard Perception of John Wyclif', in *From Ockham to Wyclif*, ed. Anne Hudson and Michael Wilks, Studies in Church History, subsidia ser. 5 (1987), 429–43, citing the anonymous authors of *Jack Upland's Rejoinder* and of British Library, Additional MS 24202. Here and hereafter, the spelling and word-forms in quotations have been modernized.

[28] Von Nolcken, 'Another Kind of Saint', 432–3, 434–5.

[29] See Matti Peikola, *Congregation of the Elect: Patterns of Self-Fashioning in English Lollard Writings*, Anglicana Turkuensia No. 21 (Turku, Finland: University of Turku Press, 2000).

[30] Hudson, *The Premature Reformation*, 318.

critique of the church's material wealth with the demand that Lords and Commons debar clergy of all ranks from holding any kind of temporal office. The Disendowment Bill presented to Parliament in 1407 or 1410 took Lollard aspirations a good distance farther in a bold vision of reform centering on the confiscation of all 'temporalities'—income derived from land or tenements rather than 'spiritualities', income derived from benefices, tithes, and fees for ecclesiastical offices—that bishops and monastic houses regularly received. Specifying the amounts that could be expected to accrue to the crown from named bishoprics and monasteries, the Disendowment Bill proposed that the money be applied to enlarge the numbers of secular nobility, to establish an almshouse in every town, and to endow new universities.[31] While redistribution of power would accompany the redistribution of money, the church of England would remain a recognizable institution as it discharged its defining spiritual functions, now suitably purified.

Neither church nor crown would have been recognizable, however, in the England envisaged by Sir John Oldcastle, Lord Cobham, who led an abortive Lollard uprising in 1414. As detailed in the subsequent judicial proceedings, Oldcastle's objectives aimed at full-scale revolution: 'wholly to annul the royal estate as well as the estate and office of prelates and religious orders in England' by killing Henry V and his brothers as well as ranking bishops and other magnates of the realm, 'to turn men of religion, after they had abandoned divine worship and religious observances, to secular occupations', and 'totally to despoil cathedrals and other churches and religious houses of their relics and other ecclesiastical goods, and to level them completely to the ground'. With the monarchy extirpated, Oldcastle would exercise the role of regent for 'a people without a head'.[32] When an anticipated gathering of 20,000 men in St Giles' Fields, London, marshalled only some two hundred supporters, a manhunt for the ringleader ensued. Although Oldcastle escaped from detention for a while, he was eventually tried, condemned, and executed for high treason. Unstinting suppression thereafter by crown and church drove the Lollards underground as a movement, casting the seeds of their future influence into dormancy. But, as von Nolcken notes regarding the historiographical consensus that has formed among scholars during the last half century,

> The Lollards first perceived Wyclif as saint—and, I have suggested, one of a new kind—, then also as martyr. In creating for themselves such a symbol of the possibility of salvation they were anticipating what was to be done very self-consciously to figures like Oldcastle by the sixteenth-century Reformers [a note refers to John Bale and John Foxe]. Their definition of what saints were is one that has

[31] Hudson, *The Premature Reformation*, 334, 339.

[32] The National Archives, MS K.B. 27/613, cited in Margaret Aston, *Lollards and Reformers: Images and Literacy in Late Medieval Religion* (London: Hambledon Press, 1984), 25.

become familiar to us from later Puritan usage. It is becoming clear that there was a good deal of continuity between Lollardy and Protestantism.[33]

It might have been supposed that the advent of the Reformation and the concomitant rupture with papal authority would advance the revolutionary Lollard objectives for the church in England—the more so because the initial agents of reform were prominently lay powers: Henry VIII, his chief minister Thomas Cromwell, and the king's compliant parliaments of 1529–36. Certain Lollard objectives were reinvented and pursued as Reformation initiatives: the dismantling of monasteries and nunneries, the confiscation of their properties, and the dissolution of the vows of members of religious orders; subsequently, chantries and payments to priests who said masses for the souls of the dead met their end.[34] It was newly licit to denounce the pope (reductively styled 'the bishop of Rome') and the Roman *curia* as Antichrist and his minions. Cromwell's and archbishop Thomas Cranmer's adroit representations to Henry VIII secured royal authorization to print and circulate the scriptures in English; the result was the Great Bible of 1538–9. In 1547 the accession of the boy-king Edward VI and his forthrightly Protestant elder uncle, Edward Seymour, duke of Somerset, as his protector increased the momentum of the Reformation and convergent influences from the Lollard inheritance on several fronts. Cranmer's English Book of Common Prayer (1549, 1552) stripped the non-biblical saints out of the ecclesiastical calendar, while iconoclasm—the despoiling of shrines and images of saints in churches—became crown policy under Henry and Edward.[35] From their London pulpits Robert Crowley and Thomas Lever inveighed against covetousness and the decay of learning, calling for the expropriated resources of the nationalized church to be applied towards founding almshouses, hospitals, and schools.[36]

Such proposals had been the substance of two provisions of the Lollard Disendowment Bill. In the event, however, in Edward's reign no less than in Henry's, the

[33] Von Nolcken, 'Another Kind of Saint', 436, 443, citing pertinent scholarship including Christopher Hill, 'From Lollards to Levellers', in *Rebels and Their Causes: Essays in Honour of A. L. Morton*, ed. Maurice Cornforth (Atlantic Highlands, NJ: Humanities Press, 1979), 49–67. Also see J. F. Davis, 'Lollardy and the Reformation in England', *Archiv für Reformationsgeschichte*, 73 (1982); reprinted in *The Impact of the English Reformation, 1500–1640*, ed. Peter Marshall (London: Arnold and New York: St. Martin's Press, 1997), 37–54. Richard Rex has recently disputed claimed continuities between Lollardy and the English Reformation in *The Lollards* (New York: Palgrave, 2002).

[34] Hudson, *The Premature Reformation*, 508–9. In the specific (and different) area of theology, Carl R. Trueman surveys convergences and commonalities in the two movements, concluding by emphasizing the difficulty of definitive assessment: 'If Lollardy was an initial influence upon the shape of English Reformation theology, this influence was rendered invisible by the overwhelming impact of more recent and more sophisticated theological developments' (*Luther's Legacy: Salvation and English Reformers, 1525–1556* (Oxford: Clarendon Press, 1994), 44).

[35] Simpson, *Reform and Cultural Revolution*, 384–8, 457.

[36] Janel Mueller, 'Literature and the Church: the Tudor Era from the Reformation to Elizabeth I', in *The Cambridge History of Early Modern English Literature*, ed. David Loewenstein and Janel Mueller (Cambridge: Cambridge University Press, 2002), 257–309.

former wealth of the Church was channelled in the direction envisaged in a third provision of that Bill: the augmentation of the estates, wealth, and power of the nobility and the crown. In by far its largest measure, the Tudor Reformation remained traditionalist and conservative regarding the Church as an institution under the supreme headship of the sovereign monarch. Despite the reduction of the bishops' wealth and the greater role of the laity in the governance of the realm, there was no impetus to restructure the Church of England and refashion its members in accordance with their primitive Christian prototypes, as Wyclif and his Lollard supporters had advocated with such zeal.

Correspondingly, the use of the term 'saints' in the writings of Church of England clergy in Henry's and Edward's reign displays a preponderantly conventional range of reference.[37] 'This word saints is diversely taken', notes Hugh Latimer, bishop of Worcester for a time under Henry; 'images of saints are called saints and inhabiters of heaven are called saints'. The prolific and popular dialogue-writer Thomas Becon, Cranmer's chaplain and a prebendary of Canterbury, endlessly ridicules praying to images of saints, while John Hooper, bishop of Gloucester and Worcester under Edward, prohibits depictions of saints in any church windows or on any church walls in his diocese. Hooper stakes his principled stand on the First Commandment (Exodus 20:3): 'I say that these superstitious persons that maketh their patrons or singular helpers of the saints, differ nothing in this point from the heathen or gentile ... Praised be the mercy of God! I hear say, and believe it, that Englishmen hath resigned St. George's usurped title to the living God.'[38] William Tyndale likewise applies a stringent scripture-only criterion in repeatedly challenging Thomas More on the intercessory powers and miracles ascribed to saints by the Roman church: the benefits alleged 'to confirm praying to saints do not confirm God's doctrine, but man's imaginations', and the so-called saints of 'the pope's kingdom' can do no miracles after their deaths, for 'miracles have ceased' and 'faith is to be grounded only upon the word of God'.[39]

To the infrequent extent that writers of the Henrician and Edwardine church acknowledge the Pauline conception of saints as the true church of God, they tend

[37] See the comprehensive listing under 'Saints' in Henry Gough, *General Index to the Publications of the Parker Society* (Cambridge: Cambridge University Press, 1855), 56: 678–9.

[38] Hugh Latimer, 'Articles imputed to Latimer in John Foxe's *Acts and Monuments* (1563)', in *Sermons and Remains*, ed. George Elwes Corrie, Publications of the Parker Society 28 (1845): 233–4; Thomas Becon, 'The Pathway unto Prayer' and 'The Governance of Virtue', in *Early Works*, ed. John Ayre, Parker Society 2 (1843): 134–5, 138–9, 420; Becon, 'A New Catechism', 'The Jewel of Joy', and 'A Treatise of Fasting', in *Later Works*, ed. Ayre, Parker Society 3 (1844): 144, 414, 536; John Hooper, 'Injunctions', in *Later Writings*, ed. Charles Nevinson, Parker Society 21 (1852), 138–9, and 'A Declaration of the Ten Commandments' in *Early Writings*, ed. Samuel Carr, Parker Society 20 (1843), 314.

[39] William Tyndale, *An Answer vnto Sir Thomas Mores Dialoge*, ed. Anne M. O'Donnell, S.N.D. and Jared Wicks, S.J., vol. 3 of *The Independent Works of William Tyndale* (Washington: The Catholic University of America Press, 2000), 118, 131–2.

notably to locate it either in New Testament times or in an invisible spiritual community that spans time and place. The historically inclined John Jewel, who would become bishop of Salisbury under Elizabeth, reflects from his pulpit: 'So the Christian men in the beginning repented themselves and changed their whole life, and therefore were called saints, as St. Paul useth in many places to name them.' Latimer reflects transhistorically from his pulpit: 'We thought only those to be saints and holy, that be gone out of this world; but it is not so. All they that believe in our Saviour Christ, that call upon his name, and look to be saved by him, those same be the Lord's saints.' Becon gives a comparable definition in 'A New Catechism': 'The holy universal church is, verily, a company of saints or of holy and godly-disposed persons knit together by one Spirit, in one faith, in one hope, in one love, in one doctrine, having one head, which is Christ Jesus, and serving one God, which is the Father of our Lord Jesus Christ.'[40]

While the content of such affirmations is unexceptionable, the tonality borders on patness, even platitude. If the conception of the saints was to regain its this-worldly dynamism, it would need recharging somehow. John Bale, self-exiled in Germany after Thomas Cromwell's fall from power brought religious conservatives to new ascendancy in England, sought to rekindle Augustinian and Lollard fervour.[41] His commentary on Revelation, *The Image of Both Churches*, offers a narrative shape and affective model for a new figuration of English nationhood as the bride of Christ, 'the undefiled spouse', who will defy and triumphantly outface the whore of Babylon, 'the paramour of Antichrist'—that is, the 'carnality' and 'idolatry' of the Roman Church and its temporal dominions.[42] Equally intemperate against 'popish' power but more incisively radical in its implications for English history and history-writing, Bale's 'Brief Chronicle concerning the examination and death of the blessed martyr of Christ, sir John Oldcastle, lord Cobham' casts the surviving records of Oldcastle's interrogation and condemnation as a composite fiendish parody of the gospel account of Jesus's betrayal by Judas, arraignment before Pilate, and eventual guiltless execution as a criminal.[43]

[40] John Jewel, 'Sermon on Haggai 1:24' in *Works*, ed. John Ayre, Parker Society 24 (1847), 1002; Latimer, 'Sermons Preached in Lincolnshire, no. 3', in *Sermons*, ed. Corrie, Parker Society 27 (1844), 507; Becon, 'A New Catechism', 43. Becon's catechism is indebted in structure and substance to Luther's *Greater Catechism*; see Derrick Sherwin Bailey, *Thomas Becon and the Reformation of the Church of England* (Edinburgh: Oliver and Boyd, 1952), 136–7.

[41] After Bale obtained a manuscript of *Fasciculi Zizaniorum*, the Carmelite collection of documents relating to Wyclif and the early Lollards, around 1538, his conception of the church and of the book of Revelation as prophetic history began to manifest distinct Lollard influences. See Leslie P. Fairfield, *John Bale: Mythmaker for the English Reformation* (West Lafayette, IN: Purdue University Press, 1976), 70–1, 78, 94.

[42] Claire McEachern, *The Poetics of English Nationhood, 1590–1612* (Cambridge: Cambridge University Press, 1996), 27.

[43] John Bale, 'Brief Chronicle', in *Select Works*, ed. Henry Christmas, Parker Society 1 (1849), 5–59.

Bale's precedent in accounting this Lollard lord a martyr-saint would be massively enlarged and indelibly inscribed in the English Protestant imagination by John Foxe's *Acts and Monuments of the English Church*, popularly known as the 'Book of Martyrs'. Foxe undertook to authenticate and memorialize the witnessings unto death by burning at the stake enacted by hundreds of English men, women, and youths, whose heresy interrogations Mary Tudor licensed when she and her compliant parliament returned the realm of England to papal jurisdiction after her accession as queen in 1553. These latter-day saints hold fast in their bible-based faith, refusing to recant and subscribe to the formulations of Catholic inquisitors, most of whom are native English, like those they interrogate. For subsequent generations of English Protestant readers the effect of Foxe's gripping narrations has been to find inward sustenance for what are often quite different and less spectacular trials of their own faith.[44]

Not the Marian martyrs, however, but the Marian self-exiles who escaped the threat of persecution by fleeing to John Calvin's Geneva would initiate the process of cultural innovation that assumed transformative shape and force in English Puritanism. The underlying coordinates of Calvin's thought are familiar. Like Paul and Augustine, he begins from the primal fact of the Fall and the universal human condition of total depravity, brought on through wilful creaturely disobedience of the sovereign will of God the creator. But, unlike Paul and Augustine, Calvin does not proceed to envisage a company of those foreknown, elect, and predestined by God for salvation. While crediting foreknowledge, election, and predestination as truths of scripture—for Calvin affirms as unconditionally as does Wyclif the absolute reality of God's being, will, and word—he nevertheless refuses to inquire into the unfathomable mystery of God's ultimate purposes for his saints at the end of time.[45]

Instead Calvin trains his attention on what he registers as the unruly, aggressive, fearful, insecure realities of human conduct and life in the here and now. He commits himself to devising 'a doctrine of discipline and obedience', at once mental and moral, that would produce 'systematic innovation' in forms of organization and governance for the church, in the first instance, and by extension, for

[44] See John N. King, *Foxe's Book of Martyrs and Early Modern Print Culture* (Cambridge: Cambridge University Press, 2006); and Brian Cummings, 'Images in Books: Foxe *Eikonoklastes*', in *Art Re-formed: Re-assessing the Impact of the Reformation on the Visual Arts*, ed. Tara Hamling and Richard L. Williams (Newcastle, UK: Cambridge Scholars Publishing, 2007), 183–200, who remarks at 188: 'The book of martyrs is quite obviously, among other things, itself a form of cult of the saints. Foxe applies his own iconography of sainthood, and mediates his own ideal of a proper understanding of his imagery, a proper form of worship among his readership.... Despite counter-propaganda, he is not at all afraid of the word "saint" or unself-conscious of the fact that his opponents will affect surprise at this.'

[45] See the expositions of 'election' and 'predestination' in François Wendel, *Calvin: Origins and Development of His Religious Thought*, trans. Philip Mairet (Durham, NC: Labyrinth Press, 1987), 263–84.

the state. A crucial ambiguity lurks in the Calvinist view of human institutions as means willed by God for containing human sin; in principle, this could justify the creation of any kind of regime. But Calvin repeatedly aims for more than the minimum, particularly in the constitution of the Church: the enterprising agents had to be instruments of the divine will. As he conceives the saints, they know themselves to be such instruments because God has put his mark upon them in the form of conscience—what Michael Walzer characterizes as 'a piece of divine willfulness implanted in man'.[46] Conscience is the saints' warrant to act in the cause of order and reform; successful action would be the sign from God justifying what they did. The precariousness that defined individual and social life could be controlled by applying one's will in systematically regulating one's own conduct and, in association with like-willed others, applying the will of the group to society as a whole. This deliberate self-investment in formulating practical, programmatic measures for institution building and saint making is what most clearly distinguishes Calvin from all of his predecessors. It is also what unleashes his revolutionary implications for church and state.[47]

Calvin sought in the institution of the church and, by extension, the Christian commonwealth an outcome qualitatively different from the formation of a secular state. Since God claims voluntary obedience, the saints should be subjects as well as the objects of organizational control. Conscience and coercion are to converge.

> Calvin was acutely aware of the vast increase in social control that would result if human beings could be made to will that control themselves and to consent to it in their hearts... This is what the Calvinist saints actually did in their private lives, in their churches and congregations, and in those states and commonwealths where they managed to seize power....
>
> As a prelude to admitting the state to the world of religious purpose, Calvin admitted politics to religion. He often described the church as a commonwealth, and the metaphor is a significant key to his thought.[48]

Of the some 800 English Protestants who fled the realm after Mary came to the throne, about half were clergymen, or students from Cambridge and Oxford. They were of modest origins and limited means. The next largest group, about a third, were gentlemen. The predominance of clerical intellectuals and the participation of the gentry invested the Marian experience of exile with ideological and practical

[46] Michael Walzer, *The Revolution of the Saints: A Study in the Origins of Radical Politics* (Cambridge, MA: Harvard University Press, 1965), 23–4, 58–9.

[47] On the English Puritan assimilation of the Calvinist binding of individual and community in the concept of 'vocation' or 'calling', see William Ames, *The Marrow of Theology*, ed. and trans. John D. Eusden (Grand Rapids, MI: Baker Books, 1968), 29–33, 157–60, 322–3; and William Perkins, 'A Treatise of the Vocations or Callings of Men', in *The Work of William Perkins*, ed. Ian Breward (Abingdon, UK: Sutton Courtenay Press, 1970), 443–76.

[48] Walzer, *Revolution of the Saints*, 47, 51. See further Ronald S. Wallace, *Calvin, Geneva and the Reformation* (Edinburgh: Scottish Academic Press, 1988), Chapters 3, 7–10.

importance. Wherever the exiles went in the Reformed cities of south Germany and Switzerland, they lived apart, 'outside the limits of any effective jurisdiction . . . free to come and go as they chose . . . above all free to order the internal affairs of their own little communities as they chose'.[49] After a dispute in the English community at Frankfurt over the use of the Book of Common Prayer, the defeated party, the Puritans of the future, relocated in Calvin's Geneva.

They found the Calvinist Church to be an inclusive organization of professing Christians, governed by a select committee of ministers and laymen. The admission of laymen to the government of the Church was an outcome of Reformation emphases on the equality of all believers before God and on individual accountability for the state of one's soul. This new equality might have yielded a new democracy in the Church, for the congregation supposedly chose the lay elders, who were always a majority, and who sat alongside the ministers. In actuality, unless there was 'godly' opposition, considerable deference was paid to the existing Church leadership. None the less, the organizational value of lay participation was considerable. Elders and deacons contributed to the integration and cohesion of a church polity that no longer depended on a binary relation of superior and inferior, a pastor and his parishioners. Walzer comments:

> Calvin . . . designed the moral discipline to tighten and stabilize the bonds of fellowship. The assembly of ministers and elders was given great powers of investigation and . . . censure, enforced by the power of excommunication. But such power . . . would be impossible without lay participation . . . The investigations of the church elders depended upon the 'mutual surveillance' of the church members. Calvinist discipline required a direct and willful obedience to the Word of God as represented in the regulations of the consistory . . . The saints were a tightly disciplined group, the supreme example of the new ideology's organising power. As they had proven their regeneracy by their rigorous self-control, so they acted it out in the world . . . The saint was the militant Christian activist, and his activity carried him outside the church. He not only participated in congregational government, he also created the holy commonwealth.[50]

The contracting of the saints with God and with one another in church and commonwealth attained formal realization in Calvin's idea of the covenant, first enacted in Geneva in 1537 when he led the ministers in demanding that the entire city make a public profession of its dual identity. The people swore to keep their new faith and to obey the Ten Commandments; they also swore their loyalty to the city. Clearly modelled on biblical antecedents, the Calvinist covenant combined

[49] Constance M. Garrett, *The Marian Exiles* (Cambridge: Cambridge University Press, 1938), 18. See further Andrew Pettegree, *Marian Protestantism: Six Studies* (Aldershot, UK, and Brookfield, VT: Scolar Press, 1996); and Diarmaid MacCullough, *The Later Reformation in England, 1547–1603* (New York: St. Martin's Press, 1990).

[50] Walzer, *Revolution of the Saints*, 53–4; also see Wendel on 'the church' in *Calvin: Origins and Development of His Religious Thought*, 291–311.

elements of law and grace. Since no human being could perfectly obey the Mosaic law, God extended his grace to the ancient Israelites no less than to later Christians. There is, however, a distinction: the Old Testament covenant was national and communal, but God offered his grace to individuals in the New Testament. Calvin's theological emphasis alternated: law, then grace, then law again—with the significant difference that those who receive grace in the third stage inwardly accept the law. Since the grace to accept law reforms a community, the alternation can be redescribed as communal, then personal, then communal again. In the final stage, a covenanting individual wills his or her obedience to God. But such self-submission is equally a communal act, subject to communal enforcement in God's name. With the introduction of the covenant, Christian discipline acquires the force of an absolute dominion—at once outwardly recognizable as godly and embraced freely by the conscience. The concept affords crucial insight into the complex workings of order and control that, for Calvin, define and direct the this-worldly associations and activities of the saints.[51] Transmuting the theology of salvation into concrete social and political practice, civic and national covenants accordingly become hallmarks of the Puritanism of old and New England.[52]

The bulk of Walzer's account in *The Revolution of the Saints* details the stages by which, first, the alienated, rootless, suggestible Marian exiles in Geneva adopt Calvinist ideology and institutional forms as normative for themselves. The clerical intellectuals are prolific in print. Christopher Goodman and John Knox carry Calvin's theories of resistance to rulers who countermand God's will beyond limits countenanced by Calvin: they justify armed resistance and even the forcible removal of an ungodly prince. Although Goodman's and Knox's target was Mary Tudor, the clash of royalist and parliamentarian armies in the civil war begun in 1642 did not lie beyond the eventual horizon of imagination. In his *Tenure of Kings and Magistrates* (1649) John Milton cites by name a group of Genevan exiles including Goodman and Knox as 'the true Protestant Divines of *England,* our fathers in the faith we hold'.[53]

In the next stage of development English Puritanism acquires its name, as returned radical clergy and their associates agitate for the purifying of the Church of England from 'popish' and 'idolatrous' vestments and ceremonies as well as for the use of extemporaneous praying and preaching in public worship. This agitation climaxes in John Field's and Thomas Wilcox's *Admonition to Parliament* (1572), a call for reform that Queen Elizabeth had declined to heed—and in Thomas Cartwright's *Second Admonition* (1574) and other polemic promoting Calvinist

[51] Walzer, *Revolution of the Saints*, 55–7, citing John Calvin, *Institutes of the Christian Religion*, 2.10.2, 3.17.5–6.

[52] Walzer, *Revolution of the Saints*, 166–71.

[53] John Milton, *The Tenure of Kings and Magistrates*, ed. Merritt Y. Hughes in *Complete Prose Works of John Milton* (New Haven, CT: Yale University Press, 1962), 3: 251.

church organization and government.[54] Groups of radical clergy convene unauthorized discussions of scripture ('prophesyings') and unauthorized consultations on doctrine and policy ('conferences'). Job Throckmorton's secret press rolls out 'Martin Marprelate's' scurrilous attacks on the bishops. The tactics recall the Lollards, as does the outcome—official suppression of all such activities by the early 1590s.

In a more extended, gradual, and overlapping stage of development, English Puritanism makes inroads into the social fabric as synergies develop between the clergy and conscientious laypersons—country gentry and London lawyers and merchants—who discover obligation and opportunity in the participatory regimens of Calvinism.[55] Spanning at least five decades from the 1580s to the 1630s, this stage of development proves strikingly effective on the institutional level. Puritan clergy and laymen cooperate in the 'Feoffees of Impropriation', a dubiously legal corporation that bought up church livings and lectureships to bestow on suitably godly recipients. The godly Puritan household emerges, its literary staple the Geneva Bible (1560) with its virulently Protestant glosses, its own literary genre the self-examining personal journal. The universities, particularly Cambridge, make Puritanism an exciting intellectual and moral adventure. Such eminences as William Perkins at Christ's College and Laurence Chaderton at Emmanuel train a generation of graduates—a number of whom take part in the 'Great Migration' of the 1630s and work to found God's 'city on a hill' in New England. Others including Milton and Oliver Cromwell hear and heed the call to remake old England anew.[56]

At the level of ideology and action alike, cultural innovations mark the ascendancy gained by the Puritan saints—Presbyterians and Independents, Parliament and army—during the eighteen-year period of civil war and commonwealth. Their ideology proves outstandingly innovative in two instances: the capital criminal charges brought against Charles I (1649) for voiding his coronation oath and taking up arms against his own people, whose welfare he had sworn to protect; the army debates at Putney (October–November 1647), where what qualifies an

[54] Patrick Collinson provides a definitive account of the controversy over *Admonition* in *The Elizabethan Puritan Movement* (Berkeley: University of California Press, 1967; rpt. Oxford: Clarendon Press, 1990), 101–49; A. F. Scott Pearson has surveyed the broader sweep of godly activism and its curtailment in *Thomas Cartwright and Elizabethan Puritanism, 1535–1603* (Cambridge: Cambridge University Press, 1925).

[55] John Stachniewski, *The Persecutory Imagination: English Puritanism and the Literature of Religious Despair* (Oxford: Clarendon Press, 1991), probes the dark underside of this era: the unassuageable doubts experienced by some aspiring saints regarding their own election and justification.

[56] See Steve Hindle's chapters on 'The Reformation of Manners' and 'The Governance of the Parish' in *The State and Social Change in Early Modern England, c. 1550–1640* (Basingstoke, UK: Macmillan Press and New York: St. Martin's Press, 2000), 176–230; and William Hunt, *The Puritan Moment: The Coming of Revolution in an English County* (Cambridge, MA: Harvard University Press, 1983).

individual as a political subject with rights of political participation and expression is freely explored without preconceived limits.[57] Action proves comparably innovative in the formidably effective organization and tactics of Cromwell's New Model Army and in the execution of Charles I.[58] The guilty verdict climaxed by the king's beheading, the mode of execution used on traitors, dealt the conception of sacred monarchy a no less lethal blow. Yet with regard to their two greatest objectives, the Puritan saints failed both to remodel the national church and to establish a national republic. Having failed in these, the Puritan saints, individuals and communities, found their subsequent places as a minority among the people of England—the proportion of their actual numbers all along. As a unified movement with an imperative agenda for politics and society, Puritanism reached its limits, although its hold in New England would last somewhat longer.[59]

Reaching limits of a potential for institutional reform, however, is one thing; spending the force of an ideology is quite another. Historians continue to argue that the precedent of the Puritan saints has been influential in the shaping of modern selfhood and the conduct of industrial and post-industrial life. They detect an enduring residue of Puritan self-discipline in such generally assumed societal norms as methodical working habits, dependable contractual relations, and impersonal arrangements for cooperation created by mutual agreement on means and ends. Most influentially, perhaps, Max Weber has claimed an origin in Puritan self-discipline for the acquisitive drive of 'capitalist man'—the pursuit of ever improved business techniques and more and more profit. Weber's claim, however, is contradicted by conspicuous historical facts: the frugality of the saints, their modest style of living and dressing, and their charitable disposal of surplus income. As Walzer observes, 'The moral discipline of the saints . . . was not in itself capitalist.'[60]

He himself locates the significance of the Puritan saints in what he calls 'an ideology of transition' that meets 'the human needs that arise whenever traditional controls give way and hierarchical status and corporate privileges are called into question'. These needs, Walzer contends, 'are met most effectively by doctrines that encourage a vigorous self-control and a narrowing of energies in a bold effort to shape a new personality against the background of social unsettledness. Once such a personality has been achieved, the saints proceed to shape society in the image of their own salvation'—that is, through group control and self-control exerted in

[57] *Puritanism and Liberty, Being the Army Debates (1647–9) from the Clarke Manuscripts with Supplementary Documents*, ed. A. S. P. Woodhouse (London: J.M. Dent, 1938; rpt. 1974, 1986).

[58] Antonia Fraser, *Cromwell, Our Chief of Men* (London: Weidenfeld and Nicolson, 1973), Part 2: 'War and Peace', Part 3: 'The Commonwealth of England'.

[59] Edmund S. Morgan, *Visible Saints: The History of a Puritan Idea* (New York: New York University Press, 1963) remains a classic account of the separatist ecclesiology of Puritan New England.

[60] Walzer, *Revolution of the Saints*, 304, quoting Max Weber, *The Protestant Ethic and the Spirit of Capitalism*, trans. Talcott Parsons (New York: Charles Scribner, 1958), 171.

new institutional forms. The surpassing value of sainthood and the core of its revolutionary character, in Walzer's view, is the mediation it models for 'the dangerous shift from one social routine to another'.[61]

Walzer's heavily psychologized assessment of the value of the model of Puritan sainthood in present-day circumstances restricts the potential contributions of that model to the level of ideology, making no allowance for potential contributions on the institutional level. Such a restriction looks untenable, however, in the wake of September 11, 2001, and the emergence of a culture of surveillance in the United States and the United Kingdom. Its institutional innovations are striking: a new Federal Department of Homeland Security; ubiquitous installations of CCTV cameras; routine breaches of privacy by airport security personnel; a prison at Guantánamo that flouts not only *habeas corpus* but the most basic human rights. Few if any contemporary Americans and Britons are likely to subscribe to Calvin's extreme notions of human depravity and rampant wilfulness or to his insistence that regulation, control, punishment, and correction are the functions that justify and define every political and social arrangement. Yet in acquiescing in the new institutions of our contemporary culture of surveillance, we as individuals and as collectivities demonstrably do accept the implications of Calvin's notions and Calvin's insistence. We behave as if we are more in touch with our own 'inner Puritan saint' than we may care to admit.

FURTHER READING

Brown, Peter. *The Cult of the Saints: its Rise and Function in Latin Christianity* (Chicago, 1981)

Walzer, Michael. *The Revolution of the Saints: A Study in the Origins of Radical Politics* (New York, 1965)

[61] Walzer, *Revolution of the Saints*, 312, 316.

CHAPTER 11

VERNACULAR THEOLOGY

THOMAS BETTERIDGE

> Being asked his name, or whether he was not called James Nayler, he replied: 'The men of this world call me "James Nayler"'.
>
> Q. Art thou not the man that rid on horseback into Bristol, a woman leading thy horse, and others singing before thee 'Holy, holy, holy, Hosannah'.
>
> A. I did ride into town, but what its name was I know not, and by the Spirit a woman was commanded to hold my horse's bridle; and some there were that cast down clothes, and sang praises to the Lord, such songs as the Lord put into their hearts; and its like it might be the song of 'Holy, holy, holy'.
>
> Q. Whether or no didst thou reprove those women?
>
> A. Nay, but I bade them take heed that they sang nothing but what they were moved to of the Lord.
>
> *The Examination of James Nayler*, 1656.[1]

This exchange between James Nayler and his examiners over the events that took place in Bristol 1656 illustrates the problems, but also the importance, of vernacular theology as a category of analysis for the study of social and cultural change during the period between Lollardy and the English Civil War. Nayler and his followers were moved by a mystical desire to experience a direct union with God embodied in their creation of a true sign that transcended particular times, places, and individuals. Nayler and his supporters were not re-enacting or staging Christ's entry into Jerusalem. They were engaged in a moment of embodied mysticism. It is easy to see Nayler as a radical, even a fanatic. His mysticism, however, simply pushed the logic of early Quaker thought to its limit. Indeed Nayler's desire to fully know Christ, to escape the coils of the world and the body, is fully explicable in terms of the Puritan privileging of an experimental understanding of Christ. Nayler was simply making real the Protestant promise of escape from the riddling allegories and false hermeneutic tropes of Papistry. His mistake was, therefore, not doctrinal as much as temporal. From a Calvinist, and Augustinian, perspective

[1] Quoted in Leopold Damrosch, *The Sorrows of the Quaker Jesus: James Nayler and the Puritan Crackdown on the Free Spirit* (London: Harvard University Press, 1996), 150.

he failed to appreciate that ultimately there can be no escape from the false allegories of this world within the scope of human time.[2]

It would, however, be a mistake to see Nayler's behaviour as simply aberrant since the events in Bristol in 1656 embody what Michel de Certeau has argued is a defining characteristic of post-Reformation Christian mysticism. De Certeau comments that, 'Mysticism is the anti-Babel. It is a search for a common language, after language has been shattered.'[3] Nayler and his followers were fully committed to the mystical ideal of escaping the curse of Babel, of experiencing a moment of oneness with God that went beyond the limitations of human language. At one level they can therefore be seen as representing, albeit in a particularly radical form, an important aspect of mainstream post-Reformation religious *praxis*.[4]

This chapter was initially entitled 'Mysticism'. Nayler's example, however, illustrates some of the scholarly problems that I have encountered in producing this piece.[5] Is Nayler a mystic? In what ways can one usefully compare Nayler's mysticism with that of fourteenth-century writers like Julian of Norwich? Is it possible to compare *The Cloud of Unknowing* and Nayler's entry into Bristol in 1656 without being seriously historically reductive? Above all, the different status accorded mystical writing by medieval and Renaissance scholars means that to compare medieval and early modern mysticism would be to reproduce existing narratives of religious and social change. For this reason, the editors and I have agreed to entitle this chapter 'Vernacular Theology'.[6] This is a compromise. The change to 'vernacular theology' reflects the problems caused by the asymmetrical status of mysticism across the period divide medieval and Renaissance. It is also, however, the product of the ideological imperative to defend the constancy and continuity of explanatory categories within traditional historiography. Mysticism as a category cannot easily or unproblematically cross from the medieval to the early modern;

[2] Thomas H. Luxon, '"Not I, But Christ": Allegory and the Puritan Self', *English Literary History*, 60 (1993), 899–937.

[3] Michel de Certeau, *Heterologies: Discourse on the Other*, trans. Brian Massumi (Minneapolis: University of Minnesota Press, 1986), 88.

[4] For a discussion of an emerging post-Reformation hermeneutic norm see James Simpson, *Burning to Read: English Fundamentalism and its Reformation Opponents* (Cambridge, MA: Harvard University Press, 2007).

[5] Nicholas Watson has recently expressed doubts about the usefulness of the term 'mysticism'. With reference to his contribution to the *Cambridge History of Medieval English Literature*, he writes that, 'the overarching theme of this chapter... is that both the cannon of "Middle English mystics" and the term "mysticism" itself have largely outlived their usefulness to scholars'; Nicholas Watson, 'The Middle English Mystics', in *Cambridge History of Medieval English Literature*, ed. David Wallace (Cambridge: Cambridge University Press, 1999), 539–65, at 539.

[6] Vernacular theology is a problematic but productive term; for an introduction to this category in relation to medieval literature see Vincent Gillespie, 'Vernacular Theology', in *Middle English*, ed. Paul Strohm, Oxford Twenty-First Century Approaches to Literature (Oxford: Oxford University Press, 2007), 401–20.

it cannot carry the weight of this crossing while retaining its purity as a historical category.[7]

Mysticism's failure, albeit within a historiography that demands constancy and continuity from the categories that it deploys, raises questions about the amount of ideological work, the erasure and eliding of cultural and social conflicts, that is being performed by those categories which can pass with their virtue intact between the medieval and Renaissance. In particular, what became clear to me when trying to explore the connections between religious works written across the period between Lollardy and the English Civil War was how powerful the temptation was to deploy confessional religious identities, Protestant and Roman Catholic, to explain the relationship between, for example, Julian of Norwich's *Showings* and George Herbert's poetry. Using these terms was tempting because it would work. It would produce acceptable scholarly work within a clear historiographic tradition. Protestantism and Roman Catholicism are, however, the product of the religious changes that took place during the sixteenth century. If the ideological solution to the cultural and social conflicts of the period between 1350 and 1550 was the emergence of a number of religious confessions that, while having different content, were structurally and formally identical, then to use terms like Protestant and Roman Catholic to explain these changes would be to simply confuse an effect for a cause.[8] Indeed it would be to make an effect, for example Protestantism, into a cause. Not surprisingly this does work—as the development, or lack of it, of Reformation historiography from *Acts and Monuments* to A. G. Dickens and from Nicholas Sanders to *The Stripping of the Altars* clearly demonstrates. It could hardly do otherwise since it was precisely in order to explain, and explain away, the real causes and effects of social and cultural change, that confessionalization generated Protestantism and Roman Catholicism. These terms, however, have always been effects masquerading as causes.

In his seminal article, 'Censorship and Cultural Change in Late-medieval England: Vernacular Theology, the Oxford Translation Debate, and Arundel's *Constitutions* of 1409', Nicholas Watson argued that the period 1340–1410 witnessed a blossoming of vernacular theology and the emergence of a tradition of English religious writing that was stopped in its tracks in 1409 when Archbishop Arundel issued the Constitutions.[9] Eamon Duffy, among others, has rightly

[7] Michel Foucault, 'Nietzsche, Genealogy, History', in *The Foucault Reader*, ed. Paul Rabinow (London: Penguin, 1984), 76–100.

[8] On confessionalization, see Heinz Schilling, *Religion, Political Culture, and the Emergence of Early Modern Society* (Leiden: E.J. Brill, 1992) and Wolfgang Reinhard, 'Reformation, Counter-Reformation, and the Early Modern State: A Reassessment', *The Catholic Historical Review*, 75 (1989), 383–404, at 391.

[9] Nicholas Watson, 'Censorship and Cultural Change in Late-medieval England: Vernacular Theology, the Oxford Translation Debate, and Arundel's Constitutions of 1409', *Speculum*, 70 (1995), 822–64.

criticized Watson's article for over-emphasizing the effects of the *Constitutions*, however, it is undoubtedly the case that Arundel's aim in 1409 was to impose new and sweeping restrictions on religious writing in England.[10] For example, Article 8 of *The Constitutions* states that, 'almighty God can not bee expressed with any Philosophical termes . . . invented of man' and goes on to proscribe the use of 'curious words or terms' to defend any proposition regardless of its truthfulness.[11] The real problem with Watson's argument is that he fails to take into account the extent to which the censoring persecutionary desire articulated in Arundel's *Constitutions* is an important element of the vernacular theology produced during the period 1340–1410. In particular, while it is the case that a number of works produced during this period do, as Watson has suggested, deploy 'the vernacular as an emblem of universality', others, particularly those written within the mystical tradition of *via negativa* (the way of negation) articulate a scepticism towards human wisdom and in particular language that Arundel would undoubtedly have approved.[12] For example, *The Cloud of Unknowing* consistently emphasizes the need to strip away all human reasoning and feeling and enter into a state of darkness or unknowing.[13] *The Cloud* is particularly critical of human language, constructing it as inherently corrupt and corrupting. Its author recommends to his readers that in their prayers they concentrate on two simple words—Sin and God.

> sithen it so is that alle yvelles ben comprehended in synne . . . lat us therfore, whan we wyll ententifly preie for remowyng of yvelles, outher sey or think or mene nought elles, ne no mo wordes, bot this lityl worde SYNNE. And if we will ententifly preie for getyng of goodes, lat us crie, outher with worde or with thought or with desire, nought elles, ne no mo wordes, bot this worde GOD.[14]

The Cloud consistently emphasizes the inability of human language to do anything other than occlude God. The author tells the reader that they should, 'Study thou not for no wordes, for so schuldest thou never come to thi purpos ne to this werk, for it is never getyn by stody, bot al only be grace.'[15] *The Cloud*'s emphasis on the complete redundancy of human wit, of study, for those wishing to grow closer to God is shared by a number of works produced during the period 1340–1410. For example, Sir John Clanvowe's *The Two Ways* condemns with an absolutist fervour

[10] Eamon Duffy, 'Religious Belief', in *A Social History of England, 1200–1500*, ed. Rosemary Horrox and W. Mark Ormrod (Cambridge: Cambridge University Press, 2006), 293–339, at 330–1.

[11] John Foxe, *Acts and Monuments* (London, 1570), 627.

[12] Nicholas Watson, 'Conceptions of the Word: The Mother Tongue and the Incarnation of God', *New Medieval Literatures*, 1 (1997), 85–124, at 108.

[13] James Simpson has recently emphasized this aspect of *The Cloud*, in particular its 'interior iconoclasm': James Simpson, *Reform and Cultural Revolution* (Oxford: Oxford University Press, 2002), 452.

[14] *The Cloud of Unknowing*, ed. Phyllis Hodgson, EETS 218 (Oxford: H. Milford, Oxford University Press, 1944), 77.

[15] *The Cloud of Unknowing*, ed. Hodgson, 77.

the ways of the world, while the 'Instructions for a Devout and Literate Layman', with its injunction that the family should spend meal-times reading edifying works and its prohibition of 'all spectacles, that is to say, dances, buckler-play, dicing, wrestling, and the like', conjures up an image of a fifteenth-century Puritan household.[16] Arundel's *Constitutions* embody a desire for religious control and order driven by a deeply pessimistic and conservative version of Christianity that is a central element of vernacular theology throughout the period between Lollardy and the English Civil War. Indeed it is arguable that the history of religious and social struggle in this period, once the misleading lens provided by post-Reformation confessions has been removed, is one of peaks of vernacular theology followed by moments of intense persecution, literal or imagined. The period between 1470 and 1530 witnessed another blossoming of vernacular theology, particular in drama and in the work of Thomas More, that was followed by the Henrician Reformation. The explosion of religious printing that followed Edward VI's succession produced a backlash that was already gathering steam before Mary Tudor came to the throne. And the religious experimentation of the period 1630–60 was followed by a final attempt to close down the vernacular religious sphere.

Vernacular theology throughout the period between Lollardy and the English Civil War was torn between a deeply pessimistic attitude towards human reason and a desire to embrace the productivity of human language; between emphasizing human sinfulness and celebrating Christ's message of salvation; between silence and speech. In these terms it grappled with issues that are at the heart of Catholic Christianity. For example, St Augustine is sometimes regarded as advocating the way of negation and certainly the ideal of silence is central to his thought. At the same time, however, in works like *On Christian Doctrine* (*De Doctrina Christiana*), Augustine emphasizes the potential of sensuous human activity, and in particular language, for Christians as they seek to grow towards God. In *On the Trinity* (*De Trinitate*), Augustine wrote that

> renewal [of the image of God] ... is not brought about in the one moment of the conversion itself, as in Baptism that renewal is brought about in one moment by the remission of all sins, for there does not remain even one sin, however small it may, that is not forgiven. But just as it is one thing to be free from fevers, and another to recover from the weakness which has resulted from the fevers ... so the first step in a cure is to remove the cause of the disease, which is done through the remission of all sins; the second is to heal the disease itself, which is done gradually by making progress in the renewal of this image [of God].[17]

[16] John Clanvowe, 'The Two Ways', in *The Works of Sir John Clanvowe*, ed. V. J. Scattergood (Cambridge: D.S. Brewer, 1965), 57–80; W. A. Pantin, 'Instructions for a Devout and Literate Layman', in *Medieval Learning and Literature*, ed. J. J. G. Alexander and M. T. Gibson (Oxford: Oxford University Press, 1976), 398–422, at 400.

[17] St Augustine, *On the Trinity, Books 8–15*, ed. Gareth B. Matthews and trans. Stephen McKenna (Cambridge: Cambridge University Press, 2002), 162.

For Augustine the renewal of the individual as the image of God was at the heart of Christian devotion. This process could not start, however, until after a person's sins had been forgiven. Augustine explicitly states that this forgiveness is total and precedes human agency. It is a freely given absolute gift of God that transforms a person's life from pointless, meaningless existence into a narrative of devotional renewal: a godly story that sweeps the Christian along. The fall of language can be seen as a curse but it can also be seen as creating a field of possibilities. In particular, Augustine saw language as a key weapon for Christians in their attempts to renew themselves as images of God. And it is the potential of language as a tool for Christian renewal that is at the heart of the religious writings of Julian of Norwich and George Herbert.

Julian of Norwich and George Herbert

Julian of Norwich wrote two accounts of her revelations: the short text was probably written shortly after the event; and a much longer version was the product of almost twenty years' reflection and thought. It is the later version that will be the focus of this discussion. Julian of Norwich's *Showings* perform the creation of understanding through reasoned reading. The *Showings* opens with a bald statement of what the text contains:

> This is a revelacion of love that Jhesu Christ, our endless blisse, made in xvi shewynges, of which the first is of this precious crownyng of thrones.[18]

Julian goes on to tell the reader that she experienced the showings when she was thirty, seriously ill, and expecting to die.

> I would that that sicknes were so hard as to the death that I might in that sicknes have undertaken all my rightes of the holie church, my selfe weenyng that I should have died, and that all creatures might suppose the same that saw me, for I would no maner of comforte of fleshly ne erthely life in that sicknes.[19]

It was at this moment of the crisis that Julian received her first revelation. She had sixteen revelations in all. In the long text of the *Showings* each account of a specific revelation is followed by detailed explications of Julian's vision and what it means. The basic pattern of the text is therefore a continuous round of mystical vision rendered into text, rendered into explanation, rendered into narrative. This process is, however, neither naïve nor un-self-reflective. Elisabeth Dutton has analysed in depth Julian's *Showings* and has demonstrated that it is a complex web of different voices that draws upon the tradition of religious compilations and deploys a

[18] Julian of Norwich, *The Showings of Julian of Norwich*, ed. Denise N. Baker (New York: Norton, 2005), 3.

[19] Julian of Norwich, *The Showings*, ed. Baker, 5.

consciously constructed 'textual voice'.[20] Julian is not only conscious of losses and gains arising from the process of textualizing her visions. She uses the possibilities offered by it to encourage the reader to identify and participate in her text's production of meaning.

Revelation 13, for example, focuses on the question of sin. Julian tells the reader that:

> And after thys oure Lord brought to my mynde the longyng that I had to hym before. And I saw nothyng lettyd my but synne, and so I behelde generally in us alle. And me thought yf synne had nott be, we shulde alle have be clene and lyke to oure Lorde as he made us. And thus in my foly before thys tyme often I wondryd why, by the grete forseyng wysdom of God, the begynnyng of synne was nott lettyd. For then thought me that all shulde have be wele.[21]

The perplexity that Julian felt in the face of sin is answered in the vision by Christ who tells her that, 'Synne is behovely, but alle shalle be wele, and alle shalle be wele, and all maner of thynge shalle be wele.'[22] Revelation 13 ends with Julian commenting that:

> These wordes were shewde fulle tenderly, shewyng no maner of blame to me ne to none that shalle be safe. Than were it great unkyndnesse of me to blame or wonder on God for my synne, sythen he blamyth nott me for synne. And in theyse same wordes I saw an hygh, mervelous prevyte hyd in God, whyche pryvyte he shalle opynly make and shalle be knowen to us un hevyn. In which knowyng we shalle verily se the cause why he sufferde synne to come, in whych syght we shalle endlessly have joye. [23]

Revelation 13 is a complex mystical moment. It addresses a central Christian issue. During the course of this revelation, Julian tells the reader that, 'I saw nott synne, for I beleve it had no maner of substaunce, ne not part of beyng, ne it myght not be knowen but by the payne that is caused therof.'[24] Julian's belief in the non-being of sin is entirely orthodox and Augustinian. It does, however, in practice undermine a dominant mode of fourteenth- and fifteenth-century religious writing and teaching which, in its focus upon sin and its effects, effectively gave sin being. An exemplary text in this context is Geoffrey Chaucer's *The Parson's Tale*, with its careful discussion of different sins and their baneful effects. In its detail and its rejection of the poetic norms of the rest of the *Canterbury Tales*—it is one of only two tales in prose and it explicitly contrasts its form with the fictionality of the other *Tales*—*The Parson's Tale* seeks to address the problem of sin through textual ordering. In the figure of the Parson, Chaucer reflects upon religious implications

[20] Elisabeth Dutton, *Julian of Norwich: The Influence of Late-Medieval Devotional Compilations* (Cambridge: D.S. Brewer, 2008), 98.

[21] Julian of Norwich, *The Showings*, ed. Baker, 39.

[22] Julian of Norwich, *The Showings*, ed. Baker, 39.

[23] Julian of Norwich, *The Showings*, ed. Baker, 40.

[24] Julian of Norwich, *The Showings*, ed. Baker, 40.

of focusing upon the description, ordering, and labelling of sins as a pastoral tool. *The Parson's Tale* prefigures Arundel's *Constitutions* in its rejection of fiction and its ultimately pessimistic view of human wit in relation to salvation. The Parson's teaching, which is entirely orthodox, is that humans are so immersed in sin that the best that one can hope for is containment and ultimately silence. Julian's Revelation 13, albeit implicitly, clearly undermines this tradition of Christian teaching. At the heart of Revelation 13 is a mystical promise of universal salvation. All will be well. Sin shall have no dominion.

Julian is, however, very conscious that Revelation 13, and indeed her whole status as a mystic, placed her in a difficult position as regards the Church. In particular, the *Showings* articulate a constant anxiety about the relation between mystical revelation and clerical authority embodied in the Church. Julian does not, although this would be an option, claim for herself any part of the Church's authority. Instead she consistently marks the tension between her revelations and the Church by asserting in her text that there is no conflict between them. Referring to Revelation 13 she comments,

> For though the revelation was shewde of goodnes, in whych was made lytylle mencion of evylle, yett I was nott drawen therby from ony poynt of the feyth that holy chyrch techith me to beleve.[25]

The implication of what Julian writes here is that if Revelation 13 had made more mention of evil it would have been more orthodox. It is its 'little mention' of evil that provokes Julian to assert that it did not draw her away from orthodox teaching. Holy Church appears in the *Showings* as a marker of orthodoxy, but also as alien to the communal world of Julian's text. The anxiety and tentativeness of this comment is typical of those moments when Julian directly refers to the Church.

In her meditation on Revelation 14 Julian comments that:

> in all this tyme, fro the begynnyng to the ende, I had ii maner of beholdinges. That one was endlesse, countynaunt love with suernesse of kepyng and blysful salvacion, for of this was all the shewyng. That othyr was the comyn techyng of holy chyrch, of whych I was befor enformyd and groundyd and wilfully havyng in use and in understondyng.[26]

Julian asserts here an equivalence between her showings and the common teaching that the entire text of the *Showings* consistently belies. Ultimately Julian cannot reconcile either the message of her revelations nor her own status as a mystic with the 'Holi Church'. She has to consistently fall back into empty, albeit confident, assertions that the contradictions that the *Showings* appear to display between her mystical experience and orthodoxy are simply a product of a failure of understanding.

[25] Julian of Norwich, *The Showings*, ed. Baker, 46.
[26] Julian of Norwich, *The Showings*, ed. Baker, 63.

They are not real in much the same sense that sin has no being, except in terms of its baneful effects on the individual Christian.

The problem with this strategy, however, is that the *Showings* embody a radical confidence in human reason to produce Christian meaning. In particular, the text of the *Showings*, its combination of revelations and meditations, stresses the importance of reading as a form of devotional practice. The *Showings* invite their reader to repeat Julian's experimental engagement with God as a kind of textual pilgrimage in which each stopping point or revelation is followed by more meditation, more narrative, drawing the reader through the same devotional journey as Julian embarked upon when writing the *Showings*. Lynn Staley has recently stressed the importance of the language of penitence and images of the Passion in Julian's *Showings*. She comments that for Julian the Passion is not 'affective theatre' but is rather an 'active and charged drama of redemption'.[27] Julian does not simply invite her readers to consume her text, to gaze with the mixture of affective fascination, pity, and voyeurism on the images of Christ's passion that readers were incited to indulge in with some fourteenth- and fifteenth-century texts (most obviously Nicholas Love's *The Mirror of the Blessed Life of Jesus Christ*). The *Showings*, like the York Corpus Christi plays, insist on the importance of form. In contrast to other religious texts from the period (for example *The Cloud*), the *Showings* and the Corpus Christi plays construct their material forms, textual and theatrical, as not only *not* negative but as actually *positive*. For Julian, the truth she wishes to communicate is embodied in the devotional labour of reading her text. The *Showings* do not invite one to smash the shell to reach the kernel. They insist that the kernel and shell are one. In the process, however, the *Showings* effectively undermine any claim to religious authority that is not universal and open to all. The implication of Julian's text is that anyone can follow in her footsteps, anyone can come to realize with her that in Christ all are forgiven.

At one level the affinity between George Herbert's poetry and the *Showings* could be seem as simply vaguely thematic—they are both Christian writers concerned with questions of faith and salvation. What links them more profoundly is a shared rejection of the way of negation—of the pessimism towards human language articulated in works like *The Cloud*. Herbert's work embraces the world of Babel. Like the *Showings*, *The Temple* is at one level a meditation on the problems of Christian speaking, post-Babel, that is ultimately positive. This is not to suggest that Herbert is unaware of the paradoxes of Christian language, in particular in relation to grace. Brian Cummings comments that Herbert's poetry attempts to capture 'what could hardly be captured. In a way which was never quite possible in academic theology, he subverted the ordinary rules of language to express the

[27] Lynn Staley, 'The Penitential Psalms: Conversion and the Limits of Lordship', *Journal of Medieval and Early Modern Studies*, 37 (2007), 221–70, at 243.

strangeness of the gift.'[28] Herbert's poems are poised between celebrating the potential of texts to teach spiritual reading and fear of the protean confusion of textuality run wild. He consistently produces lyrics, like 'Jordan II', in which the ability of texts to burnish, sprout, and swell, to 'curl with metaphors a plain intention', occludes God. At the same time *The Temple* offers the reader a plenitude of religious thoughts, tropes, and images with the confidence that the reader will be able to find a path through to understanding. For example, in 'The Bag', Herbert produces an important development on an idea from the Book of the Crucifix—that Christ's passion, and in particular his tortured body on the Cross, can be read as a text—with Christ's wounds seen as the letters written on the book of his body. 'The Bag' gives a condensed narrative of Christ's life. It ends with two verses in which Christ directly addresses the reader.

> If ye have anything to send or write,
> I have no bag, but here is room:
> Unto my Father's hands and sight,
> Believe me, it shall safely come.
> That I shall mind, what you impart,
> Look, you may put it very near my heart.
> Or if hereafter any of my friends
> Will use me in this kind, the door
> Shall still be open; what he sends
> I will present, and somewhat more,
> Not to his hurt. Sighs will convey
> Anything to me. Hark, Despair away.[29]

In 'The Bag', Herbert creates a metonymic, not metaphoric, relationship between his poem as a bag and Christ's body. In the process he creates a devotional text that explicitly resists the idea that Christ's body is an already written closed book. Herbert's Christ, like Julian's, is a potential source of salvation for all since the text of his Passion is still open, it is still being written. It is the status of Herbert's text as a graphic textual image, a 'bag', that creates and protects its ideal of Christ as open to all while at the same time finessing through its poetic form the problem of human agency. 'The Bag' as an empty container is an image of human language in which the individual and the meaning are less important than the form.

The poem that follows 'The Bag' in *The Temple* is 'The Jews'. The second stanza of this poem is a call for the second coming and the conversion of the Jews; however, the first stanza is more complicated.

[28] Brian Cummings, *The Literary Culture of the Reformation: Grammar and Grace* (Oxford: Oxford University Press, 2002), 327.

[29] George Herbert, *George Herbert and Henry Vaughan*, ed. Louis L. Martz (Oxford: Oxford University Press, 1985), 137.

> Poor nation, whose sweet sap and juice
> Our scions have purloined, and left you dry:
> Whose streams we got by the Apostles sluice,
> And use in baptism, while ye pine and die:
> Who by not keeping once, become a debtor;
> And now by keeping lose the letter.[30]

What is particularly striking about this verse is the concluding couplet. One would perhaps expect Herbert to deploy the Pauline trope in order to construct Christianity as the spirit of the letter of the Judaic law. But instead Herbert stresses not only the Jew's loss of the sweet spirit of Christ's teaching but also the extent to which they have lost the letter as well. This 'letter' could refer to the letters that Christ is imagined as taking to heaven in 'The Bag'. Herbert is, however, also stressing the materiality of Christ's teaching, that for him it is form and grace, spirit and letter. For Herbert the Jews' failure to be part of the textual community created by the image of Christ's Passion as an open communal text is not some kind of cosmic punishment. It is a tragedy that leaves both Jews and Christians impoverished.

What links Julian of Norwich and George Herbert is a shared desire to embrace the effects of Babel and a rejection of the kind of pessimism as regards human reason articulated in works like *The Cloud*. It is important to note, however, that Herbert was writing in a period in which religious reform, and in particular confessionalization, had further complicated the relationship between language, grace, and salvation.

Reform and vernacular theology

The period between Lollardy and the English Civil War witnessed a redrawing, and reduction, of the religious sphere in western Europe. John Bossy has argued that 'Divorces between the sacred and the body social were to be everyday events in the sixteenth century'; however, the seeds of Bossy's divorces were planted well before the sixteenth century. [31] They can be seen, for example, in the late medieval Church's attempts to regain control of the Eucharist by preventing lay acts of appropriation and in the increasing insistence by the Church that sainthood was a purely spiritual notion.[32] The effect of religious reform, and in particular

[30] Herbert, *George Herbert and Henry Vaughan*, ed. Martz, 138.

[31] John Bossy, *Christianity in the West 1400–1700* (Oxford: Oxford University Press, 1985), 154.

[32] Miri Rubin, 'The Eucharist and the Construction of Medieval Identities', in *Culture and History, 1350–1600: Essays on English Communities, Identities and Writings*, ed. David Aers (Hemel Hempstead and Detroit, MI: Wayne State University Press, 1992), 43–63, at 59.
59. André Vauchez, *Sainthood in the Later Middle Ages*, trans. Jean Birrell (Cambridge: Cambridge University Press, 1997), 538.

confessionalization, upon vernacular theology was most keenly felt in the redrawing of the lines between the social and religious. For example, in relation to religious writing this led to a focus upon questions of form and decorum. The mixing of genres and voices that typified late medieval mystical and devotional writing was from the reformers' point of view completely unacceptable. Works like the prose story *Mary of Nimmegen* with its story of the three iron rings that the Pope, after seeking 'some manner of knowledge from God', imposed upon Mary as a penance—one for each arm and one for her neck—simply became impossible to take seriously as religious works recounting a mystic's life story.[33] Equally impossible became works like the Digby *Mary Magdalene*. In both cases it is important to note that what was 'wrong' transcended the division between Protestantism and Roman Catholicism. All reformers rejected the mixing of the spiritual and the profane and sought to place mysticism within a clearly defined religious sphere and emphasized the way of negation, mysticism as anti-Babel, as normative. All reformers sought to undermine the potential for the vernacular to become, in Watson's words, 'an emblem of universality'.

The effects of the Reformation on religious writing can be illustrated by looking briefly at one of the few moments of figurative language in *The Cloud*, when its author creates a striking image of the Devil:

> as I have conceyvid by som disciples of nygromauncye, the whiche han it in science for to make advocacion of wickyd spirites, and by som unto whom the feende hath appereth in bodily licnes; that in what bodily licnes the feend appereth, evermore he hath bot o nose-therel, and that is grete and wyde. And he wil gladly kast it up, that a man may see in therate to his brayne up in his heed. The whiche brayn is not elles bot the fire of helle, for the feende may have none other brayn. And if he might make a man loke in therate, he kepeth no beter; for at that lokyng he shuld lese his witte for ever.[34]

This level of detail stands in marked contrast to *The Cloud*'s absolute insistence on the ineffability of God. The Devil can be seen, and given bodily form, God cannot. The Devil's fiery brain is an image of the imagination when not occupied by an absolute monological focus upon SIN and GOD; it is the human brain filled with distracting, erroneous, sensuous words.

Augustine Baker was a Roman Catholic monk and spiritual adviser to the English nuns at Cambrai. In this post, he played an important role in mediating texts like Julian's *Showings* and *The Cloud* to post-Reformation Roman Catholicism. Baker produced commentaries on both texts. Dutton has pointed out that Baker's response to the *Showings* was to reduce their 'optimistic inclusivity' and to

[33] Mariken van Nieumeghen, *Mary of Nimmegen*, introduction by Harry Morgan Ayres and Adriaan Jacob Barnouw (Cambridge, MA: Harvard University Press, 1932), c.i (3v).

[34] *The Cloud of Unknowing*, ed. Hodgson, 80.

change the focus of the *Showings* from a concern with the 'mysterious thought of God', and to instead focus upon 'the secret of the mystic's knowing of God'.[35] Baker's approach to Julian's text is almost identical to that adopted by Protestant historians like John Bale and John Foxe who, when dealing with fourteenth- and fifteenth-century texts, made them historical by focusing on the author or narrator. They treated late medieval texts as historical not living, of interest for what they can tell about the writer not for their teaching. Baker's commentary on *The Cloud*, his *Secretum*, is a strange text. Baker opens by stating that:

> Upon further Consideration of [the] matters Contained in our Treatise Called *The Clowd*, I am come to be of the mind [that] it will not be convenient for me to take in hand an Exposition. For in doing so, the matter being merely Spiritual [and] Mystick, my Exposition (So far as I could make any) would prove to be as mystick [and] obscure (if not Obscurer) as is *The Clowd* itself.[36]

Baker seems to assume that there is a direct relationship between mysticism and obscurity. In particular, he lacks any confidence that his words will be anything other than another veil further occluding God from the reader. Despite this, Baker did go on to produce a commentary which is at once a guide and a reading of *The Cloud*. Baker's approach is to emphasize the chastity of *The Cloud*, the absoluteness of its *via negativa* mysticism. For example, he comments on the fourteenth chapter that,

> There he [*The Cloud* author] speaketh further about *One Word of One Syllable*, but I rather wish you to remember [the] freedom he gave you in the precedent chapter of Using no word at all, if you be / not interiorly moved to it.[37]

For Baker, the only thing better than one word is no words. Julian's sense of the potential of texts to create through their very textuality a community united in and through devotional reading is completely alien to Baker. Equally alien is the religious *praxis* reflected in one of the few moments when the *Cloud* author uses figurative language to describe the Devil's fiery mind in Chapter 55. Baker's comment on Chapters 55 and 56 is,

> I note nothing Speciall in them.[38]

Baker's response to *The Cloud*, and in particular his anxiety or lack of interest in its very few moments of figurative language, is exemplary of post-Reformation responses to earlier devotional and mystical works. Baker confessionalizes

[35] Elisabeth Dutton, 'The Seventeenth-Century Manuscript Tradition and the Influence of Augustine Baker', in *A Companion to Julian of Norwich*, ed. Liz Herbert McAvoy (Cambridge: Boydell and Brewer, 2008), 127–38, at 136.

[36] Augustine Baker, *Secretum*, ed. John Clark, Analecta Cartusiana, 119 (Salzburg: Institut für Anglistik und Amerikanistik, Universität Salzburg, 1997), 19.

[37] Baker, *Secretum*, ed. Clark, 154.

[38] Baker, *Secretum*, ed. Clark, 175.

The Cloud, and Julian's *Showings*—turning them into Roman Catholic texts. In the process he reduces their scope so that they fit more easily into the norms of Tridentine mysticism. The implications and costs of this process are at the heart of William Shakespeare's *The Winter's Tale.*

There is nothing special in *The Cloud*'s description of the Devil's fiery mind for Leontes either. This is his reality. He shares completely the post-Reformation religious desire for a world beyond Babel— before language was shattered. In *The Winter's Tale*, William Shakespeare stages a confrontation between two forms of religious praxis: Leontes', which is individualist, confessional, and dismissive of the power of human rationality; and Paulina's, which emphasizes the power of collective acts of faith and displays an Augustinian confidence in the godly potential of sensuous human activity. In *On Christian Teaching*, Augustine commented that, 'the human condition would be wretched indeed if God appeared unwilling to minister his word to human beings through human agency'.[39] It is, however, precisely this wretchedness that drives Baker's suggestion that the ideal religious state is one without words. It is also what lies behind Leontes' phobia of language, and in particular language's communal and collective nature.

The Winter's Tale is a meditation on the effects of reform and in particular confessionalization on the shape of religion in post-Reformation England. Sarah Beckwith has recently argued that:

> Shakespeare's theater does not represent the supersession and succession of religion, purgatory, and ritual action by a disenchanted theater, but the persistence of its historical concerns in the incarnation of performance.[40]

Leontes is a product of reform. He is a godly Puritan/Jesuit. Like them, and like the *Cloud* author, he has no time or tolerance for the play of religion. Leontes' fall, in a parodic version of Henry VIII, is the product of a sudden entirely personal leap to judgement, the discovery of a scruple that turns his, and everyone else's, world upside down. At the same time the ultimate cause of Leontes' fall is adherence to a particularly wretched understanding of the human condition, one that is theorized and explained by his friend Polixenes who tells Hermione that when he and Leontes were boys,

> POLIXENES
> We were as twinn'd lambs that did frisk i' th' sun,
> And bleat the one at th'other: what we chang'd
> Was innocence for innocence: we knew not
> The doctrine of ill-doing, nor dream'd
> That any did. Had we pursu'd that life,

[39] St Augustine, *On Christian Teaching*, trans. R. P. H. Green (Oxford: Oxford University Press, 1997), 5.

[40] Sarah Beckwith, 'Stephen Greenblatt's *Hamlet* and the Forms of Oblivion', *Journal of Medieval and Early Modern Studies*, 33 (2003), 261–80, at 275.

And our weak spirits ne' er been higher rear'd
With stronger blood, we should have answer'd heaven
Boldly 'not guilty', the imposition clear'd
Hereditary ours.
HERMIONE
By this we gather
You have tripp'd since.
POLIXENES
O my most sacred lady,
Temptations have since then been born to's: for
In those unfledg'd days was my wife a girl;
Your precious self had then not cross'd the eyes
Of my young play-fellow. (1.2.66–80)

Polixenes conjures an image of a world entirely free from sin. It is also one without words. For him the fall into temptation, sin, and words is a product of sexual knowledge. Bizarrely Polixenes seems to expect Hermione will regard this speech as complimentary. She, however, has no illusions concerning the implications of Polixenes' fantasy, 'Of this make no conclusion, lest you say / Your queen and I are devils.' (1.2.81–2). Leontes looks into Hermione's eyes and what he sees is a mirror image of his fears, hatreds, and desires.

Leontes' fall into madness takes place within the world of *The Cloud*. He is caught between a desire for order, fixity, and silence and an overwhelming fear of sin, of the power of words to mislead and corrupt. Above all Leontes, like the *Cloud* author, fears the proteanness of textuality—the ability of texts to grow, mutate, and change; to give the human imagination body and form.

LEONTES
Affection! thy intention stabs the centre:
Thou dost make possible things not so held,
Communicat'st with dreams; how can this be?—
With what's unreal thou coactive art,
And fellow'st nothing: then 'tis very credent
Thou may'st co-join with something; and thou dost
(And that beyond commission) and I find it,
(And that to the infection of my brains
And hard'ning of my brows). (1.2.138–45)

Leontes fears the materiality of words: their collective and communal nature. At the heart of his madness is a fear of being reduced to a topic, an object, in someone else's conversation.

LEONTES
You, my lords,
Look on her, mark her well: be but about
To say 'she is a goodly lady', and
The justice of your hearts will thereto add
''Tis pity she's not honest, honorable':

Praise her but for this her without-door form
(Which on my faith deserves high speech) and straight
The shrug, the hum or ha, these petty brands
That calumny doth use— (2.1.64–72).

Leontes occupies the same basically wretched world as the *Cloud* author. For them the ability of words, and in particular graphic text, to give expression to a collective sensuous humanity is not a sign of God's preparedness to 'minister his word through human agency', but simply a further indication of the language's irredeemably corporeal sinfulness.

Leontes' redemption happens when he goes from the world of *The Cloud* to that of the *Showings*. What Paulina offers him at the end of the play is above all redemption through participation in precisely the kind of mystical textual community that Julian evokes in her work.

PAULINA
It is requir'd
You do awake your faith. Then all stand still:
Or—those that think it is unlawful business
I am about, let them depart. (5.3.94–7)

Having restored Hermione to life, Paulina rejects Polixenes' demand that she explains what she has done, telling him, 'That she is living, / Were it but told you, should be hooted at / Like an old tale' (5.3.115–17). The play, however, ends precisely with an old tale being told.

LEONTES
Good Paulina,
Lead us hence, where we may leisurely
Each one demand, and answer to his part
Perform'd in this wide gap of time, since first
We were dissever'd: hastily lead away. (5.3.151–5).

The Winter's Tale ends with an image of a textual community coming together through telling a story that has at its centre a resurrection that is either a theatrical trick or a piece of magic but which certainly requires an act of faith. Stanley Cavell comments, in relation *The Winter's Tale*, that

> this theater is contesting the distinction between saying and showing. If the concluding scene of this theater is telling something, it is not something antecedently known; it is rather instituting knowledge, reconceiving, reconstituting knowledge, along with the world.[41]

The Winter's Tale is a religious experiment. It invites its audience to engage in the production of an experimental faith. Paulina, like Julian, creates a space in which religious knowledge can be created and she achieves this by teaching Leontes, and

[41] Stanley Cavell, *Disowning Knowledge in Seven Plays of Shakespeare* (Cambridge: Cambridge University Press, 2003; first published 1987), 204.

the audience, that telling a tale, narrating a story, is simply another way of showing God's promise of renewal.

Conclusion

John Bunyan would have regarded Nayler as acting out of human arrogance but he undoubtedly would have shared the desire to escape the human world of allegory, or play, into the truth of God. As he tells the reader of *Grace Abounding to the Chief of Sinners*,

> I could... have stepped into a style much higher than this in which I have here discoursed... but I dare not: God did not play in convincing of me; the devil did not play in tempting me; neither did I play when I sunk as into a bottomless pit.[42]

Playing is, however, precisely what Bunyan does in his most famous work, *The Pilgrim's Progress*. In his preface to *The Pilgrim's Progress*, 'The Author's Apology for his Book', Bunyan recounts how, having sat down to write another book, he found himself, before he was aware, writing *The Pilgrim's Progress*.

> And thus it was: I writing of the Way
> And Race of Saints in this our Gospel Day,
> Fell suddenly into an Allegory
> About their Journey, and the way to Glory,
> In more than twenty things, which I set down;
> This done, I twenty more had in my Crown,
> And they again began to multiply,
> Like sparks that from the coals of Fire do flie.
> Nay then, thought I, if that you breed so fast,
> I'll put you by your selves, lest you at last
> Should prove ad infinitum, and eat out
> The Book that I already am about.[43]

Bunyan is surprised by allegory. He decides that in order to prevent the fast-breeding fiery thoughts filling his head from destroying the work he has already begun that he will write for them a book of their own, *The Pilgrim's Progress*. This work is a classic of Protestant mysticism. Its relationship to the orthodoxies of Calvinism is in many ways identical to the relationship between Holi Church and the *Showings*. Bunyan was committed to the doctrine of election but the whole form and ethos of *The Pilgrim's Progress* pushes towards an image of a textual community created through the act of reading: the textual labour of collective pilgrimage.

[42] John Bunyan, *Grace Abounding to the Chief of Sinners*, ed. W. R. Owens (Harmondsworth: Penguin), 3.

[43] John Bunyan, *The Pilgrim's Progress* (1678), ed. N. H. Keeble (Oxford: Oxford University Press, 1984), 1.

Allegory in *The Pilgrim's Progress* becomes an emblem for universality—to be able to read Bunyan's work, to accept one's status as a reader, is to participate in Christian's journey of renewal and salvation.

Being anti-Babel can take two diametrically opposed forms. It can mean, like the *Cloud* author or Leontes, assuming that language is irredeemably corrupt and flawed and that therefore the truth can never be spoken or known. Silence is the best we can hope for. There is, however, an alternative in which Babel did not shatter language but instead liberated it. Rowan Williams has recently suggested that,

> part of the theologian's task in the Church may be to urge that we stand aside from some of the words we think we know, so that we may see better what our language is *for*—keeping open the door to the promises of God.[44]

This is precisely what a central strand of vernacular theology consistently attempted to do throughout the period between Lollardy and the English Civil War, sometimes in spite of itself and often against what it knew to be the Church's teaching. By focusing on what Christian language is *for*, it created texts that promised—to those prepared to awaken their faith—the renewal of God's image through human reason, through the devotional labour of reading and writing.

FURTHER READING

Cummings, Brian. *The Literary Culture of the Reformation: Grammar and Grace* (Oxford: Oxford University Press, 2002)

Gillespie, Vincent. 'Vernacular Theology', in *Middle English*, ed. Paul Strohm, Oxford Twenty-First Century Approaches to Literature (Oxford: Oxford University Press, 2007), 401–20

Simpson, James. *Reform and Cultural Revolution* (Oxford: Oxford University Press, 2002)

Watson, Nicholas. 'Conceptions of the Word: The Mother Tongue and the Incarnation of God', *New Medieval Literatures*, 1 (1997), 85–124

—— 'Visions of Inclusion: Universal Salvation and Vernacular Theology in Pre-Reformation England', *Journal of Medieval and Early Modern Studies*, 27 (1997), 145–87

44 Rowan Williams, *On Christian Theology* (Oxford: Blackwell, 2000), 85.

CHAPTER 12

CONSCIENCE

PAUL STROHM

An exchange between judge James Hales and Marian chancellor Stephen Gardiner illustrates the fraught situation surrounding matters of conscience in the mid-sixteenth century. Hales had enjoyed preferment during the reign of Edward VI, including a post on the commission which had tried Gardiner for anti-Reformation activities in 1550–1. Even so, as the only Edwardian jurist to withhold his signature from a statement supporting Jane Grey's succession, he was regarded with initial favor by the Marian establishment. He had refused to sign the anti-Marian statement on the ground that only Parliament could decide such matters, but then, stiff-necked in both directions, he immediately forfeited Mary's favor by applying Edwardian Nonconformity laws to Catholics illegally celebrating Mass in Kent. When he presented himself to Gardiner in October 1553 to be sworn as justice of common pleas, he was challenged and subjected to hostile examination. Accounts of his examination, first published as a separate tract,[1] and then republished with additional commentary by Foxe,[2] describe him as defending his actions on grounds of conscience. Even Gardiner is represented as willing, albeit rather impatiently, to grant truth to this claim, saying, 'Ye Maister Hales, your conscience is knowen well inough. I knowe ye lacke no conscience.' Still on the offensive, Hales tartly rejoins by asserting the autonomy of individual conscience: 'ye maye do well to serch your owne conscience. For mine is better knowen to my selfe then to you.'

Both evangelically leaning Hales and Catholic Gardiner bandy the word 'conscience' back and forth as if they were talking about the same thing. To some extent, of course, they are, but not entirely. Gardiner speaks of conscience as a recognizable and unproblematic entity. Even though his concession to Hales is hedged with

[1] *The communication betwene my Lord Chauncelor and iudge Hales being among other iudges to take his oth in VVestminster hall. Anno. M.D. Liii. Vi of October.* EEBO/TCP. Although Gardiner is named as author of this tract, it seems to me even-handed, if not explicitly supportive of Hales, and unlikely to have been authored by Gardiner himself.

[2] <http://www.hrionline.ac.uk/johnfoxe/main/11_1563.jsp. pages 1114-7>. Hereafter, cited as Foxe Edition. I want to thank David Loewenstein for directing me to the subject of conscience in Foxe.

sarcasm, he regards conscience as possessed of evident properties which allow its confident identification. Hales takes a different view, understanding conscience as a private matter, a personal secret, unknowable to any other person. The Catholic Gardiner understands conscience more or less as it had been understood for a millennium: that, as its etymology of *con + sciencia* would suggest, it references commonly held beliefs, matters on which all Christendom might communally and consensually agree. The evangelically leaning Hales employs the word in a more inward and private sense peculiar to the sixteenth century and beyond, according to which each person must look to his own conscience because he cannot know another's. The tipoff to Hales's new understanding is his insistence on distinguishing between 'my' conscience and 'yours'—an insistence on the singularity of each conscience which had become commonplace only in recent decades and would have seemed novel and objectionable to the more traditional Gardiner.

The novelty of Hales's view becomes even clearer in the aftermath of the interview. Conscience had always goaded, bit, and gnawed, but, in the middle ages, its promptings were normally bent toward the individual's self-reformation and reintegration into the larger community of the faith. By contrast, Hales's conscience is profoundly individuating, first by encouraging his resistance to Gardiner and his estrangement from the new Marian order, and eventually in a more self-isolative and destructive sense. Foxe reports that, imprisoned, he ultimately gave way to various importunities and persuasions. Evidently forswearing his faith, he is said to have fallen 'in a great dump, and sorow with him self'. The consequence is a desperation induced 'by the worme of his conscience', inducing 'a greate repentaunce of the deede, and . . . a terror of conscience therby'. First unsuccessfully attempting suicide by wounding himself 'wyth a penknife . . . in divers places', he returned to his home a broken man in 1555, put his affairs in order, and then committed suicide by 'casting hym self into a shallow ryver'.

Gardiner's moralization of this event may be inferred from his comment on a parallel case. Laurence Saunders, examined by Gardiner in the year of Hale's death, describes himself as motived by conscience. Gardiner replies, crying of Saunders and his fellows, 'Conscience? you have none at all, but pride and arrogancy, deviding your selves by singularitye from the Church.'[3] Here he takes an even stronger view than he took with Hales: conscience which divides from the Church and abets singularity is not just misdirected, but no conscience at all.

To say that a *wholly* new view of conscience emerged in the sixteenth century would undervalue the subtlety and diversity of more than a millennium of previous consideration, and would underrate the unevenness with which such changes occur. Even so, several marked new currents are evident in the sixteenth century. People like Hales were seeing conscience less as a haven of consensual views and more as a locus of singular opinions; less as an ally in the task of self-reconciliation

[3] Foxe Edition, 1498.

with ecclesiastical authority and more as a hectoring, troubling, and divisive presence; less as a body of ecclesiastical precepts imported from the 'outside in', and more as a set of deeply lodged convictions speaking from the 'inside out'. Some of these matters of new emphasis will become clearer in historical perspective.

Conscience, 400–1500

Despite later variations and refinements, the main outlines of what might broadly be called a 'Christian' view of conscience were in place when Augustine wrote his *Confessions.* On the brink of conversion but still hesitant, Augustine is chided by his own conscience:

> The day came when I was naked to myself and my conscience angrily spoke out within me [*increparet in me conscientia mea*]: 'where is my tongue? indeed you have said, how that you would not cast off the burden of vanity for an uncertain truth... yet others have not exhausted themselves in such a quest, or spent ten years or more thinking about it.' Thus I was inwardly gnawed [*rodebar intus*] and violently confused with horrible shame.[4]

Confidently as Augustine's voice addresses him, it speaks from a complicated enunciative position. It speaks in a voice something like his own, but not entirely his own. Although intimately acquainted with Augustine's own prevarications and evasions in the matter of conversation, it is also well informed about public norms and expectations as expressed by what 'other' Christians are doing. In this sense, it operates from without as well as within, expressing public consensus as well as private inclination.

Augustine's conscience has its own complicated prehistory. One of its elements, as a staunch truth-teller and ally in the quest for self improvement, may be traced to Jerome's choice of Latin *conscientia* as the best equivalent to Greek *syneidesis/ synderesis*—an indwelling spark of natural reason—for the translation of Paul's epistles in the vulgate Bible. In this aspect, although speaking inwardly, conscience proceeds according to general principles of reasonable analysis available not just to one person but to all persons. At the same time, the commingling of *synderesis* with *conscientia* introduced complexities which were never quite to be resolved. C. A. Pierce has perceptively observed of Jerome's choice that 'use [of *conscientia*] in translation could not fail to reduce what was for the New Testament writers a precise, indeed somewhat narrow, idea into a conception so broad, vague and formless as to confuse rather than clarify all ethical discussion from that moment forward'.[5] Unlike *synderesis*, for example, Latin *conscientia* was complexly tied to

[4] St Augustine, *St. Augustine's Confessions*, trans. William Watts, 2 vols. (London: Heinemann, 1960), 1: 441.

[5] C. A. Pierce, *Conscience in the New Testament* (London: SCM Press, 1955), 118.

public expectation and the public sphere, pertaining in one of its elements to prosecutorial knowledge mobilized in adverse judicial testimony.[6] This classical and Ciceronian conscience directed its observations within, but its admonitions were ultimately derived from exterior norms and standards. Augustine's conscience is thus supported by varied and potentially contradictory Greek and Roman traditions, all reworked within a new Christian emphasis upon evaluation of personal and subjective dispositions and motivations.

This mixed heritage guarantees the medieval conscience a high level of complexity in all its operations. As a voice straddling the inner and the outer, it is alternately friend and foe, at some times supportively encouraging and at other times harshly corrective. It knows one's worst foibles, but it addresses them within broadly entertained and rationally accessible norms. It simultaneously institutes a strengthened sense of selfhood on the one hand and a permanent division of that self between private inclination and public consensus on the other. Whether based upon natural reason, social practice, or gift of God, medieval conscience is never the sole property of its subject, but is intersubjectively held.

This medieval conscience, variously balancing public and private, consensual and distinctive, is on view in a host of texts, including Langland's *Piers Plowman*. Langland's Conscience is, of course, a quality of mind, and hence an inward faculty, but its closest allegiances—instructed by Kynde Wit and supported by Reson (3.284)[7]—suggest that Conscience is never Will's sole property; that, like Greek *synderesis*, it operates on generally accessible and widely shared principles. Moreover, Conscience's sphere of operations is very much in and of the world. Always well informed, and ready to report to the king and others on matters of consensual understanding (3. 230, 7.134), he acts in a number of what might be considered 'public'—and very few entirely private—capacities. Thus, we find Conscience repeatedly sermonizing Will, reminding him of what he ought to know, already implicitly 'knowest wel' (19.26), because it is embodied in received lore and official Church history, about which Conscience is thoroughly informed. The official and public nature of Conscience's duties is emphasized in his various capacities and titles; he is a sound 'counseilor' (19.200), he is 'kepere and gyour [guide] / Over kynde Cristene and Cardynale Vertues' (20.72–3), he is 'conestable' of the castle of Unity (20.214).

Although the public and exterior involvements of Conscience tend mainly to inform and stabilize his views, his activities also remind us that public involvement has its perils. Forced to make decisions in a compromised public sphere, Conscience reveals fallibilities which might otherwise have gone unsuspected. He draws

[6] This idea is elaborated in Michael G. Baylor, *Action and Person: Conscience in Late Scholasticism and the Young Luther* (Leiden: Brill, 1977), especially 22–9.

[7] William Langland, *The Vision of Piers Plowman*, 2nd edn, ed. A. V. C. Schmidt (London: Everyman, 1995; first published 1978).

up a questionable guest list for his dinner party in passus 13 and finally needs to clear his head by walking out on his own guests; we see him scramble against external foes in passus 19–20; he is at times befuddled (19.351), and, despite warnings to the contrary, he makes the disastrous mistake of admitting Friars to the castle of Unity (20.230). The poem's ending suggests that, as wayfarer and pilgrim Conscience might be better off in a less 'institutionalized' capacity, even as that capacity remains tantalizingly unexplored. But in the world of the poem Conscience has no choice but to grapple with flawed alternatives as he enacts his higher responsibility as an arbiter of Christian consensus.

In the contexts in which we have seen him, Conscience speaks for doctrinal consensus and against deviant norms or interpretations formed outside the Church—certainly not as an apologist for, or defender of, subjective or potentially idiosyncratic conclusions. In Langland's poem, Conscience may be seen, as Morton Bloomfield so forcefully argued, not as a power expressed by or through individuals, but as a possession of collective Christian society; it is a house of wisdom and God's dwelling-place within the Christian soul, but its walls are built of such external materials as the four cardinal virtues and other consensual beliefs.[8] This is, we might say, an *inherently* orthodox Conscience. It might misjudge once in a while but, as a matter of *definition*, it could never embrace or even entertain a heterodox belief.[9]

Conscience is thus at once Will's particular conscience and an entity generalized across all Christendom. Indicatively, Will never speaks of 'my conscience', even as, in the medieval centuries generally, references to a personalized conscience are extremely rare. Only occasionally—and then, in my experience, late in the period—do such references occur, and normally in situations of some duress, as when an accusation of treason or heresy has left an individual somehow stranded or isolated from the commonalties of political adherence or shared faith. For example, Thomas Usk, composing his *Testament of Love* under accusations of bad faith and, eventually, treason, speaks exceptionally of a deeply interior and highly personalized faculty which he styles 'the precious secré of my conscience'.[10] Accused Lollard Purvey, under the equivalent pressure of a heresy accusation, argues that the

[8] Morton Bloomfield, *Piers Plowman as a Fourteenth Century Apocalypse* (New Brunswick, NJ: Rutgers University Press, 1961), 167–9.

[9] I refer here, and throughout most of this essay, to views of conscience commonly and broadly entertained. In Thomistic theology, however, conscience was always understood to be an 'applied' or secondary, and thus potentially errant, process, as opposed to *synderesis*, the locus of pure reason. In *Summa Theologica*, 1.79.13, Thomas treats *synderesis* as a natural habit, conscience as an act; as an act, conscience may either be laid aside or be liable to error, as in the case of the misguided heretic. At the same time, Thomas acknowledges the frequent confusion of conscience and *synderesis*, noting that 'Jerome calls *synderesis* conscience', and observing that 'it is customary for causes and effects to be called after one another'. See Thomas Aquinas, *Summa Theologica*, trans. Fathers of the English Dominican Province, vol. 1 (New York: Benziger Brothers, 1947), 1.79.12–13, 407–8; Thomas Aquinas, *Summa Theologiae*, *Sancti Thomae de Aquino Opera Omnia*, vol. 5 (Paris: Vrin, 1989), 1.79.12–13, 279–81. I thank Brian Cummings for his stimulating correspondence on this subject.

[10] Thomas Usk, *The Testament of Love*, ed. R. Allen Shoaf (Kalamazoo, MI: TEAMS, 1998), 1.1.644.

Christian 'ought to commit him to the governaunce of the holy Ghoste, and of his owne conscience' (Foxe Edition, 1563, 141). Unregenerate Lollard Thorpe declares himself moved by 'my conscience' to record his Testimony,[11] and he refuses to name names 'bi the dom of [my] conscience' (35). The only possessor of a personalized conscience in Chaucer is old January of the 'Merchant's Tale', who finds that 'o thyng' (that marriage to May might confer more happiness than he can stand) 'priketh in my conscience'[12]—but this claim to possess a distinctive conscience is typical of the eccentricity and stubborn solipsism of January's views and behavior throughout.[13] Only in the sixteenth century will references to 'my conscience' become commonplace.[14] Their first profuse occurrence is triggered by the self-representations of a most unlikely 'man of conscience', Henry VIII.

My conscience / your conscience

Like most people in the earlier sixteenth century, Henry VIII deployed conscience in traditional as well as innovative ways. His reliance upon tradition is perhaps most amusingly illustrated when, at the consequential moment of 1526–7, he enlisted Wolsey to write chidingly to his sister Margaret, queen of Scotland, who either just had or was about to gain papal permission for *her* divorce. At this juncture, Henry urged his sister to preserve her marriage and—richer still—her daughter's legitimacy. As ventriloquized by Wolsey, he thunders against her intention: 'what charge of conscience, what grudge and fretyng, ye[a] what daunger of dampnacyon shuld that be to your soule with perpetuall infamye of your renounce'.[15] Conscience here informs Margaret of broadly accepted ideas: what everybody knows, and Henry knows, and she should know, on the topics of marriage, parenthood, and succession.

[11] William Taylor and William Thorpe, *Two Wycliffite Texts*, ed. Anne Hudson, EETS, original series, 310 (Oxford: Oxford University Press, 1993), 25.

[12] Geoffrey Chaucer, *The Merchant's Tale*, in *The Riverside Chaucer*, 3rd edn, general editor, Larry D. Benson (Boston, MA: Houghton Mifflin, 1987), 4: 1635.

[13] Already rare, these occurrences are often clouded by textual circumstance. Thorpe's principal reference to the judgment of 'my' conscience, although present in three of four witnesses, is omitted in favor of simple 'conscience' in MS Rawlinson C.208, the base manuscript of Hudson's edition. Usk's references to the secret of his conscience may possibly reflect subsequent interventions in his text, of which the original is missing and only a sixteenth-century print version survives.

[14] The *OED* anticipates me in this matter, suggesting that the individualization or privatization of conscience as a personal judgment of one's own actions was a gradual development, signaled by the emergent sense in which '*my conscience, your conscience*, was understood to mean no longer our respective shares or amounts of the common quality *conscience*, but to be two distinct individual *consciences*, mine and yours'. Only in and after the sixteenth century does one speak of conscience*s*, the plural acknowledging the existence of alternate views of any one matter. *OED* online <http://dictionary.oed.com> : 'conscience' *n.* def. 1.2 and def. 4.9.

[15] BL MS Caligula B. VI, fol. 226; edited in *The Letters of King Henry VIII*, ed. Muriel St Clare Byrne (New York: Funk & Wagnalls, 1936), 67–8.

Soon after this letter was composed, or even as it was in composition, Henry was doing some more innovative thinking about his *own* conscience, and *it* was instructing him to swim upstream, against prevailing currents of understanding. The spring and summer of 1527 were, of course, the months of Henry's amorous dalliance with Anne Boleyn and his gathering resolve to seek a divorce from Queen Catherine. His grounds were to be scriptural and legal-jurisdictional, bearing on the illegitimacy of his marriage to his brother's widow (either because the papal dispensation was faulty in origin, or because of its offence against natural law). But his *rationale* involved the torments of his *scrupulum conscienciae* or scrupulous conscience, a conscience responsible neither to papal approval, nor conciliar authority, nor the opinions of the public at large.[16] This scrupulous conscience alternately pierces and burdens, but, either way, sounds a call to action.[17]

Earlier discussions of conscience undoubtedly occurred in closed session, but, as far as the written record goes, in December 1527 Wolsey explains to one of the King's emissaries that

> the King, partly by his assiduous study and learning, and partly by conference with theologians, has found his conscience somewhat burthened with his present marriage; and out of regard to the quiet of his soul, and next to the security of his succession . . . he considers it would be offensive to God and man if he were to persist in it, and with great remorse of conscience has now for a long time felt that he is living under the offense of the Almighty.[18]

Nor did Henry stray from this alibi; near the end of it all, in a letter of 16 April 1533, the Emperor's envoy Chapuys, describing an interview in which Henry proved steadily obstinate and disclosed that he had already privately married Anne Boleyn, says that he begged Henry, no respecter of other men, at least to respect God: 'He told me that he did so, and that God and his conscience were on very good terms.'[19]

To be sure, the coincidental convenience of Henry's suddenly qualmous conscience to his plan to displace Catherine did not fail to impress itself on some of his more skeptical observers. A 1531 confidential report to the Emperor describes Henry as having put forward the whole notion of his conscience merely to serve as

[16] On the chronology of Henry's involvement with Anne Boleyn, and the character of the theological arguments mounted in his behalf, see J. J. Scarisbrick, *Henry VIII* (New Haven, CT, and London: Yale University Press, 1997), 147–240.

[17] *Scrupulum* is alternately rendered into English as *scrupulous* or *scripelous* conscience—the former from Latin *scrupulus*, a small pointed stone; the latter from Latin *scripulum*, a small weight.

[18] *L&P*, 4: item 3641. See also BL MS Vitellius B ix, fol. 189.
See also *L&P*, 4: item 3913. In fact, Wolsey appears to have been quite active in coining apposite terminology. A note in his own handwriting corrects one draft, in which Henry's divorce is to be conducted in conformity with God's laws and those of the Church, with 'It shall be to the safe of his conscience, for the surety of his person, of his succession, and for the weal of his realm.' Nicholas Pocock (ed.), *Records of the Reformation: The Divorce, 1527–1533* (Oxford: Clarendon Press, 1870), 1: 214.

[19] *L&P*, 6: item 351.

pretext (*pretexere*; from verb *praetexo*) for his intended actions.[20] Murmur to this effect was evidently widely current, in England as well as on the Continent, and Chapuys reports to the Emperor in 1531 that Henry succeeded in getting still-chancellor Thomas More to frame a reply to his critics: 'the Chancellor set forth by command that there were some who had said that the King pursued this divorce out of love for some lady, and not out of any scruple of conscience; and this was not true, for he was only moved thereto in discharge of his conscience'.[21] Among the leading skeptics must be mentioned Queen Catherine herself. As Edward Hall reports the matter, when Henry, failing in his importunities to the Pope, sought the Queen's consent to an English adjudication of the matter 'for the quyetnesse of the Kynges conscience', she accompanied her refusal with barbed irony: 'I praye God sende his grace a quyet conscience.'[22]

But the point is not whether Henry was *really* troubled in his conscience, or (as seems more likely) in some other part of his body. The point is that, even if his conscience-talk was a 'pretext', he was remarkably successful at drawing people into the discussion, on terms which admitted a possibility that he had some sort of conscience-claim. He got partial concessions, at least early on, even from staunch people like John Fisher. In or around 1528, we find Fisher writing (nervously but hopefully), 'I am convinced that the royal wish is not at all to reject the laws of God. That, if on account of Levitical prohibitions, he has yielded to a scruple of conscience [*conscienciae scrupulum*] he will rightly set it aside if, as is truly becoming for a Christian and orthodox prince, he will submit himself to the Pope's interpretation.'[23] The Pope himself might have hatched a short-lived scheme by which Henry would have two wives, with the goal that Henry's conscience might be satisfied.[24] So, too, do we find More, during his 1529–32 Chancellorship, bending to accommodate varied conscience-claims. More's own rather contorted position during his term of office was that he would assist the King in matters not unacceptable to his own conscience, but that other persons than himself might be enlisted to prosecute the great matter of the divorce, their number to include 'onely those (of whom his Grace had good nombre) whose conscience his Grace perceived well and fully persuaded uppon that parte'. More's early hope (which he would ruefully revise during the events of 1532–4) had been that Henry would find a way 'never... to put eny man in ruffle or trowble of his conscience' in this matter; that

[20] *L&P*, 5: item 354; BL MS Add. 28,585, fol. 200.

[21] *L&P*, 5: item 171. See also Edward Hall, *The vnion of the two noble and illustre famelies of Lancastre [and] Yorke*, in which More as Chancellor explains to Parliament that the King, 'like a vertuous prince willyng to be satisfied in his conscience', had sought advice from great clerks and chief universities on the matter of his marriage to his brother's wife and on the extent of the Pope's power to have authorized such a marriage in the first place [1548]. EEBO/TCP, 185.

[22] Hall, *Vnion*, 185.

[23] PRO State Papers 1/42, fol.166v. Cited in Richard Rex, *The Theology of John Fisher* (Cambridge: Cambridge University Press, 1991), 261.

[24] Letter from Sir Gregory Cassali to the King, *Records of the Reformation*, 1: 428 and 95.

each participant's distinctive conscience would be sacrosanct.[25] Thus we find even ultimate doubters like Fisher and More ready to bend at least part way toward an emergent discourse about the sanctity of individual conscience, a discourse non-existent or, at best, dimly adumbrated in preceding decades.[26]

Henry's own shift from a universally accessible conscience to an individualized one was not left untheorized. Early on, he participated personally in the composition of the *Censurae*, a 1531 pamphlet of determinations favorable to his divorce.[27] Citing various biblical and learned opinions on the abomination of marriage to the wife of a deceased brother, this pamphlet's argument progresses to a consideration of one's pained conscience upon discovering himself in such a marriage. The pivot of the Henrician argument rests on a distinction between public and private law: a public or common law confirmed in the writings of the fathers and a private law written in men's hearts. Quoting from a nearly contemporaneous English translation of the original Latin, 'the public law is that, whiche hath ben confirmed by writynge of the holye fathers. The private lawe is the lawe that is written in mennes harts by the inspiration of the holye goste as thapostoll seaketh of certeyne, WHICHE have the lawe of god written in theyr hartes [*in corde hominum scribitur*].'[28] When one declares oneself moved by conscience, and the conscientious interpretation of a supervening law of God, external tests in common law or the writings of the fathers or any other element of the Magisterium fall by the wayside: 'if we folowe the motion of the holy spirite and of our conscience we be not undeer the commune lawe whiche ever ouchte [*ought*] to give place to the pryvate lawe. For in tho thinges that be forbidden by the lawe of god we must obey our conscience: and in other thinges the churche' (266–9). Thus, men moved by *privata conscientia* or 'private conscience' may act *impune* or 'without any ieopardie' in their own behalf, with the church relegated to decide upon matters of lesser import (268–9).[29]

[25] Thomas More, *The Correspondence of Sir Thomas More*, ed. Elizabeth Frances Rogers (Princeton, NJ: Princeton University Press, 1947), 495–6. Hereafter, cited as *Correspondence.*

[26] Not only was Henry wildly successful at putting the scrupled state of his conscience forward as a subject of public conjecture and debate, but he was no less successful at getting everybody talking and thinking in the language of personal conscience and its requirements. Despite her doubts about the character of Henry's conscience, Queen Catherine counters his scruples with a conscience-claim of her own: that 'she never would have wished, nor did wish, to live a moment with him contrary to her conscience' (*L&P*, 5: item 287).

[27] An early draft closest to Henry's own language and presumed views is preserved as PRO MS SP 1/63, fols. 244–64.

[28] *Censurae*, printed as *The Divorce Tracts of Henry VIII*, ed. Edward Surtz and Virginia Murphy (Angers: Moreana, 1988), 266–7.

[29] The treatise offers the example of a priest who, moved by private conscience, may change bishoprics against his ecclesiastical superior's will. Abetting this view of conscience as a personal or private matter is the discussion of legal theorist St German, composed *c.*1528 in Latin with a nearly contemporaneous English translation. He says that 'as a lyght is sette in a lanterne that all that is in the

The chiding, but non-renegade, conscience of the Middle Ages obviously had more to offer to the embattled sixteenth-century Church of Rome than did the subjective and unruly *privata conscientia* favored by Henry VIII and his advisers. Henry's *Censurae*, with their argument that conscience can exist as a matter of private knowledge, written on a man's heart, was necessarily and promptly engaged by Cardinal Fisher, in his 1531–2 *Apologia*.[30] Fisher reiterates the Henrician distinction between a public or common law, confirmed in the writings of the fathers, and a private law which is written in men's hearts, and grants that Pope Urban conceded the two kinds of law (*una publica, altera privata*). But he emphatically affirms that neither kind of law was ever meant to overturn divine law. Moreover, he says, as far as this business about private law being written on man's heart, nobody ever has access to it except at the sacrifice of their reason (*nemo non perspicit, nisi qui ratione destitutus est*). Furthermore, with respect to following inner promptings as opposed to outer counsel, he reminds us of the possibility of self-deception: 'For, as Paul said, an angel of Satan may sometimes transform himself into an angel of light' (*angelus Satanae non numquam transfigurat se in angelum lucis*).[31] What Fisher correctly intuits in Henry's argument, and seeks to ward off, is the emergence of a new situation in which personal conscience-claims are treated as immune to papal or institutional correction and seek authority in their own right.

More himself came to realize the dangers of an unrestricted conscience-claim. We saw him, in the early years of his chancellorship, displaying some deference to the emergent view, and assigning more than an ordinary degree of latitude to personal, and potentially divergent, conscience. Not only, with respect to the oaths of Supremacy and Succession, did he rely on his optimistic expectation that no man might be put 'in ruffle or trowble of his conscience', but he also refused personally to 'condemn the conscience of any other man' who had sworn.[32] His iterations of the fact that he speaks only of his own conscience and seeks not to dictate to others were frequent, and in fact persist nearly to the end of his life.[33]

house may be seen therby so almyghty god hathe sette conscyence in the myddes of every resonable soule as a lyght wherby he may dyscerne and know what he ought to do: and what he ought not to do': Christopher St German, *Dialogus de Fundamentis Legum Anglie et de Conscientia, Doctor and Student*, ed. T. F. T. Plucknett and J. L. Barton (London: Selden Society, 1974), 94–5.

[30] *Matrimonii... brevis Apologia*, British Museum MS Arundel 151, fols. 202–339, at fols. 334v–335r.

[31] BL MS Arundel 151, fols. 334v–335r. Fisher's treatise is summarized in nearly contemporary English in Nicholas Harpsfield, *A Treatise on the Pretended Divorce between Henry VIII and Catherine of Aragon*, Camden Society, second series (1878), 127: 116–17.

[32] *Correspondence*, 502, 526.

[33] For instance, *Correspondence*, 505, 507, 547, 549, 559. In his tale of 'good company', he imagines ALL those who keep to their own conscience to be heaven-bound—even as, in a later illustration, he assumes both St Bernard and St Anselm to be together in heaven, even though they held to different and conscience-bound positions on the Immaculate Conception (*Correspondence*, 526).

This is not to say, however, that More's view of conscience was ever purely private or subjective; his view always possessed an outer, as well as inner, component, a social as well as individual dimension, and in 1532–34 this view would come to the fore. Thus, while granting considerable latitude to conscience, he concurrently believed that conscience could go utterly wrong if misdirected by the idiosyncratic or heretical individual against matters of common faith. Writing to Margaret, he speaks to this matter in the case of a man who would 'take away by hym self upon his owne minde alone, or with some fewe, or with never so many, against an evident trouthe appearing by the common faith of Christendome', finding that 'this conscience is very damnable'. In his later vicissitudes, More placed increasing emphasis on the idea of an external community of right belief. In the *Dialogue of Comfort*, for example, he recommends that the rule of conscience be submitted to external correction, if only in the limited form of advice from some other good man.[34]

In extremis, More found his way back to a still more traditional and consensual view of conscience. In his last months in prison, most radically isolated and estranged from the advice of a good man or men and more than usually pressured by circumstance to rely upon the promptings of his own conscience, he found a way to introduce a guard-rail of external authority. This was to create his own inner voice or wise man and his own public or community. This community is unpresent, drawn not from persons to whose conversation he enjoyed access, but from what might be considered a 'moveable' body of synods, saints, and apostles, whose approval—and, if necessary, correction—he sought. He makes this point eloquently in his post-condemnation speech, as reported in Chastelman's *Memoirs*:

> The Chancellor interrupting him said, 'What, More, you wish to be considered wiser and of better conscience than all the bishops and nobles of the realm?' To this More replied, 'My lord, for one bishop of your opinion I have a hundred saints of mine; and for one parliament of yours, and God knows of what kind, I have all the General Councils for 1,000 years, and for one kingdom I have France and all the kingdoms of Christendom.'[35]

Despite staking some of his earlier arguments on tolerance for singular conscience-claims, More came at the end of it all to rest in a more traditional view of conscience as consensual and authoritative rather than individual and potentially erratic.[36]

[34] Thomas More, *The Dialogue of Comfort*, ed. Louis Martz and Frank Manley, in *The Complete Works of St Thomas More*, vol. 12 (New Haven: Yale University Press, 1976), 112–21.

[35] *L&P*, 8: item 996.

[36] For a differently inflected, but I think broadly compatible, view of the tension between More's view of conscience as voice of doctrinal truth on the one hand and personal belief on the other, see Brian Cummings, 'The Conscience of Thomas More', in *Representing Religious Pluralization in Early Modern Europe*, ed. Andreas Höfele *et al.* (Münster: Lit Verlag, 2007), 1–14.

A 'Reformation' conscience?

In the cases of Henry and More, and Hales and Gardiner, we encounter contemporaries who hold the word conscience in common but mean different things by it. Hales and other mid-century evangelicals laid unprecedented emphasis on its interiority, singularity, and the rigorousness of 'my' conscience's demands—a development undoubtedly intimately related to the situation of doctrinal contestation, and occasional danger, in which these advocates of new religious arrangements found themselves. If Gardiner's irascible acknowledgment of his conscience-claims is any indication, Hales seems to have developed his reliance upon private conscience into a new and perhaps even slightly ostentatious public identity. Does this identity express a distinctively 'Protestant' or 'Reformation' conscience? Probably so, and we may assume that, by the mid-century, this conscience was bolstered and supplemented by Continental example.

The strong current of specifically Protestant interest in conscience flowing England's way may be briefly epitomized in the writings of Luther, with his unequivocal emphasis on *conscientia mea*. This emphasis is brought to particular focus in his celebrated declaration at Worms:

> [my] conscience is captive to the words of God; I cannot nor will I retract anything, since it is never safe nor virtuous to go against conscience.
> (*capta conscientia in verbis dei, revocare neque possum nec volo quicquam, cum contra conscientiam agere neque tutum neque integrum sit.*)[37]

Luther's centralization of his conscience-claims could hardly go unmarked. No sooner, in fact, had he spoken than Johann Eck, secretary to the proceedings, cried out, in his own account of the matter: 'Lay aside your conscience, Martin! (*Depone conscientiam, Martine!*) You must lay it aside because it is in error.'[38] Of course, Luther had no intention of laying his conscience aside, because he was confident that his position was already validated in scripture (*in verbis dei*). In this respect, Luther avoided a purely solipsistic or idiosyncratic position, admitting the text of scripture as his external 'control'. Yet what distressed the papal representatives was his refusal to grant intermediary authorities—the conclusions of councils and synods, for example—any role as arbiters of relations between the personal and the divine.

Luther was announcing, and in a sense formalizing, a new understanding of conscience, a shift from the institutionally bound conscience of Catholicism to what may indeed be considered a 'Reformation' conscience, bound only by its direct communication with God as revealed in scripture. Despite the introduction

[37] Martin Luther, *D. Martin Luthers Werke, kritische Gesamtausgabe*, 7 (Weimar, Böhlaus, 1897), 838.

[38] Luther, *Werke*, 7: 839.

of scripture as a final authority, his insistence on personal rather than institutional or collective scriptural interpretation meant that, from the point of view of the institution-minded representatives of the Roman Church, he was not really significantly bound at all.[39] Virtue was, in consequence, radically interiorized, belittling the role of the Church as arbiter of relations between the personal and the divine.[40] Luther was far from regarding himself as an advocate for an entirely subjective conscience; he would have poured anathema on such a position. But Luther's stand on conscience had the undoubted *effect* of enhancing potentially singular belief at the expense of traditional and collective authority.[41] Those influenced—especially at second or third hand—by Luther's radical personalization of conscience could hardly be expected to grasp the particulars of his confidence in scripture as a check against idiosyncratic conclusions.

Too long in the body

Conscience is always, to one degree or another, stationed within, but the character of its interiority shifts with the Reformation. Medieval conscience operates inwardly, but it enters from without, as a gift of God or as a matter of doctrinal consensus. Recall that Conscience, in *Piers Plowman*, is represented not as a long-term resident, but an outsider: the King describes him as 'a knight, Conscience, cam late fro biyond' (3.110).[42] Far from belonging solely to Will, Conscience often serves as something like an ambassador from God, or a diplomat on a posting, or a bureaucratic functionary on special assignment, as when he operates within Anima or the soul as 'Goddes clerk and his notarie' (15, line 32). Serving in such provisional capacities, medieval conscience is less likely to 'go native' or desert to the 'other side'—less likely to give way to the promptings of the body within which it dwells.

When medieval conscience does go astray, however, it is likely to have been besmirched as a consequence of having spent too long in the body. The evocatively entitled *Ayenbite of Inwyt*, for example, gives us *inwyt* or conscience serving in a variety of capacities. Some of its functions are neutral with respect to embodiment, as when *inwyt* is described as the Christian's amanuensis or record-keeper, recording his findings in a book which is, indeed, skin-bound, but by the skin of a sheep rather than a human: 'ine the boc of his inwyt: þanne ine ane seepes scinne' ('in the

[39] See the reasoned formulation of Baylor, *Action and Person*, 261–70.

[40] Norman Jones, *The English Reformation: Religion and Cultural Adaptation* (Oxford: Blackwell, 2002), 173.

[41] Michael G. Baylor observes that 'the authority of the church to act as an instructor and guide of conscience received a shock from which it never recovered' (*Action and Person*, 270).

[42] I am indebted to Jennifer Lichtblau for this observation.

book of his conscience, bound in a sheep's skin').[43] Even so, *inwyt* still maintains his 'chombre' within the body, and serves there as the bed of the soul, and a bed, liable to be fouled, must be well cleansed (171–3). *Inwyt* must, in other words, *be* examined rather than conduct the examination, and prayers launched from within a soiled chamber will be ignored because they come 'of inwyt vol of velthe and of zenne' ('full of filth and sin') (217).

Despite such occasional instances, a thoroughly corrupt conscience—as opposed to an ignored or temporarily deceived but properly oriented one—remains a comparative rarity in the Middle Ages. The Reformation conscience, lingering longer and dwelling more deeply within, faces new challenges and temptations. Consider the particular language in which George Cavendish represents Henry VIII, hearing a French ambassador's comment about her prior marriage to his brother, recoiling from his queen: 'thes wordes ware so conceyved within my scripulous concyence that it brede a doughtfull prike within my brest whiche dought prykked vexed & trobled so my mynd'.[44] Here, in a small but telling reversal of direction, conscience abdicates its responsibility to prick the guilty, and is *itself* penetrated by doubt. *Being* pricked, conscience turns out to have a bodily self, and a self subject to impregnation; conception having occurred, it reproduced, and 'bred' a prick within Henry's own breast. This passive conscience—a conscience susceptible to violation from within—is on the way to becoming something like a body part, with all attendant liabilities. And this is what, in Shakespeare's consideration of Henry's case, it does become.

Shakespeare and Fletcher's *King Henry VIII (All is True)* uses the word *conscience* twenty-four times, twice as often as any other in the Shakespeare canon. Many of its appearances are quite traditional, persisting in the early modern period in what I have called a 'medieval' sense. But, in its most significant appearances, this play's corrupted conscience is no longer an opponent, or even (as in the historical Henry's case) a facilitator of desires, but is *itself* invaded and fatally disfigured by desire. This play's conscience has dwelt too long within the body, has been corrupted by the hermetic environment in which it lives. Henry's is a physically vulnerable conscience, one which sustains wounds (2.2.73).[45] It is, consequently, a 'tender place'. Speaking of his severance from Catherine, he exclaims,

> But conscience, conscience—
> O, 'tis a tender place, and I must leave her. (2.2.141–2)

[43] Dan Michel, *Ayenbite of Inwyt*, ed. Pamela Gradon, EETS, original series, 23, 2 vols. (Oxford: Oxford University Press, 1965; first published 1866), 1: 44. I want to thank Emily Cersonsky for greatly expanding my understanding of this text.

[44] George Cavendish, *The Life and Death of Cardinal Wolsey*, ed. Richard Sylvester, EETS, original series, 243 (London, New York: Oxford University Press, 1959), 83.

[45] William Shakespeare and John Fletcher, *King Henry VIII* (*All is True*), ed. Gordon McMullan (London: Arden Shakespeare, 2002).

Henry's conscience is constantly trembling and quailing, and here its tenderness is manifest in the physical pain he feels over the impending separation from his 'sweet bedfellow', Catherine. Yet a palpable conscience is also, in some respects, a corruptible one, and this 'tender place' runs afoul of a syntactic ambiguity: is the conscience *itself* a tender place, or has Henry's own attention drifted to the tender place of his desires, Anne Bullen's own sexual parts? This sexual undertone is sustained in 2.3.66 when Anne, receiving honors from Henry, imagines that they entail obedience and wonders 'What kind of my obedience I should tender'—the 'tender' being, as her Old Lady interlocutor soon specifies, sexual in nature. The Old Lady has previously debunked Anne's 'mincing', suggesting that she can accommodate Henry's gifts, which gifts

> . . . the capacity
> Of your soft cheverel conscience would receive,
> If you might please to stretch it. (2.3.31–3)

Gordon McMullan, whose observations about the sexual imagery of these passages precede and inform mine, notes that the pliancy of cheverel leather had made it proverbial for a flexible conscience, but also underwrites its accompanying allusion to Anne's pliant genitalia.[46] In this case, Anne's conscience is so embodied that it behaves like—in fact becomes inseparable from—a vagina, stretching itself open to receive Henry's bounty.

Meanwhile, the vicissitudes of Henry's conscience continue. Rehearsing his decision to divorce Catherine, he describes the occasion when his 'conscience first received a tenderness, / Scruple and prick' (2.4.167–8)—not only a phallic pun, but, as in Cavendish, a reformulation of the medieval understanding in which conscience 'pricks' its guilty host, with conscience now seen as an organ or body-part capable of *being* pricked, as liable to its own corrupted kind of embodiment.[47] Late in the play, at the queen's coronation, a mocking gentleman comments to another,

> Our King has all the Indies in his arms,
> And more, and richer, when he strains that lady.
> I cannot blame his conscience. (4.1.46–7).

In this evocation of Henry 'straining' his lady—that is, straining her in his arms in the act of intercourse—conscience is invoked as the historical Henry invoked it, as a pretext for or enabler of his desires. But in this new situation, conscience is no longer simply an alibi or absent cause, but rather becomes an active accomplice of

[46] See especially notes to Shakespeare and Fletcher, *King Henry VIII (All is True)*, ed. McMullan, 2.2.16–17 and 2.3.32.

[47] Note the same reversal in Holinshed: 'a certeine scrupulositie that pricked my conscience'; Geoffrey Bullough, *Narrative and Dramatic Sources of Shakespeare*, 4 (London: Routledge and Kegan Paul, 1966), 468.

Henry's embraces. This participatory or volitional conscience has been evident since the very first of the play's conscience-quibbles:

CHAMBERLAIN
It seems the marriage with his brother's wife
Has crept too near his conscience.
SUFFOLK
No, his conscience
Has crept too near another lady. (2.2.14–15)

This exchange could be read as a simple play on the two traditional senses of 'conscience', still fused in early modern English: his 'conscience' in its sense of guilty self-reproach bothers him, even as his 'consciousness' drifts to a new object. But, in a more incriminating and post-medieval way, conscience in any or all of its senses is not just operating within Henry's mind, but as an extension of his bodily desires: insinuatingly creeping around, actively participating in the production of sexual opportunities.

Our play's Henry is conscience-driven, but his conscience is itself a greedy, overfleshly, and desirous place. In comparison, the historical Henry of the *Censurae* and elsewhere seems almost quaint in his desire for external and theological corroboration, in his professed deference to the opinions of university centers, theologians, and the published word. The historical Henry was, in this sense, caught between emergent and older conceptions. As innovator, he enlisted the promptings of his conscience as an abettor of his singular desires; as traditionalist, he sought external verification and ratification of his conscience's contents. Whereas the play's Henry possesses a conscience wholly unapologetic in its solipsism, utterly indwelling and seeking or requiring nothing in the way of external corroboration or restraint. In this sense, the play's Henry possesses a full development of what I am calling a 'Reformation' conscience—although in a highly problematic form, suggestive of aberrations to which a conscience emancipated from external authority and conciliar constraint had become subject.

The problem of aberrant conscience is registered differently—but nevertheless registered—within some of the theological tendencies of the day. The literary view of a corruptible, and fully corrupted, conscience has its own counterparts within Reformation theology, and even at that movement's Geneva epicenter. For sheer mistrust of conscience—seen not as a site of calm self-assessment and fair reckoning but as polluted ground wracked by agitation and stupefied by terror—Jean Calvin enjoys an unchallengeable pre-eminence. These emphases are reproduced and, if anything, underscored in Thomas Norton's influential 1561 Englishing of his text.

Calvin writes his *Institutes* with a broad awareness of previous traditions; he draws extensively on Paul's Epistles and other collectively important sources. In consequence, he makes a variety of familiar points about such matters as conscience's divine inspiration ('engraven of God in the myndes of men': 4.20, 166).[48] Like Langland and many medieval commentators, he presents a view of conscience working inside and outside, peculiar to the individual but also assigned the traditional, stern duty to offer testimony or even indictment to God on Judgment Day. Conscience is 'joined' to its host, but with an external loyalty requiring the errant Christian to be drawn *by* conscience to the bar of justice: 'as a witnesse ioyned with them whiche doth not suffer them to hide their synnes but that they be drawen accused to the iudgement seate of God, that same felyng is called Conscience' (3.19, 213). This conscience fully revives its latent classical sense as a giver of adverse testimony, hounding its host to professions of guilt: 'it is a certayne meane betwene God and man, bicause it suffreth not to man to suppresse in himselfe that whiche he knoweth, but pursueth him so farre till it bryng him to giltinesse' (3.19, 213).

Despite these acknowledgments of conscience as man's divine part and guarantee of God's interest in man, and even despite the resolute astringency with which conscience will act as bailiff and witness at the bar of God, Calvin's conscience runs its own simultaneous risk of a disturbing naturalization within its bodily home. No wonder that we find conscience constantly battered, tremulous, lacerated, shaken to the core, because, no longer just God's emissary to the Christian, this conscience now bears the brunt of God's wrath. How, Calvin asks, given God's implacable anger, can conscience fail to collapse under the strain of divine disapproval: 'When oure conscience beholdeth onely indignation and vengeance, howe canne it butte tremble and quake for feare' (3.2, 110)? This is a load-bearing conscience, a conscience oppressed by sin and guilt: 'oure owne conscience oppressed with heavy burden of sinnes lying upon it [*Ipsa praecipue conscientia incumbente peccatorum mole oppressa*[49]], dothe sometime lament and grone with it selfe, and sometime accuseth it selfe: sometime secretely murmureth, and sometime is openly troubled' (3: 2, 117). Such consciences can hardly be expected to retain their composure, for they struggle endlessly with their own mistrust of salvation. This tremulous, self-accusing, and sin-burdened conscience quakes and awaits God within the body, and its deprivations are metaphorically expressed as bodily wounds. Speaking of inward, as opposed to public, confession, Calvin urges, after Chrysostom, 'rehearse & utter thy conscience before God. Shewe thy woundes to the Lord [*Domino*... *ostende vulnera*], the best surgeon, and aske salve of him. Shew to him that... wil moste gently heale thee'. This is an ulcerated conscience, and God, as physician, offers to 'heale thy sore' (*ut samen ulcus*) (3.4, 141; ccel 409). Only an 'evell conscience' (3.4, 144) would require such ministration, and its evil is deeply involved in the circumstances of its bodily sojourn. No longer a spark of reason, or a staunch friend, or even God's neutral account-keeper, Calvin's

[48] Jean Calvin, *The institution of Christian religion by maister Ihon Caluin* (1561), trans. Thomas Norton, EEBO/TCP.

[49] Jean Calvin, *Institutes of the Christian Religion*, Christian Classics Ethereal Library (<http://www.ccel.org>), 2: 3, 367.

conscience—in his original and also as Norton renders it—often acts like one of those corrupted cops in *The Wire* or *Fort Apache, the Bronx*: embattled, besmirched, smack dab in the middle of troubles it would have once been summoned to solve.

FURTHER READING

Baylor, Michael G. *Action and Person: Conscience in Late Scholasticism and the Young Luther* (Leiden: Brill, 1977)
Cummings, Brian. 'Conscience and the Law in Thomas More', *Renaissance Studies*, 23.4 (2009), 463–85 (this issue, dedicated to 'The Renaissance Conscience' is generally useful)
Pierce, C. A. *Conscience in the New Testament* (London: SCM Press, 1955)
Ricoeur, Paul. *Oneself as Another* (Chicago: University of Chicago Press, 1999)
Taylor, Charles. *Sources of the Self* (Cambridge, MA: Harvard University Press, 1989)

PART IV

LEGALITIES

CHAPTER 13

THEATRE

LORNA HUTSON

Post-Reformation theatre in England is more generally known to us as 'Renaissance theatre' or even, nowadays, 'Shakespearean theatre'. I am going to argue that this Renaissance or post-Reformation theatre has continuities with the sacramental or penitential theatre of the previous century in that it is concerned with the questions of sin, restitution, and forgiveness that were once at the heart of the sacrament of penance. But I am also going to argue that post-Reformation or Renaissance theatre is, in certain aspects, neoclassical. Its neoclassicism, moreover, is part of a formal and spiritual transformation of medieval penitential culture. This latter contention is controversial. Argument for continuities between late medieval Corpus Christi drama and Shakespeare are predicated on the extent to which Shakespearean drama is *not* humanist or neoclassical. Helen Cooper has recently written that Shakespeare's theatre is, like medieval theatre, an art of 'enactment, not description', and that it is 'that element of enactment . . . that . . . decisively separates' such theatre 'from humanist or classical drama'.[1] The purpose of this chapter is not to deny the continuity between Shakespeare and medieval theatre, but to argue that we can only understand it fully by acknowledging the neoclassicism that is, in however modified a sense, its vehicle, the means by which a penitential jurisdiction over the interior (the soul) is transformed and made a vital part of the post-Reformation and Counter-Reformation theatrical world. If medieval theatre comes out of what Sarah Beckwith calls the literature and culture of 'handling sin', Renaissance theatre adapts the 'handling' of sin as it assimilates the rhetorical lessons of a classical dramaturgy.[2]

This chapter will consider first, briefly, the recent debate among Renaissance critics and medievalists on the theoretical question of theatre's relation to ritual

[1] Helen Cooper, 'Shakespeare and the Mystery Plays', in *Shakespeare and Elizabethan Popular Culture*, ed. Stuart Gillespie and Neil Rhodes (London: Arden, 2006) 18–41, at 19.

[2] Sarah Beckwith, 'Medieval Penance, Reformation Repentance and *Measure for Measure*', in *Reading the Medieval in Early Modern England*, ed. Gordon McMullan and David Matthews (Cambridge: Cambridge University Press, 2007) 193–204, at 193.

and sacrament, and the historical question of the effects of the Reformation on the experience of this relation. It will then consider two English plays, one from the mid-fifteenth century (*Mankind*, *c.*1460), and one from the mid-sixteenth century (*Gammer Gurton's Needle*, *c.*1560), both of which clearly constitute the community both on- and offstage as one whose relations are founded on the premise of acknowledging sinfulness and being forgiven. *Gammer Gurton's Needle* will serve as an example of the Reformation humanism's forensic transformations of penitential culture, as well as of its neoclassical transformations of the stagecraft and dramaturgy of penitential theatre. I hope to show that reforming authors adapted Latin intrigue comedy less out of concern with the putative Aristotelian 'unities' than out of a desire to educate audiences in the forms of ethical and intellectual inquiry that are involved in the following of an intricate plot. In doing so, they transformed and democratized the discursive strategies once devoted to the private, priestly handling and discerning of sin, turning these into the ethical and hermeneutic accommodations of the audience's equitable judgement. Mid-sixteenth-century experiments in neoclassical intrigue plots, which Anglo-American critics have all too often dismissed or overlooked as representing a sterile Continental neoclassicism, were profoundly involved in the very questions of interior and exterior jurisdiction that precipitated the Reformation, as well as being excitingly generative of what we might call new 'reality effects' in the craft and discourse of theatrical representation.

Theatre, sacrament, belief

Theatre and ritual are not absolutely different in kind, but they do differ in the nature and degree of audience participation, and in the forms of emotional, intellectual, and sensory (and, hence, spiritual) transformation they achieve. Scholars have engaged in a variety of ways with the apparent paradox that such a vital and emotive theatrical culture should emerge in post-Reformation England, in spite of Protestant iconoclasm and a general 'Protestant distrust of artifice and imagination'.[3] The most probing and insightful work of this kind has been done, over a period of years, by Stephen Greenblatt, who since the mid-1980s has been interpreting what happens onstage in Shakespeare's plays in terms of a wider cultural struggle over 'the definition of the sacred' in late sixteenth- and early seventeenth-century England.[4] Greenblatt explored the boundaries of theatre and sacred rite, suggesting that these are themselves by-products of the cultural trauma of Protestantism. He showed, for example, how the Protestant Samuel Harsnett

[3] Huston Diehl, *Staging Reform, Reforming the Stage: Protestantism and Popular Theater in Early Modern England* (Ithaca, NY: Cornell University Press, 1997), 71.

[4] Stephen Greenblatt, *Shakespearean Negotiations* (Oxford: Clarendon Press, 1988), 95.

exposed Jesuit exorcism as a theatrical performance that conceals its inauthenticity and hence deprives spectators 'of the rational disenchantment that frames the experience of a play'.[5] Shakespeare's *King Lear*, he went on to argue, builds this rational disenchantment into the emotional work performed by its exorcisms; characters in the play are 'haunted by a sense of rituals and beliefs that are no longer efficacious, that have been *emptied out*'.[6] Later, in his study of the relationship of Shakespeare's drama to the reformers' rejection of Purgatory, Greenblatt characterized Shakespeare as 'fascinated by what we might call evacuated ghost beliefs'.[7] These hollowed-out rites and beliefs are, in Greenblatt's account, forms of emotional and spiritual longing, forms of susceptibility from which belief in ritual efficacy springs. Shakespeare, he implies, has characters in the plays fill out the spaces vacated by the efficacy and presence of sacred rites with their own powerfully affecting fictions, so that the creative humanity of Shakespearean theatre may be said to be predicated on the loss of belief.

A difficulty with Greenblatt's account for medievalists, however, is the fact that it depends on the very structural opposition between sacred rite and theatre, or sacrament and theatre, which is said to be a product of the Reformation. 'Unless we put sacrament and theater back into relation with one another', as Sarah Beckwith has observed, 'pre-Reformation theater is unacknowledgeable'.[8] What pre-Reformation theatre has in common with sacred rite, Beckwith shows, turns not on degrees of belief or scepticism, but on the nature of *participation* in the symbolic act. Eucharistic real presence, which was to become the subject of the most vexed and grotesque post-Reformation debate, is enacted in fifteenth-century Corpus Christi theatre across the body of the actor playing Christ in the crucifixion scenes, a body at once semiotic and phenomenal, experiencing real physical risk. 'The host, the little biscuit', comments Beckwith, 'is returned in this theater to a relation that is fully intersubjective, discovering Christ as the encounter between humanity and God'.[9] But if participation in the symbolic act unites the theatre of Corpus Christi with the sacrament of Corpus Christi, or the Eucharist, it does so only because that latter is fully implicated in the community's struggle over and adjudication of its own relations of sin and forgiveness. For, as Beckwith shows, the mystery of Eucharistic real presence could not, in the fifteenth century, be separated from the 'most awkwardly but productively dialogic of the sacraments', the sacrament of penance.[10] The Easter Eucharist, as Beckwith put it,

> was a communion, not a spectacle. The eucharist as the body of Christ is thus judge as well as redeemer. Preparation of the soul and reconciliation were central to worthy

[5] Greenblatt, *Shakespearean Negotiations*, 106.

[6] Greenblatt, *Shakespearean Negotiations*, 119.

[7] Greenblatt, *Shakespeare in Purgatory*, 157.

[8] Sarah Beckwith, *Signifying God: Social Relation and Symbolic Act in the York Corpus Christi Plays* (Chicago: University of Chicago Press, 2001), xvii.

[9] Beckwith, *Signifying God*, 68–70.

[10] Beckwith, *Signifying God*, 90.

> reception because receiving the eucharist meant enacting the body of Christ through living relations of love as known (and forgiven) creatures. This entailed not merely self-examination but actually restoring the damaged bonds of love between people.[11]

To say that fifteenth-century English vernacular theatre is penitential or sacramental theatre, then, is to say that it, too, enacts the body of Christ as a divine jurisdiction exercised through community reconciliation and mutual forgiveness of sins. Neither the theatrical quality of the sacrament nor the sacramental quality of theatre is part of a con trick. People don't need to be persuaded into belief, or deprived of rational disenchantment: they *participate* in symbolic enactments of their own communality, their own membership of a body bound by a divine love that can only be expressed through human and material signs.

Beckwith's book thus counters prevalent new historical accounts of Renaissance theatre as evacuated Catholic ritual by insisting on the *communal* and *juridical* dimensions of the Eucharist and of Purgatory (that is, by insisting on confession and penance as acts that involve forgiveness, transgression, and satisfaction made for wrongs done to neighbours). The importance of this insistence can hardly be overstated. It suggests that the real distinction between a sacramental and a non-sacramental theatre (theatre pre- and post-Reformation) may turn less on degrees of scepticism and belief per se than on the way in which a community imagines its own human participation in a divine jurisdiction.

Participation, forgiveness, judgement: Mankind

Confession and private penance became established as sacraments in the twelfth century. By the end of the twelfth century, as Elizabeth Fowler has written, 'confession was considered to be a formal legal jurisdiction complementary to that of the external forum of the ecclesiastical courts'. In 1215, as is well known, the Fourth Lateran Council 'institutionalized the regulation of the interior' by requiring all Christians to confess to a priest at least once a year.[12] Medievalists have emphasized the continuities between the literature of this sacrament—manuals of guidance for priests and penitents, detailing the species and circumstances of sins, and their attendant remedies—and other dramatic and literary productions from the thirteenth to the fifteenth centuries. Drama, in particular, presents 'the acknowledgement, confession and forgiveness of sin, institutionalised ... as the sacrament of penance'.[13] But if this sense of Eucharistic participation through the drama of penance precludes distinctions between sacrament and theatre, between credulous populace

[11] Beckwith, *Signifying God*, 92.

[12] Elizabeth Fowler, *Literary Character: The Human Figure in Early English Writing* (Ithaca, NY: Cornell University Press, 2003), 49.

[13] Robert Potter, *The English Morality Play: Origins, History and Influence of a Dramatic Tradition* (London: Routledge and Kegan Paul, 1975) 16.

and dramaturgical priesthood, it clearly sets up its own tensions and contradictions. In the fifteenth-century play of *Mankind*, for example, it is the audience's participation in the carnivalesque 'game' of the drama itself that precipitates the recognition of its own spiritual plight, its profound need to be forgiven. But this, in turn, involves a rejection of that very participation at the level of the body that originally constituted the audience as a community.

Mankind is unequivocally associated with the sacrament of penance. Not only is the play centrally concerned with Shrovetide or shriving-tide—with the need to confess sins and do penance in preparation for the Easter houseling—it has even been specifically linked to the penitential treatise, *Jacob's Well*, which seems to have been composed as a series of sermons for delivery from Ash Wednesday to the vigil of Pentecost.[14] From the outset of the play, the audience is directly addressed by a priest-figure, identified as 'Mercy', who reminds them that God sent 'hys own son to be torn and crucyfyede' for their 'dysobedyenc'.[15] His preaching becomes more urgent: he reminds us all ('soverens' and 'brothern', sitting and standing) that our Saviour is the only food to save us from our ancient bond with the devil, which bodes evil for us at the Last Judgement, when 'ther xall be a streyt examinacyon / The corn xall be savyde, the chaffe xall be brente' (ll. 29–44). This reminder of the eschatological drama of exclusion is, to the audience's relief, interrupted by a carnival joker ('Myscheff') who comes on and mockingly reappropriates Mercy's spiritual metaphors for the acoustic pleasure of punning. His wordplay expresses the body's resourceful carnality, its resistance to the terrifying spiritual distinctions on which Mercy insists: 'Leve yowr chaffe, leve yowr corn, leve yowr dalyacyon... Corn servit bredibus, chaffe horsibus, straw fyrybusque. / Thys ys as moche to say, to yowr leude wndyrstondynge, / As the corn xall serve to brede at the nexte bakynge...When a man ys forcolde the straw may be brent, / And so forth, et cetera' (ll. 46, 57–63).

Thereafter, the audience is drawn in to the sensory pleasures of what Myscheff calls the 'game' (l. 69). Three of his companions come on and call in 'mynstrellys' to play music, trying to make Mercy dance and continuing in Myscheff's vein of materializing and debasing the 'Englysch Laten' that fills the priest's 'mowth' and 'body' (ll. 124, 132). When these comedians fail to tempt the audience's surrogate, Mankind, away from his work (he hits out at them with his spade), they mingle among the audience, collecting money for the next great attraction—the spectacle of Tytivillus, the Devil himself: 'worshypfull soverence', New Gyse wheedles, 'We intende to gather mony, yf yt plesse yowr neclygence / For a man wyth a hede

[14] See W. K. Smart, 'Some Notes on Mankind', *Modern Philology*, 14 (1916) 45–8; Sister Mary Philippa Coogan, *An Interpretation of the Moral Play, Mankind* (Washington, DC: Catholic University of America Press, 1947) 1–21; Leo M. Carruthers, 'The Liturgical Setting of *Jacob's Well*', *English Language Notes*, 24:4 (1987), 11–24.

[15] *Mankind*, lines 3–4, in *The Macro Plays*, ed. Mark Eccles, EETS, 262 (Oxford: Oxford University Press, 1969), 155. Hereafter references to line numbers of the play in this edition will appear in the text.

that is of grett omnipotens' (l.459–61). As many critics have noted, Tytivillus's entrance, accompanied by the traditional request to make room, recalls older non-mimetic dramatic forms of mumming and masking.

Anticipating the audience's joyful reception of the spectacle of the devil, as well as eliciting its laughter and pleasure in the antics of the singing and dancing Vices who poke fun at their parish priest is, of course, part of the emotional design of this powerful penitential drama. The audience, like Mankind, draws ever closer to the Vices, and eventually finds itself choking on its own laughter when Mankind dutifully recites a mock catechism that begins with promising never to get up early to go to church, and ends with vowing to cut men's throats by the highway. But if there is a sense of collective guilt which unites the audience with Mankind as he finally recognizes his profound need of Christ's mercy, it is one which emphatically does not draw on dramatic resources to represent the communal and reconciliatory aspects of penance, 'the restoring of damaged bonds of love between people'.

For the drawing of the audience into a recognition of their guilt, and their collective need for mercy, can only be achieved by a lack of dramatic interest in the traditional questions posed by confessors regarding the relation of act to intention, and the circumstances of sin. Tytivillus was famed in sermon literature as the devil who recorded 'the woordys of the peple, whiche thei iangledyn & rownedyn in cherche' and who collected them in a 'gret sacche full of youre ydell woordys'.[16] In the play over which he presides, the 'idle' speech (whether blasphemous, or merely non-referential) that initially constitutes the audience's carnival entertainment leads directly to the offstage murders, robberies, and rapes boastfully recounted by Myscheff and the Vices towards the end. Tytivillus, the cause of Mankind's capitulation to sin, is a devil primarily associated with inattention, with minds which wander in church, with gossip during sermons, with lack of concentration at prayer. The play explicitly equates such negligence with the most heinous premeditated crimes. Idle speech, says Mercy, 'ys wers than ony felony or treson. / How may it be excusyde befor the Justyce of all / When for euery ydyll worde we must yelde a reson?' (ll. 171–4). If, as Anthony Gash has suggested, the roles of Mercy and Tytivillus might have been played by the same actor, then such a symbolic doubling at the level of the actor's body would also expose the tension at the heart of the play's invocation of the Judgement Day, and God's justice.[17] If 'the Justyce of all' requires 'euery ydyll worde' be weighed against each human soul, then its exactions seem diabolically undiscriminating, a Tytivillus whose alter ego is the 'Mercy' that embraces all Mankind and forgives it for having been 'audyence' (l. 299) to idle words and curses at a play.

[16] *Jacob's Well, An English Treatise on the Cleansing of Man's Conscience* [*c*.1440], ed. Arthur Brandeis (London: EETS, o.s., no. 23, 1900), 114–15.

[17] Anthony Gash, 'Carnival and the Poetics of Reversal', in *New Directions in Theatre*, ed. Julian Hilton (New York: St Martin's Press, 1993) 87–119, at 100.

Interiority after penance: the spread of 'circumstantial' inquiry

The Reformation in England did away with the primary jurisdictional division of canon law, the distinction between internal and external fora. How are we to interpret the effects of this on drama? Historians and literary critics have argued that Protestantism exteriorized penance and transformed the complex production of interiority associated with penitential discourse into a political tool of the state, an instrument of a politicized criminal justice system. According to this account, 'the abolition of mandatory auricular confession reduced the complexity and permeability of the boundary between public and private adjudicated by the parish priest', and confession was reduced to a form of moral propaganda for the state, 'relegated to the last dying speech of the criminal penitent'.[18]

At the same time there has been, and continues to be, a tendency among Anglophone literary critics to regard post-Reformation experimentation with classical drama as a premature rejection of the 'incarnational aesthetic' of native sacred drama and a misguided attempt to replace it with a Latin tradition of plays that 'locate their action offstage, and so privilege the spoken word' to the exclusion of enactment and embodiment.[19] Neither of these commonplaces can possibly tell the whole story. The abolition of the Church's jurisdiction over the interior via the confessional coincided with the dramatic realization of *more*, not less, complex representations of human interiority. And the transformation of the jurisdictional relations of church and state fostered the growth of jurisdictional and political communities that 'maintain[ed] neighbourliness' and ordered and governed themselves within the commonwealth—at the parish level.[20] This different sense of community is enabled by the different kinds of actor–plot–audience relationship fostered by neoclassical experimentation. We need to tell a more complicated story about the jurisdictional transformations brought about by the Reformation.

The effects of the Reformation on ecclesiastical law and parish life cannot be isolated from the larger jurisdictional interrelations of canon and common law. The main legal impact of the Reformation involved a seismic shift in the relative power and moral authority of spiritual and temporal jurisdictions.[21] While ecclesiastical courts enjoyed a revival from 1570 to 1640, their work had become

[18] Beckwith, 'Medieval Penance, Reformation Repentance', 198; Peter Lake, with Michael Questier, *The Antichrist's Lewd Hat: Protestants, Papists and Players in Post-Reformation England* (New Haven, CT: Yale University Press, 2002).

[19] Cooper, 'Shakespeare and the Mystery Plays', 19.

[20] See, for example, Steve Hindle, 'The Governance of the Parish', in *The State and Social Change in Early Modern England 1540–1660* (Houndmills: Palgrave, 2002), 204–30, at 205.

[21] See *The Reports of Sir John Spelman*, ed. J. H. Baker, 2 vols. (London: Selden Society, 1977, 1978), 2: 327–34.

collaborative with that of constables, justices of the peace, and other non-professional local common law officers working through the institutions of local and parish governance.[22] Ecclesiastical jurisdiction no longer represented a sacramental alternative to the jurisdiction of the common law; rather, both had become instrumental in achieving administrative and judicial 'commonweal' at a local level.

This is not, however, to say that this work of local governance was merely authoritarian or merely instrumental to the wishes of the political centre. Village officers—whether churchwardens or constables—exercised discretion in presenting offenders, and were, as Keith Wrightson writes, reluctant to present any 'other than those who had scandalized, threatened or alienated the greater part of the community'.[23] Steve Hindle notes how, in the parish of Swallowfield, Wiltshire, in 1596, the vestry passed 'an extraordinary series of measures designed to maintain neighbourliness: for instance 'that non of us shall disdayne one another'.[24] The second half of the sixteenth century in England saw the beginning of a 'a general quickening of the tempo of local administration', the key to which was the linking of justices, constables of hundreds, and parish officers in effective channels of communication and collaboration.[25] Local governance was administered by voluntary, unpaid officers, and required that laypeople at every level—Justices, churchwardens, constables, and members of juries—use their discretion to make judgements in particular and contingent circumstances.

One effect of the increase of local governance in the sixteenth and seventeenth centuries was to promulgate and vernacularize certain habits of circumstantial inquiry into the facts. And here the vernacular literature of voluntary and participatory legal office—handbooks for justices and, latterly, for grand and petty juries—drew, remarkably enough, on the same ancient rhetorical topics of inquiry that had once pervaded the literature written for priests in confession. When the Fourth Lateran Council originally mandated annual confession to a priest as a more nuanced way of adjudicating guilt than had been possible by means of judicial ordeal, it also stipulated that confessors should inquire into the *circumstances* of sin. To guide confessors in their consideration of circumstances, treatises on confession and penance made use of the rhetorical *circumstantiae* employed by Latin authors on forensic rhetoric. These took the mnemonic form of a series of questions: '*Quis, quid, ubi, quibus auxiliis, cur, quomodo, quando*' ('Who, what,

[22] Martin Ingram, *Church Courts, Sex and Marriage in England, 1570–1640* (Cambridge: Cambridge University Press, 1987), 29.

[23] Keith Wrightson, 'Two Concepts of Order: Justices, Constables and Jurymen in Seventeenth-Century England', in *An Ungovernable People: The English and their Law in the Seventeenth and Eighteenth Centuries*, ed. J. Brewer and J. Styles (London: Hutchinson, 1979), 21–46.

[24] Hindle, *State and Social Change*, 205.

[25] Anthony Fletcher, *Reform in the Provinces: The Government of Stuart England* (New Haven, CT: Yale University Press, 1986), 116–42.

where, with what help, why, how, when').[26] William Lyndwood in his *Provincials* of 1433 makes the *circumstantiae* central to the question of adjudicating penance:

> The priest ought dylygently to note and marke the circumstances of the cryme, the qualyte of the persone, the kynde of the synne, tyme and place cause and continuaunce in the synne the devout mynd of the penitent. And these thynges consydered and dylygently weyed and dyscretely, let hym inioyne the penytent the greater or lesse penaunce.[27]

Circumstantial inquiry in the internal forum could be devoted to complex discriminations between kinds and degrees of affect—of contrition, for example—because factual questions of proof, of cognizance by the law, were not at issue. The *Speculum Sacerdotale* thus allows secret penance in a range of cases, such as incest and manslaughter, where the wrongdoing is not, as the author puts it, 'aknowe in the lawe', or legally known.[28] But the *circumstantiae* had in fact originated as techniques of forensic argument, of arousing suspicion or proving guilt or innocence, in cases where the facts were in dispute.[29]

At the same time as these rhetorical *circumstantiae* were adapted for confession, they had also entered the external forum of Roman canon law as the *indiciae*, or circumstantial evidence, that enabled judges to decide about cases when credible eyewitnesses or confessions were lacking.[30] After the Reformation in England, when it was still hoped that it would be possible to compile a reformed corpus of English canon law, Archbishop Cranmer wrote, in the draft of the chapter '*de probationis*', that a 'wise judge will easily figure out (after the weighing of the circumstances of matters and persons) how much of what each one says is to be believed' (*facile existimabit, pensatis rerum et personarum circumstantiis, quatenus cuique credendum sit*).[31]

England's secular justice system had long been participatory, involving juries as sworn neighbour witnesses. Already by the mid-fifteenth century, however, juries were no longer being empanelled from the vicinity, and had to gain their knowledge from the evidence presented at trial.[32] Bailiffs and justices of the peace took

[26] D. W. Robertson, 'A Note on the Classical Origin of "Circumstances" in the Medieval Confessional', *Studies in Philology* (1946), 6–14.

[27] William Lyndwood, *Constitutions prouincialles and of Otho and Octhobone Translated in to Englyshe* (Robert Redman, Fleetstreet, 1534), fol. 95^{v}.

[28] *Speculum Sacerdotale*, ed. Edward H. Weatherly (London: EETS, o.s., no. 200, 1936) 76, 77–8.

[29] Robertson, 'Classical Origin of "Circumstances"', 9–10.

[30] Barbara J. Shapiro, 'Classical Rhetoric and the English Law of Evidence', in *Rhetoric and Law in Early Modern Europe*, ed. Victoria Kahn and Lorna Hutson (New Haven, CT: Yale University Press, 2000), 59–61.

[31] Gerald Bray, *Tudor Church Reform: The Henrician Canons of 1535 and the Reformatio Legum Ecclesiasticarum* (Church of England Record Society: Boydell Press, 2000), 650–1, 562–3.

[32] Edward Powell, 'Jury Trial at Gaol Delivery in the Late Middle Ages: the Midland Circuit, 1400–1429', in *Twelve Good Men and True: The Criminal Jury in England, 1200–1800*, ed. J. S. Cockburn and Thomas A. Green (Princeton, NJ: Princeton University Press, 1988), 78–116.

pre-trial examinations; Thomas More asserts that these were offered in evidence to the jury at bar, 'with such contrarye othes and all the cyrcumstaunces therwith'.[33] By the mid-sixteenth century, the circumstantial pre-trial examination had become a statutory requirement.[34] Juries were soon also exhorted by Justices to evaluate the circumstances of a case: Steve Hindle quotes Sir Francis Willoughby telling trial jurors in the 1580s that 'the trueth lieth hid in evidence as fier in ashes & he which will find fier must stirre ashes'.[35]

As the rhetorical *circumstantiae* entered the procedures and language of English common law, they ceased to be part of a Latin, professional legal culture and became part of a popular mental disposition, readiness to inquire into probability for the good of the community. When William Lambarde revised his handbook for Justices of the Peace in 1592, he set out the circumstantial topics of time, place, occasion, motive as part of a Ramist analytical diagram.[36] Other justicing handbooks took over these topics.[37] What's more, legal and literary treatments of the *circumstantiae* closely resemble one another. As Justices were adapting the *circumstantiae* to their purposes, so were grammar school pedagogues. Reinhard Lorichius's sixteenth-century Latin edition of Aphthonius's *Progymnasmata*—an elementary textbook on composition—added a lot of new material from Latin legal rhetoric. In the lesson on narrative, Lorichius refers to its use 'to set out the circumstances of a case', and adds as example the narrative of the facts from one of Cicero's murder trials.[38] Lorichius's setting out of the topics of *narratio* likewise derives from judicial rhetoric. 'Narrative', he writes, is

> concerned with circumstances which are listed in this little verse: who, what, where, with what help, why, how, when. It can be made more copious if you amplify and dwell on the circumstances and carefully describe the time, the place, the manner, the instrument and lastly the reason [*causa*] for which something was done.[39]

The topics that Lorichius deemed essential to student composition of credible narrative were simultaneously being framed as aids to its sceptical evaluation. Everywhere in the sixteenth and seventeenth centuries rhetorical treatises and justicing manuals were simultaneously teaching men, on the one hand, how to

[33] J. G. Bellamy, *The Criminal Trial in Later Medieval England: Felony before the Courts from Edward I to the Sixteenth Century* (Thrupp: Sutton Publishing, 1998), 107.

[34] John H. Langbein, *Prosecuting Crime in the Renaissance: England, Germany, France* (Cambridge, MA: Harvard University Press, 1974), 122.

[35] Hindle, *State and Social Change*, 129.

[36] William Lambarde, *Eirenarcha: or of the office of the Justices of the Peace* (London: 1592), 218–19.

[37] Michael Dalton, *The Country Justice* (London, 1635), 295; *The Complete Justice. A Compendium of the particulars incident to Justices of the Peace... Abstracted and cited Alphabetically* (London, 1637), 67–8.

[38] Peter Mack, *Elizabethan Rhetoric: Theory and Practice* (Cambridge: Cambridge University Press, 2002), 27, 36–7.

[39] *Aphthonii Sophistae Progymnasmata... cum luculentis & utilibus in eadem scholijs Reinhardi Lorichii Hadamarii* (London, 1583), fol. 17r-v; the translation is Mack's, *Elizabethan Rhetoric*, 37.

use circumstances to give credibility to a narrative, and, on the other, how to use them to inquire into that narrative for inconsistencies and improbabilities. In Erasmus's *De copia*, for example, the eleventh method of rhetorical amplification, is 'taken from circumstances', and John Hoskins's *Directions for Speech and Style* recommends that in amplifying a narrative 'you inquire in every controversy for the circumstances', which are these: 'the persons who and to whom, the matter, the intent, the time, the place, the manner, the consequences'.[40] Conversely, Richard Bernard's *Guide to Grand-Jury Men* advises men evaluating evidence of witchcraft to 'weigh seriously the occasion' of the victim's alleged sufferings, along with 'all the circumstances, before whom, at what time, in what place, who those be which are about him or her', and so forth.[41]

The circumstances and the neoclassical-penitential stage

In the third act of *Gammer Gurton's Needle*, the eponymous Gammer, by this time thoroughly exhausted, exasperated, and convinced (on what she thinks is very good evidence) that her neighbour, Dame Chat, is maliciously withholding her needle from her, naturally thinks of settling the dispute and regaining her property by summoning the parish priest to administer shrift and penance. 'We have', she says to Hodge, 'a parson',

> . . . a man esteemed wise.
> Mast' Doctor Rat; chill for him send and let me hear his advice.
> He will her shrive for all this gear, and give her penance strait:
> Wes' have our nee'le, else Dame Chat comes ne'er within heaven gate!
>
> (3.3.59–62)

Gammer clearly exploits the concept of sacrament of penance as a mode of 'conflict-solving exercised by the clergy', though, like most parishioners, according to John Bossy, she is readier 'to tell the priest about the sins of [her] neighbours than about [her] own'.[42] But, as anyone familiar with the play of *Gammer Gurton* knows, Doctor Rat, the parish priest, not only fails to settle the dispute and bring Dame Chat and Gammer back into charity with one another, but actively escalates the levels of mutual suspicion, hostility, and violence until he himself is pressing

40 Desiderius Erasmus, *On Copia of Words and Ideas*, trans. Donald B. King and H. David Rix (Milwaukee, WI: Marquette University Press), 57; John Hoskins, *Directions for Speech and Style*, ed. Hoyt T. Hudson (Princeton, NJ: Princeton University Press, 1935), 28.

41 Richard Bernard, *A Guide to Grand-Jury men, Divided into Two Bookes* (London, 1627), 43.

42 John Bossy, 'The Social History of Confession in the Age of Reformation', *Transactions of the Royal Historical Society*, Fifth Series, 25 (1975), 21–38.

charges of murder against Dame Chat for bashing him on the head when he attempted to creep into her house to catch her red-handed (4.4.53–6).

Critics have interpreted the play as Protestant satire against an unreformed clergy, or simply as scholarly laughter at the dung-mired yokels.[43] It is true that Doctor Rat is said to have been located 'at Hob Filcher's shop . . . a cup of ale in his hand (3.3.74), that he thinks less of his parishioners' souls than of his tithes (4.1.12), and that at the end, Master Bailey rebukes him for wishing to see Diccon punished by hanging: 'A spiritual man to be so extreme! . . . you must both learn and teach us to forgive' (5.2.240, 254). But to call this play an academic farce, or even a Reformation satire, is to mistake completely where its formally experimental excitement lies, and, with that, its serious ethical engagements.

The play seems to have been first performed in Christ's College, Cambridge, either in 1553–4 or in 1559–60. Performances of a play by a 'Mr Stephenson' exist in the college accounts for both dates; advocates of the former take the phrase 'in the king's name' at 5.2.234 as referring to Edward VI, while advocates of the latter note that the printer, Thomas Colwell, originally entered the play in the Stationers' Register in 1562, and that the title page of the play as finally printed in 1575 says it was played in Christ's College 'not long ago'.[44] What is clear is that the play is either Edwardian or very early Elizabethan, a product of a reforming dramatist and musician working in the college that became the most Puritan of all the Cambridge colleges.[45]

William Stevenson, who is plausibly identified as the 'Mr S. Mr of Art' on the quarto's title page, became B.A. in 1549–50, M.A. in 1553, and B.D. in 1560. He was later appointed prebendary of Durham in 1560–1 and died in 1575.[46] Stevenson is thus an early example of the phenomenal increase of university-educated clergy as a response to the Reformation's undermining of the priest's sacramental function.[47] If he is the author of *Gammer Gurton*, he is also exemplary of the reformed clergy's interest in the specifically forensic or probabilistic reasoning characteristic of the intrigue plots of Roman New Comedy. Other examples of this interest may be seen in the trial scenes of John Foxe's comedy of *Titus et Gesippus*, and in the legal vocabulary used by Richard Bernard, the Nonconformist vicar of Worksop, in his translation of Terence's plays, first published in 1598.[48] Both Foxe and Bernard

[43] See H. F. N. Brett-Smith, 'Introduction', *Gammer Gurton's Needle* (Oxford: Basil Blackwell, 1920), vii.

[44] Charles Whitworth, 'Introduction' of *Gammer Gurton's Needle*, xvii, in *Three Sixteenth-Century Comedies*, ed. Charles Walters Whitworth (London: W.W. Norton, 1984).

[45] *Records of Early English Drama : Cambridge*, ed. Alan Nelson (Toronto: University of Toronto Press, 1989), 173, 184, 897.

[46] Henry Bradley, 'William Stevenson', in *Representative English Comedies*, ed. Charles Mills Gayley (New York: Macmillan, 1903), 199.

[47] Rosemary O'Day, *The English Clergy: The Emergence and Consolidation of a Profession 1558–1642* (Leicester University Press, 1979), 126–43.

[48] John Foxe, *Titus et Gesippus* in *Two Latin Comedies by John Foxe the Martyrologist*, ed. John Hazel Smith (Ithaca, NY: Cornell University Press); Richard Bernard, *Terence in English* (London, 1629), 286, 371–3, 421–3, and *passim*; Richard L. Greaves, 'Bernard, Richard (*bap.* 1568, *d.* 1641)', *ODNB.*

were interested in how the *circumstantiae* functioned as techniques for the invention of proof in erudite comic dramaturgy and legal trials. Foxe prepared and annotated Cranmer's draft of the *Reformation of Ecclesiastical Laws*, and Bernard introduced the language of circumstantial probability to vernacular guides for grand jurymen.[49] In other words, where an earlier generation of clergy had applied the *circumstantiae* as modes of qualitative inquiry—inquiry into the nature of the penitent's act and intent—these reformed clergymen were interested in their use as modes of factual inquiry—inquiry into the question of exactly what it was that happened.

Gammer Gurton's Needle is both a brilliant dramatization of such a factual inquiry, and a brilliant theatrical comment on the power of such inquiry to generate fictions of interiority—interior domestic spaces, as well as the inwardness of intent, motive, and meaning. The play depicts, as many critics have noted, a rural village (Girton in Cambridgeshire) of Brueghelesque vitality and specificity. Even critics disdainful of its 'rudimentary...humour'[50] have conceded its life-likeness, and most have praised its 'realistic' depiction of life in a Tudor village—'the miry winter weather, the impassable roads, the sluttishly kept houses...the rude comfort which does not lack a slip of bacon, a draught of ale, and a game of trump by the fire—all these are real enough'.[51] More perceptive critics have noted extraordinary dramaturgical innovation in the play's ability to 'create a sense of places elsewhere, out of sight, beyond the confines of space defined by the stage's boundaries'.[52] What I would argue, however, is that the play's ability to evoke 'spatial relations between places' and a sense of the particularity of village life is actually bound up with its spiritual project of revealing to all of us what breeds about all our hearts, as we, like these villagers, tend to snatch at images and likelihoods conjured by our own fears and desires, and take them, quite uncharitably, for true representations of our neighbour's acts and intentions. The invention of *circumstantiae* as topics of inquiry into the fact of the needle's loss is both a source of the play's intensely vivid evocation of the village as local habitation, and of an audience's insight into the inwardness of its local habitants.

The play opens with Diccon, newly discharged from St Mary of Bethlehem's hospital for lunatics (Bedlam), telling us about the mysterious clamour and crying he hears coming from 'here within this house'—Gammer's house—the doorway of which appears on the stage. Diccon's reaction to the noise is both wondering ('I marvel in my mind what the devil they ail'), and pragmatic. When no-one answers

[49] For Foxe, see Bray, *Tudor Church Reform*, lxxx–lxxxi; for Bernard, Barbara J. Shapiro, *'Beyond Reasonable Doubt' and 'Probable Cause': Historical Perspectives on the Anglo-American Law of Evidence* (Berkeley, CA: University of California Press, 1991), 52.

[50] Henry Bradley, 'William Stevenson', 203.

[51] Brett-Smith, 'Introduction', *Gammer Gurton's Needle*, viii.

[52] Charles Whitworth, 'Reporting Offstage Events in Early Tudor Drama', in *Tudor Theatre: 'Let There be Covenants...': Convention et Théâtre*, ed. Andre Lascombes (Bern: Peter Lang, 1977), 45–6.

his inquiries at the doorway, he tells us he 'caught a slip of bacon when I saw that none spied me / Which I intend not far hence, unless my purpose fail / Shall serve for a shoeing-horn to draw two pots of ale' (1.1.22–4).

How Diccon will fulfil the proverb, and turn this particular theft of bacon into a further opportunity for two pots of ale remains for the audience to discern, but this slight adumbration of plot in itself reminds us, as Richard Andrews has noted in an Italian context, that the play's spectators 'had (literally, never) had to absorb and remember a brand-new intrigue in performance conditions', a fact easy to forget with the subsequent rapid development of vernacular intrigue plots.[53] The bacon resurfaces later in the first scene of Act 2, when Diccon, returning from Mother Chat's alehouse, the better for a pint, meets Hodge complaining that he's had no dinner but dry horse-bread. 'Why?' asks Diccon innocently—and Hodge immediately offers a fairly detailed, circumstantial account of how Gib the cat not only licked the milk pan clean, ''twas not washed so well this seven year' (2.1.26), but must—apparently—have 'eat the bacon too'. A note to the reader in the 1575 quarto reminds the reader: '*Which bacon Diccon stole, as is declared before*'. The note should remind us that in 1575, readers were no more used than audiences to following a brand-new intrigue plot in the vernacular.

The realistic depiction of 'sluttishly kept houses' praised by former critics are thus, in fact, evidential reconstructions of the facts and circumstances—the scenes of domestic crimes—which audiences and readers might well invent or construe as such. The reason Hodge assumes that Gib has eaten the bacon, rather than suspecting that Diccon has stolen it, has to do with the circumstances associated with the central mystery of the plot—the disappearance of Gammer's needle while she was sewing. Gammer had just sat down, as Tib, the maid, tells Hodge, and taken a few stitches on Hodge's breeches, when

> by chance aside she leers,
> And Gib, our cat, in the milk pan she spied, over head and ears.
> 'Ah whore! Out thief!', she cried aloud, and swapped the breeches down;
> Up went her staff and out leapt Gib at doors into the town,
> And since that time was never wight could set their eyes upon it... (1.3.32–5)

All critics realize, of course, that the loss of the needle is both central to the intrigue, and trivial in itself, but most conclude that this, again, is an instance of its scholarly hubris and disdain for village life. Charles Whitworth, for example, imagines a wager: 'I'll bet you that I can write a five-act comedy on any subject you care to name... How about—a needle?'[54] I prefer the interpretation offered by J. W. Robinson, who finds a deeper moral sense in the proverbial associations of a

[53] Richard Andrews, *Scripts and Scenarios: The Performance of Comedy in Renaissance Italy* (Cambridge: Cambridge University Press, 1993), 43.

[54] Charles Whitworth, 'Introduction', *Gammer Gurton's Needle*, xxii.

needle as 'something both trivial and elusive'—'needles are notoriously hard to find, whether really lost or not. One is usually advised not to bother to search', he notes.[55] The villagers, in an uproar about the loss of something not worth seeking, are misdirecting their spiritual energies and endangering their souls. Diccon the bedlam, coming across this situation and failing to receive the charity that a licensed beggar should receive from parishioners, 'sees into the darkness and disharmony of the lives of the uncharitable villagers'[56] and proceeds to 'make a play' (2.2.10) of what he finds by exacerbating the hostility that 'lieth in . . . [the] hearts' (2.3.4) of these neighbours.

How does Diccon elicit the false inferences from the villagers that finally result in a full-scale murder inquiry conducted by the temporal magistrate? His tactics are brilliantly nuanced, brilliantly responsive to the disposition of each interlocutor, and thus capable of revealing something of their inwardness to us. Hodge, for example, reveals his superstitious self-centredness when his only reaction to Diccon's description of signs of sorrow and anxiety in the faces of Gammer and Tib is first to dismiss the news—'tis their daily look'—and then to insist that he'd foreseen some trouble this very morning, when he noticed the strange antics of Tom Tankard's cow: 'chave heard some say such tokens do not fail' (1.2.36). As Hodge gets drawn into the search for the needle—not out of sympathy for Gammer, but out of irritability and anger about her domestic incompetence ('Gog's death, how shall my breeches be sewed?' 1.4.18)—he is easily persuaded by Diccon that the needle's loss, as well as that of the bacon, signify that he in particular is suffering from the curse of some ill sprite. Swearing him to secrecy, Diccon promises to conjure up the devil to reveal the culprit and the needle's whereabouts. Hodge is literally too shit-scared to stick around for the actual appearance of the devil—'ich must beray the hall', he calls out to the audience. But crucially, his failure to witness any actual devil is no bar to the putative devil's becoming reliable evidence, in both his and later Gammer's minds, of the undoubted guilt of Dame Chat in the mystery of the needle's disappearance. First Diccon berates Hodge for spoiling the conjuring by his fearful flight, and then—with a stroke of genius—he offers the 'doubtful' evidence proffered by the devil as a result in such a way as to make it far more suggestive—far more like corroborative circumstantial evidence—than a coherent pronouncement would have been. 'Ye foolish dolt', he scolds Hodge, 'ye were to seek ere we had got our ground! / Therefore his tale so doubtful was that I could not perceive it' (2.3.12–13). Hodge snatches at this in his general longing for news of the devil: 'Then ich see well something was said . . . But Diccon, Diccon, did not the devil cry "Ho, ho, ho"?' (2.3.14–15). Hodge begins to persuade himself that he *did* hear something:

[55] J. W. Robinson, 'The Art and Meaning of *Gammer Gurton's Needle*', *Renaissance Drama*, 14 (1983), 45–77, at 65.

[56] Robinson, 'Art and Meaning', 58.

'Durst swear of a book, cheard him roar, straight after ich was gone! / But tell me, Diccon, what said the knave?' (2.3.17–18). What follows is Diccon's brilliant improvisation of diabolically ambiguous testimony:

> The whoreson talked to me, I know not well of what:
> One while his tongue it ran and paltered of a cat,
> Another while it stammered still upon a rat,
> Last of all there was nothing but every word, 'Chat, Chat'.
> ... Now whether Gib the cat have it eat in her maw,
> Or Doctor Rat our curate have found it in the straw,
> Or this Dame Chat your neighbour have stolen it, God he knoweth ... (2.3.19–27)

Diccon's proffering of multiple, competing scenarios as possible interpretations of the Devil's imputed testimony is all the more persuasive for being impressionistic and suggestive. Diccon's tale then acquires the status of corroborative evidence to his own false witness against Dame Chat when, in Act 3, Gammer informs Hodge that she knows—because Diccon told her—that Dame Chat was seen picking up her needle at the doorway to her house. Hodge's response is first to endorse Diccon's status as a witness by virtue of his capacity to conjure, and then, as if in independent corroboration of Diccon's witness against Dame Chat, to invoke Diccon's report of the devil's testimony. Especially delightful in this scene is the way in which Hodge's complete failure to witness the devil is transformed into precise accounts of his dimensions, how he sounded, etc.:

> HODGE
> Diccon? It is a vengeable knave, Gammer, 'tis a bonable whoreson,
> ... By the mass, ich saw him of late call up a great black devil!
> 'O', the knave cried, 'Ho, ho!' He roared and he thundered!
> And ye 'ad been here, cham sure you'ld murrainely ha' wondered ...
> GAMMER
> But Hodge, had he no horns to push?
> HODGE
> As long as your two arms! Saw ye never Friar Rush
> Painted on a cloth, with a sidelong cow's tail,
> And crooked cloven feet, and many a hooked nail?
> For all the world, if I should judge, chwould reckon him his brother;
> Look, even what face Friar Rush had, the devil had such another!
> ... Nay, Gammer, hear me speak; chill tell you a greater thing.
> The devil, when Diccon bad him (ich heard him wondrous well)
> Said plainly here before us, that Dame Chat had your nee'le. (3.2.10–26)

Gammer feels able, on hearing this, to bluster to Chat that she can 'prove it well / Thou fet my good even from my door' (3.3.13), and when, after an inconclusive brawl, she hits on the plan of calling Doctor Rat to shrive her neighbour, Hodge's memory of the devil's stammerings seems to endorse this course of action: 'The sooner Doctor Rat be here, the sooner we's ha' an end', crows Hodge, 'And hear,

Gammer! Diccon's devil, as ich remember well, / Of Cat, and Chat, and Doctor Rat a felonious tale did tell; / Chold you forty pound that is the way your nee'le to get again' (3.3.64–7). Where Tytivillus, the devil of idle speech and false report, actually appeared to star in *Mankind*, his features are more acutely delineated in *Gammer Gurton*, where the audience's own longing to see the devil, though frustrated, prompts them to see more clearly the connection between such desire and the reality effects of malicious rumour.

If Diccon plays on Hodge's self-importance and credulity, his technique with Dame Chat, the alehouse keeper, is rather to exploit the rational, calculating, and sceptical habit of her mind. And the scene in which he does this also vividly exemplifies the claim I made earlier about the way in which the play's innovation in conjuring up domestic interiors—inner spaces which the audience can never really 'see'—is simultaneously an innovation in inviting the audience to infer, through these preoccupations with objects and spaces, the inwardness of intent and motive, and 'what lieth about . . . their hearts'.

More than one critic has noted the remarkable number of references to doors and doorposts in *Gammer Gurton's Needle*.[57] As Alan Nelson has pointed out, it is a characteristic of sixteenth-century academic theatre that locales—entrances and exits—are fixed by a single identity throughout the performance—'a particular exit is understood as leading to a particular forum or port, and nowhere else'.[58] One of the ways in which this restricts the action is that it becomes impossible to stage an interior scene—characters are frequently reduced to giving elaborate explanations as to why their private conversations are occurring out of doors.[59] Rather than seeing this solely as a restriction, though, we might well see this dramatic problem as generative of certain kinds of mimesis—in particular, the evocation of the invisible interior, or the 'mute' character, who never appears onstage (Gib the cat, who has a very vivid and dynamic fictional presence 'behind the door' [3.4.2] in *Gammer Gurton*, is one such character). Such an evocation takes place when Diccon calls out to Dame Chat, 'Dame Chat, I say, where be ye! Within?' (2.2.19), and she responds from the doorway: 'What Diccon? Come near, ye be no stranger. / We be fast set at trump, man, hard by the fire; / Thou shalt set on the king if thou come a little nigher' (2.2.22–4). This is the hearthside game of trump that was felt to be so 'real' as to redeem the play from its imperfections, but it evokes more than firelight on the faces of the card-players. Diccon refuses to join the game, and titillates Chat's curiosity by telling he has a word for her 'in counsel' (2.2.26).

[57] Richard Southern, *The Staging of Plays before Shakespeare* (London: Faber and Faber, 1973), 403–11.

[58] Alan Nelson, 'The Universities: Early Staging in Cambridge', in *A New History of English Drama*, ed. John D. Cox and David Scott Kastan (New York: Columbia University Press, 1997), 59–67, at 64.

[59] Nelson, 'The Universities: Early Staging in Cambridge', 64; Peter Womack, 'The Comical Scene: Renaissance Civility on the Renaissance Stage', *Representations*, 101 (2008), 32–56, at 42–4.

She calls to a 'mute' character—her maid, called 'Doll'—to take her place in the game while she steps outside for a word with Diccon. In her words to Doll, we gain a sudden insight:

> DAME CHAT
> Come hither, Doll! Doll, sit down and play this game,
> And as thou sawest me do, see thou do even the same.
> There is five trumps beside the queen, the hindmost thou shalt find her.
> Take heed of Sim Glover's wife—she hath an eye behind her! (2.2.27–30)

Delegating her hand to Doll, Dame Chat can't resist advising her to 'take heed' of the keen sight of their neighbour, Sim Glover's wife, who's likely to note any sleights of hand with the five trumps and the queen. It's not Dame Chat's credulity, then, but her suspicion, and readiness to attribute suspicion, that makes her fall so easily for Diccon's outrageous story of how Gammer and Tib both suspect and accuse her of having stolen and eaten Gammer's 'goodly fair cock' with 'the yellow legs that nightly crowed so just' (2.2.38). 'Tib', confides Diccon, 'hath tickled in Gammer's ear that you should steal the cock' (2.2.43), and he goes on, warming to the theme, to produce a full-blown narrative of the facts of the murder, disposal of the body, etc., even implicating the hapless Doll:

> for well I heard Tib say
> The cock was roasted in your house to breakfast yesterday,
> And when ye had the carcass eaten, the feathers ye out flung
> And Doll, your maid, the legs she hid a foot deep in the dung. (2.2.62–5)

The otiose forensic circumstantiality of Diccon's account—detailing where and when the cock was roasted, and for what occasion, along with the corroborative detail of where and by whom the evidence was then concealed—is simultaneously comic, mimetic, and persuasive. We begin to see how thoroughly William Stevenson—if he it was—enjoys revealing the affinities between these false evidential scenarios and the *tours de force* of dramatic mimesis that make us believe in the characters and the play.

Other critics have done justice to the magnificently plotted epitasis (or complication), and catastrophe (or clearing up of errors) that follow in acts four and five. First, Doctor Rat, having been brought on to shrive and give penance to Dame Chat, finds himself too easily crediting the likelihood of her guilt, and is persuaded by Diccon to enter by a 'hole' into her house to catch 'the bitchfox and the nee'le together' as if in illicit liaison (4.4.33). Dame Chat, alerted by Diccon that Hodge is planning to sneak in and steal her hens, thrashes the interloper soundly, and the furious Doctor Rat then sends for Master Bailey 'to snaffle these murderers' and see them punished (4.4.54). As Joel Altman writes:

> The *status* [issue] is conjectural. Doctor Rat, suffering from contusions acquired while breaking into Chat's house, accuses Dame Chat of attempted murder. Dame

> Chat denies the charge flatly, claiming that she has not even seen the curate in seven weeks—he has been too busy with his minions, she adds spitefully. He offers his wounded head in evidence. She insists rightfully that it does not prove it was she who hit him. The Bailly then attempts to fix the time of the alleged injury: two hours since.[60]

The proof is invented out of the circumstantial topic of time: 'within less than these two hours', says Doctor Rat, and Dame Chat admits there was 'a knave not far / Who caught one good fillip on the brow with a door bar' at about that time, but denies it was Rat (5.2.33). The circumstantial topics of time and place, of course, have also contributed playfully to dramatic mimesis throughout, as when, in Act 2, Scene 4, Gammer is persuaded by Diccon's false witness against Chat because he adds the detail of her stooping 'even by this post', where Gammer is convinced she lost the needle (2.4.20). This, in turn, recalls Hodge earlier, asking Gammer where she had been since she lost her needle: 'Within the house and at the door, sitting by this same post', she had replied, 'Where I was looking a long hour before these folks came here' (1.4.33–4). Just as there is no 'within the house', so there was no 'long hour' before the audience arrived in which a needle was sought—but the circumstantial topics of time and place both help the characters to delude themselves and help us invent the sense of the play's fictionality stretching beyond the stage and the two hours' duration of the performance.

The bailiff does manage to unravel the knot of accusations and reveal that it is Diccon who has misled them all. The characters appropriate to the offices of priest and bailiff, spiritual and temporal, are reversed as Doctor Rat swears 'By all hallows' that Diccon's punishment 'if I may judge, shall be naught else but the gallows' (5.2.238–9), while Master Bailey, on the contrary, seems to want merely to assign penance:

> MASTER BAILEY
> Since Diccon hath confession made and is so clean shrive,
> If you will consent, to amend this heavy chance,
> I will enjoin him here to some open kind of penance. (5.2.255–7)

The penance assigned to Diccon, however, is no public humiliation, but a carnivalesque reminder to the parish of the charity they owe to bedlam beggars. Diccon is to swear upon Hodge's breeches that he will let Doctor Rat pay for all, and never insist that Dame Chat take his money or forsake a free drink, and finally, in a parody of the legal formula, to be 'of good abearing' to Gib, Gammer's great cat, while never mistaking Hodge for a gentleman (5.2.283). Diccon's compliance with this instruction by hitting Hodge on the buttocks is the action that discovers the needle, lodged in his breeches all this time. But the important point to note here is

[60] John Altman, *The Tudor Play of Mind: Rhetorical Inquiry and the Development of Elizabethan Drama* (Berkeley: University of California Press, 1978), 153–4.

that *Gammer Gurton's Needle*, far from exteriorizing penance, or reducing theatre to rhetoric, adapts the devices of intrigue comedy to the penitential concerns with what is '*in interiore homine*'. The play enables the audience to infer what is 'within' the hearts of all the *dramatis personae* caught up in the confusions, inviting the audience to judge each equitably, according to the circumstances in which they speak and act, and the intentions and passions these reveal. Intrigue—or circumstantial invention of plot—releases or 'makes evident' that which is dark and hidden within.

The wider significance of insisting that *Gammer Gurton* is a Reformation play involves the credit we are willing to grant to thesis that the great theatre of the popular stage—the theatre of Shakespeare—owes just as much to this neoclassical experimentation with the mimetic and moral possibilities of Roman forensic comedy as it does to the ritual doubleness of the body in sacramental theatre. *Gammer Gurton* exemplifies the power of forensic rhetoric and circumstantial invention both to generate pleasurable fictions, and to reveal to us our complicity in their production. This form of theatre does not eradicate community, but rather constitutes relations of community as relations built on the capacity to judge sceptically and respond empathetically and with delight to the 'evidence' of one another's narrations, through which, no less than through our embodiedness, we become 'present' to one another.

FURTHER READING

Beckwith, Sarah. *Signifying God: Social Relation and Symbolic Act in the York Corpus Christi Plays* (Chicago: University of Chicago Press, 2001)

Cormack, Bradin. *A Power to Do Justice: Jurisdiction, English Literature and the Rise of Common Law, 1509–1625* (Chicago: Chicago University Press, 2008)

Fowler, Elizabeth. *Literary Character: The Human Figure in Early English Writing* (Ithaca, NY: Cornell University Press, 2003)

Hutson, Lorna. *The Invention of Suspicion: Law and Mimesis in Shakespeare and Renaissance Drama* (Oxford: Oxford University Press, 2007)

CHAPTER 14

WHEN ENGLISH BECAME LATIN

TIM WILLIAM MACHAN

Language periodization

From a structural point of view, there's no doubt that a major break occurred in the English language, at all grammatical levels, between 1377 and 1642. Perhaps most famously, at least among those who allow that phonological change can ever be famous, is the Great Vowel Shift, a push-chain co-varying shift that completely rearranged the long tense vowel system of English and began and was completed entirely within this period. But the language's inflectional morphology changed just as significantly, with the atrophy of the few residual adjectival and substantival endings. And between the learning of humanism and the global explorations of colonialism, both of which produced new vocabulary to suit new experiences, the lexicon of English increased dramatically through contact with languages not even known to exist in the Middle Ages—such as Algonquian and later, a bit after 1642, Zulu and Maori.

What I have described, of course, is the transition from Middle to Modern English. This transition was gradual, so that some precocious Middle English speakers might already have used Modern English forms, while some sluggard Modern English ones might have hung onto Middle English forms. If some precision in dating is required, critics often identify 1500 as the key transitional moment; if still greater precision is required, 1476 and Caxton's establishment of a printing press at Westminster generally suffices. Periodizations like this are useful to historical linguists, both because they respond to demonstrable grammatical specifics of phonology, morphology, lexis, and syntax, and because they provide a heuristic for organizing and interpreting such data. Having decided on the structural definitions of early Modern English, linguists can proceed to ask questions about whether particular speakers were in fact old-fashioned or advanced and about how certain works validate or qualify the historical periods of the language.

When non-grammatical issues have figured in the definition of a historical stage of English, they have often done so merely as mnemonic devices, so that the Norman Conquest marks the beginning of Middle English and, as I've just noted, Caxton's printing press its end.

All this makes good sense. Yet language is more than a structured code. For speakers, language is a lived experience, used to accomplish real tasks in real time. And in view of this quality, what speakers do with a language, or how they think about it, may prove as significant as structure in defining what the language is. A theoretical framework like this might confirm periodization based solely on structure, but it also might complicate it in important ways.

The shift from Middle to Modern English is a case in point. As categorical as I have described this to be from a structural perspective, from a sociolinguistic one it's rather less so. It's true enough, on one hand, that metaphors like the triumph of English or the rise of vernacular culture emphasize genuinely new roles for English in powerful domains of the early modern period; these roles harmonize with structural changes to project clear, multifaceted breaks in the use, status, and character of English between the fourteenth and seventeenth centuries. On the other, it's also true that certain sociolinguistic considerations suggest that something familiar, something constant, persists all the way from Middle though early Modern to contemporary Modern English. And it is this unfamiliar constancy that I want to consider here in questioning the existence of a neat and decisive shift in the English language between the medieval and early modern epochs. My focus is early modern metalinguistic discussion, and my framework is the sense that what transpired linguistically amounted to a version of a larger heuristic of reform and revolution that animated the fifteenth and sixteenth centuries.[1] More particularly, I want to argue that during this period, alongside a wholesale reconfiguration of English's grammar and social uses, there was also a retention of what might be called England's sociolinguistic infrastructure. Put rather archly, the linguistic facts may have changed, but the linguistic repertoire they constructed in 1642 had much in common with the one constructed by another set of facts in 1377.

Regulating language

One unfamiliar constancy involved the object of grammatical inquiry in early modern England. Unfamiliarity describes, of course, the interest in characterizing the origin, growth, and structure not of Latin, as had been the predominant case in western grammatical discussions for over a millennium, but of English. Beginning with William Bullokar's 1586 *Pamphlet for Grammar*, the first extant full grammar

[1] James Simpson, *Reform and Cultural Revolution*, The Oxford English Literary History, vol. 2: *1350–1547* (Oxford: Oxford University Press, 2002).

of English, this interest in English developed quickly, with over thirty such grammars appearing by 1700, along with nearly twenty dictionaries after Robert Cawdrey's 1604 *A Table Alphabeticall*. Such interest in codification bespeaks not an abstruse academic topic but a discipline that, to the early modernists, formed the foundation of culture. When critics like More and Tyndale argued over the sense of a passage from the Hebrew Bible, in fact, linguistic issues impinged on doctrine and even national identity. And as the new cultivation of English grammar rejected long-standing assumptions about language and culture, so it advanced a more general cultivation of a new England.[2]

At the same time, there's something very familiar in the way such discussions remained consonant with the Latin grammatical tradition by preserving long-standing presumptions about linguistic regularity and its relation to non-linguistic issues. English grammarians, that is, did not so much reject or revolutionize grammatical discussion as appropriate it for English. The very premises of English discussion retain not simply Dante's famous notion of grammar as a stay against change—which therefore marks regional and social variation as error—but also the traditional sense, of a writer like Quintilian, that grammar is the art of writing and speaking well.[3] In his 1582 *The First Part of the Elementarie*, Richard Mulcaster thus states that one of grammar's purposes is 'to reduce our English tung to som certain rule, for writing and reading, for words and speaking, for sentence and ornament, that men maie know, when theie write or speak right'.[4] And if Mulcaster sounds like Quintilian, so the schoolrooms where English eventually would be taught resembled their medieval predecessors with their emphases on invention, composition, and recitation. The medium was in the process of changing from Latin to English, but the foundational principles were remaining the same.

Of greater consequence is the persistence of the notion that some languages—and not all of them (certainly not Irish or Algonquian)—could merit such treatment because of their intrinsic rhetorical capabilities and because of what they (and these capabilities) might project about those who speak them. For Latin, this notion had emerged from political as well as exegetical traditions. The language of imperial Rome, Latin provided the means for the most expansive, ambitious, and

[2] See Ian Michael, *English Grammatical Categories and the Tradition to 1800* (Cambridge: Cambridge University Press, 1970); Manfred Görlach, *Explorations in English Historical Linguistics* (Heidelberg: C. Winter, 2002), 137–212; and DeWitt T. Starnes and Gertrude E. Noyes, *The English Dictionary from Cawdrey to Johnson, 1604–1755* (Chapel Hill, NC: University of North Carolina Press, 1946). For the significance of grammar, see Brian Cummings, *The Literary Culture of the Reformation: Grammar and Grace* (Oxford: Oxford University Press, 2002), 20–6 and 190–213. On English and national identity, see Cathy Shrank, *Writing the Nation in Reformation England, 1530–1580* (Oxford: Oxford University Press, 2004).

[3] For Dante's discussion, see *De vulgari eloquentia*, in *Classical and Medieval Literary Criticism: Translations and Interpretations*, ed. and trans. Alex Preminger et al. (New York: Frederick Ungar, 1974), 412–46, at 420–1.

[4] Richard Mulcaster, *The First Part of the Elementarie* (1582; rpt. Menston: Scolar Press, 1970), 50.

successful government in the Middle East and European West. It was also the language of Virgil and Ovid, whose works provided the literary equivalents to such political models. And if Hebrew was the language of Adam and Eve, as St Augustine and other exegetes believed, Latin was the language of the Vulgate Bible and the schools and commentaries that accrued to it. For the Middle Ages, when God gave the power of speech to Adam, he spoke in Latin, as did Christ, when He promised rebirth in a kingdom yet to come. In a fundamental way, as the medium of the most powerful western traditions, Latin was self-evidently an inherently expressive language and vehicle for cultural achievement.

In the later Middle Ages, English, just as self-evidently, was none of these things. Though English had been the language of government in much of the Anglo-Saxon period, Latin and then French had characterized this domain since the Conquest, with English of the fifteenth century only beginning to figure in legal and administrative actions. And England itself, in any case, could make no claim to rival the territorial and political achievements of imperial or Christian Rome. As for literature, as accomplished as we, and even the fifteenth and sixteenth centuries, might think Chaucer, Gower, and Lydgate, throughout the early modern period none could truly rival the status of Virgil and Ovid. It would be well into the twentieth century before school syllabi and learned commentary might indicate that at least Chaucer had achieved this status, though even so, no one (I think) has ever called Homer the Chaucer of Greek.

By presuming for English the implications of the Latin traditions, early English grammarians thereby achieved a kind of sleight of hand. If Latin's cultural worth was self-evident and empirically demonstrable, the value of English, particularly given its role in a developing sense of nationhood, would seem to require some kind of supporting argument. But not only did these grammarians not assemble proof that would justify the conclusion that as much had been achieved in English as in Latin; neither did they construct an alternate argument that would lead to the same conclusion by offering competing rather than comparable proof. Instead, almost by fiat and without addressing the historical practices through which Latin had achieved its status, these grammarians largely preserved and simply transferred this status to English, where they looked for—and saw—the characteristics that had made Latin great. Through various tactics they managed to maintain the idea that a language might be both cultural achievement and confirmation of political consequence, but, in bypassing the means by which Latin had attained that prominence, also to clear the way for English to substitute for Latin.

One tactic was the mere assertion that English was in fact a great language. Richard Verstegan thus invokes a frequent early modern anxiety over the borrowing of foreign words and the creation of arch 'inkhorn' terms. These he regards as not merely affectations and sources of confusion but also, in view of the expressiveness of English, superfluities: 'But doubtlesse yf our selues pleased to use the treasurie of our own toung, wee should as litle need to borrow woords, from any language, extravagant from ours, as any such borroweth from us: our toung in it self beeing sufficient and copious enough, without this dayly borrowing from somany as take scorne to borrow any from us.'[5] In his *Elementarie*, Mulcaster seems to establish a standard of proof by claiming that the best tongues 'ar so termed, bycause they are so estemed, for the prerogatiue of that use, which we find to be in them'. And via a metaphor, he constructs an argument that seems to point necessarily to the conclusion that English has attained cultural and linguistic greatness. Art, Mulcaster maintains, takes responsibility for writing in any period that is 'of most and best account, and therefor fittest to be made a pattern for others to follow, and pleasantest for his self to travell and toill in'. In ancient Greece, this was during Demosthenes' lifetime, and in ancient Rome during Cicero's. 'Such a period in the English tung' he concludes, 'I take this to be in our daies, for both the pen and the speche'.

But Mulcaster's proof for these conclusions amounts to something far less than the demonstrable achievements of Latin. Ultimately, in fact, it operates as much by fiat and assertion as do his conclusions. Like Verstegan, he asserts that 'the tung it self hath matter enough in it self, to furnish out an art, & that the same mean, which hath bene used in the reducing of other tungs to their right, will serve this of ours, both for generalitie of precept, and certaintie of ground'. And English has these resources because it has 'those thinges... which make anie tung to be of account, which things I take to be thre, the autoritie of the peple which speak it, the matter & argument, wherein the speche dealeth, [and] the manifold use, for which the speche serveth. For all which thre, our tung nedeth not to give place, to anie of her peres.' In each case, Mulcaster's reasoning shifts between circular and iterative forms. English can't be an obscure language, for instance, because foreign chronicles talk about it; and the fact that the language has been used in war and trade and thereby been introduced to new locales where there are new topics for writing means that English learning and martial achievement have long given matter for writing in English. All this means (to Mulcaster) that those who speak it have authority.

The language's matter and argument qualify English for pre-eminent status among languages in just as circular a fashion—because the language is used to talk about matters and arguments that are of consequence to many people: 'If the spreading sea, and the spacious land could use anie speche, theie would both shew you, where, and in how manie strange places, theie have sene our peple, and also give you to wit, that theie deall in as much, and as great varietie of matters, as anie other peple do, whether at home or abrode'. All together, these qualities 'seme to infer no base witted peple, not to amplify it with more, bycause it is not for foulls to be so well learned, to be so warrious, to be so well practised'. English, in short, is a language of 'account' because it accomplishes the linguistic tasks such languages

5 Richard Verstegan, *A Restitution of Decayed Intelligence* (1605; rpt. Ilkey: Scolar Press, 1976), 206.

accomplish, and these are in turn tasks of account because they're the things for which a people of account use language. Like the medieval status of Latin, all of this Mulcaster sees as self-evident, and by saying so, he eliminates the need for any additional evidence: 'I shall not nede to prove anie of these my positions, either by foren or home histories: seing my reader stranger, will not strive with me for them, and mine own nation, will not gainsaie me in them, I think, which knoweth them to be trew, and maie use them for their honor.'[6]

Another grammatical tactic that Mulcaster uses to assert the cultural achievement and political consequence of English focuses attention on the prestigious desire of foreigners to learn the language. Perhaps not coincidentally, at the very moment when both Anglophones and non-Anglophones claimed that the pronunciation of Latin by the English was so idiosyncratic as to be incomprehensible abroad, the desirability of English as a second language thus became a prominent feature of metalinguistic discourse.[7] Throughout the Middle Ages, of course, *all* of those conversant with Latin had necessarily learned it as a second language. They did so for the reasons I noted above, but the fact that they took the trouble to do so could itself serve as another credit to the status of the language and its learners; into the twentieth century, indeed, knowledge of Latin in many ways remained the mark of an educated person.

Without addressing any differences between why one sixteenth-century speaker might want to learn Latin and another English, Mulcaster simply emphasizes that English is as desirable a second language as Latin. In the old days, he says, people mostly stayed at home and thus had no need of a foreign grammar, but in the contemporary period, with its more mobile populations, grammars have become measures of international consequence.[8] For John Hart, one of the pre-eminent reasons for regularizing English spelling is just this audience of foreigners, whose efforts to learn spoken English could be compromised by the language's chaotic spelling. His linguistic comparison is to Welsh and Irish, which he sees as characterized by unintelligible orthographies, but his imagined audience might be better compared to that learning Latin, for whom, at least outside of universities and church settings, the spoken language was always secondary to the written.[9] And bluntly connecting the desirability of a language to that of its people and culture, the French diplomat Hubert Languet wrote to Sir Philip Sidney that it seemed 'quite absurd' to him that the English 'should make such a point of speaking Italian well, since, as far as I know, you derive no advantage from them; on the other hand, they derive the greatest from you, and therefore out to learn

[6] Richard Mulcaster, *The First Part of the Elementarie*, 62, 75, 79, 80, 81–2, 253–4.

[7] See, for example, John Hart, *An Orthographie* (1569; rpt. Menston: Scolar, 1969), Bii^{r}. More generally, see Paula Blank, 'The Babel of Renaissance English', in *The Oxford History of English*, ed. Lynda Mugglestone (Oxford: Oxford University Press, 2006), 212–39, at 223–4.

[8] Richard Mulcaster, *The First Part of the Elementarie*, 51.

[9] Hart, *An Orthographie*, 4^{v}.

your language.'[10] In all these ways, this audience for English as a second language is thus made parallel to the generations that had learned Latin from grammar books. Its very existence imputes similar status to both languages. And this happens despite the fact that the practical, mercantile concerns that would make English into a popular global language shared nothing with the cultural ones that fashioned a role for Latin.

Language and hierarchy

A second unfamiliar constancy between Middle and Modern English involves the character of England's linguistic repertoire. The pre-eminent organizing principle for this repertoire in the Middle Ages was diglossia, or the functional distribution of distinct languages. For medieval England this meant that Latin, conventionally, was the High Language used in the Church, education, exegesis, and much government; French, a less High though still prestigious language, eventually used in many monasteries, education, legal activity, business, literature, and, perhaps most importantly, aristocratic households and the court; and English, the Low Language, spoken in the vast majority of domestic domains and increasingly used for ephemeral kinds of literature.

In the sixteenth century, this diglossia had already been fundamentally reconfigured. In particular, the introduction of English into the domains of theology, business, and even the court meant the destabilization of long-standing distinctions among languages and the social functions they performed. The characteristics and cultural significance of Latin had also certainly changed from the days of scholasticism to those of humanism, though its general prestige and social power continued into the eighteenth century. By 1600, however, French had become very much a foreign language, useful for international travel and activity though no longer significant in England's linguistic repertoire outside of restricted uses in, for example, courts of law.[11] But as consequential as these many changes were, the point I wish to emphasize is that like Bottom, in the early modern period diglossia was not so much gone as changed. In an essential way, despite the shifting statuses of English, French, and Latin, something remained the same in England's linguistic repertoire: the functional distribution and stratification of language varieties as a foundational feature of English social dynamics. But no longer drawing its social meanings from its relations with primarily Latin and French, English of the early

[10] Quoted in Michael Wyatt, *The Italian Encounter with Tudor England: a Cultural Politics of Translation* (Cambridge: Cambridge University Press, 2005), 157.

[11] See further Tim Machan, 'French, English, and the Late Medieval Linguistics Repertoire', in *Language and Culture in Medieval Britain: The French of England, c1100–c1500*, ed. Jocelyn Wogan Browne (Woodbridge, UK: York Medieval Press, 2009), 363–72.

modern period fostered instead a repertoire shaped by regional varieties of English, sociolects of English, and indigenous colonial languages.

Prior to even 1500, comments on regional dialects of English are only brief and sporadic, such as William of Malmesbury's observation, eventually echoed in the fourteenth century by both Higden and Trevisa, that 'the entire language of the Northumbrians, especially in York, grates so stridently that none of us southerners is able to understand it', or Caxton's observation that 'our langage now used varyeth ferre from that which was used and spoken whan I was borne'.[12] Throughout the Middle Ages, indeed, the most meaningful relationships in England's linguistic repertoire—the ones with the greatest sociolinguistic consequence—were not among varieties of English but between English and other languages, especially Latin and French. And so long as this remained the case, there was no motivation to develop any coherent metalinguistic discourse about regional or social variation. It's important to recognize, I think, that as English became more socially nuanced in early modern England, it might well have done so without the development among English dialects of some new version of diglossia, which is by no means a linguistic universal. For a millennium, English had in fact thrived without the functional distribution of its regional varieties and sociolects.

Yet a revised version of diglossia is exactly what did take shape, and this reformation is described in great detail by early grammarians. For George Puttenham, a clear distinction exists between a preferred urban language and the variety that occurs outside urban areas, whether in the marches or among academics. The aspiring poet, says Puttenham, should avoid the language of universities, 'where Schollers use much peeuish affectation of words out of the primative languages, or finally, in any uplandish village or corner of a Realme, where is no resort but of poore rusticall or uncivill people'.[13] Both Verstegan and Carew likewise draw distinctions between the speech of Londoners and 'the countrey people' in particular.[14] And Alexander Gill's 1621 *Logonomia Anglica* begins with the premise that throughout its history English has been a changeable language and moves on to the period's most detailed account of current regional variation, identifying six distinct dialects of English.[15] It's thus not surprising that though the first dialect dictionary of English falls slightly outside of our chronological limits (dating to 1674), the first

[12] William of Malmesbury, *De Gestis Pontificum Anglorum*, ed. N. E. S. A. Hamilton, Rolls Series 52 (London: Longman, 1870), 209; W. J. B. Crotch (ed.), *The Prologues and Epilogues of William Caxton*, EETS o.s. 176 (1928; rpt. New York: Burt Franklin, 1971), 108. Many of the other scattered medieval metalinguistic comments are collected in Jocelyn Wogan-Browne et al., *The Idea of the Vernacular: An Anthology of Middle English Literary Theory, 1280–1520* (University Park: Pennsylvania State University Press, 1999).

[13] George Puttenham, *The Arte of English Poesie* (1589; rpt. Menston, England, 1968), 120.

[14] Richard Verstegan, *A Restitution of Decayed Intelligence*, 195; Richard Carew, 'The Excellency of the English Tongue', in William Camden's *Remains Concerning Britain* (1606; rpt. Yorkshire: EP Publishing, 1974), 42–51, at 49.

[15] Alexander Gill, *Logonomia Anglica*, 2nd. edn (1621; Menston: Scolar Press, 1968), B1r, 16–19.

English dictionary to define *dialect* and thereby give it a kind of formal status was John Bullokar's *English Expositor*, published in 1616.[16]

If there's no grammatical imperative for diglossia to exist—no structural reasons, of syntax or morphology, for example, that would compel Anglophones to adapt diglossia in this way—the enthusiasm and extent of this metalinguistic discourse suggests that there were nonetheless reasons enough to do so. And as these comments also suggest, these reasons lay in the way that diglossia could map social forms onto linguistic ones and in the process articulate and maintain cultural institutions and stratifications. By serving as a learned High Language, characteristic of powerful domains and accessible only to those speakers already judged acceptable by virtue of social rank, religion, and sex, Latin had offered a way for all speakers, from peasant to king, to define each other's place in the hierarchy of English society. And since the opportunity to acquire and use Latin was socially restricted, the language had offered this way to maintain prevailing cultural practices and institutions alongside the disingenuous notion that linguistic knowledge somehow existed independently of other kinds of knowledge and of other social issues. Theoretically, a peasant fully conversant with Latin grammar, literature, and theology would have been a peasant to whom the highest echelon of medieval Christendom would have been accessible. But while William Wykeham rose from humble origins to become Bishop of Winchester, for the most part humble medieval beginnings led to humble ends.

English grammatical discussions extended the discriminations that Latin made possible by tying together social and regional variation and implicating social prestige in both. Puttenham, again, proscribes 'uncivill' speakers alongside 'uplandish' locales, as does Verstegan, who predicates knowledge of Latin and French on whether or not a speaker resides in the 'countrey'. For his part, while Gill can describe the phonology of the various regional dialects with genuine scholarly detachment, he can also say of the 'Occidentalium' dialect in particular that it is the 'greatest barbarity. And in fact if you should hear a farmer in Somerset, you would easily wonder whether English or some foreign tongue was being spoken.'[17] For Thomas Wilson, in his 1553 *Arte of Rhetorique*, recognition of the hierarchical arrangement of varieties of English is necessary for the prescription of a cultivated style: 'either we must make a difference of Englishe, and saie some is learned Englishe, and other some is rude Englishe, or the one is courte talke, the other is countrey speache, or else we must of necessitee, banishe al suche affected Rhetorique, and use altogether one maner of language'. And if the correct use of Latinate diction serves as a way for an elite rank to identify itself, its incorrect use

[16] See John Ray's *A Collection of English Words* (London: H. Bruges, 1674). Also see Bullokar, *An English Expositor: Teaching the Interpretation of the Hardest Words Used in Our Language* (London: John Legatt, 1616), s.v. *dialect*. Blank identifies this as the earliest such definition ('The Babel', 214).

[17] Gill, *Logonomia Anglica*, 18.

equally exposes any pretensions that rustics or clowns might have: 'And thus we see that poore simple men are muche troubled, and talke oftentymes, thei knowe not what, for lacke of wit and want of Latine & Frenche, wherof many of our straunge woordes full often are derived.'[18] Citing Cicero on stylistic decorum, Wilson thereby uses rhetorical appropriateness as justification for social order. The entire inkhorn controversy might be seen in this light—as an attempt to control the vocabulary of English and thereby, through the limited ways to gain access to a select portion of this vocabulary, to reinforce social hierarchies and degrees that had become increasingly difficult to maintain in early modern England.[19] As social and geographic mobility proliferated in the early modern period, it thus produced increased language contact and increased opportunities to mediate social status through linguistic variation, even as print and economic development provided greater motivation for London speakers to distinguish their standard language from non-standard regional varieties.[20]

The increased production of grammars and dictionaries in this period did more than simply codify English, then. It also fostered the ideology of standardization and, more particularly, of a nascent standard written English that perversely required the identification and maintenance of non-standard forms against which the standard ones might be distinguished. If less invested in geography than some of the regional observations I have considered, this ideology nonetheless reproduced the social distinctions inherent in these comments and thus helped maintain in its own way the reformed diglossia that came to characterize English in the early modern period. Increased proscriptions against blasphemy—specifically in the form of Puritan censorship of bad language—served much the same purpose, as did the identification of cant as the specific kind of language that one social group would use to mislead and cozen another, higher one.[21] In all these ways, varieties of English came to assume the stratification once maintained by Latin, French, and English.

As this new version of intralinguistic diglossia developed, however, interlinguistic diglossia did not disappear, though it, too, appeared in a new guise. When the statuses of Latin, French, and English changed in relation to one another, they did

[18] Thomas Wilson, *The Arte of Rhetorique* (1553; rpt. Gainesville, FL: Scholars' Facsimiles & Reprints, 1962) at 87^r, 87^v.

[19] Joseph M. Williams, '"O! When Degree is Shak'd": Sixteenth-Century Anticipations of Some Modern Attitudes toward Usage', in *English in Its Social Contexts*, ed. Tim William Machan and Charles T. Scott (New York: Oxford University Press, 1992), 69–101; and Blank, 'The Babel of Renaissance English'. It is this investment of linguistic forms in social structure that sharply differentiates inkhorn vocabulary from the earlier aureate diction of poets like Lydgate and Dunbar.

[20] Terttu Nevalainen and Helena Raumolin-Brunberg, *Historical Sociolinguistics: Language Change in Tudor and Stewart England* (London: Longman, 2003), 30–43.

[21] Tony McEnery, *Swearing in English: Bad Language, Purity and Power from 1586 to the Present* (London: Routledge, 2006); Julie Coleman, *A History of Cant and Slang Dictionaries*, vol. 1: *1567–1784* (Oxford: Oxford University Press, 2004).

so in part because, through colonial and business activities, English of the early modern and modern periods came into increasing and increasingly socially charged contact with a number of *other* languages: in the British Isles, Irish, Welsh, and Gaelic; in North America, Spanish, German, Swedish, and various African and Native American languages; in the South Pacific, Maori, Hawaiian, and Aboriginal languages; and in Asia, Hindi, Punjabi, and Cantonese. In effect, the interlinguistic diglossia of English reformed not merely because French had become a foreign language, Latin the language of a rejected religion and bureaucracy, and English the language of aspirant nationalism. To a large extent, it reformed because these new languages, mediating mercantile and governmental issues absent in the Middle Ages, revolutionized the English linguistic repertoire. If medieval diglossia rested on presumptive social and cultural truths, the early modern variety rested on technology and business. Just as an urban, increasingly standardized variety of English would come to stand hierarchically above various regional and (eventually) other national varieties of English, then, so English in general would stand above the indigenous languages it contacted as Anglophone colonists and merchants traveled around the globe.

Roger Williams's 1643 *A Key into the Language of America*, one of the earliest substantial accounts of a Native American language, offers an apt illustration. Devoting itself to the vocabulary and phrases for the events of daily life, such as housing, clothing, and hunting, the *Key* provides a kind of through-the-looking-glass version of Walter of Bibbesworth's *Tretiz*. Williams wants to inform Anglophones about Narragansett not to facilitate the Anglicization of the Indians, nor to foster bilingual Anglophones, nor, above all, to champion the linguistic and cultural achievements of Native American languages. He wants to write about the language before its speakers, their society, and the language itself disappear.[22]

Language and self-definition

The third unfamiliar constancy in English between the years 1377 and 1642 that I want to consider here relates to the cultural significance that English was understood to project as an emerging High Language. For medieval Latin and French, this significance had lain in the broad acceptance of certain cultural truths: that language, while it may have fallen with a fallen world, was still a divine gift utilized in the construction and maintenance of a divinely sanctioned order;[23] that the goal of this language, as of all human activity, was salvation; that the language of God

[22] Roger Williams, *A Key into the Language of America* (1643; 5th edn 1936; rpt Bedford, MA: Applewood Books, 1997).

[23] John Fyler, *Language and the Declining World in Chaucer, Dante, and Jean de Meun* (Cambridge: Cambridge University Press, 2007), 1–59.

and the institutions inspired by and designed to honor Him was in effect Latin; and that the language of cultural prestige, affluence, and gentility was French. And as truths, these claims were so well-established that they had become fundamentally implicit; they were horizons of linguistic expectation that generally did not require to be affirmed, addressed, or even noticed.

With the possible exception of prestige and affluence, at least within colonial regions, none of this, of course, could be true of English in the early modern period. Even the Reformation claimed not that English was the only language of God but that, alongside other vernaculars, it could and should be used for religious purposes. One of the priorities of Protestant missionaries to North America, indeed, was the transliteration of Native American languages, followed by the translation and publication of the Bible in them.[24] And so, if English was to subsume the dominant status that Latin and French had held in medieval England, it required some other theoretical justification, some other means to the end of Latin prestige. A self-conscious sense of England, religiously and politically consolidated through the Reformation and emerging for the first time as a world power, provided just this justification. Beyond any of the assertions of linguistic relativity that I considered above, early grammarians furthered a burgeoning sense of national identity by insisting on the value of England as underwriting the value of English. In doing so, they replaced divinely sanctioned order with earthly politics as the explanation for why English should be a High Language.

Mulcaster, for instance, makes a point of saying not only that there is in English 'great and sufficient stuf for Art', but that he has identified this art 'without anie foren help, and with those rules onelie, which ar, and maie be gathered out of our own ordinarie writing'. Even if English were not spoken anywhere else, it is spoken in England, and that's reason enough to use and cultivate it.[25] To Hart, the transcendent merits of England and its language are so apparent that it could well be the case that foreigners might see English as a model language for themselves. And also for Hart, the magnanimity of the English people requires that they share the wealth of their language and culture: 'I trust there is none English man but would be contented that any nation should borowe of our language part or all: and use it both in their speach and writing, as they mought best serve and please themselves therewith. What should it grieve us; but even as the shining of the sunne upon any other countrie besides ours.'[26]

Bullokar shares Hart's nationalistic magnanimity, for even though he invents new graphs specifically suited to English, he acknowledges that those speaking other languages might benefit from his system:

[24] Edward G. Gray, *New World Babel: Languages and Nations in Early America* (Princeton, NJ: Princeton University Press, 1999).

[25] Mulcaster, *The First Part of the Elementarie*, 77, 256.

[26] Hart, *An Orthographie*, 17^{v}.

> if some of our special figures or letters, may be used also of any nation, in the same sound...they neede not to be ashamed, to thinke this our amendment ready for them to use, as wel where we agree with them in soundes, as where we have some speciall sound in voice, which they have not.

At the same time, by identifying linguistically and ethically limited non-Anglophones as the source of certain solecisms in English, Bullokar equates English, England, clarity, and even virtue:

> Let us Inglish not be ashamed, to wipe away, the dirt, filth, and dust, negligently suffered long time on the picture of our speech, nor be afraid to correct the unskilfull liniaments, coulers, and shadowes, laied thereon by straungers, who never coulde enter in the perfect divisions of the soundes of our speech, and much lesse make perfect figures, and letters for the same: by which negligence of our selves, or unskilfulnesse of straungers, or both, this deformite either began, or hath crept in.[27]

And Carew takes this nationalistic pride one step further, claiming for English the status often still claimed today for Latin: that knowing it facilitates the learning of other languages. Many Italians, says Carew, can't pronounce French correctly, and many French can't pronounce Italian, 'but turn an Englishman at any time of his age into what Countrey soever, allowing him due respite, and you shall see him profit so well, that the imitation of his utterance will in nothing differ from the pattern of that Native Language'.[28]

For several early grammarians, the alleged confluence of English, England, and virtue acquires the kind of self-righteousness of an affirmation beyond challenge and without need of proof. Though Gill claims only that 'The English nation and language have one origin: they go back to the Saxon and Angle peoples of Germany', Camden sees this derivation as (circular) evidence of both English and German superiority: 'The English tongue is extracted, as the nation, from the Germans, the most glorious of al now extant in Europe for their moral and martial vertues, and preserving the liberty entire, as also for propagating their language by happy victories in France by the Francs and Burgundians.'[29] With a distinctly nationalistic sentiment, Camden understands the Teutonic–English connection to be so strong and so determinative as by itself to constitute resistance to any foreign influences, linguistic or cultural: 'Great, verily, was the glory of our tongue, before the Norman Conquest, in this—that the old English could express most aptly all the conceits of the mind in their own tongue without borrowing from any.' In order to justify this view of English as a self-determined, self-affirming language, Camden manages to rewrite linguistic history in ways that should have strained credibility, even in the days before the *OED*, by claiming that

[27] William Bullokar, *The Amendment of Orthographie for English Speech* (1580; rpt Amsterdam: Theatrum Orbis Terrarum, 1968), 20^{r}, 14^{r}.

[28] Carew, 'The Excellency of the English Tongue', 46.

[29] Gill, *Logonomia Anglica*, no sig; Camden, *Remains concerning Britain*, 24.

in the 300 years between the Conquest and the reign of Edward III, the 'Conquerors . . . intermingled very few French-Norman words, except some terms of law, hunting, hawking, and dicing; when as we within these 60 years have incorporated so many Latine and French, as the third part of our tongue consisteth now in them.'[30]

Verstegan carries this argument even a stage further, suggesting a connection between language and nation that is generally more characteristic of the eighteenth century. At Babel, he observes, each 'troop',

> having a natural desyre to remain by it self, seperated from the others whose language it understood not, caused that they all resolved to departe divers wayes to seek themselves new and severall habitacions . . . [they] were now become meer strangers the one unto the other, & thence-forward dayly grew unto more & more alienation.

Since each 'troop' naturally segregated itself by language, their ethnic identities seem almost primeval, predating the languages by which they are known. German—and by extension English—has remained among the 'moste noble', because the Germans, whose language dated to the big bang of Babel, 'have ever kept themselves unmixed with forrain people, and their language without mixing it with any forrain toung'. The Normans, by contrast, *did* shift languages, and it is therefore not coincidental that they proved to be a brutal and deceitful people who fabricated the notion that some arrangement had been made for William to succeed Edward the Confessor and who after the Conquest revealed their true character in their disdain of the English. The inherent virtue of the English eventually won over the Normans, however, softening their attitude and leading them to teach English to their children. But inasmuch as the Normans had initially spoken another *Germanic* language prior to their arrival in northern France, by shifting to English they in effect returned 'again unto themselves'. For this reason—that the Normans were somehow both cruelly foreign and never far from the English anyway—the English and Normans assimilated with one another in short order:

> And thus by one meanes or other may they have bin somuch worne away and diminished, that I think the one half of them, yf it were observed (as by their surnames it best might bee) would not bee found to have remayned two ages after, and scarse the one quarter of them to bee remayning at this present.'

English and England thereby emerge as not only morally upright but ethnically and linguistically pure from time immemorial. 'Some do call us a mixed nation by reason of these Danes and Normannes coming in among us', Verstegan notes, but Danes, Norwegians, and the English all 'were once one same people with the Germans, as were also the Saxons'.[31] In all this, a new horizon of linguistic

[30] Camden, *Remains concerning Britain*, 29, 35.

[31] Verstegan, *A Restitution of Decayed Intelligence*, 6, 43, 170–1, 182–3, 186–7, 188.

expectation emerges, as English assumes the status of Latin without also having to demonstrate the same justifications that had produced that status. English is the High Language not because God ordained it to be so, nor because He speaks in it, nor even because a landed aristocracy does. English is the High Language because it embodies the character of its speakers and their nation, both of which are self-evidently virtuous.

How Middle English became modern

When we use the linguistic periodizations Middle English and Modern English, we certainly do refer to empirical realities, which involved empirical ruptures. And these realities reflect not simply English but natural languages more generally. The grammatical heuristic that accounts for the history of English by invoking the traditional Old, Middle, and Modern stages of the language, that is, replicates the histories of at least other Germanic languages, all of which embody similar patterns in the atrophy of inflectional endings.[32] No amount of discussion about continuities can make these empirical facts and ruptures go away.

At the same time, as I have suggested here, some important features of language use in England do remain the same throughout this period. When English moved from the Middle Ages into the early modern period, its speakers and uses—to fudge agency for a bit—adjusted the status of the language in several ways, but they did not simply cast away the inherited sociolinguistic frameworks that shaped language in medieval England. To do so, to throw out diglossia alongside the use of French and Latin or the definition of grammar as a stay against change, *would* have been to achieve a true revolution of paradigm as well as type. Rather, they preserved and reformed what I have called the infrastructure of medieval England's linguistic repertoire by allowing English, in effect, to become Latin, with its grammar and rhetoric the focus of critical discussion, its varieties arrayed vertically in a version of diglossia, and its value rooted in the transcendent value of the English nation. English speakers and grammarians not only absorbed the implication of social identity in language that *rusticus* implies, then. Despite the steadily increasing evidence of spoken and written English traditions, they also absorbed Latin's proscription of inevitable, natural variation as something that is, in several senses, simply wrong. And they did this even though it also meant disregarding the cultural bulwarks that had maintained the pre-eminence of Latin and, for the most part, simply taking the status of English as a given. In this way, English ironically became a language that aspired to be and act as Latin, even while its

[32] Roger Lass, 'Language Periodization and the Concept "Middle"', in *Placing Middle English in Context: Selected Papers from the Second Middle English Conference*, ed. Irma Taavitsainen et al. (Berlin: Mouton de Gruyter, 2000), 7–41.

grammarians avoided the arguments by which Latin had achieved its status and turned Latinate terms in English into the object of derision.

But the tricky question about agency remains: *who* or *what* did all this? I think it least productive to attribute any of this linguistic reformation simply to some vast sociolinguistic conspiracy propelled by insecure nobles, whispering bureaucrats, or any of the other usual suspects for channeling social power. As the Académie Française and any other language-governing body continually learns, speakers are too wilful and language too intractable for that kind of malfeasance to be effective. Through targeted change, speakers can certainly instigate and propel linguistic transformation, but this is typically very limited, such as the ameliorization of an offensive word. At least in the history of English, large changes in status have tended to occur as means to some other larger non-linguistic goal—like mining Welsh valleys or displacing indigenous populations—and not as ends in themselves.

Rather than point a finger at any person, group, or institution I'd like in closing briefly to consider how what I've discussed here relates to some generalities about language and society. As I suggested at the outset, the structure of a language has typically been given primacy in defining both that language and any synchronic or diachronic varieties it might experience. We might remember the beginning of Middle English by the Battle of Hastings, for example, but histories will present its real beginning in a set of grammatical changes involving gender, adjectival inflections, and so forth. Roger Lass, one of the very best historical linguists, even sounds triumphant in noting that his analysis of Middle English is based 'entirely on intralinguistic structural criteria', without 'reference to the Norman Conquest or loanwords or standardization'.[33] As valuable as structurally based insights may be, however, there can also be something circular in this line of reasoning. Beginning with a definition of language as a set of structured phenomena irrespective of those who use it and how they do so, such reasoning necessarily identifies both the ontology of language and therefore any modifications to this ontology in these phenomena.

But as a form of cultural display—what Halliday calls a social semiotic—language perhaps inevitably, perhaps necessarily, also encodes varying social meanings in its varying forms and usages. In the more concise version I used above, speakers map social variation onto linguistic variation. From this perspective the uses of a language would be not simply and tautologically what one does with the language but rather a fundamental feature of the language itself. Whether diachronically or synchronically, then, English is a collection of forms. But it is also a collection of pragmatic effects that themselves can vary historically or remain constant. And in this way, pragmatics and sociolinguistic activity become not just extralinguistic phenomena—like invasions and printing presses—by which

[33] Lass, 'Language Periodization and the Concept "Middle"', 32.

we might remember developments in the real language but rather intrinsic features of that language. English became Latin, then, not so much because of a change initiated by any group or individual as through the maintenance of traditional patterns for thinking about language. Rather than (anthropomorphically) fashioning a triumph over Latin, English simply ceased to compete with it and instead appropriated its metalinguistic discourse to frame a new role in the vernacular's new linguistic repertoire. One might even say that by becoming Latin, English helped make it possible for a modern England to come into being.

A perspective like this opens up subtleties that can be hidden by period labels such as Middle and Modern English. Yes, the grammar of English changed significantly between 1377 and 1642, but the sociolinguistic infrastructure in which English figured did not. In fact, just when it did change is an intriguing question, since the kind of reformed diglossia that I have described—with Standard English hierarchically situated above regional dialects and colonial and immigrant contact languages—persists well into the twentieth century, played out again and again in the Anglophone repertoires of post-colonial speech communities. This persistence in sociolinguistic infrastructure doesn't of course mean that we still speak Middle English; indeed, we'd have little success trying to converse with a revenant Chaucer. But this persistence does mean that our own analytical tools and frames, as necessary as they obviously are, can sometimes obscure the character both of historical language use and natural language in general. If language periodization is defined solely by structural criteria, we can lose some surprising continuities and complexities. And with them we lose something of the nuanced way in which speakers, their languages, and their culture interact.

FURTHER READING

Labov, William. *Principles of Linguistic Change*, vol. 2: *Social Factors* (Oxford: Blackwell, 2001)

Lass, Roger (ed.). *The Cambridge History of the English Language*, Vol. 3: *1476–1776* (Cambridge: Cambridge University Press, 1999)

Machan, Tim William. *Language Anxiety: Conflict and Change in the History of English* (Oxford: Oxford University Press, 2009)

Milroy, James and Lesley Milroy. *Authority in Standard Language: Investigating Standard English*, 3rd edn (London: Routledge, 1999)

Nevalainen, Terttu and Helena Raumolin-Brunberg. *Historical Sociolinguistics: Language Change in Tudor and Stewart England* (London: Longman, 2003)

CHAPTER 15

HERESY AND TREASON

DAVID LOEWENSTEIN

In this essay I examine the specter of heresy, especially in that porous boundary between the medieval and early modern periods. I will focus on two periods of acute religious crisis when the specter of heresies proliferating in England was especially troublesome: the 1520s and 1530s, when Thomas More devoted so much of his energies to attempting to eradicate new heresies which threatened thousands of souls; and the 1640s and 1650s, when the fragmentation of Protestantism generated powerful new fears of unchecked heresies and a wealth of anti-heretical writings. However, underpinning More's own anti-heresy writings lies the authority of late medieval anti-heresy legislation, although this does not fully explain the savagery of More's responses and the tensions generated by it. Anti-heresy writings of the English Civil War and Interregnum also need to be understood in the context of new legislation enacted by Parliament to control the proliferation of religious error and its contagious impact on society and on political and ecclesiastical institutions. Moreover, during the upheavals of the English Revolution, the language of contamination and disease associated with heresy is as potent as it ever was during the Middle Ages and during the decades of religious confrontation in More's England. This essay examines the powerful cultural fears generated by the heated religious imagination. It examines continuities between the late Middle Ages and early modern period, while also emphasizing what was distinctive about the imaginings of heretics and heresies during those unstable decades when the English Reformation was emerging and those decades when the religious ferment of the English Revolution stimulated powerful new anti-heretical fantasies and fears.

Fear and anti-heresy polemic in Thomas More's England

I focus on Thomas More in the first part of this essay because he became frighteningly obsessed with the spread of heresy and because in this volume, devoted to traversing the pre- and post-Reformation boundary or the boundary between the medieval and early modern periods, More proves especially challenging to assess. How do we situate the highly sophisticated Renaissance humanist writer in relation to the scourge of heretics fiercely committed, as More was, to keeping the pre-Reformation Church from becoming dismembered? A complex and contradictory figure, More in some sense straddles two worlds, reminding us that we need to question polarized distinctions between medieval and humanist world views; this includes the distinction between the world of Renaissance humanism, which opened up imaginative possibilities brilliantly explored in More's *Utopia*, and the religious world of the pre-Reformation Church which More staunchly defended in major vernacular prose works and by invoking medieval anti-heresy legislation. In our post-9/11 world of religious phobias, it is More the scourge of heretics who most disturbs us and who clashes with the man of 'unspotted conscience... more pure... than the whitest snow', as More's early biographer, William Roper, represented him—the More canonized in the twentieth century.[1] Further, as we address the feverish campaign to eradicate heresy in More's England, we might ask: what does that campaign suggest about the emergence of the English Reformation and the bitter, tragic cultural, political, and religious conflicts it generated?

Appointed Lord Chancellor in 1529, More played a central role in the escalating war against heresy—and evangelical books contributing to it—during the 1520s and early 1530s, since heresy, imperiling thousands of souls, was in his view 'as great a cryme as treason' against God and Church, as well as a heinous crime against the king.[2] More's efforts to combat the nation's descent into the madness of heresy—for so he regarded the frightening threat to the pre-Reformation Church in his darkening age—generated his most controversial and bitter vernacular writings, and fueled a new kind of religious warfare. More envisioned the mighty struggle against heresy as a 'batayle that is to [know] the questyon whyche is the chyrche',[3] and he believed that the campaign to eradicate evangelical reform, doctrine, and texts, along with the urgent need to control biblical exegesis, was nothing less than a battle for the very soul of England.[4]

[1] William Roper, *The Life of Sir Thomas More*, in *Two Early Tudor Lives*, ed. Richard S. Sylvester and Davis P. Harding (New Haven, CT: Yale University Press, 1962), 197.

[2] Thomas More, *The Apology*, in *The Complete Works of St. Thomas More*, general editors Louis L. Martz, Richard S. Sylvester, and Clarence Miller, 15 vols. (London and New Haven, CT: Yale University Press, 1963–97), 9:136. Unless otherwise noted, subsequent quotations from More's works are taken from the Yale edition, hereafter *CW*.

[3] See the preface to More, *The Confutation of Tyndale's Answer*, *CW*, 8: 34.

[4] The justification for the term 'evangelical' to describe the religious reformism which developed in England during the 1520s and 1530s has been made most persuasively by Diarmaid MacCulloch: see e.g. *Thomas Cranmer* (New Haven, CT: Yale University Press, 1996), 2–3. The term refers to the faithful return to the spirit of the Gospel, the good news or *evangelium*. See also Alec Ryrie, *The Gospel and Henry VIII: Evangelicals in the Early English Reformation* (Cambridge: Cambridge University Press, 2003).

For twenty-first-century readers, constantly reminded that the world is still plagued by religious divisiveness and intolerance, the More who used his pen and power to demonize heretics remains an uncomfortable figure. It is surely easier to admire the urbane, flexible, international humanist writer—the wise, supremely intelligent More who takes pleasure in a merry tale and an Erasmian jest,[5] and whose most famous piece of writing is a tentative, paradoxical utopian text that concludes inconclusively by promising further discussion of its radical social, political, and religious ideals. This witty humanist side of More can of course complement the devotional More, the man of conscience and integrity who eventually became a Christian martyr for refusing to succumb to the tyranny of Henry VIII. Yet we also have More the relentless defender of the old faith and the persecutor of heretics, a view of More emphasized by one of his principal biographers, Richard Marius, and originally addressed by the studies of G. R. Elton with their own strong pro-Protestant bias.[6] I too wish to reconsider More the scourge of heretics, but, more than Marius or Elton, I highlight here a deeply conflicted, unstable More. Scholars have (understandably) preferred the witty, open-ended, reform-minded humanist thinker who seems willing to entertain, at least in the realm of fiction, radical alternative perspectives to the highly imperfect political, economic, and social conditions of sixteenth-century Europe and Henrician England. In *Utopia*, More the character and flexible public figure appears accommodating when it comes to adapting to his imperfect, Machiavellian political world in contrast to the humorless and visionary Platonic traveler Raphael Hythloday who gives voice to vehement, uncompromising views about European political conduct and social mores: 'I was not sure', More observes at the end of *Utopia*, that 'he could take contradiction in these matters'.[7] Yet one might make the same observation about Thomas More himself when, in the 1520s and 1530s, it came to his unbending loyalty to the pre-Reformation Church fueling his implacable hatred of heretics.

Of course, one might observe that More's Utopians are themselves inconsistent when it comes to matters of religious difference (not to mention matters of warfare, where their shrewd tactics resemble Machiavellian European behavior).

[5] See Erasmus's letter to Ulrich Von Hutten in *Epistles of Erasmus*, trans. Francis Nichols (London: Longman Green, 1917), 387–99.

[6] Richard Marius, *Thomas More: A Biography* (New York: Knopf, 1984), xxiv: 'His fury at the Protestant heretics... has a touch of hysteria about it... for he cried for them to be burned alive, and he rejoiced when some of them went to the fire. This fury was... almost the essence of the man'. See also Elton, *Studies in Tudor and Stuart Politics and Government*, 2 vols. (Cambridge: Cambridge University Press, 1974), 1: 129–54; and 'The Real Thomas More?', in *Reformation Principle and Practice*, ed. Peter Newman Brooks (London: Scolar Press, 1980), 23–31. See also John Guy, *The Public Career of Sir Thomas More* (New Haven, CT: Yale University Press, 1980), for an account of More's activities as a prosecutor of heretics.

[7] Thomas More, *Utopia: Latin Text and English Translation*, ed. George Logan, Robert M. Adams, and Clarence Miller (Cambridge: Cambridge University Press, 2005), 249.

On the one hand, they seem to practice religious toleration: 'For it is one of their oldest rules', Raphael relates, 'that no one should suffer for his religion'. In order to placate the different sects on the island and the fighting amongst them, King Utopus realizes that toleration is the best way to prevent civil strife and that it is a mistake to enforce conformity in religion by means of abuse, threats, or violence; otherwise, 'implacable hatreds' are likely to develop, so that 'in matters of religion, [Utopus] was not at all quick to dogmatize'. Yet despite 'allowing each person to choose what he would believe', Utopus does show some dogmatism when it comes to any person who adheres to a heretical belief like mortalism, as well as those who reject the belief that the universe is ruled by divine providence. Indeed, in the communal culture of Utopia, the non-believer is subject to public shaming and barred from public office: 'a person who holds such views is offered no honours, entrusted with no offices, and given no public responsibility; he is generally regarded as utterly contemptible'.[8] By enabling attentive readers of his text to note such inconsistencies when it comes to religious toleration, More prompts them to view the Utopians and their practices from a more skeptical, tentative perspective. Nonetheless, despite religious tensions which existed before the arrival of King Utopus, the world of the Utopians is not torn apart by the 'implacable hatreds' created by fears of heresy and religious difference. Yet in the decade following the publication of his utopian book envisioning religious pluralism (however qualified), More would emerge as one of the most implacable hunters of heretics in England, employing his considerable verbal resources to wage that vitriolic campaign.[9]

To support his anti-heresy campaign, including his assaults on evangelical preaching and books, More invoked late medieval legislation as his legal weapon. Heretics, after all, had been actively sought out and burned in England since 1401, when Parliament, in the statute *De heretico comburendo* ('On Burning Heretics'), responded to the perceived threat of seditious Lollard doctrines not only by prohibiting books and preaching 'contrary to the Catholic faith or determination of the Holy Church' and by empowering bishops to arrest and imprison heretics (and ordering sheriffs and municipal officers to assist the episcopal powers), but also by instituting death by fire for persons who refused to abjure their heretical opinions. The punitive statute was an instrument of terror: the burning of heretics 'before the people' and 'in a high place' was intended to 'strike fear [*metum*] to the minds of others'.[10] The statute, which equated heresy with treason and spiritual

[8] More, *Utopia*, ed. Logan et. al., 223, 225; I have slightly altered the translation from the Latin.

[9] For the view that there are consistencies between More's views voiced in *Utopia* and his later intolerance of heresy, see also G. R. Elton, 'Persecution and Toleration in the English Reformation', in *Persecution and Toleration*, ed. W. J. Sheils, Studies in Church History, 21 (Oxford: Basil Blackwell, 1984), 165–8, 171.

[10] *De heretico comburendo*, in *Documents of the Christian Church*, ed. Henry Bettenson and Chris Maunder, 3rd edn (Oxford: Oxford University Press, 1999), 198–202. For the Latin, see *CW*, 9: 254.

dissent with political disobedience, was strengthened in Henry V's reign by a supplementary act of 1414 (prompted by the abortive revolt of Sir John Oldcastle) ordering secular authorities from the Lord Chancellor downward to assist in the detection of heresy and punishment of heretics;[11] indeed, Cardinal Wolsey began the anti-heresy proclamation of March 1529, a response to the crisis of evangelicalism, by invoking the authority of medieval anti-heresy statutes enacted by Henry VIII's 'noble progenitors'.[12] More himself identified Oldcastle's heresy with treason, and it was essentially under the medieval act *De heretico comburendo*, which had turned Henry IV's England into a suspicious, persecuting state, that More himself justified the burning of heretics who refused to abjure; as the character More observes in *A Dialogue Concerning Heresies*, 'in England... a good catholyke realme, [heresy] hath bene longe punyshed by deth in the fyre' including—and here More raises the specter of the Oldcastle revolt—the famous case of Lord Cobham 'taken in Wales and burned in London' (*CW*, 6: 409).

More was using medieval legislation, a response to the religious crisis generated by the heretical Lollard movement, to combat a new type of heresy: Lutheran heresy and the doctrine of justification. Yet More's bitter reactions against those whom he considered pernicious new heretics were not only a consequence of diligently enforcing the law as Lord Chancellor, defending the rigor of episcopal jurisdiction, and carrying out a divinely ordained obligation in order to safeguard his society and kingdom. Nor was his severity towards heretics simply an expression of 'fatherly chastisement of the Lord' towards sinners, a means of enacting a kind of 'charitable hatred'.[13] His war against heresy was fed by a current of hatred that ran deeper than this; it was profoundly visceral and irrational, fueled by dark, violent fantasies about heretics. 'I find that breed of men', he wrote of heretics in his last extant letter to Erasmus, 'absolutely loathsome'—and he combated heresy with a language and rhetoric sometimes terrifying in their virulence.[14]

Among recent scholars, Louis Martz eloquently attempts to counter the image of the severe More by stressing the gentle, wise, and devotional More depicted in Holbein's family portraits and in Nicholas Harpsfield's early biography

See also A. K. McHardy, '*De heretico comburendo*, 1401', in *Lollardy and Gentry in the Later Middle Ages*, ed. Margaret Aston and Colin Richmond (Stroud: Sutton, 1997), 112–26.

11 For More's own association of Oldcastle, 'the captayne of heretykes', with treason, see *CW*, 10: 110; on More's response to the revolt, see also *CW*, 9: 162. Also see Ian Forrest, *The Detection of Heresy in Late Medieval England* (Oxford: Clarendon Press, 2005), 43–6, 150.

12 *Tudor Royal Proclamations*, ed. Paul L. Hughes and James F. Larkin, 2 vols. (New Haven, CT: Yale University Press, 1964, 1969), 1: 182–3.

13 Alexandra Walsham, *Charitable Hatred: Tolerance and Intolerance in England, 1500–1700* (Manchester: Manchester University Press, 2006), 2.

14 See More's letter to Erasmus, *c.*June 1533, in Thomas More, *St. Thomas More: Selected Letters*, ed. and trans. Elizabeth Frances Rogers (New Haven, CT: Yale University Press, 1961), 180.

(where More's piety is amply highlighted).[15] Martz defends the image of the humane More—the man of conscience devoted to his family and friends and to his work as lawyer and judge—shaped by the classic twentieth-century biography by R. W. Chambers (published in 1935, the year of More's canonization) and projected by Robert Bolt in his biographical play about More, *A Man for All Seasons* (1960). The more resolute qualities of More the lawyer, judge, royal counsellor, and statesman can be reconciled, Martz argues, with the sensitive More depicted by Holbein. While highlighting that More indeed had many sides to him, Martz nonetheless remains profoundly uncomfortable with More's ruthless side. My own view stresses a more contradictory, unstable writer whose heated religious imagination becomes unchecked—a More whose war against heresy could be combined with his humanism and disputatious wit (as in *A Dialogue Concerning Heresies*) and a More whose controversial venom could at times become unbridled and terrifying (as in his massive *Confutation of Tyndale's Answer*). More may have regained some of his composure and wit in his last works written in the Tower; nevertheless, his anti-heresy campaign was obsessive and sometimes ferocious. We should not let his final achievements, including his touching letters to his daughter Margaret, obscure this dimension of More, even if it leaves us in the end with a more ambiguous, troubling writer and man.

More's most significant vernacular anti-heresy writings were prompted by the Bishop of London, Cuthbert Tunstall, who licensed More in March 1528 to enter the war against heresy by reading heretical books and combating them with his formidable literary skills. In a prohibition issued in October 1526 and addressed to officials in his diocese, Tunstall conveyed a sense of grave crisis, warning that heresy would rapidly infect London, destroying thousands of souls, unless combated vigorously: Tyndale's New Testament and many Lutheran texts were 'dispersed throughout our diocese of London in great number' and would 'contaminate the flock... with most deadly poison to the grievous peril of souls committed to our charge'. The language of contamination, disease, plague, and lethal poison—metaphors and analogies used to express alarm about heresy and its workings in the Middle Ages—were reinvigorated, expressing a new climate of fear about the invasion of insidious heresy during these unstable decades of the sixteenth century.[16] Tunstall regarded the struggle against the epidemic of heresy as a war

[15] Louis L. Martz, *Thomas More: The Search for the Inner Man* (New Haven, CT: Yale University Press, 1990), 4, which considers the mixture of 'severity and charity'. For the devotional qualities in the young More, see Nicholas Harpsfield, *The Life and Death of Sir Thomas Moore*, EETS, original series, 186, ed. E. V. Hitchcock and R. W. Chambers (London: Published for the Early English Text Society by H. Milford, Oxford University Press, 1932), 17–18. Harpsfield's life was presented to William Roper in 1557 or 1558 but was not printed; it was not published until 1932.

[16] On metaphors of disease and contamination in medieval Europe, see especially R. I. Moore, *The Formation of a Persecuting Society: Authority and Deviance in Western Europe 950–1250*, 2nd edn

against treacherous Satanic forces, believing that some kind of homeland security and pre-emptive activity were urgently required to contain the threat. The immediate result of Tunstall's commission—and More's own determination to combat the spread of heresy—was More's *Dialogue Concerning Heresies*, a substantial, skillful work that appeared in June 1529, shortly before More became Lord Chancellor. It illustrates the uneasy relation between the sophisticated humanist writer and the ruthless hunter of heretics.

On one level, More's *Dialogue* displays the attractive side of the humanist More: the persona of More as a witty, wise figure of authority and learning who enjoys a merry jest or tale in the familiar setting of his study or in the leisurely setting of his garden as he converses with a young, evangelically-minded, nameless Messenger, a fictional interlocutor (sent to More by a fictional friend), about the old Church and its traditions and about the impact of evangelical beliefs, books, preaching, and interpretation. Yet *A Dialogue*'s subject is also deadly serious: the dangerous spread of heretical ideas and texts, as well as the protean, menacing behavior of heretics. Underneath the 'mery disputacion' (*CW*, 6: 250) between two interlocutors, there emerges an author who, despite using the potentially more open-ended dialogue form, will not take contradiction in matters concerning the preservation of the old faith and pre-Reformation Church. On one level, then, More's *Dialogue* seems like a lively exchange of differing religious viewpoints; on another, it registers a profound sense of religious insecurity and fear. Yet the self-consciously fictional nature of the work also allows More the author to maintain rhetorical control over his subject matter: the blight of contagious new heresies.

A 'letter of credence' at the beginning of *A Dialogue* reinforces the fictive situation, while making the fiction seem all the more real, as do the humanist letters published along with *Utopia*. The Messenger, we discover, is more than 'meanly learned': he is not tongue-tied; he is a 'mery wytte' (*CW*, 6: 25) like More himself; and his master has encouraged him to express freely what he thinks. More thus creates a situation where wit and serious dialogue mingle; this is another example of *serio ludere*, except that in this case the issue is heresy and its increasingly dangerous impact in England and abroad. Here More appears as the wiser, more experienced man—an urbane, assured interlocutor who draws easily upon a wealth of Church authorities to make his arguments against heresies—versus the young, studious, sometimes feisty evangelically-minded Messenger. But since the situation is self-consciously fictional, the reader is aware that More is arguing here (as in the first book of *Utopia*) with no man and that More remains in rhetorical control of the imagined debate—much as he hopes to control the menacing spread of heresy.

(Oxford: Blackwell, 2007). See also R.I. Moore, 'Heresy as Disease', in *The Concept of Heresy in the Middle Ages: (11th–13th c.)*, ed. W. Lordaux and D. Verhelst, Medievalia Lovaniensia, series 1 *Studia* 4 (Leuven and The Hague, 1976), 1–11.

Central to More's fictional *Dialogue* are concerns about the destabilizing impact of so-called 'heretics'. In 1530, a year after More's *Dialogue* was published, new, sharply worded royal proclamations—the work of More himself—evoked fears of contamination and its consequences, denouncing the spread of Lutheran heresy by means of 'pestiferous English books, printed in other regions and sent into this realm to pervert the people from the true faith of Christ, to stir them to sedition against their princes, [and] to cause them to contemn all good laws, [and] customs ... to the desolation of this noble realm'.[17] Heretics may have been far from numerous in 1529 or 1530—revisionist historians like to tell us that at this moment there were indeed 'few signs of a future Reformation'[18]—but fears about contagious heresies raging out of control by means of books and the exegesis of the vernacular Bible were surely deepening and tell a different story.

Members of More's family, after all, had been contaminated by the disease of heresy by reading evangelical texts—including books by Luther 'apte to infecte the reder' (*CW*, 6: 348). More's son-in-law, William Roper, a young lawyer, was one of the first English converts to the new faith and became, according to Harpsfield's life of More, 'so bewitched [by evangelical texts] that he then did beleeve every matter sett forth by Luther to be true', including 'his doctrine that faith onely did justifie' and 'that the workes of man did nothing profite' when it came to salvation.[19] Roper's enthusiasm for Lutheran heresies reached the Church authorities and he was brought before Cardinal Wolsey 'but [was] discharged' (Harpsfield records) 'with a friendly warning'—no doubt a consequence of More's position—and eventually, having learned how to survive in a world of religious change and confusion, he was brought back to the Catholic faith.

Roper's fall into Lutheran heresy thus becomes a kind of *felix culpa* narrative with a happy ending.[20] Moreover, his adaptation in a world of religious uncertainty is in a larger sense emblematic of his generation.[21] Nevertheless, before this happy conclusion, More himself struggled to bring his son-in-law back to the mainstream Church, attempting to reason with the stubborn Roper much as More in *A Dialogue* attempts to reason with the fictional Messenger; as More told his daughter Margaret (whom Roper married in 1521): 'I have borne a long time with thy husbande; I have reasoned with him in those pointes of religion ... but I perceive none of all this able to call him home; and therefore, Megge, I will no longer dispute

[17] I quote from the proclamation prohibiting erroneous books and Bible translations dated 22 June 1530: *Tudor Royal Proclamations*, ed. Hughes and Larkin, 1: 193–7.

[18] Christopher Haigh, *English Reformations: Religion, Politics, and Society under the Tudors* (Oxford: Clarendon Press, 1993), 55.

[19] Harpsfield, *The Life and Death of Sir Thomas Moore*, 84–6. See also *A Dialogue concerning Heresies*, *CW*, 6: 444, 491–2, on Roper as a model for the Messenger.

[20] *The Life and Death of Sir Thomas Moore*, 86–7.

[21] Norman Jones, *The English Reformation: Religion and Cultural Adaptation* (Oxford: Blackwell, 2002), 3, 15.

with him, but will . . . praye for him'.[22] More, however, would not always respond so charitably to heretics 'bewitched' by Lutheran books and novelties; later in the 1520s he would prosecute them with savagery and persistence, interrogating some at his house in Chelsea, often in the company of Tunstall.[23] As More bluntly puts it near the end of *A Dialogue*, signaling that his punitive measures are sanctioned by the late medieval anti-heresy statute *De heretico comburendo*: 'The author sheweth his oppynyon concernynge the burnynge of heretykes and that it is lawfull, necessary, and well done' (*CW*, 6: 405–6).

The fictional Messenger's views verge on Reformation ones which troubled More; yet the Messenger is not quite a radical evangelical (even if Roper temporarily was), and he is certainly not the kind of obstinate new heretic More would wish to burn, although upon first meeting him More is 'somewhat in doubte whether he were (as yonge scolers be somtyme prone to newe fantasyes) fallen in to luthers secte' (*CW*, 6: 34). A suspicious though amiable More realizes that he must do everything in his rhetorical power to confute the near-Reformation positions of the younger man who, questioning the rituals of the Old Church, disputes the value of ceremonial practices and ostentatious outward observance, including venerating saints, worshiping images and relics, and going on pilgrimages, while also raising skeptical questions about miracles. When it comes to reading scripture, the Messenger's perspective is close to a Reformation view of the Bible as the principal authority for God's will rather than the weight of the pre-Reformation Church and the tradition of interpretation—written and unwritten—associated with it. From More's perspective, evangelical readers or 'new gospellers',[24] are themselves unbridled young men and women carried away by their newfangled fantasies and by their subjective interpretations of the Bible, turning it into a highly unpredictable force.

Yet More also worries about heresy as an insidious, hidden danger hard to be discerned; he portrays heretics as cunning operators who employ dissimulation, verbal prevarication, covert tactics, and protean behavior. Heresy statutes well known to More from the reigns of Richard II and Henry IV had warned about malicious heretics, including itinerant preachers, spreading 'new doctrines and wicked, heretical, and erroneous opinions', 'under the colour of dissembled holiness'.[25] More, however, significantly develops the association of heretics with seductive theatricalism. His view of heretics preaching to the people as a beguiling

[22] Harpsfield, *The Life and Death of Sir Thomas Moore*, 87.

[23] For More examining heretics at Chelsea, see Marius, *Thomas More*, 232, 395, 402–3, 404–5.

[24] See More's use of this phrase in *The Apology*, *CW*, 9: 5.

[25] See the heresy statute of Richard II (1382) on 'plusours malveies persones deinz le dit Roialme' who travel from county to county and town to town 'en certains habitz souz dissimulation de grant saintitee' (*CW*, 9: 249); and see the original Latin of *De heretico comburendo* which refers to those who maliciously preach new doctrines in diverse places in the realm 'sub simulate sancitatis colore' (*CW*, 9: 251).

theatrical performance suggests that they are particularly skilled at putting on a 'saintly shew' that conceals 'deep malice'.[26] Concerning Lutheran preachers who 'beare two faces in one hoode', More observes of their cunning behavior: 'I never sawe any that more veryly play that pagaunt, than do this kynde of suche prechours. For in prechynge to the people they make a vysage as though they came strayght from heven to teche them a new better way & more trew than the chyrche techeth' (*CW*, 6: 399). Seductive theatrical behavior exploited by reformers conceals, in More's view, a deeper treachery, for when 'that falshode of theyr cloked collusyon is pulled off, then appereth there all the . . . poyson they put forth under the cloke of hony' (*CW*, 6: 399). We might expect evangelical or Protestant writers scornful of popish ceremonialism to voice such sharp anti-theatricalism in the war of religion;[27] but clearly More could employ the language of anti-theatricalism as his own weapon. Although More hopes to expose guileful behavior exploited by evangelical activists, his repeated association of the heretic with cunning theatricalism conveys considerable anxiety: skillful dissimulation suggests that heretics possess a potent means of seducing the simple and unlearned.

More's fear that manipulative, vicious heretics threaten to dismember the church can disrupt the merry disputation of *A Dialogue*: determined to prevent the pre-Reformation Church from being 'severed a sunder', More depicts the aggressive new heretics of his age as savage animals: 'For though they have dystroyed & shal dystroy many of the chyrch . . . the church shall stand & be by god preserved in despyte of all theyr teth' (*CW*, 6: 203, 204). More's vision of church history, unity, and order thus has no place for a multi-theological England—yet that is what England would become in the subsequent decades of religious confusion.[28] From More's perspective, the influx of heresies and heretics, generating alternative churches and contradictory religious messages, was creating an uncertain, fractured, violent religious world in which all coherence was in genuine danger of being lost.

There remains a tension in More's *Dialogue*, then, between its ominous subject—the frightening specter of heresy—and its playful fictional dialogue created by the sophisticated author More. In that fictional world, explosive religious beliefs can be contained and diffused: there More can engage in 'mery disputacion'; and there the reformist-minded Messenger, in the end, can be brought around to More's own anti-evangelical viewpoint: 'by my trouthe quod he whan I . . . rede Luthers wordes & Tyndales . . . I can not but wonder that eyther any Almayne [i.e. German] coulde lyke the one / or any englysshe man the other' (*CW*, 6: 432).

[26] I quote from John Milton, *Paradise Lost*, ed. Barbara Lewalski (Malden, MA: Blackwell, 2007), 4.122–3, line 121, where the poet exposes Satan as the 'Artificer of fraud'.

[27] See e.g. More's response to Tyndale's use of the term 'mummynge' to characterize the mass: *Confutation*, *CW*, 8: 110.

[28] On multi-theological sixteenth-century England, see Jones, *The English Reformation*, 3.

A Dialogue creates a fictional situation in which the seductive allure of heresy—'the false enchauntementes of all these heretykes' (6: 435)—can be stripped away and in which More, magisterial defender of the old faith, can imagine overcoming the subversive forces of an increasingly uncertain religious world. The fiction may be over and the debate concluded in favor of the character More, yet the author More's fictional work against heresy was a short-lived fantasy of control and containment.

The rhetoric of hysteria and savagery became more strident in More's massive *Confutation of Tyndale's Answer* (1532–3); though no work of fiction, it reveals much about More's violent fantasies concerning heretics. Here his preoccupation with heretics becomes a terrifying obsession and there is little room for any kind of playful wit. This brutal verbal assault on heresy and heretics is a sprawling work in which the enraged More loses control over his subject matter. More's immediate polemical opponent, moreover, is no lightweight—as in the case of the fictional Messenger. Rather, Tyndale's New Testament, with its scriptural appeal to individual lay judgment and with its translation of Paul's epistles (emphasizing justification by faith alone), has made the printed Bible a highly unpredictable force, the cause of a potentially dangerous, destabilizing cultural revolution by encouraging the novelty of heretical opinions; even before Tyndale was burned in 1536 as many as sixteen thousand copies of his translation may have been imported into England (then with a population of no more than two and half million people).[29] More, who feared the religious and political consequences of losing control over the interpretation of scripture, regarded Tyndale as the 'captain of our English heretics', representing him as sexually perverse, bestial, monstrous and mad, his 'trewthes . . . starke develyshe heresyses'.[30] A work full of *ad hominem* attacks and savage mockery, More's *Confutation* conveys even greater anxiety about the difficulty of eradicating the venomous spread of heresy, for once the insidious infection has become an epidemic, More observes, 'Heresie is harde to be cured' (*CW*, 8:28).

Behind the *Confutation* lies an increasingly dark view of 'this wretched world' overtaken by heresy and its demonic agents—'yt be badde ynough all redye', a troubled More laments—which 'wold yet wax then mich worse' (*CW*, 8: 58) if the contagion spreads.[31] Just as heresy and its transmission by texts seem frightful to More, so his verbal response is truly terrifying in its own way—a kind of textual *sparagmos* or dismemberment.[32] More violently dismembers Tyndale's texts, responding point by point to Tyndale's statements and arguments, especially

[29] Orlaith O'Sullivan (ed.), *The Bible as Book: The Reformation* (London: British Library, 2000), 47; Diarmaid MacCulloch, *The Reformation: A History* (New York: Viking, 2004), 197–8.

[30] See also Patrick Collinson, 'William Tyndale and the Course of the English Reformation', *Reformation*, 1 (1996), 72–98, at 72.

[31] Cf. More's reference to 'these latter dayes of thys blynde worlde' (*CW*, 8: 63).

[32] For a study of anxieties about and uses of *sparagmos*, see Michael Lieb, *Milton and the Culture of Violence* (Ithaca, NY: Cornell University Press, 1994).

those in *An Answer unto Sir Thomas More's Dialogue made by William Tyndale* (1531), a work in which Tyndale had insisted that scripture should be the test of the Church and then had gone on to refute, often by means of direct dialogue, More's own *Dialogue.* The vast size of More's *Confutation*—over three-quarters of a million words—reveals the exhausting strain of his brutal efforts to stop the blight of heresy and destroy Tyndale's theological authority by dismembering his words and arguments, including the vernacular language of his New Testament. It reveals as well the paranoia and hysteria that the specter of heresy could generate—not unlike, say, the atmosphere of hysteria generated by the specter of communism during the twentieth century. More's gigantic work, full of anti-heretical venom and fear, was in fact never completed; instead, it was abandoned after the second part appeared in a large volume in 1533. In its incompleteness and vast size, the *Confutation* stands as a fitting literary monument to the uncontrollable fears and imaginings heresy could generate in More's age—and to More's inability to contain the darker forces of heresy.

There are thus violent dimensions to More's character and works of religious controversy that cannot simply be softened by appealing to his humane qualities or by appealing to his final meditative works and witty letters written in the Tower of London under sentence of death.[33] The witty, devotional, humanist More—the man of great literary sensibility and conscience—is clearly a more attractive figure than More the inflexible, savage heretic-hunter for whom the preoccupation with heresy became a terrifying obsession, so that in his violent, apocalyptic fantasies about heretics he envisioned 'theyr bodyes... burned in erthe wyth [William Tyndale's] bokes, and theyr soulys burned in helle wyth hys heresyes' (*CW,* 8: 219). Yet they were the same man and the same writer, and we need to acknowledge and explain the coexistence of these conflicting sides of the multifaceted More. I have sought to highlight the unstable, contradictory sides of More, especially More the scourge of heretics, whose vernacular writings and fierce loyalty to a pre-Reformation religious culture challenge schematic conceptions of medieval versus humanist world views and whose expressions of religious extremism contribute to his ambiguous legacy. More remains a richly complex figure. Indeed, for twenty-first-century readers, living in an anxious time haunted by the specter of terrorism and plagued by religious intolerance and violence, the controversy over how to assess More the scourge of heretics is likely to assume renewed significance.[34] In Thomas More's case, his war against heresy eerily resonates at the beginning

[33] Cf. Martz, who wishes to reconcile these divergent sides of More: 'Fury against heresy there certainly was in his writings, but our assessment of this quality needs to be tempered by the humane, humanist, Socratic portrait drawn by Chambers and by the devotional, humanist, juridical, and statesmanlike portraits drawn by Holbein' (Martz, *Thomas More,* 19).

[34] One powerful study that has already begun to do this is James Simpson, *Burning to Read: English Fundamentalism and Its Reformation Opponents* (Cambridge, MA: Harvard University Press, 2007).

of the twenty-first century: conducted at times with savage intensity, it illustrates, in sixteenth-century terms, how the unchecked, heated religious imagination can create a dark, persecuting world plagued by suspicion, fear, and intolerance.

Heresy fears in Civil War and Interregnum England

Although separated by more than a century from More's world, Civil War and Interregnum England is another period in early modern history and culture when fearful fantasies about heresy and heretics became unusually acute, and when writers themselves contributed notably to the specter of heresy. A new and rapidly escalating war against the insidious spread of heresy erupted with fury as Protestant unity fragmented during the 1640s and 1650s, generating fears of political chaos, moral confusion, and religious anarchy. What was distinctive about this unsettled period is that the godly were furiously demonizing other Protestants. The specter of monstrous heresy and its atmosphere of hysteria and religious phobia were especially generated by orthodox Puritan writers, including Thomas Edwards, Ephraim Pagitt, Daniel Featley, Robert Baillie, and James Cranford (to mention just a few of these authors), who produced large printed catalogues of heresies and heretics as well as other anti-heretical writings—frantic texts full of shrill rhetoric in which acute fears of religious otherness, dark fantasies about heretics, and the power of the heated religious imagination interacted. Their preoccupation with heresy, its rapid spread, and its power to disfigure the Church and endanger the kingdom became a terrifying obsession. The term 'heretic' was once again built up as a particularly terrible and frightening label.

To be sure, there existed notable catalogues of heretics in sixteenth-century Europe;[35] but the impulse to catalogue heresies and excoriate heretics took on new urgency in the middle decades of seventeenth-century England, unsettled by civil war, the splintering of Protestant unity, and experimental governments. And with the new specter of heresy came a new climate of fear. The outburst of violent anti-heretical discourses, the unbridled language and shocking images they employed, and the frightening specter of heresy they generated have received little sustained attention from literary scholars, although a leading historian has given us a first-rate account of Edwards's *Gangraena* and the struggle for the English Revolution.[36]

[35] See e.g. Bernard de Luxembourg, *Catalogus haereticorum* (Cologne, 1522); Gabriel de Preau, *Se vitis, sectis et dogmatibus omnium haereticorum* (Cologne, 1569).

[36] Ann Hughes, *Gangraena and the Struggle for the English Revolution* (Oxford: Oxford University Press, 2004). See also Sammy Basu, ' "We are in strange hands, and things are come to a strange passé": Argument and Rhetoric against Heresy in Thomas Edwards's *Gangraena* (1646)', in *Histories of Heresy in Early Modern Europe: For, Against, Beyond Persecution and Toleration*, ed. John Christian Laursen (Basingstoke: Palgrave-Macmillan, 2002), 11–32.

No doubt this is because these books or catalogues of errors—for example, Edwards's book or Pagitt's *Heresiography*—do not necessarily seem 'literary' in the ways that we usually think of the term. Yet there are features in these important religious texts from the mid-seventeenth century—works whose ferocious rhetoric and alarming images demonize heretics and generate dark fantasies about them—that are indeed worthy of rigorous attention by the literary historian. These texts reveal much about the unchecked, heated religious imagination during the mid-seventeenth-century crisis in England.

In this section I examine the violent rhetoric and emotionally charged images and language of religious fear these writers employed in order to generate a new specter of heresy during the English Revolution. One trope godly writers employed regularly was that of warfare. This was a period in which the war of religion was especially intense, fueled by fears of religious fragmentation and spreading heresies which were undermining hierarchy and the authority of university-educated and formally ordained ministers.[37] These writers perceived their propaganda campaign against heresy—a campaign conducted in a climate of fear, crisis, and uncertainty—as a form of aggressive warfare requiring the besieged godly to maintain a militant and vigilant stance against swarms of treacherous heretics invading the body politic and threatening not only its security but its very existence: the London minister and press licenser James Cranford entitled his 1645 text *Haereseo-Machia*, since the mighty campaign against heresy was a bitter fight for the soul of England; the Scottish Presbyterian writer Robert Baillie presented himself in the same year as 'among the weakest of Christ's soldiers' engaged in 'warfare' against the dangerous errors of the times; and the prominent London Presbyterian minister Thomas Edwards urged Parliament in 1646 to 'become terrible as an Army' in the war 'both against schisms that may arise from within, and the assaults of enemies without'.[38] Published in three massive parts, Edwards's *Gangraena: Or a Catalogue and Discovery of many of the Errours, Heresies, and Blasphemies and Pernicious Practices of the Sectaries of this Time*—the most popular, influential, and ambitious heresiography of the period—did much to encourage and generate the new, terrifying specter of heresy proliferating in Civil War England.

Proliferating at an alarming rate and deforming religion, heresy seemed like a many-headed, monstrous Hydra which had 'sprung up in these times in *England*'.[39]

[37] On the war of religion during the English Revolution, see esp. John Morrill, *The Nature of the English Revolution* (London: Longman, 1993), Part 1; see also Christopher Durston and Judith Maltby (eds.) *Religion in Revolutionary England* (Manchester: Manchester University Press, 2006).

[38] Robert Baillie, *A Dissuasive from the Errours of the Time* (London, 1645), 'The Epistle Dedicatory', sig.*2^r; Thomas Edwards, *Gangraena: Or a Catalogue and Discovery of many of the Errours, Heresies, Blasphemies and Pernicious Practices of the Sectaries of this Time* (London, 1646), Part 1, 'The Epistle Dedicatory', sig. a4^v (I quote, unless noted otherwise, from the first edition).

[39] Edwards, *Gangraena*, Part 1, 'The Preface', sig. B^v. See also Thomas Edwards, *The Second Part of Gangraena: A Fresh and Further Discovery of the Errors, Heresies, Blasphemies, and Dangerous*

Edwards warned that the spread of heresy had been particularly acute and uncontrolled 'in *England* within these last four years' leading up to the publication of his *Gangraena* in 1646; consequently, he found himself forced to produce 'a Catalogue of errours now in being, alive in these present times'. The task seemed truly daunting. Indeed, heresies and errors were spreading so fast, thanks to 'all the books of the Sectaries', he warned his readers, that he was producing a 'Catalogue of *many of the Errours*' (emphasis added)—but not 'of all the erroneous opinions' since 'a great volume would not contain the errours, prodigious opinions, and strange practices of these times'.[40]

Edwards's gargantuan efforts to record the mass of errors and heresies of his age—he kept adding more and more material to his heresiography—suggests both the alarming size of the challenge and the overwhelming number of errors he believed were endangering his world.[41] As the most popular and formidable heresy hunter writing in mid-seventeenth-century England, Edwards is therefore notable because he provides, in the three massive parts of his *Gangraena*, the most expansive and seemingly precise exposition of monstrous heresies in the period—nearly three hundred errors and (in Part 1) sixteen varieties of so-called sects or denominations—in terms of a deadly gangrene infecting the body politic:

> 1. Independents. 2. Brownists. 3. Chiliasts, or Millenaries. 4. Antinomians. 5. Anabaptists. 6. Manifestarians or Arminians. 7. Libertines. 8. Familists. 9. Enthusiasts. 10. Seekers and Waiters. 11. Perfectists. 12. Socinians. 13. Arians. 14. Antitrinitarians. 15. Antiscripturists. 16. Scepticks and Questionists.[42]

The very act of attempting to list the great and seemingly growing multitude of heresies, errors, and sects was a desperate attempt to impose order on the frightening phenomenon of religious schism.

In this climate of intense religious fear and anxiety, religious and political stability thus seemed more fragile and elusive than ever, although outraged writers like Edwards and Pagitt would do their utmost to combat and contain the bewildering onslaught of errors. The spread of heresy in Civil War England,

Proceedings of the Sectaries of this Time (London, 1646), 'To the Christian Reader' and 'The Preface', sigs. A^{v}, A3^{v} ; James Cranford, *Haereseo-Machia* (London, 1645), 6.

[40] Edwards, *Gangraena*, Part 1: title page, 1–3; cf. 41. In the third part of *Gangraena*, Edwards warns that he has 'so large a field to walke in' that he 'might make a fourth part' (Part 3, 218); he never did, of course, although he did still manage to produce the most popular and 'the fullest [Catalogue] that hath yet been made of these times' (Part 1, 3).

[41] *Gangraena*, Part 1: 3.

[42] In *The Third Part of Gangraena*, published in December 1646, Edwards notes that he has catalogued 214 errors in the first and second parts, and that his third part expands upon these to 'neer upon three hundred' (1). See also Edwards, *Gangraena*, Part 1: 15, 18–36; Part 2: 1–3; Part 3: 2–17; and Cranford, *Haereseo-Machia*, noting that London and England 'in so short a space' have 'entertained above 160 errours, many of them damnable' (5).

moreover, seemed particularly alarming because it was primarily taking place within the kingdom—it was an internal invasion, as it were, as new sects and heresies seemed to spring up overnight, fueling faction and generating religious chaos.[43] Heresiographies were consequently often expanded and went through multiple editions as they obsessively catalogued new heresies and innumerable sects rapidly spreading like a gangrene insidiously infecting the body politic and proliferating out of control, as though it were a terrible outbreak of spiritual AIDS.[44] The analogy of heresy as disease may have been ubiquitous in English and continental writings about religious error (and it was certainly widely used during the Middle Ages, as we noted above), but heresiographers in Civil War England applied it with renewed force and vividness as a way of conveying the enormous threat to the health and stability of the body politic as Protestant sects were proliferating. Once again, fear was expressed powerfully in the language and imagery of contamination.

Parliament issued its own series of ordinances and acts aimed at suppressing heresy and fuelling a sense of religious crisis that was endangering godliness and reformation. 'An Ordinance concerning the growth and spreading of Errors, Heresies, and Blasphemies', issued on 4 February 1646/7 by the Presbyterian-dominated Parliament, warned of the deepening crisis, employing the language of plague, contamination, and seduction to reinforce a sense of acute urgency and danger; seeking a day of Public Humiliation, the 'godly leaders of Parliament'

> Have thought fit (lest we partake in other men's sins, and *thereby be in danger to receive of their plagues*) to set forth this our deepe sense of the great dishonour of God, and perilous condition that this Kingdome is in, through the abominable blasphemies, and damnable heresies, vented and spread abroad therein, tending to the subversion of the Faith, contempt of the Ministry and Ordinance of Christ.

The language of the ordinance echoes the words of the Apostle Paul: do not 'be partaker of other men's sins' (1 Timothy 5:22), a reminder that to admit sinners—or heretics since heresy was considered an especially heinous species of sin—into one's company was also to share in their sin and suffer defilement. Moreover, here it was not the king who was dishonored by the subversive and treasonous behavior of heretics (since Parliament was still engaged in conflict with Charles I) but God Himself; 'swift destruction', Parliament's ordinance warned, would befall all the souls who succumb to the 'seducing Spirits' of heretics and sectarians.[45]

[43] See Cranford, *Haereseo-Machia*, 34.

[44] Patrick Collinson has commented on heresy as a 'deadly infection, a kind of spiritual AIDS' in the age of More and Tyndale: 'William Tyndale and the Course of the English Reformation', 82. The comparison surely applies just as well to the prominence of the trope of heresy as deadly infection during the middle decades of the seventeenth century.

[45] C. H. Firth and R. S. Rait (eds.), *Acts and Ordinances of the Interregnum, 1642–1660*, 3 vols. (London, 1911), 1: 913; my emphasis.

By May 1648 Parliament would issue another ordinance for 'the preventing of the growth and spreading of Heresie and Blasphemy' by means of 'Preaching, Teaching, Printing, or Writing', a piece of legislation that threatened obstinate heretics—including those who denied God's omnipotence or omniscience and those who professed anti-Trinitarianism, Arminianism, anabaptism, and mortalism, among other errors—with imprisonment and, in some cases, capital punishment.[46] And in August 1650, the Parliament of the experimental Republic, attempting to reinforce orthodox godliness, issued the Blasphemy Act. Aimed at suppressing the shocking behavior and heresies of the Ranters, who dared to claim, for example, that sin exists only in the imagination, Parliament's Act suggested that this small antinomian and licentious group of individuals 'distempered with sickness, or distracted in brain' was truly a menacing threat to the health and stability of the Commonwealth and human society.[47] Nevertheless, it was the godly anti-heresy writers themselves who did the most during this period to engage in scaremongering and generate a frightening specter of heresy. This was despite the occasional warnings of moderate Presbyterian voices about the shrill rhetoric of heresy hunting, its reliance on fear and the creation of hysteria, its easy conflation of error and heresy ('every Errour is not Haeresie'), and its loose employment of vilifying labels, including 'the abuse of this name [heretic], and throwing it about at random' so 'that *haerisie* and *schisme* are two theologicall scare-crowes, many times set up to scare people and affright them'.[48]

Yet making nuanced discriminations about the dangers posed by different kinds of erroneous opinions—determining which ones fundamentally threatened the church and state and the souls of individuals and which ones were much less menacing—was not the aim of outraged heresy hunters and their alarmist assaults on heretics. Ephraim Pagitt's *Heresiography: or, A Description of the Hereticks and Sectaries of These Latter Times*, first published in 1645 and eventually going through six enlarged editions (the last published in 1661) and three issues (1647, 1648, 1662), is, along with Edward's *Gangraena*, one of the most notable printed assaults on heresy to emerge during the English Revolution; indeed, its title gives us the name of this new, frenetic form of writing attempting to catalogue the proliferation of heresies and heretics during the religious ferment of the 1640s.

Addressing his text to the aldermen and Lord Mayor of London, and appealing to Parliament for assistance, Pagitt reminds them of earlier forms of heresy (for example, sacramentarianism or denying the real presence, for which Anne Askew had been burned a century before), but then he quickly modulates to the new

[46] See *Acts and Ordinances*, ed. Firth and Rait, 1: 1133–6.

[47] *Acts and Ordinances*, ed. Firth and Rait, 2: 409–12.

[48] Richard Vines, *The Authours, Nature, and Danger of Haeresie* (London, 1647), 31 (invoking Augustine: *non omnis error est haeresis*), 49–50; this was a sermon preached before the House of Commons.

dangers of the present decade, drawing upon Revelation 9 and its imagery of eschatological calamities to heighten the sense of immediate urgency and the need for aggressive vigilance: 'Behold suddenly a numerous company of other *Hereticks* stole in upon us like the locusts.'[49] The emotionally charged language of religious fear and caustic metaphors Pagitt employs—that of cannibalism, madness, fire, infestation, monstrosity, lethal poison, or infection—convey his horror, as well as his irrational fears and imaginings, occasioned by the destructive spread of both new and old heresies and heretics within England, including (he asserts) Anabaptists, Brownists, Familists, Antinomians, Arminians, Independents, Socianians, Antitrinitarians, Mortalists, and many others. Pagitt's language and analogies register his anxiety over whether this terrible blight and deadly force can ever be contained—whether, as another contemporary text from this alarming pamphlet war announced, truth could ever proclaim 'Victory against Heresie'.[50] Beset by a swarm of heretics and heresies, England exists in a state of internal warfare and savagery, as Pagitt's disturbing language of cannibalism suggests: men now 'imbrue their hands in the bloud one of another with no lesse inhumanity then Cannibals or Men-eaters, without any reluctation at all; the Sonne against the Father, and the Father against the Son, being involved in a most cruell War without any hopes of peace'.[51]

The taxonomies of popular heresies and sects we find in Pagitt, Edwards, and the writings of other heresy hunters rarely discriminate with any nuance or judiciousness, despite *the appearance* in their books of conceptual precision, objectivity, and orderly presentation. There is no attempt, for example, to assess the differing sects, 'heresies', and 'heretics' in terms of just how gravely each one poses a threat to the Church and state or to individuals; trivial errors, moreover, regularly get conflated with more serious ones. Rather, the taxonomies which appear in heresiographies suggest the overwhelming danger posed by the shattering of religious unity among the godly during the mid-seventeenth century, and the urgent need to make some sense of the nightmarish growth of heresies as a result. They suggest as well the desperate need to impose some kind of order on the chaos of religious fragmentation, even as such large catalogues of errors surely helped to advertise them and, paradoxically, encourage their dissemination, fueling a greater sense of fear and hysteria about heresy.[52] This strategy for attempting to reduce the fear of

[49] Ephraim Pagitt, *Heresiography: Or, A Description of the Heretickes and Sectaries of These Latter Times* (London, 1645), 'The Epistle Dedicatory', sig. A2^{r}; quotations from Pagitt here and elsewhere in this essay are from the first edition. William Lee, the publisher of the third and subsequent editions of Pagitt's work, added Ranters and Quakers to this heresiography after Pagitt's death in 1647.

[50] John Graunt of Bucklersbury, *Truths Victory against Heresie* (London, 1645), in which Truth is depicted as eventually triumphant against the great and multiple forces of Heresy.

[51] *Heresiography*, sig. A4^{r}.

[52] See Edwards's remarks about his need to impose an order on 'a rude and undigested Chaos' of strange opinions: *Gangraena*, Part 1: 4. On cataloguing of errors and their dissemination, see Barry

heresy—cataloguing its many and changing permutations—only called attention to it further, intensifying anxiety. It was this new and frightening specter of heresy that Milton referred to in 1644 as the 'fantastic terrors of sect and schism'.[53]

In Pagitt's alarmist account of heresies and heretical books, contagious texts by the separatist Roger Williams and Milton the Divorcer get indiscriminately and hastily lumped together ('for books, *vide* the bloody Tenet, witnesse a tractate of divorce in which the bonds are let loose to inordinate lust'), along with Richard Overton's *Mans Mortalitie* (a book which argues that 'the soul is laid asleepe from the houre of death unto the houre of judgement', the heresy of mortalism condemned in More's *Utopia* and found in Milton).[54] The dramatic growth of heresy means not only the collapse of the social and religious order, but the disintegration of sexual mores and boundaries (since heresy was often sexualized in the early modern period), an obsession in Thomas More's unbridled assaults on heretics more than a century earlier and in Thomas Edwards's frenetic writing against licentious, deviant sectarian behavior.[55] And as traditional religious authorities lose control and disintegrate, so does any kind of religious order, social hierarchy, and regulated scriptural exegesis, resulting in seditious violence and blasphemous behavior: now, it seems, anyone can preach, not only women who preach regularly causing 'confusion and disorder in Church-matters both of opinions and practices', but also 'Shoo-makers, Coblers, Buttonmakers, Hostlers and such like... expound the holy Scriptures, intrude into our Pulpits, and vent strange doctrine, tending to faction, sedition, and blasphemie'.[56]

In the eyes of Civil War heresiographers, the world of religion, however, was not only confused, fragmented, and turned upside down. It had become a strange, alien place—'a world of strange errours' in the words of Thomas Edwards—where any kind of religious doctrine, no matter how extreme, could flourish.[57] In a world where heretics themselves were not just strange but out of bounds, there were no longer any clearly defined boundaries for religious behavior—all coherence was indeed gone. An England overrun with a vast number of heresies and new sects, encouraged by monstrous proponents of religious toleration, was, in Edwards's view, a land where one encountered (as in the case of Parliament's own New Model Army infected with heresies) 'strange monsters, having their heads of Enthusiasme,

Reay, *Radical Religion in the English Revolution*, ed. J. F. McGregor and B. Reay (Oxford: Oxford University Press, 1984), 14; and *Histories of Heresy in Early Modern Europe*, ed. Laursen, 8.

[53] See John Milton, *Areopagitica*, in *Complete Prose Works of John Milton*, general editor Don M. Wolfe, 8 vols. (New Haven, CT: Yale University Press, 1953–82), 2: 554.

[54] Pagitt, *Heresiography*, sig. A3^{v}. See also Norman T. Burns, *Christian Mortalism from Tyndale to Milton* (Cambridge, MA: Harvard University Press, 1972).

[55] For More, see e.g. *CW*, 6: 165, 286; 8: 141, 164, 181, 251, 359.

[56] Edwards, *Gangraena*, Part 1: 84; Pagitt, *Heresiography*, sig. A3^{v}.

[57] Edwards, *Gangraena*, Part 1: 3.

their bodies of Antinomianisme, their thighs of Familisme, their leggs and feet of Anabaptisme, their hands of Arminianisme, and Libertinisme, as the great vein going thorow the whole'.[58] This specter of menacing heresy figured as a monstrous body was meant to shock and unsettle godly readers: to make them fearful and alarmed by what seemed like a rapidly changing, unsettled world where religion was not only disintegrating but taking on new and unanticipated manifestations and combinations. Such images of monstrosity convey deepening anxieties about a religious world exploding, falling apart, and metamorphosing in unprecedented ways. At the same time, this language of monstrosity, which conveys the culture's darkest fantasies about heretics, also served to dehumanize heretics—making the violent rhetorical assaults of heretic hunters appear more justified and, indeed, a natural response to an unnatural calamity.

The trope of protean change employed by Edwards conveys the anxiety and lack of control felt so acutely by orthodox Puritan writers during this period, especially their sense of how difficult it was to grasp the slippery behavior and proliferations of the new sectarians and heretics:

> They, *Proteus*-like, turne themselves into all shapes and forms, and according to severall occasions and times, have different humours and tempers, sometimes complying so that one would thinke all difference would quickly be at an end and they were ours, sometimes so far off and back again, as causes wonder and amazement in the beholders.[59]

In the unstable and rapidly changing religious world of England during the 1640s, Proteus had assumed new powers, making it difficult to get a handle on all the multitude of sectaries who had suddenly emerged and all the heresies and errors they were generating. In this world of dizzying religious change the term 'innovation' was itself fluid and subject to new applications. If Archbishop William Laud and his followers had been condemned by Puritans for being 'great Innovators' (a codeword for encouraging High Church ceremonies) who aimed to weaken Protestant unity and were generating fear and horror, now it was the new, audacious sectaries who had become 'great Innovatours, as changeable as the Moon, bringing into their Churches new opinions daily, new practices, taking away the old used in all Reformed Churches, and substituting new'.[60] The undisciplined size of Edwards's *Gangraena* itself reflects the protean nature of his subject: error completely out of control, assuming ever new forms and shapes, and overrunning the kingdom.

[58] Edwards, *Gangraena*, Part 1: 16–17. On the bitter struggle for toleration in relation to the spread of heresy during the Civil War years, see David Loewenstein, 'Toleration and the Specter of Heresy in Milton's England', in *Milton and Toleration*, ed. Sharon Achinstein and Elizabeth Sauer (Oxford: Oxford University Press, 2007), 45–71.

[59] Edwards, *Gangraena*, Part 1: 41.

[60] Edwards, *Gangraena*, Part 1: 51; see also Cranford, *Haereseo-Machia*, 9.

Fears of heresy raging out of control and infecting the nation like a contagious plague were likewise voiced during the volatile religious and political years of the Interregnum when further sectarianism developed, including the most significant heretical movement to emerge during this period: the terrifying Quakers who rapidly spread from the north to the south of England (and beyond) during the 1650s, generating fierce hostility. The heated religious imagination of godly Puritans fueled one of the most acute political and religious crises over heretical behavior and symbolism during seventeenth-century England: the debates in Parliament in late 1656 over the alarming behavior of James Nayler, the flamboyant and charismatic Quaker leader who, riding into Bristol on a horse in October 1656, had dared, according to hostile observers, to re-enact with a small group of enthusiastic followers Christ's entry into Jerusalem on Psalm Sunday. Recorded by the diarist Thomas Burton, these intense debates reveal the degree to which irrational fears of heresy and blasphemy (the two were regularly conflated in the period), as well as anxieties about the dangers of liberty of conscience, could result in bitter intolerance and savagery.[61] Nayler's gesture prompted many furious MPs, as well as Richard Cromwell (Oliver's son), to cry out for nothing less than the death penalty.[62] Indeed, the medieval statute *De heretico comburendo*, which More invoked in his anti-heresy campaign, was by no means forgotten during the Civil War and Interregnum years. It was invoked and discussed in these heated parliamentary debates over just how severely to punish the 'horrid blasphemer' Nayler for his egregious behavior, and for making himself nothing less than 'a traitor' by setting himself up 'as a Saviour'.[63]

In the eyes of orthodox Puritans, Quakers threatening ministry and magistracy were a menace whose immediate danger the most alarming analogies could barely convey: Quakerism seemed 'as infectious as the plague' or as dangerous as leprosy or like a poison which was spreading to many others; regarded as enemies of the state, the Quakers swarming all over the nation in 'every county' and 'every parish' were 'vipers' who had 'crept into the bowels of [the] Commonwealth, and the government too'.[64] Aggressive sectarianism meant that England was becoming a

[61] Thomas Burton, *The Diary of Thomas Burton*, ed. John T. Rutt, 4 vols. (London, 1828). Parliament spent eleven days in December 1656 debating Nayler's crimes.

[62] For Oliver Cromwell's son's support of the death penalty for Nayler, see Burton, *Diary*, ed. Rutt, 1: 126.

[63] During the heated Nayler debates, one member of Parliament observed: 'I know no law or statute which has repealed that law *de heretico comburendo*': Burton, *Diary*, ed. Rutt, 1: 141. Another MP in the Nayler debates argued that 'you cannot go to less than the punishment by death. It is death by the common law, blasphemy and heresy, and it is true till 2d *Henry* IV' (118); for further references to the medieval anti-heresy law, see also 119, 123, 133, 137. For Nayler's treason, see 28, also 60–1.

[64] Burton, *Diary*, ed. Rutt, 1: 155; one MP recommended 'perpetual imprisonment' so that Nayler 'not spread his leprosy' (98; cf. 35–6). On Nayler spreading poison, see 74; on Quakers as vipers, see 96. On Quakers perceived as enemies of the state, see also Ralph Josselin, *The Diary of Ralph Josselin, 1616–1683*, ed. Alan Macfarlane (London: The British Academy, 1976), 349 (entry for 15 July 1655).

particularly fertile breeding ground for heresy—'the great nursery of blasphemies and heresies'.[65] Moreover, in the eyes of hostile observers, Nayler confirmed once again the association of heretics with seductive theatricalism, powers which needed to be exposed and stripped away by the state: the Quaker leader, who had performed 'a horrid piece of pageantry', was pronounced 'a grand imposter, and a great seducer of the people'.[66] Nayler's shocking behavior was startling evidence that only the most punitive measures would stop the pestilent spread of this major radical sect, the largest and most successful of the English Revolution;[67] 'let him not longer infect the nation', urged one MP, furious that the Quaker leader had tried 'to make himself equal with God'.[68]

During the intense debates over the Nayler episode, some orthodox godly MPs, looking to the Bible for guidance, invoked the law of Leviticus 24 which recommended punishing blasphemers by stoning them to death;[69] some invoked the authority of the Blasphemy Act of 1650;[70] and a few invoked and debated the authority of the medieval statute *De heretico comburendo*, an act not officially repealed until 1677.[71] Because the Nayler episode was so disturbing to orthodox Puritans, it prompted enraged MPs to seek any kind of legal or scriptural authority to punish, as severely as possible, the shocking and spectacular behavior of this notorious Quaker whose symbolic actions seemed beyond the pale and were misconstrued. Most godly participants in the debates were outraged that Nayler had 'assumed the gesture, words, names, and attributes of our Saviour Christ' and had made himself God. Only a handful of less hot-headed ones, worried about meting out a savage punishment, observed about Nayler that 'he hath not said he is Christ, but only a sign';[72] in other words, his symbolic gesture illustrated Quaker doctrine that Christ is within all men and women and that he is a prophet or sign of the Second Coming of Christ. In the end, Nayler did indeed suffer a brutal punishment: he was whipped, pilloried, and placed in solitary confinement; he

On Quakerism in general during the Interregnum, see Barry Reay, *The Quakers and the English Revolution* (London: Temple Smith, 1985).

[65] Burton, *Diary*, ed. Rutt, 1: 86. [66] Burton, *Diary*, ed. Rutt, 1: 72, 79.

[67] The Quakers may have reached as many as 60,000 by the time of the Restoration: Reay, *Quakers and the English Revolution*, 27.

[68] Burton, *Diary*, ed. Rutt, 1: 39–40.

[69] As one member of the debates observed: 'I think that law made against blasphemy in *Leviticus*, is as binding to us at this day, as surely as that against murder, which follows in the next verse', a reference to Lev. 24:16–17 (Burton, *Diary*, ed. Rutt, 1: 113); for Leviticus's law, see also 55, 75, 87, 99–100, 103, 112, 121, 128–9, 132–3, 134.

[70] Burton, *Diary*, ed. Rutt, 1: 29, 38, 125, 146; see also 124 where one MP's language (i.e. that Nayler's 'principles and practices are destructive to human society') echoes the Blasphemy Act.

[71] See John Marshall, *Locke, Toleration and Early Enlightenment Culture* (Cambridge: Cambridge University Press, 2006), 126–7, on the statute during the Restoration.

[72] Burton, *Diary*, ed. Rutt, 1: 24, 151; on Nayler as a 'sign', see also 48, 65.

was bored through the tongue with a red-hot iron and branded with a 'B' on his forehead for blasphemer.[73] Nayler could have faced even more savage punishment—execution—if some MPs had gotten their way (the death penalty was narrowly defeated by 96 to 82 votes),[74] but the punishment he did receive expressed the fury of MPs at the spread of sectarianism, anger at Oliver Cromwell for not coming down hard enough on disruptive religious radicals during the Interregnum, and primordial fears that heretics were capable of destroying the political, religious, and social order.

The examples and texts I have discussed in this essay—late medieval anti-heresy legislation in England, More's polemical warfare against Lutheran and evangelical heresy, and the exacerbation of dark imaginings about new heretics during the English Revolution—illustrate how the convergence of fears of heresy, the treatment of heresy as treason, and the heated religious imagination could generate enormous anxieties, savagery, and bitter religious contention and polarization. As I have attempted to show, there are striking continuities between the late medieval and early modern periods with regard to heresy, treason, fears, and the unbridled religious imagination. At the same time, each of the moments of religious crisis I have highlighted needs to be understood in terms of its particular cultural and historical contexts and pressures. Yet as we continue in the twenty-first century to struggle with a world unsettled by religious fears, suspicion, extremism, and intolerance, we can see in the examples I have chosen to consider the makings of the disturbing legacy we have inherited.

FURTHER READING

Forrest, Ian. *The Detection of Heresy in Late Medieval England* (Oxford: Clarendon Press, 2005)

Laursen, John Christian (ed.). *Histories of Heresy in Early Modern Europe: For, Against, Beyond Persecution and Toleration* (Basingstoke: Palgrave Macmillan, 2002)

Moore, R. I. *The Formation of a Persecuting Society: Authority and Deviance in Western Europe 950–1250*, 2nd edn (Oxford: Blackwell 2007)

Simpson, James. *Burning to Read: English Fundamentalism and Its Reformation Opponents* (Cambridge, MA: Harvard University Press, 2007)

[73] Burton, *Diary*, ed. Rutt, 1: 96–8; *Journal of the House of Commons*, 7: 468.

[74] Burton, *Diary*, ed. Rutt, 1: 152.

CHAPTER 16

NAUGHTY PRINTED BOOKS

DAVID SCOTT KASTAN

In an exhibition on censorship in the library at Princeton in 1984, the first case presented paired pages of what are generally taken to be the poles of the discussion: the *Index librorum prohibitorum* and Milton's *Areopagitica*.[1] The Catholic Church's official effort (first issued in 1559) to ban certain books was juxtaposed with the stirring Euripidean defense of the Protestant writer's tract: 'This is true Liberty when free born men / Having to advise the public may speak free.'[2] It is not a surprising contrast. Indeed it articulates the familiar binary that has commonly served to define the very nature of the interaction we define as censorship: the Catholic Church as a repressive agent of authority; the heroic individual as the dissenting voice of freedom.

But the opposition is more a function of a modern desire than of historical fact. Even beyond the unexamined Protestant triumphalism implicit in the juxtaposition, which Milton, of course, would have himself endorsed—'the whole Discourse propos'd will be a certaine testimony, if not a Trophey', to all those 'who wish and promote their Countries liberty' (487)—the real problem is that the two texts do not so much display this reassuring opposition as demonstrate their unnerving similarity. Both, one might say with only minimal perversity, are documents of censorship.

Milton, of course, has understandably been read as censorship's first great opponent, with *Areopagitica* as the foundational text of a modern notion of freedom of expression. (At most American law schools, the always popular course on

[1] Similarly, see William Zeisel's catalogue of an exhibition at the New York Public Library: *Censorship: 500 Years of Conflict* (New York: New York Public Library, 1984), which, while not so directly juxtaposing the two books, uses them similarly to represent the polar positions: the *Index* as 'the first list of prohibited books published by the Roman Catholic Church' (30); *Areopagitica* as 'the English speaking world's first great statement urging freedom of expression' (55).

[2] John Milton, *Areopagitica* (London, 1644), title page. Further references are cited parenthetically from *The Complete Prose Works of John Milton*, ed. Ernest Sirluck, general editor Don M. Wolfe, vol. 2 (New Haven, CT: Yale University Press, 1959).

the First Amendment begins with Milton's tract, usually ignoring or explaining away as an inescapable but inessential historical constraint the fact that his notion of a free press is tendentiously limited.) Within the sphere of Protestant sectarianism, Milton is happy to endorse the gains to truth from 'much arguing, much writing, many opinions' (554). But it is only within the shared space of Protestant doctrine that this is so. Beyond that he is hardly open-minded: 'I mean not tolerated Popery, and open superstition, which as it extirpats [i.e. destroys] all religions and civill supremacies, so it self should be extirpat' (565). 'Opinion', may be, as he says, 'but knowledge in the making' (554); nonetheless, clearly some opinions are beyond the pale, not knowledge *in potentia* but existing obstacles to truth—and for these 'the fire and the executioner will be found the timeliest and most effectuall remedy' (569).

The seeming contradiction within the tract is less an inconsistency in Milton's argument than a misunderstanding of it—or, what is in fact the same thing, a miscontextualizing of it. For a set of overdetermined reasons, we have tended to consider *Areopagitica* a political document rather than a religious tract. It is more likely to be viewed as, in Catherine Belsey's words, 'one of the founding and canonical texts of modern liberalism'[3] than as an idiosyncratic expression of early modern religious polemic. Unquestionably it has taken its place in the canon of modern liberalism, but that has more to do with the intentions of those who have established that canon than those of Milton himself. Milton, however, was not a Habermasian *avant la lettre*, interested in the promotion of the free expression of ideas as a necessary precondition of critical debate, and the tract cannot quite be a 'celebration of a public sphere', as David Norbrook has termed it,[4] as it would fiercely restrict what is available for debate and contestation only to the opinions and beliefs of the godly. In spite of his genuine opposition to monopolistic publishing practices and to pre-publication licensing, Milton's fundamental commitment is not to *open* debate, but to debate open only within a predetermined field of acceptability, even if that field is wider than what crown or clergy would allow. And it is on the *grounds* of the exclusion, not the *fact* of it, that he reveals himself as something other than a proto-liberal.

Milton's desire, which *Areopagitica* both announces and would help bring about, is not to establish a public sphere of rational, critical debate, but, rather, to form—or reform—a godly nation in which 'all the Lords people are become prophets' (556). That 'all', however, is less inclusive than it promises. Certainly Milton does

[3] Catherine Belsey, *John Milton: Language, Gender, Power* (Oxford: Basil Blackwell, 1988), 78. That Milton's tract does not easily fulfill the role historians of free speech have asked it to play has long been known to Miltonists, certainly as early as David Masson's *Life of John Milton*, 7 vols. (London: Macmillan, 1871–80). See Michael Wilding, 'Milton's *Areopagitica*: Liberty for the Sects', *Prose Studies*, 9 (1986), 7–38.

[4] David Norbrook, *Writing the English Republic* (Cambridge: Cambridge University Press, 1999), 118–19.

commit himself to extending the range of Protestant thought that can be incorporated, invoking a 'spirituall architecture' that, like the building of the Temple of Solomon, achieves its excellence in spite of the 'many schisms and many dissections made in the quarry and in the timber' (555). Indeed its very 'perfection consists in this, that out of many moderat varieties and brotherly dissimilitudes that are not vastly disproportionall arises the goodly and gracefull symmetry that commends the whole pile and structure' (555). The godly nation must include the 'schismaticks and sectaries' that are 'cry'd out against', but the 'mansion house of liberty' (554) is not quite as open and hospitable as modern readers might wish. Pointedly, the 'dissimilitudes' he welcomes are only those that are 'brotherly', those that are already related, even as each is distinct, in a common commitment to the godly nation.[5] Dissimilitudes, however, that are not 'brotherly', or that are 'vastly disproportional', cannot participate in this 'perfection'. Indeed these are exactly what must be 'extirpat', since what 'is impious or evil absolutely either against faith or maners no law can possibly permit, that intends not to unlaw it self' (565).

For Milton, then, the argument for censorship is inevitable and unembarrassing. It doesn't betray or compromise his principles; it emerges from and confirms them. To the degree he is interested in freedom of expression it is only insofar as such freedom advances the religio-political project for which he speaks, 'the reforming of Reformation it self' (553). What obstructs or threatens that project is readily condemned. Should a book prove 'a Monster', he says, 'who denies, but that it was justly burnt, or sunk into the Sea' (505). The exception to his tolerance, that which proves 'a Monster', is, then, actually what defines and naturalizes his fundamental commitment, even as it disqualifies his tract from serving as an example of what it never was intended to be.

But perhaps it is always thus. Ironically (or is it 'necessarily'?), the logic of his exclusion exactly reproduces the logic of the Catholic *Index*. The 1559 *Index* was not the first Catholic effort to restrict access to certain books (the honor for that probably goes to a 1479 bull of Sixtus V authorizing sanctions against the publishing, selling, or reading of heretical books in Cologne),[6] but it was the first to be prepared in Rome and whose scope was intended to be universal. Such Indices were continuously updated and issued until 1948. While the *Index* obviously did not offer itself up as a defense of press freedom, in fact it might have made virtually the same argument as Milton does in *Areopagitica*. Indeed Milton's tract, rather than being taken, as it usually is, as the imperfect prototype of the argument for a free

[5] See Milton's call for 'one generall and brotherly search after Truth' in John Milton, *Complete Works*, ed. Sirluck, 2: 554; William Kolbrenner's essay on the tract in his *Milton's Warring Angels* (Cambridge: Cambridge University Press, 1997), 11–27, brilliantly takes up this aspect of Milton's argument.

[6] See Gigliola Fragnito (ed.), *Church, Censorship, and Culture in Early Modern Italy*, trans. Adrian Belton (Cambridge: Cambridge University Press, 2001).

press, could in fact be taken as a sophisticated example of the primitive argument for censorship that the early Catholic Indices make.

Milton's confident justification that certain ideas are so thoroughly hostile to the values of the community that, in order to protect that community, they must be 'extirpat', is exactly the logic of the Catholic censors. Even before the first *Index* was issued, an English Catholic answered the claim that Protestant books should be allowed on the seemingly reasonable grounds that by knowing what is said 'men may for their own surety better choose and hold the right way', with the counter-claim that this would be true only if 'it were now doubtful... whether the Church of Christ were in the right rule of doctrine or not'. But, as it is certain that 'Christ's church hath the true doctrine already', there is no point, and indeed much risk, in allowing the pointless debate.[7] This is Thomas More, in his *Dialogue Concerning Heresies* (1529), articulating the position that the Catholic Church has used since the first *Index* to justify the restriction of access to certain books. But the Protestant Milton, exactly like the Catholic More, is certain about 'true doctrine', and neither is tolerant of the expression of ideas that contradict his conviction of it. Milton may insist that what 'purifies us is triall and triall is by what is contrary' (515), but both he and More would rule out of court what is truly contrary and not contiguous.

Nonetheless, the purpose of this introduction is not to disparage Milton (though it is, if only incidentally, to remind us of how unstable is the position he has been asked to fill in various genealogies of modern liberalism). It is, rather, to attempt to undo some of the easy oppositions that have structured most of the scholarly discussion on the subject of censorship: Catholic versus Protestant, state versus individual, repression versus freedom. All of these play their role in an undeniably appealing, whiggish history of liberty and toleration, but it is not a history that has much purchase in early modern England.

Ages of faith in which salvation is held to depend upon nice points of doctrine do not produce compelling documents of toleration, and a Protestant England was no more likely to do so than was a Catholic Rome. Christopher Hill points to *Areopagitica* as 'one of many tracts... glorifying the freedom of the press',[8] but Hill is wrong about both claims. *Areopagitica* does not glorify the freedom of the press, nor are there 'many' others that do.[9] Indeed I know only two in English (though no doubt there are others): the earliest by an obscure Baptist, Leonard Busher,

[7] Thomas More, *A Dialogue Concerning Heresies*, ed. T. M. C. Lawler, Germain Marc'hadour, and Richard Marius, 2 Parts, in *The Complete Works of St Thomas More*, vol. 6 (New Haven, CT: Yale University Press, 1981), Part 1: 345–6.

[8] Christopher Hill, 'Censorship and English Literature', in *The Collected Essays of Christopher Hill* (Amherst, MA: University of Massachusetts Press, 1985), 50.

[9] Deborah Shuger similarly notes Hill's willful distortion, claiming that there are 'no principled defenses of freedom of the press', in her provocative *Censorship and Cultural Sensibility: The Regulation of Language in Tudor-Stuart England* (Philadelphia: University of Pennsylvania Press, 2006), 1. Shuger argues that the logic of early English censorship is not primarily to restrict heresy or treason but to promote civility by limiting corrosive defamation.

published first in Amsterdam in 1614 and reprinted in 1646, which insists that it should 'bee lawfull for every person or persons, yea Jewes and Papists, to write, dispute, confer, and reason, print and publish any matter touching Religion, either for or against whomsoever', with the only proviso being that 'they alledge no Fathers for proof of any point of religion, but only the holy Scriptures'.[10] The other is a Leveller petition in early 1649 that argues that it is incumbent upon the King and Parliament 'to hear all voices and judgments, which they can never do but by given freedom to the Press'.[11] The argument protesting 'even the least restraint upon the Press' was motivated less by some generalized commitment to the free exchange of ideas than by a not unreasonable fear of the government's efforts to prohibit the dissenters' own manifestoes. But both of these calls for freedom of the press exist within broad tolerationist programs, revealing again how uneasily the example of Milton fits within any history of modern liberalism and perhaps distracts us from what we should be looking at as we consider early modern censorship.

Historians of early modern England have not been loath to engage the issue of censorship, but the scholarly debate has largely circled around the question of how efficiently censorship in early modern England worked. Was it the ruthless and robust agent of an authoritarian regime, as the oft-cited examples of John Stubbs or William Prynne might suggest, or was it the far more desultory activity of a state, as Blair Worden has written, that 'lacked not merely the power, but the inclination, to impose conditions of writing that can helpfully be called "repressive" '?[12] My own sense is that the truth lies somewhere in between—or, rather, *overall* the truth lies somewhere in between, but that in any particular case of censorship the truth might fall anywhere on the scale between draconian repression and a kind of 'benign censorship', in Anthony Milton's phrase (as, say, in Daniel Featley's 1625 licensing of William Crompton's *Saint Austins Summes*, after which Featley said, 'although I found many errors... for which I might have rejected the book', he 'chose rather *to purge those errors, and mend those faults*', clearly in this case working more as an advocate than an antagonist).[13] Therefore, rather than try to articulate some more

[10] Leonard Busher, *Religions Peace* (London, 1646), sig. D3^{r-v}.

[11] Don M. Wolfe (ed.), *Leveller Manifestoes of the Puritan Revolution* (New York: Humanities Press, 1967), 328–9.

[12] A. Blair Worden, 'Literature and Political Censorship in Early Modern England', in *Too Mighty to be Free: Censorship and the Press in Britain and the Netherlands*, ed. A. C. Duke and C. Tamse, Britain and the Netherlands, 9 (Zutphen: Walburg Press, 1988), 48. For enormously valuable overviews of the principles and procedures of early modern English censorship, see David Loades, *Politics, Censorship and the English Reformation* (London and New York: Pinter, 1991) and three volumes by Cyndia Susan Clegg: *Press Censorship in Elizabethan England* (Cambridge: Cambridge University Press, 1997); *Press Censorship in Jacobean England* (Cambridge: Cambridge University Press, 2001); and *Press Censorship in Caroline England* (Cambridge: Cambridge University Press, 2008).

[13] See A. Milton, 'Licensing Censorship, and Religious Orthodoxy', *The Historical Journal*, 41 (1998), 629; see also Arnold Hunt, 'Licensing and Religious Censorship in Early Modern England',

precise middle way that might at once acknowledge the chilling authoritarian impulses of early modern censorship while also allowing for its unsystematic and often inefficient practices (though a useful synecdoche could be found for such an enterprise in the example of the Catholic Robert Southwell, executed for treason in February 1595, while his book, *St. Peter's Complaint*, was licensed and published in April of that year and reprinted thirteen times in the next forty years), I want to suggest that it might prove more useful to ask a different question about censorship in early modern England, one that seems to me logically prior: not 'were they any good at it?' but 'what did they think they were trying to do?'

The simple answer is, of course, that they (putting aside for a moment the question of exactly who 'they' might be) were trying to prevent certain books from circulating. My title here comes from one such effort, a royal proclamation dated 16 November 1538 in which the King expresses his 'high discontention and displeasure' at 'the sundry contentions and sinister opinions' that, by virtue of 'wrong teaching and naughty printed books', have 'increased and grown within this his realm of England... contrary to the true faith, reverence and due observation of such sacraments, sacramentals, laudable rites and ceremonies as heretofore have been used and accustomed within the Church of England'.[14] In response to the threat posed by the circulation of these naughty printed books, Henry orders that no one 'of what estate, degree, or condition soever' shall '(without his majesty's special license) transport... into this his realm of England, or any other his grace's dominions, any manner books printed in the English tongue, nor sell, give, utter, or publish any such books from henceforth to be brought into this realm'. In addition, the proclamation orders that 'no person or persons in this realm shall from henceforth print any book in the English tongue, unless upon examination made by some of his grace's Privy Council, or other such as his highness shall appoint, they shall have license to do so' (Hughes and Larkin, 1: 271–2). Offenders against this order risked not only Henry's 'most high displeasure and indignation' but also the forfeit of all 'their goods and chattels and have imprisonment at his grace's will' (Hughes and Larkin, 1: 271).

This was not the first attempt by the crown in England to stop the spread of 'naughty books'. Arguably that distinction belongs to a proclamation in the second year of the reign of Henry V that orders the arrest of 'all them which hold out any error or heresies, as Lollards, and which be their... Common writers of such Books, as well as of [the] sermons'.[15] It is not even the first effort in the reign of

in *Literature and Censorship in Renaissance England*, ed. Andrew Hadfield (Houndsmill, Basingstoke: Palgrave, 2001), 127–48.

14 Paul L. Hughes and James F. Larkin (eds.), *Tudor Royal Proclamations* (New Haven and London: Yale University Press, 1964), 1: 270. Hereafter cited by volume and page number parenthetically in the text.

15 *SR*, 2 Henry V, 1. c. 7 (2.182–3). In 1382, the first censoring proclamation was issued against the (unnamed) Lollards, prohibiting the preaching of heresy in 'open places'. See Nicholas Watson,

Henry VIII. That came in March of 1529, nominally continuing the campaign against 'heretics and Lollards', but by which it is clear it now means Lutherans, a proclamation of interest not least for its list of fifteen books that it orders 'prohibited', as well as for its optimistic demands that anyone having any of these will 'bring the said book or work to the bishop of the diocese without concealment or fraud', and, even, that anyone knowing someone who has these books 'shall detect them to the said bishop, all favor and affection laid aside' (Hughes and Larkin, 1: 185). But the 1538 proclamation is the first to name the object of its censoring efforts 'naughty printed books'. And it is with a discussion of that phrase that I want to begin ('yet once more', as Milton might say), for perhaps in discovering what might make a printed book naughty we can get a clearer sense of the motives of early modern censorship.

The word is an interesting one, with a range of negative meanings from the proclamation's seemingly intended 'sinful' or 'wicked', which is how it is also used, for example, in Humphrey Gifford's poetic 'Will or Testament', where he renounces his 'wicked thoughts, / [His] vile and naughty waies'[16] (the three adjectives virtually synonymous in a conventional display of *copia*), to other, weaker forms of disparagement. Nicholas Udall, the Tudor translator of Erasmus's *Apophthegms* (1542) has the Dutchman say that self-indulgent men suffer not only bodily harm but also 'the tormentes of their owne naughtye conscience' (sig. A4r), but the thirteenth chapter of Christopher Langton's *Introduction into Physicke* (1545) has a chapter entitled 'Of naughty flegme' (f. xlv), while another early medical textbook advises against using leeches that were 'founde in noughty waters'[17] (sig. O2v). Philip Stubbes protests the behavior of certain dishonest wool merchants who knowingly sell 'naughty wool',[18] a usage like that in a statute of 1543 that prohibits the weaving of substandard woolen blankets and 'putting the same naughty ware to sale secretly' (*SR*, 34 & 35 Henry VIII c. 10 § 2). In the 1535 Coverdale Bible, Jeremiah's vision of fig baskets compares the wholesome figs of the offerings of those who will receive God's blessing with 'the very naughty figs' (24:2) that God refuses as unfit for consumption. Shakespeare's fool in the midst of the

'Censorship and Cultural Change in late Medieval England: Vernacular Theology, The Oxford Translation Debate, and Arundel's Constitutions of 1409', *Speculum*, 70 (1995), 822–64. For a broader consideration of censorship in the period 1350–1550, see James Simpson, *Reform and Cultural Revolution*, The Oxford English Literary History, Vol. 2: *1350–1547* (Oxford: Oxford University Press, 2002), 333–43. See also Kathryn Kerby-Fulton, *Books Under Suspicion: Censorship and Tolerance of Revelatory Writing in Late Medieval England* (Notre Dame, IN: University of Notre Dame Press, 2006) for an important argument both about the impossibility of effective censorship even in an age of manuscript circulation, as well as a challenge to the near exclusivity of Lollardy in scholarly accounts of intellectual radicalism in the period.

16 Humphrey Gifford, *A Posie of Gilloflowers* (London, 1580), sig. L1r.

17 Guy de Chauliac, *The Questionary of Cyrurgens*, trans. Robert Copeland (London, 1542), sig. O2^{v}.

18 Philip Stubbes, *Anatomy of Abuses* (London, 1583) 2, sig. D7^{v}.

storm urges Lear not to tear off his clothes, as it is 'a naughty night to swim in' (3.4.107). 'Naughty' animals were uncontrollable, like Angel Day's 'naughty' ox that seems regularly to have gored his cow,[19] and some disagreeable plants might also be thought naughty, like some species of marigolds which are, in Henry Lyte's phrase, 'both in their leaves and flowers of a naughtie strong & unpleasaunt savour'.[20] Cupid is inevitably a 'naughty boy', a usage that leads to its modern weak form in which it usually means something not much more critical than 'mischievous'.

It is, then, a word that from its earliest uses quickly begins to diminish in force, deflating the degree of censoriousness even as its strong meaning remains available. Arguably the very breadth of its semantic field makes it a poor choice for the adjective chosen to name the quality that would be eradicated. Still, the usage in this context is hardly unique. In 1550, in Johannes Carrion's *Three Bokes of Chronicles... gathered with great diligence of the best authors*, there is a short account of the recantation of Edward Crome at Paul's Cross on June 27, 1546, 'affirming openly that he hade bene seduced by noughty books'. In 1554, the London diarist Henry Machyn notes that John Day was sent to the Tower on October 16 of that year 'for printing of noythy books',[21] the Protestant works he published from the clandestine 'Michael Wood' press. In both cases, the word must mean almost exactly what it did in the 1538 proclamation: that is, 'wicked', or more precisely, 'heretical' (though in the case of Day the particular doctrinal wickedness exactly reverses what it was for Crome). But in both of these later examples, it is easy enough to assign a value to it if not a precise meaning, and in neither case does the account have the force of law.

In the proclamation, however, it does (or, rather, almost does, though the exact relation of royal prerogative to statutory authority is complex and can be seen to be, not entirely successfully, negotiated in the notorious 1539 'Act that Proclamations Made by the King Shall be Obeyed'[22]). But whatever the exact legal status of proclamations, if only from their status as royal writ one might expect a precision that 'naughty' here seems to unsettle. In fact its meaning seems contextually clear enough; that is, what sorts of texts it wishes to prohibit can be determined from the context, and we can reason backwards to determine what the word must mean. In its focus on 'wrong teaching and naughty printed books', it is not unlike the aforementioned statute of 1414 that would seek out the writers of heretical sermons and books. The specific heresy is different: not the Lollardy that the

[19] Angel Day, *The English Secretorie* (London, 1592), sig. U2^{v}.

[20] Rembert Dodoens, *A Niewe Herball*, trans. Henry Lyte (London, 1578), sig. P4^{v}.

[21] Henry Machyn, *The Diary of Henry Machyn*, ed. John Gough Nichols (London: Camden Society, 1848), 72. I am grateful to Tom Freeman for this reference and for his overall contribution to my understanding of the issues in this essay.

[22] Hughes and Larkin, 1: 545–9; see M. L. Bush, 'The Act of Proclamations: A Reinterpretation', *The American Journal of Legal History*, 27 (1983), 33–53.

1414 statute names but here the 'Anabaptists and Sacramentaries' (Hughes and Larkin, 1: 270). But if it is the seriousness of the threat of heresy that motivates the proclamation, one might ask why choose a word that is neither clear nor particularly common. (A quick search on EEBO turned up 377 uses of the word between 1535 and 1550, while there were 3,214 of 'wicked'.)

There were alternatives available. The 1529 proclamation against heresy refers to 'erroneous books' (Hughes and Larkin, 1: 182), as does a 1536 order demanding the surrender of writings by John Fisher (Hughes and Larkin, 1: 235). These declare their opposition to the prohibited writings on the ground that they are incorrect (though the 'error' in the two examples is a function of contrasting doctrinal commitments), but perhaps also on the ground, as the word's etymology suggests, that they circulate (from the Latin *errare*, to wander). The 1538 proclamation, however, stakes its opposition on the grounds that the books are wicked, moving the discourse into a different register, from reason to morality (though few would admit an absolute difference), and also exploiting the word's etymology, here as 'no thing'. But if it is no thing or nothing, in its available sense of 'worthless', then it should need no prohibition, and if it is 'nought' at all, there should be nothing to prohibit. It is, then, not merely that there has been an amelioration of the word's pejorative sense, a common enough linguistic process, but that even in its pejorative sense the word does not clearly suggest why what is named is objectionable, only that it is. 'Naughty' modifying 'books' always means 'wicked', but the fact that it so easily could carry any of the word's many weaker depreciative forms does not allow the word to carry much specific content. 'Naughty' books are prohibited, and the elusiveness of the word's meaning inhibits any discussion about what makes them so. What makes them naughty can only be inferred from the efforts to ban them, yet arguably, in the vertiginous religious world of the late 1530s, this might be its greatest advantage.

Focusing on 'naughty' perhaps, then, only reveals that there was enormous anxiety about these books and that the efforts to censor them were motivated mainly by the desire to prevent the spread of the dissident religious ideas and the civil unrest that they might provoke, rather than targeting explicitly political discourse. After 1534, of course, the difference between religion and politics begins to blur, since, as the 1539 statute has it, 'the king's most excellent Majesty is by God's law supreme head immediately under Him of this whole Church and congregation of England'.[23] Once Henry becomes the head of the Church of England, heresy and treason become difficult to separate. But if the definition of

[23] In Edward Arber (ed.), *A Transcript of the Registers of the Company of Stationers of London 1554–1640*, 5 vols. (London, privately printed, 1875–94), 3: 739. See James Simpson, *Burning to Read: English Fundamentalism and its Reformation Opponents* (Cambridge, MA: Harvard University Press, 2007), 266–7, for a fuller account of the blurring of treason and heresy after 1534.

heresy did come to depend on governmental statute rather than ecclesiastical injunction, it was for the most part religious writing that was proscribed.[24]

The other adjective modifying 'books' in the proclamation, while less semiotically intriguing than 'naughty', is arguably more illuminating in spite of its seeming banality: 'printed'. In our world, 'printed books' has until very recently been almost a tautology. Now the increasing availability of digital books means that 'printed' is again a useful qualifying adjective to describe the particular material form in which a text circulates. That was certainly true in early modern England, when texts circulated both in manuscript and print (and in either form could be properly considered books). But what makes it of concern that these are '*printed* books' is exactly the material advantage of print over manuscript: in the familiar Humanist adage, *Imprimit una dies quantum non scribatur anno* ('he can print in one day what could not be transcribed in a year').

Print vastly increased the range of a text's influence and complicated any effort to control it. The new 'artificial writing' (*artificialiter scribere*) was a revolutionary technique of textual production and dissemination. In William Caxton's prologue to Raoul Le Fevre's *The Recuyell of the Histories of Troy* (1475?), the first printed book in the English language, he notes that the book was in great demand and thus it was 'not wreton with penne and ynke as bokes ben', but printed 'to thende that every man may have them attones'.[25] Single manuscript copies did not any more have to pass hand to hand. Every man might indeed have some desired book 'attones'. While the effects of print were slow to be felt at first—initially print was just an improved means of textual production, even reproducing the letter forms of script—already by 1500, according to Antonia McLean's estimate, over twenty million individual books had been issued from the presses in Europe.[26] The very scale of production makes it clear that print is a revolutionary new information technology, not a mere refinement of an existing one. Written material was now available in hitherto unimaginable quantities and circulating into hitherto unreachable segments of the social world. Where, previously, desiring readers had to find books, books, it might be said, now found (and even made) readers.[27]

Yet, we must be careful not to embrace an unconsidered technological determinism as we consider the impact of print. Too readily the new technology has been

[24] One of the few exceptions is the 1544 proclamation to suppress the publication of rumors in 'printed books' about 'the prosperous success of the King's majesty's army in Scotland; wherein although the effect of the victory be indeed true, yet the circumstances in divers points be in some part overslenderly, in some parts untruly and amiss, reported' (Hughes and Larkin, 1: 329).

[25] William Caxton, *The Prologues and Epilogues of William Caxton*, ed. W. J. B. Crotch, EETS, original series, 176 (London: H.Milford, Oxford University Press, 1928), 7.

[26] Antonia McLean, *Humanism and the Rise of Science in Tudor England* (London: Heinemann, 1972), 14.

[27] The most consequential account of the impact of print is, of course, Elizabeth L. Eisenstein, *The Printing Press as an Agent of Change*, 2 vols. (Cambridge: Cambridge University Press, 1979). It is important, however, to register Eisenstein's own insistence that she regards 'printing as an agent, not

accorded a power of its own to produce powerful social effects, as though the agency rested in the technology itself rather than in its products and its users, even as scholars disagree about its valence: whether it functions to reinforce pre-existent forms of power or to allow those forms to be subjected to a previously unknown public scrutiny. Surely, however, print brought about various, unpredictable, and often contradictory effects, all consequences more of the uses to which it was put than of the techniques of its production.

One certain effect, however, was that, as a result of its astonishing productivity, print demanded new understandings and new strategies of censorship. In the early fifteenth century, the number of manuscripts of an individual text was relatively small, restricted both by the effort of reproduction and the number of potential readers in an age of limited literacy (though one can easily underestimate the efficiency of manuscript production and the resilience of its texts: in spite of various official efforts to forbid the availability of translated bibles, about 250 manuscript copies of the Wyclif bible survive in various collections, interestingly almost exactly the number of surviving printed copies of Shakespeare's First Folio). The flood of printed books meant that the old strategies of prohibition could no longer be effective. Convinced that at one time he could have staunched the tide of heretical texts, Bishop Nix of Norwich nonetheless admitted in 1530 that 'it passeth my power, or that of any spiritual man, to hinder it now, and if this continue much longer it will undo us all'.[28] By the end of Elizabeth's reign at least 500,000 bibles were in print. Whether or not the political nation was in any sense undone by the spread of vernacular scripture, certainly the English bible promoted the spread of literacy, creating a nation of readers that did resist the monopoly on scriptural interpretation claimed by crown and clergy.[29]

It quickly became obvious that tactics that could inhibit the circulation of offending books in manuscript or of printed ones when, as a statute of 1535 says, 'there were but fewe bokes and fewe printers within this realme',[30] would no longer work when books seemed to be almost everywhere. In 1548, Philip Nichols remarked with delight on 'the nu[m]bre of bookes ther be abrode in every ma[n]s

the agent, let alone the only agent, of change in Western Europe'; see her redaction of the earlier book, *The Printing Revolution in Early Modern Europe* (Cambridge: Cambridge University Press, 1983), xiii. For a critique of Eisenstein, though one focused mainly on the later seventeenth century, see Adrian Johns, *The Nature of the Book: Print and Knowledge in the Making* (Chicago: University of Chicago Press, 1998). See also David Kastan, 'Print, Literary Culture and the Book Trade', in *Cambridge History of Early Modern English Literature*, ed. David Loewenstein and Janel Mueller (Cambridge: Cambridge University Press, 2002), 81–116, from which a few sentences have been borrowed here.

[28] *L&P*, 5: 297.

[29] For a fuller account, see David Kastan, ' "The Noyse of the New Bible": Reaction and Reform in Henrician England', in *Religion and Culture in Early Modern England*, ed. Claire McEachern and Deborah Shugar (Cambridge: Cambridge University Press, 1997), 46–68, from which a few sentences have been borrowed here.

[30] *SR*, 25 Henry VIII, c. 15.

hand',[31] but the very proliferation and dissemination that provoked Nichols's wonder provoked official worry. Administrative machinery that had been more or less successful dealing with Lollardy in the fifteenth century proved itself incapable of responding effectively to the new world of print.

This, of course, is not to say that print replaced manuscript; the two systems of textual production, as is well known, worked side-by-side well into the seventeenth century and beyond, sometimes in the very same book. But although manuscript copies of prohibited books continued to be produced and circulated, it was mainly printed works that became the object of official censor. Clearly, then, it was not content alone that was disturbing but even more so their means of production, a fact that Brian Cummings has brilliantly recognized in the language of epidemiology that marks these proclamations,[32] a trope I will borrow and slightly refine to focus on their disturbing *infectivity*, a specific epidemiological term describing the ability of a pathogen to enter, survive, and multiply in the host. This seems to me an almost exact metaphor for the anxiety produced by print. The early censorship proclamations of course identify the cultural pathogen as some form of heresy, but it would be of little concern could it easily be contained. The heresies are 'venomous... intolerable to the clean ears of any Christian man', but they are 'sent into this realm' by heretics and 'sown and spread' within the land, 'whereby the King's subjects are likely to be corrupted' (Hughes and Larkin, 1: 182). Cuthbert Tunstall, the Archbishop of London, notes the 'pestiferous and most pernicious poison dispersed throughout all our diocesse of London in great number: which truly, without it be spedely foreseene, without doubt wyl contaminate and infect the flock committed unto us, with most deadly poison and heresie'.[33]

An infection is identified, its virulence asserted, and the efforts to isolate it prescribed. Censorship laws offer themselves as 'ordinances for the maintenance and defense' of the nation against the invasion of the 'pestiferous English books... sent into this realm' that must be isolated and 'put in perpetual oblivion' (Hughes and Larkin, 1: 194). Like some kind of cultural center for disease control, the King, 'intending the safeguard of this his realm' and 'the preservation of his subjects', commits considerable resources to 'the extirpation, suppressing, and withstanding of the said heresies' (Hughes and Larkin, 1: 182).

As with any highly contagious disease, containment and eradication are difficult. One might command that no one write, print, or publish any work contrary to the

[31] Philip Nicolls, *Here Begynneth a Godly Newe Story of .xii. Men that Moyses Sent to Spye Owt the Land of Canaan* (London, 1548), sig. A3^{v}.

[32] See Brian Cummings, 'Reformed Literature and Literature Reformed', in *The Cambridge History of Medieval English Literature*, ed. David Wallace (Cambridge: Cambridge University Press, 1999), 821–51, at 831. I thank him for authorizing my borrowing here and in general for helping clarify my thinking on these matters in the following paragraphs.

[33] Simon Fish, *Four Supplications: 1529–1553 A.D.*, ed. F. J. Furnivall, EETS, extra series, 13 (London: Early English Text Society, 1871), xiii, xi.

'faith Catholic', or 'presume to bring into this realm' any such book, or even, 'buy, receive, or have' it (Hughes and Larkin, 1: 194), but it is easier to detect the problem than to stop its spread. Harsh penalties are ordered for those in violation of the edicts, but the dictate that any person having any book proscribed 'do immediately bring the same book or books, or cause the same to be brought, to the bishop of the diocese where he dwelleth' (Hughes and Larkin, 1: 196) seems unlikely to be effective. It is hard to imagine that many thought it better to turn in such books than to keep them even more carefully out of common view.

Though authorities were clearly serious about their efforts to censor offending texts (More, for example, bringing cases to Star Chamber[34]), their own rhetoric reveals the difficulty in combating the threat they faced. At the Westminster conference in May 1530, the King and his advisors sought to protect the nation against the 'contagion of wrong opinions',[35] by banning books and ordering subjects to 'detest them, abhorre them, keep them not in your hands, [and] deliver them to the superiours'. They realize, however, that it may be too late, that people have already been exposed, and, once infected, they would prove difficult to treat. No wonder-drugs existed to fight the infection; the best that could be offered was the advice that 'if by reding of them heretofore any thing remeanyth in the breasts of that teching, ether forget it, or by enformacyon of the truthe expel it and purge it'.[36]

Efforts focused, then, more on prevention than cure. Symbolic book burnings took place, like that at the recantation of the evangelical Robert Barnes in 1526 in St Paul's, where he and four German merchants were marched through the Cathedral carrying faggots as a sign of the fate they had escaped and then led three times around a fire burning at the North door in which 'great baskets full of [prohibited Lutheran] books' were burned. But fire, they knew, was not a practical solution to the threat of unruly print. Famously in Ray Bradbury's *Fahrenheit 451*, Guy Montag describes his work as a 'fireman' systematically ridding the nation of books: 'Monday burn Millay, Wednesday Whitman, Friday Faulkner, burn 'em to ashes, then burn the ashes. That's our official slogan.'[37] Bradbury's title refers of course to the temperature at which paper burns. But book burning in Henrician England (even if it had the authority of Acts 19:19) was something different; it was not intended in fact to rid the nation of offending books (however desirable that might seem to some), but was, as in the case of Barnes, a carefully choreographed spectacle asserting state power and church orthodoxy, but also an unwitting sign of a desire that could not be realized in fact.[38]

[34] John Guy, *The Public Career of Thomas More* (New Haven, CT: Yale University Press, 1980), 173–4.

[35] *Concilia Magnae Britanniae et Hiberniae*, ed. David Wilkins, 4 vols. (London: Bowyer, Richardson, Purser, 1737), 3: 727.

[36] *Concilia*, ed. Wilkins, 3: 735.

[37] Ray Bradbury, *Farenheit 451* (New York: Ballantine Books, 1953), 8.

[38] See David Cressy, 'Book Burning in Tudor–Stuart England', *Sixteenth-Century Journal*, 36 (2005), 359–74.

The anxious awareness of the threat of print and the recognition that it was virtually impossible to stop its spread demanded new forms of regulation attempting to control what was produced. If books, both in terms of access and impact, seemed impossible to control once they were dispersed, a system of control had to be developed to regulate what could reach print in the first place. The old technologies of regulation—banning, burning, and expurgation—would no longer work. In 1535, in an effort to abolish papal authority, Cranmer had ordered the clergy to erase all mentions of the pope from all 'books used in the churches' (Hughes and Larkin, 1: 231) but the difficulty in enforcing even this quickly became clear. In the aftermath of the proclamation, many churches were visited and the expurgations checked, but conformity was haphazard. In one church, the vicar had pasted over some offending passages with strips of paper, which were easily removed, leaving visible what was meant to be expurgated 'as fair as it ever was and as legible', though many more passages were left entirely untouched. When questioned, he defended his desultory compliance on the grounds that 'they are but fools that so will destroy their books, for this world will not ever last'.[39]

If the churches themselves could not establish an effective system of post-publication censorship, there was little chance it would work in the country at large. As early as 1407, Archbishop Arundel's Constitutions tried to prohibit English bibles, forbidding translation and insisting that existing copies be inspected and approved. Only one authorized New Testament survives, a copy from the 1460s, with the claim that 'This booke . . . was overseyn and redd by doctor Thomas Ebbrall and Doctor Yve.'[40] It isn't clear why this copy was approved or, in fact, if indeed it was (it is a comment by the book owner), but in any case it is obvious that the new medium of print made impractical the idea of authorizing individual copies of books rather than the texts themselves prior to their publication. Proclamations regulating printed books began to insist that books on controversial subjects could not be printed 'until such time as the same book or books be examined and approved by the ordinary of the diocese where the said books shall be printed; and that the printer thereof, upon every of the said books being so examined, do set the name of the examiner or examiners, with also his own name upon the said books' (Hughes and Larkin, 1: 195). Though specific terms and forms would change, as well as the ultimate source of its authority, a system of pre-publication licensing was set in motion that would be in place until 1641, be abandoned for a short time at the beginning of the Civil Wars, and then be reestablished in 1643, remaining in effect until it was allowed to lapse in 1695.

[39] Quoted in G. R. Elton, *Policy and the Police: The Enforcement of the Reformation in the Age of Cromwell* (Cambridge: Cambridge University Press, 1972), 131.

[40] See Ralph Hanna, *London Literature, 1300–1380* (Cambridge: Cambridge University Press, 2005), 308; see also Anne Hudson, *Lollards and Their Books* (London and Ronceverte: Hambeldon Press, 1985), esp. 141–64. I am grateful to Andrew Kraebel for raising this point.

The most consequential, as well as the most poorly understood, of the early formulations comes from the proclamation of 1538 with which we began:

> Item, that no person or persons in this realm shall from henceforth print any book in the English tongue, unless upon examination made by some of his grace's Privy Council, or other such his highness shall appoint, they shall have license so to do; and yet so having, not to put these words *cum privilegio regali*, without adding *ad imprimendum solum*, and that whole copy, or else at least the effect of his license and privilege be therewith printed, and plainly declared and expressed in the English tongue underneath them. (Hughes and Larkin, 1: 271–2)

Privileges were common enough in the emerging book trade, granted by the crown in lieu of a system of copyright to protect the investment of publishers. The oldest surviving privileges are from Henry VIII to Richard Pynson for the publishing of two Latin sermons—one by Cuthbert Tunstall, then Prebendary of York and the other by Richard Pace, Dean of St Paul's—both of which Pynson printed in 1518. The privileges appear on the colophon: *Cum privilegio a rege ne quis hanc orationem infra biennium in regno Angliae imprimat aut alibi impressam at importatam in eodem regno Angliae vendat* ('with privilege granted by the King so no one may print this sermon within two years in the kingdom of England or sell it if printed elsewhere and imported'). The function is clear and it seems to have worked, as others soon sought similar exclusivity for their projects and either petitioned for or purchased a monopoly on their books for specific lengths of time. Thomas Berthelet held a six-year patent for publishing Thomas Elyot's English–Latin dictionary, granted most likely to justify the expense of production. Enterprising publishers sometimes sought privileges not merely for individual titles but for whole classes of books: Richard Tottel, for example, in 1552 was granted a monopoly for seven years on the publication of law books.

Nonetheless, protecting the financial investment of publishers clearly was not much on the mind of the authors of the licensing procedures specified by the 1538 proclamation, though it was written with full awareness that such a system of privileges did exist, along with an economic justification for it. The Latin tags are evidence of this, though their meaning has been debated by scholars. W. W. Greg has argued that '*ad imprimendum solum*' means 'for sole, or exclusive, printing' (that is, that the additional phrase reserves for the publisher a unique proprietary right to the text in question), but this seems to me an unlikely understanding, if only from its tautological force as interpreted. More likely is A. W. Pollard's earlier interpretation: that the phrase means 'only for printing'.[41] The proclamation went through several drafts, with Henry himself revising the last and adding in his own hand the debated phrase. It seems certain from these drafts that the proclamation's

[41] W. W. Greg, '*Ad Imprimendum Solum*' (1954), in *Collected Papers*, ed. J. C. Maxwell (Oxford: Oxford University Press, 1966), 407–8; A. W. Pollard, '*Ad Imprimendum Solum*', *The Library*, 10 (1919), 57–63.

phrasing here was a function of a two-part recognition: first, that, on account of the system of privileges, books would appear with the phrase *cum privilegio regali* as a mark of the publisher's exclusive right to the title, but, then, realizing that such a *privilege* might be taken as a *licence*, an additional phrase was demanded, *ad imprimendum solum*, to clarify that the first phrase refers only to the exclusivity of the publisher's right to publish the book rather than to any authorization of its contents, which had to be made separately by 'examination'. It is to preserve the function of the 'licence' that the qualification to the 'privilege' is insisted upon, no doubt because books published with privileges were inevitably those of some considerable consequence and the crown did not want to run the risk that a privilege granted on economic grounds might unwittingly be used to allow a publisher to escape the requisite examination of the copy to be 'made by some of his grace's Privy Council, or other such as his highness shall appoint', that now seemed to crown and clergy the last, best hope to contain the spreading infection of 'naughty printed books'.

But this may bring us full circle to *Areopagitica*, for it was of course pre-publication licensing that attracted Milton's ire, though the irony that he became a licenser in 1649 has often been noted. The great nineteenth-century biographer David Masson quickly assures his readers that Milton's licensing work was but 'friendly superintendence',[42] but Milton's commitment was always to truth rather than to liberty and in this he was little different than Archbishop Arundel or Thomas More. If Milton would have protested the Henrician license, on the ground that it 'hinders and retards the importation of our richest Marchandize, Truth' (548), no less than they, he knows that our understanding of this Truth, whose 'perfect shape' will not be fully known 'till her Masters second comming' (549), for now can be defined most clearly by what it feels it must exclude. Orthodoxy is defined by its opposition to what it constructs as falsity, its 'everything' defined by the other's 'nought'.

FURTHER READING

Clegg, Cyndia. *Press Censorship in Elizabethan England* (Cambridge: Cambridge University Press, 1997)

Loades, David. *Politics, Censorship and the English Reformation* (London and New York: Pinter Press, 1991)

Shuger, Debora. *Censorship and Cultural Sensibility: The Reformation of Language in Tudor–Stuart England* (Philadelphia: University of Pennsylvania Press, 2006)

Simpson, James. *Burning to Read: English Fundamentalism and its Reformation Opponents* (Cambridge, MA, and London: Harvard University Press, 2007)

[42] Masson, *Life of John Milton*, 4: 326.

PART V

OUTSIDE THE LAW

CHAPTER 17

UTOPIAN PLEASURE

STEPHEN GREENBLATT

In 1417, in a monastic library in Germany, an Italian humanist and book-hunter, Poggio Bracciolini, found a manuscript of Lucretius's philosophical poem *De rerum natura.*[1] Italian humanists recognized at once that *De rerum natura* was written in remarkably beautiful verse, verse dating from the most prestigious moment of the classical past by which they had become obsessed. But though Lucretius's style was dazzling, it was by no means easy for Poggio and his contemporaries to absorb the philosophical lessons that this didactic masterpiece set out to teach.[2] Ambrogio Traversari's translation into Latin a few years later of Diogenes Laertius's Greek *Lives of the Poets* only made matters worse.[3] The philosopher Epicurus, a hero to both Lucretius and Diogenes Laertius, was virtually a by-word for everything most hateful to good Christians: programmatic pleasure-seeking as the highest goal of existence, the exaltation of the care of the body above the care of the soul, an insistence on the superiority of reason over faith, a steadfast refusal of pious fear, a thoroughgoing, indeed dogmatic atomistic materialism, a belief in the mortality of the soul, a concomitant refusal to believe in

[1] Ernst Walser, *Poggius Florentinus: Leben und Werke* (Hildesheim: George Olms, 1974), 56.

[2] See Eugenio Garin, *La cultura filosofica del Rinascimento italiano* (Florence: Sansoni, 1979). On the general issue of reception, see George D. Hadzsits, *Lucretius and His Influence* (New York: Longmans, Green & Co, 1935); L. D. Reynolds and N. G. Wilson, *Scribes and Scholars: A Guide to the Transmission of Greek and Latin Literature* (London: Oxford University Press, 1968); Charles Trinkaus, *In Our Image and Likeness*, 2 vols. (Chicago: University of Chicago Press, 1970); L. D. Reynolds, *Texts and Transmission: A Survey of the Latin Classics* (Oxford: Clarendon, 1983); Antony Grafton, *Commerce with the Classics: Ancient Books and Renaissance Readers* (Ann Arbor: University of Michigan Press, 1997); Pat Duffy Hutcheon, *The Road to Reason: Landmarks in the Evolution of Humanist Thought* (Ottowa: Canadian Humanist Publications, 2001); Susanna Gambino Longo, *Savoir de la nature et poésie des choses: Lucrèce et épicure à la Renaissance Italienne* (Paris: Honoré Champion, 2004).

[3] Cf. Charles L. Stinger, *Humanism and the Church Fathers: Ambrogio Taversari* (1386–1439) and *Christian Antiquity in the Italian Renaissance* (Albany: State University of New York Press, 1977).

any afterlife at all, a claim that the universe has existed forever and that it exists and will continue to exist eternally without the slightest intervention from any god.[4]

This set of convictions was virtually a textbook—or, better still, an inquisitor's—definition of atheism. Its eruption into Renaissance intellectual life elicited an array of anxious responses precisely from those most powerfully responsive to it. One such response—let us call it 'The Renunciation of Youthful Indiscretion'— was that of the great mid-fifteenth-century Florentine Marsilio Ficino. In his twenties, Ficino, deeply impressed by the poet he called 'our Lucretius, the most brilliant of the Epicurean philosophers', undertook to write a commentary on *De rerum natura*. But, coming to his senses—that is, returning to his faith—Ficino burned this commentary and spent much of his life adapting Plato to construct a subtle philosophical defense of religion and, specifically, of Christianity.[5]

A second response—let us call it 'The Divorce Settlement'—was to separate Lucretius's poetic style from his ideas. This separation seems to have been Poggio's own tactic: he took pride in his discovery, as in the others he made, but he never associated himself or even grappled openly with Lucretian thought. Poggio and close friends like the humanist Niccolò Niccoli could borrow elegant diction and turns of phrase from *De rerum natura* but at the same time hold themselves aloof from its dangerous ideas.[6] Indeed, later in his career Poggio did not hesitate to accuse his bitter rival, Lorenzo Valla, of a heretical adherence to Epicureanism.[7]

This public charge—part of a startlingly vicious quarrel—was potentially dangerous, and Valla's reply allows us to glimpse a third type of response to the ferment caused by the recovery of Lucretius's poem. The strategy is what we might call 'Dialogical Disavowal'. The ideas Poggio attacked were present in his writing, Valla conceded, but they were not his own ideas but rather those of a spokesman for Epicureanism in a literary dialogue, *De voluptate* (1431). Indeed that spokesman, not a fictional character but the contemporary poet Maffeo Vegio, makes it clear that even he is not really an Epicurean, but that he is willing to play the role of a defender of pleasure in order to refute Stoical arguments for virtue as the highest

[4] On Epicurus's core ideas, see A. A. Long, *Hellenistic Philosophy: Stoics, Epicureans, Sceptics*, 2nd edn (Berkeley: University of California Press, 1986); A. A. Long and D. N. Sedley, *The Hellenistic Philosophers*, 2 vols. (Cambridge: Cambridge University Press, 1987); Epicurus, *The Epicurus Reader: Selected Writings and Testimonia*, trans. and ed. Brad Inwood and L. P. Gerson (Indianapolis: Hackett, 1994).

[5] See J. Hankins, 'Ficino's Theology and the Critique of Lucretius', forthcoming in the proceedings of the conference *Platonic Theology: Ancient, Medieval and Renaissance*, held at the Villa I Tatti and the Istituto Nazionale di Studi sul Rinascimento, Florence, 26–27 April 2007.

[6] For the correspondence of these two remarkable friends, see Poggio Bracciolini, *Two Renaissance Book Hunters: The Letters of Poggius Bracciolini to Nicolaus De Niccolis*, trans. Phyllis Walter Goodhart Gordan (New York: Columbia University Press, 1974).

[7] On the controversy, see Salvatore I. Camporeale, 'Poggio Bracciolini contro Lorenzo Valla. Le "Orationes in L. Vallam"', in *Poggio Bracciolini, 1380–1980*, Istituto Nazionale di Studi sul Rinascimento: Studi e testi, vol. 8 (Florence: Sansoni, 1982), 137–61.

good, arguments that, in his view, represent a far more serious threat to Christian orthodoxy. And that orthodoxy, voiced in the dialogue by the monk Antonio Raudense, is announced as the clear victor.[8]

And yet, at the center of *De voluptate* Valla delivers, in Vegio's voice, a more vigorous and sustained defense of Epicurean philosophy than had been penned in more than a thousand years. That defense directly quotes Lucretius and rehearses many of the key positions in *De rerum natura*: the wisdom of withdrawing from competitive striving into the tranquil garden of philosophy, the advantages of moderation, the perverse unnaturalness of sexual abstinence, the denial of any afterlife, the refusal of fear, the pursuit of pleasure.

It is possible to argue that Valla voiced these views only to show them crushed by the sober admonitions of the monkish Raudense. But Valla's contemporary Poggio, as we have seen, reached the opposite conclusion: the Christian framework and the dialogic form served, in his view, only as a convenient cover to permit Valla to make public his scandalous and subversive assault on Christian doctrine. What is the correct interpretation? It is exceedingly unlikely that at this distance we will discover the evidence that might enable us definitively to answer this question—if such evidence ever existed. Indeed the question itself implies a programmatic certainty and clarity that may bear little relation to the actual situation of intellectuals in the fifteenth and sixteenth centuries. A very small number of people—perhaps the soldier-poet Marullus who drowned in the Cecina river, near Volterra, in 1500 with a copy of Lucretius in his pocket, or Giordano Bruno, burned at the stake in Rome a century later—may have fully embraced radical Epicureanism, as far as they understood it, in its entirety.[9] But for many of the most daring speculative minds of the Renaissance, the ideas that surged up in 1417, with the recovery of Lucretius's poem, did not constitute a fully formed philosophical or ideological system. Couched in its beautiful, seductive poetry, the Lucretian vision was a profound intellectual and creative challenge, and the key question is not whether it was formally embraced as a coherent set of propositions but when and in what forms it reentered circulation.

[8] Lorenzo Valla, *De vero falsoque bono/On Pleasure*, trans. A. Kent Hieatt and Maristella Lorch (New York: Abaris Books, 1977). I will use the better known title, *De voluptate*, throughout.

The text of Valla's in question actually deploys several different strategies in addition to Dialogical Disavowal to protect its author from the charge of Epicureanism. Valla has good grounds then for indignantly rejecting Poggio's charge of Epicureanism. The Lucretian arguments that take up the entire second book of *De voluptate* and much of the first are carefully framed by proper Christian doctrines, doctrines that the narrator and the other interlocutors unanimously declare have carried the day.

[9] See Michele Marullo, *Inni Naturali* (Florence: Casa Editrice le Lettere, 1995); on Bruno and Epicureanism, see, among other works, Hans Blumenberg, *The Legitimacy of the Modern Age*, trans. Robert M. Wallace (Cambridge, MA: MIT Press, 1983; first published as *Die Legitimität der Neuzeit*, 1966).

The principal issue is not adherence but mobility—the renewed mobility of a poem that had been resting untouched in monastic libraries for many centuries, the mobility of Epicurean arguments that had been silenced first by hostile pagans and then by hostile Christians, the mobility of daydreams, half-formed speculations, whispered doubts, dangerous thoughts. Poggio Bracciolini may have distanced himself from the content of *De rerum natura*, but he took the crucial first step in pulling the poem off the shelf, having it copied, and sending the copy to his friends in Florence. Such literal mobility was the essential precondition for the strikingly uneven yet momentous history of reception that followed. And that history of reception may, in the long run, have been as important, for the *cultural* reformation that is our central concern, as the bitter doctrinal disagreements that provoked the religious reformation of the sixteenth century. While fierce debates about the exact status of the bread and wine of communion raged across Europe, something else, inspired by the recovery of Lucretius, was brewing in the shadows, something that would in time lead to Montaigne and Hobbes, Gassendi and Spinoza, Darwin, Freud, and Einstein.

In 1419, Poggio accepted the post of secretary to the powerful and immensely wealthy Henry Beaufort, Bishop of Winchester.[10] Poggio's years in England were deeply disappointing to him personally, but his presence there was one of the earliest signs of an interest among the English elite in Italian humanism. English appetite for classical texts did not begin stirring in earnest until at least a generation later, under the patronage of Beaufort's bitter enemy, the powerful and immensely wealthy Humphrey, Duke of Gloucester (d. 1447), and it was not until the sinister career of the powerful and immensely wealthy John Tiptoft, Earl of Worcester (executed 1470), that the books that could assuage this appetite began to be shipped back to England in crates from Padua, Ferrara, and Florence.[11]

The link between humanism, wealth, and the exercise of power in England is worth stressing, because it conditioned the most remarkable Renaissance English response to Lucretius and to everything Lucretius brought back into circulation, Thomas More's *Utopia* (1516). 'Having carefully considered and weighed the matter', More's character Hythloday reports, the Utopians maintain 'that all our actions, and even the very virtues exercised in them, look at last to pleasure as their end and happiness.'[12]

[10] On Poggio's decision to accept this post, see Walser, *Poggius Florentinus*, 71ff.

[11] R. Weiss, *Humanism in England during the Fifteenth Century* (Oxford: Basil Blackwell, 1967). See Clare Carroll, 'Humanism and English Literature in the Fifteenth and Sixteenth Centuries', in *The Cambridge Companion to Renaissance Humanism*, ed. Jill Kraye (Cambridge: Cambridge University Press, 1996), 246–68; David Rundle, 'Humanism Before the Tudors: On Nobility and the Reception of the *studia humanitatis* in Fifteenth-Century England', in *Reassessing Tudor Humanism*, ed. Jonathan Woolfson (London: Palgrave, 2002), 22–42.

[12] Thomas More, *Utopia*, ed. Edward Surtz, S.J. and J. H. Hexter, in *The Complete Works of St Thomas More*, vol. 4 (New Haven, CT: Yale University Press, 1965), 167. On More and Epicureanism, see especially Edward Surtz, S. J., *The Praise of Pleasure: Philosophy, Education, and Communism in*

As More imagines it then, an entire society—not simply a philosophical viewpoint but a complex set of laws and institutional arrangements—could be founded explicitly on Epicurean principles. Like Valla almost a century earlier, More places a defense of pleasure as the highest good at the center of a dialogue that gives him both the space to expound and the rhetorical occasion to disavow the dangerous ideas he sympathetically explores. Like Valla he sets this dialogue in a garden, where busy men find a few hours of leisure to take recreation in speculative exchange. And like Valla he carefully frames the most heterodox speculations with qualifications, conservative objections, and direct personal demurrals. But, quite unlike Valla, More insists that the discussion of philosophical ideas, Epicurean or other, must be set in relation to the pressure of the actual world he inhabited and tried to understand, the world of the blood-soaked statesman and book collector, John Tiptoft, or of his own royal master, the blood-soaked monarch and occasional dabbler in humanism, Henry VIII.

Utopia opens with a vivid evocation of this pressure through the words of a fictive character, Raphael Hythloday, with whom More says he conversed in the course of a long, quiet afternoon in Antwerp. The name 'Hythloday' is a Greek coinage for 'expert in nonsense', so More is deploying and intensifying the strategy of disavowal he found in Valla and others. But this intensification only liberates More to be startlingly, brutally frank. '"What!" I asked, "Were you ever in our country?"' (59). Hythloday's reply is a searing account of poverty, unemployment, crime, conspiracy, greed, corruption, ambition, murderous violence, civil strife, expansionist wars, and foreign invasions. The England he describes is a place where noblemen, living idly off the labor of others, bleed their tenants white by constantly raising their rents, where land enclosures for sheep-raising throw untold thousands of poor people into an existence of starvation or crime, where the cities are ringed by gibbets on which thieves are hanged by the score without the slightest indication that the draconian punishment deters anyone from committing the same crimes.

Valla was certainly aware of comparable nightmares: the world of fourteenth-century Florence and Rome was turbulent, unstable, and frequently violent. But very little of that world seeps into *De voluptate*. Instead Valla follows Epicurus himself in enacting at least a temporary withdrawal into the tranquil realm of the garden. Epicurus urged that this withdrawal should be made as complete and permanent as possible, precisely because the surrounding social, economic, and political struggles were so intractable and vicious. There is, he argued, nothing out there worth fighting for. The pursuit of pleasure necessitates an abandonment of the life of civic engagement.

More's Utopia (Cambridge, MA: Harvard University Press, 1957); and George Logan, *The Meaning of More's Utopia* (Princeton, NJ: Princeton University Press, 1983).

This issue is raised directly at the beginning of *Utopia*, when More (as a character in his own dialogue) asks Hythloday why he does not devote his time and energy to public affairs by becoming a counselor to a king. Hythloday's reply, a highly detailed and bitter indictment of the state of England and of Europe, sets the stage for a withdrawal from the blind and ignorant social world, just such a withdrawal as Epicurus counseled. And in some sense this trajectory is what follows. Hythloday definitively refuses a life of service, which would be indistinguishable, in his view, from a life of servitude. He turns instead to the famous description of the realm apart, Utopia or No-place, whose inhabitants are convinced that 'either the whole or the chief part of human happiness' (161) lies in the pursuit of pleasure. He has found his epicurean garden.

Utopia is literally set apart from the rest of the world in a way that Lucretius and Valla, urbane inhabitants of ancient Rome and Renaissance Rome, could scarcely have imagined. The astonishing New World encounters, in the decades just before More wrote his work, had changed the whole way of conceiving terrestrial space. The alternative for humanist speculation is no longer located in an enclosed garden, with the everyday sounds of the street barely stilled, or even a remote country estate; it is an altogether different part of the globe, hitherto unknown to Europe and completely untouched by its history and culture. Reading Amerigo Vespucci, More realized that he could use this space to explore some of the disturbing ideas that he had encountered in Plato and the still more disturbing ideas that had returned to circulation with Diogenes Laertius and Lucretius. In particular, he seized upon one of Vespucci's observations about the peoples in the newfound lands that, thanks to Martin Waldseemüller's map, had come to bear the name America: 'Since their life is so entirely given over to pleasure', Vespucci had written, 'I should style it Epicurean.'[13] More chooses to make the link to the Italian explorer explicit: Hythloday, we are told at the beginning of the work, 'joined Amerigo Vespucci and was his constant companion in the last three of his four voyages, which are now universally read of, but on the final voyage he did not return with him' (51). He was instead one of those left behind, at his own urging, in a garrison at the farthest point of the explorers' venture into the unknown.

The setting, in the remotest part of the remotest part of the world, enables More to convey a sense that was extremely difficult for his contemporaries to articulate: a sense that the ancient texts recovered by the humanists were at once compellingly vital and at the same time utterly weird. They had been reinjected into the intellectual bloodstream of Europe after long centuries in which they were almost entirely forgotten, and they represented not continuity or recovery but rather a

[13] Cited in Thomas More, *Utopia*, ed. George M. Logan and Robert M. Adams (Cambridge: Cambridge University Press, revised edition 2002; originally published 1989), 68. On More and Vespucci, see Alfred Cave, 'Thomas More and the New World', *Albion*, 23 (1991), 209–29; and Louis Marin, 'Frontiers of Utopia: Past and Present', *Critical Inquiry*, 19 (1993), 397–420.

deep disturbance. They were in effect voices from another world, a world as different as Vespucci's Brazil was to England, and their power derived as much from their distance as their eloquent lucidity.[14]

The invocation of the New World allows More to articulate a second key response to the texts that fascinated the humanists. He insists that these texts be understood not as isolated philosophical ideas but as expressions of a whole way of life lived in particular physical, historical, cultural, and social circumstances. The description of the Epicureanism of the Utopians only makes sense for More in the larger context of an entire existence: it is embedded in a detailed account of the island, its relation to the surrounding territories, its history, its modes of production, its family structure, its beliefs and rituals, and so forth. This understanding of the context of thought has long and complex roots, reaching back at least to Plato's *Laws*, but it received in More an astonishingly rich elaboration that anticipated and to some extent helped to shape the historical and anthropological scholarship of the ensuing centuries, including our own.[15]

For More an interest in Epicureanism only makes sense to the extent that it can address life experience, most centrally his own. The world of England is depicted in such vivid terms in the first part of *Utopia* not as the mere setting for a retreat into the utopian version of the Epicurean garden—the description goes on far too long to serve that purpose alone—but rather as the set of conditions to which More believes that any strong philosophical system, if it is to prove itself worthy of respect, would have to respond. Hence when the second part of the work shifts to the description of Utopia, it does not leave behind the catastrophic social problems that Hythloday had depicted; rather, it attempts to address those problems by proposing in detail ways in which they could be solved.

More could have used the new world setting to imagine a transformation of human nature or the physical environment. But instead he deliberately chose simply to replicate the natural givenness of things of the world as he knew it, including the topography of his own land. And precisely by doing so, he highlights

[14] More plays a characteristically brilliant and self-conscious game in *Utopia* with these issues, including the role of sheer accident in the transmission or loss of cultural sources:

> When about to go on the fourth voyage [Hythloday remarks], I put on board, in place of wares to sell, a fairly large package of books, having made up my mind never to return rather than to come back soon. They received from me most of Plato's works, several of Aristotle's, as well as Theophrastus on plants, which I regret to say was mutilated in parts. During the voyage an ape found the book, left lying carelessly about, and in wanton sport tore out and destroyed several pages in various sections. (181)

[15] More's relation to this intuition is characteristically complex and elusive. On the one hand, it seems, as I have suggested, to be the whole point of Utopia, as described by Hythloday. On the other hand, Hythloday describes Utopia precisely in justifying his refusal to participate in the political life of his own society. It would only be in a society organized on completely different principles—principles found in No-Place—that a philosophical stance such as his own could be integrated into the world.

the crucial significance of Utopian institutions and values, institutions and values deeply shaped—as his characterization of Hythloday makes clear—by a passionate humanistic engagement with classical texts.[16]

The Utopian theory of the nature of pleasure, carefully expounded by Hythloday, is close to the sober spirit of the Greek philosopher presented by Diogenes Laertius. 'When we say, then, that pleasure is the end and aim', Epicurus wrote in his letter to Menoeceus, 'we do not mean the pleasures of the prodigal or the pleasures of sensuality.' It is not 'an unbroken succession of drinking-bouts and of revelry, not sexual love', and not indulgence at the dinner table that leads to true happiness: 'By pleasure we mean the absence of pain in the body and of trouble in the soul.'[17] Just so, the Utopian pursuit of pleasure does not confuse riotous excess with enduring and worthwhile delights. The Utopians certainly do not condemn the pleasures of the flesh—on the contrary, they recognize and enjoy the satisfaction that comes with eating or excreting or scratching an itch. But they understand that such experiences must be ranked lower than the deep joys of good health, a quiet conscience, or the contemplation of the truth.

More is not concerned with getting Epicurus right, though he has in fact managed to get at the essential sobriety and discipline of the philosopher's thought and his life, nor is he concerned with reconstructing the actual society that helped produced Epicurean thought or, for that matter, the thought of Plato, Seneca, Cicero, or Lucretius. His unwavering interest is in his own world and how that world might be illuminated and possibly changed by encountering a new and radical set of ideas. More himself had evidently been grappling intensely with those ideas and was well aware of how much they pulled against some of his own most cherished values.

This inner tension is reflected in the otherwise incomprehensible existence in Utopia of the ascetic religious sect called the Buthrescae, a sect committed to suffering, abjection, and the rigorous punishment of the flesh. The existence of this striking exception to what was said to be the Utopian rule—the celebration of pleasure as 'either the whole or the chief part of human happiness'—is a sign of More's complex response to Epicureanism. He places it at the center of his imaginary realm and thus posits it as the most rational and enlightened philosophy, but he is wary about its implications. A good Christian had ample reason to be wary. After all, the core of Epicurus's teaching, as Lucretius makes clear, is a denial of any afterlife whatever. The soul dies with the body, and there is no judgment, no reward for good or punishment for evil, no pleasure or pain, after death. It is this basic recognition—that all we have is the material body, and nothing more—that gives the embrace of pleasure its meaning.

16 This Raphael, Peter Giles tells More, 'is no bad Latin scholar, and most learned in Greek' (49).

17 Diogenes Laertius, *Lives of Eminent Philosophers*, trans. R. D. Hicks, 2 vols. (Cambridge, MA: Harvard University Press, 1925), 2: 657.

More cannot permit this recognition, even in a geographically distant, explicitly non-Christian, entirely fictive Noplace described by a character whose name means Expert-in-Nonsense. Hence the deliberate crack in the Utopian logic, the introduction of the Buthrescae whose asceticism is grounded on the fact that they 'long only for the future life by means of their watching and sweat' (227). Far from laughing at this hope, the Utopians applaud it, for, as Hythloday explains, they insist urgently and dogmatically on the existence of an afterlife.

Here too we confront a further startling exception to a Utopian norm, in this case the norm of religious toleration. Fearing that wrangling and hatred over religious differences would threaten the survival of the state, the founder Utopus had ruled—astonishingly, from the perspective of More's Europe—that 'it should be lawful for every man to follow the religion of his choice, that each might strive to bring others over to his own, provided that he quietly and modestly supported his own by reasons nor bitterly demolished all others if his persuasions were not successful nor used any violence and refrained from abuse' (221).[18] But one position is not merely discouraged but emphatically prohibited: Utopus 'conscientiously and strictly gave injunction that no one should fall so far below the dignity of human nature as to believe that souls likewise perish with the body or that the world is the mere sport of chance and not governed by any divine providence' (221). These principles—the mortality of the soul and the absence of any providential order in the endless recycling of matter—happen, not by coincidence, to be the twin pillars of Epicureanism. In effect, the Utopian authorities have established a rule: this much of Epicureanism you can and should believe in; any further, and you are transgressing and will pay the consequences.

Hythloday does not make clear how Utopians ordinarily discover such thought-crime, but once they do, their response is extreme: a person who is found not to believe in post-mortem punishment and rewards is no longer counted as a citizen or indeed as a human being. Such a person, despised by everyone, is denied all honors, given no offices, and entrusted with no public responsibilities. We have reached the limit of what the Utopians, nominally open to all schools of thought, will tolerate.

Why does More go out of his way to place Epicureanism at the center of Utopia, if at the same time he cuts out its core denial of the afterlife? Some half-century ago Edward Surtz proposed an answer: More was writing as 'a Catholic reformer who was drawing a humanistic picture of an ideal commonwealth' (6). He freely adapted elements from the pagan Greek philosophers whom he had been reading to articulate a vision of what could be done to purify Catholic practice, shore up

[18] There is a tension that More does not attempt to resolve between this injunction to use 'reason' to justify religious conviction and the honoring of the Buthrescae's asceticism precisely because they do not attempt to use reason to justify it.

Catholic confessional unity, and forge a Catholic social community. Epicurus represents no real disturbance, no alien vision that has reentered European thought to disrupt the core beliefs. 'The author of *Utopia*', as Surtz puts it with special emphasis, 'writes as a *Catholic* to Catholics'.[19]

But several elements of *Utopia* seem to pull sharply against this account. More does not Christianize Epicureanism (or Platonism). Utopia is an explicitly non-Christian realm with an explicitly non-Christian system of values based on communism and the pursuit of pleasure as the highest good. Hythloday does not rule out the possibility that its inhabitants may ultimately be converted—when Hythloday and his fellow voyagers expound their faith, some of the Utopians quickly embrace it. But there is no miraculous mass conversion and very little likelihood of one. When one of the Christian converts becomes too vehement in the condemnation of other faiths, he is arrested and exiled, and the Utopian churches of all sects bear strikingly little resemblance to Catholic churches: 'No image of the gods is seen in the temple so that the individual may be free to conceive of God with the most ardent devotion in any form he pleases' (233).

If More's absorption of pagan culture is less seamless and untroubled than Surtz implies, there is an alternative explanation. More—'the future martyr and saint', as Surtz calls him[20]—may have been highly sensitive to and concerned about the heretical implications of the pagan texts to which he and other humanist intellectuals were drawn. He could have attacked these implications directly, but that would have meant a repudiation of a whole intellectual world in which he and his closest friends had eagerly participated. Instead he chose neither to condemn pagan philosophy nor to convert it to Christianity but rather to refashion it, as it were, from the inside. By reassembling the elements and, specifically, by transforming or repudiating the most dangerous principles, More could get control of the potentially threatening currents in a philosophical inheritance he valued.

For More this control is not a matter of blithely ignoring the threat and cherry-picking the features that seemed to him most welcome for the cause of Christian reform. And it would not do, as in Valla, simply to allow the subversive voice to be

[19] Surtz, *Praise of Pleasure*, 2. In Surtz's account, *Utopia* was written in the last moment of Catholic unity.

> In spite of the survival and strength of the Waldenses, the Lollards, and the Hussites, the one world of western Europe is Roman Catholic in its length and breadth. For all classes and peoples there are still the same faith, the same sacraments, the same vicar of Christ. This one world has its weakness and its rottenness, but it has within itself also the means for the preservation of unity and the restoration of integrity. Ultimately the antagonistic and rival camps which it will spawn are to spring up as result of betrayal from within and violence from without.

Quite apart from the startling erasure of Europe's Jews, this vision of 'the one world of western Europe' is open to serious challenge.

[20] Surtz, *Praise of Pleasure*, 3.

heard and then to claim, whether disingenuously or in all seriousness, that it lost the argument. More's design instead calls for a careful identification and eradication of beliefs that are absolutely impermissible. Those Utopians who assert the death of the soul and therefore do not believe in post-mortem punishments and rewards assigned by divine providence are immediately arrested as threats to the community.[21]

Hythloday does not disclose what happens to those freethinkers who are not cured of their 'madness'. (In the actual practice of More's time, they were handed over to the authorities for execution.) Utopian heretics could conceivably be enslaved. But such enslavement would be a relatively mild fate, one assigned to prisoners of war or to those penniless drudges from other countries who actually request hard labor in Utopia. Utopians, Hythloday explains, deal with their own countrymen more harshly than with others, 'since their conduct is regarded as all the more regrettable and deserving a more severe punishment as an object lesson because, having had an excellent rearing to a virtuous life, they still could not be restrained from crime' (185).

Something exemplary then would have to be in store for those who fail to return to their senses and instead insist that there is neither divine providence nor an afterlife. The principal example Hythloday chooses to give of the harshest punishment comes very close to the way in which recalcitrant or backsliding freethinkers would presumably have to be treated: adulterers, he reports, are punished by statute with 'the strictest form of slavery' (191). No explanation is given for the exceptional rigor of this penalty: as with the denier of the soul's immortality, the adulterer has crossed a line that the Utopians defend with the full force of the state. And, if anyone is foolish enough to commit—or to attempt to commit—the crime again, Utopian law is unequivocal. For other crimes, even heinous ones, the punishment is enslavement, with varying degrees of strictness. But in this instance the Utopians forego the free labor: a second conviction for adultery 'involves the penalty of death' (191).[22]

As the punishments make clear, More adopts Epicurus's pursuit of pleasure but rejects the key philosophical principles on which the Epicurean pursuit was based. The project of *Utopia* then, it is possible to argue, is to get control of the humanist texts in which More had immersed himself by subtly betraying them, at once embracing them and stripping them of their foundational principles.

[21] In book 10 of the *Inferno*, Dante consigns the Epicureans to a place set apart from the other heretics, for only the Epicureans believed that the soul dies with the body. Commenting on this passage in 1481, Cristoforo Landino explained that this belief in the death of the soul removed the entire foundation for a just life in civil society—'ogni fondamento al giusto vivere civile'—as well as for true religion.

[22] Apart from a second adultery conviction and slave rebellion (discussed below), there is one other offense in Utopia that brings the death penalty: 'To take counsel on matters of common interest outside the senate or the popular assembly is considered a capital offense' (125). (*Extra senatum, aut comitia publica de rebus communibus inire consilia capitale habetur* (124).) I cite the Latin because, as George Logan has pointed out to me, the Yale *Complete Works* translation is potentially misleading. Surtz translates the key phrase *inire consilia* as 'to take counsel', but it actually has the force of 'to form plans' or 'to enter into schemes'.

I have represented this view as an alternative to Surtz's account of More as Catholic reformer, but it is in fact only an intensification and darkening of his account: what it means for More to be 'a *Catholic* writing to Catholics', as Surtz puts it, is that he must inevitably and necessarily cut the heart out of the classical doctrines he appears so warmly to embrace. As a humanist, More does not adopt the stance of violent struggle against pagan antiquity—he is at a far remove from St Cyril of Alexandria and the monks howling for the murder of Hypatia and the torching of the great library—but instead smilingly represents a spirit of recovery and accommodation. Reactionaries regarded this spirit as a dangerous flirtation with wickedness. But More, viewing the old order as sclerotic and ignorant, wants to address the spirit of inquiry and the longing for spiritual and social transformation he exemplified in himself and warmly shared with others.[23] He does this in *Utopia* by brilliantly fashioning an imaginative appropriation—of Plato, of Epicurus, of the most radical thinking of his generation—that is at the same time a cunning, systematic stifling, an embrace that kills.

It is difficult to disprove this melancholy view of More's project, but I want to close by offering an alternative account of the place of Epicureanism in *Utopia*, one that would lay greater emphasis on the work's innovative and open-ended character and would emphasize a cultural, rather than Catholic or Protestant, reformation. More looked around him and insisted on truly taking in the spectacle of offenders strung up, often for grotesquely minor offenses. He despised the stupidity of those who expressed surprise that so many thieves continue to spring up everywhere when so few of them escape hanging. And he despised even more the bad faith, linked to stupidity, of those who insisted, 'There are manual crafts. There is farming. They might maintain themselves by these pursuits if they did not voluntarily prefer to be rascals' (61). He understood that the problems were structural, deeply rooted in the design of the economy and the organization of society. Above all, he observed the extent to which, in response to these structural problems, the social order of Henry VIII's England was based on punishment and fear.

Because More was a truly radical and original thinker—because he had brooded on the meaning of Plato and Epicurus and taken in the unnerving significance of Vespucci's reports—he was not content to imagine a kindlier, gentler version of the existing order of things. He allowed himself to reflect on the fact that the crushing weight of punishment and fear extended from the secular realm he had watched with mingled personal ambition and contempt to the spiritual realm to which he

[23] See, especially, More's 'Letter to Martin Dorp', in St Thomas More, *In Defense of Humanism*, ed. Daniel Kinney, in *The Yale Edition of the Complete Works of St. Thomas More*, vol. 15 (New Haven, CT: Yale University Press, 1986). More's position is specifically associated with the revival of interest in Greek literature: cf. Eric Nelson, *The Greek Tradition in Republican Thought* (Cambridge: Cambridge University Press, 2004).

was deeply drawn. That is, he understood that much of the religious world to which he was committed had been colonized and fashioned by the identical impulse to string up sinners on gibbets and then express astonishment that more sinners arose to take their place.[24] How would it ever stop?

The answer, More thought, could be found in the most unlikely place, in a commonwealth inclined to the belief that the pursuit of pleasure, rather than the threat of punishment, is the soundest basis of a just social order. He presented this idea in a garden setting that recalled Epicurus's philosophical retreat, and his spokesman Hythloday rejects civic engagement, just as Epicurus had counseled. But it is here that the borrowing stops, and the process of transformation begins that we have characterized as the dismantling of the foundations of Epicurus's philosophy, even in the act of embracing it.

That dismantling can be described, as we have suggested, as the effect of the Catholic in Catholic humanism. But it can also be described as the only way More could conceive of the pursuit of pleasure actually realized by more than a tiny elite who have withdrawn from public life. For a whole society to be organized around the pursuit of pleasure, More believed that private property would have been abolished—otherwise the avidity of human beings, their longing for 'nobility, magnificence, splendor and majesty' (245) would inevitably lead to the unequal distribution of wealth that consigns a large portion of the population to lives of misery, resentment, and crime. But communism, in More's view, was not enough: people would have to believe, at a bare minimum, that there was an overarching providential design—not only in the state but in the very structure of the universe itself—and they would have to believe as well that the hierarchical norms by which they are meant to regulate their pursuit of pleasure and hence discipline their behavior were reinforced by this providential design. The way that this reinforcement would work would be through a belief in rewards and punishments in an afterlife—otherwise, in More's view, it would be impossible drastically to reduce, as he wished, both the terrible temporal punishments and the extravagant temporal rewards that kept his own unjust society in order.

More is trying to think through a paradox in Epicureanism: how is it possible to counsel a way of life that would require a withdrawal from the world, when the basic conditions of that world—a modicum of order, a reasonable and reliable plenty of goods and services, a stable city at peace—would seem to be necessary for the happiness that the philosopher seeks as the highest good? How would it be possible to conjoin Epicurean ideas to the ethical notion of a self-regulating society? This project—to turn Epicureanism from the philosophy of a privileged few to the principle of a just society—leads More to introduce the key change we

[24] See Jean Delumeau, *Sin and Fear: The Emergence of a Western Guilt Culture, 13th–18th Centuries*, trans. Eric Nicholson (New York: St. Martin's Press, 1990).

have examined: the Utopian view that anyone who denies providence or the afterlife has fallen from the sublimity of the human soul to the level of a miserable beast. More does not propose that this view is only and entirely instrumental, but he carefully highlights its instrumental function. The Utopians will regard a freethinker as less than a man, he writes; still less will they count him 'among their citizens whose laws and customs he would treat as worthless if it were not for fear' (221).

'If it were not for fear': fear might be eliminated in the philosopher's garden, among a tiny, enlightened elite, but it cannot be eliminated from an entire society, if that society is to be imagined as inhabited by the range of people who actually exist in the world as it has always been known. Why? Because even with the full force of Utopian social conditioning, human nature, More believed, would inevitably lead men in pursuit of their desires to resort to force or fraud in order to overcome the obstacles erected by laws and customs. The Utopians train their citizens, from the time they are children, to distinguish between higher and lower pleasures, to abstain from self-destructive or anti-social impulses, to forgo lesser satisfactions in order to secure greater ones, to defer immediate gratification in the interest of more lasting rewards. They have eliminated distinctions of social class, universalized access to authority, erased coveted marks of status conferred by dress or ornaments, and abolished private property. But they cannot abolish what More calls 'private desires' (*priuatim cupiditati*) (223).[25] Therefore none of the training is enough, in his view, to secure for an entire population the stable, balanced, disciplined life that Epicurus thought he could bring by freeing men from fear of the gods, dismantling belief in providence, eliminating the fantasy of an afterlife, and teaching men, in Auden's phrase, 'to find the mortal world enough'.

More is trying to imagine what it would take not for certain individuals to be enlightened but for a whole commonwealth to do away with cruelty and disorder, tear down the gibbets, share the goods of life equitably, and organize itself around the pursuit of pleasure. And the answer, he concluded, would have to include what he calls fear beyond the law (*ultra leges metus*) and hope beyond the body (*ultra corpus spe[s]*). Without these supplements the social order would inevitably collapse, with each individual attempting to fulfill his wishes: 'Who can doubt that he will strive either to evade by craft the public laws of his country or to break them by violence in order to serve his private desires when he has nothing to fear but laws and no hope beyond the body?' (221–3). The gibbets, all but a few, could be dismantled, More thought, only if people were persuaded to imagine gibbets (and rewards) in some other life.

[25] The ineradicable persistence of private desires is exemplified in adultery, and here too More's Utopians are not confident in the efficacy of training and rational persuasion. Hence the death penalty for repeat offenders.

This conclusion has less to do, I think, with a Catholic writing to Catholics than it does with a more wide-ranging and diverse set of conversations in the course of the cultural reformation: between conservatives and radicals, Latin-oriented humanists and Greek-oriented humanists, Augustinians and Epicureans, and many other interlocutors that resist convenient labels. What is most striking is the extent to which More can distribute himself across so many of these positions, as if in different aspects of his very complex being he felt himself drawn to them all, or as if he were rehearsing the whole range of strategies—Renunciation of Youthful Indiscretion, Divorce Settlement, Dialogical Disavowal in the interest of containment, and Dialogical Disavowal in the interest of subversion—with which humanists responded to the disturbing power of what they were recovering.

Hence perhaps the strange, telltale loop in More's logic. His Hythloday describes a world in which a philosophical principle—the Epicurean pursuit of pleasure—can at last be integrated into a whole mode of life, active, productive, and engaged, and no longer withhold itself by withdrawing into contemplative aloofness. But he describes this world as a way of explaining why he steadfastly refuses to be integrated into a whole mode of life, namely, the life of his own culture, to which 'Morus' urges him to make a productive contribution. And a society organized for the pursuit of pleasure, and not for the defense of property secured by a regime of punishment, can only be realized if its citizens are compelled to abjure key elements of the very philosophy that society is meant to embody. That is, the citizens must embrace strict monogamy and a belief both in providence and in post-mortem punishments, an embrace secured, if necessary, by the enslavement or execution of dissenters.

More understood perfectly well—as Valla understood—that the Epicurean vision of pleasure as the highest good, reintroduced by the translation of Diogenes Laertius and the recovery of Lucretius, posed a profound challenge to central elements in Christian belief. Specifically, it challenged More's own deep longing for an ascetic Christianity centering on spiritual discipline, penitential suffering, and the punishing of the flesh. Valla allowed this challenge to voice itself and then be defeated by orthodoxy. But More took it seriously enough to attempt to construct a whole alternative world around it. If that world turned out to renounce certain key Epicurean principles, the renunciation was in the service not of Christian orthodoxy but of practical success. That is, More was in some sense writing as an Epicurean to other Epicureans. In the long run, the most interesting story is not his conservative recuperation of Catholic doctrines but his explosive release of an Epicurean vision that, in a world full of crazed suicide bombers, fervent believers in the Rapture, plutocratic billionaires, and overflowing prisons, still seems a radical alternative to anything we know.

FURTHER READING

Grafton, Anthony. *Commerce with the Classics: Ancient Books and Renaissance Readers* (Ann Arbor: University of Michigan Press, 1997)

Logan, George. *The Meaning of More's 'Utopia'* (Princeton, NJ: Princeton University Press, 1983)

Marin, Louis. 'Frontiers of Utopia: Past and Present', *Critical Inquiry*, 19 (1993): 397–420

Surtz, Edward, S. J. *The Praise of Pleasure: Philosophy, Education, and Communism in More's Utopia* (Cambridge, MA: Harvard University Press, 1957)

CHAPTER 18

FOLLY

GREG WALKER

Gallows Humour[1]

The chronicler Edward Hall's final judgement on Sir Thomas More makes intriguing reading. Given that More was executed for denying the Royal Supremacy, we might expect a loyal Henrician like Hall to focus on his treason. Curiously, after briefly noting his papalism and persecution of evangelicals, he instead concentrates on More's frivolous lack of decorum, most notably on the scaffold itself:

> I cannot tell whether I should call him a foolish wise-man or a wise foolish-man, for undoubtedly he, beside his learning, had a great wit, but it was so mingled with taunting and mocking that it seemed to them that best knew him that he thought nothing to be well spoken except he had ministered some mock in the communication, in so much as at his coming to the Tower, one of the officers demanded his upper garment for his fee, meaning his gown, and he answered he should have it, and took [gave] him his cap, saying it was the uppermost garment that he had.[2]

Elsewhere Hall describes More as:

> A man well learned in the tongues and also in the Common Law, whose wit was fine, and full of imaginations, by reason whereof he was too much given to mocking, which was to his gravity a great blemish.[3]

Far from passing over this blemish, however, Hall was clearly fascinated by it, to the extent that his account of More's death becomes an extended catalogue of his witticisms.

[1] I am grateful to Anne Marie D'Arcy, Sarah Knight, John McGavin, David Salter, and the editors for help while writing this essay.

[2] Edward Halle, *The Union of the Two Noble Families of Lancaster and York* (1550), facsimile edition (London: Scolar Press, 1970), fol. ccxxvi and verso.

[3] Halle, *The Union of the Two Noble Families*, clxxxiv and verso.

> Likewise, even going to his death at the Tower gate, a poor woman... besought him to declare that he had certain evidences of hers in the time that he was in office... He answered, 'Good woman, have patience a little while, for the King is good unto me that even within this half hour he will discharge me of all businesses and help thee himself'. Also, when he went up the stair on the scaffold, he desired one of the sheriff's officers to give him his hand to help him up, and said, 'When I come down again, let me shift for myself as well as I can'. Also the hangman kneeled down to him, asking him forgiveness of his death (as the manner is) to whom he said, 'I forgive thee, but I promise thee that thou shalt never have honesty of the striking off my head, my neck is so short'. Also, even when he should lay down his head on the block, he, having a great grey beard, striked [stretched] out his beard, and said to the hangman, 'I pray you let me lay my beard over the block lest ye should cut it': thus with a mock he ended his life.[4]

Hall's sense of the excessive, transgressive quality of More's jesting is evident in his syntax. The sheer quantity of the jokes, emphasized by the anaphoric 'Also... Also... Also', is supplemented by the implied indignation of the 'evens'. *Even* entering the place of execution, *even* climbing the scaffold, *even* with his head on the block itself, he still found time for another ill-judged jest unbefitting a statesman at such a moment.

More's evangelical opponents made similar points. William Tyndale criticized him for 'mocking' and 'laughing' at matters which warranted more sober treatment—a habit he attributed to More's vocation as a 'poet' (i.e. a writer of fiction) rather than a theologian, while in *The Supper of The Lord* he claimed that it 'is no Christian matter... [to]... trifle out the truth with taunts and mocks as Master More doth'.[5] Far from trying to refute such accusations, More's friends were seemingly happy to endorse them. The same quips that in Hall attest to More's indecorous 'mocking' were repeated by William Roper, Nicholas Harpsfield, and Thomas Stapleton in their biographies as evidence of their subject's amiable, witty disposition.[6]

Thus More's mirth became a critical issue in the struggle over his reputation and legacy—as perhaps it was always destined to. (How his life might have differed had he not been saddled with a surname, 'Morus', that inevitably suggested the Greek word for 'folly' is not a wholly flippant question). This essay looks at how the ideas of mirth and folly are woven through both More's public career and the life of his close contemporary, the playwright John Heywood. I suggest how each man

4 Halle, *The Union of the Two Noble Families*, ccxxvi and verso.

5 William Tyndale, *An Answere Unto Sir Thomas More's Dialogue*, ed. A. M. O'Donnell, S. N. D. and J. Wicks, S. J. (Washington, DC: Catholic University of America Press, 2000), 108; and *The Supper of The Lord*, ed. Henry Walter, Parker Society (Cambridge: Cambridge University Press, 1850), 263. See John Foxe, *Acts and Monuments*, IV, ed. Rev. J. Pratt (London: Religious Tract Society, 1841), 198 and 652; and James Simpson, *Burning to Read: English Fundamentalism and its Reformation Opponents* (Cambridge, MA: Harvard University Press, 2007) for the controversial context.

6 William Roper, *The Lyfe of Sir Thomas Moore, Knight*, ed. E.V. Hitchcock, EETS, original series, 197 (Oxford: Oxford University Press, 1935 for 1934), 75–7, 102–3.

adopted and adapted classical and medieval notions of foolishness and comedy for their own ends in the perilous years of Henry VIII's Reformation.

The key term in the sympathetic version of More's character is 'merry': a word with an interesting contemporary semantic range, stretching from merely 'amusing' or 'playful' in texts such as *The Hundred Merry Tales*[7] to encompass human good fellowship of all kinds, including, in More's own usage, the spiritual fellowship of the saved souls in heaven. Roper, Stapleton, and Harpsfield all use it, the last speaking of More's 'special notable gift of eloquence, merry and pleasant talk, and yet without any gall or bitterness, hurt or slander in his jesting'.[8] Erasmus similarly described his friend as 'disposed to be merry rather than serious or solemn' and addicted to jesting.[9] In Stapleton's *Life*, a central element of More's humour is his ability to keep those around him uncertain whether he is joking or serious. Thus,

> in the midst of jokes he kept so grave a face, and even when those around him were laughing heartily, looked so solemn, that neither his wife nor any other member of his family could tell from his countenance whether he was speaking seriously or in jest.[10]

Reading More's intentions was, then, a tricky business; so Hall's bafflement at his behaviour on the scaffold is perhaps understandable. But the fact that the chronicler accused him of a lapse of public decorum in the quasi-theatrical setting of a state execution is particularly curious given the scholar's well-known interest in theatrical performance, and his stress on the demand it makes on performers precisely to tailor their conduct to the dramatic context.

The clearest statement of this principle (termed *convenientia* by rhetoricians) is the advice regarding counselling kings given by More's alter ego to Hythlodaeus in Book 1 of *Utopia*, where the 'philosophy more practical for statesmen, which knows its stage, adapts itself to the play in hand, and performs its role neatly and appropriately' is contrasted to the rigid approach that would commit its advocates always to speak with the same gravity, even in the middle of a Plautine comedy.[11]

[7] *A Hundred Merry Tales: The Earliest English Jest-Book*, ed. W. C. Hazlitt (London: J. W. Jarvis & Son, 1887).

[8] Nicholas Harpsfield, *The Life and Death of Sir Thomas Moore*, ed. E. V. Hitchcock, EETS, o.s., 186 (Oxford: Oxford University Press, 1932), 74.

[9] Erasmus, *Opus Epistolarum des. Erasmi*, ed. P. S. Allen, H. M. Allen, and H. W. Garrod (Oxford: Oxford University Press, 1906–58), 7: 17, 18–19; Harpsfield, *Life*, 74–5. By celebrating jesting as convivial, More, Heywood, and their allies were resisting the conventional link between laughter and scorn. See Quentin Skinner, *Visions of Politics*, 3 vols. (Cambridge: Cambridge University Press, 2001–2), 3: 142–76.

[10] Thomas Stapleton, *The Life and Illustrious Martyrdom of Sir Thomas More*, ed. E. E. Reynolds (London: Catholic Book Club, 1966), 127. See More's *Apology*, ed. J. B. Trapp, in *The Yale Edition of the Complete Works of St. Thomas More* [Hereafter '*CWM*'], vol. 9 (New Haven, CT: Yale University Press, 1979), 170.

[11] *CWM*, vol. 4, ed. E. Surtz, S. J. and J. H. Hexter (1965), 99; James Simpson, 'Rhetoric, Conscience and the Playful Positions of Sir Thomas More', *The Oxford Handbook to Tudor Literature, 1485–1603*, ed. M. Pincombe and C. Shrank (Oxford: Oxford University Press, 2009), 121–36.

This fictional advice echoes an equally well-known anecdote recorded by Roper, which also talks about stepping into a theatrical performance and acting appropriately to the play in hand. While More was serving in the household of Cardinal John Morton, Roper observes,

> Though he was young in years, yet would he at Christmastide suddenly sometimes step in among the players, and never studying for the matter, make a part of his own there presently among them, which made the lookers on more sport then all the players beside.[12]

In life as in literature, then, More was adept at judging the effects that personal performances might have, both on his own reputation as a player and on the wider social and dramatic situation.[13] How, then, might we account for what Hall saw as his lapse in judgement during that most dramatic public performance at his own execution? And what might this suggest about the uses of mirth in premodern culture more generally? In order to discuss these questions, we need to look at More's attitude towards theatrical performance a little more closely.

All the World's a Stage?

The analogy of life to a play was, of course, not new in the sixteenth century. More himself would have encountered it in his reading of the cynic satirist Lucian of Samosata (2nd cent. CE), a number of whose dialogues he and Erasmus translated in 1505–6. In *Menippus: Or the Decent to Hades*, Lucian's eponymous protagonist, confronted by the bones of the dead on the Acherusian fields, declares that human life seems merely a pageant directed by Fortune:

> Taking one person, it may be she attires him royally, placing a tiara upon his head... but on another she puts the costume of a slave... And often in the middle of the pageant she exchanges the costumes of several players... And when at length the play comes to an end, each of them strips off his gold-bespangled robe, lays aside his mask, steps out of his buskins and goes about in poverty and humility.[14]

This notion that human beings are essentially actors and worldly identity merely a matter of costume evidently had an impact upon More. He would rehearse it several times throughout his career.[15] That an actor could become, temporarily, the role he was playing (and the fact that classical actors wore masks would have made

[12] Roper, *Lyfe*, 5.

[13] H. B. Norland, 'The Role of Drama in More's Literary Career', *Sixteenth Century Journal*, 13 (1982), 59–75.

[14] More, *CWM*, vol. 3 (i), ed. C. R. Thompson (1974), 176–7.

[15] *The History of Richard III* in *CWM*, vol. 2, ed. R. S. Sylvester (1963), 80–2; *CWM*, vol. 1, ed. A. S. G. Edwards, K. G. Rodgers, and C. Miller (1997), 153–6; *The Treatise Upon the Passion* in *CWM*, vol. 13, ed. G. E. Haupt (1976), 157, *CWM*, vol. 3 (i): 204.

both their immersion in role and their artifice more striking) carried a powerful charge. In a society regulated by entrenched assumptions about class and position, the kind of mobility that allowed a mere tradesman (which actors ultimately were) to become a king at one minute and a slave the next, seems to have had a queasily intoxicating appeal to More, who would not have expected to experience either social extreme in his lifetime.

But, as Roper's anecdote suggests, More's association with plays and impromptu performances predated his translation of Lucian. And what is most striking about these stories is not so much that More reached readily for dramatic metaphors to describe important principles or took part in household entertainments, but that in each case he saw a play as something to be freely stepped in and out of. Where the weight of Lucian's anecdote lies upon the all-encompassing nature of the worldly interlude—everyone is trapped within the play Fortune is directing—for More the human actor is free to make of the play what he will. As Robert Bracht Branham observes, if Lucian's moral is that the only course for the wise is to retreat into stoic detachment, More's concerns the 'practical value of role-playing'.[16] Moreover, let us dwell for a moment on the nature of the scenario that More envisages in *Utopia*. What he chooses to highlight is not the danger of introducing undue levity into a serious scene (the offence with which Hall would charge him) but that of inappropriate gravity—of delivering a speech from Senecan tragedy in a Plautine comedy. Role-playing for More, it is tempting to suggest, always seemed more successful when it involved an essentially comic intervention. And a closer look at the surviving accounts of his life suggest that such interventions did indeed provide him, not only with a means of tempering the more formal performances of his public career,[17] but also of structuring and making sense of more private events in the final phase of his life.

While More's biographers took pains to present him as immunized to the whims of Fortune, always able to step back from worldly affairs into stoic contemplation,[18] they also provide ample evidence of his use of comic role-playing to take control of shifts in his personal fortunes. Rather than stepping out of the worldly play, More, as the earlier anecdotes suggest, habitually thought of stepping into it, and of making a part there for himself. Thus, as Roper records, as his material fortunes declined following his resignation of the Chancellorship, More reasserted a sense of his own agency by briefly finding a new role for himself in events—a role with echoes of his celebrated interventions in Morton's household—as a comic servant:

> And, whereas upon the holidays during his high Chancellorship, one of his gentlemen, when service at the church was done, ordinarily used to come to my lady his wife's pew, and say [unto her], 'Madam, my lord is gone', the next holiday after the

[16] R. B. Branham, 'Utopian Laughter', *Moreana*, 86 (1985), 23–43, at 38.

[17] See his performances as Speaker of the House of Commons in Roper, *Lyfe*, 14–15 ff.

[18] Roper, *Lyfe*, 55–6; Harpsfield, *Life*, 66, 77.

surrender of his office and departure of his gentlemen, he came unto my lady his wife's pew himself, and making a low curtsy, said unto her, 'Madam, my lord is gone.'[19]

Thus with a jest, and no doubt an awkward laugh from the redoubtable Dame Alice, More stepped in among the earnest events of his newly-impoverished life and structured them on a more gamesome pattern, even if only momentarily.

This sense of More scripting his own life as a drama is also evident in the more momentous scenes of his last years. As he was leaving his house in Chelsea to take the boat for the meeting at Lambeth at which he knew he must mark himself out for imprisonment and death by refusing to take Henry VIII's Succession oath, he again choreographed his actions carefully, this time into a more sombre scene. As Roper records, rather than let his wife and children accompany him to the quay, '[More would] suffer none of them forth of the gate to follow him, but pulled the wicket after him, and shut them all from him', before stepping into the boat:

Wherein, sitting still sadly [soberly] a while, at the last he . . . rounded [whispered] me in the ear, and said, 'Son Roper, I thank our Lord the field is won'. What he meant thereby I then wist not. But as I conjectured afterward, it was . . . [that] the love he had to God wrought in him so effectively that it conquered all his carnal affections utterly.[20]

The deliberate exclusion of his family from even the first stage of his journey, the richly symbolic stepping through the wicket gate alone and closing it behind him, and the lengthy pause after stepping into the boat: all these actions mark out More's departure as a formal movement out of one scene and into another, opening a new and wholly more serious act in his life story in which he would have to conquer his worldly appetites definitively and prepare himself for death.

It is in the light of such carefully dramatized moments that we might reconsider More's behaviour at his execution. Far from being the ill-considered rupture of decorum that Hall suggests, it seems likely that More's jesting on the scaffold signalled precisely what he intended his audience to make of the last act of his life. Having now conquered what he saw as the sins that threatened his resolution—fear of death, love of family, delight in material pleasures—More's life had now become a comedy (in the sense of a narrative ending in felicity) once more. He must have hoped that he was bound for a better place—although he would resist that insidious form of pride that assumed he was surely among the saved[21]—and was signalling this through the lengths he went to arouse convivial laughter among the witnesses of his death. Rather than excluding those around him, he invited them to touch him (the *noli me tangere* of Chelsea is replaced by the request for the

[19] Roper, *Lyfe*, 55. [20] Roper, *Lyfe*, 72–3.

[21] *CWM*, vol. 1: 153–6; *CWM*, vol. 12, ed. L. Martz and F. Manley (1976), 39, 129–32.

physical support of the sheriff's officers); rather than sitting silently, he filled the air with flippant chatter. This might be dismissed as the understandable nervousness of a man about to die, but, given what we know of More, it seems more likely that here again he was finding a role for himself to perform, and significantly one that did *not* conform to the play that Henry VIII had in hand. The royal script called for the sombre last act of a traitor justly punished; More's intervention sought to rewrite the story in a merrier, comic vein.

John Heywood Treads the Boards

On 7 March 1544, another witty Catholic writer, More's nephew, the playwright and epigrammatist John Heywood, ascended another Henrician scaffold similarly accused of the capital crime of denying the Royal Supremacy. Unlike More, however, Heywood was pardoned at the last moment and walked free. A timely offer to recant and the intervention of a well-placed ally seem to have won him the reprieve. On 26 June, Heywood was granted a general pardon,[22] and on 9 July, nine years to the day after More's death, he delivered a formal recantation at Paul's Cross, acknowledging that

> for lack of grace I have most wilfully and obstinately suffered myself to fall to such blindness that I have not only thought that the bishop of Rome hath been and ought to be taken the chief and supreme head of the universal church of Christ here in earth, but also, like no true subject, concealed and favoured such as I have known and thought to be of the [same] opinion.[23]

Heywood's sober performance clearly struck John Foxe as more in keeping with the occasion than More's flippant asides had seemed to Hall, for he quoted the confession in its entirety in his *Acts and Monuments*. But at least one commentator felt that it was actually Heywood's jests and good humour that had finally saved him. In *The Metamorphosis of Ajax*, Sir John Harrington asked,

> What think you by Heywood, that 'scaped hanging with his mirth, the King being graciously and (as I think) truly persuaded, that a man that wrate so pleasant and harmless verses could not have any harmful conceit against his proceeding and so by the honest motion of a Gentleman of his Chamber, saved him from the jerk of the six stringed whip.[24]

Heywood, like More, was a writer who enjoyed—indeed cultivated—a reputation for merriness in his life and work. Contemporaries spoke of his 'wit and invention',

[22] *L&P*, 19 (i): 812 (109). [23] Foxe, *Acts and Monuments*, V, 628.

[24] *Sir John Harrington's A New Discourse of a Stale Subject Called the Metamorphosis of Ajax*, ed. E. S. Donno (London: Routledge and Kegan Paul, 1962), 102. The 'six stringed whip' was the Act of Six Articles (1539).

later commentators of his 'mirth and quickness of conceit'.[25] His plays declare their allegiance to mirth on their very title pages: 'A merry play' (*Johan Johan*, 1533), 'A new and a very merry interlude' (*The Four PP*, ?1533, and *The Play of the Weather*, 1533). His poems laud amiability and moderation:

> In such things as we cannot flee,
> But needs they must abiden be,
> Let contentation [contentment] be decree,
> Make virtue of necessity,
> Be merry, friends![26]

And his hugely popular collections of epigrams and proverbs reinforce his abiding reputation as a wit with a penchant for modesty and self-deprecation:

> 'Art thou Heywood, that hath made many plays?'
> 'Yea, many plays, few good works in all my days.'[27]

But, like More, Heywood did not eschew controversy; rather, his 'harmless' merriness allowed him to engage with the most contentious issues of his day. The appeals for moderation voiced in his dramatic and poetic works were performed in a courtly community traumatized by the divisive 'Great Matter' of Henry VIII's divorce and the assault on conventional religion instigated by the Royal Supremacy. His lyrics lauding reconciliation were written in the household of Princess Mary, who had been cast aside by her father—a collateral casualty of the divorce proceedings and the break with Rome. As the king drifted ever further into despotic immoderation and the body politic seemed increasingly divided into mutually antipathetic factions, Heywood's tenacious advocacy of the merry mean and a generosity of spirit which might encompass and supersede differences of religious practice was a clear political statement, albeit one voiced in terms to which few could take serious exception.[28]

In *The Four PP*, for example, the Pedlar enjoins characters and spectators alike to leave ecclesiastical reform to the church authorities. Where it is obvious that

[25] *The Autobiography of Thomas Wythorne*, ed. J. M. Osborn (Oxford: Clarendon Press, 1961), 13; Thomas Puttenham, *The Art of Poesie*, ed. G. D. Willcock and A. Walker (Cambridge: Cambridge University Press, 1936), 60; cited in R. Axton and P. Happé (eds.), *The Plays of John Heywood* (Cambridge: D.S. Brewer, 1991), 1–3. 'Merry John Heywood' was already a cliché when Puttenham used it in *The Art* (275–6). See John Bale, *Illustrium majoris Brittaniae scriptorum summarium* (Wessel, 1548), 235; Bale, *Scriptorum illustrium majoris Brytannie Catalogus* (Basle, 1557–9), 2: 110.

[26] BL MS Add. 15233, ff. 43a–43b (ll. 46–50); *John Heywood's Works and Miscellaneous Short Poems*, ed. B. A. Milligan (Urbana, IL: University of Illinois Press, 1956), 260.

[27] Epigram 100, *The Fifth Hundred of Epigrams* (1562), quoted in Axton and Happé, *Plays*, 1.

[28] See Greg Walker, *Writing Under Tyranny: English Literature and the Henrician Reformation* (Oxford: Oxford University Press, 2005), 100–19; and Walker, *The Politics of Performance in Early Renaissance Drama* (Cambridge: Cambridge University Press, 1998), 76–116.

pardons, relics, or shrines are fraudulent, he suggests, there is no obligation to do them reverence:

> But where ye doubt, the truth not knowing,
> Believing the best, good may be growing...
> ...best in these things it seemeth to me,
> To make no judgment upon ye;
> But as the church doth judge or take them,
> So do ye receive or forsake them. (1203–4, 1207–10)

Taken in isolation, such sentiments are anodyne commonplaces; but the artful injunction to look on the best side of tricky theological questions has a long pedigree in English reformist and satirical writings.[29] To argue for the authority of the institutional church over the validation of relics, pilgrimages, and pardons at a time when evangelical preachers were challenging their theological basis was to do rather more than rehearse a timeless platitude. It was to take sides in a matter of intense controversy. Yet, by wrapping his partisanship in the blanket of 'believing the best' of all people, Heywood was smoothing the potentially abrasive edges from the suggestion, leaving it with the appearance of simply amiable good counsel.[30] Hence perhaps his ability to escape his uncle's fate, and to survive through the reigns of Henry, Edward, and Mary, writing and publishing for a range of audiences that spanned the widening confessional divide.

Menippean Satire

The very different fates of More and Heywood have largely forestalled attempts to consider them together. Yet they were both highly moral men, engaged in the defence of Catholic values in a period of violent change, who each in his own way deployed 'mirth' as a conspicuous part of his public persona. How might we reconcile their striking conflation of the serious with the jocular? Why did 'merriness' prove so congenial to them at this time? And how did they employ it in their wholly more serious engagements with Henrician politics?

Jests, witticisms, and maxims were, of course, all part of the orator's rhetorical arsenal, as anyone familiar with Cicero or Quintilian would know.[31] So More and Heywood may have learnt the persuasive value of humour in the schoolroom. But

[29] William Langland, *The Vision of Piers Plowman*, ed. A. V. C. Schmidt (London: J. M. Dent, 1978), ll. 199–229. For the wider context, see Brian Cummings, *The Literary Culture of the Reformation: Grammar and Grace* (Oxford: Oxford University Press, 2002).

[30] Candace Lines, '"To Take on Them Judgemente": Absolutism and Debate in John Heywood's Plays', *Studies in Philology*, 97 (2000), 401–32.

[31] Cicero, *On The Ideal Orator*, ed. and trans. J. M. May and J. Wisse (Oxford: Oxford University Press, 2001), 2.237–90; Quintilianus, Marcus Fabius, *Institutio Oratoria*, trans. H. E. Butler (New Haven, CT: Loeb Classical Library, 1920), 6.3; D. Marsh, 'Aesop and the Humanist Apologue',

there was more to their deployment of mirth than simple adherence to humanist rhetorical training. They shared, in addition to their family ties, a number of important literary affiliations. They clearly knew and admired Chaucer, that consummate mixer of 'earnestness' and 'game', and deployed ideas and tropes from his work—most obviously the *Pardoner's Prologue* and the *General Prologue* to *The Canterbury Tales*—in their own writings.[32] They evidently saw in Chaucer a kindred spirit, a liberal, reforming Catholic who, while thoroughly orthodox in doctrine, also had no time for the grosser abuses of the established church.

Moreover, Chaucer offered a striking example of a writer who could address the issues close to More's and Heywood's hearts while maintaining a persona which was amiably, self-effacingly 'merry'. His disarmingly self-deprecating comments go beyond conventional modesty topoi to present a 'Geoffrey Chaucer' who is seemingly hardly qualified to discuss serious matters of morality or politics at all. Nowhere is this more obvious than in *The Canterbury Tales*, his most sustained exercise in social observation and commentary. The *Tales*, newly available in 1532 in William Thynne's monumental edition of Chaucer's *Works*, also offered More and Heywood a masterclass in the uses of merry ambiguity, suggesting how humour and irony, once loosed in a text, could hover mischievously over even the most seemingly straightforward utterances. The wry understatements and knowingly provocative naiveties of the *General Prologue*, for example, have an unsettling afterlife in the work, drawing within their destabilising purview everything that follows. When, for example, the narrator intervenes directly in the portrait of the ambitious Monk to observe 'And I seyde his opinion was good' (*General Prologue*, l.183), one senses the presence of ironic effects that potentially encompass not only the Monk and narrator but the reader as well.

But how secure is any reader in their reading at this point? We might laugh comfortably at the Monk, confident that he is the unwitting butt of an unspoken critique, but how do we stand vis-à-vis the narrator? Are we being invited to laugh with the author at a naïve misjudgement, or is the narrator's comment itself delivered with a knowing wink in our direction? Our uncertainty about the precise scope of the joke betrays the fact that we are not in full command of the effects at play here—and the only recourse, short of despair, is to delight in the ambiguities we experience. Thus, through calculated ambivalence and the multiplication of narrators and characters, Chaucer is able to broach highly contentious issues such as clerical immorality, the status of relics and pardons or the efficacy of sacraments administered by a sinful priest, without appearing to side openly with either the criticisms of the Lollards or the reactions of their orthodox opponents. The strategy

Renaissance Studies, 17 (2003), 9–26; and B. C. Bowen, 'Ciceronian Wit and Renaissance Rhetoric', *Rhetorica*, 16 (1998), 409–29.

[32] See *CWM*, vol. 6 (i), ed. T. M. C. Lawler, G. Marc'hadour, and R. Marius (1981), 6, 98, 217; Axton and Happé, *Plays*, 38–40; Walker, *Writing*, 73–99.

was one which More and Heywood would each use to their advantage a century and a half later.

Beyond Chaucer, More and Heywood, as we have seen, shared a delight in the comic potential of the manipulation of dramatic personae.[33] But recent scholarship has traced the curious mixture of seriousness and comedy, in More's case at least, to his encounter with another text, mentioned earlier: Lucian's dialogues. Like Erasmus, who was to create a Lucianic classic in his *Praise of Folly*, More, it is argued, discovered a new and more satisfactory way of approaching serious issues when he set about translating a number of the satirist's works.[34] The key to Lucian's comedy, as it is for Chaucer's, is a 'serio-comic' (*spoudogeloion*) approach that flouts conventional generic and cultural distinctions and exposes serious matters to playful ridicule. As More describes it, this mode of satire allows its exponent to castigate vice without causing offence, even to those whose vices he castigates:

> He [Lucian] everywhere reprimands and censures, with very honest and at the same time entertaining wit... And this he does so cleverly and effectively that, although no one pricks more deeply, nobody resents his stinging.[35]

As we shall see, this description suits More's *Utopia* as readily as Lucian's dialogues, but it is arguably to Heywood that we should look to find the most sustained and consistent use of Lucianic models in Henrician literature.

At the heart of Lucianic serio-comedy is an ability to laugh with as well as at the target of one's satire, while inviting laughter at one's own expense as well—an expansive quality that allowed writers to have it all ways, as Erasmus said of More, speaking the truth while laughing and laughing while speaking the truth.[36] This attitude is embodied in the characteristic literary genre of Lucian and the cynics, the Menippean satire, named after Menippus of Gadara, whose own works, lost since classical times, were said by Diogenes Laertius to have been '*spoudogeloion*'.[37] As we have seen, Lucian borrowed the earlier cynic's name and serio-comic attitude for the central character in two of his best-known dialogues, sending his fictional Menippus to consult the shades of the dead, or up to Olympus to petition Zeus in *Icaromenippus*. In each case the traveller's irreverent account of the journey allows

[33] *Opus Epistolarum des. Erasmi*, 6: 16.

[34] Alistair Fox, *Thomas More: History and Providence* (Oxford: Blackwell, 1982), 36, 41, 43.

[35] *CWM*, vol. 3 (i): 3. These were also the qualities admirers saw in More and Heywood. See Harpsfield, *Life*, 74, 76, and *CWM*, vol. 3 (ii), ed. C.H. Miller, L. Bradner, C. A. Lynch, and R. P. Oliver (1984), 75.

[36] *Opus Epistolarum*, 1: 425.45–426.46; 422.16; C. S. Thompson, *CWM*, vol. 3 (i): 1, fn. 1; Daniel Kinney, 'Heirs of the Dog: Cynic Selfhood in Medieval and Renaissance Culture', in *The Cynics: The Cynical Movement in Antiquity and its Legacy*, ed. R. B. Branham and Marie-Odile Goulet-Caze (Berkeley: University of California Press, 1996), 294–328; and in the same volume, J. L. Moles, 'Cynic Cosmopolitanism', 105–20.

[37] Diogenes Laertius, *Lives of the Eminent Philosophers*, ed. R. D. Hicks (Cambridge, MA: Harvard University Press, 1931), 102–5; D. R. Dudley, *A History of Cynicism from Diogenes to the Sixth Century AD* (London: Methuen, 1937), 69–70.

the author to subject serious theological and philosophical subjects (the fate of the dead, the nature of existence, the role of Fortune, and divine intervention in human affairs) to audacious scrutiny, while seeming only to poke gentle fun at the pomposities of the great and the simplicity of the narrator. By describing fantastical realms, which are unlike conventional society yet comment on it in ironic ways, these texts can suggest portentous, serious intentions. Yet they habitually end in comic anticlimax, modestly pointing back to their status as merely merry jests. In the *Menippus*, for example, the only advice which the protagonist finally receives from the seer Tiresias turns out to be to live for the moment, have a good time, and take nothing seriously.[38] In the *Icaromennipus*, Zeus, having been encouraged to visit terrible destruction on all philosophers for their temerity in slandering the Olympians, suddenly recalls that it is a festival day and so postpones any action until the Spring. Epic journeys have been undertaken and momentous expectations aroused, but in the end nothing changes.

What the Menippean mode also generates is a disorienting sense that no speaker, however earnest or plausible, delivers the final word on a subject. Rather than act as vehicles for the direct exposition of truth in the mode of the Socratic dialogue, the Lucianic form thus problematizes the notion that any single truth can be found. Meaning is always a matter for readers to discern for themselves from among contending claims. Even in a Menippean monologue there are always unspoken objections to what is being said that press for the reader's attention, and other realms of experience mobilized to complicate the claims being advanced. Hence reading a Menippean text is always coloured by a profound, and usually pleasurable, sense of ambivalence.[39]

The final feature of Menippean satire of interest here is its delight in paradox. As Scott Blanchard observes, it is 'an immensely learned form that is at the same time... anti-intellectual'.[40] And, although it relies upon in-jokes, parodies, and ironies that are accessible only to an intellectual elite, it is not as a consequence smug about its own elitism. Rather, as Anne Payne suggests, 'if it exposes fools and knaves, it also democratically exposes the presumptions of those who piously expose them'.[41] Just as no set of values is safe from its gaze, so no one is free from its implied allegations of folly and hypocrisy.[42] These twin aspects of the Menippean mode—the intellectual maturity and humility inherent in its refusal to endorse any single view of the human condition (a tendency that might initially appear merely irresponsible), and its refusal to exempt anyone, even the author,

[38] *CWM*, vol. 3 (i): 179.

[39] Branham, 'Utopian Laughter', 23–43; Fox, *Thomas More*, 38–41; M. A. Screech, *Laughter at the Foot of the Cross* (London: Penguin, 1997), 141–60.

[40] W. S. Blanchard, *Scholars' Bedlam: Menippean Satire in the Renaissance* (Lewisburg: Bucknell University Press, 1995), 14 and 27.

[41] F. A. Payne, *Chaucer and Menippean Satire* (Madison: University of Wisconsin Press, 1981), 5.

[42] Payne, *Chaucer and Menippean Satire*, 5.

from its ironic, satirical gaze—are probably the features that initially drew More so powerfully to it as a way of writing and thinking about the world.

In *Utopia*, More takes the venerable idea of the description of an ideal state—a genre traceable to Plato's *Republic*—and rewrites it in a Menippean spirit. Its nature is hinted at on its title page, which describes it as *festivus* (festive/merry),[43] and in the text's playful use of Greek proper names (*Anydrus*, the river 'without water', *Ademus*, the ruler 'without people'), which signal to the cognoscenti that Utopia is both an attempt to imagine the happiest of commonwealths (*eutopia*) and 'No-Place', a never-land of the author's fancy.[44] As Edward Surtz suggests, it, like most Menippean satires, is a coterie text, aimed primarily at European humanists who could decode and appreciate its allusions and quibbles. And on one level it gives those readers exactly what they wanted to hear. In Raphael Hythlodaeus it presents a spokesman for humanist values and aspirations of 'almost heroic stature',[45] whose narrative can be read as a direct critique of those aspects of contemporary society (ignorant, self-seeking clergymen, unjust laws, the celebration of warfare) which men like Erasmus, the book's dedicatee Peter Giles, and More himself most criticized.[46]

But in the true Menippean spirit, *Utopia* is not only a satire for humanists, but a satire *of* them too. It espouses many of their cherished values, but also gently mocks them, suggesting the naivety of expecting them to prosper in a fallen world.[47] As Surtz argues, Hythlodaeus (whose name implies 'nonsense-spreader') remains convinced that Utopia represents the best and only true form of social organization, but, as with the zealous protagonist of Lucian's *Cynic*, it gradually becomes clear as he speaks that 'something is not wholly satisfactory about either the substance of his claims, or the certainty with which he advances them'.[48] The Utopians can appear too perfect. Only a people so virtuous and self-disciplined, one might think, could enjoy a regimen of self-denial and communal uniformity that most mortals would find intolerable. Yet they are also less than perfect in other aspects of their lives, often alarmingly so. Could More really have looked with equanimity on a culture (even a pagan one) that practised suicide for the incurably ill, licensed divorce for lay-folk and the marriage of priests, all notions that he condemned with abhorrence elsewhere? One is, perhaps, inclined to detect a degree of sincerity in the comment offered by his fictional namesake at the end of Hythlodaeus's account, that 'many things' in the narrative seemed to him 'very absurdly established in the customs and laws of the people described'. Yet any sense of security we might feel in even that judgement is quickly problematized by the suggestion that it aligns us with 'the estimation of the common people', that

[43] B. C. Bowen, 'Festive Humanism: The Case of Luscinus', in Bowen, *Humour and Humanism in the Renaissance* (Aldershot: Ashgate, 2004), VII, 1–18.

[44] *CWM*, vol. 4: cxlviii and 117–19. [45] *CWM*, vol. 4: cxlviii. [46] *CWM*, vol. 4: 231.

[47] *CWM*, vol. 4: clii. [48] *CWM*, vol. 4: cxxxii–cxxxiii.

many-headed mob whose instincts are rarely to be trusted by wiser folk.[49] Thus, as with the *Cynic*, we are left with a dialogue in which neither antagonist nor protagonist emerges fully vindicated.[50]

The greatest attraction of the Menippean mode for More, was, as I have suggested, probably that the writer himself would always be contained in its implied critique, always exposing his own limitations along with those of his subjects. Thus, in *Utopia* he creates two disputants who, in part at least, expose different aspects of his own personality, his naïve zeal for moral and social reform in Hythlodaeus, in Morus the desire for the place in royal service which would allow him to put his aspirations into practice. And he allows each aspect to expose the other's flaws in a no-holds-barred debate. Thus, while Hythlodaeus can appear inflexibly fundamentalist in his demands, he is nonetheless able to land the telling blow that Morus's willingness to adapt himself to 'the play in hand' runs contrary to Christ's own teachings.[51] The text thus works to unsettle the intellectual, spiritual, and social complacencies that are the breeding grounds of pride and the gateway to sin. It prompts reader and writer alike to question both those values on display in the text and those which they bring to the viewing, offering an implicit invitation to reject any that do not stand the test of this exercise in merry self-scrutiny.

In *Utopia*, then, More deploys the full range of serio-comic, ambivalent effects that Menippean satire offers, to tease, surprise, and delight his intended scholarly readership. And his pleasure in the confusion which it caused those readers not privy to its ironies is evident in the stories, gleefully repeated by his friends, about those literalists who eagerly sought the whereabouts of the island.[52] But *Utopia* was the last of More's sustained literary evocations of the Menippean spirit. Thereafter he used irony and mirth more sparingly, deploying them as occasional rhetorical devices rather than structuring principles in his works. In part, of course, this was a result of shifts in his intended readership. By the time he began *The Dialogue Concerning Heresies* (1528) he was no longer writing for a Latinate readership united (however fractious their disagreements over minutiae) around a core of shared intellectual values. His polemical English works were written for a wider, less homogeneous readership that was considerably less predictable in its reactions. The tricks and subtleties of the Menippean mode that had been vital in engaging scholarly readers were less appropriate in this new context. What had been a pleasantly provoking ambivalence or a playful piece of misdirection might be a dangerous hostage to fortune among a popular audience, a source of either genuine misunderstanding by the unschooled or deliberate misuse by his enemies. Hence the playfulness evident in the text was subordinated more obviously to its argumentative

[49] *CWM*, vol. 4: 245.

[50] *CWM*, vol. 4: cxxxviii. But see Skinner, *Visions of Politics*, vol. 2: 213–14.

[51] Fox, *Thomas More*, 65.

[52] Harpsfield, *Life*, 102–4.

purpose.[53] Moreover, by the early 1530s 'Lucianism' itself had become a term of abuse, bandied between evangelicals and conservatives as a synonym for scoffing scepticism or sophistry, and needed to be treated with care.[54]

In his public and private lives, however, More was still, as we have seen, wedded to a mirthful persona. And this suggests that 'merriness' for him was always rather more than just a literary strategy learned from Lucian—or rather that his reading of Lucian and the cynics suggested more to him than simply a way of meeting Horace's dictum that the author should both instruct and delight.[55]

Cynics and Holy Fools

The cynic tradition was, of course, available to Renaissance readers in a number of forms. The Church Fathers, while censoring the more radically anti-social aspects of the cynics' lifestyle, were nonetheless keen to co-opt them among the classical precursors of Christian asceticism.[56] Thus, when Latin accounts of the life and sayings of Diogenes became available in print in the latter half of the fifteenth century, Christian readers possessed a ready-made interpretative framework through which to read them.[57] This stressed the cynic's rejection of materialism and pointed nonconformity in the face of hypocritical worldly values, his personal austerity and the boldness with which he criticized the conduct of those around him—especially those in authority. In this way the irreverent, 'foolish' cynic could be readily accommodated to the Christian ascetic model of 'folly for Christ's sake', a mode of radical *imitatio Christi*, especially popular in the Eastern Church, that rejected the trappings of worldly civilization and favoured the life of the humble mendicant.

[53] Brian Cummings, 'Reformed Literature and Literature Reformed', in *The Cambridge History of Medieval English Literature*, ed. D. Wallace (Cambridge: Cambridge University Press, 1999), 821–51. See *The Confutation of Tyndale's Answer* (1532), *CWM*, vol. 8 (3), ed. L. A. Schuster, R. C. Marius, J. P. Lusardi, and R. J. Schoek (1973), 178; Stephen Greenblatt, *Renaissance Self-Fashioning From More to Shakespeare* (Chicago: University of Chicago Press, 1980), 74–114; Simpson, *Burning to Read*, 277–82.

[54] John Frith called More 'another Lucian, neither regarding God nor man': *The Works of the English Reformers William Tyndale and John Frith*, vol. 3, ed. T. Russell (Whitefish, MT: Kessinger Publishing reprint, 2007), 267; *CWM*, vol. 3 (i): xxiv.

[55] *CWM*, vol. 3 (i): 3.

[56] Derek Krueger, 'Diogenes the Cynic Among the Fourth-Century Fathers', *Vigiliae Christianae*, 4 (1993), 24–49, at 35 and 40–4; Krueger, 'The Bawdy and Society: The Shamelessness of Diogenes in Roman Imperial Culture', in Branham and Goulet-Caze, *The Cynics*, 222–38; S. Matton, 'Cynics and Christianity from the Middle Ages to the Renaissance', in *The Cynics*, 240–56, at 243–5.

[57] A Latin text of Diogenes Laertius's *Lives* was printed in Rome in 1472. Another source, Plutarch's *Moralia*, appeared in Venice in 1509. Matton, 'Cynics', 242; Kinney, 'Heirs', 306–7; David Marsh, *Lucian and the Latins* (Ann Arbor: University of Michigan Press, 1998), 5; Krueger, 'Diogenes', 29–30.

This higher, Christian folly, vaunted by St Paul,[58] offered its adherents two distinct forms of foolishness, what we might think of as a 'merry', gamesome stream and a more earnest one. The former is evident in the near-ecstatic joy which characterized the piety of western mystics such as St Columba, 'happy in his inmost heart in the joy of the Holy Spirit'; or St Bruno, the founder of the Carthusian Order that More himself considered joining in his youth, who practised his devotions with 'a mirthful expression on his face'.[59] This was, arguably, the path that Heywood chose to follow. More's inclinations, however, drew him increasingly, as he became set on confrontation with the King, to the alternative stream of holy folly that placed its adherents not at the centre of convivial fellowship but on the margins of the political community, distanced from the indulgences of regular society and from many of its defining features. It was this 'salonic' (foolish) strand to More's merry persona that allowed him to adapt so readily from the Lucianic comic mode of his earlier writings to the path of the man of conscience and ultimately the martyr.

Figures such as the seventh-century Simeon Salos of Emesa, who publicly flaunted social proprieties, threw nuts in church, and ran naked into the female bathhouse, or the later example of St Francis of Assisi, who lived as a beggar, preaching to animals, have much in common with the version of Diogenes bequeathed to medieval Christians by the Fathers.[60] Rather than rely on worldly wisdom, such men sought to live out the Pauline dictum that 'the foolish things of the world hath God chosen that he may confound the wise' (1 Corinthians 1:27). For them, adopting the life of the foolish outcast was the most direct and overt means of subduing the flesh and the egotistical will-to-pride that seeks the good opinion of one's peers and neighbours. Though they were originally neither poor nor foolish, they adopted the personae of the low and laughable as conscious choices.[61]

What the cynics and holy fools shared was a commitment to *askesis*, the self-discipline that renders the subject immune to the lures of Fortune and the Devil.[62] As John Saward eloquently describes it, the asceticism of the holy fools was designed to help them 'to . . . conquer pride, renounce self, and live only to the Lord; folly for them is the last stage or highest grade of humility—the loss of all reputation and esteem'.[63]

58 'If any man among you seem to be wise in this world, let him become a fool, that he may be wise. For the wisdom of this world is foolishness with God.' (1 Corinthians 3:18–20); Screech, *Laughter*, 116–40.

59 John Saward, *Perfect Fools: Folly for Christ's Sake in Catholic and Orthodox Spirituality* (Oxford: Oxford University Press, 1980), 46–7, 58, and 95.

60 Krueger, 'Bawdy', 231; Peter Brown, 'The Function of the Holy Man in Late Antiquity', *Journal of Roman Studies*, 61 (1971), 80–101; Saward, *Perfect Fools*, 12–25.

61 Saward, *Perfect Fools*, 3–4 and 18–20.

62 Introduction in Branham and Goulet-Caze, *Cynics*, 7–9; Brown, 'Function', 80–101.

63 Saward, *Perfect Fools*, 29.

One of the most valuable aspects of the serio-comic mode for More was thus, as Daniel Kinney notes, precisely that it allowed him to expose his own flaws to the same 'mocking' scrutiny that it trained on the flaws of others. While the laughter he sought to provoke evoked a convivial sense of fellowship amid the terrible events of his later life, it nonetheless established More himself as the butt of many of the jokes—the fool who is laughed at as well as with. This 'ironic self-exposure'[64] was the literary equivalent of his famous hair-shirt, with the crucial difference that it, like the scandalous self-exposures of the fools for Christ, was worn openly and in public. The two seemingly contradictory aspects of More's persona (i.e. the public 'merry' folly and the pious private mortification) might thus better be seen as two aspects of the same ascetic strategy, each aimed distinctly at the mortification of pride. More 'acted the fool' in public to live out the reminder (to himself and others) that all humankind is foolish in the eyes of God, and that to realize this is the all-important first step in the process of redemption. Significantly he identified himself as such a fool in a letter written from the Tower in 1534, telling his daughter Margaret that 'I trust my lord reckoneth me among the fools, and so I reckon myself, as my name is in Greek. And I find, thank God, causes not a few wherefore I should in very deed.'[65]

The Denial of Malice

For Heywood, the channels of Lucianic merriness ran along different channels. Rather than follow the ascetic aspects of cynic philosophy into holy folly, he seems to have followed the Menippean strain from Lucian to Chaucer, and thence to the later Lucianic imitators of the Italian Renaissance such as Leon Battista Alberti.[66] In imitating them he found a means to pursue his critique of Henrician government even in the heart of the royal court, attempting through laughter to counsel Henry VIII back to moderation.

When language itself becomes the subject of explicit political scrutiny, and key terms in the religious and political lexicons are the focus of anxious policing, then the Menippean mode, with its ambivalences and indirections, becomes a useful tool for an author with dangerous ideas to explore. This was the situation in the 1390s, when Chaucer's Menippean irony allowed him to navigate a satirical path through the thickets of religious controversy in *The Canterbury Tales*, offering memorable representations of what the Lollards condemned as scandalous clerical

[64] Kinney, 'Heirs', 323–4; D. R. Smith, 'Portrait and Counter-portrait in Holbein's "The Family of Sir Thomas More"', *The Art Bulletin*, 87 (2005), 484–507.

[65] E. F. Rogers, *The Correspondence of Sir Thomas More* (Princeton, NJ: University of Princeton Press, 1947), 519.

[66] Walker, *Writing*, 110–11.

abuses while not appearing to advance dangerous views either directly or in his own voice. It was still more obviously the situation in the 1530s, when the Henrician Treason Act (1534) made it a capital offence to

> Maliciously wish, will or desire by words or writing, or by craft imagine, invent, practise, or attempt any bodily harm to be done or committed to the king's most royal person, the queen's or their heirs apparent, or to deprive them . . . of the dignity, title, or name of their royal estates, or slanderously and maliciously publish and pronounce by express writing or words that the king . . . should be heretic, schismatic, tyrant, infidel or usurper of the Crown.[67]

The Act thus made words alone treasonable, albeit, it was said, the common lawyers in Parliament had insisted that such words had to be 'maliciously' spoken.[68] Hence it was necessary to prove authorial intention if words alone were to provide evidence of guilt. But well before this Act cemented royal paranoia into statute, the use of words, especially in writing, was a matter of profound political unease. The Proclamation against Heretical Books, issued prior to 6 March 1529, for example, made it illegal not only to import, sell, or receive any text, printed or handwritten, that impugned the Catholic faith or the decrees and ordinances of the Church, but also any that might be thought to 'reproach, rebuke, or slander . . . the King, his honourable Council, or his lords spiritual or temporal',[69] a stipulation which, if interpreted strictly, would criminalize most forms of social or religious satire and complaint. Similarly the Proclamation Prohibiting Erroneous Books of 22 June 1530 condemned texts printed in English abroad and circulated in England, 'to the intent as well to pervert and withdraw the people from the catholic and true faith of Christ, as also to stir and incense them to sedition and disobedience against their princes, sovereigns, and heads, as also to condemn and neglect all good laws, customs, and virtuous manners'.[70]

In such an environment a wide range of critical opinion was potentially drawn within the definition of seditious writings, yet it was essential for the intentions of the authors or circulators of texts to be proved to be malicious for the ordinances to apply. The crucial ambivalence of the Menippean mode therefore gave authors a freedom (limited and fraught though it might be) to suggest the otherwise unspeakable and explore otherwise dangerous ideas. It gave them leave to hint and suggest rather than to state outright, to imply rather more (or less) than they seemed to say, and ultimately to pass the burden of interpretation of their works to their readers. With such texts it would be very difficult to determine the precise intentions of their authors, and so the blunt instrument of Henrician statute might potentially be checked.

[67] *SR*, 3: 508–9. [68] *L&P*, 8: 856.

[69] P. L. Hughes and J. F. Larkin (eds.), *Tudor Royal Proclamations*, Vol. 1: *The Early Tudors, 1485–1553* (New Haven, CT: Yale University Press, 1964), 185.

[70] Hughes and Larkin, *The Early Tudors*, 193–5; Cummings, 'Reformed Literature', 839–47.

Thus, while More retreated into silence on the key issues proscribed by statute, refusing either to swear to the Oath of Succession or to say why he would not swear, Heywood continued to speak, and speak volubly. For a writer like him, who was willing to acknowledge abuses within the church and argue for their reform, yet wished fervently to oppose the threat of evangelical religion which was gaining ground under the Royal Supremacy, the Menippean mode allowed him to mock what he saw as the follies of current policies while not exposing himself to the charge of malicious or seditious intent. Unlike the more conventional Socratic dialogue, the Menippean text identified no speaker as the author's surrogate, so no single speech could be extracted as evidence of his views. A character in Heywood's interludes might appear to be speaking persuasively at one point but foolishly elsewhere, while the apparent meaning of any given utterance might depend either upon its overt logical consistency or on its emotional impact upon the reader, with the two not always coinciding and the text not signalling which faculty should have priority.

Nor was Menippean irony, unlike its more straightforward cousin, readily susceptible to decoding. While a reader might well feel that the text is saying one thing but meaning another, it is not always possible to say exactly what that other thing might be. Simply reversing the logic of what is said does not always reveal the truth. Thus the Menippean author had a ready-made defence against the kind of allegation of malicious intent which Henry VIII's interrogators put to John Skip, Anne Boleyn's chaplain, when on Passion Sunday 1536 he preached a wittily critical sermon about the failings of the King's councillors and parliament in the guise of an encomium of their wisdom. As his interrogators reminded themselves in the list of questions they would ask him, it was easy to decode such 'mockish' irony, as it simply said the opposite of what the speaker really meant.

> Item, let the preacher be examined upon his oath whether he spake not all this sentence *ironice* and mockishly in displeasure and rebuke of the parliament: 'where be a great number of sad and discrete men which love the commonwealth... [etc.]', albeit the preacher meaneth the contrary by his irony, for in all ironies the meaning is contrary to the words. And so all the foresaid sentence is to be taken clean contrary to the words, whereby it may appear the preacher greatly to be blamed if he be examined particularly upon everything contained in the said sentence.[71]

It would be far harder to examine Heywood 'particularly' on the content of a text like his *Play of the Weather*, which delivered its ironies with a far subtler hand. Did its wry portrayal of King Jupiter imply that Henry VIII was a usurper or tyrant, or mock his claim to supreme headship of the church? Did it seek, through ridicule, to stir its audiences to disobedience to their 'princes, sovereigns, and heads'? It would be hard to see how this could be established definitively, despite the play's amused

[71] National Archives, Kew, State Papers 1/103 ff. 80^{v}–81. See Cummings, *Literary Culture*, 223–31, for the analogous case of Thomas Wyatt.

account of the god-king's claim to have taken supreme authority to benefit everyone but himself, and its ribald jokes about heads and headship in the commonwealth.[72] Or, did it mock Henry's claims that only the highest motives drove him to seek an annulment of his first marriage (claims that he declared his subjects should not question) through its hints that Jupiter was fashioning a fresh 'new moon' to replace a leaky, old one; in its allusions to the name 'Anne' or its talk of a hurried Olympian wedding at a time when the King's marriage to the pregnant Anne Boleyn was an open courtly secret?[73] Again, spectators might suspect as much, but the text offered no point of purchase for an investigator wishing to prove it. In a world in which treason might lie in 'words alone' and proving authorial intention might be a matter of life and death, the Menippean mode's insistence that meaning was never delivered merely by words, and intention was always in the eye of the beholder, offered a limited space in which literature could still perform its traditional cultural work of speaking truth to power.

As this brief examination of two very different Henrician 'merry men' has suggested, the roots of their mirthful, foolish personae were many and diverse, some stretching back to classical precepts and biblical injunctions, others to medieval traditions or recent humanist experiments. 'Acting merrily' might encompass the most profound questions of religious and personal identity, or social and political issues of striking topicality, or both at once. It might lead its exponent either to a reputation for conviviality or to marginalization and a martyr's death. More's jests on the scaffold might thus be read in various ways. For Hall, as we saw, they were a curious contradiction, a blemish on the character of an otherwise sagacious man. For Tyndale and Foxe they were evidence of More's lack of integrity, of a piece with his capacity to retreat into 'poetic' fictions if he could not win an argument by reason alone. For More's defenders, by contrast, they set him in an honourable tradition of martyrdom, being perhaps milder, more accommodating versions of the tricks with which earlier saintly victims had turned the tables on their persecutors.

For More himself, 'merriness', however congenial, was always a means to an end—part of a considered approach to public life that remained contingent upon the moral and theological questions that dominated his thinking. He could jest until the point of death, but always mindful of the role that jesting played in his intention to make a good end. His last jokes thus contributed both to what he hoped would be the perception of his death as a happy event and to his private determination to subdue any vestiges of pride that his final public performance might prompt. In Heywood's case, conversely, the commitment to merriness as an end in itself was perhaps more complete, more closely tied to his perception of himself as a courtly maker of plays, part of the same community as the sovereign he

[72] See *Weather*, lines 296–328, in Axton and Happé, *Plays of John Heywood*.
[73] Halle, *The Union of the Two Noble Families*, clxxx; *Weather*, ll. 780–5, 797–811.

criticized. Hence he would resist the ultimate earnestness of his own encounter with the wicket gate and the point of no return, not finally giving up the struggle to laugh the kingdom back into moderation until his old age and the death of Queen Mary.

FURTHER READING

Blanchard, W. S. *Scholars' Bedlam: Menippean Satire in the Renaissance* (Lewisburg, PA: Bucknell University Press, 1995)

Fox, Alistair. *Thomas More: History and Providence* (Oxford: Blackwell, 1982)

Simpson, James. *Burning to Read: English Fundamentalism and its Reformation Opponents* (Cambridge, MA: Harvard University Press, 2007)

Walker, Greg. *Writing Under Tyranny: English Literature and the Henrician Reformation* (Oxford: Oxford University Press, 2005)

CHAPTER 19

DESPAIR

NICHOLAS WATSON

This essay, as much a contribution to the history of emotion as to that of theology, is an investigation of the relationship between the late medieval understanding of despair and its post-Reformation career as a key concern of Protestant theology and narrative. The standard view of this relationship is that it is tenuous. For example, in an important 1992 study around which a good deal of this paper moves, Michael McDonald argues that despair, 'an overwhelming sense of rejection, helplessness, and guilt *with respect to God*', was a 'normal . . . experience' in the early modern period, in large part because it had been constructed (by several types of Reformed theology) as a stage through which Puritans, Methodists, and others must pass during their early spiritual development, as 'wakened, but not yet saved'. In the Middle Ages, on the other hand, McDonald asserts that despair was normatively linked to *acedia* or sloth, and as such constituted an 'abnormal and wholly negative' experience that might befall people at any point in their lives.[1] This experience is said to have been without shape or intrinsic meaning, consisting, in this rather straightforward understanding of *acedia*, more of a sense of blankness, an absence of experience, than of 'rejection, helplessness, and guilt'; more by the lack of any awareness of God at all than by the overwhelming and terrified sense of his angry presence.[2] Here, as in other areas of affect, by reconfiguring the theological structure within which Christians directed their lives towards salvation, the Reformation is claimed equally to have reconfigured the terrain of the Christian psyche, making urgent, energetic, and individual an emotion that was previously experienced as torpid, purposeless, and generalized.

[1] For more complex understandings of sloth, see Siegfried Wenzel, *The Sin of Sloth: Acedia in Medieval Thought and Literature* (Chapel Hill: University of North Carolina Press, 1967); and Giorgio Agamben, *Stanzas: Word and Phantasm in Western Culture*, trans. Ronald L. Martinez (Minneapolis: University of Minnesota Press, 1993).

[2] Michael McDonald, '*The Fearefull Estate of Francis Spira*: Narrative, Emotion, and Identity in Early Modern England', *Journal of British Studies*, 31 (1992), 32–61, at 59 (italics his).

In the Middle Ages, on this view, despair was merely one sin on the penitential tree, a perilous sin if not repented—indeed, according to Aquinas, formally the most dangerous of sins, for its capacity to render the sinner incapable of recognizing the dire nature of her or his spiritual state[3]—but readily treatable by a mixture of fear and hope, the virtues best able to infuse the soul with the energy to seek forgiveness. If the struggle with this sin had any special life-stage, it belonged to old age, when the medieval sinful were roused, in part by the creeping despair that threatened the unprepared, to win last-minute pardon. Thus in the final passus of *Piers Plowman*, Sloth's slingshot full of 'drede of dispair' (despairing fear) causes Conscience to enlist Elde in the fight against Wanhope, a miasmic presence who, for all his sinister power, is quickly subdued by Elde's surprising display of energy, invigorated as Elde is by the accessibility of penitential rituals and the virtue of Hope:

> For care Conscience tho cride upon Elde, And bad him
> fonde to fighte and afere Wanhope. And *[stir himself; frighten; Despair]*
> Elde hente Good Hope, and hastiliche he shifte hym, *[seized; confessed himself]*
> And waived awey Wanhope [. . .][4]

While Langland does not regard Wanhope as 'abnormal', he does seem to treat it as a 'wholly negative' branch of the sin of sloth, if also as fully curable once a cure is sought. According to the Good Samaritan in Passus 17, even on deathbeds where 'Drede of desperacion . . . driveth awey grace', the dying can expect to find God's mercy 'gretter/ Thanne alle our wikkede werkes, as Holy Writ telleth: *Misericordia eius super omnia opera eius* [his mercy is above all his works]' (Psalm 144:9, *juxta LXX*).[5] Only those guilty of 'unkindnesse', the ungenerosity that is Langland's version of the sin against the Holy Spirit, have cause to fear once it is too late for them to do restitution; and even here 'sorwe is satisfaccion for [swich] that may noght paye'.[6] Where Aquinas describes despair on a theoretical level as a *generator* of sins, a sin that, once embraced, gives birth to an ever expanding range of sins,[7] Langland treats it practically, as a *consequence* of sins: a pastoral problem to be sure, especially at deathbeds, but not a major or independent part of the soul's spiritual journey.

In its account of despair as a phenomenon associated with the deathbed, *Piers Plowman* represents one late-medieval pastoral mainstream. This had moved

[3] Thomas Aquinas, *Summa Theologiae*, cura fratrum eiusdem ordinis (Madrid: La Editorial Católica, 1961), 2.2.20, art. 3.

[4] William Langland, *Piers Plowman: A Parallel-Text edition of the A, B, C, and Z Versions*, ed. A. V. C. Schmidt (London: Longman, 1995), B.20.165–68. Spellings slightly normalized.

[5] Jerome's translation of the Septuagint, used in liturgical contexts. Compare Jerome's Vulgate translation from the Hebrew: 'Misericordia eius in universa opera eius'. Authorized Version Psalm 145:9 is notably closer to the Septuagint version: 'His tender mercies are over all his works'.

[6] Langland, *Piers Plowman*, ed. Schmidt, B.17.310–16. See also B.13.420–40, B.5.279–83.

[7] Aquinas, *Summa Theologiae*, 2.2.20, art. 1.

gradually away from an earlier monastic understanding of *acedia* as the 'noon-day demon', the insidious undermining of vocation, hope, and finally faith that was the shadow side of the ascetic rigours of monastic *disciplina*—from a version of which our crude modern picture of medieval *acedia* as mere torpor derives—and towards a laicized understanding of the sin as, exactly, a difficult passage in life's journey.[8] Despair in this lay context had become a compound of personal panic and intellectual error for which it was crucial and possible to prepare in advance and which friends of the dying gathered around the deathbed for the very purpose of 'waiv[ing] awey', along with the clustered demonic presences that urged 'wanhope' on the departing soul.[9] Even for Aquinas (scholarly representative of a new, activist contemplative order, the Dominicans) *acedia* was already becoming part of this penitential nexus, and to this extent McDonald is right in thinking it held no special urgency for him. While *Piers Plowman* does not bear out the claim that late medieval despair was essentially unpatterned, a casual rather than a systemic experience, the poem's association of despair with Elde might support McDonald's more fundamental contention that early modern despair was an historically 'distinct emotion', coming into being as part of the larger reconfiguration of selfhood often ascribed to the period.

But there was also a second late medieval tradition of thinking about despair: as a spiritual problem affecting, not ordinary people on their deathbeds, but religious specialists engaged in contemplative living. Writers in this tradition maintained strong roots in the earlier conceptualization of *acedia* articulated by monastic writers from Cassian in the fifth century to Bernard of Clairvaux in the twelfth, and so understood (as many modern commentators do not) the existential nature of this sin, close kin as it was to the great theological sin of unbelief. Yet this tradition had also come to associate despair with a specific set of temptations that have a markedly post-Reformation ring, including doubt, blasphemy, an over-scrupulous sense of sinfulness, and terror at an implacably predestining divine justice. While, as we shall see, writers in this tradition finally understood despair differently from most Protestant theologies, in this case such differences were of the intimate kind that suggests an underlying commonality of feeling and thought. It seems possible, in other words, that the Protestant experience of despair, in whatever senses it may indeed be distinct to the early modern period, was also

[8] For the 'noon-day demon', see Vulgate Psalm 90:6, which offers protection 'a sagitta volante in die...ab incursu et daemonio meridiano' (compare Authorized Version Psalm 91:6, 'the destruction that wasteth at noonday'); Bernard of Clairvaux, *Qui Habitat Sermo 1*, in *Sancti Bernardi Opera*, ed. Jean Leclercq et al., 8 vols. (Rome: Editiones Cistercienses, 1957–77), 4: 10–12; discussed with reference to Cassian's centrally important *Institutes* in Agamben, *Stanzas*, trans. Martinez, 3–10.

[9] A ritual described in detail, using both ritual and textual materials related to *The Visitation of the Sick*, in the early chapters of both versions of Julian of Norwich's *Revelation of Love*. See Amy Appleford, 'The "Comene Course of Prayers": Julian of Norwich and Late Medieval Death Culture', *Journal of English and Germanic Philology*, 107 (2008), 190–214.

continuous with a specific medieval tradition, much as this tradition was itself continuous with an ancient one associated with monasticism.

In pursuing this possibility here, I focus on two sets of works: a series of narrative treatments of despair written in England in the century after 1580 related to the death of the apostate Francesco Spiera in 1548, which form the kernel of McDonald's argument and are described as a group below; and a set of 'remedy' texts, also written in England, the earliest of which is the Augustinian Friar William Flete's *De remediis contra temptaciones* from the 1350s, the latest *The Book of Margery Kempe*, finished in the 1430s (although it is significant that, as is also the case with *Piers Plowman*, many of these works remained in print or manuscript circulation throughout the sixteenth and seventeenth centuries). Scarcely known now except to scholars of English mysticism—and still lacking any edition of its original, Latin text—the *De remediis* was likely written before Flete left England in 1359 to pursue a career in Italy as a hermit and close associate of Catherine of Siena.[10] A powerful influence on Walter Hilton in his *Scale of Perfection* and well known to the author of *The Cloud of Unknowing* amongst others, the *De remediis*, brief as it is, stands at the head of a series of accounts of despair that include passages of Julian of Norwich's *Revelation of Love* (1380s–?1400s), *Fervor Amoris* (*c.*1400), *The Chastising of God's Children* (?1390s), and an important expansion of the *De remediis* called *The Remedy Ayenst the Troubles of Temptacyons* (? before 1400), the third of three Middle English versions of the work.[11] While this group of works takes many positions antipathetic to most sixteenth- and seventeenth-century Protestant theologies—for example, agreeing with Langland over the ease with which God forgives sin and holding that, in all temptations, 'mannes will . . . may not be constrained' by evil, but remains wholly unsullied by any sin to which it does not yield[12]—they do treat despair as a serious spiritual problem, one as important to the lives of their readers as it became to the Reformers. They thereby offer us a chance to think through the relationship between pre- and post-Reformation attitudes to despair with a fuller sense of what the term might signify to a late medieval thinker than was available to McDonald.

*

[10] The modern authority on Flete, Father Benedict Hackett, recently died, leaving a long-awaited edition in draft; it is being completed by Jerry Hackett. The major study of the work remains Michael Benedict Hackett, '*William Flete's De remediis contra temptationes* in its Latin and English Recensions: The Growth of a Text', *Mediaeval Studies*, 26 (1964), 210–30.

[11] This is the title given by Wynkyn de Worde in his editions of 1508 and 1519, as edited by C. Horstmann in his *Yorkshire Writers: Richard Rolle of Hampole and His Followers* (London: Swan Sonnenschein, 1895–6, reprinted by Cambridge: D. S. Brewer, 1999), 2: 106–23, from which the work is quoted here. De Worde's title page ascribes the work to Richard Rolle. For an edition from one of the three surviving manuscripts, with an account of the influence of the *De remediis* on later writings, see Edmund Colledge and Noel Chadwick, 'Remedies Against Temptations: The Third English Version of William Flete', *Archivio Italiano per la Storia della Pietà*, 5 (1968), 201–40.

[12] *Remedy Ayenst the Troubles*, ed. Horstmann, 2: 108.

First, however, to early modern despair, which in its most distinctive Reformed articulation was associated with a predestinarian theology that affirmed a doctrine of 'double election', in which God not only foreknew the identity of those who are to be damned but actually excluded them from his grace, predestining them to damnation as he predestined the elect to salvation. This doctrine, derived by John Calvin during the 1540s from a tradition of thinking about divine omnipotence whose roots lay in fourteenth-century scholasticism,[13] generated a two-hundred-year fascination with the condition of reprobation, in which the possibility that one might know oneself reprobate—in the same way both late medieval 'lovers of God' such as Rolle and many sixteenth- and seventeenth-century believers knew themselves saved—was figured in treatises, sermons, spiritual autobiographies, and admonitory narratives.[14] Calvin himself opened the door to this possibility by his reinterpretation of the sin against the Holy Ghost (Matthew 12:31–2), to commit which is *ipso facto* to forfeit the possibility of mercy, as neither obduracy (as for Augustine) nor ungenerosity (as for Langland) but apostasy: the conscious turning away from truth and embrace of error.[15]

Calvin's argument found early narrative expression in the bestselling accounts of the death of the apostate Italian Protestant Francesco Spiera in 1548 written by Pier Paolo Vergerio, Matteo Gribaldi, and others and collected in a *Francisci Spierae... historia* published in Basle in 1550, with a preface by Calvin. This collection quickly became available in England, later found a place in Foxe's *Book of Martyrs* (1563), and became sufficiently notorious to influence the denouement of *Dr. Faustus* (1588), make a cameo appearance in Thomas Beard's *Theatre of God's Judgements* (1597), and inform a passage of Robert Burton's *Anatomy of Melancholy* (1621).[16] According to these accounts, 'Spira' (as the English punningly called him) spent his last days on his deathbed, lamenting his renunciation of his faith at the hands of the Inquisition and defending the view that he had committed the

[13] See John Calvin, *De Eterna dei predestinatione* (1552), translated as *A Treatise of the Eternal Predestination of God*, by Henry Cole (Grand Rapids, MI: Eerdmans, 1956). For a helpful study, see Richard A. Muller, *The Unaccommodated Calvin: Studies in the Foundation of a Theological Tradition*, Oxford Studies in Historical Theology (New York: Oxford University Press, 2000).

[14] See R. T. Kendall, *Calvin and English Calvinism to 1649* (Oxford: Clarendon, 1979). John Stachniewski, *The Persecutory Imagination: English Puritanism and the Literature of Religious Despair* (Oxford: Clarendon, 1991), is useful although his conclusions have been criticized. A more moderate account is Jeremy Schmidt, *Melancholy and the Care of the Soul: Religion, Moral Philosophy, and Madness in Early Modern England* (Aldershot: Ashgate, 2007).

[15] See Baird Tipson, 'A Dark Side of English Seventeenth-Century Protestantism: The Sin Against the Holy Spirit', *Harvard Theological Journal*, 77 (1984), 301–30.

[16] For references, see McDonald, 'Fearefull Estate', 34. On Spiera and *Dr. Faustus*, see Lily B. Campbell, 'Doctor Faustus: A Case of Conscience', *PMLA*, 67 (1952), 219–39. Other studies of the narrative and its history include M. A. Overell, 'The Exploitation of Francesco Spiera', *Sixteenth Century Journal*, 26 (1995), 619–37, and 'Recantation and Retribution: "Remembering Francis Spira", 1548–1638', in *Retribution, Repentance, and Reconciliation*, ed. Catherine Fales Cooper and Jeremy Gregory (Cambridge: Boydell, 2004), 159–68.

unforgivable sin and was beyond the reach of God's mercy: '*My sinne*', he says in Nathaniel Bacon's synthesizing *Relation of the Fearfull Estate of Francis Spira* (1638), '*is greater than the mercy of God.* Nay, answered they, the mercy of God is above all sin; God would have all men to be saved; *It is true* (quoth he) *hee would have all that he hath elected, to bee saved, he would not have damned reprobates to be saved; I am one of that number; I know it* [. . .]'[17]

Even though there were many who believed that Spira's damnable sin here was not apostasy but obduracy—in other words, that his despairing certainty of damnation was the very thing that sealed that damnation—Calvin was only one of those who thought Spira's despair justified, and many retellings leave this possibility open or focus on the sophistication of his theology, not its fallaciousness. The 1581 rime-royale morality play, *The Conflict of Conscience*, by the Norwich clergyman Nathaniell Woodes, even has it both ways, being published in two versions, one of which damns Spira while the other saves him, as alternative divine responses to the admirable rigor of the doctrine of double election he affirms:

> *Gisbertus*: O father, rest your selfe in God, and all thing shalbe well.
> *Philologus* [i.e. Spira]: A dredfull name, which when I heere, to sigh it mee compell:
> God is against mee I perceive, he is none of my God,
> Unlesse in this, that he will beat, and plague mee with his rod.
> And though his mercy doth surpasse, the sinnes of all the worlde,
> Yet shall it not once profit me, or pardon mine offence,
> I am refused utterly, I quite from God am whorld: [*whirled*]
> My name within the Boke of Life, had never residence,
> Christ payed not, Christ suffered not, my sinnes to recompence:
> But only for the Lordes elect, of which sort I am none,
> I feele his justice towardes me, his mercy all is gone.[18]

Converting many to Calvinist belief by his insistence on the truth of a double predestinarianism that damns him, against an erroneous Catholic penitentialism that believed itself capable of saving him, the Spira of these accounts is at once a modern figure of despair to set alongside his biblical antetypes, Cain and Judas, and a kind of martyr to a new theological order, his *legenda* as compelling a witness to the rigors of the new soteriology, the theology of salvation, as the legend of the apostate but forgiven Theophilus was to the misericordist soteriology of the later

[17] Nathaniel Bacon, *A Relation of the Fearfull Estate of Francis Spira, in the Year, 1548* (London: Printed by I. L. for Phil. Stephens, and Christoph. Meredith, at the golden Lyon in Paul's Church-yard, 1638), 41 (STC 1126). Besides, again, Psalm 144:9, see I Timothy 2:4.

[18] Nathaniell Woodes, *The Conflict of Conscience* (London: Printed by Richard Bradocke Dwelling in Alermanburie, 1581), V.i (STC 404). For an account of both versions, see the edition of *The Conflict of Conscience* prepared by F. P. Wilson and Herbert Davis (Oxford: Oxford University Press for the Malone Society, 1952).

Middle Ages.[19] One might damn Spira with Calvin, or one might save him with Woodes, with Arminius, who firmly read the story against the grain of Calvinist theology, or with William Perkins, who saw Spira's ability to perceive 'the hardnesse of his heart' in 'the very middest of his desperation' as a paradoxical sign of grace, claiming that 'They are much overseene that write of him as a damned creature.'[20] Either way, Spira gave narrative form to the concepts of apostasy, despair, reprobation, and the sin against the Holy Ghost itself: a form, according to McDonald, that remained influential throughout the seventeenth century and beyond.

McDonald is clearly right to suggest that the Spira story helped despair to become a 'normal experience' amongst Calvinists and other kinds of Protestant, one that might befall, not only literal apostates as they renounced one of the many versions of the faith now available for another, but also any kind of backslider frightened that her or his sin might count as apostasy and so incur Spira's experience of living damnation. By the late seventeenth century such fear was also generally seen as temporary, part of an early stage of the spiritual life. Works such as *The Second Spira* (1693), *Spira Respirans* (1694), and *A True Second Spira* (1697) describe the slide into despair through threat of atheism—and all, learning from Spira's error, also describe the resolute climb back from the edge of damnation and the spiritual growth that accompanies it.[21] Rather as with monastic *acedia*, despair in these narratives is again a combination of existential doubt and intellectual error, but has also become self-correcting, already beginning its long slide into mere angst.

The Spira story also explicitly provides a negative reference point for the most famous such spiritual autobiography, John Bunyan's *Grace Abounding to the Chief of Sinners* (1666), with its pattern of repeated doubt, terror of apostasy, fear of the unforgivable sin, and ultimate confirmation in faith:

> About this time, I did light on that dreadful story of that miserable mortal, *Francis Spira*; a book that was to my troubled spirit as salt, when rubbed into a fresh wound; every sentence in that book, every groan of that man, with all the rest of his actions in his dolors, as his tears, his prayers, his gnashing of teeth, his wringing of hands, his twining and twisting, languishing and pining away under that mighty hand of God that was upon him, was as knives and daggers in my soul; especially that sentence of his was frightful to me, *Man knows the beginning of sin, but who bounds the issues thereof*?[22]

[19] See, e.g., Gautier de Coinci, *Le miracle de Théophile*, ed. and trans. Annette Garnier (Paris: H. Champion, 1998). I coin 'misericordist' from Augustine's use of the word *misericordes* in the *City of God*, 21.17, where it denotes those who believe almost nobody is damned eternally: Saint Augustine, *City of God*, trans. R. W. Dyson (Cambridge: Cambridge University Press, 1998), 21.7: 1076–90.

[20] See James Arminius, *On the Sin Against the Holy Ghost* (1599), in *The Works of James Arminius, D. D.*, trans. James Nichols and W. R. Bagnall (Auburn, NY: Derby and Miller, 1853), 511; William Perkins, *A Treatise Tending Unto a Declaration, Whether A Man Be in the Estate of Damnation or in the Estate of Grace*, in *The Workes of... William Perkins*, Vol. 1 (London: John Legatt, 1612), 378.

[21] References in McDonald, 'Fearefull Estate', 44 n. 37.

[22] In John Bunyan, *Grace Abounding to the Chief of Sinners* and *The Pilgrim's Progress*, ed. Roger Sharrock (London: Oxford University Press 1966), §163, 51–2.

Repudiating the Spira pattern as Bunyan determinedly seeks out assurance of salvation, *Grace Abounding* goes far towards normalizing the experience of despair to the point at which it becomes synonymous with any spiritual difficulty involving doubt or what Catholic theologians had long called 'scrupulosity', the too strict appraisal of conscience. In *The Pilgrim's Progress* (1676), accordingly, Giant Despair has become one of the lesser dangers Christian faces on his pilgrimage, both because he is sustained by his fellowship with Hopeful—who represents the same Cardinal Virtue that Elde summons in dispelling Wanhope near the end of *Piers Plowman*—and because he carries a key called Promise 'that will [. . .] open any Lock in *Doubting-Castle*'. Travelling almost alone, Christian can long forget that he holds this key, giving the Giant more power than he ought. But in this strikingly Langlandian theological world, the presence of an active Christian community once again makes such unmindfulness almost impossible. When Christian's wife comes by in Book 2 (1684), her band of trusty companions thus demolish Doubting Castle and behead its Giant.[23]

Yet it is also Bunyan who, in *The Pilgrim's Progress*'s other treatment of despair, gives the lie to any claim that despair became so conformable to Puritan election narratives—so 'normal' an 'experience' in MacDonald's phrase—as to lose the horror the Spira story articulates. For it is someone much like Spira, once 'a fair and flourishing professor' but now a Man of Despair in an iron cage, that Christian meets in the Interpreter's house as a sign of the doctrine of reprobation:

> *Man*: I left off to watch, and be sober; I laid the reins upon the neck of my lusts; I sinned against the light of the Word, and the goodness of God: I have grieved the Spirit, and he is gone; I tempted the Devil, and he is come to me; I have provoked God to anger, and he has left me; I have so hardened my heart, that I *cannot* repent.
> Then said *Christian* to the *Interpreter*, But is there no hopes for such a Man as this?
> Ask him, said the *Interpreter*. Nay, said *Christian*, pray Sir, do you.
> Christian: Then said *Christian*, Is there no hope, but you must be kept in this Iron Cage of Despair?
> *Man*: No, none at all.[24]

Despair here is not the consequence of the Man's imprisonment but the imprisoning iron cage itself, a detail that leaves it possible that the Man's damning sin is not apostasy but obduracy: that the Man could repent if he could only believe in God's mercy. Yet in keeping the Interpreter silent here, so that Christian and the Man address one another directly, Bunyan also allows for the rigorist Calvinist reading that would identify the Man's apostasy with the sin against the Holy Ghost and so confirm the Man's despair as objective and legitimate, as well as subjective and self-damning. Recall Bunyan's comment in the earlier *Grace Abounding* that 'the hand of God' was heavy on Spira. In 'double election' predestinarianism, divine

[23] Bunyan, *Pilgrim's Progress*, ed. Sharrock, 1: 234, 374.
[24] Bunyan, *Pilgrim's Progress*, ed. Sharrock, 1: 166–7.

prescience works with predestination both to foreordain and to foreknow the wickedness that will condemn the reprobate to a fate determined for them before the creation of the world. This is why the reprobates invariably choose the path they are predestined to follow, working with divine justice towards their own damnation almost as the elect cooperate with divine grace in their salvation. God's ineffable presence is thus as fully manifested in the despair of the reprobate as in the joy of the elect. Indeed, even as it at once produces and is produced by the inexorable fact of their eternal separation, despair itself is here a place of spiritual conjunction between the human subject and the divine object, reprobate soul and its creator and judge. This is the wholly 'abnormal' image that lies like a shadow across the Protestant experience of despair: the fear that one might become, like Spira, not a moral example but a prophetic sign: a sign of the workings of divine justice, terrible beyond all terrors to those who experience it from within, but to the elect who see its intricately circular patterning from without, also wonderful to behold.[25]

*

In turning to the late medieval precursors of Protestant despair, I note first that McDonald tends to underrate the general resemblances between the two. Those who seek to argue themselves or others out of despair in Protestant narratives use the same battery of energizing scriptural promises and point in the same way to the Christian obligation to hope as the medievals. Both Bacon and Woodes cite the verse central to medieval remedy literature, the same verse with which Langland's Good Samaritan offers hope of salvation to all, Repentance comforts a despairing Envy as he contemplates suicide, and Scripture comforts an anxious Will after her sermon on predestination, Psalm 144:9: 'His mercy is above all his works', in the Septuagint version (see note 5).[26] Woodes also invokes another formula of remedy literature, used as a leitmotif of a more famous earlier religious work from Norwich, Julian's *Revelation of Love*, 'all thing shalbe well'.[27] Despite their awareness of double predestination, the vernacular Spira texts are clear that to succumb to a belief in one's own reprobation is to sin *even though that belief may be true*, and that the remedy is a deliberate turning away from introspection towards hope and good cheer, shunning one's despair on the assumption it is inspired by Satan. According to Bacon, '*Spira's* principall Errors... were to dispute with Satan over

[25] On Bunyan's theology, see Christopher Hill, *A Turbulent, Seditious, and Factious People: John Bunyan and his Church 1628–1688* (Oxford: Clarendon, 1988), 155–93. On Bunyan and election, see Stachniewski, *Persecutory Imagination*, 168–216.

[26] Bacon, *Fearefull Estate*, 41: 'the mercy of God is above all sin'; Woodes, *Conflict of Conscience*, V.i: 'though his mercy doth surpasse, the sinnes of all the worlde.' Langland, *Piers Plowman*, ed. Schmidt, B.17.314, 283, B.11.139.

[27] See 'A Revelation' in Julian of Norwich, *The Writings of Julian of Norwich: A Vision Showed to a Devout Woman and A Revelation of Love*, ed. Nicholas Watson and Jacqueline Jenkins (University Park: Pennsylvania State University Press, 2006), Chapter 27.

busily in time of weaknesse: especially to reason, and conclude from present sense: to Gods past Reprobation, and future Damnation.'[28] Any late medieval treatise on temptation would have agreed.

Indeed, this is very much where Flete's *De remediis* makes its opening stand against despair:

> Forasmech as th'apostle saith that we may not pleise God without good faith and bileve [Heb. 11.6], therfore it is to wite [*it is to be known*] that oure olde enmye the devill besieth him what he may with fals suggestions and divers imaginacions to hinder and destroy ful faith, that is beginning and grounde of all good werkinge: ... that is to wite, with all manere fantasies, mislikinges, and misconceitis, and al the filthe of blasphemye ... Wherfore a man shall not tarye ne dwelle in suche thoughtes, Ne wonnder moche on theim, neither enserche theim in his soule, ne dispute the causes of theim. For the more besely that he medleth him with suche errours and falsenes for to avaide [*avoid*] theim only by sovereintee of his owne witte, the more and also the ferder in he wadeth in to hem warde [*into them*].[29]

'Fals suggestions' about 'good faith and bileve' that occur unexpectedly in the minds of the devout, along with 'al the filthe of blasphemye', all liable to 'hinder and destroy ful faith', are to be understood as diabolical in origin and one should not 'dispute the causes of theim'. Flete declares that the devil uses 'divers imaginacions', not theological truths, to assault the soul, a view in tune with a wider concern in the medieval remedy tradition on the imagination as a seat of error. But apart from this difference of emphasis, his strategy—in the case of his use of the word 'dispute', even his language—is much the same as the one advocated by Bacon.

Such continuities of sound advice over what to do about despair would not have surprised Calvin or his English followers, though they might surprise scholars such as McDonald, as might the degree of continuity over the causes of despair and sense of its consequences. As the opening of the *De remediis* suggests—with its focus on demonic attempts to make the soul 'dispute' the faith, 'torment[ing] so mannes thoughte with diseases of suche manere temptacions that a man falleth almost in wanhope'[30]—the disputatious nature of fourteenth-century scholastic thought was an acknowledged problem for the religious and lay contemplatives who formed the work's initial audience. In the *De remediis* and the vernacular tradition that stems from the work, this problem gradually became a preoccupation of accounts of tribulation and despair, particularly in relation to

[28] Bacon, *Fearefull Estate*, 133.

[29] For want of a Latin edition, I quote the *De remediis* from the second Middle English translation, as edited, along with *The Chastising of God's Children*, by Wynkyn de Worde in his *Prouffytable Boke For Mannes Soule* (Westminster: Printed by Wynkyn de Worde, ?1493), fos. G.iv^{r}–H.iii^{r} (STC 5065), checking it for general resemblance to the Latin against Benedict Hackett's translation of an unattributed Latin manuscript in his *William Flete, O.S.A and Catherine of Siena: Masters of Fourteenth-Century Spirituality*, Augustinian Series 15 (Villanova, PA: Augustinian Press, 1992). This passage occurs on G.iv^{r}, with spelling, punctuation, and capitalization slightly modified.

[30] Flete, *De remediis*, G.iv^{v}.

questions of salvation. This likely had something to do with the role of soteriology in contemporary scholastic thought as a focus of discussions of one of the most significant theological themes of the era, divine power.

During the 1340s, the important theologian, Gregory of Rimini—like Flete, as well as Luther, an Augustinian Friar—taught a version of double predestination in a commentary on Lombard's *Sentences.* Gregory's contention that the reprobate play no causal role in their own reprobation had a clear influence on Luther and especially Calvin, in some ways the direct heir of this moment in scholastic theology.[31] Whether or not they agreed with Gregory's stand on double predestination, theological systems emphasizing divine power and challenging what used to be termed the 'semi-Pelagian' consensus on divine grace remained a regular, if controversial, feature of fourteenth-century scholastic thought,[32] a feature with particularly difficult implications for pastoral theology and its necessary emphasis on the predictability of the divine judgment.

The *De remediis* was likely written between the time Flete finished his own *Sentences* commentary, as part of his progress towards becoming a Master of Theology at Cambridge in the mid-1350s, and his departure for Italy in 1359, having decided not to proceed to his degree.[33] Flete's commentary is lost but will have engaged at some level with the influential thought of his great Augustinian predecessor, among others. It is possible that the emphasis in the *De remediis* on the need to avoid tormenting thoughts formed part of Flete's wider rejection of academic theology, even his public statement of that rejection. Views like Flete's certainly became increasingly explicit in vernacular texts during the late Middle Ages, most notably exemplified in the works of one of Flete's Cambridge near-contemporaries, the eremitic author of *The Cloud of Unknowing*, who used the vernacular as an antidote to the damnable curiosity his writings attribute to scholasticism and whose *Discretion of Stirrings* makes use of the *De remediis.*[34]

[31] See Paul Vignaux, *Justification et prédestination au XIVe siècle: Duns Scot, Pierre d'Auriole, Guillaume d'Occam, Grégoire de Rimini* (Paris: Librairie Philosophique J. Vrin, 1981, first published 1934); Heiko Obermann, *The Reformation: Roots and Ramifications*, trans. Andrew Gow (Grand Rapids, MI: Eerdmans, 1994). Still useful is Gordon Leff, *Gregory of Rimini: Tradition and Innovation in Fourteenth-Century Thought* (Manchester: Manchester University Press, 1961).

[32] See William J. Courtenay, *Schools and Scholars in Fourteenth-Century England* (Princeton, NJ: Princeton University Press, 1987); and his *Capacity and Volition: A History of the Distinction of Absolute and Ordained Power* (Bergao: P. Lubrina, 1990).

[33] M. B. Hackett, 'William Flete and the *De remediis contra temptationes*', in *Medieval Studies Presented to Aubrey Gwynn*, ed. J. A. Watt et al. (Dublin: Lochlainn, 1961), 330–48; building on Aubrey Gwynn, *The English Austin Friars in the Time of Wyclif* (London: Oxford University Press, 1940).

[34] For the *Cloud* author and Cambridge, see John Clark, 'Late Fourteenth-Century Cambridge Theology and the English Mystical Tradition', in *The Medieval Mystical Tradition in England: Exeter Symposium V*, ed. Marion Glasscoe (Cambridge: Brewer, 1992), 1–16. For the *Cloud* author's learned repudiation of scholasticism, see Nicholas Watson, 'The Middle English Mystics', in *The Cambridge History of Medieval English Literature*, ed. David Wallace (Cambridge: Cambridge University Press 1999), 539–65, at 552–4.

Indeed, the *De remediis* tradition as a whole is partly about keeping at bay some of the same threatening theological ideas—'wordes that ye have herde or redde in bookes by the whiche ye doute of salvacion', as the expanded *Remedy Ayenst the Troubles of Temptacyons* puts it—that were to inform the Protestant understanding of despair.[35]

Admittedly, the *De remediis* is also positively influenced by Flete's Augustinian learning, even by his awareness of predestinarian thought. Indeed, most works in the *De remediis* tradition directly depend on a doctrine of single predestination—a doctrine, that is, of election—to assure readers in a state of moral or intellectual confusion that their salvation is sure *because* their election means they can take the ultimate goodness of their wills for granted. Flete writes that 'to a man that willith to be faithfull, suche manere temptacion [i.e. temptation against faith or hope] is displeising, and moche ayenst his will. Wherfore it is painful to him but not giltfull of sinne, sith every sinne is wilfull, or elles no sinne, as saith saint Austin [*De vera religione*]'.[36] This position is perhaps best understood in relation to a common-sense definition of predestination such as is provided by the *Chastising of God's Children*, which lays careful, characteristic, and very un-Calvinist emphasis on human agency and perseverance: 'Predestinacion is begon by the ordenaunce of God. and it is holpen by the prayer of saintes, and it is ended by a mannis owne werking.'[37] Yet in his determination to rescue the devout from diabolically induced anxieties, Flete nonetheless permitted a degree of unconcern about inner doubts and perversities unusual in an age dominated by penitential theology.

Two of his successors push this unconcern further. Trying to find a place for the penitential idea of venial sin—sin that does not damn since it is done without full consent of the will—while protecting Flete's notion of the purity of the elect will, *The Remedy Ayenst the Troubles of Temptacyons* goes so far as to distinguish 'two willes, a good will and an evill' in the soul of 'every man and woman'. The first 'evill will cometh of sensualite [that is, is associated with the mutable body], the whiche is ever inclininge downwarde to sinne; and the good will cometh of grace, whiche alwaye stireth the soul upwarde to all goodness'. Inclinations to 'wicked thoughtes and sterynges' belong entirely to the 'sensualite' and do not involve 'consent' of the soul; rather, 'it is the sensualite that dooth it in you, and your good will abideth in you still unbroken'.[38] From something like this passage, Julian of Norwich forged her celebrated doctrine that 'in every soule that shalle be saved is a godly wille that never assented to sinne, nor never shalle', a

35 *Remedy Ayenst the Troubles*, ed. Horstmann, 2: 112.

36 *Remedy Ayenst the Troubles*, ed. Horstmann, 2: 112.

37 *Chastising*, Chapter 15, as edited in *Prouffytable Boke*, by Wynkyn de Worde, C.v^{v}. There is a scholarly edition by Eric Colledge and Joyce Bazire (eds.), *The Chastising of God's Children: and the Treatise of Perfection of the Sons of God* (Oxford: Blackwell, 1957).

38 *Remedy Ayenst the Troubles*, ed. Horstmann, 2: 114.

doctrine that similarly incorporates a strict separation in the soul between a 'bestely wille in the lower party that may wille no good' and a 'godly will in the higher party, which wille is so good that it may never will eville, but ever good'.[39] This doctrine explicitly invokes a predestinarian soteriology in affirming Julian's claim that what she elsewhere calls the 'substance' of the souls of the elect remains hidden and eternally sinless in God, awaiting the redemption of the 'sensuality' at death.[40] But as in the *Chastising*, predestination is here completed, and made secure, by a deliberate and thus knowable act of human choice: 'What man or woman wilfully choseth God in this life for love, he may be seker that he is loved without end, with endless love that werketh in him that grace.'[41] This combination of predestinarianism with a strong sense of the power of human choice evident in the *De remediis* tradition was hard to defend in Protestant theologies, at least before Arminius. But the cliché that late medieval theology was 'semi-Pelagian' compared to its Reformation successor should not blind us to Julian's dependance on a predestinarian view of salvation, nor on its many distinctively Augustinian (and Fletian) resonances.

If predestination was surprisingly congenial to writers in the *De remediis* tradition, however, *double* predestination was not, returning only in repressed form as the despair that threatens to be induced by what Flete calls 'fals suggestions and divers imaginacions'. These phrases are deliberately vague, potentially referring to a variety of errors besides doubt of salvation or heresy. Yet some of Flete's successors took this language to apply to the doubts that arose from and generated the growing fear of reprobation in particular, the same fear Will feels in Passus B.11 of *Piers Plowman* after hearing Scripture preach on the theme 'Many are called and few are chosen' (Matthew 22:14):

> Al for tene of hir text trembled min herte, [*anguish*]
> And in a weer gan I wexe, and with myself to dispute [*panic*]
> Wheither I were chose or noght chose.[42]

Thus the *Chastising* writes of those 'traveiled' not only 'with pointes of the faith' but also those who 'will imagine of the predestinacion and of the prescience or of the foreknowinge of God', who can be so 'dredful for sinnes done before' that they 'agayn her will ben traveyled with dispeire, notwithstondyng they knowe well our lordes mercy passeth all her sinnes'. To someone in this state, double predestination generates a tormenting, circular anxiety: 'In predestinacion he doubteth whether God hath ordeined him to be saved. And in imaginacion of the prescience of God,

[39] Julian of Norwich, *Revelation of Love*, ed. Watson and Jenkins, 37.14–18. It may be that *The Remedy Ayenst the Troubles* is adapting material from Julian, not the other way around.

[40] Julian of Norwich, *Revelation of Love*, ed. Watson and Jenkins, e.g. Chapter 45.

[41] Julian of Norwich, *Revelation of Love*, ed. Watson and Jenkins, 61.1–2.

[42] Langland, *Piers Plowman*, ed. Schmidt, B.11.115–17. Compare B.10.371–4 and C.12.207–10, which complains of preachers arguing that all souls are already 'prodestinat'.

he doubteth to be dampned.'[43] The extended *Remedy Ayenst the Troubles of Temptacyons*, which lists 'doubtes of the faith and dredes of salvacion' as types of diabolic temptation specific to its own era (they occur 'specially now in these dayes'), links fear of reprobation even more precisely with the terrifying fear one has committed the sin against the Holy Ghost:

> But some men, whan they have drede of salvacion or be tempted to dispaire by visions or ghostly steringes of their owne frailtye, they wene anone that they have sinned in the sinne of the Holy Ghoost, and than the fende putteth in them that they may never be saved nor forgiven of their trespaces... so feringe [frightening] sume good creatures that they wene to goo out of their mindes.[44]

Although the *Remedy* reassuringly defines the sin against the Holy Ghost as 'infinite without repentaunce', the fear it seeks to quell here is exactly that felt by Spiera and Bunyan.

True to her Fletian interest in doubt, even Julian lists 'dispair or doughtfulle drede' as one of two 'specialle' sins treated by her revelation—along with 'unpaciens or slouth'—devoting Chapters 73 and 74 of *A Revelation* to distinguishing this sinful fear, 'a foule blindhede and a wekenesse', from the 'reverent drede' which God deserves. These chapters associate 'doughtfulle drede' with scrupulosity—the 'beholding of ourselfe and of oure sinne afore done'—more than intellectual doubt or fear of reprobation.[45] Yet both these latter are present elsewhere in the text in the universalized form Julian's thought always prefers. Christ speaks the key phrase 'alle shalle be wele' in answer to her doubt as to 'why the beginning of sinne was not letted', and after courteously treating this doubt as legitimate, not sinful, and answering it with a set of mysterious promises, makes it known that God himself does not engage in too much reflection on the condition of the reprobate:

> I saw the deville is reproved of God and endlessly dampned. In which sight I understond that alle the creatures that be of the devilles condition in this life, and therin ende, ther is no more mention made of them before God and alle his holen [saints] then of the deville, notwithstonding that they be of mankinde... And as long as we be in this life, what time that we by oure foly turne us to the beholding of the reproved, tenderly oure lorde toucheth us... seyeng in oure soule: 'Let me alone, my derwurdy childe, intende to me, I am inogh to the'.[46]

Just as Julian's revelation allows for endless intellectual exploration in a form it is still possible to defend as 'in the faith and in the beleve',[47] contributing to

[43] *Chastising*, Chapters 6 and 15, B.I^{r-v} and C.VI^{r}. Chapter 15 deals wholly with 'predestinacion and prescience of God and of hem that ben traveyled wyth suche manere materis' (C.V^{v}). It may be the most extensive such discussion in Middle English.

[44] *Remedy Ayenst the Troubles*, ed. Horstmann, 2: 107 and 110.

[45] Julian of Norwich, *Revelation of Love*, ed. Watson and Jenkins, 73.28–9.

[46] Julian of Norwich, *Revelation of Love*, ed. Watson and Jenkins, 33.7–11, 36.37–40.

[47] Julian of Norwich, *Revelation of Love*, ed. Watson and Jenkins, 53.12.

the reader's salvation rather than inducing 'doughtfulle drede', so the idea of reprobation is here allowed into the text in a form in which its presence can be acknowledged without any fear it will give rise to 'dispair'.

*

An investigation of the *De remediis* tradition thus opens up an area of late medieval English religiosity—an area not normally regarded, like Wycliffism, as proto-Protestant—whose thinking about despair has more in common with those we encounter in the sixteenth and seventeenth centuries than might have been expected (and, one might add, vice versa). Puritans aware of the Spira story probably were more inclined to term experiences of spiritual desolation 'despair' than their medieval predecessors, and conceivably lived under a theological regime that made despair harder to overcome and thus, it may be, more meaningful when it was overcome. But we can be confident that readers of *De remediis* and its successors would have understood the Spira story in detail, and could have articulated this understanding in terms that made sense in turn to that story's historical readers.

Not only do *De remediis* texts share a good deal of common thought and vocabulary with Spira texts, but the immediate relevance of *De remediis* texts to post-Reformation thought about despair and predestination is demonstrated by their continuing history of circulation in Catholic circles. The *De remediis* itself was known both to Thomas More, who borrowed from it in his own 'remedy' text, the *Dialogue of Comfort*, and to the seventeenth-century mystical theologian Augustine Baker, as well as to the nuns of Cambrai and Paris who likely copied both the key surviving manuscripts of Julian's *Revelation* and may have provided the exemplar for Serenus Cressy's 1670 edition.[48] A version of the opening passage of the *De remediis* may even have been known to Spiera himself, through its use in Chapter 2 of the extremely widely dispersed treatise on dying, *De arte bene moriendi* (after 1405) which warns those on their deathbeds, like Spiera, precisely of threats to their orthodoxy and the dangers of despair: 'supersticiose and false errouris or herisies' and 'disperacion' caused by fear of sin, as the English translation of the *De arte*, the early fifteenth-century *Book of the Craft of Dying* puts it.[49] Spira texts thus did not simply come after *De remediis* texts in a straightforward historical progression. Rather, these two groups of texts, whose theological origins were in many ways so curiously analogous even as their conclusions differed, remained in dialogue for a period of nearly two hundred years.

[48] On the post-medieval circulation of the *De remediis*, see Hackett (trans.), *William Flete, OSA and Catherine of Siena*, 119–20. On that of Julian's *Revelation*, see *Writings of Julian of Norwich*, ed. Watson and Jenkins, 12–17, 437–55.

[49] *Book of the Craft of Dying*, in *Yorkshire Writers*, ed. Horstmann, 2: 409. On the *De arte*, see Mary Catherine O'Connor, *The Art of Dying Well: The Development of the Ars Moriendi* (New York: Columbia University Press, 1942). On Spiera and the *ars moriendi*, see Overell, 'Exploitation of Francesco Spiera'. The dependence of Chapter 2 of the *De arte* on Flete's *De remediis* has not, to my knowledge, previously been noticed and deserves more investigation.

Did Calvin's contribution to the discourse of despair—his argument that the sin against the Holy Ghost is apostasy—therefore make early modern despair a 'distinct emotion', as McDonald claims? Perhaps so. Spira's story clearly belongs to its theological moment: we would have to look to visionary meetings with the damned in hell to find a medieval equivalent, and the shock of Spira—the shock that prevented early modern despair from becoming normalized to the point its threat was lost—resides exactly in the fact that, in the Spira narratives, he is *not* in hell but might as well be so. Yet I am still not sure how confidently we could distinguish the unease that fear of reprobation bestows on the moment-by-moment movement of Bunyan's early life told in *Grace Abounding* from the unease, equally caused by fear of reprobation, that gives such restless energy to *The Book of Margery Kempe*: a work in which we see the lessons of the *De remediis* tradition repeatedly applied and as repeatedly come unstuck. Its protagonist is a lay woman whose status and past life long makes the assurance of election the lover of God is meant to feel an unsteady ground on which to stand; the *Book* represents the long journey, very much like Bunyan's, the protagonist must undertake to rid herself of the temptation to despair—whether caused by her early lechery, her fear that the signs of grace she receives are diabolical illusions, or her occasional refusal of that grace—and to become, at last, a bulwark against despair for her community and the *Book*'s readers. The *Book* is as full of horror at the possibility of damnation and as repetitive in its search for assurance as any Protestant autobiography. What is more, as fear of reprobation slowly gives way to spiritual confidence, the *Book* describes the birth of that confidence in terms that could as easily belong to early modern Protestantism as to affective late medieval devotionalism: 'I have ronnin awey fro the, and thou hast ronnin aftir me; I wold fallin in dispeir, and thu woldist not suffer me,' she says to her loving, ferocious, and heavy-handed God.[50] Bunyan would have recognized both the vocabulary and the sentiment.

FURTHER READING

Agamben, Giorgio. *Stanzas: Word and Phantasm in Western Culture*, trans. Ronald L. Martinez (Minneapolis: University of Minnesota Press, 1993)

Hackett, Benedict (trans.). *William Flete, OSA and Catherine of Siena: Masters of Fourteenth-Century Spirituality*, Augustinian Series 15 (Villanova, PA: Augustinian Press, 1992)

McDonald, Michael. '*The Fearefull Estate of Francis Spira*: Narrative, Emotion, and Identity in Early Modern England', *Journal of British Studies*, 31 (1992), 32–61

Wenzel, Siegfried. *The Sin of Sloth: Acedia in Medieval Thought and Literature* (Chapel Hill: University of North Carolina Press, 1967)

[50] Margery Kempe, *Book of Margery Kempe*, ed. Barry Windeatt (New York: Longman, 2000), Chapter 22 with orthography slightly modified.

PART VI

LITERATURE

CHAPTER 20

POETIC FAME

HELEN COOPER

Poetry is nothing without fame: it needs to be known. If in addition it carries the name of a famous poet, then that itself authorizes and validates the work. When an early modern poet, a humanist poet, wanted to write in English, he looked for such validation: for a model of fame that would not only give him something to emulate or imitate, important as that was, but that would authorize his work in the eyes of his reading public. Throughout the sixteenth century as in the fifteenth, one such poet was chosen with impressive consistency: Geoffrey Chaucer.

That choice might seem surprising to recent critics. Chaucer has largely been written out of early modern criticism, even in areas (poetic laureateship, though he was universally praised as a laureate poet; the writing of England, though he was the supreme model for vernacular authorship) where he should figure most prominently. It might also in some respects have surprised fifteenth- and early sixteenth-century writers, who combined a massive admiration for Chaucer as a model of eloquence and rhetoric with some doubts as to his ethical weight, largely derived from his own refusal to claim storytelling as carrying any absolute authority. There is a further problem in bringing together his poetic mastery and his refusal of authority in relation to modern theories of canon formation. In John Guillory's formulation, entry into the canon depends on the ideological need of the moment, with authors being promoted to suit current intellectual or political agendas.[1] Yet for all that Chaucer was the main author who offers himself—and was offered in the sixteenth century—as the validation for English poetry, he does not quite fit Guillory's template.

At first glance he seems to fit perfectly. He was appropriated not only, and most famously, by the Protestants, who had their own theological reasons for welcoming a vernacular authority, but also by humanists and Catholics; and explicitly too in

[1] John Guillory, *Cultural Capital: The Problem of Literary Canon Formation* (Chicago: Chicago University Press, 1993).

the whole process of the writing of England, the construction of nationhood. That very multiplicity, however, creates problems for Guillory's model, for it suggests that Chaucer's fame came first, preceding his entry into the canon on ideological grounds. Guillory's criteria of canon formation, in Chaucer's case, operate largely retrospectively, to harness the fact that he was already so widely read. In the intense debates of the sixteenth century—over religion, the definition of England and Englishness, the nature and function of literature (teaching or delighting), the proper nature of the language—Chaucer was called on as a witness, or a focus. He could not be disregarded, for all that he had lived before humanism had, in the views of the humanists, transformed the practice of letters, before the Reformation had opened men's eyes to true religion, and before Calvinist habits of thought had set more severe standards for the duty of literature to subordinate pleasure to instruction.

Chaucer's fame was so taken for granted that it has to be demonstrated largely by example rather than statement. There is one striking assertion of it, however, by no less a witness than Shakespeare. What was probably his very last play, a dramatization of Chaucer's *Knight's Tale*, opened with a eulogy of England's greatest poet. The play, it declares,

> ... has a noble breeder, and a pure,
> A learned, and a poet never went
> More famous yet twixt Po and silver Trent.
> Chaucer, of all admired, the story gives:
> There constant to eternity it lives.[2]

This Chaucer, in other words, outranks in fame every poet from Petrarch (for the Po) to the whole flood of Elizabethan and Jacobean poets who came from south of the Trent (Shakespeare himself, Spenser, all the Londoners). It may be objected that this is advertising propaganda rather than a serious statement of belief, but advertising works by enlisting the predispositions of its audience: if by 1613 Chaucer had ceased to be an enticement, the prologue would presumably not have been written at all, or not like this. It may be objected too that the lines may well not be by Shakespeare but by his collaborator in the play, John Fletcher; but Shakespeare had already worked with the *Knight's Tale* earlier, with his gloriously free adaptation of the newly married Duke Theseus, the lovers fighting in the wood outside Athens and their supernatural puppetmasters in *A Midsummer Night's Dream*. The *Dream* was probably composed shortly after the Admiral's Men, with whom Shakespeare's own company had recently ended a joint operation, had staged a *Palamon and Arcite* of their own,[3] and was quite possibly written as a

[2] *The Two Noble Kinsmen*, Prologue 10–14, in *William Shakespeare: The Complete Works*, general editors Stanley Wells and Gary Taylor, 2nd edn (Oxford: Clarendon Press, 2005).

[3] Recorded in Henslowe's diary for September 1594; most fully discussed by E. K. Chambers, *The Elizabethan Stage*, 4 vols. (Oxford: Clarendon Press, 1923), 2: 138–46.

response to it, or an overgoing of it. Chaucer was the dominant inspiration too behind *Troilus and Cressida*, for *Troilus and Criseyde* was the sole full version of the love story available in England, and the only one to make Pandarus Criseyde's uncle and a strikingly un-Classical key character. Shakespeare thus derived three of his plays from Chaucer, a number that suggests he would not have been inclined to disagree with the lines even if Fletcher (who also dramatized *The Wife of Bath's Tale*) actually wrote them. Chaucer comes a narrow second to Plutarch as an inspiration for Shakespeare; yet hogsheads more of critical ink has been spilled over the classical Plutarch as a Shakespearean source than the medieval Chaucer.[4]

Shakespeare's attitude to Chaucer thus becomes something of a test case for the contrast between how he was received in the sixteenth century, and the widespread modern refusal to recognize his continuing centrality as the laureate poet of England. Yet Chaucer was distinguished by having six folio editions of his complete works printed between 1532 and 1602—folio, therefore large and expensive, and assuming sufficient eager readers ready to make the necessary outlay for every new edition and reprint; and printed, moreover, under the title *Works*, an Englishing of the Latin 'opera' that was normally reserved for the acknowledged Latin and Greek classics. No other English author was given such an unqualified 'works' until Ben Jonson published his own, to some derision, in 1616; Shakespeare had to wait until the eighteenth century until he was granted the accolade of such a title. Jonson was, moreover, for all his better-known classicizing, something of a Chaucer devotee. He brought him on stage (with Gower, Lydgate, and Spenser) in his 1615 masque *The Golden Age restor'd*, to personify the golden age of poetry, and had Inigo Jones design a temple of Fame 'to follow that noble description, made by *Chaucer*' for his *Masque of Queens* (1609).[5] He drew on the *Canon's Yeoman's Tale* in *The Alchemist*; he chose Chaucer as one of his exemplars of English grammar (*c.*1637); and he quotes or alludes to him in a number of his plays in a way that suggests a long immersion in his poetry. Those allusions moreover assume that his audience will pick them up. As late as *The New Inn* of 1629, he will have a character interrupt another to condemn

[4] The two major studies are Ann Thompson, *Shakespeare's Chaucer: A Study in Literary Origins* (Liverpool: Liverpool University Press, 1978); and E. Talbot Donaldson, *The Swan at the Well: Shakespeare Reading Chaucer* (New Haven, CT: Yale University Press, 1985).

[5] Some 1,500 allusions to Chaucer from before the Civil War are collected by Caroline F. E. Spurgeon, *Five Hundred Years of Chaucer Criticism and Allusion (1357–1900)*, 3 vols. (London: Chaucer Society, 1914–25); and by Jackson Campbell Boswell and Sylvia Wallace Holton, *Chaucer's Fame in England: STC Chauceriana, 1475–1640* (New York: Modern Language Association of America, 2004), who revise and extend Spurgeon's list and provide translations of Latin but exclude unprinted material. Both organize their lists by date (though some dates are conjectural, or refer to printing rather than composition), so most dates given here serve as references to both collections to enable detailed identification. The criticism collected by Derek Brewer in *Chaucer: The Critical Heritage*, vol. 1: *1385–1837* (London: Routledge and Kegan Paul, 1978) is also organized chronologically.

flye-blowne Latin,
After the School–
Of Stratford o' the Bow,
For Lillies Latine, is to him unknow.

It is even possible that in choosing the title *Works* for his own volume, he was aiming to place himself not only in the Classical tradition, but in the Chaucerian one, as a Son of Geoffrey.

The tributes given to Chaucer by Shakespeare and Fletcher and Jonson, moreover, were replicated by just about every significant writer, and a host of minor ones, throughout the sixteenth and early seventeenth centuries. Roger Ascham called him 'our English Homer' (1545), an epithet acknowledging both his quality and his foundational status, and one that was frequently repeated. To Spenser he was the 'god of shepheards', the English Virgil. Sidney (1581?) confessed himself baffled as to 'whether to marvel more, that he in that misty time could see so clearly, or that we in this clear age walk so stumblingly after him'. To Gabriel Harvey (1585), he was 'above all other' as a poet, and not a mere 'superficial humanist' but an 'exquisite artist' and 'curious universal scholar'. The theorist William Webbe (1586) called him the god of English poets; Robert Greene (1592) turned him into the patron saint of English letters. Drayton devoted twelve lines of eulogy to him (1627), apparently recalling fond evenings spent with a friend discussing him and other poets, and wrote an imitation of *Sir Thopas*. And in 1622, Henry Peacham specified a familiarity with the *Canterbury Tales*, *Troilus*, the *Romaunt of the Rose*, and the *Treatise of the Astrolabe* as an essential part of a gentleman's cultural literacy.

If such a pattern of allusion is noted at all, it is often assumed that praise of Chaucer was a mere convention and does not prove that any of the eulogists had any first-hand acquaintance with his work. A second look decisively dispels any such notion. Of the numerous writers who nodded a brief compliment in Chaucer's direction, some may indeed be doing so because it seemed to be the thing to do, just as the triumvirate of Chaucer, Gower, and Lydgate became something of a reflex response to a call for a history of English literature; similarly, three Chaucerian couples—Troilus and Cressida, January and May, and Chauntecleer and Pertelote—took on a proverbial life of their own beyond Chaucer's text. Dozens more writers, however, alluded to textual specifics of the entire range of his works, quoted them, or rewrote them for print or the stage.[6] Sir Thomas More and his daughter Margaret Roper borrowed a phrase from *Troilus* in 1535 to share with a friend. Hakluyt (1596) quotes the portrait of the Knight to prove how long and how far Englishmen had been travelling. Milton in *Il Penseroso* assumed that

[6] Boswell and Holton's index of allusions by work runs to twenty double columns (381–90). A list and brief discussion of adaptations of the *Tales* is given in Helen Cooper, *Oxford Guides to Chaucer: The Canterbury Tales*, 2nd edn (Oxford: Clarendon Press, 1996), 420–7.

his readers would not need telling who it was who 'left half told / The story of Cambuskan bold', though both Spenser and another poet, John Lane, had already had a shot at completing it.

The first dramatizations, of *Melibee* and the *Clerk's Tale*, were made into Latin around 1550, for the grammar school at Hitchin, and before the closing of the theatres at least ten adaptations for the English stage followed, of six tales plus *Troilus*—more, if the criteria of closeness are relaxed. The most faithful dramatization of *Troilus* (together with Henryson's *Testament of Cresseid*, its regular companion in the prints), was made into Welsh.[7] Chaucer was given his own voice on a number of occasions: by William Bullein in 1564, when he speaks a satirical verse on the state of the times; by Robert Greene in 1592, who gives him an entire prose fabliau on the model of the *Miller's Tale* and puts him in extended debate with 'moral' Gower (Chaucer loses); in verse spoken in the first person to accompany the portrait of him in the 1598 edition of his works; and as a ghost by Richard Braithwait in 1617, when 'Chaucer' notes that his works should be esteemed 'like Sybillas Oracles' in view of how many of his characters

> though moulded in another age,
> Have rais'd new Subjects both for *Presse* and *Stage*.

Even as they walked the streets of London, Elizabethan citizens could have heard various ballads of Troilus being sung, and Jacobeans could have added others on Griselda, the loathly lady, and what happened to the Wife of Bath when she tried to get access to Heaven. And the list could go on, and on. In contrast to the modern critical silence, in fact, what one finds when one looks back four or five hundred years is something more like a cultural saturation with Chaucer: a confirmation of those lines about there never being a poet more famous.

If Chaucer's symbolic capital lay in his being the pre-eminent linguistic and rhetorical model for poets, his actual capital lay in his commercial success, and that was led simply by enjoyment. Printer after printer from Caxton forwards fed the market for his works, initially in individual prints (the *Canterbury Tales* was one of the first works, perhaps the very first, to come from Caxton's press after he moved to Westminster in 1476), then in the large collected editions. Editors and printers and readers all started from the premise that he *was* famous: that was a given that they had inherited. Far from the processes of canon formation setting the seal of approval on him and offering him entry, there was a scramble to enlist his fame for each particular cause. His position at the top of the

[7] *Troelus a Chresyd*, ed. W. Beynon Davies (Cardiff: University of Wales Press, 1976): perhaps from the 1560s, though the one manuscript is seventeenth-century.

canon of English literature was a fact, but it had to be justified in terms of some further measure of cultural capital relevant to each new stage of a fast-changing century. Not only did his works have to be given an interpretation that suited the agenda of whoever was promoting him, but he had to be enlisted as himself an active promoter of that ideology. None of the other English works of literature inherited from the Middle Ages carried with them this kind of cultural urgency. Many were anonymous, so did not carry the burden of implied authority. Gower and Lydgate, associated with Chaucer as the triumvirate of great English poets since the mid-fifteenth century, were never made the focus of any comparable fight for appropriation, though Lydgate's epithet as 'the monk of Bury' seems to have quietly contributed to his demise over the decades after the death of Mary Tudor.

There is a certain irony in all this, in that Chaucer's own attitude to fame was unusually sceptical. Dante and Petrarch saw poetic fame as an absolute, a way of preserving their names against the ravages of time, and later poets followed suit. Chaucer, by contrast, derived his own idea of Fame more from the monstrous figures portrayed by Virgil and Ovid, which have as much to do with the instabilities of rumour and scandal as with proper renown. His *House of Fame* presents a personification of Fame who is distinguished by her complete arbitrariness: of the nine groups of people who come before her, only one is accorded fame in return for being worthy of it. The other eight are consigned to oblivion despite their worth, or accorded renown they have done nothing to deserve, or given the wrong reputation. The narrative does put on record the names of famous poets—Homer, Ovid, Virgil, and so on—but they are presented as quarrelling with each other, and their own status as authorities falls with that, just as the dreamer's vision had opened by setting Virgil's and Ovid's versions of the story of Dido at loggerheads. Chaucer himself makes a named appearance, as 'Geoffrey', but that happens when he is being carried up to the heavens by an eagle and strenuously resisting its attempts to instruct him in the wonders of the cosmos, as if to deny himself any plausible reputation for anything. If the reference to 'English Gaufride' in his list of writers on Troy is indeed a reference to himself, as seems likely (all his other uses of 'English' refer to the language, and the poem may well date from the mid-1380s), any bid for fame there signally failed to achieve its object, since the identification has remained almost entirely unrecognized.

Chaucer is notoriously self-deprecating in his own poetry. He names himself as 'Chaucer' only in the Man of Law's rather irritated remarks about how Chaucer has stolen all the good stories—a kind of self-compliment, but one that serves to eliminate any sense of him as the actual creator of his most famous work, the Canterbury stories. The contributions he makes to those in his own voice as pilgrim, *Sir Thopas*, and the prose Melibee, likewise serve to write him out of consideration as a serious poet: as his 1598 editor commented, *Sir Thopas* is 'purposely uttered by Chaucer, in a differing rime and stile from the other tales, as though he himselfe were not the author, but only the reporter of the rest'.[8] It is unsurprising that Henryson's *Testament of Cresseid* was printed as his despite its early question, 'Who wot if al that Chaucer wrate was trewe?' It is just the kind of denial of responsibility he makes elsewhere on his own account; and it was not easy to promote the authority of a man who so strenuously insisted on his own inadequacy.

Humanist Chaucer

The very recurrence of these denials of his standing none the less indicates a self-assurance greater than other poets' declarations of their own fame, as if Chaucer can take the recognition of his poetic pre-eminence for granted. He has subtler, and more telling, ways to indicate that than to announce it directly. He is the first English poet to invoke, or indeed to mention, the Muses. As early as *The Book of the Duchess*, he gave the hunting aristocrat who rides back to his long castle on a rich hill—Lancaster and Richmond, John of Gaunt's titles—the name of Octavian, Virgil's patron. At the end of *Troilus*, in imitation of Dante and Boccaccio, he famously places himself as the sixth in line after Homer, Virgil, Ovid, Lucan, and Statius, even if ostensibly to kiss their steps. And in the *The House of Fame* and *The Legend of Good Women*, he disagrees with Virgil outright (to the horror of the *Aeneid*'s translator Gavin Douglas). The humanists' classical training might be expected to have placed them best to understand the high claim that Chaucer was making for himself, but the form that took could work to the opposite effect. Their own self-definition required them to reject Chaucer's challenge to Virgil's authority, and to regard the classical languages as superior to the vernacular and the pre-humanist age as barbaric.

Yet the new humanist focus on the practice of letters, on eloquence as a high mark of civilization and on rhetoric as the benchmark of learning, made it especially important that England should have a poet of its own, and one who could demonstrate eloquence in the vernacular. Caxton, who attached his reputation and his financial future to promoting works in the English language, was among the foremost to urge Chaucer's claims. He praises him in his prefaces, especially to the 1478/9 *Boece* (the most classical of his works), and he printed there too a Latin epitaph he had commissioned from the humanist Stephen Surigo. He perhaps also told him what he wanted it to say: that Chaucer enhances the fame of the same poetic Muse that inspired Virgil; admiration for his learning and wisdom;

[8] From the 'Arguments to the Tales', reproduced with the supplementary material at the end of *Geoffrey Chaucer: The Works 1532*, facsimile intro. D. S. Brewer (London: Scolar Press, 1978), 1598 edn. Cv.a.

his refining of the English language. William Thynne's 1532 *Works* invoked the classics not only in its title but in the editorial labour put into establishing a correct text: its preface contains the first recorded usage of 'collation' in this textual sense, along with an account of the development of language that derives English from Greek and Latin.[9]

Later scholars sometimes solved the problem of Chaucer's writing the wrong language twice over (the vernacular, and an outmoded form of that) by according him a place equivalent to the more archaic writers of Greece and Rome, as England's Homer or Ennius. Comparisons with Petrarch or Virgil were more likely to come from creative writers. Spenser, for all that he modelled his own poetic career, from eclogues to epic, on Virgil's, redefined Tityrus, Virgil's name for himself, as Chaucer, the master-poet of England. He turned Chaucer into a kind of personified fount of Helicon, a 'well of English undefyled', and claimed that Chaucer's spirit lived on in him.[10] His invention of a poetic diction based on Chaucer's is of a piece with this, as his work presented the only model of poetry in English that could stand comparison with the classics. The experiment was, however, received with some caution, not least because by the late sixteenth century the language had changed so much that readers were finding Chaucer's work increasingly difficult of access. Speght added a glossary to his 1598 edition of the *Works* and expanded it in 1602, but that was the last edition to be published until 1687. Jonson, for all his admiration for Chaucer, expressed a concern that too much and too early an exposure to him might spoil the style of the young through an affectation of antiquity (*Timber*, ?1620–35, printed 1640). Although some admirers suspected that complaints about his difficulty were just an excuse for not bothering to read him at all, the problems were large enough to require action. In 1630 Jonathan Sidnam 'paraphrased' the first three books of *Troilus* into modern English (see Spurgeon), and in 1635 Francis Kynaston published a translation of the first two books into Latin, not just to preserve them for the future, but because for the educated Latin was easier to understand than Chaucer's English. The accompanying flock of commendatory verses make the point clear:

> Our Natiue was become an vnknowne tongue,
> And homebred *Chaucer* vnto vs was such,
> As if he had bin written in High Dutch,

whereas the Latin means that

[9] James E. Blodgett, 'William Thynne', in *Editing Chaucer: The Great Tradition*, ed. Paul G. Ruggiers (Norman, OK: Pilgrim Books, 1984), 35–52, at 47.

[10] *The Poetical Works of Edmund Spenser*, ed. J. C. Smith and E. de Selincourt (Oxford: Oxford University Press, 1912, numerous reprints), *Calender, February* 91–9, *June* 81–6, *Faerie Queene* IV. ii.32, 34.

wee
Read *Chaucer* now without a Dictionary.[11]

It needed Dryden's translations of him to bring him back into full public consciousness; and those appeared in his *Fables* of 1700 alongside other translations from Homer and Ovid. Chaucer's Restoration was as a classical author.

Protestant Chaucer

Arguing for Chaucer as a great poet on the Classical model, however, or even as a learned poet, did not solve all the problems. 'What a gods name haue ye a booke in your hand?' inquires a character in Sir Thomas Elyot's dialogue *Pasquill the Playne* of 1533. It turns out to be a New Testament; but his companion is also hiding another, less reputable book inside his jacket: 'What is here? Troylus and Chreseid? Lorde what discord is bytwene these two bokes.' The first is described as a *Novum Testamentum*, so it may be a Catholic Latin rather than a Protestant English text; but the sense of disapproval of Chaucer as a poet incompatible with piety, of any colour whatsoever, is unmistakable. William Tyndale (1528) was convinced that a reading of love-stories such as *Troilus* would 'corrupte the myndes of youth with all clene contrary to the doctrine of christ and of his apostles', and he was not the only one to hold such a view. It was not obvious how to find a place for Chaucer within the new mood of religious fervour that was sweeping Henrician England, and it took some creative accounting on the part of editors and commentators before they worked out how to incorporate him. He was, it was evident, no friend to monks and friars, and did not seem to take the pilgrimage to St Thomas Becket too seriously; but his recognized works included a Life of St Cecilia, an advocacy of pilgrimage as a legitimate part of penance in the course of the Parson's lengthy discussion of confession, a good scatter of references to the Virgin, and the misascribed *Lamentations of Mary Magdalene*—a plausible attribution, since Chaucer himself claimed to have written something on the same subject. The 1532 *Works* added to those 'A Balade in Commendation of our Lady', though not the authentic *ABC to the Virgin*; that had to wait until 1602 for inclusion, when its presence required some skillful footwork on the part of its editor (a work of his youth, 'made, as some say, at the request of Blanch, Duchesse of Lancaster, as a praier for her privat use, being a woman in her religion very devout'[12]) to explain it away.

[11] By William Barker and William Cartwright; full texts (and translations of the Latin commendations) in Boswell and Holton, no. 1265 (322–35).

[12] In the 1602 supplementary material (f. 347) to the *Works 1532* facsimile.

The 1532 volume claimed Chaucer for England rather than for Protestantism.[13] Its preface, an extended dedication to Henry VIII, was ghostwritten for Thynne by his fellow bureaucrat Sir Brian Tuke. Both men were officers in the royal household, and Tuke in particular seems to have retained Catholic sympathies throughout his successful career under Henry; what is interesting here is that the preface should make religion an issue at all. It starts innocuously enough, in effect as a reply to the unstated humanist objection that Chaucer did not write in Latin, by eulogizing language in general and 'that noble and famous clerke Geffray Chaucer' in particular, whose works Thynne therefore intends to publish 'to the laude and honour of this your noble realme' and out of his own love for his country. It concludes, however, with a further address to Henry as

> Most gracious, victorious, and of god most electe and worthy prince, my most dradde soveraygne lorde, in whom of very merite and successyon is renewed the glorious tytell of Defensor of the christen faithe whiche by your noble progenytour the great Constantyne, somtyme kyng of this realme and emperour of Rome, was nexte god and his apostels chefely maynteyned, corroborate and defended.[14]

The terms fit well with Henry's imperialist ambitions, and they almost sound like praise of him as a faithful son of the Church; but there is one loud omission, in the absence of any mention of the pope between 'god and his apostels' and the Emperor. A reference to Constantine and the maintenance of the Church should bring to mind his Donation, the document by which he had supposedly given the pope supreme secular authority; but Lorenzo Valla's demonstration that it was a forgery was by this date widely known, in England as elsewhere. The King had not yet broken with Rome, but the omission is perhaps a straw in the wind, a hedging of bets on the part of the editors. Just how far this prefatory matter could be read as Protestant is indicated by its continuing appearance in the editions published both under Edward VI in 1550 and by John Stow in 1561.

Things changed decisively over the decade following that first *Works*, as the King moved further towards Protestantism and Chaucer was reformulated to match. Around 1536/8, a little volume entitled *The Court of Venus* appeared, which included a narrative entitled *The Pilgrim's Tale*. Set at Sempringham Abbey, this recounts how the narrator is addressed at length by a priest (a good priest, on the model of Chaucer's Parson) about the misbehaviour and general godlessness of monks and friars, concluding with an extensive prophecy developed from the later variations of Geoffrey of Monmouth's *Prophecies of Merlin*. The work associates itself with Chaucer implicitly in the title and extensively through its pattern of allusions and semi-quotations; in addition, it quotes six lines from a comparable

[13] The point is argued in detail by Greg Walker, *Writing under Tyranny: English Literature and the Henrician Reformation* (Oxford: Oxford University Press, 2005), 56–99.

[14] Quotations from the *Works 1532* facsimile, sig. Aii–iii.

passage of apocalyptic ecclesiastical satire from the *Romaunt of the Rose*, complete with a reference to precisely where in the 1532 *Works* it can be found.[15] The *Romaunt* was known to be a translation from Jean de Meun, and the passage in question, from Fragment C, is now known not to be by Chaucer at all; no one in the sixteenth century, however, had any reason to doubt the attribution, and furthermore the placing of the *Romaunt* immediately after the *Tales* gave it a prominence that it tends not to have in modern editions. All of a sudden, Chaucer was being promoted as the poet who wrote

Whyle Peter hath mastery,
May never John show well his myght

—in Reformation terms, that true evangelisation could never happen under the dominance of the pope. *The Pilgrim's Tale* was never reprinted, perhaps because of the government's fierce suppression of prophecy as much as its outspokenness on religious matters, and it had disappeared from sight by the end of the century. It none the less both illustrated and promoted the move to attach Chaucer firmly to the Protestant cause.

That move was taken further in two other works published under Chaucer's name at around the same time: *Jack Upland* and *The Plowman's Tale*, both Lollard in origin. The latter consists of a recent frame associating it with the *Canterbury Tales*, which enfolds an early fifteenth-century 'tale' in the form of a dialogue attacking the wealth and corruption of the Church between a pelican, representing the Lollards, and a griffin 'on the Popes syde'. When the *Works* was reprinted in 1542, the *Tale* was inserted as an addition, after the Parson's; in later editions, it was moved forward to precede the Parson's, so offering itself as an integral part of the *Tales* as Chaucer had written them. *Jack Upland* had to wait until 1602 to be incorporated into Chaucer's *Works*, but by that time its place as part of the canon had been authorized by John Foxe in his *Ecclesiastical History* (better known as the *Book of Martyrs*), where it is reprinted in full in the 1570 and later editions as further evidence that he was indeed a 'right Wiclevian', a fully-fledged proto-Protestant. Foxe also cited *The Testament of Love*, also regularly printed as Chaucer's. In contrast to the attempts of modern scholarship to identify Lollard sympathies in his works, in fact, the proto-Protestantism of the post-1536 Chaucer rested almost entirely in misattributions. If the almost-Catholic paratext of 1532 remained in place through the next three editions, the Chaucer portrayed by the contents changed decisively.

[15] *Francis Thynne's Animadversions on Speght's first edition of Chaucer's Works*, ed. G. H. Kingsley, revised by F. J. Furnivall, EETS, o.s. 9 (1965; first published 1875), Appendix I, lines 721–46 (742–3 quoted; cf. *Romaunt* 7165–70).

The idea that Thynne already had a Protestant agenda in mind for the 1532 edition was so firmly entrenched by the end of the century that his son Francis described with generous authenticating detail the battle over its ideological programme, in an account that, on the grounds of the dates involved, is simply impossible. His father, he claims, had intended to include the *Pilgrim's Tale*, 'a thinge more odious to the Clergye, then the speche of the plowmanne'; but

> This tale, when kinge henrye the eighte had redde, he called my father unto hym, sayinge, 'Williame Thynne! I dobte this will not be allowed; for I suspecte the Byshoppes will call the in questione for yt.' to whome my father, beinge in great favore with his prince... sayed, 'yf your grace be not offended, I hoope to be protected by yo'; whereuppon the kinge bydd hym goo his waye, and fear not.

Despite that, he says, the combined resistance of the bishops and Cardinal Wolsey forced the reprinting of the volume without the tale, though the *Plowman's Tale* was 'with muche ado permitted to pass with the reste'.[16] The contents and dating of the *Pilgrim's Tale*, as well as the absence of the *Plowman's Tale*, rule this out as an account of the 1532 volume; it is possible that Francis Thynne was confusing the second edition with the first, though there is otherwise no evidence for his father's continuing involvement with the volume after its initial publication, and Wolsey was long dead by then. What the story does attest is the belief that Henry in some sense had a vested interest in the printing of Chaucer, and a strongly Protestant one at that. Famously, 'Canterburye tales, Chaucers books' were exempted, along with chronicles, official service books, laws of the realm, the works of Gower and 'stories of mennes lieves', from the Act for the Advancement of True Religion of 1542–3 that aimed to repress printing in English. Francis Thynne thought Chaucer got past the bishops because his works were 'counted but fables', and the fact that by this date 'canterbury tale' could be used as a term for a cock-and-bull story might support that. The ambiguity did prove useful for the new edition, since a marginal note was added alongside the Parson's advocacy of pilgrimage, 'Thys is a Canterbury tale': it is both spoken in the Parson's own voice, and fantastic nonsense.[17] There are, however, other reasons why the bishops might have allowed its printing: because of Chaucer's standing as a poet of English; because they did not realize that the 1542 *Works* was being transformed into religious polemic; or perhaps because they did. As Foxe's comments confirm, a Protestant Chaucer was becoming an essential part of developing an English ancestry for the new English church. Chaucer's works were thus allowed not because they were innocuous, but because they were not.

[16] Ibid., 8–10.

[17] Alexandra Gillespie, *Print Culture and the Medieval Author: Chaucer, Lydgate, and their Books 1473–1557* (Oxford: Oxford University Press, 2006), 190–1.

Even among the reformers, there were strikingly different attitudes towards him. A number called on or quoted the *Plowman's Tale* as evidence against the Catholic Church. Others cited the Wife of Bath's equation of friars and incubi as an argument against friars, though Reginald Scot (1584) used it as an argument against incubi. There were a number of complaints that the time spent reading the *Canterbury Tales* would be better spent on the Bible; but if part of the point of reading the Bible rather than the *Tales* was, as Edmund Becke believed (1549), in order to bring about a reduction in 'blasphemyes, swearing, carding, dysing', later reformers, who knew their Chaucer better (Becke may indeed have used the title in the generic sense), would happily quote the *Pardoner's Tale* at length as showing Chaucer's proper opposition to such vices, among them the fiercely polemical opponent of the stage, John Northbrooke (1577). Other homilists seem to have been unable to resist seduction despite their best efforts. Meredith Hanmer, in the preface to his 1576 translation of Eusebius, condemns those who had rather read a whole shoal of secular works, from King Arthur and Gargantua through Chaucer to *Bevis of Hampton* and the *Hundred Merry Tales*, rather than 'bookes of divinitie'; but rather like the Pardoner whose condemnation of drinking turns into a handbook for wine buffs, he finds himself advertising Chaucer as full of 'excellent wit, good reading, and good decorum', and goes on to quote with approval *Lack of Steadfastness* and the prophecy (or statement of the obvious) 'When fayth fayleth in priestes sawes' that had become a standard item prefacing every complete works. The key lines of 'Chaucer's prophecy',

> Then shall the land of Albion
> Come to great confusion,

reappear in *King Lear* (at the end of the Folio text of 3.2), where the Fool describes them as a prophecy of Merlin; they seem to have been circulating in various forms, but it is not impossible that Shakespeare adapted them out of his Chaucer. His own first line, 'When priests are more in word than matter', would resonate well with an audience brought up on long Protestant sermons.

Catholic Chaucer

The protestantizing of Chaucer in turn fuelled Catholic attempts to assert him as orthodox, or to reclaim him from the opposition. Before the mid-1530s, with the appearance of the misascribed works, there was no need to do so: Chaucer appeared as a good Catholic author, and if he inveighed against ecclesiastical abuses, he was doing no more than many sons of the Church had done for many centuries, Jean de Meun among them. A thoroughly orthodox Miracle of the Virgin by Thomas Hoccleve was incorporated into one manuscript as the first attempt to provide a tale for the Ploughman, and no one would have found it inappropriate: the *Tales* did, after all, already include another such miracle story, from the Prioress. Furthermore, a poem in the form of an appeal to the king and the Knights of the Garter to support the true faith of Holy Church appeared in every edition from 1532 to 1602, initially after Tuke's preface, but in 1598/1602 with the poems implicitly ascribed to Chaucer that followed the list of contents. It was in fact written by Hoccleve to Henry V to urge him to repress Lollardy, but it was never clear that it was anything other than a first-person statement of Chaucer's own orthodoxy (John Selden still assumed his authorship in 1612), and so strongly invited a Catholic interpretation.

Mary Tudor seems to have had no problem with thinking of Chaucer as a congenial spirit. A homiletic work in rhyme royal entitled *A Lytell Treatyse in Englysshe, called the Extripacion of Ignorancy*, on fearing and loving God and honouring the King, was dedicated to her in 1526 by the priest Paul Bushe (see Boswell and Holton), with a dedication invoking the 'dropes of the lycour laureate / Which sprang of Chaucer, the fountayne of oratours', though what follows that is more Hawes than Chaucer. One of the most interesting, and the most thoughtful, of all the sixteenth-century adaptations of Chaucer was written with Mary as its primary, perhaps almost sole, intended reader. This is *The History of Grisilde the Second*, completed and presented to her in 1558 by her chaplain William Forrest; the sole surviving copy, a delicate presentation-style manuscript with an embroidered cover, may well be the original.[18]

The work is a version of the Griselda story, like Chaucer's in rhyme royal, in which Catherine of Aragon, Mary's mother, is given the role of 'Grisilde the second', and Henry VIII that of Walter. The fit of the two stories is remarkably close, except of course for the final reconciliation offered in the original. Catherine, despite her obedience and good wifehood, suffered the death of her son and the removal from her of her daughter before herself being cast off by her husband. Forrest knew Petrarch's version as well as Chaucer's, but despite Petrarch's largely approving treatment of the husband, who becomes an analogy if not an allegory for God, Forrest takes even further Chaucer's presentation of him as something more like a psychopath. The only possible happy ending for Catherine lies in what amounts to a martyr's death and her entry into everlasting queenship, a 'perdurable Coronation', in heaven. His work was never published, and was probably never intended for publication: its attack on the previous monarch, the father of the incumbent queen, was not the kind of thing any Tudor sovereign would want broadcast, and Mary's

[18] Oxford, Bodleian Library MS Wood. empt. 2; ed. W. D. Macray, *The History of Grisilde the Second* (Roxburghe Club, 1875).

death soon after its completion removed all possibility of disseminating such a supportive reading of the events of her mother's marriage.

Altogether more visible as a move towards incorporating Chaucer within the new regime was the erection of a tomb for him in Westminster Abbey, newly restored to its Catholic status. He had been buried in the south aisle near the entrance to St Benedict's Chapel, but there was no monument to him until (or unless: the account is unclear) Caxton had Surigo's epitaph affixed to a nearby pillar. In 1556, Nicholas Brigham set out to change that, with a full-size tomb ornamented with both a portrait and an inscription. As Derek Pearsall puts it,

> The place where someone is buried may or may not be important, but the place where someone is reburied is always important, not of course in this latter case to the person reburied, but to the reburier. The movement of someone's remains constitutes a significant political statement, or is a form of propaganda, or a way of shaping public opinion.[19]

The tomb is of a design fashionable in the 1550s that allowed space for a priest to stand at the end beneath the canopy to pray for the dead, in true Catholic fashion. The installation of the tomb thus showed a double piety: piety towards Chaucer, and also towards orthodox Catholicism, in this church newly restored to its full Catholic function as an abbey. Even so, if the later illustrations of the tomb represent its original appearance, he himself was depicted not with a rosary, as in the portraits drawn for Hoccleve's *Regiment of Princes* and used for the 1598 *Works*, but holding a pile of books: as a learned author, not as a devout Catholic. The new prominence given to him none the less asserted a Chaucer who could be seen as supporting the monarch's duty to defend Holy Church, as the attaching of Hoccleve's address to Henry V that prefaced the printed *Works* affirmed. The tomb doubled initially as a semi-official place for the payment of debts, but the decision to bury Spenser alongside Chaucer, 'closest to him in spirit and likewise in his grave',[20] turned the single tomb into the foundation for Poets' Corner, and the site for more secular pilgrimage.

Chaucer's Lineage

The generation of poets who immediately followed Chaucer were unanimous in the terms by which they praised him. He was the exemplar of eloquence, 'the noble Rethor, poete of Brytayne',

[19] Derek Pearsall, 'Chaucer's Tomb: The Politics of Reburial', *Medium Ævum*, 64 (1995), 31–73, at 31, for a full discussion of the tomb.

[20] Latin epitaph recorded by Camden, 1600.

> That made firste, to distille and rayne
> The golde dewe dropes of speche and eloquence
> Into our tunge, thurgh his excellence.[21]

Most of the poets of the fifteenth century acknowledged Chaucer as their master. Hoccleve, who claims to have known him personally, further addresses him repeatedly as 'fadir', and the term remained a commonplace conveying both respect and affection: one should, as a matter of course, 'of English Poets of our owne Nation, esteeme *Sir Geoffrey Chaucer* the father' (1622), the man at the root of the family tree of English letters. The very fact that he was the first major poet whose name was known underlined the point. Most poetry before the 1360s was anonymous, and so was impossible to father on anyone; most poetry after Chaucer carried the name of the author with it, and with that a claim to higher status than anonymous verse had possessed. Later poets may not have carried his patronymic, but they inherited from him the right to carry their own.

For his most ardent sixteenth-century heir, Spenser, poetic descent was not enough. He borrowed the initiating episode of the central action of the whole *Faerie Queene*, Arthur's dream of his destined love Gloriana (I.ix.13–15), from the tale Chaucer tells in his own voice, *Sir Thopas*. Through the mediation of Chaucer's elf-queen, Spenser thus grounds the symbolic lineage of both the nation and the poem in the father of English poetry, as a supplement in terms of poetic heritage to the founding of Britain by the descendants of Aeneas: as a new myth of origin.

Genealogy was an important business in the sixteenth century: in Chaucer's case, too important to leave with his poetic descendants alone. A move to write him into the political history of England, as well as its linguistic and literary history, started as early as the 1532 *Works*, and reached its culmination in the editions of 1598 and 1602. Tuke's preface writes English into the great descent of language from its classical roots, and then goes on to draw Chaucer into that great tradition, as one of those Englishmen who 'have right well and notably endevoyred and employed themselves to the beautifyeng and bettryng of th'englysh tonge'. With the King's blessing, the volume can go out into the world like the martial princes of the English past, to 'prevayle over those that wolde blemysshe, deface and in many thynges clerely abolyssh the laude, renoume and glorie heretofore compared and meritoriously adquired by dyvers princes and other of this said most noble yle'. Even the invocation of Constantine at the end of the Preface is phrased in genealogical terms, as Constantine, who had a British mother, is cast as Henry's progenitor. The genealogy of the royal house of England, and the Tudors in particular, gives them dominance over both empire and Church. The next stage in the process was to write Chaucer more explicitly into that genealogy.

[21] From *The Life of our Lady*, one of many such encomia offered to Chaucer by Lydgate (1409–11).

The process started in Stow's edition of 1561, which provided for the *Canterbury Tales* a sub-titlepage originally cut for Halle's *Union of the Noble Houses of Lancaster and York*, showing a family tree (or, more accurately, a family rosebush) for the Tudors curling around the title in the central panel.[22] At its double root, sleeping, are John of Gaunt and Edmund of Langley; arising from them, to clasp hands across the top of the title, are their respective descendants Henry VII and Elizabeth of York; and at the top is Henry VIII himself. Chaucer is there only by implication in the title.

The page appears again in Speght's editions, but by that time it had been discovered that Chaucer himself apparently had royal connections, through his marriage to the sister of Katherine Swynford, John of Gaunt's mistress and ancestress of the Tudors. John Speed, the man famous for the mapping of England, accordingly provided a portrait page that made those connections so prominent as to govern the reading of all the works that follow. Here the centre of the page is taken by a full-length, and tall, Chaucer: a man of literal stature. Below him is an engraving of the tomb of his son Thomas, ornamented with twenty-four coats of arms, eight of which bear some variant on the royal arms of England. Across the top and down each side is a genealogy, of the Lancastrians and Tudors to the left, and Chaucer's own descendants, the de la Pole dukes of Suffolk, to the right. It is headed 'The Progenie of Geffrey Chaucer', and one has to look quite hard to see that the name at the head of both lines is not in fact Chaucer himself but his father-in-law, Payne Roet. (Interestingly, it omits John de la Pole, earl of Lincoln, who as the potential heir to Richard III after the death of his own son was the closest any of Chaucer's descendants ever came to the throne itself: his inclusion in the right-hand line might have come too close to questioning the legitimacy of the Tudors on the left.)

What the portrait page declares is that Chaucer is embedded in the great tradition of the nation in part by his close incorporation into the royal and aristocratic history of England. That had begun with the chance of his marrying a Roet daughter, but the process worked towards its culmination over the two centuries after his death, with the acknowledgement of his supremacy in English, the comparison of him to the great classical authors in the *Works*, the patronage of Henry VIII, the tussle to claim him for each religion, the triumph of his misidentification as a forerunner of English Protestantism, and the erection of his tomb close to those of England's monarchs. The portrait makes literal what Spenser had suggested as metaphor in his deriving of Gloriana from Chaucer. As the praise and the imitations testify, however, whatever the ideological justifications for honouring him may have been, it was his qualities as a model of poetry and a fountain of eternally living stories that ensured his fame as the great poet of England.

[22] R. B. McKerrow and F. S. Ferguson, *Title-Page Borders used in England and Scotland 1485–1640* (London: Oxford University Press for the Bibliographical Society, 1932), no. 75.

FURTHER READING

Donaldson, E. Talbot. *The Swan at the Well: Shakespeare Reading Chaucer* (New Haven, CT: Yale University Press, 1985)

Gillespie, Alexandra. *Print Culture and the Medieval Author: Chaucer, Lydgate and their Books 1473–1557* (Oxford: Oxford University Press, 2006)

Pearsall, Derek. 'Chaucer's Tomb: The Politics of Reburial', *Medium Ævum*, 64 (1995): 31–73

Thompson, Ann. *Shakespeare's Chaucer: A Study in Literary Origins* (Liverpool: Liverpool University Press, 1978)

CHAPTER 21

'LITERATURE'

GORDON TESKEY *

In reflecting on storytelling in Britain on either side of the Protestant Reformation I shall myself be retelling two stories of two unfortunate, though imaginary, heroines: Robert Henryson's Cresseid, 'sumtyme countit the flour of womanheid', who becomes a leper, and Thomas Lodge's Scylla, a beautiful nymph who is also unpleasantly transformed, becoming a monster in the Straits of Messina, between Sicily and the Italian mainland.[1] Lodge does not mention Charybdis, the sucking gulf on the opposite shore of the strait, a bow-shot away as Homer tells us. Nor does Lodge give Scylla the full complement of horrors she has in ancient literature from Homer to Ovid: six man-eating heads with three sets of teeth in each head, twelve legs, and howling wolves around her loins, this last being the nasty inspiration of Milton's Sin. Even so, what happens to Lodge's Scylla isn't pretty: she becomes a natural feature of the straits along what Milton called 'the hoarse Trinacrian shore', a deadly combination of sandbars and reefs: 'hir locks / Are chang'd', Lodge says, 'with wonder into hideous sands, / And hard as flint become her snow-white hands.'[2]

* This essay is dedicated to the memory of my teachers, Denton Fox and James Winny.

[1] *The Testament of Cresseid*, line 608, cited hereafter in the text from *Robert Henryson, The Poems*, ed. Denton Fox (Oxford: Clarendon Press, 1981). On Henryson, see James Simpson, *Reform and Cultural Revolution*, The Oxford English Literary History, vol. 2: *1350–1547* (Oxford: Oxford University Press, 2002), 187–90.

[2] *Scillaes Metamorphosis*, lines 736–8, hereafter cited in text from Nigel Alexander (ed.), *Elizabethan Narrative Verse*, Stratford-Upon-Avon Library, 3 (London: Butler and Tanner, 1967). The phrase 'hoarse Trinacrian shore' is from John Milton, *Paradise Lost*, ed. Gordon Teskey (New York: W.W. Norton, 2005), Book 2, line 661. *Scillaes Metamorphosis* appears also in the important selection of Elizabethan narrative works by Elizabeth Story Donno (ed.), *Elizabethan Minor Epics* (New York: Columbia University Press, 1963). Scholars have been uncertain what generic name to apply to the erotic narrative poems by Marlowe, Shakespeare, Chapman, Drayton, Marston, Willoby, Daniel, Heywood, Beaumont, Fletcher, Weever, and others that were written in the wake of *Scillaes Metamorphoses*. 'Erotic epyllion', despite its shortcomings, still seems the best: 'minor epic' will not do—there is nothing epic about these poems, even in a minor sense—and 'narrative verse' is evasive. As Douglas Bush notes, in *Mythology and the Renaissance Tradition in English Poetry*, 2nd edn

My subject, however, is not so much the stories themselves as the circumstances in which they were told, or rather retold, Henryson pretending to draw skeptically from his authority—'Quha wait gif all that Chauceir wrait was trew?' (line 604)—Lodge amplifying on Ovid, who is for him not so much an authority, a source of truth, as a model of attitude and style. What are their relative truth claims? One story purports to be 'historical' and is grounded in the world by its authority, Geoffrey Chaucer, author of *Troilus and Criseyde*, who also claims historical truth for his tale, and whose veracity is a matter of pretended concern to the later poet. Although Henryson has invented his tale in its exact verbal form, part of his tale's fiction is that it has not been invented but found in an old book, which is the first step on a trail of evidence leading back (through Boccaccio, Guido delle Colonne, and others) to a witnessed, historical event at the time of the Trojan War. Fiction—the literary power of invention, of simply making things up—is deeply denied.

The other story is grounded, if that is the right word, in nothing more substantial than literary discourse, that is, in poetic fictions and figures of speech making up an imaginary, independent environment, one that is felt to be distinct from our own. 'Discourse was steersman', Lodge says, 'while my barke did saile, / My ship conceit, and fancie was my bay' (lines 686–7). His whole voyage—and Lodge, it should be recalled, was a real sailor too, a tough one, who endured a winter in the Straits of Magellan—is within the realm of literary performance without reference to anything outside it. The ship he sails in is 'conceit', which I take to mean a structure of poetical ideas not yet arranged in sequential order (in rhetoric, *inventio*). The ship is directed by 'discourse', or the marshaling of ideas into such an order (*dispositio*), followed by their elaboration (*amplificatio*). The goal or 'bay' is not a place to drop anchor, making contact with the world: it is 'fancie', a realm of imaginative pleasure quite apart from the world.

Cresseid's story was told by Henryson in the third quarter of the fifteenth century in Scotland, probably in Dunfermline, Scylla's by Lodge in London in 1589, at the outset of the Elizabethan golden age (if C. S. Lewis's controversial term may be allowed here). They are thus told about a century apart and on either side of the Protestant Reformation, although they both fall within the long Tudor century, from the victory of Henry Tudor at Bosworth Field in 1485 to the death of the last Tudor, Henry's granddaughter, Elizabeth, in 1603. The Protestant Reformation came first from Luther's Germany and then, still more powerfully for England, from Calvin's Geneva, to which the Marian refugees fled and from which they returned after Queen Mary's death and Elizabeth's accession in 1558, bringing a more radical Protestantism with them, soon to be known as Puritanism.

(New York: W.W. Norton, 1963), 85, there is much in Lodge's form to recall the medieval dream poem and amorous complaint. For C. S. Lewis's valuable comparisons between Marlowe, Shakespeare, and Lodge, see his *English Literature in the Sixteenth Century Excluding Drama* (New York: Oxford University Press, 1954), 486–9.

The Protestant Reformation in England, when mixed with the powerful stimulants of English nationalism and insular distrust of foreigners, especially Italians, and most especially Italian priests (consider Shakespeare's *King John*), was immensely important for literature. The greatest and, at the same time, the most representative product of the Protestant Reformation in England was Spenser's nationalistic epic (it is many other things, too, but it is certainly that), *The Faerie Queene.* In addition to fueling English nationalism, the Protestant Reformation saw the translation of the Bible into English and the conduct of divine service with an English Book of Common Prayer, factors which immediately and profoundly influenced authors, who heard readings from the Bible and the Book of Common Prayer at least twice a week. The radical Protestant idea that salvation depends upon scripture alone contributed to the emergence of a different, more private and unmediated conception of reading in which much was at stake—indeed, for the religious, everything. The seriousness with which solitary reading of the Bible was conducted spread to reading in general, especially of 'poesy', or what we now call 'literature'. Texts read in solitude began to have the narcotic and mesmerizing power Milton describes in his poem on Shakespeare, which imagines Shakespeare's plays as a single, priceless, or 'unvalued book', open for solitary reading: 'Then thou our fancy of itself bereaving, / Dost make us marble with too much conceiving'.[3]

It is hard to overestimate the importance of the Protestant Reformation to every area of consciousness and social practice in England, not excluding the rise of a phenomenon I mentioned just above, one that grows out of popular culture but will come to make higher, even transcendent claims for itself: literature. Long before Matthew Arnold, at least from William Blake, literature would bid fair to replace religion altogether as a medium of prophetic truth to which it has access because of its disconnection from the world and its grounding in imaginative forms—forms, it is important to add, that are independent of Christian revelation. Classical culture provided part of this realm of independent literary forms, as we see in Chaucer and Henryson as much as in Lodge, although not in Langland, for whom the underlying imaginative forms do belong to Christian revelation.

The rise of literature is also the rise of a complex social event that is perhaps too dynamic to be called an 'institution', one consisting of many independent but synergistic practices embedded in a rapidly changing culture, all of them supported by the new technology of printing with moveable type. These practices extend from elementary reading and writing to university study; literary theory (initially imported from Italy); secretary-ships; discussion groups such as those around Philip Sidney, Walter Raleigh, and Lodowick Bryskett; translation of ancient and modern literary texts; writing for the theatre and going to plays; political lobbying

[3] John Milton, 'On Shakespeare', in *John Milton, Complete Shorter Poems*, 2nd edn, ed. John Carey (Edinburgh Gate, Harlow: Pearson-Longman, 1997), lines 13–14. The particular 'unvalued book' (line 11) for which this poem was composed is the Shakespeare Second Folio (1632).

and status-seeking (or, in Sir Walter Raleigh's case, status-recovering), both of which demanded the composition of poems; and the elaborate rituals of dedicatory sonnets and epistles. The rise of literature as a social event was too broad an occurrence to have been brought about by a handful of authors of genius—Marlowe, Spenser, Shakespeare, and Donne (much of whose poetry was written in the 1590s)—plus a crowd of lesser but considerable talents, Lodge among them. Large social and political factors were in play. It will therefore be worth taking a few moments to consider in still broader terms the changes that took place in the European world during the long Tudor century, from 1485 to 1603.

With the discovery of America and of the sea route around Africa to India, and with the opening of the Pacific Ocean and the circumnavigation of the earth, the old, basin-like, Mediterranean world wherein the lands enclose a sea—*mare nostrum*, as the Romans called it—became a new, vastly enlarged globe on which the seas encircle all the lands. Formerly, countries such as Portugal, Spain and England, and of course Henryson's Scotland, were marginal and unimportant. Now these countries were central, if one may use that word when speaking of a globe, because they were not locked up in the Mediterranean but advantageously situated on the Atlantic Ocean. The high seas were dominated first by the Portuguese, then by the Spanish and then, when the Baltic trade was becoming important, by the English and the Dutch, whose striving for the upper hand would continue up to the eighteenth century, when British sea power was supreme. The great Venetian Republic shrank to irrelevance and over its long Tudor century England was transformed from an unimportant Roman Catholic nation on the edge of the known world, where the Church owned almost a third of the land, into a militantly Protestant, bourgeois state with global power, international ports, colonies in North America, a rich, East India trade, an advanced scientific community, and, in its theatres, the beginnings of popular entertainment as a profitable commercial venture.

The all-encompassing administrative power of the old aristocracy was exhausted in the lethal Wars of the Roses and under Henry VII, who has been credited with inventing a rudimentary civil service, new men from the upper middle classes rose to positions of power, doing so on the strength of learning rather than of social rank. As to learning, practical subjects, such as mapmaking, deepwater navigation, and double-entry bookkeeping gained prestige over theology, which remained queen of the sciences only in name, and not long in name, either. With the coming of the Protestant Reformation, theology had to descend into the arena of debate and international politics.

'Modern' literature, that is, literature in the contemporary languages of Europe, especially French, Italian, and Spanish, had been important since Chaucer's day and before, in the bilingual culture of Anglo-Norman England. Even such a work as *Sir Gawain and the Green Knight*, contemporary with Chaucer but from the remote, Welsh border area, far enough north to be rich in words derived from

Old Norse, shows the powerful international influence of vernacular French culture long before the Renaissance.

Of course, England had a rich vernacular literature before Henry Tudor reached Bosworth Field: Chaucer, Langland, and Malory were its stars, among others who were stars in their day, if not now. But it was in the long Tudor century that broad claims began to be made not for individual authors in English but for the English language itself as a medium capable of the highest literary aspiration. The very strange idea that something so impersonal as a language, considered in grammatical abstraction from its users, could be judged suitable for literary expression—or not—was a consequence of the new studies in ancient Latin and Greek, and of astonishment at the treasures reposing in those ancient tongues. Might English be strong enough to have its own Aeschylus and Homer, or at least its own Seneca and Virgil? A major cultural effort of inestimable importance in extending the range and flexibility of English, but also in freeing energies already there in the language, was the translation of popular, late ancient authors—among whom, Heliodorus, translated by Thomas Underdowne (1569?), Apuleius, translated by William Adlington (1566), and Plutarch, some of whose moral works were translated by Sir Thomas Wyatt (1528) and by Sir Thomas Elyot (1553 and 1535?), and whose *Lives of the Noble Grecians and Romans* was translated by Thomas North (1579). There were also translations of signal modern European works, such as Castiglione's *Courtier*, brilliantly recreated in English by Sir Thomas Hoby (1561).[4]

*

The long Tudor century also brought an event that was as momentous for what we call 'literature' as it was also for popular culture: the art of printing with moveable type. The new medium altered the nature of stories. They appeared in print, at the higher end of the scale, in quarto books like Lodge's *Scillaes Metamorphosis* or, near the summit, the first three books of Spenser's *Faerie Queene*, published the following year, in 1590. At the summit were the deluxe, folio editions of Virgil printed on the continent, massive in their authority, lavishly illustrated and difficult to print, the poetry hedged in on the page by the commentaries of Donatus, Servius, and others. They were imitated, although in quarto, in the elaborately illustrated and still more elaborately commented-upon first edition of Spenser's *Shepeardes Calender*, published in 1579.

Folios were rare in the sixteenth century. Spenser would be published in folio editions between 1609 and 1617. Ben Jonson published his works in a two-volume folio in 1617 and the Shakespeare First Folio, an immense task for English printing

[4] For examples and discussion, see James Winny, *Elizabethan Prose Translation* (Cambridge: Cambridge University Press, 1960). For a full list, see George Watson (ed.), *New Cambridge Bibliography of English Literature*, Vol. 1: *600–1600* (Cambridge: Cambridge University Press, 1974), cols. 2165–92.

of the period, was published in 1623. Of course the most prestigious book of the period was published in folio in 1611, the Authorized Version of the Bible. The smaller, cheaper octavo format was less prestigious as an object, but this does not necessarily reflect on the prestige of the contents. Classical texts from the Aldine press in Venice and from the Estiennes in France, being intended for scholarly use instead of display, were mostly octavos. Like our Loeb editions, the smaller format, saving space and expense, made it possible to build up private libraries on a scale that was unimaginable before printing with moveable type. From thence printed matter descends in prestige from 'literature' in the quasi-official sense to popular plays published in quarto and, lower still in prestige, cheap, popular broadsides such as we see in Shakespeare's *Winter's Tale*—single sheets of folio paper printed with ballads and tabloid-quality news.

What are the consequences of printing for stories? They are (1) isolation from other stories, as 'works'; and (2) dematerialization, or abstraction from their medium, making them quasi-transcendent, imaginative productions. Formerly, a story was the latest, slow-emerging leaf on a branch that reaches back in time through earlier versions, at last descending the great bole of stories to an event rooted in the soil of the world. Whether it was literally true or not, stories were thought of as existing on a stemma of witnesses going back in time. Because stories in a manuscript culture notionally existed in single copies, they were more closely identified with their physical medium, the 'book'. Even after the invention of printing with moveable type stories must have been thought of for some time in this way, as identifiable with the books in which they appear. In 'The Letter to Raleigh', for example, Spenser refers to *The Faerie Queene* as 'all the booke', although whoever wrote the editorial head-note calls it a 'worke'. But once the consequences of printing were felt, stories were cut off from their stemmata to become independent units, published works unrelated to other stories or even to other versions of the same story. Such works were not connected to the world through a chain of witnesses leading back an original event in the world. They were connected instead to their 'authors', who were not *auctors* in the medieval sense of 'authorities', 'experts', but *authors* in our originative sense of the word: free creators of works of art.

Yet even as stories came to seem more isolated from other stories, as independent 'works', another, almost contrary result was the viral multiplication of one particular telling of a story in simultaneous and notionally identical copies, as many as a thousand. Suddenly, a story could be anywhere at once, or everywhere at once, all over London. The effect of this multiplication, however, was to further dematerialize and isolate the story, freeing it from its medium, the book, and making the story as told by this author something at least potentially transcendent. The notion that literature in general—not just some literary works, such as the *Commedia*, but literature in general—may have something to do with the transcendent, the unearthly, and the otherworldly, or simply with what is higher, the sublime, emerges into view at this moment. But what also emerges into view is great anxiety concerning the insubstantiality and unanchoredness of stories.

I have suggested that literature emerges from popular culture. What makes it different, and what is peculiar to literature as a social phenomenon? I would define 'literature' as the telling of stories with self-conscious verbal craft and the preservation of those stories in a medium (in the period we are concerned with, writing and printing) so that not just the stories but also their craft—the exact words used in the exact order they were used—is preserved and disseminated. Literature is the telling of stories in an exact verbal form that is preserved by one practice and disseminated by another. (Making copies of a manuscript is a practice different from composition, although both employ writing.) Literature is a peculiar activity that is hard to justify, given the social resources required to sustain it, except for the pleasure it gives. In the relentlessly materializing, puritan culture of sixteenth-century England the enemies of pleasure understood this well, attacking literature—not just plays, but also poems, and especially romances—as an excuse for idleness and an incitement to lust, erotic pleasures having long been associated with literary ones.

The defenses of literature (or, as they called it, of 'poesy', from Greek *poiein* 'to fabricate'), Sidney's *Defense of Poesie* and Spenser's 'Letter to Raleigh', divided the operation of literature into two, complementary streams, as Horace had taught: moral instruction and fictive delight. A tale that is 'pleasant', as it says on the title page of *Scillaes Metamorphosis*, must also be 'pithie'. Like a sugared pill, a simile repeated *ad nauseam* in the Renaissance but rarely, so far as I can tell, in the Middle Ages, delight is necessary to the conveying of instruction. Sidney's more elegant term is a 'medicine of Cheries'.[5] Earlier in the same passage he writes,

> even as the child is often brought to take most wholesome things by hiding them in such other as have a pleasant taste... so it is in men (most of which, are childish in the best things, til they be cradled in their graves) glad they will be to heare the tales of *Hercules, Achilles, Cyrus, Aeneas*, and hearing them, must needs heare the right description of wisdom, value, and justice; which if they had been barely (that is to say Philosophically) set out, they would 'sweare they be brought to schoole againe.[6]

Spenser's 'Letter to Raleigh' develops the same, morally improving theme in relation to the epic tradition in particular: 'The generall end therefore of all the booke', he says of *The Faerie Queene*, 'is to fashion a gentleman or noble person in virtuous and gentle discipline: Which for that I conceived shoulde be most plausible and pleasing, being coloured with an historicall fiction, the which the most part of men delight to read, rather for variety of matter, then for profite of the ensample.' Spenser goes on to say that his hero Arthur unites in himself the exemplary

[5] *Defence of Poesie*, in *The Prose Works of Sir Philip Sidney*, Vol. 3, ed. Albert Feuillerat (Cambridge: Cambridge Uuniversity Press, 1968), 21.

[6] Sidney, *Defense of Poesie*, ed. Albert Feuillerat, 20.

qualities of a good governor and a virtuous man. Homer distributed government and virtue between Agamemnon and Ulysses; Virgil united them in Aeneas, as did Ariosto in Orlando; and Tasso 'dissevered' them again into 'that part which they in Philosophy call Ethice, or vertues of a private man, coloured in his Rinaldo: The other named Politice in his Godfredo.'[7] The only character of whom this seems remotely true is Virgil's Aeneas.

Tasso did retroactively, and for the most part insincerely, allegorize his own poem so as to justify to critics his miraculous episodes and purely poetical flights. But in the 'Allegoria del poema' appended to his *Gierusalemme* [sic] *Liberata* in 1581, a totalizing scheme is invented wherein Tasso identifies Rinaldo and Godfredo as ethical and political virtue and ties up the romantic and supernatural episodes as allegorical commentaries on this unifying scheme.[8] This was the immediate model for Spenser's 'Letter to Raleigh', appended to the 1590 *Faerie Queene*, although there was a long tradition, going back to antiquity, of submitting the adventures of Odysseus to moral allegorizing, a practice extensively applied to Ariosto's *Orlando Furioso* long before Tasso composed his 'Allegoria del poema' or Spenser his 'Letter to Raleigh'.[9] The sense of literature of which I am speaking—the Renaissance sense of the literary, of the fictive—has to be defended from the outset, and self-defense appears to be a part of its nature.[10] But the deeper point of such defenses is not the claim that literature does some good, developing minds or improving morals. The deeper point is to affirm that the reason for the existence of stories is something more real than the aimless pleasure of wandering a short distance—or a long distance—down the path of not-being.

Behind the moral objection to pure narrative, therefore, was something more, or something other than the anxiety that stories are an incitement to idleness and lust. In the relentlessly materializing culture of England in the sixteenth century, the

[7] Edmund Spenser, 'Letter to Raleigh', in *The Faerie Queene*, 2nd edn, ed. A. C. Hamilton, Hiroshi Yamashita, and Toshiyuki Suzuki (Edinburgh Gate, Harlow: Pearson-Longman, 2007), 714–15. Compare Sidney's longer and less schematic treatment of such figures in *Defence of Poesie*, 14–15.

[8] Torquato Tasso, *Gierusalemme liberata ... con l'allegoria dello stesso autore*, ed. Febo Bonnà (Ferrara, 1581). The spelling of 'Gierusalemme' is intended to evoke Greek *hieros* 'sacred'. In his famous 'poetic letters' Tasso says he had no idea as he wrote of there being any allegorical meaning in his supernatural, or 'marvelous', episodes, which he says conform with the demands of poetry in itself ('convengono a la poesia per sè'), without allegory. But he adds that his poetry will be more favorably judged by censorious readers, the *severi*, if it is supposed that beneath the fiction there lies, as he dryly puts it, 'some good and saintly allegory' ('alcuna buona e santa allegoria'). Torquato Tasso, Letter 48, 'to Scipione Gonzaga', 4 October 1785 in *Le Lettere di Torquato Tasso*, ed. Cesare Guasti, 5 vols. (Naples: G. Rondinella, 1857), 1: 114–15.

[9] The most extensive was a two-volume allegorical commentary, or *La Spositione*, on the *Orlando Furioso* by Simone Fornari, bound together but with independent signatures, published in Florence in 1549 and 1550. For a broader view of these developments, see Daniel Javitch, *Proclaiming a Classic: The Canonization of 'Orlando Furioso'* (Princeton, NJ: Princeton University Press, 1991).

[10] See Margaret W. Ferguson, *Trials of Desire: Renaissance Defenses of Poetry* (New Haven, CT: Yale University Press, 1983).

objection to stories was raised by their disturbing immateriality, their dubious ontological status. What kind of being, or, in Greek, ὄν, does a story have? We may recall that Marlowe's Doctor Faustus rejects the study of metaphysics, of 'being and not-being'—'bid *Oncaymaeon* farewell' (ὂν καὶ μὴ ὄν)—in favor of real power in the real and present world: 'A sound Magician is a mighty God.'[11] But the discipline of literary study is always working the boundary between being and not being, or that rather less rigorous version of this boundary known as the real and the fictive, seeking lines of connection between them. In Chaucer and Langland's day the easiest way to talk about this connection was by appealing to the theory of dreams, which are a convenient stand-in for the literary. But by the end of the sixteenth century framing a story as a dream was regarded as hopelessly old-fashioned. The interest was no longer in the literary and the fictive as vision, such as a dream might afford—a *visio* in Macrobius's terms—but rather in the literary as an art, a *techne*, a product of making, of fabrication, of *poiesis*. The line was drawn therefore not between dreaming and waking but between the fictive and the real.

In Chaucer's day, this other world of the literary, being composed of stories and of rhetorical figures, was associated either with allegory—the discourse of abstract truth in a figurative form, as in the *Romaunt of the Rose*—or with dreams, the status and kinds of which were matters of great concern to anyone preoccupied with the literary, as of course Chaucer was. In each of his three important dream poems—*The Bok of the Duchesse*, *The Hous of Fame*, and *The Parlement of Foules*—Chaucer takes time to reflect on the theory of dreams, which he has from Macrobius's commentary on the *Somnium Scipionis*, as if to reassure us that the visions with which he confronts us have some connection to the real world, justifying their otherwise tenuous existence and their disturbing insubstantiality, their status as what would now be called *epiphenomena*.

But Chaucer's most lively interest is in mimesis, imitating the energies of the real world so well as not to seem fictive at all. In his greatest work he puts an energetic frame of real persons around the stories told, stories which appertain to the very in-the-world behavior and lives of the Canterbury pilgrims. These energies—in the Miller and the Reeve, in the Pardoner, in the Wife of Bath, in the Host, Harry Bailly, and even in the chubby, abashed incompetent who narrates the Tale of Sir Thopas—may well have their imaginative source in whatever it is we are being shown in that tumultuous vision of the crowd at the conclusion of *The Hous of Fame*, a heap of whelming bodies:

> And whan they were alle on an hepe,
> Tho behynde begunne up lepe,
> And clamben up on other faste,
> And up the nose and yën kaste,

[11] *Doctor Faustus*, lines 42 and 92 in the A-Text, in *Marlowe's 'Doctor Faustus', 1604–1616*, ed. W. W. Greg (Oxford: Clarendon Press, 1950), A Text: lines 42 and 92.

And troden faste on others heles,
And stampen, as men doon aftir eles.[12]

There then appears a man who 'semed for to be / A man of gret auctorite' (lines 2157–8) who will presumably impose order on the tumult. The poem then breaks off, but James Winny is surely right to see the man of great authority as Chaucer's figure for the shaping force of the creative imagination, and to see the energies of the crowd as the unconscious materials on which imagination works.[13] The *Hous of Fame* is a fascinating meditation on the impermanence and insubstantiality of the fictive, which is essentially what Chaucer means by the word 'fame'. Yet for all its insubstantiality it has the power to soar up into the heavens, away from the earth, despite its author's weight, of which the eagle of fiction complains.

But the energies we see in the mob at the conclusion of the *Hous of Fame* are of greatest interest to Chaucer as an artist when they are freed from the unconscious and are distributed out on the surface of experience. Tumult, as in the riotous conclusion to the 'Miller's Tale', has been untangled enough to be set forth in time, in a sequence, a narrative, a telling. Of course, Chaucer said this much better in 'The Nun's Priest's Tale', where the most negligible of stories—a cock caught by a fox outfoxes the fox—is almost ground to pieces in the machinery of its justificatory apparatus. If a central purpose of literature is to show the division between the fictive and the real, without canceling the reality of fiction itself as a compulsive human need, then Chaucer is the most central of literary artists.

But the peculiar sense of the literary as constituting an autonomous world, one that might be related to ours through various ingenious operations, such as allegory, but that is wholly distinct nevertheless, was something new in the long Tudor century, even if many elements that went into it existed before. Kant's famous definition of the aesthetic as purposiveness without purpose—'Zweckmässigkeit ohne Zweck'—is a modern idea that has its origin here, in London, in the second half of the sixteenth century. For what are Protestant good works, since they have no salvific force, but an aesthetic activity, performed for their beauty? They are not done in the hope that they will prove a sign of God's grace but rather to provide an aesthetic escape from the terrible regime of that grace. Which way shall we fly from an inscrutable, predestining God? Eighteenth-century aesthetics had an answer to

[12] Geoffrey Chaucer, *The Hous of Fame*, in *The Riverside Chaucer*, general editor Larry D. Benson, 3rd edn (Oxford: Oxford University Press, 1987), lines 2149–54.

[13]

> Had Chaucer been a contemporary of Coleridge he might have written explicitly on the creative working of the imagination. Being a medieval poet, he made *The Hous of Fame* express his awareness of this crucial process in a manner typical of his art: through metaphors of celestial flight, a whirling house, a gabbling multitude, and the figure of authority who arrives at the point where Chaucer finds it impossible, or unnecessary, to continue his exploration of his creative consciousness.

James Winny, *Chaucer's Dream Poems* (London: Chatto and Windus, 1973), 110.

that question: into the beautiful and the sublime. But in Lodge's day, the path of flight from the Protestant God led straight into Ovid, the unconscious of the Renaissance. Lodge could write a poem about a world without God—though gods are everywhere in it, in every bush and stream—but he still had to find a way to make that other world connected to the one in which we live.

*

Robert Henryson is a graver figure than Lodge, at least the young Lodge who wrote *Scillaes Metamorphosis*. Henryson was a schoolteacher, a notary public and, at the time he composed the *Testament of Cresseid*, 'ane man of age' (line 29). He's an attractive and talented poet, too, vigorous, witty, and psychologically acute. He describes himself, as the poem opens, outdoors on a winter night in Scotland, when 'the northin wind had purifyit the air / And sched the mistie cloudis fra the sky' (lines 17–18). He's watching the planet Venus and hoping the withered stump that is his heart will put forth shoots again and experience love. But it's cold, so he goes indoors, stokes the fire, surveys his books, takes a drink to arm him from the cold and then, to shorten the long night, picks up a *quair* of *Troilus and Criseyde*:

> I mend the fyre and beikit me about,
> Than tuik ane drink, my spreitis to comfort,
> And armit me weill fra the cauld thairout.
> To cut the winter nicht and mak it schort
> I tuik ane quair—and left all uther sport—
> Written be worthie Chaucer glorious
> Of fair Creisseid and worthie Troylus. lines 36–42

But he finds an 'uther quair' (line 61) unknown to him before, which goes beyond the tale we know from Chaucer. In this new tale Cresseid, having been abandoned by Troilus's successor Diomeid, is taken in by her father Chalchas, who is not a priest of Apollo, as in Homer, but of 'Venus and hir sone Cupido' (line 108). Performing in the temple's oratorio the usual rites to Venus and Cupid, Cresseid has the temerity to complain of their cruelty and to say 'Allace, that ever I maid yow sacrifice!' (line 126). This was unwise. She falls immediately into an ecstasy and dreams a dream, one in which Cupid arraigns her for impiety and, ringing his silver bell, 'Quhilk men micht heir fra hevin unto hell' (line 145), calls down the seven planets from their spheres to try Cresseid for her crime.

A spectacular description of them follows, from Saturn, 'with auster luik and cheir' (line 154) to Venus, who laughs with one eye and weeps with the other—'In taikning that all fleschlie paramour... Is sum tyme sweit, sum tyme bitter and sour' (lines 232–4)—and Mercury, with laurel crown and red hood, bearing book, pen and ink, 'Lyke to ane poeit of the auld fassoun' (line 245). No sooner is Cresseid accused than she is condemned and sentenced: no plea is entered, no evidence cited, no defense mounted. Saturn and Cynthia strike her with poverty, ugliness, age and disease, in particular, leprosy, and the dream ends with Cynthia's conclusion: 'This [i.e. 'thus'] sall thow go begging fra hous to hous / With cop and clapper lyke ane lazarous' (lines 342–3). Cresseid wakes from her ecstasy, looks in the mirror, sees the sentence fulfilled, condoles with her father and is delivered to a 'spitaill hous' (line 391) half a mile away, from whence she goes out daily with the lepers to beg, although her father daily sends her a share of his alms—'and daylie sent hir part of his almous' (line 392). What Elizabethan poet would have been troubled with such an interesting detail? Understandably depressed, and having sung a long, formal 'complaint', she is unexpectedly taken up short by a fellow 'lipper lady', who puts to her this practical question: 'Why spurnis thow againis the wall / To sla thy self and mend nathing at all?' (lines 475–6). Such cameo appearances—another is the child sent to summon Cresseid to dinner (lines 358–64)—are one of Henryson's strengths, giving us the feeling that the action is taking place in a complete world. The past is not another country, certainly not another culture, that ethnographic hallucination: in Henryson, we meet the past and it is us.

The climax of the tale is when the troop of lepers runs into Troilus himself, who meets Cresseid's eyes: 'and with ane blenk it come into his thoucht / That he sumtime hir face befoir had sene' (lines 499–500). Neither recognizes the other: 'nat ane ane uther knew' (line 518). But both are strangely moved. Why? Here follows Henryson's theory of the emotions, as well as his theory, if he could have had one, of the literary:

> The idole of ane thing in cace may be
> Sa deip imprentit in the fantasy
> That it deludes the wittis outwardly,
> And sa appeiris in forme and lyke estait
> Within the mynd as it was figurait. lines 507–11

The passage seems to me almost Lucretian. When an image flies into the mind it can, like a palimpsest, delude us about the outer world. But the fantasies are in the mind, not outside it, and so have their place in the hierarchy of the world, as being lower than the outwardly real. Still, the literary 'deludes the wittis outwardly'.

Troilus tosses gold into Cresseid's skirt and rides off, sighing and nearly swooning with 'greit care', as is his wont (line 525). The gold is distributed equally—there's a utopian theory lurking in Henryson's troop of lepers, who are scrupulously egalitarian and, as we shall see, honest—and Cresseid asks them who the lord is who has 'done to us so greit humanitie' (line 534). Hearing the truth, she delivers herself of a final lament, 'With mony cairfull cry and cald ochane' (line 541), urging lovers to hold to *treuth* (line 573), that great Chaucerian word, and blaming herself for her fate: 'Nane but my self as now I will accuse' (line 574). She then composes the 'testament' (line 576) for which the poem is named, leaving her cup and clapper to the lepers, with enough gold to pay for her burial, leaving her body 'with wormies and with taidis to be rent' (line 578), and leaving her soul to the goddess Diana to wander among the woods and the streams: 'My spreit I leif to Diane, quhair scho dwellis, / To walk with hir in waist woddis and wellis' (lines 587–8). The last article in the testament is a ruby ring Troilus gave her long ago, which a 'lipper man' (line 592) faithfully returns to the prince, at her request. Receiving it, Troilus exclaims, as he swoons, 'Scho was untrew and wo is me thairfoir' (line 602). It is a famous but to my mind shockingly self-pitying line, but it does show another of the qualities of Henryson's art: a noble Roman *brevitas*, which is also seen in the words on his heroine's tomb: 'Lo, fair ladyis, Cresseid of Troy the toun, / Sumtyme countit the flour of womanheid, / Under this stane, lait lipper, lyis deid' (lines 607–9). In the final line the poet ends abruptly, 'sen scho is deid, I speik of hir no moir' (line 616).

Nothing is out of place in Henryson's hierarchical world. Rationality and realism, sharply defined human details, and what I have not yet mentioned, a strong sense of decorum suitable for a tale of antiquity (Cresseid bequeaths her soul to a pagan goddess)—all these things belong to the enframement of poetic narrative in the rich and demanding culture of late scholasticism and the international gothic. In the soaring, empty spaces of this world, a single tone of lament, of 'cald ochane', of painful regret eloquently spoken reverberates in the distant spheres and reverberates again in our hearts: 'I am by lovers left, and all forlorn!' ('And I fra luifferis left, and all forlane') (line 140). It is a world of hard granite hills and brittle pines where, after watching Venus in the evening sky, it is good to go into one's study and settle in with drink and book, after stoking the fire. But the lepers, who have no fire or food, and no books to escape into, are driven outside by cold and hunger, begging for the means of life and sounding their clappers, as they were required to do. The gods of the warmer, Mediterranean world—a world of limestone, not granite—may visit the poet in his Scottish redoubt, but they descend to his sight from the astrological spheres to which they had removed over a thousand years before. They are not the lively gods of Homer or Ovid but of Macrobius and Martianus Capella, and they are narrowly confined to their allegorical functions, like parts of a smoothly working machine. Just beyond the poet's fire and his book, everything is cold.

*

Lodge was a comparatively young man of about thirty-one years when he wrote *Scillaes Metamorphosis*. He was the son of a bankrupt Lord Mayor, and was a scholar, like Spenser, of the Merchant Taylors' School, and also of Trinity College Oxford, after which he was resident in Lincoln's Inn and like his fellow resident there, John Donne, was less interested in the law than in literature and in cutting a figure as a man about town. He fled to the continent in 1597, driven thither by the compounded liabilities of heavy debt (he would write a monitory pamphlet on the subject) and Roman Catholicism, to which he had converted, imprudently. His *curriculum vitae* includes Ovidian poet, euphuist romancer, satirical hack, playwright, sailor—I have mentioned he endured a winter in the Straits of Magellan—and, in his years of discretion, medical doctor and translator both of Seneca's philosophical works and of Josephus's *Jewish History*—considerable tasks! One cannot but feel Lodge deserves more fame than he has now in literary history, in which he is known chiefly as the author of the prose romance, *Rosalynde*, the source of *As You Like It*. But that's not bad.

Scillae's Metamorphosis is also in stanzas, not in rhyme royal but less imposing hexaines. There any similarity with Henryson's *Testament of Cresseid* ends. Instead of granite and pine, Lodge's fictive world feels as if it's made up of myths right down to its foundations, if it has any. It reminds me of one of Calvino's invisible cities, suspended in a great net stretched like a hammock between mountain peaks and swaying over an abyss. Lodge's heterocosm is a reticulated world of interwoven myths, one in which every movement—brushing a thorn bush, walking along a reedy stream back, or sailing past a sandbar—starts a myth out of hiding and provokes it to speak. It is not an allegorical but an aetiological world, a world of 'just-so stories', and we do not have to spend very long there before we begin to suspect that the order of explanation needs to be reversed. I mean that the stories are not there to explain the existence of objects in the world. Objects in the world are being used to explain—or to anchor—the troubling existence of stories.

As the poem opens the poet describes himself walking by the upper Thames, the Isis, lamenting his unhappiness in love. Suddenly, with no dream-frame to warn us we are passing onto another plane of existence, the sea god Glaucus rises from the stream to assert that sorrow is general in the world and unavoidable in life, adding, illogically, 'Then mourn no more, but moan my hapless state' (line 42). The two sit down amiably and the sea god reposes his head on the poet's knee to tell him all about his sorrow when the nymph Scylla spurned him. The trees shed their leaves at his tale, and the rest of nature mourns. Other nymphs, themselves potential tales, rise from the 'weeds and sallows neare the bancke' (line 52) and at a wave of Glaucus's finger are still, upon which he 'orderlie his hideous harmes recited' (line 226), the chief of which is of course that Scylla is unaccountably indifferent to his considerable charms: 'Was any Nimph, you Nimphes', he challenges them, 'that tangled not her fingers in my tresses?' (lines 265–6). 'Tresses' seems an odd word for the hair of a masculine god, but perhaps not for one who moves his head from the poet's knee to his lap, and then snuggles up on his chest, wailing and complaining all the time. He is particularly outraged that he has fulfilled, to no purpose, all the requirements of wooing: 'Eache office of a lover I performed' (line 368). This is a theme that will be sounded in the moral at the end, and his outrage comes from the feeling that a contractual obligation has been treated with insulting indifference: 'Was ever amorous Sea-god scornèd thus?' (line 360).

Enough is enough. Glaucus's mother Thetis appears with still more comely nymphs, in order to lure her son away to the pleasures of the sea, where yet more nymphs are held in reserve. When this fails Thetis summons Venus, who is spectacularly described in her ivory coach, her golden locks barely concealing her bosom, her silken robe adorned with stories of Adonis and Leda, her cheeks giving off the odor of carnations, her eyes shining with mischief, and on her head the crown in which the poor Amyntas is a star (lines 505–28). She is attired in stories. Cupid is with her, looking for trouble, but his first task is to cure Glaucus, shooting a homeopathic arrow into the wound in Glaucus's heart—'to cure the wound that it had carv'd before'—which takes immediate effect: 'And sodeinly the Sea-god started up; / Revivde, relievd, and free from Fancies cup' (lines 544–6). Whereupon Scylla appears, only to be shot by Cupid's flaming dart, causing her to fall in love with Glaucus: 'Lord how her lippes do dwell upon his cheekes; / And how she lookes for babies in his eies!' (lines 619–20). She is gleefully spurned by Glaucus and flies back to Sicily in despair, followed by the entire, gloating crowd, including the poet and Glaucus, who ride side by side on two dolphins, holding hands and singing amorous ditties as they go:

> What neede I talke the order of my way,
> Discourse was steersman while my barke did saile,
> My ship conceit, and fancie was my bay:
> If these faile me, then faint my Muse and faile,
> Hast brought us where the hapless Nimph sojourned,
> Beating the weeping waves that for her mourned. lines 685–90

When they get to Sicily they find Scylla transformed, as was noted at the outset, into a more rationalistic sandbar and a reef, instead of the Homeric and Ovidian monster:

> The Sea-man wandring by that famous Isle
> Shuns all with feare despairing *Scillaes* bowre;
> Nimphes, Sea-gods, Syrens when they list to smile
> Forsake the haunt of *Scilla* in that stowre:
> Ah Nimphes thought I, if everie coy one felt
> The like misshapes, their flintie hearts would melt. lines 739–50

There is general rejoicing at Scylla's torment and everyone is invited home by Thetis to her husband Neptune's palace—he's a tolerant husband—there to drink nectar and feast on ambrosia, but not before Glaucus gives the sweaty nymphs a wash: 'Glaucus let flie a daintie Christall baine / That washt the Nimphs with labour tir'd before' (lines 764–5). Forgetting the party at Neptune's, Glaucus takes the poet up on a dolphin and double-rides him back to England, leaving him on shore, but not before extracting a promise that the poet will no longer write for money, which he has presumably done here, but only for fame. Then the moral is stated: 'nimphs must yeeld!'

Ladies he left me, trust me I missay not,
But so he left me, as he wild me tell you:
That Nimphs must yeeld, when faithful lovers straie not,
Least through contempt, almightie love compel you
With *Scilla* in the rockes to make your biding
A cursed plague, for womens proud back-sliding. lines 781–6

I love that 'back-sliding', the opposite of sliding forward into a commodious posture for love. Slide forward, girls! This advice seems somehow less useful, and less real, than Henryson's sensible, if unremarkable message, that it is on the whole wise to be faithful in love. Henryson's purpose, however, is not to draw a moral. It is to give us the world as it is and our passions as they are, but in a form in which we can see them more clearly. That's a lot.

*

What makes literature different from storytelling, that great and ancient human reservoir, perhaps 100,000 years old, on which literature very sparingly draws? I have said already that literature is the telling of stories in an exact verbal form that is preserved in that form and disseminated. But what makes literature different from stories told orally is something more than this definition implies. Literature seems to carry with it the feeling that it must also account for the strange *eventuation* of stories. Why do we tell them? Where do stories come from? Where do they repose when they are not being told? What binding relations do stories have to our world? These are naïve questions, but such questions are often the deepest ones we can ask. It is tempting to give immediate, impatient answers, followed by increasingly technical ones outside the competence of literary scholars. Stories come from and return to the brain, anciently called *Mneme*, the mother of invention. Brain science will tell us more, in its own good time, if we pay some brain scientists to share our perplexity for a moment, and explain it away. Naïve questions invite technical answers. Why look into it further than that?

First, I suppose, because the reproduction of stories—copying them down onto paper, printing them in books, recording them on wax for UNESCO, filming and televising them, digitizing and feeding them into computers, storing them on retrievable disks and storing on readable disks the older technologies of reproduction, manuscripts and printed books—is a social activity requiring complex social arrangements interfacing with technology, which is itself a social arrangement, but much more than that, too. It takes brains to make technology work, lots of brains, but brains in the aggregate, embodied in people and in communication with one another through the processes of social desire. Such networks are more than a brain, and less than one, too.

The technology of printing brought about a profound alteration in our sense of the whatness of stories. Print runs were small in Lodge's day. Even so, as we noted, when a story is printed it can be physically present in many places simultaneously, in hundreds of copies all over London. With Henryson, the story has a physical presence. He knows exactly where his story is and can grasp it with his hand: 'an uther quair I tuik' (line 61). What about Lodge? The multiplying of the story's physical presence in printed books has an idealizing and abstracting effect, which means the story no longer coincides with the physical book. The story becomes what we call 'information', which like mathematical phenomena is not joined to any of its physical manifestations but merely borrows them, as a geometric figure borrows chalk and slate. How can a story, with its unbearable lightness, be brought down again and connected to us—we who suppose we are more real? How can the escapism and insubstantiality of the literary be repaired? This does not seem to be a problem for Henryson, for whom the literary is never insubstantial, and if it is escapist it is so for good reason: the Scottish winter night is long and cold, and the author is alone. It is time for two reliable stimulants, a drink and a book.

The most famous successor to Lodge's *Scillaes Metamorphosis* was Shakespeare's *Venus and Adonis* (1592), which was also written in hexaines, and there again the resemblance ends. In Shakespeare's poem we never feel what we do in Lodge: that every object in its landscape, every bush and stream bank, is a story ready to burst into sight, imposing itself on our attention and appealing for pity, for understanding, or for simple recognition, simple hearing. Like the dreamlike apparitions in Giorgione's paintings, placed in uncannily real settings, Shakespeare's fabulous, naked goddess and the boy she loves, soon to be an Asiatic flower, enact their ancient story in a landscape that is discordantly real and contemporary, resembling the Warwickshire hills. Shakespeare's fiction appears to be happily situated in a world to which it does not belong, explaining nothing and allegorizing nothing, floating before us as we read it, simply for the pleasure it gives. This pleasure is to a considerable degree erotic—the censorious Lord Burleigh and his like had a point—but then erotic pleasure, in its full intensity, is no easier to account for in practical terms than is our other compulsive joy, reading stories.

FURTHER READING

Barkan, Leonard. *The Gods Made Flesh: Metamorphosis and the Pursuit of Paganism* (New Haven, CT: Yale University Press, 1986)

Bush, Douglas. *Mythology and the Renaissance Tradition in English Poetry*, 2nd edn (New York: Norton, 1963)

Ferguson, Margaret W. *Trials of Desire: Renaissance Defenses of Poetry* (New Haven, CT: Yale University Press, 1983)

Henryson, Robert. *The Poems*, ed. Denton Fox (Oxford: Clarendon Press, 1981). Extremely valuable introduction and editorial material

Winny, James. *Chaucer's Dream Poems* (London: Chatto and Windus, 1973)

CHAPTER 22

STYLE

MAURA NOLAN

It might be said that the analysis of poetic style begins with the smallest measurable units of poetry. Scrutiny of such units reveals habits and models among them that produce more abstract notions of style—historical, religious, economic, political, and so on. Style, then, as it has come to be understood over the past century, has two often contradictory aspects, the particular and the general. The first of these can be characterized in the words of Roland Barthes, as a 'self-sufficient language . . . which has its roots only in the depths of the author's personal and secret mythology'.[1] Style is individual. It comes from the body and the history of the poet. It is often a secret even to him or her; 'it is the writer's "thing", his glory and his prison'.[2] This concept of individual style is intimately connected to the micro-level of the writer's work; it is at that level that difference and variation appear in their most vivid and distinct forms. As Marshall Brown has put it, 'A writers' style is the way he or she continues to differ from anything you have yet said about her or him'.[3] And Fredric Jameson remarks that style 'is the very element of individuality itself, that mode through which the individual consciousness seeks to distinguish itself, to affirm its incomparable originality'.[4]

This notion of style must be distinguished from 'fashion' or 'personal style'; it is rather, as Barthes suggests, a deeply embedded 'vertical and lonely dimension of *thought*' (emphasis added).[5] For a poet, it is that 'subnature of expression . . . where once and for all the great verbal themes of his existence come to be installed' that is not available to consciousness; it is expressed only through the poems themselves

[1] Roland Barthes, *Writing Degree Zero*, trans. Annette Lavers and Colin Smith (New York: Hill and Wang, 1967), 10, 12.

[2] Barthes, *Writing Degree Zero*, 11.

[3] Marshall Brown, '"Le Style est l'homme même": The Action of Literature', *College English*, 59 (1997), 801–9, at 807.

[4] Fredric Jameson, *Marxism and Form: Twentieth-century Dialectical Theories of Literature* (Princeton, NJ: Princeton University Press, 1971), 334.

[5] Barthes, *Writing Degree Zero*, 11.

and cannot be articulated in simple everyday lists of 'influences' or 'writing habits' or in answer to questions like 'why do you write?'[6] We have all read the deeply unsatisfying answers of poets to questions about their own work. Style makes itself present in the words of a poet's oeuvre—and those words and the patterns they form stand as the essential basis for critical commentary on that poet's style. The 'great verbal themes of [a poet's] existence' are not only made manifest in the images, metaphors, characters, and proverbs that make up the overt features of a poem or set of poems. Instead they are revealed in delicate selections of words, syllables, letters, stresses, and pauses—multiple acts of choice that demand from readers, especially critics and scholars, a degree of attention that accounts for the variations and subtleties that fundamentally structure the poetic work. This attention constitutes the kind of reading traditionally called 'close' but that might be called 'intensive' or 'slow'; it creates an intimacy between the reader and the poem (sometimes mistaken for an intimacy between reader and poet) that allows style to declare itself—to make itself palpable and real in such a way that it can be assessed in critical, not to say demystified, terms.

The point of connection between this first aspect of style and the second aspect I will shortly describe is what Barthes calls the 'closed recollection' of the poet. With this last phrase, he describes the sum total of verbal and written engagements that any one poet has had in her life, the storehouse in her mind of words, metaphors, metonymies, images, sentences, and other manipulations of language—including patterns of sound, rhythms, grammars, syntaxes, and phrasings. This kind of storehouse is locked away. The poet cannot make exhaustive lists of all the words and sentences he has heard or read, though they nestle in the memory and surface when jostled—by the remembered scent, the trill of the once-familiar song, the old photograph, a rhythm or a rhyme. These collections of words are often partially reconstructed by scholars in search of influences and sources, those significant texts absorbed by poets during their lifetimes and to which they allude (consciously or unconsciously) in their works.

Because poets live at certain moments in time, at certain places and in specific communities of people and texts, their styles are also forged by history in a particular way. As Heinrich Wölfflin, writing about visual art, puts it, 'Every artist finds certain visual possibilities before him, to which he is bound. Not everything is possible at all times'.[7] It is in the investigation of what is possible at a particular time that a local, or period, or epochal style may be discerned and elaborated. This aspect of style is what people traditionally mean when they refer to a 'medieval' or 'Renaissance' style of art, and even though such broadly essentializing labels have

[6] Barthes, *Writing Degree Zero*, 10.

[7] Heinrich Wölfflin, *Principles of Art History: The Problem of the Development of Style in Later Art*, trans. M. D. Hottinger (New York: Henry Holt, 1932), 11; see also Frederic Schwartz, 'Cathedrals and Shoes: Concepts of Style in Wöllflin and Adorno', *New German Critique*, 76 (1999): 3–48.

gone out of fashion, the idea that style is delimited by place and time undergirds much critical thinking about the history of art, whether it be painting, architecture, poetry, music, or some other mode of artistic expression.

The poet, sculptor, painter, musician, or other artist engages in his or her making from within history, and it is history that sets limits not only on the legibility of concepts and the recognizability of artistic practices, but also on what can be made—what is craftable, composable, paintable, or writeable. All art is the art of the possible; when epochal shifts or sudden breakthroughs in art occur, they do so because makers of art have recognized a hidden or emergent possibility. One crucial feature of what I am calling, following Wölfflin, 'the possible', is the fact that it is comprised of other works of art (or, to use a different vocabulary, other modes and forms of cultural production) rather than being a horizon defined by events and the natural world. An artist's environment and what happens in it are critical to the work of art, to be sure, but its tools—its forms and modes of expressivity—depend on a deep well of experience made manifest in artistic tradition. That tradition, that 'collectivity of art', is the medium through which style relates to and engages history, both history-as-event, and such notions as 'epochality' or 'periodicity'. As Wölfflin, describing Raphael, puts it:

> And yet the tectonics of Raphael are not entirely to be attributed to an intention born of a state of mind: it is rather a question of a representational form of his epoch which he only perfected in a certain way and used for his own ends.[8]

Here we see the oscillating quality of style, in which both poles of an endless alternation share the same name: style is a characteristic of eras, a generalizing concept, at the same time as it stands for a notion of resistance to generalization—for an embodied particularity that cannot be assimilated by a larger organism or type. What makes this opposition productive—what makes energy crackle between the two electrodes of the circuit—is exemplified by what Wölfflin describes above as Raphael's 'perfection' of a 'form of his epoch' instead of his 'intention born of a state of mind'. The particularity of style, that is, does not arise wholly from an individual's deliberate production of difference, or from his or her determined opposition to the dominant artistic modes of the age. Rather, style can only be apprehended or defined as the intersection of the individual with the possible—of individual style with epochal style, or of the creative will with the collectivity of art as it has been transmitted, unconsciously absorbed, secretly passed down, or painstakingly reconstructed.

This essay meditates on the question of style in both of its aspects by juxtaposing three poets, three centuries, and two literary-historical periods. The relationship between the Middle Ages and the Renaissance, and the embeddedness of Chaucer, Lydgate, and Wyatt in those periods, are explored here in stylistic terms and

[8] Wölfflin, *Principles of Art History*, 12.

deployed as illustrations of an alternative way of thinking about literary style: one that neither glamorizes the poet as an emblem of particularity nor deadens the poetry by demonstrating its essentially 'medieval' or 'Renaissance' character. To start, I bracket the pressing question of periodization, setting aside the shift from 'medieval' to 'Renaissance' poetry in order to clear a space for the consideration of style apart from the epochal assumptions that periodizing labels inevitably bring to bear on literary analysis.

By bracketing such epochal questions, of course, I subject my account of style to various risks: there is no denying that the overwhelming social and cultural changes that occurred in the first half of the sixteenth century had an effect on poetic style. Nor do I wish to ignore the fact that the notion of style itself underwent various alterations over the years between Chaucer and Wyatt. As James Simpson has recently argued, the Reformation produced very deep changes in ways of reading and modes of interpretation, changes that inevitably shaped the styles of writers who knew they would be read according to new hermeneutic models.[9] But for this essay, I wish to stipulate those historical shifts in order to experiment with a mode of reading capable of acknowledging both the particular and the general elements of style itself. This method of reading depends on an intimacy with its subjects—the poems themselves—that paradoxically creates a kind of 'alienation effect' in relation to epochality. The more intently scrutinized is a poem, the less typical or generalizable it becomes—a lesson that deconstruction, for example, taught very well. However, even as these poems by Chaucer, Lydgate, and Wyatt are made strange to their historical moments, they become familiar to each other. That is to say, bracketing the history of the transition from the Middle Ages to the Renaissance allows the deep echoes of Chaucer in Lydgate and both of those poets in Wyatt to be heard—and those echoes resonate with poetic style.

A close reading that registers the micro-level of poetic effects in poems by Chaucer, Lydgate, and Wyatt provides the raw material for a new way of seeing poetic style—a way of seeing that is not, as I will show, alienated from history but instead reveals the secretive way that history works in art. I have chosen, in this very short space, to read three poems for *sound*—to explore the troublesome poetic terrain of stresses, absences of stress, feet, and meter as a way of examining the 'styles' of Chaucer, Lydgate, and Wyatt. By arranging these poets in chronological order and drawing a picture of their relationships based on sound and stress, I have begun to map something I will call a 'strong sequence'—a sort of 'minor tradition'—within the 'collectivity of art' I describe above. My mapping of this 'strong sequence' is intended to demonstrate a critical reading practice that engages as fully as possible with the 'smallest possible units of poetry' mentioned in my opening. In so doing, I suggest that thinking about literary style ought to produce

[9] James Simpson, *Burning to Read: English Fundamentalism and its Reformation Opponents* (Cambridge, MA: Harvard University Press, 2007), especially Chapter 4: 106–41, and Chapter 7: 222–59.

two paradoxical and simultaneous moves. First, it should shrink the distance between the critic and the text, so that the observer can evaluate the style and import of the words (including letters and syllables) on the page. Second, it should also retreat somewhat from the text, far enough away to see the firmness of the boundaries between literary-historical eras and to ponder the ways in which those boundaries might obscure connections among texts that come to light during the scrutiny of style produced by this new intimacy with the poet's words.

The example I have chosen here to illustrate this paradoxical double movement is a 'strong sequence' beginning with Chaucer's 'Truth', continuing through Lydgate's 'The World is Variable', and culminating in Wyatt's rondeau, 'What Vaileth Trouth'. These poems share a common theme—the instability of the world and the danger of false speaking—and they all rely on thematic conventions embodied in Chaucer's poem. Wyatt necessarily stands as the central figure here, because he embodies the transition from one period to the other as both a courtier and a poet. At one level this essay is designed to illustrate what Wyatt saw when he looked back to his poetic predecessors and to demonstrate how he responded to and revised their work. But while it is certainly possible to write an account of Wyatt's 'reformed' style, or to argue that the crushing weight of his role as a courtier in a despotic and cruel regime formed and deformed his poetic identity and thus his very notions of what poetry could do and should be, the goal of this essay is instead to shine a light on poetic style that illuminates *both* its epochal character *and* its individual, particular, perhaps 'secret' aspect.

I do not offer an historical account of stylistic change, nor yet a conclusive description of Chaucer's, Lydgate's, or Wyatt's distinctive styles. In contrast, I have experimented with a method of reading for style that is founded on the principle that style comes into being at the intersection of minute poetic choices with the array of possibilities disclosed by history, possibilities that Wyatt would have encountered in the textual traces left by his poetic predecessors Chaucer and Lydgate. The 'strong sequence' I have defined here is a record of what was possible at a particular juncture in time, and the style that this sequence makes manifest has much to tell us about the place of poetic art in medieval and Renaissance culture. The questions of epochal style and individual style, while undeniably pressing, can also obscure the more associative, allusive, and chancy workings of poetic language over time. These non-linear, subterranean energies surface in various constellations at different moments in the hands of different poets—and when they emerge, they testify to the engagement of the typical with the idiosyncratic. Put another way, such constellations embody the dialectic of epochal style and individual choice, the perpetual engagement of the style that history dictates with the style that individuals (both consciously and unconsciously) select for themselves. The 'strong sequence' of Chaucer, Lydgate, and Wyatt is not a metonym for the progression of medieval to Renaissance style, nor is it a portrait of style before and after the trauma of the Reformation. It is rather a demonstration of how style is produced over time and at the micro-level of poetics—produced not only by acts of differentiation (Wyatt makes choices that Lydgate and Chaucer do not) but also by ventriloquism, as if poems tune themselves to the sounds of other poems, precisely calibrating their notes to create striking echoes and reverberations. Oddly, these echoes constitute the building blocks of literary tradition—oddly, because it is often by silencing them that the scholarly guardians of tradition demarcate one period from another, setting in places definitions of style based on definite boundaries and clear historical causation. Heeding these very specific stylistic echoes and repetitions, which link these texts at the level of the syllable and the stress in the realms of sound and style, forges a chain of literary links that stretches across the period divide and demonstrates how fragile that boundary appears when viewed from the perspective of a figure like Wyatt, a poet with one foot firmly in the past even as he strides toward the future.

Chaucer's 'Truth' and metrical variation

In defining a sequence of the type I wish to articulate here, one must choose a meaningful starting point, in this case, Chaucer. Chaucer was an explicitly acknowledged influence for both Lydgate and Wyatt: both understood themselves to be inheritors and practitioners of Chaucerian poetics and styles. Both poets owed Chaucer a metrical debt, and it is in part to assess that debt that I have examined one of Chaucer's most metrically complex poems, 'Truth':[10]

Balade de Bon Conseyl

Flee fro the prees and dwelle with sothfastnesse; [*crowd*]
Suffyce unto thy thing, though it be smal, [*possessions*]
For hord hath hate, and climbing tikelnesse, [*avarice; instability*]
Prees hath envye, and wele blent overal. [*blinds*]
Savour no more than thee bihove shal,
Reule wel thyself that other folk canst rede, [*interpret*]
And trouthe thee shal delivere, it is no drede.

Tempest thee noght al croked to redresse [*trouble yourself; wrong things*]
In trust of hir that turneth as a bal; [*i.e. Fortune*]
Gret reste stant in litel besinesse.
Be war therfore to sporne ayeyns an al, [*kick; awl*]
Stryve not, as doth the crokke with the wal. [*crock*]
Daunte thyself, that dauntest otheres dede, [*rule*]
And trouthe thee shal delivere, it is no drede.

[10] See Morris Halle and Samuel Jay Keyser, 'Chaucer and the Study of Prosody', *College English*, 28 (1966), 187–219. For an account that focuses on continuities between Chaucer's prosody and that of fifteenth- and sixteenth-century poets like Lydgate and Wyatt, see Ian Robinson, *Chaucer's Prosody: A Study of the Middle English Verse Tradition* (London: Cambridge University Press, 1971).

That thee is sent, receyve in buxumnesse; [*obedience*]
The wrastling for this world axeth a fal.
Her is non hoom, her nis but wildernesse:
Forth, pilgrim, forth! Forth, beste, out of thy stal!
Know thy contree, look up, thank God of al;
Hold the heye wey and lat thy gost thee lede, [*main road*]
And trouthe thee shal delivere, it is no drede.

Envoy

Therfore, thou Vache, leve thyn old wrecchednesse; [*cease*]
Unto the world leve now to be thral.
Crye him mercy, that of his hy goodnesse
Made thee of noght, and in especial
Draw unto him, and pray in general
For thee, and eek for other, hevenlich mede; [*reward*]
And trouthe thee shal delivere, it is no drede.[11]

The aspect of this dense poem that I wish to highlight here is its metrical variation, manifested in three different types of iambic pentameter line and wielded by Chaucer with impeccable control. I have cited the version of 'Truth' that appears in the *Riverside Chaucer* for the sake of simplicity, but of course a more thorough account of metrical variation would have to explore different manuscript readings. For my purposes here, however, the snapshot of Chaucer's meter found in the edited 'Truth' is more than adequate to illustrate my larger point about the use of stress within the English poetic line. The first type of pentameter I will illustrate, unsurprisingly, is the standard version, of which line 2 is a good example:

- / - / - / - / - /
Suf**fyce** un**to** thy **thing**, though **it** be **smal**
(line 2)

Out of twenty-eight lines, sixteen conform to this pattern. Another group of nine lines is fundamentally iambic, but each line is distinguished by a trochaic substitution at its start, brought about by the use of the imperative voice. These inversions create a disruption in the meter that Chaucer is able to manipulate with seeming ease, as these examples show:

/ - - / - / - / - /
Flee fro the **prees** and **dwelle** with **soth**fast**nesse**
(line 1)

/ - - / - / - / - /
Hold the heye **way** and **lat** thy **gost** thee **lede**
(line 20)

[11] Geoffrey Chaucer, *The Riverside Chaucer*, general editor Larry D. Benson, 3rd edn (Oxford: Oxford University Press; Boston: Houghton Mifflin, 1987), 653. Subsequent references to the poem will be in the text by line number.

But there are also three lines that fit neither of these categories. One is an exceptional line I will discuss shortly; the other two are characterized by the infamous 'broken-backed' meter frequently used by Lydgate. These two lines appear in the envoy to the poem, which itself appears in only one of the twenty-four manuscript copies of the lyric, and could very well have been a later addition.[12] Wyatt, for example, would almost certainly never have seen the envoy—it does not appear in early printed editions—but for now, its 'broken-backed' lines serve as useful exemplars:

- / - / / - - / - /
Ther**fore**, thou **Vache**, **leve** thyn old **wrecchednesse**
(line 22)

- / - / /- / - - /
Un**to** the **world leve now** to be **thral**
(line 23)

In line 22, we see two iambs before the caesura, and a trochee and two further iambs after it; in line 23, the same two iambs appear in the first half, but the second portion of the line now shows two trochees and one iamb. In both cases, the mid-line use of the imperative 'leve' demands a pause at the caesura, which acts to simulate the direct address implied by 'thou Vache'. This pause, plus the inverted foot created by the stress on the imperative verb, creates the 'broken back'.

One last line from 'Truth' remains to be discussed, because it shows us Chaucer *performing* meter with clear deliberation and force:

/ / - / / / - / - /
Forth, **pilgrim**, **forth**! **Forth**, **beste**, out **of** thy **stal**!
(line 18)

I suggest that the line has seven stresses, but would argue that it remains fundamentally a pentameter, with two double stresses in place of a single stress at the beginning and caesura of the line. Thus we have 'Forth, pilgrim, forth' (stress, stress, unstress, stress), followed by 'Forth, beste, out of' (stress, stress, unstress, stress). The stresses are doubled in two crucial feet, but the syllable count remains the same, so that the line remains parallel to the remaining lines in the poem. This line is a remarkable example of the controlled use of stress; it *displays* its deployment of forms and techniques drawn from the 'collectivity of art' at Chaucer's poetic fingertips. There is much more that could be said about 'Truth', one of the most brilliantly complex Middle English lyrics that survives. Chaucer's use of Boethian and scriptural allusions, for example, would take many pages to explore.

[12] The manuscript is London, British Library MS Additional 10340; see the textual notes to the *Riverside Chaucer*, 1189, as well as Ralph Hanna, *Pursuing History: Middle English Manuscripts and Their Texts* (Stanford: Stanford University Press, 1996), 159–73.

Here, however, 'Truth' functions as a short index to the metrical complexity of which Chaucer was capable. It is this complexity that yields a crucial clue to the parameters of 'the possible' for a figure like Wyatt, a brilliant inheritor of the Chaucerian line, as he engaged with the 'collectivity of art' available to him and sought to articulate his own artistic vision. As I will show, it is obvious from reading Wyatt's 'What Vaileth Trouth' that he had read a version of Chaucer's poem; it seems very likely that the sounds of 'Truth's' variable meter were ringing in his ears as he crafted his lines of verse.

Lydgate: Counterfeit style and variation

Chaucer was not the only poet whose voice Wyatt would have heard, however. In the fifteenth century, Lydgate emerged as the dominant successor to Chaucer—and it is clear from reading Lydgate's verse that he is steeped in his predecessor's language to an extent that suggests a much deeper notion of influence than 'imitation' alone. I have chosen Lydgate's short poem, 'The World is Variable', as the second text in the 'strong sequence' I am defining here because it articulates the Boethian themes of Chaucer's 'Truth' and simultaneously exploits that poem's metrical variations as a way of reinforcing and amplifying those themes for the reader.

What a close look at 'The World is Variable' shows is that meter does not function in a purely instrumental fashion, as the servant of meaning or the handmaiden of proverbial wisdom. Lydgate's meter has long been considered a negative aspect of his style. But I will suggest here that he not only takes over Chaucerian metrical variations, but also retrospectively reads Chaucer as an imitable stylist of variation. The 'strong sequence' of poems I have highlighted illustrates how Lydgate's notion of variation looks both backward and forward, constructing Chaucer, being constructed by Chaucer, and creating a style that looks ahead to Wyatt. At first glance, however, Lydgate's verses seem to be simply a confused and confusing morass. The syllables and stresses simply do not scan like Chaucer's pentameter. To help us think through Lydgate's metrics, we have at hand Josef Schick's five-part system for classifying Lydgate's lines, and Derek Pearsall's assurance that, surprisingly, the system seems to work for the most part.[13]

As I will show, the effort to construct a system that entirely accounts for Lydgate's metrical variability is somewhat misguided: Lydgate was not a systematic poet and did not strategize his use of stress in the manner of a general plotting the

[13] John Lydgate, *Temple of Glas*, ed. Josef Schick, EETS extra series, 60 (London: Kegan Paul, Trench, Trübner & Co, 1891), lvii–lix; Derek Pearsall, *John Lydgate* (London: Routledge & Kegan Paul, 1970), 60–1. See also John Stevens, *Music and Poetry in the Early Tudor Court* (London: Methuen, 1961), 16; C. S. Lewis, 'The Fifteenth-Century Heroic Line', in *Selected Literary Essays*, ed. Walter Hooper (Cambridge: Cambridge University Press, 1969), 45–57.

positions of his forces. To carry through the metaphor, Lydgate instead used metrical *tactics*, responding to poetic crisis after poetic crisis by adopting different formations from moment to moment. A model like Schick's, which depends on a notion of the poet as a careful planner utterly in control of his unfolding poems, cannot reflect the flexibility and spontaneity of Lydgate's poetic practice. What it can do is provide a set of broad classifications into which Lydgate's meter can be sorted as a way of discerning the general shape of his thinking about metrics. To illustrate how such sorting might work, I have analyzed the fourteen eight-line stanzas of 'The World is Variable' in relation to Schick's system. I found that, while some lines had characteristics of two or three of Schick's categories, and some did not fit precisely, overall the poem can be organized into a version of his system that is streamlined and less strict.

In order to make my readings in this essay as clear as possible, I have used the labels for metrical phenomena most familiar to literary critics, the Greek names for different metrical feet, such as iamb, trochee, spondee, or anapest. Middle English and Early Modern English poetry often does not fit these labels precisely, because it is apt to include 'extra' unstressed syllables (for example, Chaucer's use of final *-e* often produces one of these syllables). Many scholars have argued that, in fact, English is a language of stresses for which the counting of syllables—produced by the labeling of 'feet'—is inappropriate and distorting.[14] As Derek Attridge has remarked, 'foot prosody brings with it the danger... of developing elaborate accounts of poetic lines, or finding tricky problems in metrical analysis, on the basis of units that are more of a theoretical convenience than an experiential reality'.[15] However, for ease of reference in this essay I have chosen to use the familiar Greek names as the easiest way of dissecting the verses under consideration, with the goal of demonstrating precisely Attridge's point that 'metrical language is language written in such a way as to make possible the experiencing of *beats*, bursts of energy that produce repeated and structured patterns'.[16]

Because the poetic tradition I am describing, beginning with Chaucer, is ordinarily labeled 'iambic pentameter', it is easiest to show how that label breaks down by identifying the intrusion of alternative 'feet' (trochees, anapests, and the like) into the supposedly regular sequence of iambs that should comprise each line. Further, although poets like Chaucer, Lydgate, and Wyatt may not have set out to write verse constrained by fixed feet and numbers of syllables, they certainly understood the idea of metrical regularity (made evident by the sheer volume of metrically regular lines in each poet's work) and therefore understood what it meant to create metrical variation. The simplest way to describe the workings of

[14] This argument is often made using Chaucer as an example; see the work of Halle and Keyser, and Robinson, cited above.

[15] Derek Attridge, *Poetic Rhythm: An Introduction* (Cambridge and New York: Cambridge University Press, 1995), 141.

[16] Attridge, *Poetic Rhythm*, 19.

such variation, it seems to me, is to use a vocabulary commonly known to readers as a workable lexicon for the analysis of meter. It is an imperfect solution to the problem of analyzing early English meter, to be sure, but my goal here is not to produce a new system of metrical analysis. Indeed, the myriad difficulties of such metrical analysis have created a situation in which meter is hardly mentioned by literary critics, for fear of inviting critique and igniting controversy. This fear is worth overcoming, because meter forms such a significant element of early English poetics: it is not possible to understand figures like Chaucer, Lydgate, and Wyatt in stylistic or formal terms without grappling with their use of meter—nor is it possible to describe the development of the English poetic line across the boundary between the Middle Ages and the Renaissance without analyzing the 'repeated and structured patterns' of stress that fundamentally shape it. This essay is an experiment in thinking metrically, based on the premise that such thinking will yield crucial insights into the nature and history of poetic style. As such, I have used the available tools for parsing meter, limited as they may be, and will argue that such parsing clarifies the links among Chaucer, Lydgate, and Wyatt in profoundly important ways.

In the case of Lydgate's 'The World is Variable', I have classified the lines in three basic groups: the standard iambic pentameter line, with room for extra syllables in the middle or end; the 'broken-backed' line, with two successive stresses, usually at the caesura; and the line with either an initial trochaic substitution and an extra unstressed syllable or two to follow, or an absent initial unstressed syllable (the 'headless' line). It should be evident by now that my grouping of lines in Lydgate's verses bears a strong resemblance to the variants we saw in 'Truth'—standard iambic pentameter, initial trochaic substitution, and the line with the 'broken back'. In this sense, my analysis confirms Pearsall's assertion that Lydgate reified variants in Chaucer into 'types' of lines, which he then repeated with some frequency.[17] In the 112 lines of 'The World is Variable', I found 61 lines of standard iambic pentameter, 36 lines with an initial trochaic substitution, 6 'broken-backed' lines, and 9 lines that are both 'broken-backed' and contain an initial trochaic inversion. Proportionally, then, these stanzas look a lot like 'Truth', in which approximately half of the verses are standard pentameter lines and half are variants. This outline gives a rough, but not complete account of the extent of Lydgate's metrical variations, because I have flexibly defined the 'standard' iambic line to include extra syllables, which produce occasional anapests. A more thorough way of analyzing Lydgate's variation concentrates on metrical feet: out of 560 metrical feet, 369 are iambs, 110 are anapests, 65 are trochees, ten contain a single stress, and only 6 are spondees.

But this kind of analytical work has to be a starting point, not a conclusion, for any critical engagement with style. Once the metrical structure of

[17] Pearsall, *John Lydgate*, 62.

Lydgate's poem has been sketched, even in the cursory way that I have treated it here, the question of style in relation to technique becomes a bit more fraught. Can Lydgate's adoptions of Chaucerian variants be regarded as clues to his style, to 'the way he . . . continues to differ from any thing you have yet said about her or him', or are they merely evidence of imitation?[18] This question can only be answered by subjecting Lydgate's verse to the same kind of intense scrutiny, line by line, that Chaucer's poems have traditionally received. I have chosen stanza 12 of 'The World is Variable' because it addresses the problems of 'truth' and 'false speaking' that so dominate 'Truth', but confronts those questions in a distinctive and surprising way. It shows that metrical variation functions as a defining element of Lydgate's poetic style, and points toward the conclusion that such variation is a generalizable feature of some late medieval and early modern verse, represented here by the 'strong sequence' of poems I have collected. Stanza 12 begins:

- / - / - - / - / - - /
A**geyn** Au**ror**a the **cok** doth **mer**yly **crowe**,
/ - / - / - - / /
Which for **en**vye **re**dily **doth** **fight**,
/ - / - / - / - - /
Countir**feet** poetis **seed**ys doun **sowe**,
- / - / - - / / - /
In **mynde** **imag**yned a**geyn** **trouthe** & **right.**[19]

These lines compare cocks, who 'meryly crowe *ageyn* Aurora' to 'countirfeet poetis', who 'sowe seedys *ageyn* trouth & right'. The seeming equivalence of Aurora, symbol of dawn, and moral concepts like 'trouthe & right', is undermined by the unstable meaning of 'ageyn', which connotes both 'facing toward' and 'in opposition to'.[20] Readers of the whole poem are especially primed to recognize this double meaning, because its first lines describe the narrator walking alone 'toward Aurora' (lines 1–2). As a result, we see a resemblance between the metaphorical cock of stanza 12 and the poem's narrator—and thus a further resemblance to the 'countirfeet poetis' to which the cock is analogized. The narrator's walking becomes the cock's crowing becomes the 'seed sowing' of false poets, creating a moment of agonized self-reflexivity for Lydgate, summed up in the adjective 'countirfeet'.

[18] Marshall Brown, 'The Action of Literature', 807.

[19] *The Minor Poems of John Lydgate*, ed. Henry Noble MacCracken, EETS, o.s., 192, 2 (London: Oxford University Press, 1934), 844–7, lines 89–92. Subsequent references to the poem will be in the text by line number.

[20] *MED*, s.v. 'ayen(e)s', 1, 4.

It should be no surprise that this stanza comprises one of Lydgate's most metrically challenging sets of lines, beginning with the twelve syllables of the first line and continuing with a series of variations. We move from an iambic line (89)

- /   - / - - / - / - - /
Ageyn Aurora the **cok** doth **meryly** **crowe,**

to two trochaic lines (90–91),

/ - / - / - - / /
Which for **envye** **redily** **doth fight,**
/ - / - / - / - - /
Countirfeet poetis seedys doun **sowe,**

to a broken-backed line (92),

- / - / - - / / - /
In **mynde** imagyned **ageyn** **trouthe** & **right,**

to two iambic lines (93–94),

- / - / - / - / - /
Al **is** not **goold** which **shynyth** **cleer** & **bright**
- / - / - / - - / - /
A **beggere** **to** a **lord** is not **comperable,**

a further trochaic line (95)

/ - - / - / - / - - /
Lyk in **apparaylle** **which** apperyth to **sight,**

and a last iambic line (96),

- / - / - - / - / - /
Ex**sperience** **shewith** the **wourld** is **varyable.**

In just eight lines we find four 'regular' iambic pentameter lines (with some extra stresses), three primarily trochaic lines, and a broken-backed line. This metrical variation is intimately connected to the unfolding meaning of the self-referential gesture contained in the line 'Countirfeet poetis seedys doun sowe' (91). That line is comprised of a series of trochees, or inverted iambs; Lydgate has turned the iambic pentameter line inside out in order to reflect in a formal way his insistence that other poets are 'countirfeet'—and signaled this inversion with the strong pun on 'countirfeet', or 'counter-feet'. The whole stanza literally contains 'counter-feet': its three trochaic lines function as inversions of, and counters to, Chaucer's iambic foot. Metrical form thus becomes a self-consciously deployed technique of ironic self-reference. Lydgate seems to be winking at his readers, as if to say, 'I'll show you counterfeit poetry by showing you counter-feet'—a self-indicting message on the surface, to be sure, but in another sense a powerful statement about metrical intention: the trochaic inversion displays the *willed* character of Lydgate's metrical variation, with his stylish pun on 'feet' performing for readers the deliberation underlying the poem's metrical structure.

We tend to think of the Lydgatean aesthetic as 'rhetorical'—bound up with amplification and ornamentation—and indeed, rhetoric plays an important role in Lydgate's poetics.[21] But I would like to draw attention to another feature of his verse as a bridge to my reading of Wyatt, the idea of a counter-rhythm. In the line 'Countirfeet poetis seedys doun sowe' (91), we find a very complex use of internal rhyme and consonance. Every syllable, in fact, with one exception, rhymes with another across the caesura:

> **coun**tirfeet–**doun**; countir**feet**–poetis–**see**dys; **po**etis–**so**we; poet**is**–see**dys**.

These rhymes visually create a mirroring effect from the first to the second half of the line, and aurally produce a set of echoes that lends to the line a regular beat dependent on, but also separate from, the pattern of stressed and unstressed syllables. These internal rhymes are extended further by consonances throughout the line, divided by the caesura: in the first half, we find repeated 't's' (countirfeet poetis), while in the second half we have the sibilance of 'seedys doun sowe'. Thus a tension emerges between an *external* notion of meter, established by Chaucer's pentameter line and copied (and inverted) by Lydgate, and an *internal* beat, unconsciously absorbed by Lydgate after deep immersion in Chaucerian verse, and manifesting itself as a kind of sonic saturation in the poetry overall. This tension only emerges at the level of the syllable, deep within the formal layers of the verse, and it guides us inward as we approach the final poem in the sequence, 'What Vaileth Trouth'.

Wyatt and style: Counter-rhythm and refrain

I have chosen Wyatt's 'What Vaileth Trouth' as the third poem in the sequence I am defining because it echoes Chaucer's 'Truth' and thus parallels Lydgate's own echoes of that poem.[22] Wyatt's poem takes the form of the rondeau, which includes three stanzas, two rhymes, and a refrain created by the first half line of the poem:

[21] See Pearsall, *John Lydgate*, 64–6, 143–51.

[22] For other poems of Wyatt's that respond to 'Truth', see Helen Cooper, 'Wyatt and Chaucer: A Re-Appraisal', *Leeds Studies in English*, new series, 13 (1982), 104–23. For a recent discussion of Wyatt and style that reaches very different conclusions than mine, see Jeff Dolven, 'Reading Wyatt for the Style', *Modern Philology*, 105 (2007), 65–86. Brian Cummings has written a helpful account of Wyatt's life and works; see his 'Thomas Wyatt', in *The Oxford Encyclopedia of British Literature*, 5, ed. Dana Scott Kastan (Oxford: Oxford University Press, 2006), 346–50.

What vaileth trouth or by it to take payn
to stryve by stedfastnes for to attayne
to be iuste & true & fle from dowblenes
sythens all alike where rueleth craftines [*since*]
rewarded is boeth fals & plain
sonest he spedeth that moost can fain [*pretend*]
true meanyng hert is had in disdayn
against deceipt & dowblenes
What vaileth trouth

Deceved is he by crafty trayn [*trick*]
that meaneth no gile & doeth remayn
within the trapp without redresse
but for to love lo suche a maisteres [*mistress*]
whose crueltie nothing can refrayn
What vaileth trouth.

The version of the poem copied above is taken from Richard Harrier's transcription of British Library MS Egerton 2711; I have silently expanded abbreviations and eliminated scribal flourishes but have otherwise copied the text exactly, with one exception.[23] Though there have been many printed versions of 'What Vaileth Trouth', starting with Richard Tottel's in 1557, all of the editorial decisions about punctuation, capitalization, and various corrections made to the Egerton MS impose a level of interpretation that I wish to strip away as a means of assessing questions of meter, phrasing, rhyme, and syllable-count.[24] Some of these markings and changes date from Wyatt's own lifetime or shortly thereafter; for example, Nicholas Grimald, his contemporary, engaged in heavy orthographic alteration to

[23] Richard Harrier, *The Canon of Sir Thomas Wyatt's Poetry* (Cambridge, MA: Harvard University Press, 1975), 98–9. The poem appears on folio 4, recto and verso, of the manuscript, and it is the second poem in the collection. I have not reproduced Harrier's exact rendition of line 2, which records the variant reading 'for to be tayne', of which 'be' was deleted and above which 'at' was inserted to create 'for to attayne'. Most published versions of the poem use the latter formulation, because the correction was clearly made very early, probably by the original copyist; see Harrier, 99; see also Joost Daalder, 'Are Wyatt's Poems in Egerton MS 2711 in Chronological Order?', *English Studies*, 69 (1988), 205–23. 'What Vaileth Trouth' appears in all modern editions of Wyatt. For the most recent scholarly edition, see R. A. Rebholz (ed.), *Sir Thomas Wyatt: the Complete Poems* (New Haven, CT: Yale University Press, 1978), 72, which also contains a useful survey of critical approaches to Wyatt's meter, 44–55. I do not have space to cite fully the many editions of Wyatt printed during the nineteeth and twentieth centuries or to map out the contentious history of the editing of Wyatt; for example, one edition by Kenneth Muir and Patricia Thomson, *Collected Poems of Sir Thomas Wyatt* (Liverpool: Liverpool University Press, 1969), inspired a book of correction in response. See H. A. Mason, *Editing Wyatt: An Examination of Collected Poems of Sir Thomas Wyatt* (Cambridge: Cambridge Quarterly Publications, 1972), in which the author lists the many errors of transcription from the manuscripts in the Muir and Thomson edition, and sets forth his own principles for editing Wyatt.

[24] Hyder Edward Rollins (ed.), *Tottel's Miscellany (1557–1587)*, rev. edn (Cambridge, MA: Harvard University Press, 1966); 'What Vaileth Trouth' is titled 'Complaint for true loue vnrequited' (#70, p. 51, vol. 1).

the Egerton MS.[25] Punctuation imposes syntax and erases ambiguities central to Wyatt's style—which tends to layer clause upon clause in order to establish a series of tensions (syntactical, metrical, prosodic, thematic) upon which each poem depends. I have turned to the manuscript transcription here because the modern edited versions of the poem are so at odds as to make the kind of close analysis I am undertaking impossible. In contrast, I have used edited versions of Chaucer's and Lydgate's poems, both because there is greater consensus about the texts and because the earlier poems are cited in order to identify certain habits of style that reappear in Wyatt's poetry, which forms the centerpiece of this essay and thereby garners more sustained attention here.

In the first and second parts of this project, I heuristically identified three forms of iambic pentameter, based on the system proposed by Josef Schick: the simple series of five iambs; the line beginning with a trochaic inversion (or simply headless); and the 'broken-backed' line, with two stresses in sequence in the middle of the line. All three appear in Chaucer's 'Truth', and turn up again, much elaborated, in Lydgate's 'The World is Variable' as well as in the rest of Lydgate's oeuvre. George Wright has applied Schick's scheme to Wyatt's verse, expanding it to eight categories that account for all of Wyatt's metrical habits. But Wright's most important insight is not his elaborate scheme. It is rather the crucial attention he draws to the caesura in each line and to Wyatt's use of the *phrase* within the line. These aspects of Wyatt's verse best clarify his relationship to Chaucer and Lydgate, and in general to the English poetic tradition.

Pre-sixteenth-century poetry, Wright suggests, is characterized by a strong caesura (a legacy of the alliterative line) and by the use of phrases, short units of two or three stresses joined together to build the pentameter line.[26] What he calls the 'jointed line' depends upon variation, on constant changes in stress patterns and degrees of emphasis, but it is not *irregular.* John Stevens similarly argues that, for courtly poetry at least, there is a continuous tradition stretching from Chaucer to Wyatt, based not on the smooth iambic line, but rather on rhythmical varation organized around a pause in the middle of the line. This pause created a line 'balanced' on two sides, which Stevens argues was rather mysteriously replaced by the simplified, 'easily flowing' iambic line around the middle of the sixteenth century.[27] In 'What

[25] The Egerton MS contains many poems (though not 'Trouth') that were copied by Wyatt himself, and he also made corrections to many of the poems he did not copy. See Harrier, *Canon*, 3–5; and Daalder, 'Wyatt's Poems in Egerton MS 2711', 206–9. For Grimald's alterations in general, see Harrier, *Canon*, 5–15; for the specific alterations to 'Trouth', see Harrier, *Cannon*, 99. Ruth Hughey identified Grimald's hand; see Ruth Hughey, 'The Harington Manuscript at Arundel Castle and Related Documents', *The Library*, Fourth series, 15 (1935), 413–44, at 415–16 and 426–30.

[26] George Wright, 'Wyatt's Decasyllabic Line', *Studies in Philology*, 82 (1985), 129–56, at 137 and 147. See also John Thompson, *The Founding of English Metre* (London: Routledge & Kegan Paul, 1961), 1–37; D. W. Harding, 'The Rhythmical Intention in Wyatt's Poetry', *Scrutiny*, 14 (1946), 90–102.

[27] John Stevens, *Music and Poetry in the Early Tudor Court* (London: Methuen, 1961); see pages 16, and 93, 156, n. 13.

Vaileth Trouth', this phrasal quality is both produced and enhanced by the poem's meter. Its overarching structure fundamentally relies on variation: it begins with four iambic pentameter lines (of ten or eleven syllables), then shifts in line five to a four-stress line, with eight or nine syllables. Further, each refrain (lines nine and fifteen) has four syllables and two stresses, and produces a counter-rhythm to the dominant iambic character of the verses when read as an interrogative sentence. This counter-rhythm consists of a trochee plus an iamb—'**What** vaileth **trouth**?'—and Wyatt deploys it throughout the poem as a way of shaping the meanings of various lines or sequences of lines. The line can be read iambically as well—'What **vail**eth **trouth**', which drains away its interrogative sense and transforms the phrase into a flat, declarative statement, thus producing a crucial tension between rhythm and counter-rhythm. To illustrate how this phrasal counter-rhythm works, I have turned to the final stanza of the poem, particularly the final three lines, in which we see a series of such phrases working both with and against each other:

- / - - / - / - /
De**ceved** is **he** by **crafty** **trayn**
- / - - / - / - /
That **mean**eth no **gile** & **doeth** re**mayn**
- / - / - / - /
With**in** the **trapp** with**out** re**dress**e
/ - - / - / - - /
But for to **love** lo **suche** a mais**teres**
- / - / - / - /
Whose **cruel**tie **no**thing **can** re**frayn**
/ - - /
What vaileth **trouth.**
(lines 10–15)

The pattern I am describing appears in lines 10, 11, 13, and 15, and consists of the sequence 'stress–unstress–unstress–stress', which emerges from the coupling of an iamb plus an anapest, or a trochee plus an iamb, or a spondee and an anapest—all sequences we find in Lydgate and elsewhere in Wyatt, and all seemingly irregular and rough. We first saw this pattern in Chaucer's 'Truth', where it came into being as an effect of the use of the imperative, which often created the pairing of a trochee with an iamb. Instead of the trotting iambic beat (- / - / - / - / - /), we find a more emphatic, processional stomping: / - - / | / - - / | / - - /, produced by the doubling of stresses when an iamb meets a trochee or anapest. To show how this rhythmic pattern works in tandem (and sometimes in tension) with the unfolding meaning of the poem, I have reconstructed its final three lines in syntactic order—in other words, as a sentence:

What vaileth **trouth**
but for to **love**
lo, **suche** a maisteres
whose **cruel**ty **no**thing **can** refrayn?

Here we see the signature metrical phrase of the poem—trochee-plus-iamb or iamb-plus-anapest—recurring again and again. Read aloud, the sequence of phrases with its variable feet creates an alternation between flowing and marching, between the smooth liquidity of successive iambs and the clash of incompatible feet: trochees, anapests, and out-of-place iambs. The major turn in the poem, the point at which it pivots to show us its theme in summary form, or to reveal a hidden import, or to spring a trap, comes when Wyatt begins line 13 with 'But'. Here he creates a very tricky line, with two possible shift-markers, 'but' and 'lo', both obvious. 'But' either implies 'only', as in 'his only redress is to love' or it functions as a conjunction that invalidates what comes before it—'he is deceived... but in order to love (he does something different)'. It is clear that the second of these uses for 'but' does not apply here; the turn is not from despair to hope ('But love will change everything'), but from a world of untruthfulness to a world of cruel mistresses, two worlds that sometimes seem to merge in the poet's mind to become one tyrannical whole.

Wyatt's craftiness extends from the doubled shift markers ('But' and 'lo') to the variability of the meter *within* the phrase itself. Reading the iambs of line 12 ('within the trapp, without redresse') creates a springy forward motion that takes the next phrase in its stride, encouraging us to hear it as an iambic extension of the line: 'with**out** re**dresse** but **for** to **love**'. When 'but for to love' is read in this way, it contains a small seed of optimism, the idea that love can provide an answer, a solution, a way of breaking free from the 'cruel trayn' that is Wyatt's world. But when we reach the second half-line, 'lo, such a maisteres', the syntactical object of the verb 'to love', the beginning of the line becomes detached from 'without redresse' and reattached to the final sequence of lines in the poem. Instead of iambs ('But **for** to **love**'), we hear the trochaic inversion at the start ('**But** for to **love**'), which draws the energy of the verse forward toward its grammatical conclusion, the subject–verb–object phrase ('What vaileth trouth') demanded by the combination of 'but' and the dangling infinitive, 'to love'. '**But** for to **love**' then mirrors perfectly its missing half, '**what** vaileth **trouth**', as well as its object, '**suche** a mai**steres**', and the stomping cadence of those phrases sounds out the sheer misery of the poem's conclusion.

This metrical account of the final lines of the poem is not the only possible analysis. But it illustrates both the surgical skill with which Wyatt wields the tool of metrical variation, and the extent of the ambiguity he is willing to allow into his verses. Indeed, 'What Vaileth Trouth' traffics in ambiguity by embracing the phrase as a central unit of poetic composition, creating a poem in which stable 'trouth' is forever elusive, always lurking behind another ambiguity and refusing to play a part in the world of feigning, deception, cruelty, and falsity Wyatt describes.

Having illustrated two aspects of Wyatt's style shared with the other poems in the 'strong sequence' I have defined here—his use of the phrase and his manipulation of the pattern of stresses introduced by Chaucer's trochaic inversions (stress–unstress–unstress–stress), let me turn by way of conclusion to a further aspect of style that emerges very subtly in all three poems. In 'What Vaileth Trouth' we find it in the metrically inconspicuous line that appears sandwiched between the final staccato phrases of the poem, 'whose crueltie nothing can refrayn' (14). This sequence of iambs functions syntactically as an adverbial phrase modifying 'maisteres', and it reads as if it were in parentheses: 'But to love such a mistress (whose cruelty can't be restrained)'. The line ends with a crucial word, 'refrayn'. In a literal sense, 'refrayn' here means 'to restrain', a transitive sense of the verb that was current in Middle English and Early Modern English; Nicholas Grimald certainly recognized its meaning when he altered the Egerton MS to read 'restrayn'.[28] This alteration would seem to be in keeping with Grimald's tendency to pin down the meaning of the poem by adding punctuation and diminishing verbal ambiguities (substituting 'troth' for 'trouth', for example). Here, he has eliminated the alternate sense of 'refrayn', its familiar meaning as the 'chorus' or 'burden' of a song or poem. Chaucer also used the word with this meaning, and it clearly would resonate in a form—the rondeau—in which the refrain dominates, both opening and closing the poem and providing a hinge in the middle.[29]

Wyatt's use of the word 'refrayn' thus turns the poem in on itself, dissolving the already tenuous distinction between form and content, and creating a startling equivalence among the several layers of meaning that the verses contain: the restraint of a cruel mistress; the failure to restrain deceit and doubleness, feigning and falsity; and finally the restraint of words and phrases provided by the recurrent refrain. The poem's form thus becomes an illustration—a demonstration—of the kind of control truth (or 'troth') should provide. Or so it might seem. The word 'refrayn' appears in a semantically negative sense—'nothing can *refrayn* the cruelty of such a mistress'—and is enjambed with the actual *refrain* of the poem, thus creating a curious double, a pair of fraternal twins: 'refrayne' as noun and verb. Behind the grammatical functions of the word are different etymological origins; 'to refrayne' comes from the Old French 'refrener' and ultimately from the Latin 'frenare' (to bridle), while 'refrain' can be traced to the Old French 'refrein', to the

[28] *OED*, s.v. 'refrain, v', I, 1.

[29] We find the word in *Troilus and Criseyde*: see *The Riverside Chaucer*, 2: 1571 ('But evere mo "Alas!" was his refreyn'). Lydgate uses the similar word, 'refreyd' or 'refrete'; see the *MED*, s.v. 'refrete', from the French 'refrait, refret, refreit'. Ardis Butterfield has thoroughly explored the role of the refrain in French poetry and music from the thirteenth century forward, starting with its simplest appearances (in rondeaux) and tracing it through a variety of genres, in order to show that the refrain itself became both an authoritative form and 'an emblem of *mouvance* in the period... authoritative yet formally mobile'. See Ardis Butterfield, 'Repetition and Variation in the Thirteenth-Century Refrain', *Journal of Royal Music Association*, 116 (1991), 1–23, at 23; as well as her more extended treatment of the refrain in *Poetry and Music in Medieval France: From Jean Renart to Guillaume Machaut* (Cambridge: Cambridge University Press, 2002). The relationship of Wyatt to French sources is a complex one and lies outside the scope of this essay, but it is well worth considering, as his use of the French genre of rondeau indicates.

Provencal 'refranh' and again to the Latin, 'frangere' (to break).[30] These dual meanings are mirrored by the metrical variations in which Wyatt embeds them. At first, it would appear that the purity of the poem's penultimate line is stunningly encapsulated in its final word, the iamb 're**frayn**', which constitutes a metrical foot by itself. Syllables and foot, content and form, glide together seamlessly so that the word shines through its metrical container—its meaning of 'restraint' captured by the formal restraint of the meter with which it is self-identical.

But that glimmering moment of semantic clarity is instantly shattered by the poem's final line. It is shattered because we have learned over the course of the rondeau that 'What vaileth trouth'—apart from its literal meaning—is a *refrain*. Indeed, if we are sophisticated readers of rondeaux, we have known from the poem's first half-line that those three words were imbued with a special meaning and function for the remainder of the poem. Paradoxically, the phrase serves not only to bring order to the verses (to 'refrayn' or to 'bridle' them), but also to *break* them: to make divisions among them, to induce stopping and starting. The metrical regularity of 'whose crueltie nothing can refrayn' is thus firmly halted by the 'refrayn' of the poem. The beautiful union among metrical form (the iamb), syllabic structure ('re-**frayn**') and signification ('to restrain'), staged as the final utterance of the verse proper, is dissolved by the pushy intrusion of the poetic gesture that completes the rondeau form: the refrain, the very same word in a different guise. Once 'to refrayn' has been paired with its nominal twin ('to restrain' with poetic refrain), the metrical perfection of the iambic line is revealed as only one half of a poetic oscillation between order and disorder, between the regular rise and fall of successive iambs and the ambiguous and changeable patterns of stress that cluster around and within the poem's refrain ('**But** for to **love**'; '**What** vaileth **trouth**'). The refrain brings order; the refrain also shatters, breaking the poem and refusing metrical regularity. Wyatt's choice of this oddly doubled word to conclude the poem creates a brilliant moment of poetic self-reflection, an electric moment at which forms and meanings stand face to face. The poem cannot fix the meaning of 'truth'; the poem cannot even fix its own refrain.

We have seen moments of self-referentiality like this one before. Lydgate too showed us 'countirfeet poetis' and 'counter-feet': a seeming indictment of false versifiers that becomes a virtuoso display of poetic proficiency when Lydgate inverts the meter of the line to create a pun where none existed. Chaucer's 'Truth', with its spectacular metrical variation and control, also displays the inner workings of the iambic pentameter line by repeatedly violating its regularity and wrapping those violations back into the orderly cadence of the poem. When Chaucer's most dramatic line arrives, poetic and spiritual advice come together in an explosion of stresses that exhort the listener to *act*: 'Forth, pilgrim, forth! Forth, beste, out of thy stal!' This supercharged line stretches iambic pentameter as

[30] *OED*, s.v. 'refrain, v' and 'refrain, n[1]'.

far as it will go, much as Lydgate's 'counter-feet' and Wyatt's 'refrayn' press against the ordering limits of form by drawing our attention inexorably to moments of formal breakdown.

It is no coincidence that each of these poets should test those limits in this way. Moments at which a form is overloaded and threatened with breakdown are parallel to meta-poetic moments at which a poet draws attention to his verse *as verse*, in that both constitute occasions at which the two functions of style I have described (individual style and general style) come together. Charles Altieri has labeled such moments 'demonstrative': instances in which poetic language *displays* how it works and what it can do, given the limits of 'the possible' described by Wölfflin:

> Demonstratives do not propose assertions that something is true but instead show that something is happening or is possible. The fundamental demonstrative claim is that I am showing you how I do something so that you can do it or at least understand how it is done. Style then becomes the display of possible uses of a medium—as innovation in relation to tradition and as shaping possible ways that manner effects matter.... [in the case of the demonstrative], stylistically one exemplifies possible powers of a medium to intensify or realize what the agent is engaging. By using the category of the demonstrative we show how intentional qualities can be attributed to making.[31]

In the work of all three of the poets I have described here, the demonstrative functions in precisely this way; each text displays inherited forms at the very limits of their capacities. This demonstrative function appears regardless of a poet's conscious intention, because it is the very nature of style to display the 'intentional qualities' of making. It cannot be said that Wyatt—whose poetry is perhaps the most 'demonstrative' of the three poets—*set out* to test the boundaries of form in a self-conscious and deliberate way. There is no way to support such a claim. It *can* be said, however, that Wyatt exhausts the capacity for meaning-making of the rondeau, its refrain, and the iamb, leaving readers with no message or lesson, no platitude to apply to their own lives. The answer to 'What Vaileth Trouth?' is indeed 'nothing'—but as a stylistic display, the poem is rife with possibilities for poetic re-making, re-writing, and re-thinking. Perhaps in Wyatt the Lydgatean line, with its strong caesura and its use of the phrase as building-block, reached a stylistic endpoint. But as the sequence of poetic examples I have described here shows, stylistic endpoints last only until a new Wyatt or Chaucer arrives on the scene to re-imagine the limits of style and to demonstrate its new possibilities.

For each of the poems I have read here, much more could be said about meaning. Each poet deploys a discourse of truth and falsity—false-speaking and imposture, uncertainty and variability—at widely separated moments in time for different purposes. Another kind of essay would be required to show how, for

[31] Charles Altieri, 'Style', in *The Oxford Handbook of Philosophy and Literature*, ed. Richard Eldridge (New York: Oxford University Press, 2009), 420–41.

example, the terminal ambiguity of Wyatt's rondeau was produced by a particular courtly and political situation.[32] What I have shown, however, is how the 'strong sequence' I set forth here embodies a particular style of writing poetry, with various common formal characteristics that appear beneath the level of shared diction, in the most foundational elements of the poetic line. I have concentrated especially on forms of metrical variation and the ways in which variation creates counter-rhythms within the line. These counter-rhythms expose a tension between the metrical drive to regularity implied by iambic pentameter and each poet's desire to manipulate meaning by ringing changes on the rhythms of his verse.

This 'strong sequence' thus reveals a style of writing verse that is shared, to varying degrees, by all three poets. It is a style dependent upon variation and a certain metrical freedom, one that relies heavily on sound—stresses, beats, consonances, assonances, rhymes—to lend to its content an intensity and emphasis that regular iambs cannot deliver. This style is most fully exploited by Wyatt, who firmly links metrical variation and rhythmic change to semantic ambiguity, creating the apotheosis of a style fitted to a world of feigning, false speech, deceit, and dissimulation. It is perhaps Wyatt's combination of the style he shares with Chaucer and Lydgate with his well-known commitment to 'plainness'—simplicity of diction, lack of aureate embellishment, and a deceptive limpidity—that makes him distinctly a figure of his age.[33] Part of my aim in this essay has been to show how even Wyatt's 'plainness' consists of careful arrangements of the smallest parts of the line, wrought with ceaseless care to create a simplicity subject to variation. No half-line could be plainer than 'But for to love', but, as we have seen, no phrase could be more subject to ambiguity or express more variability. Thus, in Altieri's terms, it is the demonstrative character of metrical variation that allows Wyatt's style to do its work of revealing the capacities of his medium, the poetic line he inherited from Chaucer and Lydgate. In its clarity and frugality, 'plainness' then becomes the stark backdrop against which the English poetic line displays itself and its limits.

The 'style' I have explored here is the product of a compromise between the individual styles of poets and the notion of a style that can be labeled 'medieval', 'Renaissance', 'Ricardian', 'Lancastrian', or 'Drab Age'. Far from being a purely

[32] For discussions that address these questions, see Stephen Greenblatt, *Renaissance Self-Fashioning from More to Shakespeare* (Chicago: University of Chicago Press, 1980), 115–56; Jonathan Crewe, *Trials of Authorship: Anterior Forms and Poetic Reconstruction from Wyatt to Shakespeare* (Berkeley: University of California Press, 1990), 23–47; James Simpson, *Reform and Cultural Revolution*, The Oxford English Literary History, Vol. 2: *1350–1547* (Oxford: Oxford University Press, 2002), 157–60.

[33] For representative discussions of Wyatt's 'plainness', see Douglas L. Peterson, *The English Lyric from Wyatt to Donne: A History of the Plain and Eloquent Styles* (Princeton, NJ: Princeton University Press, 1967), 87–119; Kenneth J. E. Graham, 'The Performance of Conviction: Wyatt's Antirhetorical Plainness', *Style*, 23 (1989), 374–94; Catherine Bates, '"A mild admonisher": Sir Thomas Wyatt and Sixteenth-Century Satire', *Huntington Library Quarterly*, 56 (1993), 243–58; Elizabeth Heale, '"An owl in a sack troubles no man": Proverbs, Plainness, and Wyatt', *Renaissance Studies*, 11 (1997), 420–33.

formal or ahistorical concept, style is uniquely situated between the particular and the general, the poet and his age or era. As such, it is critical to literary-historical scholarship, especially because it respects both historical boundaries and larger narrations of epochal identity, while illuminating the details of the poetic work (or any other art object) with the strongest possible light—even when those details threaten to undermine the coherence or consistency of generalized accounts of 'period style' or literary history more broadly. Style is a flexible concept that allows the critic or scholar to move between different levels of thought—especially from conceptual to concrete and back again—with relative ease, revising either in light of the other as needed. Focusing on style means that we can begin to match the intensity, the sheer force of will, contained and displayed syllable by syllable in such poems as 'Truth', 'The World is Variable', and 'What Vaileth Trouth?'. As Wyatt himself once wrote while imprisoned for treason at a moment of great danger,

> For in some lyttell thynge may apere the truthe which I dare saye you seke for your consciens sake. And besydys that, yt is a smale thynge in alteringe of one syllable ether with penne or worde that may mayk in the conceavinge of the truthe myche matter or error. For in thys thynge 'I fere', or 'I truste', semethe but one smale syllable chaynged, and yet it makethe a great dyfferaunce, and may be of an herer wronge conceaved and worse reported, and yet worste of all altered by an examyner. Agayne 'fall owte', 'caste owte', or 'lefte owte' makethe dyfferaunce, yea and the settinge of the wordes one in an others place may mayke greate dyfferaunce, tho the wordes were all one—as 'a myll horse' and 'a horse myll'.[34]

These words of Wyatt's are the key to style: the blueprint for a critical practice in which we seek the 'lyttell thynges' through which the truths of an age, an era, or simply a sequence are endlessly confirmed, impeached, reaffirmed, and shattered. Wyatt describes a world in which 'lytell thynges' are both an instrument of tyranny and the only possible remedy for tyranny. What James Simpson has called a 'world of pretty much ubiquitous verbal mistrust'—the Henrician court, the Tudor realm—demanded that readers and writers strive for ever greater precision, focusing on ever smaller units of interpretation (the word, the syllable, the letter).[35] Style, however, interrupts this tyranny of the detail. It does so in part by answering fragment with fragment, syllable with syllable; it embraces the particular. But style is also, as I have shown, radically double, always signaling differences while perpetually demonstrating the limits of the possible, poised between the poet's will and the history within which that will displays its potential to create. Style demonstrates, without ever rendering explicit, the agency inherent in the choice of

[34] Thomas Wyatt, 'Defence: To the Iudges after the Indictment and the evidence', in Kenneth Muir, *Life and Letters of Sir Thomas Wyatt* (Liverpool: Liverpool University Press, 1963), item no. 37, 197. Wyatt was arrested on 17 January 1541 and charged with treason; he was freed at the end of March. There is no evidence that he ever delivered his 'Defence'.

[35] Simpson, *Burning to Read*, 227.

'lyttell thynges'—and in so doing, it unveils precisely the human capacity for making that tyranny would subdue.

FURTHER READING

Altieri, Charles. 'Style', in *The Oxford Handbook of Philosophy and Literature*, ed. Richard Eldridge (New York: Oxford University Press, 2009), 420–41

Barthes, Roland. *Writing Degree Zero*, trans. Annette Lavers and Colin Smith (New York: Hill and Wang, 1967)

Jameson, Fredric. *Marxism and Form: Twentieth-century Dialectical Theories of Literature* (Princeton, NJ: Princeton University Press, 1971)

Stevens, John. *Music and Poetry in the Early Tudor Court* (London: Methuen; Lincoln, NE: University of Nebraska Press, 1961)

Wölfflin, Heinrich. *Principles of Art History: The Problem of the Development of Style in Later Art*, trans. M. D. Hottinger (New York: Henry Holt, 1932)

CHAPTER 23

LONDON BOOKS AND LONDON READERS

JULIA BOFFEY

'London thou art of Townes *A per se*', wrote a visitor to the city, apparently in 1501–2. The well-known encomium which follows, praising London's 'renown, riches and royalte', commands attention not just as one of very few late medieval descriptions of the city, but because its origins and preservation point to so much that is characteristic of metropolitan textual production and transmission during the period when—from the vantage-point of the twenty-first century—the Middle Ages were becoming early modern.[1] Conceived or commissioned for delivery at a ceremonial feast, the poem is a powerful statement of the city's multitudinousness, invoking the many different groups that populate it, and making special and frequent reference to merchants and above all to the 'famowse mayre' (Edmund Shaa), whose praise occupies the whole of the final stanza. Its probable status as the work of a visitor to the city (a Scot, according to some manuscripts)[2] bears witness to the cosmopolitan mix of London's populace; and its role in a ceremony associated either with Prince Arthur's marriage to Katharine of Aragon or with the negotiations for the marriage of Arthur's sister Margaret to James IV of Scotland, both of which took place in the winter months of 1501–2, demonstrates something of the city's busy ceremonial life.

The poem has been preserved in contexts whose range is usefully suggestive of the variously civic, social, politico-economic, and more personal functions served by London textual practices. In two manuscripts (London, BL Cotton Vitellius A XVI and London, Guildhall Library MS 3313) the poem is included in chronicles,

[1] Quotations are from the edition in Oxford, Balliol College, MS 354, compiled by the London grocer Richard Hill; see Richard Hill, *Songs, Carols and Other Miscellaneous Poems from the Balliol MS 354, Richard Hill's Commonplace-Book*, ed. Roman Dyboski, EETS, extra series, 101 (London: Oxford University Press, 1908), 100–2.

[2] The long-standing attribution to Dunbar is now held to be 'dubious'; see Priscilla Bawcutt, *Dunbar the Makar* (Oxford: Clarendon Press, 1992), 44, 82.

with introductions securely placing it in its ceremonial context. In two others (Oxford, Balliol College 354 and the rather later BL Lansdowne 762) it has been collected by individuals seemingly concerned not just with civic events but also with business affairs and matters of local government, and whose miscellanies have something of the flavour of personal archives. The fifth witness, a manuscript fragment of two leaves (now New York, Pierpont Morgan Library MA 717), seems at an early stage in its life to have been combined in a volume with a printed book—Caxton's 1479 edition of the *Cordiale* or 'four last things', translated by Anthony Woodville, Earl Rivers (STC 5758)—from which it was later separated.[3]

Many questions are prompted by the fact that this hand-written copy, introduced as if with insider knowledge as a 'balad mayde at London when my Lorde Prince Arthur was wed, by a Scotte havyng muche money of dyverse lordes for hys Indytyng', was at an early stage conjoined with a product of the still new technology of printing with moveable type. How would the differences between the manuscript poem and the printed book have been perceived by an early owner or reader? Would perceptions of difference focus largely on material aspects, or might they concern less visible or less palpable features of the manuscript and the printed book? The aim of this discussion is to explore some of the contexts in which manuscript and print were brought together, or conversely kept apart, in the decades which immediately followed the introduction of printing to England by Caxton in *c.*1476, and to do so in relation to some categories of text which announce particular London connections. The justification for pursuing this search with a metropolitan focus is of course that London's size, its role as a port, its proximity to the centre of government, all ensured that its book trade was both nationally important and multifaceted. Its bishop, and its many parish churches and religious houses and fraternities, were influential on the texts generated and read there, just as its important livery companies, its trading connections, and its centrality to the machinery of law and training of lawyers shaped other features of what was copied and printed.

In the first decade of the sixteenth century the printers Wynkyn de Worde and Richard Pynson moved their businesses to Fleet Street, de Worde from Caxton's old premises in Westminster, to join an established community of producers of manuscript books located close by, around St Paul's churchyard.[4] They retained their connections with royal patrons (de Worde with Lady Margaret Beaufort, Pynson from 1506–7 as printer to the king), but also increasingly took on city

[3] See Curt F. Bühler, 'London Thow Art the Flowre of Cytes All', *Review of English Studies*, 13 (1937), 1–9.

[4] STC, 3: 140–1 and 3: 187–8; C. Paul Christianson, 'The rise of London's book-trade', in *The Cambridge History of the Book in Britain, Volume 3: 1400–1557*, ed. Lotte Hellinga and Joseph B. Trapp (Cambridge: Cambridge University Press, 1999), 128–47.

commissions.[5] Their example would draw a succession of other printers to the locality of St Paul's, and significantly marks an interesting coalescence of different means of book production in the one area.

London readers enjoyed access to the written or printed word in many contexts.[6] Words were visible on notices and libels, on indulgences and other forms of public document; in school books, law books, liturgical books, and works of practical information; in learned or pious treatises, popular songs and carols, and sophisticated works of literary diversion. Texts could be copied by hand for one's own personal use, obtained through bequests, or borrowed from acquaintances; they could be commissioned from a scribe, or bought in printed or manuscript form from a stationer or from a printer's premises, or perhaps from a haberdasher or a mercer. Texts from abroad, imported through London, were readily available from these latter sources; texts from other parts of England could have been procured from travellers and itinerant salesmen. Books were important to corporate bodies such as parish fraternities: BL MS Add. 37664, the guild book of the Fraternity of the Trinity and Saints Fabian and Sebastian in St Botolph's church, Aldersgate, lists members from the reign of Edward III through to that of Edward VI, and amongst its book-related payments records outgoings on a missal, a black register book, and a vellum roll containing pageants.[7] Libraries, whether substantial collections like that in the Guildhall, or smaller school or parish libraries, must have serviced some needs: from the period preceding 1603, lists of books survive from thirty parishes;[8] both a library and a grammar school were attached to St Peter's Cornhill in the medieval period, with books that included a Latin manuscript bible (now deposited in the Guildhall).[9] What specifically London-connected texts did these readers encounter? And in what ways—if at all—were the different modes of manuscript and print distinctive for them?

[5] Letters of confraternity, for example (see STC 14077c.51–60A), and proclamations concerning the city and its governance (STC 7764, 7767).

[6] For a long view, see Lawrence Manley, *Literature and Culture in Early Modern London* (Cambridge: Cambridge University Press, 1995).

[7] See *Catalogue of Additions to the Manuscripts in the British Museum 1906–1910* (London: British Museum, 1912), 95–6; and John Stow, *A Survey of London*, ed. Charles Lethbridge Kingsford, 2 vols. (Oxford: Clarendon Press, 1908), 1: 309.

[8] Fiona Kisby, 'Books in London Parish Churches before 1603: Some Preliminary Observations', in *The Church and Learning in Late Medieval Society: Studies in Honour of Professor R. B. Dobson*, ed. Caroline Barron and Jenny Stratford, Harlaxton Medieval Studies, 11 (Donington, Lincs: Shaun Tyas, 2002), 305–26.

[9] Michael Perkin, *A Directory of the Parochial Libraries of the Church of England and the Church in Wales* (London: Bibliographical Society, 2004), 274; Neil Ripley Ker, *Medieval Manuscripts in British Libraries: London*, 5 vols. (Oxford: Oxford University Press, 1969), 1: 262–3. On the provision of books in schools, see C. M. Barron, 'The Expansion of Education in Fifteenth-Century London', in *The Cloister and the World: Essays in Medieval History in Honour of Barbara Harvey*, ed. John Blair and Brian Golding (Oxford: Oxford University Press, 1996), 219–45.

Ralph Hanna's exploration of the London literature of earlier centuries has made clear the growing importance assumed in the city's textual culture by its governance and by records associated with that.[10] In the later period under consideration here, while the anonymous author of 'London thou art of Townes *A per se*' celebrated the city's legendary Trojan origins ('Citie that sumtyme called was Newe Troye!'), other more bureaucratic forms of energy were devoted to compiling and archiving accounts of administrative and legal matters: meetings of the common council, the court of aldermen, business falling to the chamberlain and the common clerk.[11] Some of this material concerning laws and customs was copied for official or semi-official purposes at the instigation of civic notables: just as the fishmonger and city chamberlain Andrew Horn had in the fourteenth century prompted the collection of a 'Liber custumarum' and 'Liber Horn', city registers for preservation in the Guildhall, so John Carpenter, town clerk 1417–*c.*1438, brought into being the collection known as the 'Liber Albus', for example.[12] Collections of these materials were also procured by individual readers: BL MS Add. 38131 and BL MS Egerton 2885 are collections of statutes, proclamations, and customs seemingly owned by Londoners in the late fourteenth or fifteenth centuries, the first by Richard Drax, a sergeant-at-arms, and the second probably by a fishmonger.[13] Such material also leaked in smaller ways into other contexts. A largely religious anthology of English and Latin prose and verse (now MS Bodley 596, part I), with the arms of the exchequer official William Baron, concludes with some London notes and an account of the deposition of Richard II;[14] a register of pleas in Latin, largely from the time of Richard II but with additions to the time of Edward IV (BL MS Add. 34783), concludes on fol. 173^{v} with a note recording the English words of the mayoral oath.

Annalistic chronicles of London history, sometimes so brief as to be barely more than records of successive sheriffs, mayors, and aldermen, are among the clearest forms of evidence for a growing interest in the city's identity and heritage.[15] Increasing numbers of literate Londoners kept their own informal records in

[10] Ralph Hanna, *London Literature, 1300–1380* (Cambridge: Cambridge University Press, 2005), especially 44–103; Sheila Lindenbaum, 'London texts and literate practice', in *The Cambridge History of Medieval English Literature*, ed. David Wallace (Cambridge: Cambridge University Press, 1999), 284–309.

[11] See Caroline M. Barron, *London in the Later Middle Ages: Government and People, 1200–1500* (Oxford: Oxford University Press, 2004), 173–98.

[12] All now in the Corporation of London Record Office. The *Liber Albus* was completed in 1419; see Henry T. Riley (ed. and trans.), *Liber Albus: The White Book of the City of London* (London: (S. I.) Griffin, 1861).

[13] Lindenbaum, 'London texts and literate practice', 308.

[14] On Baron, see A. I. Doyle, 'Books Connected with the Vere Family and Barking Abbey', *Essex Archaeological Society Transactions*, new series, 25 (1958), 222–43.

[15] Mary-Rose McLaren, *The London Chronicles of the Fifteenth Century: A Revolution in English Writing* (Cambridge: D. S. Brewer, 2002), and 'Reading, Writing and Recording: Literacy and the London Chronicles in the Fifteenth Century', in *London and the Kingdom: Essays in Honour of Caroline*

which city chronicles figure alongside other kinds of useful civic information or documents. Such assortments of material are found in large, well-produced manuscript volumes such as London, BL MS Egerton 1995, which includes a chronicle begun by the skinner and mayor William Gregory and continued independently after his death in 1467, but also in much smaller and even sometimes scrappier assemblages.[16] A thirty-two-page booklet which now forms part of BL MS Harley 541, for example, contains alongside some verses and personalized information the names of mayors and sheriffs, and lists of London churches, religious houses, and companies, with blank pages apparently designed for do-it-yourself completion.[17] The existence of a developed market for London-centred compilations is attested by the printing of successive editions of 'Arnold's Chronicle', a collection of miscellaneous and in part London-focused material apparently put together by a London haberdasher (d. *c.*1521), whose mercantile connections with Flanders perhaps explain why the first surviving edition was one printed around 1503 in Antwerp, by A. van Berghen; only in 1525 was the compilation printed actually in London, by Treveris.[18]

M. Barron, ed. Matthew Davies and Andrew Prescott, Harlaxton Medieval Studies, 16 (Donington: Shaun Tyas, 2008), 346–65.

[16] 'Gregory's Chronicle' in *Historical Collections of a London Citizen*, ed. James Gairdner, Camden Society Publications, new series, 17 (London: Printed for the Camden Society, 1876). For examples of less formal collections, see Carol M. Meale, 'The Compiler at Work: John Colyns and BL MS Harley 2252', in *Manuscripts and Readers in Fifteenth-Century England: The Literary Implications of Manuscript Study. Essays from the 1981 Conference at the University of York*, ed. Derek Pearsall (Cambridge: D. S. Brewer, 1983), 82–103; Julia Boffey and Carol M. Meale, 'Selecting the text: Rawlinson C. 86 and some other books for London readers', in *Regionalism in Late Medieval Manuscripts and Texts: Essays Celebrating the Publication of 'A Linguistic Atlas of Late Mediaeval English'. Proceedings of the 1989 York Manuscripts Conference*, ed. Felicity Riddy, York Manuscripts Conferences: Proceedings Series, 2 (Cambridge: D. S. Brewer, 1991), 143–69; David R. Parker, *The Commonplace Book in Tudor London: An Examination of BL MSS Egerton 1995, Harley 2252, Lansdowne 762, and Oxford, Balliol College MS 354* (Lanham, MD, and Oxford: University Press of America, 1998). The most arresting forms of historical record are also sometimes the most unsophisticated. BL MS Add. 37075, a schoolbook of which substantial parts seem to have been compiled by the schoolboy John Claveryng, eventually to become an early sixteenth-century rector of St Christopher by the Stocks, contains on folios 188^{v}–198^{v} a group of practice Latin sentences which include a reference to the recent burning of heretical books (fol. 197^{v}). For a description, see David Thomson, *A Descriptive Catalogue of Middle English Grammatical Texts* (New York: Garland, 1979), 219–32.

[17] Anne F. Sutton and Livia Visser-Fuchs, 'The Making of a Minor London Chronicle in the Household of Sir Thomas Frowyk (died 1485)', *The Ricardian*, 10 (1994–6), 86–103, 198–9.

[18] STC 782 and 783. See Richard Arnold, *The Customs of London, otherwise called, Arnold's Chronicle*, ed. Francis Douce (London: F. C. & J. Rivington, 1811). Extracts from these editions were also to appear in later prints up to *c.*1550 (see STC 5952.5, 9270.5, 17297); and material from Arnold's chronicle was copied into manuscript collections such as Balliol MS 354 (see above, n. 1), Bodl. MS Tanner 2, and Wriothesley's Chronicle (of which the MS is now lost; see Charles Wriothesley, *A Chronicle of England during the Reigns of the Tudors from AD 1485 to 1559*, ed. W. D. Hamilton, Camden Society Publications, new series, 11, 2 vols. (1875), 1: i–xlviii).

While maintaining their interest in these books about their local history and customs, London readers were also a significant audience for texts of wider national significance—sometimes, but not always, as a result of the metropolitan origins or early circulation of many such works. Study of the transmission of *The Libelle of Englysshe Polycye* has demonstrated how this poem, which came into being as a response to the besieging of Calais by Burgundian forces after the Franco-Burgundian alliance ratified at the Treaty of Arras in 1436, held a special interest for London mercantile readers alarmed by a threat to trading routes. On the evidence of a copy made in the mid-sixteenth century (Manchester, Rylands Library Eng. 955), its appeal seems to have been long-lasting.[19] A whole collection of works dealing with issues of national concern was assembled in a late fifteenth-century London volume which is now BL MS Royal 17 D XV: the 'Somnium vigilantis', a defence of the proscription of Yorkists (probably dating from before July 1463); Sir John Fortescue's 'Declaration' (refuting his anti-Yorkist writings, and produced at the order of Edward IV); a verse 'Ballett' on Edward IV's recovery of the throne; and a printed text of 1483 called *The promisse of matrimonie*, largely taken up with the terms of the 1475 Treaty of Picqigny made between Edward IV and Louis XI of France.[20] The scribe responsible for the manuscript sections was active in London in the second part of the fifteenth century and is known to have produced copies of the statutes, of works by Lydgate and Hoccleve, treatises on science, medicine, heraldry, and ceremony, and (in Cambridge, Trinity College MS O.3.11) a miscellany of material very similar in its London focus to Arnold's chronicle. His connections, which included a London stationer named Thomas Multon and members of the household of the London draper, alderman, and mayor Sir Thomas Cook, suggest the interpenetrating worlds of business, politics, ceremony, and diversion which fuelled metropolitan textual production.[21]

BL MS Royal 17 D XV contains manuscript material, a printed fragment, and (in its 'ballett') a work which may well have had an oral circulation: its contents reflect several of the modes by which texts could be transmitted in late medieval London.

[19] Carol M. Meale, '*The Libelle of Englyshe Polycye* and Mercantile Literary Culture in Late-Medieval London', in *London and Europe in the Later Middle Ages*, ed. Julia Boffey and Pamela King (London: Westfield Publications in Medieval Studies, 1995), 181–227. Other such texts include *Brut* chronicles and universal histories such as the *Polychronicon*, both also printed at a fairly early stage.

[20] For descriptions, see J. M. Manly and E. Rickert, *The Text of the Canterbury Tales*, 8 vols. (Chicago: Chicago University Press, 1940), 1: 476–84. The printed section (STC 9176) was removed from the manuscript in 1850.

[21] The most recent account of the work of this scribe (the so-called 'Hammond scribe') is provided by Linne R. Mooney, 'A New Manuscript of the Hammond Scribe Discovered by Jeremy Griffiths', in *The English Medieval Book: Studies in Memory of Jeremy Griffiths*, ed. A. S. G. Edwards, Vincent Gillespie, and Ralph Hanna (London: The British Library, 2000), 113–23. On Multon and Cook, see Margaret Lucille Kekewich *et al.* (eds.), *The Politics of Fifteenth Century England: John Vale's Book* (Stroud: Alan Sutton/Richard III and Yorkist History Trust, 1995), 107–11. The career of the legal scrivener Robert Bale further illustrates such interpenetrating networks; see Anne F. Sutton, 'Robert Bale, Scrivener and Chronicler of London', *English Manuscript Studies*, 14 (2008), 180–206.

The book of documents compiled after Sir Thomas Cook's death by his factotum John Vale (now BL MS Add. 48031A) similarly draws together texts whose first 'publication' took a variety of forms. One item is a copy of a letter written by Warwick and Clarence in 1470 to the commons of England, 'the whiche letre above wretyn divers copies were made and sette upon the standard in Chepe, upon the stulpes [stone gate posts] on London brigge and upon divers chirche doris in London and in other places in Englonde'. Its public airing came to an end when 'Richard Lee, grocer, thane being mair... toke downe the seide letres and wolde not suffer theime to be openly knowen ner seen to the commones.' The copy in BL MS Add. 48031A was presumably transcribed during the period of public display, or taken from an exemplar made at that time.[22] Many of the other items in this compilation reproduce letters, documents, grants, manifestos, and memoranda—texts of different forms and shapes whose transmission into written copies may have involved a variety of agents and processes; it includes, furthermore, a manuscript copy of the same *promisse of matrimonie* which is found in printed form in BL MS Royal 17 D XV.

A companion of the young Vale, during his apprenticeship to Sir Thomas Cook, was apparently one of the authors of a work known as *The Great Chronicle of London*, now in the Guildhall Library (MS 3313): a large and well-presented volume containing an annalistic history of the city from 1189 to 1439, with a continuation to 1512.[23] This *Great Chronicle* is connected in a number of ways with another chronicle which survives in both manuscript and printed copies (BL Cotton Nero C XI and Holkham Hall MS 671; STC 10659 and 10660).[24] No reference is made to its author in the manuscripts or in the first printed edition, made by Richard Pynson in 1516, and called simply 'The new cronycles of England and Fraunce'; but in the second edition (by Rastell, in 1533), it is called 'Fabyans cronycle newly prynted', and thus attributable to Robert Fabyan, a London sheriff and alderman, and Master of the Drapers' Company in 1495–6 and again in

[22] Kekewich *et al.*, *The Politics of Fifteenth-Century England*, 219. Stow copied this entry (along with others) into BL MS Harley 543.

[23] Arthur H. Thomas and Isobel D. Thornley (eds.), *The Great Chronicle of London (Guildhall Library MS 3313)* (London: George W. Jones, 1938). See also McLaren, *London Chronicles*, 26–8; Edward Donald Kennedy, 'Chronicles and Other Historical Writing', in *A Manual of the Writings in Middle English 1050–1500*, general editor Albert E. Hartung, vol. 8 (New Haven, CT: Connecticut Academy of Arts and Sciences, 1989), 2647–56. The association with Cook's household is clear from what the author has to say about Cook's 'troubles' when he was impeached for treason in 1468: 'In the tyme of his ffyrst trowble I was his apprentyze and abowth the age of xvii or xviii yerys and therabowth' (*Great Chronicle*, ed. Thomas and Thornley, 205); the incompleteness of the Drapers' Company Wardens' Accounts, together with the fact that Cook's 'troubles' meant that his business folded for a while, impede any attempts to identify this apprentice turned chronicler.

[24] Even though comparison of the content of their latter portions is confused by the fact that various continuations were added to both works at various points, there seems to be considerable overlap between the two. Fabyan is known to have been apprenticed to a master called William Holme, but may have changed at some stage to work for Thomas Cook.

1501–2.[25] Stow and other sixteenth-century authorities certainly believed that Fabyan was the author of both works,[26] and the fact that one particular scribe's hand appears in the manuscripts of both the *Great Chronicle* and the *New cronycles* certainly supports the likelihood of a close connection.[27] These two works neatly illustrate London interests in both locally focused and national, even international, history: where the *Great Chronicle* is annalistic and London-centred, the *Newe Cronycles*, organized into a series of seven books following the Seven Joys of Mary, deals more comprehensively with the larger histories of both England and France.

The various surviving copies of these two works have a great deal to tell us about the interpenetration of different forms of book production in London at the start of the sixteenth century. All three manuscripts—the two separate volumes of the *New cronycles*, and the Guildhall manuscript of the *Great Chronicle*—have been distinctively 'enhanced' with pasted-in engraved initials. Added to the Holkham Hall manuscript of the *New cronycles*, in addition, are woodcut scenes and borders cut from two Parisian books of hours, further cut-out embellishments both xylographic and engraved, and two miniatures, hand-painted on vellum.[28] Thus right from the start these works took material form as varieties of hybrid book, produced by a combination of available technologies. The *Great Chronicle* seems not to have reached print in the form preserved by Guildhall MS 3313, although it certainly continued to be available to London readers: the sixteenth-century chronicler Edward Hall may have used it, and it clearly passed through the hands of John Foxe and John Stowe.[29] But the question of Pynson's setting-copy for his 1516 edition of the *New cronycles* is a tantalizing one. While it is possible that he used the Cotton and Holkham Hall manuscripts,[30] there survives another manuscript copy of the *New cronycles* (Harvard University, Houghton Library MS Eng 766) whose relationship to the print awaits proper study.[31] Was it used by Pynson, perhaps as

[25] Fabyan could probably have been mayor had he not suffered financial difficulties which caused him to resign his aldermanship in 1503; see M.-R. McLaren, 'Fabyan, Robert (*d.* 1513)', *ODNB* (accessed 13 January 2009).

[26] 'He wrote a chronicle of London, England, and of France, beginning at the creation and endynge in the third of Henry the 8, which both I have in written hand'; see Stow, *A Survey of London*, ed. Kingsford, 2: 305–6.

[27] It has occasionally been supposed that this main hand could be Fabyan's own; but more likely, perhaps, that the scribe was copying on behalf of the author (or authors).

[28] *Great Chronicle*, ed. Thomas and Thornley, l–li; William O. Hassall, *The Holkham Library: Illuminations and Illustrations in the Manuscript Library of the Earl of Leicester*, Roxburghe Club Publications, 234 (London: Printed for the Roxburghe Club, 1970), plates 16 and 17; Mary C. Erler, 'Pasted-In Embellishments in English Manuscripts and Printed Books *c.* 1480–1533', *The Library*, sixth series, 14 (1992), 185–206.

[29] *Great Chronicle*, ed. Thomas and Thornley, xv–xviii.

[30] *Great Chronicle*, ed. Thomas and Thornley, lxiv.

[31] See Linda E. Voigts, 'A Handlist of Middle English in Harvard Manuscripts', *Harvard Library Bulletin*, 33 (1985), 32–8.

working or setting copy? Or was it rather made after the printed edition, and copied from it?

In terms of what fed into their composition, both of these works are strikingly heterogeneous. Like John Vale's book, the *Great Chronicle* and the *Newe Chronicles* drew together materials that must have reached their compiler(s) in a variety of forms. Fabyan is known to have borrowed manuscripts from the Guildhall Library: some while after his death the man his widow married returned to the library the 'grete boke of the Chroniques of Fraunce Wreton in Frensh', noted by a clerk as 'long time in the kepyng of the sayd M. Fabyan'.[32] But printed and orally circulating materials, equally, were important to the construction of these works. The French portions of the *Newe Cronycles* were drawn from a Paris print of 1497 (Robert Gaguin, *Compendium super Francorum Gestis*), and both the *Great Chronicle* and the *New cronycles* include accounts of texts pinned up for public reading, such as the famous couplet about Richard III posted in 1484:

> In these dayes were chieff Rulers abowth the kyng, The lord lovell, and ij Gentylmen beyng named Mr Ratclyff & Mr Catysby, Of the whych personys was made a sedicious Ryme & fastenyd upon the crosse In Chepe & othir placys of the Cyte whereof the Sentence was as folowyth, The Catt the ratt, and lovell owyr dogge Rulyn all Engeland, undyr an hogge[33]
>
> . . . of that affynite was one named Wyllyam Colyngbourne taken. And after he had ben holden a season in pryson he wyth another gentylman named Turbyrvyle were brought unto Guyldehalle and ther areygned. But the sayd Turbyrvyle was repryed to pryson, and that other was caste for sondry treasons & for a ryme, whyche was layde to his charge that he shulde make in derysyon of the kyng and his counsayll as foloweth: The catte the ratte and Lovell our dogge / Rulyth all England under a hogge.[34]

These materials were to reappear throughout the sixteenth century in successive redactions, both manuscript and print: John Rastell's *The pastyme of people* (1530?, STC 20724), Halle's *Vnion of the two noble and illustrate families of Lancastre and Yorke* (1548, STC 12721), and through these a number of subsequent sixteenth-century histories, owe a debt to the *Newe Cronycles.*[35]

Accounts of more formal public events central to civic life feature in some numbers, and in a diversity of forms, in London-produced books. As with Vale's documents and Stow's later copies, there is a distinction to be made here between accounts produced contemporaneously with the events recorded, and those made at a later date, in the context of retrospective histories. Lydgate's London

[32] *Great Chronicle*, ed. Thomas and Thornley, xxiii.

[33] Guildhall MS fol. 212; *Great Chronicle*, 236.

[34] *Fabyans croncyle*, Rastell 1533, STC 10660; II, fol.CCXXVII^{v}.

[35] Elias Ashmole transcribed parts of the *Newe Cronycles* in 1672; Hakluyt appears to have known both these and the *Great Chronicle*; see Kennedy, 'Chronicles and Other Historical Writing', 2853, 2858.

'mummings', for example (for the Mercers' and Goldsmiths' companies, and a sheriffs' dinner), were copied by the London scribe John Shirley, who may have known Lydgate, in the first half of the fifteenth century, and they were then retranscribed by John Stow a century later, in BL MS Add. 29729.[36] A version of Lydgate's verses commemorating the pageants marking Henry VI's entry into London in 1432 was copied by John Carpenter into the city's letter-book, but other formulations of the material are preserved in London chronicles of much later dates, and indeed in the printed *New cronycles* of 1516. From a later edition of this (printed by Grafton for Bonham in 1542, STC 10661), portions were then appropriated for Edward VI's coronation in 1547.[37]

The growing acknowledgement of the usefulness of print in public, civic contexts is manifest in relation to the ceremonies following Catherine of Aragon's arrival in England in 1500 to marry Henry VII's elder son Prince Arthur. The ordinances for the princess's reception, in the form of Privy Council orders, survive in a series of contemporary manuscript copies (BL Cotton Vitellius C XI, College of Arms 1st M. 13, BL Cotton Vespasian C XIV). Contemporary accounts of the events themselves are preserved in manuscript chronicles (the *Great Chronicle*, London, Guildhall 3313; BL Cotton Vitellius A XVI), and in an eyewitness account made perhaps by a member of the royal household.[38] But printed versions of the ordinances were also produced by Pynson, as *The traduction & mariage of the princesse* (STC 4814).[39] As king's printer, Pynson was to undertake other tasks of this kind: when an embassy was sent by the Emperor Maximilian to finalize arrangements for the marriage of Henry VII's daughter Mary to Charles, prince of Castile, in 1508, Pynson printed a Latin account of its reception (STC 4659), followed a year later by an English translation (*the solempnities. & triumphes doon at the spousells of the kings doughter*; STC 17558).[40] When Mary married Louis XII of France in 1514, the ceremonies in Paris were recorded in both a Parisian printed

[36] See Derek Pearsall, *John Lydgate (1371–1449): A Bio-bibliography*, English Literary Studies Monograph Series, 71 (Victoria, BC: University of Victoria, 1997), 29.

[37] Henry N. MacCracken, 'King Henry's Triumphal Entry into London: Lydgate's Poem and Carpenter's Letter', *Archiv für das Studium der neueren Sprachen und Literaturen*, 126 (1911), 75–102; Sydney Anglo, *Spectacle, Pageantry and Early Tudor Policy* (Oxford: Clarendon Press, 1969), 283–94 at 283n. (where it is noted that a contemporary manuscript account of the 1547 ceremonies survives in the College of Arms).

[38] Gordon Kipling (ed.), *The Receyt of the Ladie Kateryne*, EETS, o.s., 296 (Oxford: Oxford University Press, 1990); brief details of the sequence of accounts are on xi–xii.

[39] Kate Harris, 'Richard Pynson's *Remembraunce for the Traduction of the Princesse Kateryne*: the Printer's Contribution to the Reception of Catharine of Aragon', *The Library*, sixth series, 12 (1990), 89–109.

[40] Petrus Carmelianus, '"The Spousells" of the Princess Mary, daughter of Henry VII, to Charles prince of Castile, A.D. 1508', ed. James Gairdner, *Camden Miscellany*, Vol. 9, Works of the Camden Society, new series, Vol. 53 (London: Nichols & Sons, 1895); see also Pamela Neville-Sington, 'Press, Politics and Religion', in *The Cambridge History of the Book in Britain*, vol. 3, ed. Hellinga and Trapp, 576–607, at 579.

version and a special *de luxe* manuscript account, which was brought back to England (BL Cotton Vespasian B II).[41]

Much of what can be recovered about city pageantry, and about musical and dramatic performances of other kinds, resides in accounts and other documents rather than in the form of surviving texts: especially in the early part of the period we are considering, the 'publication' of material of this sort seems to have been unusual unless (as in the items just discussed) for reasons of propaganda. Copies of fifteenth-century texts used in entertainments sponsored by the great livery companies, or by smaller trade or parish-centred associations, or from the households of civic dignitaries, aristocrats, and prelates, have (with odd exceptions, like Lydgate's mummings) mostly not survived.[42] Sixteenth-century printers, however, seem to have perceived some new economic potential in the publication of dramatic interludes, from Pynson's edition of *Everyman* (*c.*1515: STC 10604) onwards. The appeal of some of these works, *Everyman* especially, may have been the fact that they could be read as morally instructive treatises just as easily as dramatic interludes.[43] Some had other attractions as well: the edition of Skelton's *Magnificence* printed *c.*1530 by Treveris for John Rastell (STC 22607) is introduced as 'a goodly interlude and a mery', with a cast list, but its title page also stresses its newsworthiness, and thus its commercial potential, in the form of its associations with 'Mayster Skelton, poet laureate late deceasyd'. Rastell's access to the textual records of civic and court entertainment is likely to have been relatively direct: he was a lawyer, a printer and stationer, the brother-in-law of Sir Thomas More and the father-in-law of the playwright John Heywood, and involved at various levels in the supply and the printing of material appropriate for London performance and London circulation.

Interludes such as *Hycke Scorner*, printed by de Worde (STC 14039), and featuring episodes of urban debauchery in London locations, may in printed

[41] Pierre Gringore, *Pierre Gringore's Pageants for the Entry of Mary Tudor into Paris: An Unpublished Manuscript*, ed. Charles Read Baskervill (Chicago: University of Chicago Press, 1934).

[42] Anne Lancashire, 'Medieval to Renaissance: Plays and the London Drapers' Company to 1558', in *The Centre and its Compass: Studies in Medieval Literature in Honor of Professor John Leyerle*, ed. Robert A. Taylor et al., Studies in Medieval Culture, 33 (Kalamazoo: Western Michigan University, 1993), 297–313; Anne Lancashire, 'Continuing Civic Ceremonies of 1530s London', in *Civic Ritual and Drama*, ed. Alexandra F. Johnston and Wim Hüsken, *Ludus*, 2 (Amsterdam: Rodopi, 1997), 81–105; see also Edward Wilson, 'The Debate of the Carpenter's Tools', *Review of English Studies*, new series, 38 (1987), 445–70, for more general discussion of entertainments at company feasts. Sheila Lindenbaum, 'Ceremony and Oligarchy: the London Midsummer Watch', in *City and Spectacle in Medieval Europe*, ed. Barbara K. Hanawalt and Kathryn L. Reyerson, (Minneapolis: University of Minnesota Press, 1994), 171–88, and Mary C. Erler (ed.), *Ecclesiastical London*, Records of Early English Drama (Toronto: Toronto University Press, 2008), contain information pertaining to other forms of London performance.

[43] Julie Stone Peters, *Theatre of the Book 1480–1880: Print, Text, and Performance in Europe* (Oxford: Oxford University Press, 2000), 15–40.

form have functioned more as comic satires than as scripts for dramatic performance.[44] *Hycke Scorner*'s presentation, in quarto form and with factotum woodcuts, seems to link it with works like *Cocke Lorell's Bote*, a miniature, London-specific *Ship of Fools*. Two early de Worde editions of this work have survived (STC 5456, 5456.3), and it appeared in later sixteenth-century reprintings in the context of a collection called *The Fraternity of Vagabonds* (STC 993 etc.). Cock Lorell's vessel carries a motley civic fraternity from Newgate, Ludgate, Clerkenwell, and Lothbury, licensed by a joke pre-embarkation pardon to drink copiously and to behave in comprehensively indecent ways; some of the fraternity have generic joke names ('Alan Maltson'), but others sound like real individuals. A popular verse satire called the *Treatise of a Galaunt*, printed in several quarto editions by de Worde, seems to have been considered a London text, since de Worde eventually incorporated with it another poem called *The maryage of the bosse of Byllyngesgate vnto London stone* (STC 24240–24242.3).[45] The 'bosse', according to Stow, was 'a Bosse of spring water continually running which standeth by Billinsgate... sometimes made by the executors of Richard Whittington'; the origins of London stone, a nearby 'great stone... fixed in the ground verie deepe, fastned with bars of iron', are a matter of some speculation, but it attracted sightseers until by 1798 it was no more than a stump and had to be removed and built into the wall of St Swithin's church.[46]

The Treatise of a Galaunt had an established manuscript circulation in the later part of the fifteenth century, and the printed editions may simply have given readers the option of acquiring it in another form. It is not possible to detect a trend by which manuscript versions of such popular texts were completely superseded by printed ones. Other comic satires featuring city or immediately suburban locations—texts like *Piers of Fulham* and *Colyn Blobol's Testament*—survive only in manuscript; *Jyl of Braintfords Testament* only in printed editions of the 1560s (STC 5730 and 5731).[47] One of the most famous, *London Lickpenny*, although dated to the fifteenth century on the grounds of linguistic evidence, is extant only in sixteenth-century manuscripts, one a copy made by Stow. The hapless narrator of this satire is assailed in various city locations and in Westminster by rapacious lawyers, chancery clerks, foreign salesmen, cooks, and taverners, before returning

[44] Ian Lancashire (ed.), *Two Tudor Interludes: The Interlude of Youth, Hick Scorner* (Manchester: Manchester University Press, 1980), 32, 154.

[45] Julia Boffey, '*The Treatise of a Galaunt* in Manuscript and Print', *The Library*, sixth series, 15 (1993), 175–86.

[46] Stow, *A Survey of London*, ed. Kingsford, 1: 208, 224–5.

[47] *Piers of Fulham* and *Colyn Blobol's Testament* appear in Bodl. MS Rawlinson C. 86 (see above, note 16); see James Orchard Halliwell-Phillipps (ed.), *Nugae Poeticae* (London: John Russell Smith, 1844), 1–12. *Jyl of Braintfords Testament* is edited by Frederick James Furnivall in *Jyl of Brentford's Testament by Robert Copland, Boke-prynter... and Other Short Pieces* (London: printed for private circulation, 1871).

to Kent to his plough, praying 'Jesus save London'.[48] As well as making his manuscript copy, Stow invoked the poem in his *Survey of London* 'to proove this Eastcheape to bee a place replenished with Cookes'.[49] Like *Cocke Lorell's Bote*, and seemingly like other popular London poems, *London Lickpenny* seems to have had a long life. The burlesque *Turnement of Totenham*, whose manuscript circulation is attested by three fifteenth-century copies, was still being printed over a century later, in 1631 (STC 19925).[50]

While the appeal of some burlesques and satires appears to have endured, it is necessarily harder to find pious metropolitan texts which survived the fractures brought about by religious reform, although here as elsewhere it is possible to identify a symbiotic relationship between script and print which was to continue on into the seventeenth century. Simple statistics explain London's centrality to the production and circulation of religious texts.[51] The city's jurisdiction covered over a hundred parishes and (until *c.*1540) thirty-nine religious houses: the provision of liturgical, pastoral, and devotional books for such a large number of institutions and congregations must have significantly stimulated processes of production and supply, many reliant on local labour and resources.[52] The growing centrality of London to the production and transmission of religious writings throughout the fifteenth and sixteenth centuries also went alongside a growing geographical concentration of interested parties—in the area around St Paul's, which attracted both the personnel associated with the manuscript book trade and after 1501 the major printers—and a consolidation of its import trade in continentally produced books. Paul Christianson's work on the fifteenth-century production of manuscript books in London makes clear just how much business was generated by corporate bodies such as churches and schools as well as by civic, governmental, and royal business.[53]

The works of William Lichefeld (d. 1448), vicar of All Hallows, Thames Street, conveniently illustrate some features of the pre-Reformation London production

[48] See Eleanor P. Hammond, *English Verse between Chaucer and Surrey* (Durham, NC: Duke University Press, 1927), 237–9 and Russell H. Robbins (ed.), *Historical Poems of the XIVth and XVth Centuries* (New York: Columbia University Press, 1959), 130–4.

[49] Stow, *A Survey of London*, ed. Kingsford, 1: 217 (where it is attributed to Lydgate). Stow's manuscript is BL MS Harley 542; the copy in BL MS Harley 367 also has an attribution to Lydgate.

[50] On the manuscript copies, see Carol M. Meale, 'Romance and its Anti-Type? *The Turnament of Totenham*, the Carnivalesque, and Popular Culture', in *Middle English Poetry: Texts and Traditions. Essays in Honour of Derek Pearsall*, ed. A. J. Minnis (York: York Medieval Press, 2001), 103–27.

[51] As Clive Burgess notes: 'We are well accustomed to conceiving of London as the pivot both of England's government and its economy by the later Middle Ages; but conspicuous devotional provision had also secured its position at the heart of the spiritual realm'; see Clive Burgess, 'London, the Church and the Kingdom', in *London and the Kingdom*, ed. Davies and Prescott, 98–117, at 109.

[52] See Kisby, 'Books in London Parish Churches before 1603'.

[53] C. Paul Christianson, 'Evidence for the Study of London's Late Medieval Manuscript-book Trade', in *Book Production and Publishing in Britain, 1375–1475*, ed. Jeremy Griffiths and Derek Pearsall (Cambridge: Cambridge University Press, 1989), 87–108, especially 99–100.

and circulation of pious texts.[54] Lichefeld was, according to Stow, 'a great student, and compiled many bookes both moral and divine, in prose and verse'. These included an expansion of part of a much earlier work, *Ancrene Riwle*, as 'De quinque sensibus' (in BL MS Royal 8 C I), and the composition of no less than 3,083 sermons, of which—extraordinarily—no material trace is left.[55] He was an acquaintance of John Carpenter and of the religious author and bishop Reginald Pecock, for some years master of the London college of priests founded by Richard Whittington. Both Lichefeld and Pecock were responsible at Carpenter's death in 1441 for selecting books from his private collection for the Guildhall library, although their acquaintance presumably soured at the end of the decade when Pecock's activities began to attract suspicions of heresy and Lichefeld was among those charged with opposing him.[56] Lichefeld's short verse 'Complaint of God' has fared better than his sermons, surviving in at least twelve manuscripts, several of which (on the evidence of their scribes or of other signs of provenance) have London associations.[57] Although it appears consistently in these contexts as an anthology component rather than a free-standing work, it was printed by de Worde in at least three editions between about 1510 and 1535 as a short pamphlet (STC 20881.3–20882; possibly designed to be bound with other booklets of similar size and length), and clearly accommodated itself readily to various modes of transmission.

The 'Complaint' is a handily short prompt to affective devotion, made easily memorable by the fact of its composition in verse, and with its instructive function underlined in the printed editions by a prefatory woodcut. Its orthodox nature, together with Lichefeld's possible reputation as an opponent of heresy, may have both assured its success and eventually limited its shelf-life. More generally, London textual production seems to have been able both to participate in and adapt to the changes brought about by religious reform. Despite ceremonial book-burnings—Pecock's at St Paul's Cross in 1457, for example, after he publicly recanted what had been deemed to be heretical beliefs; the burning of Lutheran books in 1521, and of Tyndale's New Testament in 1526—access to proscribed material remained possible by a variety of means, whether through do-it-yourself manuscript production (perhaps sometimes by the 'common-profit' networks studied by Wendy Scase),[58] or (increasingly) the procurement of texts printed

54 R. M. Ball, 'Lichefeld, William (*d.* 1448)', *ODNB* (accessed 15 December 2008).

55 Stow, *A Survey of London*, 1: 235; 2: 321n.

56 Wendy Scase, 'Pecock, Reginald (*b.* *c.*1392, *d.* in or after 1459)', *ODNB* (accessed 16 December 2008).

57 See Francis Lee Utley, 'Dialogues, Debates and Catechisms', in *A Manual of the Writings in Middle English*, vol. 3, ed. A. E. Hartung (Hamden, CT: Connecticut Academy of Arts and Sciences, 1972), 840.

58 Wendy Scase, 'Reginald Pecock, John Carpenter and John Colop's "Common-Profit" Book: Aspects of Book Ownership and Circulation in Fifteenth-Century London', *Medium Ævum*, 61 (1992), 261–74; see also Anne Hudson, 'Lollard book production', in *Book Production and Publishing*, ed. Griffiths and Pearsall, 125–42.

abroad. As Alexandra Walsham has noted, 'The condition of proscription stimulated creative and imaginative use of the pen and the press in a culture in which communication was still predominantly oral and in which modes of scribal publication continued to thrive alongside the technology of typographical reproduction.'[59] Established London printers like de Worde seem anyway to have been able to weather many of the changes that the sixteenth century was to bring. At least one of de Worde's books concludes with a note signalling that it was 'approved' for publication by John Colet,[60] but he was unaffected by the fact that Colet fell from favour and was in 1513 banned from preaching.[61] His business continued apparently unscathed after an incident in 1525 when he was ordered to recall copies of a work called *The ymage of loue* (STC 21471.5), of which he had both sold copies and sent a consignment to the nuns of Syon;[62] still more strikingly, his associate in this venture, John Gough, who had translated *The ymage*, was able to print it (STC 21472) and other more obviously reformist works under Cromwell's patronage in the 1530s. De Worde's associate Skot survived a brush with Cromwell in 1533 over the printing of a book attributed to the nun of Kent, Elizabeth Barton, the manuscript of which had been brought to him by her spiritual advisor Edward Bocking; those involved were forced to confess their crimes in a public reading at St Paul's which apparently involved copies of both the preliminary manuscript and the print.[63]

The introduction of printing undoubtedly revolutionized the business of supplying the market for service books, and for indulgences: one need only look at the lists of these in STC to gain some understanding of the scale of this change, and its implications for those employed in the manuscript book trade. Print also had an incomparably dynamic role in polemic, as the pamphlet wars of the later sixteenth century were to prove. But manuscript retained its uses. The last work of Miles Huggard, an unreformed arch-pamphleteer who had begun adult life as a hosier in Pudding Lane, was presented to Queen Mary not in the printed form used for most of his publications, but in manuscript ('A Mirroure of Myserie'; San Marino, Huntington Library MS HM 121). The poignant numbers of handwritten treatises, translations, complaints, and letters which issued from prisoners in the Tower and

[59] Alexandra Walsham, 'Preaching without Speaking: Script, Print and Religious Dissent', in *The Uses of Script and Print, 1300–1700*, ed. Julia Crick and Alexandra Walsham (Cambridge: Cambridge University Press, 2004), 211–34; see also in the same volume Thomas S. Freeman, 'Publish and Perish: The Scribal Culture of the Marian Martyrs', 235–54.

[60] William de Melton, *Sermo exhortationis* (STC 17806, ?1510): 'hunc sermone*m* legi diligenter at lectu*m* approbaui: et decreui imprimi posse sine periculo. Joannes Colet' (sig. [viij^{v}]).

[61] Susan Brigden, *London and the Reformation* (Oxford: Clarendon Press, 1989), 70.

[62] Arthur W. Reed, *Early Tudor Drama: Medwall, the Rastells, Heywood and the More Circle* (London: Methuen, 1926), 166–9.

[63] Neither copy survives, except in the form of notes made later in the sixteenth century by William Lambarde. See E. J. Devereux, 'Elizabeth Barton and Tudor Censorship', *Bulletin of the John Rylands Library*, 49 (1966–7), 91–106.

elsewhere are another reminder of the continuing vitality of manuscript production: the manuscript account of Anne Askew's experiences was smuggled out of England to be printed abroad by John Bale (STC 848), who noted 'Scripsit haec propria manu, quos & ego praefationibus ac scholiis illustravi' ('she wrote this in her own hand and I illustrated it with prefaces and notes').[64]

The transmission of another of these prison texts, a poem written in the Fleet in 1543 by Henry Howard, Earl of Surrey, effectively illustrates the continuing possibilities of coterie circulation that were to remain available to the producers and consumers of London texts. 'London hast thow accused me / of breache of lawes?' was a comic rather than poignant attempt by Surrey to justify the behaviour for which he had been briefly imprisoned—'walking in the night abowght the streets and breaking with stonebowes off certeyne wyndowes'.[65] The city of London features in this poem as a new Babylon, Surrey himself (building ludicrously on the acts of vandalism which provoked his arrest) as a scourge of God sent to strike 'thie prowd towers and turrettes hye' and extinguish sin. The work survives in a copy made for John Harington of Stepney (the Arundel Harington MS) in a volume where it keeps company with epigrams, satirical libels, translations, other poems by Surrey and by fellow Tudor courtiers like Wyatt, and such topical pieces as 'Verses made by a Catholiq; in prayse of Campion that was executed at Tyburne for Treason as ys made known by Proclamation'. Harington's access to the poem was probably fairly direct—it has been suggested that he came into possession of Surrey's papers after the latter's execution in 1547, possibly even during one of his own periods of imprisonment—and the text's circulation seems to have remained within the Harington family circle rather than reaching any wider London readership: the only other known copy is in a later family collection associated with John Harington's son (BL MS Add. 36529).[66]

While Harington was busy accumulating texts for his manuscript collection, a more obscure individual named William Samuel was occupied with the composition of scriptural translations and abridgements, and with Protestant verse tracts, all of which survive only in printed form. In a quarto pamphlet called *A warnyng for the cittie of London. That the dwellers, there in may repent their evyll lyues for*

[64] Quoted in John N. King, *English Reformation Literature: The Tudor Origins of the Protestant Tradition* (Princeton, NJ: Princeton University Press, 1982), 75; see further Oliver Wort, 'The Double Life of Anne: John Bale's *Examinations* and *Diue Anne Uitam (sic)*', *Review of English Studies*, 58 (2007), 633–56. Cf. More's letters and works copied in the Tower in 1534–5 (BL MS Royal 17.D.xiv); Sir Thomas Smith's translations of some of the Psalms (after 1551; BL MS Royal 17.A.xvii).

[65] For the text, see Ruth Hughey (ed.), *The Arundel Harington Manuscript of Tudor Poetry*, 2 vols. (Columbus, OH: Ohio State University Press, 1960), 1: 119–21 (with notes in 2: 89–90); the accusation brought by the Privy Council is quoted in Henry Howard, *The Poems of Henry Howard, Earl of Surrey*, ed. Frederick M. Padelford (Seattle: University of Washington Press, 1920), 190.

[66] Hughey, *Arundel Harington Manuscript*, 1: 63–7, where it is suggested that Harington came into possession of Surrey's papers. The copy of the poem in BL MS Add. 28635 is a nineteenth-century transcript.

feare of Goddes plages (STC 21690.8, 1550?) Samuel offers a counterpart to Surrey's address to London. But where Surrey draws on contemporary religious polemic and constructs his image of London as a new Babylon for the purposes of wit, Samuel by contrast uses the image as the starting-point for a grim series of Protestant-inflected warnings, punctuating the end of each four-line stanza with the refrain 'Repent ye sittizyns of London'.[67] Some of what is here simply echoes the conventions of traditional urban satire: London's whores and lechers, its swindlers and fashion victims, appear here as they do in *London Lickpenny*. But other details are more specific, whether those of contemporary vernacular architecture (elaborate overhanging pentices, unnecessarily fussy black paint) or of recent burnings in Smithfield ('the good creature of God, called An Askewe', for instance). Most particularly, Samuels uses London's own civic structures as the framework for his critique:

Whan dyd any Mayer knowe his juste dowtie?
Whan dyd any shereffe do his office truly?
Whan dyd any sargant use him selfe godly?
Repent ye citizyns of London.

Whan dyd any Constable see good order kepte?
Whan dyd any bedells loke to povertie that wepte?
Whan hard ye of Kepers that fro*m* crueltie slepte?
Repent ye citizyns of London. (sig. [iii^{r}])

The capacious and fluid nature of textual production in late medieval and early modern London accommodated the open printing and circulation of this piece just as it did any number of other kinds of writing: ballads, broadsheets, indulgences, libels, coterie poems, works sanctioned and unsanctioned by ecclesiastical or state authority, ancient works in new dress, legal texts, schoolbooks, service books, bibles of different kinds. Print was inevitably to establish itself as the preferred means of publication for some categories of text (works required in large quantities, like school and law books, service books, and some forms of government publication), while manuscript retained its primacy in coterie contexts and for some other specific purposes. But instances of interpenetration between the modes—whether in the form of hybrid books made up of both manuscript and printed sections, or the ways that composite printed books (*Sammelbände*) mimicked compilations of manuscript booklets, or the printing of originally 'coterie' material in contexts like Tottel's *Songes and sonettes* (STC 13860 etc., 1557)—demonstrate extraordinary imagination, not to mention commercial acumen. The range of available modes of textual production in London was large in

[67] On Samuel, see King, *English Reformation Literature*, 112–13; and Brian Cummings, 'Samuel, William (*fl.* 1551–1569)', *ODNB* (accessed 13 January 2009). His other works are STC 21690, 21690.2, 21690.4, 21690.6.

the fifteenth century, before the advent of print; by the sixteenth century (supplemented by a flourishing trade in the importation of books) it was still further extended, not least through the ways in which it responded to the challenge of a series of religious reforms of extraordinary speed and contradictoriness. Book producers were endlessly resourceful, whether in locating copy or finding forms and ways in which it might be disseminated; and the city itself—its history, topography, governance, populace—was a most fruitful subject.

FURTHER READING

Brigden, Susan. *London and the Reformation* (Oxford: Clarendon Press, 1989)

Christianson, C. Paul. 'The rise of London's book trade', in *The Cambridge History of the Book in Britain*, vol. 3: *1400–1557*, ed. Lotte Hellinga and J. B. Trapp (Cambridge University Press: Cambridge, 1999), 128–47

Lindenbaum, Sheila. 'London texts and literate practice?', in *The Cambridge History of Medieval English Literature*, ed. David Wallace (Cambridge: Cambridge University Press, 1999), 284–309

Manley, Lawrence. *Literature and Culture in Early Modern London* (Cambridge: Cambridge University Press, 1995)

PART VII

COMMUNITIES

CHAPTER 24

COMMUNITY

CATHY SHRANK*

In 1590, Edward Allde produced for John Perrin a slim quarto of thirty-six leaves containing *The Serpent of Devision . . . Whereunto is annexed the Tragedye of Gorboduc*. No author was named on the title page. Nonetheless, at least some readers would have known *Serpent* to be by John Lydgate, whose authorship was acknowledged at the end of an edition printed by Owen Rogers in 1559, while a second internal title page to *Gorboduc* ascribes the play (performed in January 1562) to Thomas Norton and Thomas Sackville.[1] The joint publication of the two works—neither of which was new in 1590—serves as a useful starting point from which to consider the extent, and nature, of the 'cultural reformations' experienced by late medieval and Tudor England. This essay examines three types of community: first, the national communities of Gorboduc's Britain and Caesar's Rome, whose fracturing we see depicted. Secondly, we have the imagined communities of readers/spectators that these texts address, as they warn against the dangers of division. Thirdly, the type of audiences these texts assume, and therefore encourage to act, tell us something about the identity of those who constitute the third community discussed, namely the *political* community—those with, or who should have, a role in ensuring the safe-keeping of the community under threat. The essay divides into three sections: first, an introduction to the often interrelated processes of religious, social, political, technological, and cultural change witnessed in the period. The second section examines the fifteenth-century *Serpent* and its revision in 1590; the

* Thanks to Dermot Cavanagh, Alex Gillespie, Mike Pincombe, Jessica Winston, Phil Withington, and participants at 'Cultural Reformations' (Harvard, September 2008) for comments on earlier drafts.

[1] As in William Griffith's 1565 edition, the first three acts are credited to Norton; the final two to Sackville; however, this attribution is not upheld by John Day's 'authorized' edition of 1570, and stylistic analysis is inconclusive on this point. When title pages of editions of *Gorboduc* refer to its performance at court on 'xviii. daye of Januarie 1561', they are using old-style dating (where the year begins on 25 March); I have amended this to new style (i.e. 1562).

final section turns to *Gorboduc*, the text with which this reworked *Serpent* was juxtaposed.

I

Undoubtedly the most far-reaching change during the 170-odd years between the composition of Lydgate's *Serpent* and its final early modern publication in 1590 was religious. Lydgate lived in a realm which adhered to the medieval church; Norton and Sackville in one where, by 1590, it was commonplace to equate Protestantism not just with loyalty to the crown but with Englishness itself. For Norton, writing in 1570 in the aftermath of the Northern Rising, 'true Christians' were synonymous with 'true English subjectes', and every 'English Papist' was not merely 'a traytor to the Queene of England' but to 'the realme of England'.[2] Yet religious reform is just one strand in a complicated weft of social and cultural changes: developments which have distinct trajectories and yet are so entangled that tugging one string warps the weave.

The difference between the cultural landscapes in which and for which *Serpent* and *Gorboduc* were produced can be illustrated in terms of their authors' institutional affiliations. Lydgate was a monk, educated at the monastery school in Bury St Edmunds, and—after studying at Oxford University—he returned to the monastery there.[3] Norton (son of a prosperous London grocer) and Sackville (later first Baron Buckhurst and first earl of Dorset) attended the Universities of Cambridge and Oxford and the Inns of Court; both went on to pursue political careers—Norton in the House of Commons, Sackville as an administrator, diplomat, and, eventually, Lord High Treasurer.[4] This difference symbolizes the shift from religious to secular educational establishments; it also highlights the rise of an administrative class, which the humanist and legal education enjoyed at the universities and Inns was designed to equip. This is not to say that medieval England lacked an administrative body: Ethan Knapp has drawn attention to the 'joint development of lay administrations and literary vernaculars' in the late fourteenth and early fifteenth century.[5] However, the increasing machinery of state over the

[2] Thomas Norton, *To the Quenes Majesties poor deceived Subjectes of the North Countrey*, in *All such treatises as have been lately published by Thomas Norton* (London: John Day, 1570), B4^{r-v}. For further evidence of Norton's Protestantism, and his acquaintance with notable reformers such as Thomas Becon, Thomas Cranmer, and William Turner, see Michael A. R. Graves, *Thomas Norton: The Parliament Man* (Oxford: Blackwell, 1994), 18–20.

[3] Derek Pearsall, 'John Lydgate (1371–1449): A Bio-bibliography', *English Literary Studies*, 71 (1997), 13; Douglas Gray, 'Lydgate, John', *ODNB* (accessed 29 April 2008).

[4] Graves, *Thomas Norton*, 17 and 27; Rivkah Zim, 'Sackville, Thomas', *ODNB* (accessed 29 April 2008).

[5] Ethan Knapp, *The Bureaucratic Muse: Thomas Hoccleve and the Literature of Late Medieval England* (University Park, PA: Pennsylvania State University Press, 2001), 6.

course of the sixteenth century intensified the demand for office-holders, as did the rapid proliferation of incorporated towns and boroughs.[6] These corporate communities enjoyed a degree of legislative autonomy from the crown; they also had numerous offices—'places'—which they needed local men to fill. Early modern England, in other words, needed people (men) to be involved in governance. This hunger for office-holders meant that those groomed for public service came from socially varied, and often humble, backgrounds. For the Elizabethan schoolmaster Richard Mulcaster, the purpose of education was that those 'which ar of the universitie' might 'serve . . . in publik functions of the common weal', and the students fittest for such a training were sons of 'the midle sorte of parentes which neither welter in to much wealthe, nor wrastle with to much want'.[7] This mobility (within a stratified society) was not simply theoretical, as the careers of Thomas Smith and Thomas Wilson demonstrate: both these Elizabethan secretaries of state rose from the provincial yeomanry via grammar school and university.[8]

Norton and Sackville thus operated in a world where the political domain had expanded. Whilst parliament certainly in no way resembled or was even destined to become a democratic body, from the Magna Carta on, it seems commonplace to comment on the ways in which it strengthened its role in law-making and financial regulation.[9] Certainly, its rhetorical authority was bolstered by the need to pass sufficiently authoritative legislation to effect Henry VIII's split from the Church of Rome in the 1530s; as Geoffrey Elton put it, 'time and again, respect for disconcerting change was demanded on the grounds that it had been agreed in Parliament'.[10] But parliament was not the only forum for political discussion. The role of the printing press in spreading religious reform has been subject to some revision in recent years. Whilst it is certainly true that reformers did not have a monopoly of the printed word, it is nonetheless evident that the dissemination of ideas was facilitated by the arrival of print.[11] Books could be produced faster, in greater

[6] Michael Braddick, *State Formation in Early Modern England, c.1550–1700* (Cambridge: Cambridge University Press, 2000); Phil Withington, *The Politics of Commonwealth: Citizens and Freemen in Early Modern England* (Cambridge: Cambridge University Press, 2005).

[7] Richard Mulcaster, *The first part of the elementarie* (London: Thomas Vautrollier, 1582), ¶2^{v}; Richard Mulcaster, *Positions wherin those primitive circumstances be examined, which are necessarie for the training up of children* (London: Thomas Vautrollier for Thomas Chard, 1581), 140.

[8] Ian W. Archer, 'Smith, Thomas'; Susan Doran and Jonathan Woolfson, 'Wilson, Thomas'; both cited from *ODNB* (accessed 29 April 2008).

[9] Alfred L. Brown, *The Governance of Late Medieval England, 1272–1461* (London: Arnold, 1989), 156–237.

[10] Geoffrey R. Elton, *Reform and Renewal: Thomas Cromwell and the Commonweal* (Cambridge: Cambridge University Press, 1973), 66–7.

[11] For the perceived importance, at the time, of books—especially printed books—to processes of Reformation, see Brian Cummings, 'Reformed Literature and Literature Reformed', in *The Cambridge History of Medieval English Literature*, ed. David Wallace (Cambridge: Cambridge University Press, 1999), 821–51.

numbers, at lower prices, and evangelicals such as John Bale and John Foxe were not slow to salute the new technology—'this mooste worthye science'—for its perceived role in advancing the 'true' faith.[12] With its talismanic stress on the written word and vernacular worship, reformed religion also contributed to increased levels of literacy among significant sections of the population.[13]

All the indications are that Lydgate's *Serpent* circulated within relatively limited and elite circles: two of the four remaining manuscripts are on vellum.[14] That alone reveals little: documents on vellum have a much greater survival rate (partly because of the durability of the material, partly because of their value, and therefore the care with which they are kept). Nonetheless, the remarkable consistency of the four manuscript witnesses also points to a small circulation. As none of the extant manuscripts are contemporaneous with the composition of the work, the paucity of major variants would imply that they are copied from a common ancestor, and that—with few copies disseminated—its readership must have been necessarily limited (in contrast to a near-contemporaneous text like Thomas Hoccleve's *Regiment of Princes*, the survival of which in over forty manuscripts—ranging from the 'magnificent' to the 'small, unadorned'—points to an audience 'by no means restricted to the circle of Prince Henry's intimates', for whom it had originally been composed).[15] Norton and Sackville belonged to an age where the written word had proliferated still further and access to it broadened. The possibilities of print not only fuelled religious Reformation (and Counter-Reformation), that is: they also enabled and cultivated a more extensive discursive domain, as pamphlets and broadsides publicly debated affairs of state, engaging readers beyond the political elite and closed doors of court and parliament.[16]

This discursiveness was also fed by another fundamental change in the political milieu inhabited by Lydgate in the 1420s, and by Norton and Sackville in the second half of the sixteenth century: namely, the rise of the vocabulary and rhetoric of 'commonweal'. The term dominates socio-political discourse in Tudor England, employed (often simultaneously) both as a synonym for 'realm' and to denote a state in which government serves the interests of the whole polity. Yet, as David

[12] John Foxe, *Actes and Monuments of these latter and perillous dayes* (London: John Day, 1563), 362, <http://www.hrionline.ac.uk/johnfoxe> (accessed 8 May 2008). Cf. John Bale, *The laboryouse Journey & serche of Johan Leylande* (London: Stephen Mierdman for John Bale, 1549), C2^{r}.

[13] Ian Green, *Print and Protestantism in Early Modern England* (Oxford: Oxford University Press, 2000), 26–7.

[14] Fitzwilliam Museum, McLean MS 181; Magdalene College, Cambridge, Pepys MS 2006.

[15] Nicholas Perkins, *Hoccleve's 'Regiment of Princes': Counsel and Constraint* (Cambridge: D.S. Brewer, 2001), 151–2, and 190.

[16] Cathy Shrank, 'Trollers and Dreamers: Defining the Citizen-Subject in Sixteenth-Century Cheap Print', *Yearbook of English Studies*, 38 (2008), 102–18; Cathy Shrank, '1553', in *Oxford History of Popular Print*, ed. Joad Raymond, vol. 1 (Oxford: Oxford University Press, forthcoming).

Starkey demonstrates, the word was scarcely used before 1450.[17] 'Common profit' was regularly invoked, but that is not quite the same thing as 'commonweal', with its convenient ability both to mean 'common good' and to stand in for the polity itself. Strikingly, though, in the last forty years of the fifteenth century, 'commonweal' rapidly became the preferred term. Crucially, this newly dominant ideology of commonweal invited and legitimated political participation—be it through the metaphors of ship and body used to explain and analyse it (whereby keeping the ship/body safe entails the full, if varied, involvement of all)—or through the valorization of debate as the best means of deciding policy, found in the writings of humanist statesmen-scholars such as Thomas Smith. As Norton himself stated in the House of Commons, 'in consultacions convenient it is to have contrary opinions, contrary reasoninges and contradiccions, thereby the rather to wrest out the best'.[18] 'Commonweal', that is, embodies a sense of community: the government of a polity which calls itself a commonweal should be in the interest of the wider community, but in turn, the health of that polity is only maintained by the proper contribution of the people who comprise it. It is against this backdrop of socio-political, as much as religious, change that this essay considers the ways in which *Serpent* and *Gorboduc* construct the imperilled communities they depict.

II

Lydgate's *Serpent of Division* probably dates from 1422.[19] Produced, the author's valedictory remarks inform us, 'bi commaundement of my moste worschipfull maistere & sovereyne',[20] it was possibly commissioned by Humphrey, Duke of Gloucester, Lord Protector, as a vernacular counterpart to the Latin life of Henry V,

[17] David Starkey, 'Which Age of Reform?', in *Revolution Reassessed: Revisions in the History of Tudor Government and Administration*, ed. Christopher Coleman and David Starkey (Oxford: Clarendon Press, 1986), 14–27. Cf. Paul Strohm, *Politique: Languages of Statecraft between Chaucer and Shakespeare* (Notre Dame, IN: University of Notre Dame Press, 2005), 13–15. The *MED* cites one example *c.*1400; the next usage cited is *c.*1450: *MED*, 'Communewele', sense 'b'. I am also indebted here to John Watts, 'Common weal to commonwealth', presented at 'Early Modern Texts', Virtual Research Environment, 14 November 2007.

[18] *Proceedings in the Parliaments of Elizabeth I*, Vol. 1: *1558–1581*, ed. T. E. Hartley (Leicester: Leicester University Press, 1981), 241.

[19] For a summary of arguments regarding dating, see Maura B. Nolan, 'The Art of History Writing: Lydgate's *Serpent of Division*', *Speculum*, 78 (2003), 99–127, at n. 100. BL MS Add. 48031A gives two dates on 175^{v}: the first (presumably correct, due to internal evidence) dates it, 'the month of decembre, the Firste yere of oure souvereigne Lorde that now ys king henry the .vi^{te}' (i.e. 1422); since the second is in Roman numerals ('M^{l} iiii^{C}', i.e. 1400), it may be that the copyist has mistakenly left the date unfinished.

[20] John Lydgate, *The Serpent of Division*, ed. Henry Noble MacCracken (London: Henry Frowde, 1911), 66. Unless otherwise stated, quotations will be from this edition.

then being produced by Gloucester's secretary, Tito Livio.[21] Certainly, by 1422 Lydgate had a patronage relationship with Gloucester, as his poem on Gloucester's marriage to Jacqueline of Hainault that same year evidences.[22] As *Serpent* charts the collapse of the Roman republic, its warnings against civil discord hold particular resonance in the years immediately following Henry V's premature death, when he left a nine-month-old heir (the future Henry VI) and power divided—as in the late republican Rome described by Lydgate—between a triumvirate comprising two of Henry VI's uncles—Gloucester, and John, Duke of Bedford—and his great-uncle, Cardinal Henry Beaufort, Bishop of Winchester. The subsequent uncertainty created by quarrels between Gloucester and both Bedford and Beaufort, and then the internecine struggles of the 'Wars of the Roses' (1455–85) ensured that the text, which warns repeatedly how 'every kingdome b[y] division is conveied to his distruccion', maintained an unfortunate pertinence over the ensuing decades (50).

Three of the four surviving manuscripts place *Serpent* amongst works which concur with its self-categorization as 'a mirror' for 'wise governours' (65). Fitzwilliam Museum McLean MS 181 sets it alongside envoys from *The Fall of Princes*, a version of *The Governance of Kings and Princes* (both by Lydgate) and Hoccleve's *Regiment*; Harvard Houghton MS Eng 530 sees it juxtaposed with *The Governance of Princes* and *Brut*; and in BL MS Add. 48031A, it rubs shoulders with political papers—letters patent, diplomatic correspondence, details of Richard, Duke of York's claim to the throne—and advice for princes, such as its immediate companion, 'The xxij right wisnesses belonging to a kyng', possibly by Sir John Fortescue (164^{v}–165^{r}). The exception is Magdalene College Pepys MS 2006, where it features in a more literary collection, alongside Chaucer and some of Lydgate's poetry. The regular transcription of *Serpent* into collections of advice literature reflects an understandable fifteenth-century anxiety about civil discord. This same concern struck a deep chord with sixteenth-century readers, as they experienced the turmoil of Reformation and Counter-Reformation, which pitted evangelicals and papists against each other, and (in the later Elizabethan period) lived under the shadow of an unsettled succession. *Serpent* consequently saw four sixteenth-century imprintings: a lost edition by Peter Treverys (*c.*1530),[23] by Robert Redman (*c.*1535), Rogers in 1559, and Allde in 1590.

Despite its title, the ruinous effects of division—or the responsibility of the senators, knights, or people of Rome to eschew it—are curiously missing from much of Lydgate's narrative. There is one key scene, set in the forum (a site embodying community), where a philosopher demonstrates the dangers of

21 Walter F. Schirmer, *John Lydgate*, trans. Ann E. Keep (London: Metheun, 1961), 82.

22 Gray, 'Lydgate', *ODNB*. Cf. Larry Scanlon and James Simpson (eds.), *John Lydgate: Poetry, Culture, and Lancastrian England* (Notre Dame, IN: Notre Dame University Press, 2006).

23 A fragment of Treverys's edition is transcribed in Egerton Brydges, *Censura Literaria*, 10 vols. (London: Longman, 1805–1809), 9: 369–72.

division by challenging the strongest man in Rome to pull out a horse's tail; whilst he cannot do it in one, the 'meanest beggar' successfully plucks it bare, by removing the hairs one by one (59). For much of the text, Lydgate's moralizing targets not so much division as the cardinal sins which cause it: Caesar's 'ambicious pride'; Pompey's 'envie'; Crassus's 'covetise' (65). The focus is on important men, not the community harmed by their actions. By the envoy, the text teeters towards a version of history in which the rise and fall of great ones is almost inevitable: 'Hit is full hard in fortune to assure,/ Here whele so ofte turnith up and downe' (66).

That Lydgate tells the history of great men is highlighted by comparing *Serpent* to Lucan's *Pharsalia*, from which the material is ultimately derived (via French sources). Book 1 of *Pharsalia* gives a vivid portrait of a crumbling civilization—cities deserted, houses crumbling, fields unploughed.[24] The power struggles of the triumvirs that ensue are thus framed by a reminder of the ultimate victims of civil discord. However, if Lucan's verse attends to this universal distress, it also exposes the people's answerability for it. 'Why this rage, citizens, this great desire for war?' the poem demands: 'does it please you to fight [civil] wars that can win no triumphs?' ('Quis furor, o cives, quae tanta licentia ferri?/ . . . Bella geri placuit nullos habitura triumphos', 1.8–12). The absence of this same sense of wider accountability in Lydgate's text—that others besides Caesar and Pompey play a part—is momentarily exposed in the 1590 edition, where unlike the fifteenth-century manuscripts and earlier imprints, Lady Rome's oration at the Rubicon is addressed to the army as a whole. The directive 'to Julius' omitted, she appeals to plural 'hartes' (B3^{r}), not a single Julian 'herte' (56). Similarly, the 1590 version accentuates the cost of discord for the populace at large, through the way in which the final paragraphs—in which *Serpent* finally acknowledges 'the dethe . . . of many a thowsande other more than I can tell' (65)—are gathered under the heading 'The Conclusion' and distinguished from the main text by appearing in Roman rather than black letter type (C4^{r}). Since the 1590 text also ignores the envoy,[25] the effect is to make the endpoint the impact of civil war and the fate of Rome and its inhabitants, rather than Pompey and Caesar, subject to the whirligig of Fortune's wheel.

This attempt to shift the focus from the doings and decisions of great men to the responsibility of, and effect on, the community is one indication that the 1590 edition has departed from its predecessors (in manuscript and print). Both the 1535 and 1559 imprints are sold to us as texts bearing a generally applicable moral. The 1559 title page makes no mention of Rome; rather, 'The Serpent of division' is something 'whych hath ever bene yet the chefest undoer of any Region or Citie'. The 1535 title page similarly pushes this universal message, announcing 'the

[24] Lucan, *Lucan*, ed. James D. Duff (Cambridge, MA: Harvard University Press, 1951), 1: 24–9.

[25] The envoy is also missing in the BL and Harvard manuscripts.

damage and Destruction in Realmes/ caused by the Serpente of Division'. In contrast, rather than conveying this sense of a universal pattern or endlessly repeating design, the 1590 title page stresses the analogy that Rome offers: it is a 'mappe'—'a detailed representation in epitome'—from which its readers are invited to learn.[26]

The 1559 edition also stresses its faithfulness to a manuscript witness: the work is 'set forth after the Auctours old copy/ by J. S.' (probably the antiquarian John Stow, who also edited Chaucer).[27] The 1590 editor sheds that appeal to aged authenticity: rather than staking his authority on his fidelity to an earlier text, he plays fast and loose with Lydgate's prose, producing a thoroughly modernized text. As George Puttenham recommends, 'our makar... at these dayes shall not follow *Piers plowman* nor *Gower* nor *Lydgate* nor yet *Chaucer*, for their language is now out of use with us.'[28] Words which, by 1590, risked sounding archaic are consistently removed: 'surquedous'/'surquedrance' is deleted or replaced four times; 'manner' and 'effect' are seven times substituted for 'wise', which is eradicated altogether on two further occasions; the emphatic 'full' (as in 'ful advisedly') is omitted eleven times, and twice changed for other intensifiers ('most', 'arch'). Other antiquated vocabulary eliminated includes 'stondmele', 'gwerdon', and 'platly'. Double negatives are struck out six times; double superlatives ('most fairest', 'most highest') twice; 'the which', six times (replaced by 'which' or 'who'). Tautology is avoided: Lydgate uses the phrase 'manly man' seven times; the 1590 editor once, substituting synonyms for 'man' such as 'warriour' or 'victor'. Elsewhere, diction is made more Latinate ('splendent' replaces 'flouring'; 'turned into' is 'converted'; 'not devided' becomes 'conjoined'; 'stock', 'progeny'). The syntax is also made more varied, deploying more dependent clauses to avoid Lydgate's paratactic prose.

The liberties taken with Lydgate's text extend to more than localized tweakings of vocabulary or syntax. Revisions to the 1590 *Serpent* suggest a different attitude to the material. Perhaps bowing to a sense of national pride, for example, the ancient Britons receive a consistently more favourable write-up.[29] The bonds of Britain are made 'beautious' in 1590 (A4^{r}); Caesar cannot 'vanquish the least part', let alone all of the Britons; this 'foresaid Cassybelan [Cassivellaunus]' (51) is redescribed as 'this woorthy Brittaine king'; and whereas in earlier versions 'Britons' are told that they 'ought ful wel to complaine' of the death of Cassivellaunus's brother (51), the 1590 editor assures us that they 'mourned many a day' (A4^{v}). Lydgate's frequent

[26] *OED, Map,* n. *def.* II. †5.a. *fig.* <http://dictionary.oed.com> (accessed 16 November 2008).

[27] William Ringler, 'Lydgate's *Serpent of Division,* 1559, edited by John Stow', *Studies in Bibliography,* 14 (1961), 201–3.

[28] [George Puttenham], *The Arte of English Poesie* (London: Richard Field, 1589), R2^{v}.

[29] For the investment of writers such as Bale and John Leland in the recovery of a British past, see Cathy Shrank, *Writing the Nation in Reformation England, 1530–1580* (Oxford: Oxford University Press, 2004), especially 69–90; Philip Schwyzer, *Literature, Nationalism, and Memory in Early Modern England and Wales* (Cambridge: Cambridge University Press, 2004).

asides on the transience of life and fickleness of fame and prosperity are recurrently pruned, not just by excluding the envoy with its meditations on fortune's wheel, but throughout the text. Where previous versions made Crassus's death an exemplum—'Lo here ye may considryn and se the schorte and the momentay[rie] tyme, transitorie and not abidynge, of *all* th[ese] werreowrs' (52)—in 1590, it becomes the 'momentary end of *this* covetous warriour', alone (A4^{v}, emphases added). Elsewhere, digressions on transience or contrarious fortune are simply stripped out, reducing the impression of *de casibus* tragedy and placing more direct responsibility on the choices made by the protagonists.[30]

The 1590 text also displays a different attitude to authority. As Maura Nolan argues, Lydgate's 'five invocations—Lucan, Eusebius, Vincent, Valerius, and Chaucer—reveal far less about the background of *Serpent of Division* than about Lydgate's vision of cultural authority'.[31] In the same light, the 1590 editor's perception of cultural authority is demonstrated by the way he sloughs off the habit of appealing to others' expertise. He repeatedly cuts tags such as 'as seithe myne auctowre' (51), 'as the stori rehersith' (52), or 'bi discripcioun of Auctours' (62). He happily cites alleged sources by name, but the relationship with these predecessors is less subservient: Lucan is just 'Lucan' (B2^{v}), not 'myne autoure Lucan' (55); Chaucer is 'famous and worthy' (C3^{v}) rather than 'my maistere Chaucere' (65); and no reference is made to 'clerkis' to justify introducing a phrase such as 'Bellum Civile' (56).

These alterations do not just tell us about the editor. They also reveal information about his anticipated readership: his community of readers. He expects them to take pride in a British past, to be sufficiently *au fait* with Roman history to know what augurs are (C1^{v}), and to follow his prose without the crutch of signposting words and phrases like 'foresaid' or 'as is specified to forne' (thirteen such expressions are removed). Thanks to the greater amount of paratextual material in the 1590 edition, this community of readers is also made much more present than in earlier versions.

The type of readers addressed in 1590 is indicated by the title page, where six lines of verse sum up *Serpent*, concluding '*England* take heede, such chaunce to thee may come:/ *Foelix quem faciunt aliena pericula cautum*' ('happy the man made cautious by other people's misfortunes'). The Latin here works in two ways. First, it requires that readers understand it; without that, the admonitory poem remains incomplete, although those with rustier, schoolroom Latin are aided by the fact that the quotation is proverbial. Secondly, the motto links the 1590 *Serpent* to *The*

[30] Compare, for example, 1559, A5^{v} (on 'contrary and perverse' fortune) with 1590, A3^{r}; and 1559, B5^{r} (on 'the blossomes of transitorie riches') with 1590, B2^{v}. For the emergence, in the second half of the fifteenth century, of statecraft that equipped princes to master Fortune, see Strohm, *Politique: Languages of Statecraft.*

[31] Nolan, 'Art of History Writing', 106.

Mirror for Magistrates (a collaborative work to which Thomas Sackville contributed), whose title page it adorned in all editions from 1559 to 1578. Openly indebted to another of Lydgate's works (*The Fall of Princes*), the *Mirror* shares *Serpent*'s vilification of ambition as the major vice in office-holders because it is detrimental to the community—the 'common weale'—they should tend; the audience the *Mirror* conceives, however, comprises not just 'the noblitye' but 'all other in office'.[32]

In view of this explicit acknowledgement that political power and responsibility extend beyond the aristocracy, it is significant that the 1590 edition, which aligns itself with the *Mirror*, portrays the Roman senate as a legislative body, like the English parliament: it is described as an 'assembly' (B1^{r}) rather than the more ambiguous 'court' (53), and the formula 'the assent of senate' is three times rewritten as 'assent and decree', inserting a reference to its status as a law-making institution. Unlike all previous versions, the 1590 text also places 'citizens' at that symbolic scene in the forum, where the wise philosopher demonstrates the dangers of division through the example of the horse's tail. The term is not used to identify all Romans, however, but to differentiate 'citizens' from the 'Lords' with whom they gather (B4^{v}). As such, it is used—as it was in sixteenth-century England—to denote enfranchised inhabitants of incorporated towns and cities, and (in the light of the stress on wide political participation) proves a suggestive variant to the more predictable formula 'Lords and Commons'.[33]

The 1590 editor's assumption of politically capable and (at least moderately) learned readers is borne out by the prefatory material unique to this version (the others plunge straight into *Serpent* itself). Opening with an erudite, if convoluted, comparison of the act of publishing Caesar's story to Darius's dishonouring of Alexander, and composed in long, periodic sentences, the preface indicates from the outset the sophisticated reader it desires. The cautionary verse on the title page notwithstanding, the tone established initially seems far from urgent; England might be 'in danger and dread' (A2^{v}), but that is not going to impede an elegant turn of phrase. The preface risks pulling in contrary directions. On the one hand, it evokes a leisurely atmosphere in which its 'Gentlemen Readers'—whose social status depends on their ability to 'live idly'[34]—might 'sit... downe and patiently with a Mer-maides eye peruse this small volume'. On the other, what begins as an invitation to unhurried pleasure transmutes into an instruction to 'compare our state with Romes'. Yet the urbane manner endorses, rather than conflicts with, the political message. As the preface recurrently addresses its audience in terms of

[32] William Baldwin, *A Myrroure for Magistrates* (London: Thomas Marshe, 1559), A1^{r}, [uncial C] 2^{r}. This dedication remained in all editions until 1610.

[33] Thomas Smith, *De Republica Anglorum* (London: Henry Middleton for Gregory Seton, 1583), E3^{r}. Cf. Withington, *Politics of Commonwealth*.

[34] Smith, *De Republica Anglorum*, E2^{r}.

sociability—as 'gentle and frendly' (A2^{r}) and 'affable' (A2^{v}), framing them as social equals with the familiar pronouns 'thee' and 'thou'—it deploys terms which are the very antidote of the discord against which the book seeks to warn. The toleration readers are then asked to extend to the work—regarding it indulgently, with a 'Mer-maides eye'—symbolizes the sort of generosity and understanding which mitigates against contention.[35]

The self-conscious blend of seemingly otiose learning and political seriousness found in the 1590 preface is reminiscent of Day's address, 'The P[rinter] to the reader', in his 1570 edition of *Gorboduc*, in which Norton and Sackville's text—now entitled *The Tragidie of Ferrex and Porrex*—is presented as a fallen woman, shamefully undone by her previous, unscrupulous printer (William Griffith). Despite Day's insistence that he has rescued the text from the 'disfigured' state of its previous imprinting (A2^{r}), his text is almost identical to Griffith's 1565 edition, bar the title prioritizing Gorboduc's fratricidal sons and the omission of eight lines advocating non-resistance to tyrants.[36] Day's preface—like that of the 1590 *Serpent/Gorboduc*—seeks a novel way of requesting the benevolence of its readers, imagined here as an 'honest companie', who will welcome the text and not reproach her 'with her former missehap'. Yet in the process, the analogy constructed serves more than the immediate purpose for which it was designed (namely, begging readers' goodwill). Day frames the text as 'Lucrece', who, if rebuked, will 'of her self die for shame'. In doing so, he conjures the foundational moment of the Roman republic; Lucrece's suicide is the catalyst which provokes an elite, male group to action.[37] On one level, Day's evocation of Lucrece is *de trop*; on the other, to humanistically trained readers it immediately suggests a collective responsibility (among men of a certain sphere) to act on behalf of the wider community. The readerships of both the 1570 and 1590 texts, in other words, are fashioned as a select company of like-minded, like-educated men: men with leisure time, who are also obliged to serve the state.

Serpent and *Gorboduc* are consequently linked, as the 1590 edition recognizes, by their common concern to alert readers to the perils of division. They also share an assumption that, in dealing with affairs of state, the audience they engage is predominantly male, although, in 1590—long into the reign of a queen who often proved obdurate to men's advice—this gendering of politics as masculine needs to be made overt. The next section examines the ways in which different

[35] The phrase is uncommon, but does appear in Christopher Marlowe's *Dido, Queen of Carthage*, when Dido asks Anna to dissuade Aeneas from leaving. *Dido* was not printed until 1594, so possibly the author of the 1590 preface is remembering the lines 'Call him not wicked, sister, speak him fair,/ And look upon him with a mermaid's eye', out of context, so that the mermaid's eye becomes forgiving, rather than seductive (Christopher Marlowe, *The Complete Plays*, ed. Mark Thornton Burnett [London: J. M. Dent, 1999], 5.200–1).

[36] Graves, *Thomas Norton*, 118.

[37] See Stephanie H. Jed, *Chaste Thinking: The Rape of Lucretia and the Birth of Humanism* (Bloomington: Indiana University Press, 1989).

versions of *Gorboduc* invoke this political community, before returning to the question of how *Serpent* is inflected by its juxtaposition with this mid-Tudor text.

III

Gorboduc, like *King Lear*, tells the story of a monarch who abdicates, dividing his dominions between his offspring, with disastrous results for him, his family, and his former realm. (Not insignificantly, both narratives are drawn from Geoffrey of Monmouth's *Historia Regum Britanniae*, to which Tudor writers repeatedly returned when they wanted to understand their present through the prism of their past.[38]) From the outset, *Gorboduc* stresses the dangers of a fractured community. The opening dumb show, which introduces the play as well as the first act it precedes, enacts a scene analogous to that of the horse's tail in *Serpent* (reprinted two years earlier in 1559), as six wild men demonstrate how faggots—indestructible when 'conjoyned'—are 'easilie' broken 'beynge severed'.[39]

This initial stress on strength-through-unity is endorsed by the ensuing drama, which is punctuated by the term *kind* and its cognates (kindliness, kindly, unkind, and so on): there are five instances on the opening leaf of Act 1 alone (A3^{r-v}), firmly establishing the importance of the concept. What we see, though, is the repeated violation of kind, the unnaturalness of civil discord emphasized by the fact that the wider national story is depicted through the tale of a family destroying itself—brother assassinating brother, mother slaying son—just as the people will kill their rightful king, 'the father of our common weale' (A8^{v}).[40] Videna, Gorboduc's murderous queen, holds a perverted mirror to '*Brittaine* Land the Mother of ye all' (E1^{v}). In the mouth of Mandud, duke of Leogris, the motif appeals to a complex set of affective bonds:

> Yet now the common mother of us all
> Our native land, our country that containes
> Our wives, children, kindred, our selves and all
> That ever is or may be dear to man,
> Cries unto us to help our selves and her. (E1^{r})

The double figuring of familial love and duty—the motherland and kin that, womb-like, she enfolds—intensifies Mandud's emotive plea. Moreover, those

[38] Helen Cooper, *The English Romance in Time: Transforming Motifs from Geoffrey of Monmouth to the Death of Shakespeare* (Oxford: Oxford University Press, 2004), 23–4.

[39] Thomas Norton and Thomas Sackville, *The Tragedie of Gorboduc* (London: William Griffith, 1565), A2^{v}. Unless otherwise stated, quotations will be from this edition.

[40] For an examination of the interplay between *oikos* and *polis*, see James Emmanuel Berg, '*Gorboduc* as a Tragic Discovery of "Feudalism"', *Studies in English Literature, 1500–1900*, 40 (2000), 199–226.

addressed are both called upon for, and in need of aid—a basic trope of commonweal rhetoric, whereby the failing of the body politic or the floundering of the ship of state is to the detriment of all. Limbs cannot survive without the body; the vessel sinks with all on board.

The exemplum offered by the 'torne estate' (E2^{r}) of Gorboduc's former realm is all the more striking because the native soil is that of the audience too. As Nolan indicates, when composing *Serpent*, Lydgate added material about Britain, 'making it relevant to English readers'.[41] Lydgate also ensures that this interpolation acts as a reflection, in miniature, of the piece as a whole, by blaming the Britons' defeat on dissension between Cassivellaunus and the duke of Cornwall. Indeed, it is in the dismembering of Cassivellaunus's heroic brother—'rofe . . . atweyne' (51)—that we see the destruction of the body politic fleetingly figured—a mutilation still more explicit in 1590, where Caesar's death blow (which seals the Britons' fate) 'clave his bodye in partes' (A4^{v}). Norton and Sackville move the entire sphere of action close to home, lending the story of the maimed community added pathos because it happened here, in this land. Certainly the sufferings of the people receive more attention than in *Serpent*, as in Mandud's depiction of the unnatural fruits born of civil war: 'the wide and hugie [sic] fieldes/ With bloud & bodie spred . . . / The lustie trees clothed with corpses dead' (D8^{v}). The effect of witnessing the unkindness rife within, and enacted upon, one's ancestors and motherland is especially resonant when we consider that the first performance, at the Inner Temple on Twelfth Night 1562, was part of a festival—the annual Christmas revels—celebrated through feasting (the epitome of community) as well as theatrical entertainments, the production of which would have been a communal and collaborative act.[42] This is not to see community through rose-tinted spectacles. Communities are established by exclusion as well as inclusion.[43] The merrymaking at the Inner Temple in winter 1561–2 carried a particularly triumphant note because it also marked the end of an argument between the Inner and Middle Temples about the jurisdiction of a subsidiary inn of chancery, Lyons Inn, which—due to the mediation of Elizabeth I's favourite Robert Dudley, earl of Leicester—the Inner Temple had retained; to thank him for his support, Dudley was appointed lord of misrule at the subsequent festivities.[44]

The particular circumstances of these revels remind us that *Gorboduc*'s various audiences and readers belonged to no single community. When the Innsmen observed the warning against division performed in their hall, it was both as

[41] Nolan, 'Art of History Writing', 120.

[42] Jessica Winston, 'Expanding the Political Nation: *Gorboduc* at the Inns of Court and Succession Revisited', *Early Theatre*, 8 (2005), 11–34, at 1–16.

[43] Phil Withington and Alexandra Shepard, 'Introduction', in *Communities in Early Modern England*, ed. Withington and Shepard (Manchester: Manchester University Press, 2000), 1–15, at 6–7.

[44] Winston, 'Expanding the Political Nation', 13–14.

members of an institution which had recently resolved a dispute, and of a realm they expected to serve. The tragedy would have a different, additional context for them than for the 'm[a]ny of the [privy] conselle' present as their guests.[45] It would have a different context again when replayed, twelve days later, at court for Elizabeth herself. Indeed, the openness of drama to subjective interpretation is demonstrated by an eyewitness account of the Inner Temple performance, which focuses on three of the five dumb shows. The message derived from the second dumb show in particular is remarkably precise, and at odds with the interpretation provided by the chorus and prose description ('the order and signification of the domme shewe') in all three printed editions (1565, 1570, 1590). The mime depicts a king refusing a glass of wine offered by a 'grave and aged Gentilman', instead accepting 'a Cup of Golde filled with poison', presented by 'a brave and lustie yong Gentleman'; drinking this, the king dies (B3^{r}). Where both the prose explanation and chorus (C1^{r}) explain that the liquid in the gold goblet represents flattery while the transparent glass symbolises good counsel (clarification underscored by the fact that the glass is proffered by an archetype of mature experience), the anonymous spectator declares that it signifies 'howe that men refused the certen and toocke the uncerten, wherby was ment that yt was better for the Quene to marye with the L[ord] R[obert, i.e Dudley] knowen th[a]n with the K[ing] of Sweden', in the early 1560s both candidates for Elizabeth's hand.[46] One potential justification for the discrepancy is that a more pro-Dudleian version was performed at the Inner Temple, where Dudley was guest of honour.[47] Yet you do not necessarily need a different text to produce different interpretations, just a different set of eyes, ears, beliefs, or circumstances.

That the situation in which a work is presented can alter its reception is demonstrated by Day's 1570 publication of *Gorboduc*. In the immediate aftermath of the Northern Rising—which sought to release Mary Queen of Scots from imprisonment and restore the old faith, with her as sovereign—the figure of Fergus, the double-dealing duke of Albany (i.e. Scotland), assumes added significance, as he works to subdue Britain not just by conquest but by 'secret practise' (D7^{r}). Jacqueline Vanhoutte has stressed *Gorboduc*'s stigmatization of 'foreign interlopers' and emphasis on native birth as a prerequisite for rightful rulers,[48]

[45] Henry Machyn, *The Diary of Henry Machyn*, ed. John Gough Nichols, Camden Society Publications, 42 (London: J. B. Nichols and Son, 1848), 273–4; cited in Winston, 'Expanding the Political Nation', 14.

[46] BL MS Add. 48023, 359^{v}, cited in Henry James and Greg Walker, 'The Politics of *Gorboduc*', *English Historical Review*, 110 (1995), 109–21, at 112–13.

[47] James and Walker, 'Politics of *Gorboduc*', 120–1; but see also Mike Pincombe, 'Robert Dudley, *Gorboduc*, and "The masque of Beauty and Desire": A Reconsideration of the Evidence for Political Intervention', *Parergon*, 20 (2003), 19–44.

[48] Jacqueline Vanhoutte, 'Community, Authority, and the Motherland in Sackville and Norton's "Gorboduc"', *Studies in English Literature, 1500–1900*, 40 (2000), 227–39, at 235.

and Englishness was at this period becoming increasingly equated with Protestantism (as Norton's own statement about 'true subjectes' reveals). Yet the play not only reflects how national identities calcified along religious lines: it participates in that process. Day issued it in two formats: singly, or bound into *All such treatises as have been lately published by Thomas Norton*, a collection of tracts lambasting the Northern rebels and papistry. The company the play here keeps styles it too as a work demonstrating the threat from the north and from Catholicism, helping to propagate a sense that proper Englishmen were loyal Protestants; community is thus established by excluding foreigners *and* those so-called Englishmen and women who owed allegiance to a foreign potentate, the pope. In a similar vein, it is pertinent that the only publication of *Gorboduc* between 1590 and the nineteenth century was in 1736, as support grew for Charles Stuart (the Young Pretender) and the Porteous Riot in Edinburgh that April was regarded by many as a Jacobite plot.

Gorboduc, then—like *Serpent*—offers 'a Myrrour... to Princes all' (B3^{r}), demonstrating the same interest in political literature evinced by Sackville's 'Induction' and 'Complaint of Buckingham', which appeared in the 1563 *Mirror for Magistrates*. Yet the message in the glass varies, depending on the political landscape it reflects. If in 1570 and 1736, it depicted papists invading from the north, then probably in 1590—with Elizabeth well past childbearing years—it would have been the play's emphasis on the uncertain succession resulting from 'want of Issue' (A1^{v}) that loomed largest. *Gorboduc*'s political valency is not confined to one topic, and despite recurrent critical interest in *Gorboduc* as a play about whom Elizabeth should marry, it is more illuminating to view it, following Dermot Cavanagh, as a 'critical meditation' on counsel itself.[49] Cavanagh's choice of the adjective 'critical' is revealing: counsel is not idealized. *Gorboduc* shows no illusions about the fallibility of monarchs, but it is equally candid about the impotence of counsellors—usually presented in Tudor political theory as the necessary check and balance to monarchical incompetence—to do anything about this.[50] Gorboduc's blind faith in the power of advisers to curb his sons is shown to be fatally misguided. Well-meaning men, such as Arostus (signifying 'weak') or Philander ('philanthropist'), give bad advice; sound opinions—those of Eubulus ('good counsellor')—go unregarded; counsellors are impotent if those they warn will not listen; and rulers are vulnerable to flattery, the bogeyman of Tudor politics.[51]

49 See, for example, William R. Orwen, 'Spenser and the *Serpent of Division*', *Studies in Philology*, 38 (1941), 198–210; Marie Axton, *The Queen's Two Bodies: Drama and the Elizabethan Succession* (London: Royal Historical Society, 1977), 11–25, 38–72; James and Walker, 'Politics of *Gorboduc*'; Dermot Cavanagh, *Language and Politics in the Sixteenth-Century History Play* (Basingstoke: Palgrave Macmillan, 2003), 43.

50 Shrank, *Writing the Nation*, 164–5, 168–9. For the importance of counsel to late fourteenth- and fifteenth-century political thought, see Perkins, *Hoccleve's 'Regiment of Princes'*, 61–70.

51 See Kevin Dunn, 'Representing Counsel: *Gorboduc* and the Elizabethan Privy Council', *English Literary Renaissance*, 33 (2003), 279–308.

Gorboduc is not a play on which Lorna Hutson focuses in her account of how the participatory nature of the English judicial system impacted on the development of English drama, but it could have been—and its primary audience was, of course, legally trained.[52] *Gorboduc*'s audience is given an active role, weighing up different advice and advice-givers. An attentive listener/reader, for example, might note that the concept of commonweal is missing from Act 2, scene 1, an absence all the more stark because of the frequency with which the word occurred in the previous scene, when Gorboduc and his counsellors—however wrong-headedly—at least considered their duty to the 'tender care of commen weale' (A6^{v}). As the obsequious hanger-on Hermon goads Ferrex to provoke his brother, the loyal counsellor Dordan plays into his hands. Trying to placate Ferrex, by arguing that his half of the realm is sufficient, Dordan reduces the language of weal (well-being and prosperity) into one of riches alone, affluence which furthermore belongs to the monarch: Ferrex's portion has 'abounding store / Of things that serve to make a welthie realme'; 'in flowing welth', it 'dooth passe the double value of the part / That *Porrex* hath' (B4^{r-v}).

Gorboduc's use of dialogue is a crucial factor in casting the audience in an adjudicatory role. Where *Serpent* features orations, not conversations, and 'debate' is used solely in the negative sense of 'strife', *Gorboduc* places discussion at the heart of its depiction of governance. The difference is not purely generic: plenty of mid-Tudor plays (for example, those by Bale), make statements rather than stage deliberations. *Gorboduc* also leaves the audience space to assess the contrary opinions propounded, to notice that history (for example, Brutus's division of the kingdom) can be used to support conflicting arguments (A7^{r}, B1^{r}). Admittedly, audience responses are to some extent prescribed by the dumb shows which precede each act and by the Chorus. These 'Foure auncient and Sage men of *Brittayne*' (A2^{r}), who epitomize the play's ideal of experienced male counsel rooted in a sense of national community, provide a summary at the end of Acts 1–4, endorsing or correcting judgements made by audience members in the intervening period. Crucially, though, the final act, dominated by the debate about how to settle the succession in an acephalous realm, is uniquely left without the Chorus' guiding conclusion, inviting the audience to continue deliberating beyond the end of the play.

These deliberations are, however, constrained by the fact that *Gorboduc*'s initial audiences, watching private performances at the Inner Temple and Whitehall, comprised lawyers and courtiers. Their inclusion in the debate is thus legitimated by the fact that they are men who had, or were acquiring, the requisite 'skyll' to govern, as Eubulus, the wisest counsellor, advocates (B2^{r}). Print publication enlarges that political community, as Day's anxiety about prostituting the

[52] Lorna Hutson, *The Invention of Suspicion: Law and Mimesis in Shakespeare and Renaissance Drama* (Oxford: Oxford University Press, 2007).

Lucrece-like text indicates. The 1590 preface thus tries to restrict its appeal by constructing an appropriate, gentlemanly readership. There is consequently a conservative impulse present, in different ways, in both the staged and printed texts. Moreover, even as *Gorboduc* 'pushe[s] to expand legitimate political discourse beyond the centre of national power', the advice it propounds is based on precedent and tradition.[53] When Eubulus ends the play, prophesying a world turned upside down—where the suckling child is slaughtered at its mother's breast, and fathers and sons 'unwitting' slay each other—he attributes the chaos to the way in which the various political players have failed in their customary roles:

> Hereto it comes when kinges will not consent,
> To grave advise, but folow wilfull wyll:
> This is the ende, when in yonge Princes hartes
> Flattery prevayles, and sage rede hath no place:
> . . .
> This, this ensues when noble men do faile
> In loyall trouthe, and subiectes will be kinges. (E3^{v})

Eubulus spares no estate from blame, but nor does he challenge the established hierarchy. When the play rallies its audience to act and learn from Gorboduc's failure to call parliament to appoint an heir 'of establisshed righte' while the prince still lives (E3^{v}), it calls not for regime change (as in the story of Lucrece invoked in Day's preface) but for maintenance of the status quo, even as it dares to suggest which path Elizabeth should take. Socio-political change—like other cultural reformations experienced in sixteenth-century England (not least among them religious reformation)—thus depends on a complex interplay between tradition and innovation, each dressed in the other's clothing, and oscillates between conflicting impulses to cultivate and limit individual agency (be it the right to a political voice, or to interpret the Bible).

IV

When Allde printed *Serpent* alongside *Gorboduc* in 1590, he juxtaposed two texts warning against civil discord; he did so when England was confronted by the fact that, since Elizabeth refused to name an heir and prohibited discussion of the matter, the country faced an uncertain future. The two texts share a concern for the political health of the nation, but the 1590 context for *Serpent* is far removed from the circumstances of its composition, differences which are highlighted by the community each version evokes and addresses. The perceived threat to national stability in late Elizabethan England came not just from foreign

[53] Winston, 'Expanding the Political Nation', 28.

invasion (enabled by internal division), but from the feared overthrow of the 'true Christian religion' which would result. Protecting the faith was thus a key aim behind the Bond of Association (1584)—a declaration of loyalty to Elizabeth signed by freeholders and tradesmen as well as gentry and aristocrats—and the subsequent Act of Association (1585), which made provision for the continued governance of the realm in case of her untimely death. Patrick Collinson argues that the Bond provides 'vivid insight into both the autonomous political capacity of the Elizabethan republic and its extent and social depth'.[54]

The same is true—to a lesser degree—of Allde's 1590 edition. Lydgate's *Serpent* had been addressed to a class of noblemen epitomized by his patron Gloucester, a focus which befitted its concentration on the moral failings of powerful leaders. It was now joined with *Gorboduc*, a text which embodies the desirability of wider political involvement, not by telling its audience/readers, but by implicating them in the process of evaluation and adjudication. Community exists on the margins of *Serpent*: *Gorboduc* pulls it centre-stage. As Howard Baker states, the play makes 'the commonwealth the protagonist'.[55] By this Baker means that, lacking one person on whose tribulations we concentrate (as Day's alternative title exposes), it is the sufferings of the commonweal which provide a consistent focus otherwise missing. Yet commonweal is not just a body on which things are inflicted, but is composed of individual bodies capable of action. The ideology of commonweal invests community with a sense of agency. When the 1590 editor reworked *Serpent*, its overhaul was more than cosmetic: in the company of a commonweal text like *Gorboduc*, he taught it to speak—not just in Elizabethan prose—but also in the language of Tudor politics: of confessionalization, commonweal, and the virtues of a mixed constitution.

FURTHER READING

Cavanagh, Dermot. *Language and Politics in the Sixteenth-Century History Play* (Basingstoke: Palgrave Macmillan, 2003)

Nolan, Maura B. 'The Art of History Writing: Lydgate's *Serpent of Division*', *Speculum*, 78:1 (2003), 99–127. A later version of this article appears as Chapter 1 of Maura Nolan, *John Lydgate and the Making of Public Culture* (Cambridge: Cambridge University Press, 2005)

Strohm, Paul. *Politique: Languages of Statecraft between Chaucer and Shakespeare* (Notre Dame, IN: University of Notre Dame Press, 2005)

Winston, Jessica. 'Expanding the Political Nation: *Gorboduc* at the Inns of Court and Succession Revisited', *Early Theatre*, 8:1 (2005), 11–34

[54] Patrick Collinson, 'The Monarchical Republic of Elizabeth I', in *The Tudor Monarchy*, ed. John Guy (London: Arnold, 1997), 110–35, at 123.

[55] Howard Baker, *Induction to Tragedy* (Baton Rouge: Louisiana State University, 1939), 295.

CHAPTER 25

THE REFORMATION OF THE HOUSEHOLD

COLIN BURROW

Spenser's *Faerie Queene* is full of curious and abrupt transitions. Perhaps the most curious and abrupt of them all happens between cantos viii and ix of Book VI. At the end of canto viii Serena is captured by cannibals, who strip her naked and salivate over her body. The cannibals' priest then tells them not to defile her because her blood is intended as a sacrifice to their god. She is duly prepared for sacrifice. The Priest 'with naked armes full net / Approching nigh, and murdrous knife well whet, / Gan mutter close a certaine secret charme, / With other divelish ceremonies met' (VI.viii.45.4–7).[1] In the nick of time Sir Calepine comes to Serena's rescue. He does his own bit of sacrificial slaughter by butchering the cannibals, and 'swarmes of damned soules to hell he sends' (VI.viii.49.7) in the course of releasing the lady. The episode is a more than usually naked (so to speak) allegory of anti-Catholicism: the Real Presence becomes a piece of savage flesh-eating theatre, accompanied by 'divelish ceremonies', and the means of Reformation is the sword.

The next canto begins in a completely different realm, as though it is projected by revulsion away from the erotic and fleshly excesses of the Catholic cannibals. The narrative returns to the nominal hero of the book, Sir Calidore (last seen five cantos before), who has fled from the court to the 'private farmes' (VI.ix.3.9) and 'litle cots' (VI.ix.4.8) of a pastoral realm. Here there is no cannibalism, though there is a little genteelly Protestant-sounding idolatry. Shepherds sit around a little hillock, admiring the (fully clad) Pastorella as 'their soveraine goddesse' (VI.ix.9.7). The representation of this pastoral society is quite distinctive and unusual in *The Faerie Queene* because it is centred on the small-scale household and on the kinds of hospitality which it fosters: Meliboee invites the errant knight into his 'cottage

[1] Quotations from Edmund Spenser, *The Faerie Queene*, ed. A. C. Hamilton., H. Yamashita, and T. Suzuki (Harlow: Pearson Education, 2001).

clad with lome' (VI.ix.16.5), and we are miles away, suddenly, from the large magnate households which dominate the earlier cantos of Book VI.[2] That abrupt shift of worlds, from cannibalistic Catholics to pastoral piety, from a godless outdoors to the small-scale courtesies of the godly household, is a paradigm of Protestant self-representation. It suggests that the act of violent religious Reformation suddenly brings about a cultural reformation, which radically alters the scale and style of social organization. The Reformation, it seems, was followed by a reformation of the household.

The fact that Spenser expresses this myth of cultural reform by means of a gap and a shift of heroes is significant. It indicates how very difficult it is to explain how the religious Reformation did actually influence an institution as various and complex as the household. Literary historians have on the whole not attempted to fill in his gap, or have done so in ways which leave the narrative almost as incomplete as Spenser's version of it. Indeed there are effectively two dominant stories about literary representations of households in the sixteenth and seventeenth centuries which in various and revealing ways do not quite overlap with each other.

The first is a story about royal and magnate households. David Starkey—who describes the literature of late Plantagenet and early Tudor England as 'The Age of the Household'—has told the most influential story of this kind. Large and incidentally Catholic magnate households, he argues, go into a sharp decline after the reign of Richard III as members of the nobility are drawn towards the court. They shed their retainers and have to rely on personal charm, style, and machismo to win advancement under the Tudors. Membership of Henry VIII's Privy Chamber was, Starkey suggests, the best way to get on in the blokish early reign of the second Tudor monarch; and that intimate inner circle within the royal household fostered competitive display between its members, which was the fashioning energy behind the English Renaissance.[3] Henrician literature was court literature, and the household that really mattered was the household of the king. Starkey does not take the story forward into the later sixteenth century except to

[2] On cottages in Spenser, see Christopher Burlinson, *Allegory, Space and the Material World in the Writings of Edmund Spenser* (Woodbridge: Brewer, 2006), 195–219.

[3] David Starkey, 'The Age of the Household: Politics, Society and the Arts c.1350–1550', in *The Context of English Literature: The Later Middle Ages*, ed. Stephen Medcalf (London: Methuen, 1981), 225–90, at 277:

> The court not only stripped the leading members of the political nation of the protective cocoon of their own households; it also brought them—as individuals—face to face with each other in a lively and often viciously competitive society... The world of the Tudor court, in short, reproduced the crucial features of the Italian city, which historians of the Renaissance now see as the cradle of the great cultural changes of the fourteenth and fifteenth centuries.

For the decline of magnate households in the sixteenth century, see Kate Mertes, *The English Noble Household, 1250–1600: Good Governance and Politic Rule*, Family, Sexuality and Social Relations in Past Times (Oxford: Basil Blackwell, 1988), 187–8.

suggest that the Reformation helped the emergence of Shakespeare's 'bewildering variety', which he contrasts with the simple certainty of Cardinal Wolsey's biographer George Cavendish 'that Wolsey was above criticism because he was the greatest householder of his day'.[4]

At the other end of the sixteenth century and on up to the Civil War we find a rather different kind of story. The focus here tends to be on small-scale (and sometimes only incidentally Protestant) households, and on the politics of domesticity and household relationships. The star texts to consider here might be *Gammer Gurton's Needle* and the domestic tragedies of the Elizabethan and Jacobean periods.[5] The domestic-scale households of the late century used to be seen as haunts of patriarchal primacy, or as the Puritan William Perkins described it 'a Seminarie of all other societies' ordered by 'the written word of God',[6] and governed by God's ordained agents, the 'father and mother, master and mistresse'.[7] More often than not scholars today emphasize the strong role such households played within the national economy (the word 'oeconomy' in this period refers to the management of household affairs), and the productive and regulatory role played in them by women—themes which can in fact be traced back well into the Middle Ages.[8] This second kind of story tends to focus on non-royal, non-magnate households, and is particularly favoured by critics of early modern drama who might argue, with Wendy Wall, that 'a "middle class" national identity was generated out of reflections on the material realities of household work'.[9] This kind of narrative might draw on evidence of widespread rebuilding and restructuring of domestic houses in the later sixteenth century and on the economic changes which underpinned these architectural transformations,[10] and it might often gesture forwards to the growing tendency to identify household government with national government in the Civil War. As Milton put it, a nation cannot pretend to

[4] Starkey, 'Age of the Household', 286.

[5] See, e.g., Wendy Wall, *Staging Domesticity: Household Work and English Identity in Early Modern Drama*, Cambridge Studies in Renaissance Literature and Culture (Cambridge: Cambridge University Press, 2002); Heather Dubrow, *Shakespeare and Domestic Loss: Forms of Deprivation, Mourning, and Recuperation*, Cambridge Studies in Renaissance Literature and Culture (Cambridge: Cambridge University Press, 1999).

[6] William Perkins, *Christian Oeconomie, or, A Short Survey of the Right Manner of Erecting and Ordering a Familie According to the Scriptures* (London: Imprinted by Felix Kyngston, 1609), sigs. A3^r–B1^r.

[7] Robert Cleaver and John Dod, *A Godly Forme of Houshold Gouernment* (London: Printed by the assignes of Thomas Man, 1630), sig. A8^r.

[8] See, e.g., Wall, *Staging Domesticity*; Keith Wrightson, *Earthly Necessities: Economic Lives in Early Modern Britain, 1470–1750* (New Haven, CT: Yale University Press, 2002), 30–68; and for the earlier period David Herlihy, *Medieval Households* (Cambridge, MA: Harvard University Press, 1985).

[9] Wall, *Staging Domesticity*, 6.

[10] W. G. Hoskins, 'The Rebuilding of Rural England 1570–1640', *Past and Present*, 4 (1953), 44–57, as qualified by Robert Machin, 'The Great Rebuilding: A Reassessment', *Past and Present*, 77 (1977), 35–9; and Colin Platt, *The Great Rebuildings of Tudor and Stuart England: Revolutions in Architectural Taste* (London: UCL Press, 1994).

be free while 'wanting that power, which is the root and sourse of all liberty, to dispose and *oeconomize* in the Land which God hath giv'n them, as Maisters of Family in thir own house and free inheritance'.[11]

It is perhaps not surprising that these two stories do not meet in the middle, since they are about two completely different kinds of institutions which happen to share the same name and the same century. Well into the sixteenth century, royal and major magnate households were massive organizations with their own formal protocols and hierarchies. The Earl of Derby's household ordinances for 1568 stipulate 'that one Gentleman Vssher shall alwayes be attendaunte', they list elaborate hierarchies of household servants, and they even descend to details such as the rule 'that no Doggs of any sorte goe abroade in the house especiallie at meale tymes'.[12] 'Domestic' structures, by contrast, were on a vastly smaller scale and operated by fluid systems and relationships, the volatility of which was the principal reason for their appeal to dramatists. These might be predominantly nuclear—consisting of a married couple and children—or be extended by the inclusion of apprentices or servants, and they might be domains in which men and women enjoyed different forms of variously questioned and tested supremacy. They might be places of exchange, rivalry, and of economic activity, in which women might play a central role; and they might be represented (as they are in Thomas Dekker's *The Shoemaker's Holiday*, for example) as sites which manifest the energies and aspirations of urban citizens.

Representations of these two very different kinds of institution tend to occur in very different writing milieux. Early Tudor writing, we are led to believe, was dominated by the dramatic events of the Tudor court in the 1530s, and the writers of note were almost all courtiers, or else aspiring to the condition of courtiers.[13] By the early seventeenth century professional writers for the public stage were presenting a set of images of household life—articulate women, male jealousies, irascible fathers—which had some points of affinity with the world to which their largely urban audience would return at the end of the show. So these two different stories not only concern different institutions but are represented by different types of writer (courtly vs. professional) for different types of audience (courtly elites vs. citizens). Literary history tends to be driven by a conviction that there is a story to tell, so it is tempting for a literary historian to assume that somewhere in between these two periods England becomes bourgeois and

[11] John Milton, *Complete Prose Works*, ed. D. M. Wolfe et al. (New Haven, CT: Yale University Press, 1953–82), 3: 237.

[12] Francis Robert Raines (ed.), *The Derby Household Books*, The Stanley Papers, Part 2 (Manchester: Chetham Society, 1853), 8, 22.

[13] The strongest and most explicit examples of this emphasis are Greg Walker, *Writing under Tyranny: English Literature and the Henrician Reformation* (Oxford: Oxford University Press, 2005); and James Simpson, *Reform and Cultural Revolution*, The Oxford English Literary History, Vol. 2: *1350–1547* (Oxford: Oxford University Press, 2002).

Protestant, and probably a place in which companionate marriages flourished too. A myth of this kind provides an easy way of understanding how we move, say, from the coterie humanistic drama of *Fulgens and Lucrece*, performed before the elaborate clerical household of Cardinal Morton some time in the 1490s, to *Arden of Faversham*, *Othello*, and the high uplands of Jacobean household tragedy, which dramatize domestic conflicts on the public stage. We might explain those shifts through the metamorphosis of the household into a patriarchal nuclear unit, and link that to the devolution of piety, social affect, and authority brought about by the Reformation.[14]

Making the story work in this way, however, depends on some of the worst vices of traditional sixteenth-century literary historians. It requires underplaying the complexity of sixteenth-century religious beliefs and their cultural consequences, and it also requires a systematic fuzziness about what happens between the early sixteenth century and its end. And as a result of these vices Spenser's gap between an act of reforming zeal and the miraculous emergence of small-scale domesticity remains a gap in the literary and cultural history of the sixteenth century. The chronological equivalent to this hole in the story is roughly those awkward messy years around 1550–60, when England saw three monarchs and at least two official religions, and of which traditional literary histories were scandalously neglectful or straightforwardly dismissive.

In order to pull together the literary history of households in the sixteenth and early seventeenth centuries three things need to be done, and those things have large consequences for how we understand the entire period. First of all we need to allow in a wider chronological perspective. The arts of representing the inner workings of households—both the social exchanges which go on within them and the larger economic structures in which they participate—are central to late medieval writing, much of which depends upon capturing the spaces, economic relationships, and social gestures associated with a wide range of households, from the elaborate games of exchange in Bertilak's castle in *Sir Gawain and the Green Knight*, through the large-scale economic visions of *Piers Ploughman*, and right into the intricately imagined courtly and non-courtly interiors of *Troilus and Criseide* and *The Canterbury Tales*.[15]

Then, even from the narrower temporal perspective of the sixteenth century, we should give less exclusive coverage to the literature of the royal household in the early Tudor period, and open our ears to moments when other households are speaking. Non-royal households still retained a powerful hold on the imaginations of poets in the early Tudor years, and played an important part in attempts in the

[14] Hence the appeal of Lawrence Stone, *The Family, Sex and Marriage in England 1500–1800* (London: Weidenfeld & Nicolson, 1977); for a critique of which, see J. A. Sharpe, *Early Modern England: A Social History 1550–1700* (London: Edward Arnold, 1987), 56–76.

[15] See D. Vance Smith, *Arts of Possession: The Middle English Household Imaginary*, Medieval Cultures, vol. 33 (Minneapolis: University of Minnesota Press, 2003).

period to suggest, invent, or wishfully imagine some kind of autonomy for the poet. Skelton attracted odium for apparently having had 'Calliope' embroidered on his livery, which he claimed indicated that he belonged not to the household of the Howards or of the King, but to that of the Muse: 'Of her I holde / And her housholde', he declared in 'Calliope' (lines 13–14).[16] And in 'Why Come Ye Nat to Courte' from November 1522 he asks, rhetorically, 'To whyche courte?' should he come, 'the kynges courte, / Or to Hampton Court?' (lines 402–4). Even households less grandiose than Wolsey's, which at its height is thought to have numbered about 500, could by the 1530s present alternative sites of loyalty to the royal household. Sir Thomas Wyatt, who is often presented as a selfish self, fashioned purely by the pressures of the late Tudor court, also has room for a household perspective which is not simply a courtly perspective. He positions himself within his own household at Allington Castle in Kent in his satirical attack on the court:

> But here I ame in Kent and Christendome
> Emong the muses where I rede and ryme. (lines 100–1)[17]

This is not simply a frustrated courtier's way of compensating himself for misadventures at and possible exile from the royal household. It locates Wyatt in a social space which was his own possession in the middle of a county in which his family (originally from Yorkshire) was establishing an extensive affinity. A deep and long-standing element within anti-court satire is the belief that home, one's own proper household, was a personal domain. Alain Chartier voiced this common view when he wrote early in the fifteenth century to persuade a friend not to come to court: 'thou lyvest in thyn hous lyke an Emperour, thou regnest as a kyng paysyble under the couverte of thyn hous', whereas at court 'we tremble for drede to dysplayse the lordes of hye houses'.[18] There is necessarily an intimate dialectical relationship between enduring the rule of an irascible monarch at court and the fantasy of ruling one's own domain at home, but that dialectic should not simply be collapsed into the claim that the court was supreme source of all authority and power, the fashioning energy of the nation. Households apart from the royal household mattered in the sixteenth century, and a proper recognition of that fact would enrich and devolve the obsessively court-centred emphasis of the first of our two stories about the period. This in turn would make us less prone to see a major break or lacuna in mid-century. Even early Tudor courtly writing is overlaid by an imaginary vision of a longed-for domestic space, in which the courtier can be himself a ruler.

[16] Quotations from John Skelton, *The Complete English Poems*, ed. J. Scattergood (Harmondsworth: Penguin Books, 1983).

[17] Quotations from Thomas Wyatt, *Collected Poems of Sir Thomas Wyatt*, ed. K. Muir and P. Thomson (Liverpool: Liverpool University Press, 1969).

[18] Alain Chartier, *The Curial Made by Maystere Alain Charretier*, ed. F. J. Furnivall, EETS, extra series, 54 (London: N. Trübner & co., 1888), 8.

That leads on to the third injunction to literary historians of the household: that they attend carefully to the writing of the mid-sixteenth century and its distinctive features. Doing so reveals some surprising continuities in the representations of households across the century and across religious divides. And as we shall see, attending closely to the nature of mid-century writing can also, oddly enough, help to explain why literary historians have tended to ignore or downplay the significance of that period.

*

The most vivid representation of a household and its workings in the mid-sixteenth century is George Cavendish's *Life and Death of Cardinal Wolsey.* This has generally been seen as a medieval throwback.[19] It was written between 1554 and 1558 by Cardinal Wolsey's former Gentleman Usher—that is, the officer in his household who oversaw dining arrangements, and who made sure that each man was treated according to his rank. The *Life* principally relates the events that led up to Wolsey's fall and death in 1530. It is therefore about the politicking that preceded the English Reformation and about its impact on what was (only just, as Skelton indicates) the second largest household in the land during that period.

Cavendish's principal aim is to defend Wolsey. He denies that his master was persistently corrupt, insists that he was a good lord to his household, and rebuts rumours that he sought his own death when he fell from favour. Cavendish is also keen to make clear that the royal divorce was not Wolsey's idea. His *Life* was described by A. F. Pollard as 'the classic example of history as it appears to a gentleman-usher'[20] because of its fondness for listing household effects. Certainly Cavendish does indeed like a good fabric ('Nowe in his privy kytchen he had a Mr Cooke whoe went dayly in Dammaske, Satten or velvett wt a chayn of gold abought his nekke' [19]), but Pollard's snobbish description quite unfairly suggests that his *Life* was little more than an early modern *Remains of the Day*, an expurgated account of his former master by a loyal retainer.

Cavendish was in fact well-born, shrewd, and Cambridge-educated. The period in which he wrote the *Life*, the mid-to-late 1550s, had an entirely distinctive literary flavour, and Cavendish knew just what that flavour was. The major discursive task of these years (and this is true of writers on both sides of the religious divide) was

[19] Quotations from George Cavendish, *The Life and Death of Cardinal Wolsey*, ed. R. S. Sylvester, EETS, o.s., 243 (London: Oxford University Press, 1959). 'This is perhaps the last work written in English which belongs completely to the Middle Ages', C. S. Lewis, *English Literature in the Sixteenth Century, Excluding Drama* (Oxford: Clarendon Press, 1954), 288.

[20] A. F. Pollard, *Wolsey* (London: Longmans Green, 1929), 2. More sympathetic views are in Richard Standish Sylvester, 'Cavendish's *Life of Wolsey*: The Artistry of a Tudor Biographer', *Studies in Philology*, 57 (1960), 44–71; Warren W. Wooden, 'The Art of Partisan Biography: George Cavendish's "Life of Wolsey"', *Renaissance and Reformation / Renaissance et Réforme*, 1 (1977), 24–35; and Judith H. Anderson, *Biographical Truth: The Representation of Historical Persons in Tudor-Stuart Writing* (New Haven, CT and London: Yale University Press, 1984), 27–39.

to provide a way of understanding what the Reformation was, and to suggest that it created a major rupture in English culture. English Counter-Reformation literature of the 1550s is playing this game just as much as English Reformation literature from the reign of Edward VI and after. Both literary projects work principally by erasure of the 1540s. Marian writing is particularly prone to go back to the 1530s and rethink them, rather than to dwell on its own age. This has left a major literary historical legacy: the tendency of writing from this period to look backwards has effectively convinced the majority of literary historians that the 1550s are themselves a hiatus, a gap in the middle of the century.

The two most major literary events of the 1550s are both retrospective volumes. The first was the publication of *Tottel's Miscellany*, or *Songes and Sonettes written by the right honorable Lorde Henry Haward late Earle of Surrey, and other*—which represents itself as principally containing works from the 1530s and early 1540s—in 1557. The second was the printing of the collected edition of the *English Works* of Sir Thomas More in the same year by a consortium of printers which included Richard Tottel. This volume (one of few English printed books in the vernacular to enjoy significant sales abroad)[21] marked the return to England of a group of Catholic associates of More who had been in exile during the reign of Edward VI. Both works sought in various ways to revisit what by the 1550s looked like the terrible mistakes of the 1530s, and to tap the energy of Henrician literature afresh. It might be an exaggeration to call the very end of the Marian period a Catholic renaissance, or to find in it a literature of the Counter-Reformation; but these high-profile Tottel publications showed a clear ambition to edit out the reign of Edward VI, and to align present-day literary activity with Henrician and in particular pre-Reformation court culture.[22]

In this period George Cavendish, who had been living in effective retirement in Suffolk since the death of Wolsey in 1530, chose to write a life of his former master. Why did he do so, and why did he present a far more positive view of Wolsey than he had done in his metrical vision of the life and death of the Cardinal, which he had composed in around 1552–4?[23] The traditional answer is that this loyal retainer was prompted to write the *Life* by the hostile portrait of Wolsey in Hall's *Chronicle* of 1548—a view which rests on his own statement that 'synce his [Wolsey's] deathe I have hard dyvers sundry surmysis & Imagyned tales made of his procedynges & doynges, w[che] I my selfe have perfightly knowen to be most untrewe'

[21] Lotte Hellinga and J. B. Trapp (eds.), *The Cambridge History of the Book in Britain*, vol. 3: *1400–1557* (Cambridge: Cambridge University Press, 1999), 23–4.

[22] On the parallel attempts of the Marian Church to assert continuity with the Henrician era, see Eamon Duffy and D. M. Loades (eds.), *The Church of Mary Tudor* (Aldershot: Ashgate, 2006), 232–5; on the propaganda campaign of the Marian counter-reformation, see Eamon Duffy, *Fires of Faith: Catholic England under Mary Tudor* (New Haven, CT and London: Yale University Press, 2009), 57–78.

[23] Date conjectured in George Cavendish, *Metrical Visions*, ed. A. S. G. Edwards (Columbia, SC: Published for the Newberry Library by the University of South Carolina Press, 1980), 8.

(4). Most commentators take this remark entirely at face value, and have believed that Cavendish wanted to correct hostile reforming accounts of Wolsey's actions.[24] They may be naïve to do so. Cavendish was no backwoodsman. He had an ear for fashion in the capital. His *Metrical Visions, de casibus* monologues which brought Lydgate's *Fall of Princes* up to the Reformation, were composed at almost exactly the same time that the first edition of *A Mirror for Magistrates* was being suppressed.[25] His *Life* was written just as Nicholas Harpsfield was at work preparing a *Life of More* with a view to its accompanying the Rastell edition of the *English Works*. These could be coincidences, but in all probability they indicate Cavendish's connections with points west and south of his home. Suffolk was not the back of beyond in the 1550s. It had its own distinct governmental structures and religious culture,[26] and had of course provided Mary with the small army which enabled her to proclaim herself Queen in 1553. Its gentry networks were, partly as a result of their involvement in Mary's accession, well connected with the capital and the court. And George Cavendish, as (probably) resident in Glemsford in Suffolk, half way between Cavendish (the place, that is) and Long Melford, would certainly have been in a good position to join the group of Suffolk gentry who rallied to Framlingham in support of Mary when she raised her standard there in July 1553.[27] Indeed if Robert Wingfield, the Suffolk gentleman who wrote the earliest life of Mary, is to be believed, Cavendish was exactly the kind of middling Suffolk gentry who flocked to her cause.[28]

Cavendish's family ties also link him very closely with the household of the Queen. His brother Sir William Cavendish had become Treasurer of the Chamber in 1546, and remained in that office (despite its chaotic finances) through Mary's reign.[29] As a former aid of Thomas Cromwell, Sir William Cavendish might well

[24] Cavendish, *Life of Wolsey*, ed. Sylvester, xxx–xxxi; MacCulloch suggests that he was inspired to write by his fellow Suffolk gentleman Robert Wingfield's *Vita* of Mary: Robert Wingfield, '"The Vita Mariae Reginae" of Robert Wingfield', in *Camden Miscellany XXVIII*, ed. D. MacCulloch (London: Camden Society, 1984), 187–8.

[25] Cavendish, *Metrical Visions*, ed. Edwards, 12 proposes the date of 1552–4, and favours the hypothesis that they anticipated the *Mirror*. If the first edition of the *Mirror* was suppressed in 1554 (William Baldwin, *The Mirror for Magistrates*, ed. L. B. Campbell (Cambridge: Cambridge University Press, 1938), 4) it must have been written at the same time as Cavendish's work.

[26] See Diarmaid MacCulloch, *Suffolk and the Tudors: Politics and Religion in an English County, 1500–1600* (Oxford: Clarendon Press, 1986).

[27] MacCulloch, *Suffolk and the Tudors*, 79.

[28] Wingfield, 'Vita Mariae', 257. 'It is possible that Robert's work inspired Cavendish to write down his memories' (MacCulloch, *Suffolk and the Tudors*, 187).

[29] The Treasurer of the Chamber under Henry VII had enjoyed considerable intimacy with the monarch; by 1546, when Cavendish's brother took over the office, its business had expanded and personal audits by the monarch of the accounts had become less regular. See Walter Cecil Richardson, *Tudor Chamber Administration, 1485–1547* (Baton Rouge: Louisiana State University Press, 1952), 216–48. Richardson records that Cavendish was 'ambitiously working for advancement' (245). On the relatively high degree of continuity in office-holding under Mary, see D. M. Loades, *The Reign of Mary Tudor: Politics, Government and Religion in England, 1553–58* (London: Longman, 1991), 41–56.

have had a particular need to establish his credentials as a good Catholic in the reign of Mary. He also might have had other motives to encourage his brother to write works of retrospect and historical reappraisal. The accounts of the Treasury of the Chamber were under investigation in the latter part of 1557. William Cavendish had to appeal to the Queen and Council to overlook the glaring inefficiency and probable corruption of his account-keeping.[30] Cavendish's *Life* may be history as told by a gentleman usher, but the chances are that it is also a conscious work of Catholic memorialization, encouraged, perhaps even commissioned, by a member of the royal household, the Treasurer of the Chamber.[31] The *Life*, and the metrical visions which preceded it, probably remained unprinted because William Cavendish died in October 1557, an event which instantly deprived his brother George of his immediate point of access to the royal household.[32] By the time the *Life* was completed on 24 June 1558 its moment had passed, and Mary herself was beginning her slow decline towards death.

Cavendish's *Life* is a modish work of Catholic revivalism from the mid-1550s rather than a rustic throwback. But it is also a representation, and a remarkably vivid one, of the pressures which the political aspects of the Reformation put on one particularly large household in the later 1520s. Those pressures allow the household to speak not just as a social unit, but as a socially delicate space, full of boundaries, hidden thresholds, and above all of affective ties. That household is presented as a centre of loyalty which is—for a while at least—an alternative to the King's household. The work has another remarkable feature. Cavendish's instinctive understanding of what might be called social geography means that he imagines internal scenes in ways that are acutely aware of the spatial disposition and social relations of their participants. Perhaps the most brilliant example of this occurs at a climactic moment in the prehistory of the Reformation, when Wolsey and Cardinal Campeggio visit Catherine of Aragon to urge her to accept the divorce. Cavendish the gentleman usher clearly has his eye on his equivalent officer in the Queen's household:

> the gentilman ussher Advertised the quene ther of / Incontynent wt that she came owt of hir privye Chamber wt a skayn of whight thred abought hir neke in to the chamber of presence / where the Cardynalles ware gevyng of attendaunce uppon hir Commyng (87)

[30] Richardson, *Tudor Chamber Administration*, 246–8.

[31] It is noteworthy that BL MS Add. 48066, which includes both Cavendish's *Life* and Nicholas Harpsfield's *Life of Sir Thomas More*, derives from the collection of the Elizabethan clerk to the Privy Council Robert Beale, who was a native of Woodbridge. The *Life* therefore may have enjoyed limited circulation among the Suffolk gentry. See Wingfield, 'Vita Mariae', 182.

[32] Cavendish's autograph, MS Egerton 2402, appears to have entered the collection of Francis Henry Egerton by gift of the son of Clement Rossington of Dronfield. It therefore was not originally owned by the Lord Chancellor, Sir Thomas Egerton (1540–1617), Baron Ellesmere, and Viscount Brackley, and so probably never found a courtly readership.

Most Tudor palaces had both a 'presence' and a 'privy' chamber, and the movement from one to the other is one of the most significant moments in the social performances of the period. Movement into the presence chamber brings with it the full theatre of public display; while retreat into the privy chamber stages a performance of intimacy. The Cardinals then ask Catherine to retire with them into a privy chamber. She refuses, insisting

> Yf ye have any thyng to say speke it opynly byfore all thes folkes ffor I feare no thyng that ye can sey or allege ayenst me / but that I wold all the world shold bothe here & se it / therfor I pray you speke yor mynd opynly / Than began my lord to speake / to hir in latten // Nay good my lord / qd she / speke to me in Englysshe I beseche you (88)

This is pure drama of the household. At the critical enabling moment of the Reformation Catherine refuses to be bundled off into her privy chamber to be bullied or manipulated, and insists on discussing the King's great matter in front of her household and in the vernacular. The drama is interpersonal, between a woman who is at that particular moment in control of her household and what happens in it, and men who are in control of the nation (or who want to think they are). But there is also a historical battle going on between styles of conducting public and social interchanges, almost between different forms of social architecture. Catherine needs to maintain the idea of public life in a household which consists of a large body of retainers and potential witnesses in order to prevent her visitors having their say and their way. For Wolsey's style of negotiation to succeed he needs to exploit the social geography of both house and household, to find a place of privacy and retreat, where he can cajole and threaten off the record. Catherine (the mother, of course, of Cavendish's Queen) is so touching here partly because she is historically on the wrong side: her kind of public household was in long-term decline, and Wolsey was the master of using conversations in the privy areas of a house to manipulate the front of house outcome. His own building-works very often included a gallery which was a dead end rather than a passageway from one area of the building to another.[33] He worked architectural space to create zones in which he could corner his interlocutors.

Catherine claims that 'I cannot so sodenly [answer] for I was sett among my maydens at worke thynkyng full littill of any suche matter' (88), but she does eventually agree to listen to them:

> And wt that she toke my lord by the hand and led hyme in to hyr privye chamber wt tother Carndynall / where they ware in long Commynycacion / we in the other Chamber myght some tyme here the quene speke very lowde but what it was we could not understand (88–9)

[33] S. J. Gunn and Phillip Lindley (eds.), *Cardinal Wolsey: Church, State and Art* (Cambridge: Cambridge University Press, 1991), 97.

According to a 'Breviate Touching the Order and Governmente of a Nobleman's House' dating from 1605, Gentlemen Ushers had a particular responsibility to prevent eavesdropping. They were 'to give notice to all wayters, that they give noe eare to table taulke, for that withdraweth the eie and minde from respecte of theire service'.[34] Cavendish's *Life* testifies to the repeated flapping of its author's ears, but the closed door to the privy chamber almost always baffles further speculation about what is going on behind it.

In Cavendish's *Life* space becomes charged with emotion, and political events, favours, and interpersonal attitudes are expressed through meticulously observed movement between front-stage and back-stage zones of the household. And all of this is the result of his ability to read movements within the household as a social language. When he describes the early stages of Wolsey's fall, Cavendish represents all the moment-by-moment revolutions of fortune of a Tudor statesman through social geography. At first the Cardinal is summoned to the presence chamber 'where the lordes of the Councell stode in a Rowe'—as though about to judge him:

> Than Immedyatly after came the kyng in to the Chamber / and standyng there under the Clothe of estate / my lord kneled down byfore hyme who toke my lord by the hand (and so he dyd the other Cardynall) than he toke my lord uppe by bothe Armez & caused hyme to stand uppe / whome the kyng receyved wt as amyable a chere as ever he dyd / & called hyme a side and led hyme by the hand to a great wyndowe where he talked wt hyme And caused hyme to be Covered (93–4)

Cavendish is initially delighted to see his master's enemies so discountenanced by this public display of favour. Then the performance of intimacy by Henry begins to seem little more than a performance put on in order to confront Wolsey with evidence of treachery:

> I hard the kyng say / howe can that be / is not this yor owen hand / and plukked owt frome hys bosome a letter or writyng and shewed hyme the same / and as I perceyved that it was answerd so by my lord that the kyng had no more to say (94)[35]

Wolsey then dines in public, while the King 'dynned that same day wt mrs Anne Boleyn in hir chamber', and, by implication, has his ears further poisoned by the black crow. The Gentleman Usher, though, has many ears: 'And as I hard it reported by them that wayted uppon the kyng at dynner that Mrs Anne Bolleyn was myche offendyd wt the kyng' (94–5). Immediately after this, Henry goes back to the presence chamber where the lords are dining 'And at the last the kyng toke my lord by the hand and led hyme in to his privye Chamber syttyng there in

[34] Joseph Banks, 'A Breviate Touching the Order and Governmente of a Nobleman's House', *Archaeologia*, 13 (1800), 315–89, at 323.

[35] This was 19 September 1529. Pollard, *Wolsey*, 239–40, suggests that the document was a letter from Wolsey to Stephen Gardiner which implied the former was pursuing his own designs in his dealings with the Pope and the Emperor.

Consultacion wt hyme all a lone/ wtout any other of the lordes of the Councell untill it was nyght' (95). Cavendish is not transcribing the truth here (much of what he says is out of historical sequence or simply muddled) but is constructing household drama, in which being in and out of favour is related to how much intimacy you enjoy with the King; but in which a final level of intimacy—being alone with your monarch late at night, after he has dined with the mistress whom you know hates you—might well be the last thing you want or need, or even the last thing that you do. The setting of the drama is the royal household, but the awareness of spatial dynamics and of the changing relationships between its characters is the strongest anticipation we have of the social theatre of late Elizabethan England. It is a domestic drama enacted in a magnate household.

Cavendish does not simply have an eye for the social significance of intimacy. Household loyalty emerges as the main ethical and emotional tie, and comes to stand in for something even greater. After Wolsey's fall, as his household is about to be dissolved, Cavendish lightly and contemptuously sketches the rise of Thomas Cromwell, the master of what might be called the second reign of Henry VIII. One of Wolsey's trusted advisors, but without a formal role in his household, Cromwell was the kind of misfit who would not appeal to the hierarchically minded Cavendish, and his description of Cromwell's mediations between the Cardinal and the King are rarely untinged by suspicion. We first meet him in Cavendish's *Life* in the kind of staged privacy which is exactly suited to a snake from a new age:

> I found master Cromwell leanyng in the great wyndowe wt a prymer in his hand sayeng of our lady mattens (wche had byn synce a very straynge syght) he prayed not more earnestly / than the teares distilled frome his eyes / whome I bad god morowe / And wt that I perceyved the teares uppon his chekes (104)

Cromwell is weeping not for his master but because he fears he will lose his status as a result of his loyalty to the wrong person, despite all his hard work. That venomous parenthetical allusion to his future as a reformer suggests that even the prayer book in his hand is the prop of a hypocrite, of a disloyal servant of the household who emerges out of the intimate, staged seclusion of a fashionable oriel window to take charge of the nation and its religion. Those who betray the household are the real villains of Cavendish's *Life*. They are the people who also betray their religion.

Wolsey is represented as a man who betrays neither his household nor his faith. So, immediately before his arrest, the Cardinal greets the Earl of Northumberland and congratulates him on the number of loyal retainers which surround him:

> Ah my lord I perceyve well that ye have observed my old preceptes & Instruccions wche I gave you whan ye ware abydyng wt me in yor youthe / wche was to cheryshe yor fathers old servauntes ... Thys sayd / he toke therle by the hand & led hyme in to hys bedd chamber and they beyng there all alone (save oonly I that kepte the doore / accordyng to my dewtie beyng gentilman ussher) thes ij lordes standyng at a

> wyndowe / by the chymney in my lordes bedd chamber / therle tremlyng sayed wt a very faynt & softe voyce / unto my lord / layeng his hand uppon his arme / My lord / qd he / I arrest you of hyghe treason (155)

Brought up in Wolsey's household, Northumberland receives Cavendish's deepest implicit condemnation: he is the disloyal retainer, the Judas, the man who keeps his own household around him while betraying that of his friend and teacher.

History as told from the viewpoint of a gentleman usher. Yes; but a history of the Henrician Reformation as told from the viewpoint of a major member of Wolsey's household has a massive ideological charge. It pushes the royal household off centre. It gives huge weight to Catherine of Aragon. It generates domestic immediacy out of the formal architecture of early Tudor palaces. And it implicitly tags as traitors those who are loyal to the King and Queen Anne rather than to the master of the household to which they belong. And here the fact that Cavendish's *Life* was composed in Mary's reign, perhaps at the request of her Treasurer, gives a wider significance to its household allegiances. In the later 1550s a defence of Wolsey's household is not just a defence of Wolsey's household: the household perspective is effectively aligned with resistance to the Reformation.

*

The household of Sir Thomas More was a rather different sort of establishment from Cardinal Wolsey's quasi-regal court. Erasmus famously described this godly and learned, but decidedly uncourtly, institution in his letter to Ulrich von Hutten on 23 July 1519 as a place which 'seems to enjoy a kind of natural felicity, for no one has ever been a member of it without bettering his fortune later, and no one has ever earned the least shadow on his reputation'.[36] Holbein of course memorialized More's household in the group portrait of which only sketches survive, a portrait which presents More *homo oeconomicus*, a household man among a group of readers and doers, a striking proportion of whom are women, and several of whom piously hold Books of Hours.[37] All are positioned within an almost ostentatiously small interior, tucked into a corner with books, furniture, and (as Holbein's notes on the draft indicate) in the lost final version musical instruments.

Armed with this picture and a little knowledge of More's life it is easy enough, in a simple-minded way, to place him within a larger narrative about the evolution of households. He spent the years 1489–92 in the household of Cardinal Morton—one of the most lavish clerical households of the reigns of Richard III and Henry VII—where, Roper famously relates, 'wold he at Christmas tyde sodenly sometimes steppe in among the players, and never studying for the matter, make a parte of his

[36] Desiderius Erasmus, *The Correspondence of Erasmus*, vol. 7, ed. R. A. B. Mynors and P. G. Bietenholz, *The Collected Works of Erasmus* (Toronto: University of Toronto Press, 1987), 24.

[37] See John Rowlands, *Holbein: the Paintings of Hans Holbein the Younger* (Oxford: Phaidon, 1985), 69–71; Eamon Duffy, *Marking the Hours: English People and their Prayers, 1240–1570* (New Haven, CT, and London: Yale University Press, 2006), 58.

owne there presently among them'.[38] The association of that particular household with free speech, and especially anti-tyrannical speech, runs through *Richard III*, and, of course, the fictional setting for part of Book I of *Utopia* (1516) is a conversation at Cardinal Morton's table. Despite that loyalty to Morton's household, Book I of *Utopia* itself is explicitly opposed to large magnate households and their troupes of badged retainers, while the political landscape of Book II is in large measure shaped by the complete absence of royal and noble households from Utopian society.[39] One could go a little further: Utopian society (particularly as represented in Ralph Robinson's 1551 translation) presents a model of devolved government which gives remarkable weight to the medium-scale household, and reminds us that there is nothing particularly Protestant about such forms of social organization:

> Habent ruri per omnes agros commode dispositas domos, rusticis instrumentis instructas. Hae habitantur ciuibus per uices eo commigrantibus. Nulla familia rustica in uiris mulieribus pauciores habet, quam quadraginta praetor duos ascriptitios seruos, quibus pater materque familias graues ac mature praeficiuntur, & singulis tricenis familijs phylarchus unus. (114)[40]

> They have in the country in all parts of the shire houses or farms builded, well appointed and furnished with all sorts of instruments and tools belonging to husbandry. These houses be inhabited of the citizens, which come thither to dwell by course. No household or farm in the country hath fewer than forty persons, men and women, besides two bondmen which be all under the rule and order of the good man and the good wife of the house, being both very sage and discreet persons. And every thirty farms or families have one head ruler, which is called a Philarch, being as it were a head bailiff. (51)[41]

Indeed the reciprocal give and take which shapes the relationship between Utopian cities indicates that 'ita tota insula uelut una familia est' (148), which Robinson renders as 'the whole island is as it were one family, or household' (69). *Utopia* is an attempt to fuse together economics—in its etymological sense of government of the household—with ethics and politics by imagining a society in which government depends on 'the rule and order of the good man, and the good wife of the house'. In this respect Utopian society resembles an extended version of

[38] William Roper, *The Lyfe of Sir Thomas Moore, Knighte*, ed. Elsie Vaughan Hitchcock, EETS, o.s., 197 (London: Oxford University Press, 1998; first published 1935), 5.

[39] See Felicity Heal, *Hospitality in Early Modern England* (Oxford: Clarendon Press, 1990), 95–7; and Colin Burrow, 'The Experience of Exclusion: Literature and Politics in the Reigns of Henry VII and Henry VIII', in *The Cambridge History of Medieval English Literature*, ed. David Wallace (Cambridge: Cambridge University Press, 1999), 793–820, at 805.

[40] Quotations from Thomas More, *Utopia*, ed. J. H. Hexter and E. Surtz, in *The Complete Works of St. Thomas More*, 4 (New Haven, CT: Yale University Press, 1965).

[41] Quotations from Thomas More et al., *Three Early Modern Utopias*, ed. Susan Bruce (Oxford: Oxford University Press, 1999).

More's own relatively small-scale household, which is grounded, not in the nuclear family, but in the interpersonal ethics and economics of household membership.

Roper's *Lyfe of Sir Thomas More* is a product of More's household. Roper was Sir Thomas More's son-in-law, and had since around 1518 been resident in More's household, first in Old Barge, Bucklesbury, and then from around 1526 in Chelsea. He ended up, by a legal accident, retaining his house on More's estate even after the remainder of More's possessions were seized by the crown. His *Life* was a set of notes intended to assist Nicholas Harpsfield in drafting his biography of More, a fact that marks it as belonging to exactly the same culture of retrospect as Cavendish's *Life*. The good lawyer Roper presents his work as a set of quasi-legal depositions (its first word is 'Forasmuche'), which record what he has himself witnessed or received on the testimony of good men and women. The *Life* is not exactly hagiographical, but it does throughout present More as a man who believes in Papal supremacy (he makes his name as a lawyer by successfully ensuring the release of one of the Pope's ships which had been taken as a forfeit by Henry VIII), and in the absolute unconditional subordination of secular to sacred authority. This is clearly designed to make More into a hero for the age of Mary. So much is obvious.

But the *Life* also contains a very strong and effectively competing perspective. And that is the perspective of a member of More's household, whose material well-being depended on More's physical survival. Erasmus claimed in 1519 that there was an entirely equable and symmetrical relationship between More the virtuous ruler of his household and More the politician—that, as it were, the virtues manifested in the household of Sir Thomas More leeched naturally into those of the household of Henry VIII: 'Such are the men whom that most intelligent king admits to his household and his privy chamber; admits, yes, and invites, and even forces them to come.'[42] Nearly four decades later Roper presents the relationship between these two asymmetrically powerful households from the viewpoint of someone who might be destroyed by the conflict between them. As a result his *Life* is charged with both energy and irony, as it shuttles between the political, the religious, and the economic perspectives. The traditional view is that Roper regarded More's refusal to subscribe to the Oath of Supremacy as an act of simple heroism, in which the martyr will not subordinate divine to secular authority. That is at best half of Roper's story. He himself took the Oath. Furthermore his economic and personal entanglement with More's household meant that his father-in-law's stubbornness would also be the source of personal and domestic ruin, the overturning of his 'oeconomie' in both the early modern and the modern senses. His economic well-being depended on More reconciling his conscience to the Oath. This perspective is most visible when Roper describes the events surrounding the Nun of Kent in March 1534. At that date More had been included in a draft

[42] Erasmus, *Correspondence*, 7, ed. Mynors and Bietenholz, 24.

parliamentary act which indicted him for having had treasonous communication with Elizabeth Barton, the Kentish visionary nun who had predicted that Henry's reign would not last more than a month if he remarried.[43] More was examined for treasonable intent by Cromwell, the Duke of Norfolk, the Lord Chancellor Thomas Audley, and the Archbishop of Canterbury. On his return he walks with Roper in the garden of the Chelsea house. Seeing that More is merry, Roper asks him:

> 'Are you then put out of the parliament bill?' said I. 'By my trothe, sonne Roper,' quothe he, 'I never remembred it.' 'Never remembred it, Sir,' sayd I, 'A case that toucheth your self so neere, and us all for your sake. I am sory to heare it; For I veryly trusted, when I sawe you so meerye, that all had bine well.' Then said he: 'Wilte thow knowe, sonne Roper, why I was so meery?' 'That wold I gladly, Sir,' quoth I. 'In good faithe, I reioyced, sonne,' quoth he, 'that I had geven the divell a fowle fall, and that with those Lordes I had gone so farre, as without greate shame I could never goe back agayne.' At which wordes waxed I very sad, for thoughe himself liked it well, yet liked it me but a litle. (69–70)[44]

The *Life* depends on a mild level of self-ironization on Roper's part: he is the loyal member of More's household who is concerned for its head, whose fate 'toucheth ... us all for your sake'. But 'toucheth' of course does not just mean 'moves'. It also means 'materially implicates'. This pun enables Roper to be at once the concerned family member and also the slightly self-interested son-in-law who is appalled that his father-in-law can be irresponsible enough not particularly to care if he ruins his wife, children, and extended family by seeking death. This gives the *Life* a twin perspective: the More who merrily rejoices in his loyalty to God is also the head of the household who destroys all those who love him.

As with Cavendish's *Life*, the historical gap between the period at which Roper's life was written and that which it describes is extremely important, and the erasure of those intervening years—the blank into which Marian literature sought to turn the Reforming years of Edward VI—is a major part of its overall aim. But this temporal gap functions here in a slightly different way from the corresponding gap in Cavendish's work. In Roper's *Life* the household perspective is throughout presented almost as a historical anachronism. It is a viewpoint which More (and implicitly also the Marian reader of the *Life*) has abandoned, while those around him are stuck within its limiting confines. And this presence of the partially cancelled perspective of the household is in large measure what makes Roper's *Life* so affecting. More's self-sacrifice is dramatized as the discarding of his household and dependants, and part of Roper—the Roper of 1534 at any rate—sees that act as almost a wilful sacrifice of others in order to ensure personal salvation. As in Cavendish's *Life*, this complex of emotions is often evoked by delicate

[43] 25 Henry VIII, *c*.12. [44] Roper, *The Lyfe of Sir Thomas Moore.*

manipulation of spatial relationships. So, when More is summoned to take the oath of supremacy he quite literally shuts the gate on his household:

> And whereas he evermore used before, at his departure from his wife and children, whom he tenderly loved, to have them bring him to his boate, and there to kisse them all, and bidd them farewell, Then wold he Suffer none of them forthe of the gate to followe him, but pulled the wickatt after him, and shutt them all from him; and with an heavy harte, as by his countenaunce it appeared, with me and our foure servantes there tooke he his boate towards Lambithe. Wherein sitting still sadly a while, at the last he [sodainely] rounded me in the yeare, and said: 'Sonne Roper, I thancke our Lord the feild is wonne.' What he ment thereby I then wist not, yeat loth to seeme ignorant, I awneswered: 'Sir, I am therof very glad.' (72–3)

The Roper of 1534 is carefully presented as naïve. His humdrum household perspective is represented as a limiting point of view which has been transcended by the time of writing, and which throughout the work becomes increasingly comic and inadequate, as a new world opens up before it.

The final stage of this process is effected by, or perhaps even creates, the figure of More's second wife Dame Alice. She visits her husband in the Tower and, like Roper only more garrulously and more comically, cannot understand how More could possibly want to forgo his house rather than swear an oath which learned people have duly accepted:

> 'And seinge you have at Chelsey a [right] faire house, your library, your bookes, your gallery, your garden, your orchard, and all other necessaries so handsome about you, where you might in the company of me your wife, [your] children, and howshold be meerye, I muse what a gods name you meane heare still thus fondly to tarye'.
>
> (82–3)

Dame Alice has gone down in history as a shrew and simpleton, but Roper's testimony to her voice should not be taken at face value. The portrait is probably malicious, since the charming lawyer Roper engaged his step-mother-in-law in a lawsuit over some elements of More's estate after his execution. But Dame Alice is also a rhetorical necessity: she takes over from Roper himself as the voice of the household. Her concern for all those lovely orchards and books reduces that institution to a purely material and social set of relationships. This representation of Dame Alice also enables the voice of (surely almost by now) Saint Thomas More (for whom, as the *Life* progresses, being 'meery' is something you do only in heaven) to ask 'is not this house [i.e. the Tower] as nighe heaven as my owne?' (83). That voice has gone beyond the world. The household has become merely a physical space which might just as well be exchanged for the physical space of the Tower. The affect of the work follows its household perspective, which both its readers and its author have to work out of their systems. Roper's *Life* has all Cavendish's sense of witness, all his eye and eavesdropping ear for the connections between spaces, interiors, and emotions; but its overall force is almost diametrically opposite to Cavendish's. It implies that resistance to the Reformation requires giving up the household.

*

How do these two works fit into a larger historical framework? Both Roper's *Life* of More and Cavendish's *Life* of Wolsey show the pressure placed on the great but non-noble households of Henry VIII's major office-holders as a result of the political events which preceded the Reformation. Those households—different in scale, distinct in their gender balance, distinct in the architecture within which they developed—become as a result of the break with Rome sources of allegiance and of quiet resistance. That in itself makes these works important. They provide a strong counterweight to the widespread tendency among literary historians to totalize or even totalitarianize the Henrician regime, and to see the royal household as the all-encompassing centre of early Tudor writing. They also remind us that not only Protestant nuclear households gave rise to affect and conflict. But these works do not simply tell us more about the oppositional force of non-royal households in the 1520s and 1530s. Both are historically binocular: they look back to the period about which they are written as well as out towards the time at which they were composed. Each of them uses the time-lag between the present Counter-Reformation and the past Henrician Reformation in different ways. The Suffolk gentleman makes household loyalty a marker of religious loyalty. The metropolitan lawyer gives affective force to More's household in order to show More's strength in renouncing it. Both works, in their different ways, bring their readers to identify with a household perspective as part of establishing a Counter-Reformation perspective.

This means in turn that Roper and Cavendish make both a bridge and a gulf between the two narratives about households with which this essay began. They make a bridge because the pressures of the Reformation force their authors to think in minute detail about the political relationships and perspectives of particular people within particular household spaces, and to do so in a quasi-theatrical manner. As a result Cavendish and Roper could be seen as partly at least filling in the gap between the two stories about household literature in the sixteenth century. They relate the events which occurred in large-scale households during the Reformation in a manner that would make sense to the dramatists of the later century. But at the same time as bridging the gap between early and later Tudor writing they also play a part in constructing that gap. Because they look backwards they make it appear that representations of households from little more than a decade later actually belong to a different age. A glance forward will illustrate this point. George Gascoigne (who, curiously enough, was the grandson of Cardinal Wolsey's household Treasurer) in 1573 set *The Adventures of Master F.J.* in a smartly Italianate English household. But despite its apparent modernity, Gascoigne's novella, with its sexual encounters in long galleries and its intimate scenes in private bedchambers, springs from the same awareness of social spaces that we find developing in Roper and Cavendish.

What is different about literary works set in larger households in the later century is their tendency to focus on intimate servants (and in particular the learned intimate servants) of those households. One of the principals in *The Adventures of Master F.J.* is the mistress's secretary, who returns to supplant our hero in his mistress's affection. The central figure in the (so-called) *Autobiography* of Thomas Whythorne (1576) is a music master,[45] whose many misadventures in the various households to which he is attached are the pretexts for a variety of lyrics. Here too (perhaps under the influence of Gascoigne) sexual and social aspiration, rather than urgent political and religious realignments, are the main forces released by residence in a household. Later literary representations of households show a similar tendency to dramatize the actions and aspirations of characters who occupy socially ambiguous positions within them—schoolmasters like Holofernes, stewards like Malvolio in *Twelfth Night*, moderately unwelcome guests like Toby Belch, or Lucentio and Hortensio in *The Taming of the Shrew*, who impersonate a schoolmaster and a music master in order to penetrate a mercantile household.

The crucial point here is that these representational changes were not simple reflections of changes in the ways in which households were shaped and organized, and they were not the consequences of a social revolution or a cultural reformation. They were largely the result of much smaller-scale changes. These works were written by people who did not have a formal place within the larger scale households of the upper gentry and nobility of a kind which was enjoyed by Cavendish and Roper. A failed lawyer like Gascoigne, a glover's son like Shakespeare, George Chapman (author of *The Gentleman Usher* and a grandson of the man who looked after Henry VIII's dogs), all of whom made their ways by their wits, might see a household as a place of comic confluences in which to explore social and sexual aspirations. For these later writers, socially edgy figures—stewards, secretaries, gentleman ushers—provided the most sympathetic angles from which to focalize their household fictions. Households were places into which you tried to worm, and within which you tried to rise.

*

What light does all this cast on Spenser's strange jump from the (Catholic) cannibals to the (Protestant) shepherds and their hospitable cottages between cantos viii and ix of book VI? Spenser's thinking is on the whole geographical rather than historical, or spatial rather than chronological (though none of these terms fits him very well, since he tends to elide distinctions between space and time). This means that the rituals of the salivating cannibals are contemporaneous

45 Thomas Whythorne, *The Autobiography of Thomas Whythorne*, ed. J. M. Osborne (Oxford: Oxford University Press, 1961).

with Meliboee and his virtuous cottages, but occur in a different place. This is probably done with polemical intent: Spenser may well wish to suggest that in the wilds of Ireland ritualized flesh-eating continues at the same time as Meliboee and his companions chastely worship virgin goddesses in their godly cottages. This is a salutary reminder that any history of literary representations of households in the sixteenth century has to be alive to geography, and, in a less narrowly physical sense, to where people stand: a Suffolk Catholic in the mid-century finds it natural to align household allegiance with Catholicism, while an urban lawyer like Roper sees the household perspective as an earthly alternative to the viewpoint of a saint. It is perhaps the case that *where* you stand matters as much or more than *when* you stand.

There is also a larger and more paradoxical point that emerges from this discussion, though, which would have appalled Spenser. His gap—which implies that a religious Reformation as if by magic brings about a reformation of the household—was partly created by the habitual erasures of the mid-century by *both* Reformation and Counter-Reformation writing. Like his Marian predecessors, he wants the story of the Reformation to be a story of a radical break or gulf in time, and he does not concentrate too closely on the complex and unpredictable processes (including shifts in the nature of Catholic households) which might have gradually and in haphazard ways led a religious Reformation to contribute to cultural change. It is by going back to that Marian writing that we can hope (at last) to see the sixteenth century as a whole, and see beyond the Reformation and Counter-Reformation myths, gaps, and occlusions which still shape our vision of it.

FURTHER READING

Heal, Felicity. *Hospitality in Early Modern England* (Oxford: Clarendon Press, 1990)

Mertes, Kate. *The English Noble Household, 1250–1600: Good Governance and Politic Rule*, Family, Sexuality and Social Relations in Past Times (Oxford: Basil Blackwell, 1988)

Smith, D. Vance. *Arts of Possession: The Middle English Household Imaginary*, Medieval Cultures (Minneapolis: University of Minnesota Press, 2003)

Starkey, David. 'The Age of the Household: Politics, Society and the Arts *c.*1350–1550', in *The Context of English Literature: The Later Middle Ages*, ed. S. Medcalf (London: Methuen, 1981), 225–90

Wall, Wendy. *Staging Domesticity: Household Work and English Identity in Early Modern Drama*, Cambridge Studies in Renaissance Literature and Culture (Cambridge: Cambridge University Press, 2002)

CHAPTER 26

MONASTICISM

VINCENT GILLESPIE

As royal last words go, they do not have the pithy and alliterative force of George V's 'Bugger Bognor'. But there is much to puzzle over and savour in the reputed final words of Henry VIII: 'I trust in the merits of Christ. All is lost! Monks, monks, monks. So, now all is gone—Empire, Body, and Soul!'[1] The messages are wonderfully mixed: the impeccably Protestant acknowledgement of the merits of Christ as the means of justification and salvation; the distress at the loss of worldly power (with the politically correct recognition of his kingdom as a closed-crown Empire); the traditional lament for transience: all these might confidently have been scripted by one of his courtiers. But the anxiety over a soul feared lost, and the repeated invocation of a religious group who had not been seen in his kingdom for seven years are more puzzling. Was he suffering a vengeful deathbed visitation from those whom he had suppressed, dissolved, and dispersed, or pitifully realizing that he was the first of his line of kings to die without the benefit of their prayers and intercessions for his soul? Though absent from his kingdom, the monks were seemingly not absent from his thoughts, rising up from his subconscious as he faced his own dissolution.

There is a famous image of Henry VIII on his deathbed, gesturing to the young Edward VI as the Pope slumps defeated in the foreground with two shifty looking monks or friars trying to overturn the dais on which Edward VI sits, the whole marked 'Feyned Holines'.[2] One of these religious has features reminiscent of that other type of the unacceptable and untrustworthy outsider, the tormenting and spitting Jew of the medieval *Arma Christi* tradition. Professed religious have become demonized as emblems of an alien Other to be rejected, ejected, and

[1] The words have become legendary, but Thomas Fuller, *The Church-History of Britain from the Birth of Jesus until the year M.DC. XLVIII* (London: Printed for John Williams, 1655), Cent. xvi, Book v, 254, attributes versions of them to the sixteenth-century Catholic apologists Nicholas Sanders and Richard Hall. I am indebted to Margaret Aston for this reference.

[2] For discussion of the image, see Margaret Aston, *The King's Bedpost: Reformation and Iconography in a Tudor Group Portrait* (Cambridge: Cambridge University Press, 1993).

despised. Through the window or in the vignette in the top right hand corner is a scene of iconoclasm and the fall of Babylon, representing the radical shifts of emphasis in Edward's reign that led to a sustained wave of destruction of Catholic imagery. The right of the portrait shows Edward's Council of Regency, including Archbishop Cranmer and Bishop Tunstall, under whom the reformist nature of the Edwardian church had emerged more powerfully, soberly represented as the best of church and state unified in common purpose. This image was probably executed *c.*1570, under Elizabeth. By this date, after the few and frail refoundations of the Marian period had once again been swept away, monasticism could safely be presented as definitively 'foreign', historically sealed in Henry's time. The frontispiece to the 1570 version of John Foxe's *Acts and Monuments* similarly shows monks in disarray at the feet of Henry's throne. Monks are a thing of the past, an emblem of a church long gone.[3]

The 1570s are the decade in which the nature of English Catholicism changed irrevocably, as Catholic clergy trained in England died, retired, or conformed, and as the first waves of Englishmen trained in the new continental 'seminaries' as Catholic secular priests became symbols of the hostile and foreign nature of the Counter-Reformation church militant.[4] In the 1580s this hostility was extended to the Jesuits, who provided potent and powerful hate figures for propagandists of the Elizabethan settlements. These priests no longer saw themselves as servants of the *ecclesia anglicana*—a Bedan term brought back into use in England from Henry V's time at least—but swore allegiance to the universal Church and to the Pope as missionaries for Christ.[5] In this period traditional European and coenobitic monasticism was eclipsed by the new orders such as the Theatines, the Capuchins, and, most notably, the Jesuits, *milites Christi* fighting for an institution in crisis, spiritual stormtroopers of the Counter-Reformation.

Perhaps because they were cloisterers whose way of life was primarily intended to foster a 'hid divinite', monks do not feature heavily in the satiric literature of the post-dissolution period. Most frequently they occur as part of a strangely static taxonomy of reviled religious usually listed in the order of 'monks, chanouns, friars and nunnes'. Friars remained targets of literary satire of the Sir Penetrans Domos kind, especially in the drama of the sixteenth and early seventeenth century. They were joined by moustache-twirling and Machiavellian cardinals as part of a line-up

[3] For reasons of space, reference is usually made to current scholarship as a starting point for further reading. The best recent discussions of the religious changes in sixteenth-century England are Christopher Haigh, *English Reformations: Religion, Politics, and Society under the Tudors* (Oxford: Clarendon Press, 1993) and G. W. Bernard, *The King's Reformation: Henry VIII and the Remaking of the English Church* (New Haven, CT: Yale University Press, 2005).

[4] Lucy E. C. Wooding, *Rethinking Catholicism in Reformation England* (Oxford: Clarendon Press; New York: Oxford University Press, 2000).

[5] Roy Martin Haines, *Ecclesia Anglicana: Studies in the English Church of the Later Middle Ages* (Toronto: University of Toronto Press, 1989).

of two-dimensional villains, often in the pay of foreign powers, under the sway of papal obedience, and typically engaged in some licentious skullduggery, perfidious necromancy, or plain malicious mischief making. The locus of their thrillingly subversive actions was usually safely 'overseas'. But once the suppressions were completed, satirists and propagandists seemed largely content to allow monks to slide off their agenda of agitation and outrage. Monastic ruins instead speedily came to symbolize a world that had passed.[6] For the most part the monks had gone quietly, and then gone quiet.[7] Because monasticism seemed no longer to pose a threat to society or the stability of the realm, it could be treated more gently, more tolerantly, and perhaps even more affectionately:

> I do love these ancient ruins:
> We never tread upon them, but we set
> Our foot upon some reverend history.
> And questionless, here in this open court,
> Which now lies naked to the injuries
> Of stormy weather, some men lie interred
> Loved the church so well, and gave so largely to't,
> They thought it should have canopied their bones
> Till doomsday; but all things have their end.[8]

When John Webster's *The Duchess of Malfi* was first performed in 1612–13, Britain was still littered with the ruins of monastic houses suppressed or surrendered in the 1530s. Many of these had been turned into private residences ('This fortification grew from the ruins of an ancient abbey', says Delio, Antonio's companion in this scene). Others were abandoned to the ravages of time and weather and the opportunistic depredations of local builders.[9] The 'reverend history' sensed by Antonio, his sense of inevitable change, and the sympathy he feels for those who 'lov'd the church so well' articulate the doubleness that characterizes the post-dissolution view of monasticism.

[6] Philip Schwyzer, *Archaeologies of English Renaissance Literature* (Oxford: Oxford University Press, 2007); Margaret Aston, 'English Ruins and English History: The Dissolution and the Sense of the Past', *Journal of the Warburg and Courtauld Institutes*, 36 (1973), 231–55; reprinted in Margaret Aston, *Lollards and Reformers: Images and Literacy in Late Medieval Religion* (London: Hambledon Press, 1984), 313–37; Cathy Shrank, *Writing the Nation in Reformation England, 1530–1580* (Oxford: Oxford University Press, 2004), 65–103.

[7] Peter Cunich, 'Dissolution and De-Conversion: Institutional Change and Individual Response in the 1530s', in *The Vocation of Service to God and Neighbour*, ed. Joan Greatrex (Turnhout: Brepols, 1998), 25–42; Peter Cunich, 'The Ex-Religious in Post-Dissolution Society: Symptoms of Post-Traumatic Stress Disorder?', in *The Religious Orders in Pre-Reformation England*, ed. James G. Clark (Woodbridge: The Boydell Press, 2002), 227–38.

[8] *The Duchess of Malfi*, 5.3.9–17: *John Webster, The Duchess of Malfi*, 4th edn, ed. Brian Gibbons (London: A. & C. Black, 2001; First published 1993), 123.

[9] David R. M. Gaimster and Roberta Gilchrist (eds.), *The Archeology of Reformation 1480–1580: Papers Given at the Archeology of Reformation Conference, February 2001* (Leeds: Maney, 2003).

There are no living people in these desolate landscapes. It is the 'ancient ruins' that speak to Antonio of 'reverend history', and it is they that lie naked and vulnerable to the injuries of the weather. The monk has evaporated as a signifier. It is as if the dissolution had been a neutron bomb. One of the most eloquent dissolution accounts comes from one of the last suppressions:

> And the year of Our Lord 1540 the monastery of Evesham was suppressed by King Henry VIII, the xxxi year of his reign the 30 day of January at evensongs, the convent being in their choir at this verse *Deposuit potentes* ['He has put down the mighty from their seats, and the rich he has sent empty away'] . . . And they would not suffer them to make an end.[10]

Written in the hand of John Alcester, late sacristan of the abbey, the note is found on the flyleaf of a copy of the 1537 Matthew Bible, a potent symbol of the new order, and a touching vehicle for recording the dissolution of the old. So apt as to be almost artful, the idea that the pomp and ceremony of the abbey should be suddenly overthrown during the *Magnificat* by an act of Biblical peripeteia typifies the sense of sudden evaporation: 'And they would not suffer them to make an end.'

According to Walter Benjamin, 'Allegories are, in the realm of thoughts, what ruins are in the realm of things.'[11] In Thomas Storer's *The Life and Death of Thomas Wolsey* (1599), Wolsey's Boethian deathbed lament makes an allegorical linkage between the fall of the cardinal and the ruin of the monasteries:

> Behold my grave, where scarce lies any stone
> To cover me, nor roofe to cover it,
> And when thou seest our ruines both in one,
> One *Epitaph* will equally befit
> The church and me, let never man of wit
> Be usde therein; paint on the churches wall,
> Here lies an Abbey, there a Cardinall.[12]

'Our ruines both in one': Wolsey symbolizes the old religion in all its garishly hubristic pomp, while the Abbey stands as a synecdoche or metonym for the monastic life it nurtured. In real life, the resulting landscape was often harsh and

[10] Joyce A. Youings, *The Dissolution of the Monasteries*, Historical Problems: Studies and Documents (London: Allen and Unwin, 1971), 195. On the end of monastic life at Durham, see now Geoffrey Moorhouse, *The Last Office: 1539 and the Dissolution of a Monastery* (London: Weidenfeld and Nicolson, 2008), largely drawing on materials preserved in *A Description or Brief Declaration of All the Ancient Monuments, Rites and, Customes Belonginge or Beinge within the Monastical Church of Durham before the Suppression, Written in 1593,* ed. James Raine (Surtees Society, London: J. B. Nichols and Son, 1842).

[11] Walter Benjamin, *The Origin of German Tragic Drama,* trans. John Osborne (London: Verso, 1977), 178.

[12] Thomas Storer, *The Life and Death of Thomas Wolsey* (London: [Valentine Simmes for] Thomas Dawson, 1599) (STC 23294), lines 1345–51.

chaotic. Thomas Starkey wrote to Henry VIII in 1536 warning of the dangers of brutally putting down the monastic houses:

> Pity it were that so much fair housing and goodly building, which might with commodity be maintained to the comfort of man should be left to fall to ruin and decay, whereby our country might appear to be so defaced as it had been lately overrun with enemies in time of war[13]

But in literature, the architecture of monasticism is more gently remembered by Shakespeare's 'Bare ruined choirs, where late the sweet birds sang' or Donne's 'when winds in our ruin'd Abbeyes rore', or by Surrey's powerful paraphrase of Ecclesiastes, 'Auncient walles to race is our unstable guyse/ And of their wetherbeten stones to buylde some new devyse'; or in the plangent recusant lament for Walsingham:

> Levell levell with the ground
> The towres doe lye
> Which with their golden, glitteringe tops
> Pearsed once to the skye.[14]

Even the Elizabethan polemicist Barnabe Googe's sustained and sarcastic (if translated) attacks on monasticism in *The Popish Kingdome* (1570) conjure a counter-intuitive imaginative envy of the architecture they left behind in the richness and opulence of this description:

> There standes the stately Towres aloft, and dredfull shot within,
> Or deckt with curious furniture to feast and banquet in,
> In eyery place the Counduites runne, within continually
> And gardens here with pleasaunt herbes, and flowers furnisht ly
> With Cloysters square, and arbours that procure a pleasaunt shade.
> In fine it seems a paradice such as th'almightie made.[15]

[13] Youings, *Dissolution*, 169. Other contemporary comments on the chaos of the urban and rural landscape are found in Leland's *Itinerary*, discussed in Shrank, *Writing the Nation*, 100–1, and in Jennifer Summit, 'Leland's Itinerary and the Remains of the Medieval Past', in *Reading the Medieval in Early Modern England*, ed. Gordon McMullan and David Matthews (Cambridge: Cambridge University Press, 2007), 159–76; Jennifer Summit, *Memory's Library: Medieval Books in Early Modern England* (Chicago: University of Chicago Press, 2008). See also Michael Sherbrook's *The Fall of Religious Houses*, ed. A. G. Dickens, *Tudor Treatises*, Record Series, vol. 125 (Wakefield: Yorkshire Archaeological Society, 1959), 89–142. The spoil of monastic libraries was famously lamented by Bale and Leland; see Timothy Graham and Andrew G. Watson, *The Recovery of the Past in Early Elizabethan England: Documents by John Bale and John Joscelyn from the Circle of Matthew Parker*, Cambridge Bibliographical Society Monograph, 13 (Cambridge: Cambridge Bibliographical Society, 1998).

[14] For discussion and text, see Schwyzer, *Archaeologies*, 84–92.

[15] Thomas Neogeorg, *The Popish Kingdome or Reigne of Antichrist, written in Latin verse by Thomas Naogeorgus, and englyshed by Barnabe Googe* (London: Henry Denham for Richard Watkins, 1570) (STC 15011), Book 2, lines 465–70.

There is a distinct doubleness here, a sense of wonder, tempered by the overarching polemic of the rest of the text. In fact, the satirical freight of this mock-Edenic portrait is clearly in the tradition of medieval anti-monastic estates satire. Compare, for example, the setting of the early fourteenth-century Anglo-Irish satire *The Land of Cokayne*, which begins as architectural fast food and ends with imagery comparable to *Pearl*'s paradisal setting:

Ther is a wel fair abbei
Of white monkes and of grei.
Ther beth bowris and halles.
Al of pasteiis beth the walles,
Of fleis, of fisse and rich met,
The likfullist that man mai et. [*most delightful*[
Fluren cakes beth the schingles alle [*floury cakes*]
Of cherch, cloister, boure, and halle,
The pinnes beth fat podinges, [*nails*]
Rich met to princez and kinges.
Man mai ther-of et inogh
Al with right and noght with wogh. [*justly and not wrongly*]
Al is commune to yung and old,
To stoute and sterne, mek and bold.
Ther is a cloister fair and light,
Brod and lang of sembli sight. [*beautiful*]
The pilers of that cloister alle
Beth iturned of cristale.
With har bas and capitale [*their*]
Of grene Jaspe and rede corale.[16]

Such hyperboles articulate the strange imaginative tension generated between the (sometimes grudging) admiration for and curiosity about coenobitic monastic life, and the natural tendency to suspect, resent, and challenge the hidden reality of that life. Attitudes to monasticism had always been ambivalent and conflicted, poised as anti-clericalism often is between contempt and reverence. For medieval audiences, the very visibility of monks was a sign that all was not well: a monk out of his cloister was like a fish out of water went the old aphorism.[17] For the post-dissolution audience, monks soon became as culturally invisible as they were physically absent. In both cases, their buildings substituted for them in the imaginative landscape.

[16] J. A. W. Bennett and G. V. Smithers (eds.), *Early Middle English Verse and Prose*, 2nd edn (Oxford: Clarendon Press; Oxford University Press, 1968), 40, lines 51–70.

[17] See, for example, Chaucer's use of it as a commonplace in the General Prologue to *The Canterbury Tales*, lines 179–81: Geoffrey Chaucer, *The Riverside Chaucer*, general editor Larry D. Benson, 3rd edn (Oxford: Oxford University Press, 1987), 26. It goes back at least as far as the *Vitae Patrum*, and is also used by Wyclif, Langland, and Gower.

When texts of interior religion came to be produced or adapted for laymen in later medieval England, they often borrowed as their dominant spatial allegory the architecture of a monastic community:

> Blessid is that religioun of whiche the temple is holynes, the scole soothnes, and the cloister stilnes, the chapilte of equite, the dortoir of chastite, and the fermary pitee, the fraitir sobirnes and the hostrie largenes and charite. Therfore who that hath these viij placis goostly in his soule and outward in hise werkis, his religioun is perfight.
>
> (*The Eight Ghostly Dwelling Places*)[18]

For those lay readers who used such texts as part of the burgeoning market for vernacular devotional miscellanies and common-profit books, monasticism existed as powerfully and perhaps more purely within the mental framework of architectural allegory than as an institutional reality to be aspired to, as popular texts like *The Abbey of the Holy Ghost* reveal:

> I make here a book of relygyon of the herte, that is the abbey of the Holi Goost that all tho that mow nout been in bodylyche relygyon the mow been in gostly.... yyf thow wolt holde the in gostly relygyon, and be in rest of soule and swetnesse of herte, holde the withinne and steke thy gates.[19]

But as the monastic ideal moved into the realm of spatial consciousness and interior spiritual enclosures, this left the contemporary reality of monastic life dangerously exposed, vulnerable to criticism and at risk of appearing irrelevant. In the spiritual economy of later medieval England, monastic life could appear sterile and fruitless, even if the monasteries themselves remained useful as family mausoleums, places of pilgrimage to relics and images, and sources of indulgence, intercessory prayer, and masses after death.[20] These were, of course, precisely and quite deliberately the areas that the religious reforms of 1535–8 addressed, effectively rendering monastic life purposeless as the focus of religious observance and spiritual aspiration moved decisively to the parish church. But even in the

[18] John W. Conlee, '*The Abbey of the Holy Ghost* and *The Eight Ghostly Dwelling Places* of Huntington Library HM 744', *Medium Ævum*, 44 (1975), 137–44. On such allegories, see now Christiania Whitehead, *Castles of the Mind: A Study of Medieval Architectural Allegory*, Religion and Culture in the Middle Ages (Cardiff: University of Wales Press, 2003).

[19] N. F. Blake (ed.), *Middle English Religious Prose*, York Medieval Texts (London: Edward Arnold, 1972), 89–91; Nicole Rice, 'Spiritual Ambition and the Translation of the Cloister: *The Abbey* and *Charter of the Holy Ghost*', *Viator*, 33 (2002), 221–60; and the discussions in Nicole Rice, *Lay Piety and Religious Discipline in Middle English Literature*, Cambridge Studies in Medieval Literature, 73 (Cambridge: Cambridge University Press, 2009).

[20] Eamon Duffy, *The Stripping of the Altars: Traditional Religion in England c.1400–c.1580* (London: Yale University Press, 1992); Eamon Duffy, 'Religious Belief', in *A Social History of England 1200–1500*, ed. Rosemary Horrox and W. M. Ormrod (Cambridge: Cambridge University Press, 2006), 293–339; Eamon Duffy, *Marking the Hours: English People and Their Prayers 1240–1570* (New Haven, CT and London: Yale University Press, 2006); Karen Stöber, *Late Medieval Monasteries and Their Patrons: England and Wales, c.1300–1540*, Studies in the History of Medieval Religion, 29 (Woodbridge: The Boydell Press, 2007).

fourteenth and fifteenth centuries some sections of the laity were coming to see that perfection might more readily be achieved by a spiritual pilgrimage inwards and by enclosing oneself in the love and service of God than by the actual adoption of monastic habits and vows. This process was already under way before Wyclif and Lollardy, but was undoubtedly fuelled by the polemical views of both. The mood was already turning against traditional (i.e. Benedictine and Cistercian) monasticism in later medieval England. The best days of monasticism were always already in the past.[21]

There is a strikingly idealistic account of coenobitic monasticism in passus 10 of the B text of *Piers Plowman*:

> For if hevene be on this erthe, and ese to any soule,
> It is in cloistre or in scole, by manye skiles I fynde.
> For in cloistre cometh no man to chide ne to fighte,
> But al is buxomnesse there and bokes, to rede and to lerne.
> In scole there is scorn but if a clerk wol lerne,
> And gret love and likyng, for ech of hem l[er]eth oother. (B. 10.296–302)[22]

But this apparent idealism is soon undercut by a catalogue of criticisms of contemporary monastic practice drawn straight from the repertoire of medieval anti-monastic satire:

> Ac now is Religion a rydere, a romere by stretes,
> A ledere of lovedayes and a lond buggere,
> A prikere on a palfrey fro manere to manere,
> An heep of houndes at his ers as he a lord were. (B. 10.303–6)

Chaucer used the same satirical repertoire in the portrait of his Monk.[23] But while Chaucer, almost uniquely, tries to give his monk a local habitation and a name, the habit of his order and the *habitus* of a real person, Langland's wandering monk is flattened by his allegoresis as 'Religion'. Medieval representations of monasticism scarcely ever aspire to escape from the schematic and the allegorical: they remain

[21] But for some evidence of the actual vitality of late medieval English monastic life, in addition to Duffy, *Stripping of the Altars*, see also James G. Clark (ed.), *The Religious Orders in Pre-Reformation England*, Studies in the History of Medieval Religion, 18 (Woodbridge: The Boydell Press, 2002); James G. Clark (ed.), *The Culture of Medieval English Monasticism*, Studies in the History of Medieval Religion, 30 (Woodbridge: The Boydell Press, 2007). Martin Heale, 'Training in Superstition? Monasteries and Popular Religion in Late Medieval and Reformation England', *Journal of Ecclesiastical History*, 58 (2007), 417–39, argues for the continuing importance of monasteries as places of pilgrimage.

[22] William Langland, *The Vision of Piers Plowman: A Critical Edition of the B-Text Based on Trinity College Cambridge Ms. B.15.17*, ed. A. V. C. Schmidt (London: Dent, 1978), 111.

[23] The classic discussion is Jill Mann, *Chaucer and Medieval Estates Satire: The Literature of Social Classes and the 'General Prologue' to the Canterbury Tales* (Cambridge: Cambridge University Press, 1973), 17–37.

conveniently flat surfaces onto which can be projected the prejudices, fantasies, and idealisms of contemporary society, and this flatness was later exploited in the dissolution polemics.

Langland's passus 10 account culminates in this apocalyptic warning:

> Ac ther shal come a kyng and confesse yow religiouses,
> And bete yow, as the Bible telleth, for brekynge of youre rule,
> And amende monyals, monkes and chanons,
> And puten hem to hir penaunce—
> *Ad pristinum statum ire.* (B 10.314–7)

The need for a strong king who would reform monasticism would have been seen by Langland's London readers in the fifteenth century as prophetic of the hard line taken by Henry V against laxity in religious life, part of the contemporary reform of the church 'in head and members', culminating in 1421 in a Benedictine general chapter presided over by the king himself, and shown by his personal preference for strictly eremitic orders such as Carthusians and Birgittines.[24] But in the sixteenth century these lines encouraged the anti-Catholic polemicist Robert Crowley to hear pre-echoes of the attitudes of his own time and to add against this passage in the third imprint of his edition: 'Reade thys /The suppression of Abbayes', or to place against a similar warning at Passus 5.46–7: 'The suppression of Abbayes/ Good counsel'.[25]

No major new monasteries were founded in England after Henry V's royal foundations of the Carthusians at Sheen and the Birgittines at Syon, both strictly enclosed and notably austere orders that were largely untainted by contemporary criticisms of monastic life. Instead royal, noble, and gentry patronage turned towards chantries, colleges, grammar schools, and other 'mixed life' foundations, whose religious engagement was both more transparent and more tangibly useful to a literate laity increasingly striving to exercise and develop their own actual and

[24] On Langland's fifteenth-century London readership, see Kathryn Kerby-Fulton and Steven Justice, 'Langlandian Reading Circles, and the Civil Service in London and Dublin, 1380–1427', *New Medieval Literatures*, 1 (1997), 60–83. On Henry V's religious reforms, see the classic short account by J. I. Catto, 'Religious Change under Henry V', in *Henry V: The Practice of Kingship*, ed. G. L. Harriss (Oxford: Oxford University Press, 1985; reprinted Stroud: Sutton, 1993), 97–115; Vincent Gillespie, 'The Mole in the Vineyard: Wyclif at Syon in the Fifteenth Century', in *Text and Controversy from Wyclif to Bale: Essays in Honour of Anne Hudson*, ed. Helen Barr and Ann M. Hutchison, Medieval Church Studies, 4 (Turnhout: Brepols, 2005), 131–62; Ian Forrest, *The Detection of Heresy in Late Medieval England* (Oxford: Oxford University Press, 2005).

[25] *The vision of pierce Plowman nowe the second time imprinted by Roberte Crowlye dwellynge in Elye rentes in Holburne whereunto are added certayne notes and cotations in the mergyne, geuyng light to the reader* (London: [R. Grafton for] Robert Crowley, [1550]) (STC 19907), fols. 21^{r}, 50^{r}. See the important recent discussion of Crowley's *marginalia* in Larry Scanlon, 'Langland, Apocalypse and the Early Modern Editor', in *Reading the Medieval in Early Modern England*, ed. Gordon McMullan and David Matthews (Cambridge: Cambridge University Press, 2007), 51–73, at 72.

devotional literacy, and increasingly demanding better standards of preaching and pastoral care.[26]

The Augustinian canon John Audelay, in his sequence of poems *The Council of Conscience* completed by 1426, powerfully addresses the growing sense of deficiency in traditional monasticism:

> I move these mater to monkys in a meke maner
> And to al relegyous that beth i-blest by Goddis ordynans;
> Forst Saynt Benet hom enformyd to kepe her cloyster
> In povert and in prayers in preve penawns,
> And to abeyde abstinens and foresake abundans...
>
> Fore in the rewle of relygyous ther may ye rede
> Hou the graceous goodys of God schuld be spend...
> Ye schuld have no propurte; on the pore hit schuld be spend;
> And hold up youre houshold and youre housyng,
> And let hem not adoune,
> And herbore the pore pur charyte
> And yef mete and dreng to the nede
> And cumford hem that woful be,
> Ellis be ye no relegyon.[27]

Reading the change of mood and temper in popular sentiment towards monasticism, Audelay also praises the newly founded Birgittines for the superlative aspirations of their vocation:

> Was never holeer order preveleged in no plas
> Fore to red al the rollis of relegyown.[28]

In the divinely dictated *Regula salvatoris*, Christ characterizes Birgitta's new order as a fresh beginning for monasticism in response to the decay and dissolution of older forms:

> But nowe I playne me that the wall of the vyneyerdes is distroyed, the kepers slepe, and thevys entyr in, the rotys arn undyr dolvyn of mollis, the braunches arn wedryd by drynesse and the smale brawnches that the grapys shulde growe on are born downe wyth

[26] For recent work on this, see Clive Burgess and Eamon Duffy, *The Parish in Late Medieval England: Proceedings of the 2002 Harlaxton Symposium*, Harlaxton Medieval Studies, 14 (Donington: Shaun Tyas, 2006); Clive Burgess and Martin Heale, *The Late Medieval English College and Its Context* (Woodbridge: York Medieval Press, 2008); and the collection of documents in R. N. Swanson, *Catholic England: Faith, Religion, and Observance before the Reformation* (Manchester: Manchester University Press, 1993).

[27] John Audelay, *The Poems of John Audelay*, ed. Ella Keats Whiting, EETS, o.s., 184 (London: Oxford University Press, 1931), poem 2, 16–17. A new edition of Audelay's poems, edited by Susanna Fein, is forthcoming; see also *My Wyl and my Wrytyng: Essays on John the Blind Audelay*, ed. Susanna Fein (Kalamazoo, MI: Western Institute Publications, 2009).

[28] Saint Bridget of Sweden, *Revelations of St. Birgitta*, ed. W. P. Cumming, EETS, o.s., 178 (London: Oxford University Press, 1929), xxxv.

> the wynde and trode under the fete. Therfore lees that wyne shuld fayle in alle wyse, I shal plante me a vyneyerde of newe in which thoue shalt bere the brawnches of my wordes my freende shall sett them and I my self god schall put the*m* to fastnesse of grace.[29]

The early fifteenth-century English Benedictines were certainly aware of this change of sentiment.[30] In *The declaryng of religion*, the Benedictine author of the lyrics in Digby 102 offers an account of monasticism as a state of purity and idealistic commitment, characterized by internal motivation rather than external show:

> Tonsure, abyte, ne no wede
> Nes no cause of religeon.
> Ne wakyng, ne fastyng, ne almesdede,
> Ne preyere, ne oreson,
> But the herte therto take hede
> With werkys of discrecion.
> Devocion maketh soules to spede
> With werkis of contemplacion.[31]

These words respond directly to the Wycliffite challenges to monastic life, but, more remarkably, they prefigure in surprisingly close terms the 1535 Injunctions to Monastic Visitors:

> [T]rue religion is not contained in apparell, manner of going, shaven heads, and such other marks, nor in silence, fasting, uprising in the night, singing, and such other kinds of ceremonies, but in cleanness of mind, pureness of living, Christ's faith not feigned, and brotherly charity, and true honouring of God in spirit and verity.
>
> (Injunction 18)[32]

Monasticism exists in the late medieval English *imaginaire* as an absent presence every bit as powerfully as it does in the post-dissolution world. The bizarre late

29 *Regula Salvatoris*, 'prologue', in *The Rewyll of Seynt Sauioure and Other Middle English Brigittine Legislative Texts*, ed. James Hogg, 4 vols, Salzburger Studien zur Anglistik und Amerikanistik (Salzburg: Institut für Englische Sprache und Literatur, 1978–80), 2: 1–58, at 6. The standard edition of the versions of the Latin is *Regula Salvatoris*, ed. S. Eklund, Den Heliga Birgitta Opera Minora 1, Samlingar utgivna av Svenska Fornskriftsällskapet, Andra Serien, *Latinska Skrifter*, 8.1 (Lund: Lund University Press, 1975).

30 See, for example, James G. Clark, *A Monastic Renaissance at St. Albans: Thomas Walsingham and His Circle, c. 1350–1440* (Oxford: Clarendon Press; New York: Oxford University Press, 2004).

31 D. J. Kail (ed.), *Twenty-six Political and Other Poems (Including 'Petty Job') from the Oxford Mss. Digby 102 and Douce 322*, EETS, o.s., 124 (London: Kegan Paul, Trench, Trübner, 1904), 84. A new edition of the lyrics of MS Digby 102 by Helen Barr appeared in 2009 from Exeter Medieval Texts and Studies. The lyrics, dating from the reign of Henry V, are probably by the same well-connected Benedictine author responsible for a set of politically aware macaronic sermons: Patrick Horner (ed.), *A Macaronic Sermon Collection from Late Medieval England: Oxford, MS Bodley 649*, Studies and Texts, 153 (Toronto: Pontifical Institute of Mediaeval Studies, 2006).

32 Translation cited from G. W. Bernard, *The King's Reformation: Henry VIII and the Remaking of the English Church* (New Haven, CT: Yale University Press, 2005), 253; cf. Youings, *Dissolution*, 151. The Latin text is in David Wilkins (ed.), *Concilia Magnae Britanniae*, 4 Vols. (London, 1737), 3: 789–91.

fifteenth-century version of the Life of Buddha, *Barlam and Iosaphat*, celebrates an extreme eremitic form of monasticism rooted in an unattainably distant past and an unimaginable geographical remoteness:

> What tyme that abbeis were first ordeyned and monkis were first gadered togydre, al the world spake of here good conversacion, and of here gostly lyf and holy, that thei leved in. For here good loos, and here good fame, spredde thorough-out the world. For many of hem forsoke al that thei had, and went and dwelled in deserte, to put away the lustis of the flessh, and of the world, there to lede here lyf in holy contemplacion.... That tyme, as the glorious use and manere was of Crysten monkis, thei dispsised the fals ydolatrie of the kynge, and dredde nat ne lefte for no thretenynge, but prechid Goddis worde opinly and taught besely the pepele to lyve in good lyf, and in Goddis worship.[33]

In the world of fifteenth-century English monasticism, this portrait only chimes with the rigorous pastoral and ascetic life of the brethren of Syon Abbey (whom Birgitta in any case always calls *sacerdoti* rather than *monachi*), and the eremitic aspirations of the Carthusian foundations. They represent the one strand of English monasticism that generated tradeable cultural capital, and retained broad popular credibility right up to the dissolution.[34] As the reformers of the 1530s found to their cost and difficulty, these were precisely the houses that retained popular respect, and recruited men of nobility of spirit and bravery of conscience like Richard Reynolds and John Houghton.[35]

The doubleness of the medieval response to monasticism is also well attested in early sixteenth-century orthodox writing. As in the early fifteenth century, new educational imperatives were beginning to assert themselves, more sharply pointed by the New Learning (including Erasmus's well documented reservations about monastic life). In 1514, Bishop Richard Foxe of Winchester, a close adviser of

[33] John C. Hirsh (ed.), *Barlam and Iosaphat: A Middle English Life of Buddha*, EETS, o.s., 290 (Oxford: Oxford University Press, 1986), 3.

[34] William Tyndale felt it necessary directly to attack 'Sion and the Carterhouse of Shene': see William Tyndale, *An exposicion vppon the v. vi. vii. chapters of Mathew, which thre chaptres are the keye and the dore of the scripture* ([Antwerp?], 1533) (STC 24440), fols. 70^{r-v}. Thomas Cromwell's commissioners spent much time and energy in monitoring and persuading both orders to accept Henry's divorce from Catherine of Aragon and subsequently the Royal Supremacy. Their letters to him report in riveting detail their views of the state of the English monasteries, and the mechanics of their suppression and surrender: Thomas Wright (ed.), *Three Chapters of Letters Relating to the Suppression of Monasteries*, Camden Society Publications, 26 (London: John Bowyer Nichols and Son, 1843); George Henry Cook, *Letters to Cromwell and Others on the Suppression of the Monasteries* (London: John Baker, 1965). Geoffrey Baskerville, *English Monks and Suppression of the Monasteries* (Jonathan Cape: London, 1937) still offers some useful materials.

[35] For a sixteenth-century account of the execution of the Birgittine Richard Reynolds and the Carthusian John Houghton on 4 May 1535, see Maurice Chauncy, *The Various Versions of the Historia Aliquot Martyrum Anglorum Maxime Octodecim Cartusianorum Sub Rege Henrico Octavo Ob Fidei Confessionem Et Summa Pontificis Jura Vindicanda Interemptorum by Dom Maurice Chauncy*, 3 vols., ed. John Clark, Analecta Cartusiana, 86 (Salzburg: Institut für Anglistik und Amerikanistik, 2007).

Henry VIII, had intended to found Corpus Christi College Oxford as a college for monks, but had been allegedly persuaded by Bishop Hugh Oldham of Exeter not to

> build houses and provide livelihood for a company of bussing monks whose end and fall we may live to see. No, no it is more meet a great deal that we should have care to provide for the increase of learning and for such as by their learning should do good in the church and the commonwealth.[36]

The evangelical humanism of early sixteenth-century Catholicism was fuelling changes of temper and of mood towards monastic life similar if more moderate than those that would later inspire the Protestant reformers.[37] Hythlodaeus in More's *Utopia* (1516) suggests that the Utopians' interest in Christianity was partly fired by their discovery that 'Christ approved of life in common for his disciples, and that it is still practised among the most genuine Christian communities.' This communalism is close to an idealized form of monastic life, as is the Utopian religious sect which is

> celibate and not only abstains from any sexual activity but also eats no meat (and some of them no animal products at all), totally rejecting the pleasures of this life as harmful, longing only for those of the world to come, which they strive to obtain by toil and vigils.[38]

But More's utopian view of monasticism depended on an expansion of the monastic confines to encompass a whole society. Such views robbed monastic life of its spiritual cachet and clerical distinctiveness, to the extent that Erasmus could provocatively ask in the prologue to the 1518 edition of his *Enchiridion* 'What is the state but a great monastery?' Even ecclesiological traditionalists seemed to be doubting the worth of monastic life. Thomas Starkey's *Dialogue between Pole and Lupset*, composed between 1529 and 1532, attributes to Pole the view that the laxness of contemporary monasticism was the 'ground & mother of al mysordur in the church . . . of thys fountayn springyth al the sklandur of the church'.[39] He argues that admission after proof of life should only be granted to those over the age of 30 years, and, reflecting the high status of eremitic orders, that the life should be austere and ascetically contemplative:

[36] Cited Cook, *Letters to Cromwell*, 13.

[37] See, for example, Richard Rex, *The Theology of John Fisher* (Cambridge: Cambridge University Press, 1991); Brendan Bradshaw and Eamon Duffy (eds.), *Humanism, Reform and the Reformation: The Career of Bishop John Fisher* (Cambridge: Cambridge University Press, 1989).

[38] Thomas More, *Utopia*, ed. Clarence H. Miller (New Haven: Yale University Press, 2001), 122; Walter M. Gordon, 'The Monastic Achievement and More's Utopian Dream', *Medievalia et Humanistica*, New Series, 9 (1979), 199–214.

[39] Thomas Starkey, *A Dialogue between Pole and Lupset*, ed. Thomas F. Mayer, Camden Society Fourth Series, 37 (London: Offices of the Royal Historical Society, University College London, 1989), 135.

> I wold not that thes relygyouse men wyth theyr monasterys schold utturly be take away, but only some gud reformatyon to be had to them, & schortly to say I wold thynke in that behalfe chefely thys to be a gud remedy that youth schold have no place therein at al but only such men as by fervent love of relygyon movyd therto flying the daungerys & snarys of the world, schold ther have place & yf that gape were onys stoppyd I dare wel say theyr nombur wold not be over grete we schold have fewar in nombur relygouse men but bettur in lyfe. (103–4)

In real life, Pole seems to have held very similar views, and to have recommended them as part of a curial commission to the Pope in 1537, the *Consilium de emendanda ecclesia.*[40]

By contrast, the English Protestant reformers in the 1520s and 1530s sought to present traditional monasticism as a form of life contrary to scripture and the traditions of the early church, which they argued had been introduced into England in 597 by Augustine of Canterbury. John Bale in *The Actes of the English Votaryes* argued that Augustine of Canterbury was 'not of the ordre of Christ as was Peter but of the superstityeyouse secte of Benet'. Simon Fish's translation of *The summe of holy scripture* (first published 1529) asserts that 'in tymes passed there were no holyer parsones than monkes...so was then the lyfe of monkes the fontaygne of christendome'.[41] He argues that the first monks took no vows, were not constrained to chastity, and willingly subordinated themselves to their abbot. As the cloisters of monks multiplied, argues Fish, so all charity among them diminished: 'the lyfe of monks as it is nowe used in the worlde is none other thing but a secte and theryn lyeth no more holynesse than in the lyfe of a good housholder'. Indeed in contrast to the productively 'mixed life' of householders, the fruits of a monastic life given over to ceremonies and outward show is vanity, vainglory, and inflated self-esteem. 'Monks', a term originally meaning solitaries, should now be called 'religious' (or 'bound persons'), 'for whate is now the life of the religious but a supersticious subjection unto certayn vayne ceremonyes'.[42]

[40] John C. Olin, 'The *Consilium De Emendanda Ecclesia,* 1537', in his *Catholic Reform: From Cardinal Ximenes to the Council of Trent, 1495–1563* (New York: Fordham University Press, 1990), 65–79.

[41] John Bale, *The actes of Englysh votaryes comprehendynge their vnchast practyses and examples by all ages, from the worldes begynnynge to thys present yeare, collected out of their owne legendes and chronycles by Iohan Bale* (Wesel (i.e. Antwerp), 1546) (STC 1270), fol. 23^{v}; (Henricus Bomelius, trans. Simon Fish), *The summe of the holye scripture: and ordinarye of the Christen teachyng, the true Christen faithe, by the whiche we be all iustified* ((Antwerp), 1529) (STC 3036), cap. 16.

[42] For discussion of the literary explorations of anti-monastic polemic, the standard resources are Alistair Fox, *Politics and Literature in the Reigns of Henry VII and Henry VIII* (Oxford: Blackwell, 1989); Greg Walker, *Persuasive Fictions: Faction, Faith, and Political Culture in the Reign of Henry VIII* (Aldershot: Scolar Press, 1996); Thomas Betteridge, *Literature and Politics in the English Reformation* (Manchester: Manchester University Press, 2004); Greg Walker, *Writing under Tyranny: English Literature and the Henrician Reformation* (Oxford: Oxford University Press, 2005).

John Foxe, in the 1570 version of the *Acts and Monuments*, elaborating his praise of Thomas Cromwell as '*malleus monachorum*' and 'our christian Camyllus', argues that the monasticism destroyed by Henry was both a powerful deviation from its original character and identity and, more seriously, responsible for the wholesale deformation of English Christianity:

> [L]et us nowe come to the first institution of these orders and houses of Munkerye, and consider how and to what ende they were first instituted and erected here among the Saxons, at the first foundation of them, about the tyme 666 . . . for as the trade of their lives was too wretched and bestiall, so the profession of their doctrine was intollerable, fraught with all superstition, full of much idolatrie, and utterly contrarye to the grace of the Gospell, and doctrine of Christ . . . yet notwithstandyng the Monkes of those dayes were not lyke to the Monkes of our tyme, nor their houses then, lyke to our Abbayes now . . . as ignoraunce and superstition with tyme increased: so the number and swarme of Monkes still more and more multiplied in such sort . . . Of whiche number began Austen the first Archbyshop of the Sea of Canterbury, and the most parte of all other Archbyshops after hym, vntill the tyme of the Conquest, and after.[43]

This attempt to appeal to the ancient purity of the English church is of course a hallmark of English Reformation polemic and self-invention, where the adjective 'monkish' becomes a byword for devious and deceitful.[44] But the historical identity that was articulated by the reformers borrows heavily from that already crafted for the *ecclesia anglicana* by the English delegates at the Council of Constance under the leadership of Henry Chichele and under the inspired nationalism of Henry V, just as the political advisors of Henry VIII, and the king himself, based many of their territorial and imperial claims and modelled their kingly persona on that of Henry V. The continuities in ecclesiastical critique and political self-presentation between early fifteenth-century and early modern England are powerful and sustained. There are few manoeuvres employed by the sixteenth-century reformers that had not already been deployed by their medieval predecessors.[45]

The historical consciousness of the monastic reformers in the sixteenth century is frequently revealed in their writings and comments. Thomas Cromwell had been part of Wolsey's *familia* when the cardinal had suppressed monastic

[43] John Foxe, *Actes and Monuments of These Latter and Perillous Dayes, Touching Matters of the Church, Wherein Ar Comprehended and Described the Great Persecutions, Horrible Troubles, That Have Bene Wrought and Practised by the Romishe Prelates, Speciallye in This Realme of England and Scotlande, from the Yeare of Our Lorde, a Thousande, Unto the Tyme Nowe Present. Gathered and Collected According to the True Copies* (London, 1570), Book 8, 1349–51. Consulted online at <http://www.hrionline.ac.uk/johnfoxe/main/8_1570_1349>.

[44] Thomas Betteridge, *Tudor Histories of the English Reformation, 1530–83*, St Andrews Studies in Reformation History (Aldershot: Ashgate, 1999); Helen L. Parish, *Monks, Miracles, and Magic: Reformation Representations of the Medieval Church* (London: Routledge, 2005).

[45] For a recent overview of this period, see James Simpson, *Reform and Cultural Revolution*, The Oxford English Literary History, Vol 2: 1350–1547 (Oxford: Oxford University Press, 2002).

houses to endow his proposed new colleges in Ipswich and Oxford and to fund proposed new dioceses.[46] The 1536 Act of Suppression positions itself as merely the latest in a sequence of visitations and reformations of monastic life reaching back into the Middle Ages. Ostensibly, therefore, the campaign of the 1530s was not to destroy monasticism but to reform it. The 1536 Act for the Suppression of Smaller Monasteries speaks of the 'manifest sin, vicious, carnal, and abominable living' to be found in small houses, while acknowledging that in the 'divers and great solemn monasteries of this realm... religion is right well kept and observed.'[47] But by the time that the preamble to an Act of 1539 was drafted in Henry VIII's own hand, it is possible for him to remark in a studiedly understated manner:

> Forasmuch as it is not unknown the slothful and ungodly life which hath been used amongst all those sort which have borne the name of religious folk...[48]

Certain truths about monasticism are now self-evident ('not unknown' is a nice touch), while the entire cadre of monks ('all those sort') who practised this slothful and ungodly life are consigned to an already sealed off past ('hath been used... have borne'). The 'pastness' of monasticism has become part of the propaganda in favour of its own present destruction. As the Pilgrimage of Grace showed, the invisibility of monastic life made effective public rebuttal almost impossible. The already empty signifier of monasticism could be filled with innuendo and exaggeration against 'Abbey lubbers' or what Foxe called 'the vnprofytable multitude of idle Epicures' (*Actes and Monumentes*, 1563, Book 3, 596).

As early as 1528, *Rede me and be not wroth* was already deploying the main themes of the anti-monastic attack.[49] In this 'brefe Dialoge betwene two prestes servauntes / named Watkyn and Ieffraye', Ieffraye fuels the prurient curiosity of Watkyn with his accounts of life inside the monastery. He attacks monastic ceremonies and liturgy by claiming that choir monks sing words that they do not understand. He outlines 'the intollerabel enormitie' (line 969) of religious persons who in their greed for goods and possessions seduce 'the peoples simplicite' (line 978) with their apparent 'wilfull poverte'. Watkyn responds:

> I marvayle men make no restraynt
> Their dissaytfulnes to attaynt
> Whyls it is open and aperte. (lines 979–81)

To which Ieffraye replies, in a clearly coat-trailing reference to Henry VIII:

[46] On Wolsey's monastic reforms and suppressions, see Peter Gwyn, *The King's Cardinal: The Rise and Fall of Thomas Wolsey* (London: Pimlico, 1992).

[47] Youings, *Dissolution*, 155; Bernard, *King's Reformation*, 267–76.

[48] Cited from Wooding, *Rethinking Catholicism*, 65; Bernard, *King's Reformation*, 457.

[49] Jerome Barlow, *Rede Me and Be Nott Wrothe* (Strasburg: J. Schott, 1528) (STC 1462.7), part 2, subsequent references by line number from LION (Literature Online <http://lion.chadwyck.co.uk>).

Daniel is not yett come
Which shall obtayne the roume
Their fraudfull wayes to subuerte. (lines 982–4)

Watkyn follows the thought through to its logical (if at this stage still radical) conclusion:

I se then he werre a very chylde
Which wolde eny mo abbeys bylde
Yf the goodes shuld be so yll spent. (lines 1060–2)

To which Ieffraye delivers the telling punchline:

It werre fare better I suppose
To plucke downe a grett sorte of those
Which are all redy of costly bildynge. (lines 1063–5)

Watkyn, parroting the usual defence of the role of the monasteries in the life of the church, is alarmed at this prospect because of the effect it will have on hospitality for wayfarers, care for the sick, charity, and the good governance of landholdings. But Ieffraye argues that this is all sham and show and that the monks behave like cormorants, leaving little for the poor and needy, while systematically fleecing the laity though phoney shrines, images, and relics, worshipping

paynted stockes and stones
With shrynes/full of rotten bones
To the whiche they make oblacion. (lines 1423–5)

Ieffraye's trump card in support of the need for suppression is the example of Wolsey's actions against the houses recently put down:

I am sure thou hast hearde spoken
What monasteries he hath broken
With out their fownders consentes.
He subverteth churches / and chappells
Takynge a waye bokes and bells
With chalesces / and vestmentes.
He plucketh downe the costly leades
That it maye rayne on saynctes heades
Not sparynge god nor oure ladye.
Where as they red servyce divyne
There is groutynge of pigges and swyne
With lowynge of oxen and kyne.
The aultres of their celebracions
Are made pearches for hens and capons
Defoylynge theym with their durt. (lines 1693–707)

Although reporting this in politic tones of disapproval, and calling the hubristic Wolsey 'the Englisshe Lucifer' (line 1373), Barlow is also mapping out the way that Wolsey's precedent provides the script for a scenario of destruction that will be re-enacted many times over the next twelve years.

Although most post-dissolution public literature quickly 'let the monasteries go', as Foxe had encouraged in 1570 (Book 8, 1351), allowing them to become symbolically unpeopled ciphers, the various Reformation treatments of King John's typologically prophetic battle with the Church grant the monks a real (if unflattering) role. John's campaign of hostility towards papal power and against the riches and privileges of the monasteries offered irresistibly easy parallels with Henry VIII's travails. In John Bale's pantomimic *King Johan*, dating from 1538 or 1539, in the white heat of the suppressions and perhaps written for and performed before Archbishop Cranmer, the medieval tradition of personification allegory in the morality play allows Sedicyon to appear as a monastic deceiver:[50]

> I am Sedicyon playne
> In every relygyon and munkysh secte I rayne
> Havyng you prynces in scorne, hate and dysdayne. (lines 186–8)

Reflecting the revised historiography of the English Reformation, John wants a pure and reformed Church restored to the idealism of its earliest and most glorious period:

> Yes I wold have a church, not of dysgysyd shavelynges
> But of faythfull hartes and charytable doynges
> For whan Christes chyrch was in her hyeste glory
> She knoew neyther thes sectes nor ther ipocrysy. (lines 429–32)

And when Clergye, misglossing Scripture, describes the church as 'beawtyfull, decked with many holy relygyons' (line 440) and presents him with a comically elongated list of fifty-seven orders of monks, canons, and friars, John soberly remarks:

> I wonder that yow for such veyne popych baggage
> Can suffyre Englond to be impoveryshyd
> And mad a beggar; ye are very yll advysyd. (lines 477–9)

Later on, when confronting Treason (a capital crime widely alleged against and prosecuted on monks by Henrician agents in the period of the suppressions), John criticizes Latinate mumbo jumbo and pointedly asks

> Hast thu knowne such wayes and sought no reformacyon?

50 All references are by line number to John Bale, *King Johan*, ed. Barry B. Adams (San Marino, CA: The Huntington Library, 1969).

to which Treason replies:

> It is the lyvynge of our hole congregacyon,
> If supersticyons and ceremonyes from us fall
> Farwele monke and chanon, priest, fryer, bishopp and all. (lines 1843–6)

Bale's play labours under the considerable limitations of his own dramatic competency, and of the creaky allegoresis that haunts medieval and early modern explorations of monasticism. But, except for Shakespeare, the story of King John provided an imaginative place where issues and ideas could be rehearsed, explored, and reinforced, as John Foxe well knew.[51] Coming from much later in the process of religious transformation, part 2 of the 1591 *Troublesome Raigne of Iohn King of England* uses the image of the reforming monarch and the demonization of monks in a much more subtle and theatrical manner.[52] John's purpose in sequestering monastic lands is now articulated in the crisp lexis of well honed nationalistic propaganda:

> Ile ceaze the lazie Abbey lubbers lands
> Into my hands to pay my men of warre.
> The Pope and Popelings shall not grease themselves
> With golde and groates, that are the souldiers due.

But the keystone encounter between the proto-Reformation ruler and his monastic adversaries is staged when the king arrives, sick and weary, at Swinestead abbey to rest overnight. John's arrival is overseen by a disgruntled monk whose soliloquy on whether to assassinate the king is a virtuoso piece of blatantly treasonable self-justification:

> Is this the King that never loud a Frier?
> Is this the man that doth contemne the Pope?
> Is this the man that robd the holy Church,
> And yet will flye unto a Friory?
> Is this the King that aymes at Abbeys lands?
> Is this the man whome all the world abhorres,
> And yet will flye unto a Friory?
> Accurst be Swinsteed Abbey, Abbot, Friers,
> Moncks, Nuns, and Clarks, and all that dwells therein,
> If wicked *Iohn* escape alive away.
> Now if that thou wilt looke to merit heaven,
> And be canonizd for a holy Saint:
> To please the world with a deserving worke,

[51] There is an engraving of the Swinestead Abbey episode designed for binding at p. 256 of the 1570 edition of the *Actes and Monumentes*.

[52] *The Troublesome Raigne of Iohn King of England with the Discouerie of King Richard Cordelions Base Sonne (Vulgarly Named, the Bastard Fawconbridge): Also the Death of King Iohn at Swinstead Abbey* (London: Sampson Clarke, 1591) (STC 14644), sig. B3^{v}.

Be thou the man to set thy cuntrey free,
And murder him that seekes to murder thee.[53]

Potent as this is in its Marlovian malevolence, even here the author needs to borrow satirical velocity in his portrayal of the treasonous monk from the still virulent hostility to meddling and devious friars, who are much more visible as contemporary hate figures. And in the murderous threat to the person of the King there is surely an echo of the widespread perception that Jesuits were all vowed to murder the Queen. So eroded is the cultural knowledge of monasticism by this date that the Abbot of Swinestead finds himself speaking classic anti-Catholic rebukes in his questions to the monk: 'What, at thy *mumpsimus*?' Monks in the Reformation version of the King John story are little more than comic hybrids from a variety of anti-Catholic *topoi* of the period. Monasticism itself remains the empty signifier that it rapidly became after the houses were put down.

One of the main reasons for this imaginative vacancy was that, as Foxe had exultantly pointed out, Mary had had neither the money nor the political leverage to restore more than a handful of monastic houses in her short reign, and, in keeping with the changed times, these were only of the most austere and eremitical orders. Nor did her Archbishop, Reginald Pole, have the theological will to go for a wholesale restoration. In a sermon to the citizens of London, he argued that the restoration of parochial life was a much higher priority than the return of the monasteries,

> And yf you were able, and had suche a gay mynde to restore the ruynes of the chyrches, yet there be other chyrches that are nowe fyrst to be helpen, and these be your parryshe-chyrches; whiche albeyt they have not byn cast downe by coloure of authoryte, as the abbayes were, yet they have byn sufferede to fawle downe of themselves maynye, and yn lyke maner spoyled as the monasteryes were. And to thys I exhorte you furthewyth to sett your hande, the whyche you maye yn no wyse fayle to doo, excepte you wyll haue your people wax brutyshe and wylde, and your commonwealthe wythout foundacion.[54]

No doubt the refusal—indeed the economic and political inability—of the Marian restoration to reconstruct the monastic realm as it had been before 1535, and the limiting of the handful of restored houses to the most austere and eremitic orders, meant that the Elizabethan onslaught against the symbols and practices of restored Marian Catholicism could afford to be largely silent on the subject of monasticism. In the waterman John Taylor's early Jacobean paean to the Queen, where Elizabeth was praised for purifying England and establishing a new vernacular religious order, the abbeys get only a passing mention:

[53] *The First and Second Part of the Troublesome Raigne of Iohn King of England with the Discouerie of King Richard Cordelions Base Sonne (Vulgarly Named, the Bastard Fawconbridge:) Also, the Death of King Iohn at Swinstead Abbey.* (London: By Valentine Simmes for Iohn Helme, 1611) (STC 14646), sig. Li^{r}.

[54] John Strype, *Ecclesiastical Memorials: Relating Chiefly to Religion and the Reformation of It, and the Emergencies of the Church of England*, 3 vols. (Oxford: Clarendon Press, 1822), 3: 237–56, at 237–8.

She did repurifie this Land once more,
From the infection of the Romish whore.
Now Abbies, Abbots, Fri'rs, Monks, Nuns & Stews,
Masses, and Masse-priests, that mens soules abuse,
Were all cast downe, Lamps, Tapers, Relikes, Beads,
And Superstitions that mans soule misse-leads,
All Popish pardons, Buls, Confessions,
With Crossings, Cristening bels, Saints, Intercessions,
The Altars, Idols, Images downe cast,
All Pilgrimage, and Superstitious Fast,
Th'acknowledging the Pope for supreme head,
The holy water, and the god of bread,
The mumbling Mattins, and the pickpurse Masse,
These bables this good Queene did turne to grasse.
She caus'd *Gods* service to be said and sung,
In our owne understanding English tongue.[55]

By the turn of the century, the 'reverend history' of monks had become the stuff of picturesque architectural and antiquarian regret, or the butt of knockabout dramatic humour. Their studiedly invisible life became the subject of epigrams and emblem books, using imported continental images, and passively remodelled into static and distantly historical allegories of the kinds of reclusion and retreat from the world that would soon power so much pastoral poetry in the seventeenth century:

If thou desire to cherish true *Content*,
And in a troublous time that course to take,
Which may be likely mischieves to prevent,
Some use, of this our *Hieroglyphick*, make.
The *Fryers Habit*, seemeth to import,
That, thou (as ancient *Monkes* and *Fryers* did)
Shouldst live remote, from places of resort,
And, in *retyrednesse*, lye closely hid.
...
Let this our *Emblem*, therefore, counsell thee,
Thy life in safe *Retyrednesse*, to spend.[56]

[55] John Taylor, 'Queene Elizabeth An. Dom. 1558', part of *A Memorial of all the English Monarchs, being in number 150. from Brute to King James. In Heroyicall verse*, in his *All the Workes of Iohn Taylor the Water-Poet. Beeing Sixty and Three in Number. Collected into One Volume by the Author: With Sundry New Additions, Corrected, Etc* (London: Printed by I. B. for Iames Boler, 1630).

[56] George Wither and Alexander Dalrymple, *A Collection of Emblemes, Ancient and Modern: Quickened with Metricall Illustrations, Both Morall and Divine; and Disposed into Lotteries... The First(-Fourth) Booke* (Printed by A. M. for R. Milbourne: London, 1635), Book 2, Illustration XI, p. 73, available online at <http://emblem.libraries.psu.edu/withe073.htm>.

What is presented here is the recluded monasticism of the desert fathers, and the eremitic orders, that part of monasticism's cultural capital that had avoided devaluation in the reforms of the previous century. And by 1626, Nicholas Ferrar had already begin the work of re-imagining a Protestant para-monastic community at Little Gidding.

FURTHER READING

Bernard, G. W. *The King's Reformation: Henry VIII and the Remaking of the English Church* (New Haven, CT: Yale University Press, 2005)

Clark, James G. (ed.). *The Religious Orders in Pre-Reformation England*, Studies in the History of Medieval Religion, 18 (Woodbridge: The Boydell Press, 2002)

—— (ed.). *The Culture of Medieval English Monasticism*, Studies in the History of Medieval Religion, 30 (Woodbridge: The Boydell Press, 2007)

Parish, Helen L. *Monks, Miracles, and Magic: Reformation Representations of the Medieval Church* (London: Routledge, 2005)

Swanson, R. N. *Catholic England: Faith, Religion, and Observance before the Reformation* (Manchester: Manchester University Press, 1993)

Youings, Joyce A. *The Dissolution of the Monasteries*, Historical Problems: Studies and Documents (London: Allen and Unwin, 1971)

CHAPTER 27

NUNS

DAVID WALLACE

> Oh, brother, all the nuns are dead! Let's bury them.
>
> Marlowe, *The Jew of Malta*

The summer of 1651 saw Andrew Marvell tutoring Maria Fairfax at Nun Appleton, Yorkshire. Maria's father, Baron Fairfax, had quit commanding Parliamentary forces in favour of country retirement, reading and writing, and contemplating a grand new house. As Marvell writes *Upon Appleton House*, however, this new edifice has yet to rise: the house he contemplates, standing next to a ruined church, had been seized from Cistercian nuns in 1536. His poem soon finds its way back to Appleton's nunnery days as Isabel Thwaites, destined to marry William Fairfax in 1518, finds herself sucked into cloistered life by a smooth-tongued sister.[1] The nunnery resists young Fairfax's *raptus* of Maria with 'wooden saints', an 'old holy-water brush' and 'the jingling chain-shot' of rosary beads,

> But the glad youth away her bears,
> And to the nuns bequeaths her tears:
> Who guiltily their prize bemoan,
> Like gypsies that a child had stol'n.
> Thenceforth (as when th'enchantment ends,
> The castle vanishes or rends)
> The wasting cloister with the rest
> Was in one instant dispossessed. (lines 265–72)

The suggestion that the nunnery and all its works disappear 'in one instant', like a bad conjuring trick, is iconic both of English Renaissance imaginings and of modern scholarship: for one would think, surveying most contemporary anthologies of Renaissance writing, that English nuns vanish the instant they are chased from their buildings. 'Dissolution' is itself complicit with such suggestions in

[1] 'The nun's smooth tongue has sucked her in': 'Upon Appleton House, To My Lord Fairfax', in *The Poems of Andrew Marvell*, ed. Nigel Smith (London: Longman, 2003), line 200.

denoting 'liquefaction', or (as Trevisa employs it in 1398) 'melting upon the tongue'.[2] Yet as Marvell's poem immediately acknowledges, such displacement of persons, of nuns, requires acts of destruction and legal argument:

> At the demolishing, this seat
> To Fairfax fell as by escheat. (lines 273–4)

Marvell's poem suggests both that English nuns never really were, and that their presence abides both in names—'Nun Appleton', 'Nuneaton', 'Quinton'—and material fabric.[3] Protestant girls, inspired by their large post-Reformation houses, might channel nuns: as at Welbeck Abbey, where in 1645 Elizabeth and Jane Cavendish enter a play of their own devising dressed in 'white sheet of Innocence'.[4] Ghostly nuns haunting sometime Catholic sites in teenage drama complement actual English nuns living closer to London than Nun Appleton or Welbeck: nuns in the Spanish Netherlands, hopeful of return once England becomes Catholic again. Such compounding of mysterious absence with excessive presence might seem peculiar to Protestant English imagining. But such complexity in many ways compares, I shall argue, with medieval Catholic thinking and feeling about nuns. For sometimes we know too little about a particular nun, as with the Second Nun of *The Canterbury Tales*, and sometimes too much, *à la* Madame Eglentyne. This mystery of too little or too much acquaintance with nuns in Catholic culture involves *enclosure*, the extent to which female religious can be known to the world. It also touches on fascination with the nunly body: for whereas the priestly *corpus* might supposedly exchange sexuality for depersonalized public functions, the body of the nun remains fully sexualized (in or out of the cloister).[5] It is important to grasp, however, that the paradigm of enclosure for medieval English nuns was never static: indeed, struggles over its defining and policing continued long after they went into exile. Ironically, representations of nuns on English Renaissance stages habitually fail to evoke the kinds of lives, and conditions of enclosure,

[2] *OED*, *dissolution*, n. def. 1. *OED*'s first recorded sense of *dissolution* as the termination of the existence of a constituted body of persons (e.g. of the monasteries, and now especially of Parliament) dates from 1535 (Act 27 Hen. VIII, c. 26. §26).

[3] On the derivation of 'Quinton' (Warwickshire) from 'Quinentune', 'the manor of the nuns', see Roberta Gilchrist, *Gender and Material Culture: The Archaeology of Religious Women* (London: Routledge, 1994), 35.

[4] Nathan Comfort Starr, '*The Concealed Fancies:* A Play by Lady Jane Cavendish and Lady Elizabeth Brackley', *PMLA*, 46 (1931), 802–38, at 5.2.13. The stage direction at the beginning of 5.2 is 'Enter the 2 Nunns mallencholy speakeing to one another' (830). Welbeck Abbey had been home not to nuns, but to Premonstratensian Canons; they did, however, wear white.

[5] See Peter Brown, 'Late Antiquity', in *A History of Private Life*, ed. Paul Veyne, general editors Philippe Ariès and Georges Duby, 5 vols. (Harvard: Belknap Press, 1987), 1: 235–311, at 270; Gilchrist, *Gender and Material Culture*, 18; Claire M. Waters, *Preaching, Performance, and Gender in the Later Middle Ages* (Philadelphia: University of Pennsylvania Press, 2004), 26.

actually known to nuns in England; popular English imaginings of nunnish life have ever since possessed a strong Counter-Reformation flavor.

Nuns' influence upon English literary imagining is out of all proportion to their actual numbers. In medieval England they occupied only 153 known sites and were outnumbered by monks and friars by about six to one; there were about 2,000 nuns in England and Wales in the early 1500s.[6] These numbers are small. There were, for example, more than ten times as many German nuns; and whereas England had just the one house of Dominican nuns, at Dartford, Germany had seventy (with seven at Strasbourg alone).[7] Each of these English houses, nonetheless, was of considerable local importance: for just as Marvell imagines the Appleton House doorway adorned by 'a stately frontispiece of poor' (65), so did nuns, observant of their Benedictine or Augustinian rules, count themselves obliged to offer hospitality and alms. Women of all ages might be accommodated. Illegitimate girls, such as the parson's daughter who marries Chaucer's miller of Trumpington, could acquire *nortelrie* in the *nonnerie* (1.3967–8). Nine-year-old nunlets whispering in choir might need to be chastened by ghost stories; zealous girls competing over their studies realized that the nunnery, following the rise of universities, represented their best chance of educational advancement.[8] Girls from more prosperous families might notice nuns living longer than wives: texts such as *Hali Meithhad* were on hand to evoke 'that cruel distressing anguish, that fierce and stabbing pain, that incessant misery, that torment upon torment, that wailing outcry that is childbirth'.[9] Widows, perhaps childbirth survivors, might retire to a convent as a lodger or corrodian or take the veil as a mature nun.[10] The Queen of England might choose to visit any convent as often as she pleased with 'a suite of fifty honest persons of either sex'.[11]

6 See Gilchrist, *Gender and Material Culture*, 36 and 61; Barry Collett (ed.), *Female Monastic Life in Early Tudor England. With an Edition of Richard Fox's Translation of the Benedictine Rule for Women, 1517* (Aldershot: Ashgate, 2002), 16.

7 See Anne Winston-Allen, *Convent Chronicles: Women Writing About Women and Reform in the Late Middle Ages* (University Park, PA: Penn State University Press, 2004), 2 and 3; David N. Bell, *What Nuns Read: Books and Libraries in Medieval English Nunneries* (Kalamazoo, MI: Cistercian Publications, 1995), 62; Nancy Warren, *Spiritual Economies: Female Monasticism in Later Medieval England* (Philadelphia: University of Pennsylvania Press), *passim.*

8 See Caesarius of Heisterbach, *The Dialogue on Miracles*, trans. H. von E. Scott and C. C. Swinton Bland, introd. G. G. Coulton, 2 vols. (London: Routledge, 1929), 2: 323–5; 1: 222.

9 *Hali Meithhad*, in *Medieval English Prose for Women*, ed. and trans. Bella Millett and Jocelyn Wogan-Browne (Oxford: Clarendon Press, 1990), 1–43, at 33. The average lifespan of medieval abbesses exceeded that of women outside the cloister by almost thirty years; see Winston-Allen, *Convent Chronicles*, 28.

10 For an account of widows and virgins taking the veil together, see Caesarius, *Dialogue*, 2: 82–3.

11 Such was the indult granted to Anne of Bohemia in 1391; see Graciela S. Daichman, *Wayward Nuns in Medieval Literature* (Syracuse: Syracuse University Press, 1986), 24, citing a papal letter of Boniface IX; see further Elizabeth Makowski, *Canon Law and Cloistered Women: Periculoso and its Commentators, 1298–1545* (Washington, DC: Catholic University of America Press, 1997), 117.

Medieval convent permeability flowed outwards as well as inwards: for it was understood that nuns would keep in touch with families and benefactors, and that abbesses and prioresses, especially, must travel. Gifts acquired by nuns abroad were to be declared to the prioress on their return: should they be kept by the individual, or devoted to common use?[12] Some such gifts were books. Donors might specify that a certain text be used by a particular nun for the term of her life, and then pass to the convent.[13] Spiritual benefits for donors are cannily calculated here: personal prayers of one nun, perhaps a daughter or relative, might later be supplemented by collective intercession. Nuns could be just as proactive: as when a newly-elected abbess, 'symple and yonge of age', writes hoping that Denny might be refounded by sharing in the Fastolf inheritance.[14] The model of religio-economic *commonweal* operative here envisions fairly free passage between cloister and wider community.[15] Local communities, in London and elsewhere, seem generally happy with their end of the bargain.[16]

The intercessory prayers of nuns, it seems, count as much if not more than those of their religious brethren; burial plots in convent churches were especially prized. Some nuns, particularly those of Syon, were especially esteemed for powers of prayer: obits might be offered for dry weather, sailors, the heathen, the king and queen, and special friends.[17] Worshipping nuns were more often heard than seen (thus enhancing their spiritual mystique); conventual churches were sometimes modified, more so than monastic ones, so parishioners might listen up and join in.[18] The occasional pastoral visit suggests borders between cloister and city street sometimes becoming *too* porous: as when Dean Kentwode found too many guests, dogs, and fancy clothes and dancing at the Benedictine nunnery of St Helen's, Bishopsgate, *c.*1432. But the enthusiasm of London's merchants, mayors, and guildsmen for this particular convent was obviously very great.[19]

[12] See John Tillotson, 'Visitation and Reform of the Yorkshire Nunneries in the Fourteenth Centuries', *Northern History*, 30 (1994), 1–21, at 13.

[13] For example, the Middle English *Golden Legend* given by John Burton, London mercer, to his daughter Kateryne was to pass to her convent at Holywell, London, after her death: see Bell, *What Nuns Read*, 148–9.

[14] See 'From Joan Keteryche, Abbess of Denny, to John Paston I', in *Women's Writing in Middle English*, ed. Alexandra Barratt (London: Longman, 1992), 257–60, at 258. This petition was unsuccessful; most of the Fastolf inheritance found its way eventually to Magdalen College, Oxford.

[15] See Warren, *Spiritual Economies.*

[16] See Catherine Paxton, 'The Nunneries of London and its Environs in the Later Middle Ages'. Unpublished PhD dissertation, Oxford University, 1992.

[17] See Bell, *What Nuns Read*, 189.

[18] See Marilyn Oliva, *The Convent and the Community in Late Medieval England: Female Monasteries in the Diocese of Norwich, 1350–1540* (Woodbridge: Boydell, 1998), 148.

[19] See William Page (ed.), *The Victoria History of London* (London: Constable, 1909), 1: 458–9. A roundel to the grocer Sir John Crosby and his wife survived here until the IRA truck bombing of 24 April 1993.

Two great protagonists of Malory's *Morte Darthur* derive their exceptional powers from convent education. 'Morgan le Fey', we learn early on, 'was put to scole in a nonnery, and ther she lerned so moche that she was a grete clerke of nygromancye'; and twelve nuns proudly present Galahad as 'thys chylde the whycch we have norysshed'.[20] The 'fayr felyship' that unarms Lancelot in the 'abbey of nunnys' where he meets his son, Galahad, proves as technically adroit as any coven of courtly maidens; nuns generally seem relaxedly at home with Arthurian knights. Perceval's sister, never named, seems nun-like even when sailing with three men in a boat (578–87). But the most powerful figure actually to become a nun is Guenevere: the final part of the *Morte* opens with 'the queen in Amysbery, a nunne in whyght clothys and blak—and there she was abbas and rular, as reson w[o]lde' (718). The 'reson' dictating Guenevere's rulership here bases itself upon social rank, not moral standing; sharp differentiations of class structured convent life. By the fifteenth century, certainly, the franchise had widened: the aristocratic women who had earlier been the mainstay of English convent life now often preferred marriage; girls from gentry and mercantile backgrounds increasingly took their place. Nuns remained, nonetheless, a cut above: medieval parish priests were, for the most part, more akin to their dung-booted parishioners.[21]

The history of Amesbury, while not quite stretching back to abbess Guenevere, is long and distinctive. Founded in 979, it was refounded as a priory of Fontrevault in 1177 with thirty nuns. By the early fourteenth century there were more than a hundred, including Mary, daughter of Edward I, who entered aged six to keep her grandmother company (Queen Eleanor of Provence). In 1535 Amesbury was still one of England's five wealthiest nunneries; it was dissolved in 1539.[22] Two of the others lay close by: Shaftesbury (whose nuns at the Dissolution included a daughter of Cardinal Wolsey),[23] and Wilton. In fact, all but two of the late Anglo-Saxon nunneries were founded in Wessex: when Guenevere heads to Amesbury, then, she seeks out the heartland of English conventual life. But to what extent might English nuns have known the depth and rootedness of their pedigree? Nicholas Trevet, ordinarily a Latin author, took to Anglo-Norman chronicling for the princess Marie (sometime of Shaftesbury); the saintly Custance of Chaucer's *Man of Law's Tale* is his best-known heroine. And in a remarkable poem preserved by British Library Cotton Vespasian D.IX, a female dreamer called Kateryne finds renewed

[20] See Thomas Malory, *Morte Darthur*, in *Works*, ed. Eugène Vinaver, 2nd edn (London: Oxford University Press, 1971), 3, 516.

[21] See Eamon Duffy, *Faith of Our Fathers: Reflections on Catholic Tradition* (London: Continuum, 2004), 100; Oliva, *The Convent and the Community*, 52–61. Class differentiation ruled within convents in the distinction between choir sisters, who sang Divine Office, and lay sisters, who performed manual labor.

[22] See Nikolaus Pevsner, *Wiltshire*, revised by Bridget Cherry, The Buildings of England (New Haven, CT: Yale University Press, 2002), 89; Collett (ed.), *Female Monastic Life*, 26; J. H. Bettey, *The Suppression of Monasteries in the West Country* (Gloucester: Alan Sutton, 1989), 84–6.

[23] See Daichman, *Wayward Nuns*, 15.

inspiration in contemplating a long succession of illustrious Anglo-Saxon and Anglo-Norman nuns.[24] At first, having fallen asleep upon 'a benche of camomylle' (line 114), she is discouraged by disorderly scenes in a nunnery ('Dame lust, dame wantowne, and dame nyce', line 236). But she is encouraged at the last to recall 'Fulle holy vyrgynes many a store who leveyden here relygyiusly': these include saints Edith of Wilton, Radegund, Etheldreda of Ely, Frideswide of Oxford, Withburga of Dereham, Sexburga of Sheppey, and Ermengild (lines 381–91).

The long history of convent literacies in England, leading from Anglo-Saxon and Latin to Anglo-Norman and English, effects gradual separation of women from the literacy of the clerical elite: women must increasingly translate, or be translated to. The nuns of Barking, for whom the Anglo-Saxon Latin poet Aldhelm wrote his *De virginitate*, *c.*700, corresponded in Latin and studied Latin metrics; Bede and Alcuin wrote Latin works of theology in response to women. Nuns of Barking continued reading and translating from Latin before and after the Norman conquest.[25] Wilton, too, consolidated its reputation as a vital center of Latin-based education for women of the elite. Edith (961–84), daughter of Wulfthryh and King Edgar, spent her whole short life at Wilton (where her mother became abbess). Her later devotees included kings Cnut (who built a shrine to her at Wilton), William the Conqueror, Henry III, and Edward I (whose daughter, Mary, popped over from Amesbury to offer seven shillings and a gold clasp at her shrine).[26] Muriel of Wilton was celebrated as *versificatrix*, Eve of Wilton inspired Goscelin's *Liber Confortatorius*, and queen-to-be Matilda, at Wilton, 'litteris quoque foemineum pectus exercuit'.[27] While ancient establishments such as Wilton and Barking continued to flourish, however, there were few new foundations after 1066: monasteries for men formed better options for alliance and land reclamation for incoming Norman barons. The translation of Aelred of Rievaulx's *Life of St Edward the Confessor* in the 1160s from Latin into Anglo-Norman verse by an anonymous nun of Barking coincides both with the originating of French

[24] See F. J. Furnivall (ed.), *Early English Poems and Lives of the Saints* (Berlin: The Philological Society, 1862), 138–48. According to Thomas Warton, who misattributes the poem to 'one Bertram Walton', the poem 'is without wit, and almost without numbers' and depicts 'the usual degeneracy': Warton, *History of English Poetry*, ed. Richard Price, 3 vols. (London: Thomas Tegg, 1840), 2: 361.

[25] See Jane Stevenson, 'Anglo-Latin Poets', in *Latin Learning and English Lore: Studies in Anglo-Saxon Literature for Michael Lapidge*, ed. Katherine O'Brien O'Keeffe and Andy Orchard, 2 vols. (Toronto: University of Toronto Press, 2005), 2: 86–107, at 87, 94.

[26] See O'Brien O'Keefe, 'Edith's Choice', in *Latin Learning*, 2: 253–74, at 254; Elizabeth Critall, 'The Abbey of Wilton', in *Wiltshire*, Volume 3, ed. R. B. Pugh and Elizabeth Crittall, Victoria County History (London: Oxford University Press, 1956), 231–42 at 231–4. A poem from the first half of the fifteenth century, likely written at Wilton and based upon Goscelin's life of St Edith, lays out much of the early history (BL Cotton Faustus B. III).

[27] See J. S. P. Tatlock, 'Muriel: The Earliest English Poetess', *PMLA*, 48 (1933), 317–21; Stephanie Hollis et al. (eds.), *Writing the Wilton Women: Goscelin's Legend of Edith and Liber confortatorius* (Turnhout: Brepols, 2004); William of Malmesbury, *De Gestis Regum Anglorum*, ed. William Stubbs, 2 vols., Rolls Series, 90 (London: HMSO, 1887–9), 2: 493 ('learned letters and womanly wiles').

romance and a wave of conventual foundations. Many of the first-generation nuns came from France. French became the first language of English convents, and its use endured remarkably: the nuns of Lacock, Wiltshire, were in 1535 found to be 'very perfitt' in French.[28]

Transition to an English conventual *lingua franca* was eventually made. More than two-thirds of all books surviving from English nunneries date from 1400 or later; two-thirds of these, excluding liturgical works, are in English.[29] Convent Latinity becomes more precarious: in 1481, Jane Fisher of Dartford is allowed to have a teacher of Latin; but in 1533, no nun at Little Marlowe is found competent to teach the son of Thomas Cromwell.[30] Some prioresses at the Dissolution signed documents that they could not read; some nuns embracing foreign exile will speak of 'the aching loss of our native land, families and mother tongue'.[31] Tellingly, the iconic female translator of psalms and psalm commentary from the later fifteenth century, Lady Eleanor Hull, works not from the Vulgate but from French into English.[32] Such increasing reliance upon translations and clerical mediation inevitably draws nuns closer to ordinary lay literacy. It is thus not surprising that the poor Benedictines of Thetford should own a Wycliffite New Testament, inscribed *Katherina Methwold, monaca.*[33]

English medieval nunneries successfully resisted one major clerical assault on their liberties: the concept of *aut virum aut murum*, implying that women should either marry or be permanently immured. Requirements for enclosure had been fairly equal across genders until the coming of mendicancy: but whereas male Dominicans and Franciscans were free to roam the land in pairs, preaching and befriending animals, their female counterparts were strictly enclosed. In 1298 Boniface VIII, Dante's least favourite pope, sought to drive this principle further with *Periculoso*, an edict folded into a bull imposing strict enclosure upon nuns of all orders. It was argued that this represented only the enforcement of prior legislation, but this was spurious: neither the Benedictine nor Augustineian rules speak of perpetual *clausura*, and a watertight convent could hardly perform those acts of almsgiving and hospitality that these rules do require. Many nuns refused

[28] John ap Rice, writing to Thomas Cromwell, observes that the French of Lacock 'varieth from the vulgare frenche that is nowe used, and is moche like the frenche that the common Lawe i[s] writen in'; Bell, *What Nuns Read*, 68.

[29] See Bell, *What Nuns Read*, 71.

[30] See Bell, *What Nuns Read*, 63; Valerie G. Spear, *Leadership in Medieval English Nunneries* (Woodbridge: Boydell, 2005), 141.

[31] 'La grande falta de nuestra patria, parientes, y lenguage': thus the exiled nuns of Syon in the 1620s, as cited in Christopher de Hamel, *Syon Abbey: The Library of the Bridgettine Nuns and their Peregrinations after the Reformation. With the Manuscript at Arundel Castle* (London: The Roxburghe Club, 1991), 13.

[32] See Alexandra Barratt, 'Hull [*née* Malet], Eleanor, Lady Hull (*c.*1394–1460)', *ODNB.*

[33] See Bell, *What Nuns Read*, 211.

subjection to restrictions that had formed no part of their original religious confession. British and Irish bishops in the opening decades of the fourteenth century did attempt to enforce such legislation; they met general resistance and, at Markyate, outright rebellion.[34] Bishops could themselves see the unfeasibility of total *clausura*: most English convents were poor, and without maintaining contacts with local families, donors, and infrastructure (helping out with the harvest, joining fraternities) they would likely perish. In Yorkshire, one visit per year to friends and family was soon allowed again, and then two; lodgers could be readmitted to help impoverished convents; recreations and relaxations were (Archbishop Melton decreed in 1318) to be encouraged.[35]

One senses cross-gendered solidarity in resistance to *Periculoso*: for why should female religious suffer restrictions that their male counterparts could escape? Even the Carthusians, a strict monastic order, were required (for sanity and hygiene) to walk on Mondays beyond their cloister.[36] *Into Great Silence*, Philip Gröning's 2006 filmic account of the Grande Chartreuse, sees carefree monks sliding down snowy hillsides; it obviously seemed unjust to imagine a world with no equivalent female frolics. The Middle English *Land of Cokaygne* sees nuns skinny-dipping 'When hi beth fur from the abbei'; there are reports from Basle of female Dominicans romping in the Rhine (as citizens watch from a bridge).[37]

Caesarius of Heisterbach's highly-influential *Dialogus Miracolorum*, a compilation of miniature ascetic romances penned for Cistercian novice monks, shows similar cross-gendered sympathy. Monks as well as nuns feel the impulse to throw themselves into rivers or down wells when religious life gets too oppressive; monks as well as nuns, the young male novice of the *Dialogus* concedes, may damage kneecaps through excessive genuflection or feel sudden, inexplicable terrors.[38] Caesarius knows how enclosure may be defeated: by climbing over walls or through windows; by meeting in convent orchards or becoming a keyholder. One assignation between an English nun and her male mentor takes place in a garden shed (a prototype for Langland's convent henhouse); another sees a nun raped at an outlying grange.[39] Caesarius, writing some seventy years before *Periculoso* (with Thomas of Canterbury the greatest of contemporary martyr-heroes), nowhere

[34] See Makowski, *Canon Law*, 1–6, 114 (for Markyate); Dianne Hall, *Women and the Church in Medieval Ireland, c.1140–1540* (Dublin: Four Courts Press, 2003), 161–4, 175; Francesca Medioli, 'An Unequal Law: The Enforcement of *clausura* Before and After the Council of Trent', in *Women in Renaissance and Early Modern Europe*, ed. Christine Meek (Dublin: Four Courts Press, 2000), 136–52, at 138–9 and 145.

[35] See Tillotson, 'Visitation and Reform of the Yorkshire Nunneries', 10–11.

[36] See Medioli, 'Unequal Law', 139.

[37] See *The Land of Cokaygne*, from BL MS 913, in *Early English Poems*, ed. Furnivall, 156–61, at line 155; Winston-Allen, *Convent Chronicles*, 44.

[38] See Caesarius of Heisterbach, *The Dialogue on Miracles*, 1: 237–41; 1: 387–8; 1: 532–3.

[39] Caesarius of Heisterbach, *The Dialogue on Miracles*, 1: 311–12; 2: 315–16.

becomes exercised over female *clausura*. He is himself a frightful gossip, a monkish Froissart dependent upon conversations with men and women alike ('a certain nun of our Order named Petrissa told me that one day at matins...').[40] Similarly relaxed in spirit is a poem in BL Harley 78 that sees a young prioress wooed by a knight, a parish priest, and 'a burges of a borrow':

Make you mery alle and sone,
And I shalle telle you of a noone,
The fayryst creator under the sone,
Was pryorys of a plase.[41]

The next lines of this strangely-metered poem immediately declare this nun's aristocratic pedigree, her moral integrity, and her attraction for men of all estates:

The lady that was lovely, a lorddes dowter she was,
Full pewer and fulle precyous provyd in every plase;
Lordes and laymen and spryttualle her gave chase. (108)

The knight, who hopes 'under neth your comly cowle to have myn intent', must clearly be respected, the prioress insists, as 'ower lorde, ower patron, and ower precedent' (110). But her use of 'we' henceforth evokes the concerns not of her priory, but of her blood family; she is never again referred to as 'nun' or 'prioress', but only as 'the lady'. Kisses are exchanged, but purely in the medieval spirit of sealing agreements: 'that knyght kyssyd the lady gent, the bargen was made' (110). The three suitors have free access to her ('they goo and com'), and she shows brilliant command of worldly strategy in deflating the libido of all three men at once. Having threatened to betray the borough burgess's folly to his wife—'And proclam ytte in the markyt towene'—she induces him to endow her priory. She thus remains both lady and prioress, negotiating two worlds, to the very end of the poem. Her *salvyng* touches both worlds, bringing sexual healing to men and economic salvation to her convent:

Thus the lady ded fre,
She kepythe her vyrgenyté,
And indewed the place with ffee,
And salyvyd them of ther soore. (117)

There were always differing degrees of enclosure for different orders of nuns: Benedictine and Augustinian rules were more relaxed, Bridgettine and Poor Clare regimens more exacting. Stricter enclosure might, by force of necessity, sharpen literary skill. Joan Keteryche, abbess of Denny, deliberately adverts to her strict

[40] Caesarius of Heisterbach, *The Dialogue on Miracles*, 2: 70–2 (for Thomas), 1: 387 (for Petrissa).

[41] See John Lydgate, *A Selection from the Minor Poems of Lydgate*, ed. James O. Halliwell, Early English Poetry, 2 (London: Percy Society, 1842), 107–17, at 108 (note this poem is not by Lydgate).

Franciscan regimen: 'consydre how we be closyd wythinne the ston wallys', she appeals to John Paston I, 'and may non odyryvse speke wyth you but only be wrytynge' (258); her sophisticated hypotaxis bespeaks schooling in literary, rather than oral, communication. Nuns in Germany and the Netherlands who proved more accepting of *Periculoso* were granted, through a holy *Teufelspakt*,[42] exceptional literary freedoms: the copying of sermons by house preachers and guest preachers, the writing of convent chronicles and histories, translation from the Latin, and exchanges with other houses through inter-library loan. Thousands of texts were produced; the sisters of St Katharina, Nuremburg, alone copied some three hundred volumes.[43] Nothing remotely on this scale transpired in England or Wales, Scotland or Ireland; the remains of nuns' own writings here remain frugal to the point of non-existence. Chaucer, nonetheless, does include a nun-translator in his *Canterbury Tales* as the nameless subordinate of his Prioress, madame Eglentyne.

The first nun featured in Caesarius's *Dialogus* is also nameless and anonymous: all we learn of her is that she is nobly born and raped (1: 38). The second nun, however, is Hildegund: a local girl who embarks on vast, picaresque adventures before dying as a Cistercian monk at Schoenau on 20 April 1188 (1: 51–7). Chaucer, similarly, tells us much about one of his nuns and nothing about the other.[44] The first is Prioress of St Leonard's, Stratford, a Benedictine house just outside London. This was a house of middling prosperity that attracted the daughters of London guildsmen (while lacking the deeply rooted, royal pedigree of nearby Barking Abbey). Chaucer knew St Leonard's: his first master, Lionel Duke of Clarence, had an aunt who was a nun there; the *House of Fame* compares Chaucer's soporific state to the weariness of a man making the two mile trip to 'the corseynt Leonard' (about the distance from Chaucer's Aldgate lodgings to Stratford-atte-Bow). Chaucer humorously portrays a woman habitually moving *between* court and cloister: her physical description and her smiling 'ful simple and coy' come straight from the lexicon of French romance.[45] Chaucer never

[42] The 10 percent of houses accepting this conservative Observance produced 90 percent of the surviving manuscripts from this period; see Winston-Allen, *Convent Chronicles*, 11.

[43] See Winston-Allen, *Convent Chronicles*, xii, 5–6, 159–60. German Dominican sister-books were written by women for women with negligible masculine oversight; the nine surviving exemplars narrate some 300 female lives; see Rebecca Garber, *Feminine Figurae: Representations of Gender in Religious Texts by Medieval German Women Writers 1100–1475*, Studies in Medieval Literature and Culture, 10 (London: Routledge, 2002), 61–6.

[44] This paradigm of telling too little or too much about particular nuns recurs, perhaps reflecting the prurient ambivalence of male authors prying into female lives. E. T. Donaldson famously spoke of Chaucer's infatuation with his Prioress without ever analyzing his own engagement with Chaucerian 'women of style'; see Donaldson, *Speaking of Chaucer* (London: Athlone Press, 1970), 3; see also Carolyn Dinshaw, *Chaucer's Sexual Poetics* (Madison: University of Wisconsin Press, 1989), 28–64.

[45] *House of Fame*, line 117; Jill Mann, *Chaucer and Medieval Estates Satire* (Cambridge: Cambridge University Press, 1973), 128.

implies that she *belongs* in the cloister: such a heavy-handed judgment, made by many Chaucerians, unconsciously adopts post-Reformation expectations of strict *clausura*. The Prioress has been further censured for possessing 'perfectly dainty table manners, a refinement hardly expected in a religious woman'.[46] But *cleannesse* is a core Catholic virtue: table manners originate as a form of bodily ascesis practiced in convents and monasteries and then carried outward (like so much else) to an emulative secular world. The circulation of values between cities, courts, and convents makes Chaucer's Prioress portrait seem gently observational rather than strongly satirical: an affectionate account of the way we live now.

Chaucer's second nun, the translator, leaves her convent because nuns (even Prioresses) rarely travel alone. We know nothing of her beyond the 'leveful bisynesse' (8.5) of her translating. Her anonymity suggests total immersion in *opus Dei*: an ideal pursued by both monks and nuns. Her authorial posture suggests self-subjection to a single, authoritative literary source (even as her *Prologue* actually synthesizes from French, Latin, and Italian sources that include Dante and the *Legenda Aurea*). Her heroine Cecilie, however, lives a radically different life: of apostolic activity in the world; of face-to-face interrogation in a Roman court of law; of preaching on the Trinity (the most difficult of exegetical subjects). At the end, as she teaches and bleeds for three days, Cecelie begins to resemble an anchoress, living between life and death. Her house finally becomes a church: the first stage of the bureaucratizing process that connects this heroic time of Pope Urban I ('the goode Urban', 8.177) to the Second Nun's present of Urban VI (Pope of Rome 1378–89, followed by the English in this time of schism). The *Second Nun's Tale* is, by the standard of all other *Canterbury Tales*, strictly literal: that is, even in narrating the life of a woman so given to preaching and instruction, it avoids anything remotely interpretive. Such work of exegesis belongs to the third member of the Canterbury convent *troika*: the Nun's Priest who preaches in their convent church. His comic tale of chickens proposes that females of the species are ineluctably literal-minded. Exegesis—as practiced by his surrogate, Chauntecleer—is wasted on them; dreams, as read by 'damoysele Pertelote', are but effects of the body. The Nun's Priest revels in his role as rhetor and exegete: his verbal showboating reaches its zenith with

> *Mulier est hominis confusio*—
> Madame, the sentence of this Latyn is,
> 'Womman is mannes joye and al his blis'. (7.3164–66)

Comedy here seals relations of power as men, male religious, exult in their translating and glossing of Latin texts for women; female communities—of nuns

[46] Daichman, *Wayward Nuns*, 141; and see further, despite the comic veneer, Donaldson, *Speaking of Chaucer*, 60–1.

as of chickens—may be deluded by their dependency.[47] But perhaps the Nun's Priest will be found out: the Second Nun, who speaks next in Ellesmere order, knows Latin; her *Prologue* translates from '*Frater Jacobus Januensis in Legenda*' (263).

Gender relations at Syon, the most powerful religious foundation in England between Conquest and Dissolution, were certainly delicate and complex. Syon Abbey was established by a charter of Henry V on 3 March 1415 as a Bridgettine double monastery of sixty women and twenty-five men, led by a 'sovereyn' abbess. Monks and nuns lived separately, followed different routines of worship, and coincided only at daily mass. The abbey church, dedicated in 1488, provided a mezzanine gallery for the nuns; they could thus be heard, but not seen, by the monks and visitors below. Carthusian monks, just across the Thames at Sheen, supplied their textual needs: transcriptions of Latin texts, translations, and works of liturgy.[48] When Shakespeare's Henry V recalls having built 'two chantries, where the sad and solemn priests / sing still for Richard's soul' (4.1.298–9) he is evoking Syon and Sheen: these sites fulfill Henry IV's pledge of 1408 to found monastic houses by way of expiating bloodshed.[49]

The singing that really counted in the Syon–Sheen complex, however, was not that of priests, but of nuns. Their life was entirely dedicated to singing, reading, and prayer; the two adjunct sets of monks functioned chiefly as service providers (with the men of Syon adept especially as crowd controllers and 'marketing managers for the Syon brand').[50] One early translator for the nuns identifies himself only as 'I synfulle, unworthi to bere ony name': anonymity is the correct masculine attitude when Englishing the work of Catherine of Siena—'whiche was write as sche endited in her moder tunge'—for the 'religyous modir & devoute sustren' of Syon.[51] Bridgettine nuns, he well knew, sang a special Office of the Virgin, as revealed to St Bridget herself, that never varied from one week to the next; the Blessed Virgin is thus 'youre moost sovereyne lady and cheef abbes of hir holy co[n]vent' (1).

[47] A tale of Caesarius suggests how masculine exulting over female literal-mindedness may have tragic consequences. A priest's concubine is jokingly told that she cannot be saved unless she pass through a burning furnace; she flings herself into a bread oven, and so dies. God honours her, illuminating her tomb; see Caesarius, *Dialogue on Miracles*, 1: 448–9.

[48] See Vincent Gillespie (ed.), *Syon Abbey*, Corpus of British Medieval Library Catalogues, 9 (London: British Library, 2001), xxix–xxx; de Hamel, *Syon Abbey: The Library of the Bridgettine Nuns*, 53 and 62.

[49] See *Syon Abbey*, ed. Gillespie, xxix; David Knowles, *The Religious Orders in England*, 3 vols. (Cambridge: Cambridge University Press, 1950–59), 2: 175–81. In lieu of the singing nuns of Syon, Shakespeare's Henry V has 'Five hundred poor... in yearly pay, / Who twice a day their withered hands hold up / Toward heaven to pardon blood' (4.1.295–7): a substitution that mirrors the shift from seven conventual offices a day to the morning and evening prayer of Protestant England.

[50] *Syon Abbey*, ed. Gillespie, xxxiii.

[51] See St Catherine of Siena, *The Orcherd of Syon*, vol. 1: *Text*, ed. Phyllis Hodgson and Gabriel M. Liegey, EETS, o.s., 258 (London: Oxford University Press, 1966), 18.

A mysterious feminine sanctity, then, formed the heart of Syon: a house that attracted women of the highest pedigree and became a fashionable place of resort for London-based religious enthusiasts (such as Margery Kempe in 1434). Such sanctity performed vital ideological work for the Lancastrians at a time when Richard II, dead but unburied, still walked the land.[52] It is telling that they chose not to refound an ancient and royal foundation close to London, such as Barking, but rather to invent a new one (inspired by a woman who was foreign, royal, and newly sainted). The Visconti of Milan, a contemporary despotic dynasty, first decided to restore their ancient basilica but then to destroy it and build anew. The Lancastrians, a dynasty of similarly recent and illegitimate origins, also elect to build *ex nihilo*: Syon is thus, in Simpsonian terms, a revolutionary edifice *avant la lettre*.[53]

The nuns of Syon are complicit with this legitimizing project: but no more than was Petrarch during his eight closeted and protected years at Milan. The prayers and song of Syon nuns were considered spiritually potent and efficacious; but so too was their reading, to which much time was devoted. At Barking, the ancient and venerable Benedictine abbey on the far side of London, nuns were expected to get through one volume per year. On the Monday of the first week of Lent, the *libraria* (female librarian) would spread out a carpet in the Chapter House and call up nuns with the books they had received the previous year. Each nun would replace her book on the carpet, crying *mea culpa* to the abbess if she had not managed to finish it; new books were then distributed.[54] Barking would need about forty volumes to make this work; at Syon, where turnover was faster and numbers greater, many more books were needed. The *Rewyll* governing Syon's nuns early on insists that they are to own 'no manere thing, be it nevere so lityll' before later conceding that 'bookes they shall have as many as they wyll in whiche ys to lerne or to studye'.[55] *The Orcherd of Syon*'s anonymous male author hopes that the sisters will read his *whole* book—'assaye & serche the hool orcherd'—but knows that, once handed over, his volume will be read as they choose (as 'ye savouren best, as ye ben disposid', 1).

Confessors could exert some influence over female exegesis; but huddling too close over books might threaten disaster (sexual relations between confessed religious being classed as incest). The close involvement of Sheen Carthusian James Grenehalgh with Syon novice and nun Joanna Sewell emerges through a whole series of monograms and annotations that read like love notes: 'See well' he

[52] See Paul Strohm, *England's Empty Throne* (New Haven, CT: Yale University Press, 1998), 101–27.

[53] See David Wallace, *Chaucerian Polity* (Stanford: Stanford University Press, 1997); James Simpson, *Reform and Cultural Revolution*, The Oxford English Literary History, Vol. 2: *1350–1547* (Oxford: Oxford University Press, 2002).

[54] See Bell, *What Nuns Read*, 41–2.

[55] James Hogg (ed.), *The Rewyll of Seynt Sauioure and other Middle English Brigittine Legislative Texts* (Salzburg: Universität Salzburg, 1978), 9 and 50.

puns to her at one point; and then (to himself) 'Forsake Sewell'.[56] This last prefaces a passage of Rolle's *Contra Amatores Mundi* that denounces, *inter alia*, 'the cloistered monks who are occupied with the love of fleshly friends' (101). Grenehalgh was, quite literally, sent to Coventry: he was dispatched from Sheen to the Charterhouse there in 1507 or 1508, never to return. The right to private reading at Syon was thus strongly defended. Texts consumed included Hilton's *Scale of Perfection* (as annotated by Grenehalgh for Sewell), Englished continental mystics, such as Mechtild of Hackeborn and (so it seems) Englished bibles and the works of Julian of Norwich and Margery Kempe.[57] Not every book presented to Syon was necessarily read by the nuns: the community could not accept gifts of money, so books were often donated or bequeathed. But *The Siege of Thebes* and *The Parliament of Fowls* were certainly there to be read (Bodleian MS Laud misc. 416); and there is no mistaking the ferocity with which Margaret Winsor, 'Domina de Syon', lays claim—in both English and French—to her copy of Boccaccio, *De la ruine des nobles homes et femmes* (Lyons, 1483).[58]

Falls of great men and women interested Syon, a flourishing royal foundation nine miles upriver from Westminster. But relations with the city were important, too: Wynkyn de Worde, who presented two of his own editions to the abbey, published *The Orcharde of Syon* in 1519. Bridgettine Elyzabeth Stryckland owned a copy[59] that was to become the first Syon book to pass into secular hands after the Dissolution; but any Londoner seeking out de Worde in Fleet Street might obtain a copy long before this. Pious laypeople, such as Margery Kempe, had always looked to professed religious for inspirations not found in parish life. In and after 1519, however, the private intensities of closeted devotion were writ large in the public sphere: such, at any rate, seems to be de Worde's intuition in designing his *Orcherd*. His first full page woodcut portrays St Catherine of Siena as abbess of an orderly convent: six nuns stand behind on her left, and six on her right. The woodcut that opens *tertia pars*, however, shows the saint vigorously at prayer in a turbulent world (Figure 1): some find the bridge to salvation, some drown; devils keep watch on the dying and drag down the unchosen.

The rubric above this image claims that every man intuits his eternal destiny *as he lies dying*: for 'every soule in the last ende of his lyfe shall tast and fele by knowynge or he fully pas/ What peyne or joye he shall have after he is passed'.[60]

[56] See Michael G. Sargent, *James Grenehalgh as Textual Critic*, Analecta Cartusiana 85, 2 vols. (Salzburg: Universität Salzburg, 1984), 1: 89, 101.

[57] See Ann M. Hutchison, 'What the Nuns Read: Literary Evidence from the English Bridgettine House, Syon Abbey', *Mediaeval Studies*, 57 (1995), 205–22, at 210, 220.

[58] Now New York, Pierpont Morgan Library, 600; see Hutchison, 'What Nuns Read', 215–16; de Hamel, *Syon Abbey: The Library of the Bridgettine Nuns*, 80–1, 97.

[59] New York, Public Library, Spencer Collection, Eng. 1519; see Bell, *What Nuns Read*, 192–3.

[60] *The Orcharde of Syon* (London: Wynkyn de Worde, 1519), BL C.11.b.6; this language lightly amends and carries forward the wording of the Kalender with which the *Orcherd* opens: compare Catherine of Siena, *Orcherd of Syon*, ed. Hodgson and Liegey, 1:6.

Tertia.

¶ The fyrste chapytre of the .iii. party / sheweth of ẏ profyte of temptacyons / and how euery soule in ẏ last ende of his lyfe shall tast and fele by knowynge or he fully pas / what peyne or ioye he shall haue after he is passed.

¶ The .iii. boke.

¶ Also how ẏ fende catcheth soules vnder the coloure of some goodnes / also this boke maketh mencyon of a vysyō that this blyssed vyrgyn had with dyuers and many maters / as it is rehersed before ī the kalender.

Ca. i.

The fende a mynystre ordeyned of my ryghtwysenesse to tourment soules / whiche greuously offende me. ¶ And I ordeyned theym in this lyfe / that they sholde tempte and do greate greuaunce to my creatures. ¶ Not for my creatures shol

Figure 1 *St Catherine of Siena at Prayer*, woodcut from *The Orcherd of Syon* (Wynkyn de Worde, 1519), opening of *tertia pars*

Bishop Richard Fox, counselor to Henry VIII, had begun worrying over the state of his soul just a few years earlier: 'my lord', he told his sometime protégé Wolsey in 1516, 'to serve worldly with damnacion of my saule and many other sawles whereof I have the cure, I am sure ye woll not desire'.[61] Self-cure was essayed through serving nuns: following an invitation from abbesses of the Winchester diocese, Fox joined a long line of translators of the Benedictine Rule stretching back to Aethelwold. Fox's humane imagining draws him deeply into collective female life. Early risers should not make sleepier sisters feel bad, he suggests, but 'shall make som softe and sobre styrynge, with the so[u]nde of their mouthes, or of their fete, or knockynge uppo[n] the beddes sides, to wake theym that be sluggards' (D.iii.r). Fox died aged 80 in 1528 and Wolsey followed him two years later; Cromwell's commissioners began visiting west country convents in 1535.

In 1500, a luxurious text copied for young Prince Arthur, betrothed since he was three to Catherine of Aragon, proffered advice on love by abbess Heloise; a handsome Flemish-style miniature shows Heloise in nun's habit teaching her masculine pupil *art d'amour*.[62] Forty years later, by the authority of Arthur's brother, nuns were banished. Their disappearing was more absolute than that of their male peers: monks might join cathedral chapters, abbots become bishops, or priests parsons, but nuns could not slide sideways into Protestant England. Their loss is traumatic: for the prophetic voice of a Catherine of Siena, sounding through de Worde's 1519 *Orcharde*, cannot now be heard; and a sin-soaked careerist like Richard Fox cannot serve or borrow the sanctity of nuns.

The efforts of Cromwell's commissioners to besmirch nuns just confirm, in a sense, why nuns were so admired. For from Heloise to the *Morte Darthur*, nuns struggle harder for salvation (by conquering femaleness): priest Lancelot floats effortlessly to glory, hymned by the archbishop of Canterbury (724), whereas abbess Guenevere fights grimly to save her soul (722). Conventual life certainly amplified the status of Elizabeth Barton: a sickly serving girl who, locally famous for visionary predictions and cures, entered a Benedictine convent at Canterbury in 1526. Bridget and Catherine of Siena became role models; her revelations, some of them in rudimentary rhyme, passed to Henry VIII and she enjoyed royal favor and acclaim, for a time, as 'our holy Nun of Kent'.[63] Opposition to the king's divorce, however, sealed her demise: in April 1534 her head was impaled on London bridge. Five of her clerical teachers and followers died with her at Tyburn, and many other learned men were implicated (including More and Fisher). Thomas More actually counseled Barton in 1533 at Syon: the same year that Anne Boleyn came to censure

[61] *Female Monastic Life*, ed. Collett, 14–15.

[62] BL Royal MS 16 F II, f. 137r; Leslie C. Brook, *Two Late Medieval Love Treatises* (Oxford: Society for the Study of Mediaeval Languages and Literatures, 1993).

[63] Diane Watt, 'Barton, Elizabeth (*c.*1506–1534)', *ODNB.*

the nuns for 'ygnoraunt praying upon their Laten prymars'.[64] The mysterious power of this convent space continued to allure; even Henry VIII came to Syon in 1547.[65]

On 25 March 1539 the abbess of Wilton surrendered and was granted a house at Fovant, a pension, and a weekly cartload of wood.[66] The abbey passed to Sir William Herbert in 1541; his daughter-in-law Mary waited out the Spanish Armada there through the summer of 1588. Mary Sidney, Countess of Pembroke, may not have known that learned noblewomen had awaited invasion at Wilton in 1066.[67] But remains of the convent at Wilton, plus those of Amesbury just eight miles away, were familiar sights to her. So too Lacock, on the far side of Wiltshire, owned by the Talbots: the remains of this Anglo-Norman nunnery, the most complete in England, must have impressed a Countess with pretensions to Anglo-Norman lineage.[68] 'In her time', says John Aubrey of Sidney, 'Wilton House was like a College, there were so many learned and ingeniose persons. She was the greatest Patronesse of wit and learning of any Lady.'[69] Nicolas Breton remembers Mary Sidney's Wilton as a place where 'God [was] daily served, religion trulie preached, all quarrels avoided, peace carefully preserved'.[70] Mary Sidney, in sum, presides over a pious, learned, and aristocratic culture in Wessex, the ancient heartland of female monasticism. As a Calvinist Protestant she would not imagine herself as *abbess*, although this characterization seems more germane than Breton's 'Duchesse of Urbina' (13). When her brother Philip suffered a martyr's death in 1586, Mary withdrew to Wilton for two years of pious reclusion. Lady Eleanor Hull, similarly, retired to Sopwell Priory as a widow and then to Cannington Priory, Somerset, when her son died in the last battle of the Hundred Years War (1453). The nuns of Wilton were by 1379 following a French, rather than a Latin, Rule.[71] Mary Sidney's psalm translating, like that of Eleanor Hull and numerous Catholic nuns, is from the French; like Chaucer's Second Nun, she translates closely and diligently.[72]

[64] Anne Boleyn, as reported by Latymer in de Hamel, *Syon Abbey: The Library of the Bridgettine Nuns*, 99.

[65] As a corpse, en route from Westminster to Windsor.

[66] See Crittall, 'The Abbey of Wilton', 240a. [67] See O'Keeffe, 'Edith's Choice', 253.

[68] See Pevsner, *Wiltshire*, rev. Cherry, 285; William Herbert, Mary's son, married Mary Talbot in 1604. The Sidney genealogy (based on forged documents) traced the family back to William de Sidne, a French knight granted land by Henry II; they were actually of English yeoman stock.

[69] John Aubrey, *Brief Lives*, ed. Oliver Lawson-Dick (London: Mandarin, 1992), 138.

[70] *Wits Trenchmour*, as cited in Mary Sidney Herbert, *The Collected Works of Mary Sidney Herbert, Countess of Pembroke*, ed. Margaret P. Hannay, Noel J. Kinnamon, and Michael G. Brennan, 2 vols. (Oxford: Clarendon Press, 1998), 2: 13–14.

[71] See Crittall, 'The Abbey of Wilton', 238b.

[72] Dame Eleanor Hull, *The Seven Psalms: A Commentary on the Penitential Psalms translated from the French into English by Dame Eleanor Hull*, ed. Alexandra Barratt, EETS, o.s., 307 (Oxford: Oxford University Press, 1995), xiv; Sidney Herbert, *The Collected Works of Mary Sidney Herbert*, ed. Hannay et al., 268 (a comparison with Morley). Sidney's brilliant invention of verb forms—such as 'dishedge', 'rebecome', 'impearl', 'eternize'—seems Dantean (65).

Her verse forms are often medieval: *terza rima*, *ottava rima*, *sonetti*, and Chaucerian *rhyme royal*.

John Aubrey (1626–97), a notable historian of Wiltshire, felt the loss of 'the Nunneries, where [young mayds] learnt needlework, the art of confectionary, surgery, (anciently no apothecaries or Surgeons—the gentlewoemen did cure their poore neighbours ...)'.[73] Aubrey recognizes that poor people simply head for the big house when desperate, whatever that house might be: so it was that on 26 August 1601 Margaret Hoby performed drastic surgery on her kitchen table upon a poor child born with no anus.[74] Hoby, like her sometime sister-in-law Mary Sidney, was devoutly Protestant; her husband hunted down Catholics across the Yorkshire countryside. But in terms of *social function*, Hoby and Sidney lived out roles performed earlier by female heads of religious houses. Big houses, local landmarks, would provide the next, post-Reformation generation of English nuns.[75] Mary Ward, born in 1585, was educated in Yorkshire Catholic houses where women took prominent roles (with men often on the run and the priests in the attic). At 21, she crossed to Spanish Flanders and became a Poor Clare. Through a series of revelations, however, Mary deduced that her vocation was *not* to be enclosed: what was needed was a female apostolate of the streets—especially in England, where poor rural Catholics often died alone. This brought her serious trouble: Rome kept her under close surveillance, and in 1631 her movement of English Ladies was suppressed by papal bull. Enclosure was again the sticking point: the Council of Trent had been determined to enforce *Periculoso*; Pius V passed more stringent measures yet in 1566 with *Circa Pastoralis*.[76] So it is that plays such as *Measure for Measure* present a strongly Counter-Reformationist view of religious enclosure. A nun, says Lucio, is 'a thing enskied, and sainted' by her 'renouncement' (1.4.33–4); the minds of nuns, says Isabel, 'are dedicate/ to nothing temporal' (2.2.158–9). The *absolute* character of Poor Clare Isabel is thought to mirror that of Angelo, her pursuer: but the play's truest *absolutism* is that of the Duke, aggregating all forms and observances of religion to his personal authority.

Mary Ward makes a cameo appearance, as the Black Queen's pawn, in Thomas Middleton's *A Game at Chesse*, a play of 1624 inspired by the possible marriage of Prince Charles (the White Knight) to Maria, the Spanish *infanta*.[77] These developments were cheered on from Lisbon by the Bridgettines of Syon: for such a

73 As cited in Sylvia Crawley, *Twelve Centuries of Wilton House* (Warminster: Coates and Parker, 1933), 3.

74 Margaret Hoby, *Diary of Lady Margaret Hoby, 1599–1605*, ed. Dorothy M. Meads (London: Routledge, 1930), 184.

75 See David Wallace, 'Periodizing Women: Mary Ward (1585–1645) and the Premodern Canon', *Journal of Medieval and Early Modern Studies*, 36 (2006), 395–451, at 412–18.

76 See Medioli, 'Unequal law', *Women in Renaissance and Early Modern Europe*, ed. Meek 138–9, 144–52.

77 Thomas Middleton, *A Game at Chesse*, ed. R. C. Bald (Cambridge: Cambridge University Press, 1929), 1.1.46–50.

match might spell the end 'deste nuestro destierro' ('of this our exile'), returning them to their Thameside home.[78] So they commissioned an artist and fashioned a text for Maria, *Señora Prinçesa de Walia.* Mixing biblical, classical, and romance terms of reference, in stiff-jointed Spanish, the sisters tell of long wanderings and picaresque adventures over seventy years. Nine colourful illustrations begin with their foundress Bridget, herself a great traveler, under the rubric 'Peregrinacion'. The second sees Henry V in medieval garb, assisted by two nuns, directing the building of Syon; the third depicts nuns leaving London by boat in 1539. The fourth image, 'Recogidas a Londres', is the most arresting: Philip II of Spain, with Queen Mary nowhere in sight, welcomes the nuns back to Syon in 1557 (Figure 2). The remaining images depict exilic travels through Flanders and France before settlement in Lisbon, ending with prayerful hope of return under Spanish protection. Such hopes never materialized, and the book was never sent; it was brought to England from Lisbon by nuns fleeing Napoleon in 1809.[79]

Elizabeth Tanfield was born *c.*1585 to Protestant parents in Catholic space: Burford Priory, purchased by her father before 1580, had been home to Augustinian hospitalers since *c.*1226. Elizabeth married Henry Cary in 1602, showed brilliant early promise with her *Tragedie of Mariam* (*c.*1605) and then in 1622 followed her husband, with seven children, to Dublin. On 14 November 1626, having left Henry racking priests in Dublin castle, Elizabeth scandalously converted to Catholicism in some stables on Drury Lane. Henry, writing to Charles I as his Lord Deputy of Ireland, denounced his wife's 'Apostacy' and other 'horrid treasons' committed by 'these Locusts of Rome'.[80] But Elizabeth had made Henry a more perfect royal vicar, or deputy: for, as with the royal household, the Protestant husband was now married to a Catholic wife. Four of Elizabeth's daughters, having followed their mother into Catholicism in 1634, became Benedictine nuns at Cambrai: Mary as Dame Maria, Lucy as Dame Magdalena, Elizabeth as Elizabetha and Anne as Clementia. Our Lady of Consolation, Cambrai, had been founded in 1623 by the great-great-granddaughter of Sir Thomas, Gertrude More (1606–33); the class of 1640, that of the Cary sisters, proved especially brilliant in producing original poems and prose and in translating and transcribing.[81] The Welsh Benedictine Augustine Baker had supplied Cambrai with texts of medieval English spirituality, much of it excavated from Sir Robert Cotton's library in London, such as *The Cloud of Unknowing*, works of Hilton, and William Flete's *De Remedis*;

[78] De Hamel, *Syon Abbey: The Library of the Bridgettine Nuns*, 13.

[79] The book has resided in Arundel Castle library since 1856; see de Hamel, *Syon Abbey: The Library of the Bridgettine Nuns*, 9–10.

[80] Elizabeth Cary, *Lady Falkland, Life and Letters*, ed. Heather Wolfe (Cambridge: RTM, 2001), 268–9.

[81] See Augustine Baker OSB, *The Life and Death of Dame Gertrude More*, ed. Ben Wekking, Analecta Cartusiana 119.19 (Salzburg: Universität Salzburg, 2002), ix–xxiv; Cary, *Life and Letters*, ed. Wolfe, 45–8.

Figure 2 *Received in London, 1557*, from a history commissioned by the Syon Nuns (Lisbon, 1620s)

the two most important Julian of Norwich manuscripts are associated with this milieu.[82] Middle English mysticism, as we read it today, owes much to seventeenth-century English nuns hoping perpetually, as Gertrude More has it, to 'Returne from whence we came'.[83]

Mary Ward, after twenty years overseas, returned to London in 1639 and then, as civil war loomed, home to Yorkshire. She traveled first to Mount Grace and then to York, dying in 1645. Her *English Life* was soon written and her household moved to Paris in 1650. On St George's Day 1651, Dom Placid Cary (formerly Henry, youngest brother to the Cary sisters) preached at Paris to Henrietta Maria, widowed queen of England; in November of that year Dame Clementina Cary left the fifty nuns of Cambrai to found a daughter house at Paris, Our Lady of Good Hope. Paris, then, was one of the most vibrant locales for Catholic Englishness in 1651: the year that saw Marvell, nine miles south of York, meditating upon Appleton House. The *surreality* of Marlowe's poem catches a larger sense of strangeness in this period pertaining to translations of and within houses. In Marlowe's *The Jew of Malta*, popular until the theatres closed in 1642, Jewish Abigail speaks of 'the governor placing nuns/ displacing me': a strange inversion of the fate befalling the 226 known nuns of Yorkshire in the 1530s.[84] Marlowe's imagining of how such nuns lived generates an extraordinary stanza. The nunnery bespeaks its allure for an aristocratic girl:

Each night among us to your side
Appoint a fresh and virgin bride;
Whom if Our Lord at midnight find,
Yet neither should be left behind.
Where you may lie as chaste in bed,
As pearls together billeted.
All night embracing arm in arm,
Like crystal pure with cotton warm. (lines 185–92)

The narrator can break the spell of these lines only by sounding, for a moment, more like John Foxe than his usual urbane self:

[82] Placid Spearritt, OSB, 'The Survival of Mediaeval Spirituality among the Exiled English Black Monks', in *That Mysterious Man: Essays on Augustine Baker OSB, 1575–1641*, ed. Michael Woodward, introd. Rowan Williams (Abergavenny: Three Peaks Press, 2001), 42–56, at 19–21; Julian of Norwich, *The Writings of Julian of Norwich: A Vision Showed to a Devout Woman and A Revelation of Love*, ed. Nicholas Watson and Jacqueline Jenkins (Turnhout: Brepols, 2006), 14b–15a.

[83] From her poem in Oxford, Bodleian MS Rawlinson C. 581: Augustine Baker OSB, *Confessiones Amantis: The Spiritual Exercises of the most Vertuous and Religious Dame Gertrude More*, ed. John Clark, Analecta Cartusiana 119.27 (Salzburg: Universität Salzburg, 2007), 6, at line 23. On home-sickness as a female genre, see Wallace 'Periodizing Women', 422–5.

[84] Christopher Marlowe, *The Jew of Malta*, ed. David Bevington (Manchester: Manchester University Press, 1997), 1.2.254–5; Clare Cross and Noreen Vickers, *Monks, Friars and Nuns in Sixteenth Century Yorkshire* (York: Yorkshire Archaeological Society, 1995), 5.

Hypocrite witches, hence avaunt,
Who though in prison yet enchant! (lines 205–6)

Our modern edition seems differently unsettled in mooting 'Lesbian sexual practices' (222a); the poem affirms that virginity protects and enables the particular intimacies of convent space. Women within such spaces, in England and later abroad, were trans-generationally tied to the earliest nuns of Amesbury, Barking, and Wilton. Desire to regain possibilities for female friendship, devotion, and learning will energize Protestant Englishwomen to come, from Margaret Cavendish's *Female Academy* via Mary Astell's *Serious Proposal to the Ladies* to the female foundations of Oxbridge.[85] But the last word here goes to two nun-like sisters who were inspired, in 1674, to affix an inscription in stone to their home at Aldcliffe Hall, near Lancaster. Their affirmation of Catholic Latinity defeating Time occludes complex historical relations of women and nuns to the language that framed their religion. But its *in situ* defiance, pointing many ways, is magnificent:

Catholicae virgines nos sumus: mutare vel tempore spernimus.[86]

FURTHER READING

Bell, David N. *What Nuns Read: Books and Libraries in Medieval English Nunneries* (Kalamazoo, MI: Cistercian Publications, 1995)

Gilchrist, Roberta. *Gender and Material Culture: The Archaeology of Religious Women* (London: Routledge, 1994)

Makowski, Elizabeth. *Canon Law and Cloistered Women: Periculoso and its Commentators, 1298–1545* (Washington, DC: Catholic University of America Press, 1997)

Oliva, Marilyn. *The Convent and the Community in Late Medieval England: Female Monasteries in the Diocese of Norwich, 1350–1540* (Woodbridge: Boydell Press, 1998)

Warren, Nancy. *Spiritual Economies: Female Monasticism in Later Medieval England* (Philadelphia: University of Pennsylvania Press)

[85] See Bridget Hill, 'A Refuge from Men: The Idea of a Protestant Nunnery', *Past and Present*, 117 (1987), 107–30; Wallace, 'Periodizing Women', 427–8.

[86] 'We are Catholic virgins who spurn to change with the times': Alison Shell, *Oral Culture and Catholicism in Early Modern England* (Cambridge: Cambridge University Press, 2007), 131.

PART VIII

LABOUR

CHAPTER 28

ACTIVE AND CONTEMPLATIVE LIVES

JENNIFER SUMMIT*

The debate over the *vita activa* versus the *vita contemplativa* forms a constant theme in western culture, even as the relative values and particular meanings of both terms have been subject to constant, even drastic, redefinition since the debate's classical origins.[1] This essay proposes a reconsideration of the debate across the late medieval and early modern periods, when its central terms underwent a dramatic shift. Where the Middle Ages routinely valued the contemplative life over the active, early modernity reversed this hierarchy. So, for example, where the medieval *Imitatio Christi* warns against 'worldely bysinesse' and encourages readers to 'lerne to despise outwarde thinges and to converte . . . to inwarde thinges', in 1667 John Evelyn argues the opposite case in a tract called *Publick Employment and an Active Life Prefer'd to Solitude*, which upholds the active life using terms that by then had become commonplace.[2] The debate's early modern paradigm shift has been attributed to a revolution in thinking ushered in by the rise of science and a concomitant privileging of the practical over the theoretical. Against this influential account, I find that early modern science did not render the medieval preference for contemplation over action obsolete so much as it developed out of and ultimately co-opted the medieval meaning of contemplation itself. In making this

* I am very grateful to Brian Cummings and James Simpson, editors of this volume, as well as to Nicholas Watson and the other participants in the September 2008 conference at Harvard, 'Cultural Reformations', for vital feedback on this chapter and the larger project of which it forms part. I am also grateful to the Yale English Department graduate students and faculty who heard an earlier version of this work and offered invaluable feedback.

[1] On the long history and many incarnations of this debate, see especially Giles Constable, 'The Interpretation of Mary and Martha', in *Three Studies in Medieval Religious and Social Thought* (Cambridge: Cambridge University Press, 1995), 1–142; and the essays collected in Brian Vickers (ed.), *Arbeit, Musse, Meditation: Betrachtungen zur Vita activa und Vita contemplative* (Zürich: Verlag der Fachvereine, 1985).

[2] *The Imitation of Christ*, ed. B. J. H. Biggs, EETS 309 (Oxford: Oxford University Press, 1997), 40.

argument, I aim not only to reinstate a neglected line of continuity between the medieval and early modern periods but also to illuminate the persistence through early modernity of what I take to be the medieval debate's essential function: to determine and articulate the purpose of human intellectual activity.

By measuring acts of thought and learning according to worldly or other-worldly criteria, the distinction between 'active' and 'contemplative' lives provided a fundamental rubric for organizing and evaluating the work of the human intellect. While the debate's medieval forms focus on the question of vocation—is it better to be a monk or a merchant, a clerk or a soldier?—they are underwritten by concerns about the place and application of intellectual work, concerns that attend the historical extension of learning and literacy beyond the cloister. Thus when, in *De Vita Solitaria* (1366), Petrarch contrasts the 'anxious cares, and toilsome business' of the active man with the life of the contemplative man, spent 'in the worship of God and in noble studies, in learning new things and remembering old', he articulates the novel perspective of a lay scholar, for whom the exercise of learning and literacy represents the consequence of individual choice, rather than institutional imperatives.[3] By extension, when Thomas More's Raphael Hythloday debates the possibility of applying philosophy to the public interest in *Utopia*, he voices a dilemma that was made acute by early modern humanism: what role, if any, should the learned man play in the political life of the court?[4] At the base of the late medieval and early modern debate over the active life and the contemplative life, then, I find a larger question about the nature, value, and place of learning and the intellectual. Today, the legacy of this debate reappears whenever specific academic studies or disciplines are justified along an axis that counterpoises social utility on one end and the 'life of the mind' on the other.[5] As the long history of this question suggests, the 'ways of life' debate had its most lasting impact less on ethical than on epistemic grounds, less on ways of living than on ways of knowing.[6]

[3] Francesco Petrarch, *The Life of Solitude*, trans. Jacob Zeitlin (Urbana: University of Illinois Press, 1924), 116. Brian Stock observes, in 'Reading, Writing, and the Self: Petrarch and His Forerunners', *New Literary History*, 26 (1995), 717–30, at 724: 'In Petrarch's notion of the self, the problematic relationship between the active and the contemplative life is rethought within a literary career, along with a reassessment of classical and monastic concepts of *otium* (cultivated leisure)'.

[4] Alistair Fox, 'Sir Thomas Elyot and the Humanist Dilemma', in *Reassessing the Henrician Age: Humanism, Politics, and Reform, 1500–1550*, ed. Alistair Fox and John Guy (New York: Blackwell, 1986), 52–73.

[5] Jeffrey J. Williams observes that, as justification of academic study, 'The life of the mind is a spiritual rationale, for individual edification, rather than a public one, basically following the Aristotelian justification of philosophical activity, which is valuable for its own self-contained good and pleasure': 'The Life of the Mind and the Academic Situation', in *The Institution of Literature*, ed. Jeffrey J. Williams (New York: SUNY Press, 2002), 208. See also Barbara Herrnstein Smith, 'Disciplinary Cultures and Tribal Warfare: The Sciences and the Humanities Today', in *Scandalous Knowledge: Science, Truth, and the Human* (Edinburgh: Edinburgh University Press, 2005), 108–29.

[6] See Francisco Leonardo Lisi (ed.), *The Ways of Life in Classical Political Philosophy* (Sankt Augustin, Germany: Academia, 2004), on the ethical function of this debate in Classical political philosophy.

The *vita activa* as a marker of modernity

The inversion of the traditional hierarchy of contemplative life over active life has been called the defining paradigm shift of modernity itself.[7] In the words of Hannah Arendt, 'perhaps the most momentous of the spiritual consequences of the discoveries of the modern age, and, at the same time, the only one that could not have been avoided, . . . has been the reversal of the hierarchical order between the *vita contemplativa* and the *vita activa*'.[8] This observation, which clinches the argument of Arendt's *Human Condition*, credits the Scientific Revolution for this epoch-making reversal. The rise of science, Arendt holds, resulted in the 'equation of intelligence with ingenuity' (305) and the full-scale rejection of contemplation: 'The change that took place in the seventeenth century was more radical than what a simple reversal of the established traditional order between contemplation and doing is apt to indicate. The reversal, strictly speaking, concerned only the relationship between thinking and doing, whereas contemplation, in the original sense of beholding the truth, was altogether eliminated' (291).

The central aim and achievement of Arendt's *Human Condition* lies in its redefinition of the *vita activa* as a space of civic engagement driven by intellectual responsibility. But further scrutiny deserves to be given to its underlying assertion that modernity, and modern science in particular, made contemplation, as a way of knowing and living, obsolete—an assertion that has been repeated long enough, and authoritatively enough, to be accepted as a historical given. Hans Blumenberg's *The Legitimacy of the Modern Age* offers another highly influential iteration of this same point. According to Blumenberg, modern science liberates 'curiosity' from a medieval Aristotelian bias toward 'pure theory', a development that Blumenberg substantiates with the modern, and explicitly Baconian, precept 'that knowledge can extend beyond the Pillars of Hercules, beyond the limits of normal optics and the postulate of visibility, in other words, beyond the horizons that had been assigned to man as long as he had thought that he could remain the onlooker in repose, the leisurely enjoyer of the world, taken care of by providence'.[9] Modernity

[7] This is not to say that the 'active life' is not dignified with ample discussion in the Middle Ages; but, as F. J. Steele points out, 'The Active Life is always treated in conjunction with the Contemplative' as a less perfect but still potentially virtuous pursuit; for a survey of medieval treatments of the *vita activa*, see F. J. Steele, *Towards a Spirituality for Lay-Folk: the Active Life in Middle English Religious Literature from the Thirteenth Century to the Fifteenth* (Lewiston, NY: The Edwin Mellen Press, 1995), 62.

[8] Hannah Arendt, *The Human Condition* (1958; 2nd edn, Chicago: University of Chicago Press, 1998), 289.

[9] Hans Blumenberg, *The Legitimacy of the Modern Age*, trans. Robert M. Wallace (Cambridge, MA: MIT Press, 1983), 232, 234; see also Lawrence Dickey, 'Blumenberg and Secularization: "Self-Assertion" and the Problem of Self-Realizing Theology in History', *New German Critique*, 41 (1987), 151–65; and Elizabeth Brient, *The Immanence of the Infinite: Hans Blumenberg and the Threshold to Modernity* (Washington, DC: Catholic University of America Press, 2002).

defines knowledge, in other words, as the product of active engagement with the unknown, rather than of withdrawn contemplation of a closed and ordered system. By extension, a pragmatic world-view and worldly ethical stance that value active-life virtues over contemplative ones have been seen as the inevitable by-products of the rise of science, as recent observations like Charles Taylor's suggest: 'The vision of human agency as active, constructive, shaping, isn't confined to the activities which subserve a contemplative grasp of the world, viz. science and art; it also begins to take a greater place in ethics, in the form of a new understanding of ethical improvement, of how to reach the good life'.[10]

Yet such attempts to explain the modern reversal of the contemplative/active life hierarchy as an effect of early modern science neglect the even earlier role that the Reformation had played in unsettling the cultural status of the *vita contemplativa* in England, long before science emerged as an autonomous discipline. For a Reformation-era writer like Thomas Starkey, the humanist protégé of Thomas Cromwell and later chaplain to Henry VIII, contemplation belonged to a discredited monasticism and deserved to be rejected as such. In his *Dialogue Between Reginald Pole and Thomas Lupset*, Starkey decries the occupation of 'monks... in their solitary life, which hath brought forth (with little profit to the public state) much superstition'.[11] In place of the 'idle and slumbering life' of contemplation, Starkey insists that 'the perfection of man standeth not in bare knowledge and learning without application of it to any use or profit of other; but the very perfection of man's mind resteth in the use and exercise of all virtues and honesty' (26). Starkey frames his praise of the active life, with its emphasis on 'application', 'use', and 'profit', in explicitly anti-monastic terms; in so doing, he identifies the project of intellectual reform—and 'the very perfection of man's mind' and 'learning' in the active, rather than contemplative, life—with religious reform.

Starkey's redemption of the active life owes its rhetorical stance to the so-called 'civic' humanists like Coluccio Salutati, whose work champions the practical application of knowledge through the active virtue of prudence, while adapting it to the anti-monasticism of post-Reformation England.[12] As Starkey's example makes clear, the early modern elevation of action over contemplation does not result from scientific thought and practice; rather, it draws on a humanist rhetoric of virtuous action undertaken on behalf of the public good that staked a prior claim to—and, it can be argued, established—the active-life virtues that scientific

[10] Charles Taylor, *A Secular Age* (Cambridge, MA: Bellknap Press of Harvard University Press, 2007), 99; see also Richard Rorty, 'The Legitimacy of the Modern Age' (Review), *London Review of Books*, 5:11 (16 June – 6 July 1983), 3.

[11] Thomas Starkey, *A Dialogue between Reginald Pole and Thomas Lupset*, ed. Kathleen M. Burton (London: Chatto and Windus, 1948), 171. On Starkey, see Alistair Fox, 'English Humanism and the Body Politic', in *Reassessing the Henrician Age*, ed. Fox and Guy, 34–51.

[12] See Victoria Kahn, 'Coluccio Salutati on the Active and Contemplative Lives', in *Arbeit, Musse, Meditation*, ed. Vickers, 153–80.

discourse would claim for itself later in the seventeenth century. The active life for Starkey, as for Salutati, is the life not of science (which in the sixteenth century was still a pre-disciplinary entity) but of law and letters.[13] When early modern science emerged as a distinct branch of knowledge with an ameliorative social mission, it did so less by introducing new models of thought and action than by appropriating an ideal of public service that was already central to the humanist rationale for literate learning.

If the rise of science cannot be credited with initiating an early modern triumph of the active life over the contemplative, it was likewise far from inevitable that science would be identified with active-life virtues of practical utility and prudent action. Blumenberg and his followers credit 'Baconian pragmatism' with a pivotal role in valorizing action over contemplation.[14] Yet Bacon himself conceived science not as a pragmatic tool of the active life but as a mediation of action and contemplation; and he frequently referred to his own intellectual project in explicitly contemplative terms, while critiquing utilitarian approaches to knowledge. Indeed, the very notion of 'Baconian pragmatism', rather than originating with Bacon himself, appears to have been a retroactive construction by much later works like Thomas Sprat's *History of the Royal Society* (1667), which laments the subservience of 'active men' to 'speculative men' in the former age but predicts a new order, ushered in by science: 'While the Old could only bestow on us some barren Terms and Notions, the New shall impart to us the uses of all the Creatures, and shall inrich us with all the Benefits of Fruitfulness and Plenty' (438).[15]

Yet before Sprat, this alignment of the new science with the active over the contemplative life took hold only gradually and unevenly: indeed, John Evelyn's earliest plans for the Royal Society envision its physical setting on the model of the medieval contemplative community, with a layout of 'six apartments or cells, for the members of the society... each wherof should contain a small bedchamber, an outward room, a closet, and a private garden, somewhat after the manner of the carthusians'.[16] And Robert Boyle himself describes his own scientific research as

[13] On this point, see Peter Harrison, '"The Fashioned Image of Poetry or the Regular Instruction of Philosophy?": Truth, Utility, and the Natural Sciences in Early Modern England', in *Science, Literature, and Rhetoric in Early Modern England*, ed. Juliet Cummins and David Burchell (Aldershot: Ashgate, 2007), 15–35.

[14] On 'Baconian pragmatism', see Rorty, 'The Legitimacy of the Modern Age (Review)', 3 and Nicholas Lobkowicz, *Theory and Practice: History of a Concept from Aristotle to Marx* (Notre Dame, IN: University of Notre Dame Press, 1967), who describes 'Francis Bacon's basically antitheoretical and pragmatic attitude' (115).

[15] Thomas Sprat, *History of the Royal Society* (1667), cited and discussed by Michael Hunter, *Science and Society in Restoration England* (Cambridge and New York: Cambridge University Press, 1981), 87.

[16] John Evelyn, Letter to Robert Boyle, 3 September 1659, *Diary and Correspondence*, ed. W. Bray (London, 1852), 3: 118.

the product of his 'Hermit's averseness to society'.[17] While Evelyn would go on to dissociate the quasi-cloistered conditions of the scientific 'college' from the 'superstitious' practices of the real-life Carthusians (wary of 'scandal to our design'), and Boyle would distance himself from the influence of any 'strange, hasty, Anchoritish vow', their ready use of such analogies suggests nonetheless that the rise of early modern science did not banish contemplation and contemplative models to permanent obsolescence (as Arendt and others have claimed) but, to the contrary, unexpectedly revived the medieval contemplative as a cultural analogue for the early modern scientist.[18] This can be attributed to the fact that, in its earliest incarnation, early modern science was not clearly identifiable with a single cultural value and place.[19] In seeking to assign it one, its practitioners turn to the pre-existing taxonomy of 'active life' and 'contemplative life', but they display considerable uncertainty about which of the two lives and their cultural representatives best approximate the office of the scientist: the practical virtues of 'civic' humanists, merchants, and artisans on the one hand, or the space of pure intellection and otherworldly detachment of medieval contemplatives on the other.

If, as I have suggested, early modern science revived the medieval contemplative as an intellectual model, it was nonetheless a model riddled with ambivalence. While the medieval contemplative embodies the purity of the scientist's intellectual pursuit, the figure also darkly suggests the latter's social marginality and vulnerability to the charge of confusing knowledge with belief; if the former upholds the promise of uniting human knowledge with divine, it also suggests a deep suspicion of knowledge attained through the senses, which formed the basis of experimentalism. In other words, if the figure of the medieval contemplative provided a cultural analogue for the early modern scientist, it also established a space of critique, which became more pronounced as the scientific enterprise came to align itself with active-life virtues in the later seventeenth century. In making this point, I will focus on two central texts and the pre-Reformation sources that they selectively engage, appropriate, and reconfigure for new cultural conditions: Francis Bacon's *Advancement of Learning*, which responds to Thomas More's *Utopia* and More's Christian sources (most notably, I will argue, St Augustine and Walter Hilton) to present science as a new branch of contemplative knowledge and a new object of intellectual labor, and Margaret Cavendish's novella, 'The She-Anchoret', which analogizes the early modern natural philosopher and the medieval anchoress as parallel figures of contemplative intellection.

[17] Boyle cited and discussed by Steven Shapin, 'The House of Experiment in Seventeenth-Century England', *Isis*, 79 (1988), 373–404, at 386.

[18] Evelyn, Letter to Robert Boyle, 120; Boyle, in Shapin, 'The House of Experiment in Seventeenth-Century England', 386.

[19] As Howard Marchitello observes, early Stuart 'science' was 'still embedded within a range of cultural practices' and thus not 'an already autonomous feature of early modernity': Howard Marchitello, 'Science Studies and Early Renaissance Literature', *Literature Compass*, 3 (2006), 341–65, at 345.

By revealing the continuity of medieval forms of the 'active life'/'contemplative life' debate, as opposed to classical or neoclassical versions, into the early modern period, my larger aim is to revisit the models of historical and cultural change that underlie the association of modernity with the triumph of the active life—and in particular, the claim that science necessarily eliminated contemplation (again, to recall Arendt) from its central place in the debate. To the contrary, I find that the rise of early modern science did not preclude or short-circuit the debate over active and contemplative lives but rather emerged from, and owed its social and intellectual identity to, the debate's central terms. If this argument suggests the persistence of the debate's medieval forms into the early modern period, it does so by offering them neither as the 'vacant answer positions' of Blumenberg's account nor as the essentially secularized objects of his detractors.[20] As the history of post-Reformation English Catholicism shows, medieval contemplative practices maintained a still-vivid presence long into the seventeenth century; but on a more submerged level, I argue, those practices also established and validated a space of disciplined mental activity into which scientific thought could insert itself, thus allowing science to emerge from its humanist origins as one of many subjects in the curriculum (in the form of 'natural philosophy') and to become (in the form of 'science') the defining activity of knowledge itself.[21]

Francis Bacon and the Trials of Cain: The Scientist as Contemplative (I)

Despite Bacon's later association with an anti-theoretical pragmatism, as I have noted, contemplation and the contemplative life offered a vocabulary and a conceptual framework for Bacon's sense of his own project. In an undated, early letter to his uncle William Cecil, Lord Burghley, Bacon declares, 'the contemplative planet carrieth me away wholly', and confesses, 'I have as vast contemplative ends, as I have moderate civil ends'. But he goes on to describe his project of intellectual reform, which takes both contemplative and active forms of knowledge as its objects:

> for I have taken *all knowledge* [my emphasis] to be my province; and if I could purge it of two sorts of rovers, whereof the one with frivolous disputations, confutations,

[20] On these positions, see Dickey, 'Blumenberg and Secularization'.

[21] The publications produced by the European Science Foundation's ongoing research program, *From Natural Philosophy to Science*, offer insight into this transition; see Sachiko Kusukawa and Ian Maclean (eds.), *Transmitting Knowledge: Words, Images and Instruments in Early Modern Europe* (Oxford: Oxford University Press, 2006). See also the essays collected in Tore Frängsmyr (ed.), *The Structure of Knowledge: Classifications of Science and Learning since the Renaissance* (Berkeley: University of California, Office for History of Science and Technology, 2001).

> and verbosities, the other with blind experiments and auricular traditions and impostures, hath committed so many spoils, I hope I should bring in industrious observations, grounded conclusions, and profitable inventions and discoveries; the best state of that province.[22]

Bacon's famous profession of interest in 'all knowledge' has been taken as an axiomatic claim to a universal encyclopedism; yet its broader context reveals that the statement actually refers specifically to the debate over the *vita activa* versus the *vita contemplativa*, as it concerns the forms and functions of knowledge. Bacon's 'all knowledge' is meant to bridge the gap separating contemplative and active knowledge, wisdom and prudence, while targeting the weaknesses of both, identified here as fruitless experimentalism on the one hand and empty verbosity on the other—both symptoms of method ungrounded in truth. Using similar terms in a 1609 letter to Isaac Casaubon, Bacon declares his aim to reform contemplation by reorienting it from a posture of leisured aloofness to a pursuit aligned with the goals of social order: 'For indeed to write at leisure that which is to be read at leisure matters little; but to bring about the better ordering of man's life and business, with all its troubles and difficulties, by the help of sound and true contemplations—this is the thing I aim at' (xx).

Bacon's model of an active life ordered by contemplation recalls classical antecedents such as Plato's *Republic*; but his immediate and constant touchstone is Thomas More's *Utopia* (1516), a work with demonstrably lasting effects on Bacon's thought and its treatment of the 'vita activa' versus the 'vita contemplativa'.[23] In the 'dialogue of counsel' that opens *Utopia*'s Book 1, More presents a paradigmatically humanist conflict between the life of learning and that of public service, when his central character Hythloday resists the call to sacrifice his 'own peace and quiet' to 'promote the public interest' as a royal councilor, retorting that 'there is no room for philosophy with rulers'.[24] Against this backdrop of conflict, the description of Utopia in Book 2 presents a social order that unites, to the point of utterly confusing, active pursuits and contemplative ideals. A discussion headed *vita activa* describes the Utopians' devotion to *naturae contemplationem*, 'the contemplation of nature', which they deem 'an act of worship acceptable to God' (225). The passage goes on to describe other Utopians 'who for religious motives eschew learning and scientific pursuit and yet allow themselves no leisure. It is only by keeping busy and by all good offices that they are determined to merit the

[22] Bacon, Letter to Lord Burghley, in *Francis Bacon: The Major Works*, ed. Brian Vickers (Oxford: Oxford University Press, 1996), 20. Subsequent quotations of Bacon will be taken from this text, with references cited parenthetically in the text.

[23] On Bacon's use of More, see Denise Albanese, '*The New Atlantis* and the Uses of Utopia', *ELH*, 57 (1990): 503–28.

[24] Thomas More, *Utopia*, in *The Complete Works of St. Thomas More*, vol. 4, ed. Edward Surtz, S. J. and J. H. Hexter (New Haven, CT: Yale University Press, 1965), 57, 99. Subsequent references to *Utopia* will be taken from this edition, with page numbers cited parenthetically.

happiness coming after death' (225). More's Utopians direct contemplation toward objects of the natural world, and action toward otherworldly ends.

If, as Fredric Jameson asserts, More's *Utopia* is a work dedicated to exploring 'the intellectual missions and vocations of the emergent secular intellectual', it is in the Utopians' 'contemplation of nature' that the paradoxes inherent in that figure become palpable.[25] In the 'Letter to the University of Oxford', More explains: 'Some plot their course, as it were, to the contemplation of celestial realities through the study of nature, and progress to theology by way of philosophy and the liberal arts.'[26] Yet though More articulates this view of secular study as a route to sacred ends, he never fully endorses it himself. Instead, as Lord Chancellor, More directed lay readers to late medieval works like Walter Hilton's *Scale of Perfection*—a handbook of 'contemplation in perfect love of God' that More himself had come to know through the London Carthusians.[27]

Hilton's *Scale of Perfection* offers a corrective to a modern understanding of medieval contemplation as a state of passive and anti-rational 'leisurely enjoyment' (to recall Blumenberg). Instead, Hilton's terms reveal his understanding of contemplation as a highly-developed cognitive activity, in which a well-trained human reason purifies what Hilton calls 'the thought of the heart', and, led by 'goostli love', culminates in the 'light of undirstonding'.[28] Hilton's interest in the well-trained mind substantiates Santha Bhattacharji's observation that 'by the late Middle Ages the understanding of the term "contemplation" seems to have been strongly intellectualized, so that no clear distinction is made between, say, the prayerful meditation of the monk...and the academic study of the texts going on in the recently-founded schools and universities'.[29]

But Hilton's *Scale of Perfection*, with the contemplative tradition in which it participates, sharply distinguishes the 'bodily werkes' and 'worldeli' concerns that occupy the active life from the 'goostli vertues' of the contemplative life, whose practitioners 'feelith the thought of [their] herte[s] drawe up from alle ertheli thynges' (32–3). In contrast, the Utopians' 'contemplation of nature' and busy pursuit of 'the happiness coming after death' invert the traditional aims and

25 Fredric Jameson, 'Morus: The Generic Window', *New Literary History*, 34 (2003), 431–51, at 438.

26 Thomas More, 'Letter to the University of Oxford', ed. Daniel Kinney, *In Defense of Humanism: Complete Works of St. Thomas More*, vol. 15 (New Haven, CT: Yale University Press, 1986), 139. ('Quin sunt nonnulli qui cognitionem rerum naturalium, velut viam sibi, qua transcendant in supernarum contemplationem, praestruunt, iterque per philosophiam, et liberales artes' (138)).

27 Thomas More, *The Confutation of Tyndale's Answer*, in *The Complete Works of St Thomas More*, vol. 8, ed. L. A. Schuster (New Haven, CT: Yale University Press, 1973), 37.

28 Walter Hilton, *The Scale of Perfection*, ed. Thomas H. Bestul (Kalamazoo, MI: Medieval Institute Publications, 2000), 91, 218. Subsequent references will be to this edition, with page numbers noted parenthetically.

29 Santha Bhattacharji, 'Medieval Contemplation and Mystical Experience', in *Approaching Medieval English Anchoritic and Mystical Texts*, ed. Dee Dyas et al. (Cambridge: D. S. Brewer, 2005), 51–62, at 55.

objects of the active and contemplative lives, in what I believe More means to satirize as a comic perversion.[30]

In his shrewd reading of *Utopia*, Jameson calls the work 'a manifesto' for 'new humanist intellectuals' that ironically 'does not contain any'.[31] But I find its most attentive representation of the humanist intellectual precisely in its satire of the Utopians' confusion of active and contemplative lives, which manifests what I identified earlier as the paradox of More's secular intellectual. For More, the secular intellectual is a categorical monster, who confuses the world with an object of worship and expects that worldly business will lead to his salvation.

Yet where the Utopian 'contemplation of nature' embodies the perversity of the secular intellectual for More, Bacon adopts it as a model for his scientific program. *The Advancement of Learning* advocates 'the contemplation of God's creatures and works' as the centerpiece of Bacon's intellectual project, even while acknowledging its deficiency. As Bacon puts it, 'the contemplation of God's creatures and works produceth (having regard to the works and creatures themselves) knowledge; but having regard to God, no perfect knowledge, but *wonder*, which is broken knowledge' (125; my emphasis). Like the Utopians, Bacon makes nature an object of contemplation, but Baconian contemplation avoids the Utopians' perversity by producing not worship but wonder.

The centrality of 'wonder' to early modern thought and practice has already been well established and explored; but by replacing the term into a contemplative tradition, I want to make a point slightly different from those advanced by scholars of early modern science. Baconian 'wonder' may represent the 'outermost limits' of human knowledge, as Lorraine Daston and Katharine Park contend, and possibly even the opposite of human knowledge, as Mary Baine Campbell suggests.[32] But it does so by borrowing from a Christian tradition, represented by More, in which properly directed contemplation leads to superior knowing—what Hilton calls the 'light of understanding' as distinct from the 'merkeness of unknowynge' (91) (and here Hilton differentiates himself from a work like *The Cloud of Unknowing*). Baconian 'wonder' represents an experience of the incapacity of human reason but also a goad to further knowledge: which is why Bacon calls wonder not only 'broken knowledge' but 'the seed of knowledge', because it propels the human intellect into higher understanding.

[30] See my discussion of More's *Utopia* in Jennifer Summit, *Memory's Library: Medieval Books in Early Modern England* (Chicago: University of Chicago Press, 2008), Chapter 2.

[31] Jameson, 'Morus: The Generic Window', 434.

[32] Lorraine Daston and Katharine Park, *Wonders and the Order of Nature, 1150–1750* (New York: Zone Books, 1998), 20, 11; Caroline Walker Bynum, 'Wonder', *American Historical Review*, 102 (1997), 1–26. Compare Bynum's account with Stephen Greenblatt, 'Resonance and Wonder', in *Exhibiting Cultures: The Poetics and Politics of Museum Display*, ed. Ivan Karp and Steven D. Lavine (Washington, DC: Smithsonian Institution Press, 1991), 42–56.

The vehicle of this intellectual ascent is 'pleasure'—a crucial term for Bacon that needs to be aligned with another in his intellectual lexicon, 'charity' (as 'caritas' or 'love'). As Bacon observes in *The Advancement of Learning*, 'all knowledge and wonder (which is the seed of knowledge) is an impression of pleasure in itself' (125). By making wonder the product of contemplation, driven by charitable pleasure or love, Bacon adapts the terms and ascending structure of a medieval contemplative practice that is seen by its advocates like Hilton to be not the eradication of human reason but its fulfillment. Where Hilton's contemplation is driven by the 'the thought of the heart', through 'goostli love', to culminate in an experience of the 'light of undirstonding', Bacon adapts and abstracts a similar model to imagine an intellectual experience driven by pleasure, leading to wonder, and culminating in a knowledge that transcends the native weakness of the human mind. This is where Bacon's conception of the active and contemplative lives debate departs from classical models and shows its medieval roots. Where Cicero conceives the debate over the active and contemplative lives to be a matter of ethics—concerning what is the good life and the good society—Hilton makes it a question of the mind, its workings, and its objects. And it is in the continuity of this explicitly cognitive focus that Bacon reveals himself to be Hilton's, more than Cicero's, heir.[33]

It is not quite accurate to say that Bacon secularizes contemplation, which *The Advancement of Learning* frames in explicitly biblical terms. For Bacon, the perfection of the contemplative life is exemplified in Adam's experience in Eden:

> After the creation was finished, it is set down unto us that man was placed in the garden to work therein; which work so appointed to him could be no other than work of contemplation; that is, when the end of work is but for exercise and experiment, not for necessity; for [before the Fall] man's employment must of consequence have been matter of delight in the experiment, and not matter of labour for the use. (149)

By 'experiment', Bacon means not an action undertaken for another end but one undertaken for its own sake—a meaning closer to the modern meaning of 'experience' than 'experiment' as defined by later scientific method.[34] But this model of contemplative work—that is, labor undertaken for intellectual delight rather than practical use—disappeared with the Fall, Bacon asserts, which had the

[33] Cicero's *De Officiis* in particular was a favored text among English humanists arguing in favor of the active life; but, for reasons that will become clear in this chapter, I believe that Cicero's early modern prominence disguises the medieval sources of the debate. See Catherine Anna Louise Jarrott, 'The English Humanists' Use of Cicero's De Officiis in their Evaluation of Active and Contemplative Life' Unpublished PhD dissertation, Stanford University, 1954, which examines Cicero's centrality to humanist defenses of the *vita activa*; yet compare to Steele, *Towards a Spirituality for Lay-Folk*.

[34] This was the starting point of a conference at Stanford University, 25 April 2008, 'From Experience to Experiment in Early Modern Science', co-sponsored by the Division of Literatures, Cultures, and Languages and the Stanford Center for Medieval and Early Modern Studies.

effect of separating, and placing in opposition, the active and the contemplative, labor and leisure, use and delight.

This point is illustrated in one of Bacon's most jarring uses of biblical exempla to describe 'the contemplative state and the active state':

> After the fall of man, we see . . . an image of the two estates, the contemplative state and the active state, figured in the two persons of Abel and Cain, and in the two simplest and most primitive trades of life; that of the shepherd (who, by reason of his leisure, rest in a place, and living in view of heaven, is a lively image of a contemplative life), and that of the husbandman: where we see again the favour and election of God went to the shepherd, and not to the tiller of the ground. (150)

Bacon's decision to allegorize the active and contemplative lives in the figures of Cain and Abel replaces a more traditional allegory of the active and contemplative lives, the biblical example of Martha and Mary from Luke 10:38–42. In the story of Martha and Mary, patristic and vernacular interpreters took Christ's preference for Mary's service at his feet over Martha's busy service in the kitchen as a sign of the superiority of the contemplative life over the active life.[35] Thus Hilton quotes Christ's words to Mary with a gloss praising the contemplative life: '*Maria optimam partem elegit, que non auferetur ab ea* (Luke 10.42), that Marie hadde chosen the beste partie, that is the love of God in contemplacion, for it schal nevere be taken awey fro hire' (82). Likewise Augustine glosses the story of Martha and Mary as figuring of 'the two lives': 'the life present, and the life to come, the life of labour, and the life of quiet, the life of sorrow, and the life of blessedness, the life temporal, and the life eternal'. Despite the superiority of the contemplative over the active life, Augustine insists on the two lives' essential kinship, asserting that they are 'both harmless, both, I say, praiseworthy'. Augustine holds that Martha's life of active service, if motivated by charity, could support and ultimately lead to the more perfect life of contemplation, represented by Mary as a promise of everlasting peace: 'In Martha was the image of things present, in Mary of things to come. What Martha was doing, that we are now; what Mary was doing, that we hope for.'[36]

By replacing Martha and Mary with Cain and Abel, Bacon rewrites the relationship between active and contemplative lives; in place of Martha and Mary's kinship, which is ultimately mediated and reconciled under Christ, Bacon pictures an irreconcilable sibling rivalry, leading to fratricide. In this, he follows Augustine in contrasting the two brothers with the two sisters. Unlike Martha and Mary, Cain and Abel illustrate the post-lapsarian split between 'the city of men' and 'the city of God', 'the children of the flesh' and 'the children of the promise' as one of violent

[35] See Constable, 'The Interpretation of Mary and Martha', for many examples.

[36] Saint Augustine, *The Works of Saint Augustine [electronic resource]: A Translation for the 21st Century*, Augustinian Heritage Institute, series ed. John E. Rotelle and Boniface Ramsey (Charlottesville, VA: InteLex Corporation, 2006), Sermon 54, section 4.

conflict.[37] They exemplify Augustine's complaint that 'The perishable body weighs down the soul, and the earthly habitation presses down the mind as it ponders many questions' (853). Just as the body weighs down the soul and concerns of the world force down the mind, so Cain, the child of flesh, strikes down Abel, the child of promise, when he 'discovered that God had approved his brother's sacrifice but not his own' (604).

Augustine's treatment of active and contemplative lives anticipates Bacon's to the extent that it participates in a larger consideration 'of the mind itself', which Augustine taxonomizes in regard to 'sensation and understanding', leading to 'the apprehension and awareness of truth' (853). For Augustine, in other words, the dual drives toward action versus contemplation, flesh versus spirit, structure the human mind, which operates according to a dichotomy of lower and higher functions of sensation and reason. For Bacon, whose focus on 'all knowledge' likewise frames the active versus the contemplative as habits of mind, the allegory of Cain and Abel as figures of the active and the contemplative lives provides a means for describing and taxonomizing not only intellectual functions but also intellectual labor as a social performance. Of central importance to Bacon's treatment of Cain and Abel is the distinction between their occupations as shepherd and husbandman. The distinction recalls classical treatments of active and contemplative lives by aligning them with the generic distinction between pastoral and georgic, the literary forms of leisure and work. But it also allows Bacon to present the two as opposed figures of intellectual labor, distinguishing between Abel's posture of detached watchfulness and Cain's active ingenuity. In Cain and Abel, I am arguing, Bacon finds two opposed prototypes for the thinker as a social figure: the one, aloof, contemplative, and favored by God, the other, active, worldly, and cursed.

For recent critics, Cain's worldly ingenuity and enforced marginality have made him a figure of the modern man.[38] Thus in their introduction to Jacob Burckhardt's *Civilization of the Renaissance in Italy*, Benjamin Nelson and Charles Trinkaus observe that, like Cain, '[modern] man has irrevocably been cast out—has cast himself out—of a childlike world of enchantment and undividedness'.[39] A similar identification leads Stephen Gaukroger, in the only scholarly commentary that I have been able to find on Bacon's representation of Cain and Abel, to speculate that Bacon favors Cain—because he embodies modern values of independence and ingenuity—more than God does: 'As Bacon points out, God

[37] St Augustine, *The City of God*, trans. Henry Bettenson (London: Penguin, 1972), 596–7. Augustine's discussion of Cain and Abel is developed in Book XV.

[38] Thus see Véronique Léonard-Roques, *Caïn, figure de la modernité* (Paris: Champion, 2003), and Ricardo J. Quinones, *The Changes of Cain: Violence and the Lost Brother in Cain and Abel Literature* (Princeton, NJ: Princeton University Press, 1991).

[39] Cited in Quinones, *The Changes of Cain*, 90.

favoured Abel over Cain; but it is at best ambiguous whom Bacon favours'.[40] But Bacon's treatment of Cain in *The Advancement of Learning* needs to be read against his essay, 'Of Envy', which makes Cain into a prototype of the vice it treats, condemning 'Cain's envy' as 'vile and malignant toward his brother Abel'. In the essay, Cain exemplifies Bacon's assertion that 'near kinfolks, and fellows in office, and those that have been bred together, are more apt to envy their equals when they are raised' (355), a reading that echoes Augustine's observation that 'it was certainly envy which goaded and inflamed Cain to his brother's destruction' (605).

Rather than reading Bacon as a proto-modern partisan of Cain, I suggest that we read Bacon's treatment of Cain and Abel, together with the active and contemplative lives that they exemplify, as an instance of 'Discipline Envy', which Marjorie Garber diagnoses in *Academic Instincts* as 'the wish, on the part of an academic discipline, to model itself on, or borrow from, or appropriate the terms and vocabulary and authority figures of another discipline' in key moments of its institutional formation.[41] This comparison encourages us to interpret Bacon's Cain and Abel not as figures of pre- and proto-modernity, but as prototypes of the professional thinker, modeled on a hierarchy of occupations; for Bacon, as I have argued, Cain and Abel, the tiller and the watcher, represent competing ways of knowing, both as intellectual functions and as social performances. Following on this perception, we should observe that if Cain's offense against Abel enacts his 'envy', it is an act that doesn't mark his absolute difference from his brother so much as his desire to have what he has, to emulate and take his place.

In killing his brother, Cain acts out of desire (which Augustine tells us is the root cause of envy) that is directed at his two fathers: the heavenly father, whose approval and love he seeks, and his earthly father, Adam, whose Edenic felicity, when 'employment' was undertaken for delight rather than use ('matter of delight in the experiment, and not matter of labour for the use'), God finds reflected, and rewards, in Abel, and Cain laments having lost. Bacon's version of the Cain and Abel story can thus be seen as an origin myth for the age of science. In it, the competition of the worldly and ingenious husbandman with his contemplative brother for their heavenly father's approval thematizes the competition of the disciplines for social status and recognition. This reading both recalls and corrects the modern myth of science (supported by Arendt and Blumenberg) with which I began: Cain's act against his brother, the representative of the active life against that of the contemplative life, is less an effort to eliminate than usurp him, less a devaluation of his office than a recognition of its superior status and privilege. Bacon does not identify with Cain over his contemplative brother; rather, he uses their conflict—generated by Abel's privilege and Cain's violent envy—to illustrate

[40] Stephen Gaukroger, *Francis Bacon and the Transformation of Early Modern Philosophy* (Cambridge: Cambridge University Press, 2001), 83.

[41] Marjorie Garber, *Academic Instincts* (Princeton, NJ: Princeton University Press, 2001), 62.

the volatility of the split he diagnoses between active and contemplative lives, the world of work and the life of the mind, a split he proposes to repair by inventing a new category of intellectual labor that partakes of both.

Bacon, trained in the humanist language arts, calls his project a 'Georgics of the mind', in terms that directly recall his discussion of Cain, the husbandman and 'tiller of the ground':

> And surely if the purpose be in good earnest not to write at leisure that which men may read at leisure, but really to instruct and suborn action and active life, these Georgics of the mind, concerning the husbandry and tillage thereof, are no less worthy than the heroical descriptions of Virtue, Duty, and Felicity. (244–5)

Here Bacon defends not only Virgil's 'lowly theme' in the *Georgics* but his own project of intellectual reform as set out in the *Advancement of Learning*. Where Virgil describes a world after the Golden Age, in which humans are forced out of a world of leisure into one of work, Bacon describes a post-lapsarian world in which the ends of labor and leisure are separated and at odds with one another, as exemplified in the fratricidal conflict between Cain and Abel.[42] But Bacon also envisions a possible mediation of labor and leisure, the world of Cain and that of Abel, by redefining thought and rationality as objects of work, not of leisure. Bacon's 'Georgics of the mind' applies the active but debased labor of Cain, 'husbandry and tillage', to the leisured and elevated objects of Abel, who enjoys a 'view of heaven' (150). In claiming reason as the product of work, Bacon thereby carves out a worldly sphere of intellectual labor. Here he deliberately echoes his own letter to Casaubon, in which he declares that 'to write at leisure that which is to be read at leisure matters little' and avows his desire to generate 'sound and true contemplations' that can 'bring about the better ordering of man's life and business'. Bacon's *Advancement of Learning* fulfills this promise by envisioning a new form of intellectual labor that enacts its 'husbandry and tillage' on the mind, while also appropriating the conventions of literary genre—here, the georgic—for the project of the new science.

Bacon envisions the mediation of labor and thought, the world of Cain and that of Abel, by identifying the mind and its activities with work, rather than retirement. Through Cain and Abel Bacon offers a new model not only of the contemplative and active lives, but also of historical change, imagined as a shift in privilege from the one to the other. And here, I propose, he allows us to revisit and qualify the models of Arendt and Blumenberg with which I began. Where both hold that scientific thought renders the medieval contemplative model obsolete and ushers in a modernity dominated by the active life, Bacon shows instead that the scientist's

[42] See Giordano Bruno, *The Expulsion of the Triumphant Beast*, trans. Arthur D. Imerti (Lincoln, NE: University of Nebraska, 1992), for another early modern reading of leisure and employment in light of the *Georgics* (199–215); and Anthony Low, *The Georgic Revolution* (Princeton, NJ: Princeton University Press, 1985), 137–8, on Bruno and the *Georgics*.

work is modeled on and made possible by that of the contemplative. By proposing in his 'Georgics of the mind' a mediation between contemplative practices and worldly ends, Bacon doesn't eliminate contemplation but adapts it to new conditions and objects.

Margaret Cavendish's 'The She-Anchoret' (1656): The Scientist as Contemplative (II)

Margaret Cavendish, writing in the generation after Bacon but in an era in which the Royal Society claimed the Baconian mantle, bore a relation to the scientific culture of her day that has been seen as alternately marginal and mainstream.[43] While excluded by virtue of her gender from membership in the Royal Society itself, she was allowed to visit the Society by virtue of her elevated class status, and she expressed both public and private admiration for its accomplishments and those of its members. All the same, in published works such as her *Philosophical Letters* (1664) she critiques the experimental sciences that had come to dominate the Royal Academy and develops an alternative scientific method, which she calls 'Contemplative philosophy'. In the section that follows, I examine Cavendish's appropriation of intellectual stances and methods associated with the contemplative enterprise, particularly as inherited from the medieval debate over the active versus the contemplative lives.

For Cavendish, 'contemplation' comes to model not the intellectual labor of the scientist, as it had for Bacon, but a position eccentric to, and critical of, scientific labor and its institutionalization. Cavendish's critique of experimental science was not unique, as a growing body of scholarship on her work in natural philosophy has established; but her self-conscious use of medieval forms in issuing that critique offers a historical counterpoint to the modern association of the rise of science with the triumph of the active life. Although Cavendish's better-known works, such as *The Convent of Pleasure*, appropriate forms and images with a recognizably medieval pedigree, Cavendish herself has not been widely recognized as a reader of medieval literature, despite textual evidence establishing that she was.[44] Yet I find that Cavendish not only appropriates medieval motifs in her critique of contemporary science, she does so with an unusual level of attention to the

[43] For a survey of scholarly perspectives on Margaret Cavendish and early modern science, see Eric Lewis, 'The Legacy of Margaret Cavendish', *Perspectives on Science*, 9 (2001), 341–65.

[44] See Christina Malcomson, 'Christine de Pizan's *City of Ladies* in Early Modern England', in *Debating Gender in Early Modern England*, ed. Christina Malcolmson and Mihoko Suzuki (New York: Palgrave, 2002), 15–35. On 'the memory of convents' in Margaret Cavendish's *Convent of Pleasure* and other early modern works, see David Wallace, 'Periodizing Women: Mary Ward (1585–1645) and the Premodern Canon', *Journal of Medieval and Early Modern Studies*, 36 (2006), 397–453, at 420.

medieval contemplative tradition, which has not yet been noticed or explored. By bringing to light Cavendish's tactical medievalism, I hope to establish not only that contemplation, defined as a position opposed to the *vita activa*, persisted long after it was believed to have been eliminated by the scientific revolution, but that as early modern science increasingly aligned itself with the *vita activa*, the *vita contemplativa* was re-animated as an alternative scientific practice and a position of institutional and intellectual critique.

Cavendish's monumental but under-read *Nature's Picture Drawn by Fancies Pencil* (1656) was one of her first works to be published following its author's continental exile during the English Civil War. A volume of mixed genres comprising 'several Feigned Stories, Comical, Tragical, Tragi-comical, Poetical, Romancical, Philosophical, Historical, and Moral: Some in Verse, some in Prose, some Mixt, and some by Dialogues', its longest and central piece is a novella entitled 'The She-Anchoret'.[45] The story produces an unlikely mix of romance, hagiography, and instructive prose: the daughter of a Widower promises her dying father that she will 'live chast and holy' and 'serve the Gods above', and, after his death, 'resolved to live like a kind of Anchoret's Life, living encloistered by her self alone, vowing Chastity, and a Single-life; but gave leave for any to speak to her through a Grate' (547). She soon wins fame and 'all sorts of people resorted to her, to hear her speak; and not only to hear her speak, but to get knowledge, and to learn wisdom: for she argued rationally, instructed judiciously, admonished prudently, and perswaded piously; applying and directing her Discourse according to the several Studies, Professions, Grandeurs, Ages, and Humours of her Auditory' (547–8). Her visitors come from all sectors of society—natural philosophers, physicians, moral philosophers, 'Fathers of the Church', judges, statesmen, and so forth—and her responses to their many questions ('what was chance and fortune?' (550); 'what was an idea?' (566); 'what caused sleep?' (589); 'what was the difference between the Passions and the Appetites?' (605); 'what men made the best Privy Councellors?' (636); etc.) allow Cavendish to display the wide range of her intellectual curiosity.

The novella ends in tragedy: when the anchoress's fame spreads to a neighboring monarch, who pursues her in the hope of convincing her 'to leave that inclosed life' and marry him, she emerges from her anchorhold long enough to reveal that she has just poisoned herself, deliver an auto-eulogy, and finally succumb to a public death, following which she is permanently mourned and memorialized (704–6). My focus will be less the work's literary form and achievement (though these are ripe for evaluation) than its decision to picture its central figure as an anchoress, which develops further the central question that this essay has been exploring: what is the legacy of contemplation in the age of science?

[45] Margaret Cavendish, *Natures Picture Drawn by Fancies Pencil* (London, 1656); 'The She-Anchoret' comprises pages 544–706.

Where Robert Boyle compared himself to a 'hermit' in his desire for secluded study and John Evelyn invokes the Carthusian monastery as a model for the Royal Society, Cavendish likewise appropriates the medieval contemplative as a figure for the early modern scientist. But Boyle and Evelyn do so primarily to imagine science's social place—as one held aloof from the tumultuous world of contemporary politics and defined by its exclusive masculinity—more than its intellectual project.[46] For Cavendish, on the other hand, the anchorhold defines both a social place that is explicitly female and, I will argue, a place of intellectual critique.

Anchoresses are important figures to Cavendish: in the autobiographical essay that she attaches to *Nature's Picture*, she avows that 'I could most willingly exclude my self, so as Never to see the face of any creature, but my Lord, as long as I live, inclosing my self like an Anchoret, wearing a Frize-gown, tied with a cord about my waste' ('A true Relation of my Birth, Breeding, and Life', 271). Here the anchoress figures secular enclosure, as Cavendish removes her from the anchorhold to the household, while likewise substituting her heavenly 'Lord', as the object of her devotion, with her earthly one. Before considering how the anchoress defines the scientific project for Cavendish, we must first consider what the figure of the anchoress meant to her.[47]

Anchoresses make appearances in other seventeenth-century literary texts, usually to define extreme chastity and solitude: John Ford's *'Tis Pity She's a Whore*, which was 'Acted by the Queen's Majesty's Servants' in 1633, describes 'such hands as these / would make an Anchoret Lascivious'. As maid of honor to Charles I's openly Catholic queen, Henrietta Maria, Cavendish would have encountered anchoresses and other religious figures in the plays that the Queen sponsored and enjoyed; like Ford, playwrights under Henrietta Maria's patronage learned to brandish religious imagery figuratively.[48] But Henrietta Maria's interest in anchoresses and cloistered women was not only figurative; through the Queen, Cavendish could have gained a more nuanced model of medieval anchoresses and their contemplative practices. During the Revolution, Cavendish followed the Queen in exile to Paris, where Henrietta Maria supported the Paris Benedictines. The community still bore the imprimatur of its spiritual guide, Augustine Baker, who was responsible for preserving, copying, and even editing for publication important works of medieval contemplation, including Hilton's *Scale of Perfection*,

[46] On the aloofness of Restoration science from politics, see Hunter, *Science and Society in Restoration England*, 27; on the (neo-monastic) masculinity of the early modern scientific community, see John Guillory, 'The Bachelor State: Philosophy and Sovereignty in Bacon's *New Atlantis*', in *Politics and the Passions, 1500–1850*, ed. Victoria Kahn, Neil Saccamano, and Daniela Coli (Princeton, NJ: Princeton University Press, 2006), 49–74.

[47] I discuss Margaret Cavendish's interest in anchoresses briefly in *Lost Property: The Woman Writer and English Literary History, 1380–1589* (Chicago: University of Chicago Press, 2000), 207.

[48] See Anna Battigelli, *Margaret Cavendish and the Exiles of the Mind* (Lexington: University Press of Kentucky, 1998), 14–15.

which was originally dedicated to an anchoress. The Queen also patronized the nuns' chaplain, Serenus Cressy, whose voyage to the continent she personally underwrote; he expressed his gratitude to her by dedicating his *Roman-Catholick Doctrines No Novelty* (1663) to her. Cressy is better known as the editor who brought out the first printed edition of Julian of Norwich's *Revelation of Love* in 1670, based on manuscripts preserved and copied in the exiled Benedictine community of nuns. And it is through this channel that I find it possible that Margaret Cavendish was introduced to Julian of Norwich.

While the figure of the 'anchoret' was not unknown in the seventeenth century, Cavendish is unusual in imagining hers not simply as a figure of seclusion but as one with a distinct intellectual identity, grounded in 'contemplation'. The term recurs throughout Cavendish's works, often to describe the author herself. In the same autobiographical essay in which she compares herself to an 'anchoret', Cavendish confesses, 'I was never very active, by reason I was given so much to contemplation' (268). In Cavendish's use of the term, contemplation becomes a personal character trait more than an ethical choice, as it had been defined in the classical debate over the *vita activa* versus the *vita contemplativa*. It also bears the marks of pathology—Cavendish calls herself vulnerable to 'contemplating melancholy' (269)—which fuels both her love of solitude and also her drive to write. 'I being addicted from my childhood, to contemplation rather than conversation, to solitariness rather than society, to melancholy than mirth, to write with the pen than to work with a needle' (267), she confesses, 'For my part I had rather sit at home and write, or walk, as I said, in my chamber and contemplate' (267).[49] Contemplation is also an intellectual path that is freely open to women, unlike the life of action, 'which we by Nature are not made fit for', as Cavendish observes in her preface to *The Worlds Olio* (1655).[50] While women's actions are spatially restricted, Cavendish observes, 'Thoughts are free, those can never be inslaved, for we are not hindred from studying, since we are allowed so much idle time that we know not how to pass it away, but may as well read in our Closets, as Men in their Colleges; and Contemplation is as free to us as to Men to beget clear Speculation' ($A5^r$).

Cavendish's selection of the anchoress as the mouthpiece for her 'contemplative philosophy' is grounded in a remarkably subtle reading of the medieval contemplative tradition, whose terms she adapts to the enterprise of natural philosophy. For whatever the work's interest in the mixed genres of literary history, Cavendish makes it clear that she intends the work to be read primarily as a work of natural

49 See Lara Dodds, 'Margaret Cavendish's Domestic Experiment', in *Genre and Women's Life Writing in Early Modern England*, ed. Michelle M. Dowd and Julie A. Eckerle (Aldershot: Ashgate, 2007), who examines the relationship between 'writing work' and domestic 'work' in Cavendish's autobiographical writings (156).

50 Margaret Cavendish, Duchess of Newcastle, *The Worlds Olio* (London, 1655), $A5^r$. Subsequent references to the text will be to this edition, with folio or page numbers marked parenthetically.

philosophy. So much is clear in the fact that the interviews with the natural philosophers and the physicians form the longest sections (together, they comprise nearly a third) of the work. More than this, Cavendish intends the work to serve as a serious response to the growing influence of experimental science. In 'An Epistle to be placed before my She Anchoret', Cavendish asks readers 'that when they read those parts or places which treat of the Rational and Sensitive Spirits, that they will compare those to my Book of Philosophical and Physical Opinions, being parts that should be added thereto'. In this, she offers the work as a fictional sequel to her earlier *Philosophical and Physical Opinions* (London, 1653), a voluminous work that sets out her original theory of the 'Rational and Sensitive Spirits'. This theory forms the basis of what she calls 'contemplative philosophy' and offers as an alternative to experimental science, which she critiques because of its reliance on the unreliable senses; thus she concludes, in her *Observations Upon Experimental Philosophy* (1666), that scientists ought not 'in my opinion, to condemn contemplative philosophy, nay, to prefer the experimental part before her', because contemplation arises from reason:[51]

> Reason must direct first how sense ought to work; and so much as the rational knowledge is more noble than the sensitive, so much is the speculative part of philosophy more noble than the mechanical. But our age being more for deluding experiments than rational arguments, which some call a 'tedious babble,' doth prefer sense before reason; and trusts more to the deceiving sight of their eyes, and deluding glasses, than to the perception of clear and regular reason. (196)

Cavendish shares with her contemporary and acquaintance Thomas Hobbes the belief that experimentalism, deriving from sense perception, must be subordinate to philosophy, deriving from reason.[52] But she also critiques Hobbes's assertion that 'Imagination is nothing else, but a fading or decaying sense', insisting rather that 'Imagination is a rational perception, and sense a sensitive perception.'[53] By classing imagination with reason above sense, Cavendish implicitly defends her practice of delivering natural philosophy by means of imaginative literature, as she does in the 'She-Anchoret'. Cavendish's theory of 'the rational and sensitive spirits', though it shares some features with her contemporaries such as Hobbes, represents

[51] See Cavendish's chapter, 'Further Observations Upon Experimental Philosophy, Reflecting Withal upon some Principal Subjects in Contemplative Philosophy', in her *Observations upon Experimental Philosophy*, ed. Eileen O'Neill (Cambridge: Cambridge University Press, 2001), 195–248, at 195.

[52] Sarah Hutton, 'In Dialogue with Thomas Hobbes: Margaret Cavendish's Natural Philosophy', *Women's Writing*, 4 (1997), 421–32; Eve Keller, 'Producing Petty Gods: Margaret Cavendish's Critique of Experimental Science', *ELH*, 64 (1997), 447–71; Jay Stevenson, 'The Mechanist-Vitalist Soul of Margaret Cavendish', *SEL*, 36 (1996), 527–43; John Rogers, *The Matter of Revolution: Science, Poetry, and Politics in the Age of Milton* (Ithaca, NY: Cornell University Press, 1996), Chapter 6: 'Margaret Cavendish and the Gendering of the Vitalist Utopia', 177–211.

[53] Margaret Cavendish, *Philosophical Letters* (London, 1664), 26.

a unique synthesis of Cavendish's diverse intellectual sources: in literature, contemporary politics and science, and, I will argue, medieval contemplation.

The relationship between Sense and Reason forms the central subject of the *Philosophical and Physical Opinions*; it also structures the dialogues of 'The She-Anchoret' and forms a topic to which the anchoress and her interlocutors continually return. Thus to the Natural Philosophers the anchoress observes: 'It is no great matter to conceive what the Senses present; but it is difficult to present to the Senses what the Brain conceives, making the senses the Servants or Scouts, to seek and search, by industry and experiments, and to find the truth of a Rational opinion' (587); and further, she observes to the Physicians, 'The Rational Spirites (said she) go to the creation of the Mind or Soul, the Sensitive to the body' (602). As in her earlier work, sense and reason together produce knowledge, but sense is inferior to reason and must be directed by the higher faculty. We might discern an echo of Bacon's *New Atlantis* here, in Cavendish's image of the senses as the servant-scouts of the Brain. But beneath it, I find a further echo of St Augustine and the medieval contemplative tradition that he inspired.

Cavendish's theory of 'the rational and sensitive spirits' bears comparison to Augustine's taxonomy of the mind in *The City of God*, which differentiates 'sensation and understanding' as they lead, like two distinct but complementary paths, 'to the apprehension and awareness of truth' (853), apprehension and awareness being two separate cognitive phenomena that correspond to the offices of sense and understanding. Augustine, like Cavendish, subordinates sensation to understanding as belonging to the 'perishable body', as opposed to the soul (853). Cavendish likewise elevates the soul as the seat of understanding: thus in her *Philosophical and Physical Opinions* she develops a theory of 'Rational Animate matter', which she contrasts with 'the Sensitive Animate matter' and calls 'the Infinite Mind or Soul of Infinite matter'.[54] In so doing, she adapts an essentially Augustinian distinction between sensation and understanding to differentiate between scientific methods, experimental versus rational, which she does, following Augustine, in terms emerging from the debate over the *vita activa* and the *vita contemplativa*. Furthermore, by making an anchoress the spokesperson for her theory of 'rational and sensitive spirits', Cavendish both revives and adapts the medieval tradition of anchoritic literature that translated Augustinian ideals into practice.

The subordination of the senses forms a constant theme in medieval literature directed at anchoresses. The *Speculum Inclusorum* observes that the enclosure of the anchorhold frees its inhabitant from 'occupation of the senses', which 'hinders the fruit of the contemplative life'.[55] The *Ancrene Wisse* counsels anchoresses to

[54] Margaret Cavendish, *Philosophical and Physical Opinions* (London, 1663), 14.

[55] See E. A. Jones, 'Hermits and Anchorites in Historical Context', *Approaching Medieval English Anchoritic and Mystical Texts*, ed. Dee Dyas, Valerie Edden, and Roger Ellis (Cambridge: D. S. Brewer, 2005), 3–18, at 15.

protect and cultivate 'the life of the soul' ('sawle lif') by maintaining guard over the five senses ('fif wittes').[56] Likewise, Walter Hilton warns contemplatives against 'schewynges to the bodili wittis', and against any 'bodili feelinge' that works 'to drawe oute thyn herte from biholdinge of oure Lord Jhesu Crist and fro goostli occupacions, as from preiers, and . . . fro the inward desire of vertues and of goostli knowynge and the feelinge of God' (41). Like Hilton, Julian of Norwich develops a contemplative model that begins with human rationality, rather than degrading reason as debased and necessarily distant from contemplation.[57] But to a degree greater than Hilton, Julian allows the senses a place, albeit a secondary one, within a general theory of knowledge. If, as historians of the terms remind us, 'contemplation' translates the classical term *theoria*, Julian reveals the extent to which the medieval contemplative tradition drew on and contributed to, rather than departing from, a long history of debate over the nature and disposition of human rationality.[58]

In her *Revelation of Love*, the task of describing the multi-dimensional experience of her visions forces Julian to taxonomize the faculties and perceptive organs 'by thre partes: that is to sey, by bodily sight, and by worde formede in my understonding, and by gostely sight'.[59] *A Revelation of Love* charts the progress of Julian's experience from 'bodily sight' to 'gostely sight'. While she begins by apprehending the bodily senses as a source of knowledge (when she asks for 'a bodily sight, wherin I might have more knowinge of the bodily paines of our saviour' (127)), she learns to see 'with the eye of my understanding' (139); thus she moves from lower sense to higher understanding in a way that recalls Augustine and anticipates Margaret Cavendish. In Julian's theory of rationality, the three elements of reason, sense, and soul are ultimately interdependent, albeit distinct: 'Our faith cometh of the kinde love of oure soul, and of the clere lighte of oure reson, and of the stedfaste minde which we have of God in our first making. And what time oure soule is enspired in oure body, in which we be made sensual' (299). A similar taxonomy governs the two parts of 'substance' and 'sensualite', which are distinct—the substance relating to the upper part 'in full joy and blisse', and the 'lower perty, which is sensualite' (301)—though they come together in the soul, which binds 'the heyer and the lower, which is but one soule' (299). Thus Julian finds that

[56] Robert Hasentratz (ed.), *Ancrene Wisse* (Kalamazoo, MI: Medieval Institute Publications, 2000), part 2.

[57] See Denise N. Baker, 'The Active and Contemplative Lives in Rolle, the "Cloud" Author and Hilton', in *The Medieval Mystical Tradition in England, Ireland, and Wales (Exeter Symposium VI)*, ed. Marion Glasscoe (Cambridge: D. S. Brewer, 1999), 85–102, at 99.

[58] On these terms, see Lobkowicz, *Theory and Practice*, 47–57, and Dom Jean LeClercq, *Études sur le Vocabulaire Monastique du Moyen Age* (Rome: Pontificium Institutum S. Anselmi, 1961), 81–5.

[59] Julian of Norwich, *The Writings of Julian of Norwich*, ed. Nicholas Watson and Jacqueline Jenkins (University Park, PA: Pennsylvania State University Press, 2006), 157. All subsequent references will be to this text, with page numbers cited parenthetically.

> We be double of Gods making: that is to sey, substantial and sensual. Oure substance is the hyer perty, which we have in oure fader almighty. And the seconde person of the trinite is oure moder in kind in our substantial making, in whom we be grounded and roted, and he is oure moder of mercy in oure sensualite taking. (309)

Julian's hierarchy of reason and sense establishes a medieval analogue for Margaret Cavendish's model of the 'Rational and Sensitive Spirits', which likewise come together as two distinct but interdependent avenues of knowledge. For Cavendish, the soul too has a place in guiding the sensitive body and the rational spirit. As her anchoress explains to the Physicians: 'Said she, man hath three different natures or faculties; a sensitive body, animall spirit, and a soul, this soul is a kinde of a Deity in it self, to direct and guide those things that are inferior to it, to perceive and descry those things that are far above it; and to create by invention' (281). The soul who rules as 'a kinde of a Deity' recalls Julian's assertion that 'oure soule is a made trinite like to the unmade blessed trinite' (299), which combines substance, sense, and spirit. But for Cavendish's Anchoress, the soul which directs and guides the inferior senses and creates through the force of invention resembles nothing so much as the brain itself, which sits in the body like the anchoress in her cell, dedicated to the contemplation of the truth.

Whether Margaret Cavendish actually read Julian of Norwich or encountered her only indirectly in the exiled court of Henrietta Maria, I elaborate these parallels in order to unsettle a prevailing critical assumption that the Queen and her court owed their cultural interests in 'the spiritual life of the mind' largely to the Neoplatonism of contemporary Cambridge.[60] Rather, I find that those contemplative interests, as developed in Cavendish's work, bore a closer relation to the medieval texts and practices that the Parisian nuns preserved and maintained. As I have argued, Julian's theory of knowledge grounded in contemplation parallels Cavendish's hierarchy of the rational and sensitive spirits, from which she generates a critique of experimental science. This anchoritic association with rationality above sensuality inspires Cavendish to take a 'she-anchoret' as the spokesperson of her theory of 'Rational and Sensitive Spirits', which, in terms that directly recall the medieval contemplative tradition, postulates a model of the intellect detached from sensory experience. Thus for Cavendish, natural philosophy is a contemplative exercise of reason that, in its ultimate practice, resembles mystic rapture.

Describing those who are in 'studious contemplations' so powerful that they 'will take no notice of the sensitive motions', Cavendish proceeds to describe a state of contemplation that transcends the individual senses:

[60] Although Anna Battigelli's is the only scholarly work I have found that explicitly treats Margaret Cavendish's interest in 'contemplation', it attributes that interest to Platonic, rather than medieval, influences; see her *Margaret Cavendish and the Exiles of the Mind*, 17, 22–3, 24–32.

> So in a deep contemplation, when they view objects, hear sounds, smell scents, tast and touch, the rational knowledge takes no notice of it, because the rational spirits move not to the sensitive works; so that onely the eye sees, or the ear hears, or the nose smells, or the tonge tasts, or any particular part feels, but the rational takes no notice thereof; *so that these are but particular knowledges in every particular sense, or part of the figure, and not a general knowledge*: for the sensitive knowledge, which are the sensitive spirits, are bound to parts; but the rational knowledge, which are the rational spirits, are free to all, as being free to it self, the other bound to the dull part of matter. (308–9; my emphases)

This is the heart of Cavendish's critique of experimental knowledge: bound up in the senses, it can only aspire to a fragmented and partial knowledge, while reason alone attains a 'general knowledge' that comprises but transcends the knowledge of the parts. By making an anchoress mouthpiece of such 'general knowledge', Cavendish insists that it can only be reached through contemplation.

In making this assertion, Cavendish set herself and her 'she anchoret' against the prevailing experimentalism of the Royal Society, targeting its most illustrious members for special critique. Cavendish's *Observations upon Experimental Philosophy* (1666) criticizes Robert Hooke's treatise on the microscope, *Micrographia* (1665), the first bestselling work of popular science. Hooke, the curator of experiments for the Royal Society, was compelled to defend his method against the charge that experimentalism was an exercise in useless novelty. He did this by depicting his work in terms that directly parallel Cavendish's own, but that propose experimentalism as a new form of contemplation. As he writes:

> I do not only propose this kind of Experimental Philosophy as a matter of high rapture and delight of the mind, but even as a material and sensible Pleasure. So vast is the variety of objects which will come under their Inspections, so many different wayes there are of handling them, so great is the satisfaction of finding out new things, that I dare compare the contentment which they will injoy, not only to that of contemplation, but even to that which most men prefer of the senses themselves.[61]

Imputing to experimental science a 'satisfaction' comparable to the 'high rapture and delight of the mind', Hooke replaces contemplative rapture with a 'sensible Pleasure' of an unmistakably sexual nature—'which most men prefer of the senses themselves'—and thereby secures the phallic masculinity of the scientific enterprise.[62] Hooke's language here doesn't suggest the triumph of action over contemplation so much as it attempts to usurp for experimentalism the elevated quality of contemplative knowledge, and thus, for the debased senses, the superior status of 'the delight of the mind'. The triumph of experimental science, in other words, doesn't render the notion of contemplation obsolete, but takes it as a model for material and sensitive forms.

[61] Robert Hooke, *Micrographia* (London, 1665), Preface.
[62] I owe this point to Catherine Nicholson.

Conclusion: 'Publick Employment and an Active Life Prefer'd to Solitude'

At the pre-disciplinary moment of the seventeenth century, I have been arguing, the new science's defenders, practitioners, and critics adopted conventions and terms from the long-standing debate over the *vita activa* and the *vita contemplativa*, which had come to organize ideas about intellectual activity and its applications. From the mid to late seventeenth century, contemplation shifts from a central to an eccentric position in relation to science, which was increasingly described in terms appropriated from the *vita activa*. The shift is visible even in documents that helped to found the Royal Society itself.

If John Evelyn envisioned the Royal Society as a quasi-Carthusian space in his letter to Boyle in 1659, eight years later he disavowed the monastic model and instead aligned science with the virtues of the active life. In *Publick Employment and an Active Life Prefer'd to Solitude* (1667) Evelyn responds to a work by Sir George Mackenzie, initially published anonymously in 1665, called *A Moral Essay: Preferring Solitude to Publick Employment.*[63] Mackenzie's praise of solitude recalls Petrarch's *De Vita Solitaria*, with its arguments in favor of quiet retirement and a life devoted to literary study, while Evelyn's riposte recuperates arguments in favor of the *vita activa* from Cicero's *De Officiis*, made familiar by generations of humanists, stressing the active life's benefit for the commonwealth.[64] Reversing his earlier comparison of the community of science to the monastic dwelling, Evelyn asserts that the *vita contemplativa* is no longer an option for the post-monastic world, insisting that 'were all the Universe one ample Convent, we might all be contented, and all be happy; but this is an Idea no where existant on this side Heaven' (31), and seizing the opportunity to observe that 'the most superstitious of men have been the greatest Eremites, and besides the little good they do by their Example, there is not in the world a life more repugnant to nature, and the opportunities of doing our duty' (56). Evelyn's description of 'Eremites' recalls, while repudiating, Robert Boyle's comparison of himself to a 'Hermit' in his 'averseness to society'. In contrast, Evelyn insists that 'the most useful and profitable of studies' partake of the active, rather than the contemplative, life: 'For, believe it Sir, the Wisest men are not made in Chambers and Closets crowded with shelves; but by habitudes and active Conversations' (77). Against the reign of 'letter-struck men', Evelyn insists that 'Action is the proper fruit of Science, and therefore they should quit the education of the Colledge, when fit to appear in business' (78). He concludes by enjoining his readers:

[63] On the two works, see Vickers, 'Public and Private Life in Seventeenth-Century England: The Mackensie-Evelyn Debate', in *Arbeit, Musse, Meditation*, 257–78.

[64] See Petrarch, *The Life of Solitude*, trans. Zeitlin.

> Let us therefore rather celebrate Publick Employment and an Active Life, which renders us so nearly ally'd to Virtue, defines and maintains our Being, supports Societys, preserves Kingdoms in peace, protects them in War; has discover'd new Worlds, planted the Gospel, encreases Knowledge, cultivates Arts, relieves the afflicted; and in sum, without which, the whole Universe it self had been still but a rude and indigested Caos. (115)

Evelyn's personification of such studies virtuously employed is Boyle himself: 'Since I am confident, there lives not a Person in the World, whose moments are more employ'd then Mr Boyles, and that more confirms his contemplations by his actions and experience: and if it be objected, that his employments are not publick, I can assure him, there is nothing more publick, than the good he's always doing' (119).

In Evelyn's reformulation, Boyle, rather than following the contemplative model of the Carthusian or the Hermit, with which he had been earlier allied, now exemplifies the civic-mindedness of the new science, in the service of the active life. In the volatile climate of the English mid-century, scientists like Boyle first attempted to distance themselves and their intellectual enterprise from the political sphere by envisioning a scientific community as 'one ample Convent' set apart from civic engagement. The Restoration marks a turning point in the rhetoric surrounding the new science, whose practitioners newly asserted its uses for the public good in the hope (as Michael Hunter points out) of attracting royal patronage. Evelyn's *Publick Employment and an Active Life Prefer'd to Solitude* exemplifies this shift.[65]

In elevating the public-spirited scientist over the idle *literati*, Evelyn anticipates a modern habit of projecting the hierarchy of active over contemplative lives onto the disciplines themselves, and thereby uplifting the 'active' sciences over the 'contemplative' humanities. But Evelyn's praise of civic-minded scientists, in contrast with the 'letter-struck men' in their 'Chambers and Closets crowded with shelves', buries its own debt to the neo-Ciceronian 'civic humanists', who defined the *vita activa* around the study of letters, aligned with explicitly civic and worldly ends. It also buries the earlier contemplative models that Evelyn himself had used not long before to authorize science as a place of retreat, as distinguished from the politically engaged humanist *vita activa.* Evelyn's example allows us to return to the thesis with which I started—as formulated by Arendt, Blumenberg, and Taylor—and to argue that the apparent triumph of the active life over the contemplative life was not the consequence of the rise of science but its condition, having been rhetorically crafted and made commonplace by the very humanist tradition that the new science claimed to reject. For early modern science writers from Bacon to Cavendish to Evelyn, the new science didn't short-circuit, render obsolete, or resolve the long-standing debate over the active life and the contemplative life:

[65] On this point, see Hunter, *Science and Society in Restoration England.*

rather, it demonstrated the centrality of that debate as a taxonomy of intellectual activity, from which it drew for the very terms that allowed it to come into being.

FURTHER READING

Constable, Giles. *Three Studies in Medieval Religious and Social Thought* (Cambridge: Cambridge University Press, 1995)

Cummings, Juliet and David Burchell (eds.). *Science, Literature, and Rhetoric in Early Modern England* (Aldershot: Ashgate, 2007)

Hunter, Michael. *Science and Society in Restoration England* (Cambridge/New York: Cambridge University Press, 1981)

Vickers, Brian (ed.). *Arbeit, Musse, Meditation: Betrachtungen zur Vita activa und Vita Contemplativa* (Zürich: Verlag der Fachvereine, 1985)

CHAPTER 29

CHILDBIRTH

ALEXANDRA BARRATT

The latter part of the reign of Henry VIII was a tipping point on the late medieval–early modern continuum. It saw the entrenchment of humanism, the break with Rome, and the dissolution of the monasteries. But there were subtle shifts in other, quite different, parts of the cultural landscape, such as in the discourse of childbirth. Paradigmatic of this are two editions, four years apart, of a gynaecological handbook which is the focus of this essay and which will be read in the light of vernacular versions of the standard medieval authority on childbirth, the *Trotula*.

The two editions of *The Byrth of Mankynde*[1] contain obstetrical and gynaecological lore drawn not only from their predecessor, but also from their predecessor's predecessors. The immediate source, a German treatise entitled *Der Swangern frawen und hebammen roszgarten* (*Rose Garden for Pregnant Women and Midwives*) was written right at the end of the fifteenth century but was mediated by sixteenth-century translations and read well into the seventeenth century. Ironically, this enduring popularity may have retarded and hindered the advance of midwifery. For the trajectories of science and medicine can take very different paths from those of other areas of discourse. Not only must we continue to ask, because we still have no answer, did women have a Renaissance?[2] The same question must be applied to all those implicated in the discourse of childbirth, maybe even of natural science in general. At the risk of disturbing the ghost of F. R. Leavis, let us contemplate the probability that in this period there were, indeed, at least two cultures. And the practical consequences of that great divide may well have had far more implications, on a daily and monthly basis, for the Second Sex than for their

[1] *The Birth of Mankind: Otherwise Named, the Woman's Book*, ed. Elaine Hobby (Farnham, UK: Ashgate, 2009).

[2] Joan Gadol Kelly, 'Did Women Have a Renaissance?', in *Becoming Visible: Women in European History*, ed. Renate Bridenthal and Claudia Koonz (Boston: Houghton Mifflin, 1977), 137–64.

spouses. The really profound cultural reorientation, as argued by Thomas Laqueur, did not arrive until the eighteenth century.[3]

The *Roszgarten* was composed by Eucharius Rösslin (fl. *c.*1493–1506). Rösslin was, successively, city physician of Frankfurt am Main, Worms, and then Frankfurt again; he also served for a short time at the court of Duchess Katherine of Brunswick and Lüneburg. In 1513 he published the *Roszgarten*: it proved a best-seller and was reprinted fourteen times between 1513 and 1541. In 1532 it was translated into Latin as *De Partu Hominis*, and this version in its turn was translated into Dutch, French, Spanish, Danish, Czech, and English.[4] An expanded edition prepared by Rösslin's son, entitled *Hebammenbüchlein* (*Midwives' Booklet*), was printed ten times between 1562 and 1608. In its various manifestations, therefore, the *Roszgarten* was read across Western Europe throughout the sixteenth century, and beyond: 'it became the most widely spread handbook of midwifery…and some consider it the most widespread medical book in history'.[5]

The content of Rösslin's text was traditional. He used the *Non omnes quidem*, an epitome of a Latin text by Muscio which derived ultimately from the Hellenistic gynaecologist, Soranus:[6] this is exactly the same source as many medieval texts on midwifery, including the Middle English *Knowing of Women's Kind in Childing*, which combines the Muscio epitome with extracts from the *Trotula* ensemble. His illustrations, too, come from a Muscio manuscript. As Rösslin influenced successors such as Jacob Rueff, whose 1554 book *De conceptu et generatione hominis* was translated into English as *The Expert Midwife* and published in 1637,[7] Soranus, Muscio, and their derivatives, though never mentioned by name, had a prolonged afterlife, which was not disturbed by the cultural changes associated with a fifteenth- and sixteenth-century Renaissance. They were still going strong well into the seventeenth century. Indeed, in some ways the new-found humanist respect for classical texts served only to reinforce their hegemony.

[3] Thomas Laqueur, *Making Sex: Body and Gender from the Greeks to Freud* (Cambridge, MA: Harvard University Press, 1990), 4.

[4] I am dependent for my information on Rösslin on *Eucharius Rösslin: When Midwifery Became the Male Physician's Province: The Sixteenth Century Handbook 'The Rose Garden for Pregnant Women and Midwives', Newly Englished*, trans. Wendy Arons (Jefferson, NC and London: McFarland, 1994), esp. 1–3. See also *The Byrth of Mankynde otherwyse named The Womans Booke: Embryology, Obstretrics, Gynaecology Through Four Centuries*, comp. Ove Hagelin (Stockholm: Svenska Läkarsällskapet, 1990), 12–13.

[5] *The Byrth of Mankynde*, comp. Hagelin, viii.

[6] On the elusive Soranus, see Ann Ellis Hanson and Monica H. Green, 'Soranus of Ephesus: *Methodicorum Princeps*', in *Rise and Decline of the Roman World*, ed. Wolfgang Haase and Hildegard Temporini, Part 2: Principate, Vol. 37.2 (Berlin and New York, Walter de Gruyter, 1994), 968–1074. On the *Non omnes quidem*, see Alexandra Barratt (ed.), *The Knowing of Woman's Kind in Childing: A Middle English Version of Material Derived from the Trotula and Other Sources*, Medieval Women: Texts and Contexts 4 (Turnhout: Brepols, 2001), 7.

[7] Audrey Eccles, *Obstetrics and Gynaecology in Tudor and Stuart England* (Kent, OH: Kent State University Press, 1982), 12–13.

But like many a writer of popular textbooks, Rösslin is less than candid about his use of sources. Although he claims to use 'highly learned skilful scientists / Galen / Rhazes / Avicenna / Averroes and others',[8] he was also recycling time-honoured 'truths'—relying on authority—rather than writing from experience. This is not surprising, as in early sixteenth-century Germany it would be rare (though not impossible) for a male physician to attend a confinement.[9]

There are two versions of the *De Partu Hominis* in English. The first, *The Byrth of Mankynde* (STC 21153), was translated from Latin by Richard Jonas and printed by Thomas Raynald ('T. R.') in November 1540. Opportunistically, and optimistically, Jonas dedicated the book to 'Quene Katheryne', Henry VIII's fifth wife, the ill-fated Catherine Howard, who had married him on 28 July 1540. Raynald, his printer, was also a physician and himself compiled the second edition, *The Byrth of Mankynde, otherwyse named the womans booke* (STC 21154), which appeared in 1545. It was, of course, no longer dedicated to Henry's queen, though Henry had married another Catherine, Catherine Parr, in 1543. This second, revised edition was frequently reprinted well into the seventeenth century: editions survive from 1552, 1560, 1565 (twice), 1572 (?), 1585 (?), 1588, 1598, 1613, 1625, and 1634 (STC 21155–21164). It was not superseded until the 1650s, thus extending Rösslin's influence in England by half a century.

I wish to suggest that somewhere between the two editions a major mental shift had taken place that relates to the reorientating of the place of women in the discourse of childbirth. The 1540 edition opens with a brief 'admonicion to the reader' that precedes the dedication to the queen. This includes a stern warning issued by Jonas to his male readers:

> I requyre all suche men in the name of God, which at any tyme shall chaunse to have this boke, that they use it godlye, and onely to the profet of theyr neyghbours, utterly eschuynge all rebawde and unsemely communicacion of any thynges contayned in the same, as they wyll answere before God... (sig. AB1^{v})

This is no innovation: the Middle English *Knowing of Woman's Kind* contains a similar admonitory topos, more vigorous in its defence of women and more explicit in its idea of how such books can be misused. But the thought is the same:

> And yf hit fall any man to rede hit, I pray hym and scharge hym in oure Lady be-halve that he rede hit not in no dyspyte ne sclaundure [slander] of no woman ne for no cause but for the hele and helpe of hem, dredynge that vengauns myht fall to hym as hit hath do to other that have scheuyd here prevytees in sclaundyr of hem, undyrstondynge in certeyne that they have no other evylys that nou be [f. 2] a-lyve than thoo women hade that nou be seyntys in hevyn.[10]

8 *Eucharius Rösslin*, trans. Wendy Arons, 4.

9 On this much disputed topic see Monica Green, 'Women's Medical Care in Medieval Europe', *Signs: Journal of Women in Culture and Society*, 14 (1989), 434–73.

10 *Knowing of Woman's Kind*, ed. Barratt, 42 (slightly modernized).

Both writers are concerned that such treatises might be misused, read only for their potentially prurient content or used to abuse and slander women. And if this seems ridiculous, remember that one of the texts used by Jankyn the clerk to demoralize Chaucer's Wife of Bath was the Trotula (*CT* 3: 677).

Jonas goes on to rebuke men who at inappropriate places ('at the commune tables') and in mixed company 'rudelye and leudelye' discuss childbirth and labour, subjects on which 'they ought rather to knowe muche, and to saye lytell'. He ends with a plea for sympathy with 'oure even Christians, the women which sustayne and endure for the tyme so greate dolor and payne for the byrth of mankynde' (sig. AB1^{v}). Although addressed 'to the reader', all this is clearly directed at his fellow men, implicitly treating women not as potential readers but as the Other, the objects of his discourse.

In his dedication to the queen, Jonas comments on the current popularity of English translations both of treatises on Scripture and 'other prophane artes and sciences', in particular medicine. He highlights Rösslin's book, which had been translated from German into Latin and then into French and Dutch, 'so that there be fewe matrones and women in that [*sic*] partes / but (yf they can rede) wyll have this booke alwayes in readynesse' (sig. AB2^{v}). He wishes to extend its benefits to England and has undertaken the translation as 'a very charytable and laudable dede' (sig. AB3^{v}), 'for the love of all womanhode' but particularly for the Queen. (He may have known that Rösslin had dedicated his book to the Duchess of Brunswick and Lüneburg.) He also hopes that 'all honeste & motherlye mydwyfes' (sig. AB4^{r}) will read his treatise and profit from it, even if some are far more experienced than the writer of the book.

Jonas's printer Thomas Raynald was an innovator. In 1540 *The Byrth of Mankynde* was not only the first printed book in England on midwifery, but also the first to include copper engravings—four plates of them. (Unfortunately, the copy microfilmed for *Early English Books 1475–1640* does not contain them. Either they were deliberately removed or have fallen out by accident, as apparently 'engravings were in this period usually bound in as inserted sheets rather than integrated in the pages with letterpress printing'.)[11] When he printed the second edition in 1545, Raynald described it as '[n]ewly set furth, corrected and augmented'. Certainly the book has an augmented title: *The Byrth of Mankynde, otherwyse named the womans booke*. This marks a significant change of focus: had Raynald just noticed an unmet market opportunity?

Raynald opens with a Latin epistle invoking the name of Aristarchus, whose relevance remains obscure, whether Raynald has in mind the second-century BCE literary scholar or the third-century BCE astronomer. In it, Raynald makes the commonplace humanist claim that his new edition is 'fuller, more comprehensive

[11] *Cambridge History of the Book in Britain*, vol. 3: *1400–1557*, ed. Lotte Hellinga and J. B. Trapp (Cambridge: Cambridge University Press, 1999), 106.

and freer of error' (*locupletius, auctius, emendatiusque*) than any earlier version, whether in Latin or English (sig. A1^{v}). It has been polished with 'a more demanding file' (*exactiore lima*) and he hopes for a good reception from midwives and matrons. Even in the 1540s, however, most of these would not have been able to read Latin, so this prefatory epistle is a puzzle. Perhaps it is simply a bid for respectability.

After a list of contents follows a lengthy 'prologue to the women readers', to tell them what is on the menu (his metaphor). The first edition, Raynald claims, was faithful, possibly too faithful:

> In which his translation he varyed, or declyned nothynge at all from the steppes of his Latin autor: Observynge moore fidelite in translatynge, then choyse or discretion at that tyme... (sig. B2^{r-v})

So it has been revised 'from top to too' and he hopes the now bowdlerized text will be appreciated by 'all honeste, discrete, and sage wemen' (sig. B2^{v}). He has also added a completely new, illustrated, first book on female anatomy:

> that not onely in wurdes, but also in lyvely and expresse figures, by the which every parte before in the boke describyd, maye in maner be as exactly and clearely perceavid, as thoughe ye were present at the cuttynge open or anathomye of a ded woman. (sig. B3)

Without such knowledge no one can become an 'absolute & perfeict physition'.

It may seem obvious enough to modern readers that gynaecology requires a knowledge of anatomy and physiology, but debate had raged among classical writers over this. Soranus himself had not considered it necessary for therapeutic purposes; in his *Gynaikeia* he labelled 'as useless for the midwife all discourse on medical theory or anatomy'.[12] Medieval gynaecological texts such as the *Trotula* compendium have little to say about the subject. But anatomy was 'in the air' in 1545—the Company of Barbers and Fraternity of Surgeons had merged in 1540 and a regular course in anatomy had been instituted at that time—and Raynald argues that knowledge of the subject allows the female patient to understand her physician better. She might otherwise find his answers 'obscure, darke, and straunge to be comprehended by the woman, for lacke of due knowledge of the situation, maner, and facion of the inwards [internal organs]' (sig. B4). Generally, he puts the case for patients to be better informed, and for women to make the effort to educate themselves in this area:

> Therfore myne advise and utter counsell is, that all women in whose handes this lytell book shall chaunce to come, with all dilygence do force theym selfes perfectely to the understandynge of this fyrst book: well assurynge them that they shall not repent them of theyr small paynes bestowed in that behalfe... (sig. B4^{v}–5)

[12] Hanson and Green, 'Soranus of Ephesus', 1002.

And he has made it even easier for them by providing diagrams.

Raynald then summarizes the contents of the three following books. Book 2 concerns delivery, and he has improved it especially by having 'rectified and amendyd . . . accordyng to reason, and the lawes of physike' some of the medicines given in the first edition and by adding others, 'suche as other I my selfe, or other phisitions beyng yet a-lyve at this day, have experimented and practisyd' (sig. B5^{v}), cleverly appealing to both authority and experience. He also offers remedies to regulate menstruation. The third book deals with the choice of wet nurse and with infant management, and the fourth with conception. To this are added 'certayne embellesshing recepts, concerning only honest and helthsum decoration and clendlynes' (sig. B6^{r-v}), to reinforce and maintain a woman's natural beauty; he is certainly not promoting nasty make-up or cosmetics ('fardyng, payntyng, and counterfeit cast colours', sig. B7).

Raynald next turns to defend himself from his critics. He knows that his enterprise will not find favour in the sight of all. They may condemn it sight unseen, not just carping at the details but condemning the whole enterprise:

> alledging that it is shame, and other sume [some others] that it is not mete, ne syttyng such matters to be entreatyd of, soo playnely in our mother and vulgare langage: to the dishonour (as they say) of womanhed, and the derision of theyr wount [accustomed] secreates, by the detection and discoverynge wherof, men it readynge or hearynge shal be mooved therby the moore to abhorre and loothe the company of woomen. And farther, in theyr communycations to jeste and bourde of wemens pryvitees not wont to be knowen of them. (sig. C1^{v}–2)

(This is, of course, Raynald's take on the 'shame' topos we have already encountered.) But he roundly condemns these arguments as negative. All good things can be perverted, and he draws analogies not only with fire and water but also with Holy Scripture and the 'blissyd sacrament of th'aulter' (a significant addition, perhaps, in 1545). Scripture teaches goodness, and the sacrament is a 'most present consolation and comforte of mans conscience':

> yet both hooly scripture & also the foresayd hooly sacrament have ben, be, and wyll be, the confusion and condemnation of a greate number of th'abusars, and indigne or unworthy receavars of them bothe. (sig. C3^{v})

Raynald does admit two possible abuses of his book. One is the perversion of the medicines 'to sume dyvelysshe and lewd vse': he refuses to expand but presumably he is referring to the potential use of medicines for regulating menstruation as abortifacients—an old problem. Secondly, he is concerned that the frivolous might use information from the book 'at unset & unsemely tymes: to the derysion or asshamyng of such women as shold be in presence' (sig. C5).[13] Such people, he

[13] It is interesting that *OED*'s earliest example of 'ashame' as a transitive verb, meaning 'to put to shame, to make ashamed', is as late as 1591.

points out, 'doo greate injury, dishonor, and contumely to nature, ye to the hygh God of nature' and therefore commit deadly sin. (Richard Jonas had said almost exactly the same.) As to those who think the book contains material that might lead to a disgust for women, Raynald goes onto the offensive:

> I know nothing in woman so pryve ne so secret that thei shold nede to care who knew of it: neyther is there any part in woman moore to be abhorred, then in man. (sig. C6^{r-v})

In the peroration of his prologue, Raynald expatiates on his reasons for writing. Here (sig. C7^{v}–C8) he frugally recycles material from Jonas's dedication to the Queen (sig. AB3^{r-v}), incidentally appropriating Jonas's claim to have made the translation, and interpolating Jonas's earlier material (on sig. AB2^{v}) about the text's linguistic history and its widespread readership among women on the Continent. He wishes English women to enjoy the same advantages. Indeed, he has been reliably informed that the first edition of *The Byrth of Mankynde* was well received and that many ladies and gentlewomen have attended childbeds equipped with this book, so that it could be read to the midwife and the other women present.

Raynald's 'fyrst booke' is not, of course, in Rösslin's original German. It must be the first attempt for which textual evidence survives to communicate a systematic and comprehensive knowledge of female anatomy to educated women in England. Its inclusion further implies that gynaecological knowledge is only part of a much wider natural physiological scheme with which women need to be familiar. Such knowledge, he says, is 'as a key openyng and clearyng the matters to be entreated of in the seconde [book]' (sig. D3). However, although Raynald sets out to clear up certain common misconceptions, he was at a disadvantage. Vesalius, 'the father of modern anatomy', had published his revolutionary *Fabrica* in seven books and in epitome in 1543,[14] and Thomas Gemini copied the engravings in his own work published in England two years later,[15] but Raynald is unlikely to have seen them. English editions of Vesalius did not appear until 1553 and 1559, while the works of Gabriele Falloppio (1523–1562), who first accurately described the tubes subsequently named after him, were not published until 1584.[16] Consequently Raynald's anatomy is frequently wrong. He has abandoned some medieval misconceptions, but transmits others well into the early modern period.

Raynald begins with an account of the skin, fat, muscles, peritoneum, and the internal organs. He then turns to the reproductive system and describes the uterus, which he calls indifferently 'matrix', 'mother', or 'womb'. He has some problems in fixing on vernacular terms for the delicate surrounding area, and comes up with

[14] F. J. Cole, *A History of Comparative Anatomy from Aristotle to the Eighteenth Century* (London: Macmillan; New York: Dover, 1975; first published 1949), 56.

[15] Peter Murray Jones, 'Gemini, Thomas (*fl.* 1540–1562)', *ODNB* (accessed 19 May 2008).

[16] See *The Byrth of Mankynde*, comp. Hagelin, 17.

the terms 'womb passage, or the privy passage' (sig. E3^{v}) for the cervix (though it sounds more like what we would call the vagina), and 'privy passage' and 'passage port' (sig. E3^{v}) for the vulva.[17] The womb itself, he declares, consists of a single chamber ('vault, cavite, holonesse or amplytude', sig. E6), although in the past

> dyvers clarkes have wryten, and many other have beleved, that there shold be 7 selles, or 7 distynct places in the matrix: in thre of the whiche on the right syde sholde only men chyldren be conceyvyd: and in the other 3 on the left syde wemen chyldren: and if it chaunsyd that the seede were conceaved in the seventh sell which was the myddel most, then that sholde become a monster, half a man and halfe a woman. (sig. E6^{v}–7).

This is no alarmist fantasy: Raynald is quite accurate in his recollections, for such a belief was surprisingly persistent in the Middle Ages. It is retailed in *The Knowing of Woman's Kind* as follows:

> the matrice . . . is parted into 7 vessellis, of the which 3 ar in the parte toward the right syde, and 3 are in the parte toward the lyfte syde, and the 7th even in the myddes be-twen the navill and hire pryvite . . .
>
> And yif it so be that the seed falle in-to ony of the chambris of the ryght syde, it shal be a man childe. And yif it falle in-to ony of the vessellis on the lyfte syde, it shal be a woman chylde. And if it falle in the myd vessel, it fallith owte a-yen, and perysshith fro the place of creacion. . . . And yif the seed happen ther to be conceyvyd, it shal have the token both of man and woman.[18]

This theory,[19] which did not appear until the late Middle Ages in gynaecological (as opposed to anatomical) texts, was not derived from Soranus and is not found in the Latin Trotula texts; it has been suggested that it may have arisen from misinterpretations of the reproductive system of pigs.[20] Fortunately, having ventilated it once again, Raynald dismisses it as 'lyes, dreames, and fon fantasyes'.

He goes on to describe the 'womb port' as like 'an haukes bel or other lytle mores belles', with a split across it (a morris bell is a small metal bell attached to the clothing of a morris dancer). It stays closed during intercourse, he notes, until it opens to draw the male seed into the womb. If conception takes place, then the womb port closes 'so firmely that the point of a nedle cannot entre in therat, without violence' (sig. E8^{v}) and remains closed until delivery. (This vivid image is repeated at least twice more in the book.)

On each side of the matrix are the 'stones' (ovaries), the size of a large almond, containing 'many lytell kernelles set together, betwene the which is much holones'

17 See Laqueur, *Making Sex*, 96–8, on the failure of anatomists to come up with a consistent terminology to describe the female genitalia.

18 *Knowing of Womans Kind*, ed. Barratt, 45 (adapted).

19 See further Danielle Jacquart and Claude Thomasset, *Sexuality and Medicine in the Middle Ages*, trans. Matthew Adamson (Oxford: Polity, 1988), 21.

20 See *Knowing of Woman's Kind*, ed. Barratt, 117.

(sig. F1), within which are engendered 'the seede and sparme'.[21] *OED* records the sense 'testicle' for 'stone', but not 'ovary', but clearly Raynald adhered to what Thomas Laqueur calls 'the one-sex model', that is, the view that the female reproductive system was an inverted version of the male.[22] The existence of the ova was as yet unknown: *OED*'s first quotation for *ovary* is 1653 and for *ovum* 1672. Like many of his predecessors, including Hippocrates (though notably excluding Aristotle),[23] and like his own contemporaries, Raynald believes in the existence of 'female seed' or sperm. (Descartes still held this belief.) Like men's, it is engendered by the 'stones', but unlike men's it is cold and moist. The 'seede bryngars'—possibly the fallopian tubes—consisting of two veins and two arteries, go from the 'stones' to the womb, conveying blood and 'lyvely spyrite' (sig. F6: this is a Galenic concept, for which the more usual English term is 'vital spirits'[24]), which are mixed together. The liver, the heart, the brain, and the 'stones' act as Nature's 'myne, shoppe, or workehouse' (sig. F6), the stones mixing together blood from the veins, the arteries, and the lively spirits 'engendryd in the hed', and from these producing 'seed' by passing the liquids through its numerous narrow conduits. In the process the liquid turns from red to white. The resulting female 'sparm' or 'seed' is (of course) inferior to men's:

> and yet can you not cal this any imperfection or lacke in woman: for the woman in her kynd, and for th'office and pourpose wherfor she was made is even as absolute and perfect as man in his kynd: nether is woman to be called (as sum do) unperfecter then man (for bycause the man is moore myghtyer and strong, the woman wekar, more feble . . .) (sig. G2)

If strength were all-important, camels and elephants would be superior to human beings. 'Imperfection' is a concept far more applicable to the weakness of castrated men.

Returning to the 'sede cariers', Raynald describes how they convey the seed into the womb, where it accumulates in the '2 angles or corners' (sig. G5) (he has already described the shape of the uterus as like an upside-down heart). This seed is exuded 'in wemen having great and fervent desyre to any man': he notes that Aristotle thought this phenomenon was purely to facilitate female pleasure, and if

21 See Jacquart and Thomasset, *Sexuality and Medicine in the Middle Ages*, 17, 36, 50.

22 Laqueur, *Making Sex*, *passim*.

23 See Jacquart and Thomasset, *Sexuality and Medicine in the Middle Ages*, 60–70.

24 'According to Galen . . . the three central organs of the body are the liver, heart and brain, and associated with each of these is a subtle, impalpable effluvium, having a special function in each case. The liver produces the *natural spirits*, which are found in all living organisms, and constitute the essence of growth. The heart is the laboratory of the *vital spirits*, which are necessary for movement and muscular activity, whilst the brain lodges the *animal spirits*, derived from the rete mirabile. The animal spirits account for all nervous activities and are contained in the ventricles of the brain, whence they are transmitted through the nerves to the body. He is not certain whether the animal spirits are a fluid or what we should now term a stimulus. These three imaginary substances play a considerable part in Galen's long-accepted but misguided views on the function of the vascular system' (Cole, *History of Comparative Anatomy*, 44).

the reader thinks this 'but a symple and an ydle or slender pourpose' (sig. G5^{v}), Raynald reminds her that without sexual pleasure, who would go to the trouble of childbearing, 'to the utter dekey[decay] in shorte tyme of all mankynde'. 'Such be the privye workes of God, and such be the prikes of nature: whiche never creatyth no specyall pleasyr unaccompanyed with sume sorowe' (sig. G6).

Raynald then goes on to describe the bladder, the kidneys, and the blood vessels that service the matrix before moving on to menstruation, which he calls 'termes' (cf. the euphemism 'periods', which dates from the mid-eighteenth century). He notes that others call them 'flowres' (sig. H3), which is the word regularly used in Middle English and into the seventeenth century: *OED*'s latest example in a scientific text is dated 1662 and the usage was noted as obsolete in 1859.[25] Menstruation is simply the issuing of veinous blood that has gradually accumulated in the matrice over the previous three weeks. 'Prudent lady Nature' had a good reason for this: there must be a 'commodious and convenient place', a 'house of office', where the seed can receive nourishment (sig. H5) and be watered by the blood. In the absence of a 'feature' or foetus, the woman expels the matter.

This theory of menstruation, which is accurate as far as it goes, is quite different from that propagated in the medieval *Knowing of Woman's Kind* and derived from Soranus via the *Non omnes quidam*. There, women menstruate because their 'cold and wet' nature makes them incapable of thoroughly digesting their food, leading to a noxious build-up that must be regularly purged:

> The flowris is a syknes that fallith to every woman be nature every monyth onys at a certeyn tyme, and than are they purgyd of corrupcion that risith in hem of corrupte blood.[26]

A little of this older view survives in Raynald's remark that women of 'delycate and moyst complexions' menstruate for longer than those of 'drye and collericke' complexions (sig. H7). However, after a lengthy digression on the three 'cauls' or membranes that envelop the foetus and the placenta, Raynald reverts to the subject of menstruation and goes out of his way to deny the medieval theory:

> they be greatly disceaved and abused which call the termes the womans purgation or the clensyng of there blud, as who shuld say that it were the refuce, drosse and vilar part of the outher blud remaynyng in the body... for undoutedly this blud is even as pure and holsum as all the rest of the blud in eny parte of the boody els. (sig. J6^{r-v})

Surely Nature would not allow the child to be fed with anything but the best and purest blood. He moves on to condemn even more emphatically

> the shamefull lyes & slaunders that Plynie, Albertus Magnus de secretes [*sic*] Mulierum, and dyvers othermo, have wrytten, of the venemous and daungerous infectyve nature of the womans flowers or termes: The which al be but dreames and

25 See *OED*, *s.v.* **flower**, *n.* 1.b.

26 *Knowing of Womans Kind*, ed. Barratt, 47.

> playne dotage: to reherse there fon [their foolish] wurdes here were but losse of ynke and paper. (sig. J7)

He then discusses where the menstrual blood comes from—the lower veins—and why sometimes pregnant women continue to menstruate until the retained blood, after the pregnancy is established, 'mounteth up into the brestes and becummeth mylke' (sig. Hh2^{v}). Raynald also produces two case-studies of patients of his to support his view that menstruation comes only 'out of the vaut [vault] of the matrice' and not from the veins in the neck, as maintained by some. Two women in London and Paris had accidents close to the onset of their periods and then bled for six months and a year respectively. When menstruation resumed it was regular, but they 'voided great lumps, kakes or cloddes of blud, congelyd together even lyke the lyver of a beast' (sig. Hh3). It is not clear precisely what these stories illustrate, but they do bolster Raynald's self-presentation as a practising physician, as does his reference to 'dyvers other women' (sig. Hh4^{v}) he has seen who suffered from blood clotting.

His next topic is lactation. The breasts and the womb are closely linked; the milk comes from the blood of the 'terms', which is retained 'by the prudencie and provision of Nature' and drawn into the breasts by an 'attractive powre', which physicians can help with the application of cupping glasses. All this is wrong, of course, but Raynald correctly observes that while the woman is breast-feeding her 'terms' will be 'of verye lytell or no quantite' (sig. Hh6). For the sake of brevity he refrains from attempting to explain how the colour of the blood is changed, 'with many other problemes, douts and difficulties concerning the same' (sig. Hh7^{v}), and here concludes his first book.

There follows a detailed explanation of the eleven 'fygures'. It seems they were not engraved specifically for this publication, as on several occasions the commentary dismisses lettered features of the diagrams as 'not to our entent' or 'nothinge to our purpose'. For Raynald is not interested in knowledge for its own sake, but he does have a genuine desire to communicate with his audience. This comes over not only in the provision of diagrams and his commentary on them but also in his easy manner and his care to give vernacular equivalents for Latin anatomical terms. In contrast, in 1540 Jonas had apologized for, rather than explained, the 'straunge names . . . for the which there is no Englyshe but are usyd in there owne proper names of Greke or Laten' (sig. C3).

Raynald also has a fondness for graphic images from everyday domestic life, which he presumably judged would appeal to women. In addition they are apt, even startling, and would render both familiar and memorable anatomical features not visible to the naked eye. We have already noted the comparison of the cervix to a small bell; he also describes the 'seed carriers' creeping over the ovaries 'as the yvye branches do fastyn them selve to the walls by which they crepe' (sig. G3^{v}), while a muscle closes the bladder as 'it were with a broode and flatte hoope ryng' (sig. G6^{v}), i.e. a ring consisting of a plain band; part of the bladder is like 'a payre of bellowes' (sig. G8); and one of the membranes surrounding the foetus is 'much after the shape of the outward skyn or bagge of an haggisse puddinge' (sig. H8^{v}).

The second book of the revised edition corresponds to the first book of the original edition, so at this point it becomes possible to compare the two versions directly. Book 1 of the first edition opened with a brief description of the infant in the womb wrapped in the three cauls. As Raynald has already covered this in much greater detail in his first book, he omits it. So Book 2 Cap. 1, on signs of imminent labour, of the 1545 edition corresponds to Book 1 Cap. 2 of the 1540 edition, and so on.

It must be said that Raynald's claim to have revised 'from top to toe' is mainly marketing hype: there are some verbal changes in the second edition, but they are of little significance. Rather, the most intriguing difference between the two editions lies in their use of authorities. The 1540 edition (following Rösslin) had claimed to use 'Hypocrates / Galenus / Rasis / Avicenna and divers other' (sig. P3^{v}), and we could add Albert the Great,[27] who was credited (wrongly) with the *De Secretis Mulierum*,[28] attacked as we have seen by Raynald for its superstitious view of menstruation. In fact, Jonas mentions Galen on only one occasion, when he credits him with the belief that during pregnancy the cervix is so tightly closed 'that sca[r]ce the poynte of a nedle maye enter in at it' (sig. D3^{v}); Raynald keeps the observation but removes Galen's name. This is surprising. During the Middle Ages, Galen's writings had been known mainly through Latin translations of Arabic versions made by Constantine the African, Gerard of Cremona, and Mark of Toledo, rather than from the original Greek: it was the sixteenth century that saw '[t]he establishment of the Greek texts and the editing of better Latin translations . . . gradually accomplished.'[29] In 1545 Galen's was a revered name. His numerous writings were first printed in Latin in 1490 and in Greek in 1525.[30] In England, Thomas Linacre had translated Galen directly from Greek into Latin, publishing eight treatises, including 'some of Galen's largest and most important texts for the practical physician', between 1517 and 1524.[31] As early as 1516, Erasmus had referred to Sir Anthony Cope's English translations,[32] while Sir Thomas Elyot had popularized Galen's ideas in the *Castel of Health*, published in 1541.[33] As one scholar has remarked, 'Galen's fame increased by leaps and bounds, and doctors were still swearing by him in the seventeenth century and even in the

[27] Cited twice on sig. D1^{v}.

[28] Pseudo-Albertus Magnus, *De Secretis Mulierum (On the Secrets of Women)*, trans. Helen Rodnite Lemay (Albany, NY: State University of New York, 1992).

[29] George Sarton, *Galen of Pergamon* (Lawrence, KS: University of Kansas Press, 1954), 89.

[30] Sarton, *Galen of Pergamon*, 25.

[31] Vivian Nutton, 'Linacre, Thomas (*c*.1460–1524), *ODNB* (accessed 28 July 2006).

[32] Elizabeth Allen, 'Cope, Sir Anthony (1486/7–1551)', *ODNB* (accessed 28 July 2006).

[33] Stanford Lehmberg, 'Elyot, Sir Thomas (*c*.1490–1546), *ODNB* (accessed 28 July 2006).

eighteenth.'[34] So there is no obvious explanation for Raynald's deletion of Galen's name, unless he did not want to deter his women readers by an ostentatious display of learning.

Avicenna (Ibn Sina, 930–1037), the Arab scientist and philosopher, is the authority cited most frequently by the first edition of *The Byrth of Mankynde.* Best known for his role in conveying Aristotle to the medieval west, his medical writings were equally important: as Monica Green points out, 'For practical matters of gynecological therapeutics, Latinate physicians could and did turn to the sections on reproductive diseases in such massive medical encyclopedias as Avicenna's *Canon.*'[35] In contrast to the first edition's extensive citing of Avicenna, the 1545 edition excises almost all mentions of his name, though not the pieces of information (or misinformation) which it had supported, such as the popular, and persistent, belief that children born in the eighth month were less likely to survive than children born in either the seventh or ninth months. This coyness does not reflect doubts about authenticity, for we can indeed locate most of what Jonas attributes to Avicenna in a modern translation.[36]

Raynald does keep some references to authorities, however. Both texts (1st edn, sig. P.3^{v}; 2nd edn, sig. S7^{v}) cite 'Hypocrates / Galenus / Rasis / Avicena and divers other' on the subject of infant diseases. In Book 3 of the 1595 edition (sig. S1^{v}), 'Avicenna sayth' a number of things about what can be predicted from examining the child's umbilical cord, such as the number of children the mother will bear, and at what intervals. This is all faithfully copied from the first edition into the second without alteration, but at the end Raynald adds sceptically: 'these sayings be neither in the gospel of the day, ne of the nyght' (sig. S2).

A more extensive example of Raynald's ability to have his cake and eat it occurs at the end of the volume, where Jonas had described an elaborate method of diagnosing whether the man or the woman is infertile. It is superficially similar to a test described in the late medieval (or maybe early sixteenth-century) *Book of Rota*:

> Take a lytyll erthen pott newe and put therin the mans uryn, and cast therto an handfull of bran and stere it fast with a sticke about and take an-nothe[r] newe erthen pott and put therin the womans uryne, and put bran therto and ster it as the other and let it stande so 9 dayes or 10. And loke than in whether pott that yow fynde wormes in, ther ys the defaute that is baren, be yt the man or the woman, for the baren wyl be full of wormes. The vessell that the baren uryn is in wyll stynke. And yf nether vessell be with wormes, than is neyther of them baren. (Cambridge University Library, MS Ii. vi. 33, fols. 11^{v}–12)

34 Sarton, *Galen of Pergamon*, 90.

35 Monica H. Green (ed. and trans.), *The Trotula: A Medieval Compendium of Women's Medicine* (Philadelphia: University of Pennsylvania Press, 2001), 230.

36 I have used O. Cameron Gruner, *A Treatise on the Canon of Medicine of Avicenna incorporating a translation of the first book* (New York: Augustus M. Kelley, 1970; first published 1930).

'Rota' is probably a corruption of 'Trota' or 'Trotula', and this passage comes from a genuine Trotula text, the *Liber de Sinthomatibus Mulierum*, para. 75. It has been curiously transmuted in Book 3 Cap. 4 of Jonas's 1540 edition: the man and the woman should each soak seven wheat kernels, seven barley corns, and seven beans in their own urine for twenty-four hours, then plant them in flowerpots and regularly water with urine for eight or ten days: the one whose seeds germinate is not the one who is infertile (sig. X3^{v}). Raynald repeats this rigmarole in Bk 4 Cap. 3 of the 1545 edition, only to promptly rubbish it, adding at the end, 'truste not much this farfet experiment' (sig. Y).

In contrast to the brusque treatment Raynald metes out to Galen and Avicenna, Hippocrates, called 'the ryght excellent phisitian' in the first edition (sig. X4^{v}), is still treated as a credible authority in the second (e.g. sig. L1^{v}; sig. L2^{v}; sig. L3^{v}; sig. Y1). The 'rediscovery' of Hippocrates, or rather of the group of treatises attributed to Hippocrates of Cos (460–370 BCE), the earliest of which are now known to date back to the fifth century BCE,[37] was of course part of the humanist recuperation of Greek texts. *The Byrth of Mankynde* cites the *Aphorisms* (although misspelt as *Amphorisms*) in particular. Another survival into the 1545 edition (sig. U6) is the name of 'Rasis', the ninth-century Persian physician Rhazes, whose *Liber ad Almansorem* was known in its Latin form in medieval Europe.[38] Raynald, then, still thinks authority of some sort is important: he is not an empiricist or, if he is, he has no desire to be seen as such. But he seems to be intent on presenting his text as purely Hippocratic. Other authorities are minimized and for some reason Avicenna in particular has fallen out of favour between 1540 and 1545.

A third very obvious difference between the two editions is Raynald's addition of 'beauty-care' recipes. In his prologue and again at the beginning of Book 4 Raynald promises to 'set furth certayne bellyfyinge recepts' (sig. X4^{v}): the participial adjective seems to be an invention of his own, as this is *OED*'s only example. In its final chapter, the earlier edition had provided a variety of cures for infertility, caused by an imbalance of one of the humours. These included suffumigations (a favourite medieval remedy that went back to the Greeks), baths, and suppositories. Raynald eliminates some of these and varies others, then adds an extra chapter containing the promised recipes. He is eager to stress that these are not the sort that would give any artificial beauty, such as 'al honest, and vertuous sad wemen' (sig. Y5) would despise, but are designed to remove blemishes. Using another of his domestic images, he compares the process to a gardener removing the weeds that threaten the 'good herbes' (sig. Y5^{v}); she must keep a lookout for all such weeds, which will sprout given half a chance. Evil or superfluous humours can manifest themselves in forms other than strictly health problems: for instance, they

[37] Mary P. Gianos, *Hippocrates*, Twayne's World Authors Series, 165 (New York: Twayne, 1971), 13–14.

[38] *The Trotula*, ed. Green, 54 and 228.

can cause dandruff (wash your hair at least every ten days with lye and a special rinse and dry your head carefully), superfluous hair (especially if low on the forehead, to be fixed using arsenic), freckles, warts, bad breath (look after your teeth), pimples, teeth, 'yf they be very yelow and fylthy or blackisshe' (sig. 9^{v}), and body odour, 'very tedious and lothsum' (sig. Y10^{v}) (try artichokes seethed in white wine, to be eaten rather than applied topically: Galen's authority is invoked here).

It may seem strange to us to append a set of beauty tips to a serious gynaecological treatise. But there was a precedent in that 'patchwork of sources',[39] the medieval *Trotula* ensemble.[40] Of the three constituent treatises the second, the *De Curis Mulierum*, includes some cosmetic recipes, while the third, *De Ornatu Mulierum*, is entirely devoted to cosmetics. These include several recipes for depilatories, shampoo and various hair products, including dyes (black and gold), face creams, lip colourings, and the notorious techniques for the restoration of physical virginity. And the tradition was kept up in the late medieval *Book of Rota*, which contains several versions of the latter, beginning with:

> Yf a woman be over-large beneth, to make it narower use this medicyne, for she is abhominable to her husbande as oft tymes it is sene, and for-to make her seme a made. (fol. 18^{r-v})

(Perhaps it is not coincidence that the following folio—just as the text launches on a very elaborate recipe for the same purpose—is missing. Someone disapproved.) Later in the *Book of Rota* there are recipes 'To kepe a mannes here from fallyng', 'To make here growe there non ys' ('Take a mowse and brynne her to powder and temper it with bullis blodde'), and 'For the sawsefleme' (carbuncles, the unpleasant skin disease from which Chaucer's Summoner suffered). Although some of the *Book of Rota* material does ultimately derive from the *Trotula* ensemble (for instance, the recipe 'For ichynge of handes' comes from *De Curis Mulierum* 218), these do not, but certainly the idea of combining gynaecology and beauty culture is Trotulan, and persistent.

'Health and beauty' (the phrase itself appears to be late twentieth-century) are regularly coupled in women's magazines, television programmes, and pharmacies. The implication is that the two concepts are necessarily linked, but it would require a lengthy digression to summarize the numerous ways in which throughout history and across cultures women have engaged in practices that compromised their physical health in order to pursue an ideal of beauty. Certainly, many of the Trotulan beauty recipes would have been far from health-promoting.

In conclusion, it is arguable that Raynald's new edition is more woman-focused than the original 1540 version. It makes less ostentatious use of authorities (especially of Avicenna, for whom he does not have a kind word), perhaps because

[39] *The Trotula*, ed. Green, xiii.

[40] *Trotulae... liber unicus* (Strasbourg, 1544, repr. 1566): see *The Trotula*, ed. Green, xi and 207.

the names would mean little or nothing to a female audience, and might even emphasize their exclusion from male, university-educated culture. It promotes a 'scientific' knowledge of the female body in user-friendly fashion, with plain English terminology, illustrations, and homely imagery to encourage the study of unfamiliar subjects. Possibly one could even argue that this is a book that significantly 'empowers' women. Finally, it is dedicated, not to a single high-status woman, but to all women who qualify as readers. Indeed, it may well be the earliest printed book to address 'the women readers' by name, collectively and explicitly, and to honour them with a prefatory Prologue. Perhaps further research will either reinforce, or disprove, this claim.

FURTHER READING

Barratt, Alexandra (ed.). *The Knowing of Woman's Kind in Childing: A Middle English Version of Material Derived from the Trotula and Other Sources*, Medieval Women: Texts and Contexts 4 (Turnhout: Brepols, 2001)

Eccles, Audrey. *Obstetrics and Gynaecology in Tudor and Stuart England* (Kent, OH: Kent State University Press, 1982)

Green, Monica H. (ed. and trans.). *The Trotula: A Medieval Compendium of Women's Medicine* (Philadelphia: University of Pennsylvania Press, 2001)

Hobby, Elaine (ed.). *The Birth of Mankind: Otherwise named, The Woman's Book* (Farnham: Ashgate, 2009)

CHAPTER 30

IDLENESS

JAMES KEARNEY

Condemned to live by the sweat of his brow, Milton's Adam offers a stoic shrug: 'with labor I must earn / My bread; what harm? Idleness had been worse'.[1] Most readers of *Paradise Lost* understand this seemingly cavalier attitude toward the curse of man to be a reflection of significant changes in the conception of labour in early modern thought. In Milton's Eden, of course, Adam and Eve are famously not idle but active. It is the fate of the lesser creatures to 'Rove idle unimploy'd'; mankind 'hath his daily work of body or mind / Appointed, which declares his Dignity'.[2] Brian Vickers's reading of labour in Milton's Eden as part of a new Reformation conception of work reflects a critical consensus: 'Although pre-Reformation commentators, in the Augustinian tradition, allowed prelapsarian Adam to enjoy the contemplative life, Protestant theologians declared it right that Adam "should have exercised himselfe in some honest labour, even in Paradise." '[3] To make his point, Vickers here quotes Andrew Willett's *Sixfold Commentary Upon Genesis* (1608) as representative of a widely held post-Reformation belief that the Christian Eden was characterized by prelapsarian labour.

Indeed, one finds very similar sentiments expressed in a variety of sixteenth- and seventeenth-century commentaries on Genesis. Many of these commentaries not only insist on pre-fallen work but also reflect Milton's Adam's sense that the curse of labour, however onerous, is preferable to the idleness to which God's other creatures are consigned. And strikingly, some of these commentaries are markedly less concerned with the dignity of work than with the spiritual degradation brought

[1] John Milton, *Paradise Lost*, in *Complete Poems and Major Prose*, ed. Merritt Y. Hughes (Indianapolis, IN: Bobbs-Merrill, 1957), 10.1054–5.

[2] *Paradise Lost*, 4.617–19.

[3] Brian Vickers, 'Leisure and Idleness in the Renaissance: the Ambivalence of *Otium*', *Renaissance Studies*, 4:2 (1990), 107–54, at 145.

about by idleness.[4] The remarkable fixation on the unsettling spectre of idleness that one finds in these commentaries—an idleness evidently threatening to humanity even in a prelapsarian state—remains underexplored in histories of Christian conceptions of work. To attend to the history of idleness as a theological and ideological concept would, I suggest, force us to reconsider some of the traditional historical narratives employed to make sense of changing conceptions of labour in late medieval and early modern Christian thought.

John Salkeld's *Treatise of Paradise* (1617) offers a reading of the threat of idleness in Eden that reflects the arguments of many seventeenth-century commentaries. In his *Treatise*, Salkeld asks 'to what end was Adam placed in Paradise?' Salkeld turns to Moses, ostensible author of Genesis, to answer this fundamental question: '*Moyses* answereth . . . *that the Lord tooke the man, and put him into the garden of Eden, that he might dresse it, and keepe it*; or as the vulgar hath, *that he might worke in it*'.[5] According to Salkeld, Adam was placed in paradise, quite simply, to work. Salkeld's understanding of paradise is a function of his reading of Genesis 2:15: 'And the LORD God took the man, and put him into the garden of Eden to dresse it, and to keepe it'.[6] This passage has been crucially important for notions of dominion and stewardship, property and labour in Christian thought. And a glance at the varied commentary on this passage in Christian history illustrates that Christian beliefs concerning labour are anything but uniform and that Christian conceptions of paradise have proven surprisingly malleable. In the passage itself, of course, there is a certain ambiguity to notions of dressing and keeping paradise, a happy imprecision that allows Christian thinkers a certain amount of interpretive play when imagining human activity in the garden. Many Christians, of course, conceived of a paradise in which a divinely ordained natural abundance precisely signified freedom from labour. In this traditional view, labour only entered the world with the first disobedience and the fall of man. But many Christian commentators from the Church fathers forward understood the dressing and keeping of the garden as a form of prelapsarian labour.[7]

4 For representative examples, see Genesis 2:15, *Geneva Bible* (1560), marginalia; Gervase Babington, *Certaine plaine, briefe, and comfortable notes upon everie chapter of Genesis* (London, 1592), fol. 10^r; Andrew Willet, *Hexapla in Genesin: that is, A sixfold commentarie upon Genesis* (London, 1605), 33; John Salkeld, *Treatise of Paradise, and the Principall Contents Thereof* (London, 1617), 43–6; Alexander Ross, *First booke of questions and answers upon Genesis* (London, 1620), 45; John Yates, *A Modell of Divinitie* (London, 1622), 159; Joseph Hall, *Contemplations*, in *The Works of Joseph Hall* (London, 1634), 777.

5 Salkeld, *Treatise of Paradise*, 143.

6 *The Holy Bible* (London, 1611) (King James Version).

7 For Augustine's influential reading, see *De genesi ad litteram*, in *The Works of Saint Augustine*, ed. John Rotelle (New York: New York City Press, 1992), 13: 356–7; also see George Ovitt, 'The Cultural Context of Western Technology: Early Christian Attitudes toward Manual Labor', *Technology and Culture*, 27:3 (1986), 477–500.

What is striking about the seventeenth-century commentaries under discussion here then is not that they find labour in Eden but that they return again and again to the idea that God instituted labour in paradise precisely to ward off the threat of idleness. In Salkeld's reading of Genesis, for instance, work is simply a means of fending off sloth and sin: 'lest *Adam* or his posteritie should by alluring idleness, come to... endless paine; God of his mercy placed *Adam* in paradise' so 'that hee working might keepe paradise, and paradise by the same worke might keepe him from idleness, from sinne: because that is the ordinarie cause of sinne'. Labour here offers protection from idleness and the sin that it engenders, and this protection extends from Adam to his 'posteritie'. Indeed, Adam labours in paradise precisely so that future readers of Genesis might fathom the importance and necessity of work: 'to give us to understand how much God abhorreth idleness, seeing that even in that place, where there was no neede of labour, God would not have man idle'.[8] In Salkeld's view of humanity's origins, labour is not a consequence of sin but a gift of divine mercy offered to humanity as the means of avoiding idleness, a sloth that he reads as the occasion of sin.[9] If fallen labour is more onerous in an environment in which humanity is estranged from nature and its own proper dominion, the curse of man nevertheless seems, from a certain perspective, like a blessing: 'with labor I must earn / My bread; what harm? Idleness had been worse'.[10]

It would be tempting to align Salkeld's paradise with the familiar narratives offered to explain an historical shift in the understanding of labour. It would be tempting, for instance, to align Salkeld's paradise with the emergence of Baconian natural philosophy, or with the ongoing transition to capitalism, or with the Reformation's rejection of a theology of works and the consequences of that rejection for Christian notions of labour. It would be tempting, in short, to align this shift with the venerable break from medieval to early modern. And, in fact, when I began work on this essay, I thought that it would address the Weberian conception of the 'Protestant work ethic' and its impact on Christian notions of labour.[11] My research, however, kept leading me not to Calvin or Luther or Richard Baxter, the seventeenth-century Puritan divine so central to Weber's argument, but to the fourteenth century. If Salkeld is broadly representative of a historical shift in the Christian conception of labour, I contend that that shift cannot simply be attributed to the historical rupture of the Reformation. In England the ideas that Salkeld articulates, I suggest, began to gain traction not with the dissolution of the

[8] Salkeld, *Treatise of Paradise*, 143–5.

[9] And sloth here is not, at least in the first instance, a melancholy passion that might lead to sorrow or despair, not the medieval vice of *acedia*, but simply the absence of industry. For changing notions of sloth in the later Middle Ages, see Siegfried Wenzel, *The Sin of Sloth: Acedia in Medieval Thought and Literature* (Chapel Hill: The University of North Carolina Press, 1960; 1967).

[10] *Paradise Lost*, 10.1054–5.

[11] See Max Weber, *The Protestant Ethic and the Spirit of Capitalism*, trans. Talcott Parsons (New York: Routledge, 1992; trans. first published 1930).

monasteries or the Edwardian Reformation, but in the second half of the fourteenth century, when the cataclysm of the Black Death transformed the demographics of Europe and England, bringing about a social reformation that could not help but be a cultural reformation.

That changing conceptions of labour were a crucial consequence of this historical rupture is, of course, well known. And yet our traditional historical divisions often obscure important continuities from medieval to early modern, obscure a complex and knotty genealogy of ideas about labour and idleness that extends from the fourteenth to the seventeenth centuries. By attending to idleness rather than other more familiar rubrics for addressing labour, I contend that we can see some of these continuities more clearly. My point is not that the Reformation does not have a significant effect on changing conceptions of labour; nor is it my contention that one can trace a straight conceptual or discursive line concerning labour between the fourteenth and seventeenth centuries. Rather, my point is simply that by the early sixteenth century Christian conceptions of labour were already transformed and that our familiar historical narratives obscure the effects of this transformation on later developments in the history of ideas about labour; these traditional narratives obscure the fact that writers like Salkeld inherited fraught conceptions of industry and idleness that were profoundly informed by the theological and ideological struggles of late medieval England.

Perhaps perversely, in this essay I focus neither on Milton and the seventeenth century nor on the many fourteenth-century works that speak to the issue of human work; rather, I address an early sixteenth-century text that is not often considered in either medieval or early modern histories of Christian thought about labour: Thomas More's *Utopia* (1516). My contention is that *Utopia* is fundamentally shaped by More's meditation on labour and idleness and that that meditation opens the utopian text out toward a vexed history of ideas concerning human work that extends forward from the fourteenth century. Scholars have explored the ways in which the 'Dialogue of Counsel' in the first book of *Utopia* engages in a conversation with antiquity addressing the relative merits of *otium* and *negotium*. And scholars have also attended to the ways in which More's *Utopia* responds to the economic realities of its immediate cultural and historical moment. The significance of a longer English history of labour relations to the dialogue has been less frequently discussed.

With its idiosyncratic but historically resonant meditation on human labour, More's *Utopia* represents a particularly useful vantage point from which to address the ongoing transformation of Christian conceptions of work in late medieval and early modern England. I contend that More's *Utopia* transforms expectations of the earthly paradise—newly significant with the discovery of the New World—into a humanist dream of an ethical society founded on a transformative rationalization of the labour force. Written on the eve of the Reformation, More's *Utopia* depicts the tremendous social value of a culturally inculcated work ethic, a discipline geared toward realizing the social benefits of unprecedented material production. In this essay I suggest quite simply that the changing conceptions of labour in late medieval thought shape More's text in fundamental ways. And central both to this history of ideas concerning labour and to More's text is an ideologically fraught conception of idleness. From the vantage point of More's *Utopia*, we can begin to see the significant part that the spectre of idleness played in the ongoing transformation of labour in late medieval and early modern England.

Edenic Fantasies and Christian Labour

Shaped by a humanist movement that rejected the proximate past and took its cues from antiquity, More's *Utopia* is often considered a quintessentially Renaissance text, a product of its immediate intellectual and historical context and a revival of classical forms and concepts. The one purely fictional character of any significance in *Utopia* evokes with extraordinary economy the discursive contexts to which More directs his readers. When the character More first sees Raphael Hythlodaeus, he assumes that the weathered man, with his 'sunburnt countenance and long beard' must be 'a ship's captain'. In this, Peter Giles insists, More is 'quite mistaken':

> for his sailing has not been like that of Palinurus but that of Ulysses or, rather, of Plato. Now this Raphael... is no bad Latin scholar, and most learned in Greek. He had studied that language more than Latin because he had devoted himself unreservedly to philosophy, and in that subject he found that there is nothing valuable in Latin except certain treatises of Seneca and Cicero. He left [his home]... and being eager to see the world, joined Amerigo Vespucci and was his constant companion in the last three of those four voyages which are now universally read of.[12]

Scholar and adventurer, Hythlodaeus is an intimate of sailors and philosophers, bridging the gap between Plato and Vespucci. Taking the discovery of the New World as his point of departure, More creates a dialogue between the hugely popular travel narratives of the sixteenth century and the philosophical thought experiments of antiquity. Placing *Utopia* within an historical context is then as straightforward as meeting Hythlodaeus; readers can simply follow More's lead, situating *Utopia* in relation to the discovery of the New World and the evident renaissance of classical learning brought about by men much like Hythlodaeus and More. But scholars have perhaps taken More's direction too well, as this familiar approach to *Utopia* is blind to the ways in which More folds a dynamic sense of history into his New World fiction; as I hope to show in this essay, it is a mistake to divorce either Hythlodaeus or *Utopia* from the late medieval context that shapes them.

[12] Thomas More, *Utopia*, ed. Edward Surtz and J. H. Hexter, in *The Complete Works of St Thomas More*, vol. 4 (New Haven, CT: Yale University Press, 1965), 49–50. Hereafter cited as *CWM*.

By placing his *Utopia* in dialogue with the popular New World travel narratives, More necessarily invokes the classical and medieval 'utopian' genres that inform these travel narratives, that indeed inform Europe's response to the New World: the arcadian and pastoral visions inscribed in a variety of textual and iconic forms, including everything from descriptions of the golden age and the happy isles to representations of the land of Cockaygne and the kingdom of Prester John. These narratives proved ideologically useful in this New World context, and one of the fundamental functions they performed was to help make sense of New World labour. Encountering economies and labour practices different from their own, Europeans writing about the New World frequently employed these generic fictions to translate into familiar terms what they took to be an extraordinary natural abundance and a correspondingly remarkable lack of human industry and productivity.

It is, however, not simply that the visions of human labour in these medieval genres and modes informed conceptions of the New World. Both the reception of these generic forms and the representations of the New World were shaped by the fact that human labour was at the center of crucial theological and ideological disputes of the later Middle Ages. As a result of the anti-mendicancy controversy, Christian Europe had, from the mid-thirteenth century forward, been engaged in an ongoing theological conversation about human dominion, property and poverty, the nature of prelapsarian existence, and the redemptive value of work, that would necessarily have shaped European responses to industry and idleness in the New World.[13] More immediately, the tremendous demographic changes wrought by the calamity of the Black Death in the mid-fourteenth century created a new labour economy that made defining and controlling human work one of the most contentious ideological struggles of the era. A work like More's *Utopia* is necessarily responsive to the fraught history of labour; the conceit of Hythlodaeus's New World experiences simply makes this response more relevant to the most recent wrinkle in that history.

The most powerful myth shaping European conceptions of the New World was, of course, the Biblical Garden of Eden.[14] And Eden was a central site where various struggles over the nature and purpose of human labour were being fought. In the mid-fourteenth century, Richard Fitzralph anticipated seventeenth-century Protestant figures like Milton and Salkeld by insisting not merely that Adam laboured in paradise but that he was placed there in order to work. Drawing on Genesis 2:15,

[13] On the anti-mendicancy controversy and its impact on Christian thought, see Penn Szittya, *The Antifraternal Tradition in Medieval Literature* (Princeton, NJ: Princeton University Press, 1986); and Wendy Scase, *Piers Plowman and the New Anticlericalism* (Cambridge: Cambridge University Press, 1989).

[14] On the many and shifting uses of the Garden of Eden myth in medieval and early modern thought, see Jean Delumeau, *History of Paradise: The Garden of Eden in Myth and Tradition*, trans. Matthew O'Connell (New York: Continuum, 1995), 39–154.

Fitzralph writes that 'anoon as man was made, God put hym in Paradys for he schuld worche & kepe Paradys; so hit is writen in the begynnyng of Hooly Writ'.[15] Fitzralph—Archbishop of Armagh and one-time chancellor of Oxford—had, late in life, become a scourge of the mendicant friars. As part of an ongoing critique of the fraternal orders, Fitzralph took aim at the theological foundations of mendicancy. Charged with heresy by his adversaries after a series of provocative sermons on the topic of Christian poverty at St Paul's Church from 1356 into 1357, Fitzralph was called to answer before the Pope. It was in his defence against his accusers that he made the radical claim that 'god sett man in Paradys for he schuld worche'.[16]

For Fitzralph, human labour and the wealth it produced were signs of God's grace. As David Aers notes, Fitzralph's conception of Eden 'involves an attitude to work more conventionally associated with Protestantism than with medieval Catholicism' and 'shows . . . some signs of what looks like a new work ethic in which the production of material goods and material work seems glorified as an end in itself'.[17] Fitzralph's anti-fraternal writings would prove influential in Lollard circles—where he was sometimes referred to as St Richard—and the crucial passage of Genesis 2:15 is picked up again in a Lollard tract on 'The Seven Deadly Sins', probably written in the final decades of the fourteenth century. In a discussion of the 'synne of . . . slouthe', the author of the treatise writes, 'Mon in state of innocence schulde be kept from ydelnesse, for, as Gods lawe seis, he schulde have kept Paradis.' The injunction to keep the garden in paradise should warn fallen humanity of the danger it faces:

> if monkynde in the stat of innocence, when he had in hym strength . . . schulde not be ydel bot serve his God bisily, for elles he schulde by ydelnesse have fallen from the state of innocence,—how schulde he be ydel now when peril is myche more?[18]

In this Lollard treatise, as in the passage from Salkeld quoted above, work is quite simply a means of avoiding idleness and the sin it engenders. Labour here is not a post-lapsarian phenomenon, associated with sin and death, but the means of avoiding sin both before and after the Fall. The mendicant controversy and its conceptual fallout are topics too large and complex to address here, but it should

[15] Richard Fitzralph, *Defensio curatorum*, trans. John Trevisa, *Dialogus inter Militem et Clericum*, ed. Aaron Perry, EETS, 167 (London: Oxford University Press, 1925), 39–93, at 71.

[16] Fitzralph, *Defensio curatorum*, 71. On Fitzralph see Katherine Walsh, *Richard FitzRalph in Oxford, Avignon, and Armagh: A Fourteenth-Century Scholar and Primate* (Oxford: Clarendon Press, 1981).

[17] David Aers, *Community, Gender, and Individual Identity: English Writing 1360–1430* (New York: Routledge, 1988), 25. Also see Kellie Robertson, *The Laborer's Two Bodies: Literary and Legal Productions in Britain, 1350–1500* (New York: Palgrave Macmillan, 2006), 1–2.

[18] 'On the Seven Deadly Sins', in *Select English Works of John Wyclif*, ed. Thomas Arnold, 3 vols. (Oxford: Clarendon Press, 1869–71), 3: 119–67, at 142–43. For a discussion of this treatise in relation to changing conceptions of sloth in the later Middle Ages, see Wenzel, *Sin of Sloth*, 90–2.

be noted that we have not attended enough to the consequential effects of this controversy on a long history of Christian thought concerning dominion, property, and labour.[19] Here, I simply want to establish that changing conceptions of work were embraced and disseminated within an ongoing and wide-ranging dispute on the theological nature and spiritual value of poverty in the late thirteenth and fourteenth centuries. And with the labour crisis of the second half of the fourteenth century, these ongoing controversies moved from the theological periphery to the centre of European life.

The Spectacular Rise and Rise of the Sturdy Beggar

The quintessential Renaissance text when viewed from a certain perspective, *Utopia* is also often read as an extraordinarily topical text, the product of a very local history, a work that could only be written in the London of 1516. In thinking of *Utopia* as a text very much of its immediate time and place, scholars can again simply follow More's lead. The evocation of commonplace negotiations between England and Castile over commercial interests; the placement of the character 'More' within a network of real-world minor officials; the reduction of London, Bruges, and Antwerp to commercial and political centres without mystery or menace—all of this is clearly designed to conjure a very particular time and place and class of men.

If the resolutely prosaic backdrop works to set the stage for the entrance of the extraordinary Hythlodaeus with his tales of exotic lands, it also suggests that the mundane, contemporary world that More inhabits is crucially relevant to the eventual description of Utopia. And the contemporary relevance of the text never seems more pressing than when Hythlodaeus critiques, in the first book of *Utopia*, not some hypothetical despot or exotic nation but More's own England. A traveller in Europe as well as the wider world, Hythlodaeus mentions England as one of the many places he has been, recounting an episode at a dinner hosted by Cardinal Morton, Archbishop of Canterbury. In the course of the evening an unnamed lawyer boasts of the number of thieves hanged in England, which provokes Hythlodaeus to offer a penetrating analysis of the social and economic ills plaguing England. The ensuing conversation touches on the efficacy and morality of capital punishment, the proper methods of punishing thieves and other criminals, the problem of vagrancy, the material injustices created by enclosure and engrossment, and the cruel inequity of an economic system that rewards the indolent few at the expense of the industrious many.

[19] For more on the anti-mendicancy controversy, see Szittya, *The Antifraternal Tradition* and Scase, *Piers Plowman and the New Anticlericalism*.

That the issues addressed in this wide-ranging conversation were relevant to More's early readers has been well established. To flesh out the image that More sketches, scholars have described in great depth the vagrancy problem of England in 1516. They have depicted acts of enclosure in the early sixteenth century, specifying the ways in which the ruinous social effects of enclosure correspond with some precision to Hythlodaeus's account. A recent edition of *Utopia* informs its readers in a footnote that the callous lawyer might well boast since '72,000 thieves were hanged' in England in the 'reign of Henry VIII alone'.[20] Nothing, it seems, could be more relevant to More's readers in the England of 1516 than Hythlodaeus's devastating social and economic critique. The one nagging detail that undercuts such topical analyses is the simple fact that the famous episode at Cardinal Morton's table takes place in the 1490s, roughly twenty years before the fictional conversation between More and Hythlodaeus in Antwerp, and roughly twenty years before the writing and publication of *Utopia*. One could argue then that editors should be concerned with capital punishment and the number of thieves hanged in Henry *VII's* reign; that scholars should address the fact that vagrancy had been an issue at the forefront of social policy since the fourteenth century; that readers should be made aware that the enclosing of land was a huge economic problem in the fifteenth century and that much of the land that would be enclosed in England by 1516 had, in fact, already been enclosed by 1500.[21] Indeed, Hythlodaeus's dramatic discussion of capital punishment, the criminalization of vagrancy, and the disastrous effects of enclosure could have been written virtually at any time from the fifteenth through the seventeenth centuries.

My point here is neither that readers are wrong to consider *Utopia* a topical text, nor that Hythlodaeus's analysis is irrelevant to the England of 1516. My point is rather that not enough attention has been paid to the seemingly unmotivated twenty-year wrinkle that More writes into his text. On those few occasions when the twenty-year gap separating the conversations in England and Antwerp is addressed, it is usually waved off as biographically motivated, having to do with More's affection for Cardinal Morton and the time he spent as a page at Lambeth Palace. I contend that this twenty-year gap between Hythlodaeus's trenchant critique of England and the contemporary reader—a gap that More goes out of his way to write into his *Utopia*—opens the text to history in a particular way. As More frames the issues, the problems—theft, vagrancy, enclosure, poverty—facing England in the 1490s are precisely the same as the problems facing England in 1516. The point, however, is not to collapse the difference between then and now, but to establish that these seemingly intractable issues *have* a history, a history that needs to be attended to if these issues are ever to be addressed. Rather than synchronic

[20] Thomas More, *Utopia*, ed. George Logan and Robert Adams (Cambridge: Cambridge University Press, 1989), 15 n. 17.

[21] Peter Ramsey, *Tudor Economic Problems* (London: Gollancz, 1965), 25–7.

history—a snap shot of the social and economic problems facing England at a particular moment in time—the first book of *Utopia* offers a moving picture, the imbrication of past and present, inviting the reader to attend to diachronic history. This opening out toward history is particularly significant given that Hythlodaeus's description of Utopia in Book 2 tends, more often than not, to elide history in favour of ethnographic description and the illuminating anecdote.

The debate at Cardinal Morton's table between Hythlodaeus and the lawyer is primarily concerned with an ongoing history of social strife over labour and land that has its roots in the radical demographic changes caused by the Black Death in the middle of the fourteenth century. These demographic changes transformed both labour practices and the ways in which labour was conceived.[22] After this cataclysm and repetitions on a smaller scale in the 1360s and 1370s, England's population was roughly cut in half. In the early fourteenth century, England's landowning class had enjoyed the benefits of a surplus of workers. With the labour force decimated, these same landlords and employers were faced with an emboldened working class demanding both greater remuneration and fundamental changes in labour practices. In the face of this threat, the government attempted to define the relationship of employer to labourer and worker to work. Parliament was quick to respond to the crisis: at the onset of the plague in 1349, they issued the Ordinance of Labourers, which addressed the crisis of the 'great Scarcity of Servants' by censuring those with the temerity to refuse to labour unless they received 'excessive Wages'. Aligning labourers demanding higher wages with those 'willing to beg in Idleness,' the ordinance commands workers to return to work and to 'take only the Wages, Livery, Meed, or Salary, which were accustomed to be given'.[23] This was simply the first in a series of acts by which the landowning class attempted to encode their relationship to the labour force through legislation, freezing wages, prohibiting the movement of workers, defining as criminal and deviant attempts by workers to improve their economic situation through the leverage provided by the increased market value of their labour.[24]

[22] In my understanding of these issues, I am particularly indebted to David Aers, *Community, Gender, and Individual Identity*; Chris Given-Wilson, 'The Problem of Labour in the Context of English Government, *c.*1350–1450', in *The Problem of Labour in Fourteenth-Century England*, ed. James Bothwell, P. J. P. Goldberg, and W. M. Ormrod (Woodbridge, Suffolk: York Medieval Press, 2000); Anne Middleton, 'Acts of Vagrancy: The C Version "Autobiography" and the Statute of 1388', in *Written Work: Langland, Labor, and Authorship*, ed. Steven Justice and Kathryn Kerby-Fulton (Philadelphia: University of Pennsylvania Press, 1997), 208–317; Bertha Havens Putnam, *The Enforcement of the Statutes of Labourers during the First Decade after the Black Death, 1349–1359* (New York: Columbia University, 1908); Robertson, *The Labourer's Two Bodies*; Miri Rubin, *Charity and Community in Medieval Cambridge* (Cambridge: Cambridge University Press, 1987); and James Simpson, 'Grace Abounding: Evangelical Centralization and the End of *Piers Plowman*', *Yearbook of Langland Studies*, 14 (2000), 49–73.

[23] *Statutes of the Realm* (London: Dawsons of Pall Mall, 1810–28; 1963), vol. 1: 307.

[24] See Given-Wilson, 'The Problem of Labour'.

During this crisis, Christian conceptions of work and idleness were redefined and transformed in the struggle to control workers and define the meaning of labour. Before the labour crisis and the mendicancy controversy, labour was commonly understood in Christian thought to be a consequence of the Fall, and therefore of a piece with other ills of a fallen world: pain, sin, death. Social stratification was often viewed as a sign of one's proximity to virtue: the greater the economic privilege, the farther removed from fallen labour, the more evident it was that one enjoyed God's grace. At the same time, poverty was revered as inherently virtuous, associated with Christ and the apostles; the beggar—even, perhaps especially, the able-bodied beggar who had forsaken his or her property—was a social good. Divested of possessions and embracing a virtuous asceticism, the pious beggar not only provided an image of Christ for others to meditate upon but also provided those encumbered with possessions the opportunity to earn grace through the giving of alms.[25]

Although these and similar ideas persisted throughout the period and into the modern era, during the historical crisis in question they were challenged in direct and fundamental ways. In this new climate, threatening to the profits of landowners and employers, poverty came to be seen by the governing class as wilful and sinful. As Miri Rubin notes in her study of charity in medieval Cambridge, in the bracing light of the devastating labour shortage, 'the perception of the poor developed into a general denunciation of those members of society who were not fully productive'. And as productivity came to be the key to 'determining social acceptance and moral approbation', allegedly non-productive members of society were blamed for the economic problems facing England's landowners.[26] Of course, the vilification and persecution of the non-productive or non-compliant worker was an indication of just how valuable labour had become. And as labourers increasingly recognized their value in this new demographic world, they actively resisted attempts to limit their new economic power and potential social mobility. This recognition of their own value and power was accompanied by an increased sense of the dignity of human labour. The ongoing dispute over the place of the labourer in this new demographic world—a dispute fought in fields, courthouses, and Parliament—would, of course, come to a head with the uprising of 1381.

Outside of direct confrontations like the conflict of 1381, the English government simply could not respond to worker non-compliance and political unrest with force. As Chris Given-Wilson observes, 'medieval governments lacked the apparatus to operate as police states', and so their efforts to control labour necessarily relied on ideological forms of coercion.[27] One of the crucial ideological tools seized upon by the governing culture to navigate these contentious times was

[25] See Rubin, *Charity and Community*, 54–98.

[26] Rubin, *Charity and Community*, 293.

[27] Given-Wilson, 'The Problem of Labour', 98.

the figure of the 'sturdy beggar'. The 1349 ordinance forbade the giving of alms to the so-called 'sturdy beggar' who ought to employ his or her able body to labour for the commonwealth.[28] As Anne Middleton observes in an important essay, by the 1380s England had witnessed 'the full-blown development of a complex and ideological invention, the pejorative figure of the alms-seeking able-bodied vagrant'.[29] The figure of the 'sturdy beggar', shirking his or her responsibilities to the commonwealth, was aligned with the vagrant as a means of criminalizing and vilifying workers who elected to move from one employer to another to look for the best wage. The new legislation attempted to restrict worker movement by essentially claiming that any subject travelling without the proper authority was guilty of vagrancy. As Middleton notes, the term vagrant became 'largely metonymic for social mobility more generally'.[30] With a pernicious logic that Hythlodaeus would have loved, labour legislation of the fourteenth and fifteenth centuries first worked to create vagrants by redefining the legislative categories in question and then punished these newly defined vagrants for their transgressions. And as Given-Wilson observes, over time 'the definition of vagabondage gradually expanded' until in 1446

> it was decreed that any man who had no land of his own, but who refused to accept a contract for a full year's work, was to be declared a vagabond and dealt with accordingly, and it was simultaneously decreed that if the justices of the peace ordered a servant to leave one master and serve another who, in their opinion, had greater need of his services, and if he refused, he too was to be declared a vagabond.[31]

Incited by this new legislation (among other things), the Cade rebellion of 1450 demanded the repeal of the labour statutes. But as with the uprising of 1381, the failed Cade rebellion did not bring justice or relief to labourers but only an increased sense among the governing class that workers left to 'idleness' and 'vagrancy' would become rebellious subjects. It would not be until 1495—the era of Henry VII, and Cardinal Morton, two years before the 'Cardinal Morton episode' in *Utopia*—that some of the more punitive aspects of the labour legislation of the mid-fifteenth century were scaled back. This almost certainly had less to do with the mercy of the king than changing demographics and economic circumstances.

By the time More was writing *Utopia*, the demographic situation that had prevailed in the late fourteenth century had changed dramatically. If the initial

[28] 'Because... many valiant Beggars, as long as they may live of begging, do refuse to labour, giving themselves to Idleness and Vice, and sometime to Theft and other Abominations; none upon... Pain of Imprisonment shall, under the colour of Pity or Alms, give any thing to such, which may labour... so that thereby they may be compelled to labour for their necessary Living', *Statutes of the Realm*, 1: 308.

[29] Middleton, 'Acts of Vagrancy', 229.

[30] Middleton, 'Acts of Vagrancy', 232.

[31] Given-Wilson, 'The Problem of Labour', 89.

crisis of the fourteenth century was sparked by a labour shortage, the resurgence of England's population in the fifteenth century, accompanied by the ever more prevalent practice of enclosing and engrossing land, meant that there came to be a surplus of workers and a dearth of work. The legislation and discourse addressing labour, however, maintained its punitive stance toward the unproductive and idle. Indeed, the animus against the unproductively idle and especially the spectre of the 'sturdy beggar' continued to shape both social policy and cultural production well after the initial demographic crisis had passed. The continued ideological resonance of the 'sturdy beggar'—surely one of the great success stories of reactionary politics, still familiar to us today in the figure of the 'welfare queen'—here works according to a common historical dynamic: an ideological solution to a particular social problem persists even as the underlying situation that required resolution changes.

The useful figure of the 'sturdy beggar' is here adapted to new circumstances, no longer transforming a mobile workforce into an enemy of the commonwealth but recasting the victims of economic hardship and predation as morally repugnant wastrels preying on the industrious. If the figure of the 'sturdy beggar' was initially useful to vilify presumptuous workers, in these changed circumstances the figure was useful to vilify the downtrodden poor. As the lawyer in More's *Utopia* insists, the thieves and vagabonds punished for their crimes have no one but themselves to blame as they 'voluntarily prefer to be rascals'.[32] It is this claim that occasions Hythlodaeus's justly famous critique of the economic practices of England generally and the practice of enclosure specifically. And here Hythlodaeus contests a traditional moralizing explanation of economic ills by offering a deeply informed historical analysis that must have seemed bracingly radical at the time. Hythlodaeus, however, does not simply stand outside history to comment upon it. I contend to the contrary that More wants us to understand Hythlodaeus as a figure shaped not only by his experiences travelling the world but by a discursive history of ideas. In other words, he is not simply a character with radical positions but a figure suggestively positioned within a tradition of radicalism.

From Demotic Eden to Georgic Utopia

The reader of More's *Utopia* knows that the episode at Cardinal Morton's table takes place in the final years of the fifteenth century because Hythlodaeus dates the episode rather precisely. Mentioning England as one of the many places in which he has encountered 'proud, ridiculous, and obstinate prejudices', Hythlodaeus is interrupted by More, who asks in surprise if the inveterate traveller has in fact been to England: '"Yes", he answered, "I spent several months there, not long after

[32] *CWM*, vol. 4: 61.

the disastrous end of the insurrection of western Englishmen against the king, which was put down with their pitiful slaughter.''[33] The reference to the western insurrection is clarified shortly thereafter as Hythlodaeus situates the episode at Cardinal Morton's table in relation to the Cornish rebellion of 1497.[34] Provoked by the fiscal policies of Henry VII, who imposed heavy taxes to fund his war in Scotland, the Cornish rebels marched toward London and a confrontation with the forces of the monarchy. In time-honoured fashion, they claimed to be loyal subjects, laying the responsibility for the oppressive policies at the feet of the king's counsellors, including and especially Sir Reginald Bray and Cardinal Morton himself.[35] Describing the victory of the king over the rebels as the 'disastrous end of the insurrection', Hythlodaeus is clearly sympathetic to the rebels as victims of 'pitiful slaughter' ('*miseranda... strage*').[36] Although Hythlodaeus never offers a position on either the occasion or the merits of the rebellion, his evident sympathy for the fate of the rebels marks him early on in the dialogue as a man with potentially radical ideas.

Like the twenty-year gap between episode and anecdote, the reference to the rebellion is seemingly unmotivated. Why does More position Hythlodaeus's analysis of England's social ills in relation to the Cornish rebellion? Precipitated by the heavy taxes Henry levied to fund his foreign war, the rebellion itself seems to be a consequence of the kind of royal policies that Hythlodaeus denounces in the course of his critique of kings and their counsellors. The rebellion also illustrates the bloody consequences that Hythlodaeus contends will follow from pursuing such policies:

> [Monarchs] are completely wrong in thinking that the poverty of the people is the safeguard of peace. Where will you find more quarreling than among beggars? Who is more eager for revolution than he who is discontented with his present state of life? Who is more reckless in the endeavor to upset everything... than he who has nothing to lose?[37]

We cannot know what the nineteen-year-old More thought of the spectre of a rebel mob—numbering 15,000 according to some accounts—marching on London, demanding Cardinal Morton's head. But whatever More's reaction to this menacing spectre, this would have certainly represented a consequential event to a young Londoner in 1497, a moment in which history threatened to overtake the mundane world of everyday London. In More's *Utopia*, the reference to the Cornish rebellion works, I contend, to invoke both popular rebellion and its suppression as crucial aspects of the history that the first book of *Utopia* addresses. When the Cornish

[33] *CWM*, vol. 4: 59. [34] *CWM*, vol. 4: 61.

[35] On the Cornish rebellion, see A. L. Rowse, *Tudor Cornwall* (New York: Charles Scribner's Sons, 1941), 114–40; also see J. P. D. Cooper, *Propaganda and the Tudor State: Political Culture in the Westcountry* (Oxford: Oxford University Press, 2003), 52–7.

[36] *CWM*, vol. 4: 59. [37] *CWM*, vol. 4: 95.

rebels marched on London in 1497, all involved would inevitably have thought back to other popular revolts, especially the peasant uprising of 1381 and Cade's rebellion of 1450. In fact, the Cornish rebels took a detour to Kent in a failed attempt to foment rebellion amongst those who had famously risen in these prior insurrections.

Tracing some of the satirical vigour of More's *Utopia* to carnivalesque traditions, Christopher Kendrick suggests that the learned humanist text would have been recognized as engaged in dialogue with demotic fantasies and forms of societal critique. In its treatment of labour, for instance, *Utopia* seems to take up, on its own terms, the promise of popular notions of a society with an egalitarian ethos of work. Kendrick's point of departure is the Land of Cockaygne, and for Kendrick, if Cockaygne is explicitly concerned with 'excess consumption', it is also implicitly concerned with 'the division of labour... insofar as its pleasures and delights represent a fantasy of the division of labour's end'. As Kendrick observes, the 'root message' of this fantasy of the division of labour's end is clear: 'there would be enough and more for everyone if the ruling classes were abolished'.[38]

I contend that More's invocation of the Cornish rebellion provides another context for Edenic and idyllic fantasies of a world reformed by the transformation of work: the revolutionary discourse of popular rebellion. And the discourse of popular rebellion, of course, often trafficked in nostalgic dreams of a return to a golden age when divisions of labour were unknown. As I have been suggesting in this essay, Eden in particular became contested ground in the course of the ongoing labour strife of the fourteenth and fifteenth centuries, as workers and landowners alike attempted to harness Christian notions of labour to their own advantage. When the various conflicts between labourers and landowners came to a head in the rebellion of 1381, the language of Eden was notoriously invoked by the rebel priest John Ball. It is unclear whether Ball's invocation of the egalitarian commonplace—'When Adam delve, and Eve span, / Who was then a gentleman?'—is a reference to pre- or post-lapsarian labour; in either case, the human animal is defined by labour, fallen or otherwise.[39] Ball's rhetorical turn to Genesis is a radical return to origins in which a history of servitude and subjection is erased by a common—in both senses of the term—human genealogy. And this erasure of proximate history is, of course, one of the desires that informs popular rebellion and literary utopia alike.

It is often forgotten that Hythlodaeus's description of Utopia begins with an act of regenerative violence that dramatically transforms an already existing society. Although he is a conqueror rather than a rebel, the figure of Utopus enacts the

[38] Christopher Kendrick, *Utopia, Carnival, and Commonwealth in Renaissance England* (Toronto: University of Toronto Press, 2004), 78.

[39] *The Chronica Maiora of Thomas Walsingham, 1376–1422*, trans. David Preest (Woodbridge: Boydell Press, 2005), 162.

fantasy that inspires many popular rebellions, erasing history and beginning again through violent conquest. Utopus, however, does not overthrow the Abraxans in order to return to some state of Edenic innocence. On the contrary, as James Holstun has suggested, Utopus's transformative act of violence seems to enact a rejection of the arcadian and the pastoral, the very visions that fuelled both popular rebellion and representations of the New World.[40] The society that Utopus founds is not inspired by visions of pastoral ease but by visions of georgic labour. And this violent negation of pastoral is not simply a one-time event, but a principle that informs the Utopians' understanding of the relation of land to labour.

When the population of the country exceeds a certain limit, the Utopians simply colonize a neighboring land, 'wherever the natives have much unoccupied and uncultivated land'. If the attempt to colonize provokes resistance, the Utopians 'consider it a most just cause for war when a people which does not use its soil but keeps it idle and waste nevertheless forbids the use and possession of it to others who by the rule of nature ought to be maintained by it'.[41] A non-Christian nation, the Utopians nevertheless adopt a Christian understanding of land that one can trace back to medieval theological disputes over *dominium* and forward to Locke's theory of property, an understanding in which dominion over land involves working it, involves 'dressing and keeping' it. In Hythlodaeus's account of Utopia's origin myth, the figure of Utopus is a conqueror who transforms what appears to be one of those idyllic, New World societies so confounding to Europeans into a new model Eden, an Eden informed by changing Christian conceptions of dominion, property, and work. And he does so by transforming the native population's understanding of both land and labour.

In his first act of public policy after conquering the evidently uncivilized people of Abraxa, Utopus severed the Abraxan peninsula from the mainland:

> As the report goes and as the appearance of the ground shows, the island once was not surrounded by sea. But Utopus, who as conqueror gave the island its name . . . and who brought the rude and rustic people to such a perfection of culture and humanity as makes them now superior to almost all other mortals, gained a victory at his first landing. He then ordered the excavation of fifteen miles on the side where the land was connected with the continent and caused the sea to flow around the land.[42]

This remarkable act of geographic engineering was accompanied by a bit of social engineering as Utopus used this opportunity to begin to instil in the 'rude and rustic' native population the virtues that would bring them to the 'perfection of culture and humanity' that the present-day Utopians currently enjoy: 'He set to the task not only the natives but, to prevent them from thinking the labor a disgrace, his own soldiers also'. Teaching the Abraxans the importance and material efficacy

[40] James Holstun, *A Rational Millennium: Puritan Utopias of Seventeenth-Century England and America* (New York: Oxford University Press, 1987), 67–77.

[41] *CWM*, vol. 4: 137.

[42] *CWM*, vol. 4: 113.

of labour seems to be the first step in transforming them into Utopians, 'superior to almost all other mortals'. At the end of the description of the transformation of peninsular Abraxa into insular Utopia, Hythlodaeus celebrates the efficiency of Utopian labour: 'With the work divided among so many hands, the enterprise was finished with incredible speed and struck the neighboring peoples, who at first had derided the project as vain, with wonder and terror at its success.'[43] This primal act not only separates but also distinguishes Utopia from other nations, who look on with wonder and terror at the power of efficiently organized labour. In Hythlodaeus's telling, it almost seems that Utopia's future is encoded in this initial act: this will be a nation apart, a land transformed by the work of human hands, and a society that eliminates distinction and champions the value of manual labour.

A number of years after he wrote *Utopia*—in the context of a religious conflict that he could not have imagined in 1516—More addressed the idleness of those who expect to be fed without working for their daily bread. In a discussion of the sin of sloth, More writes that God found the 'vyce' of idleness

> so noyous unto mankynd, that even when he set him in paradyse, he bad hym be occupyed in the kepyng of that pleasaunt garden. And afterward when he should be driven thence into the earth, he gave hym a necessyte to labour, makyng the earth to be such as without mans labour should not bryng hym forth hys lyving.
>
> And therefore an evyl and a perylous lyfe lyve they, that wyll in this world not labour & worke, but lyve eyther in idelness or in idle bysiness.[44]

Unlike commentaries on Genesis 2:15, More's analysis begins not with a scriptural crux but with the sin of sloth, turning to the dressing and keeping of Eden only in order to explain the threat that idleness represents to the individual Christian soul. Like many late medieval and early modern commentaries on Genesis—Protestant and Catholic—More invokes innocent labours in Eden as a function of the seemingly ineluctable propensity to idleness. There is a revealing continuum in this passage between God's bidding mankind to keep 'that pleasant gardaine' and the subsequent 'necessity to labour', a continuum that is reminiscent of Milton's Adam's claim that idleness had been worse than the prospect of fallen labour. This suggests not only that labour is essential to humanity but also that a fundamental tension between labour and idleness is part of the human condition. Sufficiently industrious to have stood, humanity is nevertheless always free to fall into the sin of idleness. The spectre of the sturdy beggar, it seems, haunts paradise.

Although it is beyond the scope of this essay to offer a full reading of Hythlodaeus's humanist version of the earthly paradise, my contention is that the figure of the sturdy beggar haunts Hythlodaeus's description of Utopia as well. The

[43] *CWM*, vol. 4: 113.

[44] Thomas More, *The answere to the fyrst parte of the poysened booke, whych a namelesse heretyke hath named the souper of the lorde* (1533), *CWM*, vol. 11: 33.

extraordinary industry of the people of Utopia ultimately functions, of course, as a critique of the shameful idleness of European populations. The economic miracle of Utopia makes more sense, claims Hythlodaeus, when we compare the labour practices of Utopia to those of Europe: 'this phenomenon you too will understand if you consider how large a part of the population in other countries exists without working'. After censuring women and priests for their indolent ways, Hythlodaeus gets to the heart of his critique, attacking both the idle rich, 'especially the masters of estates, who are commonly termed gentlemen and noblemen', and 'the lusty and sturdy beggars who make some disease an excuse for idleness'.[45] Here, 'sturdy beggars' (*valentes mendic[i]*) is the key term, loaded with the ideological baggage of a century and a half of disputes over what constitutes labour and idleness. Drawing on the long history of discourse about, and animus against, the 'sturdy beggar', More frees the term from its class valence, extending it to other social groups, especially the indolent rich. In a characteristic move, More's radical critique here simply involves taking seriously the ideological claims of his own society: first, let's get rid of all the 'sturdy beggars'. And once they have eliminated the idle among rich and poor, the Utopians harness human labour in such a way that they are able to offer an approximation of the earthly paradise in a fallen world.

This is not to say, however, that labour is unfallen in Utopia or that Utopians celebrate the dignity of work; on the contrary, Utopia is infamously a slave economy in which a criminal class is in place precisely to perform the most onerous and odious labour. A work ethic is cultivated among the Utopians because they recognize the extraordinary social utility of a rationally organized labour force. The goal of the Utopian economy is, quite straightforwardly, overproduction, and the surplus produced by the efficient Utopian labour force is collectively deployed in a variety of ways.[46] Here, I simply want to focus on the fact that this planned overproduction makes possible one of the Edenic fantasies at the heart of More's Utopia: *otium* or idleness. The efficient organization of labour in Utopia not only produces surplus wealth, but also produces a concomitant surplus of time, time free from labour. Time free from labour is, of course, not idle time in More's *Utopia*; it is, in fact, a rationally organized, remarkably industrious *otium*, infected it seems by the pervasive Utopian work ethic. And this industrious idleness mirrors the prelapsarian labour More finds in Genesis. Fittingly, the most widespread Utopian pastime is gardening.[47] With the fruits of their fallen labour, Utopians purchase a facsimile of unfallen labour, the kind of prelapsarian industry celebrated by figures ranging from Richard Fitralph,

[45] *CWM*, vol. 4: 129–31.

[46] For a brilliant reading of the logic of surplus in *Utopia*, see Richard Halpern, *The Poetics of Primitive Accumulation* (Ithaca, NY: Cornell University Press, 1991), 136–75.

[47] *CWM*, vol. 4: 121, 129.

the fourteenth-century Archbishop of Armagh, to Gerrard Winstanley, the seventeenth-century Digger.[48]

The ideologically fraught topos of Eden is contested ground in late medieval and early modern England, and contested precisely in terms of the place and function of human labour. With its cultivation of a work ethic as a social good and its profound animus against idleness of any kind, with its surveillance techniques aimed at preventing the shirking of labour and its travel restrictions preventing the possibility of vagrancy, More's fictional no-place seems to rehearse the ideological struggles occasioned by the labour crisis of the fourteenth and fifteenth centuries. My point is not that More's text perfectly reflects, or is merely responsive to, the late medieval labour crisis. Nor is it my contention that More anticipates perfectly an early modern work ethic that we have come to associate with the Reformation. My point is simply that More's text shows us some of the ways that these two historical veins—considered separately within traditional historical divisions—are part of a larger and deeper seam. More's *Utopia* apes the New World travel narrative, calling upon idyllic fantasies of Eden and Cockaygne only to rewrite the pagan and Christian pastoral as a kind of humanist georgic. Just as Utopus transforms Abraxa into Utopia, More transforms a paradise of ease into a working utopia. And both More and Utopus believe that the foundation of this second Eden is industry, a rationally organized labour that wards off the ever-present spectre of a fall into idleness.

FURTHER READING

Fumerton, Patricia. *Unsettled: The Culture of Mobility and the Working Poor in Early Modern England* (Chicago: The University of Chicago Press, 2006)

Given-Wilson, Chris. 'The Problem of Labour in the Context of English Government, c. 1350–1450', in *The Problem of Labour in Fourteenth-Century England*, ed. James Bothwell, P. J. P. Goldberg, and W. M. Ormrod (Woodbridge, Suffolk: York Medieval Press, 2000)

Middleton, Anne. 'Acts of Vagrancy: The C Version "Autobiography" and the Statute of 1388', in *Written Work: Langland, Labor, and Authorship*, ed. Steven Justice and Kathryn Kerby-Fulton (Philadelphia: University of Pennsylvania Press, 1997), 208–317

Vickers, Brian. 'Leisure and Idleness in the Renaissance: the Ambivalence of *Otium*', *Renaissance Studies* 4.2 (1990), 107–54

[48] In his attempt to design a real-world utopia in *The Law of Freedom in a Platform*, Winstanley offers a radical vision of society organized around labour. In Winstanley's utopia, there will be 'neither Beggar nor idle person'; 'idle persons and beggars will be made to work' through corporal punishment if necessary; and children will be raised to understand the importance of work and the threat of idleness. For Winstanley the freedom of man is defined as the freedom to work the land. Gerrard Winstanley, *The Law of Freedom in a Platform*, in *Works*, ed. George Sabine (Ithaca, NY: Cornell University Press, 1941), at 513, 527, 576.

PART IX

SELFHOOD

CHAPTER 31

PERSONA

JOHN PARKER

In the beginning was polytheism. To each locality a different, specific genius. Then appeared a more pronounced difference: the imperious god of today's monotheisms, jealous and insisting on supremacy (Exod. 20:3) as though he were the only divinity and others mere demons or idols (Ps 95:4–5; 115). His counter-revelation to a people with promiscuous tastes in religion ironically enough makes foreign gods a permanent element in the self-constitution of Judeo-Christianity.[1] Where pagans had erected totems in the image of man or nature, for example, Genesis has Elohim (as yet unreconstructed, and plural) explicitly reverse their procedure: 'Let us make man in *our* image' (Gen. 1:26). An early rabbinic gloss imagines Moses taking dictation but declining to write any further for fear this proposal would invite heretics to think there was more than one god. 'Write it anyhow', God says.[2] The One, in this instance, does not fret his multiple faces. They facet a unique magnificence. It is all the more glorious, and less autocratic, the more polyvalent in appearance. The last gospel follows suit with a man-god called Jesus, otherwise known as the Word (Jn 1:1), plus then a Paraclete (Jn 14:16).[3] Christians accused their heretics, too, of inferring from scripture more than one deity, yet the heresies, like deities, kept coming anyhow. The polytheistic west had become a world of wrangling monotheists. To any given faction, the others, in seeming like reversion, guaranteed its spiritual advance.

The first exegete to justify Christianity's new pantheon with the word *persona* is Tertullian—a convert from paganism and Carthaginian priest with a heart perhaps

[1] David Penchansky, *Twilight of the Gods: Polytheism in the Hebrew Bible* (Louisville, KY: Westminster John Knox, 2005); Chiara Peri, 'The Construction of Biblical Monotheism: An Unfinished Task', *Scandinavian Journal of the Old Testament*, 19 (2005), 135–42.

[2] Jacob Neusner, *Genesis Rabbah: The Judaic Commentary to the Book of Genesis*, 3 vols. (Atlanta: Scholars, 1985), 1: 81.

[3] Raymond E. Brown (trans.), *The Gospel according to John: John I–XII* (New York: Doubleday, 1966), 519–24 (on the history of Logos); and Raymond E. Brown, *The Gospel according to John: John XIII–XXI* (New York: Doubleday, 1970), 1135–44 (on the Paraclete).

less thoroughly washed in the Blood than he wanted to think: 'Vehement, irate, witty, tender, hater of shams and of culture, cultured himself... scorner of rhetoric and master of its devices, original in thought and style, champion of the Catholic faith and self-constituted prosecuting attorney against all heretics, [yet] devotee of a sect so strict and so peculiar that it landed him in heresy'[4]—Rand's old description still fits. One peculiarity of the group that Tertullian joined (which in all fairness would have seemed as Catholic at the time as many other micro-communities retroactively branded schismatic)[5] was, according to later heresiologists, their enthusiasm for channeling the Spirit in first person; that is, for taking on themselves the role of divinity. 'I am the Lord God Almighty dwelling in a human', or alternately, 'I, Lord God the Father, have come',[6] even *women* might say in preface to further revelations.[7] Presumably they were echoing the way that Montanus himself (they supposed) had echoed Jesus's own penchant: grandiose statements beginning 'I am...' (*à la* Yahweh) were the Lord's preferred mode (especially in John) when pronouncing a role for himself *beyond* the low self that appeared in the world—which very habit, Jesus furthermore predicted, later heretics in their hubris would likewise mimic.[8]

Simple people misunderstood. They gossiped, Tertullian says, that he and his fellow Montanists preached 'two or even three gods, while they, they claim, are the worshippers of one God'.[9] Satan's hostility to the truth had of course always taken the form of *aemulatio*: 'sometimes', Tertullian asserts, he has even tried 'to shatter the truth by defending it' (*Adv. Prax.* 1.1). Such tactics had led to the present impasse, where simpletons were persuaded to defend monotheism *against* the Trinitarians: thus does the devil 'champion the one Lord, almighty creator of the world, in order to make a heresy even from [God's] unity' (*Adv. Prax.* 1.1). According to Tertullian the seeds of this error had lain dormant for years, its cunning vitality hidden 'by hypocrisy' (*Adv. Prax.* 1.7), before coming to full blossom in Praxeas. People who now agree that God is strictly singular *despite* how he speaks at creation—in the first person plural—imply that he is either

[4] E. K. Rand, *Founders of the Middle Ages* (Cambridge, MA: Harvard University Press, 1928), 38.

[5] William Tabbernee, *Fake Prophecy and Polluted Sacraments: Ecclesiastical and Imperial Reactions to Montanism* (Leiden: Brill, 2007), 131, especially those he cites at note 19.

[6] St Epiphanius, *Epiphanius*, ed. Karl Holl, vol. 2, Die griechischen christlichen Schriftsteller der ersten drei Jahrhunderte, 31 (Leipzig: J. C. Hinrichs, 1922), 233, 235 (§§48.11.1 and 9); trans. Frank Williams, *The Panarion of Epiphanius of Salamis*, 2 vols. (Leiden: Brill, 1987–94), 2: 16–17; Jaroslav Pelikan, *The Emergence of the Catholic Tradition (100–600)*, volume 1 of his *The Christian Tradition: A History of the Development of Doctrine*, 5 vols. (Chicago: University of Chicago Press, 1971), 102–3.

[7] Christine Trevett, *Montanism: Gender, Authority and the New Prophecy* (Cambridge: Cambridge University Press, 1996), especially 151–97.

[8] Mt 7:15, 22–3; Mk 13:6; cf. Jn 4:26. On the connection to Montanism, see Gerd Theissen, *The Gospels in Context: Social and Political History in the Synoptic Tradition*, trans. Linda M. Maloney (Minneapolis, MN: Fortress, 1991), 152.

[9] Tertullian, *Adversus Praxean* 3.1. Annotated and trans. Ernest Evans, *Adversus Praxean Liber: Tertullian's Treatise Against Praxeas* (London: S.P.C.K, 1948).

'deceiving or playing [*fallit aut ludit*]' (*Adv. Prax.* 12.2). They unwittingly convict their god of being, at bottom, 'a liar and impostor' (*Adv. Prax.* 11.4). Tertullian's tripartite deity, by contrast, avoids the appearance of such histrionics insofar as he actively 'gave the role [*personam*] of his son to another, since all of scripture shows... the distinction of Trinity' (*Adv. Prax.* 11.4). If you consider the very 'substance of the Word... a *persona*' (*Adv. Prax.* 7.9), that is, God's plurals are never mere play-acting: they are ultimate reality.

Tertullian's adoption of *persona* to describe the internal divisions of the Trinity has been traditionally taken as a watershed moment in the development of Christian monotheism, the point at which a new orthodoxy distinguished itself from Judaism, from its own heresies, as well as drawing 'the line', in the words of Jaroslav Pelikan, 'that separated it from pagan supernaturalism'.[10] I do not see things so simply—for the simple reason that *persona* means 'mask' and, according to Christian tradition, was borrowed from theatre. A line of that sort is more like a scar: it joins what might have been otherwise severed. The treatise against Praxeas, for example, attributes to its opponent a theatricalization of scripture ('hypocrisy', 'imposture', and so forth) which might as readily describe the *personae* Tertullian proposes in correction. His attempt to rectify errors, which he himself partly imagines, looks in other words like a way of retaining and enjoying without guilt his own un-Christian aberrance. *Persona*, psychoanalytically speaking, is a symptom of the otherness internal to orthodox doctrine.

Consider for example how Tertullian speculates—against Roman spectacle—on God's special loathing for 'the art of masks [*opus personarum*]' (*Adv. spect.* 23.5).[11] Here again an object of revulsion emulates devotion: in theatre, Tertullian complains to the pagans, masks allow 'the image of some deity' to cover 'the infamous and paltry head'[12] of a mere player—or worse, of the convicts who might be 'costumed as your very gods'[13] before getting brutally punished. 'We have often witnessed in a mutilated criminal your god of Pessinum, Attis; and he who was burnt alive has played Hercules.'[14] In fact many Romans had a hard time seeing any difference between the 'Heraklistai'—a cult that worshipped a mortal who suffered terribly before being deified—and this new sect of 'Christiani'.[15] Tertullian's early

[10] Pelikan, *Christian Tradition*, 1:172, roughly repeating the position of St Basil, *Epistulae* 219.5.41, 44 (*PG*, 32: 776B–C); trans. Agnes Clare Way, *Letters*, The Fathers of the Church, vols. 13 and 28 (Washington: Catholic University of America Press, 1965–69), 28: 9.

[11] Tertullian, *Apology, De spectaculis*, trans. T. R. Glover (London: W. Heinemann; Cambridge, MA: Harvard University Press, 1931; hereafter cited as '*Adv. spect*').

[12] Tertullian, *Ad nationes* 1.10.45 (*CCSL*, 1: 29); translated in Alexander Roberts and James Donaldson (eds.), *The Ante-Nicene Fathers: Translations of the Writings of the Fathers down to A.D. 325*, 10 vols. (Grand Rapids, MI: Eerdmans, 1951; hereafter cited as '*ANF*'), 3: 120.

[13] Tertullian, *Apologia* 15.4 (*CCSL*, 1: 114; *ANF*, 3: 30).

[14] Tertullian, *Ad nationes* 1.10.47 (*CCSL*, 1: 29; *ANF*, 3: 120).

[15] Robert Wilken, *The Christians as the Romans Saw Them*, 2nd edn (New Haven, CT: Yale University Press, 2003), 44.

admiration for the re-enactment of Hercules' burning seems, by the same token, to anticipate his devotion to another felon who was also costumed, this time in a royal cloak of purple and a parodic crown of thorns (Mk 15:17), then labeled 'King of the Jews'. In Jesus's spectacular execution by Romans, Tertullian saw the *persona* of an otherwise invisible godhead.[16] He sacrificed theatre by providing in its place a more sublime form of acting.

No wonder that any number of later churchmen would feel so much rivalry between the drama of the passion—endlessly restaged in the liturgy, readings from the saints' lives, not to mention vernacular drama—and other forms of Roman *spectacula*. Like Augustine later, Tertullian essentially promoted ritual worship of the Christian *personae* as a *superior form* of the drama he used to adore before his conversion: paganism's 'end', in a word. (And not only them: Gregory of Nazianzus, to give one further example we'll soon see again, likewise condemned the stage while applying to God the most theatrical of terms, even going so far as to write—earlier generations assumed without doubt—a play of the passion.)[17] Tertullian, for his part, does not want the spectacles of Rome to disappear with the triumph of Christ. Rather, he hopes they might eternally *reward* those willing to substitute, in their present lives, the *personae* of God for theatre-masks: 'How vast a spectacle then bursts upon the eye!' Tertullian exclaims while imagining, from the viewpoint of heaven, the great games of hell. 'What there excites my admiration? What my derision? Which sight gives me joy? Which rouses me to exultation?... I shall have a better opportunity then of hearing the tragedians, louder-voiced in their own calamity; of viewing the play-actors, much more dissolute in the dissolving flame' (*Adv. spect.* 30). The costumed person of Jesus, tormented to death, turns out to prefigure 'typologically' the excruciation of masked entertainers.

I want to restate, in short, a version of what Žižek, borrowing from Chesterton, calls the 'thrilling romance of orthodoxy'.[18] The basic idea is that we have to revise 'the standard (mis)perception according to which the ancient pagan attitude'—or, I would add, the attitude of heretics—'is that of the joyful assertion of life, while

[16] Cf. Donald G. Kyle, *Spectacles of Death in Ancient Rome* (London: Routledge, 1998), 53–5.

[17] For *prosopōn* used to mean Trinitarian person, then theatre mask, see Gregory of Nazianzus, *Oratio* 42.16 and 22 in *Discours/ Grégoire de Nazianze*, ed. Jean Bernardi, Sources chrétiennes (Paris: Éditions du Cerf; hereafter cited as 'SC'), vol. 384 (1992), 84, 97; translated in *Cyril of Jerusalem, Gregory Nazianzen*, volume 7 of *Nicene and Post-Nicene Fathers*, Second Series, ed. Philip Schaff and Henry Wace, 14 vols. (hereafter cited as '*NPNF* II') (Peabody, MA: Hendrickson Publishers, 1994), 391–2. For Christ's life more generally as a 'drama', see *Oratio* 30.6, ed. Paul Gallay, in collaboration with Maurice Jourjon, SC, 250 (1978), 236; *NPNF* II, 7: 311. The play *Christos Paschon*, now of less certain authorship, is in *La Passion du Christ, tragédie*, ed. André Tuilier, SC, 149 (1969).

[18] Slavoj Žižek, *The Puppet and the Dwarf: The Perverse Core of Christianity* (Cambridge, MA: MIT Press, 2003), 35. Cf. Virginia Burrus, '"In the Theatre of This Life": The Performance of Orthodoxy in Late Antiquity', in *The Limits of Ancient Christianity: Essays on Late Antique Thought and Culture in Honor of R. A. Markus*, ed. William E. Klingshirn and Mark Vessey (Ann Arbor: University of Michigan Press, 1999), 80–96.

[orthodox] Christianity imposes a somber order of guilt and renunciation'.[19] The anti-theatrical, Trinitarian doctrine first championed by Tertullian, on the contrary, elevates to the highest ontological level the masked performance it cancels. His 'exultation' in the drama of crucifixion and the tragedy of hellfire clearly proclaims, in the words of Žižek, a gospel 'of infinite joy beneath the deceptive surface of guilt and renunciation' (47–8). Renounce the theatre, by all means, say Tertullian, Augustine, and Gregory (together with many, many others).[20] But receive in return an orthodoxy that offers 'the only frame for pagan freedom'.[21] And not just in the Christian 'fulfillment' of paganism's promise: Dionysian decadence, on this model, achieves its highest pitch specifically as a *Christian memory*, one that the chosen of any given era can cultivate simply by insisting that the wine of Dionysus still intoxicates *other*, 'heretical' Christians. At the same time the chosen manage to speak by this means a truth that applies best to themselves: 'All living Christians', as Chesterton puts it, 'are dead pagans walking about'.[22]

Certainly a lot of the Christians walking around sixteenth-century England were convinced that the theatre's huge popularity had given new life to their pre-Christian heritage. 'The providence of God many times scourgeth a man with the sin that he loved',[23] explains Stephen Gosson, a penitent playwright now firmly against 'these dancing chaplains of Bacchus' ($C3^r$), whose theatrical antics he once had choreographed. Chastised at last, he regularly turns for instruction to Tertullian, among other 'ancient Fathers of the church, which have looked very narrowly into the cause and in anguish of heart set down their judgment' ($G8^r$). Just as they had fought to free themselves from their Roman patrimony, above all a common reverence for the stage, so too did Gosson and his fellows struggle to overcome a widespread addiction to 'Italian' drama, well after the Reformation had for the most part *displaced* 'Romish' spectacle—unfortunately with plays, the Reformers thought, modeled on even more pagan conventions. 'Compare London to Rome, and England to Italy,' writes Gosson, 'you shall find the theatres of the one, the abuses of the other, to be rife among us'.[24] Like the Fathers he admires, Gosson also attempts to purify Christendom by sublating his passion for drama into anti-theatrical polemics on behalf of Jesus's person. His confutation of theatre, for example, tellingly occurs in five acts. Were anyone to see in this a clandestine

[19] Žižek, *Puppet and the Dwarf*, 47–8.

[20] Christine Catharina Schnusenberg, *The Relationship between the Church and the Theatre* (Lantham, MD: University Press of America, 1988).

[21] Žižek, *Puppet and the Dwarf*, 48; quoting G. K. Chesterton, *Orthodoxy* (San Francisco: Ignatius, 1995), 164.

[22] Chesterton, *Orthodoxy*, 156.

[23] Stephen Gosson, *Playes Confuted in Five Actions: Proving That They Are Not to Be Suffred in a Christian Common Weale*... (London, 1582), $A1^v$.

[24] Stephen Gosson, *The Schoole of Abuse*... (London, 1579), $C1^r$.

return to Christian drama at the moment of its loss in England, he has ready to hand the example of Gregory of Nazianzus, whose supposed dramatization of Christ's life (patched together from Euripides) had been written, according to Gosson, *against* 'the corruption of the Corpus Christi plays that were set out by the papists' (E5^{v}). Thus Gregory 'thought it better', explains Gosson, to compose a *closet* drama, 'that all such as delight in numerosity of speech might read it, not behold it upon the stage, where some base fellow that played Christ would bring the person of Christ into contempt' (E6^{r}).

Note that Gosson deploys the word 'person' here in its non-theatrical meaning as a countermeasure to the traditions of masking out of which Christ's theological personhood was thought to have developed. The Middle Ages owed their understanding of that development largely to an influential polemic by Boethius against the heresies of Eutyches and Nestorius.[25] 'The word *persona*', Boethius writes, 'seems to be borrowed ... from the masks [*ex personis*] which in comedies and tragedies used to represent the people concerned'.[26] He next traces the etymology to *sonus* by noting that the sound 'is necessarily the greater from the very hollowness [*concavitate*] of the mask. The Greeks, too, call these masks *prosōpa* from the fact that they are placed over the face [i.e., *pros ōpas*] and conceal the countenance from the spectator'.[27] Such concealment is what allows for the clear recognition, on stage, of the 'subsisting' individuality of the characters—in Christian idiom, their *hypostasis*. So too with the Trinitarian persons. Boethius does not seem the least worried by the implication that outright revelation—whether Father, Son, or Spirit—should reveal at most a mere persona or that the *ens realissimum* might be exclusively a matter of surface and costuming, three alternating masks the whole of whose substance was encompassed by this ongoing act of self-impersonation. In Boethius, as in every latter formulation that the councils found orthodox, there is literally nothing behind the masks of divinity (except, perhaps, for another mask). The emptiness is precisely what resonates. It opens, I think, into the Thomistic possibility of equating God with a love so all-embracing as to make him genuinely 'selfless'.[28]

[25] Mary H. Marshall, 'Boethius' Definition of *Persona* and Medieval Understanding of the Roman Theatre', *Speculum*, 25 (1950), 471–82.

[26] Boethius, *Contra Eutychen et Nestorium* 3, in *The Theological Tractates and the Consolation of Philosophy*, trans. Hugh Fraser Stewart, E. K. Rand, and S. J. Tester (Cambridge, MA: Harvard University Press, 1973), 84–6.

[27] Boethius, *Contra Eutychen et Nestorium* 3, 84–6.

[28] Hans Urs von Balthasar, *Mysterium Paschale: The Mystery of Easter*, trans. Aidan Nichols (Grand Rapids, MI: Eerdmans, 1993), 35: 'The ultimate presupposition of the Kenosis is the "selflessness" of the Persons (when considered as pure relationships) in the inner-Trinitarian life of love'; Hans Urs von Balthasar, *Theo-Drama: Theological Dramatic Theory*, trans. Graham Harrison, 5 vols. (San Francisco: Ignatius, 1988–94), 3: 208–28 (on *persona*). For Aquinas's view on *persona* and theatre, see *Summa Theologiae* 1.29.3, obj. and resp. 2 in Thomas Aquinas, *Summa Theologiae: Latin Text and English Translation* ((London): Blackfriars, 1964), vol. 6: 50ff.

Even if maskers as such disappeared from official church ritual (save for the symptom of Trinitarian doctrine), they seem to have limped along well enough in popular festival to have, at last, their renascence.[29] *This* Renaissance is medieval drama: nearly all the otherworldly characters in the English cycles and moralities wore masks, for example: angels, devils, god(s), good and bad souls—plus particularly demonic aspirants to divinity, such as Herod.[30] Nothing so distinguishes the actor playing God as a gilt face to cover human flesh. And though a new terminology had grown up around these masking traditions, you could occasionally still hear—and see—the relevance of 'person'. Cyrus, for instance—Mary Magdalene's father and a typical figure of Antichrist[31]—makes reference in his vaunting to the god-like mask he was probably wearing:

> Behold my person, glistering in gold,
> Seemly beseen of all other men!
> Cyrus is my name, by cleffys so cold!
> I command you all obedient to beyn![32]

Such commands might have come more fittingly from one of the Trinitarian 'persons' (so named in lines 809, 1472). Yet to hear them now, in the mouth of a pretender, underscores the pretense on which all Christian drama depends: the godhead could no more be shown in all its personal glory, however supposedly genuine, than could the specious beauty of 'Cyrus'. Both require the mediation of a mask, as had nearly all of divinity's rivals. Behind Cyrus's meta-theatrical pun on 'person' there stretches an etymological genealogy going far back to an Etruscan word (*phersu*) connected to rites involving some kind of mimicry on behalf of the dead.[33]

[29] E. K. Chambers, *The Mediaeval Stage*, 2 vols. (Oxford: Oxford University Press, 1903), especially vol. 1.

[30] Meg Twycross and Sarah Carpenter, *Masks and Masking in Medieval and Early Tudor England* (Aldershot: Ashgate, 2002).

[31] Theresa Coletti, 'Paupertas est donum Dei: Hagiography, Lay Religion, and the Economics of Salvation in the Digby *Mary Magdalene*', *Speculum*, 76 (2001), 337–78, at 347, n. 34; Theresa Coletti, *Mary Magdalene and the Drama of Saints: Theatre, Gender, and Religion in Late Medieval England* (Philadelphia: University of Pennsylvania Press, 2004), 194–202 (comparing the play as a whole to Chester's Antichrist).

[32] Donald C. Baker, John L. Murphy, and Louis B. Hall (eds.), *The Late Medieval Religious Plays of Bodleian MSS Digby 133 and e Museo 160*, EETS, 283 (Oxford: Oxford University Press, 1982), 25, lines 53–6. Bevington conjectures that cleffys=cliffs (anyway, a nonce phrase): *Medieval Drama*, ed. David Bevington (Boston: Houghton Mifflin, 1975).

[33] Jean-René Jannot, 'Phersu, Phersuna, Persona: à propos du masque étrusque', in *Spectacles sportifs et scéniques dans le monde étrusco-italique*, Collection de l'école française de Rome, 172 (Rome: Palais Farnèse, 1993), 281–320. See also Alois Grillmeier, *Jesus der Christus im Glauben der Kirche: Von der Apostolischen Zeit bis zum Konzil von Chalcedon (451)*, 3rd edn, vol. 1 (Freiburg: Herder, 1990), 251.

The long history does not have to scare us. Even Twycross and Carpenter, despite their pious distaste for seeing any link between Christian performance and the pagan routines it supplanted,[34] have to concede that:

> the use of God-masks is a widespread phenomenon throughout the world, and one that seems extremely powerful in religious drama, as well as religious rituals. There is clearly something about a masked face that conveys a sense of 'human-like but more than human' that is particularly appropriate to the representation of anthropomorphic divinities of all sorts.[35]

I think by now we can afford to acknowledge that the Christian religion has always had a profoundly close, if dialectical, relation to anthropomorphism; consequently that it cannot do without the concept of a mask, even where it manages to dispense with masked impersonation by means of that concept. My point is again close to Žižek: with Jesus, Christianity effectively renounces 'this God of the Beyond, this Real behind the curtain of the phenomena; it acknowledges that there is *nothing* beyond the appearance—nothing *but* the imperceptible X that changes Christ, this ordinary man, into God. In the *absolute* identity of man and God, the Divine is the pure *Schein* of another dimension that shines through Christ, this miserable creature'.[36] What this means to me, in terms of theatre history, is that the Christian religion, perhaps more than any other, embraces the mysterious differential inherent to masking as its deepest spiritual property. Which is to say, it embraces the deep play of surface—one originally achieved through the mask's uncanny, formal ability to present to viewers something more than the human standing in front of them, though only a human stands there before them. He is still a human, but, as Twycross and Carpenter put it, 'one who exists solely in the moment of appearance' (13). In the beginning was the mask.

*

Tertullian had a few further motives for integrating the *personae* of classical drama into Christian doctrine. To read even the non-prophetic books of the Hebrew Bible as nonetheless prophetic of Christianity required that in certain key passages, from Psalms especially, the speakers 'assume the role of Christ' (*Christi personam sustinent*) (*Adv. Prax.* 11.7). You could see the Spirit, too, as though on stage speaking 'to the Father and the Son as a third person' (*ex tertia persona*) (*Adv. Prax.* 11.7). This way of reading, modeled on and eventually named after a rhetorical figure called prosopopoeia (or, in Latin, *fictio personae*),[37] was not

[34] See John Parker, 'Who's Afraid of Darwin: Revisiting Chambers and Hardison . . . and Nietzsche', *Journal of Medieval and Early Modern Studies*, 40.1 (2010), 7–35.

[35] Twycross and Carpenter, *Masks and Masking*, 223.

[36] Slavoj Žižek, *On Belief* (London: Routledge, 2001), 89. Typography has been normalized.

[37] Heinrich Lausberg, *Handbook of Literary Rhetoric*, ed. David E. Orton and R. Dean Anderson (Leiden: Brill, 1998), §§826–29; plus §820–4 on *sermocinatio* or *ethopoeia*, with which *prosopopoeia*

substantially different in its agenda from typology; yet it achieved the same end by means of an explicitly theatrical vocabulary:[38] Christians who rejected the Hebrew Bible for being incompatible with the new law of Christ failed to understand, Tertullian says elsewhere, that 'Christ has been figured in the *persona* of Moses'.[39] Jewish history better prophesied the truth of Christianity when conceived of as drama.

In order to press an increasingly alien Judaism into service, that is, early Christians annexed a way of reading from learned pagans,[40] who were as concerned as the Fathers with the rightful place of theatre. The model roughly follows the tripartite division of literature, by Plato and Aristotle, into drama (or 'mimesis'), narrative ('diegesis'), and mixtures of both,[41] such that the mimetic presentation of character without any authorial 'introduction' could be imported into other, more narrative genres, even works of literature ostensibly *opposed* to theatre (such as Plato's). Thus could Proclus happily associate *The Republic* with drama by virtue of the philosopher's constant 'prosopopoeia',[42] equal to or even surpassing that of Homer, whose famed ability to create dramatic personalities Pseudo-Plutarch admired as much as Origen.[43] The Christian merely found in God a greater talent for impersonation. One lesson to learn from scripture, Origen summarizes, 'is something like this':

> the Holy Spirit uses prosopopoeia [*prosōpopoiei*] in the prophets: and if he introduces the person [*prosōpopoiēsēi*] of God, God is not the speaker, but rather the Holy Spirit speaks in the person [*ek prosōpou*] of God; and if he introduces the person of Christ, Christ is not the speaker, but rather the Holy Spirit speaks in the

sometimes overlaps. Also Jody Enders, *Rhetoric and the Origins of Medieval Drama* (Ithaca, NY: Cornell University Press, 1992), 56–61; and Gavin Alexander, 'Prosopopoeia: the Speaking Figure', in *Renaissance Figures of Speech*, ed. Sylvia Adamson et al. (Cambridge: Cambridge University Press, 2007), 97–112.

38 Marie-Josèphe Rondeau, *Exégèse prosopologique et théologie*, volume 2 of *Les commentaires patristiques du Psautier (IIIe–Ve siècles)*, Orientalia Christiana Analecta (Rome: Pontificium Institutum Studiorum Orientalium, 1985), especially 89–93 (on typological and prosopographical reading) and 126–35 (on the connection to theatre).

39 Tertullian, *Adversus Marcionem* 2.26 (*CCSL*, 1: 505; *ANF*, 3: 318).

40 Carl Andresen, 'Zur Entstehung und Geschichte des trinitarischen Personbegriffes', *Zeitschrift für die Neutestamentliche Wissenschaft und die Kunde der älteren Kirche*, 52 (1961), 1–39.

41 Plato, *Republic* 3.7 (394b–c); Aristotle, *Poetics* 3.1–3 (1448a); summarized by Bede, *De arte metrica* 25 (*CCSL*, 123A: 139–40).

42 Proclus, *In Platonis Rem Publicam Commentarii*, ed. Guilemus Kroll, 2 vols. (Amsterdam: Adolf M. Hakkert, 1965), 1: 14 (§1.2); Proclus, *Commentaire sur la République*, trans. A. J. Festugière, 3 vols. (Paris: Libraire Philosophique J. Vrin, 1970), 1: 30; cf. Demetrius, *On Style* 5.265–6, speaking of the prosopopoeia in Socrates' funeral speech (*Menexenus* 246d).

43 Ps.-Plutarch, *In vita Homeri* 66; text and translation in Plutarch, *Essay on the Life and Poetry of Homer*, ed. J. J. Keaney and Robert Lamberton (Atlanta: Scholars Press, 1996), 132–3; Origen, *Contra Celsum* 7.36, ed. and trans. Marcel Borret (SC, 150: 98); trans. Henry Chadwick, *Contra Celsum* (Cambridge: Cambridge University Press, 1953), 424.

> person of Christ... It is the Holy Spirit who impersonates [*prosōpopoioun*] all of these.[44]

The Spirit plays a prophet who plays, as it were, Christ and the Father. Likewise, according to Origen, Solomon had not written his Song of Songs *in propria persona* but rather 'in the form of a drama [*in modum dramatis*]. For we call a thing a drama... when different *personae* are introduced and the whole structure of their narrative consists in their comings and goings among themselves'.[45] In this particular case, the thing that needed explaining to Christians was not, for once, the Judaic content of the Song, since there hardly is any, but its overt eroticism—precisely the sort of secular indecency with which the Fathers invariably tarred pagan theatre. Nevertheless, throughout the Middle Ages, marginal rubrics assigned the book speech prefixes, turning the poem, which was entirely in the first person, 'into a drama'.[46]

One early medieval master of reading the Psalms in this manner—which is to say, dramatically—was Cassiodorus, Roman consul in 514 and therefore chief benefactor to 'the most spectacular of the annual games'[47] that would have been held in his name. He became quaestor several years later, then replaced Boethius, after his execution for treason, as *magister officiorum*—a position that required 'a certain priestliness',[48] he once said, prophetically enough, as he went on in retirement to found two monasteries and turn exclusively to religious writing. Before that he wrote government letters, in the first person, for higher officials. By occupation and training, in short, he was acutely practised at impersonation. 'How hard it is for a subject to assume the speech of the ruler', he once wrote in the voice of Theoderic (while explaining how great a challenge and honour it was for a quaestor to speak as the king), 'to be able to express what may be supposed my own, and, advanced to public honour, to create a glorious falsehood [*gloriosam facere falsitatem*]!'[49]

[44] Origen, *Philocalia* 7.2, in *Sur les Écritures: Philocalie*, 1–20, ed. and trans. Marguerite Harl, SC, 302 (1983), 328; trans. George Lewis, *The Philocalia of Origen* (Edinburgh: T & T Clark, 1911), 45. Cf. *C. Celsum* 1.55 (SC, 132 [1967], 226; Chadwick, 51).

[45] Origen, *In cantica canticorum*, prologue (*PG*, 13: 63A–B), preserved in the Latin of Rufinus; trans. R. P. Lawson, *The Song of Songs: Commentary and Homilies* (New York: Newman, 1957), 22. Further commentary and examples in A. J. Minnis, *The Medieval Theory of Authorship: Scholastic Literary Attitudes in the Later Middle Ages* (London: Scolar Press, 1984), 57–8.

[46] E. Ann Matter, *The Voice of My Beloved: The Song of Songs in Western Medieval Christianity* (Philadelphia: University of Pennsylvania Press, 1990), 57.

[47] James J. O'Donnell, *Cassiodorus* (Berkeley: University of California Press, 1979), 20.

[48] Cassiodorus, *Variae* 1.12.4, ed. Å. J. Fridh (*CCSL*, 96: 23); trans. Thomas Hodgkin, *The Letters of Cassiodorus, being a condensed translation of the Variae epistolae of Magnus Aurelius Cassiodorus Senator* (London: Henry Frowde, 1886), 152.

[49] *Variae* 6.5.2 (*CCSL*, 96: 230); trans. S. J. B. Barnish, *The Variae of Magnus Aurelius Cassiodorus Senator* (Liverpool: Liverpool University Press, 1992), 96.

Cassiodorus evidently had a taste for this kind of faking. He liked in particular to embellish strictly functional matters with a show of erudition so as to demonstrate the grandeur of his comparatively ignorant ruler. Again on behalf of Theoderic, for instance, he ghostwrote a letter to Symmachus, Boethius's later companion on the scaffold, informing him of a grant to refurbish the Theatre of Pompey. This he prefaced with a small history, which remains of some interest to historians of drama, however 'imperfectly erudite'[50] we might now find it. (Pompey's building was a touchstone for Gosson, too, who noted that it had been dedicated to the pagan god Venus).[51] Theatre as an art form originated, 'Theoderic' explains, when the Athenians first raised 'the rites of various deities in groves and villages . . . into an urban spectacle'.[52] Tragedy came from the Greek for 'goat-song' and owed its name to the usual reward for the best actor's singing, which would have been fortified, Cassiodorus thought, by some sort of 'echo chamber'[53]—presumably, as Boethius had said, the mask through which (*per*) the actor sounded (*sonare*) his lines. Cassiodorus probably knew nothing firsthand about Greek tragedy and had to rely on convention. About pantomimes, however, to which he next turns, he might have known a great deal, as the tradition still thrived. These actors performed solo and played all the roles. Partly by virtue of masks, 'the same body', Cassiodorus explains, could portray Hercules and Venus, a woman in a man, both soldier and king, old and young; so that in the end, he says, 'you would believe that in one man there were many, differentiated by such a variety of imitation'.[54]

By the time Cassiodorus came to his Psalm commentary these government letters were a thing of the past; a distinct preoccupation with theatrical *personae* remained, however. He describes his difficult transition to the contemplative life as at once facilitated by scripture (especially the Psalter) and obstructed by it, in that he found himself 'confronted with an obscurity which is interwoven in different *personae* and shrouded in parables'.[55] (A millennium later, Arthur Golding would prepare English Calvinists with the same warning: this book above all others in scripture 'wrappeth up things in types and figures, describing them under borrowed personages'.)[56] Several times Cassiodorus calls the Psalms—that 'record of

[50] Chambers, *Mediaeval Stage*, 1: 20. [51] Gosson, *Playes Confuted*, D7^{r-v}.

[52] *Variae* 4.51.5 (*CCSL*, 96: 177; Barnish, 80). [53] *Variae* 4.51.5 (*CCSL*, 96: 177; Barnish, 80)

[54] *Variae* 4.51.9 (*CCSL*, 96: 178; Barnish, 81). Echoing a complaint in St Jerome, *Dialogus adversus Pelagianos* 3.12, ed. C. Moreschini (*CCSL*, 80: 113); trans. John N. Hritzu, *Dogmatic and Polemical Works*, The Fathers of the Church, vol. 53 (Washington, DC: Catholic University of America Press, 1965), 365–6.

[55] Cassiodorus, *Expositio Psalmorum*, praef., ed. Marcus Adriaen, *CCSL*, 97 (1958), 3 hereafter cited as '*Exp. ps.*'; trans. P. G. Walsh, *Cassiodorus: Explanation of the Psalms*, 3 vols. (New York: Paulist Press, 1990), 1: 23. For commentary, Reinhard Schlieben, *Cassiodors Psalmenexegese* (Göppingen: Kümmerle Verlag, 1979), 40–8.

[56] Arthur Golding (trans.), *The Psalmes of David and Others: With M. Iohn Calvins Commentaries* (London, 1571), 5^{r}.

spiritual *personae*'[57]—explicitly by the name of *drama*: after all, the poems clearly fulfill the theatrical canon laid down by Origen and others, in that they proceed 'by the changing of persons [*variatione personarum*], as alternating speeches replace and succeed each other'.[58] A great deal of his commentary then takes on the prosopographical task of designating speech-prefixes, so as to provide, in the words of James O'Donnell, 'a precise understanding of who ... is speaking to whom'.[59]

These various personages speak ultimately to the mystery of Christ's own personhood insofar as Cassiodorus intended his commentary to reaffirm unambiguously the Fourth Ecumenical on Trinitarian issues: 'two natures, one *persona*' continually recurs, and yet that usage makes for a striking tension, since the Lord had inspired David to write one hundred and fifty mini-dramas requiring far more extensive personnel: the Church, prophets, sinners, and others. What does it mean to transform the speaker(s) of the psalms into *personae* while asserting, at the same time, that the book confirms the personal singularity of Jesus as God? The simultaneity seems to me to manifest in its way the conventional hope that Christ's humanity might be utterly representative, in particular of mortal wrongdoers, even while that same representation preserves his divinity from guilt or the undue finitude of dying: not even the punishment of death can end or disgrace him. It is as though Christ, who alone of the Trinitarian persons had a body, could be thought of as acting in scripture so variously, by means of further *personae*, you might believe this one innocent man contained a maculate many. That, at any rate, is one way of putting the basic mystery of Christian personhood:[60] the reader of scripture finds his or her special distinction from, and unity with, all humanity only in Jesus, this thoroughly individuated person whose particular distinction is to represent generically the whole fissured species as can no other broken individual; who in other words gives to the species, through such representation, a concrete existence and unity that social fracturing prevents in reality. Christ is Everyman *and* Jesus.

Of course different names were attached to the psalms, suggesting multiple authors, and Cassiodorus is at pains to prove that these were the musicians David had delegated to play his inspired compositions. Here, Boethius's etymology reappears in a different context: the players 'should sound forth' (*personarent*)[61] songs, written for different voices, prophesying the Christian revelation of a three-personed God. No goat-song, these—though other authorities were quick to

[57] *Exp. ps.*, praef. (*CCSL*, 97: 4; Walsh, 1: 24).

[58] *Exp. ps.*, Psalm 17, conclusion (*CCSL*, 97: 168; Walsh, 1: 195); for other references to the Psalms as 'drama', see *Exp. ps.*, praef., ordo dicendorum (*CCSL*, 97: 25; Walsh, 1: 43); *Exp. ps.*, Psalm 1, conclusion (*CCSL*, 97: 39, Walsh, 1: 57).

[59] O'Donnell, *Cassiodorus*, 151.

[60] Cf. Balthasar, *Theo-Drama*, trans. Harrison, 3: 203–8.

[61] *Exp. ps.*, praef. 2 (*CCSL*, 97: 9 Walsh, 1: 29).

point out that the Lord had allowed Jews to borrow instruments from the pagan cultures of Egypt and Greece as a concession to their spiritual weakness: 'If God received sacrifices and blood by reason of the foolishness of the men of that time', asks Isidore of Pelusium, 'why do you wonder that he should also have borne with the music of the cithara and psaltery?'[62] That last instrument had lent its name to the Psalter as a whole, according to Cassiodorus,[63] who argues that the 'irrationality' of such musical instrumentation, combined with the 'rational part of the human voice', presaged the coming of the Catholic Church, 'which by the Lord's gift was to believe with varied tongues and diverse blending in the single harmony of faith'.[64] The harmony that encompasses discord, here and elsewhere in the commentary (cf. *Exp. ps.* 97), is in other words meant to describe the Church's accommodation of converts and its co-optation of Jewish, Greek, and Roman cultural practices so as to produce a hybrid performance of 'universal' piety. Cassiodorus—who may well have been a convert himself[65]—evidently sees the instrumental element of the psalms as part of a pre-Christian legacy that had been tamed by the 'rationality' of Christians' singing.[66] The all-night vigils that the psalms made 'pleasant', according to Cassiodorus,[67] meanwhile appeared *all too* pleasurable to other authorities. They argued that these celebrations only continued under another name the pagan *pervigilium*, just as any contrafactum set sacred words to the tune of profanity.[68] Yet this was in all likelihood why so many pagans found in Christianity a suitable substitute for the rituals they were otherwise forced to give up: even followers of Bacchus could see in this communion a *more compelling* mode of performance.

The monks for whose instruction Cassiodorus composed his commentary would have committed the psalms to memory and performed them in their entirety on regular occasions during these all-night vigils. At a minimum they cycled weekly through the Psalter in carefully scripted rites, marking the hours, which regulation must have added a reassuring dose of Apollo to the psalms' bacchanalia. Here too, however, there arose a special kind of play-acting and a particular devotion to counterfactual happenings. Whoever recites the words of the Psalter, Cassiodorus explains (quoting a passage of major importance from Athanasius), 'chants them *as if* they were his own... *as though* they had been written by him... *as though* speaking about himself... [and thus] he *seems* to offer words to

[62] *Ep.* 2.176 (*PG*, 78: 628); quoted, along with others, by Johannes Quasten, *Music and Worship in Pagan and Christian Antiquity*, trans. Boniface Ramsey (Washington: National Association of Pastoral Musicians, 1983), 64–5.

[63] *Exp. ps.*, praef. 4 (*CCSL*, 97: 11; Walsh, 1: 30–1), citing Jerome.

[64] *Exp. ps.*, praef. 2 (*CCSL*, 97: 9–10; Walsh, 1: 39).

[65] O'Donnell, *Cassiodorus*, 103–30.

[66] *Exp. ps.*, praef (*CCSL*, 97: 5; Walsh, 1: 25).

[67] *Exp. ps.*, praef (*CCSL*, 97: 4; Walsh, 1: 24).

[68] E. Catherine Dunn, *The Gallican Saint's Life and the Late Roman Dramatic Tradition* (Washington, DC: The Catholic University of America Press, 1989), especially 56–9, 62, 101.

God'.[69] According to this, the most intimate, 'personal' relationship with God has to be performed, literally, when the reciter of a psalm takes on its *persona* as if it belonged to his own person. Only then, when the performer has ceased, for this fabricated moment, to be his everyday self, does he commune with the divinity that makes him the full person he really (or 'eternally') is. Alternately, one could say with Žižek, the divine here is itself nothing more than that 'unfathomable X'[70] which prevents a person—a self—from ever becoming self-identical, in that your fullest, lived selfhood is already split between a specific individuality and the phantasmatic (if not ruined) humanity that determines its nature. God is a *name* for that irreconcilable difference in identity, which, as a name, reconciles the difference—yet *only* 'in name', through a performative enunciation, as it were, at the 'mere' level of the Word.

The recitation of the psalms in any case formed the heart and soul of the medieval liturgy. Each of the five Mass Proper chants (introit, gradual, alleluia, offertory, communion) originates here, with the first and last retaining 'considerable similarity to monastic office psalmody'.[71] And though actual *personae*—I mean, masks—played little or no part in these church performances, that was partly because their dramatic function had been absorbed so deeply into the counterfactuals and contrafactuals of Christian theology and practice; by this means the masked drama of the classical age had been *replaced* with liturgy as a major pastime in the Roman empire: a psalm, explained Ambrose, 'is a kind of play [*ludus*], which produces more learning than serious discipline transmits'.[72] It was through this sort of play, rather than discipline, that Judea won Rome.

*

The empire's turn to Christianity was no turn at all in the eyes of Protestants like Gosson, who had the Fathers to prove how bankrupt and botched was the state of Christendom: apparently it had always been so. In the course of his confutation, Gosson cites Lactantius, Cyprian, Chrysostom, Ambrose, Augustine, Isidore—not

[69] *Exp. ps.*, praef. 16 (*CCSL*, 97: 22; Walsh, 1: 41); quoting Athanasius, *Epistula ad Marcellinum* 11 (*PG*, 27: 24A), trans. Robert Gregg, *The Life of Antony and The Letter to Marcellinus* (New York: Paulist Press, 1980), 110; my emphasis. Cf. Monika Otter, 'Performing the Psalms in Goscelin's *Liber confortatorius*', *Speculum*, 80 (2008), 283–302, at 293–4.

[70] Žižek, *On Belief*, 90.

[71] James W. McKinnon, 'The Book of Psalms, Monasticism and the Western Liturgy', in *The Place of the Psalms in the Intellectual Culture of the Middle Ages*, ed. Nancy van Deusen (New York: SUNY Press, 1999), 43–58, at 55.

[72] St Ambrose, *Explanatio Psalmorum XII* 1.9, ed. Michael Petschenig, *CSEL*, 64 (Vienna: Tempsky; Leipzig: Freytag, 1919), 8; trans. Íde M. Ní Riain, *Commentary of Saint Ambrose on Twelve Psalms* (Dublin: Halcyon, 2000), 5. Cf. Jerome's attack on Ambrose in *Sancti Eusebii Hieronymi Epistulae*, ed. Isidorus Hilberg, *CSEL*, 54 (Vienna: F. Tempsky, 1910–18), 697–8 (69.9.4); translated in St Jerome, *Letters and Select Works*, ed. Philip Schaff and Henry Wace, *NPNF* II, 6: 148: 'The recent patron of actors now consecrates virgins.'

to mention the church councils 'which are not the oracles of any one man but debated substantially by the heads of many' (*Playes Confuted*, G8^{r}), plus Aquinas. Clearly the trick was less to return *ad fontes* than to claim the mantle of learned tradition while accusing opponents of reverting to some version of paganism against which orthodoxy had been laboring from time immemorial. Not that everything pagan was bad: 'I answer with Tertullian', writes Gosson, 'that of things received from the heathens, some were revealed unto them by God for necessary uses and the benefit of man; some were inspired by the Devil' (B7^{v}), as for example drama of all kinds. Drama, 'Tertullian affirmeth', had been consecrated from the beginning 'unto Bacchus for the first finding out of wine' (C1^{r}).

That the most famous defense against this line of attack should come from an English Psalmist is probably no accident. The argument seems to have begun with Gosson's first anti-theatrical treatise: 'Pull off the visard that poets mask in', he advises his readers, 'you shall... bewray their vanity'.[73] He then dedicates the insult to Sidney. Like most apologists, Sidney adopts in response the terms of his enemy: the earliest philosophers in Greece, he counters, for example, 'durst not a long time appear to the world but under the masks of poets'[74]—even anti-theatrical philosophers like Plato, who is 'the most poetical' (58), 'for all standeth upon dialogues' (19). Rather than betraying Plato's vanity in any immediate sense, this debt to drama helps explain his antipathy: philosophy knows what it knows from poets, says Sidney, who 'did only teach by a divine delightfulness' (58). Their banishment speaks to the anxiety of influence: in Sidney's view, philosophers tend to behave like 'ungrateful prentices', seeking 'by all means to discredit their masters' (58). If there is finally a place in the *Defence* for poetic vanity or fraudulence, it is in poetry's freedom from the abstraction of philosophical 'precept' and the compulsions of history, which bind us 'to what is, to the particular truth of things and not to the general reason' (32). Poetry alone transmutes the particular into the general without giving up on sensuous specificity—a synthesis of philosophy and history that follows, in the end, from the *imitation* of a particularity to which poetry, as fiction, is not fully bound. However close such mimesis may place it to lying, poetry can never cross over since it is so much less substantial than deception, and even more hollow. The poet 'nothing affirms', in Sidney's formulation, 'and therefore never lieth' (52).

And only by poetic means, Sidney furthermore argues, can scripture 'imitate the inconceivable excellencies of God' (25). Just as there could have been no philosophy without 'the poets' persons' (53), that is, there could be no personal God whose particularity still rose above history: 'May I not presume a little further', writes Sidney in a crucial passage, 'and say that':

[73] Gosson, *Schoole of Abuse*, A3^{v}.

[74] Sir Philip Sidney, *A Defence of Poetry*, ed. Jan Van Dorsten (Oxford: Oxford University Press, 1966), 19.

> the holy David's Psalms are a divine poem? If I do, I shall not do it without the testimony of great learned men, both ancient and modern.... But even the name of Psalms will speak for me, which being interpreted, is nothing but songs. (22)

And more than songs, it turns out, since they regularly feature the kind of performance that earlier commentators had continually likened to *theatre*:

> for what else is the awaking his [David's] musical instruments, the often and free changing of persons, his notable *prosopopoeias*, when he maketh you, as it were, see God coming in His majesty, his telling of the beasts' joyfulness and hills leaping, but a heavenly poesy, wherein almost he showeth himself a passionate lover of that unspeakable and everlasting beauty to be seen by the eyes of the mind only cleared by faith? (22)

Sidney's appeal to the 'testimony of great learned men, both ancient and modern' on the issue of prosopopoeia links his defense to a familiar line of biblical interpreters. If nowhere else, Sidney could have read some of them for himself in a Psalter with a commentary from Athanasius and Basil compiled by his father's friend and correspondent, Archbishop Matthew Parker.[75] More than a millennium after these and other theologians took the prosopographical approach from profane literary criticism to justify the script-like qualities of scripture, it seems, Sidney *takes back* prosopopoeia and the 'free changing of persons' to justify poetry and drama, even the secular, as forms of art on par with the Bible. Now *that* is renascence.

The risk of these maneuvers occurred to Sidney as it had to his predecessors: namely, that when treated in such terms, the psalmist and prophet 'sank to the category of the writer', while the metaphysical reality of the personal God for whom they spoke might then seem 'stamped by the model of literary fiction'.[76] Hence another reason for the often-noted oscillation in Sidney between apologizing for poetry and conceding the grounds for attack; between a euphoric vision in which the poet, through sheer counterfactual artifice, 'maketh you, *as it were*, see God coming in His majesty' and the prim rejection of any poetry that might desecrate such 'unspeakable beauty' by speaking its name: 'I fear me I seem to profane that holy name, applying it to poetry, which is among us thrown down to so ridiculous an estimation' (22). You can see here a defense of poetry and drama at one with the Protestant critique, which at any rate was never a straight repudiation, since in demonizing the theatre, Protestants reaffirmed its proximity to spirit. For English playwrights, beginning already in the Middle Ages, the basic vapidity of dramatic poetry—its frivolity and lack of substance, its non-conformity with the world of fact—seemed to hold out against the work-a-day world some small vestige of

[75] Anne Lake Prescott, 'King David as a "Right Poet": Sidney and the Psalmist', *English Literary Renaissance*, 19 (1989), 131–51.

[76] Andresen, 'Zur Entstehung', 21.

transcendence, easily discredited as a grotesque falsehood the instant it was realized on stage or in a literary text as a 'merely particular' thing of this world, but a compelling force nonetheless. So compelling, in fact, that even *secular* poetry's ersatz transcendence openly rivaled religious performance, which strove for the same effects yet disavowed artifice by excoriating its competitors as 'idolators', 'pagans', 'heretics', and finally 'papists'.

The rivalry goes on to this day—perhaps most strikingly when critics argue that in place of medieval masks and wooden allegory, Renaissance playwrights first fashioned *personalities*, even more human than humanity itself had ever yet been: 'Why do his personages seem so *real* to us', Harold Bloom asks of Shakespeare, 'and how could he contrive that illusion so persuasively?'[77] For something of an answer—and an end—let us turn to where Bottom and company wonder how to stage credibly something so faint and ghostly as 'the person of Moonshine'[78] (then as now an idiom for bull). The *OED* cites this line as an instance of *person*'s theatrical meaning: the actor can present at best the *role* of the moon, by carrying a lantern. True enough, but I think that Quince, with the foolish wisdom we see also in Bottom, echoes a theology the theatre had banished. The light of the lantern, especially if reflected (let's imagine) in an actor's white mask, both represents and *is* the moon's substance to earthly beholders—namely, its shine. So too had Christ been considered God's person, disfigured on the cross but, just as impossibly, his perfect image (Col. 1:14–15; II Cor. 4:4). In this 'absolute identity', to recall Žižek, 'the Divine is the pure *Schein* of another dimension' (*On Belief*, 89), or rather 'the "almost nothing" which the sublime shines through his miserable body' (*On Belief*, 83). When the waking Bottom travesties the first letter to the Corinthians, he makes of *his* earlier dualism—half man, half... mask (all 'airy nothing')—a distant burlesque of the old artisanal revelation. Note that the miracle occurred only when the actor was wearing a prop inherited from Balaam and the ass at the manger, the ones going to Egypt and entering Jerusalem, among others.[79] From masks such as these you had earlier learned the mysteries of God, 'yea even the bottom of his secrets' (Tyndale, I Cor. 2:11).

FURTHER READING

Marshall, Mary H. 'Boethius' Definition of *Persona* and Medieval Understanding of the Roman Theatre', *Speculum*, 25 (1950), 471–82

77 Harold Bloom, *Shakespeare: The Invention of the Human* (New York: Riverhead Books, 1998), 6.

78 William Shakespeare, *A Midsummer Night's Dream*, 3.1.57, in *The Norton Shakespeare*, ed. Stephen Greenblatt et al., 2nd edn (New York: Norton, 2008).

79 J. W. Robinson, *Studies in Fifteenth-Century Stagecraft* (Kalamazoo, MI: Medieval Institute Publications, 1991), 71; Chambers, *Mediaeval Stage*, 1: 332–4; 2: 54–7.

Nicoll, Allardyce. *Masks, Mimes, and Miracles: Studies in Popular Theatre* (New York: Cooper Square Publishers, 1963)

Rondeau, Marie-Josèphe. *Les commentaires patristiques du Psautier (IIIe–Ve siècles)*, vol. 2: *Exégèse prosopologique et théologie* (Rome: Pontificium Institutum Studiorum Orientalium, 1985)

Weihe, Richard. *Die Paradoxie der Maske: Geschichte einer Form* (Munich: Wilhelm Fink Verlag, 2004)

CHAPTER 32

PASSION

RAMIE TARGOFF

When Sir Thomas Wyatt travelled to Italy in the spring of 1527, he entered a world that was preoccupied with erotic love. In the approximately 150 years between Petrarch's death and Wyatt's arrival in Venice, Italian interest in love had not faded—on the contrary, it had grown only more and more intense. In the Neoplatonic treatises of Marsilio Ficino and Pico della Mirandola, in the paintings of Botticelli and Raphael, in the *trattati d'amore* (treatises of love) by Pietro Bembo and Leone Ebreo; in the learned commentaries on the sonnets of Michelangelo and Lorenzo de Medici, in addition to Petrarch and Dante; in the many medical works on lovesickness; in all of these different discursive and aesthetic forms Renaissance Italy focused its intellectual energies on the subject of love in a manner unprecedented by any earlier or later period.

The particular focus of this obsession for Italian poets was the female beloved, who was typically idealized as a kind of *donna angelicata*, or angelic lady. Beginning with Dante's *Vita Nuova* (*c.*1295) if not earlier, the longing that the French troubadour poets of the twelfth and thirteenth centuries directed toward their beloved assumed a sacred or spiritual quality.[1] The lady was not the object of sensual appetite and affection: she was a heavenly character, inspiring goodness and virtue in the poet. Consider, for example, Dante's description of Beatrice as 'una cosa venuta / da cielo in terra a miracol mostrare' ('a thing that has descended / from heaven to earth to manifest a miracle'); or his explanation that 'quando trova alcun che degno sia / di veder lei, quei prova sua vertute / ché li avvien, ciò che li dona, in salute' ('when she finds someone who would be worthy / of beholding her, that person experiences her virtue, because what she gives him redounds to his salvation').[2] Although different from Dante in many important respects—not

[1] On the French troubadours and Occitan poets who preceded Dante, see Gordon Braden, *Petrarchan Love and the Continental Renaissance* (New Haven, CT: Yale University Press, 1999).

[2] Dante Alighieri, *La Vita Nuova*, ed. and trans. Stanley Appelbaum (Mineola, NY: Dover Publications, 2006), Chapter xxvi, '*Tanto gentile*', lines 7–8; Chapter xix, '*Donna ch'avete intelletto d'amore*', lines 37–9. 'Salute' can also mean 'health', or 'well-being'.

least in his frank acknowledgement on multiple occasions of physical desire for Laura—Petrarch nonetheless maintains Dante's sense of his beloved as angelic. He refers to Laura's eyes as 'un dolce lume che mi mostra la via ch'al ciel conduce' ('a sweet light that shows me the way that leads to Heaven'); he praises her song and words as 'angelic' ('l'angelico canto et le parole'); and he imagines her as the ideal manifestation of Nature's pattern for heavenly beauty:

In qual parte del Ciel, in quale Idea
era l'esempio onde Natura tolse
quel bel viso leggiadro in ch'ella volse
mostrar qua già quanto lassù potea?

('In what part of Heaven, in what Idea was the pattern from which Nature copied that lovely face, in which she has shown down here all that she is capable of doing up there?')[3]

In the late fifteenth century, Ficino and his followers built from this poetry a Neoplatonic philosophy of love that combined the idealization of the beloved with a belief in the power of beauty to elevate the soul. Despite the equivocations of Petrarch's *Rime Sparse*, which are by no means consistently Platonic (Petrarch himself did not know Greek, and never read the *Symposium*), Florentine philosophers extracted from his poems the materials they needed to support a wholly Neoplatonic model of love in which the lover is guided from the terrestrial to the heavenly, and from the particular to the general.[4] Indeed, Petrarch's reluctance to move beyond Laura to a more abstract, universalized mode of love is overlooked by most of these authors, who cite Petrarch even more often than Plato in their treatises.[5]

As early as the 1420s, editions of the *Rime Sparse* with elaborate commentaries began to appear, in which the poems are subjected to a level of scholarly analysis comparable to the treatment theologians gave to the Bible. By the sixteenth century no fewer than ten separate editions with their own commentaries had been published.[6] On a typical page from one of these volumes (Figure 3)[7] the poem is

[3] All quotations from Petrarch's *Rime Sparse*, and all English translations, unless otherwise noted, are from Francesco Petrarca, *Petrarch's Lyric Poems; The Rime Sparse and Other Lyrics*, ed. and trans. Robert M. Durling (Cambridge, MA: Harvard University Press, 1976). Lines above from: Poem 72, line 23; 133, line 12; 159, lines 1–4.

[4] For Petrarch's knowledge of Plato, see Christopher S. Celenza, 'The revival of Platonic philosophy', in *The Cambridge Companion to Renaissance Philosophy*, ed. James Hankins (Cambridge: Cambridge University Press, 2007), Chapter 5; and Sears Jayne, *Plato in Renaissance England* (Dordrecht: Kluwer Academic Publishers, 1995).

[5] Cited in John Charles Nelson, *Renaissance Theory of Love: The Context of Giordano Bruno's Eroici furori* (New York: Columbia University Press, 1958), 73.

[6] See William J. Kennedy, *Authorizing Petrarch* (Ithaca, NY: Cornell University Press, 1994).

[7] *Incominciano li sonetti cõ cãzoni dello egregio poeta misser Frãcesco Petrarcha cõ la interpretatione: dello eximio & excellente poeta. mis. Fran. philepho allo inuictissimo Philippo Maria duca di Millano* (Venice, 1497).

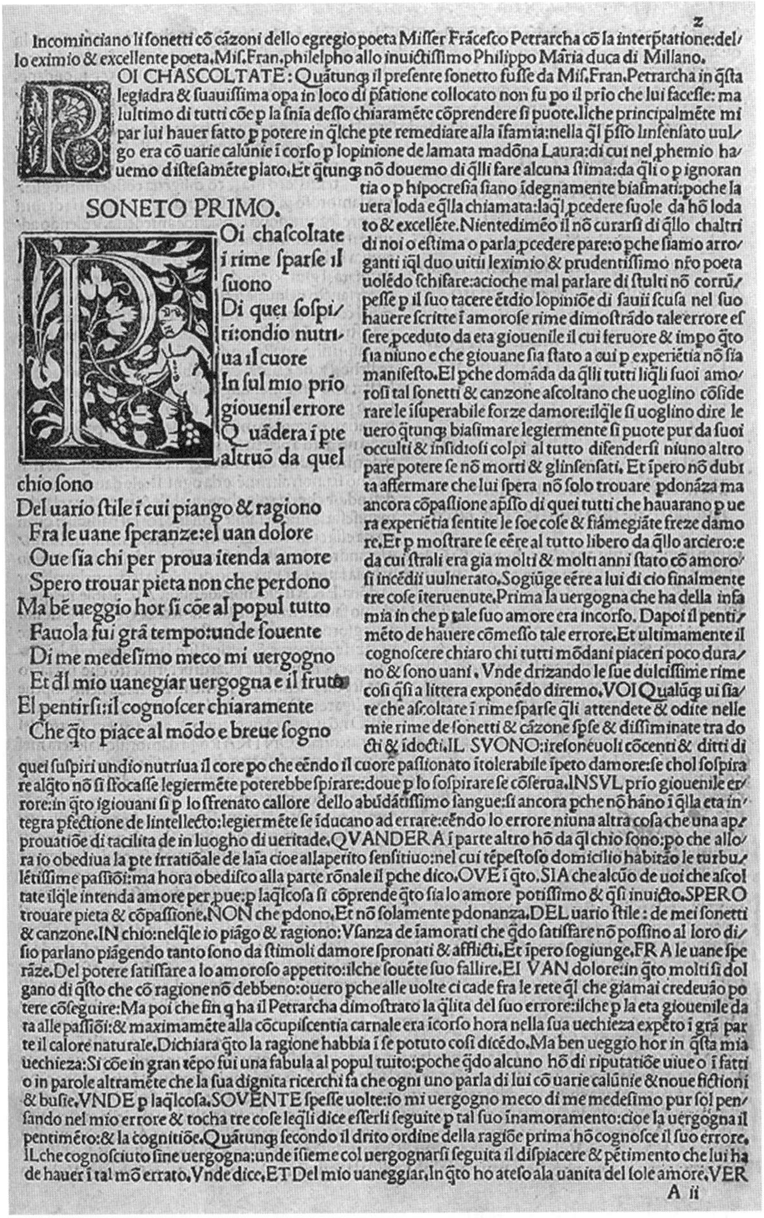

z

Incominciano li sonetti cõ cãzoni dello egregio poeta Misser Fräcesco Petrarcha cõ la interptatione: dello eximio & excellente poeta. Mis. Fran. philelpho allo inuictissimo Philippo Maria duca di Millano.

POI CHASCOLTATE: Quãtunq; il presente sonetto fusse da Mis. Fran. Petrarcha in qsta legiadra & suauissima opa in loco di pfatione collocato non fu po il prio che lui facesse: ma lultimo di tutti cõe p la snia desso chiaramẽte cõprendere si puote. Ilche principalmẽte mi par lui hauer fatto p potere in qlche pte remediare alla ĩfamia: nella ql psso linsensato uulgo era cõ uarie calũnie ĩ corso p lopinione de lamata madõna Laura: di cui nel phemio hauemo distesamẽte plato. Et qtunq; nõ douemo di qlli fare alcuna stima: da qli o p ignorantia o p hipocresia siano ĩdegnamente biasmati: poche la uera loda e qlla chiamata: laql pcedere suole da hõ lodato & excellẽte. Nientedimẽo il nõ curarsi di qllo chaltri di noi o estima o parla pcedere pare: o pche siamo arroganti ĩql duo uitii lexìmio & prudentissimo nro poeta uolẽdo schifare: acioche mal parlare di stulti nõ corrũpesse p il suo tacere ẽtdio lopiniõe di sauii scusa nel suo hauere scritte ĩ amorose rime dimostrãdo tale errore essere pceduto da eta giouenile il cui feruore & impo qto sia niuno e che giouane sia stato a cui p experiẽtia nõ sia manifesto. El pche domãda da qlli tutti liqli suoi amorosi tal sonetti & canzone ascoltano che uoglino cõsiderare le ĩsuperabile forze damore: ilqle si uoglino dire le uero qtunq; biasimare legiermente si puote pur da suoi occulti & insidiosi colpi al tutto difendersi niuno altro pare potere se nõ morti & glinsensati. Et ĩpero nõ dubita affermare che lui spera nõ solo trouare pdonãza ma ancora cõpassione apsso di quei tutti che hauarano p uera experiẽtia sentite le soe cose & fiãmegiãte freze damore. Et p mostrare se eẽre al tutto libero da qllo arciero: e da cui strali era gia molti & molti anni stato cõ amorosi incẽdii uulnerato. Sogiũge eẽre a lui di cio finalmente tre cose ĩteruenute. Prima la uergogna che ha della infamia in che p tale suo amore era incorso. Dapoi il pentimẽto de hauere cõmesso tale errore. Et ultimamente il cognoscere chiaro chi tutti mõdani piaceri poco durano & sono uani. Vnde drizando le sue dulcissime rime cosi qsi a littera exponẽdo diremo. VOI Qualũq; ui siate che ascoltate ĩ rime sparse qli attendete & odite nelle mie rime de sonetti & cãzone spse & dissiminate tra docti & ĩdocti. IL SVONO: i resoneuoli cõcenti & ditti di quei suspiri undio nutriua il core po che eẽndo il cuore passionato ĩtolerabile ĩpeto damore: se chol sospirare alqto nõ si sfocasse legiermẽte poterebbe spirare: doue p lo sospirare se cõserua. INSVL prio giouenile errore: in qto ĩgiouani si p lo sfrenato callore dello abũdãtissimo sangue: si ancora pche nõ hãno ĩ qlla eta integra pfectione de lintellecto: legiermẽte se ĩducano ad errare: eẽndo lo errore niuna altra cosa che una approuatiõe di tacilita de in luogho di ueritade. QVANDERA ĩ parte altro hõ da ql chio sono: po che allora io obediua la pte ĩrratiõale de laĩa cioe allapetito sensitiuo: nel cui tẽpestoso domicilio habitão le turbulẽtissime passiõi: ma hora obedisco alla parte rõnale il pche dico. OVE ĩ qto. SIA che alcũo de uoi che ascoltate ilqle intenda amore per pue: p laqlcosa si cõprende qto sia lo amore potissimo & qsi inuicto. SPERO trouare pieta & cõpassione. NON che pdono. Et nõ solamente pdonanza. DEL uario stile: de mei sonetti & canzone. IN chio: nelqle io piãgo & ragiono: Vsanza de ĩamorati che qdo satisfare nõ possino al loro disio parlano piãgendo tanto sono da stimoli damore spronati & afflicti. Et ĩpero sogiunge. FRA le uane sperãze. Del potere satisfare a lo amoroso appetito: ilche souẽte suo fallire. El VAN dolore: in qto molti si dolgano di qsto che cõ ragione nõ debbeno: ouero pche alle uolte ci cade fra le rete ql che giamai credeuão potere cõseguire: Ma poi che fin q ha il Petrarcha dimostrato la qlita del suo errore: ilche p la eta giouenile data alle passiõi: & maximamẽte alla cõcupiscentia carnale era ĩcorso hora nella sua uechieza expẽto ĩ grã parte il calore naturale. Dichiara qto la ragione habbia ĩ se potuto cosi dicẽdo. Ma ben ueggio hor in qsta mia uechieza: Si cõe in gran tẽpo fui una fabula al popul tuito: poche qdo alcuno hõ di riputatiõe uiue o ĩ fatti o in parole altramẽte che la sua dignita ricerchi fa che ogni uno parla di lui cõ uarie calũnie & noue fictioni & busie. VNDE p laqlcosa. SOVENTE spesse uolte: io mi uergogno meco di me medesimo pur sol pensando nel mio errore & tocha tre cose leqli dice esserli seguite p tal suo ĩnamoramento: cioe la uergogna il pentimẽto: & la cognitiõe. Quãtunq; secondo il drito ordine della ragiõe prima hõ cognosce il suo errore. ILche cognosciuto sine uergogna: unde ĩsieme col uergognarsi seguita il dispiacere & pẽtimento che lui ha de hauer ĩ tal mõ errato. Vnde dice. ET Del mio uaneggiar. In qto ho atteso ala uanita del sole amore. VER

SONETO PRIMO.

POi chascoltate ĩ rime sparse il suono
Di quei sospiri ondio nutriua il cuore
In sul mio prio giouenil errore
Quãdera ĩ pte altruõ da quel chio sono
Del uario stile ĩ cui piango & ragiono
Fra le uane speranze: el uan dolore
Oue sia chi per proua ĩtenda amore
Spero trouar pieta non che perdono
Ma bẽ ueggio hor si cõe al popul tutto
Fauola fui grã tempo: unde souente
Di me medesimo meco mi uergogno
Et dl mio uanegiar uergogna e il frutto
El pentirsi: il cognoscer chiaramente
Che qto piace al mõdo e breue sogno

A ii

Figure 3 Francesco Petrarca, *Rime* (Venice: Bartholomaeus de Zanis, 1497), f.63 (sig. Aii).

positioned near the left margin of the folio so as to allow the maximum room for extensive commentary, with each line, and sometimes each word, explained in great detail. In its physical design, these Petrarchan editions resemble biblical exegeses done in the fourteenth century in Italy—we might compare Nicholas of Lyra's *Postilia* (Figure 4), where the line of scripture is similarly fenced in by elaborate glosses.

Although scholarly interest in Petrarch was unrivalled in the period, with the obvious exception of Dante, it was by no means only Petrarch and Dante who received major critical attention. The Italian tendency to take love lyric seriously, to treat it as part of an important intellectual and philosophical development, manifests itself throughout the period. Among other notable examples: nine commentaries were written on Guido Cavalcanti's poem, *Donna mi prega*, the first of which was composed in the early 1300s by a learned doctor, Dino del Garbo, who regarded Cavalcanti's poem as a medical case history describing the appetitive passion of love;[8] Pico della Mirandola wrote an analysis of a *canzone* by the poet Benivieni as a response to Ficino's treatise on Plato's *Symposium* (*De Amore*); and in the sixteenth century, a full lecture was given by the humanist Benedetto Varchi at the Florentine Academy on a single sonnet of the poet Giovannia della Casa, in order to explicate the meaning of love.[9] Many more instances could be adduced, but the central point is clear: the Italian poet's depiction of love was deemed worthy to be the subject of humanist scholarship, as if the poems themselves were the equivalent of philosophical treatises.

When Wyatt travelled to Italy in 1527, he would have been confronted, then, by a culture whose ideas about love were profoundly different from his own. No treatises on love quoting vernacular poets were written in early sixteenth-century England; no lectures were delivered at Oxford or Cambridge on English love lyric; no elaborate editions of English erotic verse were published with commentary or annotation. To the extent that Italian philosophers like Ficino were read in England, they were read not for their thoughts on love, but for other aspects of their scholarship. John Colet, for example, the Dean of St Paul's in the early sixteenth century, admired Ficino's theological treatises and even exchanged several letters with him, but there is no evidence that Colet ever read, or expressed any interest in, Ficino's *De Amore*.[10]

Petrarch himself had a significant following in early Tudor England, but his fame likewise derived from his moral, not erotic writings. His Latin treatises were widely known and imitated, and his long vernacular poem, the *Trionfi*, was immensely popular in the Henrician court, where it was read as a moralizing tale depicting the

[8] See Nelson, *Renaissance Theory of Love*, 36–9.

[9] Nelson, *Renaissance Theory of Love*, 137. Another of Varchi's lectures was devoted to *Rime Sparse* 132, 'S'amor non è', the sonnet that Chaucer translated into twenty-one lines of rhyme royal in *Troilus and Criseyde*.

[10] See Sears Jayne, *John Colet and Marsilio Ficino* (Oxford: Oxford University Press, 1963).

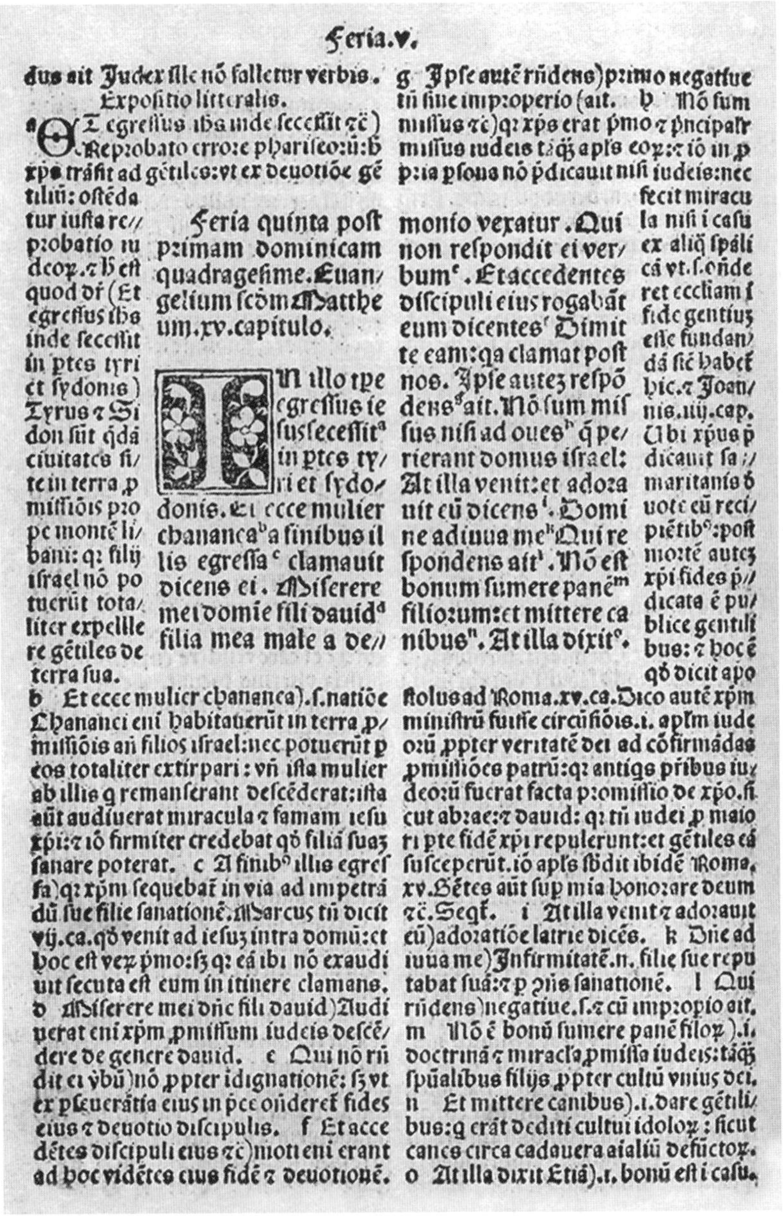

Feria.v.

dus ait Iudex ille nõ falletur verbis.

Expositio litteralis.

a Et egressus ihs inde secessit zc̃) Reprobato errore phariseorũ: h xps trãsit ad gẽtiles: vt ex deuotiõe gẽtiliũ: ostẽdatur iusta reprobatio iudeorũ. z h est quod dr (Et egressus ihs inde secessit in ptes tyri et sydonis) Tyrus z Sidon sũt q̃dã ciuitates site in terra pmissiõis prope montẽ libani: q2 filij israel nõ potuerũt totaliter expellere gẽtiles de terra sua.

Feria quinta post primam dominicam quadragesime. Euangelium scdm Matthe um.xv.capitulo.

In illo tpe egressus iesus secessit[a] in ptes tyri et sydonis. Et ecce mulier chananea[b] a finibus illis egressa[c] clamauit dicens ei. Miserere mei domie fili dauid[d] filia mea male a demonio vexatur. Qui non respondit ei verbum[e]. Et accedentes discipuli eius rogabãt eum dicentes[f] Dimitte eam: qa clamat post nos. Ipse autez respõdens[g] ait. Nõ sum missus nisi ad oues[h] q̃ perierant domus israel: At illa venit: et adorauit eũ dicens[i]. Domine adiuua me[k] Qui respondens ait[l]. Nõ est bonum sumere panẽ[m] filiorum: et mittere canibus[n]. At illa dixit[o].

b Et ecce mulier chananea). s. natiõe Chananei eni habitauerũt in terra pmissiõis añ filios israel: nec potuerũt p eos totaliter extirpari: vñ ista mulier ab illis q remanserant descẽderat: ista aũt audiuerat miracula z famam iesu xpi: z iõ firmiter credebat qd filiã suaz sanare poterat. c A finib9 illis egressa) q2 xpm sequebat in via ad impetrãdũ sue filie sanationẽ. Marcus tñ dicit vij. ca. qd venit ad iesuz intra domũ: et hoc est vez pmo: sz q2 eã ibi nõ exaudiuit secuta est eum in itinere clamans. d Miserere mei dñe fili dauid) Audiuerat eni xpm pmissum iudeis descẽdere de genere dauid. e Qui nõ rñdit ei vbũ) nõ ppter idignationẽ: sz vt ex pseuerãtia eius in pce oñderet fides eius z deuotio discipulis. f Et accedẽtes discipuli eius zc̃) moti eni erant ad hoc vidẽtes eius fidẽ z deuotionẽ.

g Ipse autẽ rñdens) primo negatiue tñ sine improperio (ait. h Nõ sum missus zc̃) q2 xps erat pmo z pncipalr missus iudeis tãq̃z apl's eoz: z iõ in pp̃ria psona nõ pdicauit nisi iudeis: nec fecit miracula nisi i casu ex aliq̃ spẽli cã vt. s. oñderet ecc̃liam i fide gentiuz esse fundandã sic habet hic. z Ioannis. iiij. cap. Ubi xp̃us pdicauit samaritanis d uote cũ recipiẽtib9: post mortẽ autez xpi fides pdicata ẽ publice gentilibus: z hoc ẽ qd dicit apostolus ad Roma. xv. ca. Dico autẽ xpm ministrũ fuisse circũsiõis. i. aplm iudeorũ pp̃ter veritatẽ dei ad cõfirmãdas pmissiões patrũ: q2 antiqs pribus iudeorũ fuerat facta promissio de xpo. sicut abrae: z dauid: q2 tñ iudei p maiori pte fidẽ xpi repulerunt: et gẽtiles eã susceperũt. iõ apl's sbdit ibidẽ Roma. xv. Gẽtes aũt sup mia honorare deum zc̃. Seqt. i At illa venit z adorauit eũ) adoratiõe latrie dicẽs. k Dñe adiuua me) Infirmitatẽ. n. filie sue reputabat suã: z p 9ñs sanationẽ. l Qui rñdens) negatiue. s. z cũ improprio ait. m Nõ ẽ bonũ sumere panẽ filioz). i. doctrinã z miracl'a pmissa iudeis: tãq̃z spũalibus filijs pp̃ter cultũ vnius dei. n Et mittere canibus). i. dare gẽtilibus: q erãt dediti cultui idoloz: sicut canes circa cadauera aialiũ defũctoz. o At illa dixit Etiã). i. bonũ est i casu.

Figure 4 Nicholas of Lyra, *Postilla super Epistolas et Euangelia quadragesimalia* (Venice: Johannes Hamman, 1494), sig. Dii[v].

triumph of eternity over time.[11] An inventory of Henry VIII's tapestries lists eleven depictions from this poem, and Cardinal Wolsey is known to have commissioned a full set of *Trionfi* tapestries for his chambers.[12] Despite the success of the *Trionfi*, however—a poem that lent itself easily to both didactic reading and triumphant wall hangings—Petrarch's other great vernacular work, the *Rime Sparse*, had no circulation whatsoever. Although the *Trionfi* was fully translated into English by Henry Parker, Lord Morley, sometime before Henry VIII's death, there was no complete English version of Petrarch's sonnets available during the sixteenth and seventeenth centuries. Love was not, in short, regarded as a serious matter for philosophical and humanistic inquiry in England as it was in Italy, and there was no equivalent cultural importance attached to the production of erotic verse.

The fact that Wyatt was writing from within a culture in which erotic love was not a celebrated subject of contemplation needs to be fully accounted for when we consider the changes he made to Petrarch's poems. These changes are perhaps best gleaned by listing some of Wyatt's most important innovations in negative terms—what Wyatt's sonnets, compared to Petrarch's, strikingly do not do:

(1) Whereas Petrarch famously idealizes Laura's virtues in a manner comparable to Dante's depiction of the heavenly Beatrice in *La Vita Nuova*, Wyatt is reluctant to praise his mistress, either physically or spiritually. There are almost no descriptions of Wyatt's mistress in any of his poems—no blazons or paeans to her beauty—and she is certainly not treated as a flawless, angelic creature.

(2) Whereas Petrarch (following again the path of Dante), depicts the death of his mistress as part of the narrative of his love, the mortality of Wyatt's mistress plays no real role in his poems. The relationships are threatened by unfaithfulness and inconstancy, not by death.

(3) Whereas Petrarch's sonnets transcend Laura's death, depicting a love that will continue in its intensity and passion once her soul has ascended to heaven, Wyatt never imagines an afterlife for love.

Literary critics have fully explored the first of these differences,[13] but they have paid little attention to the second and third, both of which address the role that death

[11] A letter survives, for example, from Edmund Bonner, the Catholic bishop of London (1540–9, 1553–9) to Thomas Cromwell, in which he reminds him that 'As you wished to make me a good Italian some time since, by promising to lend me the "Triumphs of Petrarch", I beg you to send it by Mr. Augustine's servant'; *L&P*, 4: 3.2850. Thomas More is also likely to have used the poem as the partial model for his wall hangings depicting nine pageants; six of these depict the same triumphs as Petrarch's. See Robert Coogan, 'Petrarch's *Trionfi* and the English Renaissance', in *Studies in Philology*, 67 (1970), 306–27.

[12] See Coogan for details of Lord Morley's translation. For the tapestries, see Thomas P. Campbell, *Henry VIII and the Art of Majesty* (New Haven, CT: Yale University Press, 2007), 149–53, and *passim*.

[13] See, for example, Edmund K. Chambers, *Sir Thomas Wyatt and Some Collected Studies* (London: Sidgwick & Jackson, 1933), 129; A. K. Foxwell, *The Poems of Sir Thomas Wiat*, 2 vols. (London: Hodden and Stoughton for the University of London Press, 1913), 2: 48; both cited in Patricia

plays in the poems.[14] This is a surprising, and consequential, oversight, for the fact that Wyatt never imagines an afterlife for love represents one of his most significant alterations to the Petrarchan tradition. When Wyatt translated Petrarch's poems, he stripped from them one of their most fundamental features: the idea that erotic love could transcend the beloved's death. This refusal of posthumous love was conditioned, I will argue, by the particular theological and philosophical beliefs of the world in which Wyatt lived, beliefs that have been almost entirely ignored in the critical treatment of his erotic poems. Although readers have long noted the ways that Wyatt's Protestantism affected his translation of the Penitential Psalms, no comparable account has been given of how his religion may have influenced his translations of Petrarchan lyrics.

For much of the twentieth century, literary critics generally framed the encounter between Wyatt and Petrarch as one between a textually impoverished lyric tradition in Tudor England and the richly textual poetic landscape of Renaissance Italy.[15] In his 1904 study of Elizabethan sonnets, Sidney Lee summarized Wyatt's love lyric as 'the reflection of a foreign substance', and approvingly cited George Puttenham's 1589 assessment of Wyatt and Surrey as the 'two chieftains, who having travailed into Italie . . . greatly polished our rude and homely maner of vulgar Poesie'.[16] In his classic treatment of literary imitation, *The Light in Troy*, Thomas Greene similarly described Wyatt's literary accomplishments in terms of the 'inherited poverty and willed asceticism' of English verse.[17] Wyatt's poetry, Greene argues, 'reflects the moral, social, and linguistic disarray caused by the disappearance of medieval ethical-political norms'. He labels the poems 'postfeudal' (255).

More recent studies have defended the depth and sophistication of English literary culture in the late medieval period, and have sought to establish continuity rather than rupture between Wyatt and his medieval English predecessors. Colin Burrow, for example, argues that Wyatt, 'does not make or mark a decisive break with the "medieval" past: rather he takes Chaucer's ability to explore, through a complex narrative, the range and complexity of key terms, and crushes it into the

Thomson, 'Wyatt and the Petrarchan Commentators', *The Review of English Studies*, new series, 10 (1959), 225–33. For additional comments on Wyatt's avoidance of 'descriptions of nature and of women', see Thomas Greene, *The Light in Troy: Imitation and Discovery in Renaissance Poetry* (New Haven, CT: Yale University Press, 1982), 247.

14 Indeed, with the exception of Patricia Thomson, one of Wyatt's pre-eminent editors and scholars in the mid-twentieth century, no one seems to have drawn attention to these differences directly, and Thomson herself does so only in passing; Patricia Thomson, *Sir Thomas Wyatt and his Background* (Stanford, CA: Stanford University Press, 1964), 179–80.

15 For the origins of Tudor lyric in medieval musical forms, see John Stevens, *Music and Poetry in the Early Tudor Court* (London: Methuen, 1961).

16 Sidney Lee (ed.), *Elizabethan Sonnets*, 2 vols. (Westminster: Archibald Constable, 1904), 1: xxix.

17 Greene, *The Light in Troy*, 247 and 255.

brief compass of a lyric'.[18] Derek Pearsall, speaking of Wyatt's ballades and courtly love lyrics, declares that 'there is as yet no break with the medieval tradition, and Wyatt, for all his laboured innovations elsewhere, appears here as very much the inheritor'. In these accounts, Wyatt becomes one of the last medieval poets, building from the vernacular traditions he inherited rather than making real innovations of his own.[19]

Although these two types of argument are in many ways diametrically opposed, they share a total inattention to the effect that the Protestant Reformation may have had on Wyatt's Petrarchan poems. In the first case, Wyatt represents a belated participant in the continental development of Renaissance poetry; in the second, he represents a belated participant in the English development of medieval verse. In both scenarios, Wyatt is seen as responding to poetic conventions without possessing any new theological or philosophical frameworks that would have furnished him with a different set of tools.[20] The only available alternative to the accounts put forth so far is one that reads Wyatt's Petrarchan poems as responding to the complex dynamics of social and political power at the Henrician court. This argument, first made by Stephen Greenblatt and more recently advanced, in slightly different terms, by James Simpson, is admirably attentive to the ways in which Wyatt's immediate historical context influenced his poems.[21] And yet, these critics ignore altogether the role that Protestantism may have played in shaping Wyatt's depiction of love.

To understand what happened when Wyatt translated Petrarch's sonnets, we need to recognize fully the differences between fourteenth-century Catholic and sixteenth-century Protestant approaches to love. Without acknowledging the ways in which Protestantism was fundamentally hostile not only to the idea of idolizing the female beloved, but also to the notion of a transcendent, posthumous love, we cannot begin to understand the implications of Wyatt's alterations to Petrarch's poems.[22] Far from strictly literary acts of imitation, Wyatt's translations reflect a

[18] Colin Burrow, 'The Experience of Exclusion: Literature and Politics in the Reigns of Henry VII and Henry VIII', in *The Cambridge History of Medieval English Literature*, ed. David Wallace (Cambridge: Cambridge University Press, 1999), 793–820, at 810.

[19] Derek Pearsall, *Old English and Middle English Poetry*, vol. 1 of *The Routledge History of English Poetry*, 4 vols. (Boston: Routledge & Kegan Paul, 1977), 221.

[20] Although she focuses on the nature of Wyatt's language and not on his philosophical or theological disposition, Helen Cooper wonderfully captures, and redresses, the critical tendency to explain Wyatt as beholden to either English traditions of courtly verse or to Petrarchism: 'Wyatt and Chaucer: A Re-appraisal', *Leeds Studies in English*, 13 (1982), 104–23.

[21] See Stephen Greenblatt, *Renaissance Self-Fashioning* (Chicago: University of Chicago Press, 1980); James Simpson, 'The Elegiac', Chapter 4 of *Reform and Cultural Revolution*, The Oxford English Literary History, Vol. 2, 1350–1547 (Oxford: Oxford University Press, 2002), 121–90.

[22] There were, however, sixteenth-century Italian commentators who sought to claim Petrarch as a proto-Protestant. See Kennedy, *Authorizing Petrarch*, 67–75.

profound rethinking of the relationship between love and death in the wake of the Reformation.

*

When Wyatt read Petrarch's *Rime Sparse*, he would have found the poems divided into two crucial categories: those poems that were written 'in vita di madonna Laura', when Laura was alive, and those written 'in morte di madonna Laura', following her death. This was not a division that Petrarch himself introduced to his sequence, and it is not necessarily a division that he would have embraced, so continuous were his feelings for Laura across the grave.[23] The bipartite structure for the *Rime Sparse* was introduced by Aldus Manutius in his 1501 edition, an edition overseen by the famous courtier and humanist Pietro Bembo, and it was subsequently adopted by nearly all sixteenth-century editions. Many of these editions were printed in Venice, where Wyatt arrived in the spring of 1527 on a mission for Sir John Russell. Wyatt's twentieth-century editor Patricia Thomson has convincingly shown that Wyatt most likely used the Vellutello commentary from 1525 as the basis for his translations.[24] This edition not only divided the 'in vita' and 'in morte' poems from each other, but also added a third section for those poems that did not address the poet's love for Laura directly.

What does it mean for Petrarch to have written over 100 of his 366 poems after Laura has died? As anyone who has read through the *Rime Sparse* can testify, what it does *not* mean is that the 'in morte' poems are strictly elegiac, filled with longing for someone who is irreparably lost.[25] To be sure, Petrarch elaborately mourns Laura's death, but this mourning is tempered by his anticipation of a reunion on the other side. We see this as early as poem 268, only the fifth poem in the 'in morte' series and the first to announce her death definitively. No sooner has Petrarch declared that Laura is dead than he expresses his hope to join her as soon as possible: 'Madonna è morta et à seco il mio core / Et volendol seguire / interromper conven quest'anni rei' ('My lady is dead and has my heart with her, and if I wish to follow it I must break off these cruel years,' lines 4–6). Her possession of his heart creates a bond between his earthly self and her heavenly one—it is ostensibly his heart, and not his beloved, which he longs to follow, although the two (his heart, his beloved) are completely intertwined. The pattern he establishes here, moreover—to declare a seemingly absolute end ('Madonna è morta') only to soften its finality with the hope of a future encounter ('volendol seguire')—repeats itself in the poem's very next lines. Petrarch asserts that he will

[23] In Petrarch's manuscript in the Vatican (Vat. Latin 2195), however, he left seven blank pages after poem 263, suggesting his desire to create some form of division between the poems 'in vita' and 'in morte'.

[24] Patricia Thomson, 'Wyatt and the Petrarchan Commentators'. On Wyatt's travels in Italy, see Kenneth Muir, *Life and Letters of Sir Thomas Wyatt* (Liverpool: Liverpool University Press, 1963).

[25] I use 'elegiac' here as a reference not to the classical genre of elegy, but to a poetics of mourning. For further definition of this form, see Peter M. Sacks, *The English Elegy: Studies in the Genre from Spenser to Yeats* (Baltimore, MD: Johns Hopkins University Press, 1985).

never see Laura again—'perché mai veder lei' (line 7)—only to qualify this 'mai' (never) in the enjambed next line, which begins 'di qua'(line 8): he will never see her again, from this side.

In this early 'in morte' poem, Petrarch negotiates his future with Laura, wavering between the seeming finality of their separation and the prospect of their posthumous reunion. As the sequence continues, the absoluteness of their current separation from each other disappears as a serious possibility. To return to the question of what it means for over one hundred poems to be written after Laura's death, one obvious answer is that it allows Petrarch to embark upon an entirely new phase of his relationship to her, a phase in which he speaks to her spirit on a more or less regular basis. One of the most startling features of the *Rime Sparse* is the lack of interruption in Petrarch's exchanges with Laura once she is dead. In *Rime Sparse* 279, for example, he describes Laura's responding from heaven to his heavy sighs; she instructs him in this poem not to weep for her, 'ch'e' miei dì fersi / morendo, eterni' ('for my days became eternal by dying', lines 12–13.) Or in *Rime Sparse* 282, Petrarch addresses Laura as 'Alma felice che sovente torni / a consolar le mie notti dolente / con gli occhi tuoi' ('Happy soul who often come back to console my sorrowing nights with your eyes', lines 1–3). Lest we imagine her posthumous form has been reduced merely to a set of eyes, he describes his encounter with her as if she were still embodied: 'Quando torni te conosco e'ntendo á l'andar a la voce, al volto, a' panni' ('When you return I know you by your walk, by your voice, by your face, by your dress,' lines 13–14).

Readers of Petrarch have long observed that Laura has very little, if any, voice in the *Rime Sparse*, but she is much more present in death than she ever was alive.[26] It is only in the 'in morte' poems, moreover, that Petrarch describes something like a mutuality in their affections, and suggests their ultimate destiny together. In *Rime Sparse* 302, he lifts his thoughts

> . . . in parte ov'era
> quella ch'io cerco et non ritrovo in terra
> ivi fra lor che'l terzo cerchio serra
> la rividi più bella et meno altera

('to where she was whom I seek and do not find on earth; there, among those whom the third circle encloses, I saw her more beautiful and less proud', lines 1–4). Laura's placement in the third circle of heaven—the sphere of Venus, where the souls of love poets are said to dwell—suggests already that her posthumous fate is entirely bound up with, even determined by, his own.[27] This is what Laura herself assures him:

[26] See Nancy J. Vickers, 'Diana Described: Scattered Woman and Scattered Rhyme', *Critical Inquiry*, 8 (1981), 265–79.

[27] See *Rime Sparse* 287, where Petrarch describes the love poets Guittone d'Arezzo, Cino da Pistoia, Dante, and Franceschino delgli Albizi, all resting in the third sphere.

. . . In questa spera
sarai ancor meco, se 'l desir non erra . . .
te solo aspetto, et quell che tanto amasti
et là giuso è rimaso, il mio bel velo.

('In this sphere you will be with me, if my desire is not deceived . . . I only wait for you and for that which you loved so much and which remained down there, my lovely veil', lines 5–6; 10–11). The veil is a highly complex metaphor that Petrarch uses to many different effects in the *Rime Sparse*, but in this instance it clearly refers to Laura's flesh, which shall be returned to her at the resurrection.[28] The sonnet ends with both frustrated longing, as Laura releases her hand from his, and a sense of possibility—'Deh, perchè tacque et allargò la mano?' ('why did she then become still and open her hand', line 12). Had she not done so, Petrarch laments, 'poco manco ch'io non rimasi in Cielo', ('I almost remained in heaven', line 14.)

Rime Sparse 328 provides a similar mingling of conviction, hope, and loss, as Petrarch contemplates his eventual reunion with Laura following his own death. This poem focuses on Laura's heavenly eyes, which offer reassurance to his mortal ones that they shall see one another again:

Li occhi belli, or in Ciel chiari et felici
del lume onde salute et vita piove,
lasciando i miei qui miseri et mendici,
dicean lor con faville oneste et nove:
'Rimanetevi in pace, o cari amici;
qui mai più, no, ma rivedremne altrove.'

('Her beautiful eyes, now in Heaven bright and happy in the Light that rains salvation and life, leaving my eyes here wretched and poor, With chaste, strange shining said to my eyes: "Peace be with you, dear friends; never again here, no, but we shall see each other again elsewhere" ', lines 9–14). In this final line, 'qui mai più, no, ma rivedremne altrove', we glimpse the very core of Petrarch's aspirations for his future with Laura. Here, never again. But there, *yes*.

There are times, to be sure, when Petrarch is less sanguine about the posthumous fate of his relationship to Laura. But these occasions arise in the 'in vita' poems, before Laura has died, where Petrarch tends to fantasize about his death, not hers. (It is worth noting that until Laura dies, he assumes that he will predecease her.) In *Rime Sparse* 22, he pleads to the heavens to give him a full night with his beloved wrapped in his arms, 'prima ch'i' torni a voi, lucenti stelle / o tomi giù ne l'amorosa selva / lassando il corpo che fia trita terra' ('before I return to you, bright stars, or fall down into the amorous wood, leaving my body which will be powdered earth',

[28] This is an interpretation that modern and Renaissance commentators share. Durling glosses 'my lovely veil' as 'my body', and Vellutello glosses 'il mio bel velo' as 'il bel corpo di lei': Francesco Petrarca, *Il Petrarca, con l'espositione di M. Alessandro Vellutello* (Venice, 1568).

lines 25–6). The 'amorosa selva' into which he falls is almost certainly an allusion to Virgil's 'silva magna'[29] of mourning lovers in Book 6 of the *Aeneid*; Petrarch is imagining his ultimate fate as one of the shades whom Aeneas encounters in the 'fields of mourning', those, Virgil tells us, 'whom bitter love consumed with brutal waste'.[30] This is by no means a positive affirmation of Petrarch's prospects for a posthumous reunion. It is, however, consistent with his conviction that death will not alter his condition of loving, that loving Laura will be the defining feature of his afterlife.

One of the only instances in which Petrarch does not envision, either positively or negatively, a posthumous life of loving Laura is in *Rime Sparse* 82, another 'in vita' poem in which the poet anticipates his own death. This sonnet begins:

Io non fu' d'amar voi lassato unquanco,
Madonna, né sarò mentre ch'io viva;
ma d'odiar me medesmo giunto a riva
et del continuo lagrimar so' stanco.

('I have never been weary of loving you, my Lady, nor shall I be while I live, but I have come to the end of hating myself and am weary of my constant weeping', lines 1–4). Not only does Petrarch want to bring to an end his self-loathing and despair. He also wants to ensure that his death will have no relationship to his abject condition of loving:

Voglio anzi un sepolcro bello et bianco
che 'l vostro nome a mio danno si scriva
in alcun marmo ove di spirto priva
sia la mia carne, che po star seco anco.

('I would rather have a blank tombstone than your name should be accounted to my loss on marble, when my flesh is deprived of my spirit, which now dwell together', lines 5–8)

The belief that unrequited love could cause the lover's death was not simply a poetic fancy: European physicians treated 'Amor heroes', or love-sickness, as a legitimate disease; following the views of the eleventh-century Persian philosopher and physician Avicenna, which were themselves largely derived from Galen, medieval and early modern doctors recommended some combination of baths and

[29] Virgil, *The Aeneid of Virgil*, trans. Allen Mandelbaum (Berkeley: University of California Press, 1981), 6. 451. I am indebted to Durling for this observation.

[30] Virgil, *The Aeneid*, trans. Mandelbaum, 6.582–4. The Latin reads:

Continuo auditae uoces uagitus et ingens
infantumque animae flentes, in limine primo
quos dulcis uitae exsortis et ab ubere raptos
abstulit atra dies et funere mersit acerbo;
hos iuxta falso damnati crimine mortis. (6.426–30)

topical ointments, defamation of the beloved, and, in extreme cases, coitus with an aim toward evacuating seed.[31] There is a large body of medical literature on this subject in Italy and France, with testimonials from physicians who claim their patients have indeed died of erotic love (although there is very little of this literature written in England).[32]

In *Rime Sparse* 82, Petrarch not only declares his resistance to dying of love, which was understood as a real, not phantasmic threat.[33] He also makes clear his preference not to be *remembered* as having died of love—his particular concern in this sonnet pertains to what gets inscribed on his tombstone. As someone who never married and had no legitimate children, Petrarch does not imagine his tombstone mentioning a beloved wife or offspring left behind. But he does imagine, and reject, the idea that Laura's name will be engraved in marble as the cause of his death. This fantasy does not draw upon any actual Italian funerary practice—there is no tradition of Italian gravestones that record a broken heart as the cause of death, let alone name the deceased's mistress.[34] Nor was Petrarch likely to be buried alongside Laura, although couples were regularly buried together, and joint tomb sculptures were erected for high nobility. We might consider, for example, the splendid early sixteenth-century tomb sculpture for Louis XII and Anne de Bretagne, which depicts the couple kneeling, in what Erwin Panofsky terms a *representation au vif*; and lying side by side as decaying corpses, in a *representation de la mort* or 'transi' tomb.[35] None of these options was realistically ever available for the poet laureate, although his burial was hardly a private affair. But the substantial funerary monument in the town of Arquà erected six years after his death makes no mention of Laura, or of any woman, besides the Virgin Mary.[36]

[31] The poetic tradition dates back at least to Ovid's *Remedia Amoris*, in which Ovid solicits Cupid's help in curing love-sickness by reminding him of the many deaths he has already caused; Ovid, *The Art of Love and Other Poems*, trans. J. H. Mozley (Cambridge, MA: Harvard University Press, 1929), 178–9, lines 13–22.

[32] See the immensely learned and thorough introduction to Jacques Ferrand, *A Treatise on Love-sickness*, trans. and ed. Donald A. Beecher and Massimo Ciavolella (Syracuse, NY: Syracuse University Press, 1990).

[33] For an example of an occasion in which Petrarch welcomes the idea that he could die from love, see *Rime Sparse* 126.

[34] See Giulio Ferrari, *La Tomba nellarte italiana dal periodo preromano all'odierno* (Milan: Ulrico Hoepli, 1916).

[35] Erwin Panofsky, *Tomb Sculpture: Four Lectures on its Changing Aspects from Ancient Egypt to Bernini*, ed. H. W. Janson (New York: H.N. Abrams, 1964), plates 324, 348, 349.

[36] The Latin inscription on the monument reads:

> Frigida Francisci tegit hic lapis ossa Petrarcae.
> Suscipe, Virgo parens, animam: sate Virgine, parce,
> Fessaque jam terris, coeli requiescat in arce.

('This stone protects the lifeless bones of Francesco Petrarca. Receive, O Virgin mother, [his] soul: and you begotten of the Virgin, forgive [it], Now wearied of the earth, may it rest in high heaven.') Translated by Benjamin Woodring.

The idea, however, that Petrarch would not only die of love but spend his afterlife broken-hearted is entirely compatible with his Virgilian 'amorosa selva' depicted earlier in the sequence, and it is precisely this vision of his future that he seems in *Rime Sparse* 82 to reject. The poem ends with a relatively stern ultimatum:

Però s'un cor pien d'amorosa fede
può contentarve senza farne strazio
piacciavi omai di questo aver mercede;
se 'n altro modo cerca d'esser sazio
vostro sdegno, erra, et non fia quell che crede;
di che Amor et me stesso assai ringrazio.

('Therefore if a heart full of faithful love can satisfy you without your torturing it, let it please you to have mercy on it; and if your disdain seeks to glut itself in any other way, it errs and shall not have what it seeks; for which I greatly thank Love and myself', lines 9–14). These lines reveal something with very little, if any, precedent in the *Rime Sparse*: Petrarch's desire for immediate resolution in one direction or another; his desire that his love be reciprocated *now* or cease itself to be.

*

Of the twenty-five poems Wyatt translated from Petrarch, *Rime Sparse* 82 is the only one that directly addresses the relationship between love and death. Wyatt was on the whole uninterested in the 'in morte' poems—from the 103 poems in this part of the sequence, he chose to translate only two. In one of these, the sonnet that begins 'The piller pearisht is' (236),[37] Wyatt removed all discussion of the beloved, focusing exclusively on the death of a patron (Petrarch's poem mourns two deaths— Laura's, and Cardinal Giovanni Colonna's, who died a few months after Laura in 1348). Wyatt did not engage directly, then, with Petrarch's endless imaginings of his relationship to Laura after her death. This was an important, and conscious, decision, as he almost certainly had full access to Petrarch's poems, and could pick and choose among them. But Petrarch's depiction of his love for Laura after her death was obviously not what Wyatt found compelling about the *Rime Sparse*. For the same set of reasons, he most likely regarded *Rime Sparse* 82, in which Petrarch rejects the idea that Laura's name would be inscribed on his gravestone, as worthy of his attention. (Wyatt, as it happens, was buried in an uncertain location inside a small chapel in Sherborne Abbey, where a simple commemorative stone was laid on the floor with no mention of his wife, Elizabeth Brooke, whom he disliked intensely, or his one-time mistress Anne

[37] All references to Wyatt's poems are to Thomas Wyatt, *Collected Poems of Sir Thomas Wyatt*, ed. Kenneth Muir and Patricia Thomson (Liverpool: Liverpool University Press, 1969). The parenthetical numerals cited after the titles (first lines) refer to the poem's number in the Muir and Thomson edition.

Boleyn, or his long-term mistress Elizabeth Darrell, who remained his lover until his death).[38]

If Wyatt found Petrarch's refusal to imagine Laura as the cause of his death worthy of his attention, he also found Petrarch's formulation of this refusal weaker than he would have liked. Wyatt's version of *Rime Sparse* 82, 'Was I never, yet, of your love greeved' (11), is on the whole one of his more faithful translations, but it departs from Petrarch's in the spitefulness of its tone. Beginning with his address of Laura as 'Madonna', Petrarch's tone is for the most part polite and loving; only in the last lines does he convey an uncharacteristic frustration or impatience with Laura's 'sdegno' (disdain). Wyatt assigns a much stronger degree of agency to his mistress as the wilful instigator of his demise, and he assumes a more defensive position as he protects himself from her vengeful strikes. His poem begins:

Was I never, yet, of your love greeved:
Nor never shall, while that my life doeth last:
But of hating myself that date is past:
And teares continuell sore have me weried.[39] (lines 1–4)

Petrarch's 'Io non fu' d'amar voi lassato unquanco/Madonna' ('I have never been weary of loving you, my Lady') becomes Wyatt's 'Was I never, yet, of your love greeved', and the substitution of 'greeved' for 'lassato' (weary) is far from straightforward. Wyatt's line could mean that he is not yet weary, as Petrarch suggests, or that he has not yet suffered from loving her, or that he has not yet suffered from her way of loving (or not loving) him. Whatever Wyatt means by substituting 'greeved' for 'lassato', he fundamentally alters the line by adding the 'yet', which sounds a kind of warning that this weariness or grievance might come on at any time.

Lest the force of Wyatt's 'yet' has gone unnoticed, he repeats it at the beginning of the second quatrain, where it serves not as a warning, but as a signal of defiance against his mistress's murderous intentions:

I will not yet in my grave be buried:
Nor on my tombe your name yfixed fast:
As cruell cause, that did the sperit sone hast
Ffrom th'unhappy bonys, by great sighes sterred. (lines 5–8)

Recall Petrarch's declaration, 'Voglio anzi un sepolcro bello et bianco che 'l vostro nome a mio danno si scriva' ('I would rather have a blank tombstone than that

[38] The Sherborne burial register, moreover, simply reads: 'Mensis Octobris Illo sepultus est/ Thomas Wyatt, Miles Regis Consilarius, vir venerabilis.' ('In the month of October in that place was buried Thomas Wyatt, Soldier, Counselor to the King and man of honour.') Translated by Benjamin Woodring.

[39] All references to Wyatt's poems are to Thomas Wyatt, *Collected Poems of Sir Thomas Wyatt*, ed. Kenneth Muir and Patricia Thomson (Liverpool: Liverpool University Press, 1969). The parenthetical Roman numerals cited after the titles (first lines) refer to the poem's number in the Muir and Thomson edition.

your name should be accounted to my loss'), and consider what Wyatt does with this. First, he declares his outright resistance to his mistress's killing him—'I will not yet in my grave be buried'—and then he describes as a second, separate act of resistance that her name will not be 'yfixed' on his tomb as his death's 'cruell cause' (the characterization of the cause of death as 'cruell' belongs to Wyatt alone). Petrarch's spirit parts quietly from his flesh, and he places no blame on Laura for this rupture of the self—he simply refers to the future time 'che po star seco anco' (when my flesh is deprived of my spirit, 'which are still able to live together').[40] Wyatt, by contrast, describes his 'unhappy bonys' robbed of their spirit as a result of his lady's cruelty, which in turn caused his 'great sighes', which in turn led to his death. Excessive sighing was no laughing matter in Renaissance love poetry—it was imagined to shorten one's life span by releasing too much of the spirit, which is why Donne, for example, warns his beloved in 'Sweetest love: I doe not goe' against sighing too vigorously: 'When thou sigh'st', he cautions, 'thou sigh'st not winde/ But sigh'st my soule away'.[41] Wyatt, it would seem, has not had Donne's opportunity to exchange souls with his mistress, and hence his sighs hasten only himself to the grave.

Wyatt's resistance to imagining his death as a result of love is even more pronounced in 'The long love, that in my thought doeth harbar' (4), his translation of *Rime Sparse* 140. Both Petrarch's and Wyatt's sonnets chart the beloved's angry dismissal of Love, and Love's subsequent retreat into the poet's heart. It is after this account of Love's humiliation that the two poems diverge. In Petrarch's sonnet, Love 's'asconde et non appar più fore' ('hides and no more appears outside', line 11). Petrarch's response to this is to stand by Love—'star seco infin a l'ora estrema' ('to stay with him until the last hour', line 13). This decision is not made, however, out of loyalty to Love per se. Instead, it reflects Petrarch's overarching desire in this sonnet to die from loving. In the final, aphoristic line, the poet makes this priority clear: 'che bel fin fa chi ben amando more' ('he makes a good end who dies loving well').

Wyatt subtly but definitively refuses this ending—he refuses, that is, to affirm his desire to die of love. Instead, he transforms Petrarch's pledge to the experience of love into a pledge to the figure of Love himself:

> What may I do when my maister fereth,
> But, in the felde, with him to lyve and dye?
> For goode is the liff, ending faithfully. (lines 12–14)

[40] I have made a change in Durling's translation for the phrase 'che po star seco anco'. Durling translates this as 'which now dwell together', but the Italian emphasizes that they are still able to live together, in other words, so long as he does not die of love he is able to continue living, in body and soul, for some time longer. I am indebted here and elsewhere in my readings of Petrarch to Dennis Looney.

[41] John Donne, *The Poems of John Donne*, 2 vols., ed. Herbert J. C. Grierson (Oxford: Clarendon Press, 1912), 1: 19, lines 25–6. See also 'A Valediction: of weeping', which concludes on a similar note: 'Since thou and I sigh one anothers breath/ Who e'r sighes most, is cruelest, and hasts the others death' (1: 39, lines 26–7).

In place of Petrarch's dying by 'ben amando' (loving well), Wyatt imagines dying by 'ending faithfully': the promise of faithfulness is directed to his own master, and not to the beloved. What for Petrarch was a means to an end becomes for Wyatt an end in itself: the bond between the lover and his beloved has been trumped by the bond between the lover and Love.

We have already observed that Wyatt largely ignored the 'in morte' sequence in which Petrarch imagines his relationship to Laura's posthumous self—from all of these poems, he translated only two, and from one, 'The piller pearisht', he dropped all reference to the deceased beloved. The second 'in morte' poem that he translated, however, reveals the full extent of his struggle with imposing a more earthly and temporally bound understanding of love onto the Petrarchan idea of transcendence. In the long canzone, 'Myne old dere En'mye, my forward master' (8), a translation of *Rime Sparse* 360, Wyatt found his fullest opportunity to articulate the differences between Petrarch's understanding of love and his own.

Rime Sparse 360 stages a mock trial of Love in which the 'queen of our divine nature' serves as the judge, and Petrarch plays the role of chief prosecutor.[42] Both he and Love deliver their opposing arguments to this queen, who has traditionally been understood as the personification of Reason, as to the effect that loving Laura has had on Petrarch's life. When Love makes his case, he emphasizes the ways in which he has improved Petrarch's spiritual and moral worth through his love for Laura:

> da volar sopra 'l ciel li avea dat'ali
> per le cose mortali,
> che son scala al Fattor, chi ben l'estima:
> ché mirando ei ben fiso quante et quali
> eran vertuti in quella sua speranza,
> d'una in altra sembianza
> potea levarsi a l'alta cagion prima.

('I gave him wings to fly above the heavens through mortal things, which are a ladder to the Creator, if one judges them rightly; for if he looked fixedly at how many and how great virtues were in that hope of his, from one likeness to the next he could have risen to the high First Cause', lines 137–43)

Through the mouthpiece of Love, Petrarch delivers what will become in the fifteenth century the most conventional Neoplatonic account for how love ought to work, an account that Petrarch unequivocally endorses elsewhere in the sequence.[43]

[42] 'La reina/ che la parte divina/ tien di nostra natura' ('The queen, who holds the divine part of our nature', lines 2–4).

[43] See, for example, *Rime Sparse* 306, where he describes Laura as 'Quel sol che mi mostrava il cammin destro / di gire al Ciel con gloriosi passi / tornando al sommo Sole' ('That sun which showed me the right way to go to Heaven with glorious steps, returning to the highest Sun', lines 1–3). 'Lei non trov'io', he concludes, 'ma suoi santi vestigi / tutti rivolti a la superna strada / veggio' ('her I do not find, but I see her holy footprints all turned toward the road to Heaven').

The extreme beauty and virtue of Laura was but a stepping stone, Love argues, to rise 'd'una in altra sembianza' until Petrarch could have reached 'l'alta cagion prima', and Love blames him for wasting the opportunity to climb this ladder from earthly to heavenly things. Petrarch replies in anger that Love may have given him this exceptional woman to love, but 'tosto la ritolse' (soon took her back), away from the land of the living. Love replies, 'Io no, ma chi per sé la volse' ('Not I, but One who desired her for Himself', lines 149–50). The clear implication is that the 'chi' he refers to is none other than God, who has already been invoked on multiple occasions in the poem. This interpretation corresponds to that of the Vellutello commentary that Wyatt may well have used, where the line is glossed: 'intendendo d'Iddio' ('meaning God').[44] Given the poem's placement, moreover, toward the very end of the *Rime Sparse*, and long after Laura's death, there can be little uncertainty as to either why Laura is no longer present or who has taken her away.

When Wyatt approaches this material, he confronts that aspect of Petrarchanism that was most alluring to Italian Neoplatonists: the idea that the love of one ideal being is not an end in itself, but serves as a vehicle for reaching the divine. What made the poem bearable, we might imagine, for Wyatt's purposes, is that this Neoplatonic position is voiced not by Petrarch's persona, but by his opponent—the figure of Love. (This may explain why Wyatt chose to translate this poem among the many 'in morte' poems available, for inside it Petrarch gives voice to a position Wyatt would almost certainly have embraced.) The end of *Rime Sparse* 360 is in fact entirely ambiguous as to which position—Love's, or the poet's—Petrarch wants his readers to endorse. The queen has the last line, and it is entirely inconclusive: 'piacemi aver vostre questioni udite', she exclaims, 'ma più tempo bisogna a tanta lite' ('it pleases me to have heard your pleas, but more time is needed for so great a lawsuit', lines 156–7).

Wyatt's distaste for the Neoplatonic argument that Love makes is hardly ambiguous, however, and his alterations to the poem make abundantly clear where his sympathies lie. He denies his figure of Love the most powerful argument that he makes in Petrarch's poem: that the poet's love of Laura set him on the path toward the Creator. Instead, Wyatt's Love emphasizes only the temporal nature of his gifts to the poet:

> But oon thing there is above all other:
> I gave him wynges wherewith he myght flye
> To honour and fame and if he would farther
> By mortall thinges above the starry skye. (lines 127–30)

[44] The full commentary reads: 'E che amore rispose, Non egli haversela ritolta, Ma chi a volse per se, Intendendo d'Iddio, che prima non a lui solo, ma veramente a tuto l'mondo date l'havea.' Petrarca, *Il Petrarca*, 128^{r}.

These lines omit any reference to the 'scala', the staircase or ladder that was most conspicuously associated with Neoplatonic accounts of love even before Plato's *Symposium* was available.[45] Nor is there any explicit discussion of ascending upwards until reaching the Creator. In place of the Petrarchan wings that carry him to the divine, Wyatt's wings are meant to deliver only the human rewards of 'honour and fame'. There is a vague suggestion that something more could be had, something 'above the starry skye', but it remains strikingly unarticulated.

Wyatt's final gesture of resisting the Petrarchan narrative of Laura's heavenly transcendence comes at the end of the poem, when he obfuscates the explanation that Love gives for why Laura has been taken away. In Petrarch's poem, as we have seen, Love tells the speaker that someone, presumably God, has taken Laura for himself: '*Io no, ma chi per sé la volse*' ('Not I, but One who desired her for Himself'). In place of this more or less transparent account of Laura's absence, Wyatt provides this opaque alternative:

> 'Thou gave her me' quod I, 'but, by and by
> Thou toke her streight from me, that wo worth thee!'
> 'Not I,' quod he 'but price, that is well worthy.' (lines 138–40)

The force of these lines turns on what Wyatt means by 'price', which replaces Petrarch's 'chi' as that which has taken his mistress from him. 'Price' has a number of possible meanings in the early sixteenth century, and they pull in somewhat antithetical directions. In Catholic theology, it could refer to the currency of spiritual exchange through which grace might be purchased—good works, meditative exercises, or other forms of piety.[46] But given Wyatt's Protestantism, and given more specifically his aggressive refusal to associate his mistress with the heavens above, it seems unlikely that he meant to suggest her 'worthy' adoption by God. The more common meaning of the term 'price' would have suggested the beloved's 'honour' or 'reward', terms that do not necessarily carry with them any sense of divine elevation, but merely imply that she has left him for a worthy cause. This would seem to be the most positive interpretation of Wyatt's line available, and it would keep the poem within its decidedly secular and earthly sphere.

'Price' also carries potentially negative connotations, and within Wyatt's canon there is precedent for using the term in a pejorative sense. In his song, 'Alas, the greiff and dedly wofull smert' (5), Wyatt describes his mistress's leaving him for a rival of presumably greater wealth and stature:[47]

[45] The 'scala', a scale or ladder to the divine, is an image frequently used in medieval mystical writers, such as Walter Hilton or John Climacus, and its use does not depend on direct knowledge of Plato. Knowledge of this metaphor, and others, may well have come through Neoplatonic authors such as Dionysus the Areopagite. I am indebted to James Hankins for references on this subject.

[46] For the meaning of 'price', I am indebted to private correspondence with Walter Melion.

[47] Muir and Thomson make this connection in their 'Commentary' on poem 8, 277.

I have wailed thus weping in nyghtly payne
In sobbes and sighes, Alas! and all in vayne,
In inward plaint and hertes wofull torment;
And yet, Alas, lo! crueltie and disdayn
Hath set at naught a faithfull true intent
And price hath privilege trouth to prevent. (lines 19–24)

'And price hath privilege trouth to prevent'—'price' and its privilege have come before truth, Wyatt has been 'prevented' from keeping his mistress because someone else has offered her more. This idea of being trumped by wealthy, powerful rivals also calls to mind the famous ending of 'Who so list to hounte' (7), in which the diamond necklace worn by the hind declares her to be the property of Caesar ('Noli me tangere for Cesars I ame,/ And wylde for to hold though I seme tame', lines 13–14). To return to the translation of *Rime Sparse* 360: when Love declares, 'Not I... but price that is well worthy', Wyatt seems deliberately to complicate, and compromise, Petrarch's idea that his beloved has returned to God following her death. Wyatt's mistress has not died—she has simply been taken away by someone, or something, with a stronger claim.[48]

*

The central question in Wyatt's Petrarchan poetry is this: why is it that, exposed to a tradition in which mortality posed no real obstacle to the intensity of erotic bonds, Wyatt chose to depict an exclusively earthly and transient mode of love?[49] Recent critics have not posed, let alone attempted to answer this question; it reveals something about the state of the question that the answers we have been given date back over fifty years, and are either meteorological or racial in nature. According to

[48] This is one of the interpretations that Wyatt's early nineteenth-century editor, G. F. Nott, proposes: namely, that Wyatt 'designedly departed from the original and meant to intimate that "a richer rival had taken his mistress from him"'; Thomas Wyatt and Henry Howard, *The Works of Henry Howard Earl of Surrey and Sir Thomas Wyatt the Elder*, ed. George Frederick Nott (London: Longman, Hurst, Rees, Orme, and Brown, 1816), 2: 553. H. Howarth argues that 'price' is 'power and majesty. It is Wyatt's half-concealment of a perilous matter: it is a cipher for King Henry, who took Anne Boleyn'; Howarth, 'Wyatt, Spenser, and the Canzone', *Italica*, 41 (1964), 80–1. Both glosses are cited in Muir and Thomson, 276.

[49] There is one poem among Wyatt's translations of Petrarch that does not fully fit the model I've established: the long poem, 'In Spayne', a translation of *Rime Sparse* 37. Wyatt wrote this poem from his ambassadorial post in Spain, where he lived from 1537 and 1539, so it was written probably more than a decade after the other Petrarchan translations. Petrarch's poem ends with an expression of desire to be with his mistress, in either an embodied or disembodied form: 'io sarò là tosto ch'io possa / o spirto ignudo od uom di carne et d'ossa' ('I shall be there as soon as I can, either a disembodied spirit or a man of flesh and bone'). Wyatt does not drop this reference to the possibility of his posthumous spirit visiting his beloved—his poem reads: 'Then tell her that I come she shall me shortly se / Yff that for whayte the body fayle, this sowle shall to her fle' (Muir and Thomson 98, lines 99–100). Of course, what Wyatt affirms here is his desire to see his mistress, however fleetingly, and not to spend eternity with her. In this sense, the poem is more in the spirit of Donne's 'The Relique' than of Petrarch's enduring, posthumous love.

J. W. Lever, author of *The Elizabethan Love Sonnet* (1956), the English climate is to be blamed for the lack of transcendence in the English love lyric—'the elemental foe', Lever argues, 'persisted in the northern imagination... Despite occasional touches of gaiety, the great majority of surviving lyrics view love as pitiable and frail, at the mercy of wind and weather' (9). 'Perhaps we have to do with a matter of racial temperament rather than of creed', E. K. Chambers and F. Sidgwick propose in their *Early English Lyrics* (1907), 'and it is the Anglo-Saxon melancholy that inspires so keen a sense of the transitoriness and uncertainty of all mortal things.'[50] If we take these explanations at all seriously, we are left with the idea that Wyatt's rejection of Petrarchan transcendence had little or nothing to do with his reaction to the Italian love lyric—it was merely a result of the damp, northern air that he and other naturally melancholic English poets breathed.[51]

Putting aside its racial and climatological assumptions, there is something fundamentally mistaken about an argument that regards Wyatt's rejection of transcendent love simply as his adherence to medieval English traditions. First of all, there were medieval English lyrics that directly contradict this characterization of the poetry. We might consider for example, Chaucer's 'Complaint unto Pity', in which the speaker declares his everlasting love for his deceased mistress:

> ... I wol be youres evere,
> Though ye me slee by Crueltee your foo,
> Algate my spirit shal never dissevere
> Fro youre servise, for any peyne or woo.
> Sith ye be ded—alas that hyt is soo!—
> Thus for your deth I may wel wepe and pleyne
> With herte sore and ful of besy peyne.[52]

This is a poem that Wyatt surely would have known, and it is much closer to the Petrarchan model than to the melancholic, non-transcendent lyrics that Chambers and Sidgwick describe. Second, any account of Wyatt's poems that simply absorbs his position as a continuation of certain prevalent English attitudes toward posthumous love fails to recognize the ways in which he responded forcefully and directly to the Italian texts he was self-consciously imitating. Wyatt's representation of love as insistently this-worldly needs to be understood, that is, as an active decision on his part, and this decision reflects less on the dreariness of English

50 Cited in J. W. Lever, *The Elizabethan Love Sonnet* (London: Methuen, 1956), 10.

51 Although she does not explain what aspect of Englishness (weather, race, etc.) produced this, Thomson similarly presents Wyatt's rejection of Petrarchan transcendence as entirely typical of medieval English poetry. Hence she observes: 'Wyatt is therefore no more interested than his English predecessors in the love that survives the death of a beloved mistress, purifies the lover's soul through suffering and separation, and anticipates a reunion of souls in Heaven.' (Thomson, *Sir Thomas Wyatt and his Background*, 179).

52 Geoffrey Chaucer, 'Complaint unto Pity', in *The Riverside Chaucer*, general editor Larry D. Benson, 3rd edn (Oxford: Oxford University Press, 1987), lines 113–19.

weather or temperament than on Wyatt's desire to forge a mode of love poetry—in response to the Petrarchan tradition—that would not look beyond the confines of this world.

Such a desire stems to no small degree from Wyatt's embrace of Protestantism, a religion that ultimately rejected mainstream Catholic ideas about sustaining relations with the dead. A suspicion of such relations was not an entirely new development of the Protestant Reformation: it had earlier precedents among English Lollards and Wycliffites, and hence was simmering as early as the first decades of the fifteenth century.[53] But this suspicion of speaking to the dead became a central part of the Reformers' agenda, an agenda that is made explicit in the 1552 Book of Common Prayer's service for the 'Burial for the Dead', which, unlike its pre-Reformation counterpart, eliminated prayers on behalf of the soul of the deceased as well as any direct address to the corpse.[54]

Although Wyatt did not live to see the full articulation of the Protestant position in the Prayer Book, he was exposed to the theological positions of his contemporaries, Tyndale and Luther, who criticized purgatory, among other reasons, for collapsing the necessary boundaries between this world and the next.[55] And he was part of a culture that was more broadly questioning these boundaries in ways too varied and complex to enumerate here. What matters for our purposes is this: when Wyatt read a poem like *Rime Sparse* 126, in which Petrarch expresses his hope that should he die before Laura, her sighs might force heaven to relent in his purgatorial sufferings ('faccia forza al cielo', line 38), he would have recognized a Catholic eschatology that he and his fellow Protestants were determined to overthrow.[56]

Wyatt's desire to forge a non-transcendent love lyric was not strictly bound up with his Protestantism. It must also have stemmed from his lack of sympathy for Neoplatonism. Neoplatonism, in fact, had no real following in either Catholic or Protestant England in the early sixteenth century. Ficino, as we have already observed, had very limited influence on English humanists; when he was read, it was his *Theologica Platonica* and other religious works, not his commentary on the

[53] See Anne Hudson, *The Premature Reformation: Wycliffite Texts and Lollard History* (Oxford: Clarendon Press, 1988), 309–10.

[54] See Eamon Duffy, *The Stripping of the Altars: Traditional Religion in England c.1400–c.1580* (New Haven, CT: Yale University Press, 1992), 474–5. In this respect, as in other matters, the 1549 Book of Common Prayer was much more moderate than the 1552 version.

[55] On drawing the boundaries between the living and the dead, see Stephen Greenblatt, *Hamlet in Purgatory* (Princeton, NJ: Princeton University Press, 2001), 244–5. For Tyndale's denouncements of purgatory, see William Tyndale, *An Answer to Sir Thomas More's Dialogue* (Cambridge: The Parker Society, 1850), 120–33, 142–3; for Luther, see his discussion in *Christian Songs Latin and German for Use at Funerals*, in *Works of Martin Luther*, ed. Henry Eyster Jacobs and Adolph Spaeth, 6 vols. (Philadelphia, PA: The Castle Press, 1932), 6: 288.

[56] *Rime Sparse* 126 includes this expression of hope for Laura's intervention: 'Amor l'inspiri / in guisa che sospiri / sì dolcemente che mercé m'impetre et faccia forza al cielo' ('Love will inspire her to sigh so sweetly that she will win mercy for me and force Heaven', lines 35–8).

Symposium, which garnered attention.[57] Bembo, who is given the lofty speech describing the ladder of love in Castiglione's *Cortegiano*, and whose prose dialogue, *Gli Asolani*, sought to Christianize the Platonic idea of love, would have been tainted by his deep associations with the Catholic church.[58] Born into a prominent Catholic family, Bembo served as secretary to none other than the pope, Leo X, who had in turn been a student of Ficino's, so the associations of Neoplatonism and papistry were by no means insignificant or superficial.

Plato himself had very limited circulation in early Tudor England. Although private libraries had individual works of Plato's, there was no copy of his works in the university library at Cambridge through most of the sixteenth century, and there is no evidence that Plato was being read in any sustained or thorough way until well into the Elizabethan period, when his works arrived on English soil dressed in Protestant trappings.[59] The most popular translation of Plato at this time was not Ficino's, but that of a French Calvinist, Jean de la Serre, whose 1578 translation was published by the French Protestant printer, Henri Estienne.[60] To the extent that Plato was admired by Protestants, he was praised for the compatibility of his ideas with certain strands of Christianity. This was the argument made by Luther, for example, who declared in his Heidelberg disputation of 1518 that Plato was much preferable to Aristotle because he studied the divine and immortal.[61] But Plato's *Symposium* was not the text that Protestants embraced, and his metaphysics of love had no real following among Englishmen until much later in the sixteenth century.[62]

[57] See Jayne, *Plato in Renaissance England* and Jayne, 'Ficino and the Platonism of the English Renaissance', *Comparative Literature*, 4 (1952), 214–38.

[58] There is evidence that *Il Cortegiano* was circulating at Henry VIII's court—Edmund Bonner requests it along with the *Trionfi* in the letter to Cromwell cited in note 11 above (in fact he asks 'specially if you have it [for] the *Cortigiano* in Italian').

[59] See Jayne, *Plato in Renaissance England*, 124ff. Parts of the *Timaeus* were available throughout the medieval period—see Tullio Gregory, 'The Platonic Inheritance', in *The History of Twelfth-Century Philosophy*, ed. Peter Dronke (Cambridge: Cambridge University Press, 1988), 54–80.

[60] See Sarah Hutton, 'Introduction to the Renaissance and Seventeenth Century', in *Platonism and the English Imagination*, ed. Anna Baldwin and Sarah Hutton (Cambridge: Cambridge University Press, 2005), 67–75. On the Protestants' attempt to divorce Plato from the Neoplatonists, and reclaim him for themselves, see E. N. Tigerstedt, *The Decline and Fall of the Neoplatonic Interpretation of Plato: An Outline and Some Observations*, Commentationes Humanarum Litterarum, 52 (Helinski: Societas Scientiarum Fennica, 1974).

[61] Jill Kraye, 'Moral Philosophy', in *The Cambridge History of Renaissance Philosophy*, ed. Charles Schmidt and Quentin Skinner (Cambridge: Cambridge University Press, 1988), 303–386, at 356.

[62] See Jayne, *Plato in Renaissance England*, and John Smith Harrison, *Platonism in English Poetry of the Sixteenth and Seventeenth Centuries* (Westport, CT: Greenwood Press, 1980; first published by Columbia University Press, 1903). Harrison argues (137–8) that 'the application of the tenets of Platonic theory to the writing of love lyrics in the Petrarchan manner, however, was never anything more than a courtly way of making love through exaggerated conceit and fine writing... The love of the idea of beauty... in its absolute nature is nowhere present in the mass of love lyrics written between 1590 and 1600.'

Neoplatonism was not only affiliated with the wrong religion. Its aims were also incompatible with what Wyatt seemed interested in achieving for himself as a poet. Wyatt's Petrarchan sonnets are in an important sense his attempt to liberate the love lyric from Neoplatonism's apparent shackles. For in its description of love as an experience of transcendence, moving the lover, through the beloved, ever closer toward the divine, Neoplatonism denied the possibility of real endings or closure—the possibility that the poet might conclusively and irreversibly say good-bye. This possibility was tremendously attractive to someone like Wyatt, who understood his self-possession to be linked, finally, to being on his own. As he puts it at the end of 'Madame, withouten many words': 'Ye shall another man obtain/And I mine own and yours no more.' One of the most revealing instances in all of Wyatt's Petrarchan poems is his version of this line from *Rime Sparse* 134: 'et ò in odio me stesso et amo altrui' ('and I hate myself and love another', line 11). In Wyatt's hands, the order of feelings is reversed, and the two sentiments are represented as causally linked.[63] In place of Petrarch's 'I hate myself and love another', Wyatt writes: 'I love an other and thus I hate myself.' 'And *thus* I hate myself':[64] this is perhaps the greatest insight Wyatt gives us into why he regards transcendent love and self-contentedness as mutually exclusive.

The combination of an embrace of Protestantism on the one hand, and a hostility to Neoplatonism on the other, may not fully explain Wyatt's rejection of posthumous love, but it comes closer to a full explanation than any alternative provided by our critical literature so far. It does so, moreover, by situating Wyatt firmly in the world in which he lived, a world that was balancing a new religion with new literary forms, a world that was negotiating its relationship to a European culture that it simultaneously admired and from which it sought to establish real distance.

Without these powerful factors at work, it is unlikely either that Wyatt's poems would have taken the form that they did, or that they would have had the influence that they had over subsequent generations of English poets. For the consequences of Wyatt's decision to eliminate a posthumous mode of loving can be felt in the shape that the dominant English love lyric took for the next century. Although there are plenty of poets who praise their beloved in extravagant terms, and who suffer (as Wyatt himself does) from the anguish of love, there are few, if any, lyrics written during this period that describe an erotic attachment extending beyond the realm of the mortal world.[65] In the Christian liturgy for matrimony—both in England and on the continent—marriage vows are valid until death: in the words of the Book of Common Prayer, spouses are bound to love each other 'till death us

[63] From 'I fynde no peace and all my warr is done', Poem 26, line 11.

[64] Emphasis mine.

[65] I have not yet investigated the love poems of Catholic English poets, which will be the subject of a further study.

depart'.[66] Only English poets, however, seem to adopt these liturgical limits for their non-liturgical relationships, as if they cannot imagine *any* form of erotic attachment—marital or otherwise—reaching beyond the duration of the flesh.

Petrarchism, then, was not in any straightforward sense 'the distinctive genre of the English Renaissance',[67] as several recent scholars have claimed, nor was the English Renaissance lyric merely a continuation of its fourteenth- and fifteenth-century English past, as some medievalists would like us to believe. In its direct invocation and rejection of a Petrarchan love that transcends earthly limits, Wyatt's lyrics represent a new mode of secular poetics. This secular poetics never imagines love after death except in the most spiritually reduced, and insistently corporeal, forms—think of Donne's 'bracelet of bright hair about the bone' as his greatest hope for his shared afterlife with his mistress; or of Romeo's declaration over Juliet's corpse, 'Here, here will I remain / With worms that are thy chamber-maids.'[68] (If we look at Shakespeare's source, Arthur Brooke's translation of an Italian story by Bandello, we see that Shakespeare, like Wyatt, removed any trace of the Italian text's emphasis on the reunion of the two lovers' souls—gone are Romeus and Juliet's affirmations of their destiny to meet again in heaven).[69]

This tradition of secular poetics culminates, finally, not in expressions of Neo-platonic philosophy with love as a ladder to the heavens, but in Marvell's haunting vision of a love that is destined to become only ashes and dust:

But at my back I always hear
Time's wingèd chariot hurrying near:
And yonder all before us lie
Deserts of vast eternity.
Thy beauty shall no more be found;
Nor, in thy marble vault, shall sound
My echoing song: then worms shall try
That long preserved virginity:
And your quaint honour turn to dust;
And into ashes all my lust.
The grave's a fine and private place,
But none I think do there embrace.[70]

[66] The Book of Common Prayer, *1559: The Elizabethan Prayer Book*, ed. John E. Booty (Charlottesville: University Press of Virginia for the Folger Shakespeare Library, 1976), 292.

[67] William Kerrigan and Gordon Braden, *The Idea of the Renaissance* (Baltimore, MD: Johns Hopkins University Press, 1989), 158.

[68] Donne, 'The Relique', *The Poems of John Donne*, ed. Grierson, 1: 62, line 6; Shakespeare, *Romeo and Juliet*, in *The Norton Shakespeare*, ed. Stephen Greenblatt (New York: W.W. Norton, 1997), 5.3.108–9.

[69] See Ramie Targoff, 'Posthumous Love: Joint Burial in *Romeo and Juliet*', work in progress.

[70] Andrew Marvell, 'To his Coy Mistress', in *The Poems of Andrew Marvell*, ed. Nigel Smith (Harlow, Essex: Pearson Longman, 2003), lines 21–32.

Eternity is not full of hope for reunion—it is a vast, empty desert; the marble vault is not a place for poetry, but for worms; the grave is not the site for posthumous embrace, but for solitude and privacy. What began with Wyatt's stripping of posthumous love from the Petrarchan sonnet ends with the revival of the classical genre of the *carpe diem* lyric, a profoundly secular genre that was not part of Wyatt's repertoire, but might well be considered its ultimate extension.

FURTHER READING

Cooper, Helen. 'Wyatt and Chaucer: A Re-appraisal', *Leeds Studies in English*, 13 (1982), 104–23

Kennedy, William. *Authorizing Petrarch* (Ithaca, NY: Cornell University Press, 1994)

Nelson, John Charles. *Renaissance Theory of Love: The Context of Giordano Bruno's 'Eroici furori'* (New York: Columbia University Press, 1958)

Thomson, Patricia. *Sir Thomas Wyatt and his Background* (Stanford, CA: Stanford University Press, 1964)

CHAPTER 33

AUTOBIOGRAPHY AND THE HISTORY OF READING

BRIAN CUMMINGS

Autobiography is a concept that evades history. As a word it is inescapably modern: in English it first appears in the early nineteenth century, conventionally ascribed to Robert Southey in *The Quarterly Review* in 1809, although the word can be found a few years earlier.[1] Southey's friend Isaac D'Israeli warily predicted 'an epidemical rage for auto-biography'.[2] He has not proved wrong: autobiography appears in some ways the quintessential modern genre. And yet writing of the self also seems to be as old as writing itself. In this sense, autobiography asks deep questions about the periodization of history. When does such an untimely or timeless concept come into being, and what can be said to precede it?

This is especially true of English between Lollardy and the Civil War. Southey was a champion of the romantic revival of John Bunyan, writing a *Life* as a preface to his edition of *Pilgrim's Progress* in 1830. With *Grace Abounding to the Chief of Sinners*, Southey identified the beginnings of English autobiography in 1666. In the twentieth century, a similar claim was made for *The Book of Margery Kempe* written in the 1430s. The reception of the two books dovetails neatly for us the question of autobiography's origins. Kempe and Bunyan are both self-conscious authors, and describe a spiritual awakening or 'conversion'. The narrative uses the veracity of a life to prove the validity of a religious experience. In that sense the writing of the life is always mediated. Margery's work appears in the sole surviving manuscript with two prefaces by the scribe who copied the work sometime before 1450, perhaps at the Carthusian priory of Mount Grace in Yorkshire.[3] Bunyan provided his own preface. He offers to his 'dear children', the readers of his book, this 'milk and

[1] J. Ogden, 'A Note on "Autobiography"', *Notes and Queries*, 8 (1961), 461–2.

[2] Robert Southey, 'Portuguese Literature', *The Quarterly Review* (London), 1 (1809), 386, cited in J. Ogden, 'A Note', 361.

[3] Margery Kempe, *The Book of Margery Kempe*, ed. Lynn Staley (Kalamazoo, MI: Medieval Institute Publications, 1996), Introduction.

honey' for the edification of their souls: *It is profitable for Christians to be often calling to mind the very beginnings of Grace with their Souls.*[4] Neither Kempe's nor Bunyan's work is either unspontaneous or un-self-conscious: 'Thys boke is not wretyn in ordyr, every thyng aftyr other as it wer don, but lych as the mater cam to the creatur in mend whan it schuld be wretyn.'[5]

Autobiography thus appears equally available and foreign to either a medieval or a Renaissance model of history. Yet it is also a scene of persistent rivalry in the historiography of the two periods. Since Jakob Burckhardt's *Die Kultur der Renaissance in Italien* of 1860, there has been a war of ownership over the rise of human subjectivity. Burckhardt's view of *Der Mensch des Mittelalters*, and the corresponding awakening of *Personlichkeit* in the Renaissance, is one that refuses to go away. Lee Patterson has argued that Burckhardt's theory of the emergence of individualism has survived his more general eclipse. Perhaps it is time to reassess these hoary problems in the epistemology of periodization afresh. Here the key figure is Augustine, with whom David Aers, in his polemic 'A Whisper in the Ear of Early Modernists', begins the defence of medievalism: 'The place to which anyone seeking to write a history of interiority and the subject must return is St Augustine's *Confessions*.'[6] Patterson, too, finds the history of medieval selfhood bound up in a tradition he calls 'confessional Augustinianism'.[7]

Augustine is the always, the already, in the history of autobiography. 'It is hardly an exaggeration to say', says Charles Taylor in *Sources of the Self: the Making of the Modern Identity*, 'that it was Augustine who introduced the inwardness of radical reflexivity and bequeathed it to the Western tradition of thought'.[8] As the first autobiography, Augustine's work is sometimes allowed to exist as if outside history. Augustine's *Confessions* gratifies abundantly the historian's desire to discover an exemplary movement inwards: *Et inde admonitus redire ad memet ipsum, intravi in intima mea* ('admonished to return into myself, I entered into my innermost citadel').[9] The moment of reflexivization is expressed here in an exquisite moment of grammar. Augustine draws attention to himself and at the same time draws attention to this self-attention. That loveable Latin pronoun *memet*, using the emphatic suffix *-met* (meaning 'self', as in *egomet* or *nosmet*), but in the accusative having also the character of reduplicative self-reference ('me myself'), is used three times in a cluster in the *Confessions*.[10] In this sentence the use of polyptoton

[4] John Bunyan, *Grace abounding to the chief of sinners* (London: George Larkin, 1666), A3^{v}.

[5] Kempe, *Book of Margery Kempe*, ed. Staley, 1.1.

[6] David Aers (ed.), *Culture and History 1350–1600: Essays on English Communities, Identities and Writing* (Detroit, MI: Wayne State University Press, 1992), 182.

[7] Lee Patterson, *Chaucer and the Subject of History* (London: Routledge, 1991), 9.

[8] Charles Taylor, *Sources of the Self: the Making of the Modern Identity* (Cambridge: Cambridge University Press, 1989), 131.

[9] Augustine, *Confessiones* 7.10, ed. L. Verheijen, *CCSL*, 27 (1981); see also Augustine, *Confessions*, trans. Henry Chadwick (Oxford: Oxford University Press, 1991), 123.

[10] Augustine, *Confessiones* 6.11; 7.10; 8.11.

(*in... me... me, in... in... me*) only adds to the intimate sense of self-love. There is a wider significance here. Philosophers have noted how the very concept of 'self' has resulted from turning pronouns into nouns: English 'self', of course, and German *das Selbst*, as also in a different way French *le soi* (more fashionably, *le je*), and also neologisms such as *ipseity*.[11]

Augustine's modernity is also bound up for us with the fact that self-reflection in this sentence is inspired by reading books. Brian Stock has written about how Augustine identified the reflective self with the reader, thereby inaugurating 'the age of the self-conscious reader / thinker in Western literature'.[12] The two most famous moments in the work, among modern readers, are two moments of reading. In the school of rhetoric in Carthage he comes across Cicero's *Hortensius*: 'the book changed my feelings [*ille vero liber mutavit affectum meum*]... It gave me different values and priorities' (3.4). Then in Book 8, in his garden in Milan, he is interrupted by a voice in a children's game telling him *tolle lege tolle lege* and he takes up and reads the book of scripture by which he is converted.

Augustine's book is thus not *any* book in the history of reading: it contains within itself a philosophy of such a history. In fulfilment of his prophecy of the legacy of his book, we remember Petrarch, who a thousand years later went off on a mountain walk with the *Confessions* and described it as the seminal moment of his literary life; or Rousseau, inaugurating the new condition of romantic selfhood with his own *Confessions*. Stock has named this form of introspective reading 'meditative'.[13] Several times he has commented on Petrarch as a reader of Augustine.[14] Yet he warns against turning Augustine into a modern reader, insisting how the different inflection of medieval reading practices can be read *against* the modern novelist in an armchair. This essay is written in the same spirit, as an exercise in recovering a history of the reading of Augustine, the relationship of that history to a history of religious conversion before and after the Reformation, and also therefore to a history of autobiographical writing.

The problem in such a reconstruction lies in the deep roots Augustine has established within the culture we still live in, so that we can hardly unravel our own presence from within this historical memory. In addition, we are so conscious

[11] Jerrold Seigel, *The Idea of the Self: Thought and Experience in Western Europe since the Seventeenth Century* (Cambridge: Cambridge University Press, 2005), 13–14. The *OED* online (http://dictionary.oed.com) ascribes the first use of 'self' as a noun in this sense to the end of our period (1674) (*OED*, *self*, pron., a. and n., def. 8.3); in a developed philosophical meaning only perhaps in John Locke's *Essay on Human Understanding* (1690), ed. P. H. Nidditch (Oxford: Clarendon Press, 1975), 2: c.27. §9, p. 335.

[12] Brian Stock, *After Augustine: The Meditative Reader and the Text* (Philadelphia: University of Pennsylvania Press, 2001), 13.

[13] Brian Stock, *Augustine the Reader: Meditation, Self-Knowledge, and the Ethics of Interpretation* (Cambridge, MA: Harvard University Press, 1996), 14–15.

[14] Brian Stock, 'Reading, Writing, and the Self: Petrarch and His Forerunners', *New Literary History*, 26 (1995), 717–30; also in Stock, *After Augustine*.

of his presence that we attribute to him all kinds of inauguration that are not genuine. Augustinian scholars are more wary of stating Augustine's transcendental originality. How else do we explain how Augustine came to write his book, or his contemporaries to read it? Peter Brown's classic study is at pains to provide these kinds of contextual explanations. Conversion was a familiar topic to Augustine's community of readers. Conversion was a literary *topos*; Augustine discusses this himself, when he refers to the fashion for internalizing the experience of the desert saints, for instance the hermit from Upper Egypt, St Anthony. Brown says: 'Augustine, therefore, already found himself with an audience used to intimate biography, and so, ripe for autobiography.'[15]

Yet in putting back the moment of inauguration are we merely replicating the gesture of inauguration at an earlier stage, in the process of rejecting it at a later? We might call this the 'receding Renaissance': displacing the starting point of modernity. We have equal difficulty when we approach the historicity of Augustine from the perspective of modernity. Taylor's account of Augustine is constantly on the edge of imitating the *cogito* of Descartes. This is Augustine's fault. There are three extraordinary moments in which Augustine sounds like a Cartesian, the most extended in *De civitate Dei*: *si enim fallor sum*. 'If I am mistaken, I am. Someone who is not, cannot be mistaken; therefore I am, if I am mistaken.'[16] Descartes's contemporaries wondered whether the *Discours de la méthode* had indulged in a little plagiarism. Or has Augustine been reading Descartes? Henri Marrou argued how profoundly a modern reading of Augustine has been altered by Cartesianism.[17] No wonder Augustine sounds like the birth of the modern since we have recreated him in the light of modernity.

The *Confessions* has been reread so often we no longer know what book we are reading. It contains within it the books Augustine had read, the books it has subsequently influenced, and other books which have transformed its interpretation. The *Confessions* is therefore an exemplary history of how a book has been exposed to different kinds of reading. Perhaps we could begin by stating there is no one single book, the *Confessions*, just as there is no one single Augustine. There are multiple Augustines. How do we begin to distinguish them in the history of reading? Firstly, I argue, if contentiously, that the *Confessions* has been read more extensively in the twentieth century than ever before. Furthermore, the Augustine of the 'invention of subjectivity' is a writer of a specifically twentieth-century imagination. Such a polemical statement needs some justification. Augustine was perhaps the most widely cited author between the fifth and the fifteenth centuries.

[15] Peter Brown, *Augustine of Hippo: A Biography* (London: Faber, 1967), 159.

[16] Augustine, *De civitate Dei* 11.6, ed. B. Dombart and A. Kalb, *CCSL*, 47 (1955), 345. See also *De libero arbitrio* 2.3(7), ed. W. M. Green, *CSEL*, 74 (Vienna: Hölder-Pichler-Tempsky, 1956), 38–9; and *De trinitate* 10.10 (16), ed. W. J. Mountain, *CCSL*, 50 (1968), 328–9.

[17] Henri Irénée Marrou, *Saint Augustine and his Influence through the Ages*, trans. Patrick Hepburne-Scott (London: Longman, 1957), 171.

The *Confessions* was copied plentifully throughout this period. André Wilmart produced in 1931 a list of 257 surviving manuscripts, and more have been found since; according to Lucas Verheijen, the full figure may yet approach 400.[18] Nonetheless, while this figure shows the *Confessions* was popular, it did not have the status of master-text it has now, in an age where this will be the first and often only text by Augustine known to a common reader. Manuscripts of *De civitate Dei* or *Enarrationes in Psalmos* exceed the *Confessions* in number; everything is dwarfed by the Letters and Sermons. To take an example, there are sixty-five codices of Augustine surviving from the library of the Convent of San Marco in Florence, of which only two include the *Confessions* (there is a further manuscript with excerpts, and another originally from San Marco now in the British Library).[19]

A comprehensive codicology of the *Confessions* has never yet been completed.[20] Inevitably, interest has centred on the earliest witnesses in the establishment of a modern text. Even here there are surprises: Michael Gorman judges from the scattered remains of early copies that the work 'was not especially popular among readers in the early Middle Ages'.[21] Wilmart's chronology of manuscripts shows a large rise in surviving numbers in the twelfth century (as would be expected), with similar figures for the next two centuries before another surge in the fifteenth.[22] Of eighty-one manuscripts of the *Confessions* surviving in Italian libraries, thirty-one are fifteenth century.[23] To put this more colourfully, we could say that half of the surviving examples postdate Petrarch. From bare figures alone, one other trend can tentatively be identified. Whereas more than two-thirds of fourteenth-century copies now in Italy are in collections of other works (mostly *opuscula* of several works), just over half the fifteenth-century codices are of the *Confessions* on its own. Surviving copies in British and Irish libraries show a similar pattern.[24]

[18] André Wilmart, 'La Tradition des grands ouvrages de Saint Augustin', in *Studi Agostiniani*, vol. 2 of *Miscellanea Agostiniana: Testi e studi pubblicati a cura dell'ordine eremitano di S. Agostino nel XV centenario della morte del santo dottore*, 2 vols. (Rome: Tipografia Poliglotta Vaticana, 1931), 259–68. See also the discussion in Augustine, *Confessiones*, ed. Verheijen, pp. lix–lx.

[19] M. Oberleitner (ed.), *Die handschriftliche Überlieferung der Werke des Heiligen Augustinus*, vols. 1.1 and 1.2 (Vienna: Verlag der österreichischen Akademie der Wissenschaften, 1969–70), Sitzungsberichte ÖAW, 263 and 267.

[20] The Austrian project, *Die handschriftliche Überlieferung der Werke des Heiligen Augustinus*, is not yet complete; in particular, the volume on France is keenly awaited. My analysis here is based on the volumes for Italy and for Britain and Ireland.

[21] Michael Gorman, 'The Early Manuscript Tradition of St Augustine's *Confessiones*', *The Journal of Theological Studies*, 34 (1983), 114–45, at 114.

[22] Wilmart, 'La Tradition des grands ouvrages de Saint Augustin', 266.

[23] Figures for Italy derived from Oberleitner (ed.), *Die handschriftliche Überlieferung*.

[24] Figures derived from F. Römer (ed.), *Die handschriftliche Überlieferung der Werke des Heiligen Augustinus*, vols 2.1 and 2.2: *Großbritannien und Irland*, Sitzungsberichte ÖAW, 281 and 276 (Vienna: Verlag der österreichischen Akademie der Wissenschaften, 1972). There are forty-nine MSS of the *Confessions* surviving in British and Irish libraries. Nineteen of these are from the fourteenth and fifteenth centuries; one fourteenth-century copy is of the *Confessions* alone, eight from the fifteenth century.

Can we begin to reconstruct a picture of how the *Confessions* was read?[25] The first thing to say, obviously enough, is that the image of an individual reader working through the text in one continuous sitting is a false one. Reading practices vary considerably in type and context. The *Confessions* was often copied with other theological works and was intermittently the cause of theological interest. Nevertheless, what we might take for a citation from Augustine's text has often been filtered through other sources. The Augustine of the *Sentences* is the most obvious case. Down to the time of Luther, the *Sentences*, and commentaries on them, are a major source of dissemination. The last four books of the *Confessions* are the occasion of glosses on the divine will and on creation. Equally significant is how much Augustine was known from Bede onwards as much through *florilegia* and other digests as in complete texts. Bede's *Collectaneum* extracted expositions of the Pauline epistles from forty-eight of Augustine's works, although, as Michael Lapidge points out, it is possible he, too, relied in turn on intermediary excerpts.[26] There are nine citations from the *Confessions* in the *Collectaneum*; these do not correspond with modern interests in subjectivity—the largest number are from Book 13. An enlarged version of the work was made in the ninth century by Florus, deacon of Lyons, with new citations from the *Confessions*, again mostly from Book 10 and Book 13.[27] Such compilations were widely copied for centuries.[28] A manuscript emanating from England of another example, the *Liber florum sancti Augustini* (first compiled in the eleventh or twelfth century) survives from the first quarter of the fifteenth century.[29] Later compilations were more ambitious in scope. The *Milleloquium veritatis S. Augustini* of Bartolomeo of Urbino (d.1350) is a concordance to Augustine with 15,000 excerpts from his works under useable headings such as *haeresis*, *iustitia*, *fides*, or *ecclesia*.[30]

English readers in the fourteenth century may not always have been reading what we expect. Heiko Oberman described the fascinating autobiographical account that Thomas Bradwardine gives of a conversion experience in Oxford in the late 1320s. Attending theological lectures while still on the arts course, Bradwardine says *raro solebam quicquam audire de gratia, nisi aequivoce forsan dicta* ('I rarely used to hear about grace, except in an ambiguous way').[31] A change came through reading Romans 9:16. The verse struck him like a beam of light: *velut*

[25] The fullest account of this question remains Pierre Courcelle, *Les confessions de St Augustin dans la tradition littéraire* (Paris: Collection des Études augustiniennes, 1963).

[26] Michael Lapidge, *The Anglo-Saxon Library* (Oxford: Oxford University Press, 2006), 36.

[27] Wilmart, 'La Tradition des grands ouvrages de Saint Augustin', 267–8.

[28] The manuscripts of Bede's work are listed in *Revue Bénédictine*, 38 (1926), 16–17.

[29] BL MS Burney 356. The extracts from the *Confessions* are at fol. 95^{r}.

[30] For a survey of such texts, see Joseph T. Lienhard, 'Florilegia', in *Augustine Through the Ages*, ed. Allan Fitzgerald (Grand Rapids, MI: Eerdmans, 1999), 370–1.

[31] Thomas Bradwardine, *Thomae Bradwardini de causa Dei libri tres*, ed. Henry Savile (London: John Bill, 1618), 308C.

quodam gratiae radio visitatus.[32] Oberman called this new insight 'the great conversion' of Bradwardine's life.[33] Later, he used Bradwardine's example to cast doubt on the Protestant emphasis on the uniqueness of Luther's conversion or *Turmerlebnis.* He compared a number of late medieval lives—Richard FitzRalph, Jean Gerson, Andreas Karlstadt, and Gasparo Contarini—to show a typological pattern in conversion stories.[34]

Nevertheless, it is not clear Oberman was correct in aligning Bradwardine's narrative with a specific reading of Book 8 of the *Confessions.*[35] The passage in Bradwardine's *De causa Dei* is concerned with the Pelagian heresy. The Augustinian references are to the anti-heretical works, to discussions of Pauline arguments about predestination. It is helpful to recall here that the *Confessions* was often copied alongside anti-heretical works, as for instance the twelfth-century manuscript which belonged to the Benedictine priory in Rochester, where it is combined with *De diversis haeresibus.*[36] In an *Opuscula* of a later date, also of English provenance and showing evidence of English use perhaps up to the fifteenth century, several anti-Pelagian works accompany the *Confessions.* As an indication of changing reading interests, in this copy the key moment of the conversion scene, *tolle lege,* is omitted. A manicule on the page emphasizes a standard piece of moralistic devotional cliché rather than the subjective agon of the introspective saint.[37]

Karl Morrison, in a subtle history of medieval conversion, replaces the idea of a single conversion 'pattern' with 'an ill-matched repertory of such patterns'.[38] Morrison is particularly at pains to decouple the conversion texts he is interested in from the idea of 'peripety' or sudden change from one affiliation to another, or of psychological transformation and personal struggle. These models he associates with the late antique and the post-Reformation, and are largely unknown from the twelfth to the fourteenth centuries, where conversion is a 'continuous process', indeed a process encompassing a lifetime. The *Confessions* is adapted instead for penitential purposes, to suggest a contrast between this-worldly and other-worldly

32 Bradwardine, *De causa Dei*, ed. Savile, 308D.

33 Heiko A. Oberman, *Archbishop Thomas Bradwardine, a Fourteenth-Century Augustinian: a Study of his Theology in its Historical Context* (Utrecht: Kemink, 1957), 15.

34 Heiko Oberman, '*Wie sein Pettler, Hoc est verum*: Bund und Gnade in der Theologie des Mittelalters und der Reformation', *Zeitschrift für Kirchengeschichte*, 78 (1967), 232–52, translated in Oberman, *The Reformation: Roots and Ramifications* (Edinburgh: T. &. T. Clark, 1994).

35 Heiko Oberman, '"Iustitia Christi" and "Iustitia Dei": Luther and the Scholastic Doctrines of Justification', *The Harvard Theological Review*, 59 (1966), 1–26, reprinted in Oberman, *The Dawn of the Reformation* (Edinburgh: T. &. T. Clark, 1986), 104–25, at 111.

36 BL Royal 5.B.XVI.

37 BL Royal 5.C.V (13th/14th cent.), fol. 162^{v}. There is a version of the Lord's Prayer in English in a late fourteenth/fifteenth-century hand on the endpaper.

38 Karl F. Morrison, *Understanding Conversion* (Charlottesville: University of Virginia Press, 1992), xii.

desires, to create a longing for mortality and redemptive incorporation in Christ, and a meditative framework for mysticism.

Outside the theological and mendicant schools, where the *Confessions* survives in many manuscripts as part of a collection of *opuscula* or even a virtual *opera omnia*, the main context for reading Augustine's work is monastic. Pierre Courcelle has examined this literary tradition at length. He identified in particular another Augustine, the Cistercian Augustine. The writings of Bernard of Clairvaux filter Augustine throughout the twelfth and thirteenth centuries. An example of this trend in England is Ailred of Rievaulx.[39] Cases can also be found of women readers, such as Gertrud of Helfta at Eisleben in the thirteenth century, a foundation where the Cistercian influence was strong. Gertrud appears to quote several times from the *Confessions* in Book 2 of *Legatus Divinae Pietatis.*[40] Book 2 tells the story of her 'conversion', once again to be interpreted in the mode suggested by Morrison, as an inward restitution rather than an external transformation. It is not the conversion of *Confessions* 8 to which she refers, but the meditative introspection of Book 9.[41]

'Do not omit to look into Augustine's Confessions', Goscelin of Saint Bertin advises his spiritual daughter, Eve, at the convent at Wilton in the 1080s.[42] While such advice was widespread, it is right to be mindful of where and when it was made. It can sometimes appear as if Augustine is the ubiquitous medieval author, read throughout a millennium and always in the same way, but direct access to Augustine's writing often has a specific context. The English nun Eve moved on from Wilton to join an eremitical convent in Angers in western France. There is a special affinity among the eremitical orders with the *Confessions.* The Camaldolese were early known for their devotion to Augustine's spiritual reflections. Not surprisingly, however, the order most associated with the reading of Augustine is the Augustinians. Perhaps this is an example of a fact so obvious that scholarship has hardly bothered to take notice. From the monastery of the Augustinian friars founded in Paris in 1256, the Grands-Augustins, fifty-five of the surviving two hundred manuscripts are of Augustine, including several of the *Confessions.* This is a tradition of reading much more closely related to the autobiographical Augustine. Jordan of Saxony, while a student in Paris between 1319 and 1322, composed a hagiographic manuscript which entered the monastery library. It includes three

[39] Pierre Courcelle, 'Ailred de Rievaulx à l'école des "Confessions"', *Revue des études augustiniennes*, 3 (1957), 163–74.

[40] *Legatus Divinae Pietatis* 2.1.1, 2.14.1, 2.20.12, 2.23.18, and 2.24.1; Latin text of Gertrud of Helfta, *Legatus divinae pietatis*, in *Sources Chrétiennes* (Paris: Éditions du Cerf, 1968–86), 139, 143, 255, 331. I am grateful to Alexandra Barratt for these references.

[41] Gertrud of Helfta, *The Herald of God's Loving-Kindness*, trans. Alexandra Barratt (Kalamazoo, MI: Cistercian Publications, 1991), 100.

[42] Linda Olson, 'Did Medieval English Women Read Augustine's *Confessiones*? Constructing Feminine Interiority and Literacy in the Eleventh and Twelfth Centuries', in *Learning and Literacy in Medieval England and Abroad*, ed. Sarah Rees Jones (Turnhout: Brepols, 2003), 69–96, at 69.

collections of sermons, three rules attributed to Augustine, a *Vita*, and a life of St Monica based on the *Confessions*.[43]

Filial devotion to the titular head of the order was also found among the canons regular. Walter Hilton, one of the vernacular English authors who most visibly cites the *Confessions*, was head of a house of Augustinian canons in Nottinghamshire.[44] Hilton's *Scale of Perfection* was among the most popular works of late medieval England. It was first intended for female anchorites, but manuscript evidence shows it was also disseminated in the Carthusian houses of London and Sheen and the Brigittine abbey of Syon.[45] In 1494, it was printed by Wynkyn de Worde. The Augustinians may be the conduit through which other readers became familiar with the pattern of Augustine's visionary devotion. Margery Kempe was familiar with 'Hyltons boke', listing it among her spiritual classics.[46] Julian of Norwich was secluded in St Julian's Church in Norwich just opposite the Augustinian friars, perhaps the source of some glancing references to the *Confessions* in the *Showings*.[47]

It is by this route that the story of Augustine's conversion finds its way into Middle English. John Capgrave, a native of Lynn, entered the order of Augustinian hermits and in 1453 became Provincial of the English Province. It was perhaps on a journey to Rome (before 1451) that he came across Jordan of Saxony's *Vita sancti Augustini* and translated it. It survives in a single manuscript, prepared for 'a literate but not scholarly noble-woman'.[48] The scribe (probably Capgrave himself), attests to the way the commission is motivated by devotion to the saint: 'she desired this thing of me rather than of a nother man be cause that I am of the profession for sche supposed veryly that I wold do it with the bettir wil. Sche desired eke this lif of this seynt more than of ony othir bi for sche was browt forth in to this world in hys solempne feste.'[49] The life of Augustine is copied alongside an analysis of the rule of the order. It is in this context we should understand the remarkable vernacular rendering of the climax of the conversion narrative:

> While he lay thus with grete contricion of hert and with ful sobbyng voys uttirryng alle these wordes, al sodeynly he herd a voys as though it had ben at the next hous soundyng these same wordes: 'Tak and rede, take and rede'.[50]

[43] Jordan of Saxony (alias von Quedlinburg), *Vita sancti Augustini*, Paris, Bibliothèque de l'Arsenal, MS 251.

[44] Augustinian citations in Hilton are discussed in J.P.H. Clark, 'The "Lightsome Darkness" — Aspects of Walter Hilton's Theological Background', *The Downside Review*, 95 (1977), 95–109.

[45] Michael G. Sargent, 'Walter Hilton's *Scale of Perfection*: The London Manuscript Group Reconsidered', *Medium Ævum*, 52 (1983), 189–216, at 189–90.

[46] Kempe, *Book of Margery Kempe*, ed. Staley, 1.17.

[47] Julian of Norwich, *A Shewing of God's Love*, ed. Anna Maria Reynolds (London: Sheed and Ward, 1958), xx.

[48] John Capgrave, *Life of Saint Augustine*, ed. Cyril Lawrence Smetana, Studies and Texts, 138 (Toronto: Pontifical Institute of Mediaeval Studies, 2001), 7.

[49] BL MS Add. 36704, fol. 5^{r}.

[50] Capgrave, *Life of Saint Augustine*, ed. Smetana, 36 (BL MS Add. 36704, fol. 19^{v}).

Remarkable to us, yet not in the same way as it was to its early readers. The narrative pays attention to Augustine as a saint, moralist, grammarian, and biblical expositor, not as an autobiographer.

Of all late medieval readers of Augustine, the one cited again and again is Petrarch. He has been made to symbolize the long reach of Augustine's influence, and the continuity of medieval reading practices over a thousand years.[51] Yet perhaps no reader is more singular. Medievalists and early modernists have long fought for possession of Petrarch's remains. Is his reading of Augustine an example of the emergence of Renaissance humanism, or should we call it, as Lynn Thorndike wittily suggested, a 'Prenaissance' moment?[52] Petrarch is pre-eminently the writer who challenges simplistic appeals to period descriptors and paradigm shifts.

Nevertheless, Petrarch's account of how he carried in his pocket a copy of Augustine's *Confessions,* a 'compact little volume, small indeed in size, but of infinite charm', on an arduous hike to the summit of Mont Ventoux on 26 April 1336, is a seminal episode in the history of reading.[53] It also shows it is foolish to take any such narrative at face value. This is no artless reminiscence of personal experience but a highly self-conscious exercise in literary form, placed in Book 4 of the *Epistolae familiares* some years later in 1350. The form of these letters is based on Cicero, and this particular letter quotes from Cicero, Virgil, Ovid, and Seneca as well as Augustine. The letter is addressed to Fra Dionigi, as are two others in the *Familiares* (prose and verse).[54] Dionigi is crucial to the letter not only as the recipient and implied silent auditor of everything that is said, but as the donor of the copy of Augustine's book. The identity of this pocket-book codex, so lovingly described, is the stuff of legend: Petrarch was said to have carried it with him until the last year of his life, the script so worn he could no longer read it; he left it in his will to the Florentine humanist Luigi Marsili as a token of friendship. Just as significant is the identity of Dionigi. Dionigi was a monk from the order of Augustinian hermits, originally from the convent at Borgo San Sepolcro, and later Petrarch's confessor in Avignon. He thus places the book, and Petrarch's reading, within the framework of that special form of late medieval literacy, what I have characterized as the Augustinian revival of Augustine.

Dionigi, and the reader of Petrarch's reading with him, becomes the confessor to this confession of the book. It is a wonderful example of epistolary form, artfully

[51] Douglas Gray, 'Saint Augustine and Medieval Literature', *Saint Augustine and His Influence in the Middle Ages*, ed. Edward B. King and Jacqueline T. Schaefer, Sewanee Mediæval Studies, 3 (Sewanee: Press of the University of the South, 1988), 56–8.

[52] Lynn Thorndike, 'Renaissance or Prenaissance?', *Journal of the History of Ideas*, 4 (1943), 65–74.

[53] *Epistolae familiares*, 4.1, cited from Francesco Petrarca, *Le Familiari*, ed. Ugo Dotti, 2 vols. (Urbino: Argaglia, 1974), 1: 362–77.

[54] Petrarch, *Epistolae familiares* 4.2, in *Le Familiari*, ed. Dotti; and *Epistolae metrici* 1.4, cited from Francesco Petrarca, *Epistole metriche*, ed. E. Bianchi, in *Rime, Trionfi e Poesie Latine*, general editor N. Sapegno (Milan: Ricciardi, 1951), 720–6.

improvisatory, craftily staged in its intimate revelations, a memorial transcription heavily burdened with personal allegory. It is full of Dante: the mid-life ascent of the mountain; the perilous journey of the soul as well as the body; the pellucid view from the summit; the longing for Italy from exile *ex Ponto*; the journey into memory. Yet it is also self-consciously innovative in literary method. Petrarch reveals the life of the mind as coterminous with the reading of a book:

> Then, in truth, I was satisfied that I had seen enough of the mountain; I turned my inward eye upon myself [*in me ipsum interiores oculos reflexi*], and from that time not a syllable fell from my lips until we reached the bottom again. Those words had given me occupation enough, for I could not believe that it was by a mere accident that I happened upon them. What I had there read I believed to be addressed to me and to no other [*quicquid ibi legeram, michi et non alteri dictum rebar*], remembering that Augustine had once suspected the same thing in his own case.[55]

This is presented as a moment at once solipsistic and mimetic. Petrarch discovers in Augustine a mirror image of his position, and a kind of emotional palimpsest of his book within the other book.

Petrarch places this form of self-recognition through reading within a distinctive literary tradition. He has found himself in Augustine's book, just as Augustine found himself in reading the apostle Paul. Indeed, he stretches the tradition further back, for Augustine himself, he recalls, was already working in imitation of St Anthony, who also was converted by reading. In this sense he creates what we might call a mimesis of reading, a complex rhetorical figure of self-reflection in which, like mirrors poised at an angle in relation to each other, regressive images of the self are superimposed on each other. This process reaches into the future, into the reading of Petrarch's letter. Petrarch folds his own image onto Dionigi, and then folds us as readers onto himself.

This forms a different model of conversion and of reading experience from that envisioned in Augustine. In Augustine, conversion takes places through various kinds of external agency, including the accidental presence of the children in the garden and the persuasive intervention of Alypius and Monica. The *inward* movement in Augustine is always characterized as a necessary first principle in a movement *outward* which is the real object: a movement towards true knowledge of what lies outside himself, the knowledge of God. Reflexivity has its counterpart in externalization, and the literary form of soliloquy exists in another dimension as a continual dialogue with God. Stock comments that Petrarch makes his work for the first time truly 'self-referential'; he makes it possible 'for the individual to become... his own book'.[56]

Around the same time, in *Secretum*, Petrarch extended this device into a full-scale literary dialogue between writer as self and self as reader, between Augustinus

[55] Petrarch, *Epistolae familiares* 4.1 in *Le Familiari*, ed. Ugo Dotti, 1: 375.

[56] Stock, *After Augustine*, 76.

and Franciscus. Here he completes the idea of the incorporation of a life in a book, while turning Augustine into what we might truly call a literary classic:

> FRANCISCUS
> I can see in my storm-tossed life a reflection of that difficult time in your life. For this reason, as often as I read the *Confessions*, I read them with tears of joy, caught between conflicting emotions, hope and fear. I think I am reading an account of my own wanderings instead of someone else's [*me arbitrer non alienam sed propriam meae peregrinationis historiam*].[57]

Yet whereas the *Secretum* has been described as Petrarch's *Confessions*, it is very different, much less autobiographical than the letter to Dionigi. This is part of how Petrarch turns Augustine into an epitome of antiquity and thus part of the classical inheritance of humanism.

Stock comments acutely that Petrarch's move towards interiorization is bound up with an ambiguous attitude to the monastic life: a defence of its other-worldliness combined with an assertion of the possibility of a secularized form of the religious life in the lay work of literature. Yet we can see this ambiguity within late medieval monasticism itself, in the simultaneous movements for a more idealized interiority in the eremitical traditions combined with a suspicion of the cloistered orders and a drive to new encounters with the laity. Petrarch's work, and his reading of Augustine, are not only a symptom of this, they also participate in it. Petrarch turns the pocket codex into a humanist book, for the solitary lay reader, but it began its life as a monastic copy, part of the Augustinian revival. In turn, the Petrarchized Augustine fed back into the monasteries. Marsili, who inherited this copy, later left a large legacy of Augustinian manuscripts to the Augustinian convent of Santo Spirito in Florence.[58] The library of Santo Spirito (now sadly dispersed) was an intellectual corridor between monks, the learned, and the lay. Giannozzo Manetti, who later became a politician and wrote lives of Dante, Boccaccio, and Petrarch, trained under two Augustinian friars who taught laypeople at Santo Spirito in the 1420s. He attempted to consolidate the library's Augustinian manuscripts into a systematic collection of *prima exemplaria*.

There were Augustinian collectors outside the convents. Pope Nicholas V took pride in the recovery of batches of Augustine's letters. The humanist bibliophile Niccolò Niccoli owned thirty-four Augustinian manuscripts. Yet Niccoli, too, shows the traffic between monastic and humanist learning. In his collecting he enlisted the help of Ambrogio Traversari, who entered the order of the Camaldolese at the age of fourteen in the monastery of Santa Maria degli Angeli in Florence, rapidly becoming a leading patristic theologian and Hellenist. Niccoli and

[57] Francesco Petrarca, *Secretum*, 1, ed. Enrico Carrara, in *Prose*, general editor, G. Martellotti (Milan: Ricciardi, 1955), 42.

[58] Meredith Jane Gill, *Augustine in the Italian Renaissance: Art and Philosophy from Petrarch to Michelangelo* (Cambridge: Cambridge University Press, 2005), 16. Santo Spirito was also given the bequest of Boccaccio's library; both collections are now lost.

Traversari formed an intimate friendship constructed around the *Confessions*: Traversari rebuked Niccoli for his quarrel with Leonardo Bruni via the example of St Monica at the end of Book 9, a good place to learn charity and patience.[59] Niccoli's library (he died in 1437) formed the basis of the collection of the Dominican convent of San Marco designed to be housed in 1441 in Michelozzo's library under the patronage of Cosimo de' Medici.[60]

Comparing some of the manuscripts of San Marco provenance shows the change in taste. San Marco 663, now BL MS Add. 14778, is a fourteenth-century *Opuscula* of Augustine with elegant initial letters and ornaments. It contains *De Genesi ad litteram*, *De Trinitate*, and *De doctrina Christiana* as well as the *Confessions*. There are manicules and annotations but fewer for the *Confessions* than for other works.[61] San Marco 654, now in the Biblioteca Medicea Laurenziana, on the other hand, was commissioned by Coluccio Salutati at the end of the fourteenth century and copied by Ambrogio da Firenze.[62] It organizes biographical material extracted from the *Confessions* in order to exalt the saint as a writer. This material is placed after extracts from Isidore of Seville and Cassiodorus. By this process, it turns Augustine, following the Petrarchan analysis, into a model of erudition. In the fifteenth century, Marsilio Ficino consolidated this reputation by calling Augustine the Christian writer closest to Plato. Ficino derived his idea of the typical condition of the philosopher as 'inquietudine' from the *Confessions*: *Inquietum est cor nostrum* (1; 1[1]).[63] A particularly luxurious humanist codex of the *Confessions* (and other works) is thought to have been copied by Ficino's secretary, Luca Fabiani.[64]

Salutati, who became Chancellor of Florence in 1375, owned a personal copy of the *Confessions*, bound with two pseudo-Augustinian texts of ascetic spirituality (including the *Soliloquia animae ad deum*, a work which often colours the later medieval reception of the *Confessions*), works by Jerome, and other patristic writings. The manuscript contained additional citations from Seneca and from Petrarch.[65] Salutati made personal annotations in the margin, particularly prevalent in the text of the *Confessions*. He marks out the rites of passage in the saint's life, following a biographical pattern: *Infantia* (fol. 2^{v}), *Pueritia* (fol. 3^{v}), *de*

[59] Ambrogio Traversari, *Epistulae* (Florence, 1759), 13.2 and 13.7; cited by Cesare Vasoli in *Gli umanisti e Agostino: codici in mostra*, ed. Donatella Coppini and Mariangela Regoliosi (Florence: Polistampa, 2001), 39.

[60] Charles L. Stinger, *Humanism and the Church Fathers: Ambrogio Traversari (1386–1439) and Christian Antiquity in the Italian Renaissance* (Albany: State University of New York Press, 1977), 24.

[61] BL MS Add. 14778; it was presented to San Marco by Cosimo son of Giovanni de' Medici.

[62] San Marco 654, Biblioteca Medicea Laurenziana; *Gli umanisti e Agostino*, ed. Coppini and Regoliosi, cat. 9.

[63] Marsilio Ficino, *Opera omnia* (Basle: Heinrich Petri, 1576), 769 and 665–6.

[64] Biblioteca Medicea Laurenziana, Pluteo 12.3; *Gli umanisti e Agostino*, ed. Coppini and Regoliosi, cat. 68.

[65] Biblioteca Medicea Laurenziana, Pluteo 12.23; *Gli umanisti e Agostino*, ed. Coppini and Regoliosi, cat. 13. On the *Soliloquia animae ad deum*, see F. Doveri in *Gli umanisti e Agostino*, 97–9.

adolescentia (fol. 6r). He also notes more incidental events from the life, such as Augustine's love of gladiatorial fights and musical theatre (fol. 4v). Just as significant, he marks out Augustine's classicism. In a letter to the Dominican Giovanni Dominici in 1406, he cited the Ciceronian *Hortensius* as the cause of the saint's conversion, quoting the same line that had so struck Petrarch, *ipse vero liber mutavit affectum meum*. Here in the manuscript this passage in Book 3 is marked with a marginal line and the word 'libros' (fol. 9r). From Salutati the manuscript passed into the circles of Florentine humanism, owned next by Cosimo de' Medici himself, then by Niccolò Michelozzi, son of the architect and brother of Bartolomeo, the successor to Poliziano.

One detail of this manuscript shows in special relief the Petrarchizing of the reading of Augustine. This is the placing (fol. 1v), as an epigraph prefacing the text, of Petrarch's distich on the *Confessions* from the companion volume to *Familiares*, the *Seniles*:

> Hunc celer ad fontem deserta per arida pergat
> quisquis eget lacrimis quibus impia crimina tergat.[66]

('Through arid deserts he winds his way quickly to the fountain, whoever has need of tears with which to wipe away his wicked crimes'). In this letter in the *Seniles*, Petrarch records how the *Confessions* changed his life just as the *Hortensius* had Augustine's, and cites the influence of two Augustinian friars from Padua. He tells his friend to write this distich into his copy of Augustine, as he himself has inscribed it in many of his own books. The distich reappears in other fifteenth-century manuscripts, such as BL MS Burney 289, copied in 1427 by Niccolò di Berto of San Gimignano. Niccolò has been identified as the scribe of seventeen different works, mostly classical or patristic, including a *Confessions* in Italian.[67] Here the scribe signs and dates his handiwork, providing illuminated humanistic decorated initials for each book. It is a very personal copy. There are copious annotations throughout, in red and black. Some are humanist noticings: 'Terentius' (fol. 6v), 'de Platone' (fol. 39v), 'Mathematici' (fol. 37v). There are also frequent citations of words in the text, often of an emotional nature: 'amicitia' (fol. 9r), 'lacrimas', (fol. 14r), 'talia pectore misero' (fol. 37v). The reader is a proclaimed Petrarchist: he marks the signature passage referring to Cicero's *Hortensius* and everywhere establishes his classical taste and literary temperament.

[66] *Seniles* 8.6, cited from Francesco Petrarca, *Rerum senilium*, ed. Elvira Nota, 4 vols. (Paris: Les Belles Lettres, 2002–6), 3: 82–91, at 87.

[67] Madrid, Biblioteca Nacional Vit. 22–11 (*Res.* 5a–11), with emblems of the Marquis of Santillana; a full analysis of this scribe is in Albinia de la Mare, 'New Research on Humanistic Scribes in Florence', in *Miniatura fiorentina del rinascimento, 1440–1525: un primo censimento*, ed. A. Garzelli and A. C. de la Mare, Inventari e cataloghi toscani, 18–19, 2 vols. ([Florence]: Giunta regionale toscana, 1985), 1: 395–600, at 512.

By the later fifteenth century the Petrarchan Augustine had been thoroughly assimilated into the reception of the *Confessions.* This can be seen even when there are no overt signs of humanist interpretation, in the increasing number of monastic copies of small size where the *Confessions* is the only or dominant text. British Library MS Add. 21065 was copied in 1444 by a monk of St Justina of Padua at the monastery of the Holy Ghost and St Gall outside Pavia; it is diminutive in size and shows signs of personal use; the annotations are in the same hand as the copyist. Villanova MS OM 16 is a quarto dating from after 1456, perhaps from the Dominican priory at Pistoia. Other manuscripts show evidence of new kinds of use. BL MS Add. 16588 was originally copied in a single professional fourteenth-century hand, but also contains a considerable number of annotations for which the handwriting appears to be fifteenth or even early sixteenth century. The writer in the margin is clearly theologically literate but also makes notes of a more personal interest. He endorses Augustine's comments on the uselessness of the liberal arts in the face of carnal lusts (4.16), and notes Augustine's *infirmitas* and his *perturbat[i]o[ne]s animi.*[68] He makes several marginal interventions to categorize Augustine's different comments on the processes of memory. He notes in red the passage on the palaces of memory in Book 10 (*praetoria memoriae*, fol. 114^{v}). Perhaps most strikingly of all, he is attentive to the narrative detail of Augustine's conversion in the garden, marking the words *tolle lege* with a manicule and the marginal words 'Ap[er]uit aptus et legit' (fol. 94^{v}–95^{r}).

Such a marking appears to a twenty-first century eye a commonplace, but when this manuscript was first copied in the fourteenth century the conversion scene did not have the dramatic status that it now has. A pictorial image for this scene only appears after 1464, when Benozzo Gozzoli left Florence for the hill town of San Gimignano.[69] The commission that took him there was a series of frescoes of the life of Augustine for the monastery of Sant' Agostino. This foundation dates back to 1280 but by the middle of the fifteenth century was in serious decline. In 1457 one of its friars, Fra Domenico Strambi, was asked to restore it to the ideals of scholarship, asceticism, and community embodied in the Augustinian Observant movement. In 1464, he also acquired patronal responsibility for the choir of the church, and set about the decoration of the choir in accordance with his eremitical and intellectual principles. Benozzo's seventeen narrative scenes, of considerable iconographic originality, are framed with ornate foliation similar to that in humanist books.[70]

[68] BL MS Add. 16588, fol. 48^{r} and 118^{v}.

[69] Gozzoli's cycle is the only one of the life of Augustine in the Tuscan Renaissance. The twenty-one cycles produced throughout Europe in the fourteenth and fifteenth centuries are surveyed in Jeanne and Pierre Courcelle, *Iconographie de saint Augustin—XIVe siècle* (Paris: Collection des Études augustiniennes, 1965); and *Iconographie de saint Augustin—XVe siècle* (Paris: Collection des Études augustiniennes, 1969).

[70] A full description of the cycle is given in Diane Cole Ahl, *Benozzo Gozzoli* (New Haven, CT and London: Yale University Press, 1996), cat. 78 (260–1).

For one of them, a painting the serenity of which perhaps conceals its startling philosophical distinctiveness, Benozzo and Fra Domenico chose the subject of the moment of the *tolle lege*. The composition evidently went through three stages of complex development as Benozzo created an image of the reader in action (Figure 5).[71] A motto below half-quotes from *Confessions* 8: AUDIVIT VOCEM E CELO DICENTEM SIBI. Augustine sits with his book on his lap, the lettering of the open codex visible to the viewer, the fingers of the saint's right hand marking his place on the page while his left supports his head, in rapt contemplation, a remarkable representation of intellectual introspection.

It is hard not to give in to the temptation to believe that here the conversion of Augustine is entering modernity. This is the private reader caught up in his own world and absorbed with his own self. Perhaps we can even see in it how Augustine figures his conversion in the garden in Milan as the key moment in his life, not only as a life-changing experience, not only as a change in philosophical outlook, but as a moment *of* philosophy, of coming into the possession of philosophy. Within a religious context the *topos* of conversion acquires new significance. The path to inward contemplation is transformed into a mark of external affiliation. Benozzo's image is blissfully unaware of these energies, but within fifty years it is impossible to separate conversion from two phenomena: the schism in Western Christendom making it possible to 'convert' from one form of Christianity to another, one the truth and the other a form of the Antichrist; and the New World and colonialism, with the sudden and unavoidable existence of large numbers of unconverted non-Christians.

A conventional historiography would find it natural to associate the historical liminality of Benozzo's image of reading with the two cultural transformations of the age: the Reformation and the printed book. It is salutary in this respect to recall that the revival and revision of Augustinianism of which the painting is a symptom were completed before the advent of either. And yet this does not mean continuity with medieval modes of praxis. The image of interiority in the fresco is inescapably connected with the Petrarchan tradition of the *Confessions*, and the fifteenth-century humanist manuscript copies to which Benozzo's iconography is intimately related. The reader in the library of the monastery is caught up in an imaginative world quite distinct from a reading of the *Confessions* in the early fourteenth century.[72] The history of reading Augustine thus reveals itself as a paradox, in which every reader is connected by the invisible community of the text, and yet also separated by processes that are materially distinct and yet also conceptually and emotionally fluid and variable.

[71] A preliminary drawing now in the Fogg Museum, Harvard University, and the *sinopie* to the fresco uncovered in a restoration of 1990, are described in Ahl, *Benozzo Gozzoli*, 138.

[72] Pierre Courcelle, 'Pétrarque entre saint Augustin et les Augustins du XIVe siècle', *Petrarca e il petrarchismo, Studi Petrarcheschi*, 7 (Bologna: Libreria editrice Minerva, 1961), 51–71.

Figure 5 Benozzo Gozzoli, *St Augustine Reading the Epistles of St Paul* (1464–5). Fresco, Apsidal chapel, church of Sant'Agostino, San Gimignano

What of the printed Augustine? The differences are not immediately obvious. The earliest printers in Subiaco and Rome followed the lead of Petrarchan humanism in placing Augustine, Lactantius, and the Fathers in a line with Cicero. Patristic writers were at the centre of printing projects, so that *De civitate Dei* was in 1467 one of the first Italian printed books. For the *Confessions*, on the other hand, print was at first a retrograde medium. It was a natural book for the personal luxury market of manuscript workshops. In print it returned to the bounds of the *Opuscula* and the complete works. Editions of the *Confessions* alone are rare: Jean Mentelin's Strasbourg imprint (in print by 1470) was followed by the Milanese edition of Giovanni Bono in 1475. John Shirwood, later Bishop of Durham, bought a copy of this edition in Rome in 1481.[73] Another was produced in Cologne in 1482 and another in Deventer in 1483. This compares with twenty-three incunabula of *De civitate Dei*.[74]

The impact of the Reformation on the *Confessions*, too, is ambiguous. Augustine was famously amenable to all confessional persuasions. All claimed a stake, putting pressure on the idea of conversion itself. Despite his reputation for rigorous anti-heretical orthodoxy, and perhaps even against the grain of the *Confessions* as an argument, Augustine provides a model for theological self-reinvention of enormous power. This literary impetus can readily be identified as quasi-autobiographical: it makes the experience of the individual immediate and transformative.

The initial springs for this are not revolutionary, however. Although Martin Luther's conversion became a byword for Protestant experience, and its interpretation the scene of ferocious scholarship, he was reluctant to write of his own experience as a conversion. Luther was emphatic, however, about the importance of Augustine to his thinking in his years of crisis. Most critical attention has been paid to *De spiritu et litera* and the anti-Pelagian works.[75] Yet he also made frequent reference to his reading of the *Confessions*. In his first lectures on the Psalms in Wittenberg in 1513–15, he draws an explicit comparison with the conversion in Book 8, as a way of explaining his own experience mimetically, and of attaching such a personal internalization to the meaning of the Psalm.[76]

The autobiographical trope in Luther is fully realized in his 1545 memoir appended to the complete edition of his Latin works. This magnificently obscure essay in self-analysis pores over his theological innovations by consciously

[73] Corpus Christi College, Oxford, Φ C.1.16.

[74] Comparative figures extracted from the British Library *Incunabula Short Title Catalogue*, <http://www.bl.uk/catalogues/istc/>.

[75] On the dating of Luther's reading of *De spiritu et litera*, see Brian Cummings, *The Literary Culture of the Reformation: Grammar and Grace* (Oxford: Oxford University Press, 2002), 80–3.

[76] Weimarer Ausgabe, 3.549.26–32. This passage is cited in Oberman, *Dawn*, 111. See also Pierre Courcelle, 'Luther interprète des "Confessions" de saint Augustin', *Revue d'histoire et de philosophie religieuses*, 39 (1959), 235–50.

imitating the Augustinian model. He, too, is reading a book; he is reading the same book, Paul to the Romans:

> As I meditated day and night on the words 'as it is written, the righteous person shall live by faith', I began to understand that the righteous person lives by the gift of a passive righteousness, by which the merciful God justifies us by faith. This immediately made me feel as though I had been born again, and as though I had entered through open gates into paradise itself.[77]

Augustine, we recall, read no further: 'with the last words of this sentence, it was as if a light of relief from all anxiety flooded my heart. All the shadows of doubt were dispelled' (153). Yet, while we can see this as the primal scene of the Reformation it is also a distinctly pre-Reformation mode of reading. Luther stands in the tradition of Petrarch's Dionigi. Indeed, more specifically, he is, like Fra Domenico in San Gimignano, part of the Augustinian Observant monastic revival of the late fifteenth century. Luther's spiritual father Johann von Staupitz was a key member of the German part of this movement, and Luther's famous trip to Rome in 1510 was on a mission to represent the Observants.

It is in this light, too, that we should frame the conversion experience that has often been compared with Luther's on the other side of the Alps and within the bosom of the Vatican, that of Gasparo Contarini. A minor scion of one of the oldest families in Venice, born in the same year as Luther, his spiritual crisis came at almost exactly the same time in 1511, and is attributed by him to a reading of Paul via Augustine. Only Christ's passion stands sufficient to satisfy a man's past sins, otherwise he is damned. In time, his conclusion is simpler: by no works can a man justify himself or purge his spirit, since divine grace is only matched by faith in Christ.[78]

The Lutheran phrasing in his work is startling, but Contarini's conversion also takes place through literary processes. Everything we know about it is filtered through an exchange of highly-charged letters between friends. There are thirty letters in all, written in a triangle between Contarini and two Venetian friends, Tommaso Giustianini and Vincenzo Quirini, now hermits at the Sacro Eremo high in the hillside above Camaldoli itself. The language of this literary exchange is Petrarchan, sometimes self-consciously so ('quasi nave in mezo el mar senza governo son rimasto').[79] It is suffused with the idiom of personal anxiety and decision from the Petrarchized version of the *Confessions*. Contarini's life is marked

[77] Martin Luther, 'Praefatio D. Martini Lutheri pio lectoris', *Opera Omnia*, I (1545), Weimarer Ausgabe 54.180. For a comparison of the passages in Augustine and Luther, see Cummings, *Grammar and Grace*, 60–4.

[78] Gasparo Contarini to Tommaso Giustiniani, 7 February 1523 (Letter 30), in 'Contarini und Camaldoli', ed. Hubert Jedin, *Archivio italiano per la storia della pietà*, 2 (1959), 51–119, at 117.

[79] Contarini to Giustiniani, 1 February (1511) (Letter 1), 'Contarini und Camaldoli', ed. Jedin, 61, citing Petrarch, *Rime sparse*, 277.7 ('senza governo in mar'), perhaps also referring to 189.1.

by 'la passion et noia' ('passion and trouble', 61); he yearns for the consolation provided by his spiritual confessor, 'di tanto affecto, di tanta chiareza' ('by so much feeling and clarity', 61). Tommaso plays Augustine or Dionigi to Gasparo's Franciscus. On Easter Saturday, Contarini states that his internal conflict is resolved and he experiences extraordinary release, from 'gran timor et assai tristizia' ('from great fear and much sadness'), he says, 'converso in alegreza' ('I was converted to happiness').[80]

Contarini's conversion narrative is thus bathed in the spirit of the Camaldolese devotion to the *Confessions*. Yet something, too, has changed. He lives and wakes, he says, as if ('come se... fosse') his whole life was spent in the Eremo. In fact, though, he stayed behind in Venice, 'in mezo la cità'. Contarini is a creature of a new religious world. He was a diplomat, attending the Diet of Worms in 1521 (where he carefully avoided Luther). Later he was made Cardinal by Paul III in 1535, although he was not yet ordained. He was worldly and yet attached himself readily to the new reformist orders which consciously embraced life in the midst of the laity. He encouraged revivalist religious orders, such as the Theatines; he was associated with the Oratory of Divine Love in Rome, and Ignatius Loyola regarded him as a key patron in the foundation of the Jesuits.

Both Luther and Contarini are readers of Augustine in print. It is easy to exaggerate the significance of the medium, but the portability and the transferability of the format make the printed book a natural companion for the religious world of the sixteenth century. Books pass between the confines of the spiritual and the worldly, just as readers do, and interpenetrate each other's epistemic practice. The topos of the transformational reading of a book, in the manner of Petrarch, which first happens with a small manuscript codex, migrates and expands in volume with its printed equivalent. This merges with the literary mirroring of conversion itself, in a *topos* of the convert as *writer*. Reader and writer are increasingly interchangeable, just as reading and writing become constantly mimetic of each other. These forms of self-reflection are intrinsically autobiographical. On 20 May 1521, a month after Contarini saw Luther at Worms, another young man in his twenties was badly wounded in the siege by the French of the imperial garrison at Pamplona. Confined to his bed as he recovered from a series of botched and increasingly serious operations to both of his legs, Iñigo Lopez de Loyola longed for some books to read. What else was there to do? He was hoping, he recounted years later, for fictions or 'books of chivalry'.[81] But in the house only two books were available: a life of Christ and a copy of the *Legenda Aurea*. He devoured them, 'leyendo muchas veces', reading them all the way through, again and again, until he had internalized them completely so that 'by reading he was converted'.[82]

80 Contarini to Giustiniani, 24 April (1511) (Letter 2), 'Contarini und Camaldoli', ed. Jedin, 64.

81 Ignatius of Loyola, *Autobiography*, ed. John C. Olin (New York: Harper & Row, 1974), 23.

82 Ignacio de Loyola, *Obras Completas*, ed. Ignacio Iparraguirre and Candido de Dalmases (Madrid: Biblioteca de Autores Cristianos, 1963), 94.

The material conditions and phenomenological contingencies of reading practices reverberate with Augustine's words in shifting patterns. The Augustinian phrase *tolle lege* is thrown back and forth in England between Catholic and Protestant controversialists after 1550, in Gregory Martin or Thomas Harding on the one hand, and Edward Dering or John Jewel on the other. William Alabaster, who converted in both directions, used the *Confessions* as a model. In the early seventeenth century, the *Confessions* came fully into the English language. There were two separate translations, one Catholic from the English College in St Omer, and the other, with 'the marginall notes of a former Popish translation, answered', by one of King Charles's chaplains.[83] Both books bear the marks of polemical difference on their sleeve. The recusant version, by Tobie Matthew, the Catholic convert son of the Archbishop of York, has two prefaces, the second over a hundred pages long. This presents Augustine's conversion as endorsing a particular Catholic process: a vow of chastity, entry into solitary life of the religious, a call to priesthood, the founding of a monastery.[84] At the *tolle lege* passage, a marginal note adds: 'S. Augustine converted by a miraculous calling' (395). The Protestant version answers tit for tat:

> Thus much I uttered, weeping among in the most bitter contrition of my heart: when as behold, I heard a voyce from some neighbour house, as it had beene of a Boy or Girle I know not whether, in a singing tune saying, and often repeating, TAKE UP AND READE, TAKE UP AND READE. Instantly changing my countenance thereupon. (480)

A marginal note adds: 'His conversion by a voyce from Heaven', but a further addition cannot resist replying to the Catholic version in kind. 'By this it appeares that all Popish Fryars are not divinely called, For that so few elder brothers take the vow.'

The title page of this edition shows how central the image of the conversion of Augustine had become. It bears a crude but intriguing woodcut: Augustine is kneeling; the words 'Take up and reade. Take up and reade' descend in a banderole towards him, via some cherubs; in the background is a scene in Augustine's garden. It is a strangely domesticated location, where Augustine has been translated into an English knot garden, complete with rose trellis and vegetable plot. This is not inappropriate. References in English works to the conversion scene, in English or in Latin, increase throughout the seventeenth century. The episode was known more widely than ever before. Early modern Englishwomen as well as men cited it freely.

[83] Augustine, *Saint Augustines confessions translated: and with some marginall notes illustrated*, trans. William Watts (London: John Norton, 1631), title page.

[84] Augustine, *The confessions of the incomparable doctour S. Augustine*, trans. Sir Tobie Mathew (Saint-Omer: English College, 1620), 27. The seventeenth-century versions are discussed by Molly Murray, 'Sir Tobie Matthew', *The Oxford Guide to the Historical Reception of Augustine*, ed. Bruce Gordon (Oxford: Oxford University Press, forthcoming).

The autobiography of Elizabeth Isham, written on the eve of the civil wars, declares that in the composition of her work she was 'of late imboldended [sic] by the sight of S. Austin Con[fessions]'; she makes thirteen detailed citations from Watts's *Confessions.*[85] At the funeral of Margaret Marwood in 1660, it was said by the preacher that she used to 'breakfast upon the Bible, her hand and heart being so inured to it, as if she had heard that voyce from heaven spurring her to it, 'Take up and read, take up and read.'[86]

Yet there are also new kinds of puzzle and anxiety arising from the vexed circumstances of confessional identity. Was Bunyan imagining himself in the guise of Augustine called to conversion by a children's game when Christ came to him in a game of 'Cat'?

> But the same day, as *I* was in the midst of a game at Cat, and having struck it one blow from the hole; just as I was about to strike it the second time, a voice did suddenly dart from Heaven into my Soul, which said, *Wilt thou leave thy sins, and go to Heaven? or have thy sins, and go to Hell?* At this *I* was put to an exceeding maze; wherefore leaving my Cat upon the ground, I looked up to Heaven, and was as if *I* had with the eyes of my understanding, seen the Lord Jesus looking down upon me, as being very hotly displeased with me, and as if he did severely threaten me with some grievous punishment for these, and other my ungodly practices.[87]

Bunyan prides himself on his accuracy of personal recollection as an act of humility towards God. Is he borrowing here, or has his life become his reading so much that he relives the life of his books? The seventeenth-century revolutions entered new existential territory. Autobiographical writing revelled in the extemporary, in improvised exercises of self-reinvention. Perhaps the most peculiar conversion narrative of the early modern period, Lawrence Clarkson's *The Lost Sheep Found*, purports to be a record of the life of 'the onely true converted Messenger of Christ Jesus, Creator of Heaven and Earth'.[88] Clarkson is by now a Muggletonian, for a while the only Muggletonian, since even Muggleton got it wrong. But in the past Clarkson recounts he has had no fewer than seven conversion experiences. He is the serial convert to end all series, going through the whole spectrum of seventeenth-century Christianity (discounting of course Catholicism, the only religion beyond the pale): conformist, Presbyterian, independent, Dipper, and the rest. Clarkson enters history gloriously as a member of the curious and obscure Ranter faction, but just as singular is Clarkson's narrative method, his resources as an autobiographer, by

[85] Femke Molekamp, 'Early Modern English Women,' in *Oxford Guide to the Historical Reception of Augustine*, ed. Gordon.

[86] G. Ewbancke, *The Pilgrim's Port or the Weary Man's Rest in the Grave. Opened and Improved in a Sermon, at the Funeral of the Honourable Ms Margaret Marwood* (London: Charles Tyus, 1660), 124. I owe this reference to Femke Molekamp.

[87] Bunyan, *Grace abounding*, B1^{r}.

[88] Lawrence Clarkson, *The lost sheep found, or, The prodigal returned to his fathers house, after many a sad and weary journey through many religious countreys* (London: for the author, 1660), title page.

which he is forced to reinvent his past conversions, to imagine believing things he no longer believes in, such as when he started something called the *One Flesh Society*, with the doctrine that sin only happens in the head:

> and therefore till you can lie with all women as one woman, and not judge it sin, you can do nothing but sin: now in Scripture I found a perfection spoken of, so that I understood no man could attain perfection but this way, at which Mr *Rawlinson* was much taken, and *Sarah Kullin* being then present, did invite me to make trial of what I had expressed, so as I take it, after we parted, she invited me to Mr *Wats* in *Rood-lane*, where was one or two more like herself, and as I take it, lay with me that night.
>
> (25–6)

Or later, when Clarkson imagines disbelieving altogether, 'so that I judged all was a lie, and that there was no devil at all, nor indeed no God but only nature' (32). Here we have come a long way from Augustine, yet in another sense we can see a line in the fictionalizing of past experience in order to create a meaningful narrative which is a near-perfect rendition of a conversion model. I can remake myself because I can convert into somebody completely unlike me. Yet I will still be me, whatever you make of my conversion. The pilgrimage of the fourteenth-century mystics into the self and into further self-discovery is transformed into an odyssey of personal self-fragmentation. Yet we could also say that both forms of narrative are not quite modern yet. The last move from conversion into autobiographicalization has to await another Augustinian revival in the confessional novel, in the twentieth and twenty-first century.

FURTHER READING

Coppini, Donatella and Mariangela Regoliosi (eds.). *Gli umanisti e Agostino: codici in mostra* (Florence: Polistampa, 2001)

Courcelle, Pierre. *Les confessions de St Augustin dans la tradition littéraire* (Paris: Collection des études augustiniennes, 1963)

Stock, Brian. *After Augustine: The Meditative Reader and the Text* (Philadelphia: University of Pennsylvania Press, 2001)

Wilmart, André. 'La Tradition des grands ouvrages de Saint Augustin', *Miscellanea Agostiniana: Testi e studi pubblicati a cura dell'ordine eremitano di S. Agostino nel XV centenario della morte del santo dottore* (2 vols.), vol. 2: *Studi Agostiniani* (Rome: Tipografia Poliglotta Vaticana, 1931), 259–68

INDEX